THE NAIVE AND
SENTIMENTAL LOVER

"John le Carré's superb and disturbing thrillers placed him in the company of the foremost novelists writing today. This latest book bears the stamp of his distinctive talent . . . Sad, funny, captivating and stunningly fertile, it is the most satisfying novel I have read this year."
—*Sunday Express*

"Comic and touching . . . This novel is solid, brilliant and marvelously good reading."
—*Book World*

"Splendid, original . . . Le Carré shows how endowed he is with the art of storytelling."
—*The Times*

THE NAIVE AND SENTIMENTAL LOVER

John le Carré

BANTAM BOOKS
TORONTO · NEW YORK · LONDON · SYDNEY

THE NAIVE AND SENTIMENTAL LOVER

*A Bantam Book / published by arrangement with
Alfred A. Knopf, Inc.*

PRINTING HISTORY
Knopf edition published January 1972
Bantam edition / November 1978
2nd printing .... August 1980

ISBN 0-553-13955-X

*Bantam Books are published by Bantam Books, Inc. Its trade-
mark, consisting of the words "Bantam Books" and the por-
trayal of a bantam, is Registered in U.S. Patent and Trademark
Office and in other countries. Marca Registrada. Bantam
Books, Inc., 666 Fifth Avenue, New York, New York 10103.*

PRINTED IN THE UNITED STATES OF AMERICA

11 10 9 8 7 6 5 4

*For John Miller
and Michael Truscott,
at Sancreed, with
love.*

Haverdown

1

Cassidy drove contentedly through the evening sunlight, his face as close to the windshield as the safety belt allowed, his foot alternating diffidently between accelerator and brake as he scanned the narrow lane for unseen hazards. Beside him on the passenger seat, carefully folded into a plastic envelope, lay an Ordnance Survey map of central Somerset. An oilbound compass of the newest type was fastened by suction to the walnut dashboard. At a corner of the windshield, accurately adjusted to his field of view, a copy of the Estate Agent's particulars issued under the distinguished title of Messrs. Grimble and Outhwaite of Mount Street W. was clipped to an aluminium stand of his own invention. *For the attention of Mr. Aldo Cassidy* ran the deferential inscription; for Aldo was his first name. He drove, as always, with the greatest concentration, and now and then he hummed to himself with that furtive sincerity common to the tone-deaf.

He was traversing a moor. A flimsy ground mist shifted over rhines and willow trees, slipped in little puffs across the glistening hood of his car, but ahead the sky was bright and cloudless and the spring sun made emeralds of the approaching hills. Touching a lever he lowered the electric window and leaned one side of his head into the rush of air. At once rich smells of peat and silage filled his nostrils. Over the reverent purr of the car's engine he caught the sounds of cattle and the cry of a cowhand harmlessly insulting them.

"It's an idyll," he declared aloud. "It's an absolute idyll."

Better still it was a safe idyll, for in the whole wide beautiful world Aldo Cassidy was the only person who knew where he was.

3

Beyond his conscious hearing, a closed-off chamber of his memory echoed to the awkward chords of an aspiring pianist. Sandra, wife to Aldo, is extending her artistic range.

"Good news from Bristol," Cassidy said, talking over the music. "They think they can offer us a patch of land. We'll have to level it of course."

"Good," said Sandra his wife, and carefully rearranged her hands over the keyboard.

"It's a quarter of a mile from the largest boys' school and eight hundred yards from the girls'. The city authorities say there's a fair chance that if we do the levelling and donate the changing rooms, they'll put up a footbridge on the by-pass."

She played a ragged chord.

"Not an ugly one, I hope. Town planning is *extremely* important, Aldo."

"I know."

"Can I come?"

"Well you *have* got your clinic," he reminded her with tentative severity.

Another chord.

"Yes. Yes, I've got my clinic," Sandra agreed, her voice lilting slightly in counterpoint. "So you'll have to go alone, won't you? Poor Pailthorpe."

Pailthorpe was her private name for him, he could not remember why. Pailthorpe the Bear, probably; bears were their most popular fauna.

"I'm sorry," said Cassidy.

"It's not *your* fault," said Sandra. "It's the Mayor's, isn't it? After all," she added speculatively, "he *runs* the town, doesn't he?"

"Naughty Mayor," said Cassidy.

"Naughty Mayor," Sandra agreed.

"Spank him," Cassidy suggested.

"Spank, spank," gaily said Sandra, wife to Aldo, her face in combat with its shadows.

He was a fair-haired man of thirty-eight and quite handsome in certain lights. Like his car he was groomed with loving elegance. From the left-hand buttonhole to the breast pocket of his faultless suit ran a thin gold chain of

obvious usefulness whose purpose was nevertheless undefined. Aesthetically it perfectly answered the subdued
pin stripe of the cloth behind it; as a piece of rigging it
joined the head of the man to the heart, but there was no
telling which end if either held the mastery. In both build
and looks he might have served as an architectural prototype for the middle-class Englishman privately educated
between the wars; one who had felt the wind of battle but
never the fire of it. Heavy at the waist, short in the leg,
a squire always in the making, he possessed those dogged-
ly boyish features, at once mature and retarded, which
still convey a dying hope that his pleasures may be paid
for by his parents. Not that he was effeminate. True, the
mouth was well advanced from the rest of the face and
quite deeply sculptured under the lower lip. True also
that as he drove he was guilty of certain affectations which
pointed in the female direction, such as brushing aside his
forelock or putting back his head and wrinkling his eyes
as though a sudden headache had interfered with brilliant
thoughts. But if these mannerisms meant anything at all,
then most likely they reflected a pleasing sensitivity towards a world occasionally too shrill for him, an empathy as much parental as childish, rather than any
unwelcome tendencies left over from public school.

Clearly he was no stranger to the expense account.
An untaxable affluence was legible in the thickening of
the lower waistcoat (for his safety and comfort he had
unfastened the top button of his trousers) and in the
widths of white cuff which isolated his hands from manual
labour; and there was already about his neck and complexion a sleek rich gloss, a tan almost, *flambé* rather
than sun-given, which only balloon glasses, Bunsen burn-
ers, and the fumes of *crêpes suzette* can faithfully repro-
duce. Despite this evidence of physical well-being, or
perhaps in contrast to it, the outward Cassidy possessed in
some devious way the power, even the authority to disturb. Though he was not in the slightest degree pathetic
there was something to him which caught the eye and
demanded help. Somehow he managed to convey that
the encroachments of the flesh had not yet killed the
magic of the spirit.

As if in recognition of this protective rôle which Cassidy
unconsciously imposed on his environment, the interior of

the car was provided with many important adaptations designed to spare him the distressing consequences of collision. Not only had the walls and ceiling and doors been generously upholstered with additional layers of quilt; the steering wheel, the child-proof door handles—already deeply recessed in succulent cavities of felt—the glove compartment, brake lever, even the discreetly concealed fire extinguisher, each was separately encased in hand-stitched leather and padded with a pleasing flesh-like substance calculated to reduce the most drastic impact to no more than a caress. At the rear window a sun-proof canopy, electrically operated and bordered with small silk balls, hung poised to defend at any time the good man's neck against an overzealous sun or his eyesight against the harmful dazzle of alien headlights. As to the dashboard it was a veritable medicine chest of preventive physic: from blinker lights to ice-alert, from reserve battery to reserve oil supply, from safari petrol tank to auxiliary cooling system its switches anticipated every catastrophe known to nature and the manufacturing industries. Cassidy's was a car that conveyed rather than transported; a womb, one might even have thought, from whose padded, lubricated interior the occupant had yet to make his entry into the harder world.

"How far to Haverdown, do you mind?"

"Eh?"

"Haverdown." Should he spell it? Most likely the fellow was illiterate. "Haverdown. The great house. The manor."

The lolling mouth opened and partially closed, voicelessly mimicking the name; a grimy arm struck towards the hill. "Straight on up over look."

"And is it far, would you say?" Cassidy enquired loudly, as if addressing the deaf.

"Won't take you more than five minutes, will it, not in *her?*"

"Thanks a million. Good luck to you old son."

In the mirror the yokel's brown face, frozen into an expression of comic incredulity, watched him out of sight. Well, thought Cassidy, the fellow has seen something of the world today and two shillings won't make him drunk.

All nature, it seemed, had turned out for his procession. In cottage gardens romping peasant children put aside their ancient games and turned to stare at him as he glided by. How *pastoral*, he thought; how rude, how vital. From trees and hedgerows buds of varying shades of green were bursting forth with seasonable energy, while in the fields wild daffodils mingled with other flowers he could not identify. Leaving the village, he began climbing a hill. The high banks gave way to sloping wooded glades. Below him farms, fields, churches, and rivers faded into far horizons. Lulled by such a delightful prospect he abandoned himself to the contemplation of his quest.

My pleasurable quest, as the favoured after-dinner speaker called it, my *very pleasurable* quest.

"A quest for *what?*" a nagging voice enquired inside him. "A quest *towards*, or a quest *from?*"

With an airy shake of his head, Cassidy brushed aside such pedantries. Nonsense, he told his inward audience, I have come to buy a house. Inspect it, cost it, buy it. And if I have not informed my wife, that is my own affair.

"Shall you stay all night?" Sandra remarked very casually. The piano practice temporarily interrupted, they were finishing their evening meal.

"We may not get going till five or so," Cassidy replied, avoiding the direct answer. "It depends when the Mayor's free." A clause of conciliation: "I thought I might take a book to read. If you could find me one."

Slowly, hand in hand with his cultural advisor, Cassidy the aspiring reader paraded the ranks of Sandra's bookshelves.

"Now," she mused, very earnest. "What do Pailthorpes read when they go gallivanting in Bristol?"

"It's got to be something I can manage when I'm a bit tight," he warned. They both laughed. "And not—" recalling a previous selection "—*not* Jane Austen."

They settled for non-fiction, a *straight* book suitable to a tired Pailthorpe of little fantasy.

"Sometimes," said Sandra playfully, "I wonder whether you ever really see these people at all."

"I don't," said nimble Cassidy, volleying at the net. "She's a blonde and she's eight feet tall."

"*Sexy*," said Sandra, wife to Aldo, kissing her loyal man. "What's her name?"

Haverdown.

He hoped he had pronounced the word correctly. Such things can make a difference when one arrives in a new neighbourhood.

Haverdown.

Was the *a* long or short? To have or to haver?

A pigeon was barring his approach. He sounded his horn. Prudently it withdrew.

And the *down*: what did *down* mean? A country gentleman should know his derivations. *Down* as in descent, or *down* as in the rolling downs in England? A happy repartee occurred to him, as with the exaggerated gesture of those enjoying their own company the ready wit raised his eyebrows and smiled in quiet academic superiority. Or *down* like duck-down, fluff? Answer me that if you please Messrs. Grimble and Outhwaite of Mount Street W.

Haverdown.

It was a pretty name for all that, though names of course meant nothing in such cases. Stately too. Not Hall or Court or Grange, not Haverdown Manor even. Just Haverdown: a sovereign concept, as his Oxford tutor would have said, requiring no qualification. *Haverdown.* A man might well choose it as a title if such a thing were ever asked of him. "You know young Cassidy of Haverdown? Remarkable fellow. Flourishing business in London, gave it all up, came down here. Two years later made a going thing of farming. Knew damn all about it when he began, total duffer. Mind you they do say he's a bit of a financial wizard. Locals adore him of course. Generous to a fault."

About to consult the mirror in order light-heartedly to put a face to his baronial image, Cassidy veered sharply. *The entrance is marked by a Pair of finely pointed stone gateposts surmounted by ornamental Beasts dating from the sixteenth Century.* Directly before him, two disintegrating griffins, glumly clutching armorial shields, rose into the green darkness of a beech tree. Their feet were manacled to the plinth and their shoulders hunched from fatigue. Intently, Cassidy examined their scrolled shields. An eroded diagonal cross formed the central theme, feathers or recumbent serpents filled the upper triangle. He frowned in perplexity. Feathers were Wales, that much he knew; but was not the cross Saint Andrew? And was not Saint Andrew Scotland, hence the golf course?

Shifting gears, he set off along the drive. Patience. In due course he would research the matter, it would be an occupation for the winter months. He had always fancied himself as something of a local historian, browsing in county libraries, inspiring local digs, sending postcards to learned vicars.

"Perhaps," said Sandra, wife to Aldo, as they made ready for bed, *"next* time you go, I could come?"

"Of course you can," said Cassidy. "We'll make a special trip."

"An ordinary trip will do," said Sandra and put out the light.

Briefly the coppice closed round him. Over a carpet of bluebells he caught a glint of water between the trees. The drive returned him to the sunlight, passed a derelict cottage, skirted a rusted iron fence. Now a broken signpost drunkenly divided the approach. Tradesmen left and visitors right. I'm both, Cassidy thought gaily and took the right fork. Tulips lined the verges, poking their heads between the nettles. Lot of stock there, if only he could get at the weeds in time. The pond was overgrown. Dragonflies switched across the unbroken surface of the lily leaves, bullrushes almost obscured the boathouse. How fast was nature to reclaim her own, Cassidy reflected in growing exhilaration, how inexorable, how maternal was her will!

On its own grass plateau, between a ruined chapel and the picked skeleton of a fruithouse, Haverdown rose suddenly before him.

An Historic and Scheduled FORTIFIED MANOR HOUSE AND KEEP thirty Miles from Bath (Padding-

ton one Hour forty minutes) *Haverdown is a GEN-*
TLEMAN'S RESIDENCE FULLY EQUIPPED FOR
IMMEDIATE OCCUPATION WITH FIVE LOOSE
BOXES AND FORTY ACRES OF GOOD GRAZ-
ING. The style is part Tudor part Earlier with restora-
tions dating Chiefly from the Georgian period at which
time the original Keep was substantially rebuilt under
the genius of LORD Alfred de Waldebere. His many
fine Additions include a Fine Curved Staircase in the
Style of adam and a number of Fine ITALIAN BUSTS
of great Value which are included in the Asking price.
Since Earliest Times Haverdown has been the Home
and Fortress of the de Waldebere family.

THE GEORGIAN PORTION. Perfectly sited on a
natural Spur the distinguished south Face discreetly
Masters some of the finest Scenery in Somerset. The
elevations are of old Brick, mellowed by Time and
weather to a pleasing russet Hue. The centre block
is crowned by a Shallow pediment of Bath stone. Eight
freestone Treads worn by the feet of ages lead to a fine
imposing curved Portico carried by six Individual Pil-
lars. To the West, between the Chapel and the Fruit-
house, a superb Cupola in need of Minor Repair
offsets the symmetry. The Pigeon croft is in its unspoilt
Original condition providing ample Space for heating
unit, Guesthouse or GENTLEMAN'S STUDIO RE-
TREAT. In rear GARDEN cast-lead cupid in TRA-
DITIONAL POSE, valued separately see annexe.

THE EARLIER PORTION consists of fine battle-
mented TOWER with Original steps and Bellchamber
adjoining to a Row of tudor Almshouses. Central to
these stands the castellated Great Hall and Refectory
with fine basements under and OLD MOAT ROUND.
In the Great Hall, surely one of the finest in the West
of england, a Minstrel Gallery dating from the reign of
King Edward the 1st comprises the principal Feature.
From here according to local lore, journeying Musi-
cians paid their tribute to SIR Hugo de Waldebere the
first Recorded Owner of Haverdown until the Year
1261 when he was Outlawed for felony. The House
passed to his younger Son whereafter no Tenancy is
recorded until 1760 when Lord ALFRED returned
from Foreign Parts to rebuild the Home of his Fore-
bears, probably after Catholic Persecutions had tem-

*porarily dispersed them. The Gardens are conceived
on the CLASSICAL English Pattern of containing Nature without undue Formality and are in need of upkeep all enquiries*
SOLELY THROUGH ABOVE NAMED
REFER JR/P MR. GRIMBLE

Carefully replacing the prospectus in its stand and de-
taching a light cashmere overcoat from its ingenious
hanger beside the rear window, Cassidy happened to
glance backwards past the baby seat and the silk balls of
the blind, and was subjected to a remarkable hallucination.
The drive had vanished. Thick walls of green, pierced
with dark tunnels, had closed upon his route and cut
him off from the outside world. He was alone in a magic
cave of dark green; at the pantomime, his father's guest;
in childhood, thirty years ago. . . .

Afterwards, he was well able to explain this optical illusion. A strand of vapour, he assured himself, such as lay
upon the moor, had settled below the level of his immediate vision, and by some trick of light assumed the colour
of the foliage. It had been raining (as indeed it had) and
the moisture on the drive, aided by the low sun, had set
up a green shimmer which gave it the appearance of high
grass. Or he himself, by the quick movement of his head
after the long drive, had transposed upon his own vision
images from other places . . . a natural coincidence therefore, such as mirages are made of.

Nevertheless, for an instant, and perhaps for much
longer in terms of the interior experience of Aldo Cassidy,
he had the sense of being caught up in a world that was
not as controllable as the world he was accustomed to: a
world, in short, capable of dismaying metaphysical leaps,
and although a second examination soon restored the
drive to its rightful position in the scheme of things, its
agility, or rather the remembrance of it, caused him to
remain seated for a moment while he collected himself. It
was with some distrust, therefore, as well as a lingering
sense of disconnection, that he finally opened the door and
cautiously lowered one well-shod foot on to the capricious
surface of the earth.

"And enjoy yourself," Sandra his protective spouse had warned him at breakfast in her army officer voice. "Don't let them *browbeat* you. Remember it's *you* who are doing the giving."

"I'll try," Cassidy promised with an English hero's smile.

His first impression, far from pleasurable, was that he had stepped into an air raid. A fierce evening wind had come up from the east, battering his eardrums and crashing like gunfire into the elms. Above him, recklessly swirling rooks dived and screamed at his intrusion. The house itself had already been hit. It groaned from every door and casement, waving its useless limbs in outrage, slapping them in agony against its own defenceless walls. At its base lay the débris of masonry and tiles. A fallen cable passed close over his head and ran the length of the garden. For one disgusting moment Cassidy fancied, looking up at it, that he saw a dead pigeon hanging from its frayed binding, but it was only an old shirt left behind by a careless gypsy and wound upon itself by a careless wind. Odd, he thought, recovering his composure: looks like one of mine, the kind we wore a few years back, striped, with stiff collars and a generous width of cuff.

He was extremely cold. The weather, which had looked so gentle and inviting from within the car, now assaulted him with a quite unnatural venom, inflating his thin coat with barbarous draughts and lashing at the cuffs of his tailored lightweight suit. Indeed so sudden and so fierce was the first impact of reality upon his internal reveries that Cassidy was actually tempted to return then and there to the safety of his car, and it was only a late assertion of the bulldog spirit that stayed his hand. After all, if he was to spend the rest of his life here he might as well start getting used to the climate. He had driven, by his own standards, a long way, a hundred miles or so; was he seriously proposing to turn back for a mere breeze? Resolutely fastening his collar he embarked in earnest upon the first phase of his inspection.

He called this process *taking the feel of the place*. It was one he had rehearsed often and which involved the sampling of many intangible elements. The setting for instance: is it hostile or amicable? Does it offer seclusion, which is desirable, or isolation, which is not? Does it embrace the occupant, or expose him? Was he—a vital question—born here, is *that* a feasibility?

Despite the cold, his initial impressions were not unfavourable. The park, which clearly provided the view from the principal windows of the house, had a lush pastoral quality which was distinctly soothing. The trees were deciduous (a rare advantage since he secretly found conifers too bleak) and their great age imbued them with a fatherly gentleness.

He listened.

The wind had dropped and the rooks were slowly settling. From the moor, where the sea fog still clung, the rasp of a handsaw vied with the grumbling of livestock. He examined the grazing. Good fencing there, ample space for ponies provided there was no yew to poison them. He had read somewhere, probably in Cobbett, whose *Rural Rides* he had studied for School Certificate, that yew poisoned ponies, and it was one of those aimless cruelties of nature which had remained impressed upon his memory.

Palominos, that was the word.

I shall have palominos. No need for shelter, the chestnuts will provide the shelter. The Welsh variety is best: hardy beasts, he had heard from all sides, self-sufficient and cheap to run. The right temperament too: townsmen could manhandle them without danger of reprisal.

He sniffed the air.

Woodsmoke, damp pine, and the indefinable mustiness that is fostered by neglect. I find no fault with it.

Now at last, quite coolly in his outward manner, he turned to the house and gave it his critical attention. A deep silence had fallen over the hilltop. In the trees nothing stirred. The shirt hung motionless from its cable. For long minutes he remained as if in prayer, his gloved hands loosely linked over his stomach, his shoulders well back, his fair head a little to one side, a survivor mourning his lost comrades.

Aldo Cassidy in the twilight of his thirty-ninth spring surveyed the elegant wreck of a dozen English generations.

The light was dying even as he stood there. Red shafts glinted from the buckled weather vane, touched what little glass remained in the sash windows, and were gone. A rock, he thought, with a gush of proud Victorian purple. A mountain peak against the evening sky, unscalable and immutable, an organic outcrop of English history. A rock, he repeated, his romantic heart pounding with half-remembered lines of English poetry; broken from the earth, whose name is England. A rock, fashioned by the hand of centuries, hewn by God's masons, guarded by His soldiers.

What would I not give to have been born of such a place? How much bigger, how much braver could I not be? To draw my name, my faith, my ancestry, even my profession perhaps from such a monument of heroic ages: to be a crusader still, serving not brashly but with humble courage a cause too evident to be defined? To swim in my own moat, to cook in my own refectory, to dine in my own Great Hall, to meditate in my own cell? To walk in my own crypt among the shell-torn standards of my forebears; to nurture tenants, counsel wayward servants, and till the earth in pleasingly dilapidated tweeds?

Gradually a vision formed before the dreamer's inner eye.

It is Christmas evening and the trees are bare against the early sunset. A solitary figure, no longer young, dressed in costly but unobtrusive habit, is riding through the long shadows of the chestnut avenue. The horse, well conscious of its precious burden, is docile even in sight of home. A lantern is beckoning in the portico, merry servants hasten to the door. "Pleasant ride then, Mr. Aldo?" "Not bad, Giles, not bad. No no I'll rub him down myself, thank you. Good evening, Mrs. Hopcroft. The celebrations well advanced I trust?"

And within, what then? No children, grandchildren tugging at his hand? No amiable lady in a long tweed skirt woven on the premises, no *Eve,* descending the Fine Curved Staircase in the Style of *adam,* holding a bowl of potpourri in her unhardened hands? No Sandra, younger by a dozen years, piano-less, free of her private darkness, unquestioning of Aldo's male sovereignty? Born to the gracious life, fresh to him, witty, varied, and adoring? *"Poor love you must be frozen through. I lit a fire in the library. Come, let me help you with your boots."*

There was no within. Cassidy on such occasions concerned himself resolutely with exteriors.

It was all the more surprising to him, therefore, chancing to look irritably upwards at a flock of doves whose restless fluttering had disrupted his reflections, to notice a faint but undeniable curl of woodsmoke rising from the western chimney stack and a real light, very yellow like an oil light, swinging gently in that same portico through which, in his imagination, he had that minute passed.

"Hullo lover," a pleasant voice said. "Looking for someone, are we?"

2

Now Cassidy prided himself on his aplomb at moments of crisis. In business circles he had a reputation for thinking on his feet and he considered it fairly won. "Deft" they had called him in the *Times Business News* during a recent take-over battle. "That gentle trouble-shooter." The quality derived not least from a refusal to recognise the extent of any peril, and it was backed by a solid understanding of the uses of money. Cassidy's first response therefore was to ignore the strangeness of the address and to give the man good evening.

"Jesus," the voice said, "is it?"

His second was to walk casually to his car, not by any means in order to escape but rather to identify himself as its owner and therefore, by definition, as a potential purchaser of substance. He also had in mind the agents' particulars on their aluminium stand which gave the proof, if such were needed, that he was not a wilful trespasser. He felt very badly towards the agents. It was the agents after all who had sent him, they who had given him the clearest assurances that the house was unoccupied, and they who would tomorrow pay very dearly for that error. "It's an Executors' sale, old boy," Outhwaite had croaked to him on the telephone in the fatuous tone of conspiracy which only estate agents seem to acquire. "Offer them half and they'll cut your arm off." Well, Cassidy would see who lost an arm after this adventure. Backing out of his car with the duplicated pages prominently displayed in his free hand, he became uncomfortably conscious of the fixity of his interrogator's gaze represented by the unwavering beam of the lantern.

"This is *Haverdown*, isn't it?" he asked, speaking up the steps and using the shorter *a*. His tone was precisely pitched. Puzzled but not dismayed, a dash of indignation to preserve his authority: the respectable citizen is disturbed in the conduct of his lawful business.

17

"I expect so, lover," the lantern replied not altogether playfully. "Want to buy it do we?"

The speaker's features were still hidden by the lamplight, but from the position at which the head was measured against the lintel of the door Cassidy was able to guess a person of his own height; and from the width of the shoulders, where he could define them against the interior darkness of the house, of his own build as well. The rest of his information, as he ascended the Eight freestone Treads worn by the feet of ages, was gained by ear. The man was of his own age too, but more confident, good at addressing the troops and coping with the dead. The voice, moreover, was remarkably compelling. Dramatic even, he would say. Tense. Balanced on a soft beguiling edge. Cassidy detected also—for he had a quick ear for social music—a certain regional deviation, possibly in the Gaelic direction, a brogue rather than an accent, which in no way affected his good opinion of the stranger's breeding. *The cross of Saint Andrew and the feathers of Wales:* well here, if he was not mistaken, was the harp of Ireland. He had reached the top step.

"Well I'd like to consider it certainly. Your agents, Grimble and Outhwaite sent me"—slightly moving the mimeographed sheets to indicate that the evidence was in his hand. "Did they get in touch with you by any chance?"

"Not a word," the lantern replied evenly. "Not a peep, not a funeral note."

"But I made the appointment almost a week ago! I do think they might have rung you or something. I mean don't *you?*"

"Phone's cut off, lover. It's the end of the world out here. Just the moo cows and the chickadees. And wild rooks, of course, seeking whom they may devour, the buggers."

It seemed to Cassidy more necessary than ever to preserve the line of his enquiry.

"But surely they could have *written* after all," he protested, anxious to insert between them the spectre of a common enemy. "I mean really these people *are* the end."

The answer was quite a while in coming.

"Maybe they don't know we're here."

Throughout the whole course of this exchange Cassidy had been the subject of minute scrutiny. The lamp, playing slowly over his body, had examined first his handmade shoes, then his suit, and was now engaged in deciphering the crest on his dark blue tie.

"Jesus, what's that?" the soft voice asked. "Indians?"

"A dining club actually," Cassidy confessed, grateful for the question. "A thing called the Nondescripts."

A long pause.

"Oh *no*," the voice protested at last, genuinely shocked. "Oh Jesus, what a terrible bloody name! I mean what would Nietzsche make of that, for Christ's sake? You'll be calling yourselves the Filthy Cameldrivers next."

Cassidy was not at all used to such treatment. In the places where he spent his money even his signature was an unnecessary formality, and in the ordinary way of things he would have protested vigorously against any suggestion that his credit or his person—let alone his dining club—was in doubt. But this was not the ordinary way: instead of a surge of indignation, Cassidy was once more overcome by the same uncommon feeling of disconnection. It was as though the figure behind the lamp were not a separate figure at all, but his own, mysteriously reflected from the depths of the liquid twilight; as though his swifter, freer self were examining, by the light of that unusual lantern, the features of his pedestrian other half. And after all, the Nondescripts *were* a rather seedy lot; he had thought so more than once of late. Brushing aside such bizarre inventions, he finally managed a show of heat.

"Look here," he said quite strongly. "I don't want to intrude, I can perfectly well come back another time. Assuming you *want* to sell of course," he added, to give extra sting.

The voice did not hurry to console him.

"*You're* not intruding, lover," it said at last, as if passing a considered verdict. "You're *gorgeous*, that's my view. In the first position. No fooling. We haven't had a bourgeois for years."

The beam descended. In the same moment a ray of red sunlight, reflected from the upper window of the chapel, broke like a tiny dawn over the interior of the porch and provided Cassidy with a first sight of his examiner. He was, as Cassidy had already suspected, very

handsome. Where Cassidy curved, his examiner went
straight. Where Cassidy was weak, his examiner was resolute; where concessive, zealous; where Cassidy was fluid,
the other was rock, and where he was pale and fair, his
examiner was dark and sudden and eager. From a handsome face dark eyes shone with the greatest animation; a
Gaelic smile, at once predatory and knowing, illuminated
its features.

So far so good. Still seeking, however, to assign him to
one of the social categories into which the world is naturally divided, Cassidy transferred his concentration to the
man's attire. He wore a black coat of the kind favoured
by Indian gentlemen, midway between a dinner jacket
and a military blazer, but cut with a decided oriental
flair. His feet were bare and his lower body was encased
in what appeared to be a skirt.

"Good Lord," Cassidy said involuntarily, and was about
to offer some further apology such as: "Oh my God, you
were in the middle of your bath"; or: "Oh look here this
is monstrous of me I've got you out of bed," when the lantern turned sharply away from him and shone upon the
car.

There was no need for the lantern at all—the pale
coachwork stood out excellently against the half-light, a
safety factor which Cassidy was well aware of—but the
examiner used it all the same, less to observe, perhaps,
than to stroke the pure outlines in slow caressing movements of the beam, much as a moment earlier he had
studied its owner.

"Yours is it, lover?"

"Yes it is actually."

"Your very own? All of it?"

Cassidy laughed easily, presuming a veiled reference to
hire purchase, a form of payment which (since he had no
need of it) he considered one of the ills of his generation.

"Well yes. I think it's the only way really, don't you?"

For some while the examiner made no reply but remained in deepest concentration, his body motionless, the
lantern swinging gently in his hand, his eyes intent upon
the car.

"Jesus," he whispered at last. "Jesus. There's a hearse
for a Nondescript."

Cassidy had watched people admire his car before. He
had even encouraged them. He was perfectly capable, on

a Saturday morning for instance, returning from shopping or some other semi-recreational errand, and finding a small group of enthusiasts gathered along its elegant length, of offering them some account of its history and properties, and demonstrating from a stationary position some of its more unusual modifications. He considered this democratic open-heartedness to be one of his most likeable characteristics: life had wrought its distinctions true enough, but when it came to the fellowship of the road Cassidy counted himself little better than the next man. His host's interest however was of a different sort. Once again it appeared to be an examination in principle, a fundamental questioning of certain unstated values which were inherent in the car's existence, and it only added to Cassidy's unease. Did he consider it vulgar? Was it inferior to his own? The upper classes, he knew very well, had strong views on the display of wealth, but surely the car's *specialness* put it beyond the reach of such superficial charges? Somebody has to own it, after all. Just as they have to own Haverdown, ha, ha. Perhaps he should say something, offer some deprecatory phrase? There were several which in other circumstances he might have ventured: "It's only a toy really . . . well I think of it as a sort of man's mink coat . . . of course I couldn't begin to run it without the Company . . . present from the taxpayer I'm afraid . . ." He was still considering such a move when he felt his left arm seized in a grip of unexpected force.

"Come on, lover," the voice said, beguiling. "Get your cork out, I'm freezing."

"Well, if you're sure it's not inconvenient—" Cassidy began as he almost stumbled over the rotting threshold.

He never discovered whether it was convenient or not. The heavy door had closed behind him. The lantern had gone. He was standing in the total blackness of an unknown interior with only his host's friendly grasp to guide him.

Waiting for his eyes to grow accustomed to the light, Cassidy endured many of the hallucinations which afflict the temporarily blinded. He found himself first in the Scala Cinema at Oxford, edging past rows of unseen knees, trampling apologetically on unseen feet. Some were

hard, some soft; all were hostile. There were seven cinemas at Oxford in the days when Cassidy was privileged
to receive his higher education, and he had got round
them nicely in a week. Soon, he thought, the grey rectangle will open before me and a dark-haired girl in period
costume will unbutton her blouse in French to the appreciative whistles of my fellow academics.

Before any such delight was afforded him, however,
he was abruptly translated to the Natural History Museum
in South Kensington whither one of his stepmothers had
threatened to consign him as a punishment for self-abuse.
"You're no better than an animal," she furiously assured
him. "So you'd best go and join them. For ever." Though
his vision was by now clearing, he found much evidence
to support the nightmares: prickly upholstery redolent
of cinemas, the pungent smells of moulting fur and forma-
lin, the amputated heads of elks and wildebeests which
glared down on him in the glazed terror of their last
agony, looming mammoth shapes draped in white dust
covers.

Gradually, to his relief, more familiar images reassured
him of human habitation. A grandfather clock, an oak
sideboard, a Jacobean dining table; a stone fireplace
armed with crossed muskets and the pleasingly familiar
crest of the de Waldeberes.

"My goodness," said Cassidy at last in what he hoped
was a voice of awe.

"Like it?" his companion asked. Retrieving the lantern
from Cassidy knew not where, he carelessly flicked the
beam over the uneven flagstones.

"Superb. Quite superb."

They were in the Great Hall. Chinks of grey light
marked the tall outlines of the shuttered windows. Pikes,
assagais and antlers adorned the upper levels; packing
cases and mouldering books were strewn over the floor.
Directly before them hung a gallery of dense black oak.
Behind it stone arches mouthed the openings to dismal
corridors. The smell of dry rot was unmistakable.

"Want to see the rest?"

"I'd adore to."

"The whole thing? Warts and all?"

"From top to bottom. It's fabulous. What date is the gallery by the way? I should know but I've forgotten."

"Oh Jesus, some of it was made from Noah's Ark, no kidding. So they tell me anyway."

Laughing dutifully Cassidy could not fail nevertheless to detect, above the familiar smells of antiquity, the fumes of whisky on his host's breath.

Ha la, he thought with an inward smile of recognition. Les aristos. Slice them where you will, they're all the same. Decadent, devil-may-care . . . but actually rather marvellous in an other-worldish way.

"Tell me," he asked politely, as they once more turned a corner into darkness, "is the furniture for sale too?" His voice had acquired a new Englishness as he offered it for the aristocrat's consideration.

"Not till we've moved out, lover. Got to have something to sit on, haven't we?"

"Of course. But later?"

"Sure. Have what you like."

"It would only be the smaller things," said Cassidy cautiously. "I've quite a lot already, actually. *Put by,* you know."

"Collector, eh?"

"Well a bit, certainly. But only when the price is right," he added on the same defensive note. *If there's one thing your English gentleman does understand, it's the value of money.* "I say do you think you could shine that light a little higher? I can't see a thing."

The corridor was lined with portraits of gentle soldiers and murderous civilians. The beam revealed them only capriciously, and this was unfortunate, for Cassidy was sure that, given the chance, he could have identified in their varied features traces of his eccentric escort: the brilliant erratic smile for instance, the pirate's eyes lit from within, the crop of black hair that fell so nobly over the powerful brow.

The lantern descended what appeared to be a short staircase, leaving him again in the deepest darkness.

"It's interminable," Cassidy said with a nervous laugh, and then: "I'd never have done this alone. I'm rather afraid of the dark to be honest, always have been. Some

people don't like heights, I don't like the dark." In point
of fact, Cassidy did not care for heights either, but there
seemed no point in spoiling the analogy. "Have you been
here long?" he asked, receiving no absolution for this
confession.

"Ten days."

"I meant your family."

The beam shone briefly on a rusted iron coat hanger,
then sank to the floor. "Oh Christ . . . for ever, man, for
ever." '

"And it was your father who . . ."

For an uncomfortable moment Cassidy feared he had
again trodden upon too delicate ground: a recent death,
after all, is not a subject one discusses in the dark. There
was quite a delay before he had his answer.

"My uncle *actually*," the soft voice confessed,
and gave a small revealing sigh. "But we were very
close."

"I'm sorry," Cassidy murmured.

"He was gored by a bull," his guide continued in a
more cheerful tone which reinforced the brogue. "So at
least it was quick. None of your ugly lingering, I mean,
the peasants dropping in with gruel."

"Well that's some consolation," said Cassidy. "Was he
old?"

"Very. And I mean that bull—"

"Yes?" said Cassidy, puzzled.

The lantern appeared to shake in a sudden paroxysm
of grief. "Well the bull was *terribly* old himself. I
mean it was kind of death in slow motion. Come to think
of it, I don't know how they caught each other up."

Comedy had evidently dispelled tragedy, for now a wild
boyish laughter rose to the unseen roof, the beam swayed
merrily in time to its peals, and a strong hand descended
on Cassidy's shoulder.

"Listen it's great to have you. Great. You're doing me
a power of good, and that's the honest truth. Jesus, I've
been so bored: reading John Donne to the chickadees.
Imagine. Great poet, mind, but what an audience. The
way they look at you. Jesus. Listen I've had a wee drink,
you don't mind that now?"

Very much to his surprise, Cassidy felt a definite tweak
on what the law courts call the upper thigh.

"Like a drop yourself now and then, eh?"

"Indeed yes."

"Specially when you're lonely, or down on your luck a mite?"

"And at other times too, I promise you."

"Don't do that," the stranger said shortly, with a sudden change of humour. "Don't promise a thing."

They descended two stairs.

"Who the hell do you meet round here anyway?" he resumed in his jocular tone. "Even the bloody gypsies won't talk to you. You know, Christ, it's class, class all the way."

"Oh dear," said Cassidy.

The hand still guided his shoulder. As a rule Cassidy did not like to be handled, particularly by men, but the contact disturbed him less than he might have expected.

"What about all those acres?" he asked. "Don't *they* keep you busy any more?"

The smell of woodsmoke which Cassidy had hitherto admired for its rural fragrance became suddenly oppressive.

"Ah, fuck the acres. Who the hell wants land any more? Form-filling . . . rabies . . . pollution . . . . American air bases. It's over, I'm telling you. Unless you're in mink of course. Mink are great."

"Yes," Cassidy agreed, somewhat confused by this idiosyncratic description of the farmer's problems. "Yes I hear mink can make a *lot* of money."

"Hey listen. You religious at all?"

"Well half and half . . ."

"There's this fellow in County Cork calling himself the one true living God, have you read about him? J. Flaherty of Hillside, Beohmin. All over the papers it was. Do you think there's anything in it at all?"

"I really don't know," said Cassidy.

Obedient to his companion's whim, Cassidy allowed himself to be brought to a halt. The dark face came very close to his and he was suddenly aware of tension.

"Only I wrote to him see, challenging him to a duel. I thought that's who you might be."

"Oh," said Cassidy. "Oh no, well I'm afraid I'm not."

"You've a trace of him though, all the same, you've definitely a spot of divinity in you, I could tell it a mile off."

"Oh."

"Oh yes."

They had turned a second corner and entered another corridor even longer and more derelict than the first. At its far end red firelight was playing on a stone wall and whorls of smoke were curling towards them through the open doorway. Seized by a sudden sense of lassitude, Cassidy had the eerie feeling of walking through an adverse tide. The darkness was dragging against his feet like currents of warm water. The smoke, he thought, the smoke has made me dizzy.

"Bloody chimney's bunged up. We tried to get the fellow to fix it but they never come, do they?"

"It's the same in London," Cassidy agreed warming to his favourite topic. "You can ring them, write to them, have an appointment, it makes absolutely no difference. They come *when* they want and charge *what* they want."

"Bastards. Jesus, my grandfather would have flogged the lot of them."

"You can't do that these days I'm afraid," said Cassidy loudly, in the voice of one who also yearned for a simpler social order. "They'd be down on you like a ton of bricks."

"I'll tell you this for nothing, it's time we had another bloody war. Listen, they say he's about forty-three years of age."

"Who?"

"God. This fellow in Cork. That's a bloody odd age for him to choose, don't you think so? I mean let's have him young or old, that's what I said to him see, who the hell thinks he's God at forty-three? Still, when I saw the car, then you . . . well you can't blame me can you? I mean if God *was* going to run a car, well that Bentley of yours . . ."

"How *is* the servant problem round here?" Cassidy enquired, cutting him short.

"Bloody awful. All they want is fags, telly, and fucks."

"I suppose they get lonely. Like you."

Cassidy was now quite recovered from his initial nervousness. His companion's racy tones, echoing ahead of him, were for all their quaintness pleasantly reassuring; the firelight was now definitely closer and the sight of it, after their inward journey through the successively darker chambers of the enormous mansion, gave him further cheer. His composure however was barely won before it was violently intruded upon by a new and wholly unannounced phenomenon. A sudden waft of tinny music issued from a side doorway and a girl crossed their path.

Cassidy in fact saw her twice.

Once silhouetted against the smoky firelight at the end of the corridor, and once in the direct beam of the lantern as she stopped and turned her head to look at them, at Cassidy first and then in cool question at the torchbearer. Her stare was straight and by no means welcoming. She held a towel over one arm and a small transistor radio in her hand. Her copious auburn hair was banked on top of her head as if to keep it out of the wet, and Cassidy recognised, as they briefly exchanged glances, that she was listening to the same programme which he had been playing in the car, a selection of Frank Sinatra's music on the theme of male solitude. These impressions, fragmented as they were by the wandering beam of the lantern, the flickering of the firelight, and the clouds of woodsmoke, did not by any means run consecutively. The girl's appearance, her fractional hesitation, her double glance were but flashes upon his heightened consciousness. She was gone in a moment, vanishing into another doorway, but not before Cassidy had observed, with the helpless detachment which often accompanies a wholly unexpected experience, that she was not only beautiful but naked. Indeed, so utterly improbable was the apparition, so irreconcilable its effect upon Cassidy's beleaguered fantasy, that he would have discounted her altogether—fed her at once into his ever-ready apparatus of disbelief—had not the beam of the lantern firmly pointed him the proof of her terrestrial existence.

She had been walking on tiptoe. She must have been quite used to going barefoot, for each toemark was drawn separately in round spots on the flagstone like the print of a small animal in the snow.

3

Long ago in a great restaurant an elderly lady had stolen
Cassidy's fish. She had been sitting beside him at an adjoining table facing into the room, and with one movement she had swept the fish—a sole Waleska generously
garnished with cheese and assorted seafoods—into her
open tartan handbag. Her timing was perfect. Cassidy
happened to look upwards in response to an inner call—a
girl probably, but perhaps a passing dish which he had
almost ordered in preference to his Waleska—and when
he looked down again the fish had gone and only a pink
sludge across the plate, a glutinous trail of cornflour,
cheese and particles of shrimp, marked the direction it
had taken. His first response was disbelief. He had eaten
the fish and in his distraction not even tasted it. But *how*
had he eaten it? the Great Detective asked himself. With
his fingers? His knife and fork were clean. The fish was a
mirage: the waiter had not yet brought it, Cassidy was
looking at the dirty plate left by a guest who had preceded
him.

Then he saw the tartan handbag. Its handles were
clamped tight together, but a telltale pink smear was
clearly visible on one brass ball of the clasp. Call the
waiter, he thought: "This lady has stolen my fish." Con-
front the thief, summon the police, demand that she open
her handbag.

But her posture of spinsterly composure as she continued to sip her apéritif, one hand curled lightly in her
napkin, was too much for him. Signing the bill he quietly
left the restaurant, never to return.

Following the lantern into the smoke-filled drawing room,
Cassidy underwent the same symptoms of psychic disar-
ray. Had the girl existed, or was she the creation of his
lively erotic fantasy? Was she a ghost? A de Waldebere

heiress, for instance, murdered in her bath by the reckless Sir Hugo? But family ghosts do not leave footprints nor carry transistor radios, and are certainly not constructed of such eminently persuasive flesh. Assuming then that the girl was real and that he had seen her, should he as a matter of protocol venture some casual comment suggesting he had not? Imply that he had been studying a portrait or an architectural feature at the critical moment of her appearance? Ask his host whether he was all alone here or who looked after him?

He was still wrestling with the problem when he heard himself addressed in what he took to be a foreign language.

"Alc?"

To compound Cassidy's sense of unreality he had the strong impression of being cut off by fog, for the enormous fireplace was emitting billows of cannon smoke over the stone floor and heavy palls already hung from the rafters overhead. The same fire, which seemed to consist entirely of kindling wood, provided their only source of light, for the lantern was now extinguished and the windows, like those in the Great Hall, were firmly shuttered.

"I'm awfully sorry. I don't think I understand."

"*Alc*, lover. Alcohol. *Whisky*."

"O thank you. Alcohol. Alc." He laughed. "Yes indeed I'd love an alc. It's quite a long drive from Bath actually. Well *fussy*, you know. All those narrow lanes and side turnings. *Alc*. Haha."

Mistress? Lecherous housemaid? Incestuous sister? A gypsy whore slunk in from the woods? Fiver a bang and free bath after?

"You want to try walking it." Glass in hand, the tall figure rose massively at him out of the smoke. If we were the same size, thought Cassidy, how are you now bigger? "Eight bloody hours it took us, with all God's limousines damn near running us into the hedge. It's enough to turn a man to drink, I'm telling you." The brogue was even stronger. "Still *you* wouldn't do that would you, lover? Carve us into the ditch, and not even stop to set the bone?"

A call girl perhaps, sent down by disgraceful agencies? Question: how can you call a call girl when your phone's cut off?

"Certainly not. I'm a great believer in defensive driving."

"Are you now?"

The dark eyes seemed, with this question, to invade still further Cassidy's unprotected consciousness.

"Look my name's Cassidy," he said as much to reassure himself as to inform his host.

"Cassidy? Jesus that's a lovely native name if ever I heard one. Hey, was it you robbed all those banks then? Is that where you got your money from?"

"Well I'm afraid not," said Cassidy silkily. "I had to work a little harder for it than that."

Emboldened by the aptness of his retort, Cassidy now undertook an examination of his host as frank as that which he himself had recently undergone. The garment which encased his dark legs was neither a skirt nor a bath towel nor yet a kilt, but a very old curtain embroidered with faded serpents and ripped at the edges as if by angry hands. He wore it off the hip, low at the front and higher at the back like a man about to bathe himself in the Ganges. His breast under the black jacket was bare, but garnished with clusters of rich black hair which descended in a thin line down his stomach before opening again into a frank pubic shadow.

"Like it?" his host enquired, handing him a glass.

"I beg your pardon?"

"*Shamus* is the name, lover. *Shamus.*"

Shamus. Shamus de Waldebere . . . look him up in Debrett.

From the direction of the doorway Cassidy heard Frank Sinatra singing about a girl he knew in Denver.

"Hey Helen," Shamus called over Cassidy's shoulder. "It's not Flaherty after all, it's Cassidy. *Butch* Cassidy. He's come to buy the house now poor Uncle Charlie's dead and gone. Cassidy me old friend, shake hands with a very lovely lady, lately of Troy and now reduced to the abominable state of—"

"How do you do," said Helen.

"Matrimony," said Shamus.

She was covered, if not yet fully dressed.

Wife, he thought glumly. I should have known. The Lady Helen de Waldebere, and all doors closed.

There is no established method, even to a formalist of Cassidy's stamp, of greeting a lady of great family whom you have just met naked in a corridor. The best that he could manage was a hog-like grunt, accompanied by a watery academic smile and a puckering of the eyes, designed to indicate to those familiar with his signals that he was a short-sighted person of minimal libido in the presence of someone who had hitherto escaped his notice. Helen on the other hand, with looks and breeding on her side and time to think in the dressing room, displayed a stately composure. She was even more beautiful dressed than not. She wore a housecoat of devotional simplicity. A high collar enfolded her noble neck, lace cuffs her slender wrists. Her auburn hair was combed long like Juliet's and her feet were still bare. Her breasts, which despite his simulated myopia he could not help remarking, were unsupported, and trembled delicately as she moved. Her hips were similarly unbound, and with each balanced stride a white knee, smooth as marble, peeped demurely through the division of her robe. English to the core, thought Cassidy to his relief, what an entry; what a dash she'd cut in trade. Switching off the wireless with a simple movement of her index finger and thumb, she placed it on the sofa table, smoothed the dust cover as if it were the finest linen, then gravely shook his hand and invited him to sit down. She accepted a drink and apologised for the mess in a low, almost a humble tone. Cassidy said he quite understood, he knew what it was to move, he had been through it several times in the last few years. Somehow, without trying, he managed to suggest that each move had been for the better.

"My God, even moving the *office*, when one has secretaries and assistants, even one's own workmen, it takes months. Literally *months*. So what it's like here . . ."

"Where is your office?" Helen asked politely.

Cassidy's opinion of her rose still higher.

"South Audley Street," he said promptly. "West One. Just off Park Lane, actually. We went in there last spring." He wanted to add that she might have read about it in the *Times Business News* but modestly he forebore.

"Oh how *very* nice." Chastely rearranging her skirts to cover her peerless thighs, she sat down on the sofa.

Towards her husband she showed a greater reserve. Her eyes seldom left his face and Cassidy did not fail to notice their darting expression of concern. How well, as always, did he understand a pretty woman's feelings! A drunken husband was liability enough. But who could tell what other blows her pride had suffered in the last months, the fights with lawyers, the towering death duties, the painful partings from family retainers, the tattered keepsakes in the silent desk? And how many potential purchasers in that time had swept brutally through the treasured chambers of her youth, mouthed their gross objections, and left without a word of hope?

I will ease her burden, he decided; I will take over the conversation.

Having concisely rehearsed the reasons for his unheralded arrival, he laid the blame squarely at the door of Grimble and Outhwaite:

"I've nothing against them, they're very good people in their way. I've dealt with them for a number of years and I shall go on dealing with them no doubt, but like all these old firms they get complacent. Slack." Under the velvet, the steel showed. "I mean to take this up with them in quite a big way as a matter of fact."

Shamus, who had crossed his legs under the curtain and was leaning back in an attitude of critical reflection, merely nodded with energetic approval and said, "Attaboy Cassidy," but Helen assured him that his visit was perfectly convenient, he was very welcome at any time and it made no difference really:

"*Does* it Shamus?"

"None at all, lover," said Shamus heartily. "We're having a ball."

And resumed, with a complacency amounting almost to pride of ownership, his study of his unexpected guest.

"I'm so sorry about the smoke," said Helen.

"Oh it's quite all right," said Cassidy restraining himself with difficulty from wiping away a tear. "I rather like it actually. A wood fire is one of the things we just can't buy in London. Not at any price I'm afraid."

"It's all my own fault," Shamus confessed. "We ran out of firewood so I sawed up the table."

Shamus and Cassidy laughed loudly at this good joke and Helen after a moment's doubt joined in. Her laugh, he noticed with approval, was modest and admiring; he did not care for women's humour as a rule, fearing it to be directed against himself, but Helen's was different, he could tell: she knew her place and laughed only with the men.

"Now there's a terrible thing about mahogany." Leaping to his feet, Shamus wheeled away to where the bottle stood. "It just won't bloody burn like the lower-class woods. It positively resists martyrdom. Now I count that very bad manners indeed, don't you? I mean at a certain point we should all go gentle into that good night, don't you think so, Cassidy?"

Though the question was facetious, Shamus put it with great earnestness, and waited motionless until he had his answer.

"Oh rather," said Cassidy.

"He agrees," said Shamus, with apparent relief. "Helen, he agrees."

"Of course he does," said Helen. "He's being polite." She leaned across to him. "It's weeks since he met a soul," she confided in a low voice. "He's been getting rather desperate, I'm afraid."

"Don't give it a thought," Cassidy murmured. "I love it."

"Hey Cassidy, tell her about your Bentley." Shamus' brogue was all over the words: the drink had brought it to full flower. "Hear that, Helen? Cassidy's got a Bentley, a dirty big long one with a silver tip, haven't you lover?"

"Have you really?" said Helen over the top of her glass. "Gosh."

"Well not new of course."

"But isn't that rather a good thing? I mean aren't the old ones *better* in lots of ways?"

"Oh absolutely, well in my judgment anyway," said Cassidy. "The pre-sixty-three models were a *much* superior job. Well certainly this one has turned out pretty well."

Before he knew it, with only the smallest prompting from Shamus, he was telling her the whole story, how he had been driving through Sevenoaks in his Mercedes—he'd had a Merc in those days, very functional cars of course, but no real handwriting if they knew what he meant—and had spotted a Bentley in the showroom of Caffyns.

"In Sevenoaks, hear that?" Shamus called. "Fancy buying a Bentley in *Sevenoaks*. Jesus."

"But that's half the fun of it," Cassidy insisted. "Some of the very finest models come from as far away as India. Maharajahs bought them for safaris."

"Hey, lover."

"Yes?"

"You're not a maharajah yourself by any chance?"

"I'm afraid not."

"Only in this sort of light you can't always see the colour of a person's skin. Are you a Catholic then?"

"No," said Cassidy pleasantly. "Wrong again."

"But you are holy?" he insisted, returning to an earlier theme. "You do *worship?*"

"Well," said Cassidy doubtfully, "Christmas and Easter, you know the kind of thing."

"Would you call yourself a New Testament man?"

"Please go on," said Helen. "I'm riveted."

"Or would you say you were more in favour of the barbaric and untrammelled qualities of the Ancient Jews?"

"Well . . . neither or both I suppose."

"You see this fellow Flaherty in County Cork now—"

"Please," said Helen, directing a second quelling glance at her husband.

Well, Cassidy had had this feeling that the car was *right,* he couldn't explain it really, and so in the end he'd stopped and gone back to take a second look. And anyway to cut a long story short this young salesman hadn't pushed him at all but recognised one of the breed, so to speak, and in ten minutes they'd done the deal. Cassidy wrote out a cheque for five thousand pounds dated that same day and drove away in the car.

"Goodness," Helen breathed. "How *terribly brave.*"

"Brave?" Shamus repeated. "Brave? Listen he's a lion. You should have seen him out there on the terrace. He frightened the hell out of me. I'll tell you that for nothing."

"Well of course I did have the weekend to stop the cheque," Cassidy admitted a little injudiciously, and would have gone on with a great deal more of the same thing—the Automobile Association's report for instance which had been one long paean of technical praise, the car's genealogy which he had only stumbled on months after he had bought her—if Shamus, suddenly bored, had not suggested that Helen show him round the house.

"After all, if he's a compulsive buyer, maybe he'll buy us too, eh: I mean Jesus, we can't pass over an opportunity like this. Now Cassidy have you brought your cheque book? Because if you haven't you'd best get in that grey bedpan and hurry back to the West End and fetch it, I'm telling you. I mean we don't show the house to just *anyone*, don't you know. After all, if you're not God, who *are* you?"

Once more Cassidy's seismographic spirit recorded Helen's reticence and understood it. The same worried glance troubled her serious eyes, the same innate courtesy prevented her from putting her anxiety into words. "We can hardly show it to him in the dark, darling," she said quietly.

"Of course we can show it to him in the bloody dark. We've got the lamp haven't we? Christ, he could buy the place by Braille if he felt like it, couldn't you, lover? I mean look here, Cassidy's quite clearly a *very influential person* and *very influential persons* who can wander round Sevenoaks signing cheques for five thousand pounds don't bloody well like having their time wasted, Helen, that's something you have to learn in life—"

Cassidy knew it was time for him to speak. "Oh now look here *please* don't worry. I can perfectly well come another time. You've been so good already—"

In an effort to make his intention real, he rose falteringly to his feet. The woodsmoke and the whisky had had more effect on him than he knew. His head was dizzy and his eyes were smarting.

"I can *perfectly* well come back another time," he repeated foolishly. "You must be tired out, what with all the packing and making do."

Shamus was also standing, leaning his hands on Helen's shoulders, and his dark, inward eyes were watching Cassidy intently.

"So why don't we make a date for next week?" he suggested.

"You mean you don't like the house," Shamus said in a flat, menacing tone, more as a statement than a question. Cassidy hastened to protest but Shamus rode him down. "It's not good enough for you, is that it? No cen-

tral heating, no poncy fittings like you've got in London-
town?"

"Not at all, I merely—"

"What do you want for Christ's sake? A tart's parlour?"

Cassidy in his day had handled scenes like this before.
Angry trade unionists had beaten his rosewood desk,
deprived competitors had shaken their fists in his face,
drunken maids had called him fat. But finally such situations had remained within his control, occurring for the
greater part on territory he had already bought, among
people he had yet to pay. The present situation was altogether different, and neither the whisky nor his misted
vision did anything to improve his performance.

"Of *course* I like the house. I thought I'd made that
abundantly clear, as a matter of fact it's the best I've seen
for a long time. It's got everything I've been looking for
. . . peace . . . seclusion . . . garage space."

"More," Shamus exhorted.

"Antiquity . . . what else do you want me to say?"

"Then come on with you!"

A brilliant, infecting smile had replaced the brief cloud
of anger. Grabbing the whisky bottle in one hand and
the lantern in the other, Shamus beckoned them brightly
up the great staircase. Thus for the second time that
evening Cassidy found himself conveyed, not altogether
against his liking, upon a compulsory journey that seemed
to his swimming consciousness to alternate with each new
step between past and future, illusion and reality, drunken-
ness and sobriety.

"Come, Flaherty!" Shamus cried. "God's house has
many mansions, and me and Helen will show you the
whole bloody lot, won't we, Helen?"

"Will you follow me?" Helen asked with an air hostess'
charming smile.

Sir Shamus and Lady Helen de Waldebere. It was symp-
tomatic of Cassidy's confused state that he never stopped
to consider whose heritage was actually for sale. Having cast Shamus as a kind of grounded cavalry officer
drinking away the humiliations of a horseless existence,
he vested in Helen the fortitude and dignified resignation
which properly accompany the evanescence of a Great
Line; and never asked himself how it had come about

within the probabilities of a conventional union that the two of them had passed their childhood in the same house. Even if he had hit upon the question, Helen's bearing would only have added to his bewilderment. She was in her element: the young chatelaine had stepped lightly from her portrait and was showing them her domain. Whatever restraint she had felt in the drawing room was swept aside by her transparent devotion to the task. Solemn, wistful, informative by turn, she guided him with loving familiarity through the labyrinth of mouldering corridors. Cassidy kept close behind her, led by the smell of baby soap and the contra-rotations of her firmly rounded hips; Shamus followed at a distance with the bottle and the lantern, moving on the edge of their discourse or calling after them with harsh ironic jokes. "Hey Cassidy get her to tell you about Nanny Higgins having it off with the vicar at the Servants' Ball." In the Great Hall he found a pike and fought a shadow duel with his father's ghost; in the planthouse he insisted on presenting Helen with a flowering cactus, and when she accepted it he kissed her for a long time on the nape of her neck. Helen, in her serenity, took it all in good part.

"It's the waiting and the worry," she explained to Cassidy while Shamus was chanting Gregorian plainsong in the crypt. "It's so frustrating for him."

"Please," said Cassidy. "I do understand. Really."

"Yes, I think you do," she said casting him a look of gratitude.

"What will he do now? Get a job?" Cassidy asked, in a tone which recognised that, for such as Shamus, employment was the final degradation.

"Who would have him?" Helen asked simply.

She took him everywhere. In hanging dusk with the first stars breaking they patrolled the crumbling battlements and marvelled at the empty moat. By the light of the lantern they stood in awe before worm-eaten fourposters and delved in dust-filled priest holes, they caressed mildewed screens and tapped on panelling honeycombed by beetles. They discussed the problems of heating and Cassidy said small-bore piping would do the least harm. They worked out which rooms could be sealed off with little alteration: how the rewiring could be run behind the skirting boards and how an electrolyte circuit worked perfectly as damp course.

"It turns the house into a dry battery," Cassidy explained. "It's not cheap but then what is these days?"

"You know an *awful* lot about it," said Helen. "Are you an architect by any chance?"

"I just love old things," said Cassidy.

Behind them, hands clasped, Shamus was chanting the *Magnificat*.

4

"You're a lovely man," Shamus says quietly, offering him a drink from the bottle. "You're really a lovely perfect man. Tell us, do you have any theories on the general nature of love?"

The two men are on the Minstrel Gallery. Helen stands below them, gazing through the window, her eyes upon the long view of the chestnut walk.

"Well I think I understand how you feel about the house. Let's put it that way, shall we?" Cassidy suggests with a smile.

"Oh but it's worse for *her,* though, far."

"Is it?"

"Us men, you know, we're survivors. Cope with anything really can't we? But them, eh, them."

She has her back to them still: the last light from the window shines through the thin housecoat and shows the outline of her nakedness.

"A woman needs a home," Shamus pronounces philosophically. "Cars, bank accounts. Kids. It's a crime to deprive them of it, that's my view. I mean how else are they fulfilled? That's what I say."

One black eyebrow has risen slightly and it occurs to Cassidy, but not with particular force, that Shamus is in some way mocking him, though how is not yet clear.

"I'm sure it'll work out," says Cassidy blandly.

"Tell me, have you ever had two at once?"

"Two what?"

"Women."

"I'm afraid not," says Cassidy very shocked; not by the notion, which he has quite often entertained, but by the context in which it is expressed. Could any man blessed with Helen think so base?

"Or three?"

"Not three either."

41

"Do you play golf at all?"

"Now and then."

"How about squash? Would squash be a game you play?"

"Yes, why?"

"I like you to keep fit that's all."

"Shouldn't we go down? I think she's waiting."

"Oh, lover," says Shamus softly as he takes another pull from the bottle. "A girl like that'll wait all night for the likes of you and me."

"Couldn't you give it to the National Trust?" Cassidy asked loudly in his boardroom voice as they descended the rickety staircase. "I thought there was some arrangement whereby they maintain the house and let you live in it on condition that you open it to the public so many days a year."

"Ah, the buggers would stink the place out," Shamus retorted. "We tried it once. The kids peed on the Aubusson and the parents had it off in the orangerie."

"You have to pay something for upkeep as well," Helen explained with another of those appealing glances at her husband that were so sadly eloquent of her distress.

Pee-break, Shamus called it. They had left Helen in the drawing room staunching the smoking fire and now they stood shoulder to shoulder at the edge of the moat, listening to their own water trickling over the dry stones. The night was of an alpine majesty. With shaggy splendour the black house rose in countless peaks against the pale sky, where powdery swarms of stars followed the moonlit ridges of the clouds like fireflies frozen into the eternal ice. At their feet a white dew glistened on the uncut grass.

"The heaventree of stars," said Shamus. "Hung with humid nightree fruit."

"That's beautiful," said Cassidy reverently.

"Joyce. Old girl friend. Can't get her out of my hair. Hey, lover. Watch out for frostbite for God's sake. Nip it off in a jiffy, I warn you."

"Thanks," said Cassidy with a laugh. "I will."

Shamus sidled closer. "Er . . . tell us," he enquired con-

fidingly. "Er do you think it'll do you? The house I mean
. . . will it suit you at all?"

"I don't know. I hope it will, I'll have to have a survey
of course. Get a quantity surveyor in too, probably. It'll
cost a bomb to put straight."

"Hey lover, listen."

"I'm listening."

Long pause.

"What do you want it for?"

"I'm looking for a bit of tradition, I suppose. My father
was a self-made man."

"Oh my *God*," Shamus drawled and, as if to show that
the revelation had quite put him off, stepped quickly out of
reach. "Big place all the same isn't it, for a weekend
hideaway? Twenty bedrooms or more . . ."

"I suppose it is."

"Not probing you know. Do what you like with it as far
as we're concerned, provided you pay the price. Still you
can always let a few floors I dare say."

"If I had to, yes."

"Rent out the land too, eh? Local farmer'd take it off
your hands no doubt."

"Yes I suppose he would."

"I've always thought it'd make a good school actually."

"Yes, or a school."

"Or a hotel for that matter."

"Possibly."

"Hey, what about a casino? Now there's a thought.
Some of those wicked London hostesses, eh? Get a few of
the holy fathers in for a flutter."

"I wouldn't want that," said Cassidy shortly. He was
perfectly sober but the whisky appeared to be affecting his
movements.

"Jesus why ever not?"

"I just wouldn't want it, that's all."

"Oh now for the love of God," Shamus declared in a
tone of exasperation. "Don't go telling us you're a bloody
Puritan. I mean listen, we're not giving Haverdown to the
Ironsides, lover, not even if we're crying out for a crust of
bread."

"I don't think you quite understand me," said Cassidy,
hearing himself at a distance.

Safely buttoned, he was gazing back at the great house
and the one pink window shivering with firelight. While

he watched, he saw Helen's perfect outline slip silently across it as she gravely went about her domestic duties.

"We seem to feel rather differently about these things. I'd like to put the place on its feet, certainly. I'd also like to keep it as it was."

Once more he felt Shamus' eyes watching him intently in the darkness, and he pitched his tone high to avoid the encroaching sentiment.

"I mean by that, I'd like to do some of the things that you might have done if . . . well if you'd had the chance. I expect that sounds rather silly to you, but I'm afraid that's the way I feel."

"Listen," said Shamus suddenly. "Ssh."

They stood very still while Cassidy strained his ears for an unusual rustic sound—the boom of a bittern perhaps, or the snarl of a natural predator—but all he could hear was the creaking of the house and the drowsy rustle of the treetops.

"I thought I heard someone singing," said Shamus, softly. "Doesn't matter really, does it. Maybe it was just mermaids." He was standing perfectly still, and the aggression had gone out of his voice. "Where were you?"

"Never mind."

"No, go on. I love it!"

"I was only trying to tell you," said Cassidy, "that I believe in continuity. In preserving the quality of life. Which I suppose in your book makes me rather a fool, does it?"

"You lovely gorgeous lover," Shamus whispered at last, still staring into the night.

"I don't follow you," said Cassidy.

"Ah, fuck it. Helen! Hey, Helen!"

Seizing the lower folds of his black jacket he darted bat-like in wide zigzags over the lawn until they reached the portico.

"Helen!" he shouted as he burst into the drawing room. "Get this! A most fantastic incredible epoch-making thing has happened! We are *redeemed*. Butch Cassidy has fallen in love with us. We're his *first married couple!*"

Helen was kneeling at the fireside, her hands folded in her lap, her back straight, and she had the air of someone who had taken a decision in their absence.

"He didn't get frostbite either," Shamus added, as if that were the other part of his good news. "I looked."

"Shamus," Helen said, into the fire. "I think Mr. Cassidy should go now."

"Balls. Cassidy's far too pissed to drive a Bentley. Think of the publicity."

"Let him go, Shamus," Helen said.

"Tell her," he said to Cassidy, still breathing heavily from his run. "Tell her what you told me. Out there, when we were having a pee. Helen, he doesn't *want* to go, do you, lover? You want to stay and play, I know you do! And he *is* Flaherty. I know he is, I love him, Helen, honest!"

"I don't want to hear," said Helen.

"Tell her! It's nothing filthy, honest to God, Helen. It's Cassidy's Good Housekeeping testimonial. You tell her, go *on!*"

Sweat had formed on his brow and his face was red from the exertion of the run.

"Nothing more nor less than a papal blessing," he insisted, still breathing heavily. "Cassidy admires us. Cassidy is *deeply moved*. You and me are the backbone of his Empire. The flowers of bloody England. Virginal roses. *Beaux sabreurs*. Buchan-babies. He's Flaherty, Helen, and he's come to buy Paradise. *It's true!* Tell her, for Christ's sake Cassidy, get your cock out of your mouth and *tell* her!"

Seizing Cassidy by the shoulder he forced him roughly to the centre of the room. "Tell her what you'll do with the house when you've bought it!"

"Goodbye Cassidy," Helen said quickly. "Drive carefully."

"Tell her!" Shamus insisted through harsh breaths. *"Tell her what you'll do with the house! Damn it man, you came to buy it didn't you?"*

Acutely embarrassed—not to say menaced—by the vehemence of Shamus' demand, Cassidy endeavoured to recall the main lines of his thesis.

"All right," he began. "If I buy the house I promise to, well, try and keep it in your style. Fit for a great English family with a past. . . . To honour it. I'd try to do with it whatever *you* would have done if you'd had the money. . . ."

The silence was absolute save for the long rasps of

Shamus' breathing. Even the water dripping from the ceiling fell soundlessly into its enamel pan. Helen's eyes were still lowered. Cassidy saw only the golden outline of the firelight on her cheek and the one quick movement of her shoulders as she rose, went swiftly to her husband, and buried her head in his breast.

"Please," she whispered. *"Please."*

"That was beautiful, lover," Shamus assured him with a bright diagonal nod of his head. "Really beautifully put. I'll tell you another thing. The maharajah is a fan of the great James Joyce. He quoted a whole chunk to me out there, you want to hear him."

"That was you," Cassidy protested. "That wasn't me, that was you."

"And he heard mermaids singing, Helen, and he knows the English poets back to front—"

"Shamus," Helen pleaded. *"Shamus."*

"Cassidy, listen. I've got a great idea. Spend the weekend with us! Come hunting! We can mount you."

"I'm afraid I don't ride. Otherwise I'd like to."

"Never mind! Listen, we love you, we don't care about things like that, nor does the horse! And besides you've a great leg for a boot, lover, hasn't he, Helen? Truth."

"Tell him, Shamus," Helen said quietly. "Tell him or I will."

"And in the evening—" his enthusiasm for his new friend was rising with every image "—come the evening we'll play mah-jongg, and you shall read poetry to us and tell us all about the Bentley. No need to dress up, black tie will do. And we'll dance. Nothing grand, just twenty couples or so, the County and a few earls to stiffen them, don't you know, and when finally the last coach has teetered drunkenly down the drive—"

"Shamus!"

The next moment she had crossed the room and was standing before Cassidy, arms down and hair straight like a child sent to say goodnight.

"And we'll have the Montmorencys in!" Shamus shouted. "Cassidy would love the Montmorencys! They've got *two* fucking Bentleys!"

Very softly, her hazel eyes gazing bravely into his, Helen began speaking.

"Cassidy, there's something you've got to hear. We're squatters," she said. "Voluntary squatters. Shamus doesn't believe in property, he says it's a refuge from reality, so we go from one empty house to another. He's not even Irish, he just has funny voices and a theory that God is living in County Cork disguised as a forty-three-year-old taxi driver. He's a writer, a marvellous, wonderful writer. He's altering the course of world literature and I love him. And as for you," standing on tiptoe she put her arms round his shoulders and leaned the length of her body against him. "As for Cassidy, he's the sweetest man alive, whatever he believes in."

"What does he *do*, for Christ's sake?" Shamus cried. "Ask him where he gets it all from!"

"I make accessories for prams," Cassidy replied. "Foot brakes, canopies, and chassis."

His mouth had gone quite dry and his stomach was aching. Music, he thought; someone must make music. She's holding me for dancing and the band won't play and everyone's looking at us saying we're in love.

"Cassidy's Universal Fastenings. We're quoted on the Stock Exchange, fifty-eight and sixpence for a one-pound share."

Helen is in his arms and the nestling movement of her breasts has told him she is either laughing or weeping. Shamus is taking the cap off the whisky bottle. All manner of visions are crowding upon Cassidy's troubled mind. The dance floor has given way. The soft hair of her mound is caressing him through the thin stuff of her housecoat. Swiss waterfalls alternate with tumbling castles and plunging stock prices; two-plus-two Bentleys lie wrecked along the roadside. He is in Carey Street on the steps of the Bankruptcy Court being pelted by infuriated creditors and Helen is telling them to stop. He is standing naked at a cocktail party and the pubic hair has spread over his navel, but Helen is covering him with her ball dress. Through all these intimations of catastrophe and exposure, one instinct signals to him like a beacon: she is warm and vibrant in my arms.

"I'd like to ask you both to dinner," Cassidy says. "If you promise to wear real clothes. Or is that against your religion?"

Suddenly Helen is pulled from his grasp and in her place Cassidy feels the wild heart of Shamus thumping through the black jacket; smells the sweat and woodsmoke and the fumes of whisky buried in the soft cloth; hears the dark voice breathing to him in love.

"You never wanted to buy the bloody house in the first place, did you? You were having a little dream, weren't you, lover? Truth?"

"Truth," Cassidy confesses, blushing very deeply. "I was pretending too."

Moved by a single instinct they turned to look for Helen but she had gone, taking her wireless with her. Its far strains just reached them through the doorway.

"Poor kid," said Shamus suddenly. "She really thought she owned the place."

"I expect she's getting her shoes," said Cassidy.

"Come on. Let's give her a ride in the Bentley."

"Yes," said Cassidy. "She'd like that, wouldn't she?"

5

Setting off for London early next morning in the euphoria of a painless hangover, Cassidy recalled each incident of that miraculous night.

First, to overcome a certain common shyness they drank more whisky. God alone knew where Shamus had it from. He seemed to have bottles in every pocket and to produce them like a conjuror whenever the action flagged. Hesitantly at first but with growing enthusiasm they re-enacted the brighter moments of what Cassidy called their little misunderstanding, and they made Shamus talk some more Irish for them, which he did very willingly, and Helen said it was amazing, he'd never even been to Ireland but he could just put on accents like clothes, he had the gift.

Next they made Cassidy take off his braces and they all played billiards by candlelight. There was one cue, which they shared, and one ball and one candle, so Shamus invented a game called Moth. Cassidy liked games and they agreed it was very clever of Shamus to make one up on the spot. Shamus pronounced the rules in a sergeant major's voice which Cassidy (who was by way of being a mimic himself) could still perfectly remember:

"To play Moth, you puts the candle on the centre spot, *'ere*. You then 'its the ball round the candle in a clockwise direction, and I mean clockwise. Scoring will take place in the following manner. One point for each complete circuit of the candle, five points penalty for each hinfringement of the natural borders of the table. 'Elen, kick orf."

There was a men's tee for Shamus and Cassidy and a ladies' tee for Helen. Helen won by six points, but secretly Cassidy reckoned himself the victor, because Helen twice hit the ball off the table and they hadn't counted it; but he didn't mind because it was only fun. Besides, it was a men's game; a female victory was only chivalrous.

After Moth, Shamus went and changed, and Helen

and Cassidy sat alone on the Chesterfield finishing their whisky. She was wearing a black dress and black leather boots and Cassidy thought she looked like Anna Karenina in the film.

"I think you're a wonderful gallant man," Helen told him. "And Shamus was absolutely *awful*."

"I've never met anyone like either of you," Cassidy assured Helen truthfully. "If you'd told me you were the Queen of England I wouldn't even have been *faintly* surprised."

Then Shamus returned looking very spruce indeed and said *"Take your hands off ma girl"* in a Wild West voice and they all got into the Bentley and drove to the Bird and Baby, which was Shamus' name for the Eagle and Child. The plan was to eat there, but Helen explained privately to Cassidy that they probably wouldn't eat there because Shamus didn't hold with first places.

"He likes to work his way into an evening," she said.

Shamus wanted to drive but Cassidy said unfortunately the car was only insured for him, which wasn't quite true but a sensible precaution, so Shamus sat in front with Cassidy and when Cassidy changed gear Shamus put his foot on the clutch for him so that Shamus could be co-pilot. "Wife-swapping" Shamus called it. The first time this happened they went into reverse at fifteen miles an hour but Cassidy managed to get his own foot on the clutch and no damage was done to the gearbox. Shamus was not car-minded, but he was very appreciative.

"Jesus," he kept saying, "this is the life, hey Helen can you hear me back there? . . . To hell with writing, from now on I'm going to be a big fat Gentile bourgeois. . . . Got your cheque book then, Cassidy? . . . Hey where's the cigars?"

All this in a non-stop monologue of breathless praise which made Cassidy wonder how a man who so clearly coveted property could have found the courage to renounce it.

Sure enough they had not been in the bar ten minutes before Shamus made for the door.

"This place stinks," he said in a very loud voice.

"Absolutely stinks," Helen agreed.

"The landlord stinks too," Shamus said and one or two heads turned to them in surprise.

"The landlord is a prole," Helen agreed.

"Landlord, you're a lowlander and a sheep-shagger and you come from Gerrard's Cross. Goodnight."

"Never hold him back," said Helen. They were walking to the car, going ahead in the hope that Shamus would follow. "Promise you never will."

"I wouldn't even try," Cassidy assured her. "It would be an absolute crime."

"You really feel for other people don't you?" said Helen. "I watch you doing it all the time."

"Why *Gerrard's Cross?*" asked Cassidy, who knew the place only as a desirable semi-rural dormitory town on the western fringes of Greater London.

"It's where the worst proles come from," she said. "He's been there and he knows."

"Chippenham," Shamus called from behind them.

At Chippenham railway station, they drank more whisky at the buffet. Shamus had a passion for terminals, Helen said, he saw all life as arrivals and departures, journeys to unnamed destinations.

"We have to keep moving," she said. "I mean don't you agree, Cassidy?"

"God yes," said Cassidy, and thought—the analyser in him thought—yes, that's what's exciting about them, they share a mutual desire for somewhere to go.

"The ordinary hours just aren't enough for him," Helen said. "He needs the night as well."

"I know," said Cassidy. "I can feel."

The platform ticket machine was out of order but the collector was Scottish and let them through for nothing because Shamus said he came from the Isle of Skye, and that Talisker was the best whisky in the world and that he had a friend called Flaherty who might be God. Shamus christened the collector Alastair and took him with them to the buffet.

"He's completely classless," Helen explained, while Shamus and Alastair at the other end of the bar discussed the similarities of their professions in rich Scottish accents. "He's a sort of Communist really. A Jew."

"It's fantastic," said Cassidy. "I suppose that's what makes him a writer."

"But you're like that too aren't you," Helen said, "deep down? Don't you have to get on with your workmen and that kind of thing? *They* don't put up with any side, surely?"

"I hadn't thought of that," said Cassidy.

The train arrived while they were drinking, next stop Bath, and suddenly they were all standing in a first-class compartment, waving to Alastair through the window.

"Goodbye Alastair, goodbye. God, look at him," Helen urged. "What a face in that lamplight, it's immortal."

"Fantastic," Cassidy agreed.

"Poor little sodder," said Shamus. "What a way to die."

"You know," said Helen later, when they had closed the window, "Cassidy really *notices* things." Using her arms to help, she lifted her long legs on to the cushions. "He's got a real *eye,* if only he'd use it," she added drowsily and was soon asleep.

The two men sat on the opposite bench passing the bottle and regarding her in the light of their separate experience. She lay on her side in a pose as classical as it was effortless, knees drawn and overlapping, Goya's Maja, naked and fully clothed.

"She's the most beautiful wife I've ever seen," Cassidy said.

"She's pissed," said Shamus, drinking. "Absolutely ossified."

"*Shamus* says," said Helen drowsily, "I'd be a whore if he ever let me off the lead."

"Oh my God," said Cassidy, as if that were a very shallow view.

"I wouldn't, would I, Cassidy?"

"Never."

"I would," said Helen, and turned over. "He beats me too, don't you, Shamus? I wish I had a *gentle* lover," she reflected, talking to the cushions. "Like Cassidy or Mr. Heath."

"You know," Cassidy said still contemplating her long body, "I don't care whether you own Haverdown or not. That house will belong to you for ever."

"For ever is now," said Shamus and drank some more whisky.

"Shamus," Cassidy began, as dreams and visions pressed upon him.

"What is it, lover?"

"Nothing," said Cassidy, for love has no language.

At Bath station, where the fresh air reminded Cassidy that he had drunk a great deal of neat whisky, Shamus underwent one of those sudden changes of humour which had made him such unnerving company at Haverdown. They were standing on the platform and Helen was gazing at a pile of mailbags, weeping silently into Cassidy's handkerchief.

"But what's the matter?" Cassidy insisted, not by any means for the first time. "You must *tell* us, Helen, mustn't she, Shamus?"

"They were stitched by prisoners," she cried at last, and resumed her weeping.

"For fuck's sake," Shamus shouted furiously, and rounded on Cassidy. "And you: stop curling your fingers round your cuff like that. Christopher Robin's dead, right? D'you hear that, Helen? *Dead*."

"Sorry," said Cassidy and the incident was forgotten.

Meals, in Cassidy's world, were sacrosanct. They were truces for conviviality or silence; time out, when neither passion nor hostility was allowed to mar the devout communion.

They ate at a place called Bruno's, on a slope, because Shamus was in his Italian mood and would speak no English, and because slopes (as Helen explained) have tension, a view which Cassidy found extremely profound. Bath stank, Shamus said. Bath was the lousiest city in the world. Bath was toytown, halfway between the Vatican and the Wind in the Willows, designed by Beatrix Potter for rural proles.

"Shamus is a terrific innocent really," Helen told him. "Of course anyone is a terrific innocent who is looking for love all the time, don't you agree?"

Astonished by the depth, let alone the urbanity of this observation, Cassidy agreed.

"He hates sham. He hates it more than anything in the world."

"That's absolutely what *I* hate too," said Cassidy stout-ly, and glancing surreptitiously at his watch, thought: I must ring Sandra soon or she'll wonder.

At Bruno's also they played another Shamus game called Fly, which he had invented specifically to discon-cert rural proles and uncover sham. Shamus selected the victim as he entered. He chose mainly the younger managerial type of person whom he consigned at once to certain arbitrary categories: Gerrard's Crossers, bish-ops, publishers, and, in deference to Cassidy, pram manu-facturers. These, he said, were the basic components of the Many-too-Many, the compromisers for whom freedom was a terror; these were the backcloth for the real drama of life. The purpose of the game was to demonstrate the uniformity of their responses. As soon as Shamus gave the word the three of them must stare at the prole's fly, Shamus fixedly, Helen with fluttering coyness, and Cassidy with an artful embarrassment that was particularly ef-fective. The results were varied but gratifying: a furious blush, a hurried descent of the right thumb along the telltale seam, a hasty gathering of the jacket. In one case —submerged poof, Shamus declared, typical of the pram trade these days, *real* pooves were not submerged—the victim actually retreated altogether with a distracted apol-ogy about car lights and returned minutes later after what must have been an exhaustive check.

"What would *you* do, lover," Shamus asked Cassidy quietly, "if we gave *you* the treatment?"

Not knowing what answer Shamus wanted, Cassidy took refuge in the truth.

"Oh I'd bolt," he said. "Absolutely."

There was a small silence while Helen played with her spoon.

"But what *should* I do?" Cassidy asked, suddenly con-fused. "What do you *want* me to do?"

"Flash it," said Helen promptly, very much to Cassidy's consternation, for he was not used to wit in women, nor coarseness either, even of the harmless, mannish kind.

"But then you don't know any better, do you?" Shamus said at last and gently reached for his hand across the table. "You've never seen the bloody daylight, have you lover? Jesus, I remember now, you're Flaherty."

"Oh no I'm not," Cassidy assured him modestly.

"He thinks all the time," said Helen. "I can tell."

"Who *are* you?" Shamus asked, still holding Cassidy's hand and watching his face with an expression of great puzzlement. "What have you got?"

"I don't know," said Cassidy, putting on a shy expression. "I'm sort of waiting to find out I suppose."

"It's the waiting that kills you, lover. You have to go and get it."

"Look at Alastair," Helen exhorted. "Alastair's been waiting for a train all his life. They come and go but he never hops aboard, does he, Shamus?"

"Maybe he *is* God at that," said Shamus, still studying his new friend.

"Not old enough," Helen reminded him. "God's forty-three. Cassidy's much younger, aren't you, Cassidy?"

Finding no immediate answer to these questions, Cassidy shrugged them off with a rueful, world-weary smile calculated to suggest that his problems were too profound to be resolved at a single sitting.

"Well anyway I'm very proud to be with you. I really am."

"We're very proud to be with Cassidy," said Helen after a slight pause. "Aren't we, Shamus?"

"Estatica," said Shamus in homemade Italian, and kissed him.

6

And it was at Bruno's still, just before they left for other treats, that they first touched upon the subjects of Shamus' new novel, and of Shamus' reputation as a writer. This moment was most vivid in Cassidy's recollection.

Helen talking.

"I mean honestly, Cassidy, it really is so, *so* fantastic you've no idea. I mean God, when you see the muck that *does* get well reviewed and you read this, just read it, it's ridiculous that he should worry at all. I mean I *know*."

"What's it about?" Cassidy asks.

"Oh God, *everything,* isn't it, Shamus?"

Shamus' attention has been drawn to the next table, where a blond lady from Gerrard's Cross is listening to a disguised bishop talking about The Dustbin of Ideas, which is Shamus' metaphor for politics.

"Sure," he says vaguely. "Total vision," and shifts his chair into the aisle the better to observe his quarry.

Helen resumes.

"I mean he's put his entire life into it: me and . . . well everything. I mean just the dilemma of the artist, the way he *needs* real people, I mean people like you and me, so that he can match himself against them."

"Go on," Cassidy urges. "I'm absolutely fascinated. Honestly. I've never, sort of . . . *met* this before."

"Well, you know what Henry James said, don't you?"

"Which bit exactly?"

"Our doubt is our passion and our passion is our doubt. The rest is the madness of art. That's Shamus, honestly, isn't it, Shamus? Shamus, I was talking about Henry James."

"Never heard of them," says Shamus.

The bishop, having taken the Gerrard's Crosser's hand, is apparently summoning his courage for a kiss.

"And then the identity thing," Helen continues, returning to Cassidy. "You know, who *are* we? Actually *that*

57

part of the book's rather like Dostoevsky, not a crib of course, just the sort of *concept*, isn't it, Shamus?" Still distracted, Shamus ignores her. "I mean honestly the symbolism just on this one level alone is incredible and there are so many levels, I mean I've read it half a dozen times at least and I haven't got them all yet."

"Follow, Cassidy?" Shamus enquires, over his shoulder. "Got the meat of it, have you, lover?"

Bored, finally, by the rutting habits of the Many-too-Many he pulls in his chair and helps himself to the menu, which he now reads, moving his lips in a caressing Italian murmur. "Jesus," he whispers once, "I thought *cacciatori* was a parrot."

Helen lowers her voice.

"It's the same with suffering. Look at Pascal, look at, well, anybody . . . We've *got* to suffer deeply. If we don't how *on earth* can we overcome suffering? How on earth can we create? How? That's why he simply hates the middle classes. And I mean do you blame him? They compromise the *whole* way along the line. With life, with passion, with, well . . . everything."

She is interrupted by Shamus' applause. He is clapping quite loudly and a lot of people are watching, so Cassidy changes the subject to politics: how he is thinking of standing as a candidate, how his father was a devoted parliamentarian, retired now of course, but still passionately wedded to the Cause, how Cassidy believes in enlightened self-help rather like the old-style Liberals . . .

"Meeow," says Shamus, and, losing interest, begins writing on the back of the menu, but privately, withholding his Art.

"He writes on *anything*," Helen whispers. "Envelopes, old bills, it's fantastic."

"I was a writer once," Cassidy confesses, "but only in advertising."

"Then you know what it's like," says Helen. "You've been down there in the pit."

They watch him, head bowed in the candlelight, still writing on the menu.

"How long does it take him to finish one?" Cassidy asked, still watching him.

"Oh God years . . . *Moon* was different of course,

being his first. He just sort of romped through it in four
months. Now, well he's . . . *conscious.* He demands more
of himself. He knows what he has to do to . . . justify
his success. So naturally it takes longer."

"Moon?" Cassidy repeated in bewilderment, and the
thing was out.

Before addressing herself to Cassidy's heresy, Helen cast a
fearful glance across the table to make certain Shamus
was still busy with the menu. Her voice sank to a whisper.

"You mean you didn't *know?"*

"Know what?"

"The Moon by Day. That was Shamus' first novel.
Shamus *wrote* it."

"Good Lord! . . ."

"Why?"

"But that was a *film.* I remember!" Cassidy was very
excited. "A *film,"* he repeated. "All about university, and
being in our prime and how rotten it was to have to go
into commerce . . . and about this undergraduate and his
love for this girl, who was all he had ever dreamed of,
and—"

Helen waited, pride and relief reflected equally in her
solemn eyes.

"I was his love," she said. "I was the girl."

"Good Lord," Cassidy repeated, his exhilaration gathering. "He really *is* a writer! Good *Lord.* And it was all
him?"

He gazed at Shamus, studying his profile in the candlelight, and watching with a new respect how the master's
pencil slipped smoothly across the menu.

"Good Lord," he said yet again. "That's *wonderful."*

The revelation was of great significance to Cassidy. If
there had been, until that moment, any tiny cloud of
reservation in his mind concerning his new-found friends,
then it was on this very matter of credentials; for while
Cassidy was far from being a snob, he had not for several
years been comfortable in the presence of the unsuccess-
ful. And though not by nature cynical, he had never quite
managed to overcome the prejudiced belief that the renun-
ciation of property was a gesture reserved to those who
had nothing to renounce. To learn therefore in a single
stroke that Shamus was not merely a household name—

the title had been much in circulation during Cassidy's
last year at Oxford, and he even remembered a nagging
envy for a contemporary who had made his name so soon
—but that his eccentricities were backed by solid achievement, this was a matter of great and rare joy to Cassidy
which he was quick to impart to Helen:

"But we've *all* heard of him! He was brilliant, everyone
said so. I remember my tutor raving about him . . ."

"Yes," said Helen. "Everyone did."

At this point Cassidy recalled that it was now eighteen
years since he had left Oxford.

"What's he been doing since?"

"Oh the usual things. Film scripts, television . . . even a
ghastly pageant, once. For Abingdon if you please."

"Novels?"

"The ghouls all wanted him to write *Moon* again," she
said. "Son of Moon, Moon at Easter, Moon Rides Out. . . .
Well of course he wouldn't do that would he? He wouldn't
repeat himself."

"No," said Cassidy doubtfully.

"You see he won't be vulgar. He refuses *absolutely*. He's
got that kind of integrity. Virtue," she added glancing at
him, and Cassidy somehow knew that virtue, the word as
well as the concept, was a part of their profound complicity.

"I'm sure he has," he said reverently.

"So in the end he just put a bomb under the whole lot."
With a show of brightness, Helen opened her hands, revealing the obvious solution. "Just took off. Like Gauguin,
except that I went with him of course. That was . . . years
ago."

"But good God, what happened to all the publishers and
people, the ghouls . . . didn't they come after him?"

Helen dismissed the question.

"Oh I told them he was dead," she said carelessly.

It was right that Cassidy should pay; patronage formed a
large part of his aspiring soul, affording not only protection and justification for his wealth, but also the pleasure of a public sacrifice. Calling for a settlement, using
the practised gesture of the rich—which consists of passing
an imaginary pencil over an imaginary writing pad—he
discreetly summoned his cheque book from an inner

pocket and waited in a slightly crouched position to pounce upon the bill and conceal its total before Shamus (should he prove to be that kind of guest) had a chance to object.

"God I envy him," he said, but following the waiter with his eyes.

"It needs courage at first of course," said Helen. "To be free. But then courage is what he's got. And gradually . . . you realise, well you don't need money, no one does. It's just a complete trick."

Still waiting, Cassidy shook his head at his own absurdity.

"What good did it ever do *me?*" he asked.

"We even gave up our flat in Dulwich."

"What," said Cassidy sharply. "All to be free?"

"I'm afraid so," Helen admitted a little doubtfully. "But of course we'll be *rolling* once the new book comes out. It's fabulous, it really is."

The bill came and Cassidy paid it. Far from disputing Cassidy's rôle of host, however, Shamus seemed quite unaware that the transaction had taken place. He was still busily writing on the menu. They sat and watched him, too tactful to disturb the flow.

"It's probably about Schiller," said Helen in a low aside.

"Who?"

Still waiting for her husband's mood of inspiration to pass, Helen explained.

Shamus had developed a *theory,* she said, which he had worked into his latest book. It was based on someone called Schiller who was a terrifically famous German dramatist actually but of course the English being so insular had never heard of him, and anyway Schiller had split the world in two.

"It's called being *naive,*" she said. "Or being *sentimental.* They're sort of different kinds of *thing,* and they interact."

Cassidy knew she was putting it very simply so that he could understand.

"Which am I?" he asked.

"Well Shamus is *naive,*" she replied cautiously, as if remembering a hard-learned lesson. "Because he lives life and doesn't imitate it. Feeling is knowledge," she added rather tentatively.

"So I'm the other thing."

"Yes. You're sentimental. That means you long to be *like* Shamus. You've left the natural state behind and you've become . . . well part of civilisation, sort of . . . corrupt."

"Isn't *he?*"

"No," said Helen decisively.

"Oh," said Cassidy.

"What Nietzsche calls innocence, that's what you've lost. The Old Testament is terrifically innocent, you see. But the New Testament is all corrupt and wishy-washy and that's why Nietzsche and Shamus hate it, and that's why Flaherty is such an important symbol. You have to *challenge.*"

"Challenge what?" asked Cassidy.

"Convention, morals, manners, life, God, oh I mean everything. Just everything. Flaherty's important because he *disputes*. That's why Shamus challenged him to a duel. *Now* do you understand?"

"Is that what Schiller says?" Cassidy asked again, now thoroughly confused. "Or the other one?"

"And Shamus," Helen continued, avoiding his question, "being *naive*, part of nature in fact, longs to be like *you*. It's the attraction of opposites. He's natural, you're corrupt. That's why he loves you."

"Does he?"

"I can tell," said Helen simply. "You've made a conquest, Cassidy, that's all there is to it."

"What about you, then," Cassidy enquired, only partially succeeding in hiding his gratification. "Which side are you on? Shamus' or mine?"

"I don't think it works for women," Helen replied at last. "I think they're just themselves."

"Women are eternal," Cassidy agreed as finally they got up to leave.

In return, at the pub, he told her about his accessories.

That conversation alone, in retrospect, would have made his evening unforgettable.

Even if he had never set eyes on Helen before walking into the saloon bar; if he had never seen her again after he left it, if he had simply bought her a double whisky and chatted to her in the garden, he would have counted his visit to Bath—that timeless exchange would stand for all time—among the most amazing experiences of his life.

The pub was higher up the hill—the slope of tension as Cassidy now thought of it—a leafy place with a verandah and a long view of the valley lights. The lights reached to the edge of the earth, melting together in a low haze of gold before joining the descending stars. Shamus had made straight for the public bar and was playing dominos with the naive classes, so the two of them sat outside looking into the night with eyes made wide by wisdom, mutely sharing the infinite vision. And for a moment, it seemed to Cassidy, a kind of marriage was made. For a moment, he would swear, before either one of them had spoken a word, Cassidy and Helen discovered secretly in the motionless night air a joining of their destinies and their longings, of their dreams and their enchantments. So strong was his sense of this, in fact, that he had actually turned to her in the hope of catching in her devout expression some evidence of the shared experience, when a gust of coarse laughter, issuing from inside the pub, reminded them of their companion.

"Shamus," Helen sighed, but not at all by way of criticism. "He does so adore an audience. We all do really don't we? It's no more than the warmth of human contact, when you think about it."

"I suppose it isn't," said Cassidy, who had never supposed till now that any excuse could be found for showing off.

"Ever since I've known him," she said dreamily, "he's been the complete enchanter. When we were rich it was the maid, the garage man, the milkman. And when we decided to be poor again it was . . . just anyone. Proles, Gerrard's Crossers, he magicked them all. It's the loveliest thing about him."

"But it's always been *you*," Cassidy suggested. "Rich or poor, you were his real audience, weren't you, Helen?"

She did not immediately accept the notion, but seemed to dwell on it as if it were new, and perhaps a fraction facile for her reflective nature.

"Not always. No. Just sometimes. *Sometimes* it was me. At the beginning perhaps." She drank. "In the beginning," she repeated bravely.

"But you must help him *enormously* with his work,"

said Cassidy. "Doesn't he lean on you an awful lot, on your knowledge, Helen? Your *reading?*"

"A bit," Helen said, in the same airy, questionable tone. "Now and then, sure."

"Tell me: what did you *read* at Oxford? I'll bet you're *covered* with degrees."

"Let's talk about you," Helen suggested modestly. "Shall we?"

And that was how it happened.

Deliberately, to begin with, he had emphasised the human aspect of his products, the *mother appeal* as they called it in the trade. After all, there was not a reason on earth for her to be interested in the technical side: none of his other female customers was. Cee-springs, suspension, braking mechanisms: you might as well talk to a woman about pipe tobacco as try to explain all that to her. So he had begun by telling her in simple narrative terms, albeit apocryphal, how the idea had come to him in the first place. How he had been walking one Saturday morning, in the days when walking was about the only recreation he could afford—he had just started in advertising though he had always been a meddler, if she knew what he meant, gadget-minded so to speak, handy with a screwdriver if she followed him—and he was vaguely thinking of a drink before lunch ("Tnank you," said Helen. "Just a single will be lovely") when he spotted a mother trying to cross the road.

"A *young* mother," Helen corrected him.

"How did you know?"

"Just guessed."

Cassidy smiled a little ruefully. "Well, you're right actually," he confessed. "She *was* young."

"And pretty," said Helen. "A *pretty* mother."

"Good *God* how did you—"

"Go on," said Helen.

Well of course, said Cassidy, there were no zebra crossings in those days, just the studded lines with Belisha beacons at either end, and the traffic was pretty well nonstop: "So she began probing."

"With the pram," said Helen at once.

"Yes. Exactly. She stood on the curb sort of *testing the*

water with this baby, lowering the pram into the road and pulling it out again while she waited for the traffic to stop. *And all there was between that kid and the traffic was this . . . this one footbrake.* Just a rickety bit of rodding with a rubber grip on the end," he said, meaning the footbrake still.

"Rodding?" Helen repeated, unfamiliar with the word.

"Low-grade alloy," Cassidy replied. "Virtually no stress. Metal fatigue ratio zero."

"Oh my God," said Helen.

"Well that's what I felt."

"I mean, Christ, risk your own neck if you must, but not well, God, not a child's."

"You're absolutely right. That's *precisely* what I say. I was horrified."

"You felt responsible," Helen said gravely.

Yes that was precisely what he had felt. No one had put it to him like that before, but it was true: he had felt *responsible.* So he didn't have a drink, he went home and did a spot of thinking. Responsible thinking.

"Where's home?" asked Helen.

"Oh Christ," said Cassidy, hinting at the long road and unrevealed hardships. "Where was anywhere in those days?"

And Helen nodded to show that she too understood the vagaries of an aspiring male life.

"I just thought for a moment it might have been your own wife you were watching," she said casually, not at all in the tone of someone *accusing* him of marriage, but merely recognising his state and taking it into account.

"Oh Lord no," said Cassidy, as if to say that even if he had a wife and that wife had a pram, he would certainly not waste time watching her; and plunged on with his story. So anyway, he'd had this idea: if he could build a brake, a really unbeatable, multi-systemed brake, that functioned on any pram—a brake that stayed the *hub* rather than just well Christ let's face it *dragged along the road* like your old chariot brake—

"A *disc brake,*" Helen cried. "You invented the disc brake! Cassidy!"

"That's an extremely good *analogy,*" said Cassidy after a slight pause, not quite certain whether analogy was what he meant.

"It was *your* idea," Helen said. "Not mine."

"Of course it was only prams," he reminded her. "Not grown-ups."

"Are children more important?" Helen demanded. "Or adults?"

"Well," said Cassidy very surprised. "I hadn't thought of it that way, I must say."

"I had," said Helen.

Having fetched replenishments from the bar, Cassidy returned to Helen on the verandah and continued his narrative.

So anyway: over the next few days he had done a spot of research. Nothing explicit of course, nothing that gave the show away, just taken a few soundings among reliable people he happened to know. Vital question: would a quality footbrake be universally acceptable? A twin-circuit system, for instance; something one could attach to the hubs?

"You made your mark early, didn't you?" Helen said. "Like Shamus."

"I suppose that's true," Cassidy conceded.

Be that as it might, quite soon he came up with his answer. If he could build a brake that *really* held, a one-hundred-per-cent safety brake, based on a hub-retarding principle, then he would stir up such publicity, get so much support from the Road Safety League, the Royal Society for the Prevention of Accidents, not to mention the public media, "Woman's Hour" and all the other goof programmes, that he could get the financing and clean up a fortune overnight, just on the patent alone.

"And perform a fantastic service for society," Helen reminded him.

"Yes," Cassidy said reverently. "That above all. And once it caught on, of course, I took on chaps, we expanded, grew, diversified. A *lot* of people came to us with their problems and before long . . . Look here, am I being pompous?"

Helen did not immediately reply. She looked at her drink and then through the French doors at Shamus, and finally at Cassidy with the long, frank, fearless look of a woman who knows her mind.

"I tell you this," she said. "If ever I need a pram, which I never will if Shamus has anything to do with it, it's going to be one of yours."

For a moment neither spoke.

"Do you really mean never?" Cassidy asked, embarrassed but feeling he knew her well enough.

"Well *really*," she said laughing. "Can you *imagine* Shamus going through all that? Wife and two veg, that's what he calls it. God he'd go raving mad in a week! How can an *artist* be tied to that?"

"God, you're so right," said Cassidy, and once more covertly examined his watch.

Give it ten minutes and I'll make that call.

From there it had been but a step to the technical exposition. How they had expanded to become their own customer. (*What a brilliant idea*, said Helen. *You take the profit twice!*) How they had repeatedly ploughed back profits into research, exploring ever deeper the application of these same safety principles, until Cassidy's name had become a byword, from the great hospitals to the individual housewife, for comfort and safety in your world of infant transportation. Heaven knows, he had spared her nothing. From fluid flywheels and dual braking circuits he passed with hardly a breath to the intricacies of a twin-jointed push bar and the variable suspension. Helen never faltered. He could tell by the steadiness of the sombre eyes that she took in every word; nothing, not even the universal joint, clouded their perfect comprehension. He drew for her, sketched on paper napkins until the bar was like a drawing board: gravely she sipped her drinks and gravely nodded her approval.

"Yes," she said. "You thought of everything."

Or: "But how did the competition take it?"

"Oh, the Japs had a shot at copying us as usual."

"But they couldn't," Helen said, not as a question at all but as a positive statement there was no gainsaying.

"Afraid not," Cassidy replied obligingly, preferring the spirit of the truth to the truth itself. "They put their best chaps on to it. Total failure."

"Then how did *you* take it?"

"*Me?*"

"The sudden wealth, the fame, the recognition of your talents ... didn't you go a *little* bit mad, Cassidy?"

Cassidy had met with this question often, and answered it, in his day, in many different ways, according to his mood and the requirements of the audience. Sometimes, principally within the hearing of his wife, he insisted that he was inviolate, that a natural sense of Values was too strong an answer to mere materialistic temptation, that the act of making money had shown him also its futility, he was impervious. At other times, to close male acquaintances, or strangers in railway compartments, he confessed to a deep and tragic change, a frightening loss of appetite for life.

"There's no *fun* any more," he would say. "Having money takes all the joy out of achievement."

While occasionally, in moments of great apprehension, he flatly disowned his money altogether. The British tax system was confiscatory; no honest man could keep more than a fraction of what he earned, whoever did so was on the fiddle, more should be done to control them. But in Helen's mouth the question was new, and fundamental to their relationship. Therefore, having rapidly considered many alternatives, he shrugged lightly and said, in a moment of the nicest inspiration, "A man is judged by what he looks for, Helen. Not by what he finds."

"Christ," said Helen softly.

For a long while she gazed at him with an expression of the greatest intensity. Cassidy, indeed, had difficulty in meeting it; he found his eyes drifting, or closing with the smoke of her cigarette. Until, taking a draft of whisky, she broke the spell.

"Anyway," she said, indicating an obstruction to some unspoken proposition. "How did your wife take it?"

This question also he had faced on more than one occasion. Where does she shop *now?* Did you buy her a fur coat? Once again he found the greatest difficulty in replying. Get rid of her, was his first thought. I am divorced; I am a widower. My wife died a lingering and tragic death; she recently eloped with a great pianist. The reappearance of Shamus mercifully absolved him.

It was some time now since Shamus had paid them much attention. Already at dinner his first effusive interest in Cassidy had given way to a more general interest in his fellow man, and Helen had explained that, since he went out very little as a rule when he was working, he had to cram a lot of experience into a very short period of time.

"It's being an artist," she said as they went indoors.

"He has to live terrifically intensively otherwise he just stands still."

"Which is hopeless," Cassidy agreed.

Whatever else Shamus might have been doing he was not standing still. He had a girl with him and his arm was round her waist, her upper waist as it were, his hand was cupped comfortably over her left breast and he was not at all steady on his feet.

"Hey Cassidy," he said. "Look what I got for you."

Alas, the offer is no sooner made than it is withdrawn. Two men appear from somewhere and quietly detach the nice girl from his grasp, someone in authority suggests they take a spot of fresh air, and suddenly they are playing games on a grass traffic circle, leapfrogging over posts under the gaze of a startled young policeman.

"Anyway," said Helen, as they made their way towards the next pub, "she was miles too young for Cassidy."

"Yes," said Cassidy loyally, not wishing to wound *anyone* with his private appetites, "she was."

Sequence, in Cassidy's recollection, had by now become blurred. It remained blurred for the rest of the evening. The journey to Bristol, for instance, left no clear imprint on his memory. He assumed they had a free lift—a lorry driver named Aston played a misty part, and Cassidy's suit next morning smelt strongly of diesel oil. They went there, he remembered clearly, because Shamus needed water, and he had heard from reliable sources that Bristol was a port.

"He can't survive without it," Helen explained.

"It's the sound," said Cassidy. "The lapping sound."

"*And* the permanence," Helen reminded him. "Think of undulating waves, going on for ever."

Shamus insulted Aston and called him a sodder, probably because Aston was a Methodist, and disapproving of drink. Whatever the reason, the ride ended in dissent, and Cassidy distanced himself from it. The beer hall on the other hand made a vivid impression. He perfectly remembered every white contour of the barmaid's *décolleté*—she wore a Bavarian costume which lifted the milky balls almost to her throat—and he remembered the accordion player's astonishment when Shamus, to the great pleasure of the crowd, sang all the verses of the *Horst Wessel lied* in a slow, romantic lilt.

But it was from Bath, not Bristol, that Cassidy, after a last examination of his costly gold watch, finally made that brief sojourn into a world which, in all other respects, he had for several hours rigorously banished from his thoughts.

7

A new pub, not on a slope but part of a Vatican outbuilding; the public bar because the saloon was filled with Gerrard's Crossers.

Helen and Shamus were playing darts, Smoothies versus Bumpkins, Bumpkins were all right because they were still one with nature. Shamus had drawn a pig on one side of the blackboard and a bowler on the other.

"Lovers, I am *not* asking you to vote," he assured them. "I am teaching you to read."

Helen's turn. She missed the board and nailed the poor box to the panelling. A peal of laughter shook the bar.

"Excuse me," Cassidy said confidentially to the landlord. "Have you a telephone I could use?"

"These your friends, are they?"

"Well, in a way you know."

"I don't want trouble. I like fun but I don't want trouble."

"That's all right," said Cassidy. "I'll pay for breakages."

"Mind you, I'll say this. He's a lovely boy. They don't come like him often do they? And she's a lovely girl. I haven't seen a pair like that for quite a while."

"He's a very famous television writer," Cassidy explained, intuitively adjusting Shamus' talent to the mass audience. "He's got three serials running at the moment. He's worth an absolute bomb."

"Is he though?"

"You ought to see his Bentley. It's a two-plus-two, dove grey with electric windows."

"Well I'm blessed," the landlord said. "There's not many of them about is there?"

"It's unique. Here, care for one yourself? Anything you like. How about a gold watch?" he suggested, mixing with the men.

"A *what?*"

"A Scotch," said Cassidy in a lower tone.

"That's all right son, I'll just take a shilling's worth off you, thanks. Cheers."

"Cheers," said Cassidy. "Through here is it?"

From Bath he can dial direct.

"Hi," he says. "How was the clinic?"

Sandra wife to Aldo (of Cassidy's General Fastenings) is not a quick girl. Sound takes longer to reach her, particularly on the telephone.

"All right. Where are you?"

"Just in the pub. Heather bearing up?"

It may, of course, be the other way round: that her voice takes longer to carry the distance. That she has already answered me, but the words are clogging the line. *Ay'm sorry, sah, there is a traffic jam on the M4 telephone route. Will you tray later?* That there are too many husbands apologising to too many wives on cheap rates shortly before closing time. Or that an atomic bomb has fallen, never impossible: *hurry back and shoot the children.* Alternatively that the Russians have—

"Who with?" the earpiece demands suddenly.

She has her father's military instinct for monosyllables. Montgomery's five basic questions, who, why, when, where, how? And my *God* the chaps respected him.

"The Corporation," says Cassidy. *The Corporation is with me, in full-bottomed wigs, and furs and chains, we have just given a five-year contract to the Pied Piper.* "The Corporation, the people who run the city. Great chaps, you'd love them. We only finished an hour ago."

Winged words, flying but not settling. He musters still greater enthusiasm.

"Listen it's all falling into place. The land is *absolutely* central, it needs *very* little levelling, and the boys in the Corporation assure me that the moment we raise the first twenty thousand they'll come through with the footbridge. Free. They really *believe* in it, I'm astonished."

Silence. Does *she* believe in it? For Christ's sake, Sandra, this is our meeting point. What does it matter whether it's true or not? Say *yes*, admire the achievement. What the hell?

"There's one fellow here's a contractor, in heavy machinery, all that sort of stuff. He'll level the place free and give us a cost quotation on labour for building the changing rooms."

Silence.

"They really have risen to it in a *big* way." But Sandra has not. Sandra has been cut off. Sandra has gone deaf; her mother has switched me through to an extension.

"Sandra?"

In the bar, the jukebox is playing a low tune. In the earpiece, a well-bred dog is barking. Sandra has several dogs, all are large and classically entitled. Encouraged by this sign of life, Cassidy himself rallies.

"They actually showed me a drawing, heart . . . well one *like,* you know. Off the peg, of course, but well *great,* really. Just right for kids. A *fun* bridge."

"Shut up Mummy," says Sandra. "Sorry it was Mummy, fussing about the dogs."

"Sandra, aren't you pleased?"

"What about?"

"The bridge. The playing field. For God's sake . . . "Hullo? ?"

"Don't shout."

"Are you still speaking?" the operator enquires.

"Did Hugo see the specialist?" Cassidy demands suddenly, selecting in his anger a contentious point.

A rustle in the earpiece. Her impatience sigh, unlike her sigh of frustration, is not so sharp. The impatience sigh begins with a liquid click in the roof of the mouth and is followed by a decision not to breathe, like a hunger strike, in fact, but done on air, not food.

"Just because a man can afford rooms in Harley Street," she begins, speaking off-key but with large emphasis for the sake of the untutored, "just because there are people around prepared to pay *twenty guineas* in order not to stand in a queue, it does *not* mean that a specialist is *any* better than a *perfectly* ordinary decent doctor who doesn't care about money."

"So you haven't taken him?" Cassidy says. The witness has condemned herself out of her own mouth.

"Pieces of eight," says Shamus.

He was standing in the doorway wearing a brown peaked cap and carrying a mynah bird on one finger. He had

tucked one leg under his black coat and was pretending to
be Long John Silver while he supported himself against the
lintel.

"Pieces of eight, pieces of eight," he said, talking to the
bird.

"Time," the landlord shouted from the bar, and rang a
ship's bell, dong, dong.

"Goodnight," said Cassidy, into the telephone.

"Is that all you're going to say?" Sandra demanded. "I'd
have thought it was hardly worth ringing up."

"Goodnight and thank *you*," said Shamus, taking the receiver from him and speaking in his Italian accent. " 'Ullo,
'ullo, 'ullo?"

Cassidy recovered the receiver but the line was dead. He
put it back on its cradle.

"Hullo, Shamus," he said at last, smiling. "Have a pint."

They were still in the back room. The sounds of revelry
came from all sides, but the back room was quiet all the
same; an adding machine and several wholesale boxes of
sweets lay on the baize-covered table.

"Was that the bosscow?" Shamus asked.

"The *what?*"

"Your wife. Bosscow. Queen of the herd."

"Oh I see. Well, just checking up," said Cassidy. "Can't
have her going out with the lodger, eh?"

The noise in the bar became suddenly deafening, but
neither raised his voice.

"What's the trouble?"

The mynah was also watching Cassidy. Its feathers were
almost lost against the black of Shamus' jacket, but its
eyes were jet bright.

"It's my little boy," said Cassidy. "Hugo. He broke his
leg in a skiing accident. The bone won't seem to mend."

"Poor little bugger," said Shamus not moving.

"Anyway, the specialists are looking after him."

"Sure it's not your leg?" Shamus asked.

In the saloon, someone was playing the piano, a whole
tune straight the way through.

"I don't quite understand."

"Work on it, lover, you will."

"I meant to tell you actually," Cassidy said carelessly,
with an attempt at movement. "I've got a house in Switzer-

land, a chalet. Quite modest but surprisingly comfortable for two. Place called Sainte-Angèle. It's empty most of the year. If you like tense slopes you might try that one some time."

No laughter.

"I just mean, if you ever want a place to work, to get away from it all, I'd be delighted to lend it to you for nothing. Take Helen."

"Or a substitute," Shamus suggested. "Lover."

"Yes?"

"You should have been angry with me. For barging in on that call and fucking it up. That was *very* rude."

"Should I?"

"You should have *hit* me, lover. I mean I rely on discipline. I believe in it. That's what the fucking bourgeoisie is for: to inhibit rude sodders like me."

Cassidy laughed awkwardly. "You're too strong for us," he said. Feeling in his pocket for small change, he made to open the door.

"Hey, lover."

"Yes?"

"Ever killed anyone?"

"No."

"Not even physically?"

"I don't understand," said Cassidy.

"I'll bet the bosscow does," said Shamus. "Hey, lover."

"Well?" Testily, as becomes a tired man with a crippled son.

Shamus flung out his arms. "Give us a cuddle, lover. I'm *starving*."

"I've got to pay for the call," said Cassidy.

Arms still outstretched, Shamus remained in the open doorway staring at Cassidy in astonishment while he completed his transactions at the bar; until, without waiting for the promised embrace, he swung away into the grimy crowd.

"All right you lousy filthy stinking hayseeds," he yelled. "Button your smocks, Butch Cassidy's in town!"

"Time," the landlord said quickly. "And I mean it."

After the pub, the taxi. From Bath or Bristol? No matter. They had missed the last train so Shamus ordered a radio cab in his Italian accent while they all squashed into the telephone booth. Shamus sat in the front so that he could talk to the driver, who was an old man and rather tickled to be driving drunken gentry. Quite soon the radio caught Shamus' fancy.

"Listen to her," he urges them, turning up the volume.

They all concentrate.

"Come in Peter One . . . Control calling . . . Peter Two . . . party of four at the station, no luggage, they'll sit three up at the back. Party waiting now, Peter Three. Come in Peter One, Control calling . . ."

To Cassidy she sounds as bossy and inexpert and strident and periodic as any other female announcer, but Shamus is entranced.

"She's not your daughter is she?" he asks the driver reverently.

"Not likely. She's fifty in the shade."

"She's terrific," says Shamus. "That lady is in the first position. Believe me."

"She really is," Cassidy agrees, about to doze off. Helen's head has fallen on to his shoulder and she has threaded her fingers through his hand and he is very pleased to agree to anything when suddenly they hear Shamus talking into the microphone in his Italian voice.

"I want-a you," he is whispering fervently. *"I love-a you and I want-a you. I-a long for you.* Is she dark?" he asks the driver.

"Darkish."

"Come to bed with me," Shamus breathes back at the microphone. "Fuck me."

"Here, steady," says the driver. On a tense slope, they all wait for the reply.

"She's calling the police," says Cassidy.

"She's packing her bags," says Helen.

"What a woman," says Shamus.

In a tone of incipient hysteria, the radio speaks. "Peter One . . . Peter One . . . who is that?"

"Not Peter One. Peter One is dead. My name is Dostoevsky," Shamus insists, dextrously adjusting to the deeper Russian tone. "I have just murdered Peter One without a spark of regret. It was a *crime passionel.* I want you all for myself, I love you. One night with you is worth a lifetime in Siberia." The radio pops but finds no words. "Listen I am also Nietzsche. I am no man. I am

dynamite. Don't you understand—" very thick Russian—
"that immoralism is a necessary precondition of new
values? Listen, we will found a new class together. We will
engender a world of innocent, murderous, beautiful boys!
We—"

The driver gently takes the microphone. "It's all right,
dear," he says kindly. "I've got a funny, that's all."

"Funny?" the radio screams through the interference.
"You call that funny? Bloody foreigner murdering my
drivers in the middle of—"

The driver switches her off. "She'll murder *me* in the
morning," he says, not much worried.

Shamus has fallen asleep. "Lot of woman there, boy,"
he whispers.

"I wish we could play Moth again," says Cassidy.

"Moth was super," says Helen, and gives his hand another friendly squeeze.

On the last leg home they stopped the Bentley at a phone
box and put through a call to Flaherty so that Shamus
could again test the sincerity of his conviction. "A man is
what he *thinks* he is," Helen explained, quoting the master. "That's what Shamus means by faith."

"He's absolutely right," said Cassidy.

Cassidy booked the call because he had a Post Office
credit card and Shamus, amazingly, had the number written neatly in the margin of a cutting from the *Daily Mail*.
"It's Beohmin village pub," he explained. "He's there
most evenings." FLAHERTY FOR GOD the cutting read.
They squeezed in all three together and closed the door
for comfort. Alas, Flaherty was not available. For five
minutes perhaps they listened to the number ringing out.
Cassidy was secretly quite glad—after all, it could have
been embarrassing—but Shamus was hurt and disappointed, returning to the car ahead of them and climbing
into the back without a word. For a long while they drove
in silence; while Helen, sitting beside her husband now, consoled him with kisses and small attentions.

"Sodder," Shamus declared at last, in a cracked voice.
"Shouldn't even *need* a fucking telephone."

"Of course he shouldn't," Helen agreed tenderly.

"Hey look," said Shamus, sitting up straight, watch-

ing the unnatural moonlight scatter over the hedges.
"Kolynos headlights!"

"They're iodine quartz," said Cassidy. "Halogen. The
latest thing."

"Meeow," said Shamus and went back to Helen.

Back at Haverdown—after a pause for refreshment—they
had a horse race. Shamus was Nijinsky, Cassidy was Dob-
bin. The start was unclear to him, and for once he forgot
who won, but he had the clearest recollection of the
thunder of their six feet as they galloped down uncarpeted
back staircases, and of Shamus doing his butler voice while
he charged a locked door.

" 'Ere's my lady's bedroom!" He charged it again.
"Merry bloody England, let's knock the bugger down!"

"Helen . . ." whispered Cassidy. "He'll smash himself to
pieces."

But the door it was that smashed and suddenly they
were flying, crashing into bare mattresses that smelt of
lavender and mothballs.

"Shamus, are you all right?" Helen asked.

No answer.

"Shamus is dead," she declared, not in the least alarmed.

Shamus was underneath them, groaning.

"Sounds like a broken neck," she said.

"It's a broken heart you fool," said Shamus. "For when
they butcher my masterpiece."

She was already undressing him as Cassidy left the room
to make himself a bed on the Chesterfield. For a while he
lay awake listening to the bucking of the bed as Helen
and Shamus once more consummated their perfect relationship. The next moment Helen was waking him with a
gentle shaking of his shoulder and he heard the transistor
again playing cremation music from the pocket of her
high-necked housecoat.

"No," said Helen quietly, "you can't say goodbye to him
because he works in the mornings."

She had brought a complete breakfast on a mother-ofpearl tray: a boiled egg and toast and coffee, and she carried the lantern because it was still dark. She was very neat and wore no make-up. She might have slept twelve hours and been for a country walk.

"How is he?"

"His neck's stiff," she said cheerfully. "But he likes a bit of pain."

"For the writing?" Cassidy said, being of the clan now, and Helen nodded yes.

"Were you warm enough?"

"Fine."

He sat upright, partially covering his bare paunch with the overcoats across his lap, and Helen sat beside him watching him with motherly indulgence.

"You won't leave him will you Cassidy? It's time he had a friend again."

"What happened to the others?" Cassidy said, his mouth full of toast, and they both laughed, not looking at his tummy. "But I mean why *me?* I'm mean *I'm* not much good to him."

"Shamus is *very* religious," Helen explained after a pause. "He thinks you're redeemable. Are you redeemable, Cassidy?"

"I don't know what he means." Helen waited, so he went on. "Redeemable from what?"

"What Shamus says is, any fool can *give,* it's what we take from life that matters. That's how we discover our outlines."

"Oh."

"That means . . . our identity . . . our passion."

"And our art," said Cassidy, remembering.

"He doesn't like people throwing up the struggle whether their name is Flaherty, or Christ, or Cassidy. But you *haven't* thrown up the struggle, have you Cassidy?"

"No. I haven't. I feel sometimes . . . I'm just beginning."

Very quietly, Helen said, "That's the message *we* got." She took the tray to the far end of the room, the ship's lantern lighting her face from below. *Caravaggio,* Cassidy thought, remembering Mark's postcard from Rome.

"I told him your remark about money."

"Oh . . ." said Cassidy, not knowing which remark, but wondering somewhat nervously whether it was to his credit.

"A man is judged by what he looks for, not by what he finds."

"What did he think of it?"

"He's using it," she said simply, as if there were no higher accolade. "Do you know Shamus has written his own epitaph?" she continued brightly. *"Shamus who had a lot to take.* I think it's the most super epitaph that's ever been written, don't you?"

"It's wonderful," Cassidy said. "I entirely agree. It's beautiful." Adding: "I'd like it for myself too."

"You see Shamus *loves* people. He really does. He's the difference between paddling and swimming. He's like Gatsby. He believes in the light at the end of the pier."

"I think that's what I believe in too," said Cassidy, trying to remember who Gatsby was.

"That's why he loved your remark about money," Helen explained.

She saw him to the car.

"He'll even believe in Flaherty if Flaherty will only give him a chance."

"I thought he wanted to kill him."

"Isn't that the same thing?" said Helen, giving him a very deep look.

"I suppose it is," Cassidy conceded.

"Give my love to London."

"I will. Helen."

"Yes?"

"Can I give you some money?"

"No. Shamus said you'd ask. Thanks all the same." She kissed him, not a goodbye kiss but a kiss of gratitude, swift and accurate on the blank of the cheek. "He says you're to read Dostoevsky. Not the works, just the life."

"I will. I'll start tonight." He added, "I don't read much, but when I do I really like to take my time."

"He'll be up in a week or two. As soon as he's finished the book, he'll come up and see all the managers and agents and people. He likes to be alone for that." She laughed resignedly. "He calls it charging his batteries."

"The ghouls," said Cassidy.

"The ghouls," said Helen.

The early sun sprang suddenly through the monkey puzzle trees, raising the brickwork of the mansion to a warm, flesh pink.

"Tell him to ring me at the firm," said Cassidy. "We're in the book. Any time, I'll always take the call."

"Don't worry, he will." She hesitated. "By the by, you remember last night you offered Shamus a Swiss house to work in?"

"Oh the chalet. Yes. Yes, of course. Tense slope. Ha."

"He says he might take you up on that."

"Goodness," said Cassidy gratefully, "that would be wonderful."

"He can't promise."

"No, of course."

A moment's silent plea: "Cassidy."

"Yes?"

"You won't rat, will you?"

"Of course not."

She kissed him again without fuss, on the mouth this time, the way sisters kiss brothers when they're no longer worried about incest.

So Cassidy left Haverdown with the taste of her toothpaste on his lips and the smell of her simple talc in his nostrils.

8

Bohemia.

That was his first thought and it sustained him all the way to Bath. I have visited Bohemia and got away unscathed. It was many years since he had met an artist. At Oxford in his time there had been an old house near the river that was reputed to contain a number of them and sometimes, passing on his way to the Scala Cinema, he had seen their clothes hanging from the iron balcony, or a great quantity of empty bottles sprawling out of their dustbins. On Sundays, he had heard, they congregated in the George Bar, their men in earrings and their womenfolk smoking cigars, and he imagined them saying amazing things to one another about their private parts. At public school there had been a painting master known as Whitewash, a soft man in later middle age who had worn butterfly collars and made the boys sit for each other in gym shorts, and one Wednesday Cassidy had been to tea with him alone but he had hardly spoken a word, just smiled sadly and watched him eat hot muffins. Apart from these sparse experiences, his knowledge of the breed was negligible, though he had long counted himself an honorary member.

Stopping in Bath he went to his hotel to collect his luggage and pay the bill, and found himself glancing in furtive excitement at the daylight shining on the scenes of their revel. Rotten little town, he told himself. Prole-ridden Vatican. And vowed never to return.

He had signed in as Viscount Cassidy of Mull.

"Enjoy your stay my lord?" the cashier enquired with a little more intimacy than Cassidy considered needful.

"Very much indeed, thank you," he said and gave two pounds to the porter.

The process of ratting therefore, which Helen had so accurately anticipated, did not begin until round about Devizes. For the first hour of the drive, before his hangover
had entered the retributive phase, Cassidy remained confused but still elated by his encounter with Helen and
Shamus. He had little idea of what he felt; his mood
seemed to change with the landscape. On the highroad to
Frome where blue plains reached to either side of him,
a child-like innocence gilded all he saw. His whole future
was one long adventure with his new friends: together they
would bestride the world, sail distant seas, mount the sky
on wings of laughter. In Devizes where the rain began
and a dull sickness overtook his gastric system, he remained moderately enchanted, but the sight of the morning shoppers and mothers with prams gave him food for
thought. By the time he reached Reading his head was
aching terribly and he had convinced himself that Helen
and Shamus were either a dream or a pair of fakes posing
as celebrities.

"After all," he argued, "if they're who they say they
are, why should they be interested in me?"

And later: "I am one of a row. People like me have no
part in the life of an artist."

Reconstructing Helen's *tour d'horizon* of Shamus' argument on the relationship between the artist and the bourgeois, he found it frail, confused, and poorly reasoned.

I'd have put it better, he thought, if I'd held that opinion: a lot of hot air actually.

By the time he reached the outskirts of London he had
come to certain useful conclusions. He would never hear
from Helen or Shamus again; they were probably confidence tricksters and he was lucky to get away with his wallet; and whether they reappeared or not, they belonged
with certain other phenomena to that area of Cassidy's
world which for the general peace was best not revisited.

He would have dismissed them then and there, in fact, if
a small incident had not forcibly reminded him of
Shamus' disagreeably personal perceptions.

Parked in a lay-by, he was checking the pockets of his
car for compromising souvenirs when he came upon a
crumpled sheet of paper stuffed into a glove pocket.
It was the menu from Bruno's restaurant in Bath on which,
in his simplicity, he had believed that Shamus was writing
immortal prose. Down one side of the back, done in pen-

cil, was Shamus' portrait of Cassidy with words written
at the side and arrows to show what feature they referred
to. "Baby cheeks, good at blushing; noble brow, furrowed
by vague agonies; eyes shaggy and very, very shifty." Over
the top of the head in capitals was the word WANTED
and underneath a further description of Cassidy.

NAME: Cassidy, Butch. Also known as Hopalong, Christo-
pher Robin, and Paul Getty.
CRIME: Innocence (cf, Greene: a leper without his bell).
FAITH: First Church of Christ Pessimist.
SENTENCE: Survival for life.

The other side of the menu contained a letter, addressed
to LOVER.

Dear Lover,
I hope you are well. I am. Thank you very much for
a lovely nosh. Twice or thrice had I loved thee before I
knew thy face or name. So forgive nasty drawing, can't
help the Eye but the Heart's yours for the asking. Love,
love, love
> *P. Scardanelli, alias*
> *Flaherty, alias Shamus*

What a *very* undergraduate communication thought
Cassidy indignantly; how very embarrassing. Sighing, he
threw the menu away. Talk about submerged proof . . .
Ever killed anyone lover? a voice asked from inside
him. Switching on the wireless, he turned south for Acton.
Art is all very well, he thought, but sometimes it goes a
damn sight too far.

His business in Acton was brief and useful. A wholesaler
named Dobbs, notoriously difficult but an influential connection, had been objecting to the new leather-look strollers
and was flirting with a rival manufacturer. Cassidy had
never much cared for strollers, which he regarded as an
unhappy cross between your mere pushchair and your full-
scale baby carriage, but they were a useful stand-by in the
spring when demand was capricious. Rightly he calculated
that a personal visit would end the dispute.
"Well I didn't expect Himself I will say," Dobbs con-

fessed nervously. "What's happened to the rep then, horse?"

He had lost a lot of hair, Cassidy noticed; the second marriage is wearing him out. He was a very wasted man, always perspiring, and scandal attached to him.

"I like to check on these things myself, that's all. Where a valued customer complains," Cassidy said not without a certain sternness, "I like to look into it personally."

"Now look this isn't a complaint, Mr. Cassidy. The stroller's a very elegant job and your chassis does it credit, course it does. The making of it in fact. I sell a lot of them, swear by them, course I do, horse."

"A complaint's a complaint, Andy, once it gets into the pipeline."

"It's the *folding* they don't like, Mr. Cassidy," Dobbs protested not with any real conviction. "They're doing their stockings on the links."

"Let's take a look shall we, Andy?"

They climbed the wooden steps to the warehouse and examined links.

"Yes," said Cassidy, kneeling to caress a particularly well-turned example, "I see what you mean."

"Here, watch your trousers," Dobbs cried. "That floor's filthy."

But Cassidy affected not to hear. Stretching himself at full length on the unswept floorboards he ran a devoted hand along the underpart of the pram, touching with his fingertips the nipples, threads, and couplings of his earliest and most fruitful patent.

"I'm very grateful to you, Andy," he said as they returned to the office. "I'll have my people look into it right away."

"Only they do their nylons on them you see," Dobbs repeated feebly as he brushed down Cassidy's suit. "They did on the last lot anyway."

"Know what one nylon said to the other, Andy?" Cassidy asked casually as he unloaded the crate of sherry he had ready in the trunk. Sherry, they said, was what he drank.

"What's that then?"

"There's a fellow feeling between us," said Cassidy. Their laughter covered the flurried transaction. "It's an Easter present," Cassidy explained. "We're shedding a bit of the profits from the last financial year."

"It's very decent I must say," said Dobbs.

"Not at all. Thanks for putting us on to that link."

"I get worried sometimes," Dobbs confessed, seeing him back to the Bentley. "I just think I've been forgotten."

"I understand," said Cassidy. "How's the wife then?"

"Well, you know," said Dobbs.

"I know," said Cassidy.

Changing his mind, he went to the cinema. He liked best those films which praised the British war effort or portrayed with Fearless Honesty the Intimate Sex Life of Scandinavian Teenagers. On this occasion he was fortunate enough to find a double bill.

Sandra was out. She had left a *quiche Lorraine* on the kitchen table and a note saying she had gone to her meths drinkers' clinic. The hall smelt of linseed oil. Dust sheets and painters' ladders reminded him uncomfortably of Haverdown. Adding or subtracting? He tried to remember. The mouldings, he knew, were inferior and must be taken down. The fireplace perhaps? They had bought one at Mallets a month or two ago, pine, eighteenth century, three hundred quid and fine carvings over. The fireplace was a *feature*, their architect assured them, and features, God alone knew, were what their house most needed.

Her mother was in her room. From several flights above, he heard the mellifluous tones of John Gielgud reading Héloïse and Abélard on her gramophone for the blind. The sound moved him at once to a trembling fury. *Idiot, braying idiot,* she can see perfectly well when she wants to.

Very softly he went to the nursery and by the glow of the uncurtained window tiptoed to Hugo's bedside, picking his way through the litter of toys. Why had he no night light? Cassidy was convinced he was afraid of the dark. The boy slept as if dead upon the blankets, his plastered leg shining palely in the orange light and his pyjama jacket open to the waist. On the floor beside him lay the egg whisk which he used for frisking up his bubble bath. One by one Cassidy fastened the pyjama buttons, then gently laid his open palm on the child's dry brow. Well, at least he was not overheated. He listened, studying him intently through the speckled twilight. Against the sleepless boom of traffic the boy's breath came and went in small, regular sips. Nothing wrong there apparently, but why did he suck his thumb so? A child of seven doesn't suck his thumb, not unless he's deprived of love. Inwardly, Cassidy sighed. Hugo, he thought, oh Hugo, believe me son, we all go through it. Kneeling now, he minutely examined the outer surface of the plaster, searching for the telltale ridges which might betray a second parting of the fractured bone within; but the light from the window was not enough, and all he could make out were graffiti and pictures of houses done in felt-nibbed pens.

A lorry climbed the hill. Quickly standing, he drew the curtain and closed the window against the pollution of its engine. The boy stirred, laid his forearm across his eyes. A key turned in the front door.

"Hi traveller," Sandra called.

A prepared speech, reaching for modern humour.

"Hullo," said Cassidy.

Her footsteps stopped.

"Is that all you've got to say?" she asked, still from the hall.

"What else am I supposed to say? You said hi, I said hullo. I think he should see a specialist, you don't."

He waited. She could stand like that for minutes at a time; the loser was the first to move. Losing, Sandra, wife to Aldo, went slowly upstairs to her mother.

London

9

My dear Mark,

The letter hung on him like a damp cloud. Flat, non-visual; an after-lunch letter, reaching for sustenance he did not want. A letter of the liver, rather than the heart.

The paper was headed 12 Abalone Crescent, but he wrote from South Audley Street for peace. Cassidy's office was not unlike Cassidy's car: a mahogany bastion against the non-negotiable hazards of terrestrial existence. In Audley Street he was neither Aldo nor Cassidy, but *Mister Aldo*, a Christian name treated with Christian respect. In Audley Street no foot was laid upon the ground, no door closed upon its frame but cunning pads reduced the impact. Even the several telephones on his rosewood desk had been disarmed; instead of the raucous woman's scream which from childhood had so unsettled him, the instruments emitted only a grateful purr of sexual contentment, inviting not anger, not panic, but a caress along their white, submissive spines.

Well old son how are you? I must say I envy you down there in the rural quiet of Dorset, what with all the bustle and hectic tear which more and more seems in these competitive days to be the lot of the honest merchant striving for his crust! The weather at least continues balmy (which means not daft but warm and pleasant!) but all else is activity, form-filling, and an ever-tougher struggle with foreign competition. Sometimes I fear one is inclined on reaching home to wonder whether the game is worth the candle. Even my poor efforts in the direction of doing something for the less fortunate of the community seem doomed to failure— you would be appalled at the greed and selfishness of vested local interest when asked to collaborate in a scheme to help and aid their young. Even the Bristol

Corporation, of whom I had the highest hopes, have suddenly turned tail and left us back at square one. However, soldier on, as the school motto says. We are making a great effort for the Paris Trade Fair, incidentally: if ever you come into the firm which as you know I don't want to force on you, the Foreign Desk could well be an attractive slot for you to begin at, provided always that your French comes up to scratch. . . .

A bundle of solicitors' documents caught his eye, green borders and pink ribbon. Without a pause he made a second paragraph and wrote:

Well Mark, you have probably read that we here in Commerce are all deeply worried about inflation. I thought you would be reassured to know that the Chilren's Trust, of which you and Hug are equal beneficiaries, is made up of a wide spread of equities and gilt-edged, and should be well protected from the present kind of madness. I only mention this in passing.

Having read through what he had written, Cassidy sighed, laid down his gold pen, and stared absently through the lace curtains at the pageant of smartly dressed pedestrians and shining limousines. Did Mark *care* about equities? Did he know about them? Was it even desirable that he should? Vaguely, not at all a memory man when it came to the detail of his early life, Cassidy tried to establish whether he himself had been informed about such things at the age of eleven. At eleven, most likely he was still boarded with an Aunt Nell, a gross, noisy lady with a bungalow near Pendeen Sands. Had *that* child studied the financial pages? Was the lady of a sort to encourage him to study them? He remembered only her undergarments as she waded out to sea, dragging him after her to certain death: soiled petals pink and black, flapping over sunless thighs. If he was not with Aunt Nell, he was with the Spider, a discarded mistress of his father's who kept him in bed to protect him from germs.

No. His case had no relevance to Mark's.

A deep sense of malaise informs the national scene. Everyone is counting his own chickens while the poli-

ticians exhort us to the Dunkirk spirit. Last night, the Prime Minister urged the nation to work harder for its money. Few believe that his speech will make any difference. The unions have turned their faces firmly against reconciliation. Only a showdown can result.

He put down the pen.

Ridiculous.

Tear up the letter.

Here I sit, bored stiff and what do I do? Summarise the leading articles of the *Financial Times*. Business has corrupted me: I have no relationship with my son.

A few years back he would have drawn him bears and piglets—he even kept a set of Swiss crayons handy in his desk for that very purpose. But Mark had outgrown piglets, and it was very difficult to know what else was likely to give him pleasure. Perhaps money, after all, was the answer. A promise of security never came amiss. Even if he doesn't understand in detail, the *notion* will remain with him; comfort him on dark nights when the parental world bewilders him.

Mummy will have told you that she and Heather Ast are trying to open a second all-night clinic for down-and-outs. Heather has found a disused Oxfam warehouse on the southern edge of Hampstead Heath, where many of these poor wretches spend the night sleeping fitfully under old newspaper. Heather, as you know, has suffered a great blow in her life after her husband walked out on her for no good reason. Your mother is helping to bring her round. . . .

Hearing a lighter tread on the warm pavement outside, he looked up again hopefully, but his vigilance was rewarded by a redhead, and redheads alarmed him. Also, she had a determined walk; to hear it was to know already she was not easily deflected. A heel-to-toe walk, requiring a good rotary action of the elbows and a vindictive moral purpose.

Cassidy sighed. Sandra's walk.

Should he ring her?

Much of their relationship was conducted on the telephone. It was a conceit of Cassidy's, indeed, that with time all they would need for a successful marriage was two functioning telephone boxes. . . .

No, this was not an occasion for the telephone.

Send her flowers, then?

— "Dear love please forgive me, it was well meant, I only want your happiness, Aldo."

Or the bullying tone? "Smile or get out."

Or beg?

"Sandra, you're making holes in my heart. *Please, please, please . . .*"

Please whom? What can she do that will please *me* any more?

As to myself, well I must confess that I have not had much time for anything but the papers on my desk and that bane of human existence, the telephone. . . .

As to himself, *what?*

Glumly, the unfinished letter still before him, he made the reckoning. Four weeks had passed since his visit to Haverdown. He had conducted meetings, read the trade press, composed A Word From Your Chairman on the forthcoming Paris Trade Fair, taken out new policies for private medication, retirement, and sudden death, sat with accountants over the April figures for the outgoing financial year, drafted speeches for the Annual Informal Meeting of Shareholders. He had lunched with high officials of certain charities, to whom—tentatively—he had offered large sums upon obscure conditions. He had dined with the Nondescripts and repeated, with considerable success, his nice joke about what one nylon had said to the other. He had dismissed a works foreman on suspicion of industrial espionage and by adroit diplomacy averted a walk-out. He had opened a spares depôt in Amsterdam and fought and won a savage battle with the Exports Credit Guarantee Department. He had attended a matinée spectacular in one of the smaller Soho theatres, and continued his long and costly correspondence with Somerset House about his genealogy. The discussion turned on a Cassidy who had fought at Marston Moor in Cromwell's great charge against Prince Rupert's Horse; but it appeared that the effort had exhausted him for he had never been heard of since. After six years, it now seemed to

Cassidy, the correspondence threatened to become as long and fruitless as the Civil War itself. He had taken the Bentley to Park Wards and left it there while the mechanics respectfully pursued an illusory rattle in the offside door. He had played golf with his competitors and squash with his graduate trainees. His competitors had sneered at the quantity of his clubs and the graduates said "Sorry sir" and told him how Oxford had changed. He had dictated letters to his secretary, Miss Mawdray, and quizzed her youthful shape over the rim of his unnecessary spectacles. (These spectacles were not at all to be compared with those of Sandra's mother. Cassidy's spectacles were there to give him power; Mrs. Groat's to advertise her frailty.)

His frown deepened.

There, he would admit, certain pleasurable tremors had been recorded on the Cassidy seismograph. Miss Mawdray was a trim, desirable girl, dark like Sandra but taller, with a swimmer's body and a great passion for Greece. On Fridays she wore a poncho with goat's wool tassels, and on Tuesdays she read him his horoscope, knees pressed together like little buttocks, the tips of her ears pointing through her long brown hair.

"What beastliness have you got lined up for me this week, Angie?" he had asked her yesterday morning, burying his lust in an attitude of fatherly indulgence, and listened attentively to her bold prophecies from a newspaper below his station. She had recently acquired an engagement ring, but resisted all enquiries about its origin. Fellow's probably married, Cassidy concluded with lofty disapproval; these girls are all the same nowadays.

Worse still, she had taken the day off.

On one other occasion only during this entire period had Cassidy been conscious of *impact*. Attending an ordinary meeting of his manufacturing association the distinguished member had launched, for no reason he could now determine, a searing and undeserved attack on the Board of Trade. The speech was widely considered to be out of place and for several days he had contemplated suicide. Happily, good sense prevailed and he treated himself to a great luncheon instead. He had discovered a new

restaurant in Lisle Street where they made *mille-feuilles*
with a chocolate cream, and he had two helpings with his
coffee.

What have I felt? he asked himself, gazing morosely out
of the window. What have I *learned*? In what way had
he benefitted mankind? More important still, in what way
has mankind benefitted *me*? The answer: nothing. A
vacuum. Cassidy lives in a vacuum. Poor Cassidy. Poor
Bear. Poor *Pailthorpe* Bear.

And it is probably in order to fill this vacuum, Cassidy
reflected, that I have now sinned. Grossly sinned. Mother,
against Heaven and against Thee. Against Sandra, and
(he would confess) against his own flesh too. . . .

It was too much for him. Banishing the shameful memory of his most recent and provocative marital transgres-
sion, Cassidy resumed his tribute to wise fatherhood.

*Hugo is in the pink, though of course he looks forward
very much to joining you at Hearst Leigh next year. The
other day I took him to the cinema. We rang the manager
first and he was very good and arranged for a Bath chair
in the aisle. We saw* High Noon. *Hugo loved the shooting but got very impatient with the love scenes.*

Hugo: "Is he killing her?"

Me: "No. They're hugging."

Hugo: "Why don't they shoot their guns instead?"

Me: "They will when they've finished hugging."

Collapse of all around.

*Actually, he is quite reconciled to his plaster leg, and
I really think it will be a great disappointment to him
when they remove it! Though at times, of course, particularly when the weather is as fine as it is now, and the
Elderman girls are out playing on the Heath, he gets a
bit fractious, and Father is called in to play the big bogey
man. . . .*

"Come in!"

A knock at the door. His stomach froze in panic. Tele-
gram from Sandra? I HAVE LEFT YOU FOR EVER SUPPER
IN THE FRIDGE SANDRA?

Visit from an Inland Revenue Inspector: spot check
sir, if you don't mind, here's my warrant.

Her mother, Mrs. Groat, has called, tapping her way down the corridor with her fake white stick. Hullo darling, giggle, giggle, I'm afraid she's dead, isn't she?

It was Meale, an overqualified trainee, hovering at the threshold. A goatish, unappetising boy poached from Bee-Line, their principal competitor. An author of endless schemes; charmless but thrusting. Large in the field of business studies. New. Well, Cassidy would be fair to him. Meale had had few advantages of the undefinable sort and Cassidy must make allowances. Nor did he begrudge Meale his betterment. Where would Cassidy be, after all, if he had not insisted on taking the most that the market would stand? Also, he was a distraction, and distraction was what Cassidy needed.

Affecting a small *moue* of surprise, the Chairman and Managing Director woke from his weighty deliberations.

"Ah, who's that? Meale. Good morning, Meale, sit down. Not there, over here. Coffee?"

"No thank you sir."

"I'm having some."

"Well thank you very much. I wondered whether you had had a chance to read my projection programme sir."

Manners first, Meale, manners first, I expect you to drink with me.

"Sugar?" Cassidy enquired pleasantly.

"Yes sir."

"And milk?"

"Afraid so, sir."

To the box: "Coffee, Miss Orton, will you? Milk and sugar, and the usual for me."

Switch her off. Adjust spectacles. Finger confidential papers. Squint at costly reproduction chandelier. And not find it in his heart to disappoint any man who came to ask his counsel.

"I *like* it, Meale. I think it's *good*, and I think it's *right*."

"Do you really, sir?"

"Yes. Jolly *good*. You ought to be *jolly* pleased with yourself. I am. I mean pleased with you, ha ha, not *me*."

A hiatus; a cloud of discontent, suspicion, "I say—" reaching once more for Miss Orton's provoking little button "—you don't prefer tea do you?"

"Oh *no* sir!"

"Ah."

Rearrange the hands in judicial-benevolent posture, see our photograph in *The Times* eighth March this year: *Swift but Sound. Aldo Cassidy* en poste *in his Audley Street Premises.*

"So let's go ahead with it, shall we, Meale?"

The door closed.

Nothing.

Not even a depression on the black hide chair to mark where the grateful boy had sat. Or—hm hm—perhaps had not sat? Not visited, not spoken?

With a low-burning smile of winsome superiority, Dr. Aldo Cassidy, D. Phil. and bar., Fellow of All Souls and the Chairman and Managing Director's most frequent familiar, put the proposition relating to the unvisit of the man Meale:

"There are philosophers, dear boy, and no doubt psychiatrists and mystics as well, who loudly refute any notion of a distinguishing line between our wishes and their external counterparts. That being so, dear boy: does their doctrine not also extend to people? Thus: if those we meet are unmet by an act of forgetfulness, does it not follow, dear boy, that those we retain are kept in being by acts of *remembering?* Our acts? And this is turn being so—I fear I overburden the thesis?—and this in turn being so, does not such a system impose upon each one of us a most distressing responsibility for his creations? Hm? Hm? I mean what if *you* forgot *Sandra,* would *she* exist?"

Losing the thread, Cassidy drained his cold coffee and continued, in his literary persona, his *tour d'horizon* of the domestic scene.

Well Mark, the restoration work here at home continues slow but sure. The marble fireplace for the hall is pretty well in situ *(Latin fourth declension or is it fifth?!) and Mr. Mud the Mason has succeeded, not without some stern encouragement from Mummy, in getting the mantelpiece level without breaking the supports underneath. He wanted, if you please, to cut, physically cut, a piece out of the carved pine pillar, but Mummy caught him in the act and he was duly contrite!*

Here at home.

He cast a sodden gaze round his room. Once, *this* had been his home. My *dulce domum*, my sanctuary, my refuge. His compensation for all the disagreeable rooms of his childhood. Here I administered, I dispensed, I praised; and here he received in return that glow of motherly security which no woman of Cassidy's acquaintance had come within shouting distance of providing. Once, even to approach the building had been to know peace. The brickwork, with its dull, dark red of internal flesh; the frilly wooden gables painted cream, like anonymous lifted petticoats awaiting his penetration; the glistening brass plate on the rosewood front door, brighter than any woman's smile, all these things had tantalised him with favourable sensations of purchase, conquest, and expansion. "You've go so *much*," they said to him. "And you handle it so *well*." While Miss Mawdray's murmured "Good morning, Mister Aldo," issuing, it seemed, from the depths of her youthful breasts, had reminded him of the many assets he had yet to turn to cash. Here—whatever else he left behind at 12 Abalone Crescent—*here* in this sweet deep casket, seven hours a day and five days a week, he was at peace. He could recline or sit upright. He could scowl, smile, take a drink or a bath with equal privacy and, thus cossetted, freely deploy his many God-given talents of leadership, drive, and charm.

And now it is my prison. *Pitiful* Cassidy. *Abject* Toad. *Poor* Pailthorpe.

We should have stayed in Acton, he thought, yawning after his heavy luncheon—Boulestin wasn't bad actually, he must go there more often, they were one of the few places that looked after you if you went alone—we should never have become a public company. We were pioneers then; merchant adventurers, dreamers, strivers. Lemming, the chief lieutenant, now a portly man, was then a greyhound, lithe, swift, and tireless. Faulk, his advertising manager, today a balding, flagrant queen, was in those days the sharp-tongued visualizer of unlikely stunts. Now, with recognition behind them and public audits before them, a slackening of pace, a settling of the commercial digestion as it were, had tacitly replaced their youthful frenzy. Six months ago, he himself had been the first to praise this mellowing. *Retrenching* he had called it in a lengthy interview; *steadying down* and by his own deport-

ment set the tone. *The battle is over, we have entered
the smoother waters of a long and prosperous peace,* he
had assured his shareholders at last year's meeting. Great.
And when you have retrenched? And when you have
settled down? Then what do you have? The memory, and
damn all else. "Remember the night we welded up that
first prototype?" Cassidy would say to Lemming at the
Christmas party. "In that old bike shed round behind
the toyshop? Remember how we ran out of juice and had
to knock your missus out of bed, eh Arthur?"

"Lord alive," Lemming would reply, drawing on his
cigar while the young ones waited for his words. "And
wasn't she bloody mad, and all?"

Oh, how they laughed at yesterday.

*Must rush now. Promised to pay my fortnightly visit
to Grandpa, then home to Mummy. Wonder what she's
got for supper, don't you? Hey Mark—I had a thought:
isn't it funny to think that one day, sitting at this very
desk, you may be writing these very same words to your
beloved son? Well, cheerio. Remember that life's a gift
and not a burden, and that you are still barely at the stage
of opening the wrapping.*

Dad

*P.S. Incidentally, did you read the extraordinary case of
this Irishman Flaherty, in County Cork, who goes round
claiming he is God? I am sure there is nothing in it but one
never knows. I imagine you missed it, I know you only
get the* Telegraph *down there, despite your mother's letter
to Mr. Grey.*

"Take your time," he told the driver.

Cassidy's feelings about his father varied. He lived
in a penthouse in Maida Vale, a property listed among
the assets of the Company and let to him rent free in
exchange for unspecified consultative services. From its
many large windows, it seemed to Cassidy, he followed
his son's progress through the world as once the eye of
God had followed Cain across the desert. There was no
hiding from him; his intelligence system was vast, and
where it failed, intuition served him in its place. In bad
times, Cassidy regarded him as undesirable and made elaborate plots to kill him. In good times he admired him

very much, particularly his flair. When younger, Cassidy had made copious researches about Old Hugo, interviewing lapsed acquaintances in clubs and browsing through public records; but facts about him, like facts about God, were hard to come by. In Cassidy's early childhood, it appeared, Old Hugo had been a minister of religion, most likely in the nonconformist cause. By way of corroboration, Cassidy could point to the Cromwellian connection and certain memories of a pine pulpit· on a cold day, Old Hugo wedged into it like an egg into an egg cup and the tender child alone on a forward pew a mute Christ among the elders. With time however—a very variable factor in Old Hugo's incarnations—the Lord had appeared to His shepherd in a dream and counselled him that it paid better to feed the body than the mind, and the good man had accordingly put aside the cloth in favour of the hotel trade. The source of this information, not unnaturally, was Old Hugo himself, since no one else except God had been party to the dream. Often, he insisted, he regretted his divinely inspired decision, at other times he recalled it as an act of courage; and occasionally, lamenting his misfortunes, he deeply resented the years he had wasted on the Word.

"There I was, trying to teach those cretins wisdom, and what did I get? Four old nellies and a lollipop man."

At some point in his life, he had also been a Member of Parliament, though Cassidy's enquiries of the Clerks of the House of Commons had failed to confirm the claim; and he had stood in no election that any Party Headquarters could recall. Nevertheless, the initials M.P. followed him everywhere, even on his bills; and were done in heavy ink on the nameplate below his doorbell.

It was a day for buying the Savoy Hotel.

"You can't go wrong," Old Hugo insisted. "What's a hotel, then, tell me that?"

"You tell me," said Cassidy admiringly, for he knew the answer too well.

"Bricks and mortar, food and drink, that's what a hotel is. Your basic elements, your basic facts of life. Shelter and sustenance; what more do you want?"

"It's perfectly true," said Cassidy, secretly wondering as always in these conversations how, if his father knew so much about business matters, he had managed to be penniless for twenty years. "There's a lot in what you say," he added with obedient enthusiasm.

"Forget fastenings. Fastenings are dead. So's prams. All dead. Look at the pill. Look at Vietnam. Are you going to tell me, son, that this world of ours today is a world in which men and women are going to breed their babies the way your mother and I did?"

"No," Cassidy agreed pleasantly, "I suppose not," and wrote him a cheque for a hundred pounds. "Will that do you for a bit?" he asked.

"Never forget," his father remarked, reading the words as well as the figures. "The sacrifices I made for you."

"I never could," Cassidy assured him. "Truly."

Carefully arranging his dressing gown over his bald white knees, Old Hugo shuffled to the window and surveyed the misted rooftops of Dickensian London.

"Tipping," he burst out in sudden contempt, seeing perhaps, among the chimney pots, descending generations of unpaid waiters, Cypriots from the Waldorf in Yarmouth, Anglo-Saxons at the Grand Pier in Pinner. "Tipping's *funk*, that's what tipping is. I've seen it time and again. Any fool can tip if he's got ten bob and a waistcoat."

"It's just that I know you need a little extra now and then."

"You'll *never* pay me off. *Never*. You've got assets no man can put a price on, least of all you. Where do they come from? They come from your old man. And when I'm judged as judged I shall one day surely be, as surely as night follows day, son, make no mistake about it, I shall be judged *solely and exclusively* on the many wonderful talents and attributes I have passed on to you, although you're worthless."

"It's true," said Cassidy.

"Your education, your brilliance, your inventiveness, the lot. Look at your discipline. Look at your religion. Where would *they* be if I hadn't done you right?"

"Nowhere."

"A delinquent, that's what you'd be. A pathetic delinquent, same as your mother, if I hadn't paid those boys down at Sherborne a towering fortune to put virtue and patriotism into you. You've got all the opportunity in the world. How's your French?"

"Good as ever," said Cassidy.

"That's because your mother was French. You'd never have *had* a French mother if it hadn't been for me."

"I know," said Cassidy. "I say you don't know where she is do you?"

"Well keep it up," Old Hugo urged. His bloodless palm described a magisterial arc, as if it would stop the sun from moving. "You can get anywhere with languages," he informed the cosmos. "Anywhere. Still say your prayers do you?"

"Of course."

"Still kneel down and put your hands together like a little child then?"

"Every night."

"Like hell you do," Old Hugo retorted stoutly. "Say the prayers I taught you."

"Not now," said Cassidy.

"Why not?"

"I don't feel like it."

"Don't feel like it. Christ. Don't feel like it."

He was drinking, steadying himself on the steel window frame.

"Hotels," he repeated. "That's your line. Same as it was mine; your manners alone are worth five thousand a year, you ask Hunter. Don't *feel* like it!"

Hunter was a source, now dead. Cassidy had met him secretly in the National Liberal Club, but learned nothing. Both father and son had attended his funeral.

"They're *your* manners," said Cassidy courteously.

The old man nodded approvingly and for a while seemed to forget his son altogether, giving himself wholly to his profound contemplations of the London skyline.

"There's a man in County Cork who says he's God," said Cassidy, with a sudden smile.

"It's a con," Old Hugo replied, with that prompt certainty which Cassidy adored in him. "The oldest con in the world."

Discovering the cheque still in his hand Old Hugo reread it. That's all he reads, thought Cassidy, it's all he's ever read, evening papers and cheques and a few letters diagonally, to get their drift.

"You hang on to her," Old Hugo said at last, still reading the cheque. "You'd have been a delinquent if you hadn't married a bitch."

"But she doesn't *like* me," Cassidy objected.

"Why the hell should she? You're a bigger bloody liar than I am. *You* married honesty, not me. Live with it and shut up."

"Oh I've shut up all right," said Cassidy with some spirit. "We haven't spoken for a week."

The old man rounded on him.

"What do you mean, *haven't spoken to her for a week?* Jesus, I went months with your stupid mother. *Months.* All for *your* rotten sake, because I'd given you life. You wouldn't *exist* without me. Hear?" He returned to the window. "Anyway, you shouldn't have done it."

"All right," said Cassidy meekly, "I shouldn't have done it."

"Bitch," Old Hugo declared at last, dully, but whether he meant Sandra or some other lady, Cassidy could not tell. "Bitch," he murmured yet again, and leaning the vast lilac torso as far back as it would go, poured the rest of his brandy into it as if he were filling a lamp.

"And keep away from the queers," he warned, as if they too had let him down.

Kurt was Swiss, a neutral, kindly man dressed in cautious greys. His tie was dull brown and his hair was dull honey, and he wore a pastel-shaded ruby on his pale, doctor's hands, but the rest of him was cut from slate, off-season skies, and his shoes were trellised in matt grey leather.

They sat in a plastic office beside a plastic globe, discussing great climbs they would make this summer, and studying brochures for rucksacks, crampons, and nylon ropes. Cassidy was very frightened of heights but he felt that now he owned a chalet he should come to grips with the mountains. Kurt agreed.

"You are made for it, I can tell by your shoulders you see," he said, his eyes appraising them with pale pleasure. Kurt and Cassidy would start on the smaller ones and work upwards. "Then maybe one day you climb the Eiger."

"Yes," said Cassidy, "I would like that."

Cassidy would pay, he said, if Kurt would do the arranging.

A small silence intervened. Time for business? Kurt's job had never been defined for Cassidy, but his function was undisputed. He handled money. Money as an end, a commodity, a product. He received it in England and returned it abroad, and somewhere over the Channel he took a small commission for defying tiresome English laws.

Time for a drink.

"You would like a kirsch?"

"No thank you."

"Got to get in training."

"Yes," Cassidy said. And laughed shyly, trying to anticipate the Alpine consummation. He can't want *me*, he thought; he's just *generally* queer, it's nothing local I'm sure.

"How is it?" Kurt enquired, lowering his voice to match the intimacy.

"Well. . .you know. Up and down. Down at the moment actually. She's learning the piano again."

"Ah," said Kurt. A short deprecating *ah*. A puppy has messed on my Wilton. "She is competent?"

"Not very."

"Ah."

A tiny Swiss light winked from his desk. He blew it out.

"It's just . . ." Cassidy went on. "It's just, we never talk. Except about charities and things. How about *my* charity . . . ? You know."

"Sure," said Kurt. The smile slit the pale cushions of his jaw. "My God," he remarked equably. "The piano huh?"

"The piano," Cassidy agreed. "How is it with you, Kurt?"

"Me?" The question puzzled him.

In Switzerland, Cassidy thought, they have a lot of suicides and divorces, and sometimes Kurt seemed to be the explanation for them all.

Kurt had a silver ballpoint pen. It lay like a polished bullet on his fibreglass desk. Lifting it, he peered for a long time at the tip, examining it for engineering defects.

"Thank you I am fine."

"Great."

"Is there another way I can help you, Cassidy?"

"Well if you could manage five hundred?"

"No problem. At ten to the pound okay? We rob you a few centimes."

"I'll give you a cheque," said Cassidy and wrote it out to cash, using Kurt's pen.

"You know," said Kurt, "I don't like to criticise your government but these are crazy regulations."

"I know," said Cassidy.

Old Hugo left cheques open, ready for immediate presentation, but Kurt folded them, handled them the way a card player handles cards, assuming them into the palm and emitting them through the finger and thumb.

"Then why don't you change them?" he asked.

"We should, shouldn't we? It's the silly English thing, I'm afraid. Regulations are part of our tradition. We make them, then we fall in love with them."

The expression held Kurt still for several chronometric seconds. "Fall in love?" he repeated.

"Figuratively."

Kurt saw him to the door. "Please give her my regards."

"I will. Thanks. I say, I don't know whether you read the English papers but there's a southern Irish man who's announced he's God. Not the new Christ, apparently. God."

Kurt's frown was as faint as a pencil line after the rubbing out.

"Southern Ireland is Catholic," he said.

"That's right."

"I am sorry. I am evangelical."

"Goodnight," said Cassidy.

"Goodnight," said Kurt.

For an hour, perhaps longer, he took taxis to places. Some smelt of Old Hugo's cigars, some of the scent of women he loved but had never met. It was dusk by the time he approached the Crescent and the lights were on in the houses either side. Stopping the cab he walked the last hundred yards and the Crescent was like the night they had first seen it, a treasure chest of pastel doors and antique coaching lamps, bound books, rocking chairs, and happy couples.

"You can have any one of the three. This one, this one, this one."

"Let's have them all," said Sandra, holding his hand as they stood in the rain. "Lorks, Pailthorpe—" using their

game words and giving his hand a squeeze "—whoever
will we get to fill so many rooms?"

"We'll found a dynasty," said Cassidy proudly. "We'll be
the Greeks, the Minoans, the Romans. Masses of little
Pailthorpes, fat as butter. So."

Woollen gloves she wore, and a woollen headscarf
soaked through, and the rain lay on her face like tears of
hope.

"Then there won't *never* be enough rooms," she said
proudly. "Cos I'm going to have litters of them. Ten at a
time like Sal-Sal. Till you trip over them on the stairs. *So.*"

Sal-Sal was a Labrador bitch, their first, now dead.

She had drawn the curtains early, as if she were afraid of
each day's dying. When she was young she had enjoyed
the evenings, but now the curtains made an early night
of them, and the twilight was left outside. The house stood
in darkness, a dark green column, six floors of it, one
corner stuck like a prow on to the pavement and chipped
at handlebar height where the tradesboys passed. He
hardly noticed the scaffolding any more, it had been there
so long. He saw the house like a face under the hair of it,
changing only where the masons changed it as they replaced the wooden lintels with hand-turned stone.

*We'll make it perfect. We'll make it just as it would
have been in the eighteenth century.*

And if you do decide to go into the Church, said Sandra, *we'll let it to a boys' club for peanuts.*

Yes, Cassidy agreed, *we will. So.*

Ducking under the scaffolding he unlocked the front
door and stepped inside. Bundles of Oxfam clothing in the
hall, a plastic lifeboat for putting pennies in.

Music.

She was practising a simple hymn; just the tune, no
attempt at harmony.

The day Thou gavest, Lord, is ended.

He looked for Heather's coat. Gone.

Christ, he thought; not a witness, not a referee. It'll
take them a month to find our bodies.

"Hi," he called up the stairs.

The music continued.

Sandra had her own drawing room and the piano was too large for it. It stood between her doll's house and a crate of bric-à-brac she had bought at Sotheby's and not yet unpacked, and it looked as though it had been dropped there from above like a lifeboat and no one knew where to sail it. She sat very upright before it, manning it alone, one light burning for help and the metronome ticking out a signal. On its bow, where it finally tapered to a halt, stood a pile of dusty circulars about Biafra. From under the words "Biafra the Facts," a black baby, terribly emaciated, screamed soundlessly into the crystal chandelier. Sandra wore a housecoat and her mother had put up her hair for her as if to say it wouldn't be needed any more that night. There was a hole in the wall behind her, jagged like a shell hole. Builders' dust sheets covered the floors, and a very big Afghan hound watched her from the depths of a Queen Anne winged chair.

"Hi," he said again. "What gives?"

Her concentration deepened. She was a slight, hard-bodied girl with brown, male eyes and, like the house, she wore a wistful, uninhabited look which somehow discouraged trespass and yet lamented loneliness. Something had been planted there and withered. Regarding her, and waiting for the storm to break, Cassidy had the uncomfortable feeling that that something was himself. For years he had tried to want what she wanted, and found no external reason to want anything else. But in all those years he had never quite known what she wanted. Recently, she had acquired several small accomplishments, not for herself, but to pass on to her children before she died. Yet her children wearied her, and she was frequently unkind to them in little spiritual ways, the way children are unkind to one another.

The darkness falls at Thy behest.

"You're getting on fine," Cassidy volunteered. "Who's teaching you?"

"No one," she said.

"How was trade?"

"Trade?"

"Down at the clinic. Many turn up?"

"You call that trade?" she asked.

The day Thou gavest, Lord, is ended.

"No one turned up," she said.

"Perhaps they're cured," he suggested, his voice slowing to the rhythm of the music.

The darkness falls at Thy behest.

"No. They're out there. Somewhere."

The metronome ticked slowly to a halt.

"Shall I wind it up for you?"

"No thank you," she said.

The day Thou gavest, Lord, is ended.

Awkwardly, not wishing to disturb the Afghan, he balanced one buttock on the winged chair. It was very uncomfortable and the original embroidery pricked his tender skin.

"So what did you do?"

"Baby-sat."

"Oh. Who for?"

The darkness falls at Thy behest.

"The Eldermans."

She spoke with an infinite patience, in sad acceptance of an unfathomable mystery. The Eldermans were the doctor and his wife, a hearty, treacherous couple and Sandra's closest allies.

"Well, that was nice," said Cassidy, genially. "Go to the flicks did they? What did they see?"

"I don't know. They just wanted to be together."

Very stiffly, she played a descending scale. She finished very low and the Afghan growled in discomfort.

"Sorry," said Cassidy.

"What for?"

"About Hugo. I just got worried."

"Worried what about?" she asked, frowning. "I don't think I understand."

The day Thou gavest, Lord, is ended.

In his heart, Cassidy was prepared to confess to any-thing—human crimes had no logic for him, and he readily assumed he had committed them all. Outward confession, however, was painful to him, and offensive to his notions of deportment.

"Well," he began reluctantly, "I deceived you. I took him to a specialist. I pretended I was taking him to *High Noon* and instead I took him to a specialist." Receiving not even a reply, let alone absolution, he added more crisply, "I thought that was what we've been quarrelling about for the last eight days."

The darkness falls at Thy behest.

With a noise like slopping water the Afghan began chewing at her forepaw, trying to get at something deep in the skin.

"Stop that!" Sandra bellowed; and to Cassidy: "Are we quarrelling? I'm sure we're not."

The Afghan paid her no attention.

"Oh well that's fine," said Cassidy. And being close to anger, let the hymn soothe him, both lines.

"Where's Heather?" he asked.

"Out with a boyfriend."

"I didn't know she had one."

"Oh, she has."

The day Thou gavest, Lord, is ended.

"Is he nice?"

"He cherishes her."

"Oh well that's fine."

The hole in the wall gave into what was once a study. The plan was to link the two rooms, which they agreed had been the original architect's original intention.

"What did the specialist *say?*" she enquired.

"He took another set of X-rays. He'll ring me tomorrow."

"Well let me know, won't you?"

"I'm sorry I deceived you. It was . . . emotion. I care very much for him."

She played another slow scale. "Of course you do," she said, as if accepting the inevitable. "You're very fond of your children. I know you are. It's perfectly natural, why apologise? Have you had a *good* year?" she asked politely. "Spring's the time you count your money, isn't it?"

"Useful," Cassidy replied cautiously.

"You mean you've made a lot of profit?"

"Well, before tax, you know."

Folding away her music she went to the long window and stared at things he couldn't see.

"Goodnight darling," her mother called reproachfully from upstairs.

"I'll be up in a minute," Sandra said. "Did you buy an evening paper?"

"No, no I'm afraid not."

"Or hear the news by any chance?"

He thought of telling her about Flaherty but decided

against. Religion was one of the subjects they had agreed not to discuss.

"No," he said.

She said no more but only sighed so finally he asked: "What news?"

"The Chinese have launched their own satellite."

"Oh my Lord," said Cassidy.

The political world meant nothing to either of them, Cassidy was convinced of it. Like a dead language it provided the opportunity for studying at one remove the meaning of their own. If she talked America she was objecting to his money and Cassidy would reply in kind with a reference to the falling value of the pound; if she talked world poverty she was harping upon their early days when a slender budget had forced upon them an attitude of selfless abstinence. If she talked Russia, a country for which she professed the profoundest admiration, he knew that she longed for the plainer, passionate laws of a more vigorous sex life, for a never-never land in which his own sophistries could once more be subjugated to urges he no longer felt for her.

It was only recently however that she had entered the field of Defence. Uncertain of her meaning he selected a jovial tone.

"Was it yellow?"

"I don't know what colour it was I'm afraid."

"Well I'll bet it was a flop," he said.

"It was a complete success. Jodrell Bank has confirmed the Chinese bulletin."

"Oh Lord well that'll stir things up I suppose won't it?"

"Yes. I forgot how much you enjoy sensation."

She had moved closer to the window. Her face so near the glass seemed to be lit by darkness and her voice was as lonely as if she were talking of lost love. As if the day Thou hast given her, Lord, was ended.

"You do realise don't you that the Pentagon assessment of war risk foresees an annual rise of two per cent per annum?" With the tip of her small finger she drew a triangle and crossed it out. "That gives us fifty years at the most."

"Well, not *us*," he said still striving for a cheerful note.

"I meant civilisation. Our children in case you'd forgotten them. It's not much fun is it?"

Under the piano, two cats who had till then slept peacefully in each other's arms woke and began spitting.

"Perhaps it'll change," he suggested. "Perhaps it'll go down again; it might. Like the stock market."

With a shake of her dark hair she dismissed all chances of survival.

"Well, even if it doesn't there's not much we can do about it, is there?" he added injudiciously.

"So let's just go on making money. It'll be nice for the children won't it, to die rich. They'll thank us for that, won't they?" Her voice had risen a key.

"Oh no," said Cassidy, "I don't mean that at all. God, you make me out to be a sort of monster . . ."

"But you don't propose to *do* anything do you? None of us does."

"Well . . . there are the boys' clubs . . . the playing fields . . . the Cassidy Trust . . . I mean I'm sorry they haven't *happened* yet, but they will, won't they?"

"Will they?"

"Of course they will; if I go on trying hard enough. And you encourage me enough. We got jolly close to it in Bristol, after all."

If you believe in God, he argued, surely you can believe a few simple lies like mine? Sandra, you *need* faith, scepticism ill becomes you.

"Anyway," she said. "The war will hardly be averted by a playing field, will it? But still."

"Well what about you? Biafra . . . the meths boys . . . Vietnam . . . Oxfam . . . look at that Greek petition you signed . . . you must be doing *some* good. . . ."

"Must I?" she asked of the misted window as the tears began running down her childish cheeks. "You call that *doing?*"

Somehow he had crossed the room, squeezed past the piano, and taken her unfamiliar body in his arms. Bewildered, he held her as she wept, feeling nothing but a sadness he could not change and an emptiness he could not fill, like the hunger of the screaming child on the piano.

"Take him to any specialist you like," she said at last, rolling her head on his shoulder as the tears still fell. "I don't care. Take him to the whole lot. It's you that's sick, not him."

"It's all right," Cassidy whispered, patting her. "The specialist was no better than John Elderman. Truly. Just a silly old dodderer, that's all he was. John will look after him. John will. He'll do just fine, you'll see."

For a while longer he held her until, gently releasing herself, she walked from the room, drawing her skirts after her like chains. As she opened the door, the sound of her mother's radio swept in past her, dance music from between the wars. The animals watched her leave.

Next morning trying at breakfast to keep the shadow from Sandra's eyes, he invited her to accompany him to Paris for the Trade Fair.

"It's only business," he said, "but we might get a *bit* of fun."

"Fun is what we need," said Sandra, and kissed him absently.

10

Waiting.

A time for flowers.

"In *principle* I'm all for it," Lemming insists piously. "No one more so, I dare say. But it's the details that worry me, to be frank, the details."

And it was the details which, with the cunning of an old campaigner, he was now proceeding to assault.

A Monday, balmier if possible than the last Monday, balmier than the Monday before that; Mister Aldo's prayer session, all present and correct; a day when waiting is to dream; to believe in Nietzsche and J. Flaherty.

"Nice buttonhole, Mister Aldo," said Faulk.

"Thank you, Clarence."

"Get it off a barrow?" asked Lemming coarsely.

"Moyses Stevens," said Cassidy, reminding Lemming of his membership of the Many-too-Many. "In Berkeley Square, or haven't you heard of them?"

The topic however is not flower shops but the Paris Trade Fair, now two weeks away. Lemming loathes the French more than any living thing, and next to the French he loathes exports, which he regards as synonymous with the most reckless managerial malpractice. A golden sunlight is falling in strips across the liquid surface of the eighteenth-century table and the dust rises through it in tiny stars. Miss Mawdray, dressed like a summer flower, is serving coffee and fruitcake and Lemming's lugubrious monologue is an offence against the beauty of the day.

"Take your new prototype all-aluminium chassis right? Now I admire that chassis. Properly handled I believe that chassis is going to sweep your home market. But what *I'm* saying is this: it's not going to sweep *any* ruddy market while it's lying in pieces all over the workshop floor."

And slaps the table, not too heavily, leaving pads of sweat on Mrs. Croft's Antiquax.

"Oh come on," Cassidy protests. "Of course it will be ready, they've been tinkering with that thing for months; don't be bloody silly."

Lemming's piety, Lemming's objectivity, Lemming's status do not take kindly to this rebuke, so he pulls back his chin and puts on his Trade Union Leader Voice.

"I am assured *both* by Works *and* by the Engineers," he announces in a fighting, ungrammatical statement approved by fourteen committees, "that they see no hope *whatever* at this point in time of putting together that chassis prior to last date of shipment. Thanks, dear."

And takes some more fruitcake from Miss Mawdray's ample store.

The rose in Cassidy's buttonhole smells of paradise, and freckled girls in green, arboreal overalls. *"And you can throw this in for me,"* says Gaylord Cassidy, the well-known West End beau, signing a cheque for other purposes. *"I'll fetch you a pin,"* says the freckled girl in green.

"Well that settles it," pipes queer Clarence Faulk, much under Lemming's influence these days, and does a *thing,* as he would say, with his hair. Kurt's thing, a sudden limp-wristed correction to an arrangement which only exists in the mirror. "Oh I *am* sorry Mister Aldo, I interrupted you."

"Did you?" says Cassidy. "I don't think so. Mr. Meale, what have *you* got there?"

"A rather depressing report on the sealed absorbers I'm afraid, Mister Aldo. It seems *they've* shown up badly on the testing floor too."

"Better let's have it," says Cassidy with an encouraging smile. "Take your time now." For Meale is still inclined, in conference with the great, to gabble his words and lose the sense.

Meale takes a deep breath.

"The Cassidy Easy-Clean Shock Absorber," he begins, starting rather quaintly with the title, "housed in its own PVC container and designed for all strollers and small carriages. Patent pending, fifty shillings, trade only." He stops. "Shall I read it *all?*" he asks in some embarrassment.

"If you please, Meale."

If you please Meale. Your voice, Meale, is not half as offensive as you suppose and a great deal more congenial than the voice of the prole Lemming or the sodder Faulk. There is hope in it you see, Meale. There is life, there is tomorrow, Meale. Continue with our blessing.

"The action of the spring, confined to an airtight case, has caused overheating and in one instance actual combustion. Subjected to a simulated velocity equivalent to five m.p.h.—that is, the maximum allowable pedestrian rate—the spring was observed to burst *through* the housing, whereupon a rapid deterioration of the plastic also ensued. . . ."

Whereupon, Meale, it was a free spring, burst as you rightly suggest from its unnatural housing. A bouncing jolly, vibrant spring, a liberated spring with a life to lead and a heart to give.

"Miss Mawdray."

"Yes, Mister Aldo."

Caught, you bitch.

Cassidy might have tweaked her, she turns so sharply. She had her back to him. Was stooping, generously stooping, bless the child, to freshen Meale's cup, a treacherous operation considering his own was empty, and her breasts had nudged perilously downwards almost to his neck, when Cassidy's summons recalls her to loyalty. Is that the cause of her surprise? Is that the reason she has turned to him full face, full chest, skirt tautly rucked across her pelvis, eyebrows finely raised, tongue slack upon the lip? Was there an unconscious note of urgency in his voice, of jealousy not withheld, as he saw the sunlight narrow between the two lush tips and the callow boy's hard shoulder? *Only teasing Mister Aldo.*

"Miss Mawdray—forgive me Meale—Miss Mawdray, the mail. That was *all* the mail. You're sure?"

"Yes, Mister Aldo."

"There was nothing . . . personal. No personal material?"

Like a rose, for instance?

"No."

"You've checked in the package room?"

"Yes Mister Aldo."

Back. Back to waiting. We have time to wait, time to wait.

"Well that rules the spring out, doesn't it?" said Lemming with satisfaction, jabbing one overpaid finger at Meale's report.

"Not entirely," said Cassidy. "Meale, will you continue?"

Slowly Meale, we have all the time in the world.

Waiting.

Waiting, he languished like an Edwardian girl, in flower gardens of his own remembering. Walked in morning parks and watched the first tulips open to the restive sun; wore other roses in his buttonhole, slept in the Savoy under the pretext of a charitable errand, bought Sandra several expensive gifts, including a pair of long black Anna Karenina boots and a plain, wrapover housecoat which became her adequately but not more. Waiting, he dawdled guiltily outside bookshops, teetering but somehow never daring; till one day he sent Angie out to buy a copy and put it in a drawer of his desk, and locked the drawer against his own invasion. Waiting, he took Hugo to the zoo.

"Where does *Heather* live?" Hugo asked as they rode on the waterbus under hanging beeches. He was sitting on Heather's lap, his broken leg dangling negligently between her large thighs.

"In Hampstead," said Heather. "In a teeny-weeny flat next to a milkshop."

"You ought to come and live with *us*," said Hugo, reprovingly, "because you're my friend, aren't you Heather?"

"I almost *do* live with you," said Heather, and cuddled him closer against her soft, loose body, while she munched a red apple from a bag.

She was a warm, blond creature, fortyish, once the wife of a publisher. Now she was divorced and the godmother to other marriages. Hugo seemed to prefer her to Sandra, and in a way so did Cassidy, for she possessed what he called a decent quiet, a pastoral repose to her broad, comfortable body. Sandra said divorce had broken her heart, that she wept a lot, and was given to outbursts of great anger, mainly against men, but Cassidy found no sign of this in her company.

"Look," said Heather. "Herons."

"I like herons," said Hugo. "Don't you, Daddy?"

"Very much," said Cassidy.

Heather smiled, and once more the sunlight made a gold downy line along her cheekbone.

"You're so *good* Aldo," she said. "Isn't he, Hug?"

"He's the best daddy in the world," Hugo agreed.

"You do so much for others. If *only* we could do something for you."

"I want to make people happy," said Cassidy. "That's all I care about."

From a call box within sight of the gibbons, he consulted the office switchboard. Nothing, they said. Nothing but business.

"You have the instructions?"

"Yes, Mister Aldo, we all have."

"It's the export drive," he explained to Heather emerging from the kiosk. "We're waiting for an urgent shipment."

"You work so hard," said Heather, whose smile shone straight as the sun.

And still waiting, went to Sherborne, where Old Hugo had bought him his polish and his learning.

Sat in the Abbey under the shell-torn flags of disbanded country regiments reading the names of great battles, Alma, Egypt, Sevastopol, and Plassey, and loving passionately the heritage he had never had.

And sitting thus, prayed.

Dear Lord this is Aldo Cassidy who last prayed to you under these same flags at the age of fifteen. I was then a schoolboy and not happy. The occasion was Remembrance Day; my cheeks, be it noted, ran wet with love as the Last Post played, and I specifically asked you for a quick, useful death against appalling odds. I should now like to revise my request. I don't want death any more; I want life, and only Thou, oh Lord, can provide it. So please don't let me wait too long, Amen.

And attended a Rugby match on the first fifteen field and cheered for his old school, thinking of Sandra and wondering whether he had sinned against her, fearing the answer yes. There, vaguely scanning the home team for the kind of boy he might have been, he encountered Mrs. Harabee, one of a small army of women who had tried to teach him music.

"Why it's Doubtful," cried Mrs. Harabee, a little brown lady with short hair and a beret. "Wearing a buttonhole! Doubtful, how on earth are you?"

Doubtful because he was a doubtful volunteer to music, and had remained so until she had despaired of him.

Doubtful because Old Hugo had made them an offer on the fees and scandalised the Bursar. The offer had comprised a second mortgage on a commercial hotel in Henley, but the Bursar was no friend of catering. Doubtful because . . .

"Hullo, Mrs. Harabee," said Cassidy. "How are you?" *Heard about Flaherty, Mrs. Harabee?*

And it came back to him that she had also been his mother, and housed him in a red-brick bedroom on the Yeovil Road at a time when he was in mortal conflict with Old Hugo.

"How did it all work out for you?" she asked, as if they were meeting in Heaven.

"Not too bad Mrs. Harabee. I went into advertising first, then I invented things and formed a company."

"Well done," said Mrs. Harabee in the tone she used for applauding an easy phrase of music. "And what became of that foul father of yours?"

"He died," said Cassidy, feeling it was easier to kill Old Hugo than explain him. "He went to prison and died."

"Poor lamb," said Mrs. Harabee. "I always had a *very* soft spot for him."

They walked slowly down the lane, carried by the stream of tilting straw hats.

"You can come to tea if you want," said Mrs. Harabee.

But Cassidy knew he was too old for her.

"I've got to get back I'm afraid," he said. "We've got a big deal coming off with America. I have to be on the end of a phone."

Before they parted, she became quite strict.

"Now Doubtful have you got boys?"

"Yes, Mrs. Harabee. Two. Mark and Hugo."

"Have you put them down for Sherborne?"

"Not yet, Mrs. Harabee."

"Well you must."

"I will."

"Otherwise *however* can we go on? If the Old Boys aren't loyal, who will be? And after all, you can obviously afford it."

"I'll do it next week," said Cassidy.

"Do it *now*. Run up to the porter's lodge and do it now, before you forget."

"I will," Cassidy promised and watched her up the hill, a steady pace and a healthy stride.

Walking again as the evening came, he found the narrow streets behind the Digby, and smelt the woodsmoke and the damp embracing smell of English stone; caught from the windows of schoolhouses scraps of woodwind music from half-instructed mouths; remembered the pain of loving and having no one to love; and envied Mrs. Harabee that her love could be at once so single and so diffuse.

And searched the darkening faces for the policeman's daughter.

Bella? Nellie? Ella? He no longer knew. She was fifteen, Cassidy sixteen; and since then his tastes had never seriously progressed, neither beyond her age nor the experience she gave him. Her breasts were irrepressible, her hips plump as cottage bread, and her hair was long and blond. He had her on weekdays in the summer after cricket, in the remoter bunkers of Sherborne Golf Course, lying side by side, hands only. She had never allowed him to enter her. For all he knew she was virgin to this day, for she had a terror of pregnancy and the most exaggerated notion of the agility of semen.

"They *walk*," she assured him once, as they lay in their tiny dune, her green eyes wide with sincerity. "They find the way by smell and *walk* there."

Despite these restrictions, he had never possessed anyone so fully, nor wanted anyone so urgently. She caressed him as skilfully as he caressed himself; in return he touched her as he pleased, lingered for hours over the gifts of her flesh. Her full, creaseless body was at once adolescent and maternal; her moist ovens, strained through membranes of cheap silk, were the incubators of his life and lust; as to her aweful susceptibility to his own progenital seed, it served only to deepen their relationship. As she had borne him, so she could conceive by him: mother and daughter had assumed him equally.

And thought of Sandra again, and whether he had ever loved her that way, perhaps he had, perhaps he hadn't.

In the pub, the television made its own blue firelight and a small dog barked for bacon-flavoured crisps.

"Zero," said Angie on the telephone. "Not a word."

"Not a hope," he told Sandra, pretending to call from Reading, where he had pretended to go on a pretended errand of charity; pretence being his only means of earning praise, and privacy. "Not a hope," he repeated with conviction. "The National Playing Fields Association have bagged the only possible site."

And drank six whiskies, Talisker, recently his favourite.

And bought a half-bottle of a blended malt, the flat shape, to fit into his pocket.

11

Dear Mark, he wrote in bed that night, in an old hotel in Marlborough, in the make-believe pages of his drunken fantasy. So that you never have to wonder who your parents are, or how you came to life, I am going to give you a brief rundown of how it all happened, so that you can decide for yourself how much you owe the world, and how much the world owes you.

Mummy and Daddy met in Dublin at a dance. Daddy was wearing his first dinner jacket and Grandpa Cassidy was the headwaiter. . . .

He began again. Not Dublin: Oxford. Why the hell had he thought of Dublin? *Nothing Irish about us old son, the Cassidys are English to the core.* Oxford. Oxford because Sandra was studying domestic science in a dark house in Woodstock. Oxford, that was it, a May ball, five guineas a single ticket, Old Hugo was not even on the horizon.

Mummy was a haunted, spindly girl, but very pretty in a death-wish sort of way and she wore a Cinderella dress that sometimes looked silver and sometimes seemed to be covered in ash. . . .

Hating her parents, pressing her head against his puckered shirt front as they moved to their parents' music.

Daddy gave Mummy the benefit of his conversation to which Mummy listened with melancholy intensity and later, when Daddy left her in order to dance with someone jollier, she sat in a chair and declined all other invitations. When Daddy returned, Mummy rose to him with unsmiling obedience. Early in the morning, partly out of politeness, and partly out of a sense of occasion, and partly perhaps to challenge such evident integrity, Daddy took Mummy on a punt (which is a flat boat you push along with a stick) and explained in a succession of pleasantly apologetic sentences that he had fallen in love with her.

123

He chose a confessive style modelled on a very romantic French film star named Jean Gabin whom he had recently seen at the Scala: it was a style which leaned on a sense of loss rather than of gain. It was nothing she need worry about, he assured her, she should feel no guilt or obligation, he was a man after all and would find his own way of dealing with it. Before Daddy had quite finished, Mummy seized him in a refugee's embrace and said she loved him too, and so they lay in the punt exchanging kisses, watching the sun rise over Magdalen Chapel while they strained their ears to hear the choir singing from the tower. Because you know, every first of May the choir all stand on the top of the tower and sing a song, but all *Daddy* heard was the early lorries rumbling over the bridge and the laughter of upper-class undergraduates throwing bottles into the water.

A lorry changed gear; the ceiling rocked in the half-darkness. Watch that Heaven, Flaherty.

"I love you," Mummy said, closing her eyes and breathing the words inward like a drug.

"I love *you*," Daddy assured her. "I've never said that to anyone before," which is supposed, for some reason, to make it extra true. Putting his hand inside the Cinderella dress Daddy felt the frozen pips of Mummy's bosom and it was like touching an orphan somehow, touching himself, only a lady. Then he saw the light of eternity shining in her virgin eye and was *very* gratified to think that so much animal energy was exclusively available to himself.

Flaherty was drifting round the room chanting Old Testament slogans through glistening alcoholic lips. Opening his eyes wide, Cassidy successfully despatched him.

Throughout the term, so far as I remember, we met regularly. Mummy seemed to expect it and Daddy (naturally a very polite person) was of course quite ready, when time allowed, to receive anybody's admiration, as we all are. So we met on Sunday mornings at Something Lock after Mummy had been to church, and on Wednesday evenings at the Something Restaurant after Daddy had been to the cinema. Sometimes Mummy brought one of her lovely picnics made in the domestic science kitchens. Daddy did not tell Mummy he went to the cinema because he thought she might disapprove, so he told her instead that he went to All Souls for tea with *Rowse*. Now A. L. Rowse is a very grand historian and also something of a popular name so naturally Daddy thought he would be a good person to be protected by. Rowse had taken him up, he explained, as a result of a few essays he had written, and might very well be sponsoring him for a *Fellowship*, which is something every undergraduate thinks he ought to have.

"Aren't they all *bachelors* at All Souls?" Mummy asked.

"It's changing," said Daddy, because of course bachelors aren't married, and Mummy and Daddy had to be married to have you and Hug, didn't they?

Now you may well wonder what Mummy and Daddy talked about. Well, they talked about *their* Mummy and Daddy. Grandpa Groat was in Africa (where he still is) busy completing his time. The mere mention of him made Mummy extremely angry. "He's so *stupid*," she said stamping her foot on the towpath. "And Mummy's stupid too," meaning Granny. Most of all she despised their values. Grandpa Groat, she said, cared only for his pension and Granny Groat cared only for her servants and neither of them had ever stopped to wonder what life was really all about. Mummy hoped they would stay in Africa for ever, it would serve them right for going there in the first place.

Not to be outdone, Daddy told Mummy about Grandpa Cassidy, how all his life Daddy had camped in places and never lived in them, fleeing before the wrath of Grandpa's creditors; how his housemaster at Sherborne had told him that Grandpa Cassidy was the devil, and how Grandpa Cassidy had said very much the same about his housemaster; and how Daddy had found it very hard to know whom, if either, to believe.

"I mean *God* what a way to bring somebody up," Daddy protested.

"Specially you," said Mummy and it was understood between them that their own children would get a better chance, which is you and Hug. So you see, Mummy and Daddy were child martyrs to a grown-up world and that is what I will never let you be if I can ever prevent it, I promise. They wanted to be *better* and in a way they still do. The trouble is, they never discovered how, because you can't really spread much love around unless, in a funny way, you love yourself as well. Sorry to preach, but it's true.

So Mummy and Daddy watched each other very, very closely, each waiting for the other to revert to the follies of his parents, so in the end we did, both of us, because we're inheritors, like everyone else, and because sometimes the only way to punish our parents is to imitate them. But all that came later.

So anyway.

Well, one day, Granny Groat turned up with a big trunk, all the way from Darkest Somewhere, looking not at all like the little old lady in the Babar books, which is how she looks now; oh no. She arrived with that mute, declining beauty which Daddy has always mistaken for great intelligence, and immediately Daddy loved Granny Groat, loved her more than Mummy in fact because she wasn't cross, and appointed her a Life Mother, which was very, very unwise. Mummy knew it was unwise but Daddy wouldn't listen to her, because he wanted love all round him even if he couldn't have it close. And of course, Granny got very excited because she had never had a son, and she was *specially* pleased that Daddy was blond after all the black children she'd had to look at for so long.

"You're quite *sure* you want to marry her?" she asked him with a terribly intelligent giggle. "She's such a *funny* little thing."

"I love her," said Daddy, which when you're young is a sort of snobby thing to say, and makes you feel better, particularly when you're not sure you do.

"Get out, Flaherty."

Flaherty refused to move.

"*Get out!*" Cassidy sat up sharply. Someone was banging on the wall.

"Get out!" he yelled a third time, and the figure withdrew.

Mark; contrary to all you may have heard the wedding was not a success.

Mummy wanted the Church of Saint Somebody of Somewhere, beside the lock where she and Daddy had talked so much of love. She wanted no one for herself except a seedsman called Bacon who lived in Bagshot and had been her gardener when she was a little girl, and she wanted no one for Daddy but A. L. Rowse and just ordinary witnesses brought in from the fields. Finally we were married in Bournemouth where Granny Groat had taken a flat, in a moorish red-brick church bigger even than Sherborne Abbey, with a very old organist playing "Abide with Me." I'm afraid Mr. Bacon never came. Perhaps he couldn't leave his seeds, perhaps he was dead, we never knew.

Or perhaps, Cassidy reflected, gazing at the prints of deformed race horses, he never existed at all, save in the sad, imagined places of her childhood.

A. L. Rowse never came either. He was in America giving a course of lectures. He didn't send a present but Daddy (who had intercepted the invitation) explained they knew one another far too well for that kind of silly formality. The bridesmaid was your Auntie Snaps, Mummy's sister, fifteen and very premature in low red velvet, and Auntie Snaps sulked all through the ceremony. A few weeks later, back at boarding school, she gave her maidenhead to a labourer in the potting shed. *"You* do it," she told Mummy. "So why the hell shouldn't I?"

As a religious ceremony the service reminded Daddy of his Confirmation: an awesome contract with someone he did not know. And he could not help wishing, as the processive anthems drove him into the daylight, that he had not been quite so taken with Jean Gabin.

But Mark, tell me. Is this love? After all, *you're* innocent, *you* should know. You see, just possibly it's all there is; the best the world has got, and all the rest is waiting, like Daddy is waiting now.

Goodnight, Mrs. Harabee.
Goodnight, Flaherty.
Goodnight, Sandra.
Love, goodnight.

12

And incredibly, back in London, Cassidy waited still.

"You've got a simply smashing horoscope," said Miss Mawdray.

Breasts like doves, he thought, lusting after her in his idleness, little beaks pecking the angora. Legs of a boy, hips of a whore, hoares and hips; joke. God knows what she can wear up there. No white or black to mark the spot; just the burry brown fog of a touched-out photograph, a vaginal phantom yet to be recorded . . . Ha! See how she folds her thighs to embrace the unseen member!

"I got a new book," Angie explained, meaning magazine.

He was standing at the familiar window. His desk repelled him, a symbol of sedentary inertia. Miss Mawdray, having no such inhibitions, was balanced on her babychair.

"I could do with a bit of luck," Cassidy confessed.

She began reading him a long prophecy; it must have been half a page. He heard it at a distance, believing nothing. His birth group had been singled out, she said; special consideration for the Scales. Commerce would smile on him, she promised, friendships would flourish; have courage, she exhorted, go forward, advance, thrust, brandish. Do not allow unnecessary hindrances to impede you, impediments to hinder you, obstacles to obstruct you: a rare constellation would bless all initiatives.

"*All?*" Cassidy repeated, being jocular. "Well, well, I must try some new ones."

"And in the field of love," she read, keeping her head well down and following the line with her finger as her voice became slightly louder, "Venus and Aphrodite will jointly smile on your boldest venture."

"Fine," said Cassidy. "Just fine. Why don't they clean these curtains?" he asked, tugging at the net.

"They've just been done," said Angie with spirit. "You know very well they have. You were only complaining last week they'd been taken down."

Cassidy did not care for that kind of reply.

"Tell me," he said casually, his back still turned towards her, "what's happened to your engagement ring?"

He would not have asked, but for her retaliation. "Your engagement ring," he insisted, turning now and pointing to the extra quarter-inch of nakedness. "You haven't *lost* it, have you, Angie? That would be very bad."

"I'm just not wearing it, am I?" she said in a small voice, and though she must have known that he was still facing her, did not lift her head.

"I'm sorry," he said, "I didn't mean to pry."

Hangdog, he returned to the window. A scene, he thought glumly, we're going to have a scene. I've been an oaf again and now she's hurt. The last scene had involved Meale, he remembered; Angie had wanted Cassidy to provide an excuse for her not to accept an invitation from him and he had declined.

"You must get out of it for yourself," he had told her, Cassidy the champion of plain dealing. "If you don't like him, tell him. He'll only go on asking you if you don't." Well now he had made a second, equally unfortunate sally into her private life, and he was about to pay the price.

He waited.

"I wear it when I feel like it," said Angie at last, to his back. Her voice was still quiet, but it was already breaking with anger. "And if I don't feel like it I won't bloody bother, so sod it."

"I have apologised," the Chairman reminded her.

"I don't mind if you have or not. I'm not interested in apology am I? I've gone off him, that's all, and it's none of your business."

"I'm sure it's just a tiff," Cassidy assured her. "It'll blow over, you'll see."

"It *won't*," she insisted, furious. "I don't want it to blow over. He's rotten in bed and he's rotten out of it, so why *should* I marry him if I don't want to?"

Not quite certain whether to believe the evidence of his ears, Cassidy remained silent.

"They're too young," said Angie, smacking her book on her knee. "I get bloody sick of them. They all think they're marvellous and they're just *babies*. Fucking selfish, silly *babies*."

"Well," said Cassidy stalking the safety of his desk. "I don't know about *that*," and laughed, as if ignorance were a joke. "Angie, do you often swear like that?"

She rose in a single movement, taking his cup with one hand and tugging at the hem of her skirt with the other. "Not unless I'm goaded, do I?"

"How was the dentist?" he asked, hoping by small talk to restore a certain formality.

"Smashing," she said, with a sudden very tender smile. "I could have eaten him alive, honest."

Cassidy's dentist; part of a private health scheme for the staff. A man of forty-five; married.

"Good."

He made the next question even more casual: "Any messages at all . . . nothing out of the way?"

"A daft parson rang, that's all. Wanting free prams for orphans. I put a note on your desk. Irish."

"Irish? How do you know?"

"Because he spoke Irish, silly."

"He didn't leave a message?"

"No."

Warmer. "He didn't leave his number?"

"Look, he was daft, I told you! Lay off."

She gazed at him, her hand resting on the door handle, an angel of puzzled compassion.

"If you'd tell me what it is, Aldo," she said at last very quietly, "I'd know what to look for, wouldn't I?"

The resentment, the aggression had all gone. Only a childish supplication remained. "I'm dead safe, honest, Aldo. You can tell me *anything*, they wouldn't drag it out of me, no one would. Not if it's about you."

"It's personal," said Cassidy at last, his tongue clicking awkwardly on the dry roof of his mouth. "It's something very personal. Thanks."

"Oh," said Angie.

"Sorry," said Cassidy, and returned to his curtained window on an unresponsive world.

And still waiting, went to a crucial dinner at the unstately home of Dr. John and Somebody Elderman.

Mrs. Elderman was a sublimated graduate and the leader of the local dramatic set; while to her husband fell the important rôle of Cassidy's medical advisor. The Cassidys had not so much met the Eldermans as descended to them, gone back to them, as it were, when brighter social hopes had been extinguished. John Elderman was a small man physically, and though meticulously faithful to his general practice, was known to read widely on the subject of the mind. Some years back, he had written a paper called "Positive Divorce," and the tear-sheets were still generously displayed in every avant-garde room. Since then, the Eldermans had been much consulted in the Crescent, not only by the Cassidys, and they enjoyed a great reputation in the field of marriage guidance, and in all matters relating to love. Their principle, where Cassidy had met it, was to urge self-expression in the interests of self-discipline; no one, they insisted, was *obliged* to be unhappy; love was a gift, derived from flowers and rock.

The obscurity of this advice was deepened by the figure of Mrs. Elderman, a very big woman who wore gowns of brown hemp and ran a tangled garden on lines laid down by Rudolph Steiner. Her hair, which was mainly grey, similarly flourished. Separated rather than parted, it was bonded with flax on either side, like two enormous egg-timers made of steel wool. Loathing her, Cassidy had permanently forgotten her first name.

Even before they arrived there, the occasion had taken on for Cassidy a quality of dream-like frightfulness. He had come home late, by way of the Audley Arms, after a long and exceptionally tiresome meeting of his Export Ginger Group, and Sandra accused him of smelling of drink.

"How many did you have?"

"One. But it was meths."

"How *can* you be so cheap?"

"Have one yourself. Plenty in the broom cupboard."

"You wouldn't find it *in* you, would you, to tell me what on *earth* is making you so bad-tempered?"

"Spring," said Cassidy, scrubbing his teeth. From the main drawing room came a sudden burst of machine-gun fire. "What the *hell's* that?"

"What's *what?*"

"That hammering. Who's at the gates for Christ's sake?" He knew very well what it was.

"The workmen are putting up a moulding. An eighteenth-century *moulding* which Heather and I bought two *months* ago from a breaker's yard for ten shillings. I've told you about it fifty times; but still."

"Ten bob!" He used his Jewish rag-trade voice. "Ten bob for the moulding, fine. Ten bob I can afford. But Christ Almighty what about the *labour* already?"

"Do you mind speaking properly?"

"It's after five o'clock, those lads are getting about twenty guineas an hour!"

Sandra chose silence. He returned to his East End Jewish.

"So will somebody tell me what the hell's the point of an eighteenth-century moulding in a nineteenth-century house? Everyone knows this place is Victorian except us, ask a rabbi."

Still she chose silence.

"I mean *Christ*," Cassidy demanded of the bathroom mirror, in which, like a female sentinel before the doors of Downing Street, Sandra waited vertical and motionless.

"*Christ*," he repeated, in an Irish brogue he had been working on for several days. "I mean why the hell can't we live in the *twentieth* century for a change?"

"Because you're not to be trusted with it," she snapped, and Cassidy secretly awarded her set and match. "And there's no post," she added nastily, "if that's what you're bothered about."

Cassidy, studiously applying lather, offered no reply.

"Anyway, why isn't Hugo in bed?" he asked, knowing that answer also.

"He's been invited."

"What to?"

"The Eldermans'. *As* we have. *As* you know. If there's any point in going still," she added looking at her watch.

The Eldermans had squadrons of children and dined early so that their guests could have the benefit.

"*Bloody* silly. Dinner for a kid of seven! *Needlessly exposing him to danger*: that's what it is. A doctor, I ask you. A fully fledged paid-up medic, even if he does come from Gerrard's Cross. What if Hugo falls over? What if he stubs his toe? What if he gets kicked? Hugo hates those children, you know he does. So do I. Otiose little prigs," he said.

"You know what *I* think." Sandra's mother, hovering thinly at their bedroom doorway, in blue-tinted glasses and a dress of little-girl yellow, gave a titter of terrified goodwill. "I think mercy and truth are married together."

"Shut *up*, Mummy," said Sandra.

"*Come* on, darlings," her mother begged. "*Kiss.* I would at your age."

"*Mummy*," said Sandra.

"Darling, shouldn't you give something to the workmen?"

"He did," Sandra snapped. "He gave them five pounds. He's utterly *gross*."

They left in procession, five yards between each along the pavement, Cassidy carrying Hugo in his arms like a casualty of war, and Sandra's mother bringing up the rear, jingling precariously in her cowbell jewellery.

"At least he's a *doctor*, darling," she called enticingly to Cassidy over her daughter's head.

"Aldo *hates* doctors," Sandra retorted. "You know he does. Except specialists of course," she added nastily. "*Specialists* can do no wrong, can they? Specialists are absolutely perfect, even if they do charge fifty guineas for an X-ray."

"Why's Mummy cross?" Hugo asked from inside the blanket.

"Because Daddy's been drinking," Sandra snapped.

"She's not cross," said Cassidy. "It's just Granny getting on her nerves," and pressed the bell marked "House."

"Bet you've got the wrong evening," said Sandra.

"Greetings old man!" John Elderman cried. Perhaps to augment his height, he wore a chef's hat. From beneath it pink-fringed eyes of palest blue regarded Cassidy with innocent sagacity. He stood very straight, thin shoulders braced, but the effort did him little good.

"Sorry we're late," said Cassidy.

"Smashing buttonhole," said Elderman.

"He's been wearing them all week," said Sandra, as if she were giving him in charge.

She's been briefing them, thought Cassidy; and now they're going to observe me.

Heather Ast had already arrived. He could see her kneeling in the doorway, her agreeable rump lifted towards him while she played with the Eldermans' foul children.

"Hi, Heather!" he cried cheerfully.

"Oh hullo, Sandra," said Heather, ignoring him.

"Hi, Ast," said Cassidy, but found no audience.

He was in a menagerie, he noticed, of human apes. Posturing witless apes. He had not seen the Eldermans in quite that light before, but now he realised that they were not people at all but gibbons and their children were emerging gibbons, coming on fast. The Niesthals alone escaped his censure. They were an old, stately couple dressed in black and they ran musical evenings for friendly Gentiles in a very valuable house in St. John's Wood. Cassidy loved them because they were hopeless and kind. The Niesthals had come a little late because the old man did not close his Old Master gallery till seven; and they stood among the warring children like benefactors visiting a workhouse.

"Who is this one?" Mrs. Niesthal cried, bravely handling a junior Elderman. "Ah *naturally*, it is a Cassidy, see Friedl, you can see it from the *eyes*, it is a Cassidy."

"I say John old boy," said Cassidy.

"Yes, old man."

"Those Niesthals hate kids, you know."

"Never mind. Give 'em supper and shove 'em all upstairs."

Not Hugo you won't, butcher.

"Been refreshing ourselves I hear," said Heather nastily, out of the corner of her mouth. "Who's the buttonhole in aid of, anyway?"

"Meeow," said Cassidy, rather more audibly than he intended; and two Elderman girls, picking up the note, repeated it very loud: *"Meeow, meeow."*

"Like a cat," Mrs. Niesthal explained to her husband, and they trooped into the dining room, stepping over several dogs which scavenged at the door.

Cassidy was feeling sick, and no one cared. He was sure he looked pale, and he knew he had a fever, but no one comforted him, no one lowered his voice in his proximity.

He had eaten boiled tongue, which reminded him of the Army, and he had drunk homemade wine which reminded him of nothing he had ever tasted in his life. Nettles, they made it of, apparently, foraged in Burnham Beeches and transported in their proudly distintegrating van.

"*God* it's alcoholic," one woman said. "I mean honestly John, I'm feeling *so* tipsy."

"Has it got cinnamon in it?" asked another—Mrs. Groat, in fact, for whom cinnamon was an objection, it loosened the stomach.

"No," said Cassidy, and won an embarrassed silence.

At the stove, John Elderman was adding Marc de Bourgogne to a pudding nobody wanted.

Cassidy was seated between two divorcées, a class of woman the Eldermans encouraged. To my left, Heather Ast, normally congenial to me, but tonight abhorrent, having been corrupted by the Abalone Women's Liberation Front. To my right, weighing in at about four stone one, an emaciated sea plant called Felicity, also a wine brewer, also divorced, also of the Unaligned Left, star of the Abalone Rep and famous in voluptuous rôles. The conversation however is being hogged by a Foreign Office couple; they have been brought by a child which speaks only Portuguese, it sits on one side of Hugo dressed in earrings and national costume. The wife is an improbable veteran of remote trouble spots, and very disenchanted. Who will teach Libby English? she moans. It was the price for going native; the English school in Angola was too reactionary.

"Oh, she will pick it up," said Mrs. Niesthal confidently. "Listen we also had that problem." The Niesthals laugh to one another, the rest of us are too progressive to admit that European Jews are not descended from Oliver Cromwell.

"It's such a joy," said Ast, admiring Elderman, "to find a man who can *really* cook."

"So many are just frauds," the Sea Plant agreed from his other side, waving in a slow current.

"We all are," said Cassidy.

"Frauds?" cried old Niesthal, making a joke of it. "Don't talk to me about frauds my God, I am buying them every day two dozen."

A friendly laugh went up, led by John Elderman.

"Friedl says *terrible* things," Mrs. Niesthal declared cheerfully.

"So does Heather," said Cassidy, regretting it too late.

The children had been put at the far end of the table and Hugo was reading the *Evening Standard*, his thumb wedged into his mouth like a pipe. Two Elderman girls, supine with food, clutched each other in a grimy embrace.

"Warsaw," John Elderman proposed through the steam of his concoction, referring to an earlier conversation about the Free East. "That's the place. Never seen medicine like it." He was wearing a short-sleeved shirt, and his arms were thin and silky like a girl's. "Drink deep," he exhorted, throwing back his head. "Drink deep. Be merry."

"Well," said Mrs. Groat, ever anxious to show that she was attending. "Well, not *too* deep," and giggled through the blue windows of her unnecessary spectacles.

"Well, *well*," said Cassidy, and Sandra shot him a glance of loathing. "Well, well, well, well, *well*."

The Elderman wife said she wished we could abolish private medicine. She was sitting not at the table but on the floor, half lying, a casualty of her husband's cooking, and as she spoke she pulled at her long, frizzy hair in frightful imitation of a mediaeval princess. She had recently taken up with *art nouveau* and wore a buckle of unpolished lead.

"Particularly specialists," she added, not looking at Cassidy. "I think it's so disgraceful that anyone can go in and *buy* specialist medical attention at the drop of a hat provided he's rich. It's so against the sense of it all. So *unorganic*. After all, if there *is* natural selection, it's not going to be done by money is it?"

Her face had reddened with the nettles.

"Quite right," said Sandra, and closed her mouth quickly, ready for the next round.

"Darling are you sure?" her mother asked with a frightened lowering of the jaw. "We could *never* have managed *without* in the Tropics."

"Oh *Mummy*," said Sandra in a rage.

"Sandra was born there," said Cassidy encouragingly. "Weren't you, Sandra? Why don't you tell them about it Grans, they'd like that. Tell them about the doctor who was plastered."

Hugo, turning a page, snorted into his fist.

"We were in *Nebar*," Mrs. Groat immediately began explaining to the Sea Plant. "It used to be the Gold Coast, then it was Liberia—is it Liberia, darling, I never remember these new names?—or is Liberia the *old* name?—well of course there *wasn't* any Liberia in our day!—" rather as if there wasn't penicillin either "—so it *had* to be the Gold Coast really, didn't it? We didn't have Liberia," she declared loudly with an arch smile to advertise the joke. "We had the Army instead."

"You see," Sandra hissed triumphantly to her mother, "*nobody* finds it funny. *Aldo*, shut up."

She was too late; Cassidy was already applauding. It was not a deliberate provocation. Rather, it was as if his two hands, bored with lying on the table, had decided to get up and do something of their own; not till afterwards, uncomfortably reliving the moment with Sandra, did Cassidy secretly recall a different pair of hands applauding Helen at the restaurant in Bath.

"They laugh when your father says it," her mother replied when the applause ended; and blushed.

"Coming up," said John Elderman, as a pillar of smoke shot from the overheated pan. "Who's number one?"

Ignoring him, his nameless wife rolled on her massive hip and, jamming a bottle into the mouth of an adjacent baby, raised the subject of South East Asia. Had they all had the news? she asked, naming a country Cassidy had never heard of. They had not. Well the Americans had invaded it, she said, the local government had requested intervention. They had marched in at five that morning, the Russians were threatening to retaliate.

"Up the Marines," said Cassidy, but not loud enough this time for anyone but Heather to hear.

"Hey you," Heather said softly, laying a cautionary hand on his knee. "Ease off, you'll frighten the game."

At the same moment Hugo asked his question. He had played no part in the proceedings till now, so his intervention had at least the advantage of novelty.

"Why can't you love snow?"

His thumb was still wedged in his mouth and his brows were drawn hard down over his grey unblinking eyes.

A concentrated silence preceded the volley:

"Because it melts!" Prunella Elderman shouted. "Because it's too cold, because it's all white and wet."

The other sisters joined in. A baby was screaming. A child was banging a spoon on the table, another was jumping on a chair. Seizing the carafe of nettles, Cassidy replenished his glass.

"Because it's not alive!" the velveted sisters screamed. 'Because you can't eat it! Why then? Why, why, why?"

Hugo took his time, shifted his plaster leg, turned a page of his newspaper. "Because you can't marry it," he announced gravely.

In the general groan, Shamus made his appearance.

He could not have been further from Cassidy's mind. His thoughts, he afterwards recalled with clarity, had drifted momentarily to the distressing implications of Hugo's riddle: whether it betrayed a hidden preoccupation with domestic tension, whether the pains of a fractured leg had temporarily unhinged the tender child's reason. If he had anything else in mind at all, then it was Ast's hand: was it a restraining hand? Did she know it was still on his knee; had she left it there like a handbag? Was it an olive branch after her earlier, unprovoked irascibility? Seeking perhaps the comfort of a male ally in this moment of sexual uncertainty, Cassidy transferred his attention to John Elderman, mentally selecting as he did so a topic of mutual interest, a football match, John's fascinating old van; and was therefore surprised to find in his place Shamus, not standing but suspended in the steam stirring the evil-smelling pudding with Elderman's wooden spoon, his black eyes fixed upon Cassidy across the candlelight, his moist face glowing with impish complicity.

"Hey lover," he was saying. "Isn't it a bloody bore? Urban proles having compromisers' orgy."

Simultaneously or perhaps a fraction before, since psychic experience has no equivalent in time, he heard Shamus' names, Christian name and surname both, spoken out recklessly from his left side.

"*Such* a pity he died so young," Ast declared, her hand a trifle higher on his thigh. "After all, who else *can* one read who's *modern?*"

Then John Elderman gave him his pudding and he burnt his mouth.

In retrospect, of course, Cassidy was better able to understand what had happened. His senses, taken up by Hugo's
riddle and Ast's understanding hand, had failed to remark
that a second, independent conversation was going forward between the women to either side of him: that is to
say between Ast and the Sea Plant. For some while, as he
afterwards realised, they had been exchanging murmured
intellectual commonplaces drawn from Sunday newspapers, no doubt upon the subject of the modern novel. Thus
the abrupt, unheralded mention of Shamus' name, violently intruding upon an unprotected corner of his mind, had
caused him in his confusion to imagine in the vivid frame
of Elderman the features of his banished friend. It was
also true that the four large whiskies at the Audley Arms
—not to mention a recent visit to the lavatory where Bear
had consumed a little something from a clandestine bottle
—had lingered somewhat with the monotony of the evening.

Also he had drunk a lot of nettles.

But such insights came to him too late, for while his
natural discretion implored him to be silent, he had already overcome his first experience of a ghost and was
launched into a sprightly, if injudicious, argument about
the great author.

"Dead?" he repeated as soon as he had emptied his
glass. "Dead? He's not *dead*. He's just been kicked around
so much he did a bunk. Can't blame him for *that,* can you?
As a matter of fact I happen to know he's just about to
turn in a new book—"

"I *hate* this pudding," Hugo loudly interjected but no
one paid him any notice.

Ast's hand had reached, it seemed to Cassidy, a point at
which no woman, however absent-minded, can unconsciously arrive. Abruptly, it was now withdrawn.

"—which by all accounts," he concluded confidently,
"will knock all his other books into a cocked hat. *Moon*
included."

How, so soon after the shock of Shamus' ghostly reappearance—or as now seemed possible, his reincarnation—
Cassidy found the courage to speak up so boldly was a
mystery he never solved, though he did wonder in his more
playful moments whether Shamus belonged to a small
élite known only to himself, of ghosts who had the gift of
imparting confidence rather than alarm.

"He *died* in sixty-*one*," said Ast, articulating very clearly for the benefit of the deaf. Her wide breasts, roused with anger, had lifted against their seam of harvest twine.

"He's been in hiding," said Cassidy.

"How do *you* know?" Sandra demanded. "You've never read a novel in your life."

"It's got petrol in it," said Hugo and with a clatter pushed his plate into the middle of the table.

"Shut up," said Sandra.

"I *love* it," said Prunella Elderman and put her tongue out at the Anglo-Portuguese.

At this point, Cassidy was reminded of Heather Ast's husband, a reedy, bow-tied man who, she said, had woken up one morning and decided he was queer. He thought of him very specifically in pyjamas and a nightcap, sitting up with a jolt as the tea came in. "Heather," he says, "news for you. I'm a poof." This imaginative portrait set him giggling for some time so that Sandra was beside herself with rage.

"Just know," he said, at last recovering his composure. "Just keeping a finger on the literary pulse."

"*Ooh*," said Sandra, fists clenched.

"I want more pudding," said Prunella Elderman, undeterred.

"Then eat Hugo's," yelled Somebody Elderman from the safety of the floor.

"He *died* in *France*," Ast resumed, in the low tremulous voice of a woman martyred by patience, and laying her errant hand firmly on the scrubbed table, imprisoned it with the other.

"What did he die of then?" Cassidy asked with a distinctly patronising smile. "What's the diagnosis, eh John boy?"

"Of TB I assume," snapped Ast. "Isn't that what they all die of?"

"Meeow," said Cassidy, and the children at once took it up: "Meeow, meeow, meeow."

Ast's precarious calm was fast deserting her. Within its sprawling tent of blond hair, her face, emaciated by pointless intelligence, now suddenly darkened.

"You haven't the least *idea* what they go through have you? You're so damn rich you don't even realise what it means to die abroad, penniless . . . to be denied a decent burial by some idiotic Catholic priest . . . to *rot* in some shallow common grave . . ."

"No," Cassidy agreed cheerfully. "It's true I haven't made that experience. However," he continued, slipping into his smoothest boardroom tone, "I'm afraid you're wrong. My information is incontrovertible. It may be true that he was given out for dead. It is also possible that he deliberately inspired the rumour. The reason is simple" —he let them wait a moment. "He was driven to distraction by the publishing profession." Out of the corner of his eye he saw the once-coveted shape of Ast stir and then hold still. "Whom he describes as ghouls and Gerrard's Crossers, and anything else that comes into his head. They hounded him until he could hardly think straight, let alone write. He was their golden goose and as usual they tried to kill him. Escape was the only answer," helping himself to more nettles. "Thank God he made it, says I," he added, emptying his glass. "The Queen, God bless her."

Only the Niesthals joined the toast.

"The Queen," the old man muttered. They drank looking down, a private communion.

Allowing the focus of his eyes conveniently to mist, Cassidy saw Somebody Elderman's massive fingers close round her beads, which were brown and shrivelled like nuts, and her husband put down the Marc de Bourgogne. At the same moment, Sandra's mother began talking about the rain in Nebar, how it fell much more than people realised and cleansed nothing.

"Really the smells seem to thrive on it, I don't know why." The only place was the hills, but the Brigadier her husband had not cared for heights. "So I had to have her all alone," she said. "Just a nurse and this *dreadful* drunk doctor sent up by the Commissioner. He kept dogs I remember, there was moulting hair all over his sleeves, you wouldn't do that, would you, John? She was such a funny little thing," she added when no one spoke. "All red and angry. Hugo was just the same, weren't you Hug?"

"No," said Hugo.

Sandra had evidently decided it was time to put Hugo to bed. Taking him by the wrist she marched him to the door.

"Look after him," John Elderman advised, holding her in the enveloping embrace he vouchsafed to all afflicted women. "He seems to be under a spot of strain." He was talking about Cassidy not Hugo. "Give him one of your valium now and then, calm him down. Doesn't matter if he drinks."

"Sawbones," said Cassidy. "You think you're a great big butch specialist but you're just a rotten little leech. Sodder."

"Sleep it off, I should," said Elderman, smiling sportily. "Old man."

"Flaherty is God," said Cassidy in a valiant pre-trial gesture. "Flaherty rules the earth. A man is what he thinks he is."

And threw his buttonhole to Ast.

13

The nursery was also full of flowers: he slept among them often, banished there for cheek. Floppy blue flowers in different shades of pastel. Mark's bed was very narrow, no more than a mattress laid on the linoleum and draped in a soft woollen coverlet: monkish, he liked to think, conducive to sombre thoughts. Mark's toy chest was locked and that was where Cassidy kept his paperbacks, recipes for a secret culture. Some were on ancient Greece, some were on the German High Command; others were on skills he proposed one day to acquire, how to sail, how to cook for one, how to service his own car or conduct an ideal marriage. Safely contained within the bed's narrow walls, the coverlet pulled high, Cassidy selected Kahlil Gibran's *The Prophet* and turned to the passage on love.

"Daddy," said Hugo drowsily from his cot.

"Yes."

"Daddy."

"Yes, Hug."

"If Mummy goes away, do I go with you or her?"

It was a very practical enquiry.

"No one's going away."

From upstairs, they heard her telephone Auntie Snaps in Newcastle and offer to pay her fare to London.

That's right, he thought, *raise a posse.*

"Daddy."

"Yes."

"Be Shane."

Cassidy made his Wild West voice: "I'm the sheriff around these parts and these yere's *mah* deputies."

Nonsense. Sandra was saying. *He hasn't even heard of the man. He certainly hasn't read him. He couldn't anyway, he's far too lazy to read a book. . . . Nonsense, he's not under strain at all. His parasites run the office, I run the house, and every time he wants to run away he makes up some silly lie about his charities. He did it to annoy*

Heather, and Beth and Mary and . . . Of course he loathes women, that's not his fault, it's his upbringing, I realise that, but still.

"Daddy."

"Yes Hug."

"You *have* heard of him, haven't you?"

"Yes."

"Honest?"

"Honest."

"I knew you had. Goodnight Dad."

"Goodnight old fish."

"Dad."

"Yes Hug."

"Do Sturrock."

Western again: "Okay Sturrock, you low-down lyin' Yankee, git off *mah* plantation."

"Bang," said Hugo.

"Bang," said Cassidy.

Another ping of the telephone.

John I'm most dreadfully sorry, said Sandra, *I mean I really don't know what to say . . . really . . .*

Well, reality is also a problem. Not to you of course. To me. The Eldermans. I fuck myself of the Eldermans. Who lent them six thousand quid interest free to get rid of their sitting tenants? Who lent them the chalet last year for their foul kids to rip to pieces? Who—

Martial footsteps approaching.

"It's Mummy," Hugo explained, and getting up gathered together his few necessaries.

Pogrom, thought Cassidy and dived under the bedclothes.

"Come along darling," said Sandra. "Your father's drunk." And from the doorway, whence all her Parthian shots were launched, "How on *earth* you have the *nerve* to *pretend* you *care* about your *children* when all you do is get *drunk* in front of them and *swear* and make *filthy-imputations-against-people-they-respect* . . ." She dried up, exhausted by emphasis.

"Come on," Cassidy urged, through the tartan blankets. "Let's have a main verb. Let's have some bloody grammar around the house, shall we? Set an example to the children, shall we?"

Sandra sighed and drew the door nearer to her as a shield.

"Now tell me I'm worse than my father," he suggested.

"If his leg doesn't mend," she said at last, "it will be your fault entirely."

"Night, Sturrock," said Hugo.

"Night, Shane," said Cassidy amiably.

"And in the morning," said Sandra, "I shall leave you."

Gradually the house dropped off. One by one the staircases creaked and fell silent. Her mother went to the lavatory. For a while he lay awake counting off the hours on Hugo's cuckoo clock, waiting in case she came to him. Once, still dozing, he fancied he heard again the rhythmic thudding of the fourposter and the long sharp cry of Helen's pleasure echoing down the fine curved staircase in the style of Adam. And once, struggling with the late effects of nettle wine, he discovered Shamus' strong arms locked rugger style round his aching ribs, and Helen, voice off, explaining the assault.

"You see Shamus *loves* people. It's the difference between paddling and swimming."

"When love beckons to you," wrote the Prophet, "follow him, Though his ways are hard and steep. And when his wings enfold you yield to him, Though the sword hidden among his pinions may wound you."

He fell asleep, dreaming of Hell, and Old Hugo walking over Cassidy's skull.

"Anyway," said Sandra in the morning, "I'm not going to Paris with you."

"Fine," said Cassidy.

"So you needn't think I am," said Sandra.

"I wasn't," said Cassidy.

"Don't worry," said Hugo. "You will won't you Mummy?"

Hugo is the blank slate, he thought; Hugo is me before I was written on.

He touched ninety on the motorway before the police caught up with him. For some reason they believed him when he said he had never been so fast before.

"It's my mother," he said. "She's dying."

They believed that too.

"She's at Bristol hospital," he said. "She's English born, but she's lived abroad all her life. She doesn't even speak English. She's very frightened."

"You don't own the road sir all the same," the older officer replied, embarrassed.

"What does she speak then?" the younger man asked.

"French. She's lived there all her life. She wanted to be here for the end."

"Well take it easy in future," the older one said, with a brave show of no emotion.

"I will," said Cassidy.

"What's that dial then?" the younger one asked. "The one with the orange light on it?"

"An ice-alert," said Cassidy and was about to show them how it worked when the sergeant intervened.

"Let him go, Syd," he said quietly.

"Of course. Sorry," said the constable and blushed.

He knew even before he reached the house that they had gone. The shirt was no longer hanging from the cable and the doves, hoping for food, fluttered restlessly on the portico. A tramp had left a chalk mark on the door, an arrow pointing downwards and two white crosses side by side. He pulled the iron bell and heard it clank in the Great Hall. He waited but no one came. Only the stables had word of them. A platoon of whisky bottles lay on the wet straw, shoulder to shoulder, set out by Helen's tidy hand. He picked one up. The neck was sticky with candle-wax; a film covered the mouth; at its centre, like a tiny bullet hole, a point of black carbon recalled the burnt-out flame.

His flowers were lying at the back door. "If there's no reply," he had told the girl in the green overall, "leave them on the doorstep." And there they lay, a fountain of wasted red wrapped in cellophane, big enough to com-memorate a West Country infantry regiment, with the Moyses Stevens label from the lads who'd stayed behind. They must have been there a full fortnight, and the rain had kept them alive. Roses, he had told her, fine tight buds, three dozen of your very best—a dozen for each of us you see. Had written out the label with their scratchy, unwilling pen.

Loosening the card from its sodden envelope he read his own words:

To Shamus and Helen. For the fun of a lifetime, please come back. Cassidy.

Afterwards his telephone number in London. *Do please reverse the charges.*

There was a place he knew, a green hill far away in Kensal Rise, he had found it five years ago, waiting for news of Mark's operation. It lay between a graveyard and an infant school and was known as the Valhalla. No single impulse had pointed him the way, only a sense of emptiness, of blank, contactless availability, had with God's good help guided the driven father's footsteps. He had telephoned the hospital from Marble Arch: call again at seven, they would know at seven whether the operation was a success.

Walking he had found himself in a cemetery, crouching from stone to stone in a quest for buried Cassidys. And thus searching became conscious of a drift, even of a positive direction, in the movement of the crowd. Young men dressed in their Saturday uniforms, hitherto aimlessly posted in groups, glanced at their watches, formed ranks, and walked away. Not long afterwards a portly man in a mauve dinner jacket alighted from a taxi and hurried after them carrying what seemed to be a blunderbuss in a black leatherine box.

Then a miracle happened.

Barely had the mauve jacket vanished through the small wicker gate than a flock of young girls, flouncing and trembling on long uncertain legs, bright as tropical birds in their thin blouses and bell skirts, stockingless, knickerless perhaps, fell tittering from the open heaven and landed at his feet, brushing past him on the same mysterious path. Enthralled, Cassidy followed, his fantasy vaulting from one wild vision to another. What ritual, what ceremony was here observed? A hanging? A prophet? Or an orgy on the Teenage Scandinavian pattern? Time, place, even caution had deserted him. He sensed only the proximity of fulfillment drying his tongue and tantalising his

soft loins. He was floating. A sexual vertigo conveyed him
over the municipal tarmac. Trees, ponds, fences, mothers;
in a single blur they skimmed the merest edges of his
vision, guided him along the secret line.

Peritonitis was forgotten; Mark was cured.

He lived only ahead of him in the coloured squadron, in
the lifting quarters and the plumed haunches, in the waft
of baby powder that followed in their wake. Once he
stumbled, once he heard a dog snap at him, once an old
man yelled "Hey watch out" but by then he was inside,
the three-shilling ticket lying like a wafer in his palm.
Round him coloured stars were coursing the unwindowed
church. From a raised sanctuary swaying priests pounded
music he could almost hum.

He was dancing.

Dancing at arm's length with speechless girls. In small circles round their grounded handbags. Shuffling fairy rings in
the French chalk. He never learned their names. Like nuns
sworn to silence they took him, comforted him with the
dispassion of a higher devotion, and relinquished him for
other sufferers. A few, not many, rejected him on grounds
of age; some abandoned him because he was clumsy or
when a more favoured partner intervened. Still he did not
mind: their rejection was a discipline, attaching him closer
to their impenetrable community.

"Here," said a brunette. "What's that long face for
then?"

"Sorry," said Cassidy, and smiled.

These were the girls he could love. The girls who passed
him in buses and dressed shop windows, worked for him
as secretaries, peered at him from pavements as he sat in
taxis, these were his nurses, his figureheads, agelessly
beautiful on a changing sea.

"You can take me home if you like," said a blonde, "if
you give me a nice present."

But Cassidy declined. In the world they inhabited for
him, such girls had no home but this.

He drove there now. Drove there straight from Haverdown, three and a half hours looking through a windshield. He drove there to cure himself, the same cure that

had worked for Mark. He drove there without a break, without a meal, thinking of nothing because there was nothing left. He parked at a meter and walked past the last two hundred yards. Unknown, even to himself.

The Valhalla had gone. Not requisitioned. Not bought by university or a great department store. Bombed. Eradicated. Cleaned down on both brick sides by a demolition contractor, picked away like meat from the bone by their yellow wrecking machines, and not even a doorstep left for the roses.

14

The day of the Annual Informal Meeting dawned with all the ominous tension of a first night when half the costumes are still with British Rail. Once, these meetings had been Cassidy's treasured innovation, an entirely new concept in company Management, aimed at the improvement of relations between Shareholders and Directors. Once, as from his father's pulpit, the adroit executive had addressed his faithful elders: first quarterly, then six-monthly, cleansed their souls of doubt, and refreshed them with new faith. Other companies, he had argued, gave as little information as possible; Cassidy's would reverse the trend. But time, as so often, had institutionalised the revolution: now the meeting took place once a year, an unwieldy blend of Board and Annual General, and more trouble, in Cassidy's revised opinion, than the two of them together.

By two o'clock the first arrivals had been sighted in the area of the ground-floor boardroom and report of them was brought to Cassidy by a succession of Shakespearean newsbearers. The firm's Earl, a retired steel magnate flown from Scotland, had sat for half an hour in the waiting room before being recognised, and was now in the Informal Conference Room drinking water from the carafe. Meale (good for his polish, the mawkish pup) was despatched to converse with him informally. A retired trade unionist named Aldebout, retained to pacify shopside disputes, had been seen testing the tea in the canteen.

"I told him to have it on the house," Lemming said proudly. "Those buggers'll do anything for a cup of tea."

Two brown-coated ladies from Shepton Mallet had had their mini towed away by the police.

"They tore the front bumper off too," said Angie Mawdray, who had watched the manoeuvre from her window.

A stockroom clerk was ordered to collect it and pay the fine.

Behind the scenes a condition of barely controlled chaos reigned. Today was Friday. The Fair opened on Monday. The new cee-spring chassis, finally assembled, despite Lemming's attempts at sabotage, had gone ahead air-freight to Le Bourget but the French shipping clerk telephoned to say it had been rerouted to Orly. An hour later he rang again. The chassis had been confiscated by French customs on suspicion, the shipping clerk thought, of being an instrument of war.

"Then *bribe* them! *Bribe* them for Christ's sake!" Cassidy shouted into the telephone, his maternal French having quite deserted him. "B . . . r . . ." and to Angie who was standing by with a dictionary, "What the hell's the French for bribe?"

"Bri-ber," Angie suggested promptly.

"Corrupt them!" Cassidy yelled. *"Corruptez!"* but the clerk said they were corrupt already.

Soon afterward the line went dead. A desperate telephone call to Bloburg, the Paris agent, produced no result. It was the feast of Saint Antoine of All Cities; Monsieur Bloburg was observing the local custom. By three o'clock when the meeting·opened there was still no further word from the crisis front. Elsewhere in the building a battle was being waged with the revised brochure. The first edition, hurried through the printers at the last minute after prolonged haggling between Export and Promotion, was out of register and had to be sent back. While the second edition was still anxiously awaited, Cassidy discovered to his fury that it contained no German.

"For pity's sake!" he shouted. "Do I have to remember everything myself?"

Who spoke German? Lemming had fought them in the war and remembered them only with black hatred. He refused to co-operate. Faulk, desperately willing, had no German, but would a little Italian help? A translation agency in Soho sent a lady with blue hair and no English who was at that moment closeted in the copy room while Angie Mawdray, loving the crisis, combed the Public Library for a German-English technical dictionary.

To no one's surprise therefore the proceedings began late. Fighting to introduce a sense of calm Cassidy opened with minor matters of routine. Mrs. Aldo Cassidy sent her apologies. Apologies had also been received from General Hearst-Maundy in Jamaica. They had all been sorry to learn of the untimely death of Mrs. Bannister, a longstanding and loyal member of the Board. Mrs. Allan, after seven years' service, had accepted a senior post with another firm; Cassidy moved the customary bonus of one month's pay for every complete year served. The motion was carried without comment. Only Lemming, who had achieved her dismissal after months of venomous intrigue, muttered, "Great loss to us all, very gallant little lady," and appeared to brush a tear away.

It was almost half past three, therefore, before Aldo Cassidy, son of the distinguished hotelier, the Reverend Hugo Cassidy M.P. and bar., was able to deliver his long-awaited Chairman's address on the subject of Exports. Speaking fluently and without notes, he sounded a battle cry that would have chilled Prince Rupert's heart.

"Ideals are like the stars," he told them—a favourite dictum of the great hotelier. "We cannot reach them but we profit by their presence. The Common Market—" almost ignoring the applause "—the Common Market—thank you!—the Common Market is a fact of life. We must either join it or beat it. Ladies and gentlemen, fellow shareholders old and new, Cassidy's are prepared to do both."

Having painted a somewhat paradoxical picture of a Europe crumbling under the impact of his firm's assault, but mysteriously held together by its fastenings, he came at last upon the specific matter of the Fair.

"Now I make no apology for taking a strong, a very strong selling force to Paris. We've got the guns, and we've got the troops as well!"

More cheers. Cassidy lowers his voice.

"Now we shall be spending your money and we shall be spending a lot of it. No one ever did good business with a dirty shirt. There will be two teams. I shall call them Team A and Team B. Team B, under the distinguished leadership of Mr. Faulk, whose brilliant promotional record will stand us in good stead—" loud applause "—will set sail tonight. It's a young team—" an unfriendly glance at Meale, who had recently taken to wearing pointed shoes, and humming in the corridors "—it's a tough team. It is there to sell. Man the tent, demonstrate the prototype, stimulate interest, yes. But above all, it will *sell*. And I hope that by the time the Fair opens officially on Monday one or two order books will not be quite as empty as they are at this minute. The point is this. Many of these foreign buyers have limited resources. They arrive with so much to spend, they go when they've spent it."

Lifting a folded sheet of blank paper he passed it across their enchanted vision.

"Furthermore we have done a little bit of spying. I have here a list of all the principal buyers attending the Fair, together with their addresses while they are in Paris. It seems to me, you see, that if these fellows haven't all that much to spend—" a nicely judged pause "—then the best thing they can do is spend it on Cassidy's, and *that* means before they spend it on someone else!"

As the laughter and applause gradually died, the Chairman's expression was seen to harden and his voice took on a more severe tone.

"Fellow stockholders, members of the Board, I leave you with these words." Slowly one hand rose, the fingers half uncurled as if in benediction. "A man is judged—as judged we shall all be, my friends—by what he looks for, not by what he finds. Let it never be said that the House of Cassidy has been deficient on the score of enterprise. We shall seek and we shall find. Thank you very much."

He sat down.

During the tea break the Earl as elder statesman took him aside. He was a decrepit, silvery man and he had lunched at the Connaught at Company expense.

"Listen to the advice of an old man," he said speaking very slowly through the fumes of a rare whisky. "I've seen it in steel, I've seen it in deer. Don't burn yourself out. Don't try to run the whole course before breakfast."

"I won't," Cassidy assured him, laying a steadying hand on his shoulder. "I really won't."

"What you do in your twenties you pay for in your thirties, what you do in your thirties you pay for in your forties . . ."

"Yes but look here—" they had reached the Directors' lavatory "—I've got all *you* people to worry about haven't I, sir?"

"You've not been drinking by any chance, have you?" the Earl enquired.

"Good God no!"

"You know," the Earl continued, his head propped conveniently against the cistern, "I've been watching you. You're the most terrible bloody liar. Eh, tell us," said the Earl, drawing closer and affecting to wash his hands. "You seem to be making a hell of a big profit. Do you need a dash more working capital by any chance? On the QT, you know. So's we don't have to bother the tax laddies, *you* know."

The Informal audience had thinned a little after tea, and something of Cassidy's verve had also left him. Skating over the detailed function of the B team (responsible for the *logistics of the second phase*) he for a while drifted a little glumly round problems of creating new agencies and opening spares depots.

"There is even a possibility," he said, "I speak of course of the long term here, let's have no misunderstanding about this—that Cassidy's will eventually—I refer to the distant future—arrange for local, even *regional* manufacture of their product under licence and on the basis of part profit-sharing."

This time, no one was inclined to applaud, even Informally.

"The A team incidentally will be separately accommodated in the centre of the city, where it can enjoy the advantages of mobility, separate communication, and the rest, and it will consist almost entirely—" he meant it as a joke, had even prepared it as a joke, practised the timing, shaped and reshaped the cadences "—of myself. I say *almost* because I am happy to tell you that my wife will be accompanying me."

Only the palest murmur greeted this Informal insight into family togetherness.

"Do you want to go on to any other business?" Lemming asked, quite loud. "I think they've had about enough."

From the corridor they heard a clatter of feet as someone ran for the Chairman's telephone.

"That'll be Paris," said Faulk rising.

"Please stay where you are Mr. Faulk, my secretary will call me if necessary."

Furious, but only inwardly, Cassidy picked up an agenda and glanced at the next item.

"Catering," he read aloud with an inward shiver of discomfort.

Old Hugo's pocket money. Tread gently, raise the tone to one of metallic nonchalance, look anywhere but at the Earl, who always objects to this uncomfortable entry in the ledger.

"Catering. In view of the satisfactory profit position I propose to make a retrospective one-time ex-gratia payment to—" here he took a small breath and glanced upwards as if the name had momentarily escaped him "—our valued catering consultant Mr. *Hugo* Cassidy whose wise and politic counsel has added so much cheer to the works canteen." Someone was knocking at the door. "May I take it that the payment is approved?"

"How much?" Aldebout asked.

The door opened and Angie Mawdray peeped into the room.

"One thousand pounds," Cassidy replied. "Any objection?"

"Absolutely none at all," said Clarence Faulk.

Out of the corner of his eye, he saw the Earl's white head lift, and his white eyebrows come together in a frown, and one white hand lift in tardy intervention.

"Mister Aldo, it's Paris," said Angie.

"I wonder if you will all excuse me for a moment," he asked smoothly. "I happen to know this *is* a matter which requires my personal attention."

A deferential pause.

"May I take it, ladies and gentlemen, that we can go on to the next item on the agenda? Mr. Lemming, you have that in the Informal Minutes? Mr. Faulk, perhaps you'll stand in until I come back? You might care to say a word about our Scottish promotion scheme. Mr. Meale, I may need you."

Lemming opened the door for them. "The Frogs have called it off," he hissed as Cassidy brushed past. "Pound to a penny they've called it off."

"It's a *Frenchman*," Angie Mawdray said triumphantly. "He sounds *terribly* excited."

"Did you find that technical dictionary?"

"No."

"Pity." Meale handed him the telephone. "Hullo?"

" 'Ullo, 'ullo, 'ullo!"

"Hullo," Cassidy repeated raising his voice to carry across the Channel. *"Hullo."*

" 'Ullo, 'ullo, 'ullo!"

"Hullo! Can you hear me? Meale, get hold of the exchange. Tell them to give us another line."

Meale lifted the second telephone.

"Cassidee?"

"Oui?"

"Comment ça va?"

"Listen, *écoutez, avez-vous le pram?*"

"Oui, oui, oui, oui. Tous les prams."

"Where is it? *Où?"* And to Meale, excited now, "It's okay. He's got it!"

"Cassidee?"

"Oui?"

"Comment ça va?"

"Fine. Listen, *where-is-the-pram?*"

"Ici Shamus."

"Who?"

"Jesus lover, don't say you've killed us already."

Lemming had followed him upstairs and was standing in the doorway.

"Well?" he said, hoping for bad news.

Cassidy stared at Lemming and then at the telephone. He put his hand over the mouthpiece.

"I'm sorry," he said firmly. "Do you mind shutting up? I can't conduct two conversations at once. I'll be with you in a moment. Go and hold the fort. Make yourself useful."

Scowling, Lemming withdrew. Meale trooped after him.

"Shamus," he whispered, "where are you?"

There was a slight pause before the answer came, and he thought he heard a second voice in the background as if Shamus were conferring with someone close to him.

"In bed," he said at last. "A Ladbroke Grove bed."

"Is Helen with you?"

"No, lover, it's just Daddy this time. Come and join us."

More consultation in the background, followed by a strange cajoling as between dog and master: "Say hullo to Butch . . . go on . . . *say hullo* to Butch." And much louder: "Butch, say hullo to Elsie." A soft rustle as the receiver changed hands. A girl's shy giggle, thin as rayon.

"Hullo Butch," said Elsie.

"Hullo Elsie. Elsie . . . is he all right?"

"Of course I'm all right," said Shamus. "Come round."

"I'm in the middle of a meeting."

"So am I."

"A Board Meeting," said Cassidy. "It's supposed to be my big day. They're all waiting for me downstairs."

Shamus was unimpressed. "I've been trying to ring you all week," he objected. "Didn't anyone tell you? Hey and listen: who was that sexy bitch I spoke to?"

"My secretary," said Cassidy.

"Not her, the other one."

"My wife," said Cassidy offering prayers to God.

"Lot of woman there boy. Very naive. Fond of Russians too. Want to watch out for her."

"Shamus look, I was going to write to you . . . when can I see you?"

"Tonight."

"It's no good tonight. I'm leaving for Paris on Monday, there's a convention on. We've got frightful problems with printers and God knows—"

"For *where?*"

"Paris."

"You going to *Paristown?*"

"On Monday."

"To sell prams?"

"Yes."

"I'm coming with you. And bring the Bentley, we'll need the back seat."

15

The house was in darkness when he returned. It reminded him, as he groped his way upstairs, of the day Old Hugo's father had died and the aunts had put the house into mourning. They had never had a death before but they knew exactly how to dress, both themselves and the house, where to find black and how far to draw the curtains, where there was religion on the wireless and what to do with all the smiling magazines.

The bedroom door was locked.

"She's asleep I'm afraid," Mrs. Groat called from the kitchen. "Uh-ha."

A towel was laid out on the nursery bed and his toothbrush beside it. Hugo was asleep. He undressed slowly thinking she might come in, then decided to shave to annoy his mother-in-law. The irritation dated from the birth of Mark, whom Sandra had had at home. Sandra had said there would be no pains—she had read books proscribing them—but her confidence proved unfounded. Soon the house had been filled with her sharp screams as she stubbornly rejected Pentothal and her mother sobbed in the kitchen reliving her own fights like a boxer retired from the ring. "Oh *God* you men," she shouted at Cassidy as he boiled water for purposes he dared not contemplate. "God if only you knew . . ." Ridden by guilt but furious at what he considered to be an odious display of female self-indulgence Cassidy had exercised the one male prerogative left to him. He shaved.

For similar reasons the same impulse overtook him now. Unbuttoning his shirt he rattled the razor in hot water, clanked the brush on the glass shelf, then needlessly shaved his amazingly youthful face.

Sandra kept him waiting a long time.

"I know you're awake," she said. "I can tell from your breathing."

She was standing in the nursery door, silhouetted against the landing light, and he imagined her face locked in the tension of uncomprehending resentment. She must have been there a good while for he had heard her first sigh ten minutes ago.

"You are without nobility," she continued quietly in her Ophelia voice. "You are without any scrap of decency or moral fibre or human compassion. You haven't got one instinct that is remotely honourable. I know perfectly well you're lying again. Why don't you admit it?"

Cassidy grunted and shifted one arm in a restless slumber but his mind was working fast.

I'm lying. Yes. I've always lied to you and I always will, and however many times you catch me out I'll never tell you the truth because you don't know how to deal with it any more than I do. But this time, big joke, I'm lying because I'm beginning to discover the truth and the truth, my angel, is outside us.

He waited.

Silenzio.

Or take the academic approach shall we since you have no degree? If I am without the qualities you enumerate and for the sake of argument I will largely concede that I am, why should I have the nobility, decency, and moral fibre to admit it?

Silenzio.

"I suppose you're taking A. L. Rowse," she suggested nastily, "*instead* of me."

Pulling up the blankets Cassidy did his swan act, swaying his head in the muddied water of Something Lock.

"Who was that Russian who rang you?"

I don't know.

"Who was that Russian who rang you?"

Lenin.

"Aldo!"

A business contact. How the hell should I know?

"Actually," said Sandra sadly, "he sounded rather fun."

Actually, thought Cassidy, *he is.*

Go. Grow. Stay.

"You're a complete child. Which is exactly what homosexuals are. You can't take menstruation or babies or death or *anything*. You have absolutely *no* sense of reality. You want the whole world to be pretty and tidy and full of love for Aldo."

She became grim.

"Well the world isn't like that, and *that*, my boy, is something you've got to learn. But still. *Aldo?*"

Meeow.

"The world is a tough, bitter place," she continued using her father's tone, elbows and feet apart. "A *damned* tough and bitter place. Aldo, I *know* you're awake."

I believe in Flaherty, the Father, the Son, and the little Boy.

"I'm going to leave you Aldo, I've decided. I'm going to take the children to Shropshire. Mummy has found a house near Ludlow. It's simple but it will do us perfectly well if you're not going to be there. We all live much more frugally when you're not with us. As for the children they must have father substitutes. I shall look for them in Ludlow. Thisbe and Gillian will go to kennels till we have moved."

Thisbe and Gillian were the Afghans. Bitches of course.

"I'm very sorry for you," she continued. "You know nothing about love or life and least of all women. But still."

Under the blankets Cassidy vigorously concurred. *That's why I'm going to Paris, you see. That's why I'm not taking you. I'm going to look for what you always say you've got, so fuck it. But still.*

"John Elderman says you have taken a subconscious vow to avenge yourself on your mother. You hate her for sleeping with your father. For this reason you also hate *me*. But still."

Jesus, don't say you've been having it off with Old Hugo. Well, well, well, this is a dirty house.

"So I'm very sorry for you," she repeated. "It's not your fault, there's nothing you can do. I've tried to help you but I've failed."

That's it, he thought, mentally raising one hand. *Keep it there. You have totally failed. You have failed to read my mind, my expressions, and my considerable distress in your company. You think you've got a monopoly of the metaphysics in this house but I tell you mate you wouldn't recognise God if He punched you on the jaw.*

Annoyed, apparently, that he still had not spoken, let alone contradicted her, she became more specific.

"Your responses are *entirely* homosexual," she declared, returning to an earlier charge. "Both towards your father *and* towards your sons. You don't love them as relatives—"

Relatives to what? Why can't you say relations? Why do you end all sentences with but still? Quite soon young lady you will tax me too far and I shall be obliged to fall fast asleep.

"You don't love them as relatives you love them as *men.*"

But still, Cassidy thought, *you hang around don't you?*

"Meanwhile you lie to me about those stupid charities. *I* know you're lying, *Mummy* knows you're lying, *everyone* knows. They're just a *stupid* excuse. *Bristol!* Do you really think *Bristol* needs a playing field from *you?* They wouldn't look at it if you *gave* it to them. *Footbridge. Pavilion. Levelling. Tchah!*"

She returned to her room.

Blank, he repeated.

Blank, blank, blank, blank, blank. Brainwash myself. Cassidy washes blankest. No lies, no truths, only a condition, only survival, only faith. Flaherty we need you. "If I wasn't blank," he thought, shading his eyes from darkness with his cupped hands, "I would call you an inexorable bore. You block me. I could be a writer if it wasn't for you. As it is I'm stuck in bloody prams."

The tears were back, slipping through his fingers. He named them one by one: remorse, fury, impotence, the Holy Trinity. I baptise thee in the name of apathy. He'd a good mind to go and show them to Sandra, that was what she did after all, waited till she'd got a good head of steam, then bled it all over him drip drip and boo-hoo. "I hate your fucking tears," he would shout. "Look at *mine.*"

"Good night, Daddy," said Hugo.

At breakfast as usual after such scenes Sandra made herself extremely agreeable. She kissed him maternally, vouchsafed him glances of great complicity, kept her mother in bed, and gave him tea instead of coffee, which she normally considered low.

"About what John Elderman said," Cassidy ventured as she cuddled him from behind.

"Oh don't worry about that, I was just in a bad mood," she replied lightly and kissed his head.

"Did you have a good night otherwise?"

"Fine, did you?"

"Sorry about Paristown."

"Paristown," she repeated with a smile. "What a baby you are." Kisses again. "It's going to be a real fight for you isn't it?"

"Well maybe."

"Don't be silly, I know it is. You can't fool me you know." She kissed him again. "Women *like* fighters," she said.

But Cassidy had not yet finished with John Elderman.

"You see the truth is, Sandra, I don't have motives."

"I know, I know."

More kisses. Cassidy consolidated his position. "I mean not even subconscious ones. I mean I could set up all those arguments so that they read absolutely differently."

"Of course you could," she said. "It's just John showing off. And you're *much* brighter than John, as he perfectly well realises. But still."

"I get into a fix and I react. It's got nothing to *do* with being queer."

"Of course it hasn't. And it was sweet of you to lend all that money to him," she added generously. "It's just that *sometimes* I don't understand your motives. And of course I believe in your football fields. It's just I wish those foul people would say *yes* for once."

"But Sandra, they're so *corrupt.*"

"I know, I know."

"It takes *years* to wear them down . . ."

Skilfully he set up his operational defences. I'll be out day and night . . . The Embassy's sending a car for me to the airport . . . After that anything can happen . . . Don't ring me, let *me* do it on the Company . . .

"So they *should* send a car," she said. "All their cars. Have a motorcade just for Aldo. Poop poop like Toad."

By the time he left, the charwomen were already arriving, some by taxi, some driven by their husbands. In the hall, dogs were barking, the telephone was ringing on several floors. The builders had already begun; the mason was making tea.

"I'll ring if it gets easier," he promised. "Then you take the next plane. Not the one-but-next, the next."

"Goodbye, Pailthorpe," she said. "Lover."

Turning out of her sight he glimpsed her mother standing behind her hovering like a senile nurse ready to catch her if she fell. Nearly he turned back. Nearly from a call box he rang her. Nearly he missed the plane. But Cassidy had been near to things all his life, and this time, come what may, he was going to touch them.

In Paristown.

Paris

16

Love affairs, Cassidy had always known, are timeless, and
therefore elusive of sequence. They occur, if at all, beyond
the branches of our customary trees, in certain half-lit
clouds from which day creatures are excluded; they occur
at moments when the soul, in some unfathomable way, is
more sublime than the loveliest environment, and all that
the eye perceives illustrates the inner world.

So it was with Paris.

Haverdown was a night, the Paris Fair (according to
the Pramsellers Association, Cassidy was never able to
obtain independent corroboration) lasted four days. Yet
each commanded for Cassidy the same compelling
rhythm: the same fumbling first encounter, the same blind
walk from the predictable to the unimagined; an inward
walk to the closed-off places of his heart; outward to the
closed-off places of a city. Each hung at first upon an instinct of failure; each was crowned by the same triumphal
climax; each instructed him, and left him more to learn.

They met, it was arranged, at number-two terminal, in
the departure lounge. The Many-too-Many were everywhere but Shamus had found a place to himself, a corner
reserved for bath chairs. It was some time before Cassidy
discovered him and he was beginning to panic. Shamus
sat crookedly in the steel frame, as if twisted by a terrible
injury, and he was wearing dark glasses and a beret. His
powerful shoulders were hunched forward inside the familiar black jacket and he carried nothing but an orange
which he was quietly rolling from one hand to the other
as if to bring the life back to his limbs. He spoke in a
cracked whisper. It was Elsie, he said; Elsie had made demands. Also she drank formaldehyde, which dissolved the
glottal stop and caused spasms of the vertebrae. It was the
first time Cassidy had seen him by daylight.

"How's the book going?"

"What book?"

"The novel. You were bringing it to London. Did they like it?"

Shamus knew of no novel. He wanted coffee and he wanted to be pushed round the lounge so that he could see healthy people and hear little children laughing. Over coffee —the attendants were assiduous, cleaned the table, removed unwanted chairs—Cassidy enquired after Alastair the railwayman and other characters of that great evening, but Shamus was not informative. No, he and Helen had not returned to Chippenham; the taxi-driver had gone out of their lives. No, he could not remember when they had left Haverdown. The sodders had cut the water off so they had headed for the East End of London, two friends called Hall and Sal, Hall was a boxer, the bread of life.

"He hits me," he added, as if that were a recommendation. And that was all.

"Don't hold with the past, lover, never did. Past stinks."

With quivering hands he drew the warm cup closer to his chest. Only the mention of Flaherty brought a spark to his lifeless eyes. The correspondence was flourishing, he said; he had little doubt that Flaherty's claims were justified.

They ate the orange in silence, half each. On the aeroplane, to which Shamus was assisted by burly stewards, he slept with his beret pushed up against the window like a cushion, and at Orly there was a small embarrassment. Firstly about another bath chair—the French had brought one on the runway, but Shamus indignantly refused it— secondly about luggage. Cassidy had purchased a new pigskin grip to match his globe-trotting camelhair coat, and he was watching the baggage chute fretfully because he knew what the French were. Having successfully recovered it, he found Shamus already at the barrier, empty-handed.

"Where's yours?"

"We ate it," Shamus replied. A hostess, drawn by his compelling looks, scowled at him. "Bitch," he shouted at her, and she blushed and went away.

"Hey, steady on," said Cassidy, embarrassed.

"I *loathe* air hostesses," said Shamus, and meeowed.

A limousine assumed them and for a while both were silent, stunned by beauty. The city was bathed in perfect sunlight. It fired the river, shimmered on the pink streets, and turned the golden eagles into phoenixes of present joy. Shamus sat in his favourite place beside the driver waving very slowly to the crowds, and occasionally lifting his beret. A few people waved back and a pretty girl blew him a kiss, a thing which had never happened to Cassidy in his life. At the St. Jacques they were received with all the ostentatious tolerance which French hoteliers accord to homosexuals and the unmarried. The staff assumed at once that Shamus was in charge. Cassidy had taken a suite with twin beds to cover all eventualities and the manager had sent a bowl of fruit. *Pour Monsieur et Madame,* the card read. *Avec mes compliments les plus sincères.* Shamus ordered champagne on the telephone in French, calling it shampoo, and the telephonist laughed a great deal. *"Ah, c'est vous,"* she said, as if she had already heard about him. They drank the champagne warm because the ice had melted by the time it was delivered, and afterwards they walked down the rue de Rivoli where they bought Shamus a suit and three shirts and a pair of handsome lacquered shoes.

"How's the Bentley?"

"Fine."

"Bosscow in the pink?"

"Oh yes."

"Nipper?"

"Also yes."

"Leg?"

"Leg fine. On the mend."

And a toothbrush, Shamus reminded him, so they bought a toothbrush as well, because Shamus had left his at Elsie's in case her husband needed it when he came back from prison.

"How's Helen?" Cassidy asked.

"Fine, fine."

In a minuscule flower shop, buying two carnations, Shamus kissed the girl on the nape of the neck, a salute which she received with composure. He appeared to have a way of handling women which caused them no offence, like Sandra with dogs.

"Charm the lady buyers at the Fair," he explained, as she pinned the buttonholes in place. "Worth a fortune."

At six o'clock Bloburg, Cassidy's Paris agent, lumbered massively into the foyer, exuding mad compliments even before he was through the swing door, and Shamus withdrew to the bedroom to read about prams.

"Aldo by God you are two hundred years younger how do you manage it my dear fellow look at me I am dying already! Cassidy how are you, listen tomorrow I give you a fantastic dinner, a place only the French are knowing, the best place Cassidy, the cream!"

All Bloburg's hospitality was enjoyed tomorrow. He was a sad, noisy man who had lost everything in the war, children, houses, parents. On previous visits Cassidy had made much of him, even advising him on his luckless love life.

"Cassidy you are number one! All Paris is speaking of you listen I am telling you! You are an *artist* Cassidy! All Paris is fantastic for an *artist!*"

Paris is fantastic, artists are fantastic, Cassidy is fantastic; but not even Cassidy, who could take a great deal of flattery, any longer believed in sad Bloburg as his champion.

"Let's have a drink," he suggested.

"Cassidy you are so generous! All Paris is saying . . ."

He left late, having lingered in the hope of food, but Cassidy was hardened against him. He wanted to eat with Shamus and time was important to him.

Dining in the hotel, feeling their way with one another and not yet finding the right note, they drank to the book.

"Whose book?" said Shamus, lowering his glass.

"Your book. Your new one, ass. May it be a massive success."

"Hey lover."

"Yes."

"Great brochures. Punchy, confident, persuasive. I enjoyed every word."

"Thanks."

"Write them yourself?"

"Largely."

"Great talent there lover. Want to work on it."

"Thanks," said Cassidy again and returned to his lobster. They did it very well, he thought, in a garlic butter flavoured with rosemary.

"How long since you invented that braking system?" Shamus asked.

"Oh ten years . . . more, I suppose."

"Anything since?"

"Well the sales side, you know. Manufacture, marketing, exploitation. We've even started producing our own bodies. In a small way, you know."

"Sure, sure."

Catching sight of his own reflection in the mirror, Shamus paused to admire his new suit, lifted his glass and drank to himself, then lifted his glass again to acknowledge the toast.

"But no new earth-shattering invention?" he resumed, settling back into his chair. "Huh? Huh?"

"Not really."

"What about that new folding chassis?"

Cassidy gave a confessive laugh.

"I put my name on it but I'm afraid it was my design people who dreamed it up."

"Christ," said Shamus. "You've really got it made."

Cassidy mentioned Helen. Helen was fine, said Shamus. She was staying with her mother, princesses had to be locked in towers.

"Time she was deprived," he explained. "She was getting cheeky."

"Did she enjoy London? Being with Hall and . . ."

Being not quite into the language, he had wanted to say Hall and Saul, but saved himself in time.

"Sure, sure," said Shamus, and brushing Helen aside, embarked on a somewhat desultory enquiry into the dangers of foreign competition in the Pram Trade. Was a French pram sexier? A German pram more solid? How were the Russians coming on? While he was asking these questions, Shamus' attention strayed to a young girl in the corner of the room. She was twelve years old, no more. She sat alone under a chandelier and wore Sandra's silver dress from the May ball at Oxford. She had ordered something *flambé* which required fruit and a quantity of liqueurs. Two young waiters, under the eye of the *maître d'hôtel*, were ministering to her from a trolley.

"Christ never said anything about us, did he?" he remarked suddenly. "Not a word in the whole manifesto. All we're supposed to do is keep the score."

Taken by surprise, Cassidy faltered.

"Us?"

"Writers. Who do you think?"

He was still watching her but his expression was neither

friendly nor curious, and his voice, as he continued speaking, had a trace of the familiar Irish brogue.

"I mean the pramsellers, all right: they're for the high jump. Hard luck but you know where you stand. You've got it in this world so you can sing for it in the next."

The girl was selecting bottles: not this one, that one; pointing with her small gloved hand. She wore a black band round her neck, a single diamond glittered at the centre.

"The peacemakers are laughing: they're the children of God and no one could wish for better parents. But I'm *not* a fucking peacemaker, am I?"

"You certainly are not," said Cassidy heartily, not yet fully woken to Shamus' change of tone.

"I'm a collision man. A truth-teller, that's me."

"And an Old Testament man," Cassidy reminded him, "like Hall."

Had Shamus *really* boxed? Cassidy had boxed at Sherborne. He had made the mistake of taking a bath before the contest because he wished to please his housemaster, who had an elevated view of his religious potential. Though he had stood for quite a while being hit, he was obliged to lie down in the third round, and for years afterwards leather car seats made him sick.

"Piss off," said Shamus.

"What?"

"Piss off. Shut up about Hall."

"Sorry," said Cassidy, puzzled.

It was the girl who still commanded Shamus' entire attention. The *maître d'hôtel* poured a little lemonade into her wine glass. "Enough," her frail hand said, and the bottle was removed.

"And that little bitch is all right because she's a kid," Shamus continued, still upon the subject of the saved. "And kids get blanket protection. Quite right and proper too. I'm a fervent supporter of the breed myself though I happen to reckon the age limit could come down a bit. But what do the writers get? I tell you one thing: we're not meek, thank you, so we certainly don't inherit the earth. And we're not poor in spirit either, so we can't count on the Kingdom of Heaven, for instance."

His expression hesitated at the brink of anger. Taking Cassidy's hand, he stroked it devotedly, soothing himself against it.

"Easy lover, easy . . . don't get cross . . . easy . . ." Relaxing, he smiled. "You see, lover," he explained in a gentler voice, "there's just *not enough information*, that's my view. I put this to Flaherty only last week. Flaherty, what are you going to do about the writers? I said. Do they get it now, or later? You do see my point, don't you, lover? You're the boss man after all. You're paying."

"Well you do have your *freedom*," Cassidy suggested cautiously.

Shamus rounded on him.

"Freedom from what, for fuck's sake? Freedom from all that lovely money? *That* freedom? Or was it by any chance the unbearable captivity of public recognition you were thinking of?"

Too late, Cassidy reached for his conference voice. "I suppose I was thinking more of freedom from boredom," he said easily, using a passing waiter to order brandy.

"Were you now?" said Shamus pleasantly, the Irish brogue in full flower. "You may be right about that. I will concede that freedom from boredom is a privilege I may well have overlooked. Because after all, I could sleep all day, that's true, and no bugger would raise a finger. Not everyone can say *that* now can they? I mean the warders wouldn't come and bang on the door or tell me to empty my bucket, I'd just hear the sounds of laughter that's all, and the fellows getting their exercise out in the fresh air with their girls maybe. Only trouble is, the nights are such a problem, don't you think?"

"Yes indeed," Cassidy agreed.

With child-like fascination Shamus watched him tip the waiter. It was a very large tip but Cassidy abroad believed in laying strong fences against disrespect.

"What'll you do in nineteen eighty?" Shamus asked, when the transaction was complete.

"I'm sorry?"

"World population's growing seventy million a year, lover. That's a hell of a lot of people to tip, isn't it? Even for you."

Their parting was equally enigmatic.

"You do feel *well?*" Cassidy asked doubtfully as he saw Shamus to the lobby.

"Don't worry lover, I'll be all right on the night."

"Bit too much of Elsie I expect."

"Who?"

"Elsie."

"Sure . . . Lover?"

"Yes?"

"You will let me have a go on those prams, won't you?"
An odd defencelessness had replaced the earlier menace.
"Only . . . well *you* know, it's what I came for. I feel I
could *do* it you see. Sell. I reckon I could turn it into a
real vocation. Hey lover."

"Yes."

"Thanks for the suit."

"That's all right."

"The lobster was great."

"I'm glad you liked it."

"Great bread too. Crisp outside, squidgy in the middle.
There's so much of you I could *use*," Shamus remarked
suddenly, putting his hands on Cassidy's shoulders. "Hey
listen . . . " Cassidy listened. "We got to love each other,
see. It's the great experiment, like blacks and whites and
all that shit. But if I don't have you *all*, I don't get any
of you, do I? You're such a big slimy fish. I can put
my hands on you but I don't know where you end. . . .
You're *awful*, honest. . . ."

Cassidy laughed awkwardly. "Perhaps it's just as well
you *don't* know," he said, releasing himself in case Shamus
was contemplating a public embrace. "I say you didn't
bring a copy of the book, did you?"

Somewhere in the brown darkness of Shamus' eyes, a
warning light went up, and stayed.

"What if I did?"

"It's just that I'd love to read it, that's all. If you've
brought one. What stage is it *at* actually?" he added.
Receiving no answer, he deemed a subsidiary question
politic. "Will it be a film, like *Moon?* I'll bet that's worth
a bit just by itself. Let alone the book sales. . . . Paperback, too, I suppose?" As he continued speaking, Shamus
was already backing into the lift.

"You know," Shamus said as his feet ascended into the
shaft, "if I was Flaherty I could work this thing alone."

It was midnight by the time Cassidy joined him. He had
business in the Bristol Bar and another meeting with Blo-

burg, and at eleven o'clock a public relations girl called
to check handouts. Shamus was lying like a dead onion-
seller dressed in the black coat again, flat on his stomach
on the coverlet with his face in the beret. His new suit
was hung carefully in the wardrobe with an Exhibitor's
badge pinned to the lapel. The brochures were still strewn
beside him on the floor. A ruled pad was propped on
the chimney piece.

Honourable Sir, the message read, *Kindly to wake the
undersigned tomorrow morning punctual for the Fair your
obedient humble servant Shamus P. Scardanelli* (*Vendor*).
The postscript said, Please *lover*. Please. *Major commit-
ment. And lover forgive, please forgive. Vital.*

A lorry was parked outside the window and workmen were
unloading crates on the cobble stones, shouting jokes he
couldn't understand.

I should have bought him pyjamas too, thought Cassidy.
Why does he have to wrap himself in that coat?

He sleeps like Hugo but quieter, cheeks squashed against
his forearm in a pout.

Down in the street a woman was calling, a tart by the
sound of her and drunk. Is that what I want him to do:
pimp for me? *Forgive lover, forgive.* You're so full of
truth, Cassidy thought, looking at him again, what is
there to forgive?

"Dale?"

Shamus was muttering but Cassidy couldn't hear the
words. You're dreaming, he thought, turning to look at
him again, you're dreaming of Elsie and selling prams.
Why not dream of Helen?

Suddenly Shamus cried out, a short hard cry of *"No!"*
or *"Go!"* swinging his shoulders in angry rejection.

"Shamus," Cassidy said quietly and put out his hand to
touch him. "Shamus it's all right, it's me; Cassidy. I'm
here, Shamus."

No, he thought, as Shamus settled again, better to be
just the two of us. Dream of Helen another time.

"Dale you bugger."

"It's not Dale. It's Cassidy."

A long silence.

"Can I come to the Fair?"

"Yes, you can come."

"In my new suit?"

"In your new suit."

Minutes later Shamus woke again, abruptly.

"Where's my carnation?"

"I put it in the toothmug."

"It's for the lady buyers you see. At the Fair."

"I know. It'll slay them."

"Goodnight lover."

"Goodnight Shamus."

17

The day was dull for Cassidy, for Shamus balm. The pramseller rose without haste, his ears already full of the greedy, unproductive clichés of the trade; but the great writer was already dressed save for his feet; was pacing the floor with the alacrity of the young executive bent on increasing his figures. His lacquered shoes were back with the valet; dust had been identified in the welts. Cassidy had planned to leave late, but Shamus would have none of it. Great conquests were in the air, he insisted; Cassidy and Shamus must be in the field early, breathe heart into the troops.

They arrived in fine rain; the tents were sagging dismally on their masts, smelling of rugger and changing rooms.

"Bee-Line?" Shamus cried indignantly. *"Bee-Line?* Never heard of them."

"Our main competition," said Cassidy.

Two Beefeaters guarded the entrance; halberdiers were serving bitter beer in pewter tankards.

"You mean you camp with the enemy? Jesus lover, you got to burn them down! Rape their women, nippers to the stake!"

"Take it easy," said Cassidy. "Hullo Mr. Stiles."

"Oh *hullo* Mr. Cassidy. How's business? Doing anything, are you?"

"Not much; I hear it's pretty quiet."

"I think it's the same everywhere," said Stiles with satisfaction. "I don't think devaluation's bitten the way it ought, do you?"

"I'm sure it hasn't," said Cassidy.

"Creep," said Shamus, as they left. "Toady."

"You've got to keep on terms with them," Cassidy explained. "After all, it is us against the foreigners."

The Cassidy tent restored him to humour. Introduced as an important contact of the Chairman's, Shamus tested the chassis, rode in a pushchair, flirted with the girls, and talked about Saint Francis with Meale, who had recently become extremely sullen, and was expressing a desire to take Holy Orders. They all *own* him, Cassidy thought, mystified; they all own him. If *I* was the hanger-on they'd chuck me out in minutes. A large crowd had just entered the tent, mainly Scandinavians, women of a certain age. Over luncheon, befriending a Froken Svenson from Stavanger, Shamus sold her a hundred chassis at thirteen to the dozen. She should pay when she liked, he said, Cassidy's had the large approach to money.

"Get hold of Lemming," Cassidy said quietly to Meale. "Tell him to rescind the deal."

"How?" said Meale, aggressively.

"Meale what *is* the matter with you?"

"Nothing. I happen to admire him, that's all; I think he's truthful and fine."

"Lose the order, d'you understand? Bury it. She hasn't signed anything, nor have we. We've never given thirteen to the dozen in our lives and we're not starting now."

"I made it, lover!" Shamus cried as the limousine returned them to the city. "I made it! Jesus I can swim! See the way I gave her the oil?"

"You were terrific," Cassidy agreed. "You were absolutely great."

"Jesus, that whole place, I could *die* there; I tell you, there's no better compliment than that now is there? The tent, the music, the flags . . . Lover, listen, before it goes to my head, was there anything I did wrong?"

"Nothing."

"Not too much?"

"No."

"Not too familiar? The hand on the arm?"

"Just right."

By the time they reached the St. Jacques he was even capable of reproof.

"You know lover you shouldn't have let those Japs in. I mean they were just standing there photographing the exhibits. I mean look what they did to the car trade. You should throw the sodders out, honest. Put a notice up 'No Japs,' I would."

Lying in the bath, playing with the carnations, Shamus added his own bizarre appreciation of market trends: "Hey lover, what about Paisley now? I mean if that feller's going to murder all us procreating Catholics there won't *be* any bloody babies."

"Ask Flaherty."

"You know when you come to think of it, prams are a very worthy thing to be in. I mean prams are your *ploughshares*, aren't they, for tomorrow's world. I mean there's other buggers churning out swords by the million but you and me are absolutely in the non-belligerent camp, wouldn't you say so lover?"

"See you after the party," Cassidy said benevolently.

"Why can't I come?" he demanded sulkily. "I sold the prams not you."

"Principals only," said Cassidy. "Sorry."

"Meeow," said Shamus. "Those people loved me," he continued reflectively, "and I *loved* them. A perfect marriage. A great pointer for the future." He sang a few bars of an Irish melody. "Hey, lover, you never answered my question."

"What question?"

"I asked you once: any views on the meaning of love?"

"I must say, you pick your moments, don't you?" said Cassidy with a laugh.

With his toe, Shamus guided a carnation away from the jet of the tap. "Oh do not die," he recited, apparently to the flower, "For I shall hate all women so when thou art gone. Chippie chippie, lover."

"Chippie, chippie," said Cassidy.

His last sight of Shamus was of him sitting in the bath wearing the black beret and studying stock prices in the *Herald Tribune*. He must have used the whole bottle of Cassidy's bath essence; the water was a dark green and the carnations floated on it like lilies on a stagnant pond.

The British Minister (Economic) was one of those fastidious, small, very rich, unworldly men whom, in Cassidy's experience, the Foreign Office invariably appointed to deal with trade. He cringed at one end of a long room in the shelter of a powerful wife, beside a marble fireplace stuffed with red cellophane, and he received his guests one by one after a butler had thinned them out at the door. Cassidy arrived early, second only to Mc-Kechnie of Bee-Line, and the Minister shook their hands very separately as if he would referee their fight.

"We know some Cassidys in Aldeburgh," the Minister's wife said, having listened carefully to his voice and found it phonically acceptable. "I don't expect they're any relation are they?"

"Well we are a pretty big tribe," Cassidy admitted, "but we do all seem to be related in some way."

"What does it *mean?*" the Minister complained.

"I'm told it's Norman," said Cassidy.

McKechnie, who had not been favoured with such intimacies, stood off glowering. He had brought a wife. Cassidy had met her in the tent that morning, a freckled red-headed lady in yellow and green, and she looked like all the wives he had ever met since he had begun in prams. "You stole our Meale," she had said to him, and she was getting ready to say it again. She had put her hair up and bared one shoulder. Her handbag had a long gold chain to it, enough for at least one prisoner, and she held her elbow wide in case she needed to jab anyone.

"How's the Fair going?" the Minister asked. "They're having a *Fair*," he said, for the benefit of his wife. "Out near Orsay, where poor Jenny Malloy used to walk her dog." It was more an objection than an explanation. Fairs, his tone suggested, had replaced dogs, and the change was not for the better.

"We've taken ten thousand quid in eight hours," Mrs. McKechnie said straight at Cassidy. She came from near Manchester and did not care for side. "We've not a graduate on the books, have we Mac?"

"I thought they'd all arrive together," the Minister said hopelessly. "In a charabanc or something. It is extraordinary. What about drink?"

"Two up," his wife warned. The butler announced Sanders and Meyer of Everton-Soundsleep.

"*Norman* did you say?" the Minister enquired. "Norman *French*, that kind of Norman?"

"Apparently," said Cassidy.

"You ought to tell them that. They'd like it. *We* get by because she's half a Lamey, it's the only reason. They *loathe* the rest of us like poison, always did. They loathe *us* too, really, except she's half a Lamey."

A pack of junior diplomats entered through another door.

"Can we tempt you to a drink?" they asked of Mrs. McKechnie, picking by training on the plainest woman present. One held canapés on a government tray and another asked whether she would have time for pleasure.

"She's laying it on a bit about the ten thousand," McKechnie told Cassidy aside. "It's more like two."

"There's plenty of room for both of us," said Cassidy.

"She's loyal, mind."

"I'm sure she is. Where are you staying?"

"Imperial. Here, have you had the Japs in?"

"They came this morning."

"It's got to be stopped," said McKechnie, and to Sanders who had just joined them, "I was saying to young Cassidy here, we've got to do something about the Japs."

"Japs?" said Sanders, mystified. "What Japs?"

McKechnie looked at Cassidy and Cassidy looked at McKechnie and they both looked again at Sanders, this time with pity.

"I expect it's just the big firms they go for," said McKechnie.

"I'm sure it is," said Cassidy and moved away as if in answer to a call.

They were about twelve in the room, fourteen perhaps including their hosts, but reinforcements were arriving fast. Their topic was transport. Bland and Cowdry had shared a taxi; Crosse had walked and the tarts had nearly eaten him: "Lovely some of them were, just kids, nineteen or twenty, it's a disgrace." Martenson had almost decided not to come as a protest against the Ambassador whom he thought should have been at the Opening. As soon as he returned to Leeds, he said, he proposed to complain to his Member of Parliament.

"Bloody peacock I'll have his bloody balls off. We earn it, he spends it. Look at the size of this room THEN! *One man* from Commerce: that's all you need. *One man*. You could close the whole bloody Embassy apart from him."

It was while listening to this piece of intelligence that Cassidy heard the butler call an unfamiliar name. He did not catch it precisely but it sounded like Zola; it was certainly Conte *et* Contessa, and he turned to watch them enter. Afterwards he said he had had an instinct; only instinct, he argued afterwards, could explain why he had freed himself from Crosse and Cowdry and stepped back a full pace to get a clearer view of Shamus bowing courteously over his hostess' hand.

He was wearing his rue de Rivoli suit and a pale salmon shirt belonging to Cassidy, a coveted garment which he had been keeping in reserve for a special occasion. A dark-haired girl waited at his side, one hand lightly on his arm. She was serene and very beautiful and she stood directly beneath the light. From his point of vantage Cassidy noticed, with the acuteness of perception which accompanies sudden shock, the bold imprint of a love bite on her lower neck.

"You've not had *trouble* from him?" asked McKechnie, who had joined him again. "My wife says he's queer as two left shoes."

"Who?"

"Meale."

"I'm sure not," said Cassidy. "In fact I think if anything he's too much the other way."

"It's *frightfully* enterprising of you," the Minister's wife was moaning, "to keep your own man in Warsaw. What does he *do* all the time?"

"Oh we have quite a lot of trade with them actually," Cassidy confessed modestly. "You'd be surprised."

Never hold him back, Helen whispered. *Promise you never will.*

Shamus had charmed them all. Stately and subdued he moved graciously from group to group, now talking, now listening, now gently deferring to the girl as he offered her canapés and whisky. His gestures, to those who knew him, might have seemed a little slurred; his Polish accent, where Cassidy could hear it, occasionally yielded to a faint Irish intonation, but his magic had never been more compelling.

The Minister was particularly impressed.

"If only *more* of you would look east," he complained. "Who is she?"

"Great dignity," the Minister's lady agreed. "Make a *marvellous* diplomat's wife, even in Paris."

"She's stoned out of her mind," Shamus warned him *en vol* between two admiring wives. "If we don't get her out she'll fall flat on her arse."

"Give her to me," said Cassidy.

Receiving the full weight of her he walked straight out of the room.

"Here," he heard McKechnie say, "that's the fellow who kicked my stand. Bloody well kicked it and told young Stiles our canopies were crap. He's not foreign, he's Irish!"

"Tour d'Argent," said Shamus. They were standing on the pavement watching the girl's departing taxi. Shamus looked slightly dishevelled, as if he had been pushed by several people at once.

"Shamus are you *sure?*"

"Lover," said Shamus holding his forearm in an iron grip, "I've never been hungrier in my life."

"To the suit," said Shamus.

"To the suit," said Cassidy.

"God bless her and all who sail in her."

"Amen."

Once again the unpredictable had proved itself the rule. Cassidy had claimed his corner table with the gloomiest foreboding. He did not know how much Shamus had drunk but he knew it was a lot and he was seriously wondering whether he could handle him without Helen's help. He did not know whether anyone had played Fly in the Tour d'Argent before, but he had a pretty good idea what would happen if they tried. In the cab Shamus had taken one of his quick naps and Cassidy had been obliged to wake him under the eye of the commissionaire.

Now, against all expectation, they were in paradise: Old Hugo's paradise, with food and waiters, the fragrance of angels and of heavenly flowers.

Diamonds surrounded them: hung in giant clusters in the window panes, pricked the orange night sky, were draped in the eyes of lovers and in the brown silk of women's hair. Cassidy heard nothing but the sounds of love and battle, the whispers of longing couples and the far sharpening of a knife. Vertigo seized him, stronger than Haverdown, stronger than Kensal Rise. Of all the places he had ever been, this was the most exciting, the most intoxicating. Best of all was the company of Shamus himself. Something—the drink, the girl, his conquest of the Embassy, the magic of the city—something had freed Shamus, soothed and softened him and made him young. He was alight and yet at peace, he was miraculously sober.

"Shamus."

"What is it lover?"

"*This*," said Cassidy.

Shamus' eyes were shadowed behind the candles, but Cassidy could see he was smiling.

"Shamus, it was wonderful what you did. It was just fantastic. They really believed in you . . . more than in me. You could have told them anything, just anything you wanted. You could run my whole business with your left hand."

"Great. And you write my books." They drank to that as well.

"I wish Helen was here," said Cassidy.

"Never mind lover, woods are full of them."

"What's it like being married to someone like Helen? To someone you *really* love?"

"Guess," said Shamus, but Cassidy, who had an ear for such things, sensed that he would be wiser not to.

Shamus talked.

Over linen, candles, chalices, and plate, he talked of the world and its riches. He talked of love and of Helen, and the search for happiness and the gift of life, and Cassidy, like a favoured pupil, listened to every word and remembered almost nothing but his smile and the beguiling softness of his voice. Helen is our virtue; we talk, but Helen acts. Helen is our constant; we rotate but she is still.

"I've never met a woman like her," Cassidy confessed. "She could be . . . she could be . . ."

She *is*, Shamus corrected him. Helen has no potential; Helen is fulfilled.

"Does she *mind* about . . . Elsie and people, Shamus?"

Not as long as they are called Elsie, said Shamus.

Of the obligation to live romantically and feel deeply. He talked of writing, and what a feeble task it was beside the vocation to experience.

"A book . . . Jesus. Such a *little* thing, just a handful of days. *Enoughs,* that's what a book is. Get pissed enough, get the guilts enough, get screwed enough, and suddenly . . . it's a natural. Honest, lover."

Creation was an act of moderation, but life: *life,* Shamus said, existed only in excess. Who wants *enough* for Christ's sake? Who wants the twilight when he can have the fucking sun?

"No one," said Cassidy loyally, and believed he spoke the truth.

He talked about inspiration, that much of it was genuine but useless, you left your soul out in all weathers, the birds shat on it, the rain washed it, but you had to leave it there all the same, there was no backing out, so fuck it. About equality, how there was none, and freedom, none either, it was crap, and the act of creation made it the biggest crap of all, whether God's or Shamus' creation. Because freedom meant the fulfilment of genius, and the existence of genius precluded equality. So the howl for freedom was New Testament crap, and the howl for equality was the howl of the Many-too-Many, Shamus fucked himself of them all. How he hated youth, it made an artist of every little pig who could afford a paintbrush; how he hated age, it retarded the genius of youth; how the world was in existence because Shamus witnessed it, it was certain to die without him.

And when Shamus had told him about life, he told him about Art as well. Not Vatican art, not history book art, nothing for School Certificate, attempt any two of the following questions.

Art as a destiny. As a calling and a lovely agony.

And out of the air, out of the undefined edges of Shamus' magical conversation, Cassidy discovered that Shamus was chosen.

Fatally, wonderfully chosen.

That he belonged to a body of men who never met; of the gifted early dead; and their embrace was already on him.

Whom waiters loved although they never tipped them.

That he was one of a Pack, a Few against the Many-too-Many, but each hunted alone and none had help in time of need except the comfort of knowing.

"Knowing *what*, Shamus?"

That you belonged, and nothing more.

That you were best, and could only elect yourself; that Flaherty was the only true and living God, because Flaherty was self-appointed, and Self-Appointed Man was divine, and limitless, and out of time, like love.

As to what it was exactly that joined Shamus to the others, that, as Cassidy's tutor would say, was concept rather than fact. The concept was to choose yourself very early, and to be precociously familiar with death: with premature death, romantic death, sudden and very destructive of the flesh. To live always testing the edges of your existence, the extreme outlines of your identity. To need water, not air; water defined you, there was a German poet always bathing in fountains; man is invisible until the cold waters of experience have shown him who he is, hence total immersion, violence, boxing with Hall, the Baptist church, and (somehow) Flaherty again.

Gradually, with the aid of a third bottle of wine and several names supplied by Shamus, Cassidy formed a picture of this wonderful band of brothers, this Few: a non-flying Battle of Britain squadron captained by Keats and supported by a long list of young men.

Not all of them were English.

Rather, a Free Europe Squadron, as it were, which included the pilots Novalis, Kleist, Byron, Pushkin, and Scott Fitzgerald. Their enemy was bourgeois society: the Gerrard's Crossers again, the fucking bishops in drag, the doctors, lawyers, and Jaguar drivers who thundered towards them in black, mechanical fleets; while Somewhere in England, waiting for the last Scramble, they penned fraught elegies and made up peace-loving verses in writing.

Such men by definition survived more in the promise than in the fulfilment; and commanded most respect by what they had left undone.

Also they took a lot, because it was not long before they themselves were taken.

"Who can write about life and run away from it at the same time?" Shamus wanted to know.

"No one," said Cassidy.

Of this squadron, Shamus was that night and for all the nights to come the one survivor. Cassidy believed that. He knew he would always believe it, because somehow that night and for ever Shamus had stolen into his childhood, and would stay there like a favourite place or a loved uncle. As to Cassidy himself, he was their squire, frying their bacon, carrying their helmets, and polishing their fur-lined boots; posting their last letters and giving their rings to their Helens, wiping their names off the blackboard when they didn't come back.

"You know Shamus," Cassidy said much later—they were rowing somewhere, one oar each—"I'll always be there when you need me."

He meant it. It was a promise, more real to him than marriage because it was an idea, and one that with Shamus' help he had found for himself, that night, in the Tour d'Argent in Paristown.

"Why are you crying?" Cassidy asked, as they left.

"For love," said Shamus. "You want to try it some time."

"Who's Dale?"

"Who?"

They had taken a limousine to the seventh district, Shamus had friends there.

"Dale. You talked about him in your sleep. You said he was a bugger."

"He is a bugger."

Shamus' head was very still against the window, but the lights from the street played over it like gold coins, rais-

ing him and pushing him back, so that his silhouette wore
the passive look of a man not able to control what the outside did to him.

"Then why don't you drop him down a hole?"

"Because he dropped me first, and they're the ones
you can't beat."

"Did he love you?"

"I suppose so."

"As much as . . ."

Reaching out, Shamus took Cassidy's hand in both of
his. "No lover, not like you," he assured him gently, turning his hand over and kissing the palm. "Not like you're
going to learn. You'll be the best. Number one. In the
first position. Honest."

An instinct made him say it. A moment of profoundest
empathy, of prophetic anxiety.

"Shamus . . . you're the greatest writer of our time. I
believe that. I'm very proud."

The face was turned away from him, very beautiful
and sudden against the night, against the running glitter
of the street.

"You've got me wrong lover," Shamus whispered, gently
putting away his hand. "I'm just a failed businessman."

Still in Paradise they went to Paris.

Not Cassidy's Paris of hissing vacuum doors and bad
American accents, but Shamus' Paris of hydrants and cob-
blestone streets and rotten vegetables and doors with no
name; a Paris which Cassidy had not dreamed of, not
aspired to even, since it answered appetites he did not
know he had, and showed him people he had not imagined; relaxed, gay people of unworldly wisdom who gravely shook Shamus by the hand and called him *maître*
and asked him about his work. They went to the Sulpice,
to a square full of bookshops, through a dark courtyard
buoyant with music, to a door that led straight to a lift,
and they emerged into a sea of chatter and laughing girls
and men with bare chests and beads.

"They love you, Shamus," Cassidy whispered to him,
as they drank the whisky and answered questions about

London. "Look at you," Cassidy kept saying. "You're *fa-mous.*"

"Yes," said Shamus, without bitterness. "They remember."

They went to an island, to a high grey house belonging to an American, and someone gave Shamus his own book to sign, *Moon,* a first edition, and he stood in a pulpit reading aloud from it, to sleeping couples breathing in the dark. Indians, white girls, murmured their applause. He read very quietly so that Cassidy, even had he wished, could not have heard the words, but he knew from the rhythm and the fall of them that they were the most beautiful words he had ever heard, more beautiful than Shakespeare or Kahlil Gibran or the German High Command; and he sat alone, eyes half closed, letting them go through him like the language of love, and his pride knew no bounds, pride of possession, pride of creation, pride of love.

"Shamus let's stay. Please let's stay."

"Negative."

"What about *her* then?"—for Shamus had found a girl and was gently turning her breast inside her dress.

"No good," said Shamus. "It's her house. *His* house," he corrected, indicating her husband.

The American gave them both another whisky. He was a big, kindly man, very pugnacious in his sympathy and a keen opponent of aggression.

"Get the fuck out of here," he advised them. "Have a drink and go." And to Cassidy: "I'll crucify him. He's a great guy but get him out."

"Of course," said Cassidy. "You've been very kind."

In a bright bar, drinking Chartreuse because Shamus said it had the highest killing power, shielding their eyes against the neons, they found their first whore.

"Shamus, why do you live so alone when they all want you so much?"

"Got to keep moving," Shamus said vaguely. "Can't stand still, lover, they'd get you right between the eyes. Twenty years since I wrote that book."

His gaze had drifted to the girl. A dark girl, pretty but austere; Angie Mawdray asking for a rise in salary. For a while he studied her in silence, then slowly raised his glass to her. She came to him without smiling. The barman did not even look up as they left.

18

Sitting on the curb, waiting for his master to return from the Crusade, the faithful squire watched the river and dreamed of perfect love. Of big beds made for himself and Shamus and the dark-eyed girl, of houseboats hung with lights and filled with naked bodies which never creased and never tired. White boats floating to a Hollywood Heaven of Interminable Dawn, rocking to the music of Frank Sinatra.

You see, Hug, for Shamus and the French it's different. They are lovers because they believe in love, not because they believe in people. Is that clever, Hug? They are lovers out of joy, not because they are afraid to be alone.

"I need money," Shamus said.

He was reeling a little and his face was very bright.

"How much?"

Shamus took a hundred francs.

"The passing of money," Cassidy advised him contentedly, "is a very sexual transaction."

"Piss off," said Shamus.

"Was that love?" Cassidy asked as they walked slowly away.

"Ours is for ever," said Shamus with his old smile, and put his arm round Cassidy's shoulder.

"Lover."

"Yes."

"Go soon. Paris stinks."

"Okay," said Cassidy laughing. "Wherever you like."

Fast now, and angry, a lot of drink inside them. The young squire exerting himself to keep abreast of his questing, errant master. His feet sting through his thin city shoes as the two men bound up the long stone stairway. Above them the white, incandescent dome offers its single breast to the starlit sky. Lanterns, windows lure them but

193

the master is bent on one place, one place only, a green place, it has a green door. They turn a corner; the steps make them turn a corner, and suddenly there are no houses at all, no handrail even for the height-sick apprentice, only the deep blackness of a cave, and the lights of Paris scattered over it, the walls, the ceiling, and the floor, like the wealth of buried kings. But Shamus has no eye for magic, the past is his enemy, he has his own new Vatican ahead. He is half running, thrusting onward up the endless staircase, face wet where the street lamps catch it, driving himself from the shoulders, all the body following.

"Shamus where are we going?"

"Up."

One day, maybe we climb the Eiger; and there'll be a green light waiting on the peak. One more, Shamus said. One more whore and we get out of town.

It was early for that trade, or late. A dream-like silence hung in the green glow of the table lamps and the girls of Kensal Rise sat sleepily as if they had missed the last train home, listening to Sandra's chords played on an unseen piano. Shamus, loving terminals, has entered ahead of Cassidy, his arms raised to shoulder height as if he is about to take off his coat. The girls shift to receive him, a single herd moving to the cowman.

"Monsieur ne veut pas?" a middle-aged lady enquires politely, not unlike the Minister's wife, but with a greater show of interest. *"Vous voulez quelqu' chose à boire?"* Norman, thinks Cassidy, Norman French. This part may not be happening; this part, actually, *is* a dream.

"Shamus!"

The girls have gathered to him: to Shamus the impeccable Knight. His arms are high above his head, and suddenly it is happening, it is realised, the subject of innumerable dreams. Their hands steal over him, make him their prisoner; pry, invade his knightly shirt, wrestle with the essentially English arrangement of his French waistband; rob him, strip him as the music rises, throw his absurd male clothes to the floor, divide his cloak, it is a martyrdom. Some are ugly, some are naked, but a green light makes virgins of them all, disguises their shadowed places and give a children's eagerness to their movements.

Suddenly to the thud of Sandra's slow piano, Shamus has grasped the tallest girl, a broad-buttocked, black-haired enemy, mouthed and bearded, wide-thighed. And is down on her. Has fought her down, pulling her by the arms, has forced the same arms back to pinion her. Now she averts her hips to escape the sword but Shamus is fighting with his head, shark-like, using it as a hammer to quell her white flesh.

How dark he is against her breasts, her belly, even her infernal places! Now he flings her. Has her wallowing, crying, while she holds him obediently in the scissors of her thighs.

"Shamus!"

Cassidy's voice. Who touched the light? Foul, free kick to England! The light has dimmed on their wedged bodies. This is the clinch, the hold! Wait. She stirs. Groans, draws in her breath, the sword is home! Will she resist? She writhes; shifts her spread knees, but only to admit him further.

Silence and music, one above the other.

The audience has broken ranks, drawing nearer to observe the climax. The defeated one becomes articulate.

Listen! Aha! The whore is confessing her infamy! Conceding battle, begging forgiveness, praising the everlasting king! In vain. They give her no succour. No seconds to throw in the towel; no referee to count the strokes, suppress the screams, administer the morphine. One shout is left in her.

One long-drawn sigh.

Accompanied by a frown; a grid of sexual confusion, drawn in deep fine lines at the centre of the Gallic brow. My God. My French God. My Flaherty.

He is finished? He is not finished? It is safe to approach? A typical French confusion.

Excuse me madam, do you mind?

Lights please. Lights.

Just a minute please, do you mind?

"I'll go," says Cassidy, and stepping quickly forward, helps the drenched Crusader to his feet.

"Monsieur ne veut pas?" Madame enquires again, touching the squire's keen but unproven weapon through the strained worsted.

He has to have an audience, Helen explains. *When we were rich it was the maid. Now we are poor it is Cassidy.*

Five hundred francs, traveller's cheques are acceptable. Green for go.

"I need a church, lover," Shamus whispers to the night lights of the sleeping city. "Quick! I need Flaherty and I need him express."

At High Mass in the Sacré Coeur, among more candles than they had had at the Tour d'Argent, more even than at Sherborne Abbey, Shamus and Cassidy watched the devout gestures of pure boys while covertly passing back and forth the half bottle of whisky.

Dear God this is Aldo Cassidy who last prayed to you when Helen and Shamus were missing believed killed and I faced the crime of innocence for the rest of a long and boring life. Well, since then I must tell you that my prayers have been answered and that I owe you a substantial debt of gratitude. It will take me a considerable time, in fact, to evaluate the many experiences which the reunion promises to put in my way, and in due course we shall have to get together again with Old Hugo the well-known Member of Parliament and work out between us what is the nature of love, what is good and bad, and what is the relevance of it all to our Shared Design for Living. In the meantime, once again, an interim "Thank you" for lifting me quite a few rungs very quickly in the Ladder of Beings, and all safely outside Sandra's earshot.

"It's for the fabric," Cassidy explained. "For rebuilding the church. It's falling down."

"Jesus," said Shamus, staring at the mute mouth of the offertory box. "Jesus. There must be *someone* you don't pay."

It is not easy to leave Paris when you are drunk and tired and on foot; when you are lurching through columns of yellow-lit concrete, looking for a field; when no whore knows the way and taxi drivers decline your custom. First they tried to find the Fair: they would creep into the marquee and sleep in prams. But the Fair had moved. Twice they recognised the road that led to it; each time, it led them false. So they decided to look instead for a river that would guide them to the sea, but the river path ended at a bridge, and beyond the bridge rose a forest of hideous buildings blocking their escape. At a tram station they found an empty tram, but Cassidy could not locate the power and prayers did not avail them.

"Dance," Shamus proposed. "Maybe he likes dance best."

In a cobbled alley two men of equal height, different only in their colour, are dancing. One of them is Shamus; one of them, as the ever-observant Cassidy correctly records, is himself.

It is dawn, not evening, because no one is paying attention, no one is up, no one is there. Occasionally, from Heaven, voices address them in a mother language, Flaherty presumably, or Mrs. Flaherty even, they are here incognito, a week's trip to inspect the Franco-Irish faithful. But the text of God's message, as so often alas, reaches them in garbled form, it would be rash to act on it. Their movements are for an audience; complex but perfectly performed. A divine audience; one that will transport them from a city no longer congenial to Shamus. They have completed *Swan Lake* and now they are playing Shadows, stalking one another's image along the moist stucco of an uncomplaining wall, but Shamus finds this number unrewarding, and having dealt the wall a quite unreasonable kick, bids Cassidy follow him in a dance of his own invention. Cassidy, anxious to oblige, is trying to keep time while sending many cordial greetings to his retired musical instructors, including Mrs. Harabee of Sherborne School Dorset.

Now Doubtful, think.

I am thinking Mrs. Harabee.

Well think harder Doubtful.

Yes, Mrs. Harabee.

Come on Pailthorpe, says Sandra, *you imitate people's voices, well now imitate their songs, that's all.*

I can't.

Of course you can. I've heard you singing perfectly *well in church, but still.*

But that was with other people, Sandra.

You mean you can't put up with me alone? I'm sorry.

Doubtful I shall report you to your housemaster.

"Yes Shamus."

"Well then fucking listen."

Shamus sings a line likening Helen's breasts to the twin hills of Shamaree. Obediently Cassidy tries to repeat it.

"I can't," he says, breaking off. "It's all right for you, you're artistic."

Touched by Cassidy's musical incompetence, Shamus the darker one embraces him, kissing his cheeks and mouth, twining his fingers in Cassidy's conventionally heterosexual hairstyle. Cassidy has no particular feelings at the point of oral impact, but is embarrassed by his own unshaven state. About to apologise to Shamus, who appears to have gone to sleep on his breast, the Oxford undergraduate is abruptly summoned by bells. Not merely the peal, as Shamus later said, but the bells themselves, despatched in place of thunderbolts by Flaherty's angry hand, hurtle downwards over the rooftops and smash into the courtyard in multiplying chaos, inflicting sonic tortures normally reserved for the inhabitants of Sodom. In terror, Shamus puts his hands over his ears and shouts:

"Stop it! Stop it! We repent. Pooves' penitence, Flaherty lay off! Christ, lover, you bloody fool, look what you've *done!*"

"You started it," Cassidy objects, but the great writer having already taken flight, his disciple follows.

They are running therefore, Shamus leading, his hands still over his ears, weaving and ducking to avoid the falling bells, his jacket billowing like a life belt.

"Don't look back, you fool, run! Christ why did you take us to that church, you fucking idiot! Flaherty, you live! Lover! Hell!"

Cassidy is down.

He falls probably full length, cracking his knee against the lid of a Parisian dustbin and distinctly feeling the kneecap dislodge itself and roll away into the opposing scrum. Shamus drags him to his feet. The horse is looking round at them as they unwind the brake. Of some age this horse, its face is grey, black rings surround its eyes.

The bells have stopped.

"What did I tell you?" says Shamus contentedly. "South," he tells the horse. "*Sud.* We would have shunshine."

Pulling up the blanket, he turns to Cassidy and draws him down into the leather cushions of the *fiacre*.

"Come on lover, give us a kiss."

Salt sweat joins the loved ones' faces, Old Hugo's stubble recalls a lifetime's quest.

"Jesus I hate that city," Shamus declared. "Can't think why we ever went there."

"Nor can I," said Cassidy. "It's a heap."

"Is he a good kid?" Shamus asked.

"Super. They both are."

"Can't take them with you, lover, little buggers live on. Then they want what you want. The fucks, the laughs, the drinks, the bosscows . . ."

"It'll be better for them," said Cassidy.

"It wasn't better for us, though, was it, lover?"

No answer. Cassidy is asleep. No conversation. Shamus is also asleep. Only the horse has life in him, moving ever further south.

In fact, however, Cassidy was awake. Sentient, fast-thinking, acute. His body was stiff and aching but he dared not move because Hugo was sleeping in his arms, and only sleep would mend the injured child's kneecap.

It's a *coach* Hug, he is explaining in his mind; drawn by a super grey horse, the kind they have in Sainte-Angèle only in Sainte-Angèle it's a sledge.

A coach has wheels, Hug. Wooden, wobbly wheels, and the horse is the hunter they offered me at Haverdown, a thoroughbred of great docility, sent by God to take us away from a stinking city.

"Dad how much money have you got?" Hugo enquired drowsily. "How much in the whole world?"

"Depends how the market goes," said Cassidy. "Enough," he added, thinking: who wants enough?

Stretching—and simultaneously releasing the infant Shamus from his arms—Cassidy braced himself more comfortably against the seat and, rolling up his trouser leg, cautiously examined his injured knee. It was still in place and no mark was visible. Must be internal, he thought, accepting the bottle; the bleeding is internal, and poured a little whisky on the afflicted area.

"Is it all in prams?" Shamus asked, still on the matter of money.

"God, no. It's spread."

"I was rich once," said Shamus. They were going down the ride at Haverdown: an interminable avenue of tall trees. Not south but east: red sun lay at the end of it and the tarmac was swimming red.

"I was rich once," Shamus repeated, tossing the empty bottle into the road.

"Meeow," said Cassidy, quoting the master. "I fuck myself of self-pity."

"Well done," said Shamus with approval, and pushed him on to the road. But Cassidy was ready for the assault and landed neatly thanks to his army training.

"Lover."

"Yes."

"Is Monte Carlo a place?"

"For a night or so," said Cassidy, who had never been there.

"Great. We'll go to Monte Carlo."

And gave revised instructions to the horse.

"Terrified of everything in life except the perpetuation of it," Shamus read aloud. "How's that? I've written it down about you. I'm going to make it completely permanent."

Trust your wooden wheels. Tumbrils. Aristos on the way to execution. Miss Mawdray, get on to Park Wards at once, will you, tell them I want the wheels fixed?

Dozing again, Cassidy lay this time with the elder Hugo, his father, the night they took a train to Torquay to buy the Imperial Hotel. Old Hugo was not long back in those days, a month, two perhaps, still stopping in front of doors and waiting for Cassidy to open them. They had agreed on a reconnoitre, afterwards they would discuss the finance, possibly approach one of the big people, Charles Clore or the Aga Khan, it depended on whom they could trust. On the train, waiting for the dinner call, the old man began weeping. Cassidy, who had not heard this sound before, thought at first he was choking, for the sobs came in a high-pitched retch, like one of Sandra's bitches when she had swallowed a bone.

"Here," he said, offering him a handkerchief, "Have this," and returned to his newspaper.

Then it dawned on him that Old Hugo had no bone to chew, nothing to choke on but his shame, in fact; and lowering the newspaper stared at him, at the broken figure hunched to fit so small a space, and the massive shoulders shaking in loneliness, and the bald head mottled red.

To lift the newspaper?

To go to him?

"I'll get you a drink," he said, and fetched a miniature from the bar, running all the way and crashing the queue.

"You took your time," the old man said, dead straight, when Cassidy returned. He was reading his *Standard,* the greyhound page had caught his interest. "What's *that?*" Eyeing the miniature.

"Whisky."

"When you buy whisky," the old man said, turning the little bottle in his enormous, steady hand, "buy a decent brand, or nothing."

"Sorry," said Cassidy. "I forgot."

"Lover."

"Yes, Shamus."

An hour had passed, perhaps a day. The sun had disappeared, the road was dull and dark, and the trees were black against an empty sky.

"Look at me very closely. Are you looking?"

"Sure," said Cassidy, his eyes still closed against Old Hugo's shoulder.

"Deep into the innerest recesses of my irresistible eyes?"

"Deeper."

"While you look at this picture, lover, thousands of brain cells are dying of old age. Still looking?"

"Yes," said Cassidy, thinking: this conversation came earlier actually; this is what made me think of my father.

"Now. Now. Bang! Bang! See that? Thousands dead. Spread over the cerebral battlefield. Coughing out their tiny lives."

"Don't worry," said Cassidy consolingly. "You'll go on for ever."

Long embraces under the warm blankets.

"I wasn't talking about *me,*" Shamus explained, kissing him. "I was talking about you. *My* cells get a lovely time. It's yours we're worried about. I'm writing that down too, if I remember it."

Partly, Cassidy thought, this is an inward journey. Earthbound Aldo Cassidy, *en route* to Monte Carlo, relives his life in the company of his nomadic familiar.

"Lover."

"Mmh."

"Never go back to Paristown, will we, lover?"

Shamus' voice has a note of anxiety. Not everything is play on this journey.

"Never."

"Promise?"

"Promise."

"Liar."

Cassidy, sobering, revisits the question. "Tell me Shamus, actually, why *don't* you want to go back to Paris?"

"Doesn't matter, does it? We're not going."

Partly however, as recorded, an outward journey; for when he woke again the police were keenly disputing the horse's possession.

They were near a private airfield, in a lay-by between two blue vans; a small biplane was circling to land. Everyone was talking; however, the coachman, who had arrived separately by bicycle, was talking loudest. He was an old, grey man in sailcloth trousers and a long overcoat from the war, and he was kicking the grey's front legs and cursing it for infidelity. The coachman, who shared the view of the police that Shamus was in no way to blame, would not take Cassidy's traveller's cheques so they went to a bank and the police kept guard while Cassidy signed his name ten times along the dotted line.

How did I ever cash a cheque at dawn?

"Shamus," said Cassidy, thinking of Bloburg and Meale and letters from Abalone Crescent, "isn't it time we went back?"

"Blow," said Shamus.

They blew. From the pile of twigs a thin smoke rose, but no flame. Their suits lay beside them on the shingle like dead friends; beyond them a dried-up river, just a shallow stream where they had bathed, and cracking clay imported from the moat at Haverdown. Beyond the river, the fields, beyond the fields a wood, a railway line, and a bank of Flemish sky that reached for ever.

"You'll *never* do it without paper," Cassidy objected. He was feeling cold and rather sober. "I could ring for a taxi if you'd let me dress."

A train passed over the viaduct. There were no passengers but the lights were lit in the carriages.

"I don't *want* a taxi."

"Why not?"

"Because I don't, so piss off. I don't want to go to Paris and I don't want a taxi." He blew again, shivering. "And if you try to dress I'll kill you."

"Then let me get some paper."

"No."

"Why not?"

"Shut up! *Sodder!* Shut up!"

"Meeow," said Cassidy.

The last bottle was empty so they put it on a stick and broke it with artillery fire, ten stones each, fired alternately. And that was when the boy appeared. Mark's age but younger in the face. He carried a fishing rod and a rucksack and he was sitting on a Dutch bicycle of which Cassidy owned the United Kingdom concession. First he compared their genitals, one blond one black but otherwise little to choose, then he picked up a stone and threw it hard and straight at the post where the bottle had stood.

Cassidy wrote out a shopping list and gave him twenty drenched francs.

"And mind how you cross the road," he warned him.

"You see my view is," said Cassidy cautiously, pulling the cork with his teeth—the boy, a resourceful child, had persuaded the shop to draw it halfway—"that if we called a *cab*—"

"Lover," Shamus interrupted.

"Yes."

Encouraged by several editions of the Paris press, the twigs were burning with conviction. Farther down the bank, the boy was casting for fish.

"Lover do you reckon this is a clash of egos?"

"No," said Cassidy.

"Ids?"

"No."

"Ego versus soul? Ibsen?"

"It's not a clash at all. I want to get back, *you* don't. I want a bath and a change and you're prepared to live like a troglodyte for the rest of your life—"

The stone hit him on the side of the head, the left side just behind the ear. He knew it was a stone all the way, saw it coming as he fell, saw the map on it, mainly of the Swiss Alps, the Angelhorn massif leading. The distance to the ground was much farther than he expected. He had time to throw the bottle to one side before he landed, and time to get his arm up before his head hit the shingle. Then Shamus was holding him, kissing him, pouring the wine between his teeth, forgive lover, forgive, weeping, choking like Old Hugo in the train, and the boy was pulling a small brown fish out of the water, a child's fish for a child's rod.

"What the hell did you do it for?" Cassidy asked.

Shamus was sitting apart from him in self-imposed purdah, the beret pulled over his eyes for remorse, his bare back cut in two by the grimy watermark of the depleted river. He said nothing.

"It's a bloody odd way to behave, I must say. Specially for a master of words."

The boy threw back the fish. Either he had not seen the incident, or he had seen many such incidents already, and blood did not alarm him.

"For Christ's sake stop hitting yourself with that stone," Cassidy continued irritably. "Just tell me why you did it, that's all. We did everything you wanted. Froze in the bloody river to feel our identities, ruined our new suits, caught pneumonia, and all of a sudden you stone me. *Why?*"

Silenzio. Very slightly the beret moves in rejection.

"All right, you told me: you don't want to go back to Paris. Fine. But even great lovers can't camp beside a dried-up river all their lives. Well *why* don't you want to go back? Don't you like the hotel? Are you fed up with cities all of a sudden?" A pause. "Is it something to do with Dale? With your book?"

This time the beret does not move at all, not in rejection, not in acceptance; the beret is as still as Sandra at the door, when she is cross with him for not being cosmic, for not providing her with the tragedy she was groomed for.

"Shamus for God's sake. One moment we are halfway to being pooves, the next you're trying to kill me. What the fuck's the matter with you?"

As if shaken by the wind, the bare back sways. Finally the penitent lifts the bottle, drinks.

"Here," said Cassidy, crouching beside him. "I'll have some of that." Putting out his hand he received not the wine, but the battered carnation from Shamus' buttonhole. Gently lifting the beret, Cassidy saw how the tears had collected on the rim.

"Forget it," he said softly. "It didn't hurt, I promise. I don't think you even did it. Look. Look, no lump, no throbbing, nothing. Feel, come on, put your hand there."

He lifted Shamus' muddy hand and put it against his head.

"You've *got* to love me, lover," Shamus whispered, as more tears came. "I need it, honest. That's nothing to what I'll do to you if you don't love me."

His hand was like a second Confirmation, light and full of feeling, trembling on Cassidy's scalp.

"All of you, you've got to give me *all* of you. *I* do. I've given you a blank cheque, lover. Real."

"I'm trying to understand," Cassidy promised. "I am trying. If only you'd tell me what it was."

"Fucking little bourgeois," said Shamus hopelessly. "You'll never make it. Jesus!" he cried suddenly. Relinquishing Cassidy's hand he bounded into the air. "My identity! It's ruined!"

He was pointing at a patch of scrub grass where his passport lay face downward. A dead butterfly, wings spread hopelessly for takeoff. The blue dye oozing over the grass.

"Bleeding to death," he whispered, lifting it with both hands. "Lover, get me an ambulance."

At the village post office, fully dressed, they bought a French envelope and sent their carnations to Helen. The gum tasted of peppermint and the carnations were no longer young.

And two gliders to bring them closer to Flaherty. And a kite for despatching prayers.

And a notebook because on the way back to Paris Shamus was going to start a new novel, on the theme of David and Jonathan. Also, he had lost the old one in the river, and did not hold with the past.

Roads to Paris, Cassidy wrote in his private Baedeker, in the florid prose which was yet another of Old Hugo's countless gifts, *are long and various, often doubling back upon themselves. Some are bordered by great hills from which kites and gliders may be flown and avocations made to Irish gods, some by factories filled with sad proles and the Many-too-Many mounted on brakeless bicycles; some again by inns where whores banished from the city provide great writers with mediocre glimpses of the infinite. But all these roads are slow roads, made for the dragging of feet; for Paris is no longer popular, it is menaced by the mystery of Dale.*

Lying in the barber's chair, covered in choirboy white, the weary chronicler fell asleep while being shaved, and dreamed of naked Helen standing on the beach at Dover, two dead carnations at her breasts while she launched small sailing ships in races round the world. When he woke the barber was cutting his hair.

"Shamus I don't *want* it cut!"

Shamus was sitting on the bench, writing in his notebook.

"It's good for you, lover. New life as a monk," he said vaguely, not looking up. "Necessary sacrifice."

"No!" said Cassidy, pushing the man away. God in Heaven, how to face Trumper's now? *"Non, non, non."*

Shamus continued writing.

"He wants it longer," he explained to the barber with whom he was on terms of closest friendship. *"Il le veut plus long."*

"Shamus what do you believe in?"

At the world's edge the red sun rose or sank behind the swollen grid lines of a factory. Lights lay on the fields, and the gliders were wet with dew. "What *is* the light at the end of the pier?"

"Once I believed in a whore," said Shamus, after long thought. "She worked Lord's cricket ground. I never knew anyone who loved the game better. She kept all the batting averages in her handbag."

"What else?"

He hated clergymen, he said. Hated them with the passion of a zealot.

"What else?"

He hated the past, he said, he hated convention, he hated the blind acceptance of restriction and the voluntary imprisonment of the soul.

"Isn't that all rather *negative?*" Cassidy said at last.

"I hate that too," Shamus assured him. "Essential to be positive."

They were on stolen bicycles, one side of Cassidy's head now much colder than the other. And *that*, said Shamus, was Cassidy's problem.

Meeow.

19

Who would be Shamus? Cassidy wondered, watching him write at the inn.

The city was not far away now; perhaps that was why he was writing; to arm himself against whatever threatened him in Paris. A pink glow waited at the end of the avenue, and the evening air hummed like a boiler. They sat at a table beside the road, under an umbrella advertising Coca-Cola, drinking Pernod to clear their heads. The taxi waited in a lay-by, the driver was reading pornography.

Who would live with his own recording angel, life after life recorded, distorted, straightened and rounded off? Who would be Shamus, daily chronicling his own reality? Always attacking life, never accepting it; always walking, never settling.

"Will it really be a novel?" he asked. "A full-length one, like the others?"

"Maybe."

"What about?"

"I told you. Friendship."

"Read it," said Cassidy.

"Piss off," said Shamus and read: "*Reality was what divided them, reality was what put them together. Jonathan, knowing it was there, ran away from it; but David was never sure, and went looking for it every day.*"

"Is it a fairy tale?" Cassidy asked.

"Maybe."

"Which of us is David?"

"You, you stupid sod, because you're fair. *David was a great sceptic, for he loved the present world and all its riches. Jonathan defamed the world, and was therefore the prophet of a better one; but David was too thick to understand that, and Jonathan too proud to tell him. David's world was one in which the ideals of the herd were realised, because he was of the herd, the best of the Many-*

*too-Many. Jonathan had naivety of the heart, but David
had rococo of the soul. . . ."*

"But what does it *mean*, Shamus?"

"It means you need a drink," said Shamus, "before I
stone you again for being a heretic."

To iron a passport—it is a truism of which Cassidy had
not till then been sufficiently aware—you need a whore,
whores have the most sensitive fingers.

"They're the best ironers in the world," Shamus explained. "Famous for it. And when she's ironed the passport," he added, with the pride of a time and motion
expert, "you can fuck her. It's time you lost your hymen."

So they went to the Gare du Nord, a terminal of great
attraction, to find a pair of hands.

Their return to the city had not been, could not be perhaps,
as triumphal as their flight from it. Cassidy had assumed
they would go at once to the St. Jacques. He had even
worked out a system for getting in without going through
the hall—to cross the doorman's palm and slip in by way
of the staff entrance, as becomes an hotelier's son—for
their suits, though moderately dry, were shrunk and not
at all debonair. Also he had fences to mend; the Fair
was becoming an anxiety; how about his mail and the
phone calls?

Shamus would have none of it. The city had already
darkened him; his mood was sharper and less kind.

"I'm sick of the fucking St. Jacques. It's a rotten little
death cell. It's full of fucking bishops, I know it is!"

"But Shamus you liked it before—"

"I hate it. Fuck you."

He's running away, thought Cassidy suddenly: I know
that look, it's mine.

"What are you afraid of?" he was going to ask; but
learning prudence, abstained. So they went to a place
that Shamus knew, somewhere off the rue du Bac, a white
courtyard house near an embassy; the street was lined
with diplomatic cars. Inspired by the cars perhaps,
Shamus insisted on signing their names as Burgess and
Maclean.

"Shamus are you sure?"

Of course he was bloody sure; Cassidy could mind his bloody business or do the other thing, right?

Right.

Good hands are not plentiful at the Gare du Nord, even at commuting time on a sunlit evening. There are hands that hold luggage, hands that hold umbrellas, and tender hands that are linked to lovers and cannot, alas, be parted. Being already tired from their exertions, the two friends sat on a bench and, emptying their crumpled pockets, fed remnants of bread to French pigeons. Shamus, morose, barely spoke. Cassidy's head was aching painfully and his kneecap, till recently quiescent, had started to play him up again after the cycling.

"Good," said Shamus, when he told him.

To ward off the encroaching despondency, therefore, Cassidy began singing. Not so much singing: droning. A lyric of his own invention, rendered in a modulated French monotone, a very passable imitation of Maurice Chevalier.

Which was how they found Elise, the well-known anagram of Elsie.

> *Ze leedle birds of Paris*
> *Zey 'ave a lerv'ly time*
> *Zey 'ave a lerv'ly time,*
> *Until ze snow take all zeir*
> *bread a-way . . .*
> *Until ze snow take all zeir*
> *bread a-way. . . .*

Woken from his melancholy, Shamus stared at him wide-eyed. It was the first time Cassidy had done a voice for Shamus, and Chevalier was one of his best.

"Lover go *on*. That's great. In the first position, go on! Jesus that's great, that's human. Why didn't you tell me?"

"Well your voices are so much better."

"Balls! Go *on*, you sodder, sing!"

So Cassidy continued:

> *Zey wiggle zeir feathers . . .*
> *Zey wiggle zeir pretty tails . . .*

Zey hop, and lerve, *and sing*
                    zeir leedle song . . .
Until ze snow, ze gruel snow . . .
Take all *zeir bread away.* . . .

"More, lover! Jesus that's great! Hey listen everybody,
listen to Cassidy!"

Leaping up, Shamus was about to summon a larger
audience when they saw the girl, standing, smiling at them,
wearing a smart fawn coat and a red shiny handbag like
a Swiss conductor's purse on the small trains that mount
the Angelhorn.

She was young and quite tall, hair cut short like a boy's;
a trim, fair girl with fine skin that wrinkled into crazing
when she smiled. Her toes and heels were together, and
her legs, though these were not relevant to the restoration of Shamus' identity, were very straight but not at
all thin, Angie Mawdray's legs in fact, revealed on the
same generous scale.

"Ask to look at her hands," Shamus urged.

She was smiling at Cassidy, not Shamus; she seemed to
think him more her kind of man.

"She's wearing gloves," Cassidy objected.

"Then tell her to take them off, you ape."

"Do you speak English?" Cassidy asked.

She shook her head.

"No," she said.

"For Christ's sake, lover, this is important!"

"*Vos mains,*" Cassidy said, "*nous voulons voir.* . . .
Wouldn't you like to sit down?" he asked politely, offering
her his seat.

Demurely, still smiling, she sat between them on the
bench. Lifting her right hand, Cassidy gently removed the
glove. It was of fine white nylon and it slipped off very
easily like a stocking. The hand beneath it was soft and
smooth and it curled naturally into Cassidy's.

"Now ask her whether she irons passports," said Shamus.

"I'm sure she does," said Cassidy.

"Then ask her what she charges. One passport, one
fuck. Taxes, service, the lot."

"I'd rather just pay her, Shamus. Please." And to the

girl: *"Je m'appelle Burgess,"* he explained. *"Mon ami est l'écrivain Maclean."*

"Bonjour, Maclean," said Elise politely, while her hand fluttered in Cassidy's like a tiny bird. *"Et moi je m'appelle Elise."*

At the reception desk of the white hotel Cassidy borrowed an iron, a black smoothing iron of about 1870, Sandra had one in the kitchen and preferred it to the Morphy Richards. The receptionist was an Algerian boy, a very tired accomplice, but the sight of Elise appeared to give him hope.

"She'll need blotting paper," said Shamus. "Blotting paper to put between the pages."

His temporary elation had left him.

"Okay, okay," said Cassidy.

The corridors were very narrow and dark. Through the connecting wall, a baby grizzled continuously. Cassidy helped Elise with her coat and sat her in a chair with a glass of wine to make her feel at home, and soon they were exchanging commonplaces about the weather and the hotel. Elise lived with her family, she said; it was not always convenient but it was economic and one had company. Cassidy said he lived with his family too, his father was an hotelier, the guests were sometimes tiresome. Shamus, meanwhile, deaf to such formalities, had gone straight to the window and pulled the table into the centre of the room. Tipping the electric heater on its back, he laid the flatiron on top of it.

"Ah vous avez deux chambres!" said Elise, as Shamus emerged from the bedroom with a blanket. *"Ça c'est commode, alors!"*

It was an entire suite, Cassidy assured her, and leading the way showed her the full reach of the premises. The courtyard had a vine tree and a fountain; the bathroom was lined with old marble. Elise found it romantic, but feared it was expensive to heat.

"For fuck's sake!" Shamus shouted. "She's not buying the place is she? Tell her to come and iron my bloody passport."

"She's washing," said Cassidy. "Shamus *please*—"

"Washing to hell. She's disinfecting herself. Spraying flit on her fanny, that's what they all do. Put you through a bloody sheep dip if they get half a chance. Here, take sixpence and get the blotting paper."

"What's the hurry?" Cassidy demanded, now quite cross. "What difference does it make? The iron isn't even hot yet. Relax."

"Get the blotting paper!"

Suddenly cautious, Cassidy said, "She'll be all right with you alone won't she?"

"Of course she won't. What the hell are you talking about? Do you realise that in an average working day that angel of light eats about ten of us alive? She does not observe, she does not *expect* to observe, either the inhibitions or the priorities of the English middle class. For all she cares—" They heard the flush of the lavatory; Elise returned from the bedroom. "—you and I can truss her up like a turkey and play football with her as long as we get her back on the street in good time to find two more of us."

He thrust the passport into the girl's hand.

"But Shamus, I don't think she *is* one. I think she's just an ordinary girl."

Like Heather Ast, he wanted to say; Hugo would like her very much.

Carefully, Elise turned the pages. Her fingers were slim and competent, and found their way most cleverly into narrow places.

"Mais vous vous n'appelez pas Maclean," she remarked at last, comparing Shamus with the photograph.

"Maclean, c'est son nom de plume," said Cassidy quickly, still at the door.

"Get the blotting paper!"

The stationer was across the road and Cassidy ran all the way. When he came back, out of breath, Shamus and Elise were standing at opposite sides of the room not looking at one another. Her hair was disarranged and she seemed angry.

"All right," said Shamus, looking from one to the other of them. "Have your big relationship. Christopher Robin and Wendy touch wees, go beddie-byes. But when I come back I want her *out* and that passport ironed."

"Shamus—" Cassidy called, but the door had closed on him with a bang.

"Il n'est pas gentil, votre ami," said Elise.

"He's worried," said Cassidy, and so am I. And in his best maternal French explained that Shamus was a great writer, perhaps the greatest of his time, that she was the first person in the whole world not to find him irresistible, that he had just finished his masterpiece and was naturally concerned with its reception. His anxiety in fact (Cassidy felt he could confide in her) related to a matter of business. To the film rights. The sale was made but yet to be confirmed; these deals had a way of falling through. She may have seen the film *Doctor Zhivago,* well Shamus wrote it; also *Goodbye, Mr. Chips.*

Elise listened very gravely to these explanations, but although she admired Maclean's work they did not satisfy her. Men with two names, she said, reopening his identity at the first page, were not to be trusted, and Maclean was not gentle.

"Vous êtes aussi artiste, Burgess?" she asked.

"Un peu," said Cassidy. Hearing him she smiled with shy complicity.

"Moi aussi," she murmured, with a little nod. *"Un peu artiste, mais pas . . . entièrement."*

She was a very quiet girl. He had known at once she had a decent quiet, but now in the gathering dusk she filled the room with stillness. She ironed slowly and with concentration, head cocked a little as if she were waiting for Shamus' return, and when a footfall sounded in the corridor she paused and looked in that direction. Sandra, when she ironed, put her feet wide apart and stuck out her elbow like her father the Brigadier, but Elise kept very upright, conscious only of her task.

"I thought we might go out to dinner," he said. "Just the two of us."

Her head lifted; he could not see her expression but he took it for one of doubt.

"We could go to the Tour d'Argent if you like."

She ironed another page.

"No, Burgess," she said quietly. *"Pas de Tour d'Argent."*

"Oh but I can afford it. *Je suis riche, Elise . . . vraiment.* Whatever you like, the theatre if you prefer."

"Vous n'avez pas de théâtre à Londres, Burgess?"

"Yes. We do, of course. Lots. Only I don't seem to go very much."

Again, for a time, she made no answer. Footsteps ascended the stairs but they passed without a pause, lacking Shamus' sprightliness. Closing the passport, Elise set the iron on its edge and folded the blanket on the table, then moved slowly round the room, picking up the dirty glasses and emptying the ashtrays.

"Tu veux vraiment sortir, Burgess?" she asked from the sink.

"I want to make you happy," he said. "I'd like to give you a good time. I'm quite safe, honestly."

"Bon," she said, and smiled distantly, as if his wish were no longer her concern. *"Bon, c'est comme vous voulez."*

Dear Lover, he wrote, *You are a bad-tempered sodder. Elise is taking me to her pad. Back by ten thirty.*

And left the note beside the freshly ironed passport.

At the door, letting him help her into her coat, Elise kissed him. At first it was a child's kiss, Mark beneath the mistletoe. Then, like a tiny paintbrush, her tongue traced the line between his lips, moved upwards to his eyelids.

"We could go to Allard," he said, stepping ahead of her into the corridor. It was a place which Bloburg recommended.

"Burgess . . ." Her hand was on his arm.

"Oui?"

"Je n'ai pas faim."

Cassidy laughed. "Oh, come on," he said. "You'll be hungry by the time we get there." And left another note at the desk, virtually a duplicate but ending "Love."

At Allard, he offered her a trip to London to learn the hotel trade in which, he said, his father was immensely influential. Elise was very grateful but declined: her mother, she said, forbade her to travel alone. After that they talked little. Elise ate faster than Cassidy, and when she had finished she asked for a cab, which Cassidy paid for in advance.

She would have loved to stay longer, she explained to him, but she had obligations to her family.

Somewhere, nevertheless, in a white house in Paris, in an attic lifted from the warm streets and set above a courtyard that echoed with the rifle shots of beaten carpets, in a city trembling with the energies of love, in a wide brass bed with a down comforter washed white by the moon, somewhere between dusk and dawn, in that hour which after great exertion comes before intense fatigue, alone at last in the inward world of his romantic dreams, Cassidy loved Elise.

She came to him through the window, in long strides of her sheer white legs; lit by the striped moonlight of the shutters, she stood at his bedhead whispering *Burgess*. Her body rose like a white candle out of her fallen clothes, her tiny nipples were pink stains in the wax. *Burgess are you there?* Yes Elise. *Burgess tu es tellement gentil: do you really want to marry me?* Yes Elise. *Why are you dressed, Burgess?* I was going to find you Elise. I was going to walk the streets until I found you, then take you to the Sacré Coeur, where influential priests are waiting to perform the ceremony. *That is a very sensible arrangement. But what shall we do about money?* I have secreted twenty thousand pounds at the Banque Fédérale in the Elysées. I achieved this illegally by making fictitious payments for French components. *Burgess*, she breathed.

She undressed him with gravity, loosening first his tie and lifting it in a loop wide of his ears in order not to crush the silk. *Burgess, mon artiste, my inventor, my child, my husband, my provider, is anyone as rich as you?* No, said Cassidy. But best of all it has not affected my integrity. *That is true*, said Elise. *You have great naturalness.* Sometimes, undressing him, she had to pause and settle him for her pleasure, pressing his head against her breasts or lap, his cheek into the silky odourless hair between her long closed thighs, arranging him like loved sculpture in the moonlight, commending his dimensions to unseen female friends, calling him kind and virile, gentle, brave, and virtuous. *Venez*, she whispered at last, turning to him the long plain of her back. *Follow my immaculate and pert behind, my twin watermelons which slyly conceal the crevice of forbidden love, the Secret Flower of the uninhibited Orient.* Elise, my person is protruding and erect. Will you cohabit with me? *It is my highest ambition, Burgess.* She led him from the centre, encircling his manhood with her long, domesticated fingers as they drifted back and forth over the Paris sky. *Tu aimes ça Burgess? Do I give you pleasure? Shall I do it also with my mouth? I feel what you feel Burgess. My responses are entirely homosexual.* Just the fingers thank you, Cassidy replied. The fingers will do very nicely. *Burgess, you are so pure.* Elise, who is this helping you? he asked after a moment. Do I detect *other* fingers at work as well as your own, Elise? Surely I hear Frank Sinatra singing and discern the fumes of woodsmoke in your hair? *No one,* she assured him. *They are my hands only, you are dreaming of another.* Saying this, she opened his legs and traced with her nail's edge the tiny seam that joined him front and back, once, twice, three times. *More Burgess?* A little please. That will do thank you. *And here a little attention?* Elise enquired, cradling his grateful globes, making the hair of them signal with sharp small fires, making the skin taut and loving. *Now I leave you,* she whispered, *your manhood agonisingly suspended in the darkness.* You wouldn't like to finish it off, would you, while you're here? Cassidy asked. *You know the rules,* Elise replied softly, melting into the moonlight. *See you at the Sacré Coeur.*

Don't be late, Cassidy called. Don't be late. Late. Late.

"Shamus?"

How could he face such solitude out there? What was he doing, far into the night? Out with the Few? I'm not enough for him. He needs writers; people who read his books.

An imitation ormolu clock glistening in the moonlight permanently stuck at half past two. Outside the window the bearing of carpets, tapping to nothing in slow drips.

Shamus, come back.

If only to turn me outward again; to turn my hand to better loves than me.

Darling, the outward Cassidy wrote next day, at frightful length, punishing his erring hand. It was nine o'clock in the morning, Shamus had not returned. *Things have not so far gone particularly well, and if it's any consolation to you—which I doubt!—you are well clear of the wicked city and its temptations. The Embassy people, true to form, made a complete hash of our Stand—no telephones, no separate Cassidy tent for entertainment, just all thrown together like cattle—and although we landed one big order on the first day, trade has generally been very sticky. I have a hunch that as you predicted the Vietnam war is finally having its effect—there is simply less money around, people are wary of what they buy and quite bad about settling. Our one big order—three hundred chassis—went to a very suspect lady (middle-aged) who took a thousand strollers from Bee-Line last year and still hasn't paid up. McKechnie had to recoup from the Exports Credit Guarantee people, and they won't cover her any more. (sorry!) However, it was Meale's first major triumph and I could hardly refuse to accept the order for fear of hurting his confidence, which is to say the least a delicate plant.*

Also, I have to confess that I am not much good on my own, which I suppose you knew all along. On the other hand, the alternatives to solitude are none too beguiling either. I have avoided Lemming and co. like the plague —the idea of "doing Paris" with the trade is almost physically repellant to me.

As to Bloburg he is being an absolute pest. I know you feel strongly that one should show him particular consideration, but even tolerance has its limits. Having landed me with an exhausting and frequently worthless programme of entertaining etc., he is constantly trying to "fix me up" as he calls it with female friends of his. One of these, a damsel called Elise, actually appeared at my bedroom door late at night with a note from him. Never fear—she was a very scarey lady indeed, with those very brown unblinking eyes which your mother rightly distrusts. I am convinced she was on drugs, and when I sent her off she just drifted away down the corridor as if she didn't give a damn. Very unflattering! So much then for vice and infidelity, but since I had poor McKechnie with me at the time—he and his wife are in very deep water and the poor fellow was almost in tears—the incident passed off more as a joke than anything else. I honestly feel that people who reach that pass should break it up and have done with it, don't you?

Last night, Meale disappeared in a huff after a ridiculous dispute with Lemming at the hotel—something to do with an iron, if you please, who should have it first.

Anyway, he waltzed off and I suppose that when he comes back I shall have to step in and bang their heads together.

I talk because I have nothing to say, he thought, numbering the fourth page; she would love me better if I *had* slept with Elise. Is that—rereading his turgid prose—is that in fact what I *want* her to believe?

In the few spare moments left to me, I have tried to make contact with the French playing fields people, but not much joy. Yesterday I did succeed in going out to one of the suburbs and inspecting a potential site, of all things in a dried-up riverbed—you might look into that possibility in England—what does the Water Board do with its dried-up riverbeds? But mainly it was the hair-raising drive there and back which left an impression! We did about ninety all the way—no brakes and of course no seat belts.

Incidentally, I tried to ring you last night and again this morning and just got a burr, burr, burr. Where are you all the time? I do trust you are not compensating for my absence in any inadvisable way!! I was going to propose you came out here for a few days after the Fair has ended—say on the Monday or Tuesday—and then perhaps I could give you the attention you have so long deserved, restore my somewhat frayed nerves after this silly, maddening *week, and get to know you again the way we used to. If you still know what I mean. Do you? Please give my special love to Hug. I have bought you both super presents. Can't wait to deliver them.*

                                        Pailthorpe
P.S. Incidentally: somebody stopped me in the street yesterday and asked me whether I was Guy Burgess: can you imagine? It must be my louche look. How's John E.?

Waiting again, this time with real anxiety.
   Telephone Helen? Place enquiries with the Economic Minister? *It's Cassidy the Norman Frenchman, we met in quieter times, you remember, haha. Well actually, he's going under the name of Maclean, it's hard to explain why.*

And I'm Burgess yes. Well it's a joke you see, we have an identity problem.

Waiting, Cassidy mended his fences, an excuse for great activity.

20

Leaving the white hotel gratefully behind him (notes to
Shamus posted with the boy, in the bedroom, drawing
room, and fine rococo lavatory) the President, Managing
Director, Chairman, and Most Active Principal of Cassidy's Overseas Couplings, a company recently added to
The Stock Exchange Index and widely tipped as a good
long shot for the investor looking for a flutter, straight-
ens his tie, puts his world back into shape, and fastens it
at every threatened seam. Pausing on his way to the Hotel
St. Jacques, an establishment known to him from previous
business trips to Paris, he buys with the last of his traveller's cheques a cheap but passable raincoat which disguises
the questionable condition of his suit. At the desk, where
his return is received without comment, he takes possession
of certain business mails of no pressing importance and
enquires most casually after his associate and roommate
Monsieur (note the name) not Maclean but Shamus.

The intelligence is not enlightening.

Monsieur Shamus came in yesterday evening and collected his post. Yes there was much post. Naturally:
Monsieur Shamus was a person of the highest distinction.
Thereafter Monsieur Shamus went to his room and made a
two-hour telephone call to London, the manager hoped the
cost could be covered by a separate and perhaps an earlier
payment, since he understood that Monsieur Cassidy was
charged with settling the accounts of his superior. To this
request, the cunning negotiator readily assented on the
condition that he be shown the telephonist's ticket. The
ticket gave a number in Temple Bar which the well-known
secret service agent Burgess covertly noted on the back
of the bill, but afterwards lost. Ascending in Flaherty's
lift he made quickly for the love nest and continued his
search for the absent writer.

It is here that the crime took place. The room is in disorder. Cassidy's clothes cupboard has been ransacked and the best things removed.

Feeling markedly less concerned for Shamus, Cassidy turns his attention to other clues. He had lain on his bed, no doubt to make the forty-pound telephone call. Three typewritten messages from the hotel telephonist yield identical information: a Monsieur Dale has telephoned, Shamus should ring him back. On the eiderdown, several postcards to Shamus, written and despatched by the addressee before he left London and signed variously Keats, Scardanelli, and Perseus, wish him a useful rest and congratulate him on his well-attested existence. These cards include lists of places he must visit, together with information on rivers, public fountains, and the shrines of great writers now dead. One such card cautioned him severely against venery; another, from Helen, reminded him to bring home a *terrine* and gave him the name of a shop distinguished by its fine foods.

Also on the scene of the kidnap: one volume (in German, mysteriously) of Schiller's *Uber Naive und Sentimentalische Dichtung;* one tract from Flaherty on the subject of modern heresies, citing in particular the Pope and Archbishop Ramsey; one paperback work entitled *Flying Saucers Are Hostile* ("With 16 pages of photographs and the independent laboratory analysis of UFO Residues"); and one booklet on Mystical Practices laid down by the Master Aethesius from the Planet Venus for the maintenance of health and well-being. Further: one volume of the poems of John Donne, much thumbed.

Further: one empty whisky bottle, Glen Grant 1953, by Berry Brothers and Rudd.

Temporarily putting aside his search for Shamus, Cassidy himself now made a number of telephone calls, largely of a business nature, one to an agency requesting flowers for Sandra, one to his bank requesting a further draft of funds. The business world, it appeared, had not after all disintegrated in his absence. Orders at the Fair were respectable but not dramatic; McKechnie's wife had gone home in a rage. By skilfully playing off Bloburg against Lemming, and Faulk against Meale, Cassidy gave the impression of being too busy with everyone to deal with everyone else. Shortly before lunch, having bathed, shaved,

and eaten a large plate of eggs, he actually took a limousine to the Fair and patrolled his lines with an expression of grave preoccupation.

"It's vitally important," he told Meale. "More important than you can possibly guess at this stage."

Having despatched extravagant gifts to Hugo and Mark, he
remembered a jocular promise made in South Audley
Street just before his departure and transferred a con-
signment of flowers to Miss Mawdray—no *arrière-pensée*,
the welfare of my staff is paramount—but deeming it
nevertheless wise to pay cash in order to avoid incrimi-
nating slips of paper.

On the way, however, he also remembered his dispute with
Heather Ast and, needing comfort, sent her flowers as
well. It was not a moment to nurse old grudges.

He returned to the hotel in time for the afternoon mail.

Dear Aldo,

*You asked me to write to you so I am doing so. I
trust you are all right and I presume you do not wish
me to join you as you originally suggested you might,
but still. My real reason for writing is to tell you that
last night Mummy and I were cleaning out the nursery
and came upon a collection of pornography which I
assume is yours. Please correct me if I'm wrong. You
can imagine what Mummy said. I suppose it's no good
my repeating to you yet again that I don't care what you
do as long as you tell me. If I had known you liked pornography, which in some people is perfectly normal, I
would have cleaned the nursery alone. If your soul is
imprisoned by our marriage, go away. Though I must
say, I'd like to see what you do with it when it isn't
imprisoned. I have of course no objection to your keeping a mistress, if you are not already doing so. I would
prefer not to know who it is, but if I do know it will
make no difference. Mark's report enclosed.*

                                                     Sandra

Conduct
Mark has shown a complacent, easy-going approach to

*life typical of the present British attitude of lazy fare
which is affecting the whole nation, particularly the
Unions. He picks and chooses his activities and leaves
them off halfway, he is resentful when chased, beaten, or
ticked off, he hates discipline.*

These communications drove him back into the streets
where for an hour he walked beside the Seine looking for
a good place to jump in. When he returned, Shamus was
lying on the bed, his face in the beret again, legs splayed,
as if he had never left the island.

"Your passport's on the dresser," Cassidy said.
    Ironed by loving hands.
    "One of these days," said Shamus to the black beret,
"I'll find a whore I like."

"Cassidy," said Shamus quietly, head once more buried
in the pillow.
    "Yes."
    "Go on about your mother."
    "I wasn't talking about my mother."
    "Well go on about her all the same, will you?"
    The death cell had no ormolu clock, but time had stood
still for quite a while. They had had two drinks for certain—Shamus was on cognac and Perrier, he gave no
reason for the change—but this was the first attempt that
either of them had made to speak. Shamus was using his
Haverdown voice, not quite the Irish but a little bantering.
Tense, on an edge, and slipping to either side.
    "She was a Frog. A tart, I think, knowing the old
man."
    "About how she left you. That's the bit I like."
    "She left me when I was small. Seven."
    "You said five before."
    "Five then."
    "What effect did this have on you, Cassidy?"
    "Well . . . it made me lonely I suppose . . . it sort of
. . . robbed me of my childhood."
    "What does that mean?" Shamus enquired, sitting bolt
upright.
    "What?" said Cassidy.

"What do you mean by being *robbed of childhood?*"

"Denied normal growth, I suppose," Cassidy faltered. "A sense of fun . . . I had no female reference, no one to make women . . . human."

"Normal *sexual* growth, in other words."

"Yes. It drove me in on myself. What's the matter with you?"

Placing the beret over his face, Shamus resumed his recumbent pose.

"We are not concerned with *me*, we are concerned with Cassidy. We are concerned with a man in whom the absence of maternal love has induced certain negative symptoms. I woud describe these symptoms of Cassidy's as follows. One, timidity, right?"

"Right."

"Two, guilt. Guilt arising from Cassidy's secret conviction that he drove his mother forth from the household. Possible?"

"Oh yes," said Cassidy, as ever willing, when the subject was himself, to see the force of any argument.

"Three, insecurity. The female sex, represented by Mummy, at a crucial moment rejected him. He has felt her rejection ever since, and in various disguises he has made futile attempts to regain her favour. By making money for instance, and engendering little babies. Correct?"

"I don't know," said Cassidy, very confused. "I'm not sure."

"His relations with women are accordingly apologetic, morbid, and frequently infantile. They are doomed. That is the substance, is it not, of your complaint? How was the whore?"

"Who?"

"Elise."

"Fine."

"You fucked her, did you?"

"Sure."

"She was satisfactory? She moved in mysterious ways for you? Or did you have her flog you with barbed wire?"

"Shamus, what is it? What's eating you?"

"Nothing is *eating* me. I am merely attempting a diagnosis."

Rolling on to his back he put the brandy bottle to his mouth and drank for a long time.

"That's all, lover," he said, Irish now; and gave a sudden, brilliant smile. "Just giving the devil a name, no offence. Surely to God we can't prescribe the treatment till we've diagnosed the symptoms now, can we?"

Cassidy wanted very much to ask about the two-hour telephone call to London, but he had learned by now that Shamus did not care to be questioned, so he wisely held his peace.

"You're my treatment," he said lightly. "Where shall we eat?"

After dinner, which passed largely in silence, Shamus returned to the theme of the Maternal Frog.

What did she look like, he enquired, striding purposefully at Cassidy's side through darkening streets, what were Cassidy's earliest memories of her, his last? What were her names, would he tell him; did Cassidy remember all her names?

Ella, said Cassidy.

"Did Ella have any distinguishing marks now, a walleye for instance," he required good-humouredly, but still using the Irish. "Did she have a walleye at all, the poor soul?"

They turned into a side alley.

"Not that I remember," said Cassidy laughing.

"Any mannerisms then? I'm trying to get a picture of her you see, after all Cassidy I am a writer of some stature, am I not? My subject is man, after all, in all his rich variety and complexity. I mean did she pick her nose or scratch her arse in bed?"

"She wore cashmere pullovers," Cassidy said. "She loved pink, I remember. Can we leave her alone now Shamus? I'm a bit fed up with her to be honest."

Shamus did not hear, apparently. They were walking faster, Shamus was quickening the pace, looking upwards at the street signs as he strode ahead.

"Shamus, where are we going?"

They crossed a main road, plunged into another maze of little alleys.

A light over the door said "Bar." They went in, Shamus leading.

Girls sat on a horseshoe bench, drinking and looking inward at the mirrors, studying their bodies, their reflected ghosts. A few pimps, a few customers, a slot machine for pills to stop you smoking.

"Paging Mrs. Cassidy," Shamus called, drawing Cassidy after him by the wrist. Shamus' hand was wet, but its grasp was as strong as ever. "Her small son is looking for her." At the bar, a few faces lifted. "Is *Mrs. Cassidy* here now?" He turned to Cassidy. "See her, Oedipus?" he asked.

"Please, Shamus—"

"Is she Chinese at all, is that a possibility?" indicating a lady of South East Asian extraction. "Not mainland, of course, just the fringe islands, you know."

"Shamus I want to go."

"Should have thought of that before, shouldn't you? I'm not a guest in your life, you know. I'm here to stay. I warned you, lover, don't say I didn't."

"For God's sake, Shamus, they'll murder us."

"No Chinese blood. A pure Caucasian lady. Okay I'll take your word for it. Now, will you stop that jiggering please and pay attention. Maybe you'd better have a drink?" he suggested, forcing Cassidy's hand against the wrist as he backed him into the bar.

Two tall and rather handsome elderly ladies offered refreshment to the afflicted. Cassidy wondered whether they were sisters.

"I don't want a drink."

"Er, two homosexual whiskies please miss, one with milk and sugar."

There were seats empty but Shamus preferred to stand.

"Tell us," Shamus continued still addressing the sisters, "has a wee grey-headed body come in at all, about five foot two and sixty-five years of age, somewhat fragile of build, Aryan, wears pink shirts, answers to the name of Ella?"

The sisters, shoulder to shoulder, were smiling broadly at them both. They collected miniatures, Cassidy noticed; there were several hundred on the mirrored shelves behind them; Old Hugo, himself an aficionado, would be enchanted.

"Tu es hollandais?" one asked of Cassidy.

"Anglais," said Cassidy.

"Ella!" Shamus called, cupping his hand like a lost mariner. *"Ella!"*

"Y'a pas d'Ella," a sister assured him.

With his free hand Cassidy paid for the drinks. They were ten francs each, he gave an extra ten, and when he had done so Shamus drew him close again, up and under.

"Don't you believe 'em," Shamus advised him in an undertone. "They've got her hidden upstairs." He drank. *"Mon ami s'appelle Rex,"* he announced proudly.

"Il est très *beau, Rex,"* the sisters assured him.

"Il veut dormir avec sa mère."

"Ah, bon," the sisters cried in pleasure. *"Elle est ici sa mère?"* And looked round the room for a likely candidate.

"She never ran a pub, did she, lover?" Shamus asked, close to his ear. "You know those two dykes remind me very much—"

"Shut up," said Cassidy. "Just shut up and get me out."

The double curtains which gave on to the street parted. Three men, as dark as Shamus but smaller, entered and sat down at a table. The girls round the bar did not move. The sisters were smiling more broadly than ever.

"You're a *lovely* pair," Shamus assured them, and having carefully finished his whisky, threw his glass on to the floor.

"Now I'll tell you what we'll do," Shamus murmured, drawing him yet further inward until their faces were actually touching. "We'll take it *very* easy indeed, all right? No rushing, no jumping, no dramatics."

"Couldn't we just pay them?" Cassidy whispered. "Honestly I don't mind. I'm sure they'd take cash instead."

"You see, I know damn well what they're up to. Those two dykes there: look at their faces. Know what they are? *Kidnappers*. What they have done is *transform*—by means of *plastic surgery* you understand—they have with diabolical cunning *transformed* our Ella into a person of totally different appearance."

"Shamus," Cassidy said, using the name as a prayer.

"It's all right don't worry, we'll outwit them. I made a terrible mistake when I came in here, *declaring our interest,* that's all. Now don't say a word, keep moving."

Bending Cassidy's wrist still further forward, using both hands to increase the pressure, he began walking the line of girls, brushing the bare backs of them one by one as he studied their white faces in the mirror.

"Drugged," Shamus explained, in the same conspiratorial murmur. "Look at that, drugged to the gills, every one."

He pulled back a head so that Cassidy could see her better: a German girl perhaps, strong teeth and blue eyes. Her lips parted in pain as Shamus held her hair.

"See?" he said, as if her silence only proved his point. "Listless. Stuffed, good as."

He released the head. It bent forward again, into the mirror.

"What we have therefore is a *sleeping beauty* problem."

A glass of something white, a cocktail probably, perhaps an advocaat, also a drink much favoured by Old Hugo at a certain period of his development, stood before her on the bar. Shamus drank it.

"Women," he declared in the tone of a Dublin academic, "women whose natural loves have been extinguished by strong potions. Never mind, we shall conquer yet. What mother on earth would fail to recognise the kiss of her own beloved son? Would not open her eyes and cry—" For his female impersonation he required a lot of volume:

"My Rex! My swain! My passion!"

Taking the girl's hand, he offered it to Cassidy and the girl came with it, trying to relieve the pressure.

"Here, take it," he invited. "Would not with her g-narl-ed fingers forage in the copious petticoats for a wee fondle of the familiar organ, eh Cassidy?"

Still holding her hand, he savagely swung her round on her stool. Two dull eyes, black-lidded, peered at them expressionlessly, first at Cassidy for help, then at Shamus for information.

"Tu veux?" she enquired.

"Now," Shamus urged. "Kiss her! Kiss her, call her mother! *Ella*, Aldo is *here!* Rex has come home to *Mrs. Oedipus.*"

Abruptly stooping, Shamus buried his head in her bare shoulder, black on white like an advertisement.

For a moment it seemed as if the girl would accept him. Forced forward, one hand lifted to touch him, she watched him curiously as he pastured on her flesh. Suddenly her body stiffened. Fighting loose from him she let out a sharp cry of pain, seized his hair, and with her other hand—the fingernails, Cassidy noticed, were chewed quite low—hit him, splitting his lip.

"It's worked!" Shamus cried. "We have *impact*, Cassidy! We have reaction!" Standing back, one finger to his bleeding lip, he proudly surveyed his assailant. "It's her! It's Ella! She wants *you* not me. Her Aldo! Go on, lover. Just a little peck, that's all."

The lights went out, three torches shone at them, and a man was talking politely in French.

"They want us to follow the torches," Cassidy explained.

The taxi was waiting at the curb. They helped Shamus in first and Cassidy followed. He gave them a hundred francs.

"For God's sake!" Shamus shouted. "Why didn't they hit us?"

That's a very nice place, thought Cassidy, that's the nicest place I've ever been to, and if I can remember how to find it I shall go back and apologise and offer those sisters the chalet.

"The *girl* hit you," he said, consolingly.

"Jesus, who cares about a woman?"

"Shamus, for pity's sake tell me what's the matter with you?"

"There's a place called Lipp's," said Shamus. "They'll hit me there all right, it's a writer's haven. Lipp's," he told the driver, his eye already on the radio.

"Shamus, *please*."

"Shut up."

"It's to do with Dale. You rang him for hours, I saw the messages and everything."

"If I wanted," Shamus promised him in his most detached voice, holding Cassidy's handkerchief to his mouth, "I would kill you. You know that don't you, lover?"

"Lipp," Cassidy repeated to the driver hopelessly. "*Brasserie Lipp*."

"I keep you alive for one reason only: because you are a reader. You realise that, I trust. Being a prole, you are the commercial hinterland of my genius. Know what Luther said?"

"What did Luther say?" Cassidy asked wearily.

"He said, if I were Christ, and the world had done to me what it has done to Him, I'd kick the beastly thing to pieces!"

"But Shamus," Cassidy asked, gently, when Shamus had more or less settled again, "what *has* the world done to you?"

Shamus seemed about to say something serious. He stared at Cassidy, at the blood on the handkerchief, at the passing lights, opened his split mouth as if to speak, closed it again, and sighed. "Holy God," he said at last, "it's filled itself with halfbreeds like you."

They had eaten once already that evening, a fact which Shamus had apparently forgotten. Cassidy was in no mood to remind him. The son of an hotelier and innumerable mothers had learnt long ago that there was no better sedative than good plain food, served hot.

Dining at the Brasserie Lipp, Shamus was quiet and conciliatory.

He stroked Cassidy's arm, vouchsafed him small, erratic smiles, gave the waiter ten francs from Cassidy's wallet, and generally by word and deed showed signs of regaining his lighter, affectionate mood. Observing this, Cassidy deemed it wise to take command of the conversation until the good Burgundy and the soothing, old-world atmosphere of the restaurant had completed the process of recovery.

"A writer's haven eh?" he said. "Well I'm not surprised. It's just the place not to be recognised. Can you point any out?" he asked, with a suitably conspiratorial reverence. "Any in *your* bracket, are there Shamus?"

Shamus looked round. A heavy middle-aged couple, eating slowly and apparently without implements, returned his stare. A pretty girl, out with her boyfriend, blushed, and the boy turned and scowled at Shamus, who put his thumb to his nose.

"My *bracket*," he repeated. "No I don't think so. There's Sartre over in the corner—" Rising, he bowed gravely to a gnomic, mottled gentleman of about eighty-five. "—but I think we can reasonably say I outgun Jean Paul. Has Monsieur Homer come in yet?" he asked the waiter, with that effortless complicity which Cassidy now took for granted.

"Monsieur . . . ?"

"Homer. *Omer*. Old Greek with a long white beard, looks like Father Christmas. Poof."

"Non, monsieur," the waiter regretted. *"Pas ce soir."* A ghost of a smile, too fleeting for disrespect, enlivened his elderly features.

"Well, there you are," Shamus said pleasantly, with a resigned shake of the head. "Quiet night I'm afraid. Boys all at home."

"Shamus," said Cassidy, holding with difficulty to his policy of breezy small talk, "about my soul."

"I thought you'd had it out," said Shamus.

A burst of laughter issued suddenly from the kitchen.

"No truly. Listen lover. I really do think I'm redeemable, don't you? Now, I mean. Since I met you. I don't think it's a hopeless quest any more, looking for it, do you? I know I'm reluctant. I've got a lot of bad habits but, well you have shown me the way, haven't you?" Receiving no encouragement, he added, "After all, there must be *something* there."

Shamus was playing with the water jug, dipping his finger and watching the drops fall.

"Well don't you think so? Come on."

"I am the light," said Shamus. "I am the light and the way. Follow me and you will end *on your arse*," and reaching out, turned Cassidy's face upwards and sideways, adjusting it for closer examination.

"Shamus don't . . ." said Cassidy.

"You know what you radiate, don't you? The nasty allure of an undiscovered absolute. Every poor fool who picks you up thinks he's your first friend. What they don't realise is, you were born with your legs crossed. Penetration," he concluded, carelessly releasing him, "can never take place."

A merciful waiter brought them food.

"I've never told you," said Cassidy, helping Shamus to vegetables, filling his glass, and trying now by every means to win him back from his state of hostile melancholy. "I've always been a bit dotty about writers ever since I was at school. I used to write short stories in bed after lights. I even won prizes. Hey what about that?"—with a brave if somewhat synthetic effort at enthusiasm—"Why don't I make a stab at it? Give up the firm, give up Sandra, give up my money, waste away in a garret . . . be like Renoir."

"It wasn't Renoir. It was Gauguin."

"Perhaps I'd make it . . . starve the talent out of me . . ."

Shamus had gone back to the water jug, was trailing his finger back and forth over the surface the way they had played with the sticklebacks by the river. A little resentfully, Cassidy said—it was a point he had made to Sandra not long ago—"Well if I *am* so bloody empty, why do you bother with me anyway?"

"Tell me, lover," Shamus said, very seriously, lifting the jug an inch or two off the table. "Is that smile waterproof?"

Standing up, he began pouring the water slowly over Cassidy's head, starting with a slowish trickle directed at the crown, then gradually increasing the quantity as the mood took him. Cassidy sat very still, thinking clearly about absolutely nothing; for nothing is also a concept, being neither a place nor a person but a blank, a vacuum and a tremendous help in time of trouble. He did however record that the water was running over his neck and down his spine. He did also feel it spreading over his chest, his stomach, and into his groin. His ears were full of water too, but he knew that the conversation in the restaurant had stopped because he could hear Shamus' voice and no one else's and the brogue was very strong.

"Butch Cassidy, son of Dale, in that you do earnestly repent you of your oafish ways, and faithfully promise to follow always in the paths of truth, experience, and love, we hereby baptise you in the name of . . ."

He stopped pouring. Thinking the jug was empty, Cassidy lifted his head, but Shamus was still standing over him, and there was a good half pint to come.

"Go on Butch. Hit me with your handbag."

"Please don't pour any more," Cassidy said.

He was beginning to feel quite angry, but there seemed to be nothing he could do. The injunction, however, moved Shamus unaccountably to fury.

"For Christ's sake," he shouted, pouring the rest in one

long sustained movement. "Grow, you little weed, *growl*"

The waiter was an old, kindly man, and he had the bill ready. Cassidy kept the money in his back pocket, and somehow the water had got in there too, and the notes were all stuck together. The waiter didn't mind because Cassidy gave him a lot of them.

A copper urn stood in the corner for walking sticks and umbrellas. Taking out a silver-handled cane, Shamus began piping on it, swaying from the hips like a snake charmer and emitting a low wailing noise through his nose. Everyone waited, but no snake emerged. Using the stick as a club, Shamus drove it in sudden fury against the heavy chasing.

"All right you sodder," he shouted into the urn. "Go on. Sulk. Jesus Christ, lover," he breathed as they got outside, "oh God, lover, forgive, forgive." Shaking his head, he took Cassidy's hand and held it against his tear-stained cheek. "Lover, oh lover, forgive!"

"Shamus, tell me! Please tell me. What the hell's the matter? What's happened to you? Who the hell is Dale?"

"He's the bloke who bombed Hiroshima," Shamus explained.

Shamus drunk.

Not high or tight or any other pretty word, but dirty, violent drunk. Sweating terribly, reeling and staggering as he held to Cassidy, refusing to go anywhere he knew but demanding always to move. Vomiting.

"Wander, Jew, wander," he kept saying. *"Wander."*

His arm, hooked round Cassidy's neck, is divided between destroying and embracing him. Twice they have gone down, toppled by his iron grip, and Cassidy's trouser is cut from the knee to the foot. We're all that's left of an army, the rest are dead. The night is dead too, and the dawn is limping after them. They are in a square again but not dancing any more, the dancing is over, no horses either, just an early bitch of Sandra's, long dead, eyeing them from a doorway.

Shamus is vomiting again punctuating his spasms with cries of anger.

"Fucking body," he shouts. "Do what you're bloody told! How the hell can I keep my promises if my body won't work? Tell it lover. Shamus has promises to keep. *Tell it to carry me!*"

"Come on body," Cassidy says, trying to hold its sinking weight, "Come on body, Shamus has promises to keep."

"For I have promises to keep . . ."

Shamus is trying to set the words to music. He sings

quite well in Cassidy's unmusical opinion, a very Shamus sort of singing, half talking, half humming, but with a lot of quality to the voice even when (as watchful Cassidy accurately surmises) he is out of tune.

"The night is lo-v-e-ly, dark and deep—*sing* you bugger, Dale—the night - is - lovely - dark and deep—sing!"

"I don't know the words, Shamus," Cassidy said, catching him again as he lurched forward. "I'm not Dale but I'd sing if I knew the words, I promise."

Shamus stopped dead.

"Who wouldn't?" he said at last. "Jesus, who wouldn't?" Putting both hands over Cassidy's face, he lifted it into his own. "It's singing when you *don't* know the bloody words that tears your guts out, lover."

"But you *do* know the words, Shamus."

"Oh no I don't. Oh no I bloody don't, Dale my lovely. You *think* I do. Why I love you: worshipping prole. What more can a man ask? The roar of the proles at the door, dizzy faces . . . cameras click. . . . It's all anyone wants. Queen, me, Flaherty, all of us."

Putting his whole weight on Cassidy's shoulders, Shamus forced him down on to the curb.

"Now give yourself a nice comfy rest Dale, old son," he said in Irish, "while your poor Uncle Shamus tells you the secret of the universe," and pulled the bottle of Scotch from Cassidy's inside pocket. After a couple of mouthfuls, he became quite sober but his arm was still locked round Cassidy's in case he tried to run away.

"I'm not Dale," said Cassidy again, patiently. "I'm your lover. Cassidy."

"Then I'll tell Cassidy instead. What do we have in common, you and me, Cassidy, in ourselves? Guess." He shouted very loud. "*Guess,* Cassidy! Before I turn you into Dale again, you crawling little funk!"

A window opened on the other side of the street.

"You American?" a man's voice enquired, in an American accent.

"Piss off," Shamus yelled, and back to Cassidy: "Well?"

"Well we *love* each other, if that's any help," Cassidy suggested, using one of their earlier dialogues as a working guide. "We've got *love* in common, Shamus."

"Balls," said Shamus, and brushed away a tear. "Sheer

bloody romantic bollocks, if you'll forgive me, which you will, as usual."

Two tarts were standing a few feet away from them. One of them carried a loaf of bread, and was eating mouthfuls off the end of it.

"The greedy one looks like your mother," said Shamus.

"I think we've done that one," Cassidy said wearily.

"Êtes vous la mère de mon ami?" Shamus enquired.

The tarts scowled and went away, tired of the prolonged joke.

"Well perhaps that's it. Perhaps we *are* queer," said Cassidy, still working on the false assumption that he would do best to rely on Shamus' themes, and offer them as his own.

"Zero," said Shamus. "Did I ever once venture just the smallest finger up your skirts? Not the tiniest little digit, did I?"

"No," said Cassidy, as Shamus hauled him abruptly to his feet. He was more tired than he had ever been in his life. "No, you didn't."

"Then will you listen to me please? And will you *stop* putting forward low-grade arguments, *please?*"

Cassidy had little option, for Shamus was holding him in a cruel embrace, and their faces were pressed together, rough cheek on rough cheek.

"And will you please give me your very fullest attention, Dale? What we have in common is the most dreadful, hopeless, fucking awful pessimism. Right?"

"Okay, I'll buy that."

"And the other thing we have in common is the most dreadful, awful, hopeless, fucking awful . . . mediocrity."

Real fear seized Cassidy; real unreasoning alarm.

"No Shamus, that's not true, that's absolutely not true. You're *special* Shamus, we all know that—"

"You do, do you, lover?"

The grip tightened.

"I *know.* Helen knows. We *all* know. . . ." Cassidy was going now, really frightened; holding on and desperate to survive. The Bentley was sinking in the river; Abalone Crescent was falling to its knees. "Christ you idiot you only have to walk into a room, tell a story, give them your rat's-eyes, and they *know*, we *all* know, that it's *you*, Shamus; your world. You're our chronicler, Shamus, our magus. You've got all we want, the truth, the dream, the guts. Okay you're impossible. But you're the best! You make it real for us, we *know* how good you are."

"You do?"

It was Cassidy's left arm Shamus had taken now; he had driven the upper part into the shoulder socket, and the pain was like the water at Lipp's, spreading and creeping and screaming all at once.

"Shamus you'll break it in a minute," Cassidy warned.

"You really believe that crap I tell you? Listen, I am the lousiest fucking conjuror in the business and you fall for every fucking trick. Nietzsche. Schiller. Flaherty. I never read those fucking people in my life. They're scraps. Tit-bits. Fag-ends. I pick them out of the gutter for breakfast and you poor fuckers think they're a bloody feast. *I am a bum.* You want to throw me out, pramseller: that's what you want to do. I don't work, I don't write, I don't exist! It's the fucking audience that's doing the magic, not me. *I am a fraud.* Got it? A con man. A fucking clapped-out conjuror with an audience of one."

"No!" Cassidy shouted. *"NO! NO! NO!"*

"You think I'm your friend." Shamus had found a place to lie down, so Cassidy was obliged to lie beside him, partly to hear the words and partly not to lose his arm. "Well I don't *want* a fucking friend. I don't even know how to deal with a friend. I want a fucking archaeologist, that's what I want. I'm *Troy,* not a fucking bank clerk. There are nine dead cities buried in me and each one is more rotten than the next fucker. And what do you do? You stand there like a bloody tourist and bleat, *'No! No! Shamus no.' Yes,* Cassidy. *Yes,* Shamus is a *bum.* There's a nasty smell around here. Know what it is? Failure!"

"Shamus," said Cassidy quietly. "I would swap all my fortune for your talent . . . for your life, and for your marriage . . ."

"All right," Shamus whispered, letting him loose as the tears came. "All right, lover. If I'm so bloody marvellous, why did you turn down my novel?"

Cassidy's world swung, and held still.

"It's okay, lover," Shamus whispered, seizing his arm

again and twisting it more tightly, "I'm your friend, remember."

Cassidy looked into the troubled eyes, so full of suddenness and chaos, looked at the whole iron, wild face of him, taut at the cheeks, careless at the mouth, and he wondered almost with detachment how one body could hold so much, and hold together. There seemed, as Shamus crawled slowly to his feet, still arm in arm with Cassidy, to be something cosmic in his self-destruction; as if, knowing that the creative genius of mankind was also the cause of its ruin, he had determined to make that truth personal, to take it for his own.

"He turned down the last one too," said Shamus, grinning through his tears. And releasing Cassidy's arm, fell back full length on to the cobbled street.

22

Aldo Cassidy, lately of Sherborne School and an undistinguished Oxford college, the preserver and lover of life, sometime Lieutenant Cassidy, national service subaltern in an inconspicuous English regiment of foot, secret negotiator of the world's unconquerable agonies, clandestine owner of foreign bank accounts, drew in that moment on resources of positive action which he had written off for dead.

Seizing his lover Shamus roughly by the collar of his black coat—now known to him mysteriously as the death-coat—he dragged him to a bench. He thrust the wet, hot head between the parted male knees and held the wet unshaven face while the discarded writer again vomited on to the Paris cobblestones. He loosened the discarded writer's necktie as a precaution against suffocation, and having crouched beside him, one knee on the bench in order to force down his head a second time, entered a telephone box across the square and found the right change and the right number to summon a taxi. The telephone connection being out of order, he returned to Shamus, lifted him bodily to his feet—the dejected writer's vitality, if not his actual life, lay at his feet like the milky map of his unnative Ireland—and guided him towards a fountain which however turned out to have run dry. In the course of making this short journey, he discovered Shamus to be unconscious and quickly diagnosed an excessive heart-rate and suspected alcoholic poisoning. With the aid of a passing policeman, to whom he gave at once a hundred new francs—£8.62 at the currently prevailing devalued rate, but certainly deductible from his generously viewed expense account—the Managing Director and Founder of Cassidy's Universal Fastenings finally obtained transport in the form of a green police patrol car armed with a blue light which revolved, apparently, inside the car as well as on the roof. Recumbent in the rear compartment, which was divided from the driver by a jeweller's screen of black steel, Shamus was again sick and Cassidy succeeded, during the brief spell of subsequent articulation, in obtaining from him the name of the white hotel where, as the resourceful Second Lieutenant Cassidy resourcefully remembered, two missing British diplomats had neither paid for, nor relinquished, their reserve accommodation.

To the driver and his companion, who had prudently remained in the front of the car, but were not inclined to criticise Shamus too hastily, Cassidy gave a further hundred-franc note and apologised profusely for the condition of the rear seat. His friend, he said, had been drinking in order to overcome a great personal loss. In the field of love no doubt? they enquired, examining the handsome profile. Yes, Cassidy the preserver slyly conceded, one could say it was in the field of love. *Eh bien*, Cassidy should look after his friend, supervise his recovery; with such men as this, the path was steep and slow. Cassidy promised to do his best.

The Algerian boy, keeping watch over the reception desk through the open doorway of a windowless downstairs bedroom, where he was recovering from a night of sexual exertion with a colleague he did not introduce, received a further one hundred francs for putting on his pyjamas, unlocking the front door, handing over a key, and switching on the lift, an antiquated backless box of rosewood in which Shamus attempted without success to vomit yet again. In the drawing room of their suite the small table had been replaced in its proper position in front of the window, but traces of Elise's inexpensive scent still lingered in the threadbare pile of *ancien régime* upholstery. Here Shamus, having now rejoined the ranks of the walking wounded, insisted on going alone to the bathroom, where Cassidy the preserver soon afterwards found him asleep on the floor. With a last heroic effort, Cassidy the passable rugger forward removed his sodden clothing, sponged down the naked body of his heterosexual friend, and lifted, actually *bore* him to the double bed, where he was soon well enough to sit up and request a drink of whisky.

"Lover," Shamus said brightly, clapping his hands, "what a *clever* boy. You done it all alone!"

A few hours, a few lives later the same preserver of life applied himself painstakingly to the urgent task of restoring to the bedraggled, naked figure in the bed the ideals, dimensions, and glory of his fallen familiar.

By then, the world had turned for Cassidy several times. He woke first to hear the howling of a gale and the hotel cracking like a ship and he imagined the wet pavements heaving in the torrent and the mother whores clinging to the lampposts for their lives. The storm, of Shakespearean timeliness in view of the extreme turbulence of Cassidy's immortal soul, also woke Shamus, whom Cassidy discovered at the window, leaning outwards and down, over three floors to the courtyard below. Without fuss, Cassidy went to him and gently put his arm round the powerful back.

"I dropped my fag," said Shamus.

Sixty feet below, a red ember burned miraculously in the dancing rain.

"That's all we are," Shamus said. "Bloody little glows in a great big dark."

Having by dint of his latent mechanical skill succeeded in locking the antiquated brass latch, which by means of rods and hooks uncomfortably joined the fat window frames, Cassidy returned Shamus to the bed and climbed in after him.

He did not however sleep.

The storm ended as suddenly as it had begun, it was replaced by a Sunday quietness reminiscent of the house in Abalone Crescent on the rare occasions when the builders were not on site.

Straddled across the pramseller's naked limbs, the writer was finally asleep.

Peace, thought Cassidy; Sandra has gone upstairs.

"Great night," said Shamus, not looking at him.

"Great."

The double bed. Eggs and coffee brought by the Algerian, sunlight on the eiderdown.

"Convivial, enlightening, broadening. Lover, give me a job."

"No."

"Listen, I sold those prams didn't I? I'll write you lovely brochures, lover, promise."

"No."

"Look, I drafted one the other night, want to hear it?"

"No."

"I'll be your number one. Carry your bags, answer your phone . . . I'm better than that tight-arsed secretary of yours any day. Change my name, go straight . . ."

"Get on with your eggs," said Cassidy.

While Shamus dozed, Cassidy made several telephone calls to his public world. Occasionally, hearing him mention a figure—five, tens of thousands, free on board, back it with a loan—Shamus groaned or covered his face with his hands. Sometimes he wept. And in the afternoon, still in bed, a subdued, rested, and definitely ordinary Shamus gave his own elusive version of the hellhound Dale.

How Dale was a spy, posing as one of the Few but actually a sworn supporter of the Many-too-Many. How under cover of darkness he accepted bribes from bishops and Jaguar owners, and was loyal to his frustrated wife. How *Moon* had made money, but the others hadn't; how the hardback advances had dwindled and the paperback advances ceased; and he talked quite knowledgeably of options and copyrights and things that Cassidy, being versed in Patent Law, at least marginally understood. How Dale wanted the centre pages rewritten, and would then seriously consider a second submission. And how Shamus must hurry back and shoot him, he would borrow a gun from Hall, there was not a day to lose.

"Alternatively," said Cassidy lightly, "you might rewrite the middle."

Long silence.

"I'll shoot you too," said Shamus.

"Of course I haven't read the middle. But if everything you write is perfect, that's a different matter."

Sulking, Shamus rolled to the other side of the bed. Later, however, dressing to go out, he was sufficiently revived to give Cassidy some useful instructions on the conduct of his private life.

"That bosscow."

"Yes, Shamus."

"You know, lover, you've got that lady wrong. That's a very steady and meaningful figure in your life. You want to get her back in the team."

"I'll try."

Don't try, *said Mrs. Harabee: do it.*

"Be *faithful*, lover. You're such a shit. Be *truthful*."

"Okay."

"Lot of woman there, boy."

"Sure."

"And don't read. Reading is out."

"No problem."

"And keep right away from Dostoevsky. That man was a criminal."

"A maniac."

"I need constants, lover. None of this shifting sand. How can I write if all the proles are growing long hair?"

"No way," said Cassidy.

"Listen lover, you've got to stay frustrated. The whole order is in the balance. Promise."

"Do you feel better now?" Cassidy asked as they left.

"Piss off," said Shamus. "I don't need *your* sympathy."

Walking down the rue de Rivoli, buying a second set of clothing, *terrines* for Helen, a handbag for Sandra, Shamus also counselled him on the tactic of wooing bosscows into a generous frame of mind.

"Tell her you're broke," he urged. "Cheer her up. Christopher Robin in Carey Street, all I've got left is you."

"All right," said Cassidy.

"Flood's come, fleet's all washed away, no mink, no diamonds, no Breughels—"

"No cornices," Cassidy put in. "No eighteenth-century fireplaces . . ."

"There is *nothing* that rejuvenates a lady faster, titillates her, stimulates her, jacks her up . . . better than catastrophe. Jesus, lover, I should know."

"And you'll have a go at the middle pages, won't you?" said Cassidy. "And you'll go a *tiny* bit easier?"

"Never," said Shamus.

For their last dinner, Cassidy chose Allard again. Eating there with Elise he had noticed a duck being enjoyed at a neighbouring table and he was anxious to give it a try.

Shamus' cure was complete.

"Now the first thing you've got to do, lover, is screw Angie Mawdray, right? Face to face, frenzy all the way."

"Right," said Cassidy.

"Then there's this other bird you fancy."

"Ast."

"Correct. Phase two. Proposition Ast."

"Right."

"But don't *ask*. Take. All this looking for an ideal cow. Don't do it. There's a bit of her in all of them and not much in any of them. You have to collect it wide and put it together for yourself."

"All right."

"As for your beastly wife . . ."

"Yes?"

"I hate her, lover."

"I know you do, Shamus."

"And she hates you, so why the bloody hell don't you drop her down a hole?"

"I know. I will, I will."

"Well do it. Don't just finger it, do it."

"I will, I promise."

"You know what you forgot?" said Cassidy in bed at the St. Jacques.

"What?"

"We were going to build a cairn to Flaherty. We never did."

"Do it another time," said Shamus.

"That's right," said Cassidy.

"Goodnight, lover."

"Goodnight," said Cassidy.

"Maybe I'll do those middle pages instead."

"Great," said Cassidy.

"I love you," said Shamus as they fell asleep. "I love you. And one day, I'll give you back your faith, the way you gave me mine."

Smiling in the darkness, Cassidy touched his hand.

"Poof," said Shamus. "Vandal. Bourgeois."

And made train noises, pooff, pooff, pooff, until he fell asleep.

Sandra with the sun on her looked very pretty and she smiled to see him back.

"Hullo bosscow."

"Poor love. You look worn out."

"It's all those fast Parisian women," Cassidy said with a lean smile, breathing the smells of home.

"How was the Fair?"

"Actually rather good. We took quite a few orders, considering." A char's husband emerged from the kitchen and took his suitcase. "Mind you," he added shrewdly, pursing his lips and lowering his eyes, "the revaluation of the Deutschmark helped a good deal. Those Germans are knocking the bottom out of their own market."

"Silly things," said Sandra, leading him towards the drawing room. The disputed cornice was in place. Gilded, it looked rather handsome.

"They'll begin the other wall as soon as the plaster's dry," she said.

"Fine."

They've changed her over, he thought, like they do with babies when their blood's wrong; they've just kept the outside of her and changed everything else.

"Sorry about that letter," said Sandra.

"That's okay," said Cassidy, numb-headed.

"Look! Look! Look!"

One *"look"* for every flight of stairs. Hugo's leg was out of plaster.

London

23

An unusual silence fills the house and no birds sing.

The piano is locked. The key, well out of Hugo's reach, shares a picture hook with an unknown Florentine master whose value old Niesthal has guaranteed, he does business only with friends. In the hall, the carved eighteenth-century fireplace, completed in all but the pointing, is draped in Haverdown dust sheets, a monument never to be unveiled. The unfinished section of the cornice reaches this far only; the plasterers have been sent away. On the street side, windows are closed to noisome traffic, and curtains partly drawn in mourning. In the Crescent, neighbours have been cautioned. Even the cleaning women, customarily an important element of Sandra's social life, are tamed. They Hoover like conspiratorial bees behind closed doors and tea is taken quietly; their many children have been placed elsewhere. The Austrian cook has instructions not to weep, on pain of dismissal; whether Hugo insults her or not.

As to Mrs. Groat, she addresses her departed world in a fraught whisper which passes in bands of high energy to every corner of the house. At midday her alarm clock sounds, in forty years she has not mastered it. The signal sends her galloping six full flights. Once, mistaking the occasion, she boils water, and Sandra reproves her with discreet fury. Light is also rationed. A watchful gloom illuminates the corridors, which smell of broth as well as paint. Hugo plays in the basement, pop music is proscribed. Only John Elderman is welcome. He comes twice daily on a private basis, regardless of socialism or expense.

At the antique wrought iron gate (Sotheby's again, a snip at four hundred pounds) the press waits deferentially.

"Please keep very quiet," Sandra sends out to them with dignity. "A bulletin will be issued as soon as there is anything to say."

Aldo Cassidy, alone in high fever in the sick wing of his costly London house, is dying.

A virus, said Sandra; a special virus which assailed the overworked.

A *French* virus, said Mrs. Groat, she had had it in the Tropics, Bunny Sleego's brother died of it in an hour. It was the chrysanthemums, she said; she had never held with having chrysanths in the house, the pollen could be fatal. Additionally, she blamed the London water, which the Brigadier also disapproved of.

"Though he's not here to drink it, of course. *We're* the ones who've got to drink it," she complained. "We" were the female race, discarded when we lost our looks. "*He's* out there drinking *pure* water, no wonder he's healthy, but still." In support of this theory, she crept into Cassidy's ward while Sandra was shopping and poured commercial bleach down the waste pipe of the basin.

"Don't tell Wiggie, will you darling?" she begged (Wiggie was a patronymic for her daughter) and having kissed him nervously with her pursy mouth, walked the bitches on Primrose Hill to keep them quiet and healthy.

"He's freaked out," said Snaps admiringly, younger sister to Sandra, but sexually much her senior.

Down from Newcastle, she had moved into a spare floor, where she played provocative records late into the night. Being a full girl and jolly, she brought occasional cheer to Cassidy's fading spirit. "Darling you are *all right* aren't you?" her mother would ask her in a terrified whisper behind half-opened doors, meaning "Are you pregnant?" or equally, "Are you not pregnant?" For though Mrs. Groat had no particular opinion on which her younger daughter should be, the two conditions were closely associated in her mind. In recent years Snaps had had several pregnancies; either she rang Cassidy and borrowed a hundred pounds or she went to an unmarried mothers' clinic she liked down in Bournemouth while Sandra mounted a nationwide search for the father. These attempts were seldom fruitful; when they were, the culprit too often proved unworthy of the search.

"Been on a thrash have you?" Snaps asked him, more

directly, sitting on his bed reading a comic. "Fancy little Aldo painting Paris red, didn't know you had it in you. You'll be taking a swing at me next."

"No I won't," said Cassidy, who for some years had wondered, off and on, whether such a thing would be incestuous.

Cancer, said the charladies; wherever would they go next? And poor Mrs. Cassidy, how would she ever cope, a big house all on her own?

Runny tummy, said Hugo. Daddy's got runny tummy so he can't go to work.

"I *like* it when you have runny tummy, Dad."

"So do I," said Cassidy.

They played a lot of dominos, Hugo winning.

"He's faking," said Cassidy's father, telephoning from the penthouse, needing money badly. "He's been faking all his life, *course* he has. Ask him about his spasms in Cheltenham then. Ask him about his hernia in Aberdeen! That boy's never had a genuine affliction in his life, he's as phoney as a seven-pound note—"

"You should know," said Sandra and slammed down the receiver.

In confidence, John Elderman diagnosed a mild breakdown.

He had seen it coming, he whispered, but was helpless to prevent it; and pumped up rubber tubes round Cassidy's upper arm.

"Call it psychosomatic, call it what you will, it's one of those times when the old mind puts the body to bed, and the old body just *has* to do what the old mind tells it. Eh?"

"I suppose you're right," Cassidy conceded with a weakly smile.

"Any *history* at all, old man?" asked the physician, reading "normal" for the third day running.

"A bit," Cassidy confessed, hinting at stresses overcome, brainstorms peculiar to the brilliant.

Tactfully John Elderman abstained from further question.

"Well," he remarked instead, "you've Sandra to look after you, that's one good thing, old man. *She* knows her Aldo, doesn't she?"

"Poor Pailthorpe," Sandra sighed, holding his hand on her lap and regarding her adult child with timeless love. "Poor, silly Pailthorpe, what *have* you been up to? *You* don't have to chase money like that: *we'll* get by."

It was the balance of payments, Cassidy explained; he had wanted so desperately to help the export drive. Not for Cassidy's. For the nation.

"I wanted to get Britain off the ground," he said.

"*Dear* one," said Sandra, kissing him again, lightly in order not to excite him. "You're *such* a striver. And I'm such a drag."

For an hour or more she sat with him, studying his effigy in the gloom. Her stillness was very comforting, and Cassidy loved her in return.

The malady had taken him by surprise. Had stalked him in the night and overwhelmed him with the dawn. First a nightmare, then daylit visions had assailed him; hallucinations, dialogues between the many characters of his mind. Their theme was retribution. He was striding through London over grassy, secluded squares, drawing weightless children by the hand; he was floating down the rue de Rivoli in the Bentley, driving it from the top deck; he was charging through noisy female streets, and suddenly—it could be anywhere—he would be confronted by an alp near Sainte-Angèle, the Angelhorn. No Entry, No Diversion, and No Exit. An alp of twisting jagged spires, Wilde's upturned sow; of giddy paths and incalculable embarrassments, where whores, hoteliers, tax inspectors, police officials, and coachmen leered and gesticulated from steaming caverns or hugged each other beside diminished riverbeds. Sometimes, nervously approaching its lower slopes and feeling already the onslaught of his vertigo, he saw himself opening a copy of the *Daily Express* and reading aloud from its erudite pages: *Is Pram Maker Fourth Man? Anarchist Writer also connected? Algerian porter tells of night orgy in thunderstorm; honeymoon couple claim: we heard them through wall. Writer's wife utterly innocent. Chapman Pincher Exclusive.*

Also, of his own bankruptcy, on inner pages lit in brothel green: *Are Cassidy's burnt out? Have Fastenings Come Unstuck? M.P.'s Son answers Official Receiver: "I spent it on tipping. My crime was generosity."*

"Comfort!" the wretched sinner cried miserably to the whores. "Look what has become of me!" But before he could rid himself of his cassock (a monkish sinner, this Cassidy) they ran off white-buttocked into the avalanche gullies where Shamus, already armed and disencumbered, was waiting to enjoy them.

Such a vision was not entirely of Cassidy's own invention. Its prototype hung in the ever-lit chambers of his childhood, in the days when God was still pleased to have Old Hugo feed the mind, in the kitchen of his first mother, where she sighed and ironed surplices of her husband's own design: an alp named Hades drawn by pious artists, printed in polychrome by an early process, and framed in inflammable timber. At its foot were depicted all the horrors which small boys long to commit: theft and arson; gaming and veiled lechery. On the fearful peak, black angels burned the same offenders.

He was recalled from this torment by Ast thanking him for flowers. Sitting on his bed, close, to emphasise her gratitude. Ast in ripe harvest yellow, loose fitting at the looser places.

"Did you mean it?" she asked softly. "What you wrote?"

Sandra was out buying pigs' trotters, their gravy would give him nourishment.

"With all my love," Heather recited. *"And all my sorrow.* Aldo, you *couldn't* have made that up. Sent from *Paris* too, with all those distractions."

She too held his hand; but folded, worked into the higher cushions of her thighs; at the point, on her own person, which she had reached at dinner at the Eldermans', on his. Having first closed the door against extraneous disturbance.

"You were so *right* to rebuke me," she whispered. "And I was so *pompous* wasn't I?"

Hard upon these early visions came their physical counterparts: outbreaks of sudden sweating accompanied by erratic beatings of the heart, inflammation of the ears and throat, and a hot dryness of the eyes; written calculations by Sandra to turn Fahrenheit to Centigrade.

"He's a *hundred and four*," she told John Elderman on the second visit. "He's *miles* sub," she assured him on the third. Thereafter they discussed his condition over nightly dinners in the basement, for John Elderman liked to come at seven when the rest of the world was healed.

For a while, still hovering on the brink of death, and loudly protesting his innocence of the many crimes of which, in his other mind, he constantly accused himself, Cassidy decided that Shamus was a myth. "He never existed," he told himself, and pulling the blankets to his nose, pretended he was in a sledge.

Appalled by the memories of outlandish heresies in the Sacré Coeur, he availed himself of Sandra's extensive library on the lives of holy men, and resolved, during luxurious hours in the lavatory, to follow their example.

"I've matured," he told her. "I'd like to consider going into the Church again, it's sort of fitting into place."

And later: "Let's get out of the rat race for a while, go somewhere we can think."

Sandra suggested Oxford; they had been happy there. "Or we might try Scotland. The dogs would adore it."

"Scotland would be fine," said Cassidy. Using the bedside telephone he made bookings at Gleneagles. But only in his imagination, for Scotland had no appeal for him; it lacked the company he craved.

In answer to the patient's summons, Angie Mawdray also called. She brought the mail and twelve small roses in a white tissue.

"They're for you," she said in a low voice. "To make up for the ones you sent me from Paris."

Rummaging in her Greek bag, she drew out a handwritten letter from the country which he hid under the bedclothes. She did not look at him during this transaction, and her expression discouraged conversation.

"They're from Faulk," Cassidy told Sandra, to explain the young buds. "From all of them really, but Faulk chose them."

"People really *care* about you," Sandra said generously, sniffing their elusive scent. "People really *love* you, don't they."

"Well," said Cassidy.

"We *all* do," Sandra insisted.

And settling, resumed her vigil of unblinking adoration.

For his convalescence, Cassidy wore a blue cashmere dressing gown which Sandra bought him specially from Harrods: sickness was an emergency, money could be spent on it. At first he lunched in bed and came down for an hour only, to play with Hugo.

"That's not proper billiards," said Hugo contemptuously, and reported him to Sandra for illegal practices.

"Now you listen to me, young Hugo," said Sandra with serene indulgence. "If your Daddy wants to play billiards with a candle, then that's his way of playing billiards."

"It's the *best* way too, isn't it Dad?" said Hugo proudly.

"It's called Moth," Cassidy explained. "We used to play it in the Army as a way of passing the time."

Next morning, surveying the cloth, Sandra was extremely cross.

"How on earth am I supposed to get the wax off?"

"She's baity with you for getting up," Hugo explained. "She likes you better in bed."

"Nonsense," said Cassidy.

Continuing his cautious return to normal life, the invalid went to great lengths to spare himself collision. To telephone Helen in the country, for instance, he used his credit card to avoid distressing entries on the bill; to speak with Miss Mawdray at South Audley Street he selected moments when Sandra was out shopping. Despite these precautions, he was exposed to some hard bargaining.

"But *Cassidy*," Helen insisted, not flesh yet, but an excellent telephone personality; also an angel. "You can't possibly afford it!"

"For God's sake, Helen, what's money for?"

"But Cassidy, *think* what it's going to cost you."

"Helen, look. What would *you* do if *you* were me, and loved him *my* way? Right?"

"Cassidy," said Helen, beaten down.

For the same reasons Messrs. Grimble and Outhwaite of Mount Street W. had firm instructions not to ring him at the residence. Deal only with Miss Mawdray, he told them; Miss Mawdray knows exactly what is needed.

Nonetheless, it was Cassidy who had to keep them at the wheel.

"Water," he insisted to old Grimble, speaking under the blankets. The house, though solid, had strange acoustical tricks; chimneys in particular were dangerous ducts of sound from floor to floor. "It *must* be near water. All right, use sub agents; yes of course I'll pay double commission. Good heavens it's a Company flat isn't it? Pay whatever you have to and bill Lemming for it. I mean really it's *too bad.*"

Such conversations reminded him that he was not wholly mended, for they moved him to intemperate reactions which he afterwards regretted. Sometimes, collapsing against the heaped pillows, his heart stammering with anger, his complexion red with heat, he wept to himself in the mirror. Not a sane man left in town, he told himself. And worse: they're all against me.

"The one in Chiswick's not bad," said Angie wearily, calling on him after a long day's hunting. "If you don't mind Chiswick. It's got a fabulous *gloom* and it looks right on to the river."

"Is it noisy?"

"Depends, doesn't it. Depends what you call noisy."

"Look: could you work there? Creative work I mean ... something you had to be inspired for?"

It was Angie's third day out, and her temper was running short.

"How should I know? I can't count the decibels, can I? Tell her to go and listen for herself, I should."

Sulking, she lit a cigarette from a thin box of ten.

She? Cassidy repeated to himself; what a ridiculous, disgraceful notion! Good God, she thinks I'm ...

"It's not a *she,*" he said very firmly. "It's a *he.* A writer if you must know. A married writer who needs support at a critical time in his career. Not just moral support but practical support. He's suffered a professional reverse which could seriously affect the course of—what the devil are you laughing at?"

It was not a laugh but a smile; a sudden, very pretty smile; to watch it was to smile himself.

"I'm just happy that's all. I know I'm silly; I can't help it, can I? I thought you were setting up a designing bitch, didn't I? Redhead in a leopardskin . . . dry martinis . . ."

Such was her merriment, and her pleasure, that she was obliged to take her bedridden employer's hand to steady herself; and to borrow his handkerchief from under the pillow to dry her eyes. And to return it to its proper place under the pillow again. And to take her leave of him affectionately, as became the informality of their situation. With a kiss, in fact, a neat, dry, soft, and very loving kiss, such as daughters bestow on fathers at their coming out.

"I like that lady," said Hugo, meaning Angie, who was still lingering wistfully at the gate, as if reluctant to leave. "She gives me hugs *all* the time. . . . Dad?"

"Yes Hugo."

"Do you think she's nicer than Heather?"

"Maybe."

"Nicer than Snaps?"

"Maybe."

"Nicer than Mummy?"

"Of course not," said Cassidy.

"That's what *I* think," said Hugo loyally.

Next morning early, a loud hammering filled the house in Abalone Crescent. From the hall and drawing room, unclassical male singing issued, often with improvised librettos. To the wailing of electric drills the workmen had returned.

24

Externally, Helen had not changed.

To the outward eye at least she was the same: the Anna Karenina boots were a shade more scuffed, the long brown coat a trifle more threadbare, but to Cassidy these signs of poverty only enhanced her virtue. She came down the platform first, carrying a paper parcel in both her hands as if it were a present for him, and she had that same gravity, that same essential seriousness of manner, which for Cassidy was a prerequisite of mothers and sisters alike. Her hair was also unchanged, and that was particularly fortunate since variations unnerved Cassidy; he frankly considered them fraudulent.

True, she was several feet shorter than his expectation, and the new lights at Euston Station robbed her of that angelic luminosity which candles and firelight impart. True her figure, which he remembered as fluid and noble beneath the uncomplicated Haverdown housecoat, had a certain mundanity about it when set among the Many-too-Many with whom she had been obliged to travel. But in her voice, in her embrace as she kissed him across the parcel, in her nervous laugh as she glanced behind her, he discerned at once a new intensity.

"He's been absolutely pining for you," she said.

"Look at *you*," said Shamus in his poofy voice, pulling her aside, much as he had done at Haverdown. "Fancy wearing *eelskin* at this time of year."

"Jesus," said Cassidy boldly. "Didn't know *you* were coming."

In Cassidy's glimpse of him before the long embrace, he thought it was the collar of the deathcoat. Though he remembered also thinking, as the strong arms pulled him in, that the deathcoat had no collar, or none you could

263

turn so high. Then he thought it was a bird, an Alpine chough, pitch black, swooping to peck out his eyes. Then the barricade of tiny pins pricked and broke before him, and he thought: *this is Jonathan because he's dark, he's grown a beard to be like God.*

"He's decided he's got a weak chin," said Helen, waiting for them to finish.

"Fancy it, lover?"

"It's terrific. Marvellous. How does Helen like it?"

They made the short journey by cab. The Bentley was too high-hat, Cassidy had decided; but take a plain ordinary London taxi which would not embarrass them.

Inevitably, after Cassidy's high excitement at their coming, not to speak of the countless small preparations of an administrative and domestic character—would the curtains be ready in time, had Fortnum's mistaken the address?—inevitably, that first day was something of an anticlimax. Cassidy knew that Helen, after their many clandestine telephone calls in Shamus' interest, had much to say to him; he knew also that his first duty was to Shamus, who was the reason and the driving force of their reunion.

But Shamus placed heavy burdens on their forbearance.

Having sat Helen on the jump seat so that he and Cassidy could hold hands in comfort, Shamus first showed Cassidy how to stroke his beard: he should do it this way, downwards, never against the nap. Next, he undertook a physical examination of Cassidy, searching his arms and legs for any sign of damage, smoothing his hair, and studying the palms of his hands. And finally satisfied, he resumed his admiration of Cassidy's suit, which was of Harris tweed, not eelskin, a grey houndstooth chosen for semi-formal occasions. Was it French? Was it waterproof?

"How's work?" Cassidy asked, hoping to start a diversion.

"Never tried it," said Shamus.

"He's doing wonderfully," Helen said. "*All* the news is just marvellous, isn't it, Shamus? Honestly Cassidy, he's been working marvellously since he came back, haven't you Shamus? Four, five hours a day. More sometimes, it's been just fantastic."

Her eyes said more: we owe it to you, you have made a
new man of him.

"I'm delighted," said Cassidy, while Shamus, licking a
corner of his handkerchief, wiped a smut from Cassidy's
cheek.

The best news of all, Helen confided, was that Dale had
come down from London and that he and Shamus had
had a fantastic relationship for the whole of one day.

"Great," said Cassidy with a smile, gently warding off
more intimate embraces.

"Not jealous, lover?" Shamus enquired anxiously. "Not
put out? Honest, lover? Honest?"

"I think I'll survive," said Cassidy, with another knowing glance at Helen.

"Actually," said Helen, "Dale isn't Dale at all, is he
Shamus? He's Michaelovitsch, he's a Jew, *all* the good publishers are Jews, aren't they, Shamus? Well of course they
would be really, they've got the most fantastic taste, in
art and literature, in everything, Shamus always says so."

"That's *perfectly* true," Cassidy agreed, thinking of the
Niesthals and recalling something Sandra had recently
said. "That's perfectly true," he repeated, grateful to
have a topic of conversation on which he could shine.
"It's because historically the Jews weren't allowed to own
land. Virtually throughout the *whole* of Europe, *right*
through the Middle Ages. The Dutch were marvellous to
them but then the Dutch are marvellous people anyway,
look at the way they resisted the Germans. So of course,
what happens? The Jews had to specialise in *international*
things. Like diamonds and pictures and music and whatever they could move when they were persecuted."

"Lover," said Shamus.

"Yes?"

"Fuck off."

"Please go on about Dale," said Cassidy to Helen, trying
not to laugh. "When's he actually *publishing?* That's the
point. When do we start looking in the best-seller lists?"

Helen was prevented from replying by a sudden unearthly shriek which filled the cab and caused both herself
and Cassidy to start violently. Shamus was working a
laugh machine. It was a small cylinder made of Japanese

paper, with steel ribs inside. Every time he turned it over it gave a dry cackle which, carefully controlled, slowed to a choking, tubercular cough.

"He calls it Keats," said Helen, in a tone which suggested to Cassidy that even maternal angels do not have unlimited patience.

"It's fantastic," said Cassidy, recovering from his alarm. "Mirthless and right. Carry on," he called to the driver. "It's okay, we were just laughing." He closed the partition window. "We'll be there soon," he said, with a reassuring smile at Helen.

She's tired from the journey, he thought. Shamus has probably been playing her up.

No one mentioned Paris.

It was a place on its own over a warehouse, with an outside steel staircase to the red front door. A nautical place, right on the river, with a view of two power stations and a playground to one side. Cassidy had taken it furnished for a great deal of money, and changed the furniture because it was too ordinary. There were flowers in the kitchen and more beside the bed, and there was a crate of Scotch in the broom cupboard. Talisker '54 from Berry Brothers and Rudd. There was a ship's wheel on the wall and rope for a bannister, but mainly it was the light you noticed, the upside-down light, that came off the river and lit the ceiling not the floor.

Demonstrating each tasteful feature—the new Colston washing-up machine, the coyly stowed deep-freeze in its random Iroko boarding, the draft extractors, the warm-air heating system, the Scandinavian stainless steel cutlery, not to mention the all-brass window fastenings of his own design—Cassidy felt the pride of a father who is giving the young couple a fair start in life. This is what Old Hugo would have done for me and Sandra, he thought, if he'd not been Tied Up With a Deal. Well, let's hope they show themselves worthy of it.

"Cassidy, *look,* there's even brown sugar for coffee. And serviettes, Shamus. Look, *Irish* linen. Oh my *God,* oh no, oh no . . ."

"Something wrong?" Cassidy asked.

"He's had our initials put on them," said Helen, almost crying for the sheer joy of her discovery.

He left the bedroom till last. The bedroom was his very particular pride. Green, he had wanted. Blue, Angie Mawdray had urged. Wasn't blue rather *cold?* Cassidy countered, quoting Sandra. In Harrods they found the answer: floppy blue flowers on the palest green background, the very same print which for years had given him such pleasure in Hugo's nursery at Abalone Crescent.

"Let's put it on the ceiling as well," Angie urged, with a woman's sympathy for Helen. "So they've got something to look at when they're lying on their backs."

To match, they had selected a Casa Pupo coverlet, the biggest available size to cover the biggest available bed. And sheets with a fabulous blue print, and fabulous pillowcases in the same way-out pattern. And white curtains bordered with a green-blue braid. And a fabulous white drugget to set it all off.

"Cassidy," Helen breathed, "it's the biggest bed we've ever had." And blushed, as became her modesty.

"Bathroom through there," said Cassidy, more to Shamus this time, in a very practical voice, as if bathrooms were men's work.

"Big enough for three," said Shamus, still looking at the bed.

They stood at the long window, watching the barges, Helen one side of him, Shamus the other.

"It's the loveliest place I've ever seen," said Helen. "It's the loveliest place we've ever had, or ever will have."

"I rather like *views*," said Cassidy, playing it right down to make it easy for them. "That's what first drew me to it actually."

"And the water," said Helen, understanding.

A long string of barges slid by, slow and out of step, overtaking one another as they passed the window, falling back into lines as they disappeared.

"Anyway," said Cassidy, "should be all right for a while."

"We don't want *all right*, do we, lover," Shamus quietly reminded him. It was some time since he had spoken. "Never did, never will. We want the sun, not the fucking twilight."

"Well there's plenty of sun *here*," said Helen brightly, with another confiding glance at Cassidy. "I adore picture windows. They're *so* modern."

"And free," said Cassidy.

"Exactly," said Helen.

"It needs movement," said Shamus.

Thinking he meant the river still, that he had entered their conversation with an aesthetic objection, Cassidy put his head on one side and said:

"Oh . . . *Do* you . . . ?"

"The three of us," said Shamus. "Or we'll just go into the mud."

Turning to Cassidy, he embraced him.

"Dear lover," he said softly, "that's a lovely, innocent thing you did. Bless you. Love you. Forgive."

Over Shamus' shoulder, he saw Helen shrug. *One of his moods,* her smile said. *It'll blow over.* Drawing close, she kissed him too, where he stood, held in her husband's arms.

After shampoo, which Cassidy had put ready in the High Speed Gas refrigerator, he tactfully made his excuses and left them to unpack. With the same nice tact, Helen left the two lovers to say goodbye. Shamus came down the steps with him.

"You don't know where I can buy a football, do you?" he asked, looking at the playground.

It was a dark, sullen kind of day, the grass very green and a lot of pink behind the power station as if the brickwork had stained the sky. A group of black children was playing hopscotch.

"You could try the Army and Navy," said Cassidy, a little disappointed to think he had forgotten something. "Shamus, there's nothing wrong is there? Nothing *bad* . . ."

"Moral judgment?"

"Good Lord no—" said Cassidy hastily, knowing the rules.

Again Shamus was silent.

"God took six days, lover," he said, smiling at last. "Not even Butch can do it in a morning."

"And you really got stuck into those centre pages?" Cassidy asked, wishing to end it on an upward note.

"All for you. I'm a very obedient lover these days. No booze, no whores. Enoughs all the way. Ask Helen."

"She told me," said Cassidy, injudiciously.

"Bye, lover. Great pad. Bless you. Hey, how's the boss-cow? I thought I'd ring her up some time."

Cassidy barely flinched:

"Away I'm afraid. Gone to shack up with Mum for a while."

Helen from the balcony watched them hug, a princess in her new tower, the broad moat of the river at her back. His last sight of Shamus was of him standing with the children in the queue for hopscotch, waiting to take his turn.

At home meanwhile, contrary to Cassidy's little piece of artistic licence, all was happiness and activity. Cassidy's stock was much improved; his illness had done him good, they said; John Elderman was a genius. Aldo eats well, Aldo's eye is brighter, he has a sense of purpose: the word was passed from one female mouth to another, with allowances for domestic status. The cleaning women clubbed together and bought him a backrest for the Bentley; the dogs recognised him, Hugo drew him hooray cards and illuminated them with soluble crayon. Heather Ast came almost daily, witnessing Aldo's recovery while discussing with Sandra the resuscitation of human wrecks.

"We should open a place in the country," they said, loving the summer weather. "A place where they can all dry out."

This brightening of Cassidy's domestic sky was not without its cause; for Cassidy had finally recognised his true vocation, and Sandra in particular was delighted with it. Playing fields were a dead loss, she said; one could waste whole years and get nowhere; local Councils were corrupt beyond belief.

"It's just what you need," she said. "To give you an interest."

The ideal solution, she said; the natural compromise between Church and Trade:

"I can't think *why* you didn't hit on it earlier, but still."

"It came to me while I was ill," Cassidy confessed. "I had that awful feeling I'd wasted so much of my life. I lay there, I thought *who are you?—why are you?—what will they say of you when you're dead?* I just didn't want to worry you until I was sure," he added.

"Darling," said Sandra, a little ashamed all the same, as she later admitted to Heather, that she had not been more alive to her husband's inner turmoil.

For Cassidy had decided to enter politics.

As a precaution, however, she consulted John Elderman. They went together as if their problem were bridal. Would it be too much of a strain for him? Would it get him down the way Paris had? Much travel was involved, lonely nights in dismal northern hostelries. Was John absolutely sure that Cassidy's physique could take it? After some demur, John Elderman gave the green light.

"But watch that old ticker," he warned. "The smallest tweak and you call me in. No hiding it away, right?"

"He'll hide it if he gets a chance," said Sandra, knowing her Aldo.

"Then you watch *him*," said John Elderman.

Hallowed now by a profound sense of sacrifice, they set to work in earnest. The first thing was to settle on a Party. Though Sandra's mind was absolutely made up, Cassidy, with his harsher experience of the world, his fabled understanding of the fleshly weaknesses of men in trade, had yet to reach a firm decision. Sandra thought it vital she should not influence him in *any* way, therefore (as she later told him) she witnessed in silence the dialogue between his conscience and his purse.

"I just can't get over being Socialist and rich," he said. "It doesn't seem to add up."

"You're not *that* rich," Sandra consoled him.

"Well I am really. If the market keeps up."

"Then give it away," she snapped, "if *that's* your problem."

But Cassidy felt that giving it away was too easy.

"I'm sorry, Sandra, it's just not the answer. I can't run away like that. I've got to stand for what I *am*," he told her over dinner, on the eve of Helen and Shamus' arrival. "Not for what I ought to be. Politics reflect *reality*."

"You used to say we were judged by what we looked for."

"Not in politics," said Cassidy.

"Then why not the Liberals? There are *masses* of rich Liberals, look at the Niesthals."

"But the Liberals never get in," Cassidy objected.

Better to be a free Independent than a tied Liberal, he said.

"You mean you'll only back winners?" Sandra demanded, as ever the custodian of her husband's probity.

"It's not *that*. It's just . . . well the Liberals speak with too many voices. I want a Party that knows its mind."

"Well as far as *I'm* concerned," said Sandra, "the Conservatives are absolutely *out*."

Conservatives hated the poor, she said, they had absolutely *no* sympathy for the underdog, Conservatives were *stupid*, her father had been one, and if Cassidy went anywhere *near* the Conservatives she would leave him *at once*.

"I'm absolutely damned if I'll be a Tory M.P.'s wife," she said. "Except in a country area. It's different in the country, more traditional."

Soothing her, Cassidy explained his plan of campaign. He did this very judiciously, admitting her bit by bit to a complex and delicate secret. Did she *promise* not to tell anyone?

She did.

Was she *sure?*

She was.

He didn't mind her telling Heather and the Eldermans and the cleaning women because they would all find out anyway; yes, and the Niesthals if they asked but not unless.

She understood.

Well, he had cleared the decks entirely at the office. It was the silly season, the Trade had pretty well packed up after the Paris Fair, a lot of the staff were on holiday. So anyway, Cassidy had been in touch with the Unions—

"The *Unions*," Sandra echoed, much excited. "You mean you're going to join the—"

"The Unions," Cassidy repeated patiently, brushing aside his virtue. "Now *will* you let me finish?"

Sandra would; she had not meant to interrupt.

Very well, there had been discussions. Did she remember that Wednesday he had to go to Middlesbrough and Beth Elderman said she had seen him in Harrods?

Sandra remembered it clearly.

Well, that was one of the discussions.

Sandra was contrite.

As a result of these discussions, which had ranged over several weeks, the Unions had now invited him to make a thorough examination of the whole organisation of the Labour Movement from the businessman's angle.

"Oh my *God*," Sandra breathed. "But that's *dynamite!*"

In effect (though this was highly confidential) a Business Efficiency Analysis. At the end of his researches he would put in a Paper, and if he still liked them and they still liked him, well, maybe a safe Union seat could be found . . .

"They might even publish it," Sandra said, still very excited as they undressed for bed. "Then you'd be a *writer* too. The Cassidy Report. . . . When do you start?"

"The first leg's tomorrow," said Cassidy, showing his full hand at last.

"And you're not to compromise," Sandra warned him. "Don't go saying things just to please them. Those Unions are an absolute pest."

"I'll try," said Cassidy.

"Good luck, Dad," said Hugo.

"I mean it," said Sandra.

"Politics my arse," said Old Hugo at the penthouse, receiving his secret fortnightly visit and his fortnightly cheque. "Politics my Aunt Fanny Adam. You haven't got the guts for it, take my word. You need the guts of a *lion* to be in politics today, a *lion*, Blue!"

A Mrs. Bluebridge was in residence, Old Hugo's female advisor and a longstanding mother from Cassidy's childhood. She had put a typewriter on the drawing room table—her own way of establishing respectability—and her sponge-bag in a separate bathroom, Cassidy had seen it when he went in to brush his hair. "Who's Bluebridge?" he used to ask. "Is she your wife? Your sister? Your secretary?" Once, to set a trap, he had spoken French to her, but though surprised she had not responded guiltily.

"Well I do *think*, Aldo . . ." Bluebridge began, and

drifted away into the problem of understanding the needs of young people in the world today.

A faint Scottish accent distinguished her from other members of her team. Her mouth was at the very centre of her painted lips, a frayed black line that parted and joined like a poor seam under pressure. He owes her money, Cassidy thought; he's giving her love instead. Soon she would come to him, they always did. Call at South Audley Street on a Monday morning having mulled it over all weekend, sit in the deep leather chair beside Angie Mawdray's coffee cup, twisting her fingers round old envelopes full of broken promises. *Now I don't want to say anything against your father, Aldo. Your father's a lovely man in very many ways . . .*

The young were still her concern. Having shown him her reasoning, she proceeded to announce her conclusion:

"It's sex, sex, sex, all the way, that's all they think of, truly Aldo. Politics or young girls, it's the same thing. I've seen it all my life, I have too."

"It's a carve-up," Old Hugo cried, in very high spirits, pointing to the distant outlines of Westminster. "It's a carve-up of vice, greed, and influence, that's all politics is, mark my words. You listen to Blue, Aldo; that woman has seen the world."

"Now Aldo's seen the world too, Hugo, he's not a babe any more. Well don't you agree now, Aldo, deep down?" the seam enquired.

Letting him out, she squeezed his hand and wished him luck.

"I'm so glad you're going Conservative," she whispered. "But don't do it on your dad's back, will you dear, it never lasts."

"Was *he* Conservative then?" Cassidy asked, meaning Old Hugo, and still smiling to have pleased them so exceptionally.

"Ssh," said Blue, smelling of oatcake.

At the office in South Audley Street, too, all was sunny, all was content. Meale, taking three weeks' holiday at once, had withdrawn to a monastery in Leeds; Lemming was on the Scilly Isles; Faulk had rented a cottage in Selsey and was living in much-publicised happiness with a Metropol-

itan policeman. Of his *cercle,* only Miss Mawdray had nobly stayed behind to attend the Chairman's needs. Most of
her time was spent on shopping. If she was not ordering
bound works on revolution, sanitation, and the Common
Market (either for despatch to Abalone Crescent or to
adorn the gateleg table in the waiting room) she was
engaged in the many small tasks which went towards the
welfare of her master's *protégés.* She arranged for library
facilities at Harrods and daily newspapers from a local
newsagent; for credit at a theatre ticket agency, charges
to be remitted to the Company. All this on Cassidy's instruction, all with great aplomb. She sent round stationery
from Henningham and Hollis, and arranged for typists to
be on call at an agency in Pimlico.

Having persuaded Helen (outside Shamus' hearing) to
accept a small allowance to tide them over till the new
book, Cassidy also decided she should have a credit card,
and after some difficulty and much animal persistence
Angie Mawdray succeeded in sponsoring her enrolment
with one of the major companies.

"Jesus," she said with a giggle, "she'll ruin you, I
would."

Angie's morale had never been higher. Hitherto, she had
objected to misleading Sandra on small matters of fact,
such as whether he was in London or Manchester, whether
he was still in Paris. Now, her scruple was gone, and
though Cassidy did not confide in her about his Trade
Union project, she knew enough, and guessed enough, to
protect his interests when the need arose. As to her appearance, it spoke of purest happiness. Her breasts, often
unsupported, remained sharp despite the summer heat; her
summer skirts, never long, had shrunk to a festive brevity,
and her movements seemed calculated to solicit, rather
than inhibit, his gaze.

Once, to reward her efforts, he took her to the cinema, and she held his hand in mute submission, watching
Cassidy rather than the screen, her little face flickering on
and off as the beam switched above them like wartime
searchlights.

As to his relationship with Helen and Shamus, Angie
Mawdray was neither shocked nor curious.

"If you like them, it's good enough for me," she said.

"And he's a smashing writer, truly. As good as Henry Miller, whatever the beastly critics say."

Within days of their arrival, she had learnt to recognise their voices on the telephone and put them through without enquiry. Once, using his Russian accent, Shamus asked her to go to bed with him. He was the Reverend Rasputin, he said, and tired to death of princesses.

"He would too," said Cassidy with a laugh, "if he got half a chance."

"What's so funny about that?" said Angie, stung.

But mainly he said he was Flaherty, an Irish fanatic in search of moderation.

25

Up Hall's Shamus called it.

They went there for Impact, it was better even than
water. They went there for Abstinence, it was Shamus'
new mood; to keep fit, and preserve himself to a fine
Old Testament age. They went there by bus riding at the
front on the top deck, after six, when the eastbound buses
were mainly empty. To a black-bricked warehouse behind
Cable Street, with ropes swinging from the girders, and
an old trampoline stretched above the concrete floor, and
a rope boxing ring rigged under arc lights, the canvas
blotched with blood. Cassidy wore squash kit with a little
blue laurel on the left breast, but Shamus insisted on the
deathcoat, he refused to dress for Impact. Hall wore white
ducks as broad at the cuff as they were at the waist, and
a cotton singlet with creases ironed across the shoulders.
Hall was a small, round, toothless man with quick brown
eyes and darting fists and a complexion made in squares
like an old brown eiderdown. To Cassidy, he had a lot of
the naval chaplain about him, the same shipshape philosophy and a pious way of drinking, the same way of shaking
hands while he looked for God behind you.

He called Shamus Lovely.

Not my lovely, or lovely one, but plain lovely as if it
were a noun. *Le beau*, thought Cassidy, hearing it for the
first time; the Regency tradition. Before Impact they
watched the sparring of Hall's White Hopes, and played
on the trampoline and rode the anchored bicycle. After
Impact they went up to Sal's place, which was Hall's name
for where he lived. Sal was Hall's bird, Hall's body; he
loved her better than life. She was nineteen and simple, by
profession a tart, but now in retirement owing to Hall's
insistence.

For this reason, Hall seldom allowed her out, but
banged her up to keep her safe.

"Bangs her up?" asked Cassidy.

277

Bang up was prison talk, Shamus explained proudly; Hall had been in stir. *Bang up* meant lock the cell door at night.

That's why Hall's a parson, Cassidy thought, reminded of Old Hugo; he's learnt the piety of granite walls.

For Impact, Shamus fought with Hall, when the gym was empty of all but Cassidy and a man called Ming, a blood-wiper and stone deaf.

Hall would only oblige when the gym was empty; that was his rule, that was his pride, Hall's sense of what was proper in a well-run gym, for Shamus had no art at all, and would not learn it.

"Wait," Hall would say firmly, bolting the doors. "Wait, Lovely, I'm telling you," and then duck quickly under the ropes and into the ring before Shamus could get at him.

Shamus in attack relied solely on the charge. He charged in sudden onslaughts, shouting and flailing his arms under the deathcoat: "Fucker, sodder, prole!" And if he reached his adversary, embraced him, squeezing his ribs and biting him until Hall was obliged to beat him off. Sometimes, affecting a Japanese style, he tried to kick him, then Hall took his foot and threw him on his back.

"Take it easy, Lovely, take it easy, I don't want to hurt you now," Hall would say, quite misunderstanding the purpose of the engagement.

Very rarely, provoked beyond endurance, Hall smacked him on the cheek, most frequently a backhanded blow, to deflect him from the charge. Then Shamus would stand off, very pale, frowning and smiling together, feeling the pain and rubbing his cheek with his black sleeve.

"Jesus," he would say. "Wow. Hey, go and do it to Cassidy. Cassidy, feel, it's fantastic!"

"I can imagine," Cassidy would say, laughing. "Thanks very much, Hall, all the same."

"He'd be a grand fighter," Hall declared, back at Sal's place, as they drank the Talisker out of Cassidy's brief-case. "It's his footwork, that's the trouble, it spreads him out, don't it Lovely? You're a murderous bugger though, aren't you?"

"I think he's nice," said Sal, who was very prim for her age and seldom said much else.

Hall enjoyed his whisky neat, from a tall glass so full it looked like still pale beer.

"That's how *we* should drink it," Shamus explained as they returned to Helen. "If it wasn't for me being dedicated."

"I must say," Sandra told John Elderman. Heather was present and passed it on to Cassidy. "I must say he's keeping very fit. He's lost four pounds in a week."

"It's all that Trade Union food," said John Elderman, who knew his lower classes.

"He's been taking exercise too," said Sandra, with (Heather reported) a most unusual smile.

Observing, Helen called it.

It was her own idea; she advanced it one morning while Cassidy sat on the end of the blue bed finishing up their toast from a Michael Truscott plate. He had dropped in early on his way to South Audley Street. It was the holiday season, and the business world was almost at a standstill.

The cups were also Truscott: stoneware of great delicacy, he had thought the plain form would appeal to her.

"Honestly, Shamus," she said. "He's just never lived, have you, Cassidy? He's been in London all his life and he doesn't know anything about it at all. Honestly, you ask him where anything is, or when it was built, or honestly ... *anything,* and I'll bet he doesn't know the answer. Cassidy, have you ever been to the Tate? Listen to this, Shamus. Well, Cassidy?"

So that afternoon while Shamus toiled, they went to the Tate, stopping on the way to buy Helen some sensible shoes. Finding the Tate closed they had tea at Fortnum's instead, and afterwards Helen insisted on visiting the Baby Carriage Department to inspect one of Cassidy's prams. The salesman was extremely respectful and, without knowing that Cassidy was of his audience, praised the excellence of his inventions. Also he assumed Helen and Cassidy were married and that Helen was pregnant, and this led to much secret laughter between them, and squeezes of the hand and confiding glances. Then Helen said actually it *might* be twins, there was quite a record of twins in the family, particularly on *her* side.

"My father's a twin, *and* my grandfather and my great-grandfather. . . ."

And Cassidy put in, "It led to awful trouble with the title, didn't it darling?"

So the salesman showed them a Cassidy Two-in-Hand carriage with a Cassidy Banburn canopy over the top and Helen wheeled it very solemnly up and down the carpet until she got the giggles and had to be removed.

At the zoo Helen made straight for the vultures, studying them gravely and without apparent fear. Hugo's gibbons gave her particular pleasure, causing her to laugh out loud. No, Cassidy quietly corrected her, they were not making love in the air, that was the baby holding on underneath, it was the way they carried their young, almost like kangaroos.

"Nonsense, Cassidy, don't be so prim, of *course* they're—"

"No," said Cassidy, firmly, "they're not."

In the night animals' house they watched badgers preparing a set and bats cleaning their ears and small rodents burrowing against the glass. No, said Cassidy in answer to the same question, they were just using each other's backs for steps. In the dark corridor, watched by a crowd of bleary children, Helen was moved to kiss Cassidy in gratitude for all the wonderful things he had done for Shamus; and she promised Cassidy that she loved him, in her way as faithfully as Shamus, and that he would always have a home with them however bleak the other parts of his life.

And when finally, by way of several pubs, they reached the Water Closet (Shamus' name for the flat) and found him still working, still in the beret, crouched at the river window, they told him everything they had observed, and all the fun they had had; everything in fact except the kiss, because the kiss was private and, like the actions of certain animals, liable to facile misconstruction.

"Great," said Shamus quietly, when he had heard it all. "Great," and having taken each of them in an affectionate embrace, returned to his desk.

A few days later the two men went down to Hall's for Impact and Shamus succeeded in landing Hall a painful blow on the eye. For retaliation, Hall punched him in the stomach, hard, just under the rib cage, on what boxers call the mark, and Shamus became white and sick and even more quiet than before.

With Shamus wholly given to work, abstinence, and contemplation, it was inevitable that Helen and Cassidy should spend much time observing on their own. Now in his deathcoat, now stark naked before the window, the beret pulled like a cage low on his dark brow, he would sit for hours on end, head bowed, driving his pen across the paper. Not even for *Moon*, said Helen, had he shown such zeal, such application:

"And he has *you* to thank for it. *Dear* Cassidy."

"Is it *all* rewrite?" Cassidy asked, lunching with her at Boulestin. "It looked like a whole new novel to me."

Helen said no, she was sure it was the rewrite. He had promised Cassidy he would do it, he had made the same promise to Dale: Shamus never, never forgot a promise.

"He always pays what he owes. I've never met anyone with a greater sense of honour."

She said this without drama, as a statement concerning someone they both loved; and Cassidy knew it was true, a fact beyond pretending.

London was her city.

Shamus was Paris. The Celt, the nomad, the dreamer, the practitioner: all were met in the unfathomable artistic genius of Paris. But Helen was London, and Cassidy loved her for it. She loved its worthiness, its dingy pomp and ordinary grime. And though they both subscribed to Shamus' dictum that the past was not worth discussing, Cassidy by now had learnt enough of her to know that London was where most of her life had been spent.

She led him.

She led him along wharves, past Dutch warehouses painted with impossible professions: cane importers, whalers, grinders of fine curry. She led him down dangerous Dickensian alleys, gaslit and haunted by bollards, where for twenty seconds they thrilled to a sense of being young and well-dressed and desirable to evildoers. She showed him City churches with postage-stamp edges; took him into synagogues and mosques, held his hand at the place where poets were buried in Westminster Abbey. She showed him empty markets where brown dogs ate Brussels sprouts by lamplight, and Mussolini's statue in the Imperial War Museum. She took him to the Anchor and stood him on a wooden platform and made him gaze at the sunlit outline of St. Paul's across the water; and she asked him to become Lord Mayor all in furs and chains so that she could visit him and eat roast beef by candlelight. And Cassidy knew he had never seen any of these places before, not one of them; not even the Tower of London or Piccadilly Circus, until Helen had shown them to him.

For conversation they had Shamus: their star, their parent, their lover, and their ward. How they loved him more than themselves; he was their bond. How his talent was their responsibility, their gift to the world. That to damage him in any way would be to violate a trust.

Shamus, meanwhile, had cut his beard square at the end in order to look like a rabbi.

"Solid for the Old Testament," he explained, still writing.

While at Abalone Crescent, Sandra was extremely impressed by Cassidy's portrait of dockside conditions.

"When will they realise it's the *quality* of life that matters, not the amount that people earn?" she demanded.

"Jesus," said Snaps. "Hear you."

"Still, darling, money is *nice*," countered Mrs. Groat, who had recently put her arm in a sling on the grounds that it hurt when she had it straight.

"Nonsense," said Sandra. "Money's just token. It's happiness that matters, isn't it, Aldo?"

To compensate for his prolonged absences Sandra had wisely acquired a new interest.

"What are the dockers doing about birth control?" she wanted to know. Were there advisory centres for wives? If not, she and Heather would open one *at once*. Or—a sensible thought—should they postpone their decision until Cassidy had his Seat?

"I think," said Cassidy shrewdly, after some thought, "that you might do best to wait and see where we end up."

The change in Shamus, when it came, was at first barely distinguishable from the strains of an arduous routine, and only loosely related to external events. Hall had much to do with it; yet the part he played was probably, in the end, analogous rather than contributory.

For several weeks now, Helen and Cassidy and Shamus had lived a life of quite unusual happiness. As Shamus added page after page to the neat piles of paper before him so, it seemed to Cassidy, did his own contentment rise in an ever-ascending swell of perfect companionship. Cassidy came most often after lunch, when Helen had put behind her the majority of her domestic duties. Sometimes she was still washing up—the machine, for all its simplicity, had defeated her—and in that case Cassidy would dry the glasses for her while they planned their afternoon's entertainment. Often they would consult Shamus: did he think it would rain? What did he feel about a trip to Hampton Court? Should they take the Bentley or get a car from Harrods? And when they came back, they would sit at the table hand in hand and tell him, over a frugal Talisker or a bottle of shampoo, of all their many adventures and impressions.

Occasionally, in return, Shamus read to them from his manuscript, and although Cassidy on such occasions deliberately induced in himself a kind of inner vertigo which left him only a broad impression of genius, he readily agreed it was better than Tolstoy, better even than *Moon*, and that Dale was the luckiest publisher alive.

Occasionally, Shamus said nothing at all, but rocked back and forth in his chair, letting Keats shriek for him at the funny places.

And sometimes, if Cassidy had not actually spent the night there, he would call in the morning, early enough to share their breakfast in the blue flower bedroom and in the freshness of the hour discuss with them the world's problems, or better still their own. It was a time of exceptional frankness in all matters affecting their collective relationship. The love life of Helen and Shamus, for instance, was an open book between them. Though Paris was never spoken of—indeed Cassidy sometimes wondered whether they had ever been there—Helen had made it clear that she knew Shamus in *that* mood also, and that Cassidy was not concealing from her anything that could hurt her pride. Nor was it at all unusual for Shamus or Helen to make a reference to a recent sexual encounter, often with humorous overtones.

"Christ," she said to Cassidy once as they rose from a prolonged luncheon at the Silver Grill, "he's practically broken my back," and confided to him that they had been reading the *Kamasutra* and following one of its more ambitious recommendations. From other chance remarks let slip in the ordinary line of conversation, Cassidy learned that for the same purpose they were given to using telephone booths and other public amenities; and that their most treasured achievement had taken place on a parked Lambretta in an alley behind Buckingham Palace. While in the more general way, he could not help noticing (since he quite often slept in the adjoining bedroom) that his friends enjoyed at least a daily exchange of views, and not infrequently two or three.

The first sign of a flaw in this idyllic relationship came with their visit to Greenwich. As one perfect summer's day followed another it was very natural that Helen and Cassidy should wander farther afield in search of pleasure and information. At first, they contented themselves with the larger London parks, where they flew kites and gliders and floated yachts on ponds. But the parks were full of the Many-too-Many and rutting proles in pink underclothes, and they agreed that Shamus would prefer them to find their own place, even if it took longer to get there. Therefore they took the Bentley to Greenwich, and while they were there they found themselves looking at the yacht in which Sir Francis Chichester had sailed singlehanded round the world. It was not in water, but concrete; embalmed there for ever, within a few feet of the embankment.

For some while neither spoke.

Cassidy in fact was not at all sure what his reaction should be. That the boat had superb lines, God look at those proportions? That it seemed an awful waste to put a perfectly good boat out of service, was public money involved? Or he wished they could sail away in it, just the three of them, possibly to an island?

"It's the saddest thing I've ever seen," said Helen, suddenly.

"Me too," said Cassidy.

"To think it was once *free* . . . a living, wild thing . . ."

Cassidy at once took up her argument. It was indeed a most tragic and affecting sight, he would write to the Greater London Council the moment he got back to the office.

Thrilled by the similarity of their separate responses they hurried home to share their feelings with Shamus.

"Let's all go down there one night," Cassidy suggested. "With picks, and set it free!"

"Oh do let's," said Helen.

"Jesus Christ," said Shamus and went to the lavatory, ostensibly to be sick.

Later he apologised. An unworthy thought he said, forgive, lover, forgive. He had had visions of Christopher Robin, all wrong, all wrong.

But when Cassidy, leaving for home, made his way down the steel steps, he was met by a shower of water that could only have come from the bedroom window; and he remembered Lipp's restaurant in Paris, his baptism and Shamus' pain.

The cloud, it seemed, had passed, until one day—a week later, perhaps two—Hall's gym closed. Cassidy and Shamus went down on a Monday and found the iron door locked against them and no lights burning in the air-raid-glass window.

"Gone to a fight," said Shamus, so they played football instead.

They went down again on the Thursday and the door was still locked, now with a crowbar and a curiously official-looking padlock with sealing wax over the hook.

"Gone on holiday," said Cassidy, thinking of Angie

Mawdray, who had left for Greece the day before with a
ticket bought by the Company. So they went for a run
round Battersea Park and played on the seesaw.

The third time they went, there was a notice saying
"Closed," so they rang the bell at Sal's place until she answered it. Hall was in stir, she said, very frightened, he had
clobbered an American bosun for being fresh, he was doing three months at the Scrubs. She had a bruised eye and
one hand bandaged and she shut the door on them as soon
as she had told them the news. But there was a smell of
cigar in the parlour and the sound of a radio upstairs, so
they reckoned the American bosun had not suffered ir-
reparable harm.

This news had a curious effect on Shamus. At first, he was
incensed and, like the unreformed Shamus of old, made
elaborate plans to effect his friend's escape: to kidnap
the American Ambassador, for instance, or sequester the
bosun's ship. He assembled an armoury of secret weapons:
wire nooses, files, and pieces of bicycle chain attached to
wooden handles. His plan was a mass break-out involving all inmates.

This aggressive mood was followed by one of deep melancholy and disappointment. Why had Hall allowed himself to be captured? Shamus would commit a crime in
order to be joined with him. Prison was the only place for
writers, and he fell back on the familiar examples of Dostoevsky and Voltaire.

But as the weeks passed and Hall was still not released,
Shamus gradually ceased to talk about him. He seemed instead to enter a dream world of his own from which the
excited accounts of his wife's exploits with Cassidy no
longer woke him. But he did not turn away from Hall;
to the contrary, he drew closer, developing, in some way
which Cassidy could not fully understand, an inner part-
nership with him, a secret union, as it were; to languish
with him waiting for a certain day.

Condemned still for hours at a time to the imprisonment of his novel, he even acquired, to Cassidy's skilled
eye, a prison pallor and certain prison mannerisms, a
slough of the feet and shoulders, a furtive greed at table,
and the habits of listless servility when addressed and of

following them round the room with shut-off, unwatching eyes. In conversation, when he could be drawn, he was inclined to volunteer incongruous references to atonement, hubris, and the social contract, loyalty to one's private precepts. And on one unfortunate occasion, he let slip a most damaging comparison between the sublime Helen and Hall's bird Sal.

It happened late at night.

On Cassidy's suggestion they had been to the cinema—Shamus also liked the live theatre, but he was inclined to shout at the actors—and they had seen a Western starring Paul Newman, whose features Helen had recently compared with Cassidy's. Returning by way of a couple of pubs, they had linked arms as was their custom, Helen in the middle, when Shamus suddenly interrupted Cassidy's spirited rendering of the film's key scene with a cry of:

"Hey, look there's Sal!"

Following the direction of his gaze, they looked across the road at a middle-aged woman standing alone on a street corner, under a lantern, in the classic posture of a prewar tart. Irritated by their interest, she scowled at them, turned, and toppled a few ridiculous steps along the pavement.

"Nonsense," said Helen. "She's far too old."

"You're not though, are you? You've got a few years in you, haven't you?"

For a moment no one spoke. To look for Sal they had drawn to a halt, and were standing, still linked, outside what was probably Chelsea Hospital. The windows were lighted and uncurtained. A complex of pale shadows ran outwards from their feet. Cassidy felt Helen's arm stiffen inside his own, and her bare hand turned cold.

"What the hell's that supposed to mean?" she demanded.

"Jesus," Shamus muttered. "Jesus."

Breaking away from them he hurried into a side street and returned to the flat late and very pale.

"Forgive, lover, forgive," he whispered, and having kissed Cassidy goodnight, put his arm round Helen and guided her gently, reverently to the bedroom.

On the next day the incident at football occurred.

It was for both of them conclusive. Shamus was over-worked; abstinence had gone too far.

In the absence of Impact, football had become their main recreation. They played it twice a week: on Tuesdays and Fridays. It was a fixture, always at four. On the stroke of the clock, Cassidy would roll his trousers to the knee, toss his jacket on to the blue bed, kiss Helen goodbye, and run off across the road to the playground to reserve the goal. A few moments later, dressed in the inevitable deathcoat, Shamus would descend the iron steps and after a few pre-liminary exercises on the swings take up his position either as striker or goalie according to his mood. A rigid points system was applied, and Shamus kept all manner of records in a drawer of his desk, including diagrams of intricate manoeuvres he had performed. He even spoke of publish-ing a book on method football; he would talk to Dale about it, the sodder. Generally he was better in attack than in defence. His kicking had a wild, undisciplined bril-liance to it which frequently lofted the ball far over the railings, and once into the river, for which he claimed a prize, an afternoon exchange of views with Helen. As a goalie he tended to rely on nerve tactics, which included shrill Japanese war whoops and many exotic obsceni-ties on the subject of Cassidy's bourgeois nature.

On the day in question, it was Shamus' turn to attack. Taking the ball quite close to the goal mouth, he dug a mound, set the ball on it, then stalked slowly backwards preparatory to a self-awarded free kick. Since the ball was no more than five yards from him, and the line of Shamus' run appeared to direct it at his head, Cassidy de-cided on a defensive charge, which he executed without difficulty, clearing the ball to the other side of the ground, where it was intercepted by an old man and kicked back. The next thing Cassidy knew was that Shamus had hit him on the nose, very hard, and that a stream of warm blood was running over his mouth and that his eyes were watering profusely.

"But it's the *game*," Cassidy protested, dabbing his face with his handkerchief. "That's the way it's played for God's sake!"

"You buy your own fucking ball!" Shamus shouted at

him, furious. "And keep your fucking hands off mine. Sodder."

"Here's to no rules," said Helen, back in the Water Closet, quietly observing them over her Talisker.

"Here's to *my* rules," said Shamus, not at all mollified.

"Well I wish you'd tell me what they are," said Cassidy, still smarting.

"It's the book," Helen assured him, as he left. "It's right on the brink. He always gets like this at the end."

"I think you're absolutely *wonderful,*" said Sandra, her eyes bright with excitement as she staunched the wound that same night. "You haven't hurt him *badly* have you?"

"If I have, I have," Cassidy retorted irritably. "If they want their politics rough, that's what they must expect."

Next day Helen and Shamus disappeared.

26

Waiting again.

Visiting Birmingham to discuss the Common Market with the local Liberal Party, Cassidy took Angie Mawdray, ripened by Greek suns, to dinner in Soho.

"You know what I demand of a woman?" he asked her. "A pact to live fully."

"Gosh," said Angie. "How?"

"Never to apologise, never to regret. To drink whatever life provides"—they had had a lot of retsina, Angie's favourite. "To take whatever is offered, never counting the cost."

"Why don't you?" she asked softly.

"I want to *share*," he told Heather Ast at Quaglino's the following night, a Tuesday, returning from Birmingham by way of Hull. "To cherish, to be cherished? *Yes*," he conceded. "But never to . . . live on my second stomach like a cow. A couple of glimpses of the infinite, that's all I ask. Then I'll die happy. You know what the Italians say: one day as a lion is worth a lifetime as a mouse."

"Poor Sandra," said Ast quietly. "She'd never understand."

"It's *virtue*," Cassidy insisted. "The only virtue, the only freedom, the only life. To make *wanting* the justification. For everything."

"Oh Aldo," said Ast, wistfully touching his hand. "It's such a journey, such a *lonely* journey."

"The ordinary hours are not enough," Cassidy declared to Sandra on Wednesday, driving back from a late dinner through empty streets. "I'm sick of enough. I'm sick of making *convention* an excuse for being bored."

"You mean you're bored with *me*," said Sandra.

"Christ *of course* I don't!"

"Don't swear," she said.

"I'm sure he didn't mean it, darling," said her mother from the back. "All men do it."

"What's eating you then, all of a sudden?" Snaps murmured as, ladies first, she went upstairs to bed. "You're like a bloody bitch in heat."

"We're back," said Helen, calling him at work. "Did you miss us?"

"Certainly not," said Cassidy. "I have unlimited substitutes."

"Liar," said Helen and kissed him down the telephone.

Hall was out: that was the occasion. Not sprung, as Shamus would have had it, not swapped for the American Ambassador, but out, honourably liberated with the full co-operation of the Wormwood Scrubs authorities, after remission of sentence for good conduct. His release had coincided almost to the day with the return of Shamus and Helen: valid causes both for celebration.

But surely not at the Savoy?

At the Bag o'Nails, yes. At the Victoria Palace, at one of the drag pubs which Helen liked, across the river in Battersea or Clapham. But not—in Cassidy's book at least —never for such a purpose, his beloved Savoy.

Was it Helen's idea? Cassidy doubted it.

Helen, for all her fearless virtue, had a considerable sense of decorum.

Shamus then? Was it Shamus' idea?

The finger pointed strongly in his direction. Much enlivened by his journey to the country—a tiny *lapse,* Helen said vaguely, he was cracking a bit under the book, best not refer to it—he had come back full of suggestions as to how they should celebrate. His first was a dockside firework display, the biggest London had ever seen, bigger than that of the Great Exhibition; all Cassidy's money should be devoted to it. But Cassidy claimed to remember having seen oil tankers at Egg Wharf, so that plan was dropped in favour of a *egg dancing.* Not an ordinary *dancing,* but a great ballet, written by Shamus to celebrate the virtues of passionate crime. Everyone would have a part, they would take the Albert Hall and forbid entry to Gerrard's Crossers.

To this plan, Helen had the sternest objections. He should finish the centre pages, she said, before he even *thought* of writing anything else. Moreover, he knew no choreography. If Shamus wanted to dance, why didn't they go somewhere where dancing was already available. . . . ? And from there somehow, they agreed on the Savoy.

Therefore it was most likely, but not proven, that Shamus had started the movement, and that Cassidy and Helen, as so often, joined it once it had begun.

The matter settled, it was at once their principal, indeed their only, concern. Whatever reservations Cassidy and Helen might secretly have shared were at once set aside in favour of the excitement of preparation. They planned for it, they lived for it. While naive Shamus put on his beret and settled, naked again, before the open window, the sentimental Supporters' Club took up residence in the kitchen and wrote out menus and place cards.

"Oh Cassidy, what *will* it be like? I'll bet it's absolutely *peachy*. Cassidy, can we have caviar? Say we can? Oh *Cassidy*."

News from Shamus' agent gave them fresh cause to celebrate: he had been offered a lucrative if inglorious contract to visit Lowestoft for three weeks to write a documentary on trawlermen for the Central Office of Information. The Office would pay his expenses and a fee of two hundred pounds. Helen was delighted: sea air was just what Shamus needed.

"And you *will* come and visit us, won't you Cassidy?"

"Of course."

They would leave on the morning following the party, settle in over the weekend; Shamus would start work on the Monday. Shamus called it his *Codpiece* and left the arrangements to Helen.

"But won't it interfere with his novel?" Cassidy asked, very puzzled.

Helen was oddly indifferent.

"Not madly," she said. "Anyway I want to go, and for once he can damn well do something for me."

Which left them with the vital question of what Helen would wear.

"Oh God, I'll borrow something of Mummy's, what does it *matter?*"

"Helen."

"Cassidy, *please* . . ."

So one afternoon, while Shamus was still working, they went back to Fortnum's where, in a sense, they had begun. The choice was absurd, for she gave style to everything she put on.

"Well *you* decide, Cassidy, you're buying it."

"The white one," Cassidy said promptly, "with the low back."

"But Cassidy, it costs a—"

"*Please,*" said Cassidy impatiently.

"That was the one *I* liked," said Helen.

From Piccadilly they went to the Savoy and selected a table for five and ordered a special cake with "Welcome Home Hall" in icing, a fruitcake because Helen said fruitcake would keep, they could take home what they didn't eat. Sitting in the cab again Helen became suddenly very solemn.

"Shamus must never know," she said. "Never in his whole life. Promise, Cassidy?"

"Know what?"

"About this afternoon. About the dress. About all we did, the fun we had, the laughter, and your kindness. Promise."

"But God," he protested, "this is *us,* this is friendship, it could be *you* two, or Shamus and me, or . . ."

"All the same," said Helen; and Cassidy, bowing to her superior knowledge, promised.

"But how will you explain the dress?"

Helen laughed. "God, you don't think he counts things do you?"

"Of course not," Cassidy said, ashamed by his own vulgarity.

27

Suddenly it was Friday, and they were driving in the Bentley to the river entrance.

The night was as warm as Paris; lighted candles waited on the table; the river bank was hung with white jewels palely mirrored in the stiff black water.

"Look Shamus," Cassidy breathed in his ear. "Remember?"

"Meeow," said Shamus.

Nothing in the fulfilment, it is said, matches the excitement of anticipation; yet as Cassidy took his place on Helen's left, in the most effective position, as it happened, to admire the flowers he had sent her that morning, and the scent he had given her the day before, to study with fraternal reverence the long fall of her white neck and the discreet swell of her white breasts; to admire with but a turn of the head the sudden, handsome profile of his beloved Shamus, he was filled again with that unearthly joy, that elusive ecstasy, short-lived though it would always be, which had become since Haverdown the purpose, and the occasional prize, of all his striving. This is the moment, he thought; now it is all here, under one spell, this is what was missing in Paris.

Sal seemed to have come unwillingly. She kept very close to Hall and trembled while she ate. Her choice was pale green, and a silver ring on her little finger. Addressed by any but Hall she seized the ring and turned it for a charm, but it brought her little luck.

"Come on Sal. Aren't you going to drink to Hall?" Cassidy asked in a jocular voice, coping well with the folk backstairs.

Shrugging, she drank to her man; but did not lift her eyes.

But Hall adored her. He sat beside her with a showman's pride, holding his knife and fork like the handlebars of the training cycle, smiling whenever he looked at her. The dinner jacket made no difference to him. Hall was a boxer; he had been a boxer in prison, now he was a boxer in a dinner jacket; only a tiny twinkle in each hooded eye suggested that he was temporarily off duty.

"Doing all right, Hall?"

From one clenched fist, a jointless thumb jerked into the air.

"All right, Lovely," said Hall, and winked.

As to Shamus, the evening had not come a moment too soon. The stresses of tomorrow's departure, of interrupting, if only for a few weeks, his rewrite of the novel, had once more taken a heavy toll of his humour. His manner, though benevolent, was drawn and preoccupied; Hall's release, now it had taken place, was of no further interest to him. Catching Cassidy's eye, he stared at him blankly before lifting his glass.

"Great party, lover," he murmured, with a sudden, loving smile. "Kiss kiss. Bless you lover."

"Bless you," said Cassidy.

He could not help wishing all the same that Shamus had worn a dinner jacket. He had even taken him aside the previous day and offered to buy him one, but Shamus had declined.

"Got to wear the uniform lover," he insisted. "Can't let down the regiment."

Uniform was the deathcoat and a lavishly confected bow tie of found material, a belt, perhaps, from an old black dress of Helen's. He wore it in silence, musket reversed.

To Helen and Cassidy, therefore, fell the burden of conversation; they assumed it nobly. Helen, passing olives and smiling at the ever-attentive waiters, talked brilliantly about the theatre.

"I mean how can it live? How many people *understand* Pinter; how *many?*"

"I don't," said Cassidy boldly. "I go in, I sit down, I wait for the curtain, and all I'm thinking is: God, am I up to this?"

"If only they could be more *explicit*," Helen lamented

—all this to bring in Hall and Sal. "I mean *Shakespeare* reached the masses, why can't *they?* And after all, let's face it, all of us belong to the masses when it comes to art. I mean for something to be any good, it *has* to have universality. So why can't they, well, *be* universal?"

"Take *Moon*," said Cassidy. "*Moon* was universal."

Failing by these subtle excursions to bring in either Shamus or their guests of honour, Helen wisely changed the subject.

"Tell us about your *greatest* fight," she said to Hall, over the smoked salmon. "The one you would like most to be remembered by."

"Well," said Hall, "I don't know."

"Getting Sal's knickers off," Shamus suggested. And to the wine waiter, whose attentions for some time had been annoying him, "Just bring us a bottle each and piss off."

"To Hall and Sal," said Helen quickly, lifting her champagne glass.

"To Hall and Sal," they said.

"Shamus, drink to Sal."

Obediently Shamus emptied his glass. The band was playing something fast to warm the evening up.

"Is he all right?" Cassidy asked, out of Hall's hearing.

"Dale rang," said Helen.

"Oh Christ. Not about the rewrite?"

"It's still not vulgar enough."

"I hate that man," said Cassidy. "I really hate him."

"Dear Cassidy. You're so loyal."

"What about *you* for God's sake?"

Shamus and Sal were dancing. Sal danced very upright, the way people dance on ships, away from him, watching the other people as if to copy them. Shamus' ballroom style, by contrast, was essentially his own. Having gained the centre of the floor, he set to work consolidating his position by means of a series of wide, wolf-like gyrations, while Sal waited patiently for his return.

"He's got this territorial thing," Helen explained. "He longs for land. He bought a field once, down in Dorset. We used to go and walk over it when he was feeling bad."

"What happened to it?"

"I don't know." The question seemed to puzzle her, for

she frowned and looked away. "Still there I suppose."
Cassidy waited, knowing there was more. "It had a cottage on it. We were going to convert it. That's all."

"Helen."

"Yes."

"Will you *use* the chalet? Go there, as my guests? Will
you let me do that?"

Her smile was so weary.

"Listen," he continued, "I'll *lend* him the travel money,
he can pay it back from *Codpiece* when he gets his
cheque . . ."

"It's all *owed*," she said. "It's all spent."

"Helen *please*. It would do you so much good. You'll
just *love* the mountains."

The music had stopped but Sal and Shamus were embracing under the spotlight. Sal neither resisted nor co-
operated. Shamus was kissing the nape of her neck, a
prolonged, explicit kiss which captured the attention of
the band and reminded Cassidy of the search for Mrs.
Oedipus.

"Sal likes a dance," said Hall as they finally returned.

There was no telling, from Hall's expression, whether he
was pleased or not; his face had been folded that way for
years and prison had not made it more responsive.

"So do I," said Cassidy.

The music started again. At once, Helen led him back
to the dance floor.

"Shouldn't I dance with Sal?" he asked.

"She's Hall's," said Helen, not looking at him; and
Cassidy with a small shiver remembered the American
bosun.

"Shamus seems much chirpier anyway," he said, but
for once Helen did not respond to his optimistic tone.

Dancing with Shamus' wife, he danced much better
than he had danced with Shamus in Paris, and suffered
less criticism. He had held her like this at Haverdown
when she had run to him in the woodsmoke; held him
without music; and he remembered how her breasts had
nestled on his shirt front, and how he had felt the nakedness of her through her housecoat.

"You never *really* told me about Paris, did you?" Helen
said. "Why not?"

"I thought I'd leave that to Shamus."

Helen smiled a little sadly. "I knew you'd say that," she

said. "You've *really* learnt the rules, haven't you Cassidy?"

She drew him closer in a mature, sisterly embrace.

"Lover," she said. "That's what he calls you. Let's ring lover. You're so reliable. Such a rock."

Cautiously he made a turn. Cassidy had never danced so well. He knew himself to be a bad dancer; it had not required the admonitions of the angels of Kensal Rise to tell him so; he knew he was tone-deaf and he knew he was heavy on his feet; secretly he also believed that he suffered from a rare pelvic deformation which rendered even the most elementary steps virtually impossible; yet Helen, to his astonishment, gave him the assurance of an expert. He backed, he advanced, he turned, and she neither winced nor cried out, but followed him with a skilled obedience which left him astonished by his own dexterity.

"How can we ever thank you?" she wondered. *"Dear* Cassidy."

"You're the loveliest person in the room," said Cassidy, having made cursory comparisons.

"You know what I wish?" said Helen. "Guess."

Cassidy tried, but failed.

"That we could make you *really* happy. You're so lonely. We look at you sometimes and . . . we know there are things we can never reach. It's just muscle," she said, touching his cheek. "That's all there is that's holding up this smile. . . . Cassidy?"

"Yes."

"How is it with the bosscow?"

"Grey," Cassidy conceded, in a tone which held back more than he was willing to own to.

"That's the worst," said Helen. "Greyness. That's what Shamus has been fighting all his life."

"You too," Cassidy reminded her.

"Have I?" She smiled as if her own condition were more of a memory than a present fact. "Shamus says you're frightened of her."

"Balls," said Cassidy sharply.

"That's what I told him. Cassidy, did Shamus . . ." They made another turn, this time under Helen's guidance, but she guided so gently so unobtrusively, so unlike Sandra, that Cassidy did not mind a bit. "Did Shamus," she began again, "have a *lot* of girls in Paris?"

"God, *Helen . . .*"

Again she smiled, pleased no doubt to encounter the firm borders of the two men's friendship. "Dear Cassidy," she repeated, holding him far away but keeping her gloved hands on the thickest part of his arms. "You needn't answer. I just hope they made him happy, that's all." She returned to him, laying her cheek against his shirt front. "Isn't Hall super?" she asked, dreamily, and looked past him towards the table.

"Super," Cassidy agreed.

But Hall was nowhere to be seen. Shamus was sitting alone among the bottles. He was leaning right back in Cassidy's chair, smoking a cigar, and the black beret was pulled down over his eyes, embracing his ears and nose, so that he must have been in total darkness. His feet were on the table and the cigar smoke poured out of him as if he were on fire.

"I think we'd better go back," said Cassidy.

"Hi," said Cassidy.

"Who is it?" said Shamus.

"It's your lover," said Helen, coaxingly.

"Come in," said Shamus, lifting the beret. "Nice dance?"

"Great. Where have they gone?"

"Pee-break," said Shamus vaguely.

"*You* dance with her," said Cassidy.

"Thanks," said Shamus. "Thanks very much." And lowered the beret again.

They waited for some time to see whether he would come out, but he didn't, so they danced again just to be convivial.

"It's a very long pee," said Cassidy doubtfully, wondering whether he ought to go and look for them. "You don't think they've . . ."

"They've what?"

"Well it is a *bit* of a strain for them. . . ."

"Nonsense," said Helen, "they're adoring every moment," and squeezed his hand. "And even if they aren't . . ."

Something quite hard had entered her face. In Sandra it would have been anger, but Helen was above anger. In

Sandra it would have been determination, a sudden wish to assert herself against an oppressive, though apathetic, world; but Helen, he knew, was at peace with the world.

He was about to investigate this unexpected change of mood—an outburst, almost, in relation to the bright contentment which had preceded it—when the music stopped in the middle of the tune and they heard Shamus screaming.

Looking round for him, Cassidy found himself standing beside the Niesthals. The old lady was hung in black, a mantilla perhaps. She held her husband's arm and they both craned their heads to see where the noise came from; and they wore, both of them, the sad, expert expression of people who had heard a lot of screaming in their time.

"Look," said Mrs. Niesthal, noticing Cassidy. "It is Aldo who has the musical wife."

"Hullo," said Cassidy.

"My God that poor fellow," said the old man, meaning Shamus.

He was standing on a table at the far end of the room, not their own table but someone else's; his jacket was flung aside. He was wearing a piece of red cloth over his short-sleeved tennis shirt, a cummerbund slung shoulder to waist like a military bandolier, and he was doing a sword dance among the knives and forks, not missing them.

"Oh Jesus," said Helen, frightened.

The tablecloth was screwed round one foot and he looked as though he would fall any minute. His face was scarlet and he was clapping his hands over his head. By the time Cassidy reached him, several waiters were converging and neither Hall nor Sal had reappeared.

"Shamus!" Cassidy called, upwards from the table's edge. "Hey, lover!"

Shamus stopped dancing. His eyes had that hopeless wildness that Cassidy remembered from Lipp's.

"Let *me* have a go," Cassidy said.

"What's that?" said Shamus.

Now everyone was watching Cassidy, and somehow they knew that Cassidy held the key. Even the waiters were looking at him with respect.

"I want to do a sword dance," Cassidy said.

"You can't do a fucking sword dance," Shamus replied, shaking his head. "You'll fall off the fucking table."

"I want to try."

With a sudden lovely smile, Shamus leaned forward and flung his arms round Cassidy's neck.

"Then try. Oh Jesus, try. Beg you, lover, beg you."

"You don't have to beg," said Cassidy, heaving him gently off the table. Someone came forward, old Niesthal, familiar with catastrophe; someone else was passing the deathcoat to Helen.

"Get your things together," Cassidy whispered to Helen. "We'll meet you at the door."

Once again, he was aware of Shamus' great physical strength. Half carrying him, half embracing, he led him to the lobby.

"I want a whore," said Shamus.

"Good idea," said Cassidy. And to Helen, "Take his head."

The pale assistant manager helped them to the lift. The fourteenth floor, he said; a chance vacancy. Cassidy knew him well and had once offered him the chalet. He was a tender, patient man who had learnt that certain of the rich are very humble in their needs.

"Would you like a doctor?" he asked, unlocking a door.

"He doesn't believe in them," Helen whispered, reminding him.

"No thank you," Cassidy replied. "I don't either," he added, thinking of John Elderman and not knowing why.

"You lying bugger," Shamus whispered. "You never will do that dance."

The suite was on the river side; the bowl of fruit included peaches and black grapes, but there was no card for *Monsieur et Madame;* there were telephones in the bathroom. He would not be put to bed so they laid him on the sofa, undressing him together, Shamus their common child. In the bedroom, Cassidy found an eiderdown and put it over the shaking body. Emptying out the fruit, he set the bowl on the floor in case Shamus wanted to be sick. Helen crouched in a chair watching him.

"I'm cold," she said.

So he found a blanket for her as well and put it over her shoulders. She had hunched herself together as if she had a stomach pain. From the bathroom he fetched a damp towel and wiped down Shamus' face, then held his hand.

"Where's Helen?"

"Here."

"Christ," he whispered. "Oh Christ."

The telephone rang; it was Niesthal. He had found a doctor, a damn good friend, an old fellow no longer in practice, completely discreet, look here, should they come up?

"It's very kind," said Cassidy. "But he's all right now." *I'm in Bristol,* he thought of saying, but he hadn't the nerve. Ring him in the morning, give him lunch perhaps.

"Can you get me a drink?" said Helen, still not moving.

Cassidy ordered two Scotches, yes, large ones thank you. For some reason he thought it prudent to include Shamus and rang back. Make it three.

"Have you got five shillings?" he asked Helen.

"No."

He gave the waiter a pound and saw him out.

"Water?"

"No."

"Ice?"

"No."

They sipped the whisky watching Shamus. He lay just as they had put him, one bare arm across the saffron coverlet, head turned out to them, eyes closed.

"He's asleep," said Cassidy.

Helen said nothing, just drank her whisky in small sips, nodding into the glass like a bird. She was very groomed still; more ready to go out, one would have thought, than to come home.

Cassidy switched off the overhead light. With the darkness came silence. Shamus lay so still, so young to die; only his chest moved, keeping pace with his short, fast breathing.

"He was like this in Paris, wasn't he?" said Helen.

"Sometimes."

"No wonder he loves you," she observed dully. "It used to be fun. Making hell, he called it. Not raising it, *making* it. You *make* heaven. You make hell. Make them in the same place sometimes. At the same time. As long as you make *something*. Just for a moment I wished he'd not make anything for a while. I must be getting middle-aged."

"If he didn't make hell he wouldn't make books," said Cassidy loyally.

"Other people manage," said Helen.

"Yes but look at what they write."

"You don't *know* what they write, Cassidy. You don't read, nor do I. For all you and I know there are *hundreds* of writers all with wives and two veg, churning out super books on lemon juice. For all *we* know."

"Come on," said Cassidy gently. "You don't think that really."

From the river a solitary barge sounded its horn.

"Well," said Helen, "he's got his blasted water again," and they both laughed in relief.

"Why?" she said suddenly.

"Why what?"

"Why did it hoot? It's not foggy. Why does one barge hoot at half past eleven on a fine summer night?"

"I don't know," said Cassidy.

Taking her drink with her she walked to the window and gazed out, her naked shoulders sheer and black against the London night.

"Can't even see it. Christ." She continued gazing. "Air's no good. Air's too soft for him, you know that don't you? Not enough impact."

"Like the New Testament," said Cassidy.

"Exactly like the New Testament. Masochistic, guilt-ridden, and . . ."

"And ghostwritten," said Cassidy, completing Shamus' dictum for her.

"There's a hero of his who went round bathing in fountains. Has he told you about him?"

"Can't remember," said Cassidy.

"A German poet. Spink or Krump or somebody. *The impact confirms the shape,* that's what he said, or Shamus did, I don't know who. Do you think he makes those people up?"

"It doesn't really matter, does it. He told me once he made *me* up."

"It hooted again," said Helen accusingly.

"Perhaps it was an owl," Cassidy suggested.

"Or a nightingale," said Helen, ready as ever with an erudite reference.

"Krump," said Cassidy, calling her back from reverie. "You were talking about Krump."

"The impact confirms the shape. That's why we have to collide all the time. To confirm our shape. To *feel* our outer edges." She drank. "Trouble with *that* is, if you have too much impact, you lose your shape altogether. Bash it to bits. Till there's nothing left to confirm."

"That won't happen to him," said Cassidy sternly. "Not while we're around."

"No," Helen agreed, after long reflection. "No. It mustn't must it? I wish you could sing. I'd like to do that with you. Sing with lover."

"Well I can't," said Cassidy.

Like a swimmer she lifted her arms to shoulder level, first forward, then sideways, then raised herself on her toes, as if preparing to dive out of the window.

"Funny to think of them dancing down there," she said. "To sleep while other people dance. That's not the way we used to be, me and Shamus."

Without warning, her voice changed. "Cassidy, why am I miserable?"

"Reaction," Cassidy suggested. "Shock."

"Because I'm *bloody* miserable. I'm a miserable, maudlin, middle-aged cow."

She puffed, then sniffed her breath, testing it for alcohol.

"Miserable, maudlin, middle-aged, and pissed," she confirmed. *"God* what a fool!"

"Helen—"

She was speaking too loud, loud enough to wake him in fact.

"Here I am sitting in the peachy Savoy Hotel in a peachy white dress and what am I doing?"

"Helen," Cassidy admonished, but too late; she was already taking off her shoes.

"All because my *bloody* husband blows a gasket. Dance with me."

"Helen please, we'll wake him up—"

Her arms were already round him, seeking his hand, guiding his shoulder. Lightly, tentatively, their eyes still on the prone figure of their sleeping prophet, the two disciples followed the far drumbeat of the band. The carpet was very deep and made no sound.

"Oh Cassidy," she murmured, "what a *fool* I nearly was."

Her cheek was against his, her hair was in his eyes, and all down the length of him her body swayed and trembled like his own.

"After all," she remarked, "it's what *he* would want if he was awake."

Somehow, it was not at all clear how—a common will conveyed them, neither lover steered—somehow they were in the bedroom. The connecting door was probably open: Cassidy had his eyes closed, he could not tell; and waking, as it were, and finding the angel Helen in his arms and the ominously large bed behind her (robbed of its saffron eiderdown) he saw that her eyes also were closed. Fate, therefore, must be held responsible: there was no human author.

"Wafted," Helen announced. "Is that you Cassidy?" And to confirm the identification, held her hand over his face like a muzzle.

"Bark," she said.

"I can't," said Cassidy.

Settling more comfortably into his arms, she affectionately possessed herself of his ears and fondled them between her forefinger and thumb.

"*Dear* Cassidy. How soft your fur is. Kiss me."

"No," said Cassidy.

"Seduce me."

"No," said Cassidy. "Absolutely not," and closed his eyes again.

The kiss seemed to approach from a long way off. It began far up river among the black steel forests of East India Dock, tipped the taut spanned bridges of the Embankment, skimmed the tide's smooth surface as it glowed ever larger, brighter, and more bold; until, part heat, part liquid, part light, it scaled the fourteen rigid storeys of the Savoy and found its final resting place in the inflamed interiors of Aldo Cassidy and his best friend's wife.

"Cassidy," Helen said severely, "unhand me," and putting him aside, addressed herself to the domestic task of making the bed respectable while Cassidy went to the bathroom in case he had caught her lipstick.

"I do wish I was a whore," she remarked, slapping the pillows into shape. "I'd be a damn sight better at it than Sal, I'll bet. Why *can't* I be a whore? I *like* this hotel, Cassidy. I like the food, I like the drink, and I like the people. *Very* much. I've got a *super* body too. Sturdy, workman-like, resilient. So why can't I?"

"Because you love him," said Cassidy.

"Doesn't stop *him*, does it? He fucks around. *He* seduces people, *he* goes screwing all over Europe. So why can't I?"

"I'll go and see how he is," said Cassidy. "Then perhaps we can go home."

He was in the bedroom again, but strictly in transit, making for the drawing room and safety, when Helen to his alarm suddenly sprang into the air and landed on all fours on the bed.

"Fuck him," she declared in exasperation, pulling her hair down over her eyes. "I Helen *fuck* myself of Shamus. Fuck, fuck, *fuck*. He's a reactionary, don't you realise? A drooling old Victorian fuddy-duddy. One law for him, another for us. Hogswallop. Shamus has *conned* us, Cassidy. Shamus has pulled off the biggest bloody load of hokum since . . . whoever pulled off the last load of hokum. Shamus *hates* convention. That's the message. But we mustn't. Oh no. *We've* got to love it. I'm hungry," she added, straightening her hair. "He ruined our dinner too. *Our* dinner, Cassidy, and he just stepped on it."

"Shamus," Cassidy breathed urgently, on his knees before the body. "Wake up. Please wake up." And shook him, out of her hearing, quite hard.

"The scales," Helen announced from the bedroom, "have fallen from my eyes. A revolution of one, that's me. His freedom for my freedom and fuck the consequences."

"*Shamus*," Cassidy insisted. "For Christ's sake. We need you."

But Shamus refused to wake. He was lying on his stomach, dead to the world. The coverlet had fallen to the floor and his naked back was slippery with sweat.

"Cassidy," Helen called. "Is it true? Do wicked ladies *really* have it off with waiters in hotels? Just lie prone when their Horlicks arrives, exposing their irresistible charms through diaphanous nightshirts?"

"Give me a towel," said Cassidy. "And shut up. *Lover, listen, we've got to go.*"

A damp towel flopped at his feet.

"Listen, I did things for you . . . all sorts of things. I dragged you out of the gutter didn't I? Stripped you, bought you suits, fed you, cleared up your sick . . . I believe in you. I really do. More than anyone in the world. Well, I try, anyway. Shamus, you *owe* me . . . wake up!"

"Bold," said Helen, still in the bedroom. "That's what you were tonight. Bold, bloody, and resolute. *Doughty* Cassidy. You had *grip*. I admire grip in a man. *Good* evening," she continued into the telephone. "This is suite fourteen thirty-eight. Is there *any* chance of getting a little something to eat, a snack of some sort? Two fillet steaks, a bottle of . . ." It ran on, enough to hold out for a week.

"Don't order for me," Cassidy called. "I don't want anything. *Shamus.*" Turning him over, he laid the cold towel over his face, pressing it quite roughly against his brow, his cheeks.

"You haven't any *crackers,* have you?" Helen was enquiring. "Not to eat, to pull . . ."

He heard the shuffle of her dress as she settled more comfortably on the bed.

"Are you brown, Cassidy? I always think of you as golden. Just a neat white bottom and the rest all gold." More rustles from the bed. "I'm in a sledge," she explained. "Wrapped in bearskins. *Swish, swish.* With Siberian wolves all round." A wolf howl: "Ow-oo-oo. That's a good life out there, Cassidy."

"Yes," said Cassidy, who treasured a similar fantasy.

"*You'd* protect me, wouldn't you, Cassidy? One look at you and a wolf would . . ." She lost the thread. "*Wolf-*

wood," she repeated. "Sounds like a railway station. Cassidy, which would you rather be: raped by Cossacks or torn to pieces by wolves?"

"Neither," said Cassidy.

"Me too," Helen agreed amiably. "You know gorillas rape. I wouldn't like that. Cassidy."

"Yes."

"Have you got a hairy chest? Hair's virile isn't it?"

"Supposed to be."

"You know quite little boys get erections. Even babies, it's amazing. Cassidy."

"Yes."

"I feel very *naive*. Do you?" Silence. "Or just sentimental?"

"Hullo lover," said Shamus, opening his eyes.

Seizing him by the shoulders, Cassidy set to work, patting his cheeks, sitting him upright, trying to remember what boxers' seconds did to get their champions back into the ring.

"Shamus listen, listen to me. Shamus, she's planning murder, take her away, you've *got* to . . ."

"Where's Hall?" said Shamus.

"He disappeared. Hey, let's go and find him, how about that? Go down to Cable Street, how about that? Get pissed, have a fight or two, really hit the moon for once, why not? Cable Street! That's a real place down there, not like this, all hygienic and clean—"

"Why didn't he hit me?"

"Why should he? He loves you. He's your friend, like me. You don't hit friends, you hit enemies."

"She told him," Shamus related, with sudden clarity of recall. "Sat there and told him straight out. 'Hall, Shamus has offered me five quid to have it off with him and I want to go home.' He just looked at me. Why did he do that, lover? Christ he could have killed me with one hand. Look what he did to that bosun, that fellow was maimed for life. What's wrong with me? I mean a *boxer!* If a boxer won't hit me, who the fuck will?"

Receiving no answer, but seeing perhaps Cassidy's face, fresh and nicely polished by the soap, he swung his fist at it and missed.

"Jesus!" he shouted. "Won't *anybody* hit me?" And fell back, square on to the pillow, where he closed his eyes in pain.

"Cassidy," Helen called.

"Yes."

"Didn't you hear me?"

"I don't know. No."

"I've stopped being a whore now."

"Good."

Shamus frowned. "That sounded like Helen," he said.

"It was. She's having a bath."

Listening, Cassidy heard the rustle of clear water running on the moon and casual dance music issuing from a space-born radio, school of Frank Sinatra.

"Well what the fuck is Helen doing in Paristown?" Shamus demanded testily.

"It's not Paris. It's London."

Which is the trouble really, Cassidy reflected. In Paris it would all have been tolerable, somehow. In London, I'm afraid it's not; not really.

The sound of water stopped.

"Cassidy," Helen called again.

"Yes."

"Just Cassidy," she said, with the deep content of someone lying naked in a warm bath. "It's just a pretty name, that's all. Cassidy. I like saying it, you see. Because it's a pretty name."

"Fine," said Cassidy.

"Lot of woman there, boy," said Shamus, and rolling over, fell asleep.

"Cassidy," Helen was saying. "Cassidy. Cassidy. Cassidy?"

At Sherborne, Shamus, we called it bullying.

We may not have had a very high opinion of *ourselves*—that would have been hubris and not at all to be encouraged—but we did, I think, respect one another. The nicer of us did anyway. That, it seems to me, Shamus, is the definition of a reasonable man. He doesn't mind what you do to him, but he minds what you do to other people. Sorry I'm not being clearer, but I'll get there slowly, I'm a bit of a plodder in some ways; not a flyer like you, I'm afraid, Shamus.

Sit down, will you?

There are a few things I have to explain to you, seeing you are new here and not quite our class. A *bully* is someone who picks on those who are weaker than himself. Not physically weaker necessarily; spiritually too. Emotionally also, perhaps. A *bully* performs acts of brutality against those who cannot retaliate. Our code does not like bullies. The regimental flags in the Abbey, for instance, were not scarred by unfair battles, our forebears did not march on undefended cities for their conquests. Well they may have done, but not often. Well, they wouldn't *now*.

So I'm afraid, Shamus, we do not approve. Sal may be a slut. Conceded. But Hall was your friend. He loved you and he loved Sal, and that's why he didn't hit you.

Perhaps he even loved Helen too, in a pure way.

"Cassidy," said Helen. She was trying different pronunciations. *"Cassidee,"* she said, in unconscious imitation of Elise. "Cassidy," she growled in a deep, Sinatra drawl. *"You are a* MOLE, *you live in a* HOLE. How's the patient?"

"Bearing up," said Cassidy.

"Will he live?"

"Maybe."

Hall you see, Shamus, was here in double trust. You've read *Macbeth*, haven't you. A prescribed work for O-Level English? Hall was your kinsman and your subject, or whatever it says. You appointed him to the Few, even if he wasn't really a playing member; even if the Few are by nature self-appointed. You gave him his wings and then you shot him down. Which makes you rather low and small, don't you think?

That is why you deserve to be beaten, I'm afraid; that is why, in a minute, you will be asked to lower your handsome black head into the third washbasin from the left, hold the taps firmly, and offer a passive target to myself and my under-prefects. Do you understand? Is there anything you would like to say in mitigation?

Because actually, at this precise moment in time I am very anxious to hate you.

Yes lover, said Shamus, but not aloud. Of course I've got something to say. Bags in fact. Ready? Pen poised?

Shamus, the great guru, speaks:

Never regret, never apologise. That's the upper classes.

Let's be Old Testament, lover; Old Testament's for the upper classes, New Testament's for compromisers.

To live without heed to the consequences; to give everything for today and not a damn for tomorrow: that's the upper classes.

One day as a lion is worth a lifetime as a mouse: that's the upper classes.

Never regret, never apologise.

Got to find a new innocence, lover, old one's worn out.

Those who love the world take it; those who are afraid make rules.

All relationships have to be pursued to their end. That's where the Blue Flower grows.

Immoralism, lover, is a necessary precondition for the creation of new values. . . . When I fucks, I revolts. . . . When I sleeps, I acquiesces.

Don't hold with motives, lover, never did. Act first, find the reason afterwards, that's my advice.

Acts are truth, lover. Garbage, the rest is. Horseshit.

And finally, lover, you're the biggest fucking liar in the business, you treat your wife with pig-like indifference, and you're in no position to beat anybody, see my portrait of you after Haverdown. Good morning.

"I'm not *brown*," said Helen from the bathroom. "I'm *white*."

"I know," said Cassidy, still at Shamus' side. "I saw you at Haverdown. I always wondered how you heated the water."

"Kettles," Helen explained. "We got the bath ready, but by the time we'd made love it was cold again. So we had to heat it up. That's why the fire was still going when you arrived."

"I see."

"There's an explanation for everything if you look for it."

Seizing his hand, Cassidy put his lips close to Shamus'
ear.

"*Shamus*. Lover, wake up!"

Shamus you are a terrible shit but you are our priest
and if you're not careful you'll marry us.

Shamus, I love you and you love me, I can see it in
you even when you're hating me, you long for me. Alive
or dead, Shamus, naked or in your deathcoat, screwing
in the green brothel or carrying candles in the Sacré
Coeur, you are our genius, our father, our creator. Therefore, if you love me, wake up and release me from this
improbable situation.

"Shamus. Wake up!"

I am not like you, Shamus, I am not emotional, I am
not drastic. I am an hotelier's son. I'm not anything more
than that. I am rational and I like things as they are as
long as they favour my situation. I'm a lover not of people
but of compromise and orthodoxy. You might very well
call me the archetypal victim of Fly. I'm a Jaguar driver,
a Gerrard's Crosser, a doctor, and quite frequently a
bishop in drag. I hold very much with the past, and if
I knew where I came from I would return there like a
shot. Also, you are right, I am a mother-fucker.

Now Shamus, having proved all that to me, proved it
quite conclusively, will you kindly wake up and get me out
of this!

"Cassidy? *Ici parle* Helen. *Bonjour.*"

"*Bonjour*," said Cassidy politely.

He shouldn't have poured water over me at Lipp's.

He shouldn't have hit me at football.

*He shouldn't have propositioned Sal just because he
needed a collision.*

"Forgive lover. Forgive. Please forgive."

Without opening his eyes, Shamus drew Cassidy's hand
into the bed and held it against his hot cheek.

"There's nothing to forgive," Cassidy whispered. "It's
fine. Listen, how about some more formaldehyde?"

Rising, he was about to switch on the overhead light
when Shamus spoke again, in quite a strong voice.

"Lots, lover. Lots to forgive."

"What, then?"

"Lent the Bentley to Hall. He was pissed, you see. Anyway, couldn't have him going home in a cab, could I? Got to travel in style. Not angry, lover?"

"Why should I be?"

"Not hit me?"

"Go to sleep," said Cassidy.

"Je m'appelle Hélène," Helen announced still from the bathroom. She had recently started French lessons at an academy in Chester Street.

"Hélène est mon nom. Hurrah *pour Hélène. Hélène est beau. Belle.* Fuck. Beau-belles, bow-bells, bow-bells, bow-bells!"

He sat in the dark. He had put out the lamp by the sofa so that the only light came from the bedroom and, indirectly, through the open bathroom door.

"Cassidy, I know you're listening."

Lucky I bought the place then, really. Now that I've got to live in it. The basic essentials of life, Old Hugo said. Food drink and now this. Lucky the market was looking the other way.

"Did you have lots of girls in Paris?" Helen asked, over the gentle splashing of water.

"No."

"Not even one or two?"

"No."

"Why not?"

"I don't know."

"I would if I were a man. I'd have all of us, bang bang bang. We're so *beautiful.* I wouldn't ask, I wouldn't apologise, I wouldn't care. To the victor the spoils. Fuck!" —she must have banged against something. "Why do they put the door handle on the door?"

"Carelessness," said Cassidy.

"I mean take Sal. Moronic. Totally. So why *not* be a whore? It's fun, it's profitable. I mean it's nice to do *one* thing well, don't you think? Cassidy."

She was getting out, one leg, two legs; he could hear the rubbing of the towel.

"Yes."

"What do you want most in the world?" she asked.

You maybe, thought Cassidy; maybe not.

"You," he said.

There was a knock at the door. The floor waiter wheeled in the trolley. A middle-aged man of great courtesy.

"In here, sir?" he asked, ignoring the figure on the sofa. "Or next door?"

"In here, if you would."

He set it parallel to Shamus, a hospital trolley waiting for the surgeon. Signing the bill Cassidy gave him a five-pound note.

"That's all right. That covers everything else we may need. For tips I mean."

The waiter seemed unhappy.

"I have *got* change, sir."

"All right, well give me three pounds." Transaction. "They still dancing down there?"

"Oh yes, sir."

"What time do you get off?"

"Seven o'clock, sir. I'm the night waiter, sir."

"Tough on your wife then," said Cassidy.

"She gets used to it, sir."

"Any kids?"

"One daughter, sir."

"What's she doing?"

"She's up at Oxford."

"That's fine. That's great. I was there myself. Which College?"

"At Somerville, sir. She's reading zoology."

For a moment Cassidy was on the brink of asking him to stay; to sit down with him at a long ritual dinner, to share the wine with him and eat the steak, and gossip with him about their different families and the intricacies of the hotel trade. He wanted to tell him about Hugo's leg and Mark's music, and hear his views on cantilevered extensions. He wanted to ask him about *Old* Hugo and Blue; whether he'd heard rumours, was Old Hugo still a name?

"Shall I draw the cork, sir? Or will you be doing it yourself?"

"You haven't got a toothbrush, have you, Cassidy?" Helen

called from the bathroom. "You'd think they'd provide them, wouldn't you, for people like us?"

"Just leave the corkscrew here," said Cassidy, and once more opened the door for him.

"The head porter will have a toothbrush, sir; I can send you one up if you wish."

"It's all right," said Cassidy. "Don't bother."

World population's going up seventy million lover. Lot of people to tip, lover; lot of people to tip.

"Is yours tough?" asked Helen.

"No it's fine. How's yours?"

"Fine."

They sat on opposite sides of the bed, eating steak, Helen in a bath towel and Cassidy in his dinner jacket. The towel was very long, pale green, with a rich woolly nap. She had combed out her hair. It lay in smooth auburn tresses down her bare white back. She looked very child-ish without her make-up; her skin had that luminous inno-cence which in certain women comes with the experience of recent nakedness. She smelt of soap, a nutty masculine soap, the kind that Sandra liked to put in his Christmas stocking; and she sat just as she had sat at Haverdown, on the Chesterfield in the morning twilight.

"By *want*," she said, "do you mean *love?*"

"I don't know," said Cassidy. "It was your question, not mine."

"What are the *symptoms?*" Helen pursued, being help-ful. "Apart from lust which, while we know it's lovely, doesn't really last the whole drink through, does it?"

Cassidy poured more wine.

"Is that claret?" she asked. "Or Burgundy?"

"Burgundy. You can tell by the shape. Square shoulders are claret, rounded are Burgundy. You're all I want. You're witty and beautiful and understanding . . . and you like men best."

"You mean we have that in common?" Helen enquired.

He wished very much that he had Shamus there to say it all again. Helen is our virtue; that part he remembered, that part he believed: Helen will go where her heart is, she knows no other truth. Helen is our territory; Helen is . . . Also there was a formula. Shamus had drawn it for him on the wallpaper, at a drinking in Pimlico the same night he told him about the Steppenwolf, who from the spaces of his wolfish solitude loved the security of the little bourgeois life. The formula had a fraction; why could he not remember it, Aldo Cassidy the inventor of gadgets, fastenings, and couplings? *Cassidy divided by Shamus equals Helen.* Or was it the other way round? *Helen over Cassidy equals Shamus.* Try again. *Cassidy over Helen . . .*

Somewhere in Shamus' law of human dynamics, his love for her was inevitable. But where?

"Cassidy, you still love Shamus too, don't you? I'm only trying to *diagnose* you see. Not prescribe."

"Yes. I love him, too."

"You haven't ratted?"

"No."

"Which means," she remarked contentedly, "we *both* love him. That's *excellent*. We *must* get marks for that. You see, Cassidy, I've never had a lover apart from Shamus. Nor have you, have you?"

"No."

"So I think a certain *amount* of forethought is advisable. Is that coffee?"

He poured it for her, adding cream but no sugar. He poured the cream Sandra's way, spoon upside down over the surface to prevent it from penetrating too far.

"Do you think a fair test would be: what we would give up?" Helen suggested. "Would I give up Shamus, for instance? Would you give up the bosscow and the two veg? You see, Cassidy, we are talking about ruin as well as love."

Cassidy was suddenly, if cautiously, conscious of a deep protective urge. A child might as well have talked about the world economy just then, as Helen about ruin; for she imposed a peace on him that was like a rest of arms after a long war. He perceived in her a potential honesty of companionship which till now, in all his isolated wandering, in all his attempts to live for himself, had seemed impossible. The laughter he had shared with Shamus was not gone; but in Helen he could possess it, trust it, rid it of its violence. She was smiling at him, and he knew he was smiling in return. Looking at her he knew also that it was the past that was a ruin, not the future: and he saw the empty autumn cities, the tarred warehouses, the bare road before the hood of his car, and he knew them only as the places where he had searched in vain for Helen.

"I love you," said Cassidy.

"Excellent," said Helen briskly. "I feel exactly the same."

The trolley squeaked as she pushed it. Fastening the towel more securely round her, she guided the tricky wheels skillfully through the open doorway to the drawing room.

Sitting alone on the bed, waiting for her return, Cassidy was victim to many conflicting moods. Mainly, however, they ran in the direction of terror.

First, Old Hugo addressed his Divine Employer.

Good morning Lord, he said cheerfully from the pine pulpit somewhere in England, his enormous hands folded in athletic piety. *How are you? This is Hugo Cassidy and his flock reporting from the Zion Tabernacle of East Grinstead, Sussex, offering up the prayers of our hearts this lovely Friday midnight. Look down in your goodness on young Aldo here will You, Lord? He is very much confused between sin and virtue just at the moment. My view, for what it is worth, Lord, is that he has put his hand into a snake's nest, but only Thou, oh Lord, in Thy wisdom can give a final ruling on this one; and so be it.*

There was still time. If he played his cards right, stalled a little, pleaded a small illness perhaps, such as a headache or a gastric disorder, he might very well get out of this yet. Some tricky talk perhaps to begin with—well he was good at that—some friendly kissing and making up and then get dressed, shake hands, and laugh about it later as a silly mistake they both nearly made.

Never regret, never explain, never apologise. . . .

Would she return? A sudden hope gave him solace. She's bolted. She looked at him, got the guilts, and decided to run . . .

In a towel?

Logic is my enemy, thought Cassidy; I should never have taken a degree.

He heard the door close softly and the latch slide; he heard her go back to the bathroom and he knew she was hanging up the towel because she was tidy. Suddenly, seized by panic, he imagined the total failure. He saw another Cassidy twisting, humping, recoiling, wrestling with his unrisen manhood; he heard Shamus' laughter ringing through the wall, and Helen's, Sandra's muffled grunt of irritation at his inadequacy.

The big decisions are taken for us; I have no part in this. I swim, I cannot affect the stream.

The bathroom light had gone out; Helen had put out the bathroom light. He saw the pale rectangle die on the wall before him. Economy; Jesus, does she think I pay the electricity here? I didn't really buy the place, you know.

Er, Sandra, Helen, whatever your name is, there's something you ought to know, I'm afraid: I have absolutely no expertise. If you think I can do anything for you that Shamus can't do, well (as Sandra would say) I can't finish the sentence. I don't know how you're made: that's the truth of it; none of you. I have absolutely no picture of how you're made or what gives you satisfaction. May I be absolutely specific here?

She was in bed. Cassidy had not moved, had not looked; he was preparing a speech for the Annual General Meeting:

"Now many of you have come here with the highest expectations. I know that. Many years ago I myself had similar expectations of the same act. There are certain things however that you should know, and to save you unnecessary time and trouble I will be very frank. As a lover, your Chairman is a *non-starter*. Sorry but there it is. His sexual encounters with his wife have always been essentially of the formal kind, confined to what is known within the trade as the English missionary position. Many of them, so to speak, never got off the drawing board. Your Chairman is aware that there is a distance to descend and a point at which to enter. And also, that any attempt above or below that point gives rise to discomfort and criticism. Practice has done nothing to enrich his knowledge; indeed you should know that after fifteen years of sporadic congress your Chairman can still cause Mrs. Cassidy quite unreasonable pain by entering a wrong channel, so that she has been known, not infrequently, to cry out in indignation, rearrange herself with unfriendly care; and thereafter to make no sound, but to accept your Chairman's gaucherie as the lot of every woman married into the trade."

Break. The intimate tone.

"Now I am perfectly conscious of these deficiencies. In my time I have read books, studied photographs, doodled on telephone pads, attended, during national service, army lectures; I have even, in rare moments of mutual frankness with Mrs. Cassidy, delved surreptitiously with my fingers among the perplexing folds. Yet the terrain persistently eludes me. In my imagination, it has the whorls and curlicues of a fingerprint: no two examples, the brochure reads, are ever wholly identical. I am perfectly conscious, here, of a cross fire of psychological interpretations—Dr. John Elderman, our medical consultant, will happily give you a handbook on the subject—and I have fought hard *over the years,* together with your other Directors, for a clearer orientation. In vain. Now you may very well feel that a *younger* man, less—I believe the fashionable word is inhibited is it not, Mr. Meale?—less *inhibited* might serve you better. If so, well, let me assure you that you will have the *fullest* and the most *wholehearted* co-operation of the entire Board, and no bad feelings shall be allowed to interfere with a *healthy,* a *satisfactory . . ."*

Still standing before an attentive if absent audience—a rug's width, in fact, from the edge of the double bed—he felt her gaze on him, and heard the silence of her contemplation.

"You're not very good at it, are you, Cassidy?" said Helen quietly.

"No."

"Well we're just going to have to put a lot of work in, aren't we?"

"Yes, I suppose we are."

"You can't do it in a dinner jacket," she said.

He undressed.

"Now what you do next is: you kiss me."

He kissed her, leaning across her, so that their lips met at a right angle.

"I'm afraid you'll have to get nearer," she said. And as if it were an inspiration: "Hey, how about getting into bed with me?"

He got into the bed.

"It's called foreplay," she explained. "Then there's consummation—" rather in the tone with which she had ordered dinner "—and then there's afterglow."

Swedish.

Just a Swedish episode. She probably doesn't even realise she's naked, a lot of people don't make anything of nudity at all these days, hardly know whether they're dressed or not. That was one of the things he liked about the films at the Cinephone, actually; you could look at them in their *wild state*. Might drop in there tomorrow, actually; see what they had running. Actually.

Tentatively, still listening for sounds from next door, he made the first reconnaissance. Her skin, he noticed, had a curiously flaccid texture, a cloying liquidity to the touch which he suddenly found unappealing. Her breasts particularly, which in repose largely assumed the requisite shape—and clothed were most distinguished—yielded too easily to his hand, betraying the hard bone underneath. Also, she was too white, with a whiteness that was not luminous so much as vegetable, moreover a vegetable grown underground, and entirely contrary to his appetites. Momentarily revolted by a body so shadowless and obscenely, whitely naked, he moved away from her and busied himself with the bedside light while he tried to think of something to say.

"You're not putting it *out*, are you?" Helen asked

crisply in the same tone which had earlier reminded him of Sandra.

"Of course not."

It's her purity, he told himself; this is what you feel when you sleep with a total woman.

"You're *thinking* aren't you?" Helen said sympathetically.

"Yes."

"What about?"

"Love, life . . . *us,* I suppose," Cassidy replied cautiously and lowered his head on to the pillow with a half-concealed sigh. "Shamus," he added, in a despairing appeal to her conscience.

"Would you feel better if you hated him?" she asked.

"Well it would be more Old Testament, wouldn't it?"

"That's what *he* thinks. What do you think?"

"Well . . . no."

"You haven't got the *guilts* have you, Cassidy? Because he's your lover and my husband?"

Cassidy might not understand everything, but he did know that between Shamus and Helen moral scruple was not a plea which would be accepted in evidence.

"Of course not."

"Then what is it? Touch me."

"I did."

"Touch me again."

"I am touching you."

"Only my hand."

"I love you, Helen," Cassidy said, allowing his tone to give the impression that this was only one side of an inward argument.

"But you don't want me," Helen suggested. "You've changed your mind. I must say you've picked a bloody good time."

Cassidy smiled. "God if only you knew," he said, with a poor shot at world-weariness.

"Is it *really* so difficult to take?" Helen asked. "After all the lessons we've had?"

Receiving no answer, she evidently decided to renounce the initiative and they lay in silence again for quite a long time, while Cassidy took advice from those closest to him.

"Dad."

"Yes, Hug?"

"You know, *Dad.*"

"What do I know, Hug?"

"I like this lady."

"Good."

"She's not as nice as Heather, though, is she?"

"It's just that you know Heather better. And Heather knows us better too."

"Heather's not so *pushy*. Dad."

"Yes Hug."

"I like Angie better too. *Dad.*"

"Yes Hug."

"Has Angie Mawdray seen your pennier?"

"Certainly not. Why on *earth* should she have seen it?"

"Mummy has."

"Mummy's different."

"Has Snaps?"

"No."

"Mummy's *lovely,*" said Hugo. "Goodnight."

"Goodnight Hug."

"A lot of people do it," said Sandra, standing at the door in the darkness and sighing to wake him up. "And it's *perfectly* natural. Just because you don't enjoy it, it doesn't mean everyone else doesn't, but still."

"I know."

"Well get on with it."

"It's just that I'm impotent."

"Nonsense, you're lazy and you eat too much. It's all those *ridiculous* Conservative dinners. No wonder you're bloated. Socialists don't *have* dinners. They have tea and sandwiches."

"I think I'm queer too."

"Absolute nonsense. When we were young we did it just as well as other people and we thoroughly enjoyed it. It's just that I'm a bore. Sorry, but there's nothing I can do about *that.*"

"Sandra, I love you."

Long silence.

"I love you too," she said. "But still."

*Any fool can give, lover. It's what we take from life that
matters.*

"Shall I go and look at him?" Cassidy suggested.

"To get his blessing?"

"I'm sure he's awake."

"My God," said Helen, sitting bolt upright, her anger
thoroughly aroused. "What a disgusting idea. He'd kill you
if he found out, don't you realise. He'll be *far* worse
than Hall ever was to that poor American."

"Yes, I suppose he would," Cassidy conceded.

"If he knew that you and I were in here, *naked,
lovers* . . ." Her indignation found no further expression.
"Christ!" she ended, and lay back with a thump.

"But we're not lovers, are we?" Cassidy asked cautiously. "Not yet." Meaning: penetration has not been
effected, Counsel could still put up a pretty good case; she
forced me into it.

"Do you think he cares what we *do?* It's what we *feel*
that matters." She turned to him almost desperately. "And
we *do* feel, don't we, Cassidy? Don't we? Cassidy, I've
gone the bank. What the *hell* are you putting into this?"

"Everything," he said, having briefly passed in review
all the things that had made him happy: Hugo, Mark, the
Bentley, the Night Animals House, and Sandra in a good
temper. "All I ever loved."

And suddenly was kissing her, taking her; was her master,
conjured into her and over her; and Helen, his nimble,
fluttering dying Helen, a brilliant conjunction of all his
dreams. Her touch took nothing; she steered and danced,
lay passive, rode above him; but still she only gave, and all
the while she seemed to follow him, studying him for yes
and no, testing the limits of his permission, creating in
him, of her obedience, a growing obligation to love her in
return.

"Natural break," she whispered, and lay beside him,
her eyes on his.

"Bold lover," said Helen.

"I want to laugh," said Cassidy.

"I'll have to put it to the Board," she whispered, the passion trembling in her smile.

"I love you," said Cassidy.

"Get on with your work," said Helen.

Elise and Mrs. Bluebridge floated hand in hand, intoning sweet phrases from Old Hugo's good book; respectful waiters clapped to him in rhythmic unison; sinners and strivers, toiling up God's hill, turned to watch him with approval. The chorus multiplied. *Oui, Burgess, oui. Ça te fait plaisir? Beaucoup de plaisir, Elise.* In Kensal Rise the green lights switched excitedly while the band played a Sherborne song: *Vivat rex Edwardus Sextus. Vivat!* The girls looked on, no longer dancing, studying respectfully the master's effortless technique. Now mothers with prams appeared among the crowd, waving, thanking, owing him their babies.

"Sandra!" he cried in welcome.

She had brought her meths drinkers: in crocodile, dressed for church, clean-shaven.

"You chaps!" he called to them, arresting the movement, "look here, now, you'd enjoy this; take you out of yourselves!"

"It would teach them a lesson," Sandra agreed and sighed the way she sighed when he put his dirty clothes in the wrong basket.

Grow you little weed, grow.

Oh Christ, I *am* growing. Believe me lover, I have grown, I am growing, you have taught me *anger,* you have *kindled* me, fired me deep down; the fire spreads from the root; a running, faster fire, water won't help now, my lover, I'm up there with the best of you, drenched and still bathing; better than the best of you; cooking in your place, your cave, your oven; wake if you want. For pity's sake, lover, how can you sleep when murder is being done?

She was telling him: "Cassidy, you're the best, oh Christ, oh Cassidy, oh love!"

Lights were breaking in his eyes; at his back, the movement was small and agonised. She was calling to God and to Cassidy, to Shamus and her father. Her legs were laid wide like a Buddha's, she moved in a slow trance, patting him from side to side with her crooked knees. Captain, art thou sleeping there below? I'd like to be with you now, Shamus, actually; she's joined her own dark people, she's out there with the deep feelers. Actually, Shamus, I want you back.

It was achieved. A stretching of the back, two cats upon an ironing board. It was achieved. Hey ho and fuck it: a grateful end to waiting, a settling of chairs and mirrors in the moonlight, a clearing, an evacuation of the spirit as she let him die in her, keeping her body still to drink. He stayed there, being polite, waiting for the passage of years and the boy to climb out of the water. Thinking about the Bentley and had he heard it crash? Thinking about Shamus and was he watching from the door? Thinking about being Christ caught between two thieves; about being a thief and caught between two Christs; about being a child sleeping with his parents, and a parent sleeping with his children; about needing three, and about Angie Mawdray's signs of the zodiac: "Seven and three," she said. "They're the magic numbers." About Biafran children screaming on the piano and the new lifeboat in the almost finished hall, on the right as you go in, on the Sheraton satinwood dee-shaped table with the dropped leaf six hundred guineas. A paper lifeboat, issued by the Association, with a small slit for putting in the pennies; Sandra had discovered a new affection for the drowning.

Why can't we be one person? he wondered. Why do we have to be so many, mixed together in a single womb?

Released from her, performing the thoughtful father's duty of holding her hand because she was crying, Cassidy addressed the Board for the last time during his office as President.

"Consider the arithmetic, gentlemen, of this unusual situation. (Miss Mawdray, a little more coffee for Mr. Meale perhaps, he appears a trifle tired.) You have all read Nietzsche of course; those who have not will no doubt recall the German poet Somebody. Such men, gentlemen, have devised remarkable explanations for our human behaviour. They arrange us like stars in a horoscope. Well look at us. An example may be found in the perfect arrangement of our three parallel bodies. This is how, in

our mystical assumption, we shall ultimately find our
places in the firmament. In line, with our feet pointing
east. Here, no longer in his dinner jacket, lying in his own
hotel, is a bourgeois who gave his life in search of a
dream. I will call him, tonight, on the customary Miche-
lin rating, a two-star lover; good, but not quite worth a
journey. To my left, separated from me by his wife and a
mercifully insulated wall, lies an artist broken on the wheel
of his genius: a galaxy of a man, but not organised.

"And between us, lover, between us, lies the truth.
Naked, and a little exhausted, crying like a child."

Leaving her to sleep, he unlocked the door and crept back
into the drawing room. The coverlet had fallen to the floor.
He lay even more naked than Helen, even more childish,
more young. Were his eyes open or closed? There was not
enough light to tell. Bending over him, Cassidy put his ear
as close as he dared to the bare chest and heard the restless unequal thumping of his heart.

*Lay the blanket over him, but only to the neck. Sit in
the chair and stare at him, Jonathan, my friend. Get the
towel and wipe him clean.*

Who wrote that? My book or his?
Sleep.

Outside the window, one star burned, but neither Elise nor
any other fantasy was there to welcome him. From Kensal
Rise to Abalone Crescent, from South Audley Street to the
river where it passes Pimlico, there was no one who was
not thinking of the dawn.

Dear Cassidy.

The envelope was covered in green stamps depicting
palm trees and monkeys. It was postmarked several
months ago. He must have put it in his pocket and forgotten to open it. The script like Sandra's was infantile
but adamant.

Dear Cassidy, he read, while dressing in the bathroom. *Your monthly cheque to hand with Thanks. My
daughter tells me you have elected to become a politico,*

*and that you are dabbling in lefty politics including
Communism and brawling in the docks. Don't. Your
duty is to be attentive and chivalrous to your wife and
children at all times,* not *go hobnobbing with pansy
Marxists from Balliol and treat your mother in law as a
damned cretin. I am in constant touch with Mrs. Groat
on this Matter and expect to hear of a general improvement bearing in mind she's as blind as a bat.*

It ended quaintly *P. Groat Brigadier (retd)* and
warned Cassidy in a P.S. to look after his tennis racquet:
*And Make Damn sure the press is tight P.G. (Brig.
Rtd).*

The Bentley stood in the bay where he had parked it. No,
the doorman said, jovially handing him the keys, of course
no one had taken it; not without Mr. Cassidy's consent, of
course not.

London

28

A spell of cold weather, bringing rain and unseasonable winds, coincided with Cassidy's descent into Hades. At home over the weekend he barely spoke; though he was tender to his child and noticeably protective of his wife, his outward manner remained aloof, preoccupied.

"There's trouble about the Paper," he told Sandra. "The Unions are in an ugly mood."

Concerned, she saw him to the car.

"If there's anything I can do to help, let me know. Sometimes a woman's touch is what they need."

"I will," said Cassidy, and embraced her fondly, if distractedly.

Alone in his Bentley, the louche criminal prowled the London streets, shunning the main thoroughfares and the gaze of inquisitive policemen. He drove distractedly, regarding with loathing his deceiver's eyes in the driving mirror, red-rimmed, shadowed with debauchery. Aldo Cassidy, fifty thousand pounds reward, crime innocence. I'd have drawn it better, he thought, I'd have made me more contemptible.

"You'll ring us soon, won't you?" Helen had said on the doorstep, looking into him and beyond. "Cassidy."

"Can't be soon enough, lover," Shamus whispered, shuffling ahead of them up the steel stairs. "Come and play football."

"I will."

"How about now?"

"I've got to put in time with the bosscow."

"I'll bet those bad-tempered ladies are *great* in bed," said Shamus, unlocking the kitchen door. "Helen smirks

331

too much. Too happy. Hey Helen, maybe we ought to get miserable for a bit."

"Goodbye Cassidy," said Helen, smiling.

"Good luck with *Codpiece,*" said Cassidy.

"We'll write," said Helen.

Shamus swung on her fast. "Will you? Can you do that? Maybe you could do *Codpiece* too."

"I meant letters," said Helen. "Not scripts."

Changing into his suit, Cassidy left his dinner jacket for Helen to press.

An airport drew him, possibly Heathrow. Parked in a lay-by, the loathsome sinner watched large jets take off to safety in the mist. If only he had his passport. Telephone the office, Mawdray can bring it in a taxi. For a while, coasting past petrol stations and motels, he searched for a secluded kiosk, then gave up. I'd never get away with it, they'd intercept the call, catch me at the barrier. *West End adulterer makes Airport Dash.*

Windsor, where the flag of Saint George dangled wetly over the historic stone. The obscene goat passed in un-remarked shame, gazing at shoppers, coveting their dull-ness. Tradition; what had Cassidy ever had of tradition? Where was Cromwell Cassidy now, that valiant Puritan campaigner? In the Savoy Hotel, thank you, ten pounds extra for the staff and send the bill to the Company, sleeping with his best friend's wife.

Why did no lightning strike him? This lorry, hurtling over the narrow bridge: why did its articulated trailer not slam his preening hood, shatter the glass of his unnatural im-munity? Perhaps he should kill someone; that would be an answer. A lonely cyclist, for instance, setting out for hon-est labour in the fields, mounting this very crest at the end of a long day's toil, his simple mind upon hearth and children?

Settling more comfortably into his seat, Cassidy al-lowed his ready imagination to complete the castastro-phe: the granite church, the meagre grave, the tragic group unheeding of the rain. The widow pauses at the

iron gate. Cassidy, haggard and unshaven, lays a hand upon her arm.

Send the children to Harrow, he begs her. *I have some
influence with the headmaster. I would like to care for
them as my own.*

She does not weep but only shakes her head.

Give me back my Harry, she whispers. *That's all I want.
My trouble is, I drive too carefully.*

In Aylesbury, a pretty market town not normally frequented by adulterers, the repulsive voluptuary bought his
wife a crocodile handbag and composed, over coffee in a
roadside hostelry, a letter of withdrawal to his former
friend Shamus, the well-known prophet.

> *You gave me the means to love and I have grossly
> abused your gift, turning it into a weapon of betrayal
> against yourself. No words can describe my agony; as
> high as you raised me, thus far have I fallen. I enclose a
> cheque for five thousand pounds in full settlement of
> all claims. Please keep my dinner jacket and any other
> small possessions which may be hanging around the
> flat. A banker's order takes care of the rent.*
>
> > *Your one-time friend*
> > *and eternal admirer*
> > *A. Cassidy*

To this letter, on reflection, he added a precautionary
postscript:

> *I should have told you long ago that I am subject to
> epileptic fits. These are of a very rare form. Once in
> their grip, I am powerless to resist and lose all re-
> sponsibility for my actions. If you don't believe me,
> please feel free to consult Dr. John Elderman of Aba-
> lone Crescent, whom I have instructed to pass to you
> whatever further information you may need. None but
> he and Sandra, hitherto, have been party to my secret
> grief. I beg you, whatever happens, to treat this in-
> formation in strictest confidence.*

Having sealed the letter, stamped it, and put it in his
pocket he ordered a fresh plate of hot scones and ate them

in grey despair. Now you know all, he thought; do with me
what you will.

Leaving the café, he consigned the letter to a public
litter basket. Forget, he told himself. Put nothing in
writing.

It never happened.

They never existed, he told himself. I made them up.
Come now, be honest, could I really have got away with it
so long?

Driving to Labour Party Headquarters, he enquired at the
desk how he should offer himself for adoption as a candidate. The girl did not know but promised to find out.

"It was *Labour* you wanted, wasn't it?" she asked rather
doubtfully, looking past him through the window at the
newly sprayed Bentley.

"Please," said Cassidy, and left his card.

It never happened. Forget.

So you see, Shamus is dead.
    Helen is dead.
    They never existed.
    I dreamed them.
    To nothing.

And yet, out of the pit of his agony, out of the misery of
guilt, remorse, deceit, and regret, the little weed, as Shamus would have it—also grew. For his agony was tem-
pered by a quite urgent will to live—the gift of certain
unnamed friends whose influence upon him had by no
means lost its sting.

Returning next day from an all-night debate at the
dockers' headquarters, he fulfilled an engagement at the
Elderman dinner table and won the respect of all who
heard him. Well, he said, the Report was highly confidential; he did not honestly feel he could say much about

it. Yes, it would be called the Cassidy Report. *The scope?*
It covered pretty well everything from the reception procedure at Party Headquarters to the provision of recreation
facilities in Cable Street warehouses. *Terms of reference?*
Very much as quoted in the press (a nice touch—no one
confessed to having missed the notice) with a few additions he had insisted upon for his own protection.

In bed, armed with a virility brought on by extreme
anxiety—and stimulated perhaps by certain inexplicit
memories of events which had not occurred—he astonished his wife with a succession of sexual feats.

"And get rid of your mother," he told her. "I'm sick of
having her around."

"I will," said Sandra.

"I want you to myself," he said.

"It's all that matters," Sandra agreed. *"Dear* Pailthorpe."

Grew, burgeoned, and even, mysteriously, flourished.

And felt, among many other conflicting emotions—such
as panic, for instance, such as hatred of the scarlet whore
Helen, such as a profound sympathy with the extreme
right of the Conservative Party, which protects men of
property from the vicious assaults of penurious writers
and their unprincipled wives—felt that special superiority
only found among those who live eye to eye with destiny:
alpinists, the mortally ill, and the many heroes of the war
he'd missed. The weed was of the brotherhood at last; the
élite. He understood why Helen and Shamus talked so
much about mortality. Death is the property of those
who live; they should study it with every hour.

Also the weed slept less; ate less; worked better and
more briskly.

And finding, in the passage of that fortnight, that he had
neither contracted leprosy, nor been arrested by the police, nor had served on him those ever-threatening notices
from the Inland Revenue or the Board of Trade; and
having heard nothing from either Helen or Shamus, and
made no move to reach them on his own account; and
having therefore presumed them at first missing and later
killed, he decided it was safe, in a quiet way, to explore a
little further his new exciting policy of taking.

"You know . . ," Sandra began gratefully one night.

"What do I know?"

"Even if it were all a lie, the whole thing . . . the Paper, the Party, the safe seat . . . I'd still love you. I'd still admire you. Whatever the truth was."

But Cassidy was asleep, he could tell by his breathing.

"The truth is *you*," she whispered. "Not what you say. *You*."

—

29

Time out; borrowed Time; a past unlived, too long imagined, belatedly made real; a cashing-in before the final settlement; an ascent of the emotional scale; a claiming of his rightful dues; a renewed search for the Blue Flower: who cares? Cassidy stripped, stood in the fountain, and felt the edges of his existence.

"You know what I wish, Aldo?"

"What do you wish?"

"I wish all the stars were people and all the people were stars."

"What good would that do?"

"Because then our faces would be lit up with smiles all the time. We'd twinkle at each other and never be miserable any more."

"I'm not miserable," said Cassidy stoutly. "I'm happy."

"And all the people we don't like would be masses of miles away, wouldn't they, because they'd be in the sky instead of the stars."

"We've got all night," said Cassidy. "I'm not tired or anything. I'm just happy."

"I love you so much," said Angie. "I wish you'd grin."

"Make me," said Cassidy.

"I can't. I'm not clever enough." She kissed him with placid, expert sensuality. "I never will be."

He grinned. "How's that?"

"That's good," she said. "That's very good for a beginner."

Tasting of snail garlic from the Epicure, watched by a white dog called Lettice, they lay in naked mutuality on the thin, bony bed of her attic flat in Kensington, next to the stars. Lettice was born under the sign of the bowman, she said, and Bowman was the sexiest sign out.

337

"It means cock," she explained. "Julie told me. Everything's phallic really, isn't it?"

"I suppose it is," said Cassidy.

A Che Guevara poster hung on the wall beside a tapestry woven by Cretan primitives.

"Lettice loves you too," said Angie.

"And I like him."

"Her," said Angie. "Silly."

Yesterday he knew nothing about her; today everything.

She believed in the Spirit and wore rows of mystic beads against her bare and extremely beautiful bosom. She believed in God and, like Shamus, hated the fucking clergy more than any other living thing; she was a vegetarian but thought snails were all right because they couldn't feel and anyway the birds ate them; she had loved Cassidy from the day she joined the firm. She loved him as she loved no one in the world; Meale was a stupid bugger. She had identified the actual stars which determined Cassidy's fortune, and gazed at them for nights on end. She had broad, hard thighs and her fleece grew downwards very neatly from the upper line, she called it her beard and liked him to keep his hand there, she couldn't get enough. Her right breast was erogenous, she disapproved of abortion. She adored children and hated her fucking father. As a rule, Cassidy disliked swearing in women and had been hoping, at a suitable moment, to check it in Helen. But there was a hardy familiarity to Angie's obscenities, a sublime indifference to their connotations, which somehow disinfected them of sensation.

She was twenty-three. She adored Castro but her greatest single regret was that she had not fucked Che Guevara before he died; it was for this reason she had him nearest to her bed. Greece was fabulous, and one day when she had made lots of money she was going to go back and live there and have lots of babies: "All by myself, Aldo, little brown ones that play bare on the sand."

He knew also that naked she was very beautiful and neither shy nor afraid; and it amazed him beyond words or comprehension that she had lived so long fully dressed within his reach, and that he had not put out his hand to unzip her.

"Listening?"

"Yes," said Cassidy. "Don't let go."

"Pisces, right? That's Latin. Two fishes, joined by the

astrological umbilical cord, one swimming upstream and the other swimming downstream."

"Like us," Cassidy suggested humbly.

"Not *us; me,* silly. I've got a dual personality. That's what dual personality means: two whole different people inside one head. I'm not one fish, I'm *two,* that's the whole point, silly." She continued reading. "Decisive events await you this week. Your greatest desire will come within your reach. Do not flinch. Seize the opportunity but only before the ninth or after the fifteenth, Christ what's the date?"

I love you, he thought. I love the way your ears point through your long brown hair; I love the sheerness of you, the spring and ease of your young body, I want to marry you and share the Greek beach with your babies.

"The thirteenth," he said looking at the date window of his gold watch.

"I don't care," said Angie resolutely. "They're not always right so sod them."

She lay flat on her back, pensively studying Che Guevara.

"I don't care, I don't care, *I don't fucking care,*" she repeated fiercely, staring the great revolutionary in the eye. "It's a cloud. One day the wind will come along and puff it away and I *still* won't care. Do you do it a lot, Aldo? Do you fuck lots of girls?"

"It's just the way I'm made," said Cassidy and gave a traveller's sigh, hinting at the lonely road and the wandering, and the rare moments of consolation.

"Come off it, Garbo," said Angie.

Naked, she made him cocoa, a foulmouthed goddess clattering plates in the tiny galley; a child, backlit by the orange glow from the window, preparing a dorm feast. And afterwards, she promised him, they'd do it again. She loved him, he could do it whenever he liked. Her breasts moved with her, not a tremor; her long waist had the authority of a statue. She straddled him, knees spread, making a sand castle. Bending forward, she kissed him over and over while she stirred him slowly into the thick basin of her hips.

"He was *such* a sod, my Dad," she said afterwards, still in awe, her round cheek pressed gratefully against his shoulder, her hand still lightly holding him. "But *your* kids *really* love you don't they, Aldo?"

"I love *you,*" said Cassidy, not finding it, for once, at all difficult to say.

Ast, an older lady a good three years Cassidy's senior but
not yet wholly infirm, lived nearer to the ground but in
greater affluence. In bed she was very large, about twice
her dressed weight he reckoned, thinking vaguely of Cas-
sius Clay; and when she leant on her side to talk to him her
heavy elbow staked him to the mattress.

The walls of Ast's room were hung with unframed can-
vasses by painters yet to rise; her windows faced a museum, and her interest in Cassidy, after the first round, was
essentially of the historical kind.

"When did you *know?*" she asked, in a voice which suggested that love could be proved by research. *"Frankly,
Aldo. When did you have the first inkling?"*

Frankly, Cassidy thought, never.

"Was it," she suggested, prompting his memory, "that
night at the Niesthals', at the harpsichord concert? You
looked at me. Twice. You probably don't even remember."

"Of course I do," said Cassidy politely.

"October. That gorgeous October." She sighed. "God,
one says such corny things when one's in love. I thought
you were just a boring . . . lecherous . . . merchant." Cassidy shared her amusement at this ridiculous misconception. "How wrong. How utterly wrong I was." A long,
meaningless silence. "You *love* music, don't you, Aldo?"

"Music is my favourite thing," said Cassidy.

"I could tell. Aldo, why don't you take *Sandra* to con-
certs? She's so frightfully anxious to *understand* the spirit.
You've got to help her, you know. She's nothing without
you. Nothing." The significance of her words suddenly
appalled her. "Oh God what have I said! Forgive me, say
you forgive me."

"It's quite all right," Cassidy assured her.

"God what have I said?"—She rolled on to him—"Aldo,
please, don't cut me off, please. *I forgive you.* Say *I forgive
you."*

"I forgive you," said Cassidy.

Peace returned.

"And then you went for me at the Eldermans'. I could
hardly believe it. No one had spoken to me like that for
months. You were so fluent . . . so *sure.* I felt like a child.
Just a little girl." She laughed at the pleasurable memory.
"All we stupid women could do was look insulted while
you lectured us. My mouth went dry and my heart was

going inside and I thought: he's right. He *cares* about the artist. *Publishers*," she snorted. "What do *they* know?"

"Nothing," said Cassidy, thinking of Dale.

"As to those flowers . . . well, I just never had so many flowers in my life. Cassidy?"

"Yes."

"What *prompted* you to send them?"

"Paris," Cassidy said, nimbly. "I suddenly . . . missed you. I looked everywhere . . . but you weren't there."

He must have bolted overnight, Cassidy thought, peeking surreptitiously at the uncollected pieces, the clothes-horse for his suits, the leather reading chair for rejecting manuscripts. What a master. How did he do it? Write or ring? Or did he, the Hercules, *tell* her?

They lay still, side by side, and between them a little chasm about ten thousand miles across.

White dust sheets covered the bedroom floor in one corner, and a strong smell of linseed oil lingered in the blankets. Lying on their backs, Mr. and Mrs. Aldo Cassidy admired the newly painted ceiling.

"It will be really lovely when it's finished," Cassidy said. "Like a palace or something."

"You ought to *watch* him," said Sandra, referring to Mr. Monk the mason. "He's so steady. So loyal and decent. He was in the sappers in the war."

"The sappers were a fine bunch," Cassidy remarked shrewdly, their expert on military affairs.

"He thinks he remembers Daddy. He's not sure but he thinks so. He was on bridges for a while, in Bolton. Back in thirty-nine."

"I forget which lot was stationed at Bolton," Cassidy said, as if he had been wondering. They had recently seen *Patton,* and Cassidy was still enjoying a certain reflected prestige.

"He keeps his men in order too," said Sandra approvingly. "One of them has been making eyes at Snaps."

"I'm not having that," said Cassidy sharply.

"Shush," said Sandra with a conspiratorial frown, looking upwards at the ceiling.

"Well honestly I mean the way she tarts around—"

"Aldo!"—quieting him with little kisses—"*Grizzly* Pailthorpe . . . *Aldo* . . . it's only her age. *She'll* get over it . . .

anyway, she's got a new boyfriend, a visualizer called Mel."

They both giggled.

"Oh *Christ*," said Cassidy. "Do we *have* to have visualizers?" More kisses. "How's Grans taking it?"

"Who cares?"

They lay still, listening to the slow copulative beat of Snaps' music.

"He's not up there is he?" Cassidy demanded on a sudden impulse.

"Of course he isn't," she said, restraining him.

He lay back once more, placated, the custodian still of a certain standard of virtue.

A few days later, to celebrate Cassidy's good news, he and his wife dined at the White Tower. Angie made the booking, two for eight.

They liked duck best.

They ate it crisp with a heavy Burgundy Cassidy had learnt to remember, and for a short time under the influences of meat and wine they remade the illusion of their love. First, like old friends reunited, they exchanged intelligence from their separate worlds. Sandra said Mark had asked for a new violin: the music master had written that he did not shine at the instrument but it was certainly too small. This discussion, though homely, was privately confusing to Cassidy, for he had recently once more lost his sense of time. Mark had been home last weekend, but whether from school or from some other activity Cassidy could not precisely say.

"Let's run to one more size," he proposed and Sandra smiled her assent.

"Maybe it'll encourage him," she said, fresh from the experience of the piano. "Any instrument's a drag to start with."

"It would be super if the two of you could play together," Cassidy said. "Hugo too," he added and there passed through his mind a pleasing vision of a drawing room, all the holes filled in, and Sandra sitting at a much smaller piano while her young Haydns fiddled and piped for Father.

"I'm sure I could learn to like music," he said.

"You just need to hear more. No one's *really* tone-deaf, John said so."

Next on the Chairman's informal agenda, the long-projected extension to the house. The present phase of reconstruction being almost over, it was time to consider where they should go next. An extension was the natural solution, particularly if Heather was really going to live with them permanently. Cassidy favoured a cantilevered design that left the garden unspoilt. Sandra said there would be too much shade.

"What's the point of beds," she pointed out, "if the sun never gets to them?"

Alternatively, they could revise their original plan for the conversion of the basement.

"What about a sauna?" Cassidy suggested.

It was not a welcome inspiration. Saunas were a rich man's toy, Sandra said sternly, saunas replaced abstinence and physical exercise. They agreed to consider the cantilevered extension.

"Of course we could put a swimming pool under it," Sandra said reflectively, "if we had more children."

"Children have to be foreseen," said Cassidy quickly, playing upon Sandra's recent excursions into family planning. A small lull followed this objection.

A serious matter now, the parents confer. Mark's last report: should they take it seriously, should he be punished? This was dangerous ground. Sandra believed in punishment as she believed in hell; Cassidy until recently had been sceptical of both.

"I don't *quite* see what he's done wrong," Cassidy began cautiously.

"He's shirking," Sandra retorted, and closed her mouth firmly.

But tonight was togetherness night and Cassidy would not be drawn.

"Let's give him one more term to settle in," he suggested lightly, and by way of distraction brought her up to date with the news from South Audley Street.

"I've decided to put a bomb under them."

"High time."

"Ever since Paris they've been completely out of hand.

There's no dedication, no . . . how can I say it? No sense of mission or . . . loyalty. God knows, they're on a profit-sharing basis: why don't they work, and share? That's all I ask: devotion."

"You could sack that tarty receptionist while you're about it too," said Sandra, helping herself from the bowl of *crudités*.

"Do you *mind?*" Cassidy said sharply.

"Sorry."

Smiling roguishly, she put down her carrot and touched his hand to feel the anger.

The sunny side. Despite the threat of apathy, he felt that the export drive was worthwhile, and indeed was making strides. Paris, contrary to his initial fears, had paid handsome dividends. Moreover it was an excellent way of opening the minds of his staff; moreover the national economy needed every penny.

"They should spend less on arms," Sandra interjected.

Suspecting that they had had this discussion before, and alarmed by the prospect of another debate on the British defence posture, Cassidy returned hastily to the more encompassable problems of man-management.

Faulk was becoming outrageous, always threatening to resign or cut his wrists, a real *drama queen*.

"You must *not* discriminate against homosexuals," Sandra said.

"I don't."

"It's perfectly natural."

"I know."

Meale was also a headache. Moody, brilliant, impossible; what *was* to be done with him?

"Oh *Meale*," said Sandra in a jocular voice. "There's a hardy annual if *ever* I met one!"

"He's only been with us nine months," Cassidy replied, not meaning to contradict her but lured in some way by the metaphor.

"Ha, ha," said Sandra, furious, and drank some wine, staining her mouth.

"But you're dead right: he really *is* a hardy annual, however long he's been with us. I've never known anyone so temperamental. D'you know he spent his leave in a *monastery?*"

Still scowling, Sandra took a mouthful of duck.

"You don't object to his being *religious* do you?"

"Not if it makes him happy. But it doesn't. He's come back worse than when he left."

"Probably that secretary of yours been leading him a dance. Love takes people that way, you know."

"Nonsense," said Cassidy, tersely, and returned to the more tranquil field of politics.

Harold Wilson had impressed him, he said. The burdens of recent office had aged him certainly, as they age us all; but they had not blunted his intellect. In sum, Cassidy thought him an intelligent man, sincere and well informed, even if he was a bit Gerrard's Cross. The Chancellor, on the other hand, was a type Cassidy found very hard to deal with: tremendously agreeable, and gives absolutely nothing away, which was no doubt a sound way of dealing with p.q.'s (he meant parliamentary questions), but not so well suited to off-the-record, non-attributable, round-table get-togethers.

"Then you must break him down," said Sandra.

"I know. The trouble is he's so—"

"He can't just *lie*."

"He doesn't quite do that, it's just he comes up with these bland answers you somehow can't get round."

And then mysteriously, over the *baklava*, she left him.

He ran on, giving of his best, but she slipped further and further away from him. A shadowed silence descended on her from within, causing her features suddenly to age, and sadden, her eyes to find an object to her left, and her cuffed hands to join like troubled friends before a common dread.

He played for laughs; he did his voices; he populated the political stage with a carnival of exotic personalities. Old So-and-So was a kind of Carnaby Street Hemingway, acting tough and attending his wife's deliveries, but deep down he was just a puff-ball, Cassidy had fixed him in ten minutes. Someone else was always stealing the tea out of the canteen; the secretaries walked in fear of So-and-So, he was a pincher and pounced on them from doorways. He tried to play on her concern; very few really knew how grave was our economic situation. What was the Government to *tell* us? There came a moment when by telling the truth you made the truth more real and more terrible: "I mean God, we all know *that* problem."

"Yes," said Sandra, still in her own dark place, "we do."

"And what about the people farther away?" she asked, still distracted. "Up north, or wherever you went? How were they? Also fools and knaves?"

"Oh, the Trade Union barons. Well they're *really* tough. They were a real eye-opener, believe me. I mean if you like realism, those are the boys who know what it's all about."

"I'm glad somebody does," said Sandra, still looking away from him.

Only promises remained to him.

"Look," he said. "Now it's done, finished—"

"What is?"

"The Report. The Paper. It's off my hands. I told you. That's why we're here."

"I know. I do know. You told me."

"I thought we'd take a holiday. Up sticks and away. Dump the boys with John and Beth—" for once he remembered her name "—and *go*. Wherever you like. While we're still young." To himself, he sounded like television. How did he sound to her? He could not tell.

"Just you and me," he said.

And brought her back.

Not all the way perhaps but far enough. Slowly, not all at once, the shadows withdrew from her face and a puckish, rather gallant smile took possession of her homeless features. A laugh escaped her, mocking none but herself, and she took his hand, touched it rather, sliding the tips of two very pretty fingers up and down the back.

"We could take a castle in Spain," she suggested. And

then, to his considerable concern, for he was not in any mood that night to deal with weighty matters: "You're God really, aren't you, Aldo? After all, if we don't believe in you, what *do* we believe in?"

"Listen. First we'll have a party. As soon as they've finished the drawing room. Then we'll go. Next day. Take off. Now when's the drawing room promised for?"

Details now, details gave reality. Whom they would ask: just people they liked, no one official, least of all Trade and Politics. Maybe a few of Heather's friends to brighten it up. John and Beth of course, maybe a separate room for the kids. . . . Yes, said Sandra, it would be fun to have a children's party going at the same time.

Now, about the holiday. Problem one: *Where?* All right, if she'd gone off Tito how about the Bahamas, he would even stand the cost of a trip to Bermuda.

Very cautiously, Sandra counted off her unbreakable engagements; and broke them one by one.

There was something else on Cassidy's mind: they should *do* more together.

"Perhaps that's one of the things we might think about on holiday."

As a matter of fact he had been talking to Lacon and Ollier about it, his theatre ticket people, only yesterday.

"I thought you were in Leeds yesterday," said Sandra, almost as if she were thinking about something else.

On the phone. He was actually talking to them about travel, then they got on to the question of theatre, was there *anything* worth seeing in the West End these days?

"What I was going to say was—"

"Sorry," said Sandra.

"What for?"

"Doubting you."

Checked, Cassidy glanced at her to make sure she was serious, but there was neither irony nor any other kind of insurrection in her face: only that same inward sadness, returning like a grown child to the empty houses of her youth.

"What I was going to say was: why not go to the theatre once a week *automatically* just to get a show under

one's belt so to speak? At least we'd have something to
talk about."

They agreed on Wednesdays.

"And I want to go to church again."

"For my sake?"

"Well, yours and the children's. Even if they reject it
later, it's right for them to have it now."

"Yes," said Sandra, very thoughtful again. "It will always be part of their lives, whether they reject it or not.
After all——" he thought she had finished but she had not
"——after all, if you live long enough with a dream, it *is*
real isn't it?"

Desperately he searched his imagination for stronger rem-
edies. He had heard from old Niesthal that there was a
marvellous sale at Christie's next week, no dealers would
be there because of the holidays. Why not go?

"Apparently there's some fabulous eighteenth-century
glass. You've always wanted old glass."

"Have I?"

He talked about the chalet in Sainte-Angèle; perhaps
they should drop in there on their way to Bermuda to
make sure it was still in one piece; how the children had
adored it last winter but he did wonder all the same
whether Christmas wasn't better spent at home.

"It's up to you," she said. "We'll spend it wherever you
say."

He was going to offer further thoughts on Switzerland; he
had a lot ready. He was going to suggest they retired
there, that it was a good place to die, the eternity of the
mountains gave a kind of solace; he was going to draw
her on an academic point: did mountains exist more in
time than in *space,* did something massive by definition become something of great longevity? But instead she spoke
to him on her own initiative, drawing on thoughts deep
down.

"Aldo."

"Yes."

"You know I love you, don't you?"

"Yes, of course."

"I *mean* it," she repeated, with a frown. "I actually really love you. It's a whole condition of mind. It doesn't allow for . . ."

Not being an articulate girl, she found no end to her sentence, so she got up and went to the ladies' room. Cassidy paid the bill and called a cab. The same night they made love. For her own reasons Sandra was very slow. Finally, somewhere in the darkness, she called out; but whether from pain or joy he could no longer tell.

In the morning, she was crying again and he dared not ask her why.

30

"She's here," said Angie Mawdray in a sepulchral voice, perhaps the next day; perhaps autumn, since time had lost much of its reliability.

Several possibilities occurred to Cassidy; only the certainties were excluded. Heather Ast, for instance, popping in to say hullo on the way to have her hair done; Blue-bridge wanting money, the obligatory scene; Mrs. Groat, Snaps, to discuss a new pregnancy. Heather Ast again, on a point of detail relating to Sandra's welfare.

"Who is here?" he asked, with a tolerant smile.

Angie's face, normally a treasure chest of appealing smiles and twinkling eyes, was ashen.

"You never told me she was a Beauty," she whispered.

The receptionist, a friend of Lemming, was also impressed, for she winked at Cassidy as he passed her on his way to the waiting room and Cassidy made a mental note to dismiss her very soon indeed. There had been, he remembered, an incident at last year's annual cricket match for which she had yet to pay—a matter of a locked changing room and an absent batsman—and that wink made retribution certain.

The waiting room door was ajar. She was sitting in the deepest chair, a recliner of black hide, leaning right back with her knees not quite together. Her eyes were closed and she was smiling.

"Grunt like a pig," she commanded.

Cassidy grunted.

"A lazy, non-telephoning, non-writing, head-in-the-mud pig."

He grunted again.

"That's authentic," she conceded and then she opened

her eyes and they kissed and went to tea at Fortnum's because she was ravenous after her walk.

She's here.

She's walked, he recorded, as the memories came rushing back, the fun, the laughter, the bodies tied. Tripped the country miles from cod-country to South Audley Street on her very much deteriorated Anna Karenina boots. Hitchhiked, a gorgeous lorry driver called Mason. Mason had stopped for her to pick the blue flowers, bought her tea, wrapped her blue flowers in the *Evening Standard*—she was carrying them still, on her lap, they would go beside the bed tonight—Mason had invited her to have it off with him.

"But I didn't, Cassidy, promise, just a kiss and a *thank you, Mason, I'm not that sort of girl.*"

"Very laudable," said Cassidy. "Exemplary in fact," and ordered her eggs, a second helping.

"Dear lover, are you in the pink? Can I kiss you, or will they call the lilly? That's what Mason called them, Cassidy: *lilly.* For police. Did you know? Cassidy, I love you *enormously*, that's my first vital piece of news. A blanket investment, Cassidy, not even my *toes* sticking out, Cassidy. Lock, stock, and body. Cassidy, you really *do?* Love me, I mean?"

"Really."

"God what a relief. I told Mason, I said Mason, if he stand me up you will *have* to go to bed with me, whether you like it or not it's a territorial imperative; is that the right expression? Like Schiller. To restore my pride."

She leaned forward, full of important information.

"Cassidy, you have opened me up. Is that rude? I was a toady till I met you. A lackey. A bourgeois housebeast. You have turned me into a *suffragette*, no fooling. Cassidy, *say* you love me."

"I love you."

"He loves me," Helen assured the waitress. "Him, and my husband, and a man called Mason, a lorry driver."

"Gosh," said the waitress and they all laughed.

"Cassidy, you are a *swine* not to ring me. Shamus was *very* put out. *Where's lover? Why won't lover ring?* It went on night and day until I got absolutely fed up with it. 'He's *my* lover not yours,' I told him—"

"Helen you didn't—"

"And I looked *everywhere* for the Bentley. I told Mason: Mason, if we see Cassidy's Bentley, you've got to make an emergency halt because me and Cassidy are lovers and . . . Cassidy, kiss me, you are a *total* pig."

"You could have rung *me*," Cassidy reminded her, having temporarily satisfied her needs.

"Cassidy, I did. I rang you the *whole weekend* and you just listened to it burr, burr and did absolutely nothing. Just sat there gawping at your carpet slippers."

"At the weekend?" Cassidy repeated, as iron bars gathered round his chest.

"Yes but I got the bosscow every time, so I rang off. At least I suppose it was the bosscow, she was *terribly* grey." She pulled a bovine face. "If you tell me who you *are* I *might* tell you where mah husband is," she said, in an uncomfortably good imitation of Sandra.

"I thought you were going to ring the office," said Cassidy. "I thought we agreed."

"But Cassidy it was the *weekend*."

"How's Shamus?" he asked, watching her eat the smoked salmon.

"He's absolutely *super* and I love him and *Codpiece* went like a song. I tell you, Cassidy, that fellow's on a real winning streak. Well we both are, aren't we? And *all* thanks to you."

What had happened to her? What had freed her? Did *I* do this?

"Those fishermen are *fabulous*, Cassidy, you should smell them." She ventured what Cassidy assumed was a Lowestoft accent. " '*Ya mine for the neet,*' that's what one of them said to me. I had to explain to him, Cassidy. I'm booked, I said. I've got a rich lover who invented the disc brake, and he guards me like a *lemur*. Do you like being described as a *lemur*, Cassidy?" Without a breath she returned to her other interest. "He's even been *paid*, that's how well *Codpiece* went. No rewrite, no Dale, no nothing. In fact—" indicating a little guiltily her new coat "—I'm wearing the fee. Don't worry, Cassidy"—leaning urgently forward—"I'm *nude* underneath, promise."

"Helen. Hey listen: you're completely out of control. What's come over you? You're not tight are you?"

"It's called *love*," Helen said, a little sharply. "And it's non-alcoholic."

A model moved slowly round them, a skeletal, moody girl of no attraction.

"I'm better than her anyway."

"Much," Cassidy agreed.

"He talks about you *masses*," she went on. "And he misses you *terribly*. He keeps saying, 'Is he all right? Shouldn't you ring him?' To *me!* And how he must keep faith with you because he loves you, and you gave him his, and the circle must never be broken." She lowered her voice. "And he's *terribly* ashamed about what happened at the Savoy, Cassidy."

"Oh well, I don't think he should be really."

"He's right back to self-denial. No booze, no bed, nothing. . . . Oh Cassidy he *so* missed you. He just wanted to hear you *speak*, Cassidy. He wanted to hear your *voice* and the slimy way you put sentences together when you're being boardroom." She looked round in case they were overheard. "He's imagined it, Cassidy. The whole thing, isn't he clever? Just as if he'd made us up. Cassidy, those flowers are *blue*."

"I take the point," said Cassidy, and went to the telephone.

The Minister of Labour, he told Sandra. A most mysterious summons from the Private Office; he wondered whether this might be what they were waiting for; he had heard there was a seat going begging in one of the East Anglican constituencies.

"An all-night session I expect," said Sandra.

"It looks like it," he conceded. "We're meeting in Lowestoft. I'm leaving in a couple of minutes."

"What did you mean?" he asked Helen, as they sauntered along the Embankment. "*Imagined* the whole thing? What *whole thing* exactly?"

"You and me as lovers, and himself as my husband. It's the theme of his new book, and it's *fabulous* Cassidy, honestly it is, *miles* better than the last one, you ought to read it. It's so *violent,* Cassidy. Honestly."

"That's marvellous," said Cassidy heartily. "By the way, what happened to the rewrite?"

"Oh, on the shelf marked *fragment.* You're to include it in his posthumous writings. He says you'll survive him by *decades.* Which you will, won't you Cassidy, because you're so dodgy. Dale's *livid.*"

"I'll bet he is."

"It's as good as written. He's made a complete sketch, whole chunks finished. All he has to do is put them together. I mean I could *almost* do it for him, but you know what he is. . . . A quick dash to Switzerland, record the fleeting vision, back to England in triumph. That's the plan. Oh we'll want that chalet of yours by the way, Shamus says mountains will be *just* right for it. I'm to get the key off you."

"You are?"

"Well honestly, Cassidy, he doesn't suppose I'm walking all the way to London and not seeing lover does he?"

"What's *in* the book?" Cassidy asked. *Content* had never bothered him before; had been a hindrance in fact to the pure, celestial enjoyment of Shamus' unread works; but now, for reasons too close to him yet to be defined—Helen's excitement perhaps, the imminence of certain death—he detected signs, and wished them clearly shown.

She lowered her voice again.

"Cassidy, there's the most *fabulous* murder at the end, all in Dublin. Shamus buys a gun and goes mad and all *sorts* of things, it's really *super.* . . ." She giggled, noticing his expression. "It's all *right,*" she assured him. "You kill *Shamus,* don't worry. Cassidy, I'm *happy,* are you?"

"Of course I am," said Cassidy.

"How's the bosscow?"

"Fine."

"No Thoughts?"

"Who?"

"The bosscow."

"No. No of course not."

"I want *everyone* to be happy, Cassidy. Shamus, bosscow, the veg, *all* of them. I want them to share our love and . . ."

Cassidy was suddenly laughing.

"Jesus," he said, "that *will* be the day."

Entering her embrace however—they were at the centre of the pavement, not far from Cleopatra's Needle—he was pleased to see no one he recognised, not even the Niesthals.

"Then *after* you've killed him," Helen resumed, in the taxi, holding his arm in both her hands, "you're sent to an Irish prison for life and you write a great novel thousands of pages long. *His* novel. What are Irish prisons like, Cassidy?"

"Beery I should think."

"And *very* insecure. Still, *you'll* be able to take me round one won't you? Dublin main gaol, that's his ambition for you. I'm going to do *all* his research, I've promised, and it's got to be completely authentic. He's written me the most super dedication, Cassidy. To both of us, actually."

"Marvellous."

"It's only *imagined*, Cassidy," she said, kissing him lavishly. "I haven't breathed a syllable about what *really* happened, promise. Cassidy, it was *you*, wasn't it, it wasn't a waiter? I couldn't remember whether we did it in the dark or not."

"We left the light on," said Cassidy.

"And it was me underneath?"

"Undoubtedly."

"You see *shooting him* is the only way you can survive, that's how he's worked you out. You've *got* to shoot him, for your sovereignty. He's the original, and you're the imitation, that's how he argues; so if you shoot him, you'll become an original in your own right, it's *extremely* classical. Then your genius will be liberated, but locked up in the prison so you can't piss it away, and all that lovely discipline you have will be further enhanced by—"

"I haven't *got* any genius. I'm a buffoon. I've got big hands and big feet and—"

"Don't worry, Shamus is giving you some of his. After all whoever sleeps with me *has* to be a genius, doesn't he? In Shamus' book at least. I mean it can't just be sordid and middle-class or there's no art. Hey Cassidy, I wrote you a letter."

Opening her handbag she gave it to him, and waited

while he read it. The envelope said: *To lover.* The page inside was lined, torn from one of Shamus' pads.

> *You have given me more in one night than anyone else in a lifetime.*
>
>   *Helen*

"I thought it had rhythm," she explained, watching him as he read it. "I worked on it a lot. I wanted to check it with Shamus actually but then I thought better not. After all, I'm not his creature, am I?"

"Good God no," Cassidy cried, laughing. "Rather the other way round I would have thought."

"Cassidy. Don't knock him."

"I wasn't."

"Well don't. He's your friend."

"Helen—"

"We've got to protect him for all we're worth. Because if he ever does find out it will destroy him. Totally."

The football ground was empty; the children had gone. It was a quiet day for the river too, a holiday perhaps, or a day of prayer.

Nothing had changed, but the place belonged already to the past. His dinner jacket hung in the spare room still. A light powder, either human or mineral, greyed the shoulders. The kitchen smelt of vegetable; she had forgotten to empty the rubbish. The picture window was clouded with brown grime. The desk was just as the great writer had left it, except for the yellowed paper, curled by the sunlight, and the dust thick enough to draw in. Keats lay on the blotter. The beret hung on the corner of the chair.

They embraced, kissing; kissing in the dull daylight, lips then tongues; Cassidy caressing her, mainly on the back, tracing her spine to its end and wondering whether she would mind if he continued. Lipstick tastes different in the daylight, he thought: warm and tacky.

"Cassidy," she whispered. "Oh Cassidy."

She took his fingers and kissed them and put them on her breast and glanced first at the bedroom door and then at Cassidy again, then sighed.

"Cassidy," she said.

They had left it unmade, the sheets pulled back to air,

the pillows heaped in the centre as if for one person. The
Casa Pupo coverlet lay on the floor, tossed aside in a
hurry, and the curtains were partly drawn on the side
where the neighbours overlooked. In the poor light the
blue was very dark, more black or grey than blue, and the
flowered wallpaper had a dishevelled, autumnal look
which had never been a problem with the nursery at
Abalone Crescent. Stepping over the coverlet, Cassidy
went to the window and drew the curtains.

"I should have sent someone to clear up," he said. "It
was stupid of me."

Making love to her, Cassidy smelt the familiar smell of
Shamus' sweat, and heard the clip of carpets being beaten
in the courtyard of the white hotel.

Afterwards they drank Talisker in the drawing room
and Helen began shivering for no reason, like Sandra
sometimes when he talked to her about politics.

"You haven't got *another* love nest have you?" she
asked.

Over lunch at Boulestin, their spirits fully restored, they
had a marvellous plan. They would use only sleazy boarding houses, like real illicit lovers.

*The Adastras Hotel in the neighborhood of Paddington
Station,* Cassidy wrote in his secret Baedeker, *may be
compared with a certain white hotel in Paris yet to be located by your chroniclers. It has the same elderly, un-
pretentious grace and many fine old plants long nurtured
by the management. Terminus freaks will find a haven
here; the bedrooms abut directly on to the shunting sheds,
and afford an all-night, no-holds-barred spectacle of a
little-known aspect of the British Transport system. The
hotel is particularly favoured by illicit lovers: its fine,
damp-consumed cornices dating from the nineteenth century, its marbled fire grates stuffed with yellow newspaper,
not to speak of its outrageously impertinent waiters,
who look to the unattached clientèle for the gratification of
their sexual needs, all provide a background of desolate
incongruity exceptionally conducive to high performance.*

"Shamus cramped me. He made me such a *prig. Observing.* Who the hell wants to observe? He's not a school-

master, and I'm not his pupil. It's over, all that stuff, and he's got to realise it. Fie."

"Fie."

"Pshaw."

"Pshaw."

"Meeow."

"Meeow."

"You're a bear, Cassidy. A big, wuffly bear. Cassidy, I want to be raped."

A *Pailthorpe* bear, thought Cassidy.

Cheeribye, the porter had said, seeing them to their room, mind you get your money's worth.

Do stations never sleep? he wondered. Clang-clang, clang. You must dance but I must sleep.

Got to be a lion tonight lover; mouse-time again soon.

"Cassidy."

"Yes."

"I love you."

"I love you."

"Really?"

"Really."

"I could make you the happiest man on earth."

"I am already."

"More, Cassidy."

"I *can't*. That was the full menu. *Honestly*."

"Nonsense. Put your mind to it and you can do anything. You are suffering from a thoroughly unrealised potential."

An announcer was calling the night sleeper to Penzance. Departs at midnight, Cassidy thought; a little after; his eyelids were very heavy. Bright bands of railway light lay on the papered ceiling.

"Promise?" Helen asked.

"Promise."

"For ever and ever and ever and ever?"

"And ever."

"I promise?"

"I promise."

There was no blood available so they had Talisker instead.

"What else is in that book?"

"I told you. You write the great novel in prison."

"But how does he find out?"

"Find out what?"

"That they're lovers, you and me."

"He read me that bit," Helen said gravely. "It was very spectral."

"What does that mean?"

"It was never really *dramatised*. It just happened."

"How?"

"In the book, he's called Balog. Shamus is. *Gradually Balog came to suspect what he already knew. That his virtue had gone into his friend and his friend had taken Sandra for his lover.*"

Discovering in himself physical resources he had long given up for spent, Cassidy sat up abruptly in bed.

"*Sandra?*" he repeated.

"He rather *likes* the name. He thinks it suits me."

"But that's absolutely *disgusting*. I mean everyone will . . ." He checked himself. Better to talk to Shamus directly on the matter. It's really too much. I mean, I take the man to Paris, dress him, pay his rent, and the next thing he does is lampoon my wife, make a public show of her. "Anyway," he said, in a nasty, academic tone, "how can you suspect something you already know?"

There was a long silence. "If there's one thing Shamus *does* understand," said Helen firmly, "it's the structure of the novel."

"Well it's ridiculous, that's my view. Comparing *you* with Sandra. It's insulting."

"It's art," said Helen, and turning her back lay a long way from him.

"You don't think you should ring Lowestoft do you?" Cassidy suggested. "In case he's back?"

"What would we do if he was?" Helen asked tartly. "Invite him up to join us? Cassidy, you're not *afraid* of him are you?"

"I'm worried about him if you must know. I happen to love him."

"We both do."

Gently she began kissing him. "Grinch," she whispered. "Grizzlebear, hellbeef."

Oxford, the announcer said. Your last chance to get aboard.

But by then she had decided he was in need of the ultimate comfort.

The day dawned very slowly, an internal dawn of yellow mist that gradually brightened under the sooty domes of the station roof. At first, watching through the window, Cassidy took it for the steam of locomotives. Then he remembered that locomotives had no steam any more, and he realised it was fog, a thick, venomous fog. Helen was asleep, cut off from him by the inner peace that comes with faith. No frown, no cry, no anguished whisper against the hellhound Dale: a deep repose, virtue is rewarded.

Helen *is* our virtue; Helen is eternal.

Helen can sleep.

Rising late, they spent the day visiting their favourite places but the gibbons took no pleasure in the fog, and the bust of Mussolini had been removed for cleaning.

"Probably stolen by Fascists from Gerrard's Cross."

"Probably," Cassidy agreed.

They did not go to Greenwich.

In the afternoon they saw a French film which they agreed was fabulous, and when it was over they went back to the Adastras for another exchange of views.

Afterwards, in the intimacy of shared repose, she told him with little prompting how she and Shamus had parted.

"I mean it was so easy, *Christ*. I just said, I think I'll go to town and do some shopping and see how Sal is, and tidy the flat and check on Dale and see lover, and he said fine, off you go. I mean *he* does it, why shouldn't I? Anyway he was perfectly happy. I said I'd ring him, and he said don't bother, how long would I need? I said a week and he said fine. Well that was all right, wasn't it?"

"Fine," said Cassidy. "Of course it was. Absolutely fine. Have you ever done it before?"

"Done what?" Helen asked sharply.

"Gone shopping. To London. To see Sal and people. On your own."

She thought for a long time before speaking.

"Cassidy, you have to try to understand. There is one edition of me, and one only. It belongs to you. Part of me belongs to Shamus, it's true. But not your part. Have you any questions?"

"No."

To please him however she put through a call to Lowestoft, but there was no reply.

Sandra, on the other hand, answered the telephone at once.

"They've offered me Lowestoft," he told her.

"Oh."

"Aren't you pleased?"

"Naturally. Very."

"How are the invitations going?"

For the party; the celebration. Whatever we're celebrating.

A hundred sent out, twenty so far replied, said Sandra: "We hope very much you'll be able to come."

"Thanks," said Cassidy, making a joke of it. "So do I."

31

During this exacting period of Cassidy's life—the next morning perhaps, the morning after—there occurred one of those small incidents which had little bearing upon the central destiny of the great lover but nevertheless illustrated with unpleasant force the sense of approaching reckoning which was overtaking him. Arriving at the office at about midday on one of his rare visits from the greater stage on which he had elected to perform—an unbreakable engagement, he had told Helen, a political thing and rather high level—he was met once more by the insolent gaze of the receptionist and a mauve envelope addressed to him in Angie Mawdray's handwriting.

He found her in bed, in a state of high fever, Lettice on her lap and Che Guevara on the wall.

"*How* do you know?" he insisted, holding her hand.

"I just feel it, that's all."

"But feel *what*, Angie?"

"I can feel it growing in my tummy. It's like wanting to go to the lav. I can feel its heart beating if I lie still enough."

"Listen Angie, love, have you seen a doctor?"

"I won't do that," she said.

"For a check, that's all."

"Feeling is knowledge. You said that. If you feel something it's true. My horoscope says it too. All about giving my heart to a stranger. Well if I have a baby I *do* give it a heart don't I, so sod it."

"Look," said Cassidy, urgent now. "Have you been sick?"

"No."

"Have you \ . ." he tried to remember their euphemism. "Has the Chinaman been?"

"I don't know."

363

"Of course you know!"

"Sometimes he hardly comes at all." She giggled, pulling his hand down under the bedclothes. "He just knocks and goes away. Aldo, is she *really* your mistress? Truly, Aldo?"

"Don't be daft," said Cassidy.

"Higher up," she whispered. "There, that's it . . . *now* . . . only I love you, Aldo, and I don't want you fucking other ladies."

"I know," said Cassidy. "I never will."

"I don't mind you fucking your wife if you've got to, but not Beauties like that one, it's not fair."

"Angie, believe me."

After much argument he persuaded her—a day later? two days?—to let him send a sample of her water to a place in Portsmouth that advertised on the back of Sandra's *New Statesman*. She wouldn't send much—about a miniature, no more—and she wouldn't tell him how she had got it in there. He enclosed a seven and sixpenny postal order and a stamped envelope addressed to himself at the works. The envelope never came back. Perhaps they hadn't sent enough, or perhaps—an appalling vision—the bottle had broken in the post. For a time, a part of him worried about little else; scanned the office mail for his own handwriting the moment it came in, rummaged in the package room on the pretext of having lost his watch. Gradually the danger seemed to recede.

"They only tell you if it's positive," he explained to her, and they came to agree that she probably wasn't pregnant after all.

But now and then, unawares, he surprised himself, during his moments of great passion elsewhere, by visions of Angie's pathetic offering slowly darkening on the shelf of some back-street laboratory or, still with its lemon and barley label, bobbing out to sea past the Duke of Edinburgh's yacht.

32

"Look thy last on all things lovely," Helen announced, "every hour."

"Why? What's happened?"

They were shopping in Bond Street; Helen needed gloves.

"Shamus rang."

"Rang? Rang where? How did he reach you?"

A friend, she said vaguely; he had rung the friend's house and she had happened to be there.

"Just like that?"

"Cassidy," she said wearily, "I am *not* a Russian spy."

"Where is he?"

"In Marseilles. Collecting material. He's going on to Sainte-Angèle. I'm to meet him there at the weekend."

"But you said he was in Lowestoft!"

"He got a lift."

"To Marseilles? Don't be ridiculous!"

Irritated by this interjection, Helen devoted her interest to a shop window.

"Sorry," said Cassidy. "What else?"

"He's decided to set the book in Africa instead of Ireland. He thought of getting a boat and going straight there. He changed his mind. He'll take the chalet instead."

Inside the shop a girl attendant measured her incomparable hand.

"Did he talk about me?"

"Sent you his love," she said, laying the glove against her palm.

"How did he sound?"

"Collected. Sober, I'd say."

Cautiously, she slid her fingers into the black mouth.

"Well that's great. He's probably writing hard. What else?"

"He said please buy him a dressing gown, a black one

with red piping round the collar. So we can do that now, can't we?"

"We'll take them," Cassidy told the girl and gave her his credit card.

In the street again, she added very little. No, he didn't usually go abroad without telling her; but then he wasn't a very usual person was he? No, he hadn't said anything which suggested he was suspicious; he was most insistent she should enjoy herself in London; but the week was up and she should come to him.

"Rather as if that was my ration of you. There's a place called Alderton's, do you mind? In Jermyn Street. You haven't reconsidered your investment, have you, Cassidy?" she asked in the cab.

"What in?"

"Me!"

"Of course not. Why?"

"I would very much like you to hug me. That's why."

At Alderton's, both very quiet, they selected a dressing gown and Cassidy consented to try it on.

"May he?" asked Helen. "He's *exactly* my husband's size."

They went together up a winding steel staircase. The cubicle was along one wall, behind a curtain, in what seemed to be someone's drawing room. A faded portrait of Edward VII hung beside a fox's brush. Taking him gently in her arms, she stood against him, head down, the way he remembered her at Haverdown, at the Savoy, the way he had danced with Sandra at Oxford long ago. Her body felt suddenly very weak through the mohair of the dressing gown, and her passion was no longer his enemy. She took his hands and folded them against her breast, and finally she kissed him, lips closed, for a long time. They heard the salesman's footsteps coming up the iron staircase, and Cassidy thought of prison again, nothing to say except we've still got five minutes.

"Did I give it you, Cassidy?" she asked at the airport.

"What?"

"Faith."

"You gave me love," said Cassidy.

"But did you believe in it?" she asked, crying in his

arms. "Stop patting me, I'm not a dog. *Tell me.*" She held him away. "Tell me: did you believe in it? What do I say to him if he asks?"

"I did. I did believe. I still do."

The air hostess helped her to the departure gate. She used both hands, right arm across Helen's back to help her go along and left arm short to keep her vertical. Reaching the barrier, Helen neither waved nor looked back; just joined the crowd again, and let them take her.

The party had a disjointed quietness. As if the Queen had died, thought Cassidy; part of a national dismay. On the top floor behind closed doors Snaps, in churlish non-attire, was playing sultry gramophone records to selected friends. She appeared seldom, and then only to fetch more champagne and return peevishly to her unseen entertainments. In the kitchens Sandra and Heather Ast, too busy to be present, prepared hot canapés which found no distribution; while the children, for whom costly musical instruments had been set out in the basement, made no sound whatever.

"Leave them to *themselves,*" Ast urged him with a sanity only given to the childless. "They'll be all right, you'll see."

The Eldermans had stayed away. Large parties were against their principles, they discouraged an intimate exchange.

Such guests as had arrived were stuck at the centre floors like the victims of a faulty elevator, sheepishly waiting to go up or down.

"You've given them too much drink too soon," Sandra hissed at him, storming past with a Jonathan Cafe salver piled high with *vol-au-vents.* "As *usual.* They're *drunk, look* at them."

Over her shoulder, Heather transmitted an emphatic smile.

"It's all *gorgeous,*" she assured him when Sandra had gone, and tipped his elbow with her fingers. "Gorgeous," she repeated.

Several of Heather's friends had arrived; mostly men and mostly in publishing; they were distinguished by the brightness of their clothes and they had taken over the nursery, where they were admiring Hugo's paintings. Heather, in flying visits, explained the background. Yes, Hugo was amazing for his age; well so was Mark actually, they were on a par. She was looking forward enormously to having them to herself while Sandra and Aldo were on holiday. While she spoke, her solicitor sidled over to him, the one who had managed her divorce. His name improbably was Pitt, and Oxford had made him great.

"You're so lucky," he said, "having Heather."

The largest group, however, surrounded Mrs. Groat, who was quite drunk on bitter lemon. The familiar patches of red had appeared low down on her cheeks, and her eyes were swimming wildly inside their blue lenses. She was leaning back, flapper-style, on a low Regency chair, her hands linked round one raised knee, and she was talking to the new cornice, with which she was already on coquettish terms. A black walking stick rested against her chair and her foot was bandaged against cramp. Her theme was the goatishness of all men, and the offences which they had committed against her mysteriously hardy virtue. Worst of all was Colly, a childhood friend with whom she had recently passed a weekend:

"So anyway Colly had this Hillman Minx, why he bought a Hillman I shall *never* know but of course your father had a Hillman and Colly always *wanted* to live up to him, of course." Her dialogue was addressed to her daughters, though neither was present to hear it. "Not that your father was much to live up to, not like that, but still. So anyway, we were having a perfectly ordinary nice weekend at Faulkland Saint Mary, not marvellous but what can you expect, it was a place his mother took him to when he was a child or something, only a pub with rooms of course, but still. So Colly was being perfectly reasonable, dull but quite *nice*, and we'd had *quite* a nice dinner, not Claridges but still, and my dear I was in my room writing to Snaps when in Colly waltzes, asking whether I'm warm enough and grinning all over his face. Me in well just a wrap. Ready for bed. But *Colly* of course, wearing our *mulberry* dressing gown, my dear, right down to our feet, looking *just* like your father or Noel Coward or someone but more ashamed of it. 'What *do* you mean *warm* enough,' I said. 'It's midsummer and absolutely stifling.' He knows I loathe the heat. And so my dear, he

just stands there, hovering and puffing. 'Well, *warm*
enough,' he says. '*You* know,' and my dear he *points* to it
through his dressing gown, like a beastly soldier or a tramp
or something. '*Warm* enough,' he says. 'Warm enough.
Down below.' And my dear, he was *quite* drunk, I could
tell by the way he leered although I can't see a thing but
still. I wouldn't have minded if he'd been able to carry it
off, that's a different thing altogether, I *quite* agree with
the younger generation there, I'm sure. Not with everything, but I do there."

The improbable frankness of this narrative drew no
one out; only Storm, Cassidy's accountant, was moved to
comment.

"What a *marvellous* woman," he whispered. "She's like
Dietrich, better."

"Yes," said Cassidy.

"Cassidy my dear fellow, how is your poor friend?"

It was old Niesthal. His wife, in lovely black, was nodding
brightly over his shoulder. His long, kindly face was wrinkled with concern.

"Now my dear," Mrs. Groat was saying, noticing Sandra's approach. "I was merely telling them about Colly,
I'm not flowing white raiment whatever they may think,
I'm flesh and blood my dear, it's only fair, I have my own
life to lead, it's time you knew. Darling these aren't very
hot, or is it the stairs? Still I never did hold with hot
plates did I? Colly proposed to me, so there. He wanted
me to leave your father and run away with him." She
was appealing to the company. "But of course I couldn't,
could I? Not with Snaps and Sandra to look after."

"That poor fellow, Cassidy, we were so *worried*, so
very worried."

His wife added her concern. "He was like the face of a
wild man." She turned to Sandra, accepting a *vol-au-vent*.
"Dancing on the table," she told her, evoking pity with
her eyes. "Shouting, screaming like he was being *murdered*
and the waiters not knowing how to take him. And so
brave your husband, just like a policeman—"

"Phone," said Ast.

"Thanks," said Cassidy.

"Jesus lover," said Shamus, with no accent except his own bewitching voice. "You don't half put a strain on friendship."

Next door, the children had begun to play the drums.

Sainte-Angèle

33

The enshrinement of a part of Aldo Cassidy's identity—
not to speak of a part of his fortune, illicitly yielding a tax-
free four per cent from Kantonal gilt-edged—in the remote but fashionable Swiss village of Sainte-Angèle was a
matter upon which, in less turbulent times, he would freely
have dilated. "It's my bit of aloneness," he liked to say
with a world-weary smile. "My *special* place." And would
paint a stirring picture of the Chairman and Managing
Director—was he also still President? he forgot—of Cassidy, anyway, clad in rough alpine tweeds trekking from
valley to valley, conferring with shepherds, whispering with
guides in the bazaars, as he penetrated ever deeper into
the interior of uncharted Europe on his lonely quest for
seclusion from the hurly-burly of big business. "It's
where I keep my books," he would add, leaving with his
questioners a vision of scattered cow huts and one rough-
built chalet where Cassidy, the scholar *manqué,* caught up
on his Greek philosophers.

To Helen, stretched beside him in the luxurious comfort
of the Adastras Hotel, he had emphasised the cultural
and historic appeal of his chosen section of the Alps. The
beauty of Sainte-Angèle was *fabled,* he said, quoting a
brochure he had recently read in praise of his investment.
Not a poet, not a member of the Few but had experienced
profound movements of the artistic spirit upon contemplating its incomparable peaks, its dizzy waterfalls, its
noble if rude domestic architecture. Byron, Tennyson,
Carlisle, and Goethe, to name but a handful, all had
paused here in breathless awe to sing their praises of the
apocalyptic cliffs and the uncompromising sheerness of
the valley walls: Shamus would be no exception.

"But is it *dangerous,* Cassidy?"

"Not if you know your way around. You have to get
your mountain legs, mind."

"Well, shouldn't we go bicycling first or something? To prepare?"

As to the evils of modernity, he assured her, they had barely encroached upon the place. Balanced upon the upper basements of the great Angelhorn massif, Sainte-Angèle could only be reached by a single-track railway. There was no road. Jaguars, even Bentleys, must be left at the lower station.

"In a way, it's symbolic. You leave your troubles in the valley. Once you're up there, you're on your own. The world doesn't matter any more."

"And you're leading it all to *us*," Helen breathed, reminding him that he must put off the Eldermans or they would clash. "But I mean what do we do about . . . food and things? I suppose we just manage on cheese."

"Frau Anni will look after you," Cassidy replied cheerfully, omitting to mention, in his evocation of a faithful foreign retainer, the dozen food shops which served the fifty hotels and countless tourists who for the four winter months crammed the fairy-lit streets in search of rare souvenirs not available in the cities.

In a less romantic moment—eating alone, for instance, or driving on a secret errand—Cassidy would admit to more specific reasons for his affinity with the place. He would recall how old Outhwaite of Mount Street W. had happened to mention, the very day after Cassidy had made a big killing on the Stock Exchange, that he and Grimble were handling a Swiss property for a non-residential client; a snip at twenty-five thousand, mortgage available; how Cassidy had within minutes phoned his bankers and closed on premium dollars at eighteen per cent, which in the following week had risen to forty. Warming to the narrative, he would relive his arrival in the village to inspect his purchase; the long toil up the snowy hill, the magic moment when he first saw his own house raised against the Angelhorn, the rake of its gables perfectly answered in the angles of the peak behind it; and how, sitting on the balcony and gazing upwards at the great points and saddles of the Alps, he had recognised for the first time that a certain foreignness gave him comfort; and found himself wondering whether, after all, there had not always been a foreign corner to his heart, and whether his mother had not been Swiss. The mountains of Sainte-Angèle were appalling even on a perfect afternoon; they were also a shield, placing nature between himself and his fellow man, and reminding him of the larger relationships of his heart.

His conversations of the next day with local professional men, bank managers, lawyers and the rest, opened his eyes to another extraordinary feature of the mountain life. The Swiss *revered* commercial success! They admired it; saw it as the asset of a gentleman; stranger still, they not only held wealth to be forgiveable, but desirable, moral even. Its acquisition in their unclouded eye was a social duty towards an undercapitalised world. For the Swiss, Cassidy rich was positively more admirable than Cassidy poor, a view which in his own English circle found little acceptance and much derision.

Intrigued, he decided to remain for the weekend on the pretext of a local complication. He engaged rooms at the Angèle-Kulm, the chalet not yet being ready for his occupancy. And thus, alone, made other startling discoveries. That his father owned no hotels in Sainte-Angèle, and had no penthouse aerie overlooking the curling rink. That there were no meths drinkers in Sainte-Angèle to trouble a rich man's heart, that the chalet drawing room had no space for a grand piano. That in Sainte-Angèle, as long as a man paid his bills and tipped the delivery boys, his struggle for position was over before it was joined; that thereafter he would be known, saluted, and welcomed as a person in the tradition of the English tourist, as a patron of the Alps, collecting Bartlett prints and recalling the Empire connection.

Therefore Cassidy did not let the house, as he had intended—a small tax-free income on the Continent can do a man no harm—but left it empty. By the Tuesday of his departure he was causing diligent carpenters to fit sweet-smelling pine cupboards in the bedrooms; had bought furniture from Berne and linen from Interlaken; engaged a housekeeper and fastened nameplates to the doors, this room Mark's, this room Hugo's. And every winter from that day on, and every spring when Sandra allowed it, he had taken his family there, and walked his children in the evening pageant down the high street, and bought them fur boots and *fondue*. Sandra had not gone willingly at first; Switzerland was a millionaires' playground, the women had no vote. But gradually, on its

neutral soil, they had formed a treaty of temporary co-
existence. In Sainte-Angèle, he noticed, where she had him
largely to herself, the world's agonies became markedly
less pressing for Sandra; moreover the cold made her face
pretty, she could see it in the mirror.

Lastly—though it took Cassidy a year or two to discover
this—Sainte-Angèle was English. Was administered by an
English government-in-exile, with an English cabinet re-
cruited largely from the area of Gerrard's Cross, a government that was both legislative and executive, and met daily
at a reserved table in the most popular bar, calling itself a Club, and moaning about the discourtesy of the na-
tives and the rising value of the franc. In spirit, it was a
military government, colonial, imperial, self-appointed.
Its veterans wore campaign medals and decorations for
valour; its young the uniform pullovers of English regiments. These people took decisions of immense import.
True, the governed were not even always aware of the
existence of their governors; true, the good Swiss continued
to go about their lives in the sweet illusion that they ran
their own community, and that the English were merely
tourists like any others, except a little louder and less affluent. But in terms of history it was written for all who
cared to see: the skill and power which once had bound
all India, Africa, and North America into a single Empire
had found a final enclave on this small and beautiful
alpine ledge. The village of Sainte-Angèle was the last proof-
rock of the English administrative greatness, of the super-
race of clerks and merchants. They came here every year to
own and to mispronounce it; and little by little they had
added Cassidy to their ranks. Not all at once, and never
noisily. Cassidy's desire for quiet, his un-English deference
towards the local inhabitants, his stated wish to avoid
controversy, all dictated that his function be subdued; and
so it was. On their printed lists of office-bearers, in their
announcements of annual honours and awards, his name
either did not appear or was hedged about by qualifying
adjectives: *co-opted, ex-officio, honorary.* At senate evenings
on Tuesday, Council evenings on Wednesday, Prae-
sidium conferences on Thursday, Get-Togethers on Saturday, at English Church on Sunday, his influence passed
largely unacknowledged. Only when a great matter was

in hand—the recruitment of a new member, the raising of advertisement rates in the Club magazine, or the purchase of a new piece of furniture for the gracefully disintegrating clubroom—would a small nocturnal troop of cabinet ministers and their retinue, muffled against the cold, wend its way up the narrow path for punch and wisdom at the Cassidy chalet.

"He's so awfully generous," they said, "and *such* a good committee man." Many were ladies. "He's so *rich*," they said and spoke of quite large contributions made in francs.

In the tearooms and afternoon dance-bars, in the little groups that huddled round the English notice-board at the end of the day's skiing, his prowess as an alpinist was deferentially admired. A Renaissance man, they said; an all-rounder of the alpine sports; he had climbed the Matterhorn in winter; he had won the *quatre pistes* at Val-d'Isère, he had held the bobsleigh record at St. Moritz, he had taken part in night ski-jumping in a dinner jacket and beaten all the Swiss; he had done the *haute route* with A. L. Rowse. These feats were not recorded, and Cassidy himself was too humble to own to them. But from year to year, humility or no, he had become a small monument to their collective greatness. And if he had not climbed the pedestal of his own accord, neither had he so far found reason to dismount.

Such, till now, the nature of Cassidy's foreign haven. A mountain fastness, preserving at high altitude and low temperature many of the harmless visions which comprised his aspiring English soul; an extra life, not unlike its English fellow, but rendered innocent by the vastness of the scenery which contained it. Yet on that cold, blank morning of a nameless, sunless month, Cassidy found neither pleasure nor comfort in the prospect of revisiting his mountain self.

Outside, the scenery was white and listless. What was not white was black, or chalked by cloud and squalls of gritty snow which glanced the leaking window he faced. The fog had drained the mountains of their colour; and something had drained Cassidy also, paled him, attacked the last optimism which till now had always somehow vanquished in his features. He rose because he was lifted, but his body was without motion, sketched in complementary greys against the high white desert of the sky and hills. Sometimes, as if obeying an unheard command, he intoned a note of music; and catching himself, lowered his eyes and frowned. He wore gloves; his railway ticket was stowed in the left palm, recalling a habit he had learned from a mother while travelling on trolley buses in coastal towns. He had shaved early, probably near Berne, and to himself he smelt of the many-too-many other people who used the same night sleeper from Ostend.

34

Where had he been, for how long, when?

These questions had concerned him off and on throughout the journey. They were not an obsession but much remained to disentangle, and Cassidy had a nasty feeling, particularly just before food, that he might already be dead. On the white screen of the window as it carried him indifferently upwards, a formless array of visions played before his largely uncritical eye. These pictures were his mind; his memory no longer served him, it had joined his fears. I am outside my own experience, he thought; I watch it through this window. A carriage whose name is Cassidy, peopled by empty seats. Outside me lies the desert, my destiny.

Watch. Ha!

He sits up sharply. Who is this? Mark's headmaster, carrying a number-four iron, army waterproofs over his frightful suit, a Russian fur hat clapped over his hollow face, lollops through the frosty mists. The raindrops run off him as if he were a military monument, circling his zealot's eyes and washing lighter lines over the bronze campaigner's skin. You taught me too, cried Cassidy, and you were not one day younger even in those days!

"Marazion's a tough crowd. Always were. Pity your boy's not playing."

"He is," said Cassidy, used to these confusions. "I'm Cassidy, Mark's boy," he explained, meaning father but getting it wrong.

Snow here, rain there. Battle rain, rolling across the football field in directionless, icy clouds, enveloping, not falling. Only the nearest players are visible, reeling and groping in the gas attack. A 1916 whistle blows; put on your gas masks, the Boche are coming over the top; hands on shoulders, boys, and follow me.

379

"*Think*, Saviours, *think!*" the Headmaster bellowed. "Look at that fool Meadows. Meadows you're a fool, a cretin, d'you hear? An imbecile. *You're* not Meadows are you?" the Headmaster asked.

"No," said Cassidy. "I'm Cassidy. Mark's father."

A fat child in a mud-soaked shirt hacked wildly at a sodden football.

"Sorry sir," he whispers, dying for the colonel, and rolls over, shot through the heart.

"*Use* it!" the Headmaster yelled in a quite unsimulated frenzy. "Oh my giddy aunts, my gracious Lord, don't *kick* it, use it, *keep* it! Oh my God, my God, oh *God*."

From somewhere the gas alarm sounded again and a thin burst of applause pattered wetly to nothing.

"Was it a goal?" Cassidy asked, craning his neck to show enthusiasm, as a trickle of rain slid across his collarbone. "It's very hard to see."

For some time an agonised exhalation was the only answer.

"I do tell them," the Headmaster whispers, turning to him wide-eyed with the pain of defeat. "They don't understand but I do tell them. Can't win without God. Goalie, referee, twelfth man, He's all of them. They don't understand of course. But one day they will, I'm sure. Don't you think so?"

"I believed you," Cassidy assured him. "You used to say the same to me and *I* believed you. Look, I'm Cassidy, Mark's father, I wonder whether I could talk to you for a minute about my son."

But the Headmaster is howling again, hopelessly, for God's support, as out of the fog the baleful clapping of cold, wet hands issues once more.

"Who *did* that? Who kicked it straight at their forward line? Who *was* it?"

"Cassidy," says someone.

"It's only because he's smaller than the others," says Cassidy. "He'll kick it the right way when he's bigger, I'm sure. Look, I'm going away for a bit, I wondered if I could take him out to tea."

"Keep at it *hard!* Attack, Saviours, attack! Buffoons! Oh you *stupid* little apes."

Once more the cavernous eyes turned to Cassidy, scanning him vainly for traces of divinity.

"Send him to Bryanston," he advised at last. "First class for broken homes, first class."

Turning his high thin back, the Headmaster loped forlornly into the fog.

And we Cassidys, it is a maxim of our broken home, we *always* travel first class. Beyond the window, a clump of Haverdown conifers struck suddenly out of the mist; at their foot stood a dismal pagoda painted dark brown and dusted with old snow.

"Unterwald," he read aloud.

And watched himself, seated in the locker room, smoking to defeat the smell; watching the ageing, vivid face of an eleven-year-old boy at the end of a long day's fight.

Mark.

A continental little boy, this Cassidy, confiding and easily moved; fond of touching people while he spoke to them; Mark, my lover.

"If I was a goalkeeper," Mark murmured, numbly untying his boots, "I could wear gloves."

"You did jolly well," said Cassidy, helping him.

Seeing him again after so long, Cassidy was reminded how small he was, how slender his wrists. The other boys looked on with contempt, trying to catch the traitor's actual words.

"I *loathe* football. Why do I have to play it if I loathe it? Why can't I do something gentle?"

"I loathed it too," said Cassidy to encourage him. "Always, I promise. At every school I went to."

"Then why make *me* do it?"

Following his naked son to the shower room, Cassidy thought: Only the smell is warm. The fetid, sour smell of football vests and Dorset mud, and battle dresses drying in tomorrow's sun. Mark was much thinner than the other children and his genitals were less developed: cold and shrivelled, a very jaded sex. The boys crammed in together, shorn prisoners, the whole team under one disgraceful jet.

"Mummy says she hasn't given me enough love," said Mark, over tea in the Spinning Wheel.

"That's something silly Heather said to her," said Cassidy.

The boy ate in silence.

"I'm going to Switzerland," said Cassidy.

"With Heather?"

"Alone."

"Why?"

"I thought I'd try and write a book," said Cassidy at random.

"How long will you be?"

"Few weeks."

"I don't miss Mummy. I miss you."

"You miss us both," said Cassidy.

"What's it about?" Mark asked suddenly, as if he knew already, had a hunch.

"What?"

"The book."

"It's a novel."

"Is that a story?"

"Yes."

"Tell it me."

"You can read it when you grow up."

The tea shop sold homemade sweets, fudge and chocolates with varied centres. Cassidy gave him ten shillings to make his own purchases.

"That's *miles* too much," said Mark hopelessly and gave him five back.

The boy waited at the gatepost, a slender, balancing creature, hugging himself in his grey pullover as he watched the warm Bentley glide towards him down the drive. Cassidy lowered the electric window and Mark kissed him, his small lips full upon his father's, crumby from tea, and cold from the wait in the evening air.

"I'm just not suited for this kind of education," Mark explained. "I'm not tough and I don't improve by being bullied."

"I wasn't suited to it either."

"Then take me away. It's pointless."

Mark has only a quantum of courage, he thought; I am using it up for him, spending it before he is old enough to spend it for himself.

"Here, have this," he said, and gave him his gold pencil,

sixty guineas from Asprey's, a private indulgence from another life.

"What'll *you* write with?"

"Oh a pen or something," said Cassidy, and left him, still at the gate, working the lead in and out, fair head bowed in concentration.

Sometimes it was too much for me to bear, that face, Cassidy thought, gazing back on a dead life; it was too hung in grief, too yellowed by pain and by the effort of understanding. Therefore I gave him things to turn his face away from me: gold or money, or something miniature to make him stoop.

Or perhaps, thought Cassidy consolingly, wiping the tears from the window, perhaps it wasn't Mark at all.

Perhaps—since objectivity at times of crisis is still the Managing Director's greatest single asset—perhaps this child was Aldo, back at Sherborne, the day Old Hugo called to see me on his way to Torquay; the day he ran the Great Bike Race for all comers, a nice quid for the winner and a nice ten bob note for second place.

To this moderately cohesive, moderately earthbound vision of his leavetaking, as he continued to climb the mountain, Cassidy proceeded to add others more fragmentary and less capable of verification; and in the course of this put to himself questions of a quite metaphysical nature.

Had Christmas passed, for instance? Sometimes a shadow crossed the sterile white window, closing downwards from the left corner like a drop of blood upon his field of view, and he smelt the winter evenings drawing in, and glimpsed the spectral outline of a dusk-lit pine tree frosted on its windward side, the way they grew at Christmas in the wide bow-windows of the Crescent. At Mittelwald, still pondering this question, he was not surprised to observe the face of Granny Groat appear before him, drawn and sleepless, and took it as further proof that the feast was past: for only Christmas could strain her so severely. Her head was not framed centrally—she had got it wrong in some way—and she was waiting stubbornly on the wrong side of the track, so that he felt her presence behind him and had to turn to make the recognition. Her wide, witless eyes, doubled and vulnerable, washed blue by her tinted spectacles, were bright and frightened, but the dabs of fur at her collar and the rouge at her cheeks announced quite clearly that she was on her way to church. Also, she wore a paper hat; a festive yellow creation, mannishly grotesque.

Also, she carried a Christmas cracker in her twitching hand.

Ah but for what ceremony? A funeral?

Is she wearing black for instance? The Chinese are known to loose off firecrackers for the dead.

The train lurched forward, Groat was gone.

Well, it was not so improbable; he might very well be dead; others were. Such an explanation had been in the air for several days and very many nights. A lot of people are dead and it's *perfectly* natural, but still. Nor had he far to look for the cause of death. Suppose Old Hugo's green hand grenade, contrary to Cassidy's impression at the time, had after all exploded and removed him to another life?

To *this* life, in fact?

And that instead of merely travelling to Sainte-Angèle, he was ascending to heaven; and the railway guards were angels, hence the village name?

Momentarily stirred to optimism by this small hope of non-existence, Cassidy closed his heated eyes and with each hand lightly touched the other, determining its outlines. A don experiments upon his own body, the Haldane tradition, I'll get a knighthood yet. Then in an upward movement to the face—akin to washing, such gestures are made often by men in motion—with both hands together glumly located his nose and ample eyebrows, tip of tongue and youthful forelock; confirming, if confirmation were still needed, that though his spirit might be climbing, it was still attached to its terrestrial frame.

And that Old Hugo's hand grenade, for all his loud assurances, had been, like the rest of his father's armoury, a dud.

This incident involving War Department explosives was
not, for security reasons, shown upon the white screen, but
conveyed to Cassidy by the intimate smell of wet clover
as he lay in the field somewhere in England, face downward, tampering wretchedly with the pin. Also it may
have been—but *only* may have been—a dream; this much
your Chairman will concede. Mr. Lemming, you may add
that to the Minutes.

To reconstruct: this grenade is a gift, no father can do
more. This grenade, Old Hugo has assured him, freeing it
of its oily rags and bringing it to the lightest window in
the penthouse, this poorly painted grenade, dull green
but chipping even under wraps, is not only a gift, a truly
wonderful gift, it is one of the finest grenades ever manu-
factured.

"They don't *make* a grenade like that today. You can
scour London, I'm telling you, Aldo: a grenade like that
is totally unfindable, isn't it, Blue?"

The grenade is also the climactic of a father's many
endowments to his son:

"I've given you the *final* freedom, d'you hear? Look at
that then: life and death, you owe them *all* to me. That's
the most fantastic sacrifice any father can make, and I'm
making it, right, Blue?"

But here is the nub, here is the curse of the Cassidys,
they succeed in all but the consummation: the pin has
rusted into its housing, the weakly boy cannot loosen it.

"*Pull.* Jesus Christ All Ruddy Mighty, Blue, after all I've
done for him, after all the fantastic sacrifices I made for
him, look at *that! He can't even pull the stupid pin!*"

"But he's not a *lion*, dear, is he though, not like *you*,"
Bluebridge whickers, handing him the flask. "*Go* on Aldo
dear," she begs, calling to him *sotto voce* where he lies.
"Try, Aldo, for your Daddy's sake, *please. Try.*"

"I am trying," Cassidy retorts churlishly, but still there is
no apocalypse.

Thoroughly disenchanted, the family drives home in a
temper, conversation zero till they reach the penthouse.

For a while to his great relief he thought of nothing. The
train paused at certain intermediate stations, names were
shouted and ignored. These stations offered no passengers,
and received none in return. They were stages, formalities

of religious progress as the little train continued its pilgrimage up the white hill.

Reaching a plateau, the engine relaxed its exertions and a sense of ease replaced the frenzied clatter. I am in the Bentley, Cassidy thought; I am in Superpram.

It is the Bentley which has subdued the clanging couplings and damped the eager vibrations of the cushion springs under the thin velveteen; the Bentley's English calm which has muffled the hysteria of the foreign guards.

I am inviolate.

Barely had he formulated this pleasing notion however than his sense of security was shattered by the entry of *little* Hugo (grandson of the great hotelier) who, undaunted by costly fastenings of his father's manufacture, had forced open the door and settled himself in the passenger seat. Lifting the child free, Cassidy carried him back to the house.

Hugo white, not crying, clutching a Pan Am flightbag filled with the few things he would need: a gramophone record, a new string for his toboggan.

Hugo very hot under the arms as they embraced once more on the doorstep.

Hugo white, and still not crying.

"Come along Hug," says Mrs. Groat. "Mummy wants you." At the fifth floor, Sandra's own now, John Elderman's silhouette; valium for a broken heart.

Heather Ast is hammering at the carriage window.

"I won't hear you," Cassidy assures her through the electrically closed glass of the Bentley. "I just won't. I never want to see you again, Heather. It's as bad as that."

The glass is too thick, she hears nothing.

You'll be a Groat in ten years, Heather; you'll all be Groats. Dust to dust, groat to groat, it's a woman's destiny, she has no other.

Mercifully, he has entered a tunnel, the change distracts him. At its end, five minutes away, lies Oberwald, the upper forest. After Oberwald comes Sainte-Angèle of the Peaks; there is no halt between them.

With the tunnel, a moment's dark before the lights go up. Wooden palings, painted cheap yellow by the overhead bulbs, crowd the once-white window, flick past in a bewildering curve, like the splinted fingers of a smashed hand waved across his passive face. The sounds are magnified in this long cave. History, geology, not to speak of countless set-texts from mediaeval faculties at Oxford, all deepen and intensify the underground experience. Minotaurs, hermits, martyrs, miners, incarcerated since the first constructions, howl and clank their chains, for this is under ground, where old men scratch for knowledge, gold, and death. Once, a few years ago, looking through the same window at the same dull timbers, Cassidy found himself staring into the black, patient eyes of a chamois crammed against the tunnel wall. Reaching the village he at once made representations to the station master in the interest of the local wild life. There was nothing to be done, the official said, when he had listened very carefully to the good man's case, the chamois had been dead for several days.

These yellow lights are dull; they make me sleepy.

How long since he had slept?

Was there a record of how many nights? Mr. Lemming, you might consult the Minutes.

Or was it *one* night doled out among different beds and floors? The screaming now—be forensic—where did the screaming fit in as she held my foot, Sandra my long-standing wife, to keep me in the bedroom? Held it against her head, lying full length on the tasteful curly Wilton, wetting Christ's ankle with her tears? Was that *one* incident of an eventful night, or a *whole* night by itself? Put another way, in Sandra's Women's Army voice: *Who broke the clock?* That grandfather clock. *Who broke it?* Four hundred quid's worth of sixteenth-century inlay toppled from its hall stand? *Own up! It's perfectly natural to break a clock I simply want to know who did it. I'll count five, if no culprit volunteers I shall not finish the sentence.*

One . . .

The first suspect (class has *much* to do with crime) is Snaps' libidinous visualizer, preaching free love over the bannisters in his corduroy claret suit. The resentful fellow gave the clock a push, it was his way of closing the generation gap.

But wait, Snaps has fled her lair, taking her visualizer with her. Hied herself to Bournemouth, pregnancy the cause, she likes to have them by the sea, water being ever preferable to air.

Two ...

Who else? Quick, who else?

Granny Groat, putative mother-in-law, sometime mother of the accused, floundering through dark corridors to save the electricity: *she* did it ...

Not guilty, alas. Decisive gestures are not her style, not even by mistake.

Three. I'm warning you ...

Very well: *you* did it! Sandra herself, wet-bibbed from crying, no strength left to sleep; Sandra, in her last exhaustion, lurched into the clock, toppled it, before she fell herself?

Not guilty. She would own up.

Four ...

Help! I accuse old Hugo, satanist, worker of spells, possessor of an evil eye! Staring out of the penthouse window, sipping a nice touch of brandy and ginger, the old wizard deliberately carved the air with a familiar gesture of his hand and set up waves of disturbance which found their way to Abalone Crescent and so destroyed the instrument of time!

"Father I need a bed."

"Then go home, it's waiting for you, isn't it?"

"Father, put me to bed. Please."

"Go home! You'll be a delinquent if you don't remarry that bitch, get out, get out, get out!"

The tunnel continued; to dance but not to sleep.

"Angie I need a bed."

Angie Mawdray, standing at her own front door, was dressed in a light bedwrap which did not conceal one side of her body.

"It's no good, Aldo," she said. "Honest."

"But Angie I only want to sleep."

"Then go to a hotel, Aldo, you can't come here, you know you can't, not *now*."

"But Angie."

"I'm *married*," she reminded him, rather sternly. "*You* remember, Aldo, you organised the whip-round."

"Of course," said Cassidy. "Of course I did, I'm sorry. Good evening Meale, how's it going?"

From under Che Guevara's uncompromising stare, the pallid face of Meale nodded respectfully to his master. He would have stood up no doubt, but his nakedness was against him.

"Good evening, Mister Aldo, step in, sir, do. Sorry about the mess."

"Come in the afternoons," Angie whispered. "I'm only working mornings, aren't I, *silly?*"

Went to Kurt's? Or stayed at Angie's after all? Certainly he felt a limpness round the loins, a sense of *after* rather than *before*. Did he then after all enjoy the very skilled embraces of Miss Mawdray the well-known top secretary, while Meale's apologetic eye turned sensibly away for the visit of the Chairman?

"*You've been very good to us Mister Aldo, we don't know how to thank you, I'm sure.*"

"*Think nothing of it,*" says the old boulevardier, nicely lodged among the dewy folds. "*You young people need a start in life.*"

A howl from the engine. Daylight soon? Not in Kurt's grey, uncomfortable rooms; even the windows are smoked against the sun.

"Kurt, I need a bed."

Kurt had no one in his apartment, not Angie Mawdray, not Lemming, not Snaps, not Blue, not Faulk, not even Meale. He wore a grey Swiss dressing gown of best Swiss silk, and when Cassidy was tucked unsafely in the ever-prepared spare room he came to see him with a long white cup of Swiss Ovomaltine.

"No, Kurt."

"But Cassidy my dear fellow you *know* you are one of us. Listen. *One,* you prefer the company of men, correct?"

"Correct, but—"

"*Two* your physical encounters with women have been totally without satisfaction. Cassidy, look here I mean my God I can *tell*. I can see it in your eyes, anyone can. *Three*—"

"Kurt honestly, I would if I wanted, I promise. I'm not ashamed any more. I wanted to at school but that's just because there weren't any girls about. That's the truth. I've got too much sense of humour, Kurt. I think of you lying there with nothing on, holding it, and I get the giggles. I mean *what for* . . . do you see what I'm getting at?"

"Goodnight Cassidy."

"Goodnight, Kurt. And thanks."

"And look here, one day we climb the Eiger, right?"

"Right."

Dozing, he quite hoped Kurt would come back: exhaustion erodes the moral will as well as the sense of humour. But Kurt didn't. So Cassidy listened to the traffic instead, and wondered: does he sleep, or dream of me?

Daylight, and another warning scream from the small, incorruptible engine. The train has stuck. The doors hiss and fall open. The porter is calling Sainte-Angèle.

He called it in the *patois*, it could have been Michel Angelo or England. He called it loud, above the three-toned clanging of the mountain bell; he carolled it for Christmas past or coming, in a voice of male dominance which echoed over the empty station. He called it straight at Cassidy through the smeared white window of his first-class carriage; and if you want to go farther you must change. He called it as if it were Cassidy's own name, his last walk and his last stopping place. The porter was a bearded man and wore a badge of office on his smock. His eyes were masked by heavy black brows, and by the black shadow of his black peaked cap. Answering the summons, Cassidy got up at once, stepped blithely on to the empty platform, his overnight bag swinging in his strong hand.

"Tomorrow," said the porter consolingly, "we get *plenty* snow."

"Ah but tomorrow doesn't often come, does it?" Cassidy replied, never at a loss to cap a pleasantry.

The weather which greeted Cassidy at Sainte-Angèle was like a meteorological extension of the confusion which had recently taken possession of his mind. The best of holiday resorts has its uncongenial seasons, and not even Sainte-Angèle, famed though she may be for her dependable and temperate character, is exempt from nature's immutable laws. In winter, as a rule, her snowclad village street is a jubilant carnival of bobble-hats, horse-sledges, and brilliant shop windows, where Europe's affluent swains rub shoulders with the girls of Kensal Rise, and many insincere contracts of love are closed in the surrounding forests. In summer, their less pecunious teachers and elders stride vigorously into the flower-laden slopes and refresh themselves beside Goethe's ebullient streams, while children in traditional costume chant age-old songs in praise of chastity and cattle. Spring is a sudden and lovely time, with impatient flowers bursting through the late snow; while autumn as the first snows fall brings back forgotten hours of breathless, church-like quiet between the bustle of two hectic seasons.

But there are days, as every alpine visitor must know, when this pleasing pattern is without apparent reason violently shattered; when the seasons suddenly tire of their place in the natural cycle and, using all the weapons of their armoury, do violent battle until they have reached exhaustion. In place of winter's magic the village is assailed by querulous rains and morose, unheated nights, when thunder alternates with hybrid sleet and neither stars nor sun can pierce the swirling cloud banks. Worse, a *foehn* may come, the sick south wind that strikes the mountains like a plague, rotting giant slabs of snow and poisoning the temper of both the villagers and their guests. And when at last it takes itself away, the brown patches on the hillsides are laid out like the dead, the sky is white and empty, and the birds have gone. This *foehn* is the mountains' curse; nowhere is safe from it.

The first symptoms are external: a sourceless dripping of water, a mysterious departure of air and colour. With this depletion of the atmosphere comes a gradual draining of human energy, a sense of moral listlessness, like a constipation of the mental faculties, which spreads gradually over the whole psychic body until it has blocked all outlets. At such times, waiting for the storm, a man may smoke a cigar halfway down the village street and the trace of it will be there tomorrow, the smoke and the smell lingering in the dead air at the very place where he stood. Sometimes there is no storm at all. The lull ends and the cold returns. Or a hurricane strikes: a black, raging *Walpurgisnacht* with winds of sixty, seventy miles an hour. The high street is strewn with broken sticks, the tarmac is showing through the snow, and you would think a river has slid by in the darkness on its way from the peaks to the valley.

It was the *foehn* which ruled now.

The sight reminded Cassidy of a wet day at Lord's cricket ground. The village's two porters stood together like umpires, clutching their smocks to their middles and agreeing it was impossible. Above him, but very close, the superb twin peaks of the Angelhorn hung like dirty laundry from the grey sky. The snow was mostly gone. The clock said ten-fifteen, but it might have been stuck for years. Making his way towards the restaurant he thought: *This is how we die, alone and cold and out of breath, suspended between white places.*

"Hullo lover," said Shamus quietly. "Looking for someone are we?"

"Hullo," said Cassidy.

35

Haverdown woodsmoke lingered in the damp air, antlers loomed along the brown walls. A group of dark-faced labourers sat drinking beer. Away from them, at their own sad place, the waitresses read German magazines, secretly panting from the *foehn* like patients in a doctor's waiting room.

He was sitting near the bar, in an alcove, at a big round table all to himself, under the crossed guns of the Sainte-Angèle shooting club. A silk flag, stitched by the ladies of the community, proclaimed the village loyalty to William Tell. The alcove had a Flemish darkness, homely and confiding; the pewter glinted comfortably, like well-earned coin. He was drinking *café crème* and he had lost weight. A streak of white light from the window ran down the death-coat like a recent shock. He wore no hat and no beard; his face looked bared, and vulnerable, and very pale. Cassidy moved in beside him, holding his overnight bag in his arms like Hugo's beach crocodile, then shunting it down the polished bench, then dumping it on the floor between them with a sloppy thud.

Sitting down, he saw the gun.

It lay on Shamus' lap, a sleek pet, the barrel towards Cassidy. It was essentially a military weapon, and probably an officers' issue from the First World War. Only a full-grown officer could have worn it, however, because the barrel was about twelve inches long. Or it might have been a target pistol from the days when you steadied your weapon on your left forearm, and the range sergeant yelled "Well shot sir" when you hit a man-sized target. A lanyard was fastened to the butt. From the free end dangled a pink powder-puff.

In the kitchen, the wireless was broadcasting a Swiss time signal, a very war-like noise.

Cassidy ordered coffee, *café crème,* like the gentleman's.
The waiter remembered him well. Mr. Cassidy who tips. He
brought a gingham tablecloth and spread it with affection.
He laid out cutlery and Maggi sauce and toothpicks in a
silver box. And the children, the waiter enquired, they
were well?

Fine.

They were not, for instance, suffering from the English
habit of wearing short trousers?

Not noticeably, Cassidy said.

And they were hunting, hunting the foxes and the
chamois?

At present, said Cassidy, they were at school.

Ah, said the waiter, pursing his lips, *Eton:* he had heard
that standards had fallen.

"She's waiting," said Shamus.

They set off up the hill.

Pulling with all his strength, Cassidy found that the tape
was cutting his shoulder. If he had not been wearing his
camelhair coat, in fact, it would have broken the skin.
The tape was of nylon, six foot of it and bright red, he
held it with both hands, one at the chest and one at the
waist, making a harness of it as he strained forward.
Twice he had asked Shamus to walk, but received no useful answer beyond an impatient wave of the gun barrel,
and now Shamus was sitting upright with Cassidy's overnight bag across his knee, throwing out the things he
didn't like. The silver hairbrush had already gone, sliding
like a puck backwards down the icy path, bobbing and
spinning over the half-frozen eddies of snow and ice. He
had thought he was fit: squash at the Lansdowne, tennis
at Queen's, not to mention the stairs at Abalone Crescent.
But his flannel shirt was drenched by the time they left
the railway line, and his heart, unaccustomed to the
change of altitude, was already thumping sickly. Fitness is
relative, he told himself. After all, he's at least my
weight.

Even taken downwards, the path was unsuitable for tobog-
ganing.

From the chalet, it wound at first through scattered woods where snow barely covered the boulders, and jagged tree trunks awaited the careless navigator. Crossing an avalanche gully, it descended by way of two steep bends to a poorly fenced ramp which, being much in use by pedestrians, was strewn with grit which tore at the runners and slewed them off course. If other, hardier children ignored these hazards, Cassidy's did not, for it was one of his recurring nightmares that they would have an accident here, that Hugo would skid under a train, Mark would crush his head against a signal post, and he had entirely proscribed the route on pain of punishment. Uphill, though no doubt safer, the path was even less attractive.

Shamus had chosen Mark's toboggan, probably because of the crazy daisies which were glued to its plastic base. It was a good toboggan of its kind, a prototype sent up by a Swiss correspondent for possible exploitation on the English market. At first the design had told in its favour. But soon the broad keel was dragging heavily in the slush, and Cassidy was obliged to lean far forward into the hill in order to get enough purchase. His leather-soled London shoes slipped with every step; occasionally hauling at the tapes, he slid backwards into the bow of the toboggan, grazing his frozen heels against the plastic point; and when this happened Shamus would urge him forward with a distracted oath. The night case had gone. There was nothing in it, apparently, which Shamus thought worth keeping, so he had thrown it overboard to improve the unsprung weight, and now he was aiming the gun distractedly at whatever offered itself; a bird on the roof of a hotel, a passing pedestrian, a dog.

"My dear Mr. Cassidy, how *are* you?"

Introductions; sherry on Sunday, come round after church. Shamus bows and waves the gun; shrieks of merriment. A Mrs. Horegrove or Haregrave, a senior senator of the Club.

"What a *dangerous*-looking burden!"

"It's Hugo's," Cassidy explained, panting through his smiles. "We took it to be mended. You know what he's like about guns."

"My dear, *whatever* would Sandra say?"

About Shamus or the gun? Cassidy wanted to ask, for
her eyes were moving from one to the other with mounting surprise.

"Go away," Shamus screamed at her, suddenly losing
patience, and picking up a convenient stick, threw it hard
at her feet. "Prole. Get out or I'll shoot you."

The lady withdrew.

A heap of horse manure obstructed their progress.
Cassidy took the left side, favouring the verge.

"Pull, you bugger," Shamus ordered, still angry. "Mush,
mush, *pull*."

In the forest, the going was easier. The trodden snow,
sheltered by the trees, had neither melted nor frozen;
sometimes, for short distances, they even went downhill,
so that Cassidy had to run ahead in order to remain covered by the gun. At such moments, Shamus became nervous and issued conflicting orders: lift your hands, put
them down, keep left, keep right, and Cassidy obeyed
them all, thinking of nothing, not even the hole in his back.
The trees parted, giving a view of the brown valley and
the banks of mist that rose like oil smoke from its narrow
floor. They saw the Angelhorn in a fragment of perfect
blue, its fresh snow glittering in the high sunlight.

And stopped.

"Hey, you," said Shamus quietly.

"Yes?"

"Give us a kiss."

His hands still above his head, Cassidy walked back to
the toboggan, stooped, and kissed Shamus on the cheek.

"More," said Shamus. And at last: "It's all *right*, lover,
it's all *right*," he whispered, pushing away the tears.
"Shamus fix it. Promise. We're big enough, lover. We can
make it."

"Of course we can," said Cassidy.

"Make history," said Shamus. "Be a great first, lover.
We'll beat the whole fucking system."

"Will you walk now?" Cassidy asked, after more breathless hugs. "I'm a bit tired actually."

Shamus shook his head. "Lover, I got to toughen you
up, this is a very vigorous course, very vigorous indeed.
Takes *grip*. Faith, remember? For both of us?"

"I remember," said Cassidy, and picked the tape out of the snow.

The clouds covered them. They must have left the trees without his noticing, and walked blindly into the ambush of the fog. Sightless, Cassidy lost his balance and fell forward. Not even the path existed, for its edges were lost in the downward gust of wet mist, and his hands, grasping the slope before him, were clutching an invisible enemy. He struggled forward again.

"Where are you?"

"Here."

"Pull, lover," Shamus warned. "Keep pulling, lover, or it's shootibangs."

As suddenly as it had descended the cloud cleared and the house stood clean and waiting on its own expensive patch of snowclad hillock, fifteen pounds a square meter, "Mr. and Mrs. Aldo Cassidy" framed beside the bell button and Helen wife of Shamus painted on the balcony.

Painted on the sized, white canvas of the drifting fog, in matt half-tones, a fraction out of register.

Tall, from where they looked up at her; wearing a head scarf of Sandra's; hands set apart on the rail, face turned sharply towards the path, not seeing them but hearing their footsteps in the slush, and perhaps the zigzag echo of their voices.

"Cassidy?"

"She's a bit blue," Shamus warned in a whisper coming up beside him. "Where I belted her. Sorry about that, didn't mean to damage the goods."

"Cassidy?" she repeated, still blind but guessing at the sound.

For a moment longer, she scanned the path not realising they were there beneath her. Waiting, as all women wait. Using her body to catch the sound. Waiting for a ship, or a child, or a lover; upright, taut, vibrant.

"We're just below you," said Cassidy.

The bruise was on the cheekbone, the left one, he recorded; Shamus had hit her with his right hand, a hook probably; a hard wide one from the side, not at all unlike the mark on Sal that evening they had gone to her in Cable

Street. By the time he had opened the door she was in the hall. She closed her eyes long before he touched her, the good one and the bad one, and he heard her whisper "Cassidy" as her arms came gently round him; and he felt her shaking as if she had a fever.

"On the *mouth*," Shamus shouted from behind. "Jesus. What is this, a fucking convent?"

So he kissed her on the mouth; she tasted just a little of blood, as if she had had a tooth out.

The drawing room—it was his own design—was long and perhaps too thin for comfort. The balcony ran the whole length of it, mastering the three views: the valley, the village, and the mountain range. At one end, near the kitchen, was a pine dining recess and Helen had set the table for three, using the best napkins and the beeswax candles from the top left drawer.

"She's a bit thin," Shamus explained. "Because I locked her up till you came."

"You told me," Cassidy said.

"Not *blaming* people, lover? Got to lock princesses in towers, haven't we? Can't have the bitches whoring all over the realm."

Whether she had lost weight or not, Helen's eyes had a defiant brightness, like the courage of the very sick.

"I managed to get a duck," she said. "I seem to remember it's your favourite."

"Oh," said Cassidy. "Oh thanks."

"You do still like it, don't you?" she asked very earnestly, offering him pretzels from the compartmented red plate which Sandra used for curries.

"Rather," said Cassidy.

"I thought you might have gone off it."

"No, no."

"It's only frozen. I tried to get a fresh one, but they just . . ." She dried up, then began again. "It's so difficult on the telephone, all in a foreign language . . . he wouldn't let me out, not at all. He's even burnt my passport."

"I know," said Cassidy.

She was crying a little so he led her to the kitchen, holding her under the elbow. She leaned against him, resting her head on his shoulder, and breathed very deeply, filling her lungs with the strength of his presence.

"Hello hellbeef."

"Hi."

"He just sort of . . . knew. He didn't guess, or suspect, or anything ordinary, he *knew.* What's it called when you mop it up through the pores?"

"Osmosis."

"Well he's got it. Double osmosis. I'm crying because I'm tired that's all. I'm not sad, I'm tired."

"I know."

"Are you tired, Cassidy?"

"A bit."

"He wouldn't let me lie down. I had to sleep standing up. Like a horse."

She was crying a great deal; he guessed she had been crying for several days and now it was habit, she cried when the wind changed and when the wind stopped or when it started again, and this was the *foehn,* it changed all the time.

"Cassidy."

"Yes."

"You'd have come anyway, wouldn't you? Whether he told you to or not?"

"Of course."

"He laughed. Every day you didn't come, he laughed and said you never would. Then in between he got sad. *Come on lover,* he said, *big boy now, where are you?* Then he got loving to me and told me to pray for you."

"I had a lot to do my end too."

"How did the bosscow take it?"

Through her tears he heard Sandra's scream echoing in the stairwell, up and down, like Hugo's magic bouncing ball, between the fine cornice and the flagstone floor.

"Fine. No problem. She was happier, really . . . knowing."

"It was easy here too, really . . . once he knew I loved you."

"I better go back now," said Cassidy.

"Yes. Yes he needs you."

With a little pat of encouragement she urged him on his way.

Shamus was at the long window. He had discovered Cassidy's binoculars and was trying to train them on the bedrooms of a distant hotel. Bored, he tossed them to the floor and sauntered to the bookshelves. The gun was stuck in his waistband; the powder puff dangled idly from his fingers.

"Someone's big on Ibsen," he observed distractedly.

"Sandra."

"I like that lady. Always did. Better than Helen, anyway."

While Helen cooked, the two men played Mark's mouse game. The mouse, which was plastic, was fed into a slide. After it had run about, jumped a gap, slipped through several small holes, it entered a narrow cage and tripped a bell. The bell rang, the door closed, the mouse was caught. It was not a competitive game, since there was no way of losing, and therefore none of winning either, but it was a good game in the circumstances because it enabled Shamus to keep one hand on the gun. They had not had many turns however before Shamus grew restless and, using the poker from the fireplace, smashed the outer end of the cage. After that the mouse escaped, and Shamus became easy again, and even smiled, patting Cassidy on the shoulder by way of encouragement.

"Love you, lover."

"Love you," said Cassidy.

"Shamus has been all over Europe," said Helen encouragingly, emerging from the kitchen with a dish. "Haven't you, Shamus? Marseilles he went to, Milan, Rome . . ." She rehearsed these cities as if they would spark him, much as she might sing the praises of her sullen child, but Shamus remained unresponsive. "And his book is going wonderfully, he's been working *right up to the moment when you came,* haven't you Shamus? Write, write, write from morning till evening."

"Get the fucking duck," said Shamus. "And shut up."

"Cassidy, *wine,*" Helen reminded him with a discreet smile. "We ought to have red I suppose, with poultry."

"I'll fetch it," said Cassidy, making for the door.

"Catch," said Shamus, and threw him a large bunch of keys.

Hard, so that they smashed against the wood beside his head, and smashed again, a second time, on to the wood floor.

Many were duplicates, Cassidy noticed, picking them up. He must have collected them all together when he locked her in the attic.

The oven was the problem. It didn't seem to heat like English ovens, Helen said, it didn't come on inside when you turned the knob.

"It's infrared," said Cassidy, and showed her how it worked.

Nevertheless, the bird was still raw.

"Oh dear," said Helen. "I'll put it back."

Cassidy protested: nonsense, duck *should* be red, that was exactly how he liked it.

Shamus also protested, but for different reasons. No she fucking well wouldn't. If he was going to make history, he said, he wasn't going to be delayed by an uncooked duck.

It fell to Cassidy, therefore, with his finely tuned social instinct, once again to lead the lunchtime conversation. Choosing a theme at random—it was several years since he had seen an English newspaper—he heard himself discussing the rising tide of violence in England, and more particularly the bomb outrage recently perpetrated against a Conservative Minister. He had no use for nihilists, he said. If a man had a grudge, let him speak out, Cassidy would be the first to listen. And what, after all, was the parliamentary system for if we were to be blackmailed by any Tom, Dick, and Harry who held a contrary view to our own?

"I mean what do they want to achieve, for God's sake? Apart from the destruction of society. It's the one question they can never answer. 'All right,' I'd say to them, 'fine: the world's yours. Now tell me what you're going to do with it. How you're going to cure the sick and support the old and defend us against those madmen in China?' Well don't you agree?" he asked, wondering whether he might leave the rest of his duck.

Helen and Shamus had drawn close together, and Helen was kissing and comforting him, smoothing his hair and laying her hand across his brow.

"We've rather been out of touch with English news,"

she said over his shoulder. She was cutting up his food so that he could keep hold of the gun. "Shamus tried your wireless but I'm afraid it broke, didn't it darling?"

"Never mind," said Cassidy generously.

He offered them mashed potato, but they declined.

"Hey, Cassidy," said Shamus, brightening under Helen's care, "what do you think of her cooking?"

"Well, if this is anything to go by, it's excellent," said Cassidy. "But after all, I sampled it in London too."

"Better than the bosscow's?"

"Much," Cassidy lied heartily.

While Helen cleared, Shamus delved in his pocket and produced a small leather-bound volume, which he opened on his knee. It was the size of a diary but fatter, with gold leaf at the edges. Studying it, he appeared to come across passages of particular relevance, for he marked them in heavy ink, using the gun to hold the pages flat.

"It is loaded is it?" Cassidy asked, making his question sound as casual as circumstances allowed.

"Of *course* it is," Helen called proudly from the kitchen. "Shamus never fired a blank in his life, did you darling?"

It's the wine, thought Cassidy, it's lulled him. He had chosen a heavy Burgundy, twenty-eight francs a bottle but renowned for its soporific qualities.

Waiting for Helen again, the two men went on to the balcony for target practice. Ammunition was not a problem, for the pockets of the deathcoat were filled with bullets of different bores and calibres, and though some were clearly too large, quite a number appeared to be suitable.

First, at Shamus' request, Cassidy demonstrated the safety catch.

"It's here," he said, pointing. "You push it away from you."

"Will it shoot?"

"Not when it's on, no."

"This on?"

"No. The other way."

Pointing the pistol at Cassidy's head he pulled the trigger but nothing happened.

"And if I do it this way—"

"Then it shoots. Shamus, shouldn't we wait till the fog's cleared?"

The fog in fact had thickened; beyond it, not far away, he could hear rain falling, and that mysterious grumbling of agricultural machinery which seemed always to fill the valley in times of unseasonable stillness. While they stood there, two skiers, muffled like ghostly abbots, lurched down the trail in the direction of the station and vanished, their skis rasping in the watery snow. Shamus, who was already aiming at them as they disappeared, lowered the gun with an exclamation of annoyance and peered round for other game.

"What's the range of this thing, anyway?"

"About forty yards for accuracy. It'll kill at three hundred."

"It won't fire rapid will it?"

"No."

"I tried to get dumdums but they didn't have any." He aimed the gun again, this time at a chimney on the other side of the path. "She loves you rotten."

"I know."

"And you're equally passionate about her. You pine every minute out of her sight. You can't get to sleep quick enough to dream of her, you can't wake soon enough to come and prise her from my arms. Wife, veg, Bentley are as nothing beside your overwhelming, all-consuming, all-dignifying passion for her?"

Turning his head he gazed at Cassidy over the barrel of the raised gun.

"Poor old lover, what else could we do? Couldn't let you rot out there, could we, all on your own in the cold? Not when we spend our whole fucking lives looking for just what you've found. I mean . . . what kind of man would dig twenty years for gold and not want it when he makes a strike? Eh?"

"No one."

Shamus' gaze had not left his face.

"No one," Cassidy repeated.

"Attaboy," said Shamus, thrilling to him with a sudden brilliant smile.

Taking his arm he led him back to the drawing room.

"Helen," he shouted, still holding Cassidy's arm. "Get ready, you cow! *Courage,* lover," he whispered. "Got to be brave soldier now."

Cassidy nodded.

"Otherwise Papa have to shoot you."

Again he nodded.

"Shan't be five minutes," Helen called from the bedroom.

Together they moved the table into the centre of the room.

"We need *witnesses*," said Shamus from the kitchen. "How the fuck can I be the midwife of history when there aren't any witnesses?" He emerged with a tablecloth, a white damask, part of Sandra's trousseau. "Christ, *those* could do with a rub I must say," he said, looking critically at Cassidy's shoes, which had suffered considerably from the walk from the station. "And what's with those linoleum trousers, then, what the hell are *they* all about?"

"They're cavalry twill," said Cassidy. "They're the best I've got out here."

He had bought them after he committed suicide; the others were ruined by the clover.

"I wish we had *all* the right kit," said Shamus with a sigh.

Helen was wearing a new grey suit, one of Sandra's bought in Berne last year specially for Club cocktail parties; a little old-fashioned for some tastes, but very neat all the same, with flashes of green on the collar and a matching scarf to cover her throat. She came in rather slowly, eyes shining; she had put fresh powder on her bruise and she carried a small bunch of cyclamen heads cut from the plant in the kitchen. Her mouth was stretched tight, probably a smile. The flowers trembled and she was nervous.

"That's her is it?" Shamus asked, as if he had suddenly gone blind.

He was looking out of the window, his back towards them. His shoulders had risen very high. Neither Helen nor Cassidy could see his face, but they could hear him humming in low, flat tones.

36

Shamus had changed colour.

Not blushed or paled, white to red, red to white, according to the supposed laws of mediaeval ballad; simply, his whole person appeared to have taken on the darker, stormy colours of his fervent mood. Watching him, Cassidy dully recognized what he had always known but not till now understood: that Shamus had no physical constancy, no shape or profile to be remembered by; that he was as changeful as the sky outside the window; as blustering, as calm, as light or dark, as driven or as still; and that Cassidy in his mind had spent too long defining him, mistaking his presence for a kind of familiarity; and that he might as well have tried to love the wind as tame this man for the drawing rooms where Cassidy was at home. He had known Shamus when he was six foot tall and had the softness of a dancer; when he was squat and violent, and his shoulders were rounded like a wrestler's; he had known him male and female, child and man, lover and bully; but as a single man he would never know him. That's why he wrote, thought Cassidy, placing him already in the past; he had to make one person of all that army. That's why he was so jealous of God: God has a kingdom and can absorb us all, God rejoices in the variety of his images, God has cathedrals to contain his countless likenesses; but Shamus has only this one body and must drag himself round the world pretending to be one person, that is the penalty of being Shamus, of never surrendering to one place or one woman.

Shamus was also having trouble with the gun.

His new black dressing gown, brought out by Helen, fitted him well, but the cord was not strong enough to carry the weight of such a heavy weapon. Having tried without success to strap it to his hip, he ordered Helen to knot it at the shoulder. But the gun, swinging free, interfered with his sight of the gold-edged book, and in the end he dumped it irritably on the table between the lighted candles.

"Now sit down," he commanded, indicating the sofa. "Close. Hold hands and shut up, both of you." About to go on, his eye caught Helen's beatific smile and he was moved suddenly to anger.

"Stop leering!" he shouted at her, brandishing the gun.

"I wasn't leering. I was loving you."

Replacing the gun, he draped himself in the damask tablecloth, folding it lengthways and hanging it round his neck, so that the two ends dangled forward like a long scarf.

"What the hell's that rumbling?" he muttered, looking towards the window.

"It's the central heating. It goes on and off automatically. The south wind upsets the thermostat."

"Now pay attention," said Shamus, "while I define love."

He held the small book closed in his left hand, the gold-lined pages outward.

"Love," Shamus proclaimed, as they settled nervously to silence, "love is the bridge between what we *are* and what we can *become*. Love is the measure—" looking at Helen "—of our potential. I said stop leering!"

"It's only nervousness," Helen insisted rather pathetically. "I was exactly the same at *our* wedding, you know I was."

"Shamus," said Helen softly. "Shamus."

His eye was on the long window which was now quite blanked out by fog. Raindrops were bursting on the pane like inner actions of the glass, coming from nowhere, held there, not running.

"Lover?" he said, head away from them still, with the alertness of the blind.

"Yes."

"Why did David and Jonathan break it up?"

"I thought you knew."

"I told you—" still to the window "—I told you I never read that stuff."

"Reasons of state I think. They just got divided."

"Shilling off income tax," Shamus suggested.

"Something like that. Shamus?"

"Force of circumstance?"

"Yes. Yes, I think so."

"Not a quarrel about a fifth-rate concubine, for instance?"

"Shamus, we can stop now if you like. There's no need for a service."

"No need?"

"I only mean it doesn't need the formal gesture. None of us is religious, very."

Shamus did not seem to hear him, his gaze was still on the fog, and the motionless raindrops frozen into the glass.

"There *aren't* any fucking circumstances," he said. "There are just people. *Lovely people,*" he continued, in the voice of an American Midwest hostess. *"And if everybody was lovely there wouldn't be any war would there darlings?* I never dreamed you'd make it, Cassidy, that's the truth. I never dreamed you had it in you. I must have been growing cynical. Glad you saved me, lover; no point in bitterness. After all, how often do we meet it: real, total love? Once in a lifetime if we're lucky. Twice if we're Helen."

Turning, he studied her from far away, but his shape was so black against the window that Cassidy could not have told, if he had not known, whether he was facing them or not.

"Jesus," he said, in the extraordinary quiet. "That eye of yours: it's bloody disgusting. Can't you hold a bit of steak against it or something? Cassidy's *very* squeamish."

At this point, the doorbell rang; a three-toned chime not unlike the joyful summons to worship.

"Thank God," Shamus whispered. "Flaherty's arrived at last."

Opening the door at pistol point—note the impeccable fastenings, the hand-sawn hinges, locks lathe-turned—Cassidy saw many people of his acquaintance, beginning with Mark and Hugo, who had made independent travel arrangements, and ending indeterminately with McKechnie of Bee-Line and the Swiss Chief of Police. But the sight of the Eldermans, physical, not imagined Eldermans, laden with parcels, weary from the station path, and iced up round the eyebrows, surprised him very considerably.

I'm *certain* I put them off, he thought. He had telephoned: *John, old man, trouble at the crossroads, can you possibly make it another time or will it break the kids' hearts?* He had written a letter: *Circumstances beyond my control, the chalet has been burnt down, no one is sorrier than I.* He had cabled: *Chalet destroyed in avalanche.* Evidently, however, he had done none of these things, for there they were on the doorstep, the whole tribe of them, dressed in matching woollen hats like a family of softball supporters, the little girls covered in chocolate and the parents carrying the luggage. They stood in the beam of the outside light, smiling expectantly as if he were the photographer, their twelve cheeks red with cold.

"Aldo, old man," said John Elderman.

"We knew you were home from the light," said his wife, nameless once again. And added, using one of her coarse expressions intended to put her on a footing with the Men: "That's why we pressed the tit."

"He's got a gun," one of the children announced, seeing Shamus in the background. "Can *we* play, Mister?"

They were on the doorstep still, and a host has his duties.

"Come on in," said Cassidy with a show of heartiness, and made to help them with their luggage.

Behind him, raised by a head, Shamus was standing on the bottom stair, pressed into a corner, covering them with slow arcs of the revolver while he watched their every movement.

"Who are they?" he demanded, as they crowded in from the icy, wet air.

"A doctor and his family," said Cassidy, forgetting in his confusion Shamus' great hatred of the medical profession. "Friends." And took some luggage from the wife.

"*Your* friends?"

"Sandra's."

"Hullo," said Mrs. Elderman, smiling jovially to him across the hall. "What a *gorgeous* gun. Having a kid's party?" she enquired, noticing also the dressing gown and damask stole. "You look exactly like the Dalai Lama," and gave a most injudicious laugh.

"Piss off," said Shamus.

"That's Shamus," Cassidy explained. "He's staying here too."

And busied himself with roped boxes and the usual luggage of the very mean.

"Hullo old man," said John Elderman with great cheerfulness, climbing out of his duffle coat.

Mrs. Elderman was still staring at Shamus, and neither of them had moved.

"We're a bit crowded just at the moment," Cassidy murmured confidingly, to her husband, aside. "I've had a bit of a visitation. If you wouldn't mind taking over the top floor, just for this evening . . . then tomorrow we'll sort something out."

The very unemotional voice of Mrs. Elderman cut short their conversation.

"Darling," she said, "it's a real gun," and they all looked at Shamus.

"I'm afraid it is," said Cassidy.

The children, experts in sidearms, had also remarked the gun's authenticity. They were standing round it in an admiring group; the smallest was playing with the powder puff. With a disgusted gesture, Shamus waved them back and rose hastily another stair.

"They're foul," he whispered. "They're absolutely terrible."

"Oh I don't know," said Cassidy, embarrassed.

"They'll kill us all, lover. Jesus, lover, how can you *speak* to them?"

"We were having a sort of wedding," Cassidy explained to his new guests. "That's why he's wearing those clothes."

"A *wedding*," Mrs. Elderman echoed, on whom fell all the burdens of the obvious question. "*Here?* At *this* time of day?" And before he had even time to answer, had he wished, "Nonsense. Whose wedding?"

"His," said Shamus, indicating Cassidy. "He's marrying my wife."

John Elderman took his pipe from his mouth. He screwed his infantile face into a creaseless grin.

"But old man," he objected, after quite a long silence, "old Cassidy's married already, aren't you, Aldo?"

"To Sandra what's more," said Mrs. Elderman, and

looked accusingly at Shamus. "Aldo, he's not hijacking you, is he? He looks manic to me."

"Hugo says his Mummy and Daddy are *divorced*," a larger girl announced, and offered Cassidy a toffee, part used.

"Be quiet," said her mother, and made to smack her.

If Shamus knew fear at all, this was the nature of it, these people its object. Pale and wary, he had taken up a position of extreme defensiveness at the top of the stairs, where he crouched, huddled into the dressing gown, the damask tablecloth thrown round his neck like a college scarf. They were all watching him, waiting for him to order them, but it was quite a time before their attention summoned him to action. Standing abruptly—his legs under the dressing gown were bare, Haverdown legs, and no hint of white among the higher shadows—he made a cursory wave of the gun barrel in the direction of the upper rooms.

"All right. Up here, the lot of you. One at a time, hands on your head, march. *You!*"

"Me?" John Elderman asked, grinning terribly.

"Get rid of that fucking pipe. Not going to have you smoking in church."

And thus within seconds had shooed them, parents, luggage, and children, upstairs to the drawing room. It was not only the gun which won him their obedience; he seemed to know them perfectly: how to command them, how to silence them, what foods to give their children. Within minutes, their luggage was neatly stacked along the landing wall; their children watered, fed, and relieved; and the whole family sat in descending order on the sofa, in the front pew facing the altar.

"This is absolutely disgraceful," said Mrs. Elderman, looking very critically at Helen. "Goodness, whatever happened to her eye? John—"

"Shut up," Shamus ordered her. "Camel driver's gourd! Yahoo! Shut up! You're a witness not a fucking referee!"

John Elderman, seated in the direct line of the gun, seemed disinclined, despite his wife's entreaties, to exercise his calling.

"It's damned odd," was all he would say, in the tone of one making an anthropological study. "It explains a *lot* of things."

He had put his pipe in his pocket.

Helen, meanwhile, left alone, had not altered her posture. She sat where they had left her, wearing an unclouded bridal smile, as if contemplating in the faded posy of flower heads still resting in her hand the sweet shocks of passion which the future held for her. Her other hand lay still and open, awaiting her groom's return. With the entry of the Eldermans she had risen distractedly to greet them, but her mood was reserved and aloof, as became her on her Day.

"Ah yes," she said, hearing the name, "Aldo has spoken about you."

She left the seating arrangements to her husband. Only the children caused her expression to change.

"How nice," she remarked to their mother. "How very sweet."

37

The presence of the larger congregation had had a remarkable effect on Shamus. Whatever doubts had till now
assailed him, whatever mysteries and confusions stayed his
hand, the unexpected invasion of his enemy, his sworn,
archetypal enemy, had swept them all aside. Till now, it
had seemed, his pastoral duties hung heavily on him. At
moments, even, he had appeared to question his own
faith; while his erratic changefulness of style and his frequent recourse to the revolver had much reduced the
impact of his words. No more. Now, a fever of activity
overtook him. The devil was in the house; Shamus needed
herbs, and searched the kitchen cupboards till he came upon a box of thyme which he sprinkled liberally over the
improvised altar. Candles, more candles; the Dark One was
encroaching, Shamus needed light to hold him at bay.
Receptacles were hastily assembled, and while the Eldermans looked on in sullen amazement a box of Price's
Household Candles—Sandra's provision against a power
cut—was quickly distributed. Soon the room was filled
with the smell of burning wax; the dining table a lighted
barrier behind which Shamus could take refuge from the
terrors and infections of bourgeois mediocrity.

"He's mad," said Beth Elderman.

"Quiet, darling," said her husband nervously. "He may
just be overwrought."

"Stop them!" Shamus screamed. "You know their language, reason with them!"

"Please be quiet," Cassidy said politely. "It upsets him."

Outside, the fog had temporarily lifted. In the darkening sky, the revealed peaks of the Angelhorn glittered like
giant diamonds. The first lights were going on in the village; but the peaks had their own sun still, and shone with
incongruous daylight over the twinkling darkness of the
valley.

413

The thin chimes of a servant's handbell proclaimed the ceremony begun.

"Before we *resume*," Shamus began, "I have one or two announcements to make. Sit still," he told a little girl, with a monitory wave of the gun. "Just settle down and stop fidgeting."

Her mother tugged at the child, arranging it hastily, then faced Shamus again, herself more upright.

"First," he continued, in the unctuous, pseudo-intellectual tones of a fashionable West End parson, "let me say how *happy* I am to be able to welcome *children* to our service. It is one of the pleasing signs of the abiding power of religion, that parents"—here an indulgent smile at the Eldermans—"should bring their little ones to *this place*. It does credit to the children *and* to the parents."

He glanced at a piece of paper in his hand. "The next announcement, for those who have not yet heard the tragic news, concerns a holocaust in the neighbourhood of Thailand. Last night, owing to an oversight in one of the American strategic bases, four million Asians were eliminated."

He waited, plate in one hand, gun in the other.

A short, puzzled silence was broken by the chink of a coin as Mrs. Elderman opened her handbag and distributed small change to the girls.

"*Any* currency will do. *Thank* you. *Thank* you my dear. You *are* a Christian, I trust?" he murmured to Mrs. Elderman, accepting her offering.

"As a matter of fact I'm a *humanist*," she replied. "I'm afraid my husband and I find it impossible to accept the existence of God." And stuck out her jaw. "On scientific grounds *and* psychological grounds," she added.

"You obviously have *modern* views," Shamus prompted indulgently.

"Well they're obviously not as modern as yours," said Mrs. Elderman with spirit.

"How long have you known the groom?"

"Ooh, longer than I'd like to say," she squeaked, making a nervous joke about her age, which was thirty.

"Good, good, good, *good*. The third announcement," Shamus resumed, addressing himself to the bridal pair, "concerns your travel arrangements. There's a nine-forty connecting with the night sleeper from Spiez. So don't fucking well miss it. Get that Cassidy?"

"Yes of course."

"Will you all stand?"

Helen and Cassidy were sharing the leather chair, which Shamus had pulled to the centre of the long room in order to make extra space for the newcomers. Helen was on the arm and Cassidy on the seat, but the difference in their levels made communication difficult. This arrangement had not been uncongenial to Cassidy. The extra darkness afforded by Helen's body, the opportunity to imagine himself in other places, had provided him with a temporary ease from which he was now summoned by Helen's hand drawing him gently to his feet.

"Aldo," said Shamus.

"Yes."

"Helen?"

"Yes."

"Before joining you, Aldo, and you, Helen, in holy wedlock, I feel it incumbent upon me to venture one or two *general* observations"—a smile to the Eldermans—"on the service you are about to witness."

In the simple terms becoming to a short address, Shamus briefly explained to the newcomers the difference between *social* marriage, which was the Elderman kind of marriage, rightly devised for the containment of the Many-too-Many, and *real* marriage which was something very rare and had nothing whatever to do with them. He told them about Flaherty and self-appointed divinity, and about the difference between wanting to *die* together, which was New Testament marriage, and wanting to *live* together which was Old Testament marriage. This done, he chanted a few phrases of the *Nunc Dimittis* and bowed several times to the Bartlett print that was hanging over the fireplace.

"The total passion," he announced, in a strong Irish voice, quoting, Cassidy suspected, one of Flaherty's brochures, "demands the total sacrifice—"

About to continue he was interrupted by a whispered "Amen" from Beth Elderman, followed by the higher, obedient whispers of her many daughters.

"Shut up," he told her, in suppressed fury. "Keep quiet or I'll shoot you. Jesus, lover—"

"She didn't mean any harm," said Cassidy.

Picking up the prayer book—it was held open by the weight of the gun—he read aloud:

"I require and charge you both, as ye will answer at the dreadful day of judgment when the secrets of all hearts shall be disclosed—which is *now* actually, lover. Not tomorrow, not next day, not in Christopher Robin land, but now—yes or no?"

"Yes," said Helen.

"I'm talking to *him*. I know about you, you whore, be quiet or you'll get another hit. *Him* I mean. Cassidy. Our lover. Will you or will you not have this woman for your illegally wedded wife, whether sick, pissed, maimed, imbecile, however much she whores around? Will you, forsaking all others, including the bosscow, the Veg, the Bentley, and"—he put down the prayer book—"and me, lover," he said, very softly. "Because that's the way it works."

Helen's hand was linked in Cassidy's. From behind him he heard the loose, persistent cough of his French mother and the creak of pews echoing in the vaulted ceiling. Those kids, he thought; the Elderman woman; why don't they *do* something? They're my friends, not his.

"Lover."

"Yes."

"This gun is for shooting defectors, not lovers."

"I know."

"If you say *no,* I shall shoot you for sure, because I hate you quite a lot. That's called jealousy, also an emotion. Right? But if you say yes and you don't want her, believe me that *is* . . . that really *is* . . . not polite."

Helen was looking at him and he knew her look because it was Sandra's look, it covered everything, the whole contract to live and die.

"The point being, lover, that once you drag her off to your cave Daddy won't be there to help you. You can have her, if you want her. But from that moment on you've got to find your own reason for living. I can't do more for you and you can't do more for me."

"No."

"What the hell do you mean: *no?*" Helen demanded, releasing his hand.

"I mean he can't do any more. I agree."

"You see," Shamus explained, "although she's a stupid little bitch, I love her. That's why she's so cheeky. She's got us both. So I'm offering you all I've got and all I want: and naturally, I'll be put out if you reject it. But you've got to decide. Don't let that bitch carry you. Love you, lover."

"Love you," Cassidy replied automatically.

"Then which is it? Yes please or no thank you?"

All this while Shamus had been watching him most intently through the candles, and sweat had formed on his face, which now ran like crooked tears over his shaven cheeks; but his eyes were black and steady, as if neither the pain nor the heat of his torture were relevant to his words. On Cassidy's left, Helen was whispering, urging and complaining, but he heard only Shamus; it was Shamus, most definitely, who held his attention.

"Say yes, you fool," Beth Elderman shouted suddenly from the back, and Shamus raised the gun and might well have shot her if Helen had not intervened. Instead, he came round the altar, took Cassidy by the arm, and led him into the furthest part of the room, to the corner where the table was before they moved it; to a place so dark they could barely be heard.

"She's a heavy eater, boy," he murmured. "Big grocery bills coming up. Dresses, cars; she'll want the lot."

"*Cassidy!*" Helen shouted, furious.

"She can have whatever she wants," said Cassidy loyally.

"Why not just give her the money: you don't have to put up with *her* as well. Five thousand should see her right."

With a quick, conspiratorial glance at the congregation, Shamus had drawn Cassidy towards him so that Shamus' lips were at Cassidy's ear and Shamus' lower cheek was pressed against Cassidy's temple. Coming so close to him so suddenly, Cassidy smelt Paris again, and the drink, and the garbage in the street; smelt the woodsmoke from the fireplace lingering in his dressing gown and the sweat that was on him all the time; and whatever detachment he had found was gone, because this was Shamus, who had once been Cassidy's freedom; and had loved him; who needed him and had leant on him; rested on him in his hopeless search; played with him by the river.

"For God's sake, lover," Shamus insisted. "Why screw up a friendship like ours for the sake of a bit of cunt?"

His lips stayed, their breath trembling on the membranes of his ear. Shamus' jaw was pressed against his head, and Shamus' hands were linked at his neck. Pushing Cassidy gently away from him at last, he surveyed him in his own familiar way, reading (it seemed to Cassidy) his whole life there, all its paradoxes, its evasions, and its insoluble collisions. For a moment, the sky cleared for Cassidy, and he saw the hilltop where they had flown the gliders. And he thought: *Let's go back there. From the hill I can understand it all.*

Then Shamus smiled: the broad, untrustworthy smile of a victor.

"Well?"

"There's no point," said Cassidy.

"What do you mean? *No point?* You're here because there *is* a point! There's got to be a fucking point! I had *you,* and I'm giving you to *her.* I had *her* and I'm giving her to *you!*"

"I mean there's no point in trying to talk me out of it, I love her."

"What was that?" said Shamus very quietly.

"I said I loved her."

"And still do?"

"Yes. More than you."

"More than you love me, or more than I love her?"

"Both," said Cassidy numbly.

"Again, say it again," Shamus urged, seizing him.

"I love her."

"Shout it out! Her name, everything."

"I love Helen."

"Aldo loves Helen!"

"I Aldo love Helen. I Aldo love Helen. I Aldo love Helen!"

Suddenly, without Cassidy understanding why, the rubric, the rhythm of the words took hold of him. The louder he shouted, the brighter, the more excited Shamus' smile: the louder he shouted, the larger the room became, the more it filled and echoed. Shamus was pouring water over him, Lipp-style, a jugful, purifying him in the name of the Few, Helen was kissing him, sobbing and asking why it took him so long. The sound rose; some children were clapping but one was crying, as in the eye of his imagination Cassidy saw his own drenched, stupid body upright in a pool of holy water, shouting love at a laughing world.

"I Aldo love Helen! Can you hear? I Aldo love Helen!"

John Elderman was standing, beating his hands together; his wife was holding her string gloves to her chin, weeping and laughing.

"This is *it*," John Elderman was crying. "My God this is the big league. I'll never aspire to this, never."

"If only more people could see it," said Mrs. Elderman.

But they can, Cassidy shouted, they can. Why don't you turn your head you fool? Sandra's family was packing the pews behind her, Mrs. Groat dressed in fruit and flowers, escorted by her several sisters and lady cousins; Snaps in beige velvet, her cleavage uselessly exposed. From the other side of the aisle came the tearful coughing of the Abandoned One and the plain sobs of Old Hugo, standing beside the empty place for A. L. Rowse. The strains of an organ were filling the room, "Abide With Me" and "Sheep May Safely Graze."

"I Aldo love Helen. I Aldo love Helen. I Aldo love Helen."

"Oh love, oh love," Helen sobbed; she was drying him with a tea towel; her bruise was bright again where her tears had washed away the make-up. "And he didn't stand in our way," she sobbed. "Oh Shamus, darling."

"You see lover," Shamus explained, "you're the only one I ever had. I mean Christ had twelve, didn't he, eleven good, one bad. But I've only got *you*, so you had to be right, didn't you?"

The lights had gone on. Shamus was passing around Talisker. Helen, very proud and quiet on Cassidy's arm, was receiving the congratulations of the guests. Well they had met in the West Country actually, she said; about a year ago; they had really been in love ever since, but they had agreed for Shamus' sake to keep it a secret. The speeches were short and to the point, no one became boring or untimely. Shamus, drinking heartily, the colour high on his cheeks, was the very soul of contentment: if they had children they must be brought up Catholic, he said, it was the only condition he had made.

"He's a *writer*," Beth Elderman was telling the girls, her face flushed with maternal pride. "That's a very special kind of person, that's why he knows *all* about the world. You must never, *never* compromise, do you understand? Sally listen, what did Mummy say?"

"I meet so much of it," John Elderman said shrewdly through his grown-up pipe. "Every blasted day in the surgery, three, maybe four cases, you'd be astonished. So much of it could be *avoided*," he told Shamus very confidentially, "if only they had *help*."

"And of course how he put up with the *other* one for so long," Beth Elderman said to anyone who would listen, "God alone knows. I mean *that* was *total* disaster."

38

The guests gathered on the doorstep, children at the front, grown-ups behind. The festive toboggan lay ready, Mark's again; John Elderman and Shamus had lashed the luggage to the prow. A light, sharp wind had sprung up from the north. The fog had gone for good, the rain had turned to snow, a fine, hard-driven snow that was already settling on the window sills.

For her going away, the bride wore a fitted sheepskin coat which she had found in Sandra's wardrobe, and a charming white fur hat which Mark called Mummy's rabbit's ears.

"Isn't it funny," she said in her excitement, "how everything fits me, just like that?"

Her boots were sealskin, though she did not approve of killing seals. She kissed the girls lavishly and counselled them to be good and kind, and to grow up lovely wives.

"Which you will, I know," she said, crying a little. "I just *know* you will."

To Beth Elderman, she imparted some last-minute domestic advice. The oil system was impossible to understand, the best thing to do was kick it.

"And there's cold duck in the fridge and extra milk on the sideboard. For God's *sake* don't buy the Co-op butter, it's *no* cheaper and it's absolutely foul."

"We think you're doing the right thing," said Beth.

"We know you are," said her husband.

"So long," said Shamus.

He had placed himself, modestly, at the end of the line, in the shadow of the others; he was holding a torch in one hand and a glass in the other; he was barefoot, and the skirts of his dressing gown could have been a curtain borrowed from the window in the hall.

"Is that all you've got to say?" said Helen at last. *"So long?"*

"Watch out for rabbit holes."

"I'd like to kiss you," said Helen.

"Kissin' don't last," said Shamus, in a Somerset accent which Cassidy had not heard before. "Cookin' do."

Rather hopelessly, she turned to John Elderman.

"Don't worry," said the great psychiatrist. "We'll bring him round."

With a somewhat ungainly hoist of the skirts, and a last look at Shamus, she boarded the toboggan, sitting well forward with the luggage so that Cassidy could manage the more responsible rear position.

"Are you getting divorced?" asked a little girl.

"Be quiet," said Beth Elderman.

"Hugo says he is," said the same little girl.

"Aldo," said Beth Elderman, with her plant and rock smile. "Give us a ring. We're in the book." She kissed him, smelling very slightly of ether. "Remember you're a friend as well as a patient," she added.

Her husband gave him a manly hand.

"Godspeed, Aldo. Don't overdo it. We admire you."

About to say goodbye to Shamus, Cassidy appeared to remember something.

"Crikey," he said, all boyish. "Hang on a sec." And darted past them into the house.

Hugo's room was very cold. He tested the radiator. On, but icy. Must be an airlock in the heating. His toys were put away; only a red anorak, the wet-look for this season, hung like a doll's suit from the painted hanger.

Mark's room was lined with pictures cut from magazines, mainly advertisements. The largest was a centrefold spread of a whole family smiling into the camera while they loaded fishing kit into a Range Rover. That's how he wanted us, Cassidy thought, studying the bronzed, untroubled features of the father. Mr. and Mrs. Britain sporting by the river.

"Lost something?" Shamus asked from the doorway, offering him his whisky glass. He was very relaxed. The gun, broken like a shotgun, hung vaguely over his forearm, and he had put the powder puff behind his ear like a Tahitian maiden's flower.

"My watch actually. It must be in the bathroom." He returned the glass, empty.

"Lover."

"Yes."

"Look er . . . I know you're going to keep her in the style to which you're accustomed. But don't er . . . don't let her get her hands on a lot of money. *You* know."

They tried both bathrooms, but the watch was not in either of them.

"And er . . . on the other thing."

"What other thing?"

"The other thing, you know." He bucked his pelvis. "What we did in Paris, *you* know. Watch her. She'll do anything to get pregnant, anything. We'd a flat once up in Durham, we had the builders in. She went through the whole lot of them just on the off chance. Painters, plasterers, masons, the lot."

"I don't believe you," said Cassidy.

They returned to the front door.

"You didn't hit me though, did you?"

"What will you do?" Cassidy asked after rather a long silence. "Now."

"Get pissed. Have a little drink with the Elderberries."

"Hurry up!" Helen called. "For Christ's sake, we'll miss the train!"

"You just can't alter him," they heard Beth Elderman say. "He's always been a ditherer, he always will be. He drove Sandra *mad*."

"That's why Mark's so wet," said the largest girl.

"Great people," said Shamus. "I love them all. Honest, straightforward. Might play Fly with them. Teach the kids."

"And the new book's all right, is it?"

"Finished," said Shamus, without expression. "It's all about you, actually. And immortality. The eternal survival of Aldo Cassidy."

"I'm glad I provided the material."

"I'm glad *I* did."

"Cassidy!" Helen called, very angry.

"I've got to go now," said Cassidy, taking Helen's point, "or we'll miss the train."

"Attaboy. Be brave."

"Goodbye."

"Chippie chippie," said Shamus in his poofy voice. "Love to the Bentley. Er lover."

"Yes."

"Not to miss the train but er let us in on something, will you? That waitress down at the station buffet there, the one with the tits."

"Maria," said Cassidy automatically.

"Tell us, does she oblige, do you know? I had the definite feeling yesterday that she was fumbling my hand when I gave her the coffee money."

"Well they do say she's a bit fast."

"How much?"

"Fifty francs. Maybe more."

Shamus' hand was already outstretched.

"It's for when I'm on my own you see. I'm going to need a spot of distraction." Cassidy gave him a hundred. "Thanks. Thanks very much indeed. Pay you back, lover. Promise."

"That's all right."

"And—er—on the general theme."

"Which one?" Cassidy asked, definitely *not* thinking of the train, which he definitely intended to catch, but *definitely*. The general theme of God, perhaps? Of the union of souls? Of Keats, death, taking and not giving? Of kites, or Schiller; or the threat of China to the pram trade? Or something more personal perhaps, such as the slow atrophy of a loving soul worn down to very little any more?

"Money," said Shamus.

At first, Cassidy could not recognise his smile. It belonged to other faces; faces not present, till then, in the worlds which he and Shamus had explored together. Faces weakened by need, and failure, and dependence. It was a smile that accused even while it supplicated; that haunted with its first dawning, imparting without change both allegiance and contempt; a smile from loser to winner, when both had run the same financial race. "Aldo old boy," it said. "Cassidy old man. A thousand would see me right." A shifty, sandy smile worn with a good suit fraying at the cuffs, and a silk shirt fraying at the collar: "After all old boy, we were neck and neck once, weren't we, before you hit it lucky?"

"What do you need?" Cassidy asked. His custom, till

then, had been to establish the minimum and halve it. "We'll have to be quick actually."

"Couple of thousand?" said Shamus, as if it were nothing to either of them really; just a thing that friends arranged between themselves and forgot.

"I'll make it five," said Cassidy, and wrote him a cheque, quickly because of the train.

He did not look at Shamus as he gave it him, he was too ashamed; and he never knew what Shamus did with it, whether he folded it away, Kurt-style, like a clean handkerchief, or read it after the lesson of Old Hugo, from the date to the signature, and then the back, in case. But he did hear him mutter the one word Cassidy was praying to God he wouldn't say:

"Thanks."

And he knew he had seen his first dead body, it stood for all the rest he would ever see; dead dreams, lives ended, no point.

"Just coming," he called to Helen.

"Pay you back one day lover."

"No hurry," said Cassidy, though actually there *was* a hurry in a way because Swiss trains are punctual.

He climbed on to the toboggan.

"It's on your wrist," Shamus called after him, meaning his watch.

He could not possibly have seen it, for Cassidy had pulled his cuffs right down, in the style of Christopher Robin.

"Whatever were you up to?" Helen demanded. "I've been sitting here *freezing* for hours. Look at my hair."

One of the children had found a bag of rice, and was flinging it at them in handfuls. The snow was falling steadily, the flakes thicker.

"I lost my watch," said Cassidy.

"I'd have thought you *could* have done without it for once," she said. "Seeing that it's made us miss the train."

The next moment, a dozen willing hands propelled them into the darkness, the children's merry screams of "Good luck" faded behind them, and the happy pair was hurtling ever faster down the hill, already blinded by the icy streams of racing snowflakes.

The station was empty and very cold and the train was quite indisputably gone.

The next one could be late, the guard said, there was a lot of snow higher up.

"There's a lot down here too," Cassidy replied jovially, still brushing himself clean—clean also of the guilt of dawdling—but the guard did not care for jokes apparently, nor was he of the tippable class. He was a big, rugged man, not unlike Alastair a thousand years before him, but his rocky face was set against all pleasantries.

"Well ask him *how* late," Helen told him.

"How late?" Cassidy asked, in French.

The guard made no gesture at all, neither of answering nor refusing to answer. But after staring at Helen for quite a long time, silently closed the hatch on them and locked it from the inside.

"*How late?*" Helen shouted, hammering on the little door. "The *bugger*, look at that."

They had fallen several times on the way down: Cassidy reckoned five. The first time they agreed it was funny; the second time, the suitcase came undone and Cassidy had to stumble like an Arctic explorer through the falling snow, looking for Sandra's clothes. After that, the falling was not funny at all. Helen said it was a lousy toboggan and Cassidy said you couldn't really blame it. Helen said she had thought he *knew* how to drive it, otherwise she would not have consented to come on it; she would have walked and at least remained dry. *Real* toboggans were wooden, she said, she had had one as a child. She hammered again, shouted "Bastard" through the chink, so Cassidy suggested they have a drink and try again in a few minutes.

"We can always go to Bristol," he said.

"To *where?*"

"It was a joke," said Cassidy.

"*Dithering* like that," said Helen contemptuously. "If you'd *wanted* to go away with me you'd *never* have dithered."

But still.

In the buffet, a group of English ladies in blue-banded pullovers was sitting at the English Table. Seeing Helen and Cassidy enter, a beautiful, thin lady with a deaf-aid beckoned them over.

"You old *devil*," she said cheerfully to Cassidy, taking his wrist in her thin, dry hand. "You never even told us you were coming. You're a *devil*," she repeated, as if he, not she, were deaf. "Hullo Sandra, dear, you look absolutely frozen." But men were her preference. "Darling," she asked him confidentially, "have you *heard* what Arnie's trying to do with the Championships this year?"

In a black rage, Helen accepted a glass of hot wine and drank it very slowly, staring at the clock.

"He wants a giant slalom at Mürren, my dear, can you imagine. Well I mean you know what happened *last* time we went to Mürren . . ."

Breaking away at last, Cassidy went back to the ticket office. It was still closed, there was no one in sight, and the snow was falling much harder, masking the village lights and casting a deep silence over the whole white world.

"They say about half an hour," he told Helen, who had moved to an empty table. It seemed inappropriate to give her bad news, so he had invented a small hope. "They're working flat out but at the moment it's almost beating them."

He ordered more hot wine.

"Got your passport all right?" he asked, trying to cheer her up.

"Of course I haven't. Shamus burnt it."

"Oh."

"What do you mean: *oh*. You can get a duplicate. Any consulate or legation will provide one. We can go to Berne. Once the train comes, if it ever does."

"We'll get one tomorrow," Cassidy promised her.

"I'll need more luggage too. All that stuff's *soaked*."

She began crying into her folded hands.

"Oh no," Cassidy whispered. "Oh Helen, please."

"What will we *do*, Cassidy, what will we *do*?"

"Do?" he said gallantly. "We'll do exactly what we said we'd do. We'll have a lovely holiday, then I'll go into politics and you'll be an M.P.'s wife and . . ."

From the English Table, the beautiful lady looked on with great compassion.

"Is she having a baby?" she called pleasantly. "It usually makes them odd."

Cassidy ignored her.

"It's only reaction," Cassidy promised her, holding her hand and fighting to win a smile. "Sorry about it . . . it's not because you're sad."

"Don't *apologise*," said Helen, stamping her foot. "Not *your* fault."

"Well it is in a way," Cassidy insisted. "I got you into this."

"It's not. Love's nobody's fault. It just happens. And when it happens you have to do what it says. There are winners and losers. Like in everything else. We're the winners, that's all. Although we missed the train."

"I know," Cassidy agreed. "We're very lucky." And pressed his handkerchief into her palm.

"It isn't *luck* either."

"Well what is it?" Cassidy asked.

"How should I know? Why did you take so long?"

"What for?"

"To say *yes*. It was *exactly* the same as missing the train. There they were, all waiting, and you being the ardent lover and God knows what and Shamus being so helpful, and all you do is dither while I *sit* there and look a complete fool in front of a *doctor* of all people, and his brilliant wife. Why do you have to know such brainy people?"

Drying her eyes, she saw the guard sitting at a table by the door, drinking schnapps and coffee.

"What the hell's *he* doing there?" she demanded. "He's supposed to be waiting for the train."

Off duty, the guard was quite a different man. "Hallo," he called, raising his glass. "Hallo. Cheerio. Hallo. *Ja. Bonjour.*"

"Cheers," said Cassidy. "You speak English eh? Very good. *Très bon.*"

"No train," said the guard with great satisfaction, as he drank. "Too much snows."

He drank again, as if a little more of the same could do him no harm. As he drank, he walked towards them, bent on conversation; he loomed very large and very drunk, and his eyes were on Helen, not at all on Cassidy. So when the pistol shot came it was almost a relief.

There was no other sound. None. It was not at all a question of distinguishing this bang from conflicting ones:

a door slammed, a car was backfiring; a slate from the station roof. The snow had thrown a blanket over everything; only pistols were exempt. Also, the shot was close. Not in the buffet certainly; but near to it, and it was followed by a chilling howl, midway between pain and fury; a long, baying howl of the kind that by tradition haunts deserted marshes, and ends as this howl ended with a choking, agonised sob, dwindling to nothing; a howl to chill the blood, and arrest drunken railwaymen in mid-movement.

"*My* God," he remarked, with the accent on the possessive pronoun. "They shot the bitch, I think."

He was still laughing at this apposite snatch of Americana as Cassidy raced past him into the station forecourt.

The Russian snow was tumbling crazily through the down-beams of the railway lamps. The line was covered over. A road, a path, a fence, a house, it was already buried by a new generation. *I'm Troy. There's seven fucking civilisations buried in me and each one's more rotten than the other.* Even the nearest buildings were caving in. The newspaper kiosk was on its knees; the eyes of the Hotel Angelhorn were closed and bleeding; in the high street, not a shop or church or ice palace but the remorseless snow was pounding at its doors, blotting out roofs, skirmishing in the forecourts. Wildly, hand to his eyes, Cassidy looked about him. Footprints, he thought; search for footprints. There were none but his own.

"Shamus!" He called loud. "Shamus!" he repeated. "Shamus!"

Using his intelligence too late, he looked back at the buffet window trying to think which way the noise had come from as they sat there. Helen was staggering towards him, wrapped in the sheepskin. Christ, he thought, she actually put it on before she came out to look for him. Behind her, not venturing so far, Rasputin the guard looked on from the doorway, his glass still in his hand.

"Go and look down there," Cassidy told her, pointing down an alley where a very old jeep was sinking slowly into the ground. "Look for footprints, call his name."

"What's he done?" she whispered. "Cassidy, what's he done?"

"Anything wrong?" an English lady asked from behind the porter. "I thought I heard a bang."

"I say," said another. "Did you hear that noise?"

Helen did not move. She was hugging the coat right across her body.

"Go and look for him!" he shouted at her.

Oh Christ she's frightened stiff; that's why she put on the coat, she wanted an excuse for waiting. Seizing her shoulders he shook her; her head fell stupidly from side to side.

"He's hitting her," an English lady said.

"Poor gal, she's pregnant," said the deaf one, as they all advanced into the snow.

"We've killed him," Helen whispered.

Leaving her, he ran quickly down the alley, calling Shamus. He was running directly at the snow now, he had to lower his head to see any distance at all.

He had entered a drift, the snow was in his trousers, his neck, colder than water, colder than fear and his feet were numb. Wading, he came on a pile of logs leaning against a tin roof and the snow was scratched where someone had climbed up. At first he thought the marks were handprints, each finger separate, and he had a crazy vision of Shamus doing handstands while he tried to shoot himself upside down. Then he remembered that Shamus was barefooted, and that he liked impact and a spot of pain; and he saw him sitting astride the station roof, hugging the clock as if it were his latest friend, aiming at him very deliberately, a difficult down-angle shot which mercifully missed.

"Shootibangs," said Shamus.

"Shootibangs," Cassidy agreed.

"I heard a shot! Another shot, a second one!" Helen shouted, tugging at his arm. "For Christ's sake Cassidy, find someone who can *do* something!"

"He's up there," Cassidy explained, pointing. "Shooting at me."

The bullet had passed very close; he had felt the wind of it or something, but the snow made it rather unreal, he was cold and he didn't much care.

Advancing from the buffet doorway, Rasputin the guard was screaming maternal French. Shooting on station property was absolutely forbidden, he was saying; it was doubly forbidden to foreigners.

"Look out," said an English lady to him, "or he'll shoot you too, I can tell."

Helen was scrambling up the log pile.

"Here, let me help you," he said automatically, offering his hand, but Shamus was already coming down. The dressing gown round his waist, he was sliding on his bare behind.

In a bunch, the English ladies withdrew.

"Sorry lover. Couldn't remember what her name was, the one with the tits."

"Maria," said Cassidy.

"That's it, Maria. I needed a whore, you see."

"I understand," said Cassidy.

The guard was still shouting. Irritated, Shamus fired a round at his feet and he ran to the buffet, joining Cassidy's English mothers at the door.

The three of them were standing in the station forecourt, Shamus shivering in the dressing gown, but the snow was so heavy they might have been anywhere; in Paris, in Haverdown, or here.

"Have to make world history some other time," said Shamus.

"That's it."

"What do you mean?" Helen demanded. "What are you saying?"

Cassidy felt obliged to explain.

"It's nothing, Helen. It's just that the main axis is between you two. I'm just . . ." He began again. "Maybe it's between us two, him and me. Only . . . Shamus," he said hopelessly.

"Yes lover?"

"I can't say it, I don't know the words. You're the writer, you tell her."

"Sorry lover. Your world: you end it."

"You mean you don't love me," said Helen.

"No," said Cassidy. "It's not quite that . . ."

"You love the bosscow."

"No. No, it isn't options either."

"He doesn't love *me*," Shamus explained, very simply. "He's gone off me and you're no good to him on your own." He was tearing up the cheque and throwing the pieces over the snow. "Money matter," he explained. "He walked into it with his eyes wide shut. I could shoot him if you like," he suggested to Helen, gallantly.

"I don't mind," said Cassidy. "It's up to you."

"He doesn't mind," said Shamus.

"Cassidy!" Helen cried.

"That match is rained off," Shamus said. "So shut up snivelling or you'll get a kick. I blame myself, lover. I was really going to let you go. I had it all worked out. I was going to train to be a doctor, you see. Elderberry was going to teach me how to do it. Then the bugger said it took ten years. Lover, I haven't *got* ten years. Have I?"

"No, I suppose not."

"Kept talking about the bosscow, what a bitch she was. He's the worst, that Elderberry, a bum."

"I used to hate him too."

"And his wife's a rotten fuck. I can't stand howlers. Ya, ya, ya, all that stuff. Like Swiss porters."

Cassidy nodded. "There was one like that in Paris."

"Here," said Shamus, handing him the revolver. "Souvenir. You might use it some time."

"Thanks," said Cassidy.

Shamus looked down at his bare legs, where they disappeared into the snow. He wore a white crown; a rim of white had settled over his black eyebrows.

"Jesus," he whispered, "we're a long way from home."

"Yes, we are."

"Sorry lover," Shamus said again. "You nearly made it. Come on you bitch," he said to Helen, shaking her without affection. "My feet are cold."

"It wasn't your fault," said Cassidy to Helen. "Please don't feel bad about it. It's all in me, not you."

"Quiet lover. Quiet. Bedtime now."

Coming forward, Shamus kissed him for the last time. When the kiss was over, Shamus turned away. Helen was still holding him. Then Shamus set off, vigorously, hauling her whichever way he wanted her to go, and they had actually started up the hill before she spoke.

"For a while," she said, and began again because she was crying. "For a while you really *did* care."

"Of course I did. All the time—"

"Not about me, you fool. About yourself. You put a value on yourself."

"Helen, please don't cry—"

"Shut up and listen! You put a value on *yourself*," she repeated. "That's something you never did before." Shamus was dragging her; she fell, and half got up. "For God's *sake* do it again," she shouted. "Find someone else. Don't go back into that awful dark."

"Keep trying, lover," Shamus assented, with a last careless wave. "Never regret, never apologise."

The snow had almost covered them. Sometimes he saw them, sometimes there was nothing; it was no longer possible to tell. Once, through a clearing as it were, he made out two uprights, one straight and one crooked, and either they were posts along the fencing or two people leaning together as they struggled with the very deep snow. But as they vanished finally, into the nothing that lay beyond the blizzard, he thought he heard—but could never be sure—he thought, though, that he heard her say "Goodbye, Cassidy," like a whisper alone, as if she were saying goodbye to the old year, to a decade or a lifetime, and then at last his own eyes filled with tears and he lowered his head. As he did so they seemed to go down with him, both together, like two pedestrians in the rain, before the hood of his rich man's car.

Epilogue

The retirement of Mr. Aldo Cassidy, the Founder, Chairman, Managing Director, and principal shareholder of Cassidy's General Fastenings, from active business life was noted with interest in the City press, and with some admiration. A fine example, they said, of a brilliant young businessman who put a lot into commerce and had taken a lot out, and was now retiring to enjoy the fruits. Would the lure of big business draw him back? Would the former whizz kid tire of rural charms? Only history would decide.

Those who knew him best spoke warmly of his great love for the country.

"A perfectionist," a well-known West End Estate Agent testified. "We only ever offered him the best that Britain has for sale."

It was known that the Manorship of Haverdown in Somerset had long been his ambition, not least because of the family connection: an ancient forebear of Mr. Cassidy had rested there with a detachment of Cromwell's horse. "We Cassidys have always been fighters," the Chairman recalled amid laughter and applause, explaining his decision to the shareholders; and accepted with tears in his eyes the handsome canteen of silver which had been purchased by private subscription.

The merger with Bee-Line Accessories Limited had long been in the air: City editors were confident that the inevitable streamlining was in the long-term interest of shareholders. For the new Chairman Meale, nothing but praise: a typical graduate of the tough Cassidy school, they said; a man to watch.

The sale of the house in Abalone Crescent was also noted in the property columns: *A Vision Uncompleted* ran the

435

caption. The knowledgeable named a price of forty-two thousand pounds.

How did they live there, Sandra and Aldo, for the rest of their natural lives? Did the marriage prosper? At first, they talked over their problem with great frankness. Dr. Elderman and his wife were invaluable, coming often and staying long. Sandra accepted that Cassidy had suffered spiritual death, but she was prepared, for the children's sake, to overlook it.

"He should never have had money," she concluded. "If he'd been poor, he couldn't have *afforded* to be unfaithful."

For company, she invited Heather to make Haverdown her permanent home, and Heather, though she had doubts about whether they were just being kind, finally consented to accept an empty wing. When Sandra made pickle, Heather made pickle too. When she ground her liver *pâté*, Heather ground it with her; when she went to country sales, Heather helped her to keep her head; and when she went to London to see how the clinic was progressing, Heather and Cassidy would go to bed together and talk about Sandra's limitations. Sandra was not aware of this practice, and if she had been she would have been extremely cross.

For entertainment, Cassidy browsed at the local library, where young girls attended after school; or he would drive to Bristol on a pretext and visit a dingy cinema in a railway concourse where torrid films were shown to needy peasants. In the early days, attracted by the appearance of shared happiness, he would sometimes flirt with a married couple. The curate had recently imported a plump bride from the North; a pair of Old Etonian antique dealers opened an emporium. But little came of these advances, and with time he abandoned them.

All three political parties considered him for the local council, but specific overtures were never made.

Contents

Part II Unleashing Advanced Programming Topics

Authors

Michael Amundsen

Keith D. Brophy

Richard Buhrer

Frank Font

Bill Hatfield

Mark Steven Heyman

Tim Koets

Paul W. Logston

David Medinets

Greg Perry

Ross Rothmeier

Conrad Scott

Brad Shannon

Mike Stefanik

Edward Toupin

Chuck Traywick

L. Michael Van Hoozer, Jr.

Ron West

PART

I

Unleashing the Visual Basic 4.0 Product

Visual Basic 4.0:
New and Improved

by Greg Perry

1

IN THIS CHAPTER

With the introduction of Visual Basic 4.0, Microsoft set another milestone. Not only did Microsoft create Visual Basic 4.0 to take advantage of both Windows 95's and Windows NT's 32-bit operating systems, to add development and support tools such as a code profiler and an improved image editor and resource compiler, and to support improved data access and OLE, Microsoft improved virtually every feature already found in previous versions of Visual Basic. Visual Basic 4.0 is now the development system of choice for Windows 95 and Windows NT applications.

This chapter introduces you to Visual Basic 4.0 by exploring some of its new features and features from earlier editions that have been revised in the new version. Although this chapter is not a tutorial of those new and improved features, it does present an introductory overview so that you will have a good feel for the capabilities found in Visual Basic 4.0. This chapter presents you with the big picture—a road map—of your future work with Visual Basic 4.0 so that you can feel comfortable with the new version's feature set and begin to tackle the specifics found in the rest of the book.

> **NOTE**
>
> Despite the plethora of new features in Visual Basic 4.0, all programs you've created using earlier versions of Visual Basic run without any problems under Visual Basic 4.0. In addition, programs you've written using Visual Basic for Applications version 1.0 (introduced in Microsoft Excel 5.0 and Microsoft Project 4.0) run under Visual Basic 4.0.

Visual Basic 4.0 comes in the following three editions:

- **Standard Edition.** Contains a full-featured application-creation Visual Basic 4.0 environment with which you can create stand-alone 32-bit applications for Windows 95 and Windows NT.

- **Professional Edition.** Contains the complete Standard Edition package plus additional custom controls, database support, and the Crystal Report Writer for easy report generation.

- **Enterprise Edition.** Contains the tools needed to create client/server applications: everything found in the Professional Edition plus additional tools that let project teams more easily develop advanced applications inside multiuser, multicomputer client/server environments.

The Standard Edition's New Features

The following pages present an overview of all three versions of Visual Basic 4.0. No matter which edition you use, you will spend most of your development time using the tools in the Standard Edition (and therefore in all three editions). Most of this chapter is devoted to the new and improved features of the Standard Edition because of that edition's importance for the Visual Basic 4.0 programming community.

The Interface

The Visual Basic 4.0 interface looks and acts much like previous versions of Visual Basic. You do not face a huge learning curve when moving from an earlier version, such as 3.0, to Visual Basic 4.0. The Visual Basic 4.0 interface contains the standard Windows 95 interface elements including support for long filenames in Open dialog boxes and the Windows 95 window control buttons. If you select File | Open to open a new Visual Basic 4.0 project, you see the 32-bit Windows 95 Open dialog box shown in Figure 1.1.

FIGURE 1.1.

Visual Basic 4.0 supports Windows 95 dialog boxes.

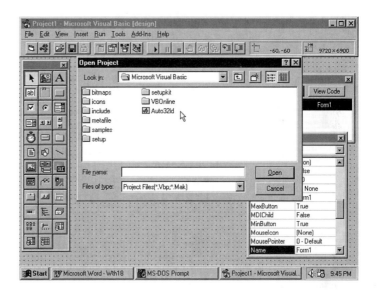

Of course, the file-related controls in Visual Basic 4.0 (such as the directory list box and the file list box controls) all support long filenames and the Windows 95 Explorer-like interface. In addition, when you use the common dialog box control for file-related support in your programs, the common dialog box control also supports the extended Windows 95 file interface.

Windows 95 supports extensive use of the right mouse button. Although some Windows 3.1 applications (such as Borland's Quattro Pro) have supported the right mouse button for several years, the only Microsoft products to use the right mouse button in a uniform fashion are those written for Windows 95. Visual Basic 4.0 is no exception. Click the right mouse button over a form, control, or property box and Visual Basic 4.0 displays a context-sensitive menu listing common tasks you may want to do with that item.

Microsoft expanded Visual Basic 4.0's online help system to support the full Windows 95-like help engine. When you request help, Visual Basic 4.0 displays a tabbed property sheet such as the one shown in Figure 1.2. The property sheet provides a Windows 95-like contents list, an index to common features, and an extensive find feature that searches across all topics for a given topic.

CAUTION

The first time you select the Find tab of the Help property sheet, Visual Basic 4.0 runs the Find Setup Wizard that lets you build the help database of find topics. If you've already had a chance to use Windows 95, you've probably been requested to build such a database in other applications. If not, you have to tell the Find Setup Wizard how you want the database built. If you have ample room on your hard disk (three or more megabytes is sufficient), select the option to maximize search capabilities. By maximizing the help system's find database, you ensure that you get the most complete help searches. If you minimize or customize the find database, you save some disk space but lose some details in the searching capabilities.

FIGURE 1.2.

Visual Basic 4.0 supports Windows 95 dialog boxes.

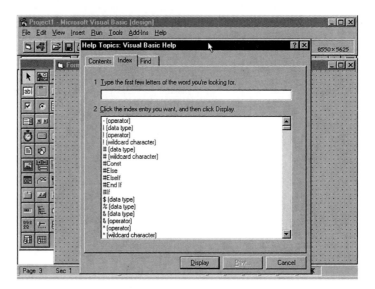

When placing controls on a form, you can now *nudge* controls to size or place them one pixel or grid unit at a time. Ctrl+arrow key moves a selected control one grid or pixel unit (if no grid is showing); Shift+arrow key resizes a selected control one grid or pixel unit.

If you click the Lock Controls toolbar button (the button with the padlock icon), Visual Basic 4.0 prevents you from moving controls elsewhere during form design. As long as the controls are locked, both current and subsequent controls placed on the form stay put; you cannot move those controls with the mouse by dragging them elsewhere. You can move the controls only by unlocking them, changing placement property location values inside the Property window, or by changing the property location values inside Visual Basic 4.0 code when you run the program.

CAUTION

All controls are locked or unlocked at the same time. You cannot lock individual controls on a form. The sizing handles on locked controls change color from black to white to indicate that you cannot move the controls. If you unlock them, the color reverts back to black.

Code-Related Support

Although little more has changed in the Visual Basic 4.0 interface, Visual Basic 4.0 has added a feature that programmers have been requesting since Visual Basic 1.0: a *line-continuation character* for the Visual Basic 4.0 text editor. When entering long lines into the editor in earlier versions, you had to keep typing the lines across the editor window no matter how long the lines got. Some Visual Basic expressions can get tediously long—but before Visual Basic 4.0, there was no way to break long lines into separate lines inside the editor.

NOTE

When you break a long Visual Basic 4.0 statement into two or more separate lines inside the text editor, that single *logical line* spans several *physical lines* in the editing window.

In pre-Visual Basic 4.0 releases, the following expression spanned a single long logical line and also a single physical line:

```
HisAnswer = "Joseph said to Carol, " + Chr$(34) + "I do!" + Chr$(34) + " Then... he
kissed her."
```

The line-continuation character is actually an underscore (_). You must always precede the underscore with a space; therefore, the line-continuation character actually requires that you type two characters (including the space). Visual Basic 4.0 considers the following two physical lines identical to the preceding long line:

```
HisAnswer = "Joseph said to Carol, " + Chr$(34) + "I do!" _
            + Chr$(34) + " Then... he kissed her."
```

This is still one logical line of code but the long physical line now spans two physical lines. Notice how these two lines eliminate the single long physical line; inside the editing window, these shorter lines make editing and debugging easier because you have to scroll the editing window left and right less often. You can continue across as many physical lines as needed to complete long logical lines of code.

CAUTION

Do not try to continue a line in the middle of a string literal using the underscore. If you do, Visual Basic 4.0 thinks that the underscore is part of the string literal and you get an error when Visual Basic 4.0 attempts to interpret the second physical line.

As you enter your Visual Basic 4.0 code, you see that the editor's scroll bars become proportional to display the relative amount of scrolling you have done. These *proportional scroll bars* are further enhancements to Visual Basic 4.0 and support a complete Windows 95 environment.

The Visual Basic 4.0 language is fully compatible with Visual Basic for Applications. (Earlier versions of Visual Basic were *almost* compatible, a fact that often caused confusion for those who programmed in both Visual Basic for Applications and Visual Basic!) To help maintain compatibility between the two similar languages, Visual Basic 4.0 supports several new language statements.

Property procedures are new kinds of procedures you can write to execute when other parts of the code access, change, or use the Set statement to modify a control property in some way. Here is the format of a property procedure:

```
[Public¦Private][Static]Property {Get¦Let¦Set} PropertyName [(Arguments)][As Type]
   One or more Visual Basic 4.0 statements
End Property
```

If you want specific code executed when a property is set, use property procedures instead of public variables. The procedures execute automatically just as other event procedures are executed; your programming overhead is decreased.

TIP

If you want one or more properties to be read-only throughout a program's execution, you can use the Property Get property procedure without any corresponding Property Let or Property Set procedure. Property Get returns the value of a control's property; Property Let changes the property value and Property Set changes the property using the Set-like mechanism.

Three new language features take advantage of *collection objects* you can create. A *collection* is actually a new data type added to Visual Basic 4.0 to augment integers, strings, and the other data types in the language. (The keyword Collection defines occurrences of collection data types in statements such as Dim and ReDim.)

A collection object lets you create a group of Visual Basic 4.0 objects, such as databases or directories, and then enumerate over that collection. For example, suppose that an application works with 25 database objects. You can store those database objects in a *collection*, which acts like an array just for those objects. The new command `For Each...Next` lets you step through (or *enumerate*) each object within the collection. Here is the format of the `For Each...Next` command:

```
For Each Element In ObjCollection
   One or more Visual Basic 4.0 statements
Next [Element]
```

The `For Each` statement cannot work with user-defined data types because Visual Basic 4.0 must be able to enumerate over variant data types; user-defined data types can never be variant.

TIP

Using OLE automation, your Visual Basic 4.0 application can easily manipulate objects from other applications such as Microsoft Excel or Microsoft Project. Visual Basic 4.0's new and improved OLE features are discussed later in this chapter and throughout this book. Part III of this book, entitled "Unleashing Component-Based Programming," explores OLE 2.0 in more detail.

Visual Basic 4.0 simplifies your work with objects not only by letting you enumerate over objects using the `For Each` statement. You can also use the `With` statement to simplify your work with both objects and user-defined data types; the format of the `With` statement is shown here:

```
With Object
   One or more Visual Basic 4.0 statements
End With
```

You could set five form properties using a qualified form name like the following:

```
frmTitle.DragMode = 0
frmTitle.Enabled = False
frmTitle.Height = 575
frmTitle.TabIndex = 3
frmTitle.Width = 1100
```

Alternatively, you can eliminate the typing of the form name by using `With`:

```
With frmTitle
    .DragMode = 0
    .Enabled = False
    .Height = 575
    .TabIndex = 3
    .Width = 1100
End With
```

As do many of Visual Basic 4.0's enhancements, the `With` statement simplifies your programming requirements and decreases development time. If you have to modify five or more property values for a control, the `With` statement is easier to use than having to qualify the object name at each assignment.

Although Visual Basic 4.0 is not a true object-oriented programming (OOP) language, you can see that each version has come closer to working with true objects. Because of the support Visual Basic 4.0 gives to objectlike programming, the new Object Browser window, shown in

Figure 1.3, lets you scan through all classes, methods, and properties and jump directly to occurrences of such objects in code. If you want additional information on any of the objects being displayed, you can jump directly to those specific help topics for more documentation and description.

FIGURE 1.3.

The hierarchical Object Browser window lets you jump directly to an object in code.

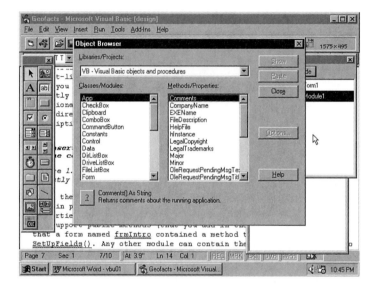

Forms themselves can now act as objects. For the first time, forms contain public properties and methods. You can call these form properties and methods from outside the form. In earlier versions of Visual Basic, forms did not support public methods. Suppose that a form named `frmIntro` contained a method you wrote named `SetUpFields()`. Any other module can contain the following statement to call that form's method:

```
frmIntro.SetUpFields
```

The way you add new properties to forms is to declare public variables inside the form's module:

```
Public DivCode As String
```

Any subsequent reference from any module to `frmIntro.DivCode`—whether on the left or right side of an assignment-like statement (called an *lvalue* or *rvalue* in C terminology)—accesses the `frmIntro`'s new property.

Better OLE Support

Windows 95 is an operating system built on a solid OLE foundation. Table 1.1 lists many of the numerous OLE-related enhancements featured in Visual Basic 4.0. Not only do the applications you create have more OLE capabilities but the Visual Basic 4.0 environment itself supports OLE and advanced drag and drop capabilities to make application development easier than ever:

■ When using Explorer, you can drag and drop files directly into the Visual Basic 4.0 Project window.

■ Visual Basic 4.0 lets you drag custom controls from other applications directly into the toolbar. If the object is an OLE-insertable object, that OLE object works as a custom control.

■ You can select one or more objects and drop those objects into a Visual Basic 4.0 OLE container during your application's design.

Table 1.1. New and improved OLE-related features in Visual Basic 4.0.

Feature	Description
OLE custom controls	Visual Basic 4.0 supports both the 16-bit VBX custom controls found in earlier versions of Visual Basic as well as 16-bit OLE controls. The 32-bit version of Visual Basic 4.0 supports OLE custom controls exclusively. An OLE custom control uses the filename extension OCX and always comes with a related OCA file that describes the control and resides in the same directory.
Automatic replacement of VBX controls with OLE controls	If you choose, you can request that Visual Basic 4.0 automatically replace all VBX custom controls with OLE custom controls so that you gain compatibility between 16-bit and 32-bit versions; this replacement also gives other applications (such as Microsoft Access and Microsoft FoxPro) access to the controls.
Error objects	When Visual Basic 4.0 encounters errors from OLE servers, you are better informed about the extent and specifics of those errors because of the more advanced error objects supported.
Visual Basic for Applications OLE support	You can easily program objects from other applications that support the Visual Basic for Applications (VBA) language from within your Visual Basic 4.0 application. Visual Basic 4.0 objects are also available outside the Visual Basic 4.0 development system from VBA-supported programs.
IDE extensibility	You can extend the functionality of Visual Basic 4.0's interactive development environment (the *IDE*) through the OLE automation interface. (You can also use the Add-Ins menu item to add items to Visual Basic 4.0's menu.)

continues

Table 1.1. continued

Feature	Description
Menu and toolbar negotiation	A form can contain compound-document OLE objects that support full, in-place activation.
OLE automation	You can create in-process OLE servers that execute as DLLs from inside the same process as a calling application. This arrangement improves performance over calling an out-of-process server that must reload each time it executes.

Some new and improved Professional Edition OLE-related features are discussed in the next section.

New Controls

Newcomers to Visual Basic 4.0 find several new controls on the toolbar. The Visual Basic 4.0 toolbar can contain any of these three kinds of tools:

- Standard controls such as the command button and option button
- Custom controls such as the common dialog box that have a VBX or OCX filename extension
- Custom controls made from insertable objects such as Microsoft Excel worksheets

The tools you see on your toolbar depend on your edition of Visual Basic 4.0 and the controls you or others have added or removed in the past or during installation. The standard controls available to all users of Visual Basic 4.0 are the pointer (on the toolbar but not considered a true control), picture box, label, text box, frame, command button, check box, option button, combo box, list box, horizontal scroll bar, vertical scroll bar, timer, drive list box, directory list box, file list box, shape, line, image, data, and OLE control.

Standard Edition users also get these custom controls: the common dialog box, the data-bound list, the data-bound combo box, the data-bound outline, and the data-bound grid control. These last four controls are now bound to data (they were not bound in earlier versions).

Many users of Visual Basic 4.0 will find additional controls. Select Tools | Custom Controls to see a list of the custom controls available with your edition of Visual Basic 4.0. "The Professional Edition's New Features," later in this chapter, describes additional controls.

Database Improvements

The Visual Basic data controls have been around for several years. However, Visual Basic 4.0 now includes an improved method for accessing external data: the Data Access Object (DAO) model. The DAO model is a new and complete interface that provides database control you can use as a supplement or even as an improved replacement over the older data controls.

The Microsoft Jet database engine appears in all three editions of Visual Basic 4.0. *Data Access Objects* are any data-related objects defined by the Jet database engine. DAOs can be tables, record sets, queries, or entire databases themselves.

CAUTION

Although Standard Edition users can access DAOs, they cannot use the Jet engine to create new databases or DAOs. The Professional Edition is required to create new databases or DAOs.

Compilation Improvements

Starting with Visual Basic 4.0, Microsoft borrowed a successful concept from C-based and C++-based Windows programs: *resource files*. Resource files contain Windows *resources* (Windows program elements) such as menus, strings, and control layouts. If you change an item inside a resource file, you do not have to recompile the Visual Basic 4.0 code that uses that resource file. One of the major advantages of resource files is that you can put every string literal in a program inside the resource file instead of inside the code. By doing so, you can easily translate the strings to other languages when you sell your application to foreign vendors. All you need to do is translate the strings inside the resource file instead of searching for and translating every string inside the program for each country.

UNICODE: VISUAL BASIC 4.0 THINKS GLOBALLY!

Visual Basic 4.0 supports the *Unicode* data definition, which allows for the globalization of character sets. Although 7-bit ASCII is fine for representing standard English and many non-English languages, some language extensions (such as technical symbols and common worldwide scripts) require too many bits to fit in a 7-bit range.

Unicode uses a 2-byte representation of data to provide enough width for those additional scripts and technical symbols. Microsoft was part of the Unicode Consortium that developed the Unicode standard; many of Microsoft's products—including the Visual Basic 4.0 runtime module—support the reading of Unicode data so that you can process data read from Unicode codes. Once read, Visual Basic 4.0 converts the Unicode into a series of 7-bit ASCII representations to work with the data internally.

Microsoft made three compilation enhancements to Visual Basic 4.0: background compilation, demand compilation, and background project loading. When you want to compile and run an application, Visual Basic 4.0 initially compiles only the initial form. The rest of the compile takes place in the background while you begin working with the running application. This background compilation feature should speed your development and debugging sessions.

> **NOTE**
>
> Beginning with Visual Basic 4.0, Microsoft changed the Visual Basic 4.0 project filename extension from MAK to VBP.

Compile on Demand lets Visual Basic 4.0 decide exactly what needs to be compiled and makes a decision that is best for you. When you choose to compile a project, Visual Basic 4.0 compiles only enough of that project to get the project up and running. Compile on Demand works just like background compilation but goes one step further. Suppose that you select an option from the running application that runs code in an entirely different module and loads a form that is not sequentially next in line to be compiled. Using Compile on Demand, Visual Basic 4.0 looks at the demand you are placing on the program and compiles and runs that needed portion of the code even though that portion was not up next for typical background compilation.

In the past, when you ran a compiled project, Visual Basic 4.0 loaded the entire project before displaying the project's first form. With version 4.0, Visual Basic now loads only the forms and files needed for you to begin running a requested project.

The Professional Edition's New Features

Most new features in all three editions of Visual Basic 4.0 were described in the first part of this chapter. The most extensive improvements were made to features found in the Standard Edition so that all users benefit from the upgrade. The new and improved features described so far in this chapter work with all versions of Visual Basic 4.0. The Professional Edition adds a few extras, however. The following short sections describe some of the new features owners of the Professional Edition can expect.

Additional Controls

The Windows 95-specific controls are available as OLE custom controls in the Professional Edition. The Windows 95 controls provide support for the image list, list view, rich text, tab strip, toolbar, tree view, progress bar, status bar, and slider controls.

If you do not see these Windows 95 controls on your toolbar, select Tools | Custom Controls to add them. Select both the Microsoft Rich Textbox and Microsoft Windows Common Controls to add these Windows 95 controls to your toolbar.

Advanced OLE Support

The Visual Basic 4.0 Professional Edition supports both the use *and creation* of OLE automation servers. Not only can you define your own servers so that you can take advantage of OLE to share code between applications, you can force an application to expose its internal objects—including elements of the Visual Basic 4.0 programming language.

Using OLE automation, you can create an OLE server to write a code package such as a compound interest calculation you can use in several different applications. As long as the other task is also written to support OLE automation, that application does not have to understand the Visual Basic 4.0 language.

Professional Database Features

As mentioned in "The Standard Edition's New Features," earlier in the chapter, the Professional Edition lets you use the Jet engine to create new databases and Data Access Objects (DAOs). Visual Basic 4.0 introduces the Jet engine version 3.0, which offers this Professional Edition database-creation feature and improves all the following database-related issues:

- Performance of database creation and access
- Improved database security
- More extensive database relationships
- Cascading updates and deletes to provide for more full recovery and auditing requirements when needed

In addition to making these improvements over the Jet engine version 2.5, Visual Basic 4.0 also adds several database-related properties and methods to give your data-related applications more power.

Additional Documentation

When you use Visual Basic 4.0's Professional Edition, you get additional documentation not available with the Standard Edition. You get bound, printed copies of the *Language Reference*, *Professional Features*, and *Crystal Reports for Visual Basic User's Manual* (the last two are not needed by Standard Edition users because the Standard Edition does not contain the Professional features or the Crystal Reports application).

The *Visual Basic Books Online* is also added to the Professional Edition and provides you with the following titles on CD-ROM:

- *Programmer's Guide.* The online version of the printed documentation that comes with Visual Basic 4.0.
- *Guide to Data Access Objects.* The online version of the printed documentation that comes with Visual Basic 4.0.

- *Crystal Reports User's Manual.* The online version of the printed documentation that comes with Visual Basic 4.0.

- *Help Compiler Guide.* An online guide that explains how to create and compile interactive help screens.

- *Data Manager Help.* An online guide that explains how to work with DAOs and the data-bound controls.

- *VisData Help.* Online help for the sample VisData database application that comes with Visual Basic 4.0.

- *BIBLIO Help.* Online help for the sample bibliography database application that comes with Visual Basic.

All online documentation supports hyperlink cross-references.

> **NOTE**
>
> Visual Basic Books Online is available by selecting Help | Visual Basic Books Online. The screen that appears (see Figure 1.4) has Explorer-like properties that let you view the contents of the online documentation in the left window and read the specific details in the right window.

FIGURE 1.4.

The Visual Basic Books Online opening screen.

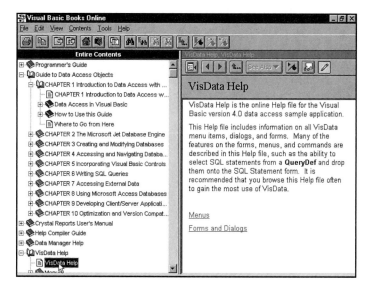

Crystal Report Writer

When you install Visual Basic 4.0, you have the option of installing the Crystal Report Writer system. Creating reports without the Crystal Report Writer is difficult because of the cumbersome nature of the Visual Basic Print command and the other language options that output data to printers. The Crystal Report Writer lets you easily design reports with headers, footers, page numbers, titles, detail lines, and additional and more fancy output features without tedious programming effort on your part.

The Crystal Report Writer works a lot like a report wizard. It presents a Report Gallery from which you can select the style of report you want Crystal Report to create. Once Crystal Reports designs the report to your specification, you can preview the report and make adjustments as needed. Refer to Chapter 8, "Reporting Mechanisms," for more information on creating reports.

The Enterprise Edition's New Features

Users of the Enterprise Edition have all the features of the Standard and Professional Editions of Visual Basic 4.0. In addition, the following support is given to the client/server environment:

- OLE Automation Controller to manage remote and local OLE objects
- Component Manager for analyzing and managing application's elements and their execution's impact in the client/server environment
- Microsoft SourceSafe version control system to ensure that test and production code does not get shuffled together when a team of programmers builds Visual Basic 4.0 applications
- Advanced client/server database management and programming tools

For example, once you create an OLE automation server using Enterprise Edition, you can use the *remote automation feature* of the Enterprise Edition to execute an OLE server on a centralized network server located far from the computer that needs the actual automation. Although a programmer may change the code inside the server, your remote application does not have to change to incorporate the updates made to the OLE automation code.

If you work with client/server technology using Visual Basic 4.0, you can use the Enterprise Edition's new Data Source Control to access and manage your remote ODBC (Open DataBase Connectivity) client/server databases from within your Visual Basic 4.0 applications.

NOTE

The Microsoft manual entitled *Building Client/Server Applications with Visual Basic* describes how the Enterprise Edition supports a multiuser client/server environment.

Summary

This chapter gave you a glimpse of the big picture. By reviewing all the new and improved Visual Basic 4.0 features, you are now ready to begin your real education as a Visual Basic 4.0 programmer. The rest of this book details the features this chapter only introduced; the book also explores several advanced ways you can make Visual Basic 4.0 work for you.

Exploiting the Features of Visual Basic 4.0

by (

Visual Basic 4.0 is an exciting new version of Visual Basic that adds many new features and enhancements to move Visual Basic to a new level in software design and development. This new version of Visual Basic uses Visual Basic for Applications (VBA) as its language engine. Several new keywords are added to the language to support the development of applications using OLE Automation. The VBX is replaced with the new generation of custom controls: the OCX. The Visual Basic interactive development environment (IDE) is significantly enhanced (see Figure 2.1); tasks such as adding a custom control to a project or viewing objects available within a project are simplified. This chapter outlines the new features of Visual Basic 4.0. Each new feature is fully explained and examples are provided where appropriate. A sample application is developed using OLE Automation and the Visual Basic 4.0 class module.

FIGURE 2.1.

The Visual Basic 4.0 interactive development environment (IDE).

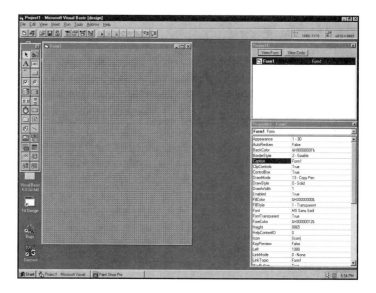

Visual Basic 4.0 also has many new features you can incorporate into existing projects. This chapter outlines the steps necessary to upgrade a project to Visual Basic 4.0 and explains some of the pitfalls you may encounter along the way. A step-by-step procedure is provided for converting a project from earlier versions of Visual Basic to VB4. Methods are covered for incorporating many new features of Visual Basic 4.0 into existing projects. Several sample programs are also provided.

Visual Basic for Applications (VBA)

Visual Basic 4.0 includes the Visual Basic for Applications (VBA) language. VBA is the language currently used in applications such as Microsoft Word and Excel. The inclusion of the language provides a new level of interaction between Visual Basic and Microsoft applications. For example, using VBA, a Visual Basic 4.0 application can create an instance of Microsoft

Excel, add a workbook, and imbed a chart in the workbook. All this can be done directly from Visual Basic *in code.* The instance of Excel and its components are created using OLE Automation. The inclusion of the VBA language allows Visual Basic to interact with other Microsoft applications without translating the language elements to something Visual Basic can understand. For example, you can use Microsoft Word to create a macro you can then copy directly to Visual Basic for inclusion in a procedure. Little or no translation is necessary to use the macro's code with Visual Basic. See Chapter 24 for more information about using Word macros in Visual Basic 4.0.

The Visual Basic Interactive Development Environment (IDE)

Many changes have been made to Visual Basic for version 4.0. The following sections cover the enhancements and changes to the Visual Basic IDE. Items that remain the same from version 3 to version 4.0 are not discussed.

The File | Make OLE DLL File Option

NOTE

The Make OLE DLL File option is available in 32-bit Visual Basic only.

The first addition to the Visual Basic IDE menu is the File | Make OLE DLL File option. This option is used to create OLE Automation objects you can expose to other applications and development environments. Once the OLE object is developed using the Visual Basic class module, the Make OLE DLL File option is used to compile the object into a DLL. The object is then added to other projects using the References dialog box (accessed by selecting Tools | References). Creating OLE automation objects using the class module is covered later in this chapter.

The Options button on the Make OLE DLL File dialog box leads to another dialog box from which you can specify a number of options such as version number, a title for the object, and the icon (if the object is visible). The OLE DLL Options dialog box is shown in Figure 2.2. The bottom section of this dialog box presents a number of different items whose information can be included in the OLE DLL. These items include Comments, Company Name, Legal Trademarks, and so on.

The OLE DLL Options dialog box allows you to place several pieces of information directly into your OLE DLL. Access the dialog box by selecting File | Make OLE DLL File from the main menu and clicking the Options button in the Make OLE DLL File dialog box.

FIGURE 2.2.

The OLE DLL Options dialog box.

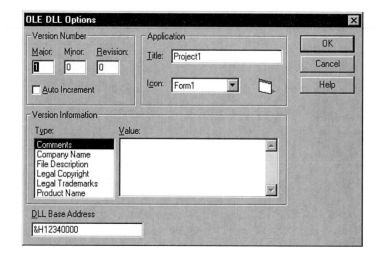

The Edit | Lock Controls Option

Another addition to the IDE is the Lock Controls feature. This option is accessed by selecting Edit | Lock Controls from the main menu. This option locks all the controls on the currently selected form. *All* the controls on the form are locked; you cannot select individual controls for locking.

There are a couple of advantages to this option. Once the design of a form is complete, you can lock the controls in place. Locking the controls marks the form as being graphically complete. You can still double-click any of the controls on the form to bring up the code window. Modifications to the code can be made without danger of changing the position of a control on a form. If you are creating a 32-bit version of an existing application (that is, you are porting an existing application from version 3 to 4), you can lock the controls to be sure that both versions of the application maintain the same graphical look.

The View | Procedure Definition Option

The View Procedure Definition feature allows you to locate the origin of a procedure. If you have used Visual C++, this feature should be familiar to you. If you call a procedure and cannot remember where the procedure definition is, this option is of great use. Imagine that you create the following function in Module1:

```
Function Hello()
    MsgBox "Have a nice day"
    Hello = 0
End Function
```

Next, you call this function from Form1's command button:

```
Private Sub Command1_Click()
    x = Hello
End Sub
```

Now suppose that your project has grown significantly (say, to 25 modules) and you can no longer remember in which module the `Hello` function resides. To solve this, do the following:

1. Open the `Private Sub Command1_Click()` procedure from Form1.

2. Click the function name (in this case, `Hello`).

3. Choose View | Procedure Definition from the main menu.

Module1 opens to display the `Hello` function. The Procedure Definition is a handy tool for large projects. Another place in which this feature has great benefit is in the modification of existing code. This feature precludes much of the searching that traditionally goes on when a programmer inherits source code written by others.

The View | Last Position Option

A helpful new feature of Visual Basic 4.0 is available by choosing View | Last Position. This action places the cursor in its previous position. This can be very helpful if you are browsing through a number of modules and want to go back to where you just were. The Last Position feature "thinks" like an undo feature but does not undo anything; instead, it merely moves the cursor back one action. Imagine that you have three modules: Module1, Module2, and Module3. You look at a procedure in each of the modules (1, 2, and then 3). Select View | Last Position; the cursor moves from the procedure being viewed in Module3 to the Module2 procedure (the one viewed just before the one you are currently viewing). Select View | Last Position again to bring up Module1's procedure. If the module is closed, Visual Basic opens it. The Last Position feature works wonders when you are stepping through large projects.

The Object Browser

Yet another addition to the Visual Basic IDE is the Object Browser. Access the Object Browser by choosing View | Object Browser (see Figure 2.3). The Object Browser presents a list of the different objects available to your application. Each of the objects lists the properties and methods it exposes.

Two types of objects are available to an application: those within Visual Basic and those provided by other applications. The objects provided by other applications are accessed through OLE Automation. To select the object you want to view, choose an object from the available items in the Libraries/Projects combo box. The Classes/Modules list box lists the items exposed by the selected object; the Methods/Properties list box displays the properties and methods exposed by the object.

FIGURE 2.3.

The Visual Basic Object Browser dialog box displays the Visual Basic for Applications (VBA) objects.

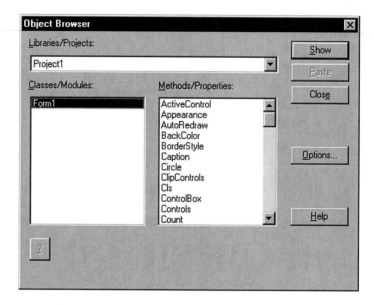

Imagine that you create a project (Project1) with one form (Form1). On the form, you place a text box. Now open the Object Browser and select Project1 from the Libraries/Projects combo box. The Classes/Modules section contains one item: Form1. The Methods/Properties section contains all the properties and methods for Form1. These are the normal properties and methods the form already includes. Scroll through the list in the Methods/Properties list box. Notice the `Text1` and `Text1_Change [Sub]` items. Because the text box is now a part of Form1, it and the properties and methods it exposes are displayed in this list as well.

Another use for the Object Browser is during the creation of a procedure using a method an object in the list exposes. Imagine that you want to create a new procedure using one of the objects VBA exposes. Using the Object Browser, you can automatically paste a Visual Basic template for the selected method or property. The following steps accomplish this:

1. Create a new project and double-click Form1 to display the code window.

2. Place the cursor in the `Form_Load` procedure (click above the `End Sub` statement).

3. Open the Object Browser and select VBA—Visual Basic for Applications from the Libraries/Projects combo box. Notice that the Collection object is highlighted in the Classes/Modules section and that the `Add` item is highlighted in the Methods/Properties list box. Click the Paste button.

The statement pasted into the `Form_Load` procedure contains the Visual Basic syntax necessary to use the `Add` method of the Collections object within VBA.

Another feature of the Object Browser is its ability to quickly locate procedures and functions within a project. Select the desired procedure or function from the browser and click the Show button; Visual Basic displays the code for that item. To use the Show feature, follow these steps:

1. Create a new project (or use the current one if you followed the steps for the last example).

2. Place a text box on the form.

3. Start the Object Browser and select Project1 from the Libraries/Projects combo box.

4. Click Form1 in the Classes/Modules list box.

5. Choose `Text1_Change [Sub]` from the Methods/Properties list box.

6. Click the Show button.

The code window for Form1 opens, displaying the `Private Sub Text1_Change()` procedure.

The Debug Window

The Visual Basic Debug Window is used to view or change the value of statements or variables at design time. The window becomes active when the interactive development environment (IDE) is in break mode (see Figure 2.4).

FIGURE 2.4.

The Visual Basic Debug Window.

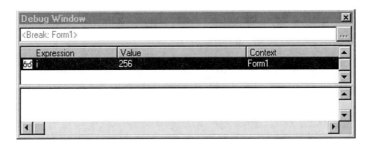

The three sections of the window are the Procedure box, the Watch pane, and the Immediate pane.

There are three major sections to the Break window. Each of these sections of the Debug Window is described in the following sections.

The Procedure Box

The Procedure box displays the Project, Module, and Procedure name that was active when the application was placed into break mode. To the right of this section is a command button with three dots; click this button to display the Calls window. The Calls window shows a list of all the procedures that were called but that have not yet completed. Using the example from the preceding section, Form1's `Private Sub Command1_Click()` procedure calls the `Hello` function in Module1. Set a break point in the middle of the `Hello` function. Once the break point is hit, the application goes into break mode and the Debug Window appears. Click the Calls button; the `Private Sub Command1_Click()` procedure appears in the Calls window because it has not yet completed. Click the Show button in the Calls window to display the code window for the selected procedure. The Calls window is especially effective when using recursive functions.

The Watch Pane

The Watch pane of the Debug window displays information about variables you have placed a watch on. To add a watch to a variable, use the mouse to select a variable in a code window (procedure, function, and so on) and choose Tools | Add Watch. The Add Watch window is displayed. The expression you want to place a watch on appears in the Expression section of this window. The center section lists the procedure, module, and project associated with the variable. The bottom section of the Add Watch window provides a choice of three types of watches. The Watch Expression displays the value of the expression in the ???Watch??? window. The Break When Value Is True option and Break When Value Changes option cause Visual Basic to go into break mode if one of those conditions occurs. Click OK to add the watch. If the application is not yet running, the Out of Context message is displayed, indicating that the variable cannot be tracked at this time. When the application is placed in break mode, the value for the selected variable is displayed.

The Immediate Pane

The immediate pane allows the getting and setting of values within the application. For example, if you did not add a variable to the watch window, you can view the value of the variable by printing it to the Debug Window's Immediate pane. To do this, type a question mark followed by the variable name. For example, to get the value of variable X, type the following in the Immediate Pane and press Enter:

```
?X
```

The value of X is displayed on the next line of the Immediate pane. You can also set a value for X using an assignment statement like the following:

```
X = 50
```

This statement sets the value of X within the program to 50. This capability is advantageous if you want to reset a loop variable to 0 during debugging.

> **NOTE**
>
> The immediate pane can be used only in Break mode.

View Color Palette

The color palette is used to set the colors for forms and controls. The palette is accessed by choosing View | Color Palette from the main menu. Foreground and background colors can be set using the palette. Follow these steps to use the color palette:

1. Open a form.
2. Open the palette by choosing View | Color Palette.
3. Use the mouse to select the form or a control on the form.
4. Click the palette's title bar to give it the focus. Notice that the palette contains a square with an inner and outer section.
5. Click the inner section of the palette's square to change the foreground color of the selected form or control. Click the outer section to set the background color.

Using the color palette is the equivalent of using the Properties dialog box to set the value for the object. However, the palette approach is quicker and more convenient. You can define custom colors by following these steps:

1. Click the Custom Colors button on the color palette.
2. Click the first color block in the section (initially, each block in the row is white).
3. Click the Define Colors button.
4. Manipulate the color using the six available categories.
5. Click Add Color to create the custom color; click Close to quit.

Start with Full Compile Command

The Run | Start with Full Compile menu option starts the Visual Basic application much like the Run menu item in Visual Basic 3.0 does. This command is used primarily when your application is acting as an OLE server. With this option, the application is fully compiled and then run. If you use only the Start command and your application has errors that show up when the application is compiled, the client applications may be left with invalid object references.

The Step to Cursor Option

The Step to Cursor option is a new element added to the Run menu. This option is used only in break mode. To use Step to Cursor, follow these steps:

1. Run your project and go into break mode.
2. Click the line you want to step to and choose Run | Step to Cursor.

The line you select must be *after* the current line. An example of Step to Cursor follows. Imagine that you have the following procedure:

```
Private Sub Command1_Click()
    Dim x As Integer
    Dim y As Integer
    Dim z As Integer
    x = 7

    For x = 1 To 100
        DoEvents
    Next x

    y = 4
    z = x + y
    y = z - x
    x = z - y
    x = x + 1
End Sub
```

There is a breakpoint set on the line x = 7. Once you are inside the procedure (execution has stopped at the break point), you decide you want to step to the line y = z - x. To avoid stepping through the very productive DoEvents loop, click the line y = z - x and choose Run | Step to Cursor. The program executes until it reaches that line and then stops.

Addition of Custom Controls

Visual Basic 4.0 has added a much needed option to its package of new features: You can now add custom controls to a project without the previous difficulty of searching the system for them. Choose Tools | Custom Controls from the main menu; the Custom Controls dialog box displays. Visual Basic automatically searches your system for a list of the available custom controls. Remember that these controls must be OCXes (VBXes are not supported under Visual Basic 4.0). To select a control to add to your project, browse the list box of available controls and click the checkbox for each control you want to add. The section at the bottom right of the dialog box allows you to choose the types of objects displayed in the dialog box. There are three categories:

- **Insertable Objects.** This option displays *insertable objects*—objects that can be inserted into a form. Some of these objects are bitmaps, media clips, Word documents, and so on.

- **Controls.** This option displays only custom OCX controls available to your application. Both selected and nonselected controls appear.

- **Selected Items Only.** This option displays only the selected controls. This option lets you view the list of items added to your project without searching the entire list of available items.

The section along the bottom of the dialog box displays the name of the current item as well as the fully qualified path to its location.

If you want to add an item to your project but that item is not displayed in the list, click the Browse button. A common dialog box is displayed, allowing you to select a specific file to add to the project.

Click OK when you have selected the items you want to add to your project. The dialog box closes and the custom controls and insertable objects are added to the toolbar. This is a much simpler method than the File | Add File method of Visual Basic 3.0.

When you open a project created in an earlier version of Visual Basic, you are asked whether the custom controls should be updated. Visual Basic 4.0 updates your project to include the OCX version of any control contained in your project. This applies to standard controls only. For third-party controls, you must either upgrade the VBX to an OCX or eliminate the control from the application. Most third-party tools vendors, such as MicroHelp, Inc., provide a complete set of OCX controls for use with Visual Basic 4.0. These controls are provided in both 16-bit and 32-bit versions.

NOTE

MicroHelp is the largest maker of third-party add-on tools for Visual Basic. MicroHelp, Inc. offers a Communications Library that is considerably faster than the 19,200 baud controls supplied with Visual Basic 4.0. The control supports numerous additional protocols and emulations and can be substituted for the Visual Basic communications control without modifying existing code. MicroHelp, Inc. also offers OLETools, a product containing more than 50 16-bit and 32-bit custom OCXes for development with Visual Basic 4.0.

You can reach MicroHelp at 1-800-922-3383 or (770) 516-0898.

The References Dialog Box

The References dialog box lets you select from a list of OLE objects to add to your project. Items in the list are OLE objects exposed for use by other applications. To select an object, check its checkbox. Remove the check to deselect that object. These objects are not actually added to your project; instead, a reference is set to the object's object library. (An *object library* contains the properties and methods an object exposes.) To view the properties and methods of an OLE object, use the Object Browser.

OLE Automation

You encounter two types of objects when creating applications for Visual Basic: objects that Visual Basic provides and objects provided by other applications. The objects Visual Basic provides are familiar to you: forms, controls, and so on. (You can also create your own objects from within Visual Basic.) The objects provided by other applications are accessed with OLE Automation. Applications create objects they expose to other applications. The term *expose* simply means to make an object or its properties and methods available for use by other applications or development environments.

An example of an application that exposes objects is Microsoft Excel. Excel exposes many different objects to applications. One of these objects is a spreadsheet. A Visual Basic application can create an instance of the spreadsheet object and manipulate it using the properties and methods the object exposes. For more information on OLE Automation with Microsoft Excel and Word, see Chapter 24, "Microsoft Office."

All the objects contained within Visual Basic are based on a hierarchy. Imagine that you are accessing objects on a form. The code you use to access the objects is in a module. To access a text box on a form, the Form object is called and then the text box is called.

```
Form1.Text1.Text = "This is an object hierarchy"
```

This line of code accesses the text box object that belongs to Form1. Another type of object in Visual Basic is one you create at runtime. For example, you can create an instance of Form1 by doing the following:

```
Sub CreateForm()
    Dim frmNew As New Form1
    Static iTop as Integer
    frmNew.Show
    iTop = iTop + 50
End Sub
```

This procedure creates a new instance of Form1 and then shows it. If this procedure is attached to a command button and you click the command button five times, five new instances of Form1 are created and then shown. The `iTop = iTop + 50` statement is used for demonstration purposes so that the forms are not stacked directly on top of each other (this may give the impression that there is only one form and the others are not being created).

This type of interaction also applies when dealing with objects another application exposes. To create and access a spreadsheet object, the hierarchy of the `application.workbook.spreadsheet` must be followed. Each application that exposes objects provides a hierarchy list of objects.

To view the list of objects for Microsoft Excel, do the following:

1. From the main Excel menu, choose Help | Contents.
2. Choose Programming with Visual Basic to jump to a screen entitled *Visual Basic Reference.*
3. Choose Microsoft Excel Object Model to jump to the listing of objects Excel exposes to other applications. You can expand an item that contains a red arrow to reveal additional objects that the item contains.

If you are planning to use an object frequently, you can add it to your project using the Custom Controls dialog box described in "Addition of Custom Controls," earlier in this chapter.

More about OLE Automation

OLE Automation allows applications to expose objects to other applications that support (or develop) OLE. Think of this functionality as an extension of Visual Basic. VB has objects (command buttons, text boxes, forms, and so on). These objects have properties and methods; for example, the text box has a `text` property (`Text1.Text = "Hello"`) and a `Change` method (`Text1_Change`). OLE Automation takes this a step—or more precisely, *several* steps—further by allowing different applications to "expose" objects to other applications. Exposing an object allows another application to see and manipulate the object. For example, the following line of Visual Basic code creates a new instance of Microsoft Excel:

```
Set objApp = CreateObject("Excel.Application")
```

The new instance of the application is stored in the variable `objApp`. The same functionality is applied to the objects Excel exposes.

The *object model* referred to in step 3 in the preceding section is a list of all the objects Microsoft Excel exposes to other applications. These objects are accessed with Visual Basic much like properties and methods for controls (`Text1.Text`, `Command1_Click`, and so on). To use an object, you must first create it with the `CreateObject` function. If the object already exists (as a saved spreadsheet, for example), you can use the `GetObject` function. Each object must be assigned to a variable; that variable is what is used in the hierarchical manipulation of the object.

```
Set objApp = CreateObject("Excel.Application")
Set objWorkBook = objApp.WorkBooks.Add
Set objSpreadSheet1 = objApp.ActiveWorkbook.ActiveSheet
```

These three lines of code create an object instance of Microsoft Excel and store it in the variable `objApp`. A new workbook is then created by using the `objApp` variable (the instance of Excel). Finally, the active spreadsheet within the workbook is assigned the variable `objSpreadSheet1`. You then access the spreadsheet by using `objApp.objWorkBook.objSpreadSheet1`.

TIP

To avoid bulky code, assign an object at the bottom of a hierarchical list its own variable name with a statement like this one:

```
Set objASheet = objApp.ActiveWorkbook.ActiveSheet
```

Now each time you use the spreadsheet, you can call it with `objASheet` instead of `objApp.ActiveWorkBook.ActiveSheet`. This saves typing time and makes the source code more readable.

Be careful that you use the proper hierarchy and that every one of the objects is a member of its parent object. Because this is not always apparent, diligence is in order. For example, to set the caption in a spreadsheet cell (or range of cells), it would seem logical to use `objSpreadSheet1Range.Caption`. However, this statement does not work because the proper structure requires the use of the `Characters` object. The spreadsheet contains the `Characters` object and the `Characters` object contains the `caption` property. Therefore, the proper statement is as follows:

```
objSpreadSheet1Range.Characters.Caption = sValue
```

In this case, `objSpreadSheet1Range` is a range of cells within the worksheet (this range can be one cell).

To find the properties and methods exposed by an object, click the object in the object model. This brings up a help sheet with two jumps: properties and methods. Using this approach, you can establish the downward order of objects within Excel. Each application should have a list that roughly follows this format. Unfortunately (at least with the object model in Excel), it is not easy to go in reverse. For example, if you know that you want to set the caption of the spreadsheet cell, it can be difficult to determine that you have to go through the `Characters` object.

All the items listed in the preceding code fragments are OLE objects exposed by Excel for use in other applications.

OLE Automation has been significantly enhanced in Visual Basic 4.0. Visual Basic for Applications (VBA) version 2.0 is included as part of Visual Basic 4.0 (it is also the language used in Microsoft Excel and Project). The inclusion of VBA provides greater control over OLE automation directly from Visual Basic.

Chapter 24 details the creation of an Excel application. In that chapter, you create an Excel workbook and set up the background color, fonts, and so on. Next, you add several command buttons to the first spreadsheet in the workbook. These command buttons are connected to a module containing functions that populate data, format cells, select cells, and so on. This module is added to the Visual Basic code. The next step adds a chart to the spreadsheet; the chart uses existing spreadsheet data for its values. A Microsoft Word document is then embedded into the spreadsheet; the document is connected to an existing Word DOC file. Finally, a title is added to the spreadsheet.

There are several interesting things to note here. Before creating the application, nothing existed in Excel. The entire application is created with code directly from Visual Basic. This is possible because of the inclusion of VBA into the language. The code includes the "wiring" of the command buttons to the functions in the module. Also, all objects (spreadsheets, charts, modules, and so on) are OLE objects created using OLE Automation.

The properties and methods of an OLE object allow one application to use functionality that resides within another application without recreating the code that does so. In Visual Basic, the class module is the mechanism used to create such objects.

Class Modules

A new feature of Visual Basic 4.0 is the class module. Before discussing class modules, a definition of the term *class* is in order. A *class* is a collection of related data objects and the functions used to manipulate them. In Visual Basic 4.0, these items are all stored in a module called a *class module*. If you are not a C++ programmer, this concept may seem a bit foreign; this section delves into this topic further.

Imagine that you are writing an application that reads data from a file, does mathematical calculations on the data, and then returns it to the file. Different calculations are performed depending on the data retrieved. To organize your application, you create two modules: FILEIO.BAS and MATH.BAS. In each of these modules, you create the necessary functions to perform the task. Each of these modules falls into a class (File I/O and Mathematics). Although you have not created classes, this analogy should help to explain the principle of classes.

Class modules somewhat resemble Visual Basic modules in that they can contain function declarations, functions, and procedures. However, class modules also allow the inclusion of property procedures and can be accessed by other applications through OLE Automation. *Property procedures* are structured like functions and are used to get and set the properties of objects within the class. Property procedures are primarily used in OLE Automation. In OLE Automation, other applications can manipulate objects your application exposes. If you have a class module with public functions, other applications can call these functions to manipulate their objects. **Remember:** In the class structure, there are objects and these objects are manipulated by their functions.

Visual Basic 4.0 provides a good example of classes in the sample application SOCCER. This application is located in the directory C:\VB4\SAMPLES\OLESERV (VB4 being the location of Visual Basic 4.0). You must have installed the samples for this directory to be present. This directory contains two projects: CLIENT.VBP and SOCCER.VBP. SOCCER.VBP is the OLE server that responds to requests from the interface CLIENT.VBP. This application is structured after a soccer league. There is one class module for each of the objects:

Class Module	Contents
LEAGUE	Data about the league
PLAYER	Data about a specific player
PLAYERS	Data about players on a team
TEAM	Data about a team
TEAMS	Data about a collection of teams

Items can be added to each of the class modules (a member can be added to a team, a team added to a league, and so on) and items can be removed. The class can be queried for information. All interaction with the SOCCER.VBP application is done using OLE Automation through CLIENT.VBP.

Several elements are involved in the creation of an OLE object using the Visual Basic 4.0 class module. Each of these elements is discussed in the following sections:

■ Properties
■ Property procedures
■ Methods

Properties

To create the properties an object exposes, the property itself must be defined. Any property to be used by another application must be declared as public. Visual Basic uses the `Public` keyword to indicate that a property can be accessed by other applications performing OLE Automation. The declaration of a property is as follows:

```
Public PropertyName as Integer
```

Any data type can be used in place of *integer*. This statement defines the property name other applications must use to interact with your OLE object. This name should be user friendly so that your library of properties and methods is easy to understand and use. The following example created a property that is difficult to read:

```
Public pLstPd as Integer
```

Remember that you are declaring the name that others have to use; the following example is easier to understand:

```
Public LastPay as Integer
```

Once the property is defined, you must then create property procedures.

Property Procedures

Property procedures are used to set and get the properties of the class module (OLE object). A *property procedure* is a function or procedure inside the class module that is called when the user gets or sets a property within the module. Imagine that you have a class module object named `Draw`. The `Draw` object has a property called `DrawItem`. To get or set the `DrawItem` property, you must first create an instance of the `Draw` object:

```
Dim objDraw as Draw
```

Then you set the object's `DrawItem` property using the standard property-setting statement:

```
objDraw.DrawItem = "Pen"
```

At this point, your class module invokes the `Property Let` method for the object and attempts to set the `DrawItem` property to `"Pen"`. The `Property Let` method validates that this is a legal setting and notifies the user appropriately.

Next, you query the `objDraw` object's `DrawItem` property for its value:

```
'Variable where we store the DrawItem property value.
Dim sWhat as String

sWhat = objDraw.DrawItem
```

Methods

Imagine that there are five objects available for drawing and that each time the `objDraw.DrawItem` property is set, one of these objects is allocated for use (also imagine that there is a `objDraw.KillItem` property that deallocates an object). You need a method that calculates how many `DrawItem` objects remain for use. If five items have been allocated and the user tries to allocate an additional item, this method should notify the user that this is not allowed. The method should be executed before the `Property Let` procedure that allocates a new drawing item. If the maximum number of drawing objects has not yet been allocated, the `Property Let` statement is executed. In this example, the `Property Let` procedure probably does something like `GetStockObject()` to create a new drawing object. When the `KillItem` property is set (for example, `ObjDraw.KillItem = "Pen"`) `DestroyObject()` is called inside the property procedure to delete the pen.

This is a very effective way to handle difficult operations in Visual Basic. The user can access your drawing object's methods and properties with simple statements such as `objDraw.DrawItem = "Pen"`. Behind the scenes, your code may be performing complex operations transparent to the user. Your OLE Automation object is therefore very effective and easy to use. Other properties may include the type of object to draw and where to draw it.

The Customer Account Example

This section creates an OLE Automation object using a class module. This module sets up and maintains an account at a local shop. The class object name is `Account`.

The properties and methods of this object allow you to set up new customers, make purchases, and query the account for information. When you process a transaction against the account, you verify that the customer is not over his or her limit.

First, create a new class module: Select Insert | Class Module from the main menu. Double-click the class module to open its code window. Press F4 to display the property window for the class module.

NOTE

The class module code window must be open to display its property sheet.

Change the Name property to Account. When a new instance of this object is created, it references the Name property (you create an instance of this object in the form procedure later).

In the general declarations section of the class module, place the following declarations:

```
Private c_CustName As String
Private c_CurrentBalance As Double
Private c_NewPurchaseAmount As Double
```

These are private variables used by the Account class to store data. These variables are called *member variables* (this term comes from the C++ language). Because they are declared as Private, they are not visible outside the class module (by other applications or even by the current VB application).

The Account class has three properties. These properties correspond to the member variables:

Property	*Member Variable*
CustomerName	c_CustName
CurrentBalance	c_CurrentBalance
NewPurchaseAmount	c_NewPurchaseAmount

NOTE

The c_ indicates that this is a private class variable not visible outside the Account object. This notation is of my choosing, but in a moment, you will see that it clarifies things significantly.

The next step is to create the property procedures to be used to get and set the properties. You create a Property Set and a Property Let procedure for each property. The Property Set procedures are invoked when a Property Set statement is used in code.

```
objAccount.NewPurchaseAmount = 500
```

This statement sets the NewPurchaseAmount property in the objAccount instance of the class Account to 500. Inside the class is a Property Let procedure that assigns the value to the c_NewPurchaseAmount member variable for storage. When the Account object is queried for the value of the NewPurchaseAmount property, the Property Get procedure returns the property value by getting the value of the member variable corresponding to the NewPurchaseAmount property: c_NewPurchaseAmount.

The first `Property Let` procedure for the `Account` class object sets the value of the customer name. The VB statement that does this is as follows:

```
objAccount.CustName = "Joe the customer"
```

Here is the `Property Let` procedure:

```
Property Let CustName(ByVal sNewCustName As String)
    c_CustName = sNewCustName
End Property
```

The next `Property Let` procedure for the `Account` class object sets the value of `CurrentBalance`. However, it is not logical to allow a direct setting of the current balance. This should be calculated by adding the current balance to any new purchases. This is done in the `NewPurchaseAmount` `Property Let` procedure. Setting the `CurrentBalance` property produces an error:

```
Property Let CurrentBalance(ByVal NewCurrentBalance As Double)
    Err.Raise vbObjectError + 2, "Project1.ShowMe", "This property is read only"
End Property
```

This statement uses the `Err.Raise` command to set an error number for this invalid property setting. In the error handler, you will check for the occurrence of `vbObjectError + 2`.

The last `Property Let` statement is `NewPurchaseAmount`. When this is set, the new purchase amount (`iPurchaseAmount`) is added to the current balance of the customer (`c_CurrentBalance`). In the procedure, you check this balance before applying any additional transactions. If the customer is over his or her limit, do not process the transaction. Here is the `NewPurchaseAmount` `Property Let` procedure:

```
Property Let NewPurchaseAmount(ByVal iPurchaseAmount As Double)
    c_NewPurchaseAmount = iPurchaseAmount
    c_CurrentBalance = c_CurrentBalance + iPurchaseAmount
End Property
```

The first `Property Get` procedure for the `Account` class object gets the value of the customer name:

```
Property Get CustName() As String
    CustName = c_CustName
End Property
```

You use the following `Property Get` procedure to get the value of the customer's current balance. For now, there is only one name in the database (so that you don't get bogged down in manipulating multiple customers and lose focus on the task at hand).

```
Property Get CurrentBalance() As Double
    CurrentBalance = c_CurrentBalance
End Property
```

When the customer makes a new purchase, it is entered by setting the `NewPurchaseAmount` property. This property retrieves the value to the `c_NewPurchaseAmount` member variable and returns it to the variable in the `Property Get` statement, as follows:

```
'Property get statement
x = objAccount.NewPurchaseAmount
```

```
'Property procedure
Property Get NewPurchaseAmount() As Double
    NewPurchaseAmount = c_NewPurchaseAmount
End Property
```

The next step is to create the user interface. For purposes of illustration, this example uses a very simple interface. It is important to concentrate on the details of object-oriented programming and not on the implementation of databases and user interfaces.

Create a form. Add three command buttons, three labels, and five text boxes to the form (see Figure 2.5). Label the command buttons as follows:

> Set Up Customer
> New Purchase
> Get Cust Info

FIGURE 2.5.

The form for the Account application.

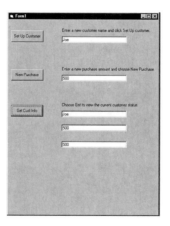

Place the following code behind the first command button (Set Up Customer). Make sure that you change the name of the command button to cmdSetUp.

```
Private Sub cmdSetUp_Click()
    If Text1.TEXT = "" Then
        MsgBox "The customer name must not be blank."
    Else
        clsAccount.CustName = Text1.TEXT
    End If
End Sub
```

This procedure adds a new customer account. For purposes of illustration, the module handles only one customer at a time. To implement additional customers, create a database file to store and retrieve information. For more information on using files to store information, see Chapter 3, "File I/O." The end of Chapter 3 explains how to store data in binary files using Visual Basic structures. The chapter also covers the use of binary chops to quickly search arrays of data for information.

The preceding procedure checks the text box to ensure that a value has been entered. If there is something in the text box, it is set as the CustName property value.

The next command button (New Purchase) posts a transaction to the account. This procedure checks the c_CurrentBalance member variable inside the Account class to ensure that the customer is not over his or her limit. In this example, the limit variable is set inside the command button's procedure. You could just as easily add a c_Limit member variable to the class to track the customer's limit. The name of this command button is cmdPostTrans; here is the procedure:

```
Private Sub cmdPostTrans_Click()
    'Set up our current balance and new purchase amount variables
    Dim iCurrentBalance As Double
    Dim iNewPurchaseAmount

    'This error handler is very important. If the transaction fails because the
    'customer's balance is greater than 5000, or if this transaction will take
    'them over the 5000 limit, the error is returned as a VB error.
    On Error GoTo ErrorHandler

    'Get the value from the text box
    iNewPurchaseAmount = Val(Text2.TEXT)

    'We check the value in the text box. If it is blank, we notify the user and
    'quit.
    If Text2.TEXT = "" Then
        MsgBox "The New Purchase Amount must not be blank."
        Exit Sub
    End If

    'Query the CurrentBalance property for its value (the Property Get
    'procedure for CurrentBalance is executed)
    iCurrentBalance = objAccount.CurrentBalance

    'We check the current balance to see if it is currently greater than $5000.
    'If it is, we notify the user that the transaction cannot be posted and quit.
    'See Raise in Visual Basic help for more information on structuring OLE errors.
    If iCurrentBalance > 5000 Then
        Err.Raise vbObjectError + 1, "Project1.ShowMe", _
        "Your balance is greater than $5000. This transaction is not allowed"
        Exit Sub
    End If

    'If the first check passed, we then check to see if this transaction will
    'cause the customer to go over $5000. If they will exceed $5000, they are
    'notified and we quit.
    If iCurrentBalance + iNewPurchaseAmount > 5000 Then
        Err.Raise vbObjectError + 2, "Project1.ShowMe", _
        "Your balance is currently " & iCurrentBalance & "." & _
        " This transaction causes your balance to exceed the limit. " & _
        " This transaction is not allowed."
        Exit Sub
    End If

    'The transaction cleared all of the checks, so we can post it.
```

```
    'We check the value
    If Val(Text2.TEXT) > 0 Then
        objAccount.NewPurchaseAmount = iNewPurchaseAmount
        MsgBox "The transaction has been posted. Your new balance is " &
objAccount.CurrentBalance
    End If
    Exit Sub

'This error handler checks for each of the OLE errors that we defined earlier.
ErrorHandler:
    Select Case Err
        Case vbObjectError + 1
            MsgBox "Your balance is greater than $5000. This transaction is not
➥allowed"
        Case vbObjectError + 2
            MsgBox "Your balance is currently " & iCurrentBalance & "." & _
            " This transaction causes your balance to exceed the limit. " & _
            " This transaction is not allowed."
        Case Else
            MsgBox "Error " & Err & " " & Error$ & "ocurred."
    End Select

    Exit Sub

End Sub
```

The final procedure queries the Account object for the value of its properties:

```
Private Sub cmdAccountStatus_Click()
    Text3.TEXT = objAccount.CustName
    Text4.TEXT = objAccount.CurrentBalance
    Text5.TEXT = objAccount.NewPurchaseAmount
End Sub
```

This implementation is simplistic so that the methodology is not lost. With small modifications, the Account object can be set up to create multiple customers. A file containing account database information can be used to store the customer information. Additional property procedures can be defined to handle overdue bills. Other applications can query this object for customer credit ratings. The list of possibilities is endless.

The result of Account class module is an interface that exposes properties and methods to other applications for use. The inner workings of this object can become extremely complex, but interacting with the object is simple.

Now that the Account object is complete, you have to turn it into an OLE Automation object other applications and development environments can access. To do this, you create an OLE DLL. This DLL is compiled from an application that houses one or many OLE Automation objects (such as the Account object.)

The first step is to create a Sub Main() procedure so that the DLL can be compiled. Sub Main() is the startup procedure for the OLE DLL. In this case, the Sub Main() procedure doesn't require any code:

```
Sub Main()

End Sub
```

Next, select Tools | Options from the main menu and select the Project tab of the Options dialog box. From the Startup Form combo box, select Sub Main. This indicates that the project does not have a form and that the `Sub Main()` procedure is the entry point to the OLE DLL. In the Start Mode section, click the OLE Server button to indicate that this application will operate as an OLE server.

Then choose File | Make OLE DLL File. Enter the filename **Account** for the project and click OK.

The OLE DLL is automatically assigned the extension DLL unless you indicate otherwise.

Once the project is compiled, you have successfully created the Account object using OLE Automation and the class module in Visual Basic 4.0.

The final step is to use the object from another application. Start a new project and select Tools | References from the main menu. This References dialog box lists the objects other applications expose. Search this list for the Account object. Place a check next to it in the list box and click OK. Although nothing appears in the toolbar, the Account object can now be accessed by your application (Visual Basic adds a reference to the object). Recall that you compiled the Account project with the form that set and queried the different properties of the object. Add this form to your new project by selecting File | Add File and selecting the form from the original project. Run the new project. The Account form creates an instance of the exposed object and then manipulates it. Even though the class module is not included in this project, you can address it because it was included in the References dialog box. As far as your application is concerned, this object is treated the same as an object from Microsoft Excel. Unlike a chart object however, this object is not visible to the user.

Another feature of OLE objects is that private data can be stored without the fear that it will be accessed by unauthorized users. The next section discusses the concept of data hiding.

Data Hiding

Data hiding is a method of setting security for the data contained in an object. The theory behind this is similar to variable scope. For example, if you create a function inside a module and declare a variable, that variable is local and can only be seen by the function:

```
Function PrivateStuff
    Dim sPrivateData as String
    ...
End Function
```

The concept of data hiding applies in the same context to objects in Visual Basic 4.0. A variable declared at the module level is available to all applications that access the module. To ensure that other applications do not have access to a module level variable, use the `Private` keyword:

```
Private sVariable
```

Because the variable is private, it can be changed or eliminated without affecting other applications that access the object. This type of variable, therefore, is internal to the object and is not seen by other processes. This arrangement is most commonly used in OLE Automation. A class module is created and its properties and methods are exposed to other applications. Many of the functions inside the class module calculate items passed in by the user and return values. Variables used in these internal workings should be private and therefore of no concern to the applications accessing the class module object.

Reusable Objects and Collections

Visual Basic 4.0 has implemented a new concept called *collections*. A *collection* is an object that organizes items used in the application. Collections are conceptually similar to arrays. The items stored in the collection object are objects themselves. An example of a collection is an assortment of bitmaps. Imagine that you have an application with four forms. Each form has a toolbar that displays different icons. You can create a collections object to store all the bitmaps and add them to your toolbar when necessary.

Create a new class module by choosing Insert | Class Module from the Visual Basic menu. At the module level, enter the following declaration:

```
Public CInstance
```

On form1, add a command button and associate the following code with its Click method:

```
Private Sub Command1_Click()
    CreateCollection
End Sub
```

Insert the following code into the class module:

```
Sub CreateCollection()
    'New collection object
    Dim CPictures As New Collection
    Dim i As Integer
    Dim sMessageText As String
    Dim sItemName, cObject, NameList

        Dim iPictures As New Class1   ' Create a new instance of Class1.
            For i = 0 To 10
                sItemName = "Item Number " & Str$(i)
                iPictures.CInstance = sItemName ' Put name in object instance.

                If iPictures.CInstance <> "" Then
                ' Add the named object to the collection.
                CPictures.Add Item:=iPictures, KEY:=CStr(i)
            End If
        Next i
End Sub
```

Several types of collections are inherent parts of Visual Basic. The Forms collection contains all the currently loaded forms. The Controls collection contains all the controls on a form.

The Printers collection contains all the available printer objects. Additionally, you can create a custom collection of objects. This type of collection is used to keep track of a group of items in your application. For example, you may want to hold a group of MDI forms in one collection. The advantage of creating a collection of these forms is that all the forms can be acted on at the same time using the For Each statement. The following example adds five forms to a collection:

```
'Module Level
Public cFormCollection as New Collection

cFormCollection.Add fForm1
cFormCollection.Add fForm2
cFormCollection.Add fForm3
cFormCollection.Add fForm4
cFormCollection.Add fForm5
```

To act on all of the forms in the collection, use the For Each statement:

```
For Each Form in cFormCollection
     Debug.Print Form.Name
Next Form
```

You can address an item in a collection in one of several ways. The cFormCollection example used earlier in this chapter can address fForm1 in any of the following ways:

```
cFormCollection("fForm1")
```

addresses fForm1.

```
cFormCollection (1)
```

In all these cases, the object is accessed by its index in the collections object. Actions can be taken on each form in the collection. For example, if you want to set the left and top of all of the forms at the same time, do the following:

```
For Each Form in cFormCollection
     Form.Top = 100
     Form.Left = 100
Next Form
```

Manipulating Controls

Visual Basic 4.0 now includes the With...End With and the For Each keywords.

The With...End With statement allows multiple actions to be taken on the same control without repeating the control name. The following example changes several properties on Form1 using the With...End With statement:

```
With Form1
     .Caption = "Form 1"
     .BackColor = H00C0C0C0&
     .Height = 8000
End With
```

The For Each statement is used to manipulate a group of controls within a loop. Imagine that you have a form with ten command buttons, two text boxes, and one label. You want to align all these controls along the left side of the form. Traditionally, the following code is used:

```
For X = 1 to 10
    Command1(X).Left = 200
Next X

For X = 1 to 2
    Text1(0).Left = 200
Next X

Label1.Left = 200
```

This code also assumes that the command buttons are contained in a control array. The manipulation of multiple controls becomes more of an issue as the number of controls on a form increases. Visual Basic 4.0 includes the For Each statement that allows manipulation of a group of controls on a form, in a collection, and so on. The same action performed by the preceding code can be accomplished using the following For Each statement:

```
For Each Control in Form1.Controls()
    Control.Left= 200
Next Control
```

All the controls on the form are set at the same time using only one statement.

Upgrading Existing Projects to Visual Basic 4.0

Projects created in earlier versions of Visual Basic can easily be upgraded to Visual Basic 4.0. During the upgrade, Visual Basic changes the format of project files so that they can be opened in version 4.0. Visual Basic 1 used a binary format; Visual Basic 2.0 and 3.0 use both text (FRM) and binary (FRX) formats for their files. This changes in Visual Basic 4.0: all project files in VB4 are in text format only. Binary project files are no longer a part of Visual Basic.

The next section explains how to upgrade to version 4.0 projects created in previous versions of Visual Basic. The quick steps are provided first and are followed by a detailed explanation of project conversion.

CAUTION

It is highly recommended that you read the detailed explanation for project conversion *before* using the quick steps. Project files converted to Visual Basic 4.0 *cannot* easily be converted back! There are several pitfalls to watch out for along the way!

Quick Steps for Upgrading a Project to Visual Basic 4.0

Follow these simple steps to convert to Visual Basic 4.0 to format a project created in an earlier version of Visual Basic:

1. Make a backup copy of your existing project (refer to the following section for important details about copying a project).

2. Update the copied project's MAK file.

3. Open the copied project in Visual Basic 4.0.

4. Choose Yes from the Custom Control Upgrade dialog box.

5. Answer OK for All in the Microsoft Visual Basic dialog box that asks whether it should upgrade project files to the new version of Visual Basic.

6. If your project uses Data Access Objects (DAOs) such as databases, Dynasets, and so on, choose Add in the next Visual Basic dialog box that appears. (This dialog box begins with the text `This project was developed in a previous version of Visual Basic`.)

7. If you have declared any arrays using the `ReDim` statement and these arrays were not first declared using either `Dim` or `Static`, VB4 produces an error. Enter the initial declarations for these variables.

It's that simple. Your project is now converted to Visual Basic 4.0 format.

If you did not use `Option Explicit` in your Visual Basic version 3.0 modules, Visual Basic 4.0 produces an error for any variables that are not declared. Select Tools | Options from the main menu and deselect the Require Variable Declaration checkbox. This should allow your project to run. Once the project runs successfully, add the variable declarations to your project and then reselect the Require Variable Declaration checkbox.

> **NOTE**
>
> You should *always* use `Option Explicit` when programming in Visual Basic. This statement prevents many errors caused by misspelling or misusing variable names and can save a great deal of time during debugging. Once your project is running smoothly, add a declaration for each variable. Then select Tools | Options from the main menu and select the Require Variable Declaration checkbox.

Project Conversion Explained

This section described several things you should consider when converting a project from a previous version of Visual Basic to Visual Basic 4.0.

More than likely, you will want to save a copy of the project in the current version's format. You must be very careful to properly copy the existing project before the conversion is undertaken. (Once a project is converted, it is not easily converted back.)

Imagine that you are converting a project from Visual Basic 3.0 to Visual Basic 4.0. The project has five forms and two modules. It also includes CONSTANT.TXT and several VBXes. Following is an example of the version 3.0 project's MAK file:

```
DATABASE.FRM
C:\VB\ABOUT.FRM
C:\VB\TOP10.FRM
TOOLBAR.FRM
C:\PROJECTS\OPEN.FRM
C:\PROJECTS\MODULE1.BAS
MODULE2.BAS
C:\VB\CONSTANT.TXT
C:\WINDOWS\SYSTEM\THREED.VBX
MHTR200.VBX
MHCOMD.VBX
ProjWinSize=75,765,254,422
ProjWinShow=2
IconForm="Project"
Title="PROJECT"
ExeName="PROJECT.EXE"
```

Let's start by saying that this is a poor way to construct a project. Note that the first entry, DATABASE.FRM, is not preceded by a path, indicating that the form file is located in the same directory as the project's MAK file. However, the second form file, C:\VB\ABOUT.FRM, is located in the C:\VB directory. In other words, the files of the project are split among several directories. Imagine that this project's MAK file is stored in the directory C:\PROJECTS\PROJECT1.

CAUTION

Do not perform the steps in the next paragraph. They are an example of how to corrupt an existing project!

To convert the project to Visual Basic 4.0, suppose that you copy all files in the directory C:\PROJECTS\PROJECT1 to the directory C:\PROJECTS\VB4PROJ (your VB4 project directory). Next, you open the project stored in C:\PROJECTS\VB4PROJ in Visual Basic 4.0. VB4 states that the project files were saved in a previous version of Visual Basic and will be converted to Visual Basic 4.0 format when saved. You answer OK to All to convert all the files in the project and then save the project.

You have just made a serious error. All the project files that were not stored in the C:\PROJECTS\PROJECT1 directory were not copied to the directory C:\PROJECTS\VB4PROJ. These files are still referenced by the MAK file in C:\PROJECTS\VB4PROJ however, and are therefore converted to VB4 format. The problem is that there is no longer a version 3.0 copy of these files; the originals have been converted to VB4's format.

The solution to this dilemma is to properly prepare the project before copying and converting it. Here are the steps:

1. Create a new directory to store the VB4 version of the project.

2. Copy all the project files in the current project directory to the new project directory.

3. Open the project's MAK file in the *new* directory. Look for any project files that reference a path (for example C:\VB\TOP10.FRM).

4. *Copy* the files that reference a path to the new project directory. In this example, copy the file C:\VB\TOP10.FRM to C:\PROJECTS\VB4PROJ. Do not copy VBX, OCX, or DLL files in the WINDOWS or WINDOWS\SYSTEM directory.

5. Remove the path statement from the project-file entries in the MAK file (for example, C:\VB\TOP10.FRM becomes TOP10.FRM). Do not remove the path from the VBX, OCX, or DLL files in the WINDOWS or WINDOWS\SYSTEM directory.

6. Remove any reference to CONSTANT.TXT. This file has been incorporated into Visual Basic 4.0 and does not need to be added. Be sure to move any items you may have added to CONSTANT.TXT to a module.

7. Save and close the project MAK file.

8. Run Visual Basic and convert the project to the Visual Basic 4.0 format.

Following is an example of the project MAK file after modification:

```
DATABASE.FRM
ABOUT.FRM
TOP10.FRM
TOOLBAR.FRM
OPEN.FRM
MODULE1.BAS
MODULE2.BAS
C:\WINDOWS\SYSTEM\THREED.VBX
MHTR200.VBX
MHCOMD.VBX
ProjWinSize=75,765,254,422
ProjWinShow=2
IconForm="Project"
Title="PROJECT"
ExeName="PROJECT.EXE"
```

If you store all your VBX, OCX, or DLL files in a common directory and all Visual Basic projects access this directory, you do not have to copy those files to the new project directory. In this case, leave the path statement on the entry in the MAK file so that it can be referenced by Visual Basic.

TIP

Visual Basic loads project files in a specific order. To speed up the loading of a project, change the order in which project files are listed in your MAK file. Place all VBX files in the MAK file first, followed by form (FRM) files, and finally by module (BAS) files. Sort the files alphabetically within each group. Projects (especially large ones) can load up to 100 percent faster with this arrangement.

In the cleaned-up project MAK file, notice that I did not remove the path from the line C:\WINDOWS\SYSTEM\THREED.VBX. The indicated directory is the natural location for this VBX because it is a part of Windows. In addition, there is no need to copy this file to the new project directory.

Upgrading Custom Controls

Visual Basic 4.0 can automatically upgrade the custom controls in a project. To choose to have Visual Basic 4.0 upgrade controls, select Tools | Options from the main menu. This displays the Options dialog box. Click the Advanced tab and select the Update Custom Controls checkbox. When this option is selected, Visual Basic searches for an updated version of the control to add to the project. This control must be an OCX file (OCXs are the new generation of custom controls for Visual Basic).

Many existing custom controls have been updated for Visual Basic 4.0 and several new controls have been added. Additionally, many of these controls provide Windows 3.1 applications with a Windows 95 look. The following sections describe custom controls you can use to improve functionality and graphical presentation. Controls available in Visual Basic 3.0 are provided because of their importance and in case you were not aware that they existed.

Communications Control

The Communications control provides a way for your applications to communicate through the serial port of the computer. A common use for the control is in the development of applications that communicate over telephone lines. If your application outputs files that are transferred from one PC to another, or calls and connects to another application through a modem, this control is a lifesaver. The Communications control simplifies the process of serial communications with an array of functions and provides an alternative to the tedious, manual operations normally required in serial communications.

The following code ensures that the modem is operational, receives data coming in over the modem, and then places the data in a file:

```
Sub Receive_Data ()
    'Select communications port 1
    Comm1.CommPort = 1
    ' Open the port.
    Comm1.PortOpen = True
    ' Set the modem to 14000 baud, Even parity, 8 data bits, 1 stop bit
    Comm1.Settings = "9600,E,8,1"
    'Set HandShaking off (default). Handshaking is a safety check to ensure that
    'data is not
    'transmitted to the input buffer faster than it can be handled, resulting in
    'the loss of data.
    Comm1.HandShaking = 0
```

```
    'We are receiving the data in 32K blocks. If I set this to 0, the entire buffer
    'is read at once.
    Comm1.InputLen = 32000
    'If there is data, receive it and place it in a file
    'Open the file
    x = FreeFile
    sFileName = "C:\PROJECT\PROJECT1\MODEM.TXT" for input as x
    'Continue placing 32000 byte chunks into sData until the modem buffer is empty.
    Do While Comm1.InBufferCount > 0
        'Input the data in sData.
        sData = Comm1.Input
        'Write the data that was received in sData and place it to the file
        Print #x, , sData
    Loop
    'Close the file
    Close x
    ' Close the serial port.
    Comm1.PortOpen = False
End Sub
```

Gauge Control

The Gauge control is a graphical tool for displaying the completion percentage of operations. There are four different styles of display, which are set using the `Style` property:

Style	Description
Horizontal Fill	The inner area is filled from left to right. This is much like a standard percentage completion bar.
Vertical Fill	The inner area is filled from bottom to top.
Semi-Needle	The needle is drawn in a semicircular arc from left to right.
Full-Needle	The needle is drawn in a full 360-degree circle from left to right.

> **NOTE**
>
> The size and shape of the inner area of the Gauge control cannot be modified by the programmer. The only control is through the `Style` property.

The following example sets up a gauge to fill with values from 0 to 100. Each of the gauge styles is demonstrated:

```
Sub UpdateStatus()
    'Set the height (Set the form's scale mode to PIXEL)
    Form1.ScaleMode = 3
    Gauge1.Height = 30
    'These 4 properties set how far from the control's edge the bar paints
    '(0 is at the edge).
    Gauge1.InnerTop = 5
```

```
Gauge1.InnerLeft = 5
Gauge1.InnerBottom = 5
Gauge1.InnerRight = 5
'Set the minimum and maximum values (if min = 100, then the status
'bar is full at 100
Gauge1.MIN = 0
Gauge1.MAX = 100
Gauge1.NeedleWidth = 10
'Set the ForeColor to red
Gauge1.ForeColor = QBColor(4)

For i = 0 To 3
    'Set the gauge to each of the fill styles
    Gauge1.Style = i
    'Fill the gauge from 0 to 100
    For x = 1 To 100
        Gauge1.VALUE = x
        'DoEvents stops and paints the control. Without this the control would
        'appear
        'at 0 throughout the operation, and then suddenly appear at 100.
        DoEvents
        'slow it down some
        For y = 1 To 10000
        Next y
    Next x
Next i End Sub
```

Graph Control

The Graph control allows you to add charts and graphs directly to your project's forms. This control has been updated in Visual Basic 4.0. Using the GraphStyle property, you can set the chart to any of the following types:

Type	Description
2-D or 3-D Pie	This chart is used for displaying percentage-related data. Each slice of the pie represents a data element.
2-D or 3-D Bar	This chart is used for displaying counts for items in a category (for example, the number of hits for each player on a baseball team). Each bar represents a data element. The items do not necessarily add up to 100 percent.
Gantt	This chart is commonly used in project management to view deadlines and dependencies. When applied in this manner, each element of the chart represents the task for a specific person on the team. Tasks and deadlines can be easily viewed. The chart also demonstrates the impact when a deadline is missed.
Line	This chart is used for plotting points. For example, each point represents the number of orders outstanding on a given day.

Type	Description
Area	The points are connected by a line that demonstrates trends. This chart is used to show data over time. Picture this as similar to a bar chart whose bars are connected. Instead of the chart's area being one color, however, the area is separated horizontally into categories. In other words, this data is stacked, and the top of the area represents the sum of all the categories. Imagine that an area chart represents sales in five categories over 12 months. The y (horizontal) axis represents the months (much like a bar chart) and the x (vertical) axis represents the number of items sold. In January, 10 items were sold in each of the categories. The total value for January is 40 (four separate colors stacked on top of each other, each representing a category). This continues throughout the year to complete the chart. Each month's data is connected (not broken like a bar chart).
ScatterGram	This type of chart is most commonly used for plotting engineering data. Another use is to demonstrate the results of a survey given to an assortment of age groups. For example, one of the axes may represent responses to questions on a survey and the other axis breaks the respondents out into different ethnic groups. Each response is represented by a dot (point) on the chart.
HLC (High, Low, Close)	The most common use for this chart is in the charting of stock market data. The chart shows the highest and lowest values for a given time period as well as the value at closing (end of the time period).

Key Status Control

When the Key Status control control is clicked, it changes the state of one of the following keys:

Caps Lock
Num Lock
Insert
Scroll Lock

This control appears as a key that can be clicked with the mouse. The `Style` property is used to set the type of key pressed by the Key Status control. The `Value` property is used to set the control's state (TRUE = On, FALSE = Off). The user can click the control with the mouse to change the state (Value) of the selected key or use the corresponding key on the keyboard.

Spin Button Control

If your application currently uses a text box or a masked edit box in which the user enters a number (for example, the number of seconds to wait before timing out an operation), the Spin Button control can come in handy. The spin button works in combination with another control (such as a text box) to allow the user to select a value. The control has an up and a down arrow. When the user click one of the arrows, the value is changed in that direction. Using the SpinUp and SpinDown events, you can control the amount by which the control is increased or decreased. The following example increases the value in the text box by 5 each time the up arrow is clicked:

```
Sub Spin1_SpinUp
    Dim iValue as Integer
    Dim iIncrementer as Integer
    iIncrementer = 5
    'Get the value out of the text box and store it in a variable
    iValue = Val(Text1.Text)
    'Increment the variable
    iValue = iValue + iIncrementer
    'Put the value back into the text box
    Text1.Text = Str$(iValue)
End Sub
```

The value placed in the text box can then be used to set the value for another control's property or to pass into a function.

SSTab Dialog Control

The SSTab Dialog control is a tab control similar to the one used in the Options section of Microsoft Word or Excel. Each tab can contain other controls. When a tab is selected, only its controls are visible; the controls on the other tabs are hidden. You have control over the number of tabs, the number of rows, and the style and size of each tab. It is also possible to display a graphic on a tab.

Status Bar Control: COMCL32.OCX (32-Bit Only)

This control is available only in Microsoft Windows 95 and Windows NT 3.51 and higher (32-bit) operating systems. The Status Bar control is placed at the bottom of a form to display information about an application. For example, in Microsoft Word, the status bar displays the current page, time, and so on. This control can be divided into as many as 16 different panel objects (sections). Each panel object is a member of a Panels collection. You can set up functions that determine what data (or picture) is displayed in each of the sections. Seven standard Style property values allow you to display data such as date and time automatically—without writing additional code. The following example adds eight panels to the status bar and sets each to a system function:

```
Sub CreateStatusBar()
    Dim iRet As Integer
    'Add 8 segments to the status bar.
    For iRet = 1 to 8
        StatusBar1.Panels.Add
    Next iRet

    'The WITH operator allows us to address the status bar panels.
    'Here we set each panel to one of the  system functions:
    With StatusBar1.Panels
        .Item(1).Style = sbrText    ' Text or picture
        .Item(2).Style = sbrCaps    ' CAPS Lock Key
        .Item(3).Style = sbrNum     ' Number Lock Key
        .Item(4).Style = sbrIns     ' Insert Key
        .Item(5).Style = sbrScrl    'Control Key (Ctrl)
        .Item(7).Style = sbrTime    'Current Time
        .Item(8).Style = sbrDate    'Current Date
    End With
End Sub
```

Slider Control: COMCL32.OCX (32-Bit Only)

The Slider control is used to set a value in a simplified manner. It is an alternative to having the user enter a value in a text box, validating the value, and then applying the value to your function. The Slider control contains a bar that can be moved across a scale with tick marks to set a value. You have control over the start and end values as well as the amount the value is incremented each time the bar is moved to a different tick mark. The bar can be moved by clicking and dragging it with the mouse, clicking on either side of it, or by using the arrow keys on the keyboard.

ImageList Control: COMCL32.OCX (32-Bit Only)

The ImageList control is designed to store images for use by other controls. For example, this control can store all the bitmaps used on all the application's toolbars. A bitmap is assigned to the button by assigning it to the picture property of the object. The following code assigns a series of bitmaps to an ImageList control. It then assigns the appropriate bitmap to the and image control at runtime:

```
'Assign the bitmaps to the ImageList object
For X = 0 to 10
    ImageList1.ListImages(x) = "C:\PROJECT\BITMAPS\BITMAP" & X " ".BMP"
Next X

'Find out which bitmap the user wants to see.
iRet = InputBox("Enter a bitmap number", "Show Bitmap", 0)

'Show the bitmap in the picture box.
Set Form1.Image1.Picture =  ImageList1.ListImages(iRet)
```

You can store bitmaps, icons, or a combination of both. The only restriction is that the images must be the same size—and you are limited there only by system memory.

ListView Control: COMCL32.OCX (32-Bit Only)

The ListView control allows you to display the items stored in an ImageList control. This control has four different views that can be set using the View property:

Large Icons
Small Icons
List
Report

The ImageList control is used to supply the icons as well as the text description for the displayed item. Keep in mind that the ListView control uses an ImageList control as the source of its data. ListView is designed to be used in conjunction with the ImageList control.

TreeView Control: COMCL32.OCX (32-Bit Only)

The TreeView control is used to display a hierarchy of information. This control resembles the functionality of the Windows 3.1 File Manager. Items can be added or removed from the list at runtime and the list can be rearranged. Items contain + and – signs to indicate whether or not the node is expanded or collapsed. Nodes can be expanded and collapsed with the mouse or by using the left-arrow and right-arrow keys. You can traverse the tree using the following properties:

Property	Description
Root	Returns a reference to the root node object of a selected node.
Parent	Returns or sets the parent object of a node object.
Child	Returns a reference to the first child of a node object.
FirstSibling	Returns a reference to the first sibling of a node object.
Next	Returns a reference to the next sibling of a node object.
Previous	Returns a reference to the previous sibling of a node object.

Bitmaps can be displayed in front of each item. The bitmaps are supplied by the ListItem control. Several different styles can alter the appearance of the control:

Style	Description
0	Text only
1	Image and text

2	Plus/minus and text
3	Plus/minus, image, and text
4	Lines and text
5	Lines, image, and text
6	Lines, plus/minus, and text
7	(Default) Lines, plus/minus, image, and text

Toolbar Control: COMCL32.OCX (32-Bit Only)

The Toolbar control allows you to create a toolbar for your application. This control uses a series of buttons contained in a Buttons collection. Each of the buttons executes an application function. Both pictures (Image property) and text (Caption property) can be placed on each button. Images are supplied through the ImageList control. At runtime, you can add a button to the toolbar or remove one using the Add or Remove method. The Button_Click() event is used to respond to a user pressing one of the toolbar buttons.

Double-clicking the toolbar at runtime brings up the Customize Toolbar dialog box. This dialog box allows you to manipulate the items on the toolbar. Items can be displayed, hidden, or re-arranged. If you set the AllowCustomize property to TRUE, users can rearrange the toolbar buttons by holding down the Shift key and dragging the buttons.

RichText Box Control: RICHTX32.OCX (32-Bit Only)

The RichText Box control is a text-editing control that is a significantly enhanced version of the text box. This control supports RTF formats (such as the one used in Microsoft Word). This control allows you to load a file directly into it, edit the contents of the file, and then save the file to disk. This is accomplished using the LoadFile and SaveFile methods. If you want to save only the portion of the text the user has selected, use the SelRTF property. The RichText Box control is a data-aware control you can bind to any memo field in a Microsoft Access database. The contents of the control can also be printed using the SelPrint method. You can also make the selected text bold and italic and set the color of the text. (Note that only the selected text can be modified.)

Another advantage this control has over the text box is that it is not limited to 64K of data. The following example loads a file into the RichText Box control. Once the user has selected some of the text, the format is changed and only the selected text is saved back to the file. Imagine that the filename C:\WORD\REPORT.DOC is passed to the function:

```
'Load the file into the control
Function OpenRTFFile(sFileName as String)
    RichTextBox1.LoadFile(sFileName, rtfRTF)
    MsgBox "Please select the text to be updated and click Update", 0, "Select
File"
```

```
End Function
```

Next, the user highlights some text and clicks Update:

```
'Updates the file. This function returns only the selected text to the file.
'All other data is erased.
Sub UpdateRTFFile()
    Open "mytext.rtf" For Output As iFileNum
    Print #1, RichTextBox1.SelRTF
    Close iFileNum
End Sub
```

ProgressBar Control: COMCL32.OCX (32-Bit Only)

The ProgressBar is a 32-bit control used to display the status of an operation. Each update segment is a small square block in the color of your choice. This control is similar to the status bar Microsoft Word uses when saving a document. The following example displays a progress bar while an array is being written to a file:

```
Sub ProgressBar()
    Dim iMin as Integer
    Dim iMax as Integer
    Dim sDataArray() as String
    Dim iIncrement as Integer
    Dim I as Integer

    'Show the progress bar
    Progress1.Visible = True
    'Fill the array with data
    ...
    'Calculate the increment
    iIncrement = UBound(sDataArray) + 1/100

    'Set up the minimum and maximum progress bar values
    ProgressBar1.Min = 0
    ProgressBar1.Max = 100

    'Open a file to write the sDataArray() to.
    x = FreeFile
    sFile = "C;\PROJECTS\PROJECT1\REPORT.TXT"
    Open sFile for output as x

    'Write the array to the file and update the progress bar
    For I = 0 to UBound (sDataArray)
        Print #x, , sDataArray(i)
        ProgressBar = iIncrement + 1
    Next I

    'Close the file
    Close x

    'Hide the progress bar
    Progress1.Visible = False

End Sub
```

The preceding sections covered some of the OCXs provided with Visual Basic 4.0.

NOTE

Visual Basic 4.0 includes a feature that allows you to lock down the controls on a form. Once you have converted your project to Visual Basic 4.0, open each of the project's forms and click the Lock Controls toolbar icon. This action prevents controls on the form from being resized or moved accidentally. Selecting this option locks *all* controls on the form. More than likely, changes you make to a project after conversion are primarily code changes. The control-lock option prevents form objects from moving and ensures that the Visual Basic 4.0 user interface matches the one developed in Visual Basic 3.0.

32-Bit Support and Conditional Compilation

Visual Basic 4.0 is available in both 16-bit and 32-bit versions. To create applications that can be used in both environments, conditional compilation has been added to the Visual Basic language. *Conditional compilation* allows you to compile certain code only under certain conditions. For example, if the executable file being created is going to be run on a 16-bit system, API functions from the 16-bit libraries must be added. To easily change the executable file for use in a 32-bit system (which requires different function declarations), use conditional compilation. When upgrading a project to Visual Basic 4.0, consider the changes required to make the application compatible with the 32-bit version of Visual Basic. Note that 32-bit applications run only on Windows 95 and Window NT operating systems.

Conditional compilation has two components: the constant definition and the compiler directive. Visual Basic provides the following constants:

- Win16: This constant has the value TRUE in a 16-bit operating system and FALSE in a 32-bit system.

- Win32: This constant has the value FALSE in a 16-bit operating system and TRUE in a 32-bit system.

You can create your own compiler constants by declaring them in the following manner:

```
#Const MyConstant = True
```

To use this constant, use the #If...#Then...#Else directive:

```
#If MyConstant = True Then
    For x% = 1 to 1000
        Print "Hello"
```

```
    Next x%
#Else
    For x% = 1 to 1000
        Print "Goodbye"
    Next x%
#End If
```

Compile the project; if the constant MyConstant equals TRUE, the first part of the #If statement is added to the executable. Otherwise, the portion after #Else is added. Under conditional compilation, any code not selected is not added to the executable file. This arrangement allows you to upgrade existing applications to 32-bit Windows platforms without writing separate versions of the project (or writing one version with a significantly larger executable file).

Another implementation of conditional compilation is for the purposes of debugging. Imagine that you want to execute a function that writes data to a file for debugging purposes. Also imagine that these data-writing functions are scattered throughout your project. Once the project is complete and ready for a final executable, it is difficult to traipse through the project and find all the debug-only code. If you use conditional compilation, however, you can easily remove these debug functions:

```
'General Declarations
#Const DebugVersion = True

Private Sub Command1_Click()
    Dim x As Integer
    Dim iRet As Integer
    Dim sFileName As String

    'Run a normal application function
    x = NormalApplicationFunction

    'If the DebugVersion constant is set to true then include the debug code in the
    'executable
    #If DebugVersion = True Then
        iRet = GetDebugStats
    #Else
        'In this case, we really don't need an #Else statement
    #End If

End Sub

Function NormalApplicationFunction

    #If DebugVersion = True Then
        Dim x as Integer
        Dim Temp as String
        Dim DebugArray()
        For x = 1 to 50
            'Place some code here that places data into the Temp variable
            ReDim Preserve DebugArray(x)
            DebugArray(x) = Temp
        Next x
    #End If
```

```
        'Normal function body

End Function

Function GetDebugStats
    #If DebugVersion = True Then
        Dim iRet as Integer
        Dim iFileNum as Integer
        Dim sFileName as String
        iFileNum = FreeFile
        Open sFileName for Output as iFileNum
        For iRet = 0 to UBound (DebugArray) 'DebugArray was previously created and
        'filled with data
            Print #x, DebugArray(iRet)
    #End If
End Function
```

Here are some considerations. First, if the DebugVersion constant is set to FALSE, the code iRet = GetDebugStats in Sub Command1_Click() is not included in the executable file. Additionally, none of the code in the function GetDebugStats is included. Although you can achieve this same functionality with standard variables, the portion of the code that executes the debug function and the debug function itself are added to the executable file, increasing its size. Second, the #Const declaration is local in scope; global #Const declarations are not allowed. The solution to this limit is to use the Advanced Options tab in the Options dialog box to declare the constant. Select Tools | Options from the Visual Basic menu and select the Advanced tab. Enter the global constant declaration in the Conditional Compilation Arguments field at the bottom of the dialog box.

Another use for conditional compilation is portability from 16-bit to 32-bit systems. Imagine that you are declaring the function OSGetPrivateProfileString. On a 16-bit system, this function is in the library KERNEL. On 32-bit systems, it is in the library Kernel32. The function used on the 32-bit system does not work on a 16-bit system. Although the 16-bit function works on a 32-bit system, it does not perform as well as the 32-bit function and is therefore not a good choice. To declare the proper function at the proper time without having to rewrite code, use the following conditional compilation statement:

```
#If Win16 Then   'Win16 (16-bit) declaration
    Declare Function OSGetPrivateProfileString% Lib "KERNEL" Alias
"GetPrivateProfileString" _
(ByVal AppName$,_
    ByVal KeyName$,_
    ByVal keydefault$,_
    ByVal ReturnString$,_
    ByVal  NumBytes As Integer, ByVal FileName$)
#Else  'Win32 declaration
    Declare Function OSGetPrivateProfileString% Lib "Kernel32" Alias
"GetPrivateProfileStringA"_
(ByVal AppName$,_
ByVal KeyName$,_
ByVal keydefault$,_
ByVal ReturnString$,_
ByVal NumBytes As Integer, ByVal FileName$)
#End If
```

It is important to understand what is actually happening here. When the source code is compiled in the 16-bit operating environment, the 16-bit portion of the code is added to the executable; the 32-bit code is omitted. When compiled in the 32-bit operating environment, the opposite occurs. The size of the executable is not increased because the project does not have to be compiled for both 16-bit and 32-bit operating systems.

Make EXE Options

Another way to take advantage of the new features of Visual Basic 4.0 is simply to recompile existing projects in Visual Basic 4.0. Visual Basic now provides an EXE Options dialog box you can use to enter information about the project directly into the executable file. This option also places a version number in the executable file for future reference. Additionally, auto-incrementing of version numbers is available. To set executable file options for a project, select File | Make EXE File. The Make EXE File dialog appears. Choose the Options button to display the EXE Options dialog box.

Enter the appropriate version information in the dialog box and choose OK. This information is then added to the executable file by Visual Basic.

Setup Wizard

Once you have upgraded your project to Visual Basic 4.0 and have created a new executable file, you can take advantage of one more new feature. Visual Basic 4.0 offers a Setup Wizard that creates installation disks for your project. This wizard allows you to choose the files to include in the project, compresses these files, and places them on floppy disks for distribution. A SETUP.EXE file is provided on the setup disk to install the application on the end user's PC. (SETUP.EXE is generated automatically by the Setup Wizard.)

To use the Setup Wizard, double-click the Application Setup Wizard (16-bit or 32-bit) icon in the Microsoft Visual Basic 4.0 program group (Program Manager), or run the program C:\VB4\setupkit\kitfiles\setupwiz.exe. Then follow these Setup Wizard steps (each of the following steps represents a new Setup Wizard dialog box):

1. Type the name of the Visual Basic project for which you want to build a setup program. Choose the ... button to open a common dialog box to choose the path. Click the Rebuild the Project's EXE File checkbox to rebuild the project. Choose the Next button.

2. If your project uses the Data control or Data Access Objects (such as Dynaset), the Setup Wizard displays the Step 2 dialog box. Choose the database drivers associated with your application. You may select more than one driver. These drivers are included in the distribution disks.

3. Select the location where the setup files are to be placed. Click either the Disk Drive or Directory option button and then select the location on that drive where you want the files to be placed.

4. If Visual Basic detects the use of OLE servers in the project, they are added to the list box in this dialog box. If an OLE server is necessary for the project but is not listed, choose Add OLE Servers to add a server to the distribution disks.

5. The wizard may display a dialog box that allows you to remove dependency files. Use this dialog box to remove any files you are not legally allowed to distribute as well as any duplicate files (files users already have on their PCs).

6. Determine the type of application being installed. The Step 6 dialog box has the following options:

   - **Install In Application Directory.** This option indicates that this is a stand-alone application to be installed in its own directory.

   - **Install as OLE Automation Shared Component.** This option indicates that this application is an OLE Automation component. If this option is selected, the application is installed in the shared components directory, \OLESVR. The 32-bit versions of Visual Basic 4.0 also have an OLE Automation Provider checkbox; when this checkbox is selected, the files AUTMGR32.EXE and AUTPRX32.DLL are added to the setup program.

7. The final step displays a list of the files to be distributed with the application and allows you to add, remove, and view the details about files. If you are unsure about the reason a certain file is included, the Dependency Of combo box displays the dependency or the reason that the file has been included. Choose Finish to place the application files on the chosen media (for example, a floppy disk). If floppy disks are the media of choice, you are prompted to insert additional disks as needed.

Once you complete step 7, your setup disks are complete and ready for distribution.

Summary

This chapter outlined many of the new features provided in Visual Basic 4.0. In particular, the following items were covered:

- The many changes and new features of the Interactive Development Environment (IDE) were covered.

- An introduction to objects using the Visual Basic class module was discussed and a basic customer account application was developed using OLE Automation.

- Several new keywords and statements added to Visual Basic 4.0 were discussed and examples were provided where necessary.

- The creation of applications in both 16-bit and 32-bit Visual Basic using conditional compilation was discussed.

■ The proper method for upgrading a project from an existing version of Visual Basic to Visual Basic 4.0 was discussed.

■ Upgrading custom controls was covered.

■ Visual Basic for Applications (VBA), the language of Microsoft Excel and Project, has been added to Visual Basic 4.0 and was discussed in this chapter.

■ The features of reusable objects and collections were covered.

■ The chapter concluded with an explanation of the enhanced Visual Basic 4.0 Setup Wizard.

File I/O

3

by Conrad Scott

IN THIS CHAPTER

Visual Basic offers an assortment of functions for the manipulation of files and directories. This chapter covers the methods that can be used to open and read from files, write to files, navigate open files, and obtain information about a file. First, the basics of file input and output (I/O) are covered, followed by more advanced topics including reading files in blocks, binary chops, and file formats.

Examples in this chapter use variables created in the following format:

Preceded with	Variable Type	Example
i	Integer	iCounter
s	String	sDirName
l	Long	lByteCount
t	Type Structure	tMyType
gc_	Global Constant	gc_MyConstant

This key should simplify the examples provided. Additionally, each example explicitly declares the variables that it uses.

File I/O Basics

This section covers the basics of file input and output (I/O) in Visual Basic. This section mirrors functionality that already exists in Visual Basic 3.0. The section is organized into keywords in two major sections: creating and deleting files and directories, and accessing files. Each statement or function discussed is fully explained and examples are provided where appropriate.

Creating and Deleting Files and Directories

Files and directories can be created and deleted using numerous Visual Basic operations. The following covers each of the functions and statements associated with directory creation and deletion. This is an area where error checking is of the utmost importance, especially when creating and deleting across network drives.

MkDir

The MkDir function is used to create a new directory on a drive. The directory to be created is passed as an argument. For example:

```
MkDir "C:\WINDOWS\MYDIR"
```

This command creates a new directory given that the path provided exists. When creating a directory, many different errors can be encountered. The following example creates a directory. The function returns a value for Err as a result. If Err does not equal 0, an error occurred.

```
Function CreateDirectory(sDirectory As String)
    'Set Up Error Handler
```

```
        On Error GoTo CreateDirectory_ErrorHandler
        'Create the directory
        MkDir sDirectory

CreateDirectory_ErrorHandler:
    Select Case Err
        Case 0
    MsgBox "Error " & Error$ Occurred
        Case 1
    MsgBox "Error " & Error$ Occurred
        Case 2
    MsgBox "Error " & Error$ Occurred
    End Select

    'Return the error as the result of the function
    CreateDirectory = Err
End Function

Usage:
Dim sDirectory As String
Dim iRet as Integer
sDirectory = "C:\PROJECTS\PROJECT1"
iRet = Createdirectory(sDirectory)
If iRet = 0 Then
    'OK to continue...
```

Name

This statement is used to move a file from one directory to another on the same drive. This statement takes the following parameters:

sFromLoc—This is the name of the source file including the fully qualified path, for example: C:\OLDDIR\FROMFILE.TXT.

sToLoc—This is the name of the target file including the fully qualified path, for example, C:\NEWDIR\TOFILE.TXT.

There are several items to note when using this statement.

1. Both sFromLoc and sToLoc must be on the same drive.
2. If sFromLoc exists and is different from sToLoc, the file in sFromLoc is moved to the directory in sToLoc. If the filename in sNewLoc is different from sFromLoc, the file is renamed before being placed in the new location.
3. You cannot move a directory using this statement, only a file.
4. You cannot move a file that is currently open.

Attempting any of these actions results in an error (Err <> 0).

The following function uses the Name statement to rename a file and checks for errors:

```
Function RenameFile(sFromLoc as String, sToLoc as String)

    Name sOldLoc To sNewLoc
```

```
    'Check for errors
    Select Case Err
        Case 0' All is well, the file was renamed.

        Case 5 'Illegal Function Call
    MsgBox "Error " & Str$(Err) & ":" & "  " & Error$ & " occurred."
        Case 68 'Device Unavailable
            MsgBox "Error " & Str$(Err) & ":" & "  " & Error$ & " occurred."
        Case 70 'Permission Denied
    MsgBox "Error " & Str$(Err) & ":" & "  " & Error$ & " occurred."
        Case 71 'Disk Not Ready
    MsgBox "Error " & Str$(Err) & ":" & "  " & Error$ & " occurred."
        Case 75 'Path/File Access Error
    MsgBox "Error " & Str$(Err) & ":" & "  " & Error$ & " occurred."
        Case 76 'Path Not Found
    MsgBox "Error " & Str$(Err) & ":" & "  " & Error$ & " occurred."
        Case Else
    MsgBox "Error " & Str$(Err) & ":" & "  " & Error$ & " occurred."
    End Select

    RenameFile = Err
End Function

Usage:
Dim sOldFile As String
Dim sNewFile As String
Dim iRet As Integer
sOldFile = "C:\PROJECTS\PROJECT1\REPORT.TXT"
sNewFile = "C:\PROJECTS\PROJECT1\REPORT.TXT"
iRet = RenameFile(sOldFile, sNewFile)
If iRet = 0 Then
    'OK to continue...
```

RmDir

This function removes a directory from the hard drive. The following example removes a directory from the hard disk and checks for errors. The function returns the error code:

```
Function RemoveDirectory(sDirName as String)
    Dim sDirName as String

    'Remove the directory
    RmDir sDirName

    'Check for errors
    Select Case Err
        Case 0' All is well, the directory was removed.

        Case 68 'Device Unavailable
            MsgBox "Error " & Str$(Err) & ":" & "  " & Error$ & " occurred."
        Case 70 'Permission Denied
    MsgBox "Error " & Str$(Err) & ":" & "  " & Error$ & " occurred."
        Case 71 'Disk Not Ready
    MsgBox "Error " & Str$(Err) & ":" & "  " & Error$ & " occurred."
        Case 75 'Path/File Access Error
    MsgBox "Error " & Str$(Err) & ":" & "  " & Error$ & " occurred."
        Case 76 'Path Not Found
```

file in Random mode, seek position 256, and read the data into your buffer using the Get statement. Data is placed into a binary file using the Put statement.

Append

The Append statement is used when you want to write data to a file and add it to the data that already exists in that file. New data is added (appended) to the bottom of the existing data. Use the Print# or Write# statements to add data to files opened in append mode.

Access Statement—Optional Component of the *Open* Statement

The Access statement decides the permissions you have when opening a file. This is a commonly ignored but very important parameter. The possible parameters are Read, Write, and Read Write. Read Write is only valid for files opened for random or binary files opened in Append mode.

Imagine you are opening a file to read some data that your program requires. You do not need to write any data to the file. Imagine you use the following code to read from the file:

```
Dim iFileNum as Integer
Dim sFileName as String
Dim sTemp as String

iFileNum = FreeFile
sFileName = "C:\PROJECTS\MYFILE.TXT"

'Open the file
Open sFileName for Input as iFileNum

'Keep going until the end of file is encountered
Do Until EOF(iFileNum)
    Line Input #iFileNum, , sTemp
    'Do some checking
    ...
Loop
```

If your file is 100 lines long, and that after 56 lines, your program encounters a GPF (this could *never* happen). The first 56 lines of the file that you were reading have been erased. This is because you opened the file for read and write. When the data was read into the sTemp variable, it was removed from the file. Solve this dilemma by opening the file for read only.

```
Open sFileName for Input Access Read as iFileNum
```

In this case you have opened the file for read only. You are still able to read data from the file and place it into the sTemp variable, but you are not endangering the source file if an error occurs. Additionally, other processes can read from this file at the same time without encountering an error. When you open a file as writable, you are "hogging" the file and no other Windows processes or applications can open it (even for read only).

Even though the file is opened as read only, you are still able to manipulate the data that is read into the sTemp variable for use within your Visual Basic application. If you need to modify data that is read from a file and then place it back into the file, you should open the file as writable. For example, imagine that you do the following (this is for example only, please don't do it):

1. Read lines of data from a file that is open for read only using the `Line Input` statement, placing the line containing the data you require data into `sTemp`.
2. Close the file.
3. Change the data that is in `sTemp`.
4. Open the file as writable.
5. Write the line of data back out to the file using the `Print#` statement.

This operation has just erased the entire contents of the file and replaced it with the one line you modified. In this case, it would have been much simpler to open the file as writable, read the entire file into an array using `Line Input`, modify the desired array element (line of the file) and then write the entire array back into the file (first close the file and then open it in the output mode).

> **NOTE**
>
> If you are reading and writing to INI files, the Visual Basic file I/O functions are *not* the best method to use. Windows offers a variety of functions designed specifically for this purpose. The most useful of these functions are `GetProfileString()` and `GetPrivateProfileString()`. See the Windows System Developers Kit (SDK) help file for information about these functions.

Lock Statement

The `Lock` statement is somewhat like the `Access` statement except that it sets permissions that other operations have for the opened file. The options are:

1. Shared—Other processes can both read and write to the file.
2. Lock Read—Other processes cannot read the open file.
3. Lock Write—Other processes cannot write to the open file.
4. Lock Read Write—Other processes cannot read or write to the file.

The difference between this statement and the `Access` statement is that you can restrict access to a file for other processes even if you open the file as read only.

This example opens a file for input and locks the file for both reading and writing (no other processes can read or write to the file until it is closed using the `Close` statement.)

```
Open sFileName for Input Lock Read Write as x
```

FreeFile

The FreeFile function allocates a new file handle. This file handle is then used to open a file. The usage is as follows:

```
Dim iFileNum As Integer
Dim sFileName As String
sFileName = "C:\PROJECTS\PROJECT1\REPORT.TXT"

iFileNum - FreeFile
Open sFileName for Input as iFileNum
```

You can use literal numbers for file handles (Open sFileName for Input as 1), but it is not recommended. This can cause conflicts if you are opening several files (if you open a file as 1, forget to close it, and try to open another file as 1, you will get an error).

Record Length

The record length variable is used when you want to specify the number of characters read in each time the file is accessed. If the file is opened in Random mode, this value is the record length. For sequential files, this is the number of characters placed in the buffer variable. For example:

```
File opened in Random mode with a Record Length of 40
Dim iFileNum As Integer
Dim sFileName As String
sFileName = "C:\PROJECTS\PROJECT1\REPORT.TXT"
iFileNum = FreeFile
Open sFileName for Random as iFileNum Len = 40

File opened in Input mode (Input and Output are sequential modes) with a record
length of 256
Dim iFileNum As Integer
Dim sFileName As String
Dim sTemp as String * 256

sFileName = "C:\PROJECTS\PROJECT1\REPORT.TXT"
Open sFileName for Input as iFileNum Len = 256
Input #iFileNum, ,sTemp
```

In this case, sTemp is 256 characters long so that is the number of characters read into the variable each time the file is accessed.

Close

This statement closes a file. Close takes one parameter, the file handle. This is the handle that was created with the FreeFile function and was used to open the file. In the following example, iFileNum is the file handle.

```
Close iFileNum
```

Multiple parameters can be used with this statement.

```
Close iFileNum1, iFileNum2, iFileNum3
```

If no parameter is used, all open files are closed. The Close statement releases all buffer space utilized by Visual Basic when the file was open.

Reset

The Reset statement closes any open files and writes the contents to disk. This statement operates the same as the Close statement without parameters.

Reading from and Writing to Files

Most of the operations on files involve the reading and writing of data. Files can also be used as databases to store information. The following section describes the functions and statements used to read from and write data to files.

Get

The Get statement is used to read data from a file and place it into a variable. The Get statement has the following syntax:

```
Dim iFileNum as Integer
Dim sData as String
iFileNum = FreeFile

Get #iFileNum, [iRecordNumber], sData
```

Depending on the mode for which the file is open, either iRecordNumber or sData is used to store the data that is read from the file. If sData is a variable length string, a 2-byte descriptor with the string length is placed in sData followed by the data. See the Visual Basic help topic "Get Statement" for additional detail on this statement.

If you choose to omit iRecordNumber, the commas must still be used.

```
Dim iFileNum as Integer
Dim sData as String
Get #FileNum,  , sData
```

Put

The Put statement writes the data from a variable into a file. This statement has the same parameters as the Get statement.

```
Dim iFileNum as Integer
Dim sData as String
sData = "This is a chunk of data being written to a file"
```

```
      MsgBox "Error " & Str$(Err) & ":" & "  " & Error$ & " occurred."
         Case Else
      MsgBox "Error " & Str$(Err) & ":" & "  " & Error$ & " occurred."
      End Select

      RemoveDirectory = Err
End Function
```

Usage:
```
Dim sDirName as String
Dim iRet as Integer
sDirName = "C:\PROJECTS\PROJECT1"
iRet = RemoveDirectory(sDirName)
If iRet = 0 Then
    'OK to continue
```

CurDir

This function returns the current directory. Imagine that the currently selected path on drive C is C:\PROJECTS, and on drive D it is D:\GAMES. The following examples denote the uses of this function:

1. `sWhereAmI = CurDir`—This returns C:\PROJECTS.

2. `sWhereAmI = CurDir ("C")`—This returns C:\PROJECTS.

3. `sWhereAmI = CurDir ("D")`—This returns D:\GAMES.

Kill

This statement deletes a file from the disk. Use `RmDir` to remove a directory. This statement accepts wildcards thus deleting multiple files at the same time. For example:

`Kill "C:\PROJECTS\DEADFILE.TXT"`	Deletes the file "C:\PROJECTS\DEADFILE.TXT"
`Kill "C:\PROJECTS\*.TXT"`	Deletes all files with the TXT extension.

Usage:
```
Dim sFile As String
sFile = "C:\PROJECTS\PROJECT1\REPORT.TXT"
Kill sFile
If Err = 0 Then
    'OK to continue...
```

Accessing Files

Files can be opened and closed programatically from Visual Basic. The following section outlines the functions used in opening and closing files as well as the modes in which they can be opened. Examples are provided for each of the statements and functions where appropriate.

Open

This statement opens a file. There are several modes for which a file can be opened (discussed below). The syntax for the Open statement is

```
Open sFileName for Mode [Access sAccess] [Lock sLockParam] as iFileNum [Len =
➥iRecordLength]
```

There are several components of this statement.

1. sFileName—The name of the file that you would like to open. This includes the fully qualified path the file.
2. Access—This decides how you will access the file (read, write, and so on).
3. Lock—This decides what other processes can do to the file while you have it open
4. iFileNum—This is a file handle assigned to the file. The file handle is created using the FreeFile function (covered later in this section).
5. Len—This is the amount of data that is to be read each time the file is accessed.

If the file in the Open statement does not exist and you are using Append, Output, Random, or Binary mode, the file is created. For example, if you open the file C:\WINDOWS\ SYSTEM\MYFILE.TXT and it does not exist, an empty file with that name is created and opened.

The following sections fully explain each of the parameters of the Open statement

File Mode—Mandatory Component of the *Open* Statement

The file mode is the manner in which the file is opened. Depending upon the type of operation you are performing (reading a file, writing to a file, and so on), the file is opened in a different mode. Visual Basic supports the following file modes: Input, Output, Random, and Binary. The following lists these modes:

Input

Sequential data input. This statement is used when you want to read data from a file. It sequentially reads the number of characters in RecLen each time the file is accessed.

Output

Sequential data output. This statement is used when you want to write data to a file. It sequentially writes the number of characters in RecLen each time the file is accessed.

Random

Binary

Binary file access is used when you want to move to a certain position in the file to retrieve or write data. For example, if you know that the data you are seeking is at position 256, open the

```
Put #FileNum, [iRecordNumber], sData
```

In this case, the data in `sData` is written to the file opened using the `Open` statement. This file is specified after the # (in this case `#iFileNum`.) This writing begins in one of the following positions within the file:

1. The first byte in the file if the file is empty and this is the first `Put` statement
2. The byte following the last `Put` statement
3. The file position set using the `Seek` function

If you choose to omit `iRecordNumber`, the comma must still be used.

```
Dim sData as String
Put #FileNumber,  , sData
```

See the Visual Basic help topic "Put Statement" for additional information.

Input Statement and Function

The `Input` statement and function are used to read data from a file and assign it to a variable. Use the `Input` function only for files opened in Input or Binary mode. The difference between the `Input` statement and the `Input` function is that the `Input` function returns all characters read from the file. This includes carriage returns, line feeds, quotes, and leading spaces. The following is the syntax for the `Input` function:

```
Dim iFileNum As Integer
Dim sFileName As String
Dim iLen As Integer
Dim sData As String
'Number of characters to read from file
Dim iChars As Integer

iFileNum = FreeFile
sFileName = "C:\PROJECTS\DATA.TXT"
Open sFileName for Input as iFileNum
iLen = LOF(iFileNum)

'If the file is less than 32000 characters, set iLen to the file size. Otherwise
set it to 32000
If iLen < 32000 Then
    iChars = LOF(iFileNum)
Else
    iChars = 32000
End If

'Input Function - get 32000 bytes and read it into sData
sData = Input iChars, #iFileNum,
```

The `Input` function reads 32,000 characters into the variable `sData`. This data includes carriage returns, line feeds, and so on.

The implementation of the `Input` statement is the same with the exception of the following line:

```
Input #x, sData
```

This statement reads the contents of the file without leading spaces, carriage returns, line feeds, and so on.

> **TIP**
>
> If you want to read bytes (instead of characters) from a file, use the `InputB` function.

Line Input

This statement reads a line at a time from a file. The end of a line is determined when a carriage return—Chr(13) or carriage return and line feed combination—Char(13) & Chr(10) is reached. The carriage return and/or line feed is not a part of the string that is read into the `sString` variable.

> **CAUTION**
>
> Do not use `Line Input` to read a binary file. There is a chance that there is no carriage return line feed in the file and therefore the Visual Basic attempts to read the entire contents of the file into the buffer at once. This can easily cause problems for your program (out of string space error messages, and so on)

The syntax for this statement is as follows:

```
Dim sData as String
Line Input #iFileNum, sData
```

This statement places the next line of the file into the variable `sData`.

Print

The `Print #` statement writes data out to a sequential file. An example of when this statement is used is for the creation of a report. The following is the syntax of the `Print #` statement:

```
Dim iFileNum as Integer
Dim sData as String
sData = 'This is a string of data being written to a file using the Print #
statement"
iFileNum = FreeFile
Print #iFileNum, sData
```

The following statement prints a blank line to the file:

```
Print #iFileNum,
```

If you are formatting data for a report, you can insert tabs and spaces so that the data is output in the correct manner. Remember to trim any leading and trailing spaces for data so that the tabs align correctly. The following line prints two columns (Name and Address) on the same line. The columns are separated by a tab.

```
Print # iFileNum, "Name"; Tab ; "Address"
```

The following line separates the Name and Address columns with two tabs.

```
Print # iFileNum, "Name"; Tab(2) ; "Address"
```

This line is the same as above, except it places 10 spaces before the Name field.

```
Print # iFileNum, Spc(10) ,"Name"; Tab(2) ; "Address"
```

This line writes the words "Have," "a," "Nice," and "Day" to the file. each word is separated by a space.

```
Print # iFileNum, "Have" ; " " ; "a" ; " " ; "Nice" ; " " ; "Day"
```

This final example writes the words "I love file I/O" to the file preceding by five tabs.

```
Print # iFileNum, Tab(5) ; "I love file I/O"
```

Data that is output using this statement is formatted for display, so the following rules apply:

1. Keywords such as Date, Time, and so on are formatted using the local settings in your Control Panel.

2. If you are printing a variable that is a result of a Boolean operation, either True or False is printed to the file.

3. If there is nothing in the list of items to print to the file (`Print #iFileNum,`), a blank line is printed.

4. If there is one variable in the list of items to be printed and that variable is `Empty` (variant that has not yet been assigned a value), nothing is printed to the file.

5. If there is one variable in the list of items to be printed and that variable is `NULL`, the word `NULL` is printed to the file.

6. If you are planning to read the data back out of the file at a later time, use `Write #` of the `Print #` statement.

File Positions

When reading and writing data to files, it is important to be able to set where in a file that operation is to take place. The following section details the functions and statements available in Visual Basic 4.0 for setting and retrieving the current position in a file. Examples are provided where appropriate.

Beginning of File (*BOF*)

Because I present the EOF function, I should explain that there is no BOF function used in Visual Basic file I/O. This function is used solely with databases to locate the first database record within a file.

EOF

This is a function that returns a Boolean (true or false) value that determines whether the file pointer has reached the end of the file. The following example demonstrates the usage of this function:

```
Dim sFileName as string
Dim iFileNum as Integer
iFileNum = FreeFile
sFileName = "C:\PROJECTS\PROJECT1\REPORT.TXT"

'Open the file
Open sFileName For Input As #iFileNum.

'Perform the following statement until the end of file has been reached.
Do While Not EOF(iFileNum)
    'Read in a line from the file and place it in sData
    Line Input #iFileNum, sData
Loop
'Close the file
Close #iFileNum
```

LOF

This function returns the size of a file in bytes that has been opened using the Open statement.

The following example demonstrates the use of the LOF function:

```
Dim sFileName as string
Dim iFileNum as Integer
iFileNum = FreeFile
sFileName = "C:\PROJECTS\PROJECT1\REPORT.TXT"

'Open the file
Open sFileName For Input As #iFileNum
'Place the length of the file into the FileLength variable
FileLength = LOF(iFileNum)
'Close the file
Close #iFileNum
```

If you want to know the length of a series of files and do not need to perform I/O, use the FileLen function, covered later in the chapter.

Loc

This function returns the current position of the file pointer within a file opened with the Open statement. The usage of this function is:

```
Dim sFileName as string
Dim iFileNum as Integer
iFileNum = FreeFile
sFileName = "C:\PROJECTS\PROJECT1\REPORT.TXT"
Dim sData as String * 256
Dim iPos as Integer

'Print the current file position to the form (before we start reading the file.)
Form1.Print "The current file position is: " & iPos

Do While iPos < LOF(iFileNum)
    'Grab 256 characters from the file and place into sData
    sData = sData & Input(256, #1)
    'Get the new file position
    iPos = Loc(iFileNum)
    Form1.Print "The current file position is: " & iPos
Loop
Close #1     ' Close file.
```

Seek Statement and Function

The Seek statement and function set and get the current position within a file. The file must have been opened using the Open statement. The Seek statement sets the position for the next read from or write to the open file. The following example opens a file for random and reads all the records into a variable. A record is comprised of a Customer type structure.

First we define a type called customer. This is done in the general declarations section of a module.

```
Type Customer
    sName As String * 30
    sAddress As String * 60
    iPurchases as Integer
End Type
```

Next, we create the function that reads the file.

```
Sub ReadCustomerFile
    Dim sFileName as String
    Dim i as Integer
    Dim iFileNum as Integer
    Dim iMax as Integer
    Dim tRecord() As Customer

    iFileNum = FreeFile
    sFileName = "C:\PROJECTS\PROJECT1\REPORT.TXT"
```

```
' Open the file
Open sFileName For Random As iFileNum Len = Len(tRecord)
'The next statement gets the number of records in the file
iMax = LOF(iFileNum) \ Len(tRecord)
' Read the records in the file and place them into the sData array
For i = 1 To Max
    Seek #1, RecordNumber    ' Set position.
    ReDim Preserve tRecord(i)
    Get #1, , tRecord(i)
Next i
Close iFileNum
```

For modes other than Random, Seek sets the position in the file where the next operation takes place.

File Information

Visual Basic 4.0 offers a variety of statements and functions for getting information about files. This section covers those and provides examples where necessary.

Dir

This function returns the name of a file meeting the specifications of the parameter passed to it. This function requires a path and allows the use of wildcards. One of the most useful places for this function is when you would like to gather a list of all files in a directory.

The following example creates a list of all files in the C:PROJECTS\PROJECT1 directory. Each file in the directory is added to the sDirList array. This listing includes all files in the directory.

```
Dim sDirectory as String
Dim sFile as String
Dim i as Integer
Dim sDirList() as String

sDirectory = "C:\PROJECTS\PROJECT1"

sFile = Dir$(sDirectory & "\*.*")
        i = 0
        Do While Len(sFile)
            ReDim Preserve sDirList(i)
            sDirList(i) = sDirectory & "\" & sFile
            sFile = Dir$
            i = i + 1
        Loop
```

This function can be modified to include only the Microsoft Word document (.DOC) files by changing one line.

```
sDirectory = "C:\PROJECTS\PROJECT1\*.DOC"
```

Additionally, this function has an attributes argument that allows you to specify the following file types:

Constant	Value	Description
vbNormal	0	Normal files
vbHidden	2	Hidden Files
vbSystem	4	System Files
vbVolume	8	Volume Label (all other attributes are ignored if this is used)
vbDirectory	16	Directory

The example is modified to screen for Hidden Files only.

```
Dim sDirectory as String
Dim sFile as String
Dim i as Integer
Dim sDirList() as String

sDirectory = "C:\PROJECTS\PROJECT1"

sFile = Dir$(sDirectory & "\*.*", 2)   '<< Hidden Files Only
        i = 0
        Do While Len(sFile)
            ReDim Preserve sDirList(i)
            sDirList(i) = sDirectory & "\" & sFile
            sFile = Dir$
            i = i + 1
        Loop
```

FileAttr (Get and Set)

The FileAttr function provides two types of information about a file opened from Visual Basic using the Open statement. This function returns either the mode for which the file was opened, or the operating system file handle (not the Visual Basic file number retrieved using FreeFile). The syntax is as follows:

```
Dim iFileNum as Integer
Dim sFileName as String
Dim iMode as Integer
Dim iHandle as Integer

iFileNum = FreeFile
sFileName = "C:\PROJECTS\PROJECT1\REPORT.TXT"

Open sFileName for Output as iFileNum

'Get the mode for which the file is opened

iMode = FileAttr(iFileNum, 1)
```

```
'Get the operating system file handle for the open file
iHandle = FileAttr(iFileNum, 2)
```

The modes are as follows:

Mode	Value
Input	1
Output	2
Random	4
Append	8
Binary	16

In using this function, it is a good idea to establish global constants for each of the values. The following example declares global constants for each of the modes and places the `FileAttr` call into a function:

```
Global Const gcI_Input = 1
Global Const gcI_Output = 2
Global Const gcI_Random = 4
Global Const gcI_Append = 8
Global Const gcI_Binary = 16

Function GetFileInfo(sFileName as String, iInfoType as Integer)
    Dim iMode as Integer
    Dim iHandle as Integer

    'Get the mode for which the file is opened
    iMode = FileAttr(iFileNum, 1)

    'Get the operating system file handle for the open file
    iHandle = FileAttr(iFileNum, 2)
End Function

'The function is called in this manner:

Dim sFileName as String
Dim iRet as Integer
Dim iHandle as Integer

sFileName = "C:\PROJECTS\PROJECT1\REPORT.TXT"
iRet = GetFileInfo(sFileName, 1)

'Check to make sure that the file is opened in the correct mode. Using global
constants makes the code
'more readable
If iRet <> gcI_Input then
    MsgBox "File opened in incorrect mode"
End If

iHandle = GetFileInfo(sFileName, 2)
```

FileLen

This function returns the length of a file in bytes. This operation is performed on a closed file. If the file is open, use the LOF function. This function can be used to add up the size of all files you choose to include so that you are sure of the total size. Additionally, the FileLen function is a good compliment to any status that you are providing to a user. For example, if you have 50,000 bytes of files to process, you can determine how far along you are after each file is completed. This can be passed to the gauge control.

The syntax for the FileLen function is as follows:

```
Dim iRet as Integer
Dim sFileName as String
sFileName = "C:\PROJECTS\PROJECT1\REPORT.TXT"

iRet = FileLen(sFileName)
```

This function is also useful in combination with the Dir function to get the size of all files selected. You modify your Dir function example.

```
Type DirInfo
    sFileName as String
    iFileSize as Integer
End Type

Dim sDirectory as String
Dim sFile as String
Dim i as Integer
Dim sDirInfo() as String

sDirectory = "C:\PROJECTS\PROJECT1"

'Get all files in the directory and place them into sDirInfo().
sFile = Dir$(sDirectory & "\*.*" )
        i = 0
        Do While Len(sFile)
            ReDim Preserve sDirList(i)
            sDirInfo(i).sFileName = sDirectory & "\" & sFile
            sDirInfo(i).iFileSize = FileLen(sDirectory & "\" & sFile)
            sFile = Dir$
            i = i + 1
        Loop
```

File Date and Time

The FileDateTime function returns a file's last modification date and time. If this file has not been modified, the return is the file creation date and time. The following builds on our FileLen example and adds the file date and time to the array of directory information:

```
Type DirInfo
    sFileName as String
    iFileSize as Integer
    iFileDateTime As Variant
End Type
```

```
Dim sDirectory as String
Dim sFile as String
Dim i as Integer
Dim sDirInfo() as String

sDirectory = "C:\PROJECTS\PROJECT1"

'Get all files in the directory and place them into sDirInfo().
sFile = Dir$(sDirectory & "\*.*" )
        i = 0
        Do While Len(sFile)
            ReDim Preserve sDirList(i)
            sDirInfo(i).sFileName = sDirectory & "\" & sFile
            sDirInfo(i).iFileSize = FileLen(sDirectory & "\" & sFile)
            sDirInfo(i).iFileDateTime = FileDateTime(sDirectory & "\" & sFile)
            sFile = Dir$
            i = i + 1
        Loop
```

File Manipulation

Now that we have covered the basics of file I/O using Visual Basic, it is time to move on to more advanced concepts. The next section of this chapter covers methods of searching a file for information, creates a database using a binary file, and delves into the realm of binary trees and binary chops.

Searching a File for Data

Now that you have opened and read data from a file, it's time to search for something. First take this from a text file point of view.

Imagine that you have a file listing the names and addresses of all employees in a company. A section of the file may look like this:

1. Joe Smith 1234 Appletree Lane Atlanta, GA 30080

2. Steve Jones 65 First Street Duluth, MN

3. Mary Stevens 150 Cumberland Avenue San Diego, CA 92102

As you can see, this file is not formatted into defined fields. Imagine that you are searching this file for Steve Jones. The following example searches the file and returns the record number:

```
Function GetRecordNumber(sLastName as String)
    Dim iFileNum as Integer
    Dim sFileName as String
    Dim sTemp as String
    Dim I as Integer
    Dim iPos as Integer
    Dim iFound as Integer

    sFileName = "C:\PROJECTS\PROJECT1\EMPLOYEE.TXT"
    iFileNum = FreeFile
```

```
    Open sFileName for Input Access Read as iFileNum

    Do Until EOF(iFileNum)
        Line Input #iFileNum, sTemp
        'Record Number Counter
        I = I + 1
        iPos = Instr(sTemp, sLastName)
        'If we find the name, set iFound to true
        If iPos Then
            iFound = True
            Exit Do
        End If
Loop

    Close iFileNum

    If iFound = True Then
        GetRecordNumber = I
    Else
        GetRecordNumber = 0
    End If
End Function
```

This example returns the record number that holds the information. The example can be modified to return any element of information contained in the line.

First, review your data:

1. Joe Smith 1234 Appletree Lane Atlanta, GA 30080
2. Steve Jones 65 First Street Duluth, MN
3. Mary Stevens 150 Cumberland Avenue San Diego, CA 92102

You are interested in getting the zip code from the customer record. Once you have the line of data from the file in sTemp, do the following:

```
Dim iZipCode as Integer

iZipCode = Right$(sTemp, 5)
```

This assumes that the zip code has five positions. If not, we have gotten incorrect data. A better implementation searches for the first space in the string starting from the right. Anything to the right of this space is the zip code. We trim the string first to ensure that there are no leading spaces.

```
Dim iZipCode as Integer
Dim iLen as Integer
Dim iFoundSpace

'Get rid of leading and trailing spaces.
sTemp = Trim$(sTemp)
'Get the length of the line and place it in iLen
iLen = Len(sTemp)

'Start at the rightmost character in the string searching for a space. step
backwards 1 space at a time.
```

```
For I = iLen to 1 Step -1
    iPos = Instr(Mid$(sTemp,I, 1), " ")
    If iPos Then
        iFoundSpace = True
    End If
    Exit For
Next I

'Once we find the space, set the characters to the right of the space to the zip
code (iPos - 1 ensures that we do not include the space in iZipCode)
If iFoundSpace = True Then
    iZipCode = Right$(sTemp, iPos - 1)
End If
```

Now, let's put it all together. The complete function searches for a last name in the list. It returns the record number, a space, and then the zip code.

```
Function GetRecordNumber(sLastName as String)
    Dim iFileNum as Integer
    Dim sFileName as String
    Dim sTemp as String
    Dim I as Integer
    Dim iPos as Integer
    Dim iFound as Integer
    Dim sZipCode as Integer
    Dim iLen as Integer
    Dim iFoundSpace

    sFileName = "C:\PROJECTS\PROJECT1\EMPLOYEE.TXT"
    iFileNum = FreeFile

    Open sFileName for Input Access Read as iFileNum

    Do Until EOF(iFileNum)
        Line Input #iFileNum, sTemp
        'Record Number Counter
        I = I + 1
        iPos = Instr(sTemp, sLastName)
        'If we find the name, set iFound to true and get the zip code.
        If iPos Then
            iFound = True
            'Get rid of leading and trailing spaces.
            sTemp = Trim$(sTemp)
            'Get the length of the line and place it in iLen
            iLen = Len(sTemp)

            'Start at the rightmost character in the string searching for a space
➥and step backwards.
        For I = iLen to 1 Step -1
            iPos = Instr(Mid$(sTemp,I, 1), " ")
            If iPos Then
                iFoundSpace = True
            End If
            Exit For
        Next I

        'Once we find the space, set the characters to the right of the space to the
➥zip code (iPos - 1ensures that we do not include the space in iZipCode)
```

```
        If iFoundSpace = True Then
                sZipCode = Right$(sTemp, iPos - 1)
        End If
                Exit Do
            End If
        Loop

        Close iFileNum

        'If we found the record, return the record number and the zip code
        If iFound = True Then
            GetRecordNumber = I & " " & sZipCode
        Else
            'We did not find the record
            GetRecordNumber = 0
        End If
End Function
```

Binary File Formatting

The section above demonstrated the reading and searching of a text file for information. Although this is possible, it is not the most efficient method of data storage. As you saw from the example above, it is clearly not the easiest to manipulate. This section discusses the structured use of binary files for the storage and retrieval of data.

The section above demonstrated a rather crude database. In this section, you use the same data but store this data in a more organized format. Start with the data

1. Joe Smith 1234 Appletree Lane Atlanta, GA 30080

2. Steve Jones 65 First Street Duluth, MN

3. Mary Stevens 150 Cumberland Avenue San Diego, CA 92102

First, create a structure in which to store the data.

```
Type CustomerRecord
    sFirstName as String * 20
    sLastName as String * 20
    sAddress as String * 50
    sCity as String * 10
    sState as String * 2
    sZipCode as String * 5
End Type
```

As you can see, this is a much more organized method of data storage. Next implement the program that adds records to the database. This assumes that the data has already been placed into the tCustomer structure by the user (added entering information into text boxes and clicking a command button, and so on).

```
Function AddRecord(sFileName as string, tCustomer as CustomerRecord)
    Dim iFileNum as Integer
```

```
      Open sFileName for Append as iFileNum
      Print # iFileNum, tCustomerRecord
      Close iFileNum
End Function
```

Remember that rather large function in the last section used to search the file for information? Implement the function again using the new file format. In this case, the following parameters are passed to the function:

1. sFileName   The database file to open.

2. sLastName   The last name to search for.

3. tCustomer   A tCustomerRecord structure to place the record in once it is found.

```
Function GetRecord(sFileName as String, sLastName as String, tCustomer as tCustomerRecord)

      Dim iFileNum as Integer
      Dim tTemp as tCustomerRecord
      Open sFileName for Input Access Read as iFileNum Len=Len(sCustomer)
      Do Until EOF(iFileNum)
          Get # iFileNum, tTemp
          'Do the compare. Uppercase and trim each string so that the comparison
➥works.
          If UCase(Trim$(tCustomerRecord.sLastName)) = UCase(Trim$(sLastName)) Then
              iFound = True
      Exit For
          Endif
      Loop

      Close iFileNum

      'If we found it, place the data from the  database into the tCustomer structure
➥which was passed into the function.
      If iFound = True Then
          tCustomer = tTemp
      Endif
End Function
```

As you can see, this is a much simpler function, and because you are not manipulating strings with Instr and Trim$, there is less chance for error. Each piece of information is stored in an element of the structure.

Binary Chops

Now that you have implemented a more structured method of storing and retrieving data, take it one step further. Let's review:

You now have a database that is comprised of type structures containing customer information. The structure is as follows:

```
Type CustomerRecord
    sFirstName as String * 20
    sLastName as String * 20
```

```
    sAddress as String * 50
    sCity as String * 10
    sState as String * 2
    sZipCode as String * 5
End Type
```

You write all the records to a file using this structure as a format. When you want to search for a record (using the last name for example), you read the records from the file into a temp structure and check to see if `Temp.LastName` is equal to what you are searching for. This is fine if the database contains a limited number of records, but what if the database contains 100,000 records? This process is slow because each record must be compared to the desired last name to see if there is a match. Additionally, if `Trim$` or `Instr` are used, the process is slowed further.

An alternative to this is to sort the records in the file and then search them. However, this does not increase the speed of the search because every record must still be checked. The answer to this dilemma is what is termed a *binary chop*.

Imagine that you have an array of 100 elements. The binary search method is structured as follows:

Divide the array by 2 to find the center and assign that value to `iIndex`. In the example, 100 elements / 2 = 50. Therefore, `iIndex` = 50. This is the place to start searching for the record.

```
Create 2 variables:
    iLBound - This is equal to the lowest element in the array or LBound(Array)
    iUBound - This is equal to the highest element in the array or UBound(Array)
```

Start searching the array at position `iIndex` (50). If what you are looking for is less than the value of the center element (in this case number 50) then you know that element number 50, as well as all elements with an array index greater than 50 are not the one that you are looking for. An example: Imagine that you are searching for `c` and that the center element is `n`. Because `c` is less than `n`, you know that `n`, and any item with an array index greater than `n` is not what you are looking for. Therefore, all elements of the array 50 and above are eliminated. To eliminate the elements, change `iUBound` to `iIndex - 1`. The `-1` eliminates element number 50 from the remaining eligible elements.

> **CAUTION**
>
> Note that you do not actually affect the array during a binary chop. No items are actually from the array by *ReDim*ming the array to a smaller size.

If what you are searching for is *greater* than the center element (`iIndex`), then you know that the center element and all elements with an array index less than it are eliminated, so we change `iLBound` to `iIndex + 1`.

Imagine that you have the following array :

```
 0  A
 1  B
 2  C
 3  D
 4  E
 5  F
 6  G
 7  H
 8  I
 9  J
10  K
```

Now, imagine that you are searching for the element "C."

Do the following:

1. Divide the array by 2 to find the center and assign that value to iIndex. In this case iIndex = 5.

2. Start searching the array at element iIndex (5) for the letter C. At index 5 you find the letter F. Because C is less than F, you know that element numbers 5 and greater are not what you are looking for, so you set iUBound to 4 (iIndex - 1). Although you have not changed the contents of the array, you are now using the following indexes to search it:

```
iLBound = 0
iUBound = 4
```

As far as your program is concerned, this array now only has five elements to search:

```
0  A
1  B
2  C
3  D
4  E
5  F
```

3. Now reset your iIndex variable and check the array again (Divide the remaining array by 2 to find the center and assign that value to iIndex.) In this case use the following calculation:

```
iIndex = CInt((UBound(Array) + LBound(Array)) / 2)
```

This results in 2. Therefore, the center of your array is now element number 2. Start the process over again. Look at element 2 and find the letter C. Because what you are searching for (C) is greater than B, you know that element 1 and any element less than 1 (just 0 in this case) are not what you are looking for. Then reset the iLBound variable to 2. As far as your program is concerned, the array now is:

2 C
3 D
4 E
5 F

When there is an even number of elements in the array it can't be exactly split in half so you must remember to use CInt when calculating the index. In this case, it makes no difference if iIndex ends up at element 3 or 4. In either case, one more iteration of the loop is necessary to find the entry that you are searching for.

So... you searched a 10-element array with only four iterations to find what you were looking for. You accomplished the same task but took only 60% of the time to do it. In many cases this percentage will be as low as 33%. This is a very effective method not only for file I/O, but for array searching in general.

The following program fully implements the binary chop function. When an item is found, its count is incremented. This function uses a typed array with a structure as follows:

```
Type Customer
    LastName as String
    iHits as Integer
End Type

Dim sArray as String
'LBound and UBound variables
iLBound = LBound(sArray)
iUbound = UBound(sArray)

    'Keep going until either iLBound and iUBound are equal, or until iLBound is
    ➥greater than iUBound (no more elements to search).
    Do Until iLBound >= iUbound
        'Reset the iIndex variable each time through the loop (since the array
        ➥is 'smaller')
        iIndex = CInt((iUbound + iLBound) / 2)
        'Compare what we are searching for to the array entry
        iVal = StrComp(sSearchFor, sArray(iIndex).LastName)

        Select Case iVal
            Case -1    'What we are searching for is less than the array
            ➥element
                iUbound = iIndex - 1

            Case 0    'We have found what we are searching for. Increment the
            ➥counter and exit the loop.
    sArray(iIndex).iHits = sArray(iIndex).Hits + 1
    Exit For
            Case 1    'What we are searching for is greater than the array
            ➥element.
                iLBound = iIndex + 1
        End Select
    Loop
```

File Formats

Now that you know the basics of file I/O from Visual Basic, you should know that many of the files on your system can be opened and read if the proper file format is known. The format for a C language type structure is:

```
typedef struct tag
TYPENAME {
    int         formatID;
    char            lenData[50];
    char            offData[65];
    int         formSize;
}TYPENAME;
```

With a very small amount of work (mostly understanding variable type conversions), these formats can be applied to Visual Basic.

```
Type TYPENAME
    formatID as Integer
    lenData as String * 50
    offData as String * 65
    formSize as Integer
End Type
```

This book provides you with an understanding of the structure of many files formats, including

1. Icon files   .ICO

2. Font files   .FNT

3. Windows metafiles .WMF

4. Clipboard view files .CLP

5. Executable files   .EXE

All these files can be opened from Visual Basic with the routines outlined in this chapter.

Additionally, when creating files for your application that you will access at a later time, it is important to ensure that you are accessing the correct file. Microsoft recommends that the first four bytes of your file contain information identifying the file as yours (this can be anything that you deem desirable. When accessing the file, ensure that you have the correct file by checking the first four bytes. The following example opens a Visual Basic 3.0 module and checks to see whether the file is saved as text. If it is, it is okay to continue.

```
Dim sFileName as String
Dim iFileNum as Integer
Dim sByte As String * 1
iFileNum = FreeFile
sFileName = "MODULE1.BAS"

Open sFileName For Binary Access Read As IFileNum
Get #iFileNum, , sByte
```

```
If sByte = Chr$(&HFC&) Then
    iRet = MsgBox("This module is saved in binary format.", 36, "Visual Basic 4
Unleashed")
ElseIf sByte = Chr$(&HFF&) Then
    iRet = MsgBox("This module is saved in text format.", 36, "Visual Basic 4
Unleashed")
End If

Close iFileNum
```

Summary

This chapter covered the basics of file input and output (I/O) in Visual Basic. First, the basics of file input and output (I/O) were covered. This included the functions and statements that Visual Basic provides for the opening, closing, and manipulation of files. This was followed by more advanced topics including the reading of files in blocks, binary chops, and file formats.

Timing Is Everything

4

by Paul W. Logston

IN THIS CHAPTER

Many programs have to respond to time in one form or another. Some programs *measure* time—they time things. An example of this type of program is one that monitors the time it takes other programs (or parts of programs) to run. Other programs are *controlled* by time—they exist to respond to "time events" external to the program itself. An example of this type of program is a scheduler.

As the remainder of this chapter demonstrates, Visual Basic 4.0 has facilities to easily create both types of programs without resorting to external C functions or Windows SDK calls.

Timing Things

The ability to measure time is an important part of any programming language. For example, games depend heavily on timing to pace the action so that they don't run too fast. Even business applications use delays to pace the application. In the technical arena, the ability to measure time is what makes code profilers possible.

Fortunately, Visual Basic provides a handy way to measure time: the built-in `Timer` function. The operation of the `Timer` function is simple: it returns the number of seconds since midnight. Although this is an arbitrary number and is not very useful to look at, it provides a way to mark a point in time. For example, if you call `Timer`, store the value it returns, and later call the function again, the difference between the two values is the elapsed time in seconds between the two calls. This simple formula is the basis for all timing done with the `Timer` function.

A Simple *Sleep* Subroutine

Probably the most simple, and common, use for `Timer` is when you need to insert a timed delay into your program. Back in the old days of GWBASIC, delays were often inserted into programs with empty `FOR...NEXT` loops like the following one:

```
FOR I = 1 TO 1000
NEXT I
```

This method is actually a poor way to insert delays. Its main flaw is that the actual amount of time it delays the program is unpredictable because it depends totally on the speed of the computer it is running on. In addition, you cannot use this method to set a specific delay even when you know which machine you are using unless you do a lot of tinkering to get the number of iterations to match the desired delay. You are likely to have to play with the number of iterations several times and may end with code like `FOR I = 1 TO 1127` to set a delay of one second—at least on your machine.

With the `Timer` function, your delays can be a little more precise. A simple example of a `Timer`-based function that delays a program for a number of seconds is as follows:

```
Sub Sleep(sngNumberOfSeconds As Single)

    Dim sngEndTime As Single

        ' compute the time until the end of the delay
```

```
sngEndTime = Timer + sngNumberOfSeconds

    'Spin until the time is up
Do
Loop Until Timer >= sngEndTime

End Sub
```

This subroutine does what was advertised—you call it and it comes back the specified number of seconds later. But it has some problems. If you run this subroutine in the 16-bit versions of Windows (Windows 3.*x*), you will notice that nothing else in the system responds during the delay loop. This is caused by the lack of a DoEvents function call inside the Do...Loop. Without a DoEvents call, nothing else in Windows can happen because that function is the heart of the cooperative multitasking architecture of 16-bit Windows. Cooperative multitasking depends on applications to be "nice" and release control so that other applications can have some processor time. The DoEvents function is the way Visual Basic applications can fulfill this requirement to be "nice" to other applications. Note that releasing time to other applications is automatic when you are just waiting for user input; however, when you are running in a tight loop, like the preceding subroutine, DoEvents is required. The revised Sleep subroutine would look like this:

```
Sub Sleep(sngNumberOfSeconds As Single)

    Dim sngEndTime As Single

        ' compute the time until the end of the delay
    sngEndTime = Timer + sngNumberOfSeconds

        ' Spin until the time is up
    Do
        DoEvents    ' Let other things happen
    Loop Until Timer >= sngEndTime

End Sub
```

> **NOTE**
>
> If you have experience with Windows SDK, note that the DoEvents function is similar to the Windows SDK Yield function.

Even in the 32-bit environments like Windows NT or Windows 95, the DoEvents function serves a purpose. Although you don't have the problem of locking up other applications by not releasing time (both Windows NT and Windows 95 preemptively multitask 32-bit applications), your applications do not receive or process any events while you are in a tight loop. Use DoEvents to allow your application to respond to events during the delay.

The next problem with the simple Sleep subroutine shown earlier is something the documentation and the help system don't really make clear: the Timer function resets at midnight. If you begin timing at 11:59 p.m. and want to wait for 180 seconds (3 minutes), the Sleep subroutine never returns. Although this isn't obvious, it becomes evident when you walk through the code:

1. At the beginning of the subroutine, Timer returns 86,340 (11:59 p.m. is 86,340 seconds from the last midnight).

2. When you add the desired delay time (180) to the initial timer value (86,340), you get the anticipated end value (86,520).

3. The subroutine loops until Timer returns a value greater than the end value of 86,520. But this condition can never be met because the maximum number of seconds in a day is 86,400. Timer can never return a value greater than 86,400. Thus, you are waiting for something that can never happen, and the loop continues to run endlessly.

In fact, any delay that goes past midnight suffers from this problem. This bug becomes even more problematic if you forget to call DoEvents in the loop: your application (and even the entire system under Windows 3.x) stops responding during that endless loop.

A More Complete *Sleep* Subroutine

The problem of timing past midnight is easily solved with a little extra code. Following is a revised Sleep subroutine that shows how to account for the passing of midnight:

```
Sub Sleep(sngNumberOfSeconds As Single)

    Const SECONDS_IN_DAY = 86400!
    Dim sngStartTime As Single, sngEndTime As Single, sngCurrentTime As Single

        ' setup the timer start and end times
    sngStartTime = Timer
    sngEndTime = sngStartTime + sngNumberOfSeconds

        ' spin until the time has elapsed
    Do
        DoEvents

            ' if the current time is less than the start time, then we know that
            ' we've passed midnight.  If that happens, apply an adjustment
            ' so the values will compare correctly.
        sngCurrentTime = Timer
        If sngCurrentTime < sngStartTime Then
            sngCurrentTime = sngCurrentTime + SECONDS_IN_DAY
        End If
    Loop Until sngCurrentTime >= sngEndTime

End Sub
```

The preceding Sleep subroutine is more complex than the simple, but flawed, one shown earlier. However, the subroutine is readily understandable when you look at it in detail:

1. The subroutine records the start time of the process and computes the desired end time.

2. The subroutine loops; on each iteration, it determines whether the end time has passed. To do this, you must see whether Timer has reset itself (you do this by seeing whether the current value of Timer is less than the value recorded when the process started). If this is true, you know that midnight has passed; you then adjust the

current value by adding a day's worth of seconds so that the value will compare correctly with the computed end time. If you haven't passed midnight, you just compare the values without modification.

Note that during the loop, the subroutine references Timer only once, storing its value in a variable for later use. Why? Besides some minor speed improvements, the subroutine has to store the Timer value because the value returned by Timer may change between the different calls. By storing the value in a program variable, you can ensure that the value is always consistent during the subroutine's computations and comparisons.

The Granularity of the *Timer* Function

In the Sleep subroutine used in the preceding section, notice that all Timer-related variables are declared as single-precision numbers. Why is that, when Timer simply returns the number of seconds since midnight? This is another fact that the documentation doesn't clearly bring out: the Timer function actually returns a fractional number of seconds. By using single-precision numbers to compute the delay, you can use the Timer function to time a fractional number of seconds. Because Sleep uses single-precision variables, all the following calls to Sleep are valid:

```
Sleep 10
Sleep .5
Sleep 2.78
```

You can demonstrate for yourself that Timer returns a fractional number of seconds by using the small program shown in Figure 4.1. The example is simple—click anywhere on the form, and the program prints the next 10 values returned by the Timer function as fast as it can. Most of the values printed are the same because the loop runs fast enough to print several Timer values before Timer increments. But you should see the Timer function increment in a few of those values.

Take note of a curious thing: the Timer values increment in steps of .03 or .04 instead of .01. This increment is the *granularity* of the Timer function (that is, the smallest amount of time Timer can measure). Keep this granularity in mind when you write programs based on the Timer function; the increment may not be as fine as you expect.

NOTE

Don't put too much faith in Timer's granularity as demonstrated in Figure 4.1. If you include a DoEvents call in the timing loop, you can never predict how much time DoEvents will take. Depending on the number of messages queued up in Windows to be processed, DoEvents may return immediately or may return minutes later. The timing granularity may also vary based on the hardware platform used. Although this is currently a concern only for Windows NT, any assumptions may limit the portability of your application.

FIGURE 4.1.

Demonstrating Timer resolution.

Measuring Time

As you saw in the first part of this chapter, an important use of the Timer function is to insert delays in a program. However, a delay is simply a piece of code that continually measures the time elapsed from its start to the desired end time. Using similar concepts, you can use the Timer function to time things other than a simple delay loop. The process is conceptually very simple: record the value returned by Timer, perform the process you want to time, and record a second Timer value. The difference between the two values is the number of seconds that elapsed while the process was being performed.

The two calls to Timer can be easily encapsulated into a pair of function calls—one to start the timer and another to calculate the difference and return it. With a little enhancement on the basic concept, you can create a useful program profiler, like the one shown in Listing 4.1.

Listing 4.1. A program profiler.

```
Option Explicit

#If PROFILING Then
    Const MAX_SECONDS = 86400    ' number of seconds at midnight

    Dim iFileHandle As Integer   ' handle for the output file
    Dim sngTimers(20) As Single  ' storage for 20 simultaneous timers
    Dim iLastTimer As Integer    ' last entry in the array used
#End If

Function StartProfiler(sFileName As String) As Integer
```

```
#If PROFILING Then
    On Error GoTo Error_StartProfiler

        ' open an output file for the timing information
    iFileHandle = FreeFile
    Open sFileName For Output As #iFileHandle

        ' initialize the counters
    iLastTimer = 0

    StartProfiler = True
    Exit Function

Error_StartProfiler:
    StartProfiler = False
    Exit Function

#Else
    StartProfiler = True
    Exit Function
#End If

End Function

Function StopProfiler() As Integer

#If PROFILING Then
    On Error GoTo Error_StopProfiler

        ' close the output file.
    Close #iFileHandle
    StopProfiler = True
    Exit Function

Error_StopProfiler:
    StopProfiler = False
    Exit Function

#Else
    StopProfiler = True
    Exit Function
#End If

End Function

Function MarkStartTime() As Integer

#If PROFILING Then
    On Error GoTo Error_MarkStartTime

    Dim i As Integer

        ' get the next entry to use
    i = iLastTimer + 1

        ' record the starting time value
    sngTimers(i) = Timer
    iLastTimer = i
```

continues

Listing 4.1. continued

```
    MarkStartTime = True
    Exit Function

Error_MarkStartTime:
    MarkStartTime = False
    Exit Function

#Else
    MarkStartTime = True
    Exit Function
#End If

End Function

Function MarkEndTime(sTag As String) As Integer

#If PROFILING Then
    On Error GoTo Error_MarkEndTime

    Dim sngEndTime As Single, sngDifference As Single

        ' record the end time and adjust for the passage of midnight
    sngEndTime = Timer
    If sngEndTime < sngTimers(iLastTimer) Then sngEndTime = sngEndTime +
➥MAX_SECONDS

        ' compute the elapsed time
    sngDifference = sngEndTime - sngTimers(iLastTimer)

        ' write it to a file, with a number of spaces that reflect
        ' its place in the stack of timers.
    Print #iFileHandle, Spc(iLastTimer); sTag; " "; sngDifference

        ' free an array entry for re-use
    iLastTimer = iLastTimer - 1

    MarkEndTime = True
    Exit Function

Error_MarkEndTime:
    MarkEndTime = False
    Exit Function

#Else
    MarkEndTime = True
    Exit Function
#End If

End Function
```

The Profiling Functions

The profiler example in Listing 4.1 works on a stack concept—multiple timers can be started, but they must be stopped in the reverse of their starting order. The reason you use multiple timers is simply so that you can time at multiple levels: You can measure the time it takes for an entire process to run and also measure the time individual portions of that process consume. The functions also record the timing information to a program-specified file rather than to any kind of window so that the functions can be inserted and have no impact on the actual user interface of the program (except for whatever speed impact they may add).

The profiling functions are globally enabled or disabled using Visual Basic 4.0's conditional compilation options. By setting the PROFILING compilation constant to a nonzero value, you enable the profiling code. When the profiling is disabled (PROFILING is either not defined or is defined as zero), all the functions return TRUE immediately and do nothing else. By immediately returning when they are not enabled, the profiling functions should have minimal impact on your program's speed. This arrangement means that you can insert the profiling functions in your application and simply disable them when you do the production compile, rather than going though your code to remove them manually.

NOTE

Conditional Compilation is a new feature in Visual Basic 4.0. Conditional Compilation works like a normal IF...THEN statement, except that the statement is evaluated when the executable is made and not at runtime. Since the condition is not evaluated when the program runs, there is no performance overhead added to the program. In fact, the false side of the #IF...#END IF doesn't even get included in the compiled program. Note that since the Conditional Compilation directives are evaluated at compile time, you can't refer to any program variables in them—their values just aren't known until the program runs!

Conditional Compilation is normally used to insert debugging code that you want to remove in the production program, or to create multiple versions of a program from the same set of source code, like versions for multiple platforms.

To add the profiler to your project, include the PROFILE.BAS module and set PROFILING=1 in the Conditional Compilation Arguments field in the Tools | Options window under the Advanced tab. Then simply insert the calls to the profiling functions in the sections of code where you want timing information, as the example in Figure 4.2 shows.

FIGURE 4.2.

Using the profiling functions.

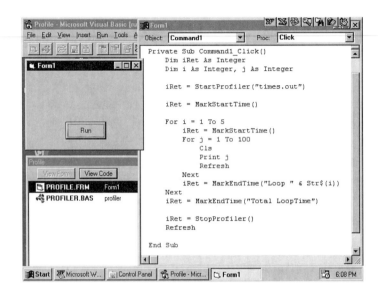

To use the profiling functions, insert the StartTimer function in your code before the first time you want to begin making profiling calls. All StartTimer does is to open the specified output file (which holds the profiling information) and to set the counter for the last timer, iLastTimer, to zero so that you begin fresh in the array. The StopTimer function is a cleanup function that closes the timing output file and returns.

The MarkStartTime and MarkEndTime functions are the ones that actually do the timing. MarkStartTime allocates a timer value from the sngTimers array and sets it to the current value of the Timer function. MarkEndTime simply computes the elapsed time based on the last entry in the sngTimers array and writes the time difference to a file, along with any programmer-specified text passed into the function. MarkEndTime then removes the used timer from the array by decrementing iLastTimer.

When you run your program, the profiling information is silently written to the file you specified so that you can examine it at your leisure.

Timing Processes with Now

There is an inherent problem with routines based on the Timer function: because Timer resets every 24 hours, you can't use it to time anything greater than 24 hours. Also, although the values returned by Timer are fine for computing the raw number of seconds a process takes, these values force the programmer to convert by hand if information is required in minutes or seconds. If these limitations are unacceptable for your purposes, consider building your timers based on the Now function.

Now returns a Date type instead of a simple number of seconds. The good news is that, because it is a Date type, you can time things for any number of days (or months and years). The bad news is that, because it is a Date type, doing computations and displaying the timing informa-tion is a little more complex: you have to use the special Visual Basic date functions.

The easiest way to get the difference between two Date values is to use the DateDiff function. With DateDiff, you can compute the difference between two Date variables in a unit of time you specify. As with the Timer function, the difference between these two variables is the elapsed time. The following is a version of the Sleep subroutine shown earlier in this chapter, but this time it uses the Now and DateDiff functions:

```
Sub Sleep(lNumberOfSeconds As Long)

    Dim dateStart As Date

        ' record the start time
    dateStart = Now()

        'Spin until the time is up
    Do
        DoEvents
    Loop Until DateDiff("s", dateStart, Now()) >= lNumberOfSeconds

End Sub
```

The preceding loop is much simpler than the Sleep subroutine used earlier in this chapter—it needs no adjustment for passing midnight. And because the example provides an S as the first parameter to the DateDiff function, the function simply returns the number of seconds be-tween the two dates—even if the number of seconds gets ridiculously large!

There are some drawbacks to this implementation:

- You cannot specify a fractional number of seconds.
- The DateDiff function is slower than even the more complex math in the Timer-based version of Sleep presented earlier in this chapter. Although this may not seem impor-tant (you are actually *delaying* the execution of a program), you are also yielding time (through DoEvents) to other processes; any time you use doing date manipulation is time other processes don't have to process events.

NOTE

DateDiff is a particularly handy function when dealing with dates in your program. Its basic function is implied by its name—it simply returns the difference between two dates. How that difference is computed depends on the first parameter to the function. That parameter is a string representing the unit of time in which you want to measure the difference. In the preceding example, we used an S to state the difference between the two dates in seconds. Other parameters include D to state the difference in days, M for months, and YYYY for years. There are still more parameters possible; look in the Visual Basic help for a complete list.

Based on these limitations, a Timer-based solution is probably the better choice unless you need to time some very long events.

Responding to Time

People are mostly time driven. We wake up, go to work, go home, and go to bed at regular times. In other words, we respond to time-based events. Some programs must function the same way to be useful. A scheduler program is a classic example of this type of program; something as simple as an animated picture in a screen saver has similar requirements. That is, they both must do something at a predetermined time or interval. Fortunately, Windows provides a set of built-in timers you can use to create this type of program.

Windows timers can be thought of as an old-fashioned grandfather clock. This type of clock chimes at regular intervals, in most cases on the hour and half-hour. Windows timers work similarly, except that you can set the "chime" interval to any value you want, and instead of an audible bell tone, you get a "Timer Event." To access built-in Windows timers in Visual Basic code, simply place a Timer control on your form.

You place a Timer control on a form in the same way as any other control: select the Timer control icon from the toolbar and place it on a form. Don't worry about the size and placement of the control; the Timer control automatically assumes a default size and becomes invisible at runtime. Figure 4.3 shows the Timer control in the toolbar and on a form.

FIGURE 4.3.

Using the Timer control.

Timer control—

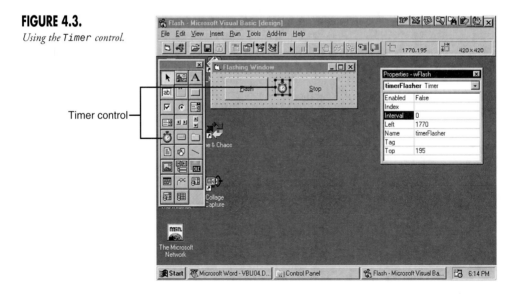

`Timer` controls have very few properties compared to other Visual Basic controls. The following chart gives a rundown on the two most important ones:

Property	Description
Enabled	Essentially turns the timer on and off. Set this property to TRUE if you want to receive `Timer` events (that is, if you want to start the timer); set this to FALSE if you don't.
Interval	Controls how often `Timer` events occur. Set this to the amount of time in milliseconds (1/1000ths of a second) you want between `Timer` events. Note that this property is ignored until `Enabled` is set to TRUE.

The `Top` and `Left` properties have no bearing on the operation of the `Timer` control because the control is be invisible at runtime and can't receive any mouse or keyboard events. The best way to position a `Timer` control is to move it to some unused part of the form and leave it (its position really doesn't matter and you might as well have it out of the way).

A `Timer` control has only one event associated with it: the `Timer` event. This event is triggered at each passing of the specified `Interval`, if the `Timer` control is `Enabled`. By placing code in the `Timer` event subroutine of the `Timer` control, you can cause something to happen on each `Interval`.

Understanding Simple Program Animation

One of the most basic uses of a timer is to add simple animation to a window. A common business use of animation is to get an operator's or user's attention during the run of a long process. Listing 4.2 uses the `Timer` control to flash the border of a window using the Windows SDK `FlashWindow` function.

Listing 4.2. A flashing window.

```
Option Explicit

' declarations differ between Windows 3.1 and Win32.
#If Win16 Then
    Private Declare Function FlashWindow Lib "User" (ByVal hWnd As Integer, ByVal
➥bInvert As Integer) As Integer
#Else
    Private Declare Function FlashWindow Lib "User32" (ByVal hWnd As Long, ByVal
➥bInvert As Long) As Long
#End If

Private Sub cbFlash_Click()
```

continues

Listing 4.2. continued

```
    timerFlasher.Interval = 500
    timerFlasher.Enabled = True

End Sub

Private Sub cbStop_Click()

    Dim iRet As Integer

        ' stop the flashing
    timerFlasher.Enabled = False

        ' Restore the window to its proper state
    iRet = FlashWindow(Me.hWnd, False)

End Sub

Private Sub Form_Load()

        ' make sure the timer isn't running when the program loads.
    timerFlasher.Enabled = False

End Sub

Private Sub timerFlasher_Timer()

    Dim iRet As Integer

        ' make the window flash
    iRet = FlashWindow(Me.hWnd, True)

End Sub
```

The FlashWindow function simply toggles the specified window's title bar and border between the Active and Inactive colors specified in the Control Panel. The hWnd parameter is the internal Windows handle for the window to be flashed. You can retrieve this value from the hWnd property on the Visual Basic Form object. When the next parameter is TRUE, it tells FlashWindow to toggle the window's title and border color, either from Active to Inactive or vice versa. If this parameter is FALSE, it returns the window to whatever color is appropriate for its current state—Active if the window is active or Inactive if the window is not active.

You'll notice the Conditional Compilation #IF...THEN that is around the declaration for the FlashWindow function. In fact, there are two declarations for FlashWindow: one that references the User library and one that references User32. This section illustrates a point about programming for multiple platforms. The first declaration of the FlashWindow function is for Windows 3.x—the 16-bit version of Windows. The second is for the 32-bit Windows versions—Windows 95 and Windows NT. You need two different declarations because Windows needs two versions of that module: one for 16-bit applications and one for 32-bit. Thus, Microsoft named them differently to prevent confusion.

Another difference between the two declarations is in the types of the parameters passed to and returned from FlashWindow. The parameters for the 32-bit versions are now Long variables instead of Integers. This is because when a machine is running a 32-bit operating system, its word size becomes a 32-bit value. Thus, the parameters are now Longs instead of Integers because an Integer is only 16-bits.

The Click event for the cbFlash button turns on the Timer control and sets the proper Interval for the flash (in this case, 500 milliseconds, or 1/2 second). The Click event for the cbStop button first shuts off the Timer and then returns the window to its proper state.

You can see that having the window flash on a Timer event doesn't keep the window from responding to other events, such as the click of a button. This kind of window is ideal for operator notification in a computer room, especially when the computer's monitor may be sitting in a row with several others. To be even more attention grabbing (or annoying), place a call to the Beep function in the Timer event.

A few caveats about the Timer control:

■ Timer controls are a limited Windows resource (you can have only 16 timers in the entire Windows environment); you can't add a Timer control to each window in your application and have them all running at once. If other ill-behaved applications have used all the available timers, none may be available when you load your form. This situation causes a runtime error. Use Timer controls with a little moderation.

■ Timer controls notify you about the passing of the Interval using a Timer event. There is nothing magical about this event; if your program is in a state in which it is not processing events (such as a tight loop with no calls to DoEvents), the code for the Timer event does not execute.

■ Other programs can affect the interval between Timer events by hogging processor time, especially under the Windows 3.*x* cooperative multitasking model. Even though you specify an Interval in milliseconds, do not assume that you will get the Timer event exactly at the specified time.

Figure 4.4 shows the variability in the regularity of the Timer event.

All the example program in Figure 4.4 does is record the elapsed time between Timer events using the Timer function. When you run this program, it prints the time in seconds that elapsed between the scheduled Timer events.

Even when the system is idling, events don't fall exactly on the scheduled time. Try running another program while looking at this display. Notice that more than the desired Interval time may pass between Timer events. This can cause some complications, especially if you are writing a program that depends on very regular Intervals. If that is a requirement, your only alternative is to time with a loop based on the Timer function.

FIGURE 4.4.

Demonstrating Timer variability.

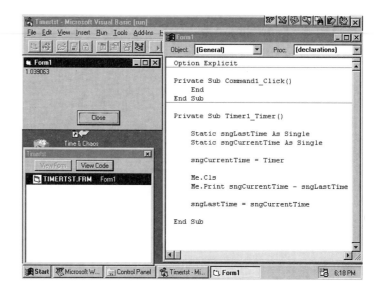

Waiting for Something

Another common use for Timer controls is to schedule applications. Such scheduler programs wait silently until there is something to do. Usually, these programs wake up at a particular time, but some look for other things such as the existence of a file.

The simplest version of this process is shown in the following example:

```
Do Until iDone
    DoEvents            ' let other events process
    IsThereAnythingToDo ' check to see if there is anything to do
Loop
```

This function works but it has some drawbacks. It is a real time waster. This loop always spins, regardless of whether or not there is anything to do—even if it just checked half a millisecond ago. Although the DoEvents function ensures that other things can happen while this loop is spinning, all the bookkeeping and event checking will be a drag to all other processes in the system.

It usually isn't necessary to check continuously to see whether there is something to do. Checking at a longer interval, perhaps once a second or once a minute, is usually fine. Following is a revised version of the preceding scheduler loop that checks for new events only once every second:

```
Do Until iDone
    DoEvents            ' let other events process
    IsThereAnythingToDo ' check to see if there is anything to do
    Sleep 1             ' snooze for a second
Loop
```

This example doesn't check to see whether there is anything to do quite so often and is less of a drag on the system's performance. However, the `Sleep` subroutine still has a loop that spins, with all the bookkeeping overhead involved. Other operating systems, such as UNIX, have a built-in `Sleep` function that places a program in a special "suspended" state for a period of time. While asleep, the operating system gives the program very little processor time until the specified duration has elapsed. Windows has no such function. The `Timer` control comes the closest to providing this capability: your application doesn't have to have any code running to check the time; all it has to do is sit back and wait for the `Timer` event to occur.

The implementation of a scheduler with the `Timer` control is a little different than the two non-`Timer` control implementations just shown. Instead of a loop, add code in the `Timer` event of the `Timer` control on the form, like this:

```
Private Sub timerScheduler_Timer()

    IsThereAnythingToDo    ' check to see if there is anything to do

End Sub
```

In the preceding example, there is no loop, no `Sleep` to delay, and no `DoEvents` call. Your program doesn't have to loop because the code in this event is executed on each passing of the specified `Interval`. Your program also doesn't have to delay itself to pace the number of checks it performs because the `Timer` control goes back to sleep when you return from this subroutine. Finally, your program doesn't need a call to `DoEvents` because, when you exit this subroutine, you automatically return control to Windows.

A Sample Scheduler Program

With the addition of a little code to build a list of things to schedule, you can have a basic scheduling program, like the one shown in Listing 4.3. Figure 4.5 shows the controls on the programs form.

Listing 4.3. A simple scheduler.

```
Option Explicit

Const SCHEDULE_DATA_FILE = "schedule.dat"

Private Type SCHEDULE_ITEM_TYPE        ' set up a structure to hold the schedule
➥entries.
    dteTime As Date
    sCommand As String
End Type

Dim strItems() As SCHEDULE_ITEM_TYPE   ' items in the schedule
Dim iCount As Integer
Dim dteLastTimeRun As Date
```

continues

Listing 4.3. continued

```
Private Sub cbClose_Click()
    End      ' end this program
End Sub

Private Sub Form_Load()

    If Not ReadScheduledItems() Then    ' fill the schedule array
        End
    End If

    dteLastTimeRun = Time

    timerScheduler.Enabled = True       ' start the timer

End Sub

Private Sub timerScheduler_Timer()

    PrintTime              ' Print the current time on the window
    IsThereAnythingToDo    ' Check the scheduled list

End Sub

Private Function ReadScheduledItems() As Integer

    Dim sFileName As String
    Dim iFile As Integer

    On Error GoTo Error_ReadScheduledItems

        ' Open the schedule file, assume that it is in the app.path
    sFileName = App.Path & "\" & SCHEDULE_DATA_FILE
    iFile = FreeFile
    Open sFileName For Input As #iFile

    iCount = 0
    Do While Not EOF(iFile)
        iCount = iCount + 1

            ' expand the structure to hold the additional item
        ReDim Preserve strItems(iCount)

            ' read it into the structure
        Input #iFile, strItems(iCount).dteTime, strItems(iCount).sCommand

    Loop

    Close #iFile

    ReadScheduledItems = True
    Exit Function

Error_ReadScheduledItems:

    ReadScheduledItems = False
    Exit Function

End Function
```

```
Private Sub IsThereAnythingToDo()

    Dim i As Integer, iRet As Integer
    Dim dteCurrentTime As Date

    On Error Resume Next

    dteCurrentTime = Time

        ' run through the array of things to do
    For i = 1 To iCount

            ' If the scheduled start time is between the time of the last run
            ' and the current time, then it is time to start the specified
            ' program.
        If strItems(i).dteTime > dteLastTimeRun And strItems(i).dteTime <=
➥dteCurrentTime Then
            iRet = Shell(strItems(i).sCommand, 1)    ' run the program
            If Err <> 0 Then
                MsgBox "Error running: " & strItems(i).sCommand
            End If
        End If
    Next

    dteLastTimeRun = dteCurrentTime

End Sub
Private Sub PrintTime()

    Dim sTime As String

        ' only print the time if the the window is not minimized
    If WindowState = 0 Then
        Me.Cls

        sTime = Format$(Time, "Long Time")                     ' format the time

        Me.CurrentX = (Me.ScaleWidth - Me.TextWidth(sTime)) / 2 ' center the time
        Me.CurrentY = Me.TextHeight(sTime) / 2
        Me.Print sTime                                         ' and print it.
    End If

End Sub
```

This example is a basic scheduler that reads a list of scheduled commands from a file and executes them at the appointed time. The user interface is simple; the program prints the current time on each Timer event and provides only a Close button that ends the program.

When the form loads, the program reads the items to be run from the file using the ReadScheduledItems function; it then starts the timer by enabling the Timer control. The only purpose for the cbClose_Click() subroutine is to force the program to end.

FIGURE 4.5.

The form for the scheduler example in Listing 4.3.

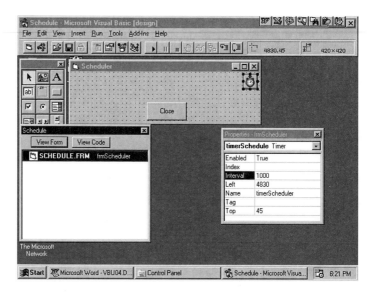

The format of the file that contains the items to be scheduled is also very simple—it was designed to be read quickly by Visual Basic's Input statement. Each line describes a schedule entry. The first parameter for each line is the time at which the command should be executed; the second parameter is a string that contains the command to be executed. An example of this file is given here:

```
#09:15:00 pm#, "calc.exe"
#09:17:00 pm#, "notepad.exe"
#09:20:00 pm#, "wordpad.exe"
```

The memory management in the ReadScheduledItems subroutine is not the best example of how to read information into a dynamic array. Calling ReDim for each element being read is slow and can cause fragmentation in the pool of memory used by Visual Basic. A better solution is to expand the array in fixed-sized extents, perhaps 10 at a time. This arrangement prevents you from going back to Windows for more memory on each iteration and eliminates a lot of the moving of data that goes on with the ReDim Preserve statement.

The heart of the scheduling engine is in the Timer event subroutine, timerScheduler_Timer(). This subroutine simply prints the current time on the form using the PrintTime subroutine and then calls the IsThereAnythingToDo subroutine, which actually runs any scheduled event whose time has come:

■ PrintTime simply prints the current time in a centered position in the window, if the window is currently visible. If you try to print the time while the window is minimized, the time prints over the icon and looks pretty bad. A possible enhancement for this program is to include the time as part of the window's caption when the window is minimized so that the current time appears regardless of the window's state.

■ `IsThereAnythingToDo` is probably the hardest piece of this code to understand. Simply put, it walks through the array of scheduled items, looking for things whose times to run have passed. When it finds an item to be run, it executes the specified command line using the `Shell` function.

How to Determine When to Run an Item

Determining when it is time to run an item is more complex than it seems. You can't simply use the following logic to compare to see whether the desired runtime is greater than the current time:

```
If Time > strItems(i).dteTime Then
```

The problem with this test is that the condition is true not only at the time the item is to be run, but also every time after that, until midnight. The command in question runs at the appointed time and at every timer interval thereafter!

The simplest way to determine when a program must be run is to see whether the desired runtime has passed between the last `Timer` event and the current one. To do this, store the time of the last `Timer` event so that you know the lower bound of the time span between the clicks. To see whether a program must be run, simply see whether it falls between the last `Timer` event and the current one:

```
If strItems(i).dteTime > dteLastTimeRun And strItems(i).dteTime <= dteCurrentTime
Then
```

The basic formula for determining whether or not an item must be run is `LastTimeRun > DesiredRunTime >= CurrentTime`. Note that one of the comparison operators in the preceding `If` statement is a "less than or equal to" operator (<=). This operator is used to accommodate the odd occasion on which a `Timer` event falls exactly on the scheduled time for an item. If you don't use this operator, events that fall exactly on the time of the `Timer` event are not executed.

Also note that you must store the real time (using the `Timer` function) of both the last `Timer` event and the current one; you cannot simply assume that just the specified `Interval` has passed. This arrangement compensates for the fact that `Timer` events don't always come at exactly the specified intervals, as demonstrated earlier in this chapter.

The *Timer* Function versus the *Timer* Control

In addition to sharing the same name, the `Timer` function and the `Timer` control also have a lot of overlap in their functionality. They both deal with time, and to some degree, can be used to replace each other.

As described earlier in this chapter, delay loops based on the `Timer` function can be used to schedule things. They aren't always the best solution, however, because they require a part of your program to always be spinning while waiting for the next scheduled time. But these delay loops are serviceable and don't depend on getting a `Timer` event from Windows. They are also reasonably accurate (as accurate as anything is in a multitasking operating system).

What may not be obvious is that the Timer control can be used to help in measuring time. By nature, the Timer control is not very good at fine time measurements (remember that it depends on your program being in a state to accept messages to work), but it is good for measuring gross time between parts of an application.

An example of a common use of a Timer control to measure time is in some of the popular disk backup programs that measure the total time the backup took; these programs also split out the amount of time the program took to actually perform the backup versus the time it spent waiting for the user. The following code fragment demonstrates one way to implement this type of timer measurement:

```
Dim sngLastTime As Single        ' the last time we record the time, for
                                   bookkeeping
Dim sngUserTime As Single        ' a bucket to hold the time spent waiting for user
                                   response
Dim sngProgramTime As Single     ' a bucket to hold the time our program has spent
                                   running

Private Sub Timer1_Timer()

    Dim sngElapsedTime As Single, sngCurrentTime As Single

    sngCurrentTime = Timer
        ' decide where to allocate this time
    If iWaitingOnUser Then
        sngUserTime = sngCurrentTime - sngLastTime
    Else
        sngProgramTime = sngCurrentTime - sngLastTime
    End If

    PrintTimes

    sngLastTime = sngCurrentTime
End Sub
```

All this code does is add the elapsed time since the last Timer event to either user time or program time, based on the iWaitingOnUser flag. By simply flipping the iWaitingOnUser flag, you can allocate time to both measurements without adding a lot of code in the application's main logic.

NOTE

The measured time, and its allocation between user and nonuser time, is far from exact because the part of the process (indicated by the iWaitingOnUser flag) that happens to be running when the Timer event hits gets credit for the entire elapsed time since the last Timer event. However, absolute accuracy is not normally a requirement for these types of timers because the elapsed time is simply a gross measurement for the user. This implementation should do fine for most applications.

Note that you still use the Timer function to actually measure the elapsed time. Again, this is because we can't depend on the Timer events to match exactly (or even come close to) the desired intervals.

Summary

The ability to measure and respond to time is an important part of any programming environment. Although it is not a very good choice for rigorous real-time applications, Visual Basic 4.0 provides some handy and easy-to-use tools for time management.

To measure time, Visual Basic 4.0 provides the Timer function to measure time in raw seconds. The Timer function is the basis for nearly all time measurement in Visual Basic. When you have to measure larger amounts of time—even potentially a number of days or weeks—Visual Basic provides the Now function.

To respond to time, Visual Basic 4.0 provides the Timer control, which lets your Visual Basic applications tap into the power of Window's timer capability and write your own animated or scheduling programs.

Error Trapping, Error Handling, and Error Reporting

5

by Richard Buhrer

IN THIS CHAPTER

Programs execute in an uncertain world. Even a completely bug-free program can encounter problems during execution. Any number of interactions between the user, the hardware (host computer and network), and other active programs in a multitasking environment can result in error conditions that stop a Visual Basic program cold.

When Visual Basic programs encounter these error conditions, they terminate immediately and unceremoniously. A user can easily lose important data. Even when the error condition is entirely caused by the user, the user's dissatisfaction and anger is directed toward the software and its author(s).

High quality software must be written with a means for intercepting errors when they occur. At best, software should provide a mechanism for remedying the error condition; at least, software should allow a graceful exit with no data loss. This process is commonly referred to as *error handling*.

An Introduction to Errors

The folks at Microsoft define *runtime errors* as "errors that occur while your code is running and that result from attempts to complete an invalid operation." These errors are reported to the program by the Visual Basic runtime engine as numerical codes. In Visual Basic 4.0, these codes are long integers. The codes (as you are probably aware) fall in the range of –2,147,483,648 to 2,147,483,647—that's approximately 4.3 billion unique errors that the system can report. There is some logic (although not a lot) to the error codes. Table 5.1 summarizes the ranges of error codes.

Table 5.1. The ranges of error codes established by Visual Basic 4.0.

Ranges	Description	Comments
3 to 94	System errors	Miscellaneous errors concerning interactions with memory, disks, and various programming errors like `Return without GoSub`.
260 to 428	DDE and form-related messages	These errors include some important interactions between programs and with Windows, such as `No timer available`.
429 to 451	OLE automation messages	These return information about the external condition of OLE automation servers, whether it can be located, if it doesnt respond in a certain amount of time, and so on. Internal conditions in servers are passed to the client program by adding an internal error code to the constant, `vbObjectError` and returning that as the error number. These are important errors to attend to if you are interested in the OLE automation client and server functions of Visual Basic 4.0.

Ranges	Description	Comments
452 to 521	Miscellaneous messages	These messages cover interactions with resource (RES) files, the Clipboard, printers, and other truly miscellaneous messages.
2055 to 3751	Data access object errors	A large range of database access errors that return error conditions from the MS Access/Jet database engine.
20476 to 28671, 31001, 32751 to 32766	Common dialog control messages	These messages are spread out over a wide range of numerical values; not a sign of careful logic in assigning error numbers.
30000 to 30017	Grid messages	Error messages from the Visual Basic grid control.
31003 to 31039	OLE control	Messages from the OLE control for Visual Basic 4.0.
32001 to 32015	DB grid messages	Error messages for the Visual Basic data-bound grid control.

The Basics of Error Handling

There are really three activities that make up error handling:

- **Trapping the error.** Disabling the compiler's normal error responses.
- **Handling the error.** Responding to the error condition in a more specific sense with corrections or presenting the user with information and instructions for correcting the problem.
- **Reporting the error.** Reporting the error condition back to the compiler for default processing if the software cannot respond.

A common example of an error condition is addressing a floppy disk drive with no disk in it. In this case, *trapping the error* means intercepting the error before Visual Basic terminates the program. In this situation, the error is Error 71, `Disk not ready`. *Handling the error* simply means instructing the user to place a disk in the drive or to close the drive door and then instructing the program to resume processing. If the error is unexpected or unrecoverable, that is, something the error handler cannot process, then the next step is *reporting the error*. This means returning the error condition to the default error-handling routines of the compiler (which cause, in this case, an unceremonious termination of the program).

There is a set of language constructs for error processing that have been present in various dialects of Basic for a number of years. Visual Basic 4.0 supports these legacy tools with which you may already be familiar. Error trapping is enabled by using the `On Error` construct, as follows:

```
On Error Goto Label1
... Error prone actions
On Error Goto 0
```

`On Error ...` is the statement that turns error handling on and off. The `On Error` statement has three forms:

- `On Error Goto` *label or line number* redirects errors from the default processing of Visual Basic to the programmer provided error handler which should follow the *label:* line or start with the *line number* line in code. The endless debate about using `Goto` does not pertain here; this is the fundamental way to manage error handling in Visual Basic.

- `On Error Resume Next` redirects the compiler to resume processing at the next line of code after the one that caused the error (see "Inline Error Handling," later in this chapter.)

- `On Error Goto 0` (zero) is a vestige of the days when Basic required line numbers. This construct returns responsibility for the management of errors back to the compiler defaults and resets or clears any errors reported before this line of code executes.

Most error-handling routines are variations on the following code skeleton:

```
Label1:
      Select Case Err
        ...Case X       ' an anticipated error
               'Fix the error
               Resume
            Case Else 'Unanticipated Errors
               Msg$ = Error$(Err)
               MsgBox Msg$
                Error Err
      End Select
Exit Sub 'or Function
```

After the label, error handling code often uses some branching structure (`If...Then...Else...End If` or `Select Case`) to process the anticipated errors; it also uses a default clause (`Else` or `Case Else`). Information about the nature of the error is retrieved from the system `Err` object that contains a long integer.

CAUTION

The nature of the system `Err` object/value is one of the big changes in Visual Basic 4.0. In Visual Basic 3.0 and earlier, the `Err` value was a global system variable of type integer. In Visual Basic 4.0, it is an OLE object with a default property of `Number` (a long integer).

Review your error-handling code in legacy code; at the least, you should change to `Long` the type of the variables used to access the `Err` value. If you don't do this, you face the possibility of generating an error (runtime error # 6, `Overflow`) in your error handler. This is not a pretty thought. The good news is that Visual Basic now has room for a much richer error-handling capability; it gives programmers the ability to identify and process errors that occur in OLE objects outside Visual Basic; it also gives programmers the ability to use the error-handling system to process programmer-defined, application-specific errors.

The `Error[$]()` function returns what Microsoft calls a *descriptive string* (these strings are still rather cryptic and may not give the programmer or the user much helpful information if the programmer relies on them solely for the information returned to the user). The `Error` statement returns the error condition to the compiler's default error processing. The syntax of the `Error` statement can take one of two forms:

```
Error Err
Error number
```

This construct is useful for the handling of unanticipated errors in an error handler. Although Visual Basic 4.0 supports both the `Error()` function and the `Error` statement, new features in Visual Basic 4.0 provider richer information and finer control of the default processing of errors. These new features are described in the following section.

New Error-Handling Features in Visual Basic 4.0

Visual Basic 4.0 introduces three new tools for managing errors and retaining the legacy error management functions. The new tools include the `Err` object (for Visual Basic errors), the Errors collection and `Error` object (for data access object errors), and options that customize the development environment's error handling behavior.

CAUTION

Although legacy code should execute correctly because of the design of the new `Err` object, it's always wise to test error-handling routines in the Visual Basic 4.0 environment.

The *Err* Object

The new `Err` object, like any OLE object, exposes properties and methods for reporting and responding to error conditions. Table 5.2 lists the properties of the `Err` object; Table 5.3 lists the methods of the `Err` object.

Table 5.2. `Err` object properties.

Property	Description
Number	The number identifying the error. This the default property of the `Err` object.
Description	The descriptive name associated with an error.
Source	The name of the object or application in which the error originated.
HelpFile	A fully qualified path to a Windows Help file.
HelpContext	A Context ID referring to a specific topic in a help file.
LastDLLError	Passes an error value returned from a dynamic link library called using the `Declare` syntax. Only available in the 32-bit version of Visual Basic (because of the error reporting capabilities of the underlying operating systems).

Table 5.3. `Err` object methods.

Method	Description
Raise	Generates a runtime error.
Clear	Resets the `Err` object, erasing any earlier error information.

WHY RAISE ERRORS?

The `Err` object gives much finer control over error reporting. Some of the potential uses are:

- **Testing your error handling code.** Set a breakpoint in your code in a `sub`, `function`, or `property` procedure where error trapping is enabled. When the program stops, you can raise error conditions simply by typing lines such as these in the Debug window

  `Err.Raise 123`

  Press the Run button or F5 and see how your error handler works.

- **Communicating between modules in your program.** If an activity in one module (for example, reading in the contents of a text file) depends on the successful completion of an activity in another module (for example, opening the file), pass information about the success or failure of that activity by using the `Raise` or `Clear` method of the `Err` object.

■ **Replacing cryptic error messages.** You can replace the less-than-cordial and informative error messages provided by Microsoft. Take, for example, Error number 71: `Drive not ready`. Now for the experienced user, it might not present a problem if you passed this message in a message box. But for less experienced users, a little hand-holding might be appropriate. You might want an error message like:

```
Excuse me, there's a little problem here: One of three things is probably wrong.
1)You might have chosen the A: drive when you meant the B: drive (or vice versa).
2)You've forgotten to put the floppy disk in the drive. Or 3)You haven't turned
the little lever on the drive up or down (closing the drive door).
```

You would build this string in a variable, for example: `strExhaustivelyPolite` and send it as a parameter to the `Raise` method:

```
Err.Raise Number:=71, Description:=strExhaustivelyPolite
```

The syntax for the `Raise` method is shown here:

```
object.Raise(Number[, Source[, Description[, HelpFile[, HelpContext]]]])
```

Note that only the first parameter, `Number`, is required. The syntax also supports named arguments. Because the default property of the Err object is the `Number` property, code using the `Error()` function and the `Error` statement still executes correctly.

TIP

The `MsgBox[()]` construct in Visual Basic 4.0 has the same capabilities as the `MsgBox[()]` construct in Visual Basic for Applications. The extended syntax is as follows:

```
MsgBox(prompt[, buttons][, title][, helpfile, context])
```

Note that `helpfile` and `context` parameters have been added. When a `helpfile` name and a `helpfile` construct are specified, the resulting message box responds to the F1 key by launching Windows Help and displaying the help context to the user. This is done without your having to use WinHelp API calls in your own application.

Consequently, you can use the following code to launch a message box:

```
Answer = MsgBox( Prompt:=Err.Description _
                          Buttons:=vbYesNO + vbCritical _
                          Title:= "Error Number " & Err.Number _
                          Helpfile:= Err.Helpfile _
                          Context:=Err.Context)
If Answer = vbYes Then ....
```

NOTE

Visual Basic 4.0 embraces the OLE 2.0 model of objects. For example, the font properties of controls in Visual Basic 3.0 and earlier (FontName, FontSize, FontBold, and so on) have been replaced by a Font object with properties (Name, Size, Bold, and so on).

Consider the following code for Visual Basic 3.0:

```
MyControl.FontName = "Arial"
MyControl.FontSize = 10
MyControl.FontBold = True
Code end
```

It is replaced by this code in Visual Basic 4.0:

```
With MyControl.Font
        .Name = "Arial"
        .Size = 10
        .Bold = True
End With
```

See Chapter 16, "OLE for the First Time," for more information on objects and their uses.

The *Error* Object and Errors Collection

The Error object reports data access object errors and is very similar to the Err object in its structure. The differences are that the Error object has no LastDLLError property and no Raise or Clear methods. Table 5.4 describes the properties of the Error object.

Table 5.4. Error object properties.

Property	Description
Number	The number identifying the error. This the default property of the Error object.
Description	The descriptive name associated with an error.
Source	The name of the object or application in which the error originated.
HelpFile	A fully qualified path to a Windows Help file.
HelpContext	A Context ID referring to a specific topic in a help file.

The Errors collection belongs to the DBEngine object. When a data access action occurs, the collection is populated with all the occurring errors. When another data access action occurs, the collection is emptied and repopulated with any new errors. Like all collections, the Errors collection has only one property: Count. By examining the Count property of the Errors collection, you can determine whether the data access action executed without error:

```
If DBEngine.Errors.Count <> 0 then
... process errors....
End If
```

Environment Options

Environment options that customize error handling are located in the Advanced tab of the Options dialog box (see Figure 5.1). To access the Options dialog box, choose Tools | Options. The error-handling options are listed here:

- Break on All Errors
- Break in OLE Server
- Break on Unhandled Errors

FIGURE 5.1.

The Advanced tab of the Options dialog box.

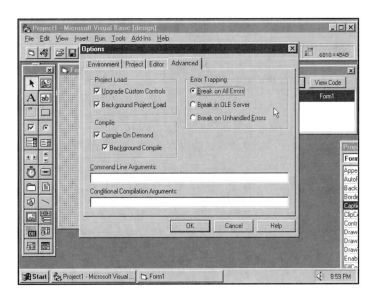

The Break on All Errors option causes the development environment to switch from Run to Break mode whenever any error occurs—whether or not an error handler is active. This setup allows the programmer to identify the occurrence of errors even when the error handler is active. Break on All Errors can be especially useful for developing and debugging the error-handling routines.

The Break on Unhandled Errors option is most useful in later debugging and testing of an application, when the programmer is more confident of the error-handling routines and is more interested in unhandled errors.

The Break in OLE Server option is most useful when debugging OLE servers created in Visual Basic. The *object application* here is another instance of Visual Basic, in which the OLE server is running in the development environment's Run mode while a test client is being run in the first instance of Visual Basic. If an error condition in the client application occurs, the server application breaks at its current position.

NOTE

Visual Basic 4.0 can be run in multiple instances (see Figure 5.2); Visual Basic 3.0 and earlier can be run only in one instance.

FIGURE 5.2.

Windows 95 with two instances of Visual Basic running.

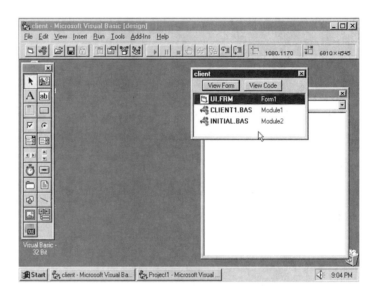

Design Issues in Error Handling

The tools and mechanics of error handling are, unfortunately, just the tip of the iceberg. There are basically three types of error handling: Inline, Local, and Centralized. The following sections explore the techniques of these different types of error handling and some of the design issues that make one type more appropriate than another in particular situations.

CAUTION

The three stages of error handling (trapping, handling, and reporting) and the three types of error handling (inline, local, and centralized) are separate concepts. Any of the three types provide all the services of the three stages.

Inline Error Handling

Inline error handling disables the default error handling of Visual Basic and checks for errors after each line of error-prone code. This emulates the behavior of languages that do not raise exceptions like the C language. C was designed to give the programmer ultimate freedom (and consequently ultimate responsibility) for the code he or she writes. Therefore, C programmers have the ability to totally ignore most if not all of the error conditions that occur in the course of execution (at his or her own risk, I hasten to add). In C you must deliberately check for errors when you expect them to occur, which is to say that you handle them inline. In Visual Basic, inline error handling always begins with the On Error Resume Next construct, which causes Visual Basic to continue with the next line of code after an error occurs. There are a variety of strategies for processing errors in this way. Microsoft mentions three in the documentation for Visual Basic to which we add a fourth:

- From Visual Basic, returning error numbers from functions
- Raising Visual Basic errors in functions and handling them in calling procedures
- Returning variants of type Error
- And additionally, anticipatory error checking

Each of these strategies is described in the following sections.

Returning Error Numbers from Functions

In this strategy, errors occurring when processing information in functions are returned as long integers or as variants from the function itself. The initiating procedure turns off error checking. The following code fragments illustrate this approach:

```
Sub DoSomethingImportant(strParameter as String)
    Dim vResult as variant
    On Error Resume Next
    vResult = MessAroundWithStrings(strParameter)
    If vResult <> 0 then 'An error occurred in the function
        ...Handle Errors...
    Else
        ...Continue Processing
    End If
    'You might include this line for completeness but it isn't required
    On Error Goto 0
End Sub

Function MessAroundWithStrings(strAString as String) as Variant
    ...Do processing...
    If Err <> 0 then
        MessAroundWithStrings = Err
    Else
        MessAroundWithStrings = 0
    End If
End Function
```

> **NOTE**
>
> Technically, you do not have to explicitly turn off error handling when you exit a sub or procedure that is controlling error handling. However, it is good technique to do so. If you develop the habit, you won't forget it when it is required.
>
> Another technique that can help reduce errors is to treat the `On Error...` to `On Error Goto 0` lines as a code block like `Do...Loop` or `For...Next`. You should indent the intervening lines to make the block more visually evident (see Figure 5.3).

FIGURE 5.3.

The Visual Basic code window with a block of error-handling code.

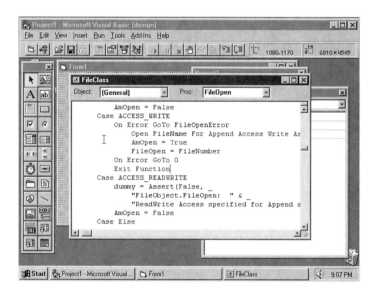

Raising Visual Basic Errors in Functions and Handling Them in Calling Procedures

In this strategy, the root procedure sets error handling to a local or centralized error handler; called subs and functions use the `Raise` method of the `Err` object (preferred) or the `Error` statement to return an error state to the root procedure for handling. In the following code, note that the function `MessAroundWithStrings` uses the `Raise` method of the `Err` object to return error conditions to the calling sub (`DoSomethingImportant`). The same action could be accomplished by using the `Error` statement (a legacy tool) with the `Err` objects default property (`Number`) substituting the line

```
Err.Raise Err.Number
```

with the line

```
Error Err.
```

```
Sub DoSomethingImportant(strParameter as String)
    Dim vResult as String
    On Error Resume Goto ErrorHandler
    vResult = MessAroundWithStrings(strParameter)
    Continue processing
    'You might include this line for completeness but it isn't required
    On Error Goto 0
    Exit Sub
ErrorHandler:
    ...Handle Error
    'If successful
    Resume 'This will resume in the sub where the error occurred
    'If not
    ...Exit gracefully...
End Sub

Function MessAroundWithStrings(strAString as String) as String
    ...Do processing on strAString...
    If Err <> 0 then
        Err.Raise Err.Number
    Else
        MessAroundWithStrings = strAString
    End If
End Function
```

This approach may be the preferred one when a programmer uses programmer-defined errors as a means of communication between procedures or processes in the application. In this way, both system and programmer-defined errors can be handled with the same code.

Returning Variants of Type Error

In this approach to error handling, the root procedure passes a variant as a parameter to the called functions and procedures. If an error occurs, the type of the variant is set to type Error and the value is set to Err.Number. In the following code, we pass a separate variant parameter (vResult) the function. MessAroundWithStrings function stores the error number (0 if none) in this parameter. The calling function checks the variant type of vResult. If it is of type vbError, check the Err object for the current error information and handle the error.

```
Sub DoSomethingImportant(strParameter as String)
    Dim vResult as Variant
    Dim strResult as String
    On Error Resume Next
    strResult = MessAroundWithStrings(strParameter, vResult)
    If VarType(vResult) = vbError then 'An error occurred in the function
        ...Handle Errors...
    Else
        ...Continue Processing
    End If
    'You might include this line for completeness but it isn't required
    On Error Goto 0
End Sub
```

```
Function MessAroundWithStrings(strAString as String, varAResult as Variant) as
➡String
Dim strBuffer as String
strBuffer = strAString
    ...Do processing on strBuffer...
    If Err <> 0 then
       varAResult = CVErr(Err.Number)
    Else
       MessAroundWithStrings = strBuffer
    End If
End Function
```

The variant parameter is another method that is useful for user-defined errors; you can set the value of the vResult parameter to a user-defined error number and set its type to vbError. Using variants of type vbError can be combined with the first strategy (returning the error value in the return parameter). A combined approach might look like the following code. Note that the function returns a variant instead of a string. In checking the return value, check first to see if it is of type vbError. Then handle the error or deal with the string information contained in the variant .

```
Sub DoSomethingImportant(strParameter as String)
    Dim vResult as variant
    On Error Resume Next
    vResult = MessAroundWithStrings(strParameter)
    If VarType(vResult) = vbError then 'An error occurred in the function
       ...Handle Errors...
    Else 'You can treat the variant as a string
       ...Continue Processing
    End If
    'You might include this line for completeness but it isn't required
    On Error Goto 0
End Sub

Function MessAroundWithStrings(strAString as String) as Variant
Dim strBuffer as String
StrBuffer = strAString
    ...Do processing on strBuffer...
    If Err <> 0 then
       MessAroundWithStrings = CVError(Err.Number)
    Else
       MessAroundWithStrings = CVar(strBuffer)
    End If
End Function
```

This is one of the uses of variants in which the overhead in memory and the loss of speed caused by using variants is probably worth the resulting simplicity and convenience of the code.

Anticipatory Error Checking

Of course, one approach to error handling (and probably the wisest approach) is to program in such a way as to identify or eliminate errors before they occur. One approach is to use this Assert() function. It is based on ASSERT macros from the C language. Here is the code for the Assert() function that I have developed and (like the *Twilight Zone*) offer for your consideration:

```
Function Assert (Condition As Boolean, Message As String,
                    Optional HelpFile as Variant, Optional Context as
                    ➥Variant) as Boolean
    If Condition = False Then
#If DebugMode Then
        Dim Style, Title
        Style =  vbStop + vbOK
        Title = "ERROR MESSAGE"
         If IsMissing(HelpFile) or IsMissing(Context) then
             MsgBox Msg, Style, Title
         Else
             MsgBox Msg, Style, Title, HelpFile, Context
        Stop
#Else
        Dim fileName As String, fileNum As Integer
        Dim buf As String
        buf = Date$ & Chr$(9) & Time$ & Chr$(9) & Message
        fileName = App.Path & "\error.log"
        fileNum = FreeFile
       Open fileName For Append As #fileNum
            Print #fileNum, Date$, Time$, Message
            Close #fileNum
        End If
#End If
    Assert = Condition
End Sub
```

NOTE

The `Assert()` function uses some of the new features of Visual Basic 4.0:

- The new variable type Boolean
- Conditional compilation directives
- Optional parameters

Visual Basic 4.0 offers a number of new variable types. Much of this is in response to the 32-bit capability of Visual Basic 4.0 and support for Unicode. In Visual Basic 3.0 and earlier, binary data was manipulated by using variables of type String. This works fine in an ANSI-based system in which characters are only one byte long. When Unicode support is added (Unicode needs two bytes per character), the manipulation of binary data no longer works correctly. Consequently, Visual Basic 4.0 adds a type Byte. You should start using Byte variables for binary data manipulation so that your code can be used across platforms.

Visual Basic now supports conditional compilation directives. These directives always begin with the # (number or pound) sign. Only two directives are supported:

- `#Const` defines a compiler constant.
- `#If...Then #Else` identifies separate blocks of code for selective compilation.

continues

> This conditional compilation feature has at least two major uses: It allows the programmer to compile debug and production executables from the same code. It also allows the programmer to use the same code between 16-bit and 32-bit versions (particularly useful when DLL or Windows API functions are used).
>
> Now you can define optional parameters in your own functions just as they are defined in native Visual Basic functions. Optional parameters must be of type Variant. Consider the Format($) function in native Visual Basic. It takes a numerical expression and converts it to a variant (or string) based on an optional parameter of representing the desired format. In Visual Basic 4.0, you can design your own subs and functions with optional parameters. You do this with (logically enough) the Optional keyword. You can search online help for optional and IsMissing for further information on this technique.

The Assert() function requires a condition parameter and a string parameter for a custom message; it optionally accepts help file and context references. The function returns a Boolean based on the condition parameter. The function is set up so that it goes into Break mode in the Visual Basic IDE after showing an informative message box. In the production executable, the information is written to an error log (so that, if program bombs on a client's computer, you have the information about errors written to disk so that you can fix the problem). The following code snippet shows how the Assert() function can anticipate errors:

```
If Not Assert(FileName <> "", "FileObject.FileRename:  FileName not initialized!")
➥Then
            'Get a valid FileName or exit gracefully
End If
```

If any attempt to open the file follows, the runtime error 76 occurs, Path not found. By checking for this condition, the error is avoided and the program can correct the condition.

Local Error Handling

Local error handling occurs in the procedure itself. The stubs of code discussed in the first part of this chapter on the basics of error handling are examples of localized error handling. Each procedure with error-prone activities has its own error-handling code. Each procedure can raise unanticipated errors, returning them step by step up the call chain for handling by calling procedures. Notice in the following example code how some error-handling code is local to the MessAroundWithStrings function. In the previous examples, the error-handling code was located completely in the calling function DoSomethingImportant.

```
Sub DoSomethingImportant(strParameter as String)
    Dim vResult as variant
    On Error Goto MyHandler
    vResult = MessAroundWithStrings(strParameter)
       ...Continue Processing
    'You might include this line for completeness but it isn't required
    On Error Goto 0
Exit Sub
```

```
MyHandler:...Handle Errors from this Sub and from the function it calls
End Sub

Function MessAroundWithStrings(strAString as String) as String
   Dim strBuffer as String
   On Error Goto SecondHandler
   StrBuffer = strAString
   ...Do processing on strBuffer...
   MessAroundWithStrings = strBuffer
   Exit Function
SecondHandler:
   Select Case Err.Number
      Case X
         ...Handle some errors but pass unhandled errors back to calling procedure:
      Case Else
         Err.Raise Number:=Err.Number
   End If
End Function
```

THE CALL TREE

The *call tree* is an important concept for error handling. Procedures can call other procedures, which in turn can call other procedures... and so on, to several levels deep.

When a procedure enables an error handler, that error handler is in effect for all subsequent procedures that the root procedure calls—as well as for all procedures those procedures call in their turn.

Figure 5.4 displays a rudimentary (and useless) Visual Basic program that shows a series of nested subs and functions; it also shows the Calls dialog box launched by clicking the Calls button on the toolbar, by selecting Tools I Calls, or by pressing Ctrl+L. The Calls dialog box is available only in Break mode.

FIGURE 5.4.

The Calls dialog box.

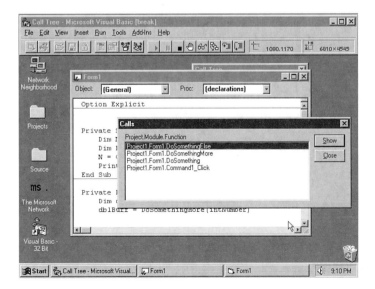

Localized error handling can invoke multiple error handlers in the same procedure, as shown in the following example:

```
Sub DoSomethingImportant(strParameter as String)
   On Error Goto StringHandler
   strParameter = MessAroundWithStrings(strParameter)
      ...Continue Processing
   On Error Goto FileHandler
   Open "Myfile.txt"for Output as #1
   ...Process File
   Close #1
   'You might include this line for completeness but it isn't required
   On Error Goto 0
Exit Sub
StringHandler:
   ...Handle string Errors
   Exit Sub
FileHandler:
   ...Handle file errors
End Sub
```

Centralized Error Handling

The final type of error handling is centralized error handling. Centralized error handling processes all errors through a single error-handling routine. Centralized error handling is difficult to implement in Visual Basic. Theoretically, if you invoke error handling from a Sub Main, you can then redirect all error handling to a centralized routine. However, this makes for a complicated and error-prone error-handling routine.

A more effective way of doing quasi-centralized error handling is to modularize code and have central error-handling code in code (.BAS), form (.FRM), or class (.CLS) modules based on the function and data of those modules. The new class modules of Visual Basic 4.0 present a great opportunity for object-oriented programming in Visual Basic.

One of the aspects of object-oriented programming is encapsulation. *Encapsulation* means isolating the data and processing in one module from all others—that is, creating a black box with clearly defined inputs and outputs. This approach allows you to develop and, more importantly, reuse error-handling code for specific types of processing.

Generating Programmer-Defined Errors

One useful strategy is to establish programmer-defined errors and then use the Visual Basic Err object and error-handling routines to trap and correct these errors. The documentation for Visual Basic 4.0 suggests that programmers define errors based on the vbObjectError offset. At press time, the specific offset of the constant has not been determined. If it is important for you to know the numerical value, you can find it by typing **? vbObjectError** in the Debug window. You should use the constant rather than a hard-coded number to maintain forward compatibility in your code.

The documentation also requires user-defined errors to be in the range of 1 to 65,535. Because this range also includes errors reported from OLE controls you may be using in your application, check the error code ranges of these controls. Nonetheless, you should have a large range of open error codes.

CAUTION

Previous versions of Visual Basic have suggested that user-defined error numbers begin at 65,535 and work downward from there. This means that legacy code with programmer-defined error values must be reviewed for compatibility.

To avoid these problems in the future, define user-defined error messages as constants. Then you only have to edit one range or set of values to update your code. But you probably already do that, right?

Suppose that an application depends on a specific data file (such as an initialization file). When the application determines that the initialization file has been deleted, the code can define and raise an error. When the error handler encounters this error, it can write a default initialization file to disk or prompt the user with a Preferences dialog box to obtain initialization information.

NOTE

Windows 95 and Windows NT recommend that programmers use the system registry to record initialization information rather than using initialization files (*.INI).

Example: A File Class

One thing I have come to hate is adding error-handling code to individual modules that perform file I/O. I also find it difficult to keep the syntax of file I/O forever straight in my head. When Visual Basic 4.0 offered the possibility of developing classes, I thought it was one area that would be very useful to me: developing class wrappers for frequently used code that can be plugged in to any project and accessed with the familiar metaphor of properties and methods. Because file and disk I/O is an especially error-prone activity, it helps to localize error handling for this activity in a single class module.

Ordinary and class modules have their own properties in Visual Basic 4.0. Figure 5.5 shows the Properties window for the `FileClass` class.

In this case, the `FileClass` object has properties of `Instancing` = 2 (Creatable Multiuse), `Public` = False, and `Name` = FileClass. This setup means that the objects of this class can be created and accessed only from within the project using the module. These objects can be created using `Dim` or `GetObject`, and there can be multiple instances of this object in use at the same time. Table 5.5 lists the properties and Table 5.6 lists the methods of the `FileClass` object.

FIGURE 5.5.

The Properties window for the FileClass *module.*

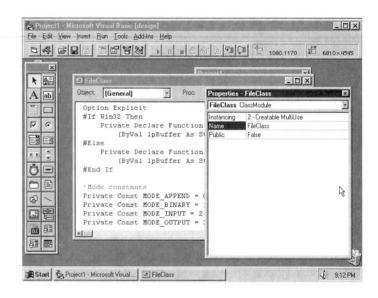

Table 5.5. Properties of a `FileClass` object.

Property (Data Type)	Description
`Name` (String)	Read/Write. This is the fully qualified path to a particular file.
`Path` (String)	Read only. This is the path segment of the filename.
`Title` (String)	Read only. This is the filename segment of the name.
`Mode` (Integer)	Read/Write. This is the mode for which the file is opened. The class supports `Input`, `Output`, `Append`, and `Binary` modes of file access.
`Access` (Integer)	Read/Write. This is the access restriction that you can optionally include in the `Open` syntax. The options include `Read`, `Write`, and `ReadWrite`.
`Length` (Long)	The number of bytes in the file.
`DateTime` (Variant)	Returns the date and time of the last revision of the file.
`FileError` (Long)	The last error returned within the file object.

Table 5.6. Methods of a `FileClass` object.

Method (Returns)	Description
`FileOpen()`	Returns an integer that is the valid file number of the open file.
`FileClose`	Closes the file wrapped in the `FileClass` object.

Method (Returns)	Description
FileMove *strNewPath*	Moves the object's file and resets the object to point at the new location for the file.
FileRename *strNewName*	Renames the object's file and resets the object to point at the new location.
FileDelete	Deletes the object's file from disk and sets a flag to remind the programmer (if necessary) that the file has been deleted.
FileCreate *strNewFile*	Creates a new null file, gives an overwrite warning, and resets the file object to point to the new file.
FileCopy *strNewName[, varRegisterNew]*	Copies the object's file to another location; optionally points the file object to the new instance of the file if the *varRegisterNew* parameter equals TRUE.
FileExists(*strFileName*)	Returns a Boolean indicating whether the specified file exists.

Declarations

The class module begins with the declarations shown in Listing 5.1.

Listing 5.1. Class module declarations.

```
Option Explicit
#If Win32 Then
    Private Declare Function GetWindowsDirectory Lib "kernel32"
        Alias "GetWindowsDirectoryA" (ByVal lpBuffer As String, _
        ByVal nSize As Long) As Long
#Else
    Private Declare Function GetWindowsDirectory Lib "Kernel" _
        (ByVal lpBuffer As String, ByVal nSize As Integer) As Integer
#End If

'Mode constants
Private Const MODE_APPEND = 0
Private Const MODE_BINARY = 1
Private Const MODE_INPUT = 2
Private Const MODE_OUTPUT = 3

'Access constants
Private Const ACCESS_READ = 0
Private Const ACCESS_WRITE = 1
Private Const ACCESS_READWRITE = 2
```

continues

Listing 5.1. continued

```
'File Object MyError Constants
Private Const FOBJ_ERROR_RESUME = 0
Private Const FOBJ_ERROR_RESUMENEXT = 1
Private Const FOBJ_ERROR_FILENAME = 2
Private Const FOBJ_ERROR_UNRECOVERABLE = 3
Private Const FOBJ_ERROR_UNRECOGNIZABLE = 4

'Constants for trappable file I/O errors
Private Const ErrOutOfMemory = 7
Private Const ErrBadFileNameOrNumber = 52
Private Const ErrFileNotFound = 53
Private Const ErrFileAlreadyOpen = 55
Private Const ErrDeviceIO = 57
Private Const ErrFileAlreadyExists = 58
Private Const ErrDiskFull = 61
Private Const ErrBadFileName = 64
Private Const ErrTooManyFiles = 67
Private Const ErrPermissionDenied = 68
Private Const ErrDiskNotReady = 71
Private Const ErrCantRename = 74
Private Const ErrPathFileAccessError = 75
Private Const ErrPathNotFound = 76
'Internal Property Variables
Private FilePath As String
Private FileTitle As String
Private FileName As String
Private FileMode As Integer
Private FileAccess As Integer
Private FileNumber As Integer
Private LastError As Long
'Flag variables
Private AmOpen As Boolean
Private AmDeleted As Boolean
```

This is pretty standard stuff: constants are defined to increase the readability and maintainability of the code. Two Visual Basic 4.0-specific features are used here: The first is the conditional compilation option; declarations are included for both the 16-bit and the 32-bit APIs. This way the module can be added to any project for either platform and compile correctly.

The second feature is the use of Public (new to Visual Basic 4.0 from VBA) instead of Global, and the deliberate use of Private variables accessed through Property methods.

Utility Subs and Functions

At the heart (not at the head) of the module are private utility functions used by the public methods (see Listing 5.2).

Listing 5.2. Private utility subs and functions.

```
'************************************************************
'
'    Private Utility Functions
'
'
'
'************************************************************

Private Sub ProcessPathTitleAndName(newName As String)

    Dim BackSlash As Integer
    If InStr(newName, "\") Then
        BackSlash = RInstr(0, newName, "\")
        FilePath = Left$(newName, BackSlash - 1)
        FileTitle = Mid$(newName, BackSlash + 1)
    ElseIf InStr(newName, ":") Then
        Dim CurDrive As String
        Dim TargetDrive As String
        TargetDrive = Left$(newName, 1)
        CurDrive = CurDir$
        If Left$(CurDrive, 1) <> TargetDrive Then
            ChDrive TargetDrive
            FilePath = CurDir$
            ChDrive CurDrive
        Else
            FilePath = CurDir$
        End If
        FileTitle = Mid$(newName, InStr(newName, ":") + 1)
    Else
        FilePath = CurDir$
        FileTitle = newName
    End If
    FileName = FilePath & "\" & FileTitle

End Sub

'=========================================================

Private Sub DoFileCopy(Source As String, Target As String, _
        Optional Overwrite As Variant)

    Dim ErrorMsg As String, SourceNum As Integer, TargetNum As Integer
    Dim buffer As String, TheLength As Long

    ErrorMsg = "FileObject.DoFileCopy: Attempting "
    ErrorMsg = ErrorMsg & "copy/move operation on non-existent file!"
    If Assert(FileExists(Source), ErrorMsg) Then
        SourceNum = FreeFile: TargetNum = FreeFile
        On Error GoTo DoFileCopyError
            Open Source For Binary Access Read As SourceNum
            TheLength = LOF(SourceNum)
            Open Source For Binary Access Read As SourceNum
            Open Target For Binary Access Write As TargetNum
```

continues

Listing 5.2. continued

```
            On Error GoTo 0
            If TheLength < 60000 Then
                'Take the file in bits
                Do Until TheLength < 60000
                    buffer = String$(0, 60000)
                    Get SourceNum, , buffer
                    Put TargetNum, , buffer
                    TheLength = TheLength - Len(buffer)
                Loop
                buffer = String$(0, TheLength)
                Get SourceNum, , buffer
                Put TargetNum, , buffer
            Else
                buffer = String$(0, TheLength)
                Get #SourceNum, , buffer
                Put TargetNum, , buffer
            End If
            Close #SourceNum
            Close #TargetNum
        End If
        Exit Sub

DoFileCopyError:
        Dim action As Integer, ErrNumber As Integer
        action = Errors()
        Select Case action
            Case 0
                Resume
            Case 1
                Resume Next
            Case 2, 3
                Exit Sub
            Case Else
                ErrNumber = Err.Number
                Err.Raise ErrNumber
    End Select

End Sub

'============================================================

Sub DeletedMsg()

    Dim msg, style
    msg = "You have deleted the file """ & FileName & "."""
    msg = msg & "  You must reinitialize the FileObject with a "
    msg = msg & "new valid file name before proceeding!"
    style = vbCritical + vbOKOnly
    MsgBox msg, style, App.Title

End Sub

'============================================================

Private Function OverwriteWarning(FileName As String) As Integer

    Dim msg As String, style As Integer
```

```
    msg = "The file, " & FileName & ", already exists in the current "
    msg = msg & "directory.  Overwrite it?"
    style = vbQuestion Or vbYesNo
    OverwriteWarning = MsgBox(msg, style, App.Title)

End Function

'============================================================

Private Function RInstr(Start As Integer, Source As String, _
    Goal As String) As Integer

    Dim Index As Integer, N As Integer

    If Start <> 0 Then Index = Start Else Index = Len(Source)
    For N = Index To 1 Step -1
        If Mid$(Source, N, 1) = Goal Then
            RInstr = N
            Exit Function
        End If
    Next
    RInstr = 0

End Function
```

Centralized Error-Handling Function

The module uses the centralized error-handling function shown in Listing 5.3.

Listing 5.3. The centralized error-handling function.

```
Private Function Errors() As Integer

    Dim MsgType As Integer, msg As String, response As Integer
    Dim NewFileNameNeeded As Boolean
    Dim DoResume As Boolean
    Dim DoResumeNext As Boolean
    'Return Value    Meaning     Return Value    Meaning
    '     0          Resume          2           Filename Error
    '     1          Resume Next     3           Unrecoverable Error
    '                                4           Unrecognized Error
    MsgType = vbExclamation
    Select Case Err.Number
        Case ErrOutOfMemory '7
            msg = "The operating system reports that there is not "
            msg = msg & "enough memory to complete this operation.  "
            msg = msg & "You can try closing some other applications and then "
            msg = msg & "click Retry to try again or you can click Cancel to exit."
            MsgType = vbExclamation + vbRetryCancel
            DoResume = True
            'Resume or Exit
```

continues

Listing 5.3. continued

```
Case ErrBadFileNameOrNumber, ErrBadFileName
    msg = "That file name is illegal!"
    NewFileNameNeeded = True
    DoResume = True
    'Resume
Case ErrFileNotFound
    msg = "That file does not exist.  Create it?"
    MsgType = vbExclamation + vbOKCancel
    DoResumeNext = True
    'Resume Next
Case ErrFileAlreadyOpen
    msg = "That file is already in use."
    MsgType = vbExclamation + vbRetryCancel
    NewFileNameNeeded = True
    'New Name
Case ErrDeviceIO
    msg = "Internal disk error."
    MsgType = vbExclamation + vbRetryCancel
    DoResume = True
    'Resume
Case ErrFileAlreadyExists
    msg = "A file with that name already exists.  "
    msg = msg & "Replace it?"
    MsgType = vbExclamation + vbOKCancel
    NewFileNameNeeded = True
    'New Name
Case ErrDiskFull
    msg = "This disk is full.  Continue?"
    MsgType = vbExclamation + vbOKCancel
    DoResume = True
    'Resume
Case ErrTooManyFiles
    msg = "The operating system reports that too "
    msg = msg & "many files are currently open.  You "
    msg = msg & "can try closing some other applications "
    msg = msg & "and then try again."
    MsgType = vbExclamation + vbRetryCancel
    DoResume = True
    'Resume
Case ErrPermissionDenied
    msg = "You have tried to write to a file that is in "
    msg = msg & "use or is designated as read-only."
    NewFileNameNeeded = True
    'New Name
Case ErrDiskNotReady
    msg = "Insert a disk in the drive and close the door."
    MsgType = vbExclamation + vbOKCancel
    DoResume = True
    'Resume
Case ErrPathFileAccessError, ErrPathNotFound
    msg = "The operating system cannot locate this file on "
    msg = msg & "this path.  Check to make sure that the file "
    msg = msg & "name and path have been entered correctly "
    msg = msg & "and then try again."
    NewFileNameNeeded = True
```

```
        Case Else
            Errors = 4
            Exit Function
    End Select
    response = MsgBox(msg, MsgType, "File Error")
    Select Case response
        Case vbRetry, vbOK
            If NewFileNameNeeded Then
                LastError = FOBJ_ERROR_FILENAME
            ElseIf DoResume Then
                LastError = FOBJ_ERROR_RESUME
            ElseIf DoResumeNext Then
                LastError = FOBJ_ERROR_RESUMENEXT
            Else
                LastError = FOBJ_ERROR_UNRECOVERABLE
            End If
        Case Else
            LastError = FOBJ_ERROR_UNRECOGNIZABLE
    End Select
    Errors = LastError

End Function
```

The `Errors()` function is adapted from the example code for centralized error handling in the *Visual Basic 4.0 Programmer's Guide*. It is changed in a few regards: it relies on constants and is a little more readable. The return values are revised so that the function can instruct various calling procedures to try for a new filename if that is an easy solution for the error condition. The function also stores the handler's assessment to a variable called `LastError`.

Properties

The properties of the `FileClass` object are accessed with the Property methods shown in Listing 5.4.

Listing 5.4. The Property procedures.

```
'*******************************************************
'
'    Property Procedures
'        Path, Name, Mode, Access,
'        Length, DateTime,
'
'
'*******************************************************

Public Property Get Path() As String

    If AmDeleted Then
        DeletedMsg
        Exit Property
```

continues

Listing 5.4. continued

```
    End If
    Path = FilePath

End Property

'=========================================================

Public Property Let Name(newName As String)

    If Not FileExists(FileName) Then
        Dim msg, style, answer
        msg = "The file, """ & newName & """ does not exist.  "
        msg = msg & "Create it?"
        style = vbQuestion Or vbYesNo
        answer = MsgBox(msg, style, App.Title)
        If answer = vbYes Then
            FileCreate newName
        Else
            Exit Property
        End If
    Else
        ProcessPathTitleAndName newName 'Checks for Drive, Directory, etc.
    End If

End Property

'=========================================================

Public Property Get Name() As String

    If AmDeleted Then
        DeletedMsg
        Exit Property
    End If
    Name = FileName

End Property

'=========================================================

Public Property Get Title() As String

    If AmDeleted Then
        DeletedMsg
        Exit Property
    End If
    Title = FileTitle

End Property

'=========================================================

Public Property Let Mode(NewMode As Integer)

    If AmDeleted Then
        DeletedMsg
        Exit Property
    End If
```

```
      If NewMode <> FileMode Then
          FileMode = NewMode
          If AmOpen Then
              Close #FileNumber
              FileOpen
          End If
      End If

End Property

'================================================================

Public Property Get Mode() As Integer

      If AmDeleted Then
          DeletedMsg
          Exit Property
      End If
      Mode = FileMode

End Property

'================================================================

Public Property Let Access(NewAccess As Integer)

      If AmDeleted Then
          DeletedMsg
          Exit Property
      End If
      If NewAccess <> FileAccess Then
          FileAccess = NewAccess
          If AmOpen Then
              Close #FileNumber
              FileOpen
          End If
      End If

End Property

'================================================================

Public Property Get Access() As Integer

      If AmDeleted Then
          DeletedMsg
          Exit Property
      End If
      Access = FileAccess

End Property

'================================================================

Public Property Get FileError() As Integer
      FileError = LastError
End Property
'================================================================
```

continues

Listing 5.4. continued

```
Public Property Get Length() As Long

    If AmDeleted Then
        DeletedMsg
        Exit Property
    End If
    Dim FileNum As Integer

    If Assert(FileName <> "", _
            "FileObject.Length:  FileName not initialized!") Then
        FileNum = FreeFile
        Open FileName For Binary Access Read As #FileNum
        Length = LOF(FileNum)
        Close FileNum
    End If

End Property

'================================================================

Public Property Get DateTime() As Variant

    If AmDeleted Then
        DeletedMsg
        Exit Property
    End If
    If Not Assert(FileName <> "", _
            "FileObject.FileOpen:  FileName not initialized!") Then
        Exit Property
    End If
    If Assert(FileExists(FileName), _
            "FileObject.DateTime:  FileName not initialized!") Then
        DateTime = FileDateTime(FileName)
    End If

End Property
```

> **NOTE**
>
> Visual Basic Applications Edition had support for the new Property procedures—and now, so does Visual Basic 4.0. `Property` is now a keyword and represents a new class of procedures along with `Sub` and `Function` procedures.

Methods

Finally, there are the method subs and functions. Note that subs and functions become methods in a class module simply by being declared as `Public` (see Listing 5.5).

Listing 5.5. The public methods of the `FileClass` object:

```
'************************************************************
'
'    Methods
'
'      FileOpen, FileClose, FileMove, FileRename,
'      FileDelete and FileError
'
'************************************************************

Public Function FileOpen() As Integer

    If AmDeleted Then
        DeletedMsg
        Exit Function
    End If

    If Not Assert(FileName <> "", _
            "FileObject.FileOpen:  FileName not initialized!") Then
        Exit Function
    End If

    If AmOpen Then Close #FileNumber
    Dim dummy As Variant
    FileNumber = FreeFile
    Select Case FileMode
        Case MODE_APPEND
            Select Case FileAccess
                Case ACCESS_READ
                    dummy = Assert(False, _
                        "FileObject.FileOpen:  " & _
                        "ReadOnly Access specified for Append action!")
                    AmOpen = False
                Case ACCESS_WRITE
                    On Error GoTo FileOpenError
                    Open FileName For Append Access Write As #FileNumber
                    AmOpen = True
                    FileOpen = FileNumber
                    On Error GoTo 0
                    Exit Function
                Case ACCESS_READWRITE
                    dummy = Assert(False, _
                        "FileObject.FileOpen:  " & _
                        "ReadWrite Access specified for Append action!")
                    AmOpen = False
                Case Else
            End Select
        Case MODE_BINARY
            Select Case FileAccess
                Case ACCESS_READ
                    On Error GoTo FileOpenError
                    Open FileName For Binary Access Write As #FileNumber
                    AmOpen = True
                    FileOpen = FileNumber
                    On Error GoTo 0
                    Exit Function
```

continues

Listing 5.5. continued

```
            Case ACCESS_WRITE
                On Error GoTo FileOpenError
                Open FileName For Binary Access Write As #FileNumber
                AmOpen = True
                FileOpen = FileNumber
                On Error GoTo 0
                Exit Function
            Case ACCESS_READWRITE
                On Error GoTo FileOpenError
                Open FileName For Binary Access Read Write As #FileNumber
                AmOpen = True
                FileOpen = FileNumber
                On Error GoTo 0
                Exit Function
            Case Else
        End Select
    Case MODE_INPUT
        Select Case FileAccess
            Case ACCESS_READ
                On Error GoTo FileOpenError
                Open FileName For Input Access Read As #FileNumber
                AmOpen = True
                FileOpen = FileNumber
                On Error GoTo 0
                Exit Function
            Case ACCESS_WRITE
                dummy = Assert(False, _
                    "FileObject.FileOpen:  " & _
                    "Attempting Access Write with Input mode!")
                Exit Function
            Case ACCESS_READWRITE
                dummy = Assert(False, _
                    "FileObject.FileOpen:  " & _
                    "Attempting Access Read Write with Input mode!")
                Exit Function
            Case Else
        End Select
    Case MODE_OUTPUT
        Select Case FileAccess
            Case ACCESS_READ
                dummy = Assert(False, _
                    "FileObject.FileOpen: " & _
                    "Attempting Access Read with Output mode!")
                Exit Function
            Case ACCESS_WRITE
                On Error GoTo FileOpenError
                Open FileName For Output Access Write As #FileNumber
                AmOpen = True
                FileOpen = FileNumber
                On Error GoTo 0
                Exit Function
            Case ACCESS_READWRITE
                dummy = Assert(False, _
                    "FileObject.FileOpen:  " & _
                    "Attempting Access Read Write with Output mode!")
                Exit Function
```

```
                    Case Else
                End Select
            Case Else
                dummy = Assert(False, _
                    "FileObject.FileOpen:  " & _
                    "Incorrect File Mode parameter set!")
                Exit Function
        End Select
FileOpenError:
    Dim action As Integer, ErrNumber As Integer
    action = Errors()
    Select Case action
        Case 0
            Resume
        Case 1
            Resume Next
        Case 2, 3
            Exit Function
        Case Else
            ErrNumber = Err.Number
            Err.Raise ErrNumber
            Err.Clear
    End Select

End Function

'==========================================================

Public Sub FileClose()

    If AmDeleted Then
        DeletedMsg
        Exit Sub
    End If

    If Not Assert(FileName <> "", _
        "FileObject.FileOpen:  FileName not initialized!") Then
        Exit Sub
    End If

    If AmOpen Then
        Close #FileNumber
        FileNumber = 0
        AmOpen = False
    End If

End Sub

'==========================================================

Public Sub FileMove(NewPath As String)

    If Not Assert(FileName <> "", _
        "FileObject.FileMove:  FileName not initialized!") Then
        Exit Sub
    End If
```

continues

Listing 5.5. continued

```
    'Check Drive Spec
    Dim newName As String, SourceNum As Integer, TargetNum As Integer
    If Right$(NewPath, 1) = "\" Then     'Get the path in shape
        newName = NewPath & FileTitle
    Else
        newName = NewPath & "\" & FileTitle
    End If
    If InStr(NewPath, ":") Then     'There is a drive spec included
        If Left$(newName, 1) <> Left$(FileName, 1) Then
            'Different drive, Name command won't work
            DoFileCopy FileName, newName
            Kill FileName
            ProcessPathTitleAndName newName
        End If
    Else
        On Error GoTo FileMoveError
        Name FileName As newName
        On Error GoTo 0
        ProcessPathTitleAndName newName
    End If
    Exit Sub

FileMoveError:
    Dim action As Integer, ErrNumber As Integer
    action = Errors()
    Select Case action
        Case 0
            Resume
        Case 1
            Resume Next
        Case 2, 3
            Exit Sub
        Case Else
            ErrNumber = Err.Number
            Err.Raise ErrNumber
            Err.Clear
    End Select

End Sub

'================================================================

Public Sub FileRename(newName As String)

    If Not Assert(FileName <> "", _
        "FileObject.FileRename:  FileName not initialized!") Then
        Exit Sub
    End If

    On Error GoTo FileRenameError
    If InStr(newName, ":") Then    'there is a drive spec
        If Left$(newName, 1) <> Left$(FileName, 1) Then
            DoFileCopy FileName, newName
            Kill FileName
        Else
            Name FileName As newName
        End If
```

```
        Else
            Name FileName As newName
        End If
        On Error GoTo 0
        ProcessPathTitleAndName newName

FileRenameError:
        Dim action As Integer, ErrNumber As Integer
        action = Errors()
        Select Case action
            Case 0
                Resume
            Case 1
                Resume Next
            Case 2, 3
                Exit Sub
            Case Else
                ErrNumber = Err.Number
                Err.Raise ErrNumber
                Err.Clear
        End Select

End Sub

'================================================================

Public Sub FileDelete()

    If Not Assert(FileName <> "", _
        "FileObject.FileOpen:  FileName not initialized!") Then
        Exit Sub
    End If

    If AmOpen Then Close #FileNumber
    If AmDeleted Then
        DeletedMsg
        Exit Sub
    End If

    Kill FileName

    AmDeleted = True
    FileNumber = 0


End Sub

'=================================================

Public Sub FileCreate(newName As String)

    Dim FileNum As Integer
    Dim choice As Integer

    If FileExists(newName) Then
        choice = OverwriteWarning(newName)
        If choice = vbNo Then Exit Sub
    End If
```

continues

Listing 5.5. continued

```
    FileNum = FreeFile
    Open newName For Output As #FileNum
    Close FileNum

    ProcessPathTitleAndName newName

End Sub

'====================================================

Public Sub FileCopy(newName As String, Optional RegisterNew As Variant)

    If Not Assert(FileName <> "", _
        "FileObject.FileOpen:  FileName not initialized!") Then
        Exit Sub
    End If

    DoFileCopy FileName, newName

    If Not IsMissing(RegisterNew) And RegisterNew = True Then
        ProcessPathTitleAndName newName
    End If

End Sub
```

Class Initialization and Termination Code

The functions shown in Listing 5.6 are called when an instance of type `FileClass` is created or destroyed.

Listing 5.6. Functions used when creating or destroying an object of type `FileClass`.

```
'************************************************************
'
'    Class Initialization and Destruction
'
'
'
'************************************************************

Private Sub Class_Initialize()

    Dim nResult As Integer
    Dim buffer As String

    'Initializes the object to an ubiquitous file
    'This works in tandem with the inifile object
    'by setting things to point to WIN.INI
    FileTitle = "WIN.INI"
    buffer = String$(200, 0)
    nResult = GetWindowsDirectory(buffer, Len(buffer))
```

```
        FilePath = Left$(buffer, nResult)
        FileName = FilePath & "\" & FileTitle
        FileMode = MODE_BINARY
        FileAccess = ACCESS_READWRITE

End Sub

Private Sub Class_Terminate()
    If FileNumber <> 0 Then
        Close #FileNumber
    End If
End Sub
```

When a file object is first initialized, the default filename, mode, and access values are set. When the object is terminated (that is, when the object variable is Set equal to Nothing or when the object variable goes out of scope), if a file is open, that file is closed.

How To Use the *FileClass* Object

To use a FileClass object in your programs, you follow these basic steps:

1. Add the FileClass.CLS file to your project.

2. Add the Assert() function to a module in your project.

3. Dim an object variable of type FileClass.

4. Use the new keyword in the dim statement or use the GetObject() function to create an instance of FileClass.

After these steps are completed, you can address the FileClass object in your code with a sequence like the following, which opens an initialization file and populates an array with all the section names in the file:

```
With myFile
        .Access = ACCESS_READ
        .Mode = MODE_INPUT
    End With
    FileNum = myFile.FileOpen()
    'Clear and refill the Sections array
    Erase mySections
    counter = 0
    Do
        Line Input #FileNum, buf
        If Len(buf) <> 0 Then
            If Left$(buf, 1) = "[" Then ' it's a section name
                ReDim Preserve mySections(counter + 1)
                Index = InStr(2, buf, "]") - 2
                mySections(counter) = Mid$(buf, 2, Index)
                counter = counter + 1
            End If
        End If
    Loop Until EOF(FileNum)
    myFile.FileClose
```

Public Constant Declarations

To take full advantage of the module, you must include the following declarations in a form or module of your program:

```
'Mode constants
Public Const MODE_APPEND = 0
Public Const MODE_BINARY = 1
Public Const MODE_INPUT = 2
Public Const MODE_OUTPUT = 3

'Access constants
Public Const ACCESS_READ = 0
Public Const ACCESS_WRITE = 1
Public Const ACCESS_READWRITE = 2

'File Object MyError Constants
Public Const FOBJ_ERROR_RESUME = 0
Public Const FOBJ_ERROR_RESUMENEXT = 1
Public Const FOBJ_ERROR_FILENAME = 2
Public Const FOBJ_ERROR_UNRECOVERABLE = 3
Public Const FOBJ_ERROR_UNRECOGNIZABLE = 4
```

This inconvenience is necessary because class modules in Visual Basic 4.0 cannot contain public constant declarations; to use constants, you have to declare them elsewhere in your application.

Summary

Error handling is an important aspect of professional-quality programming. It protects the users of your software from the mystifying disappearance of the program and from the frustrating loss of data. The basic mechanisms of error handling in Visual Basic 4.0 are similar to earlier versions and other flavors of the Basic language. Visual Basic 4.0 gives richer and finer control of error reporting through the Err object, the Error object, and Errors collection for data access and with new programming environment options. Finally, design issues like the types of errors anticipated and the modular design of the application determine which pattern of error handling (Inline, Local, or Centralized) is best for a particular situation.

Effective User Interface Design

6

by L. Michael Van Hoozer, Jr.

IN THIS CHAPTER

User interface design is probably the most overlooked subject among application developers. Most technical books that discuss development tools rarely include a chapter on this topic. But user interface design is even more important now that Windows 95 has changed the way we look at Windows.

Windows 95 has made a transformational change and has become more intuitive and easier to use. Visual Basic 4.0 has also made substantial changes to support the look and feel of this new and intriguing interface. This chapter focuses on user interface design for Windows 95 and how you can use Visual Basic 4.0 as a development tool for supporting this interface.

Principles of User Interface Design

Although the Windows 95 user interface has changed dramatically, the guiding principles of user interface design remain constant.

- **User control.** The user must always feel in control of the application. The environment should be interactive and allow the user to be proactive. The user should navigate through modeless windows whenever possible to allow for free movement within the application. *Modeless windows* allow the user to move to another window without regard to the current window.

- **Direct manipulation.** The interface should be direct and include metaphors that are self-explanatory and easily understood by the user. A *metaphor* is a paradigm that provides an implicit comparison to some object familiar to a person. For example, a folder icon can be used to indicate a placeholder for files. Use the traditional object-action paradigm to allow the user to select an object and then perform an action. The user should also be able to directly manipulate objects such as dragging and dropping a document onto a printer icon. By supporting the concept of direct manipulation, you can provide an informative environment for the user.

- **Consistency.** The interface should remain consistent throughout the application—and the operating system. The user can learn more quickly and will not be intimidated if consistency is employed for all applications within a given operating environment.

- **Forgiveness.** The interface must be willing to forgive and allow the user to recover. If the user cannot reverse an action, he or she will not be willing to explore the application. Provide warning and confirmation messages to help the user when making a potentially irreversible choice like deleting a file.

- **User feedback and assistance.** People need feedback. The interface should provide appropriate assistance and feedback for actions the user performs. This feedback should show a balance between providing the user with information and taking a back seat to the user accomplishing a task. Three ways to provide feedback are sending auditory or visual cues such as a beep, changing the mouse pointer or cursor, and displaying information in a status area on the window.

- **Aesthetics.** The interface must be visually pleasing as well as stimulating to the user's intellect. Related items should be grouped and the controls should be properly aligned. Effective spacing is also important. Users feel disorganized if the window is cluttered with numerous controls. The visual design of your application should support the 3-D look and feel of Windows 95.

- **Simple.** The interface should be simple so that it is easy to use and learn. You should design for recognition instead of recall. In other words, the user should be able to identify items from a list instead of having to recall them from memory. Providing a useful description of an item (as opposed to a cryptic code) is an example of this concept. The underlying technology should be transparent to the user.

Using these design principles as a starting point, this chapter moves on to discuss the new and improved Windows 95 interface.

What's New in 95?

The basic premise behind the Windows 95 interface is to provide an environment that is easy to learn for novices. The Windows 95 interface also allows experts to easily customize their desktop environment. In usability studies, Microsoft found that approximately 20 percent of all users choose the Alt+Tab method to switch between applications and that fewer than 50 percent use more than one application at a time. Based on these findings, a design goal for Windows 95 involved improving the interface of Windows 3.1 to be more usable. The productivity of the new interface would truly allow people to perform unpredictable tasks in any sequence. The redesigned interface offers a simple, straightforward environment that allows the user to employ multiple applications and easily switch between them. Another design goal is a neat, clean, and intuitive desktop that makes users comfortable.

Some of the new features of Windows 95 include the following:

- Taskbar and Start menu
- Object-oriented desktop
- Support for long filenames
- New system menu, and minimize, maximize, and close buttons
- Pop-up menus accessed by clicking the right mouse button
- Tabbed property sheets and dialog boxes
- New online help engine that includes the book metaphor

The Windows 95 interface is document-centric as opposed to application-centric. *Document-centric* means that the interface more clearly addresses the user's purpose for interacting with the computer—creating and using documents. The terms *documents* and *document-centric* can also be translated as *data*. The user interacts with the computer to manipulate files and data, not to work with applications. By adopting this data-centered focus, applications do not get in the way of the user's productivity but assist with accomplishing tasks.

A Better Interface

Windows 95 contains many improvements in the interface as it pertains to designing and building user applications. The following sections summarize some of the key improvements.

The Desktop Environment

The desktop represents the user's main workspace on which all objects are placed. The desktop is object oriented and has a 3-D look and feel. Two main features of the desktop are the taskbar and the Start menu. These two key features allow the user to easily accomplish tasks.

The Start menu button provides an easy starting place for the novice user to interact with the computer. Through usability testing, Microsoft discovered that users had trouble starting applications and navigating through the Program Manager hierarchy. Using Windows 95 and the Start button to start an application, participants realized speed improvements of three to nine times. This productivity improvement was the design goal behind the Start button. A novice user can quickly choose an application and begin working.

> **TIP**
>
> The user can also press Alt+S from the desktop to activate the Start button menu options.

The Start button includes the following options:

- **Programs.** This option includes all the programs that reside on the computer. The Programs menu essentially replaces the Program Manager used in Windows 3.1.
- **Documents.** This list contains the most recently accessed documents.
- **Settings.** This section includes all the applications that customize the computer's settings such as Control Panel and Printers folder.
- **Find.** The Find utility is a powerful tool for performing searches for files and information within a document.
- **Help.** This option accesses the Windows 95 online help. The Windows 95 help engine is a simplified version that uses the book metaphor and tabbed dialog boxes.
- **Run.** This option allows you to run applications.
- **Shut down.** This option provides an easy and safe method to shut down, log off, and restart the computer.

The taskbar provides a home for all applications to dock. Each time a window is opened, a representative button is placed on the taskbar. The user can easily switch between applications by using the buttons on the taskbar. The user can resize or hide the taskbar as well as move it to another edge of the screen.

Figure 6.1 shows the new desktop environment for Windows 95 emphasizing the taskbar and the choices for the Start button.

FIGURE 6.1.

The Windows 95 desktop.

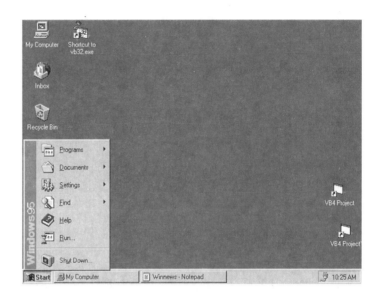

For expert users who liked using Alt+Tab to navigate in Windows 3.1, Windows 95 offers a new and improved version. The Windows 95 version displays a layout of all the icons representing active tasks. Each time you press Alt+Tab, an outline is drawn around the next task and you are given the opportunity to select that task. This layout helps prevent the task-switching endless loop that occurred for some users in Windows 3.1.

New and Improved Buttons

Several buttons have been changed for the Windows 95 interface. These buttons include the system menu, and the minimize, maximize, and close buttons, which are all displayed at the top of most primary windows. The system menu has been changed to an icon that depicts the application type. For utility applications such as the Windows calculator, a small icon representing the application should be displayed in the upper left corner of the title bar. If the user can open and save files or documents using the application, an icon depicting the document or data file type should be placed in the title bar. Figure 6.2 shows these changes to the title bar.

FIGURE 6.2.

This figure depicts an example of a window title bar.

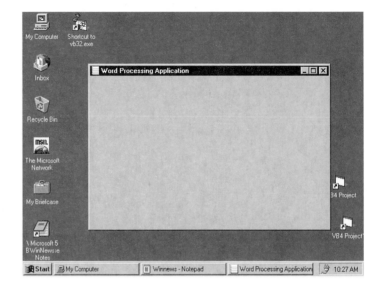

Pop-Up Menus

Pop-up menus are another new feature in Windows 95. The user activates a pop-up menu by right-clicking the mouse button. The menu options include some of the most common actions for that object. Although several Windows 3.1 applications initially introduced this functionality, Windows 95 extended the feature to include it in the operating environment.

Tabbed Property Sheets

The tabbed property sheet is something you may have used in some Windows 3.1 applications. This feature allows you to group related items in one dialog window so that the user can set a group of related properties for an object. The user moves between each group by clicking the various tabs on the window. Again, this feature has been included in the operating environment.

New Online Help

The online help for Windows 95 is more intuitive and easier to use. The online help user interface uses a book metaphor and includes tabbed dialog boxes and shortcuts to other applications. In addition, the What's This feature allows you to get context-sensitive help for individual objects on a window.

Now that you are familiar with the design principles of an effective user interface and some of the new features of the Windows 95 interface, you may be asking how this affects you as a Visual Basic developer. The rest of this chapter uses the concepts discussed so far as building blocks for designing and developing effective user interfaces in Visual Basic 4.0.

User Interface Design

Visual Basic 4.0 provides many tools for you to use to build an effective interface. This section discusses some of the basic controls that you should consider when designing your application. Along the way, I will provide guidelines to apply when using these tools.

Windows: The Foundation

Windows are the foundation of a graphical user interface (GUI) and the principal source for user interaction. There are basically two types of windows: primary and secondary. *Primary windows* include the main functionality of the application. *Secondary windows* are dialog windows that allow the user to specify options or details about objects in the primary window.

A typical primary window includes a title bar, a menu bar, and toolbar. The text section in the middle of the title bar describes the displayed object. The title bar serves as the anchor point with which the user moves the window. For Windows 95, a graphic icon replaces the system menu in the title bar. Design this icon based on the type of application you are developing. If your application allows the user to create and manipulate data or documents, design an icon that graphically represents the nature of the document or data type. If your application is a tool or utility similar to the Windows calculator, your icon should depict the application function. This design guideline is consistent with the document-centric nature of the Windows 95 interface. The title bar can also include the minimize, maximize, and close buttons.

> **NOTE**
>
> The user can display the pop-up menu for the window by clicking on the title bar with the right mouse button. The user can also press Alt+spacebar to accomplish the same task.

A status bar is often included at the bottom of a primary window. You can use the status bar to display informational messages to the user about the object or document being viewed. Scroll bars are usually included automatically if the content of the window is greater than what the user is viewing, often referred to as the *client area*. The client area extends from the menu and toolbar area at the top of the window to the bottom of the window. The client area stops at the status bar, if one is included in the window.

NOTE

If the Desktop taskbar is maintained at the bottom of the screen, the status bar will appear above the taskbar even when your application window is maximized. The user can choose to hide the taskbar. If hidden, the taskbar will only appear when the user moves the mouse cursor to the bottom of the screen.

Consider whether your windows should be sizable. Users should be able to resize most primary windows. Secondary windows are usually not resizable. By providing the ability to size the windows within your application, the user can more easily view the whole desktop area.

The window is the palette on which you design a usable interface. Controls provide the tools to make your application windows come alive. (The next section describes the various controls available.) Visual layout is the most important design consideration for your windows. You will discover that you have a plethora of controls and tools at your disposal. You must demonstrate restraint, however, concerning the number of controls you paint on your window.

Alignment is crucial to an effective interface. Think about a painting hanging crooked on a wall. Everyone has the urge to walk over to the wall and straighten the picture to bring alignment and order to the room. The same is true for your interface: the controls should be properly aligned to provide a comfortable and pleasing feeling for the user.

The layout must also contain proper spacing for clarity. The fifty-percent rule can help in your decision of whether to include the control on a window. This rule states that a control should be placed on a window if it is used fifty percent of the time; otherwise, the item should be placed on another window. You then provide a navigational path to that item. This path may include a push button, menu item, or toolbar icon.

Controls: The Building Blocks

Controls are the primary building blocks with which you construct your interface. Visual Basic includes a large set of controls that allow the application developer to develop interaction with the user. For purpose of discussion, these controls are broken into two categories:

- Menus and toolbars
- Window controls

Menus and Toolbars

Menus provide lists of actions from which the user can choose. The three types of menus are pull-down, pop-up, and cascading. The *pull-down menu* is located on the menu bar. The *menu bar* is displayed directly below the title bar and includes a list of menu titles. Each menu title includes a drop-down list of menu items that pertain to that menu title. For example, the File menu title may include the New, Open, and Save menu items. A new feature in Windows 95 allows the user to easily navigate through the menu items: Once a menu is activated, the menu items remain in view and the mouse pointer is sensitive to each item in the list. This sensitivity allows the user to more easily select a menu item as well as navigate through various submenu items.

The *pop-up menu* is a powerful feature that allows the user to invoke a choice of menu items without having to navigate to the menu bar. The pop-up menu is invoked by clicking the right mouse button over an object. The menu items vary based on where the cursor is located. For this reason, pop-up menus are often referred to as *contextual menus.* As a visual application designer, you can use pop-up menus to offer choices to a user without cluttering the screen workspace. Unlike pull-down menus, pop-up menus do not have titles. Pop-up menus should only include the most frequently used commands for that object.

A *cascading menu* allows you to include submenus underneath a particular menu item. An arrowhead to the right of a menu item indicates that a submenu exists. Visual Basic 4.0 allows you to create up to five levels of submenus. You should use cascading menus sparingly; requiring the user to navigate across several levels of submenus increases the complexity of your interface and can cause confusion. A good guideline is to include only one level of submenus. To avoid multiple levels of cascading menus, you can use a dialog box to prompt the user for action.

Here are some general guidelines for menus:

- All menu titles should be one word that represents the functionality of all of the menu items in the list. Menu items can be multiple words but should be concise.

- An access key, also called a hot key, should be defined for all menu titles. The first letter of the word is usually chosen, although a distinctive consonant or vowel in the word can also be used. The designated letter will be displayed to the user with an underline. The access key allows the user to press the Alt key and the designated letter to open the menu with the keyboard. No two menu titles should have the same access key, but menu items under different menu titles can have the same access key.

- Accelerator keys, also called shortcut keys, can also be used for menu items. Accelerator keys provide a faster shortcut for the user and usually involve function keys or a combination of the Ctrl or Shift key and a designated letter. You should only use accelerator keys for frequently performed functions such as Copy or Paste.

- Menu items should be logically grouped within the list; the groups should be divided by separator bars.

- An ellipsis (...) should follow a menu item name whose function requires more information (for example, Save As...). The ellipsis serves as an indicator to the user that a dialog box will follow to allow the input of more information. An ellipsis is not used in all cases where a menu item navigates to a dialog box. Do not use an ellipsis when selecting a menu item displays a message box.

- If a menu item becomes inappropriate for the application, the item should be disabled. If all menu items for a menu title are inappropriate, the menu title should be disabled, making all the menu items inaccessible.

- For independent menu items, a check mark should be placed to the right of the name of the item when the state of that item is turned on. For interdependent items, a bullet resembling the inner circle of a radio button should be placed to the right of the item text for an active state. These items follow the guidelines of the checkbox and radio button respectively.

Toolbars provide the user with easy access to frequently used commands and options. Toolbars are usually placed at the top of the window directly under the menu bar. Some applications require floating toolbars, which are also supported in Visual Basic 4.0. Each command on a toolbar is a graphical icon that represents the action performed when the user clicks the button. You should use ToolTips for each toolbar option that does not have a text label. ToolTips displays the name of the command in a yellow rectangular box that appears when the user rests the mouse over the button for a specified period of time. By including this feature, you can provide a straightforward text description of your visual icon.

Window Controls

Window controls are those controls you design for your window based on the needs of the user. Window controls in Visual Basic can be divided into standard controls and custom controls. *Standard controls* are those controls included in the Visual Basic executable and included by default on the Visual Basic toolbox. *Custom controls* are separate files, either in VBX or OCX format, that can be added to or removed from the toolbox to help you design specialized functionality. The OCX custom controls include Object Linking and Embedding (OLE) technology. The VBX custom controls are Dynamic Link Libraries (DLLs) compiled especially for Visual Basic; they represent functionality from previous versions of Visual Basic.

> **NOTE**
>
> OCX and VBX custom controls are included in Visual Basic 4.0. The VBX custom controls can be used only with the 16-bit version of Visual Basic. You can use OCX custom controls with either the 16-bit or the 32-bit version. The only restriction is that you use the specific controls targeted for that platform: 16-bit OCX for the 16-bit platform and 32-bit OCX for the 32-bit platform.

Figure 6.3 shows the controls included in the Visual Basic toolbox.

FIGURE 6.3.

The Visual Basic 4.0 toolbox.

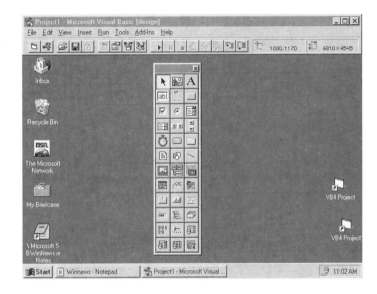

Controls that Build an Interface

The following sections discuss some of the common Visual Basic controls in the context of designing an interface. I will try to show some common design principles while walking through several examples packaged with Visual Basic.

Command or Push Button Control

The command button, often referred to as a push button, is one of the most common controls in a user interface. The user clicks the button to perform some action; the button gives the appearance that it has been pressed and released. This visual feedback is informative to the user.

The push button usually contains a label describing the action to be performed (for example, the OK button). You should provide an access key so that the user can perform the action using the keyboard. To create an access key for the push button, place an ampersand (&) before the designated letter in the button caption. The designated letter is then underlined so that the user can easily determine the access key. The user can then use the Alt+letter combination to execute the command.

If you want to use an ellipsis on a push button, refer to the guidelines for menu items in "Menus and Toolbars," earlier in this chapter. Remember that the ellipsis should be used only when the user has to supply more information, not because pressing the button leads to another window. In other words, an ellipsis is not used in a case in which clicking the command button displays a message box.

The user can also navigate to the command by pressing the Tab key; he or she can activate the button by pressing the spacebar or Enter when the button has focus. If a button is the default button for a window, the user can press Enter to execute that command. You can designate a command button as the default button by setting that button's Default property to TRUE.

People usually read top to bottom and left to right. For this reason, you should usually place command buttons at the bottom right corner of the window. The default command should be the first button, or the one furthest to the left, in the set. Place the Help button, if applicable, last in the set. Place a Cancel button last in the set but before the Help button. You can optionally place command buttons on the right side of the window from top to bottom. The same guidelines apply top to bottom as they do left to right. If a command button is exclusively associated with a single control, place that command with the control.

Label and Text Box Controls

Labels and text boxes are also familiar controls. You can use labels to display read-only text as well as to describe controls that do not have a caption. When providing a label for a text box, place the label to the left side of the text box. Related labels should be vertically aligned with the frame or group box caption, if applicable. Also, the caption for related sets of text box labels should be left aligned, and a caption should immediately follow the text.

TIP

You can use a label to protect text the user should not be allowed to edit. For read-only text, set the BorderStyle property to 1 to give the control a border similar to that of a text box. By doing so, you can design the label control to mimic the functionality of a text box and shield the contents from being manipulated. The default BorderStyle property is 0 (no outline), which is used primarily for control labels.

Text boxes allow the user to enter and edit text. To create an access key, place an ampersand before the designated letter in the caption for the text box. The text box should receive the focus when the access key (Alt+designated letter) is used. You can set the Locked property to TRUE to keep a user from directly manipulating the text while still allowing the user to select the text. The user, therefore, can select text for copying but not for cutting or pasting. The Locked property does not restrict you from manipulating the contents of the text box within your code. The text-box control defaults to a single-line text box.

You can set the MultiLine property to TRUE to support entry and display of multiple lines of text. A mulitline text box also supports word-wrapping of text. This feature functions like a word processor in that the text wraps around to the next line when the end of a line is reached. Horizontal and vertical scrolling are supported.

Figure 6.4 shows how a text box can be used in an application that requires the user to enter a password. For security reasons, each character should be masked as it is entered into the text box. The `PasswordChar` property for the text box in Figure 6.4 has been set to `*`. For every character the user types, a `*` is displayed instead.

FIGURE 6.4.

*This window displays a *
when the user enters a
character in the Password
text box.

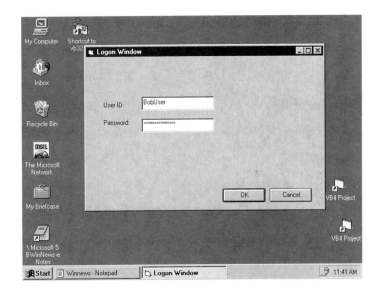

You can restrict the values a user enters into a text box as well as the number of characters. For example, you may want to limit the user to entering only numbers or only eight characters. The following code restricts the input to numbers by using the `KeyPress` event of the Age text box:

```
Private Sub txtAge_KeyPress (KeyAscii As Integer)
     If KeyAscii < Asc ("0") or KeyAscii > ("9") Then
          KeyAscii = 0
          Beep
     End If
End Sub
```

When the user types anything other than a number, the character is canceled and a beep sounds.

To restrict the number of characters a user can enter, set the `MaxChar` property to the desired number. For example, if the user can enter only eight characters for a password, set the `MaxChar` property to 8. When the user attempts to enter the ninth character, the text box does not allow it and a beep sounds.

A *rich text box* is now available in Visual Basic to support the Windows 95 interface. You can use this control only with 32-bit platforms. This control allows the user a richer set of features, such as changing the font size and making the font bold and italicized. For multiline text, paragraphs can be indented and text can be displayed as a bulleted or numbered list. OLE objects can be embedded into this control. The user can also print the contents of the text box. The rich text box is a powerful control that adds additional word processing capabilities beyond those of the standard text box.

The masked edit control provides a text box you can use to restrict the format of user input and to format the output that is displayed. This control behaves similar to a standard text box. You can define a mask or layout for the user to follow when entering information. For example, you can define a format for entering a telephone number: (###)###-####. This control can save you a lot of coding time when you are designing fields that have a predefined format.

Radio Button Control

You can use radio buttons, also referred to as option buttons, to allow the user one selection from a list of mutually exclusive items. A radio button is a circle with a caption located to the right. When the user chooses an option, a dot fills the middle of the circle. If the user selects another option within the same group, the previously selected choice becomes empty (deselected) and the newly selected option is filled with a dot.

Place a frame around a related set of option buttons. The caption for the frame should represent the type of choice; the captions for each option should represent the specific choices.

> **NOTE**
>
> You must place the frame on the window before you create the radio buttons. After you paint the frame on your window, you can place the radio buttons on the frame. By placing the radio buttons on the existing frame, you will have a group of related objects that you can move as a group.

Figure 6.5 shows the use of radio buttons to provide a choice to the user.

In this example, the user must choose only one method of payment, hence the mutually exclusive relationship.

Here are some other general guidelines for radio buttons:

- Capitalize the first letter of the first word in the caption for the frame as well as the radio buttons. This text standard is referred to as sentence capitalization.
- Design each radio button to vertically align with the text for the frame.
- Assign an access key by placing an ampersand before the designated letter in the radio button caption.
- Allow the user to double-click a radio button to select the option *and* execute the default command for the window, if applicable.

FIGURE 6.5.

Radio buttons that provide a choice to the user.

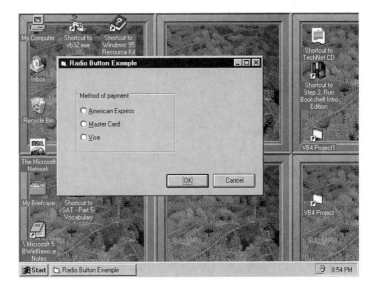

Checkbox Control

You can use checkboxes to allow the user to choose one or more options from a list of independent items. A checkbox is a square box with a caption located to the right. When the user makes a selection, the checkbox is turned on and the square is filled in with a checkmark. When the user clicks the selection again, the choice is turned off and the square becomes empty. You may also use a gray checkmark to reflect a mixed value state. A mixed value state is defined as a selection that has the properties of both states of the check box value (partially true and partially false). A common example for a mixed value state is found in word processing applications. A selection may be partially underlined; therefore, the checkbox reflecting this state would be grayed indicating the mixed state of the selection.

Place a frame around a related set of checkboxes. The caption for the frame should represent the type of choice; the captions for each option should represent the specific choices. Checkboxes are placed on a frame in the same manner as radio buttons (refer to the Note box in the preceding section).

Figure 6.6 shows an example of checkboxes that provide choices for the user.

Here are some other general guidelines for checkboxes:

- ■ Use sentence capitalization for the frame as well as the checkbox captions.
- ■ Design each checkbox to vertically align with the text for the frame.
- ■ Assign an access key by placing an ampersand before the designated letter in the checkbox caption.
- ■ The user should be able to press the spacebar to activate a checkbox if the selection has the focus.

FIGURE 6.6.

The three states of a checkbox: Off, On (checkmark), and Mixed Value (checkerboard).

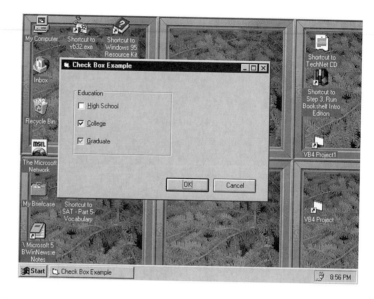

List Box Control

A list box can be used for displaying a list of choices. A typical list box displays a single list of choices vertically, although multiple columns are supported. Horizontal and vertical scroll bars are displayed automatically when the content exceeds the viewing area of the list box. For practical reasons, design the width of the list box to be equal to the list entry with the maximum possible number of characters. By using this guideline, the user can view all the text associated with an item without scrolling horizontally. If this is not possible because of limited window space, design the width of the list box to be as wide as the average width of all the items in the list box. The user can then use the horizontal scroll bar or you can place an ellipsis in the middle of an entry to support the display of the relevant information. The only scenario where you might want to use the ellipsis technique is when you need to display a file with a long directory name (five or six directory levels) which exceeds the width of the list box. The relevant information would include the root drive and maybe one or two directory levels along with the file name.

You should place a label above and to the left of the list box to describe its contents. Assign an access key to the label. When the user presses the access key, focus should be placed on the list box. A command button is sometimes associated with the list box so that the user can make a choice or choices and execute a command. Double-clicking an item should represent selecting an item and pressing the command button. The following code demonstrates how to achieve this feature:

```
Private Sub lstSelection_List_DblClick ()
     cmdSelect_Click
End Sub
```

This code example executes the click event for the Select command button when the user double-clicks the Selection list box. An alternative to this method is to set the `cmdSelect.Value` equal to `TRUE`.

A common use of the list box is to support multiple item selection. You should provide the user with the ability to contiguously and noncontiguously select items. *Contiguous items* are those items adjacent or next to each other in the list. You can use the `MultiSelect` property to support this feature. The default setting for the `MultiSelect` property is 0 (which does not permit multiple selection). Set this value to 2 for extended multiple selection. A value of 2 allows the user to employ the Shift+click combination to select all the (contiguous) items between the current item and the previous selection. For noncontiguous items, the user can employ the Ctrl+click combination to select and deselect items in the list.

Combo Box Control

The combo box is a combination of the text and list box controls. The user can type text into the combo box or select an item from the list. The three types of combo boxes are as follows:

- Drop-down
- Simple
- Drop-down list

The *drop-down* combo box is the default setting (`Style = 0`). The user can enter text directly in the combo box or select an item from the list. To open the list, the user can click the detached arrow at the right side of the control. When the control has the focus, the user can also use the Alt+down-arrow key combination to display the list. The user can press the up-arrow or down-arrow key on the keyboard to navigate the choices or can select an item by clicking the desired choice. This value is then displayed in the text portion of the text box.

> **NOTE**
>
> Windows 95 differs from Windows 3.1 in that the list of items is persistent, or remains displayed, and the mouse pointer is sensitive to the item as the user moves the cursor over the choices. This feature makes it easier for the user to select an item. This behavior is similar to menu items and is a productive design enhancement of the Windows 95 interface.

The drop-down combo box automatically supports the editing functions consistent across most applications that handle text. When the user selects an item from the list, clicking the right mouse button displays a pop-up menu for the combo box with the Cut and Copy selections enabled. The Paste option appears enabled when text has been copied and is available for pasting into the combo box. If the user types an entry into the combo box and clicks the right mouse button, the other editing functions such as Undo, Delete, and Select All are also available. Figure 6.7 shows a drop-down combo box that supports the right mouse button functionality.

FIGURE 6.7.

This window shows a drop-down combo box with the pop-up menu activated.

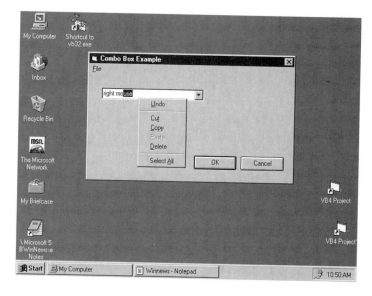

The *simple* combo box is a list displayed at all times. You can design a simple combo box by setting the Style property to 1. This box is usually drawn larger than the other two styles to display multiple entries in the list. Vertical scrolling is supported for those items that are not displayed. The user can enter text directly or select from the list, just as with the drop-down combo box.

The *drop-down list* combo box differs from the other two styles in that the user can only choose an item from the list. No text can be entered into the text portion of the control. You can design this style by setting the Style property to 2. The same navigation techniques used for the drop-down combo box apply to the drop-down list combo box.

Here are some general guidelines for combo boxes:

■ Design the width of the combo box a little larger than the average width of the items in the list.

■ Consider spacing when using combo box controls. Remember that for the drop-down and drop-down list combo boxes, the list takes up some space when opened by the user. You may not want the user to cover up other areas of the window when opening the list.

■ Most combo boxes are either the drop-down or the drop-down list style. The question to consider is user flexibility versus data integrity and control. The drop-down combo box offers the user flexibility (the user can select an item or type one if the choice is not in the list). The drop-down list offers more control over the data in the list, especially if you are using a code table to populate the list. Keep these factors in mind when designing your window.

Grid Control

The grid control is useful for displaying information that consists of rows and columns in a table format. The intersection of a row and column is called a *cell.* You can use the grid control to display text in the cells. Editing text is not supported.

> **NOTE**
>
> Several third-party vendors have created controls like the grid control and have extended the functionality of these controls to allow editing and other features. You may want to use one of these third-party spreadsheet controls if your application has to support direct editing of text in a cell as well as other features. A Data-Bound Grid control is included in Visual Basic 4.0; this control provides spreadsheet capabilities such as cell editing. You can bind the data-bound control to a database. Another option is to use OLE technology and embed a spreadsheet such as Microsoft Excel into your window. Refer to Part III, "Unleashing Component-Based Programming," later in this book, for more information on OLE.

Common Dialog Control

The common dialog control includes several standard dialog boxes you can use to offer options such as opening, saving, and printing files. You can also design this control to select colors and fonts. The behavior and functionality of this control is consistent with the standard dialog boxes found across all Windows 95 applications. Using this control can save valuable design and development time because the functionality is prepackaged.

The **Open dialog box** allows the user to choose a directory, drive, file extension, and file. The **Save As dialog box** behaves similar to the Open dialog box. The differences are the title of the dialog box and the fact that the filenames in the list of the **Save As dialog box** appear grayed out. You can specify the default drive and directory and also the default file types. New features in Windows 95 allow you to create a new folder within the dialog box. In Windows 3.1, the user had to create a new directory first in File Manager, then return to the application and save the file. Now the user can perform both operations from the same window. This feature should seem more intuitive and make the user more productive.

You can use the **Color dialog box** to provide a palette for the user to choose a color. The user can also create and select a custom color. You then can use the selected color in your application.

The **Font dialog box** allows the user to choose a font, font size, color, and style. You then can use these choices in your application.

Visual Basic Custom Controls

The Visual Basic Professional Edition contains a rich set of custom controls to enhance the features and functionality of your application. The following sections discuss some of the advanced controls and how you can use them to build an effective interface.

For the following custom controls, you must use the platform-specific (16-bit or 32-bit) control for the target platform for your application. The design guidelines pertain to Windows 95 (the 32-bit platform).

3-D Controls

The Visual Basic Professional Edition provides several 3-D controls to support the Windows 95 interface. As a general rule, all these controls should be painted onto a form that has a `BackColor` property of light gray (&H00C0C0C0&) to take advantage of the 3-D effect. Use 3-D controls to create a visual cue of depth for "actionable" objects. Command buttons are a prime example of this visual feedback. Other 3-D effects should be used sparingly, however, to enhance the overall visual effectiveness of your interface. Here is a list of the available 3-D controls, which are detailed in the following sections:

- 3-D command button
- 3-D checkbox
- 3-D radio button
- 3-D frame
- 3-D group push button
- 3-D panel

3-D Command Button Control

The 3-D command button is used in the same manner and has the same properties as the standard command button. The 3-D command button can additionally display 3-D text as well as bitmaps and icons. This button appears to be raised up off the screen to give it an enhanced visual effect.

3-D Checkbox Control

The 3-D checkbox has all the same features as a standard checkbox and also supports the 3-D look and feel of Windows 95. You can also customize the text of the checkbox to have a three-dimensional effect. Another difference between this control and the standard checkbox control involves the Value property. For the Click event, the value of this control is passed as an argument. The value for a selected checkbox is TRUE (-1); the value is FALSE (0) if the checkbox is not selected.

The 3-D checkbox can also be a data bound control. Refer to "Data Bound Controls," later in this chapter, for more information. The 3-D checkbox can be bound to a data control and display values for a Boolean data type field in your database. This control can also save values to the database.

3-D Radio Button Control

The 3-D radio button has the same features as the standard radio button with the enhanced feature of 3-D text located to the right of the control. Another difference between this control and the standard radio button involves the Value property. For both the Click and DblClick events, the value of this control is passed as an argument. A selected radio button's value is TRUE; the value is FALSE if the option is not selected.

3-D Frame Control

The 3-D frame is similar to the standard frame in that both controls provide a logical grouping of controls such as a group of radio buttons or checkboxes. The 3-D frame provides a three-dimensional look for both the frame and the text. The text can be positioned in the upper left corner, upper right corner, or centered in the middle of the frame. You can also design the frame to appear raised or inset. Use the 3-D frame over the standard frame to group 3-D controls such as radio buttons and checkboxes.

3-D Group Push Button Control

The 3-D group push button acts as a push button but also toggles between on and off when clicked. You can use this control to simulate the functionality found in applications such as word processing applications that group editing buttons. The group of push buttons acts like radio buttons in the sense that clicking on one command button deselects a previously pressed button. You can include a bitmap on the buttons for this control.

3-D Panel Control

The 3-D panel can be used as an alternative to the 3-D frame to logically group controls. You also can use the 3-D panel control to provide a three-dimensional background for other controls such as a list box. The 3-D panel supports three-dimensional text and can be sized to fit a window. You can manipulate the beveling and appearance of the panel to create some dynamic effects.

Data Bound Controls

Data bound controls represent controls that are tied or "bound" to a database. These controls allow the user to directly create, edit, and display information from the database. Refer to Part V, "Unleashing Database Programming," later in this book, for a detailed explanation of how to use these controls. The purpose of this chapter is to make you aware of these controls.

You can use the following standard controls in conjunction with the data control to bind information in the database to the control:

- Text box
- Checkbox
- List box
- Combo box
- Image control
- OLE container control
- Picture box
- Label

The following controls are OLE custom controls that already include bound data functionality:

- Data-bound list box
- Data-bound combo box
- Data-bound grid
- Masked edit control
- 3-D panel
- 3-D checkbox

Remember to consider these bound data controls when designing your application, especially if the application relies heavily on a database. These controls can save you time in your design and development and can also provide useful tools to the user.

OLE Controls

You can use the OLE container control to link or embed other OLE objects into your application. An example of OLE technology is inserting a spreadsheet object into a word processing document. Part III, "Unleashing Component-Based Programming," later in this book, covers OLE in much greater detail.

The reference to OLE in this chapter is to make you aware of an important design consideration. When you use OLE technology in your application, you can also support visual editing.

Visual editing allows the user to manipulate an embedded object within your application and not have to switch to the application that created the object—the OLE server. The design consideration for your application is to provide the menus and toolbars of the OLE server to the user within your application's window. You can accomplish this feature by using the form's NegotiateMenu property and the menu control's NegotiatePosition property.

Set the NegotiateMenu property of the form to TRUE (the default setting) to place the defined menu bar of the OLE server application on your window when the object is activated. Setting this property to FALSE prevents the OLE server application's menu bar from appearing when the object is activated. Another condition that prevents the menu from appearing is when the OLE server application does not have a defined menu bar.

Use the NegotiatePosition property of the menu control to control if and where your menu is displayed when a server object is activated. You can set this property for each menu title.

Windows 95 Custom Controls

The following controls are standard Windows 95 controls available to you in Visual Basic 4.0:

- ImageList
- ListView
- TabStrip
- ToolBar
- TreeView
- ProgressBar
- StatusBar
- Slider

ImageList Control

The ImageList control allows you to manage a collection of images such as bitmaps or icons. You can use this control when implementing a list view or tree view window which are explained next. You use the ImageList control to create and manage your images such as document icons or graphic pictures that represent your files or documents.

TreeView Control

The TreeView control allows you to mimic the left side of the Windows 95 Explorer application. You can use the TreeView control to display drives, directories, and files in a tree hierarchy. You can use the TreeView control with the ImageList control to display graphic images.

ListView Control

The ListView control simulates the right side of the Windows 95 Explorer application. You can display a list of objects such as applications, files, and folders in several different views. You can use the ListView control with the ImageList control to display graphic images.

TabStrip Control

You can use the TabStrip control to displays tabs for sections of information on a window. The tabs act as dividers in a folder. By default, a single row of tabs is created when you place this control on your window. You can select multiple rows of tabs if your application needs this functionality. The left and right arrows and the Ctrl+Tab key combination allow the user to move among the tabs.

ToolBar Control

The ToolBar control allows you to create a toolbar for the most frequently used commands. This control allows you to easily define ToolTips for each toolbar option. The ToolTip provides a textual description of the toolbar option (which is usually a graphic icon). Refer to "Menus and Toolbars," earlier in this chapter, for toolbar design considerations.

ProgressBar Control

The ProgressBar control allows you to display a visual cue to the user about the status or progress of a task. The ProgressBar is a rectangular object that fills from left to right. Use this control for tasks that take several moments to complete or for tasks that process in the background. You can also use this control to show the percentage of completion during operations such as saving or copying files.

StatusBar Control

The StatusBar control provides a way to place a status bar at the bottom of a window. The status bar area is usually used to display informational messages to the user. This area can also be used to display help or information about certain controls.

Slider Control

The slider control allows the user to adjust continuous values (for example, a volume control). The slider is a bar containing notches that represent values. An indicator is located perpendicular to the bar. This indicator is used to display the current setting and to change the value of the setting.

Effective GUI Guidelines

The following sections provide some helpful hints, lessons I have learned, and other GUI guideline considerations.

Natural Progression of a Programmer

Everyone who has moved from a mainframe environment to a graphical environment has had to make a transition both visually and programmatically. The visual transition is the one I want to touch on.

There are obvious differences between the mainframe screen and a graphical user interface such as Windows. The following textbook case shows the learning stages of a programmer making this visual design transition. Figure 6.8 shows a window designed by a programmer developing a first application in Visual Basic. This figure shows the use of controls—but in the wrong manner (notice the PF key notation on the push buttons).

FIGURE 6.8.

This window design shows a programmer in the dark concerning visual design techniques for a GUI application.

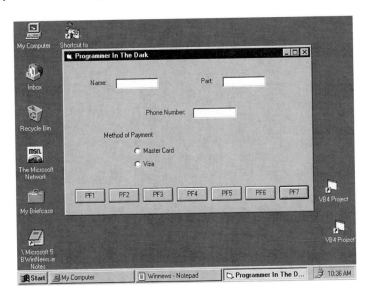

Figure 6.9 shows the next iteration of the window design. Notice that the PF key notation has been changed to reflect meaningful text. The programmer, however, is still using too many push buttons at the bottom of the window, and the controls are not properly aligned or grouped.

Figure 6.10 shows the final iteration, in which knowledge of proper window design and programmer experience is evident. Notice the use of menus and combo boxes as well as proper alignment and grouping of controls.

FIGURE 6.9.

This window design shows improvement with descriptive captions on the push buttons.

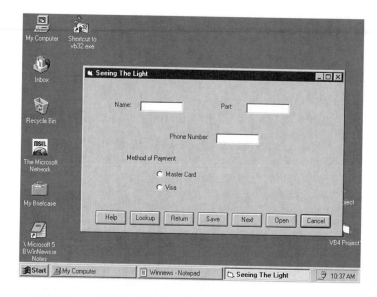

FIGURE 6.10.

This window shows how the interface is improved by alignment and proper use of controls.

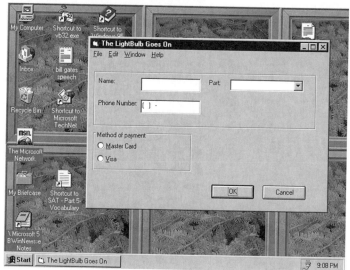

User Feedback and Assistance

This chapter has discussed the importance of providing feedback and assistance to the user. You can design this feedback in many ways, depending on the application. In some cases, auditory cues such as a beep will suffice. The status bar area is another place to provide information to the user such as descriptive messages about the activity of the window or context-sensitive descriptions about a menu item or toolbar option. ToolTips are another common way of displaying the functions of toolbar options.

Figure 6.11 shows a practical application in which visual cues provide helpful information to the user. This window shows items in a list box; the functions of the application are Add, Change, and Delete (as indicated by the push buttons). When no items are selected, the only function available is Add; when that button is selected, another dialog box displays so that information can be added. By enabling commands, you can indicate what functions are available; disabling (graying out) commands visually depicts push buttons as unavailable. In the figure, the Add button is enabled while the Change and Delete push buttons are disabled.

FIGURE 6.11.

The Change and Delete push buttons are disabled to visually inform the user that these controls are not available.

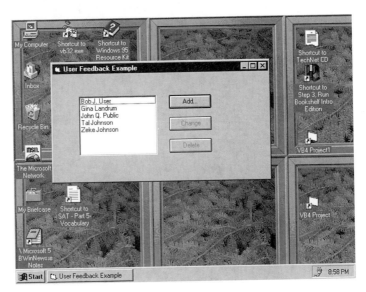

Figure 6.12 shows how all the push buttons become available when the user selects an item. This functionality supports the object-action paradigm in that the user must select an object before taking an action.

You can also provide feedback and assistance to the user by changing the mouse pointer and cursor styles depending on where the mouse is located on the window. The pointer is a symbol or shape moved by using a pointing device such as a mouse. The pointer is the primary tool that allows the user to interact with objects, controls, and the environment. The cursor conveys the current keyboard focus. Two types of cursors include the text cursor and the selection cursor. The *text cursor* allows the user to type text into a field; the *selection cursor* displays highlighted objects that can be selected. Table 6.1 shows the different mouse pointers available.

FIGURE 6.12.

The Change and Delete push buttons are enabled when an item in the list box is selected to communicate to the user that these commands are now available.

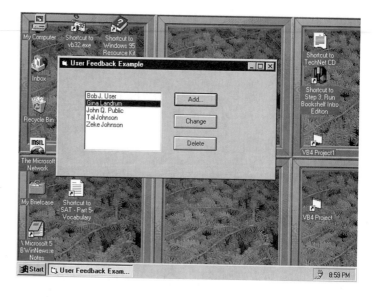

Table 6.1. Mouse pointer objects, their locations, and available actions.

Pointer	Location	Available Action
	Over most objects	Pointing, selecting, moving, resizing
	Over text	Selecting, editing text
	Over any object or location	Processing an operation
	Over any screen location	Processing in the background (application loading), but the pointer is still interactive
	Over most objects	Contextual help mode
	Inside a window	Zooming a view
	Along column gridlines	Resizing a column
	Along row gridlines	Resizing a row
	Over split box in scroll bar	Splitting a window (or adjusting a split) vertical horizontally

Pointer	Location	Available Action
↕	Over split box in horizontal scroll bar	Splitting a window (or adjusting a split) vertically
⃠	Over any object	Not available

Here are some general guidelines for pointers:

- The single arrow should be the default pointer.
- Only one cursor and the pointer should be displayed at a time.
- Use the I-beam pointer for text fields in which the user can enter or select text.
- Display the pointer with an hourglass when a background process is running.

Dialogs and Windows

Windows provide the basic interaction technique between the user and the computer. The user interacts with objects and information within the context of the window. *Window flows* describe how windows interact with each other. A *dialog* is comprised of one or more window flows. Webster's defines the word *dialog* as a "conversation between two or more people." Applying this definition to a GUI, a dialog is a conversation between two or more windows. When designing your application, you can associate a dialog with a collection of windows that accomplish a single task or business function, such as creating and saving a document or making an airline reservation.

During the design phase of your development project, consider the functionality of your application and how that translates into windows and dialogs. You will save in development time if you first spend time planning and designing your windows and how they will interact.

Modal versus Modeless

Another design consideration for your windows is whether to make them modal or modeless. Modality of a window usually becomes important when you design secondary windows. A *modal window* requires you to finish working with that window before you can continue using the rest of the application. This type of window does not offer the user much flexibility or control. Use a modal window when the user **must** answer or respond to that window before continuing. A *modeless window* offers the user more control and flexibility. A modeless window allows the user to navigate back and forth between windows in an application.

Guidelines for Window Controls

Table 6.2 shows the Window Control Matrix. This table shows some of the basic controls you can design on your windows and gives some guidelines for suggested use.

Table 6.2. Guidelines for certain controls and the suggested use and context for each control. N refers to the number of items.

Control	Suggested Use	Comments
Text box	None	No predefined list exists
Checkbox	N = 1	A static item; Used to indicate an active/inactive state
Radio buttons	1< N < 7	Static items; Must be mutually exclusive
List box	6< N < 200	Static items
	0< N <200	Dynamic items
Push button	1< N < 5	For single-action items
Menu	N < 10	For single-action items

Putting It All Together

Choosing the metaphor for your application is the single most important decision in the design process. The metaphor defines how the user will interact with your application. If you do not provide an intuitive and user-friendly interface, no one will want to use your application.

You can choose from several basic metaphors when designing your application. The following metaphors serve as suggestions to help you design an effective user interface:

- Single document interface
- Multiple document interface
- Workbooks
- Combination

Single Document Interface

Applications have become more data-centric and document-centric. The document-centric focus is a major design goal of Windows 95 applications. A single document interface supports this goal by concentrating on the data or the document rather than the application. The application becomes an enabling tool to perform tasks and is not the primary focus of attention. A single document interface involves using a single primary window with secondary windows that support the primary window with tasks such as setting properties for the primary object. Each primary window is displayed in its own application container; the window management is performed using the desktop and taskbar. The user can more easily navigate between the entries on the taskbar. Compound documents using OLE technology also represent the single document interface. The user can edit compound documents within the context of the container application without having to switch between applications.

Multiple Document Interface

Multiple document interface involves a more application-centric approach. The application becomes the main focus as child windows are displayed within one primary window. All the windows share the same menus and toolbar. This interface is useful for displaying related information through multiple views. Many Windows 3.1 word processing applications employ this interface.

Workbooks

Workbooks allow you to design an interface that uses the tab metaphor for navigating between documents. Some spreadsheet and calendar applications use this metaphor. The user can place different documents in individual sections within the workbook. The user then navigates to each document by clicking the tabs that represent each section. This interface is similar to the multiple document interface in that the menus and toolbars are still shared among the sections.

Combination

The preceding examples demonstrate a variety of user interface metaphors available to you. In some cases, you will have to create an exclusive design for a particular interface based on the functionality of your application. In other situations, a combination of these techniques can be employed to help your design.

Summary

The user interface is the most important part of your application. The underlying technology should be transparent to the person using your application. Some developers proudly say that their code is the most important aspect of the application. Although your code is important to the speed and efficiency of the application, at the end of the day, the user interface can be the stumbling block that prevents users from effectively using your application.

This chapter has discussed proper interface design considerations for building intuitive and user-friendly applications. The techniques discussed pertain to the Windows 95 interface. The first part of the chapter focused on how the Windows interface has changed. The focus then shifted to how you can use Visual Basic tools and controls to support these changes. Guidelines were given throughout the chapter and towards the end of the chapter to help you plan to use these tools.

Several stories show what the human computer interface will be in the future. I heard a quote the other day that talking to a computer was not a new concept. People have been doing this for years. The concept of the computer producing a response, however, was something new. This story shows that the human metaphor of the future for applications may be based solely on voice recognition. Another story involves several people getting on an elevator to leave the office. As one man stepped in the elevator, he reached to press the elevator button. Before he had the chance to actually push the button, the elevator doors closed. The man remarked, "You just have to point at it, and the doors close." Maybe, as this anecdote suggests, the human metaphor of the future will also involve pointing with your fingers and looking with your eyes to execute tasks.

We do not know what the future holds, but we do know what is available today. My hope is that you can use the building blocks discussed in this chapter to build the ideal interface. Let me know when you do.

Events

7

by Bill Hatfield

Visual Basic is a Visual Development Environment (VDE). In fact, it was the first VDE for Windows. A VDE is more than a programming language. It is a complete environment tailored to the needs of a programmer writing applications for a Graphical User Interface (GUI) environment.

If you have never programmed in a VDE and you are new to Visual Basic, then this new way of doing things will take some getting used to. Programming in Visual Basic is a very different experience from programming in a traditional language like C, Pascal, or COBOL. Probably the biggest difference between the two is the *event-driven paradigm.* Let me explain.

Introducing the Event-Driven Paradigm

In traditional development environments, you, as the developer, were in complete control. You determined what happened first and then what happened next. That's not to say that the users didn't have input. They did, of course. But for the most part, if the application was at step three, for example, you knew for sure that steps one and two already had been completed. You could depend on it because there was no way the user could have gotten to step three without going through the first two steps. This sort of certainty helped to simplify coding and error checking.

An application that makes use of the event-driven model works very differently. It starts up by doing some initialization code, just as the traditional system did, but at some point the application just stops. It doesn't do anything. The user stares at the application and the application stares back. And nothing happens until the user makes a move. What kind of move? Well, nearly anything qualifies. She could simply move her mouse. Or she could click a menu or a button. When she does, she sets into motion a series of events that cause the application to respond.

An Example

Let's say the user clicks a button. The operating system is monitoring very closely every move the user makes. So it doesn't fail to notice the click. The operating system also notices that the clicked button is a part of the Visual Basic application you wrote, so it sends a message to this application. *Message* here is a technical term, but it means pretty much what you might think. It is as if Windows takes out its quill pen and writes a brief note that says,

```
Dear VB Application,

The user has just clicked on the OK button that is on your main window.

Love,

Windows
```

It then drops it in the mailbox to be delivered to the application. A couple of milliseconds later when your application reads the message, it responds by generating an *event* on the appropriate object. The object, in this case, is the button on the main window. And the event is Click.

Now it just so happens that when the application was written, the programmer had an inkling that the user might click on that button. So he wrote a routine that was associated with the Click event of the OK button on the main window. In fact, that is how you will do almost all your programming in an event-driven application. You first choose an object. Then you choose an event that can happen to that object. And finally, you write a routine that will be executed at runtime when that event happens to that object.

Objects and Events

What are some examples of objects? The button in the earlier example was an object. But if there are text boxes, labels, drop-down listboxes, and other controls on the window, all of those are objects as well. Even the window itself is an object.

Events are simply things that can happen to an object. A given object can have many events. A text box can receive the focus (the GotFocus event). And it can lose the focus (LostFocus). Its text can be changed (Changed). It even can be clicked on like the button was (Click). All these are events associated with a text box control. A button shares some of these events (like Click, GotFocus, and LostFocus) but not all of them. And the button may even have a few of its own events that the text box doesn't have. Table 7.1 summarizes some often-used events common to many objects.

Table 7.1. Visual Basic common object events.

Event	Event Description
Change	Occurs again and again as changes are made in a text control.
Click	Occurs when the user presses and then releases a mouse button over an object.
DblClick	Occurs when the user rapidly presses the mouse button twice.
DragDrop	Occurs when the user presses and holds the mouse button down over a dragable object, moves the mouse to a new position, and then releases the mouse button (drops the dragged object). The DragDrop event is an event of the object that was *dropped on*, not the one being dragged.
DragOver	Occurs in an object when another object is being dragged across it.
GotFocus	Occurs when an object receives the focus. Happens when the user tabs to or clicks to move focus to the object.
KeyDown, KeyUp	Occurs when the user presses (KeyDown) or releases (KeyUp) a key while an object has the focus.

continues

Table 7.1. continued

Event	Event Description
KeyPress	Occurs when the user presses and releases a key.
LostFocus	Occurs when an object loses the focus. Happens when a user tabs to or clicks on another object.
MouseDown, MouseUp	Occurs when the user presses (MouseDown) or releases (MouseUp) a mouse button.
MouseMove	Occurs when the user moves the mouse across the screen. MouseMove is generated again and again dozens and dozens of times as the mouse moves from one place to another.

Will you, as a programmer, write code to respond to all these different events? No. In fact, you probably will write code only for a small portion of them. You will simply write for the events you think should be responded to in your application.

Do all events happen because the user did something? No. Although most events ultimately happen because of user intervention, Windows itself also can generate events based on a timer, the system clock, or the changing status of a connected peripheral.

A Shift of Control

But wait. If all your code is in these little event routines and the routines are executed only when the associated event happens, then how do you know which events will happen first? The answer is simple: You don't. And that's why event-driven programming can be more challenging than traditional development. If you are in step three, you have to check to see whether steps one and two have been done. If not, you have to decide whether they really must be done before step three. If they do, you will have to inform your users. If not, let your users do it however they like.

This points to a subtle but very important shift in priorities. You, the developer, are no longer the one in control. The user is. In fact, the user should be the center of the universe you create. This concept, called *user-centric design*, is the cornerstone to developing truly great user interfaces.

Looking at Event-Driven Gotchas

In the event-driven world, there are times when you can be writing code that looks completely harmless but causes problems when run. Look at the window in Figure 7.1.

The first text box is txtName and the second is txtPhone. Now suppose that the code in the LostFocus event of the first text box looks like Listing 7.1.

FIGURE 7.1.

A simple Visual Basic form.

Listing 7.1. The `LostFocus` event of `txtName`.

```
Private Sub txtName_LostFocus()
If txtName.Text = "" Then
    Beep
    txtName.SetFocus
End If
End Sub
```

Now suppose that the `LostFocus` event of the second text box looks like Listing 7.2.

Listing 7.2. The `LostFocus` event of `txtPhone`.

```
Private Sub txtPhone_LostFocus()
If txtPhone.Text = "" Then
    Beep
    txtPhone.SetFocus
End If
End Sub
```

Looks harmless enough. If either of these is empty, you will want your application to beep when users try to tab away and force them to enter something in the text box.

But if you run this code and simply press Tab right away, what will happen? First, the focus moves to `txtPhone`. Then the `LostFocus` event of `txtName` is executed (because it just lost the focus to `txtPhone`). `txtName`'s `LostFocus` checks to see whether `txtName` is empty. Since `txtName` is empty, it beeps and sets the focus back on `txtName`. So far so good. But setting the focus back on `txtName` causes `txtPhone` to trigger its `LostFocus` event. It goes through the same process and tries to set the focus back to it. This, in turn, triggers the `txtName LostFocus` event, creating an endless loop.

This example shows how easy it can be to unintentionally create bad situations in event-driven code. Remember that everything you do in code has the potential for triggering other events, and if those events trigger events that eventually trigger your code again, you easily can create an endless loop.

The moral of this particular story is this: Be careful when using a `SetFocus` command in a `LostFocus` or `GotFocus` event. What are some other situations to watch out for?

Table 7.2 lists some actions and corresponding events likely to be triggered.

Table 7.2. Actions and events triggered.

Action	Event(s) Triggered
Form Refresh	form's_Paint
Changing the Text property of a text box	text box's Change
Changing the Height or Width properties of a form	form's_Paint and form's_Resize

If you perform any of these actions in the event script of an event they could trigger, you risk an endless loop. If you change the height of the form in the form's Resize event, for example, you almost certainly will cause an endless loop that will generate an Out of Stack Space error. Again, these are just a few common examples. If you get an Out of Stack Space error or some other form of endless loop, be sure to check for this kind of situation.

Application Startup

So if our application is event-driven and code is only written in response to events, how do things ever get started? How your application starts depends on the setting in the Options dialog box. To access the Options dialog box, choose Options from the Tools menu. The Options tabbed dialog box appears. Now choose the Project tab. The first control is Startup Form.

Visual Basic assumes that the first thing you want to do is display a form. And, of course, this usually is correct. It further assumes that the first form you create is the one you will want to display when your application starts. This is much more likely to be a wrong assumption. After you have created several forms in your application and then want to test it, be sure to come here to the Options dialog and verify that the correct form is specified.

But what if you don't want a window to display first thing? Suppose that you want to do some initialization or checking of the system before you actually display a form? If you click on the Startup Form drop-down listbox, you will see that one of the options is Sub Main. This option enables you to create a subroutine named Main and to have it be the first thing executed. After it finishes its processing, it probably will show a form or two, but executing the subroutine first gives you a chance to verify that everything is okay before you get started.

You also would use Sub Main if you wanted to create a batch application that does all its processing behind the scenes without any user interaction. This kind of application is more unusual, but it is always good to have the option.

Application Shutdown

The next logical question is how does this whole thing end? The simplest answer is that it ends when the last form of your application is unloaded. That's the way it looks from the user's perspective. But the fact is that you still can have code executing behind the scenes long after the user thinks your application has died. So it is better to say that the application ends when the last of its components has left memory.

But that isn't very helpful from a programming perspective. How do you wrap up processing for an application in your code? The Unload command removes a form from memory. Assuming that nothing else is running, an Unload on the last form that is up shuts down the application. So generally, you don't have to worry about anything special when you are creating a simple application. Just have each form do its own cleanup in the form's Unload event.

What about larger MDI applications? Here is the process that takes place when the user indicates that he wants to close a MDI frame:

1. All the MDI child windows receive a QueryUnload event, each in turn, followed by the MDI frame's QueryUnload. In this event, each of the windows can decide whether it is OK for the application to close. This event often is used to query the user to see whether she wants to save data or cancel the close. Any of the windows can choose to cancel the close. And, in doing so, all the sheets and the frame stay open.

2. If none of the child windows cancel to the close, the Unload event occurs for each child window, and then it closes.

3. After all the child windows are closed, the frame receives an Unload event and subsequently closes. Because the MDI frame is usually the last window up at this stage, the application ends.

> **NOTE**
>
> Can't you cancel the Unload in the Unload event? Actually, yes, you can. But if you do it there, you won't know the current state of the application. Some or all of the other child windows already may have been unloaded by that time. Using the QueryUnload for canceling ensures that everything is left as it was.

What if you don't want to go through all this checking and verifying? You can stop your application cold in its tracks by executing the End command.

> **WARNING**
>
> Be careful with End. It kills the application right away. No QueryUnload—not even an Unload event—occurs. So if you have housekeeping chores or any other code in the Unload of your forms, it will not be executed.

Another way to freeze your program is by using the Stop command. This is a break. It differs from End in that it leaves all your variable values intact so that you can use the Debug window to check them. You even can restart after a Stop. You will use Stop a lot in debugging, but your final code probably will never have a need to use it.

Digging Deeper: Mapping Visual Basic Events to Windows Messages

So Visual Basic creates a visual, easy-to-use way of creating Windows applications. It receives Windows messages and converts them into events for which you can write code. But sooner or later, you are going to want to go further with your applications. Sometimes you will hear developers talk about "hitting walls" with environments like Visual Basic. Although Visual Basic makes it easy to access the most common capabilities of Windows, it doesn't really erect many walls that prevent you from going deeper. You just have to know how it's done.

Suppose that you want to make use of a Windows message that is not captured in Visual Basic. The first step is to be absolutely sure that it isn't captured in some way. Although many messages are captured as form or control events, some are captured through methods as well. Table 7.3 lists window messages and how they are captured within Visual Basic.

Table 7.3. Windows messages and how they are captured in Visual Basic.

Windows Message	VB Event/Method/ Property	Description
WM_ACTIVATE	Form_Activate	Indicates a change in the activation state
WM_ACTIVATEAPP	None	Notifies applications when a new task is activated
WM_ASKCBFORMATNAME	GetFormat() Clipboard function	Retrieves the name of the Clipboard format
WM_CANCELMODE	None	Notifies a window to cancel internal modes
WM_CHANGECBCHAIN	None	Notifies Clipboard viewer of removal from chain
WM_CHAR	Form_KeyPress, Form_KeyDown	Passes keyboard events to focus window
WM_CHARTOITEM	None, managed by Visual Basic	Provides listbox keystrokes to owner window

Windows Message	VB Event/Method/ Property	Description
WM_CHILDACTIVATE	MDIChildForm_ Activate	Notifies a child window of activation
WM_CHOOSEFONT_GETLOGFONT	None, managed by Visual Basic	Retrieves LOGFONT structure for Font dialog box
WM_CLEAR	Used as the control *object*.Clear method or Text1.Text = ""	Clears an edit or combo box
WM_CLOSE	Form_Unload, Form_QueryUnload	Signals a window or application to terminate
WM_COMMAND	*object*_Click (menu or command button)	Specifies a command message
WM_COMMNOTIFY	None	Notifies a window about the status of its queues
WM_COMPACTING	None	Indicates a low-memory condition
WM_COMPAREITEM	Used as the *object*.ListIndex method	Determines position of combo box or listbox item.
WM_COPY	Same as SetText() and SetData() Clipboard methods	Copies a selection to the Clipboard
WM_CREATE	Form_Load	Indicates that a window is being created
WM_CTLCOLOR	None	Indicates that a control is about to be drawn
WM_CUT	Used as SetText() or SetData() Clipboard methods	Deletes a selection and copies it to the Clipboard
WM_DDE_ACK		Acknowledges the receipt of a DDE transaction
WM_DDE_EXECUTE	*object*.LinkExecute()	Passes a command to a DDE server
WM_DDE_INITIATE	*object*.LinkMethod()	Initiates a DDE conversation

continues

Table 7.3. continued

Windows Message	VB Event/Method/ Property	Description
WM_DDE_POKE	object.LinkPoke()	Sends an unsolicited data item to a server
WM_DDE_REQUEST	object.LinkRequest()	Requests value of a data item from a DDE server
WM_DDE_TERMINATE	object.LinkClose()	Terminates a DDE conversation
WM_DEADCHAR	None	Indicates when a dead key is pressed
WM_DELETEITEM	None	Indicates that owner-drawn item or control is altered
WM_DESTROY	Form_QueryUnload	Indicates that window is about to be destroyed
WM_DESTROYCLIPBOARD	None	Notifies owner when Clipboard is emptied
WM_DEVMODECHANGE	None	Indicates when device-mode settings are changed
WM_DRAWCLIPBOARD	None	Indicates when Clipboard contents are changed
WM_DRAWITEM	None	Indicates when owner-drawn control or menu changes
WM_DROPFILES	object_DragDrop	Indicates when a file is dropped
WM_ENABLE	None	Indicates when enable state of window is changing
WM_ENDSESSION	None	Indicates whether the Windows session is ending
WM_ENTERIDLE	None	Indicates that a modal dialog box or menu is idle
WM_ERASEBKGND	None, closest item is the AutoRedraw property	Indicates when a window background needs erasing
WM_FONTCHANGE	None	Indicates a change in the font-resource pool
WM_GETDLGCODE	None	Allows processing of control input

Windows Message	VB Event/Method/ Property	Description
WM_GETFONT	None	Retrieves the font that a control is using
WM_GETMINMAXINFO	None, however can be linked to Form_Resize	Retrieves minimum and maximum sizing information
WM_GETTEXT	Used as GetText() or GetData() Clipboard methods	Copies the text to a corresponding window
WM_GETTEXTLENGTH	Same as Len(*object*.Text)	Determines length of text associated with a window
WM_HSCROLL	*object*.Scroll where *object* is a horizontal scroll bar	Indicates a click in a horizontal scroll bar
WM_HSCROLLCLIPBOARD	None	Prompts owner to scroll Clipboard contents
WM_ICONERASEBKGND	None	Notifies minimized window to fill icon background
WM_INITDIALOG	None	Initializes a dialog box
WM_INITMENU	None	Indicates when a menu is about to become active
WM_INITMENUPOPUP	Used as *object*.PopUpMenu method	Indicates when a pop-up menu is being created
WM_KEYDOWN	*object*_KeyDown	Indicates when a nonsystem key is pressed
WM_KEYUP	*object*_KeyUp	Indicates when a nonsystem key is released
WM_KILLFOCUS	*object*_LostFocus	Indicates window is about to lose input focus
WM_LBUTTONDBLCLK	*object*_DblClick	Indicates double-click of left mouse button
WM_LBUTTONDOWN	*object*_MouseDown	Indicates when left mouse button is pressed
WM_LBUTTONUP	*object*_MouseUp	Indicates when left mouse button is released

continues

Table 7.3. continued

Windows Message	VB Event/Method/ Property	Description
WM_MBUTTONDBLCLK	*object*_DblClick	Indicates double-click of middle mouse button
WM_MBUTTONDOWN	*object*_MouseDown	Indicates when middle mouse button is pressed
WM_MBUTTONUP	*object*_MouseUp	Indicates when middle mouse button is released
WM_MDIACTIVATE	MDIChildForm Activate	Activates a new MDI child window
WM_MDICASCADE	Used as the MDIForm.Arrange() method	Arranges MDI child windows in a cascade format
WM_MDICREATE	None	Prompts a MDI client to create a child window
WM_MDIDESTROY	MDIChildForm QueryUnload, MDIChildForm_Unload	Closes a MDI child window
WM_MDIGETACTIVE	None	Retrieves data about the active MDI child window
WM_MDIICONARRANGE	MDIForm.Arrange()	Arranges minimized MDI child windows
WM_MDIMAXIMIZE	None	Maximizes a MDI child window
WM_MDINEXT	None	Activates the next MDI child window
WM_MDIRESTORE	None	Prompts a MDI client to restore a child window
WM_MDISETMENU	None	Replaces the menu of a MDI frame window
WM_MDITILE	MDIForm.Arrange()	Arranges MDI child windows in a tiled format
WM_MEASUREITEM	None	Requests dimensions of owner-drawn control
WM_MENUCHAR	None	Indicates when unknown menu mnemonic is pressed
WM_MENUSELECT	*MenuObject*_Click	Indicates when a menu item is selected

Windows Message	VB Event/Method/ Property	Description
WM_MOUSEACTIVATE	Form_Activate	Indicates a mouse click in an inactive window
WM_MOUSEMOVE	*object*_MouseMove	Indicates mouse-cursor movement
WM_MOVE	None	Indicates the position of a window has changed
WM_NCACTIVATE	None. Visual Basic does not provide access to any non-client events	Changes the active state of a nonclient area
WM_NCCALCSIZE	Used as the ScaleWidth and ScaleHeight properties	Calculates the size of a window's client area
WM_NCCREATE	None	Indicates that a nonclient area is being created
WM_NCDESTROY	None	Indicates when nonclient area is being destroyed
WM_NCHITTEST	None	Indicates mouse-cursor movement
WM_NCLBUTTONDBLCLK	None	Indicates non-client left button double-click
WM_NCLBUTTONDOWN	None	Indicates left button pressed in nonclient area
WM_NCLBUTTONUP	None	Indicates left button released in nonclient area
WM_NCMBUTTONDBLCLK	None	Indicates middle button nonclient double-click
WM_NCMBUTTONDOWN	None	Indicates middle button pressed in nonclient area
WM_NCMBUTTONUP	None	Indicates middle button released in nonclient area
WM_NCMOUSEMOVE	None	Indicates mouse-cursor movement in nonclient area

continues

Table 7.3. continued

Windows Message	VB Event/Method/ Property	Description
WM_NCPAINT	None	Indicates that a window's frame needs painting
WM_NCRBUTTONDBLCLK	None	Indicates right button nonclient double-click
WM_NCRBUTTONDOWN	None	Indicates right button pressed in nonclient area
WM_NCRBUTTONUP	None	Indicates right button released in nonclient area
WM_NEXTDLGCTL	Used as the `SetFocus()` method	Sets focus to a different dialog box control
WM_PAINT	`Form_Paint`	Indicates that a window frame needs painting
WM_PAINTCLIPBOARD	None	Paints the specified portion of the window
WM_PALETTECHANGED	None	Indicates that focus window has realized its palette
WM_PALETTEISCHANGING	None	Informs windows about change to palette
WM_PARENTNOTIFY	None	Notifies parent of child-window activity
WM_PASTE	Used as `Text1.Text = Clipboard.GetText (vbCFText)`	Inserts Clipboard data into an edit control (text box)
WM_POWER	None	Indicates that the system is entering suspended mode
WM_QUERYDRAGICON	None	Requests a cursor handle for a minimized window
WM_QUERYENDSESSION	None	Requests that the Windows session be ended
WM_QUERYNEWPALETTE	None	Enables a window to realize its logical palette
WM_QUERYOPEN	None	Requests that a minimized window be restored
WM_QUEUESYNC	None	Delimits CBT messages

Windows Message	VB Event/Method/ Property	Description
WM_QUIT	Form_QueryUnload, Form_Unload	Requests that an application be terminated
WM_RBUTTONDBLCLK	*object*_DblClick	Indicates a double-click of right mouse button
WM_RBUTTONDOWN	*object*_MouseDown	Indicates when the right mouse button is pressed
WM_RBUTTONUP	*object*_MouseUp	Indicates when the right mouse button is released
WM_RENDERALLFORMATS	None	Notifies owner to render all Clipboard formats
WM_RENDERFORMAT	None	Notifies owner to render particular Clipboard data
WM_SETCURSOR	*object*.ScreenMouse Pointer property	Displays the appropriate mouse cursor shape
WM_SETFOCUS	*object*_GotFocus	Indicates when a window has gained input focus
WM_SETFONT	Used as the *object*.FontName property	Sets the font for a control
WM_SETREDRAW	None	Allows or prevents redrawing in a window
WM_SETTEXT	Used as the .Text or .Caption properties	Sets the text of a window
WM_SHOWWINDOW	None	Indicates that a window is about to be hidden or shown
WM_SIZE	Form_ReSize	Indicates a change in window size
WM_SIZECLIPBOARD	None	Indicates a change in Clipboard size
WM_SPOOLERSTATUS	None	Indicates when a print job is added or removed
WM_SYSCHAR	None	Indicates when a system-menu key is pressed

continues

Table 7.3. continued

Windows Message	VB Event/Method/Property	Description
WM_SYSCOLORCHANGE	None	Indicates when a system color setting is changed
WM_SYSCOMMAND	None	Indicates when a system command is requested
WM_SYSDEADCHAR	None	Indicates when a system dead key is pressed
WM_SYSKEYDOWN	*object*_KeyDown	Indicates that Alt plus another key was pressed
WM_SYSKEYUP	*object*_KeyUp	Indicates that Alt plus another key was released
WM_SYSTEMERROR	None	Indicates that a system error has occurred
WM_TIMECHANGE	None	Indicates that the system time has been set
WM_TIMER	*TimerObject*_Timer	Indicates that the time-out interval for a timer has elapsed
WM_UNDO	None	Undoes the last operation in an edit control
WM_USER	None	Indicates a range of message values
WM_VKEYTOITEM	None	Provides listbox keystrokes to owner window
WM_VSCROLL	*object*_Scroll	Indicates a click where object is a vertical scroll bar
WM_VSCROLLCLIPBOARD	None	Prompts the owner to scroll Clipboard contents
WM_WINDOWPOSCHANGED	Form_Resize	Notifies a window of a size or position change
WM_WINDOWPOSCHANGING	Form_Resize	Notifies a window of a new size or position
WM_WININICHANGE	None	Notifies applications of change to WIN.INI

As you can see, some of the Windows messages map directly to events in Visual Basic. Others map directly to methods or properties. Some loosely map to an event, method, or property that Visual Basic has chosen to handle in a more generalized way. And finally, there are some that simply are unavailable. These same things could be said of the messages associated with controls in Table 7.4.

Table 7.4. Windows messages associated with Visual Basic controls.

Windows Message	VB Event/Method/ Property	Indicates That
BN_CLICKED	CommandButton _Click	The user clicked a button
BN_DISABLE	CommandButton.Enabled	A button is disabled
BN_DOUBLECLICKED	CommandButton _DblClick	The user double-clicked a button
BN_HILITE	CommandButton _GetFocus	The user highlighted a button
BN_PAINT	None	The button should be painted
BN_UNHILITE	CommandButton_LostFocus	The highlight should be removed
CBN_CLOSEUP	None	The listbox of a combo box has closed
CBN_DBLCLK	None	The user double-clicked a string
CBN_DROPDOWN	None	The listbox of a combo box is dropping down
CBN_EDITCHANGE	ComboBox_Change	The user has changed text in the edit control
CBN_EDITUPDATE	None	Altered text is about to be displayed
CBN_ERRSPACE	None	The combo box is out of memory
CBN_KILLFOCUS	ComboBox_LostFocus	The combo box is losing the input focus
CBN_SELCHANGE	ComboBox.ListFocus	A new combo box list item is selected
CBN_SELENDCANCEL	None	The user's selection should be canceled
CBN_SELENDOK	None	The user's selection is valid
CBN_SETFOCUS	ComboBox_GotFocus	The combo box is receiving the input focus
EN_CHANGE	TextBox_Change	The display is updated after text changes

continues

Table 7.4. continued

Windows Message	VB Event/Method/ Property	Description
`EN_ERRSPACE`	None	The edit control is out of memory
`EN_HSCROLL`	None	The user clicked the scroll bar
`EN_KILLFOCUS`	`TextBox_LostFocus`	The edit control is losing the input focus
`EN_MAXTEXT`	`Text .MaxLength`	The insertion is truncated
`EN_SETFOCUS`	`TextBox_GotFocus`	The edit control is receiving the input focus
`EN_UPDATE`	None	The edit control is about to display altered text
`EN_VSCROLL`	`Vscroll_Scroll`	The user clicked the vertical scroll bar
`LBN_DBLCLK`	`ListBox_DblClick`	The user double-clicked a string
`LBN_ERRSPACE`	None	The list box is out of memory
`LBN_KILLFOCUS`	`ListBox_LostFocus`	The list box is losing the input focus
`LBN_SELCANCEL`	None	The selection is canceled
`LBN_SELCHANGE`	`ListBox_Change`	The selection is about to change
`LBN_SETFOCUS`	`ListBox_GetFocus`	The list box is receiving the input focus

Kicking Off Your Own Events

Windows sends messages to applications indicating what the user is doing, and the application responds. I also mentioned that events can be triggered by timers or the system clock. So can you, as a developer, trigger events? Can you send a message to other windows in your own application or even other applications? Well, if you just want to execute the code associated with the clicked event of your Update button, for example, you can simply code this:

```
Call cmdUpdate_Click()
```

This doesn't actually click the button (it doesn't cause the graphic to appear depressed), but it does execute the code in the `Click` event.

But what if you want to go further? You actually want to send a real Windows message to a window or control—can you do it? The answer is yes, but not in native Visual Basic. You'll have to resort to Win32.

The two primary Win32 functions you will use are `SendMessage()` and `PostMessage()`. These functions both do the same thing: They ship off a message to the window or control indicated (either in this application or in another one). The difference is that `SendMessage()` is synchronous and `PostMessage()` is asynchronous. That is, `SendMessage()` sends the message and waits until it has arrived there and has taken effect before it returns control to your application. `PostMessage()`, on the other hand, simply fires off the message and immediately returns control to your application. `SendMessage()`, then, works more like a function call. You know it is completely finished by the time the next line executes.

PostMessage

Suppose that your application wants to shut down another application. Using `PostMessage`, it is easy. First you have to declare the Win32 function, as shown in Listing 7.3.

Listing 7.3. The `PostMessage` declare statement.

```
Declare Function PostMessage Lib "user32" Alias "PostMessageA"
(ByVal hWnd As Long, _
 ByVal wMsg As Long, _
 ByVal wParam As Integer, _
 lParam As Any) As Long
```

`hWnd` identifies the window to which the message is posted. If this parameter is `HWND_BROADCAST`, the message is posted to all top-level windows, including disabled or invisible windows.

`wMsg` specifies the message to be posted.

`wParam` specifies 16 bits of additional message-dependent information. `lParam` specifies 32 bits of additional message-dependent information.

The return value is nonzero if the function is successful. The only way it would return zero is if the receiving application's message queue is full. That can happen when you send the same application many messages without giving it a chance to respond. If you run into this problem, try sprinkling a few `Yield()` statements around. You will use only `PostMessage()` with Windows. You'll see how the more flexible `SendMessage()` can be used with controls later.

After you declare `PostMessage()`, you need to declare a few other Win32 functions you'll use along the way, as shown in Listing 7.4.

Listing 7.4. Additional declarations.

```
Declare Function IsWindow Lib "User" (ByVal Hwnd As Integer) As Integer
Declare Function GetWindow Lib "User" (ByVal Hwnd As Integer, ByVal wCmd As
➡Integer) As Integer
Declare Function GetWindowLong Lib "User" (ByVal Hwnd As Integer, ByVal nIndex As
➡Integer) As Long
```

continues

Listing 7.4. continued

```
Declare Function PostMessage Lib "User" (ByVal Hwnd As Integer, ByVal wMsg As
➡Integer, ByVal wParam As Integer, ByVal lParam As Long) As Integer
Declare Function FindWindow Lib "User" (ByVal lpClassName As Any, ByVal
➡lpWindowName As String) As Integer
Const GW_OWNER = 4
Const GWL_STYLE = -16
Const WS_DISABLED = &H8000000
Const WS_CANCELMODE = &H1F
Const WM_CLOSE = &H10
```

Listing 7.5 is the EndTask function. It receives a window handle. It verifies that the window handle is valid and that it is not disabled. Then the WM_CANCELMODE and WM_CLOSE messages are passed with no parameters (0 and 0& in the word and long params).

Listing 7.5. The EndTask function.

```
Function EndTask(TargetHwnd As Integer) As Integer
    Dim X As Integer
    Dim ReturnVal As Integer
    ReturnVal = True
    If TargetHwnd = hWndMe% Or GetWindow(TargetHwnd, GW_OWNER) = hWndMe% Then
        End
    End If
    If IsWindow(TargetHwnd) = False Then
        ReturnVal = False
    Else
        If Not (GetWindowLong(TargetHwnd, GWL_STYLE) And WS_DISABLED) Then
            X = PostMessage(TargetHwnd, WM_CANCELMODE, 0, 0&)
            X = PostMessage(TargetHwnd, WM_CLOSE, 0, 0&)
            DoEvents
        End If
    End If
EndTask% = ReturnVal
End Function
```

Finally, Listing 7.6 is the Form Load event procedure, which uses EndTask to take down Notepad if it happens to be running when this window opens. You can use similar code wherever you need this functionality.

Listing 7.6. The Form Load event.

```
Sub Form_Load()
    Dim Hwnd As Integer
    Dim Y As Integer
    Hwnd = FindWindow(0&, "Notepad")
    If Hwnd = 0 Then
        MsgBox "NotePad is not running", vbInformation
        Exit Sub
    Else
        MsgBox "NotePad will now be closed", vbInformation
```

```
      End If
      Y = EndTask(Hwnd)
      If Y <> 0 Then
          MsgBox "NotePad terminated", vbInformation
      Else
          MsgBox "Error - Cannot terminate NotePad", vbInformation
      End If
End Sub
```

SendMessage

SendMessage() is the synchronous sibling of PostMessage(). Unlike PostMessage(), SendMessage() tends to get used frequently to send messages to windows and controls within the same application. Why would you want to send a message to a control on your own form? Well, it turns out that this is a good way to retrieve some of the functionality that Visual Basic steals away from you and to get around some of those "walls."

Here are some examples of things you can do with the appropriate SendMessage() that Visual Basic doesn't normally let you do:

- Setting tab stops in listboxes
- Getting a single line of text from a multiline text box
- Finding a string in a listbox

Although you can implement your own code to find a string in a listbox, you don't have to. Windows already has that functionality built right in. All you have to do is access it through SendMessage()!

The declaration and parameters are very similar to PostMessage(), as shown in Listing 7.7.

Listing 7.7. The SendMessage() declare statement.

```
Declare Function SendMessage Lib "user32" Alias "SendMessageA"
(ByVal hWnd As Long, _
 ByVal wMsg As Long, _
 ByVal wParam As Integer, _
 lParam As Any) As Long
```

hWnd identifies the window to which the message will be sent. If this parameter is HWND_BROADCAST, the message is sent to all top-level windows, including disabled or invisible unowned windows.

uMsg specifies the message to be sent.

wParam specifies 16 bits of additional message-dependent information. lParam specifies 32 bits of additional message-dependent information.

Setting Tab Stops

So how do you put it to use? Well, normally, if you include a chr$(9) (a tab character) in a string that you put in a listbox or a multiline edit, the control simply moves the following text to its next tab stop. Visual Basic gives you no way to set these tab stops to be where you want them, however. But you can with SendMessage(). Listing 7.8 shows you how.

Listing 7.8. Setting the tab stops in a listbox.

```
Dim nTabPos(3) As Integer
Dim lResult     As Long

Rem Define the positions
nTabPos(0) = 10
nTabPos(1) = 50
nTabPos(2) = 90

Rem Set the focus to the target listbox and fire away
lstExample.SetFocus
lResult = SendMessage(GetFocus(), LB_SETTABSTOPS, 0, ByVal 0&)
lResult = SendMessage(GetFocus(), LB_SETTABSTOPS, 3, nTabPos(0))
```

First, an array is created and then filled in with the desired tab positions. Then an LB_SETTABSTOPS with a 0 and ByVal 0& is used to clear any existing tab stops. Finally, LB_SETTABSTOPS with the number of array elements (3) and the first array element (nTabPos(0)) actually sets the tab stops.

You can set the tab stops in a multiline text box in the same way. Just send the message EM_SETTABSTOPS instead of LB_SETTABSTOPS.

Performing Magic with Multiline Edits

Speaking of multiline text boxes, there are several useful messages you can send to a multiline text box to get information that Visual Basic does not provide. You can send the EM_GETLINECOUNT message, for example, to get the number of lines of text in a multiline text box:

```
lLineCount = SendMessage(GetFocus(), EM_GETLINECOUNT, 0, ByVal 0&)
```

In addition, you can get the text of any individual line in a multiline text box with the message EM_GETLINE. But this message is a little tricky because it requires you to pass three parameters:

- The number of the line you want to retrieve
- The string to be filled with the contents of the line
- The length of that string

Because there are only two parameters, you will have to do a little trickery. You'll put the number of the line you want in the third parameter and the string in the fourth. But in order to tell it how long the string is, you'll have to embed the number in the first two bytes of the string, as shown in Listing 7.9.

Listing 7.9. Placing the length of the string in the first two bytes.

```
Dim nLineNum As Integer
Dim nLineLen As Integer
Dim sTemp    As String

Rem Set the max line length to 200
nLineLen = 200

Rem Fill The string with nulls and then paste the length to the front
sTemp = String$(nLinLen, vbNullChar)
sTemp = Chr$(nLinLen Mod 256) + Chr$(nLineLen \ 256) + sTemp
sTemp = Left$(sTemp, SendMessage(GetFocus(), EM_GETLINE, nLinNum, ByVal sTemp))
```

Another handy message for multiline text boxes is EM_LINESCROLL, which enables you to scroll your text boxes horizontally and vertically. Just specify the number of characters to scroll in the fourth argument of the SendMessage() function. Place the number of characters to scroll horizontally in the high order word (by multiplying by 65,536) and the number of lines to scroll vertically in the low order word. See Listing 7.10.

Listing 7.10. The ScrollText subroutine.

```
Sub ScrollText (txtSubject As TextBox, nHorizontal As Integer, nVertical As
➡Integer)

    Const EM_LINESCROLL = &HB6

    Dim lResult As Long
    Dim lScroll As Long

    lScroll = (nHorizontal * 65536) + nVertical
    txtSubject.SetFocus
    lResult = SendMessage(GetFocus(), EM_LINESCROLL, 0, ByVal lScroll)

End Sub
```

Keep in mind that this is a relative scroll. So if you use the value 3, the text box scrolls down three lines. If you use the value -65,536 (–1 times 65,536), the text box scrolls left one character.

Finding a String in a Listbox

A searching capability already is built into the listbox. But Visual Basic doesn't let you get to it. SendMessage() does. The code for FindStringInList is in Listing 7.11. It receives a string and a listbox or combo box. It returns `True` or `False`, indicating whether it succeeded in finding the string in the listbox. If it did find it, the `ListIndex` for the listbox or combo box is set to the place it was found.

Listing 7.11. Using `SendMessage()` to find a string in a listbox.

```
Function FindStringInList(sString As String, lstBox As ListBox) As Boolean

    Rem This subroutine finds the string that was passed to it and then
    Rem sets the passed combo box to that value

    Const LB_ERR = -1
    Const LB_FINDSTRING = (&H400 + 16)

    Dim lResult As Long
    Dim nZero   As Integer

    lResult = SendMessage(lstBox.hWnd, LB_FINDSTRING, 0, ByVal sString)

    If lResult = LB_ERR Then
        FindStringInList = False

    Else
        FindStringInList = True
        lstBox.ListIndex = lResult

    End If

End Function
```

Dropping Down a Listbox Automatically

Here's a neat trick for a drop-down list combo box (a combo box with the `Style` property set to 2). This code drops the list automatically when the combo box gets the focus (see Listing 7.12).

Listing 7.12. `GotFocus` drops down the listbox automatically.

```
Sub Combo1_GotFocus ()
    Rem When this control receives focus it will
    Rem automatically drop down

    Dim lResult As Long
    Const CB_SHOWDROPDOWN = WM_USER + 15

    lResult = SendMessage(GetFocus(), CB_SHOWDROPDOWN, 1, ByVal 0&)

End Sub
```

Sending messages in the GotFocus event for a control is a good technique because it enables you to avoid explicitly setting the focus to a control to get its hWnd.

Summary

This chapter was a whirlwind tour of event-driven programming and the use of events in Visual Basic. I began with a description of what it means to be event-driven in comparison to using traditional techniques. After some warnings about potential pitfalls, you explored application startup and shutdown. Then you saw the window and control events and how they applied to Visual Basic. Finally, you learned about some key Win32 functions that enable you to make use of Windows messages to get at some of the built-in Windows functionality that Visual Basic hides.

Reporting Mechanisms

8

by Conrad Scott

Visual Basic 4.0 is a powerful tool for the development of Windows applications. Many of the applications developed in Visual Basic require some sort of reporting mechanism in order to print the data associated with them. This chapter outlines reporting tools available and discusses methods of incorporating reporting into your Visual Basic applications.

Crystal Reports for Visual Basic

One tool for report development is Crystal Reports for Visual Basic. Crystal Reports is supplied with each copy of Visual Basic 4.0 (both 16 and 32 bit). This is an upgraded version of the application distributed with Visual Basic 3.

Crystal Reports is comprised of two major components. The first is the report development interface (\VB\REPORTS\CRW.EXE) (see Figure 8.1). The application icon is labeled "Crystal Reports - 16 bit" or "Crystal reports - 32 bit". This is the interface in which the report layout is designed. Designing a report includes selecting a source database, adding data fields to the report, setting record criteria, sorting, and so on. The second component is the Crystal Reports custom control (\WINDOWS\SYSTEM\CRYSTL16.OCX - 16 bit or CRYSTL32.OCX - 32 bit). This custom control is added to the Visual Basic application and handles the generation and printing of previously created reports. If you did not choose to install Crystal Reports when you initially installed Visual Basic, run Visual Basic setup again and choose Custom Installation. Choose only Crystal Reports from the list of options for installation to install Crystal Reports. This installation adds both the development interface and the OCXs to your system.

FIGURE 8.1.

The Crystal Reports development interface main application window.

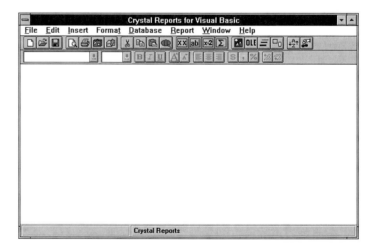

The following section outlines Crystal Reports in detail. The section begins with the steps that experienced developers can use to quickly generate a report. Following the quick steps is a detailed tour of the application, along with techniques for interfacing Crystal Reports with Visual Basic applications.

Quick Steps for Creating a Report

If you are already familiar with other reporting packages such as Microsoft Access or an earlier version of Crystal Reports, you will find creating a report in Crystal Reports intuitive. After running the Crystal Reports interface, do the following:

1. Select File | New | Report from the main menu, or click the new report icon on the toolbar (first toolbar icon). The New Report dialog is displayed.

2. Choose the type of report you would like to create from the Create new: section and the source of the report data from the from: section.

3. Choose OK. The Choose Database File dialog appears. Select a database to report against in the dialog box or choose SQL Table... to log on to a server via ODBC. If you choose to log on to a server you are returned to the Choose Database File dialog at completion of logon to select a database to report against.

4. The Choose SQL Table dialog appears. Select a table from the database to report against and choose OK. The new report is created and the Insert Database Field dialog appears.

5. Select the fields that you would like to appear on the report (extended- and multi-selection are allowed) and drag them to the report window's Details section.

6. Choose Insert | Text Field... from the main menu. The Edit Text Field dialog appears. Type in a title for the report and choose Accept. Move the mouse to the Page header section and click the left mouse to place the field on the report.

7. Choose File | Print Preview to see a preview of the report.

That's it. You have just created a report. Obviously, these are the most basic steps for report generation. Notice that although these steps do produce a report, it is not the most glamorous or eye-catching one imaginable. However, this does give you an idea of how simple creating a report can be.

The following sections examine the features of Crystal Reports in more detail. These sections include setting options for Crystal Reports, adding sections to a report, record selection, and formula creation, exporting data, OLE automation and more.

Setting Options

Select File | Options from the main menu to display the Crystal Report Options dialog (see Figure 8.2). This dialog contains a Category section with four buttons:

General

This category contains general settings for Crystal Reports (see Figure 8.2):

FIGURE 8.2.

The Options dialog displaying the General category.

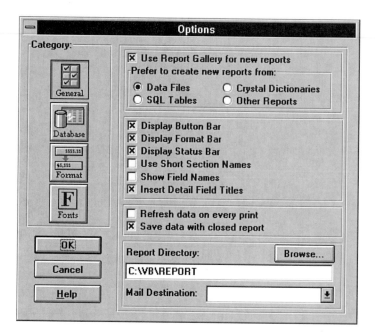

- Use Report Gallery for new reports—Choose whether to use the Report Gallery (report creation wizard) for the creation of a new report. If Report Gallery is selected, use the Prefer to Create New Reports From: section to set the default data location (Data Files, SQL table, Crystal Dictionaries, Other Reports).

The General category also contains check boxes that set whether to display the button bar, format bar, and status bar.

- Use Short Section Names—Select the Use Short Section Names check box to shorten the names of the sections in the report design window. This provides more space for the report layout. When this option is selected, the margin that displays the section names is truncated so that more of the report is visible.

- Show Field Names—When this check box is checked, Crystal Reports displays the field name in the center of each field on the report. Left unchecked, the field format is displayed.

- Insert Detail Field Titles—When a new field is added to the report and this option is checked, Crystal Reports adds a field title just above the inserted field. This field title is displayed in both design and run modes.

- Refresh Data on every print—When this option is on, Crystal Reports refreshes the report data from the selected database each time the report is printed. The report is also refreshed when it is exported to a data file or via MAPI (Mail API). Assume that this option is checked. Imagine that you are using a database that is updated frequently and you send a report via MAPI to several people in your division. If the database is updated in between mailnotes, each recipient will get a different report. This also applies if the report is sent to the printer. If multiple reports should contain the same data, uncheck this option.

- Save data with closed report—When checked, Crystal Reports saves the actual report data in a compressed format when the report is closed. When re-opened, the report data is decompressed and used to display in the report. This option can be used when the database is excessively large and only sample data is needed for report development. Another use for this is a report that is generated monthly. Once the report is generated, checking this option produces the saved month-end reporting each time the report is viewed.

- Report Directory—Sets the directory that Crystal Reports searches for existing reports. Choose Browse... to display a common dialog box in order to change the default directory.

- Mail Destination—Use this combo box to select to which mail destination to export reports. Generally, Mail via MAPI is the only selection available in this combo box.

Database

This category contains database settings for Crystal Reports.

FIGURE 8.3.

The Options dialog displaying the Database category.

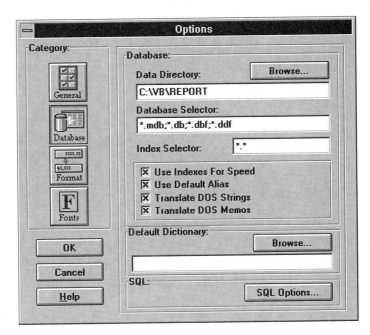

- Data Directory—The data directory sets the default directory Crystal Reports uses to list databases in the Choose Database File dialog. This common dialog appears with the current data directory set as the default (the default upon installation of Crystal Reports is \VB4\REPORT).

- Data Selector—The data selector edit box lists the database extensions to display in the Choose Database File dialog. The extensions listed in this edit box appear in the List Files Of Type combo box in the Choose Database File dialog.

- Index Selector—The index selector sets the extensions relating to indexing (Index file dialog, and so on) that appear in dialog boxes. Indexes are set by selecting Database | Links from the main menu (the Links dialog box appears) and pressing New to display the Define Link dialog. This dialog is used to link database tables using key fields. The purpose of indexing is to display reporting data from several tables at the same time.

- Use Indexes For Speed—This check box sets whether indexes defined in the Define Link dialog are used in the report generation. Using indexes speeds up the generation of a report.

- Use Default Alias—This check box indicates whether the database's 8-character filename is used as the default database name in Crystal Reports.

- Translate DOS Strings—This check box sets whether the character set used in dBASE applications (ASCII) is translated to the windows character set (ANSI). If a dBASE database's string fields contain any of the ASCII characters from 128–255 and are used to generate a report in Crystal Reports, this option should be checked so that the characters are properly translated to ANSI.

- Translate DOS Memos—This is the same as Translate DOS Strings except that it applies to memo fields.

- Default Dictionary—Allow for the use of a previously created data dictionary for the report. A data dictionary contains only pertinent report information. This is created from the reporting database prior to entering Crystal Reports. A data dictionary is essentially a data file containing the result of a query that links several tables in the reporting database and extracting only information necessary for the report.

- SQL—Choose the SQL Options... button to bring up the SQL Options dialog. This dialog is used to set default settings for SQL operations. If no options are set in this dialog box, multiple dialogs are presented during the SQL table selection process. Items covered in this dialog include the server type, server name, database, and User ID. SQL statements for tables and owners can be set in this dialog, and warnings can be set if the query yields more than a certain number of records.

Format

This category is used to set field format information for reports. There are five command buttons in this dialog (see Figure 8.4):

FIGURE 8.4.

The Options dialog displaying the Format category.

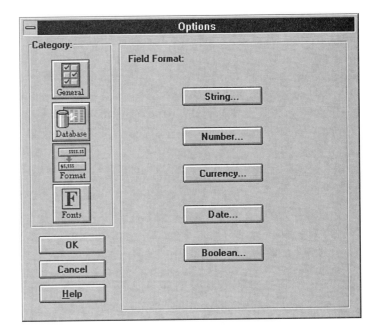

- String...—Choose this button to display the Format String dialog. This dialog contains the following controls:

  Suppress if duplicated check box—When checked, duplicate data is not printed from record to record. For example, imagine that you are creating a report that displays information about a customer order. The order contains an order number and several items. You want to display the order number only one time for each order, regardless of the number of items on the order. When the Suppress if duplicated check box is checked, the order number is listed only on the first item in an order. If the check box is unchecked, the order number appears on each item in the order.

  Hide when printing—When checked, the printing of string fields is suppressed. These fields appear in the report design window for reference.

  Alignment—Sets the alignment for text in the field (default, left, centered, right).

  Print on multiple lines—Check this check box if you would like to allow a field to print on multiple lines.

  Maximum number of lines:—If the Print on multiple lines check box is selected, enter the maximum number of lines that the field is allowed to print on (enter 0 for no limit).

- Number...—Choose this button to display the Format Number dialog. This dialog contains the following controls:

  Use Windows Default Format—Uses the Windows default date format for date fields on the report.

Suppress if Duplicated—When checked, duplicate data is not printed from record to record. For example, the order date is listed only on the first item in an order. If the check box is unchecked, the order date appears on each item in the order.

Suppress if Zero—Prevents the printing of number fields with a 0 value.

Hide When Printing—When checked, the printing of number fields is suppressed. For reference, these fields appear in the report design window.

Alignment—Sets the alignment for a number in a field (default, left, centered, right).

Decimals—Sets the number of decimal places displayed in a number field (1.0, 1.00, 1.000, and so on).

Rounding—Sets the number of places rounded to in a numeric field.

Negatives—Sets the format for the display of negative numbers in number fields (-123, 123- (123)).

Currency Symbol—Sets the currency symbol for the number fields ($, £, and so on).

One Symbol Per Page—Enabled when the Currency Symbol check box is checked. Prints the currency symbol for the first record but no others.

Fixed/Floating/Position—Sets the alignment for number fields when Currency Symbol is selected. The choices are to align the field to the dollar sign ($14,000–$400.00) or align the field to the value ($14,000–$–400.00).

Decimal Separator/Thousands Separator—Sets the characters used for the decimal and thousands separator.

Leading Zero—When checked, a zero is added to integer values less than 1 (0.2356).

- Currency...—Choose this button to display the Format Currency dialog. This dialog is exactly the same as the Number... dialog.

- Date...—Choose this button to display the Format Date dialog. Fields unique to this dialog are:

MDY/DMY/YMD—Sets the date display order for date fields.

Month/Day/Year—Sets each of these sections' display format for date fields.

- Boolean...—Choose this button to display the Format Boolean dialog. This dialog is exactly the same as the String... dialog with the following exception:

Boolean Text—Sets the display format of True and False values on a report. The options are:

True or False
T or F
Yes or No
Y or N
1 or 0

Fonts

This section contains 12 command buttons, each representing different sections of the report (see Figure 8.5). Choosing any one of these buttons displays a common font dialog that allows font settings for the selected section.

FIGURE 8.5.

The Options dialog displaying the Fonts category.

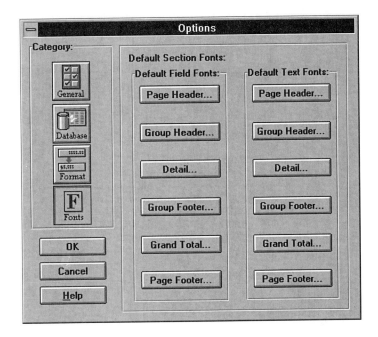

Examining the Toolbar

The Crystal Reports toolbar provides quick access to many of the most common tasks performed while creating a report. The following explains how each toolbar icon is used:

 Create a new report—The New Report dialog box is displayed asking for the type of report to be created and the source of the report data. (This assumes that Use Report Gallery for new reports in the General section of the options dialog is checked.)

 Open an existing report—A common dialog box is displayed asking for the filename of the report. Once selected, the report is opened in design mode within Crystal Reports.

 Save report—Save the report that currently has the focus. If the report has not been previously saved, the File Save As dialog appears asking for a report filename.

continues

Preview report—Previews the report in a viewer window. This option brings up the Saved Data dialog box. Choose Use Saved Data to use the current report data or Refresh Data to refresh the report using data from the selected database.

Print report to a printer—Prints the report to the default Windows printer. This option brings up the Saved Data dialog box. Choose Use Saved Data to use the current report data or Refresh Data to refresh the report using data from the selected database. The Print dialog appears when printing options can be selected.

Export a report—Export report data in one of 15 formats to either a disk file or via MAPI. Selecting this option brings up the Export dialog box where the export format and destination are selected. Once selected, the Character-Separated Values dialog, Number and Date Format Dialog, and Choose Export File dialog appear.

Mail a report—Follows the same path as the Export a report option with the exception of the Choose Export File dialog box. At this point a Send Mail window appears (similar to Microsoft Mail). Once populated, the report data is attached to a mailnote sent to the selected recipient(s).

Cut—Cut the selected item from the report and place it on the Windows Clipboard.

Copy—Copy the selected item from the report and place it on the Windows Clipboard.

Paste—Paste the contents of the Windows Clipboard at the current cursor position on the report.

Select Fields—Allows for using the mouse to select multiple fields on the report. Click this icon, hold the left mouse button down and drag to select multiple controls. During selection a rectangle is drawn around the controls. Release the mouse button to complete selection.

Insert Database Field—Brings up the Insert Database Field dialog box that allows for the addition of database fields to the report. Drag fields from this dialog to add them to the report or choose the Insert button. Choose Browse Field Data... to view a sample of the data from the highlighted field. Choose Done when field selections are complete.

Insert Text Field—Brings up the Edit Text Field dialog box. Type a name for the new text field and choose Accept. A rectangular field appears on the report. Move the mouse to position the field and click the left button to place the field in the desired location.

 Insert Formula Field—Brings up the Insert Formula dialog. Enter a name for the new formula in the edit box and press OK. The Edit Formula: @*Formula Name* dialog appears allowing for the selection of formula criteria. See the section, "The Formula Editor," later in this chapter for more information about creating formulas.

 Insert Summary Field—Brings up the Insert Summary dialog prompting for information about the new summary field. See the "Inserting Fields" section later in this chapter for more information about summary fields.

 Insert Graphic—Brings up a common dialog box asking for the name of the graphic file to insert in the report. When selected, a rectangle appears in the report design window. Move the mouse to position the graphic in the desired position and click the left mouse to place the graphic on the report. The graphic appears at both design time and run time.

 Insert OLE Object—Brings up the Insert Object dialog box. Select the type of OLE object to be inserted into the report and choose OK. When selected, a rectangle appears in the report design window. Move the mouse to position the graphic in the desired position and click the left mouse to place the graphic on the report.

 Draw a line—Changes the cursor to a pencil and allows a line to be drawn on the report.

 Draw a box—Changes the cursor to a pencil and allows a box to be drawn on the report. The box is a graphical object used for improving the look of a report. The box can act as a frame for fields (fields can be dragged inside the box area). Select the box and click the right mouse button to display a pop up menu of options for the box. Select Change Format... from the pop-up menu to display a formatting dialog.

 Record Sort Order—Brings up the Record Sort Order dialog allowing the report's primary and secondary sort order to be set.

continues

Record Selection Criteria—Brings up the Edit Formula: Record Selection Formula dialog. Use this dialog to set the criteria for what records appear on the report.

Bold—Standard toolbar icon for bolding text.

Italic—Standard toolbar icon for italicizing text.

Underline—Standard toolbar icon for underlining text.

Increase Font Size—Increases the font size of text in the selected field.

Decrease Font Size—Decreases the font size of text in the selected field.

Left Align—Left aligns the data in the selected field.

Center—Centers the data in the selected field.

Right Align—Right aligns the data in the selected field.

Currency—Enabled when a currency field is selected. Inserts a dollar sign to the left of the value ($1,000,000).

Comma—Enabled when a currency field is selected. Inserts a comma in the dollar value (1,000,000).

Percent—Enabled when a currency field is selected. Inserts a percent sign to the right of the value (1,000,000%).

Degree of Precision (Increase)—Inserts a decimal place in a currency field. The number 100.55666 is rounded to 100.56. Changing the degree of precision changes 100.56 to 100.556, 100.5666, and so on.)

Degree of Precision (Decrease)—Removes a decimal place in a currency field. The number 100.55666 is rounded to 100.56. Changing the degree of precision changes 100.556 to 100.56, and so on.)

Report Creation

This section outlines the report creation features of Crystal Reports. Items covered include accessing databases and files, The Report Gallery (Report Wizard), inserting fields, creating formulas, and inserting graphical objects.

Databases and Data Files

Crystal Reports is capable of accessing reporting data from a variety of database formats. These formats include dBASE, InterBase, Btreive, Paradox, as well as all Microsoft formats (Access, Excel, FoxPro, and so on).

If you are using a database via ODBC, you first need to log on to the ODBC server. To log on to a server, Select Database | Log On Server from the main menu. Select an ODBC server from the list and choose OK. You may log on to several ODBC servers concurrently, but you must log onto each individually. Once you are logged on to a server, you have access to all databases contained within that server.

Adding and Removing a Database from a Report

Reporting data is accessed from many different types of databases by Crystal Reports. To add a database to a report, select the Database | Add Database to Report... menu option. This brings up the Choose SQL dialog. If you are adding an additional table from the current database to the report, choose the table from the SQL Tables listbox and choose OK. To add a new database to the report, choose Database File... This option brings up a common dialog box from which you may select an additional database to add to the report. If this database is from an ODBC server that you have not logged on to, you are prompted to log on to the server.

The Report Gallery Dialog

To create a new report, select File | New from the main menu. A menu with three options appears:

1. Report
2. Cross-Tab
3. Mailing Label

Selecting any one of these options brings up the New Report dialog box. The buttons that are selected by default on this dialog depend on the menu option you selected. If you do not see the New Report dialog, select File | Options from the main menu (the Options dialog appears). In the general category, select the Use Report Gallery for new reports check box.

In the New Report dialog, select the type of report that you would like to create from the Create new: section. This section has the following buttons:

Report—Creates a detail report. A detail report has this format:

Customer Order Detail for September, 1995

Order Number	Customer Number	Serial Number
123456789	0000010123	321654987
321564987	5605640560	987906500
654056065	0987089980	654970900

Cross Tab—A crosstab report summarizes data much like a spreadsheet that compares the data in fields of one category with the data in fields of another category. A crosstab report has this format:

Number of Products by Month

	January	February	March
Product 1	1200	942	1040
Product 2	640	670	920
Product 3	80	1020	1030

Label—This options allows for the creation of mailing labels.

Inserting Fields

Inserting a field into a report is begun by selecting one of the Insert menu options. The following is an explanation of the type of fields that can be inserted into a report along with how to add each type to your report layout. Once a field is inserted into the report, right clicking on the field pops up a menu with formatting options for the field. You can also move the field from where Crystal Reports places it, to anywhere else on the report.

Database Fields

This option inserts a field from the database that you have chosen for your report. Select Insert | Database Field... from the main menu to display the Insert Database Field dialog box. Select the field(s) that you would like to add, and drag them to your design window or choose the insert button (multi-selection and extended selection are allowed). To view a sample of the data for the selected field, choose the Browse Field Data... button. This option displays a dialog box containing a sample of the data contained within the field. Choose Done when you finish adding browsing field data and when you finish adding fields choose Done from the Insert Database Field dialog.

Text Fields

To insert a text field into your report, Select Insert | Text Field... from the main menu. This option displays the Edit Text field dialog. Enter a name for the new field and choose Accept to add the field to the report.

Formula Fields

This option allows you to insert calculated fields into your report. An example of when this is useful is a field that calculates the total number of orders placed in a given month, the sum of all dollars received, and so on. Select Insert | Formula Field.. from the main menu to display the Insert formula dialog box. Enter a name for your new formula field and choose OK to bring up the Edit formula: @ Formula name dialog box. For this example, assume you are using an order entry database. The following are four sections to this dialog. Functions and fields are presented in the order you would use them.

Functions: Assume that you are interested in calculating the number of orders in your database. The first step is to select the `Count(fld)` function from the Arithmetic: section.

Fields: To select a field, double-click on it from the list of available database fields. This field is used to calculate the new formula. For our example, you select the Order Number field (ORDERNUM). Your calculation now reads: `Count ({ORDERS.ORDERNUM})`. When added to the report, this field displays the number of orders contained in the data from your database.

Operators: You need to know the current inventory amount (CURRINV) minus the number of orders received. Double-click CURRINV in the Fields list box. Next double-click Subtract in the Arithmetic section of the Operators list box. Now select the `Count(fld)` function from the Arithmetic: section and then the ORDNUM field from the Fields: section. Our finished calculation reads: `{ORDERS.CURRINV} - Count ({ORDERS.ORDERNUM})`. This field displays the available inventory after all existing orders are fulfilled.

Formula Text: As you create the formula, it is displayed in the Formula Text: section. You can edit this section manually if you wish.

When you are satisfied with your field formula, choose Accept or Check to have the Crystal compiler check the formula. If there are errors in the formula a message box appears describing the problem. After choosing Accept, the dialog closes and a field appears on the report. Move the mouse to position the field and click the left button to place the field in the desired location.

Special Fields

This option allows you to insert page numbers, record numbers, group numbers, and the date the report is printed. Selecting one of these options places the selected field on the report layout.

Record Selection Criteria

Choosing the records that you would like to appear on your report is done through the same dialog used to create formula fields. See the "Formula Fields" section earlier in this chapter for more details. Use this dialog to screen the records that you would like to appear on the report.

Sort Order

Setting a sort order for the report is done by choosing Report | Record Sort Order... This displays the Record Sort Order dialog box. The Report Fields: section of the dialog displays a list of fields that can be sorted. Fields that are currently being used for sorting are displayed in the Sort Fields: section. Select a field from the Report Fields: section and choose Add (or double-click) the field to add it for sorting. Multi-level sorting is accomplished by choosing multiple fields. For example, assume that you are using an order entry database and would like to see a detail of the orders you currently have in your database. You want this information sorted by region (REGION) and then by product (PRODUCT). Choosing REGION and then PRODUCT in the Record Sort Order dialog sorts the report in this manner:

Orders for the Month of September, 1995

Order Number	Customer Number	Product Name
Region 1		
123456789	654321987	Product AAA
564065400	320646060	Product BBB
Region 2		
65406406	5640654056	Product BBBB
5505804	6540662	Product ZZZ

Remember that you need to set up the proper sections in order to display the data in this format.

Object Linking and Embedding

Inserting an OLE object into a report is a simple task. First, select the OLE icon from the toolbar. Select from the list the type of object that you would like to insert and then select OK. There are 25 different objects that you can insert into a report, so the next step depends on which object you select. Generally, you are prompted to select the location of the object's data (a bitmap, media file, and so on). Once selected, the object is embedded into the report. Right click on the inserted object to manipulate. An example of manipulation for the Pocket CD Playlist object (CD player) is playing, pausing, and stopping the CD. This manipulation is also allowed when the report is displayed in the print preview window.

The Crystal Reports OCX

The second component of Crystal Reports is the Crystal Reports OCX (\WIN-DOWS\SYSTEM\CRYSTL16.OCX and \WINDOWS\SYSTEM\CRYSTL32.OCX). This OCX is incorporated directly in to the Visual Basic application and used to print existing Crystal Reports. This section outlines the custom control (the same for both 16 and 32 bit), and provides a sample program using the control.

Adding the OCX Control to a Visual Basic Project

To add the OCX control to a Visual Basic project, open the project and select Tools | Custom Controls... from the Visual Basic main menu. Check the Crystal Report Control item in the list box and choose OK. The Crystal Report Control is added to the Toolbox for the project. Open a form and double-click the control in the Toolbox to add it to the form. Select the control and press F4 to view its properties.

Control Properties

The Crystal Reports custom control contains the following unique properties:

Action

Description: Set this property to 1 to print a report. This property is available at runtime only.

Usage: `Form1.CrystalReport1.Action = 1`

Connect

Description: Set this property when you want to log on to a SQL server. The property has the following parameters:

1. `DSN`—Server Name
2. `UID`—User ID to log on to the SQL server
3. `PWD`—Password to log on to the SQL server
4. `DSQ`—DatabaseQualifier$

The `DatabaseQualifier` parameter is used if your server uses the database concept and is the name of the database.

Usage: `Form1.CrystalReport1.Connect = "DSN = Server1;UID = Conrad;PWD = Vacation;DSQ = Develop"`

NOTE

To use this property you must have first installed an ODBC server and have included the database in your path statement (this path should include \database\bin).

CopiesToPrinter

Description: Sets the number of report copies that are sent to the printer.

Usage: `Form1.CrystalReport1.CopiesToPrinter = 5` (sends five copies to the printer).

DataFiles

Description: Sets the database file used to generate the report. You only need to use this property if you would like to print the report from several data locations. The report has a default data location; this array property changes it.

Usage: `Form1.CrystalReport1.DataFiles(Index) = LocationOfDataFile$`

Destination

Description: Specifies the destination for the report. This property has the following settings:

  `0 - Window`—Pops up a window displaying the report.

  `1 - Printer`—Sends the report to the printer.

  `2 - File`—Prints the report to a file. When using this property you must set the `PrintFileName` and `PrintFileType` properties.

Usage: `Form1.CrystalReport1.Destination = 0`

Formula

Description: This property allows you to change an existing formula in a report. An example of this is a formula that calculates the sales tax for a state. Use this property to change the formula for a different state (this is an array property).

Usage: `Report1.Formula(State(Index)) = "Tax = {Orders.Total} * .08"` This sets the sales tax formula to 8%.

LastErrorNumber

Description: This is the number of the last error encountered on the report.

Usage: `If Form1.CrystalReport1.LastErrorNumber <> 0 Then GoTo ReportErrorHandler`

LastErrorString

Description: This is a description of the value in `LastErrorNumber`.

Usage:

```
If Form1.CrystalReport1.LastErrorNumber <> 0 Then
    ErrorNumber = Form1.CrystalReport1.LastErrorNumber
    ErrorText = Form1.CrystalReport1.LastErrorString
    MsgBox "Error Number " & ErrorNumber &  ": " & ErrorText & " encountered."
    GoTo ReportErrorHandler
Endif
```

Password

Description: Set this property to enter a password for an Access table.

Usage: `Form1.CrystalReport1.Password = "MyPassword"`

PrintFileName

Description: Sets the name of the file where the report is printed (assumes that the `Destina-tion` property is set to `2 - file`).

Usage: `Form1.CrystalReport1.Destination = 2`

`Form1.CrystalReport1.PrintFileName = "c:\vb\reports\MyReport.rpt"`

PrintFileType

Description: Use this property to set the format for printing a report to a file.

Usage: `Form1.CrystalReport1.PrintFileType = 4` (See the Help topic `PrintFileType` property in Crystal Reports for an explanation of file formats).

ReportFileName

Description: This property sets the name of the report to be printed.

Usage: `Form1.CrystalReport1.ReportFileName = "c:\vb\reports\myreport.txt"`

SelectionFormula

Description: Sets the records used when printing a report.

Usage: `Selection$ = "{Orders.Total} > 1000"`

`Form1.CrystalReport1.SelectionFormulaProperty = Selection$`

SortFields

Description: Sets the sort order for the report. This is an array property. The usage example initiates a primary and secondary sort:

Usage: `Form1.CrystalReport1.SortFields(0) = "+{ORDERS.ORDNUM}"`   `'primary`

`Form1.CrystalReport1.SortFields(1) = "+{ORDERS.ORDDATE}"`   `'secondary`

This sorts the report by order number and then by order date.

UserName

Description: Sets the user name when logging on to a protected Access database.

Usage: `Form1.CrystalReport1.UserName = "MyUserName"`

WindowBorderStyle

Description: Sets the border style for the report window. The settings are:

  0—None
  1—Fixed Single
  2—Sizable
  3—Fixed Double

Usage: `Form1.CrystalReport1.WindowBorderStyle = 1`

WindowControlBox

Description: Sets whether or not a control menu appears in the upper left hand corner of the report window. This assumes that the `Destination` property is set to `0`.

Usage: `Form1.CrystalReport1.WindowControlBox = TRUE`

WindowHeight

Description: Sets the height of the report window in pixels.

Usage: `Form1.CrystalReport1.Height = 300`

WindowLeft

Description: Sets the number of pixels from the left edge of the parent window in which the report window appears. If the report window is the parent window, this is relative to the desktop window.

Usage: `Form1.CrystalReport1.WindowLeft = 300`

WindowMaxButton

Description: Sets whether a maximize menu appears in the upper right hand corner of the report window. This assumes that the `Destination` property is set to `0`.

Usage: `Form1.CrystalReport1.WindowMaxButton = FALSE`

WindowMinButton

Description: Sets whether a minimize button appears in the upper right hand corner of the report window. This assumes that the `Destination` property is set to `0`.

Usage: `Form1.CrystalReport1.MinButton = FALSE`

WindowParentHandle

Description: Sets the handle of the parent window if the report window is a child of another window. The Usage section assumes that the report window is a child of Form1.

Usage: `Form1.CrystalReport1.ParentHandle = Form1.hWnd`

WindowTitle

Description: Sets the title for the report window. This assumes that the `Destination` property is set to `0`.

Usage: `Form1.CrystalReport1.WindowTitle = "My New Report"`

WindowTop

Description: Sets the number of pixels from the top edge of the parent window that the report window appears. If the report window is the parent window, this is relative to the desktop window.

Usage: `Form1.CrystalReport1.WindowTop = 100`

WindowWidth

Description: Sets the width of the report window in pixels. This assumes that the `Destination` property is set to `0`.

Usage: `Form1.CrystalReport1.WindowWidth = 300`

Crystal Reports OCX Examples

The following examples utilize the reporting features of the Crystal Reports OCX from within Visual Basic.

First we send a report to the printer.

```
Private Sub Print_Report Click()
    Form1.CrystalReport1.Destination = 2
    Form1.CrystalReport1.ReportFileName = "c:\vb\reports\MyReport.txt"
    Form1.CrystalReport1.Action = 1
End Sub
```

Next we send the report to the printer, then to a data file, and then open it in the report window.

```
Private Sub Print_Report Click()
    'to the printer
    Form1.CrystalReport1.Destination = 1
    Form1.CrystalReport1.ReportFileName = "c:\vb\reports\MyReport.txt"
    Form1.CrystalReport1.Action = 1

    'to a data file
    Form1.CrystalReport1.Destination = 2
    Form1.CrystalReport1.PrintFileName = "c:\vb\reports\output.txt"
    Form1.CrystalReport1.PrintFileType = 0    'Record format
    Form1.CrystalReport1.Action = 1

    'and finally the report window
    Form1.CrystalReport1.Destination = 0
    Form1.CrystalReport1.Action = 1
End Sub
```

Next we send the report to a window containing no minimize button, maximize button, or control menu. We set the window to 100 pixels from the top and left of the parent window (if there is no parent window, it is aligned based on the desktop). We also add a title.

```
Private Sub Print_Report Click()
    Form1.CrystalReport1.Destination = 0
    Form1.CrystalReport1.ReportFileName = "c:\vb\reports\MyReport.txt"
    Form1.CrystalReport1.WindowMinButton = FALSE
    Form1.CrystalReport1.WindowMaxButton = FALSE
    Form1.CrystalReport1.WindowControlBox = FALSE
    Form1.CrystalReport1.WindowTop = 100
    Form1.CrystalReport1.WindowLeft = 100
    Form1.CrystalReport1.WindowTitle = "My New Report"
    Form1.CrystalReport1.Action = 1
End Sub
```

Finally, create and print a report for each of six divisions. We sort the report by Order Number and Order Date and send it to the printer.

```
Private Sub Print_Report Click()
    'counter for loop
    Dim iRet as Integer

    'Set the number of divisions
    Dim NumDivisions as Integer
    NumDivisions = 6
```

```
        'record restriction string for each division
        Dim DivisionFormula as String

        'set the report destination and report name
        Form1.CrystalReport1.Destination = 1
        Form1.CrystalReport1.ReportFileName = "c:\vb\reports\MyReport.txt"

        'add a primary and secondary sort
        Form1.CrystalReport1.SortFields(0) = "+{ORDERS.ORDNUM}"    'primary sort
        Form1.CrystalReport1.SortFields(1) = "+{ORDERS.ORDDATE}"   'secondary sort

    For iRet = 1 to NumDivisions
        'set the division and apply it to the report
        DivisionFormula = "{ORDERS.DIVISION} = " & Str$(iRet%)
        Form1.CrystalReport1.SelectionFormula   Property = DivisionFormula

        'print the report
        Form1.CrystalReport1.Action = 1
    Next iRet
End Sub
```

Creating Reports Using VBPRINT.DLL

VBPRINT.DLL is a dynamic link library (DLL) available through the Microsoft Developer's Network (MSDN). This DLL provides a variety of formatting and drawing functions for printing from a Visual Basic application. It may be distributed royalty free with your Visual Basic applications. This DLL was ported to 32 bit (VBPRNT32.DLL) and by Paul Mahar at MicroHelp Inc. in Atlanta (Thanks, Paul!). The 16- and 32-bit DLLs, as well as the source code for each are included with this book.

VBPRINT.DLL is ideal for creating reports directly from Visual Basic using data from either a database or data file. The DLL contains functions to build a report layout. Functions included add headers and footers to your report as well as allow you to set up columns for the display of data. Rectangles, round rectangles, and lines can be placed on the report to enhance the graphical look.

NOTE

VBPRINT.DLL does not output to Visual Basic forms or to data files. This is strictly a printing DLL. If you set the printer destination to Print to File, the file created contains only printer directives.

The following section describes the ways that you can use VBPRINT.DLL to create and print reports directly from your Visual Basic application. Following the explanation is an example that incorporates the features of VBPRINT.DLL. Finally, a dictionary of the DLL's functions is provided.

Using VBPRINT

This section describes the steps necessary to design and print a report using VBPRINT.DLL. This report contains an underlined title, columns of data, and is fully formatted. The report is output to the windows default printer.

Here are the function declaration statements for VBPRINT:

```
Declare Function InitializePrinter Lib "vbprint.dll" (ByVal hWnd%) As Integer
    Declare Function PrinterSetup Lib "vbprint.dll" (ByVal hWnd%) As Integer
    Declare Function PageLayoutSetup Lib "vbprint.dll" (ByVal nTop%, ByVal nRight%,
➡ByVal nBottom%, ByVal nLeft%) As Integer
    Declare Function DonePrinting Lib "vbprint.dll" () As Integer
    Declare Function StartParagraph Lib "vbprint.dll" (ByVal szFontName$, ByVal
➡nFontSize%, ByVal nStyle%) As Integer
    Declare Function FinishParagraph Lib "vbprint.dll" () As Integer
    Declare Function PrintHeadline Lib "vbprint.dll" (ByVal szHeadLine$, ByVal
➡szFontName$, ByVal nFontSize%, ByVal nStyle%) As Integer
    Declare Function ParagraphText Lib "vbprint.dll" (ByVal szText$) As Integer
    Declare Function EjectPage Lib "vbprint.dll" () As Integer
    Declare Function PrintDLLVersion Lib "vbprint.dll" () As Integer
    Declare Function SetParagraphSpacing Lib "vbprint.dll" (ByVal nSpacingBefore%,
➡ByVal nSpacingAfter%) As Integer
    Declare Function SetUpColumns Lib "vbprint.dll" (ByVal Columns%, nC As Any,
➡ByVal szFontName$, ByVal nFontSize%, ByVal nStyle%) As Integer
    Declare Function PrintColumnText Lib "vbprint.dll" (ByVal szText$) As Integer
    Declare Function EndColumnPrinting Lib "vbprint.dll" () As Integer
    Declare Function PrintColumnHeaders Lib "vbprint.dll" (ByVal szHeader$, ByVal
➡Columns%, nC As Any, ByVal szFontName$, ByVal nFontSize%, ByVal nStyle%) As
➡Integer
    Declare Function KillJob Lib "vbprint.dll" () As Integer
    Declare Function PrinterPort Lib "vbprint.dll" (ByVal szPort$) As Integer
    Declare Function PrinterName Lib "vbprint.dll" (ByVal s$) As Integer
    Declare Function PageSizeY Lib "vbprint.dll" () As Integer
    Declare Function PageSizeX Lib "vbprint.dll" () As Integer
    Declare Function DrawLine Lib "vbprint.dll" (ByVal X1%, ByVal Y1%, ByVal X2%,
➡ByVal Y2%) As Integer
    Declare Function DrawRectangle Lib "vbprint.dll" (ByVal X1%, ByVal Y1%, ByVal
➡X2%, ByVal Y2%) As Integer
    Declare Function DrawRndRectangle Lib "vbprint.dll" (ByVal X1%, ByVal Y1%,
➡ByVal X2%, ByVal Y2%, ByVal X3%, ByVal y3%) As Integer
    Declare Function DrawEllipse Lib "vbprint.dll" (ByVal X1%, ByVal Y1%, ByVal
➡X2%, ByVal Y2%) As Integer
    Declare Function MoveYPos Lib "vbprint.dll" (ByVal nY%) As Integer
```

The first step is to create a structure to hold the data that is to be displayed on the report. The data contained in the structure is fed to the VBPRINT functions to output the data to the printer. For purposes of example we create the following structure:

```
Type OrderData
        OrderNum As String
        OrderDate As String
        CustNum As String
        SerNum As String
End Type
```

Fill this structure with data from your database (using SQL statements, file reads, and so on). The next step is to call the `InitializePrinter()` function. Pass this function the `hWnd` of the application form (the handle to a form named form1 is form1.hWnd). The `InitializePrinter` function prepares the printer to receive data from the application.

```
i% = InitializePrinter(Form1.hWnd)
```

NOTE

An `hWnd` is a handle to global information about an object (form, control, and so on). In this case, the `hWnd` denotes an instance of Form1. This handle is used by the DLL to get information from the form so that the printer can be initialized.

Next, use the `PageLayoutSetup()` function to set the margins for the page. This function sets the area in which printing is allowed. A hint here is that after you send a command to add data to the page, you can change these settings without erasing previously printed items.

```
'Set the margins for the page layout (top, right, bottom, left)
i% = PageLayoutSetup(10, 100, 100, 100)
```

The `StartParagraph()` function is then used to set the font that is used for printing, the size of the font and any number of style flags. See the `StartParagraph()` function under the function descriptions for a listing of these flags.

```
'Begin a paragraph. Set the font to Arial 12 point bold)
i% = StartParagraph("Arial", 10, BOLD_FONT)
```

Next you print a title for the report using the `PrintHeadline()` function. `szHeadline` is the text that is used for the title. Unfortunately, there does not appear to be a way to center the title. Several tabs added to the title (`Chr$(9)` & `Chr$(9)`) provide a way around that.

```
'Print a title for the report (using the font and size set in StartParagraph
 i% = PrintHeadline(szHeadLine$, "Arial", 14, BOLD_FONT)
```

After the title is printed, underline it using the `DrawLine()` function. This works the same way as the Visual Basic `Line()` function.

```
'Draw a line under the report title (left X, left Y, right X, right Y)
i% = DrawLine(100, 1500, 12000, 1500)
```

In this example, we have four columns of data to print on the report. This data is contained in the `OrderData` structure outlined above. The `SetUpColumns()` function is called to add four columns, each with a width of 100 (1 inch) using the 12 point, bold, Arial font.

```
'Set up 4 columns in which to print the reporting data.
i% = SetUpColumns(4, 100, "Arial", 12, BOLD_FONT)
```

We next use the `MoveYPos()` function to add some space between the line and the column headings. The value passed to the function is in hundredths of an inch.

```
MoveYPos (40)
```

Next we draw a line under the column headings. Usually this function is called after the column headings are printed, but I placed it here to bring up an important point. It is likely that after you print your title and underline it, you will change font sizes to print your column headings. In order to avoid having the line under the title appear bolder than the one under the column headings, draw the line before changing fonts.

```
'Draw a line under the column headings
i% = DrawLine(100, 2100, 12000, 2100)
```

To change fonts to begin printing the data, call the `FinishParagraph()` function followed by another `StartParagraph()` function. The second `StartParagraph()` function changes the font settings prior to printing the report data.

Next, we place the column titles in the variable `szHeader$`. The columns are separated by a tab (`Chr$(9)`):

```
'Construct and print the titles for the columns
szHeader$ = "Order Number" + Chr$(9) + "Order Date" + Chr$(9) + "Customer Number "
➡+ Chr$(9) + "Serial Number"
```

After the columns are set up, we call the `PrintColumnHeaders()` function:

```
i% = PrintColumnHeaders(szHeader$, 4, ColumnWidth(1), "Arial", 12, BOLD_FONT)
```

The next step is to use the `MoveYPos()` function to add some space between the column headings and the data.

```
MoveYPos (10)
```

Next we use a `For` loop to print the data to the report. This example prints 38 records (1 page) and a section label every 10 records. A space is placed after each record for readability using the `MoveYPos()` function.

```
For x% = 1 To 38
    If x% = 1 Or x% = 11 Or x% = 21 Or x% = 31 Then
        MoveYPos (20)
```

To create the column headers, divide the record number by 10 and convert the result to an integer using the `CInt()` function. If you fail to use `CInt()`, rounding causes the section numbers to be 1.1, 2.2, and so on.

```
    i% = PrintColumnHeaders("Section " & Trim$(Str$(CInt(x% / 10) + 1)), 1,
➡ColumnWidth(1), "Arial", 12, BOLD_FONT)
End If
```

The next step is to piece together the data to display in the columns on the report. We re-use the variable `szHeader` for our data and it is passed using either the `PrintColumnHeaders()` or `PrintColumnText()` function. These two functions produce the same result, but `PrintColumnHeaders()` gives you more control over changing the column width and font. In this example, we concatenate the field title with the data to displayed:

```
'Place data from database or data file into ReportData array. In this case, we use
➡the sample
'ColumnData structure.
    ReportData$ = "Order Number: " & ColumnData(x%).OrderNum & Chr$(9)
    ReportData$ = ReportData$ + "Order Date: " & ColumnData(x%).OrderDate + Chr$(9)
    ReportData$ = ReportData$ + "Customer Number: " + ColumnData(x%).CustNum +
➡Chr$(9)
    ReportData$ = ReportData$ + "Serial Number: " + ColumnData(x%).SerNum + Chr$(9)

  'Print the report data.
    i% = PrintColumnHeaders(ReportData$, 4, ColumnWidth(1), "Arial", 10, BOLD_FONT)

  'This is a trick to put more space between each line of the report
    MoveYPos (5)
Next x%

    'These functions do general cleanup.
    i% = FinishParagraph()
    i% = EndColumnPrinting
    i% = DonePrinting()
```

A Sample Printing Program Using VBPRINT.DLL

This sample program creates a report and prints it to the Windows default printer using
VBPRINT.DLL. The data for the report is created randomly and placed into a structure containing the field elements that are to be printed on the report. An underlined title is placed on
the report and columns are created to output the data. Finally the report is sent to the printer.
This sample assumes that the VBPRINT.DLL function declarations are present in the project.

```
Private Sub Command1_Click()

    'Return value for functions
    Dim i As Integer

    'Array that sets the widths of the columns on the report
    'We set the 4 column widths to 150 (1/100th of an inch, 100 = 1 inch)
    Dim ColumnWidth() As Integer
    ReDim ColumnWidth(1 To 4)

    For x% = 1 To 4
        ColumnWidth(x%) = 150
    Next x%

    'Title variable
    Dim szHeadLine As String

    szHeadLine$ = Trim$(Chr$(9) + Chr$(9) + Chr$(9) + Chr$(9) + "Customer Orders
➡for August, 1995")
    'szFontName$ = "Arial"

    'Structure that holds the reporting data
    Dim ColumnData(1 To 40) As OrderData

    'Fill the structure with bogus reporting data (this will normally come from
➡your database or data file).

    For x% = 1 To 40
```

```
        'Order Number field
        ColumnData(x%).OrderNum = ""
        ColumnData(x%).OrderNum = Trim$(Str$(x% & "000000"))

        'Order Date field
        ColumnData(x%).OrderDate = ""
        ColumnData(x%).OrderDate = Trim$(Str$(Date - x%))

        'Customer Number field
        ColumnData(x%).CustNum = ""
        ColumnData(x%).CustNum = Trim$(Str$(x% * 550))

        'Serial Number field
        ColumnData(x%).SerNum = ""
        ColumnData(x%).SerNum = Trim$(Str$(x% * 742))
    Next x%

    'Initialize the printer (pass it the handle of the main form)
    i% = InitializePrinter(Form1.hWnd)

    'Set the margins for the page layout (top, right, bottom, left)
    i% = PageLayoutSetup(10, 100, 100, 100)

    'Begin a paragraph. Set the font to Arial 12 point bold)
    i% = StartParagraph("Arial", 10, BOLD_FONT)

    'Print a title for the report (using the font and size set in StartParagraph
    i% = PrintHeadline(szHeadLine$, "Arial", 14, BOLD_FONT Or TOP_BORDER)

    'Draw a line under the report title
    i% = DrawLine(100, 1500, 12000, 1500)

    'Set up 4 columns in which to print the reporting data.
    i% = SetUpColumns(4, 100, "Arial", 12, BOLD_FONT)

    'Move down the page to place a space after the report title and before the
➥column headings
    MoveYPos (40)

    'Draw a line under the column titles
    i% = DrawLine(100, 2100, 12000, 2100)

    'Construct and print the titles for the columns
    szHeader$ = "Order Number" + Chr$(9) + "Order Date" + Chr$(9) + "Customer
➥Number " + Chr$(9) + "Serial Number"
    i% = PrintColumnHeaders(szHeader$, 4, ColumnWidth(1), "Arial", 12, BOLD_FONT)

    'Move down the page to place a space after the column headings and before the
➥report data.
    MoveYPos (10)

    'Place the reporting data into ReportData$. Concatenate the title of the column
➥with the data.
    'All of the columns for the page are assembled into the ReportData$ variable.
➥This prints the data
    'across the page when sent to the PrintColumnHeaders function.
    For x% = 1 To 38 '(38 records is one page, normally you would use
➥UBound(ReportData$)
```

```
                'Print a section label before each set of records (every 10 records in this
➡example)
        If x% = 1 Or x% = 11 Or x% = 21 Or x% = 31 Then
                'Place a space after the previous set of records and before the section
➡label
            MoveYPos (20)
                'Print a section number for the next section (CInt(x/10) is used to get
➡a heading number. Without CInt, you
                'get nice things like section 1.1 or 2.1. This is only for purposes of
➡this example.
            i% = PrintColumnHeaders("Section " & Trim$(Str$(CInt(x% / 10) + 1)), 1,
➡ColumnWidth(1), "Arial", 12, BOLD_FONT)
        End If

            'Place data from database or data file into ReportData array. In this case,
➡we use the sample
            'ColumnData structure.
        ReportData$ = "Order Number: " & ColumnData(x%).OrderNum & Chr$(9)
        ReportData$ = ReportData$ + "Order Date: " & ColumnData(x%).OrderDate +
➡Chr$(9)
        ReportData$ = ReportData$ + "Customer Number: " + ColumnData(x%).CustNum +
➡Chr$(9)
        ReportData$ = ReportData$ + "Serial Number: " + ColumnData(x%).SerNum +
➡Chr$(9)

            'Print the report data.
        i% = PrintColumnHeaders(ReportData$, 4, ColumnWidth(1), "Arial", 10,
➡BOLD_FONT)

            'This is a trick to put more space between each line of the report
        MoveYPos (5)
    Next x%

    'These functions do general cleanup.
    i% = FinishParagraph()
    i% = EndColumnPrinting
    i% = DonePrinting()

End Sub
```

The following is a sample of the report output:

```
Customer Orders for August, 1995
```

```
                        Order Number    Order Date          Customer Number
Serial Number
Section 1
Order Number:           1000000         Order Date: 6/16/95  Customer Number: 550
Serial Number: 742
Order Number:           2000000         Order Date: 6/15/95  Customer Number: 1100
Serial Number: 1484
Order Number:           3000000         Order Date: 6/14/95  Customer Number: 1650
Serial Number: 2226
Order Number:           4000000         Order Date: 6/13/95  Customer Number: 2200
Serial Number: 2968
.
.
.
```

```
Section 2
Order Number:      1100000    Order Date: 6/6/95      Customer Number: 6050
Serial Number: 8162
Order Number:      1200000    Order Date: 6/5/95      Customer Number: 6600
Serial Number: 8904
Order Number:      1300000    Order Date: 6/4/95      Customer Number: 7150
Serial Number: 9646
Order Number:      1400000    Order Date: 6/3/95      Customer Number: 7700
Serial Number: 10388
```

VBPRINT.DLL Functions

The following is an index of the functions contained within VBPRINT.DLL. The declaration is supplied for each function along with an explanation of its use.

InitializePrinter()

Declaration: `InitializePrinter(ByVal hWnd%) as integer`

Description: This is the first function called when setting up a print job. Pass the `hWnd` of the topmost application window as `hWnd%`.

Usage: `i% = InitializePrinter(Main.hWnd)`

PageLayoutSetup()

Declaration: `PageLayoutSetup(ByVal nTop%, ByVal nRight%, ByVal nBottom%, ByVal nLeft%)` as integer

Description: Sets the top, right, left, and bottom margins for the page. All printing takes place within these margins. If there is more data than can fit on one page (horizontally or vertically), additional pages are created to print the data.

Usage: `i% = PageLayoutSetup(10, 100, 100, 100)`

DonePrinting()

Declaration: `DonePrinting() as integer`

Description: This is the final function called. It is called when the print job is completed. This function performs general cleanup after the print job.

Usage: `DonePrinting()`

StartParagraph()

Declaration: `StartParagraph(ByVal szFontName$, ByVal nFontSize%, ByVal nStyle%) as integer`

Description: This function is called to set up the font for a paragraph. Call this function before sending text to the paragraph. The parameters are as follows:

szFontName—The name of the font to use for the paragraph. This is either a variable or a quoted string. For example, szFontName = "Arial"

szFontSize—The size of the font in points. This is passed as an integer (ex: 8)

nStyle—Printing specifics for the font. These are defined as follows:

```
#define BOLD_FONT        0x0001
#define ITALIC_FONT      0x0002
#define TOP_BORDER       0x0004
#define LEFT_BORDER      0x0008
#define RIGHT_BORDER     0x0010
#define BOTTOM_BORDER    0x0020
#define CHECK_BOX        0x0100
```

Usage: i% = StartParagraph("Arial", 10, BOLD_FONT)

PrintParagraphText()

Declaration: PrintParagraphText(ByVal szText$) as integer

Description: Call this function to add text to a paragraph. Call this function as many times as desired to fill the paragraph.

Usage: An example where multiple calls can be useful:

```
Dim ReportData$(1 to 20) as string

'Fill ReportData from a data file
...

'Place the text from ReportData in the paragraph
For x% = 1 to UBound(ReportData$)
    szText$ = ReportData(x%)
    PrintParagraphText(szText)
Next x%
```

This loop sequentially adds each element of the ReportData array to the current paragraph. Use FinishParagraph() and StartParagraph() to create additional paragraphs. For example:

```
'Place the text from ReportData in the paragraph
For x% = 1 to UBound(ReportData$)
        If x%%5 = 0 Then 'Do this every fifth time through the loop (when x/5 = 0)
        I% = FinishParagraph()
        i% = StartParagraph("Arial", 10, BOLD_FONT)
    Endif
    szText$ = ReportData(x%)
    PrintParagraphText(szText)
Next x%
```

FinishParagraph()

Declaration: `FinishParagraph()` as integer

Description: Called at the end of printing a paragraph to do general cleanup.

Usage: `FinishParagraph()`

PrintHeadline()

> **NOTE**
>
> The readme.txt file associated with this DLL has this function incorrectly listed as `HeadlinePrint()`.

Declaration: `PrintHeadline(ByVal szHeadLine$, ByVal szFontName$, ByVal nFontSize%, ByVal nStyle%)` as integer

Description: Prints a title for the report. This function has the following parameters:

`szHeadLine$`—Text to be printed in the title

`szFontName$`—Font name to be used in the title

`nFontSize%`—Font size as an integer (must be a valid size for the selected font)

`nStyle`—Style flags for the font. (See the `StartParagraph` function for a description of these flags.)

Usage: `i% = PrintHeadline(szHeadLine$, "Arial", 14, BOLD_FONT Or TOP_BORDER)`

SetParagraphSpacing()

Declaration: `SetParagraphSpacing(ByVal nSpacing%)` as integer

Description: This function sets the number of spaces to place between the end of one paragraph and the beginning of the next. Spacing is set in points. The default is 18 points or 1/4 inch.

Usage: `I% = SetParagraphSpacing(18)`

EjectPage()

Declaration: `EjectPage()` as integer

Description: Ejects the current page from the printer. Any text that has already been sent for printing is printed. A new page is set up for printing and the cursor is set at the top left corner of the new page.

Usage: `I% = EjectPage()`

PrintDLLVersion()

Declaration: `PrintDLLVersion()` as integer

Description: Returns the version of VBPRINT.DLL; the major version number is in the low byte number of the integer, and the minor version number is in the high byte number of the integer.

Usage: `I% = PrintDLLVersion`

SetUpColumns()

Declaration: `SetUpColumns(ByVal Columns%, ByVal nCl%, ByVal szFontName$, ByVal nFontSize%, ByVal nStyle%)` as integer

Description: This function sets columns for the report. It contains the following parameters:

`Columns%`—The number of columns to be printed on the report.

`nCl%`—An integer array, each element containing the width of a specific column. This parameter is passed to several functions to set the width of the column being printed. The settings are in hundredths of an inch. 100 = 1". The maximum number of columns allowed is 8.

`szFontName$`—A string containing the name of the font to be used in the column when printed.

`szFontSize%`—The size of the font used in the column during printing.

`nStyle%`—Style flags for the font. (See the `StartParagraph` function for a description of these flags.)

Usage: `i% = SetUpColumns(4, 100, "Arial", 12, BOLD_FONT)`

PrintColumnText()

Declaration: `PrintColumnText(ByVal szText$)` as integer

Description: Use this function to send tab delimited text into a paragraph. Used to send text into the columns.

Usage: `I% = PrintColumnText("Have" & Chr$(9) & "a" & Chr$(9) & "nice" & Chr$(9) & "day")` prints

```
Have          a          nice          day
```

EndColumnPrinting()

Declaration: `EndColumnPrinting()` as integer

Description: Used at the end of printing columns to do general cleanup.

Usage: `I% = EndColumnPrinting()`

PrintColumnHeaders()

Declaration: `PrintColumnHeaders(ByVal szHeader$, ByVal Columns%, ByVal nC1%, ByVal szFontName$, ByVal nFontSize%, ByVal nStyle%)` as integer

Description: Prints the titles of the columns on the report. This function contains the following parameters:

> `szHeader$`—The data that is printed to the column.
>
> `nC1%`—An integer array, each element containing the width of a specific column. This parameter is passed to several functions to set the width of the column being printed. The settings are in hundredths of an inch. 100 = 1". The maximum number of columns allowed is 8.
>
> `szFontName$`—A string containing the name of the font to be used in the column when printed.
>
> `szFontSize%`—The size of the font used in the column during printing.
>
> `nStyle%`—Style flags for the font. (See the `StartParagraph` function for a description of these flags.)

Usage: `i% = PrintColumnHeaders(ReportData$, 4, ColumnWidth(1), "Arial", 10, BOLD_FONT)`

MoveYPos()

Declaration: `MoveYPos( ByVal nY%)` as integer

Description: Moves the current position on the page for printing downward vertically by the value of `Y%`. `Y%` is in intervals of hundredths of an inch.

Usage: `I% = MoveYPos(30)`

DrawLine()

Declaration: `DrawLine( ByVal nX1%, ByVal nY1%, ByVal nX2%, ByVal nY2%)` as integer

Description: Draws a line from position (`nX1`, `nY1`) to (`nX2`, `nY2`). The coordinate system used for plotting is TWIPS. The parameters used in this function are:

> `nX1`—Top left vertical position
>
> `nY1`—Top left horizontal position

nX2—Bottom right vertical position

nY2—Bottom right horizontal position

Usage: i% = DrawLine(100, 2100, 12000, 2100)

DrawRectangle()

Declaration: DrawRectangle(ByVal nX1%, ByVal nY1%, ByVal nX2%, ByVal nY2%) as integer

Description: Draws a Rectangle using the following coordinates in TWIPS:

nX1—Top left vertical position
nY1—Top left horizontal position
nX2—Bottom right vertical position
nY2—Bottom right horizontal position

Usage: I% = DrawRectangle(100, 100, 5000, 5000)

DrawRndRectangle()

Declaration: DrawRndRectangle(ByVal nX1%, ByVal nY1%, ByVal nX2%, ByVal nY2%, ByVal nX3%, ByVal nY3%) as integer

Description: Draws a Rectangle with rounded corners. The following parameters are used in this function:

nX1—Top left vertical position
nY1—Top left horizontal position
nX2—Bottom right vertical position
nY2—Bottom right horizontal position
nX3—Height of the rounded corners
nY3—Width of the rounded corners

Usage: I% = DrawRndRectangle(100, 100, 5000, 5000, 500, 500)

DrawEllipse()

Declaration: DrawEllipse(ByVal nX1%, ByVal nY1%, ByVal nX2%, ByVal nY2%) as integer

Description: Draws an ellipse on the report. The parameters (in TWIPS) used in this function are:

nX1—Top left vertical position
nY1—Top left horizontal position
nX2—Bottom right vertical position
nY2—Bottom right horizontal position

Usage: I% = DrawEllipse(100, 100, 5000, 5000)

Summary

Although there are no reporting mechanisms built directly into Visual Basic, this chapter has demonstrated that there are many avenues to pursue when developing reporting for Visual Basic applications. Crystal Reports, the Crystal Reports OCX, and VBPRINT.DLL provide significant functionality and flexibility when creating quality reporting for Visual Basic applications.

PART

IN THIS PART

Unleashing Advanced Programming Topics

Multimedia

9

by Bill Hatfield

Multimedia is the buzzword of the '90s. Although there was much talk and some work done in multimedia in the late '80s, real applications that deserved that title have come into their own in just the last few years. Today you see more and more graphics, sound, music, and video being skillfully (and sometimes not so skillfully) woven together into the applications you buy. And this convergence of technologies is producing something beyond what you usually might think of as a PC. It is creating an interactive television/learning station that promises to be the cornerstone of future media.

But what about today? Can multimedia applications be put together easily, without expensive hardware? The answer is yes. With a standard PC today and a sound card, Visual Basic programmers have all they need to create and distribute high-quality multimedia applications.

And you're going to get started in this chapter. Here, I'll introduce you to an integrated and powerful control called the *Media Control Interface* (MCI), which enables you to play recorded sounds, music, and video from files inside your PC and even standard media players like audio CD players, VCRs, and video disc players. All from one simple control.

Then I'll show you how to go beyond the control and access multimedia capabilities through Win32. Although I can't hope to completely immerse you in the technology of tomorrow in just one chapter, I do hope to at least get your feet wet and point you in the right direction for your own exploration.

Introducing the Media Control Interface

The great thing about Windows is that it enables you to take advantage of all the different devices that a user might have hooked up to his or her computer without having to get elbow deep in the complexities of each. This level of abstraction is made possible through device drivers. Device drivers handle all the little details that you don't want to and provide you with a clean, simple interface to the hardware. Nowhere is this abstraction of complexity made more clear than it is in the Media Control Interface and the MCI control.

When you add the MCI control to your toolbox and then place one on your form, it doesn't immediately inspire awe (see Figure 9.1).

The MCI control looks like the controls you might see on a tape recorder or a CD player. Most media can be thought of as a tape player of some type. The play, rewind, fast-forward, pause, and stop controls just as easily can apply to an audio CD, an AVI video clip, or a WAV file.

Because you probably are eager to see this control put to work, I'll walk you through creating a simple audio CD player. Of course, this process will work only if you have a CD-ROM drive hooked up to your system. If you don't... Where've you been? Go buy one...

FIGURE 9.1.
The Media Control Interface control on a form.

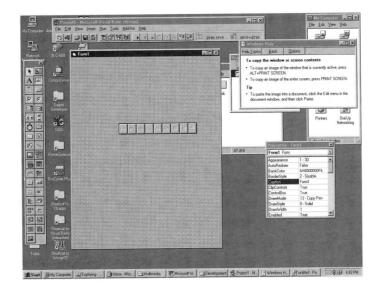

Project 1: A CD Player

"But," you protest, "I already have a nifty audio CD player that came with Windows. It even starts up automatically when I drop an audio CD into my drive! I don't *need* to create one..."

Hmm. That may be so, but I want you to say two words with me: *academic exercise.* Good.

Of course, you already have an audio CD player, but suppose that you want to add functionality to it. Or suppose that you want to integrate it with another application you are writing. In these cases, you would have to have access to the guts of the thing. And that's exactly what you'll have when you finish this little project.

To create a CD player, follow these steps:

1. Start a new project. Add WINMMSYS.TXT (in your winapi folder) to your project. It has some constant definitions you'll use later.

2. Add the MCI control to your project by choosing Custom Controls from the Tools menu (or pressing Ctrl+T). The Custom Controls dialog appears. Scroll down and click the Microsoft Multimedia Control option and click OK.

3. Drop an MDI control on the form. Now drop four labels above the control. The first label's Caption should be Track. The second label should be blank, but name it lblTrack. The third label should have the caption Of. The fourth label should be blank, but name it lblTracks (plural). Leave the default names for the first and third labels. Place a label with a blank caption centered below the MDI control, too. Name it lblStatus. You also might want to kick the point size of the font for all those labels up to 12 points. When you're done, your form should look like Figure 9.2.

FIGURE 9.2.

The CD Player form.

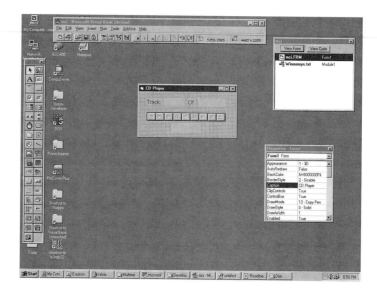

4. Set the caption of the form to CD Player. Presumptuous of us, considering it doesn't do anything, yet. But have faith—it soon will.

5. To get the application off to a good start, go to the Form Load event and type Listing 9.1.

Listing 9.1. The Form Load event.

```
Private Sub Form_Load()
MMControl1.DeviceType = "CDAudio"
MMControl1.Command = "Open"
End Sub
```

6. Just tell the application what device you want it to access and tell it to open. This control has the peculiarity of enabling you to tell it what to do by assigning strings to its Command property. There is, in fact, a whole sublanguage here that you can use. You'll explore it later in this chapter.

   Listing 9.2 shows the corresponding Form Unload event. Nice and tidy. And that's it for the form.

Listing 9.2. The Form Unload event.

```
Private Sub Form_Unload(Cancel As Integer)
MMControl1.Command = "Close"
End Sub
```

7. Double-click the control and choose the StatusUpdate event. This is an event that is tied to a built-in timer. You can set the timer's interval by using the control's UpdateInterval property. Set the UpdateInterval to 500. This number is in milliseconds (just like the timer interval), and 500 makes the StatusUpdate event fire off twice a second.

So what do you use your application for? Well, often you'll want to update controls on-screen with information coming from the multimedia driver. You might show what frame the AVI video is displaying or how many tracks are on the audio CD. Speaking of which, check out Listing 9.3.

Listing 9.3. The MCI control's StatusUpdate event.

```
Private Sub MMControl1_StatusUpdate()
If MMControl1.Mode = MCI_MODE_NOT_READY Then
    lblStatus.Caption = "Not Ready"
ElseIf MMControl1.Mode = MCI_MODE_STOP Then
    lblStatus.Caption = "Stop"
ElseIf MMControl1.Mode = MCI_MODE_PLAY Then
    lblStatus.Caption = "Play"
ElseIf MMControl1.Mode = MCI_MODE_RECORD Then
    lblStatus.Caption = "Record"
ElseIf MMControl1.Mode = MCI_MODE_SEEK Then
    lblStatus.Caption = "Seek"
ElseIf MMControl1.Mode = MCI_MODE_PAUSE Then
    lblStatus.Caption = "Pause"
ElseIf MMControl1.Mode = MCI_MODE_OPEN Then
    lblStatus.Caption = "Open"
End If

lblTrack.Caption = Str(MMControl1.Track)
lblTracks.Caption = Str(MMControl1.Tracks)

End Sub
```

The big If-Then-ElseIf figures out what mode the device is currently in and sets lblStatus appropriately. As you can see, this is where you put those constants in the WINMMSYS.TXT file to use.

8. Now just fill in the current track number and the number of total tracks.

Believe it or not, you're done. Just pop in an audio CD. If the Windows automatic CD player comes up, close it right away. Then run your application. If everything goes as planned, you should see a window that looks something like Figure 9.3.

What are you waiting for? Click Play! Try out the Skip to Next Song button (the arrow pointing to a line on the right). And the Previous Song button. Stop, Pause, and Eject should work, too. Pretty impressive for a few lines of code, aye?

FIGURE 9.3.

Your CD player in action.

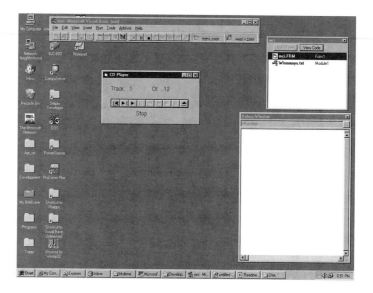

Notice how the buttons change, depending on which are disabled and which are available. This is a handy feature, and it is automatic. Well, almost automatic. You have to make sure that the MCI control's AutoEnable property is True. But because that's the default, you're set.

Your MCI can control two classes of devices. The audio CD, along with the VCR and video disc player, are called *simple devices*. WAVs and AVIs are referred to as *compound devices*, because they require you to specify a file name in order for them to work. The next section shows you how tough it would be to turn your simple device player into a compound one.

Project 2: A WAV Player

The next task is to create a WAV player. You should begin with your CD player as a base. You might want to save the project and files to a different name if you want to keep your CD player intact. When you are ready, follow these steps:

1. Delete all four Track labels above the MCI control. Drop an edit control and a button on the form. Name the edit control txtFileName and name the button cmdOpen. Set the Default property of the Open button to True. And don't forget to change the caption of the form to Wave Player. Your form now should look like Figure 9.4.

2. Take a look at the Form Load event. Change it so that it looks like Listing 9.4.

Listing 9.4. The new Form Load event.

```
Private Sub Form_Load()
MMControl1.DeviceType = "WaveAudio"
End Sub
```

FIGURE 9.4.

Moving things around to create a Wave player application.

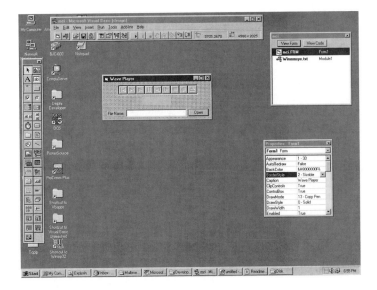

You can't open the device here like you did with the CD player because you don't have all the information you need. You still must have the file name of the WAV file. All you can do is tell it that you'll be playing WAVs.

Listing 9.5 shows the `Click` event for the Open button.

Listing 9.5. The `Click` event for the `cmdOpen` button.

```
Private Sub cmdOpen_Click()
MMControl1.filename = txtFileName.TEXT
MMControl1.Command = "Open"
End Sub
```

After the file name is known and entered into txtFileName, you can open the device and play it.

3. Finish up by going to the `StatusUpdate` event of the MCI control and deleting the lines that filled in the track information. The final event should look like Listing 9.6.

Listing 9.6. The new `StatusUpdate` event.

```
Private Sub MMControl1_StatusUpdate()
If MMControl1.Mode = MCI_MODE_NOT_READY Then
    lblStatus.Caption = "Not Ready"
ElseIf MMControl1.Mode = MCI_MODE_STOP Then
    lblStatus.Caption = "Stop"
ElseIf MMControl1.Mode = MCI_MODE_PLAY Then
    lblStatus.Caption = "Play"
```

continues

Listing 9.6. continued

```
ElseIf MMControl1.Mode = MCI_MODE_RECORD Then
    lblStatus.Caption = "Record"
ElseIf MMControl1.Mode = MCI_MODE_SEEK Then
    lblStatus.Caption = "Seek"
ElseIf MMControl1.Mode = MCI_MODE_PAUSE Then
    lblStatus.Caption = "Pause"
ElseIf MMControl1.Mode = MCI_MODE_OPEN Then
    lblStatus.Caption = "Open"
End If
End Sub
```

4. The only other event was the `Close` of the form, which sent a Close command to the MCI. This is fine as it is, so run it (see Figure 9.5).

FIGURE 9.5.

The Wave Player application.

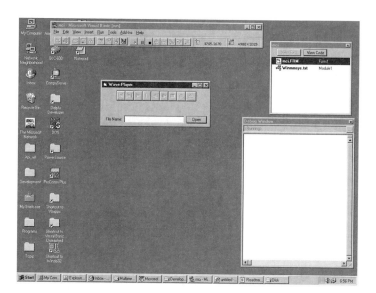

5. Notice that all the buttons are disabled when the application first comes up. This is because the Open command hasn't been executed yet. Type a path and file name of a WAV file on your hard drive. For example, type the following:

```
c:\windows\media\chimes.wav
```

6. Press Enter or click the Open button. The MCI comes to life and you can play your WAV. You'll have to rewind it to play it a second time.

Notice one other thing. There is another button that is enabled that wasn't enabled for the audio CD player. The big round circle. Yes, this is the Record button. You also can use your new little utility to record WAV files. Actually, you have no way of creating new wave files (that would take some more work), but you can record at the beginning or end of the sound file in memory and then play it back. But again, you don't have any way of saving the recording back out as it is right now. You'll see how you would go about saving recordings as new WAV files later in this chapter.

Project 3: Video

On to bigger and better players. The MCI control can do more than make your sound card chirp. It actually can play back video for your viewing pleasure. The first question you no doubt will be asking is, "*Where*, exactly, does it play this video?" Do you punch a button and it grows a screen to project it on?

Not exactly. The fact is that you need to drop another control on the form. A picture control. Then you connect the picture control to the MCI and it plays the video there.

To play back your video, follow these steps:

1. Stretch out your form window and add the picture control below the file name edit control. The form should look like Figure 9.6.

FIGURE 9.6.

The AVI video player form.

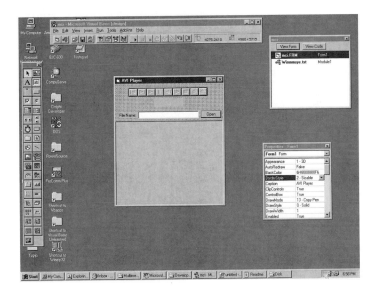

2. Name the picture control `picVid`. Don't forget to change the form caption to AVI Player.
3. Believe it or not, the only code change you need to make is in the `Form Load` event (see Listing 9.7).

Listing 9.7. The new Form Load event.

```
Private Sub Form_Load()
MMControl1.DeviceType = "AVIVideo"
MMControl1.hWndDisplay = picVid.hWnd
End Sub
```

4. Change DeviceType to AVIVideo. Then add a line to make the connection between the MCI control and the picture control. The hWnd property is the Windows handle for the picture control. Anytime you want to refer to a window or control when interfacing with a DLL or Win32, you should use this attribute. You use it here to fill in the hWndDisplay attribute of the MCI control, which always needs to be assigned the window handle of the object you want to use for the video output. This makes the connection.

5. Run your new video player (see Figure 9.7).

FIGURE 9.7.

Running the AVI video player.

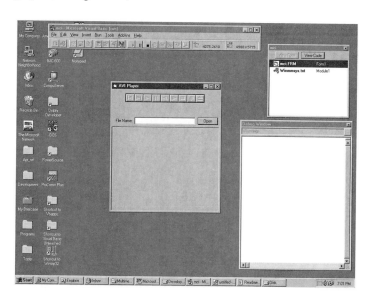

6. Again, the buttons are disabled until you type a file name and click Open. Try this one:

    c:\windows\help\whatson.avi

    Or this one:

    c:\windows\help\explorer.avi

Or, type any file name that you happen to have on your hard drive or CD-ROM. It's just that easy.

Delving Deeper into the MCI Control

So far, you have learned about the fundamental functionality available with the MCI control. You can take advantage of many more attributes and events, however, to enhance your multimedia application. In this section, you will learn about the most important enhancements you can make.

Enabled, Visible, and AutoEnable

Earlier in this chapter, you learned that when AutoEnable is set to True, it turns over the handling of the appropriate enabling and disabling of the individual buttons on the MCI control to the system. Normally, you want AutoEnable to be True. If you set AutoEnable to False, you can use the *Button*Enable properties to set the buttons yourself. (No ButtonEnable property actually exists. *Button*Enable is just an easy way to refer collectively to these nine properties: BackEnable, EjectEnable, NextEnable, PauseEnable, PlayEnable, PrevEnable, RecordEnable, StepEnable, and StopEnable.) Keep in mind that if the AutoEnable property is set to True, it overrides any *Button*Enable property settings you have explicitly set yourself. In other words, if you want to use the *Button*Enable properties, you'll have to set AutoEnable to False.

Regardless of whether you handle the enabling and disabling of the buttons or you let AutoEnable handle it for you, there will be times when you want a button to be completely invisible. The *Button*Visible properties enable you to make a button invisible. Again, *Button*Visible is shorthand for the collection of visible properties associated with each button.

A Visible property and Enabled property also exist for the entire control. These properties supersede all the Button properties and the AutoEnable property.

DeviceType and FileName

You've seen these properties already. You used DeviceType to specify what type of device you would be opening for each of the different players. For the audio CD player, you used CDAudio; for the Wave player, you used WaveAudio. And for the AVI player, you used AVIVideo. The other possible values for the DeviceType property are DAT, DigitalVideo, MMMovie, Other, Overlay, Scanner, Sequencer, VCR, and Videodisc.

FileName, of course, is used with compound devices to indicate which file they should use.

TIP

You don't have to specify the DeviceType when you are using a compound device and the extension on the file name makes it clear which device should be used.

For instance,

```
MMControl1.filename = "MyWav.WAV"
MMControl1.Command = "Open"
```

This code would cause Visual Basic to open a `WaveAudio` device even though you never set the `DeviceType` attribute because it surmised the information from the filename extension (WAV).

UpdateInterval, StatusUpdate, and Mode

As you saw from the MCI control projects earlier, at every `UpdateInterval` (specified in milliseconds), the `StatusUpdate` event is triggered. This event generally is used to update status displays on-screen, such as the mode in which you are working.

`Mode` gives you the current mode the MCI device is in, such as Stop, Play, Record, Pause, and so on. `Mode` is read-only and is available only at runtime.

Other attributes often displayed in the `StatusUpdate` event are Track, Tracks, Length, Position, TrackLength, and TrackPosition.

Track and Tracks

You've seen these properties before in this chapter. These determine the current track and the number of the final track. `Track` can be set to change the current track. `Tracks` is read-only. Both properties are available only at runtime.

UsesWindows and hWndDisplay

The `UsesWindows` property tells you whether the current device uses a window (or picture control) to present its output. This property is True for `MMMovie`, `Overlay`, `VCR`, or `AVIVideo`.

The `hWndDisplay` property, as you saw in the AVI player example, specifies which control displays the output. You always assign another control's `hWnd` property to this property.

Orientation

The `Orientation` property tells Visual Basic to lay out the buttons horizontally (0, the default) or vertically (1).

Silent

This property works like a Mute button. Set it to True, and all sound stops.

The Can-Can

The MCI control has several properties that give you information about the capabilities of the device with which you are working. These properties are `CanEject`, `CanPlay`, `CanRecord`, and `CanStep`. They are each simple True/False variables and can be read only at runtime.

In addition, you can use the `DeviceID` property to determine the ID of the currently open device at runtime.

RecordMode

When you record to a medium, you can use the `RecordMode` property to specify that it insert the recorded material in the middle of what's there (0) or simply overwrite it (1). You can tell whether a medium is recordable by enabling `CanRecord`, but no attribute exists to let you know whether the medium supports Insert, Overwrite, or both modes. You just have to try it; if one mode fails, try the other mode. Nifty. I *can* tell you that WAVs can support only Insert mode, and one would assume that VCRs would support only Overwrite mode. From there, you're on your own.

TimeFormat

Many properties are set using values based on the current `TimeFormat`. The `TimeFormat` property enables you to specify how you want to reference points in your media. Certain time formats make sense with certain media. If you assign a format with a media that doesn't make sense, the assignment is ignored. Table 9.1 lists the acceptable values for `TimeFormat`.

Table 9.1. Acceptable values for `TimeFormat`.

Constant	*Value*	*Meaning*
`mci_Format_Milliseconds`	0	Milliseconds
`mci_Format_Hms`	1	Hours, minutes, seconds
`mci_Format_Msf`	2	Minutes, seconds, frames
`mci_Format_Frames`	3	Frames
`mci_Format_Smpte_24`	4	24-frame SMPTE: Hours, minutes, seconds, frames
`mci_Format_Smpte_25`	5	25-frame SMPTE: Hours, minutes, seconds, frames
`mci_Format_Smpte_30`	6	30-frame SMPTE: Hours, minutes, seconds, frames

continues

Table 9.1. continued

Constant	Value	Meaning
mci_Format_Smpte_30Drop	7	30-drop-frame SMPTE: Hours, minutes, seconds, frames
mci_Format_Bytes	8	Number of bytes
mci_Format_Samples	9	Number of samples
mci_Format_Tmsf	10	Tracks, minutes, seconds, frames

Each of these formats stores its data in a four-byte integer. It is up to you to decode it. For example, mci_Format_Hms stores the hours, minutes, and seconds from the least-significant byte to the most-significant byte in a four-byte Long value.

If you were checking the position at 1 hour, 5 minutes, and 3 seconds, for example, it would be stored like the following:

	Most-Significant Byte 4	Byte 3	Byte 2	Least-Significant Byte 1
Decimal	0	3	5	1
Binary	00000000	00000011	00000101	00000001

Note: The last (most significant) byte is not needed.

If this looks backward to you, remember that numbers generally are read from right to left. The least-significant digit (the 1s, in decimal) always is the farthest to the right, and the digits become larger and larger (tens, hundreds, and so on) as you move to the left. This process also is used with binary numbers.

The problem is, when you check the value of the Long number, it is 197889. That's because the bytes are taken together to mean one really Long binary value. The decimal values for each of the On bits add up like this:

```
1 + 256 + 1024 + 65536 + 131072 = 197889
```

(I just love binary math.)

But the value 197889 is useless to us. How do we pry 1 hour, 5 minutes, and 3 seconds out of it? This sort of storage scheme is common for Win32 functions, and you see it more and more now in Visual Basic's native functions, too. The problem is, there is no built-in function for extracting individual byte values out of a four-byte Long value. Because this need is becoming so common, I will spend a little time here showing you how to do it. It isn't difficult, but it isn't immediately obvious, either.

All it takes is a little bit masking and some division. *Bit masking* is a way of pulling just the data you want out of a Long binary number, which happens to be just what we want to do.

To see the lowest order byte of the number in this example (the hours), you can take the following approach:

Binary:	00000000	00000011	00000101	00000001
AND	00000000	00000000	00000000	01111111
	00000000	00000000	00000000	00000001

An AND logical operator only allows a bit in the result if *both* the corresponding bits in the problem are 1. By doing an AND with a number that only has 1s in the least-significant byte, you get only the value from that byte. By the way, you only want to check the first seven bits. The eighth bit is the sign, and you won't be getting signed values back under normal circumstances.

And the answer is 1. One hour. One down, two to go.

Can you use the same trick for the minutes?

Binary:	00000000	00000011	00000101	00000001
AND	00000000	00000000	01111111	00000000
	00000000	00000000	00000101	00000000

Well, you masked out all the other bytes, but the value is still 1280 (256 + 1024). You need to shift the byte over to the least-significant value position. How do you do it? Well, if you wanted to shift the 7 in 700 to the lowest position, what would you do? Divide by 100. That would give you 7.

So you just need to divide by 100000000 (binary) or 256. 1280 divided by 256 equals 5. That's it! Five minutes. One more.

Binary:	00000000	00000011	00000101	00000001
AND	00000000	01111111	00000000	00000000
	00000000	00000011	00000000	00000000

Got the byte. 196608 is the number. Now divide by binary 10000000000000000 (16 zeros—count 'em). That's 65536 in decimal. 196608 divided by 65536 equals 3. One hour, five minutes, and three seconds. Cool.

But that seems like a lot of work just to get the position. Why couldn't they make it easier? They could have. But there is always the trade-off between efficiency and programming simplicity. This time, the programmers opted for efficiency. You can easily turn this into a function. Add Listing 9.8 to your library.

Listing 9.8. The `ByteFromLong` function.

```
Public Function ByteFromLong(LongVal As Long, Position As Integer) As Integer
Dim iTemp As Long

If Position < 1 Or Position > 4 Then
    ByteFromLong = -1
    Exit Function
End If

Select Case Position
Case 1
    ' 127 = Binary 01111111
    iTemp = LongVal And 127
Case 2
    ' 32512 = Binary 01111111 00000000
    iTemp = LongVal And 32512
    ' 256 = Binary 1 00000000
    iTemp = iTemp / 256
Case 3
    ' 8323072 = Binary 01111111 00000000 00000000
    iTemp = LongVal And 8323072
    ' 65536 = Binary 1 00000000 00000000
    iTemp = iTemp / 65536
Case 4
    ' 2130706432 = Binary 01111111 00000000 00000000 00000000
    iTemp = LongVal And 2130706432
    ' 16777216 = Binary 1 00000000 00000000 00000000
    iTemp = iTemp / 16777216
End Select

ByteFromLong = iTemp

End Function
```

On the CD that comes with this book, you will find this function as part of an application called LongDissector. The form looks like Figure 9.8.

The button's `Click` event uses the `ByteFromLong` function, as you can see in Listing 9.9.

Listing 9.9. The `Click` event of the button on the LongDissector form.

```
Private Sub cmdFigureIt_Click()
Dim iLong As Long

iLong = Val(txtLong.TEXT)

lblByte1.Caption = Str(ByteFromLong(iLong, 1))
lblByte2.Caption = Str(ByteFromLong(iLong, 2))
lblByte3.Caption = Str(ByteFromLong(iLong, 3))
lblByte4.Caption = Str(ByteFromLong(iLong, 4))

End Sub
```

FIGURE 9.8.

The form for LongDissector.

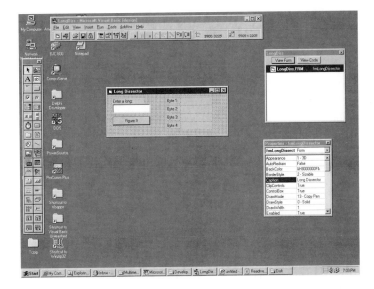

Now you easily can extract information out of a Long value for all the functions that return a value based on the TimeFormat (just as you can for any other functions in Visual Basic or Win32 that use this type of return value).

From and To

These properties can be set with values to indicate a portion of media that should be played. From and To enable you to play a snippet from the middle of a WAV or a single scene from an AVI video. You also can use From and To with the Record command.

The From and To property definitions apply only to the next command given.

These properties are specified in the format set by TimeFormat. To assign a value to these properties, you might need to pack your own Long value with specific bytes of information. You must modify the function shown in Listing 9.9 to allow it to assign a value to a given byte, rather than to retrieve it. I'll leave this one up to you to try.

Length, Position, TrackLength, TrackPosition, and Start

As their names imply, these properties give you the length and position of the currently open media or the currently specified track. Start gives you the starting position of the current media.

These properties are all read-only and available only at runtime.

Notify, NotifyValue, NotifyMessage, and the Done event

Notify is a Boolean that can be set to True to cause the next command to perform a *callback* when it is done—that is, the Done event is triggered when the next command completes its task. The Notify assignment applies only to the next command issued. If Notify is not specified before a command, that command uses its default notification. The default notification is different for each command (see "Commands and Errors," later in this chapter).

NotifyValue and NotifyMessage can be accessed in the Done event to find out exactly how the last command went. You can determine whether it was successful, whether it was aborted by the user, or whether it failed for some reason. Table 9.2 lists the constants associated with NotifyValue.

Table 9.2. Constants for NotifyValue.

Constant	Value	Meaning
mci_Notify_Successful	1	Completed successfully
mci_Notify_Superseded	2	Another command overrode this one.
mci_Notify_Aborted	4	Aborted by the user
mci_Notify_Failure	8	Failed

NotifyMessage is simply a textual description of NotifyValue. It is handy for dropping into a message box or a status bar.

Wait

Wait determines whether the next command waits until it finishes its processing before returning control to the application. The default depends on the command executed (see "Commands and Errors," later in this chapter, for a list of the commands).

Shareable

This Boolean enables you to specify whether other applications can share the currently open device.

Commands and Errors

The Command property is not used to set a value or to specify the way things should be carried out, as most properties are used. Command is a special way to tell the MCI control to do something. You already saw the most commonly used commands in the examples earlier in this chapter. In this section, I will talk briefly about each command, how it works, and what it impacts.

Open and Close

These commands open and close the device specified in `DeviceName`. If it is a compound device, `FileName` is used to locate the associated file.

Play and Record

These commands play from or record to the media. Play and Record look at the `From` and `To` properties and use the values specified there to locate the media and to determine how much of the media to work on. Record also uses `RecordMode` to determine whether it should insert or overwrite the new information.

Pause and Stop

`Pause` pauses the playback or recording. If this command is executed while in Pause mode, it acts as a toggle and attempts to resume whatever it was doing before.

`Stop` stops playing or recording.

Back, Step, Prev, and Next

`Back` and `Step` act like a Rewind and Fast Forward button on the current track. You can use the `Frames` property to fine-tune how far back and forward these commands take you.

`Prev` and `Next` move to the start of the current track and to the next track.

Seek

`Seek` moves the current location (whether the MCI control is currently playing or not) to the place specified in the `To` property. If it is playing, it continues playing at the new position.

Eject

This command ejects the media.

Sound

This command plays a sound specified in `FileName`.

Save

This command saves a currently open file on a compound device to the file name specified in `FileName`. This is what you would have needed to make the recording session with your Wave player worthwhile.

Notify and Wait

The Notify and Wait properties affect the next command given. You only need to use them, though, when you want the next command to work differently than it normally works. Table 9.3 lists the default behavior for each command.

Table 9.3. Default Notify and Wait statuses by command.

Command	Default Notify	Default Wait
Back	False	True
Close	False	True
Eject	False	True
Next	False	True
Open	False	True
Pause	False	True
Play	True	False
Prev	False	True
Record	True	False
Save	False	True
Seek	False	True
Sound	False	False
Step	False	True
Stop	False	True

Error and ErrorMessage hold the error number and error description (respectively) for the last MCI command. If there was no error, Error is zero.

Beyond the MCI Control

Consensus has it that the MCI control doesn't win any awards for beauty. But it is highly functional. And it makes something that could be very difficult very easy. To work around this appearance problem, some developers simply use the MCI control with its Visible property set to False. Any commands they want to offer to the user are provided through the developer's user interface, which is, presumably, much more attractive. Then the properties of the control are manipulated in code behind the scenes. This is a perfectly workable solution and gives you a lot of flexibility without tying you to visual controls.

If you want to go to the next level, though, you can access the MCI through Win32's multimedia API. Specifically, you can use the `mciSendString` function. Listing 9.10 shows the declaration.

Listing 9.10. The `mciSendString` declaration.

```
Declare Function mciSendString Lib "winmm" _
(ByVal lpstrCommand As String, _
ByVal lpstrReturnString As String, _
ByVal uReturnLength As Integer, _
ByVal hWndCallback As Integer) As Long
```

NOTE

Keep in mind that if you include \WinAPI\WINMMSYS.TXT as a module in your application, not only are all the multimedia constants already defined, but all the multimedia Win32 functions also are declared for you. Don't declare the functions a second time in your application.

The `lpstrCommand` argument is where you send the actual command (like Play, Stop, or Record). `lpstrReturnString` is where you receive information back from the multimedia system (like status information requested), and `uReturnLength` is where you pass the length of the string. (Actually, you want to pass the length minus 1 so that there is room for the string ending character.)

Finally, `hWndCallback` is the `hWnd` pointer to a window that will receive the callback function. This is analogous to the `Notify` property and the `Done` event of the control. Unless you trap for the `mm_Mcinotify` for a particular window (using a third-party tool to trap events Visual Basic doesn't normally trap) and then pass that window's `hWnd` property here, however, you won't be able to take advantage of it.

mciSendString returns a value if there was an error, or 0 if everything went fine. There are a large number of possible error codes that can be returned. For a complete list, open WINMMSYS.TXT (in your WinAPI directory) and search for `MCIERR_INVALID_DEVICE_ID`. This is the first error code. A long list follows this first error code.

After you declare the function, you are ready to put it to use. Listing 9.11 provides an example bit of code that opens the audio CD player and begins playing. It also shows you some status updates with the message box.

Listing 9.11. Playing the audio CD without the MCI control.

```
Dim ReturnString As String
Dim rc As Integer

'Always set your string size before sending to a DLL
ReturnString = String(128, " ")

' Opens the audio CD device.
rc = mciSendString("open CDAudio", ReturnString, 127, 0)

' Plays an audio CD.
rc = mciSendString("play CDAudio", ReturnString, 127, 0)

' Request the mode be returned
rc = mciSendString("status CDAudio mode", _
    ReturnString, 127, 0)
MsgBox (ReturnString)

' Returns the number of tracks on the current audio CD
rc = mciSendString("status CDAudio number of tracks", _
    ReturnString, 127, 0)
MsgBox (ReturnString)

' Closes the audio CD device.
rc = mciSendString("close CDAudio", ReturnString, 127, 0)
```

The commands you can specify in the lpstrCommand string can be quite extensive. The commands and options available depend on the device. Because there's no way I can provide an exhaustive list here of all the things you can do, I will show you some examples of common strings you might want to try in Listing 9.12. This isn't intended to be a sequential listing, but rather a list of separate examples of strings that you could use to control all different kinds of devices.

Listing 9.12. Some common strings to try with mciSendString.

```
play c:\windows\media\chimes.wav

open new type WaveAudio alias wave
set wave bitpersample 8
set wave samplespersec 11025
set wave channels 2
record wave

stop wave

save wave c:\mywave\mywave.wav

close wave

capability WaveAudio can save

capability CDAudio can reverse
```

```
capability AVIVideo has audio

open c:\vid.avi

play WaveAudio

play VCR fast

play VCR reverse

play VCR slow

resume CDAudio

seek CDAudio to start

set CDAudio left off

set AVIVideo time format SMPTE 24

status WaveAudio bitspersample

status CDAudio length

status CDAudio length track 5

status VCR media present

stop VCR
```

If you want a more complete list of available MCI commands, see Microsoft's *Multimedia Programmer's Reference.*

Keep in mind that more and more consumer audio and video equipment now supports MCI. So the next time you go out to buy a video disc player or a do-everything VCR or DAT tape deck, you might want to check whether it supports MCI. If you buy equipment that does support MCI, you usually can install it on a serial port.

Summary

In this chapter, you began by creating several complete multimedia players that easily went together, thanks to Visual Basic's MCI control. Then you dove deeper into the control to learn about all its rich features and capabilities. Finally, you finished by going one level deeper—using the mciSendString Win32 function. This function enabled you to send English-like strings directly to the MCI to control all the devices the MCI control accessed.

Animation

10

by Bill Hatfield

"Animation can explain whatever the mind of man can conceive. This facility makes it the most versatile and explicit means of communication yet devised for quick mass appreciation."

—Walt Disney

Walt Disney talked about cartoon animation with the voice of a true pioneer. Much of what he said rings true today to the new pioneers in the field of *computer* animation. Multimedia is touted as the education tool of the next century. Even the lowly computer game is aspiring to Interactive Fiction, but the difference is that the animated tales are not only coming to life, they are responding to our presence and bringing us into their yarns; into a place where whole worlds can be created with the flick of an artist's stylus.

Visual Basic is at the heart of it. No other tool offers both the broad flexibility of a true programming language and the development speed of an authoring tool. While Visual Basic interfaces with many, many third-party controls, utilities, and applications, you will concentrate, in this chapter, on the innate abilities of Visual Basic itself, particularly those that are new with Visual Basic 4.0.

While most of what is covered here will seem most directly applicable to games, it is equally well suited for a variety of graphical applications. The techniques, once learned, are simple enough to be included almost anywhere.

Flip-Books and Processing Efficiency

Have you ever seen a flip-book? I used to make them all the time as a kid. You just take any sufficiently fat tablet and draw a different frame of animation on each page until you have filled them all (or your hand gets very tired, whichever comes first).

Then you use your thumb to slowly, steadily flip through the pages to produce animation. The pictures run together to produce what looks like true movement.

In the animation industry, this type of animation didn't last long. How could you possibly produce a ten-minute short, let alone an hour-and-a-half movie, when you had to draw each frame of animation from scratch. It couldn't be done.

But wait. Why redraw the whole frame? Not everything moves with every frame. In fact, from one frame to the next, very few things move. So why not just move the things that move and leave the rest of it alone! This idea brought forth what animators call *cels*. Cels are clear plastic sheets laid one on top of the other, each with a component of the animated scene. Whenever one of the components moved, only that cel had to be redrawn and replaced.

So it is today in the computer world. If you want to create animation, you could simply redraw or replace the entire picture fifteen times a second, but that would produce far more work for the computer than is necessary, and your animations would be slow and choppy, even on the fastest of machines.

Today, multimedia and game developers use a technique very similar to the cartoonist's cel to optimize their animations. The technique utilizes something called *sprites*.

Sprites

What is a *sprite*? A sprite is an on-screen entity that moves around over a background bitmap without disturbing it. In addition, there are often a number of these guys on a screen at once. The programmer occupies much of his time deciding how they should move, what they should look like, how they should interact, what should happen if they bump into each other, and so forth. A sprite, in short, is a name for all the little people who inhabit your graphical world.

So where are the sprite facilities in Visual Basic. or in Windows, or in the VGA video card? It is such a basic concept, that you would think that these environments would provide all kinds of routines and data structures to support it. Unfortunately, that's not the case. Game platforms do have these facilities at the hardware level. Even my old Commodore 64 understood sprites, but PCs have not traditionally been where it's at for hot games or graphics in general. Only recently with the near domination of the PC platform, combined with the coming of age of the hardware, have serious graphics and game development moved to the PC. So only now are you starting to see more and more support of it at the various levels.

For Visual Basic, version 4.0 provides the much-needed `PaintPicture` procedure and the `ImageList` control and its associated `Overlay` and `Draw` functions (we'll talk about these later this chapter). Although there is not automatic, built-in support, you can get there with a few objects and functions of your own.

The Making of a Sprite

All right, so what does it take to make a sprite. Well, the first condition is that it be a bitmap. No problem, but it also must be able to move around on top of a background bitmap without disturbing it.

One solution might be to create a picture control and just move the picture control around on top of another, larger picture control using the `Move` method. Because the two are separate controls, this works and the background isn't disturbed.

This would work except for two objections.

1. It's too slow to do any real animation
2. Every sprite object created must be rectangular.

If you're writing a game with a warehouse setting with many boxes, maybe, but in most situations, you will not have square sprites. In fact, some folks include the words "irregularly shaped" in their definition of a sprite.

Great. So to get past the first objection, that this would be too slow, you traditionally turn to the Windows API or Win32. This was done in previous versions of Visual Basic with the `BitBlt` and `StretchBlt` functions mentioned earlier. Today, you can turn to the `PaintPicture` method.

The *PaintPicture* Method

`PaintPicture` is an exciting new method included with Visual Basic 4.0. If you have done animation in earlier versions of Visual Basic for Windows 3.1 you have probably become quite familiar with the Windows API function `BitBlt` (pronounced bit-blit) and its cousin `StretchBlt`. When you are doing animation in any language, it is essential to be able to move chunks of memory from one location to another very quickly; this is `BitBlt`'s forte. `StretchBlt` does the same thing, but offers more options, like reversing the image horizontally or vertically or, as the name implies, stretching the image out or squishing it down to a different size.

Although Win32 has new (and much faster) versions of `BitBlt` and `StretchBlt`, you probably will never need to visit them yourself. That's because the `PaintPicture` method provides an easy way to access these features without leaving the safety and comfort of Visual Basic syntax.

Syntax

Speaking of syntax, here is the syntax for `PaintPicture`.

```
DestinationObject.PaintPicture SourcePicture, DestinationX,
    DestinationY, DestinationWidth, DestinationHeight, _
    SourceX, SourceY, SourceWidth, SourceHeight, _
    BitwiseOperator
```

`DestinationObject` is either a form, a picture control, or the printer object. If omitted, the current form is the default.

`SourcePicture` is where the graphic to be painted on the destination will come from. Notice that it is a picture, not an object. Be sure and specify the Picture property of the form or picture control you want to use. This argument is, of course, required.

`DestinationX` and `DestinationY` are the coordinates on the `DestinationObject` where you want this picture painted. These are also required.

`DestinationWidth` and `DestinationHeight` describe the space into which you want to place the picture. They are used in case you want to change the size of the picture from what it was originally (to stretch or shrink it).

`SourceX`, `SourceY`, `SourceWidth`, and `SourceHeight` are used to specify a *clipping region* or smaller portion of the source to be transferred to the destination. It's just like clipping a coupon out of the middle of a newspaper page (except that the page stays intact!).

`BitwiseOperator`, also called a *raster operation* or *ROP*, is a long value that specifies how you want to copy the source to the destination. Table 10.1 shows possible values for `BitwiseOperator` and a description of each. These constants are defined in WIN32API.TXT, which you can include as a module in your project.

Table 10.1. Possible values for `BitwiseOperator`.

Name	Hex	Decimal	Operation
SRCCOPY	&HCC0020&	13369376	Copies Source directly over Destination
SRCPAINT	&HEE0086&	15597702	Bitwise OR of Source and Destination
SRCAND	&H8800C6&	8913094	Bitwise AND of Source and Destination
SRCINVERT	&H660046&	6684742	Bitwise XOR of Source and Destination
SRCERASE	&H440328&	4457256	Source AND (NOT Destination)
NOTSRCCOPY	&H330008&	3342344	NOT Source
NOTSRCERASE	&H1100A6&	1114278	NOT (Source OR Destination)
MERGEPAINT	&HBB0226&	12255782	(NOT Source) OR Destination
DSTINVERT	&H550009&	5570569	NOT Destination
BLACKNESS	&H000042&	66	Fill Destination with black
WITENESS	&HFF0062&	16711778	Fill Destination with white

Note that the `ScaleMode` used for every one of the coordinates and width/height arguments is that of the `DestinationObject`. It would be quite confusing if you have a different `ScaleMode` for the source. In general, when working with bitmaps and animation at this level, it is best to standardize on a `ScaleMode` `Pixel` for everything.

Making Sense of it

If you read a book like I do, you just skipped that last section and jumped down to this one looking for example code. Although I have tried to make the preceding description of the syntax as meaningful as possible, nothing brings it home like seeing real code. So here it is.

```
picBoard.PaintPicture picPlayer.picture, 284, 84, _
```

```
picPlayer.ScaleWidth, picPlayer.ScaleHeight, _
0, 0, picPlayer.ScaleWidth, picPlayer.ScaleHeight, _
SRCCOPY
```

What does this one do? Well, imagine a game board with graphics on it. You want to copy the representation of the player onto the game board. The game board is in the picture control picBoard, and the representation of the player is in another picture control picPlayer, so you execute the method of picBoard, because this will be your destination. The first argument specifies the source. You want to place the player at a particular position on the board, so you specify the X and Y pixel locations (assuming everything is in ScaleMode Pixel). Then you say that you are going to take up a certain amount of space on the destination indicated by the picPlayer's ScaleWidth and ScaleHeight properties. Finally, you get to the source arguments. You want the entire picPlayer picture (not some clipped-out subset of it) so you specify 0, 0 for X and Y and picPlayer ScaleWidth and ScaleHeight again for the width and height. The last argument, SRCCOPY, says just copy the source over of the destination without regard to what was there before.

Whew! Do you really have to specify each one of those things? No. Here's the short form of the same command.

```
picBoard.PaintPicture picPlayer.picture, 284, 84, , , , , _
    , , SRCCOPY
```

You do have to specify the source, destination, where on the board to put it, and how it should be placed there (SRCCOPY). But that's it, the defaults cover us for the rest of it.

Weird Shapes

Don't you run into the second objection with the PaintPicture method, too? Doesn't it just move rectangular areas of memory from one place to another? The answer is yes. It only moves rectangular areas, but the last argument of the PaintPicture method leaves an open door for us to do more.

The last argument in PaintPicture is a bitwise operator. Table 10.1 showed possible values you could assign to it, most of them confusing at best. How does it work?

Suppose your background image is one of a living room. You want to place a round ball on the sofa without removing a square chunk of the sofa in the process. The easiest way to solve this problem is with a two-step process.

First, you must create what is called a *mask*. A mask is a monochrome copy of your bitmap where everything in the picture is black and everything that should be transparent is white. For our purposes, the ball would be painted completely flat back so it was only a silhouette of its former self on a white background.

Now you execute a PaintPicture method for the destination object. The source is the mask image. The location is where you want to place the ball (on the sofa), and the bitwise operator is SRCAND. Look back at that confusing table. It tells you that SRCAND does a bitwise AND of the destination and the source bytes. White is represented by the highest possible bit values (all 1s), while black is all 0s. Anything ANDed with white is itself. Anything ANDed with black is black. So what does this do? It makes a perfectly ball-shaped black hole in our sofa!

> **NOTE**
>
> This is a note for those confused by the last paragraph because they don't know what a bitwise operator or ANDing bytes means.
>
> A byte is just a bunch of bits. So a bit-wise operator works on bytes at the bit level. For instance, here are two bytes:
>
> ```
> 01101001
> 11011000
> ```
>
> If I choose to AND these two bytes, I look at the bits in each one and if a certain bit is 1 AND its corresponding bit is 1 the result is 1. Otherwise, the result bit is 0. Here is how the AND arithmetic works out.
>
> ```
>     01101001
> AND 11011000
>     01001000
> ```
>
> ORing, then, means that if either the top number has a bit set or the bottom one does, go ahead and set the result bit. ORing would look like this.
>
> ```
>    01101001
> OR 11011000
>    11111001
> ```
>
> White is represented by 11111111 and black as 00000000. Now the statement "Anything ANDed with white is itself. Anything ANDed with black is black," should make more sense to you. ANDing any byte with 11111111 would produce that same byte as the result. ANDing anything with 00000000 always produces 00000000.

But that didn't solve our problem. Now we have no sprite on the screen and a great big hole in the couch. Don't worry, you can work this out.

Take your original bitmap (the one with a picture of a real ball on it) and change it so that everything that is *not* a ball is black. Flood-fill the background using your favorite picture editing program. Filling gives you a regular ball on a black background as your source. Using the SRCPAINT bitwise operator, do a `PaintPicture` to indicate the destination (the living room) with this ball in the correct location. If you refer back to Table 10.1, you see this basically performs an OR operation on all the bytes of color from the source to the destination. Black is zero, anything ORed with zero is itself. The background remains the same (because the area outside the ball is black), and the ball is placed neatly in the black spot, because its bits are ORed with the black of the hole.

Very nice. Now you have a sprite. Almost.

The Background

You have an irregularly shaped picture superimposed on another picture. You *would* have a sprite. *If* sprites never moved.

But sprites do move. They usually move a lot. And all that movement can cause problems. Most notably, big black spots or remnants of sprites gone by left on the background. So you want to save the background in a safe place to restore later when the sprite moves on.

Here's a test of your understanding of the `PaintPicture` method. What does the following code do?

```
picWork.PaintPicture picBoard.picture, 0, 0, _
   , , 284, 84, , , SRCCOPY

picSave.PaintPicture picWork.picture, 0, 0, _
   , , , , , , SRCCOPY

picWork.PaintPicture picMask.picture, 0, 0, _
   , , , , , , SRCAND

picWork.PaintPicture picPic.picture, 0, 0, _
   , , , , , , SRCPAINT

picBoard.PaintPicture picWork.picture, 284, 84, _
   , , , , , , SRCCOPY
```

There are five picture controls: `picWork`, `picBoard`, `picSave`, `picMask`, and `picPic`. The sprite is `picPic` and `picMask` is its associated mask. The game board where all the action takes place is `picBoard`. `picSave` is where to save the background image for use later. `picWork` is another bitmap, the same size as `picPic` and `picMask` to serve as an off-screen work area. Is that enough hints?

Here's how the code works.

1. Copy a portion of the game board to the working area.
2. Copy the working area into the `picSave` bitmap so that the background can be restored later.
3. AND the mask onto the work area and poke a sprite-shaped black hole in it.
4. OR the sprite itself into the black hole for a perfect fit.
5. Copy the image from the working area back out to the game board.

Pretty spiffy. But why go to all the extra trouble of a work area? It turns out that the number of times you copy images to the visible screen is important. If we did all these operations right on the screen, you probably wouldn't notice a difference, but if we took this same bitmap and started moving it across the screen, redrawing each step of the way, you would start to see the image flicker in and out. You have probably even seen this effect on some video games when there are a lot of sprites moving at once. This happened a lot on the old home game systems like the Atari 2600.

By moving most of the work to an off-screen buffer, you can make the animation much snappier. You do all the work in the back room and just present it when you're done.

The Final Step: Animation

Animation is more than a static image moving around the screen. Animation means that the image itself is alive with realistic (or not-so-realistic) movement. Just like in the movies, this is done by rapidly flipping through pre-created frames quickly enough that the eye perceives motion.

Easy, right? You set the timer to go off 10 or 15 times a second and in the timer event you do this:

```
Static iFrame As Integer
iFrame = iFrame + 1
If iFrame > 10 Then iFrame = 0
picClown.Picture = LoadPicture(Clown$(iFrame))
```

Assuming the `Clown$` array is filled with filenames, this works, right? Wrong. There is no disk drive anywhere that allows you to read in a new file (of any size) 15 times a second. `LoadPicture()` will be much too slow for this.

Instead, you probably should load your pictures off-screen ahead of time in their own picture controls. Then, rapidly switch among them. Assuming you had a control array of picture boxes called `picClownFrame`, this code would work fine.

```
Static iFrame As Integer
iFrame = iFrame + 1
If iFrame > 10 Then iFrame = 0
picClown.Picture = picClownFrame(iFrame)
```

All of this put together begins to get complicated. It's true that graphics applications, particularly games, are not simple beasts. But there is relief, and it comes in the form of a control. The `ImageList` control.

The *ImageList* Control

On first glance the `ImageList` control is interesting. A single control who's primary job is to contain a collection of unseen images. The images are indexed by number and, if you like, a key string. There's a handy dialog provided to set them at design time or you can use the Add method of the collection to add new images at runtime. This sounds perfect for animation. There are a couple of catches:

1. The images must all be exactly the same size. Usually this isn't a problem because frames of an animated sprite generally are going to be the same size. If they weren't, positioning them correctly would be a pain.

2. They must be either a BMP file or an ICO file. An icon can be in one of three fixed sizes: Small (16×16), Large (32×32), or Huge (48×48). BMPs can be any size as long as they all match.

The image control is much more than an image warehouse. It has two key methods that make the animator's life *much* easier.

The *Overlay* Method

The syntax for the `Overlay` method looks like this.

```
ListImageObject.Overlay (IndexKey1, IndexKey2)
```

`IndexKey1` is the numeric index or string key used to specify the image to be overlain.

`IndexKey2` is the numeric index or string key used to specify the image to be laid over `IndexKey1`, using the `MaskColor` property to identify what color is transparent.

The `Overlay` method is a function that returns a composite of the two images. This is made possible through an ImageList property called `MaskColor`. You simply fill in `MaskColor` with the image color that is supposed to be made transparent. The first image is then laid over the second image.

This is an interesting prospect, and it holds promise. It could have been used in the code we created above to combine our `picPic` image with the portion of the picBoard that we copied out to the work area.

What are the benefits? You don't have to go through the tedious process of creating a mask yourself. The `ImageList` creates an associated mask for every image it holds by using the `MaskColor` property. Then it automatically does the hole punching and copying that is necessary to create a combined image.

Believe it or not, there is an even better solution to our animation woes.

The *Draw* Method

The `Draw` method takes one of our stored images and draws it on any given device context we care to give it. Its syntax looks like this.

```
ListImageObject.Draw (DestinationhDC, DestinationX, DestinationY, DrawingStyle)
```

`DestinationhDC` is the device context of any control. A device context is just a number used by Win32 to address the drawing area on a particular window or control. When you deal with Win32 graphics commands, you always work with device contexts instead of passing picture controls around or assigning picture properties as you might do in Visual Basic programming. Visual Basic provides access to the device context through the attribute hDC which can be found on the form, `PictureBox`, and printer objects.

DestinationX and DestinationY indicate the coordinates on the destination picture where the image is to be placed. The default is 0,0.

DrawingStyle determines how the image will be drawn. Table 10.2 lists options for DrawingStyle.

Table 10.2. Options for DrawingStyle.

Constant	Value	Description
imlNormal	0	Draws the image over the destination, just as it is.
imlTransparent	1	Uses the MaskColor method to superimpose the image on the destination so that the parts colored with the value specified in MaskColor are invisible.
imlSelected	2	The image is dithered with the system highlight color to look as if it is selected.
imlFocus	3	The image is both dithered and striped with the system highlight color to appear as if it has the focus.

The exciting one, for our purposes is, of course, imgTransparent. This means that in one call, you can superimpose an image on a destination without ever having to create your own mask image. It keeps one internally for each image and does all the hard work for you.

Summary

This chapter has been a quick introduction to the concepts of animation and how it can be implemented in Visual Basic 4.0. The topic and associated examples could (and will) fill volumes. But the foundation you have gained here will give you a shove off in the right direction for experimentation on your own and a foundation for future study.

Performance Tuning

by Ke
and

If you've done much programming in Visual Basic, you have likely realized that performance gremlins are a frequent companion of the Visual Basic developer. However, it is possible to write efficient, high-performance Visual Basic programs. Better yet, this is achievable by the ordinary programmer, not just the Visual Basic guru who has been weaned on the Windows API. The world of performance encompasses such a vast number of topics and considerations that it could fill a large book in its own right. This chapter opens a door to this world by providing a look at some of the most fundamental Visual Basic performance considerations that every programmer should be aware of.

> **NOTE**
>
> Sams offers an excellent comprehensive book on performance tuning, *Visual Basic Optimization and Performance Tuning*, by Keith Brophy and Tim Koets. This book covers a much wider range of performance issues than can be addressed here and is recommended for those who wish to have an in-depth understanding of performance tuning.

When one sets out to slay performance gremlins and eliminate performance bottlenecks, it helps to have an overall understanding of performance tuning strategy. That is the focus of the first section of this chapter. A discussion of the Visual Basic Performance Paradox leads to the question, "What is performance tuning?" Likewise, the accompanying questions of when to optimize, where to optimize, and how to measure performance are discussed.

Armed with this conceptual background, we can tackle specific performance areas. An area of interest to most programmers is in the section "VB4 Considerations"—a look at specific performance tuning issues that arise with the groundbreaking, 32-bit version of the Visual Basic development tool. Other key areas addressed include related performance tuning issues as discussed in sections concerning variables, code structure, control loading, control properties and methods, math, graphics methods, and picture controls.

The material in this chapter will provide you with a fundamental understanding of basic performance issues. You may not be able to dodge every performance gremlin that pops up in your program, but you will be able to eliminate some of the most persistent ones, and you can look the remainder square in the eye with a better understanding of why they stalk you!

What Is Performance?

Application performance is traditionally thought of as the amount of time a user must wait for a program action to take place. For example, the time it takes a program at startup to fully display the first window the user can interact with, the time it takes to retrieve database data and update a display after a user clicks on a command button, or the amount of time it takes to carry out a series of complex financial calculations and show the final result are all speed issues.

Performance tuning is aimed at providing better programs to the end user. The process of making changes to improve speed or robustness is commonly called *performance tuning*.

The Cost of Poor Performance

The end user pays for poor performance. In some cases, if the end user is frustrated enough, the developer and company, too, may ultimately pay when the end user refuses to use the product. Perhaps more common than such a dramatic case, however, is the situation in which the end user tolerates a poorly performing program day after day. The developer may be on to the next product, happily coding away, believing "That widget application I did last year was awesome!" The end user, on the other hand, may spend most coffee breaks complaining to co-workers about the fact that "It takes that dumb widget program five minutes just to load!" The bottom line is if the end user perceives he has a performance problem, *he does have a problem.* This isn't to say the problem can necessarily be fixed, but the ultimate judge of determining acceptable performance is the end user.

User's Psychological Perception of Performance

The developer must often act as an advocate for the user in gauging performance, because the developer knows (or at least he thinks he knows) what is and is not technically achievable. Likewise, a user's satisfaction point is, perhaps, unreachable, because a user's ideal performance speed would be a zero wait time! However, if an application is usable, performs well enough that users are content to use it, and has taken advantage of available technology to provide the fastest performance reasonably achievable, it can be viewed as an application with adequate performance.

The decision of when this goal is reached is subjective. There is a real danger in not representing the user's viewpoint when considering performance in this manner. For example, a developer of a recipe-management application may consider performance just fine when a hierarchical bitmap-based listbox loads in less than 10 seconds. However, if the developer reached that conclusion based on a sample database of 50 recipes, but then the project ships to customers who work with databases of 50,000 recipes, they may feel differently. When the listbox takes 15 minutes to load for customers, performance would not have been successfully addressed from their standpoint.

A user's outlook on the performance of an application is also shaped largely by expectations and past experience. If the same application is provided to two businesses, workers may react to it very differently. If one business has just switched its workers from mainframe-connected terminals to PCs, and your new application is the first PC application they have ever used, they may be delighted with the performance. Compared to their terminal experience, it seems to blaze if they only have to wait five seconds to retrieve data instead of the 30 seconds they were used to.

On the other hand, if the other business has a group of users accustomed to working with fast local spreadsheets on the PC, and then they are introduced to a networked PC program that takes five seconds to retrieve data, they may be very unhappy. In the first case, the developer should consider himself fortunate. In the second case, the users should be educated to realize that network database applications have performance that is not on a par with local applications so they can downscale their expectations to be more realistic.

In many cases, even if there are performance constraints the developer can do nothing to fix, the satisfaction level of the user can still be increased by distracting them during times of system inactivity. For example, displaying a *splash screen*, or colorful startup screen, in front of the user can give him something to look at and divert his attention while a more complex form with many controls loads.

Tactics such as assessing performance from the standpoint of real-world use, educating the user in order to shape expectations, and distracting the user from performance through avenues such as splash-screens are all an important part of the strategy of addressing user performance concerns, in addition to performance tuning. The reception your program receives will involve the emotions and reactions of your users as well as the ultimate speed of your application on their computers. Therefore, performance addresses subjective perception considerations as well as objective, measurable behavior.

The Challenge of Producing Meaningful Performance Assessments

Performance is typically evaluated by collecting *timings*. These timings may be collected from the application itself, or from test applications that highlight various characteristics of the target application. In some cases, comparisons may be performed between different code techniques to determine which of various alternative methods is preferable. There are many considerations to keep in mind when carrying out performance analysis that can complicate the task considerably.

Many Factors Affect Performance

Nothing would seem to be easier on the surface than choosing the speediest car at the conclusion of the Indy 500, or the fastest runner at the finish line of the Vermont 100-Mile Trail Run. Simply point to the contestant that reached the finish line first and is carrying the trophy around, and you can say "that one is the fastest!" *Or can you...?* If you call the same field of contestants back to the starting line and rerun the race, the results may be completely different. A safer statement to make about who's the fastest is to say "that one was the fastest in the last race!"

While computers are more predictable than highly tuned race cars and exhausted runners, in some respects the process of gauging performance of Visual Basic code shares the same outcome uncertainty. The results of a trial run can vary with successive trials, subject to the influence of the environment. And coming up with a fair race that is not slanted to any one competitor is a constant concern.

Everything from memory, to disk access speed, to system swap file configuration, to other programs running, to other Windows configuration issues, and potentially hundreds more issues both minor and major beyond just your application code can affect the speed of your application. The developer must identify any areas of major significance and isolate them out of the test as much as possible. Unfortunately, if all these factors were removed from the test, there would be no PC hardware or operating environment left to test on. Therefore, performance assessment includes understanding the impact of the environment and determining which factors should be eliminated or isolated before gathering timings.

> **TIP**
>
> One performance measurement is not conclusive.

Timing Methods Can Affect Performance Assessments

Even the method used to time various performance alternatives can affect the conclusions that are reached. Different methods of timing code execution are available to the programmer. The crudest of these is simply using a wristwatch. The human error inherent in this can introduce time skew ranging from one second to several seconds. Other code-based methods could take advantage of Visual Basic time-of-day functions, VB timer capabilities, or Windows API timer functions such as GetTickCount. The choice of a timing method can be very important. For example, the underlying time behind the VB Timer function is only updated every 55 milliseconds under Windows 3.1 and Windows 95, so this timing method cannot be used to measure *brief duration* time spans of a few milliseconds. Rather, tests should be structured to be of longer duration if Timer will be used for the timings. Instead of comparing assignment times of a textbox assignment versus a label assignment, you could time 1,000 textbox assignments versus 1,000 listbox assignments, and Timer then would have adequate resolution for the longer duration task. Alternatively, higher resolution timing methods can be used, but this requires considerable knowledge of the techniques. For more precise resolution, the timeGetTime API is available, which has default resolution of around 1 millisecond under Win95 and 5 milliseconds or above under Windows NT. The other well-known timing-based API, GetTickCount, does not offer this degree of resolution. It's actual resolution will vary between Windows 3.1, Windows 95, and Windows NT, and is essentially the same as using VBs Timer function under Windows 3.1. The bottom line is that a thorough understanding of the ramifications of the timing method used is required.

Fair Tests Are Required

Another key issue in comparison testing is that tests should be fair. You need to ensure that if you are comparing two code methods, they are truly similar methods for comparing the alternatives under consideration. For example, if you were deciding between the use of a textbox or a label, comparing the two code fragments in Listings 11.1 and 11.2 would accurately judge two potentially interchangeable methods.

Listing 11.1. Fair Test Case 1.

```
TestCase #1:  where txtAuthors is defined as a textbox control
txtAuthors = "Keith Brophy and Tim Koets"
```

Listing 11.2. Fair Test Case 2.

```
TestCase#2:  where lblAuthors is defined as a label control
lblAuthors = "Keith Brophy and Tim Koets"
```

On the other hand, the test shown in Listings 11.3 and 11.4 would be unfair, because it uses the most efficient textbox update method, but would not accurately reflect the most efficient label method available.

Listing 11.3. Unfair Test Case 1.

```
TestCase #1:  where txtAuthors is defined as a textbox control
txtAuthors = "Keith Brophy and Tim Koets"
```

Listing 11.4. Unfair Test Case 2.

```
TestCase#2:  where lblAuthors is defined as a label controllblAuthors.caption =
"Keith Brophy "
lblAuthors.caption = lblAuthors.caption & " and Tim Koets"
```

The Visual Basic Performance Paradox

The paradox of Visual Basic programming is that the very characteristics that allow it to be praised as a wonderful development language can also lead to it being criticized as a language with performance drawbacks. Visual Basic allows developers to piece together programs with tremendous ease and a minimum time investment. However, the same ease of use and rapid application development technology that makes that rapid assembly possible can introduce many difficulties from a performance and optimization standpoint.

Custom Control Layers

Visual Basic programs are often built with many custom controls. These custom controls consist of pre-packaged code available to the user in a consolidated library in OCX or VBX form. Controls are typically written in a generic manner to provide maximum flexibility in the widest variety of application uses. Any one application typically exercises only a subset of the properties and methods available, and uses only a fraction of the flexibility built into the control.

That means each use of a control may carry with it more of an automatic overhead penalty than if the user had built a customized control or designed a direct implementation from the ground up.

Ease of Technology Incorporation

The ease of component incorporation in Visual Basic also means that Visual Basic programs, as much or more than programs of any other language, are likely to leverage areas of technology beyond the programming language itself. The odds are very high that a Visual Basic program makes use of a database, mail support, multimedia, or generates graphs. In each of these cases, the performance perception of the user is based on the performance of the underlying technologies: database engine speed, network load impact, the mail interface and mail server, network speed, CD speed, the graphics engine, as well as on the application itself.

Interpreted Language

Visual Basic is an interpreted language. When a Visual Basic program is running, the instructions in the Visual Basic executable file are not carried out directly by the PC's processor. Rather, the instructions are passed on as data to yet another program, the Visual Basic runtime executive, that is started along with the Visual Basic application. Runtime executive file names are listed for various versions of Visual Basic:

Visual Basic 3.0	VBRUN300.DLL
Visual Basic 4.0 16 Bit	VB40016.DLL
Visual Basic 4.0 32 Bit	VB40032.DLL

A *compiled language* such as C, Pascal, or Delphi, stores executable programs as a sequence of instructions that can be directly carried out by the PC's processor without assistance from another runtime program, avoiding the overhead of the interpreter. It has been stated by many that the performance penalty for the interpreter is relatively small, because the Visual Basic runtime program performs its interpretation very quickly and much of the time in a program is actually spent waiting on areas such as system and database response rather than on raw processing of the application's instructions. Nevertheless, there is no denying that an extra level of activity must take place to execute the program.

High-Level, Layered Building-Block Tool

Windows resource management is complicated by the presence of a high-level interpreted language. In the traditional Windows language of C and C++, management of Windows resources is directly assessable through the use of Windows APIs. In Visual Basic, the developer still has capabilities to take advantage of this low-level management, but also must depend on the fact that Visual Basic interpreter is automatically carrying out its own level of resource and memory management in support of the forms and the code that have been defined. Forms are easy to define exactly because the developer does not have to deal with these low level issues. Visual Basic addresses these issues "out of sight, out of mind." Visual Basic is a programming language that makes the task of the developer wonderfully easy because it allows work to take place at a high level by moving the tedious work of programming out of the way to lower layers. The beauty of Visual Basic carries with it an unavoidable penalty—the typical Visual Basic developer is shielded from low level details by the layers, and it is often these low level details that affect performance.

Ease of Programming and Impact on Performance

There is still another penalty area of Visual Basic development that is usually conspicuously absent from many industry discussions on Visual Basic performance, but can in some cases be one of the most significant factors that influences performance. Here it is, stated for the record:

> Visual Basic can be a sloppy language. It is easy to write sloppy programs in Visual Basic.

Whew! Now that the secret is out we can address the problem. For several reasons, inefficient code can be a serious problem in Visual Basic applications produced in certain development environments. At the top of the list is the fact that Basic is an easy language to begin programming in right away. Even those without prior knowledge of the language find the syntax quick to master with its clear identifiers (that is, End ends a program as one might expect) and lack of complexity (no pointers to explicitly deal with). However, this ease of use allows programmers to piece together programs rapidly in a "first-come, first-served" manner, using the first syntax that gets the job done without considering the ramifications.

Likewise, VB programs can be built in a piecemeal fashion. A snippet of code can be associated with one control, and later a snippet added for another control, with a variable thrown in here or there in the mix. This makes for an easy and painless development path as you add a piece of functionality at a time, but can lead to tangled, unorganized code in the end if planning and discipline are not used along the way.

Similarly, VB is the classic example of an "I'll do it later" language. It's so easy to implement functionality that it's natural for a programmer to add a quick and dirty piece of code. Such code is rarely optimized or elegantly written. Of course, the developer taking these shortcuts usually plans to revisit the code and implement it more elegantly in the future. But it is easy for the developer to forget (or choose to forget) to go back and optimize the code once a working program is in hand.

All the performance problems mentioned here are areas that can be avoided by planning, discipline, and up-front design. These problems don't just go away with experience, however. In the real world, there often remain situations where code must be done quick, dirty, and yesterday rather than today. The inevitable fallout from this mix is that there is often code that cries out for optimization.

Alternative Languages

Until very recently, in the minds of many seasoned programmers, there were two fundamental approaches to Visual Basic application performance problems.

- Write *part* of it in another, faster language
- Write *all* of it in another, faster language

Needless to say, there can be a great deal of work and inconvenience in either of these approaches, and they mitigate the advantages of using Visual Basic in the first place. The world will never know how many potential Visual Basic programs never reached fruition because of the purveyor of doom to be found in every company grumbling and overreacting "It'll never be fast enough in VB...we must rewrite it in C++!" This is *not* to say that there are never situations where another language alternative is warranted. However, in many cases there are optimization steps that can be taken short of turning to such drastic measures.

Visual Basic versus Other Languages

One issue that often arises in discussions of Visual Basic performance is that of C++ versus VB or Delphi versus VB. All too often, discussions on language performance issues lose sight of the forest for the trees as participants get bogged down in emotional views of particular languages based on their own subjective language experience. There have been industry demonstrations of highly optimized VB applications outperforming similar non-optimized C++ applications. When looked at objectively, most seasoned developers would agree that programs written in C or C++, unless special circumstances prevail, have faster performance than Visual Basic programs. However, more important than the issue of which language is faster is the question of "Can a Visual Basic program have acceptable performance to the user?" The answer is, in most cases, "Yes."

Industry Standard Advice—Write A DLL (Give Up!)

While guidelines on proper use of VB syntax and controls may be the Visual Basic performance battle cry, the white-flag wave surrender of "Write a DLL in another language!" often seems to follow closely on its heels. A program can often gain considerable speed by implementing key pieces in a block of performance-tuned, carefully crafted code that is packaged into Dynamic Link Library. This is especially true of compute-intensive pieces of code that must, for example, process many floating point numbers. Often these routines can be carried out much more efficiently in another language. However, writing a DLL in another language should be an avenue of last resort, not of first resort. Backing away from Visual Basic and into another language mitigates the very reasons that Visual Basic was used as the target language in the first place—ease of use and rapid development.

When to Optimize

Software optimization is as much of an art as a science. Optimization is not a set of rules and techniques that can be applied the same way to all applications with equally predictable results. While software developers have collected a body of general optimization techniques, the practical application of these techniques varies widely with the programming languages being used, the operating system and hardware platforms being targeted, and the end users' expectations of the software. Three key observations lend support to the assertion that software optimization is an art. The developer should understand them in order to appreciate the magnitude and scope of software optimization and its ramifications.

> **TIP**
>
> Software optimization is not just a set of techniques that can be applied at the end of software development.

If you wait until you have written all your code and then decide to optimize it, you are never likely to have a product with the highest possible efficiency. In order to properly optimize an application, you must optimize code, to some extent, as it is being written. When writing software, developers constantly face the temptation to take shortcuts in developing software. Once the actual coding effort begins, the developer is further tempted to simply get something working, and then worry about how efficient it is.

When using a language like Visual Basic, this temptation is especially alluring. One of Visual Basic's primary strengths is to make it easier for programmers to create applications, especially for those who may not have an extensive programming background. A significant penalty for this, however, is the equally high ability to write *inefficient* code. Thus, more of a burden is placed on the developer to write structured, maintainable, and efficient code.

When an application is put together hastily and without regard to performance, the developer often finds that when the program is finished, the performance is unacceptable to the user. The developer must then go back and figure out how to make the code more efficient. While it is possible for developers to spend too much time optimizing at *early* stages in software development, developers should take the time to write the code efficiently *during* development and not to just optimize it later.

> **TIP**
>
> Software optimization must be based on how users will use the application and on what kind of systems the application runs.

In order to better understand when to optimize, the developer should work closely with testers and users to see just how the application is being used. The developer may be unable to predict just how the user will use his application during a typical day, and may therefore completely overlook areas of the application the user will be dissatisfied with.

An important metric that the developer should understand up front is the multitude of hardware and operating system configurations the application may be run under. Each configuration may behave differently in terms of performance, and each one needs to be addressed separately. Often during development, the programmer fails to anticipate a unique type of hardware or operating system configuration the user may select. If this particular configuration bogs down performance and it is the only one the user wishes to use, he will be very unhappy with the program. That one configuration overlooked could cause much anxiety to you as the programmer, once you release the application.

The most effective way to overcome the failure to anticipate the user's pattern of usage with your application is to continually elicit tester feedback, and optimize and evaluate each major feature or component of functionality in the application. As the major components of functionality are built and integrated with one another, this evaluation of performance from the user's perspective must continue and broaden as the application broadens. Keep in mind the importance of optimizing in little ways as you develop and not overlooking minor housekeeping tasks to improve performance.

> **TIP**
>
> Optimization is not always appropriate.

Optimization often comes at the cost of increased difficulty in code maintenance, debugging, and reuse, as well as optimizations that compete with each other in the same application. Optimization sometimes takes code that is fairly easy to understand and makes it more complex or difficult to follow. This, in turn, can make the program more difficult to maintain, either for yourself or someone totally new to the code. While this can be minimized by careful documentation of the optimization stages, the trade-off does exist between making an application very efficient, yet with code that is very cryptic and difficult to understand.

Likewise, optimization often makes code difficult to debug. This trade-off goes hand in hand with maintenance, because code that is more difficult to understand is typically more error prone and more difficult to debug. If the programmer is careful to test the application in light of the applied optimization technique, his chances of having fewer errors are greatly improved.

Yet another area of compromise is in the area of code reuse. The goal in Visual Basic, as in any other language, is often to write reusable components of software so that they can be applied in a wide variety of projects. Optimization strategies often include techniques that can break down the modeling goals for code reuse, particularly the well-defined interface between modules. Care must be taken to preserve this interface as much as possible, avoiding any implied conditions for the programmer reusing the code.

Often performance is increased by taking certain assumptions into account, limiting the scope of the code's reusability. Herein lies the tradeoff. If certain assumptions are made, it is very important to document them thoroughly. While this can be an acceptable tradeoff, it is unwise to make too many assumptions and take out critical code such as error checking and validation. Your users will be much more upset with an efficient application that crashes than a less efficient application that runs correctly every time under every circumstance. The developer has to make the final decision by weighing the benefits of optimization with these competing factors that can make optimization prohibitive.

Where to Optimize

Optimization can be a time-consuming process, so knowing *where* to optimize is very important. A programmer can spend a great deal of time optimizing part of an application that is not critical to performance. Likewise, a programmer can overlook areas of code that are very critical to performance. If a developer does not have a good understanding of which parts of an application are critical to performance and which parts are not, he will be "shooting in the dark" when optimizing, and will be likely to optimize areas he *thinks* are critical with no quantitative justification for doing so.

When considering how Windows applications run, areas for improving performance can be classified into two main categories: *actual speed* and *perceived speed.* Actual speed represents how fast your program performs calculated operations, database access, form loads and unloads, graphical painting, and file I/O. Perceived speed represents how fast your application appears to run. These two categories provide an optimization framework that allows the programmer to break down performance tasks into these two areas, concentrating on each one as appropriate.

In order to increase the actual and perceived speeds of an application, the programmer must be intimately familiar with the application, starting with the code. Programmers can use the VBCP32 and VBCP16 profilers that come with Visual Basic, commercial profiling tools such as Avantis PinPoint, hand-inserted timings, or simple analysis to determine what segments of code are executed the most. As a general rule, one should spend the greatest amount of time optimizing the code that has the largest impact on the user, so knowing what segments of code get executed the most is critical.

In addition to understanding the code, the developer must also be aware of the amount of resources and memory the application uses. Because Visual Basic applications run in the Microsoft Windows environment, much goes on behind the scenes that has a critical impact on performance. Resource- and memory-monitoring tools can be used to find areas of excessive memory and resource usage that degrade performance.

As a result of carefully analyzing the code, memory, and resource usage in the application, the programmer will discover a collection of areas to optimize. Because time is almost always a scarce resource when developing applications, the potential optimization areas must be prioritized so that areas most critical to overall performance are addressed first, followed by less critical areas, in order of decreasing priority.

The first step in trying to make an application run faster is to see how long it takes the application to perform its tasks. Specifically, the developer must profile the code, checking to see how much time certain commands, subroutines, functions, procedures, operations, algorithms, events, and methods take. When profiling the code, it is essential to exercise all possible cases and conditions so that a realistic profile can be taken and no areas are overlooked.

One must be careful never to blindly assume the code that executes the longest must be inefficient. Just because a subroutine consumes a large amount of time in an application, for instance, does not necessarily mean it is inefficient. It simply means that the program spends most of its time in that subroutine, whether it gets carried out frequently and executes quickly, gets run infrequently but takes a long time, or somewhere in the middle. In order to determine this, the developer must go deeper.

Depending on the profiling approach you use, whether using a Windows API timing call, user perception, a commercial profiling tool, or some combination of these approaches, you should at least have some set of timings for every procedure in your application that is carried out frequently by the user or of key impact to them. The next step is to take each critical procedure and determine which ones the program spends the most amount of time executing. Those are the procedures you must pay close attention to, because they are the ones in which modifications most dramatically effect the application's overall performance.

Once you have ordered the procedures in terms of percentage of total user impact, you should take each procedure (starting with the one that gets the most execution time), break it down into components, and analyze each component separately, determining how long it takes each component to execute. The components may consist of a single line of code or modular groups of code. You will gain a good understanding of what each section is doing and how those sections individually contribute to the overall execution time.

Continue to break out sections of code within each procedure until the subsections are down to a low enough level to apply a clearly-defined optimization technique or set of techniques to that subsection. Again, the developer should maintain a prioritized list of the sections and subsections that need to be optimized based on percentage of time executed in the application.

Once every procedure and module significant to the performance of the application has been fleshed out, the developer must make a judgment call on what procedures and sections to deal with first.

How to Measure Performance

When measuring the amount of time it takes to execute a series of instructions, the resolution of the timer you use is very important. If the timer you use is not precise enough, your results will be inaccurate and probably not worth very much. The frequency that the timer "ticks down" is important. If a timer only updates once every 55 milliseconds, for example, the timing will be inaccurate if it takes 109 milliseconds for an operation to execute. The timer may only report that 55 milliseconds have elapsed, which introduces a 98% error!

Windows also makes getting accurate timings inherently difficult. This is due to the means by which Windows accomplishes tasks. Unlike their MS-DOS counterparts, which are *procedure driven,* programs written in Windows are *event-driven.* Procedure-driven code executes in a very predictable fashion, one line of code at a time, in a predetermined manner. The programmer is usually in full control of the environment. When the programmer decides it is time for the user to offer input, he allows the program to wait for the user to take an action such as entering data into a field. In Windows, however, the user can respond one of several ways, each of which is called an *event.* Each event can potentially occur in any order and must be accounted for by the software.

In order for Windows applications to be event-driven, the operating environment must inform the program what is happening. For example, when the user clicks on an OK button, Windows must tell the Visual Basic application that the click event has occurred for that button. Windows does this by passing a message to Visual Basic, telling it the OK button has been clicked on by the mouse. Visual Basic then triggers the cmdOK_Click() event, executing the code you place in that event subroutine.

Windows must rely on messages to respond to user actions, timers, screen drawing, operating system maintenance, and so on. The number of messages Windows receives at any one moment can fluctuate. At times, very few messages are being processed by Windows, and it spends most of its time waiting idly for the user to do something. At other times, the system is so busy that the user has to wait for Windows to take care of all its messages and background tasks. In addition to system messages, Windows often has *background tasks* that must be processed, such as updating disk caches or virtual memory, updating the screen, or handling network access.

The same issue of time variability can also happen when using a timer in your code. You may put the Timer statement at the beginning of a subroutine, and another one at the end. If the elapsed time during those two calls varies, it is often due to the fact that every time you execute the body of code, Windows has a particular set of background tasks to process, different memory management considerations, or, under certain conditions, Windows messages which must be immediately addressed. In other words, it may have more to do during one instance of the subroutine's execution than another.

Thus, depending on the state of the system, it may take more time in one instance of the execution than another instance simply because Windows happens to have more to take care of at the time the application is executing. Thus, you can often receive inconsistent timing values. As a programmer, you must accept the fact that Windows limits your control over the accuracy of the timings.

Various techniques can be used to take timings for measuring performance in applications. Perhaps the easiest way is to use the Visual Basic Timer function (see Listing 11.5). This is very easy to use, because it is a VB command and can be placed directly in code. This function is accurate to the nearest 55 milliseconds under Windows 3.1 and Windows 95. Resolution is significantly greater under Windows NT. The Timer call can be placed at the beginning of a series of code statements to be timed and again at the end, as in the following example. Then, the difference in reported times can be calculated in order to obtain the elapsed time for the operation or series of operations being timed. You can also rely on commercial profiling tools such as the VBCP32 and VBCP16 profilers packaged with Visual Basic, and Avanti's PinPoint, which help automate the process of inserting timing-gathering code and collecting and analyzing results.

Listing 11.5. Example of obtaining a timing.

```
Private Sub Command1_Click()

Dim sngStart As Single
Dim sngEnd As Single
Dim lngIndex As Single

 ' The timing obtained below will only be accurate to the nearest 55 milliseconds
 '    due to underlying constraints of the hardware timer interrupt dependencies
 '    on Windows 3.1 and Windows 95 Systems
sngStart = Timer

'Time text box assignments
For lngIndex = 1 To 100000
    txtField1 = "Testing
Next lngIndex

sngEnd = Timer
rc% = MsgBox("Assignments took " & Int((sngEnd - sngStart) * 1000) & "
milliseconds.")

End Sub
```

Visual Basic 4.0 Considerations: 32-Bit versus 16-Bit Code

Visual Basic 4.0 can produce either 16-bit or 32-bit code when the corresponding development environment version is used. For example, 32-bit programs can only run in 32-bit Windows environments such as Win95 and NT, while 16-bit programs can run in either 32-bit environments or 16-bit environments such as Windows 3.1 or WFW 3.11. A consideration of Visual Basic program performance, then, also entails consideration of the 32-bit and 16-bit environments in which programs will run.

A 32-bit program has inherent performance advantages because it can take full advantage of the 32-bit operating system environment and APIs. There are many complex reasons for the superiority of the 32-bit environment, including the fact that programs are freed from the shackles of the 16-bit segmented memory architecture and that preemptive multitasking can take place.

The ability of the 32-bit Win95 operating system to carry out preemptive multitasking is very significant to performance measurement. First of all, it makes assessing performance much harder. In a cooperative multitasking environment such as Windows 3.1, programs have, generally speaking, full control of the processor when they execute. Once a process gains control, no other process gets a turn until the process underway completes or explicitly yields control of the CPU. This means that programs under Windows 3.1 can "hog" the CPU, locking out other applications until their own turn is complete. This often results in programs sprinkled with DoEvents statements that cause Visual Basic to temporarily give up or share the CPU.

From a performance assessment standpoint, obtaining meaningful timings can be somewhat easier under cooperative multitasking. If you look at a piece of code that doesn't yield the CPU, and then time that code segment, system activity may have affected the timing somewhat, but you can be confident no other application was given a slice of the processor time.

With Win95, however, the ground rules are different. No longer must an application use a DoEvents to be a good neighbor and give other processes a turn during lengthy calculations. The operating system takes care of that itself if needed, temporarily cutting one process off to give another a turn. The operating system makes these decisions based on scheduling algorithms that take many factors into account. The processes that are managed are no longer in the drivers seat for juggling their own CPU time once they start to execute. Therefore, when you time a given piece of code, even if that code does not yield the CPU, the operating system may give other processes turns as well before every instruction in the timed piece of code completes, which affects the duration of your timing. There are various timing approaches that can be taken to cope with this, but the most basic guidelines are simply to ensure you have no extra tasks running when assessing performance, and always base performance analysis decisions on a series of timings, and not just one individual timing.

The performance-related choice of which environments to target for an application, 32-bit or both 16- and 32-bit, also confronts the developer. The answer is dictated by your user base, but you can count on the fact that users with 32-bit operating systems will enjoy better performance if you can provide them with 32-bit applications rather than 16-bit applications. The exact degree of speed increase of an application when it is moved from the 16-bit world to the 32-bit world is extremely application specific. However, with this disclaimer in mind, tests on a variety of small applications show that performance improvements of 50 percent are commonly achieved when code is migrated from 16-bit to 32-bit VB programs.

This is enough of a performance gain to offer considerable incentive to developers to move their applications to 32-bit format. Fortunately, the 16-bit user base does not have to be abandoned to make this a reality. The conditional compilation capability of VB 4.0 makes it feasible to maintain the same program in both 32-bit and 16-bit versions from the very same source files. Programs can automatically be compiled with one set of declarations when targeted for the 16-bit environment, and another set of declarations when targeted for the 32-bit environment. This technique, illustrated below, means that you can bring enhanced performance to your high-end users without abandoning your 16-bit holdouts.

```
#If Win32 Then ' 32-bit VB uses this Declare.
    Declare Function GetTickCount Lib "kernel32" () As Long
    Declare Function GetWindowsDirectory Lib "kernel32" Alias
    "GetWindowsDirectoryA" (ByVal lpBuffer As String, _
        ByVal nSize As Long) As Long
#Else    ' 16-bit VB uses this Declare.
    Declare Function GetTickCount Lib "User" () As Long
    Declare Function GetWindowsDirectory Lib "Kernel" _
     (ByVal lpBuffer As String, ByVal nSize As Integer) As Integer
#End If
```

There are significant performance differences between environments in terms of control loading as well. 32-bit Visual Basic load performance is dependent on the 32-bit OLE controls (sometimes referred to as OCXs) that it supports. 16-bit applications can make use of 16-bit OLE controls as well as 16-bit VBXs. A detailed discussion of this topic appears later in this chapter in the controls section.

Object Linking and Embedding (OLE)

Another very powerful technical capability of Visual Basic 4.0 is the level of integration that can be achieved with other applications through OLE, specifically embedding or linking data with the OLE container, direct insertion of OLE objects, or the use of OLE Automation Objects to control other applications. With easy access to other application objects from a VB application, and now the ability for a VB application to likewise make itself available as a server, the only limit to what a VB application can now achieve is the developer's initiative and creativity. This world of object sharing does impose some important performance considerations, however.

When you use the services of another application, you inherit their performance impact. OLE performance is much improved from early versions, and superior to DDE in most cases, but nevertheless, there is a lot more overhead that goes on to support OLE than if an application simply had internal code to achieve the same result with no external dependencies. It is incumbent on the developer to fully assess performance of the integrated piece of software before settling on it as an acceptable solution. You adopt that software object as your own when you incorporate it into your application, because from the standpoint of the user it *is* part of your application. Sometimes there will be nothing you can do about poor performance of an object driven through OLE automation. Many times, though, performance can be improved simply by gaining a better understanding of the objects methods and properties.

The same principle in reverse applies when providing services through exposed objects, OLE servers, and DLLs. If the code you develop is intended to be shared with other applications, there is an added need for performance tuning. Others will certainly be using the application, and they will be using it with additional overhead to get to the capabilities your external software provides. You should assess performance from this perspective with relevant test applications before considering any object complete and ready for public use.

In-Process versus Out-of-Process OLE Automation Servers

With the 32-bit version of Visual Basic 4.0, two types of OLE Automation Servers can be implemented: *in-process* and *out-of-process* OLE Servers. In-process servers are built from Visual Basic source code into DLLs, whereas an out-of-process server is built as an executable file. As the name implies, an in-process server can be run in the same address space as its calling application. An out-of-process server incurs the overhead of a separate address space and corresponding OLE communication issues. Therefore, the use of in-process servers can provide considerable performance benefits. This is another strength of 32-bit Visual Basic applications for which the 16-bit application has no equivalent alternative.

OLE Server Busy Timeouts and Perceived Performance

When you make use of another applications' exposed objects through OLE, you are counting on that OLE server application to be available to service your requests. However, if that application is already responding to the requests of yet another client application, your application must wait its turn. Likewise, if your application requests some action of the server that the server application is not able to fill because of its current state (for example, if it is already displaying a modal error message to an interactive user), the server will not be able to respond right at that time.

In both of these cases, Visual Basic automatically keeps trying to fulfill your request by continually retrying to give the request to the server, in hopes that the busy period is a temporary condition. Visual Basic continues these repeated efforts until a given timeout period has expired, and then it displays the "Server Busy" message to the user.

The retry duration is controlled by your application through the App.ServerBusyTimeout and App.RequestPendingTimeout properties. The ServerBusyTimeout property has a default of 10 seconds, and RequestPendingTimeout has a default of 5 seconds. While OLE communication establishment is not an area you can tune or control, this is an area that may be a perceived performance issue to your user because they are very aware that they are waiting on the software at these times.

The timeout properties raise an interesting performance question for the developer. Is it better to have faster feedback to the user with less likelihood that all operations will succeed, or to build-in longer wait times that the user may be subject too, with the payoff of more chance of OLE operations' success? Will your users' perception of the program be better if they periodically have to wait long periods of time but rarely have the application give them a busy (failure) message? If so, you may want to increase the timeout periods even more. Or, is it more likely that situations when the OLE server is tied up will be very infrequent? In this case perhaps your user would like immediate feedback in the very rare cases when the server is busy, rather than be subject to much longer waits to see the same "busy" error message? As you likely suspected, there are no stock answers to these questions. A timeout strategy that works well for one user on a blazing fast Pentium with little OLE server contention, may seem to impose insufferable waits on another user on a turtle-slow 386 where there is much contention for OLE services due to other software being used there. In general, the Visual Basic defaults serve as an effective starting point, but depending on your specific OLE server needs and target user base, you may need to tweak these to satisfy your user's robustness or acceptable wait time needs.

Objects and User-Defined Classes

Objects and the VB 4.0 capability to utilize user-defined classes from which objects can be created pose the traditional performance tradeoff. Objects are a powerful construct, and enable greatly enhanced development and maintenance. However, enhanced development often comes at the expense of speed. A very complex design based on hierarchical object implementation and built-on layers of collections and objects can have performance impact if the alternative was a flatter, simpler implementation that would require less interpretation time. The performance impact is very application specific, and in most cases the development benefits outweigh the performance penalties. The best way to assess this is to simply take measurements throughout the development lifecycle, so there are no surprises at the end of a complex project when performance is considered for the first time.

Another object consideration is to use the most specific means possible of declaring an object. The more specific the declaration, the faster performance is when that object is accessed. The following assignments give examples of slow and fast object declaration pairs:

```
Dim MyForm as New Form              ' Slower
Dim MyForm as New frmPreviouslyDefined   ' Faster - uses existing form

Dim MyThing as New Object           ' Slower
Dim MyThing as New MyObjectClass    ' Faster - uses class module def.
```

```
Dim MyControl as New Control        ' Slower
Dim MyControl as New Textbox        ' Faster - uses control class
```

The improved performance between any one change as described above is relatively small, but it will apply to subsequent object accesses as well as just the definition statement. In an object-intensive program the cumulative benefit can be noticeable. There are no significant maintenance disadvantages to this approach, and the more specific declarations could even be regarded as better programming practice. Therefore, this approach should be used as standard practice.

TIP

For faster performance, always use the explicit class name rather than the generic one when declaring objects.

Collections of Objects

In addition to the ability to use objects, we can also manipulate them much more easily in Visual Basic 4.0. A very powerful capability of Visual Basic 4.0 is the means to create collections of objects, including collections of objects defined from user-defined classes specified in class modules. Managing objects is much easier when those objects are grouped into collections. Collections can have add methods applied, remove methods applied, and be indexed by item. There are many inherent advantages to these methods, such as the fact that when an item is removed from a collection with the remove method, the collection is automatically compressed. You don't have to worry about holes left in the array sequence from deletions and writing code to carry out corresponding shifts of data or Redims.

Collections do come at a performance cost that, as usual, will vary depending on the specific application. Tests were carried out on a simple user-defined class defined in a class module. A comparison was made of creating a collection of these objects versus an array of these objects. The array approach was noticeably faster. Then another test was carried out comparing modification of a given property for every object created. The array modification loop was dramatically faster than the collection loop, as reflected in the following table:

Object Creation in Collections versus Arrays—Normalized Results

Collection	*Array*
Creation of All Instances	1.25–1.00

Object Modification in Collections vs. Arrays—Normalized Results

Collection	*Array*
Modification of All Instances	15.00–1.00

TIP

There is a performance penalty when collections are used in place of arrays. Despite this, the development/maintenance/good programming practice advantages of this approach are likely significant enough to warrant the use of collections in many cases.

Using Variables

The various data types which variables are based upon can have dramatic impacts on performance. Since some data types perform faster than others, strategies for using certain types of data types for certain uses and avoiding the general use of others is essential to making an application as efficient as possible. A brief overview of the most commonly used Visual Basic data types is discussed, followed by some general guidelines for using variables.

Visual Basic Data Types

The following lists the Visual Basic data types and their descriptions:

Integer—A variable that has been defined with the *integer* data type is a number that is two bytes in length. Because it is an integer, no fractional or decimal places can be used. Integers can range from –32,768 to 32,767. The integer is the most commonly used data type in Visual Basic. It is the standard data type for representing numbers for counting and representing quantities.

Long—Variables of data type *long* are also integers, except that they use four bytes of storage rather than two. This gives them a much higher range of –2,147,483,648 to 2,147,483,648. Because this data type is also an integer, decimal points cannot be used. If the range of an integer is not suitably represented in two bytes, it can most always be represented with four bytes. If the range exceeds even the *long* data type, a floating-point data type must be used.

Single—Some quantities or expressions cannot be easily represented without using a decimal point. Furthermore, sometimes programs require numbers with a much higher range than a long integer can provide. In either case, Visual Basic provides several floating-point data types. The first, the *single* data type, is a 4-byte value with a range of -3.4×10^{-45} to $+3.4 \times 10^{38}$. This data type is usually sufficient to represent most floating point values. While the single data type takes just as many bytes as the long integer, additional instructions are required by the computer to take the decimal place into account.

Double—When even larger floating-point values are required, the *double* data type can be used. A variable with this data type is eight bytes in length and has a range from -1.8×10^{308} to -4.9×10^{-324} and 4.9×10^{-324} to 1.8×10^{308}. When the programmer needs to use floating-point numbers, this data type should be used only when this degree of precision or range is required. Because it takes eight bytes to represent a variable, it requires more memory and takes longer in calculations.

Currency—The *currency* data type is an 8-byte number with a fixed decimal point. This data type provides a range of ±922,337,203,685,477.5808. The currency data type supports up to four digits to the right of the decimal point and up to 15 points to the left. This data type was designed for monetary calculations, because the decimal point is fixed. It does have more of a limited range than the floating-point numbers, but the smaller range makes it less susceptible to the small rounding errors that can occur with the other floating-point data types.

String—The string is a data type used to hold alphanumeric data. Strings are used extensively in most applications, because they are required to store and represent textual information. The length of a string variable depends on whether the string is declared fixed-length or variable-length. A variable-length string has four bytes of overhead along with the number of bytes it takes to represent the string (the number of characters). In the case of a fixed-length string, the user specifies the number of bytes for the string when it is declared, and no overhead bytes are required.

Variant—The variant is a "catch-all" variable that can represent any data type and automatically converts between them when necessary. Unfortunately, the variant adds a great deal of processing overhead and significantly increases the amount of time and memory used in an application. A variant used to represent a variable-length string, for example, takes 16 bytes plus one per character in the string. If a variant is used to represent a number, it requires 16 bytes of memory as opposed to 2 for an integer, 4 for a long or single, and 8 for a double.

Constants—While the Visual Basic constant is not, strictly speaking, a *data type*, it is mentioned here since it is yet another way to represent data. Constants can be used to represent numeric values and strings. While constants still require the same amount of memory to be represented in an application, they are loaded differently into memory and can help make an application more efficient.

Use Strings Instead of Variants

To compare the use of fixed-length strings, variable-length strings and variants, an application was constructed that assigns text to variants, variable-length strings, and fixed-length strings. The strings are declared and assigned as shown in Listing 11.6.

Listing 11.6. Strings versus Variants.

```
' Create an array of variable-length strings
ReDim svTest(1 To intStringCount) As String

' Assign the variables
For iCount = 1 to intStringCount
     svTest(iCount) = "Test String"
Next
```

The same type of test was carried out for fixed-length and variant strings. Timings were taken for each variable assignment separately, and the results obtained are shown in Table 11.1.

Table 11.1. String versus Variant Timing Results—Normalized Results.

Data Type	Elapsed Time
Fixed-Length String	1.00
Variable-Length String	4.50
Variant	8.00

Note that the use of fixed-length strings provides the fastest execution time. This is to be expected, because Visual Basic knows the size of the string ahead of time and doesn't need to calculate a size as it does with the variable-length string or variant. It is not always possible or desirable, however, to use a fixed-length string, so a variable-length string must be used. Even so, both are considerably faster than using a variant.

> **TIP**
>
> Use strings instead of variants.

Variants require more time due to the overhead required in handling them. Thus, the use of variants to represent strings should be avoided whenever possible. In specific cases, variants must be used to represent dates or can be used to easily convert between data types. Their use, however, should be restricted and only used when absolutely necessary.

Use Integers Whenever Possible

As discussed earlier, integers use fewer bytes than any other numeric data type. Use integer variables whenever possible rather than floating-point data types or variants. To illustrate this principle, a test application was constructed which assigns an integer value to each data type. A simplified code listing of this process is shown in Listing 11.7.

Listing 11.7. Integer data assignments.

```
' Variable Definitions
Dim intTest As Integer

' Perform the assignments
intTest = 33
```

A similar test was carried out for longs, singles, doubles, and variants. The results of each individual timing can be seen in Table 11.2.

Table 11.2. Integer versus Long, Single, Double, Variant Timing Results—Normalized Results.

Data Type	Elapsed Time
Integer	1.00
Long	1.12
Single	2.36
Double	2.40
Variant	1.24

Notice that the integer assignment has the fastest execution time, followed closely by the long data type. The floating-point data types both require approximately twice as much execution time due to the additional processing required to take into account the decimal-point and increased range capabilities of the data types.

The variant takes approximately 25 percent more time for the assignment than the integer and about 10 percent more than the long integer. While one might expect the variant to take the longest time of all the data types, Visual Basic treats the variant like an integer because the number assigned to it can be represented most efficiently by *typecasting* it into an integer. In doing so, the execution time is very close to that of an integer. Additional time is still required, however, for the overhead required in typecasting the variant into an integer. This once again supports the conclusion that the variant should be avoided unless necessary.

When using floating-point data types, the variables do not require as much space as the variant does, but the execution time is much more significant. The variant provides easy and automatic conversion between data types, but at the cost of memory. The floating-point data types provide decimal-point capability without the extra baggage of the variant's memory consumption, but they require much more time to execute than integers.

TIP

Use integers whenever possible.

Using the Currency Data Type

The currency data type is a special data type designed for monetary calculations. An application was constructed that performed a simple multiplication of dollar amounts using the currency data type as well as all the other data types. The results of the timings are shown in Table 11.3.

Table 11.3. The Currency Data Type versus all others—normalized results.

Data Type	Elapsed Time
Currency	1.63
Integer	1.00
Long	1.85
Single	1.04
Double	1.09
Variant	36.96

TIP

Use alternatives to the currency data type.

As can be seen, the use of the currency data type is slower than its floating-point counterparts. Note the dramatic increase in execution time of the variant data type. This again underscores the importance of avoiding this data type, particularly for floating-point and currency operations. Note further that the integer data types can be used to obtain even better performance. Integers cannot always be used for currency math, because currency math often uses floating-point arithmetic.

NOTE

As the book *Visual Basic Optimization and Performance Tuning* points out, alternate implementations are possible which enable the programmer to only use integer data types in place of floating point arithmetic, making the execution time of the application considerably faster.

Code Structure

Code structure can have a direct impact on speed. There are cases where the considerations for structured code based on "good programming practice" might not be the same as for structuring for "maximum speed." The structure of code effects applications in ways you may anticipate, and in ways you may not anticipate. How you package your code does make a difference, as reflected in the observations that follow.

The first observation is one that is, perhaps, intuitively obvious to many programmers: *in-line code is faster than procedure calls.* In-line code refers to placing statements that must be carried out directly in the code path rather than packaging them in a subroutine or function call. The reason for the speed is apparent—if statements are simply part of the current logic flow, no extra call overhead is incurred when the statements are carried out. If those statements are placed in a separate procedure and must be reached by a call, more low level machine instructions must be executed simply to change the flow of code from the current sequence of statements to the procedure's statements which are at a different address in memory. Accordingly, additional extra overhead is expended at the end of the procedure call to return back to the original flow of statements.

However, the modular maintenance advantages and clarity provided from packaging code in procedures are regarded as good standard programming practices. The value of in-line code must then be considered with respect to the trade-off with procedure maintainability. If a block of in-line code is used 20 different places in the code, and a bug is found in this block, a change must be made in 20 places. This is opposed to the one location where a change is needed if a procedure had been used instead of in-line code.

What type of performance advantages does VB in-line code really provide to offset these maintenance penalties? A simple timed test was carried out to provide answers to this question. The basic concept behind the test program can be observed in Listing 11.8. The same code sequence shown in this listing was packaged four different ways: in-line code, function call within the same module, subroutine call within the same module, and function call in a different module. Then a separate timing was recorded for each of the four different packaging approaches.

Listing 11.8. Code sequence to be tested.

```
For i& = 1 To txtLoops

' The sample algorithm below serves as a simple
' example of an algorithm which takes two initial values,
' performs calculations on them, and modifies a global variable
' with the product of the results.

    dblInput1 = START_VALUE1
    dblInput2 = START_VALUE2
    dblInput1 = dblInput1 * 2
    dblInput2 = dblInput2 * 3
    g_dblAnswer = dblInput1 * dblInput2

Next i&
```

This sequence was tested in each of the four scenarios with precise timing methods, and the following results were recorded:

Scenario	Normalized Time
In-line code	1.00
Function call (function in same module as call)	2.00
Subroutine call (subroutine in same module as call)	(59 milliseconds) 1.65
Subroutine call (sub in different module than call)	(60 milliseconds) 1.66

The in-line code, not surprisingly, executes the fastest of any of our tests. The next quickest procedure-based approach took 65 percent longer than the in-line method. Clearly, there are significant performance benefits that can be realized from in-line code if the code being examined makes heavy use of calls. This leads us to the following observation:

> **TIP**
>
> In-line code is significantly faster than procedure calls.

The subroutine call test (same module) is faster than the function call test (same module) by a margin that is potentially non-trivial if many function calls are made within one program and the cumulative impact on performance is great. A function call incurs the overhead of assigning its return value to the calling argument, while our subroutine call simply assigned the value to the parameter passed by reference. Of course, the exact comparison depends on the type of data returned, and whether the subroutine data is passed by reference or value. In the tests carried out here, all parameters were passed by value. The trend is significant enough to bring us to another observation.

> **TIP**
>
> Subroutines are generally somewhat faster than function calls because of efficiencies in returning data.

Notice that in our small test the subroutine call time is much the same regardless of whether the subroutine is defined in the same module as the call or a different module. Even though this module must be loaded into memory, whereas the form-defined subroutine was already in memory, the time impact difference was small. However, if you are on a memory constrained system or the module to load was very big, the impact could be more significant. A procedure in a module is loaded on-demand if that module has not already been loaded, so the code for the module must be pulled into memory when the call is made. The form, however, is already in memory along with its code, so it does not incur the same penalty. With small programs on systems without memory constraints, the impact is not likely to be significant. For large programs, there are economies of scale to grouping related procedures into one module so the whole collection can be loaded at one time.

> **TIP**
>
> There are advantages to grouping similar procedures into one module, but the performance savings may range from significant to barely noticeable depending on the program and environment.

So far our attention has focused on different types of procedure call alternatives. However, even within the same type of call, factors can affect performance. Of course the amount of data passed to a procedure will have an effect on performance: The more data passed via parameters, the greater the performance impact. However, it is not just the type and quantity of data passed that affects speed. Another often overlooked factor is the issue of *how* the data is passed into parameters.

Data can be passed by reference or by value. If the ByVal keyword is not provided in the declaration, the data is passed by reference for a given parameter. That means that variables passed in to the procedure and changed within the procedure *will* reflect the updated values back in the procedure which made the call. On the other hand, if the ByVal keyword is specified on a parameter declaration, that parameter is passed simply by value. In effect, when the procedure is called, VB looks at the master memory location and provides a copy of that to the called procedure. Then when a parameter is updated in that called procedure, only the local copy is altered, and the original variable supplied as the parameter when the call is made will be left untouched when the original flow of statements resumes after the call completes.

The explicit use of ByVal with variables that should not be altered when passed as parameters is a good programming practice and can prevent many unintended side-effect errors. Unfortunately, like many good programming practices, it comes at the cost of a slight performance penalty. Calls made with the ByVal keyword, whether function or subroutine calls, will be slower to a small extent.

A simple test program provided a look at the difference that can result. This program timed four types of procedure calls: a function call that passed parameters with ByVal; an identical function call without ByVal; a subroutine call that passed parameters with ByVal; and the identical subroutine call without ByVal.

Test Results

Test	Normalized Timing
Function Call ByVal Test	1.11
Function Call No ByVal Test	1.05
Subroutine Call ByVal Test	1.04
Subroutine Call No ByVal Test	1.00

A time cost of roughly 4 percent results from passing the two parameters by value instead of by reference for functions and subroutines. The impact of this should be carefully considered, however, before deciding to apply optimizations to this area. ByVal is slower, but 4 percent is not a big performance penalty. The cumulative effect could be large and perhaps noticeable to a user if an application makes many repetitive procedure calls. Likewise, if procedure calls use many parameters, the savings to be gained would be expected to be greater than 5 percent. However, if ByVals are eliminated to gain speed, this comes at the cost of good programming practice. Like most performance decisions, this one is not cut and dried, and will depend very much on the nature of your specific application.

TIP

Calls using parameters passed by reference are slightly faster than parameters passed by value (declared with ByVal).

Execution Time In and Out of Development Environment

So far the timings we have examined have come outside of the Visual Basic development environment. What if we were to carry out the same tests within the development environment? This is the mode many developers carry out performance testing in, because it is more convenient to modify source code and run a quick trial right in the environment than to generate an .exe and execute it. However, this is *not* the correct way to assess VB performance. Users will not be running their programs in this environment, so if performance analysis is performed in this environment, our results will be skewed and not representative of the performance issues facing the user who simply runs his .exe file. A test was carried out to determine how big of a skew the VB development environment introduces to performance assessments.

To carry out this test, the same ByVal tests covered earlier were simply repeated inside the VB development environment. The execution times for these particular tests increased significantly, with slowdowns ranging from 26 percent to 31 percent. One reason for this slowdown is that when we have the VB environment running, there is another program loaded by Windows and active at the time the program runs. Some insight into the memory layout of Visual Basic, as provided at the start of this chapter, provides further understanding. Visual Basic maintains symbol tables in data segments in the development environment that are not present in the final executable. When your program runs in the development environment, VB has stored the text name representations of your variables and constants in this symbol table. This is, in effect, optimized out when you produce your .exe. The Visual Basic development environment, in conjunction with Windows, is doing more work to make your program run than would be carried out by the interpreter and Windows if it was already in P-code, or executable, format.

On the other hand, you may have correctly perceived in the past that your programs some-times seem to load faster when run from the VB development environment. When you're in the development environment, the OCXs and VBXs required by your project are already loaded and do not have to be freshly loaded from disk when your program is started. All of these con-siderations add up to one important bottom line—don't gauge the performance your users will be faced with when in the VB environment.

> **TIP**
>
> Aside from load time, performance will be generally faster outside the VB environment.

Control Loading

Many a Visual Basic programmer has turned to his or her users after they watch the 15-second load time of the program with dismay, and said, "There's nothing I can do about that, that's just how fast the custom controls load!" Is the programmer really helpless to do anything about the speed of custom control loads? And for that matter, how much of a performance penalty is inherent in the loading of custom controls? Program load time is the time required to com-plete all load activity. To assess such activity, it is important to accurately measure starting immediately prior to load startup initialization and concluding on the last statement of the form load event. Program initialization includes the load phase where Windows loads your executable, the runtime interpreter, and carries out activity such as VBX and OCX file loading and initialization into memory. The VB run-time interpreter is also part of load time, and is loaded into memory before your first program statement is carried out. Taking a measurement within the program to encompass this Windows startup activity can pose something of a prob-lem because it is hard to have a program time itself when you must begin measurement of time before the program even has control. Therefore, a special load utility or manual timing methods must be used to gather true load time that encompasses a program's entire load span time from immediately prior to launch through the last statement in the load event. The key concept to be aware of when assessing form loads is that there is a lot more going on during a program load than just the code in your first Form_Load event.

When a form is loaded, every custom control used is loaded into memory from its OCX or VBX file. This means the more total custom controls you use, the more time is spent loading from files. The ramifications are clear.

> **TIP**
>
> If you can reduce the total number of custom controls your application uses, you will reduce form load time.

To test this, a test program with many custom controls was built. The program had no code that was carried, but was simply a container for controls. Despite doing "no real code work," the required load was significant. Simply eliminating controls drastically sped up the application, as expected. An immediate benefit is gained by each control eliminated, and if several are eliminated, the cumulative savings are very significant, with speed increases of 90 percent easily reached in such trials.

Another activity that takes place during load time is that initializations for any standard controls you have defined are carried out by the interpreter. However, standard controls do not have to be loaded from a separate OCX or VBX file, because they are along for the ride with Visual Basic executable. In this sense, standard controls have an innate performance advantage over custom controls in separate files, which leads us to our next observation.

> **TIP**
>
> To enhance performance, use standard controls in lieu of custom controls, where possible. Standard controls load faster due to reduced disk access at load time.

In many cases it may not be possible or desirable to use a standard control alternative for a custom control. Custom controls provide many rich features and functional advantages, but if your motivation is sheer performance, you would be wise to use a standard control rather than its three dimensional, multimedia, fireworks color-generating alternative.

It is to be expected that some controls will load faster than others. After all, each control is based on different underlying code with different resource requirements. One of the challenges of evaluating the performance of your applications then becomes determining which controls load faster than others.

Often this must be considered on a case-by-case basis, but one generalization can be made about the standard VB controls. Lightweight controls load faster than heavyweight controls. A lightweight control is one that carries less baggage than a heavyweight control. Specifically, a lightweight control does not have a window handle and associated hWnd property, because it is not created as a window in the system, as many controls are. Therefore, there is less overhead in creating it and it requires fewer resources. Lightweight controls include the line, shape, label, and image control. The image control is perhaps the most significant in this group because these controls can be used in place of the picture control to contain bitmaps.

A test program was carried out to measure the difference. In the first test case, heavyweight picture controls loaded by the program are defined at design-time. In other words, they were placed on the form in design mode and are automatically loaded when the form loads. This program loaded in slightly over 300 milliseconds in repeated trials.

The next step was to compare this load time with that of an equivalent program based on the lightweight image controls. This program was essentially identical to the picture control load program, except that the controls used were image controls. This program consisted of a form that had the image controls placed on it at design-time just as the picture control program did. This image control program loaded in just over 200 milliseconds in a series of trials.

The lightweight control program was roughly 100 milliseconds (33 percent) faster than the heavyweight picture control program. Windows and the VB interpreter carry out less work to create the non-window image control than they do to create the picture control which has a window handle, among other resource requirements. Thus, a clear observation emerges.

> **TIP**
>
> Lightweight controls are significantly faster than heavyweight controls.

Because lightweight controls load faster than heavyweight controls, you might think the best you can do to optimize form loading is to simply use lightweight controls when you lay out your form. However, there is yet another optimization step that can be used if the situation warrants. That is to dynamically create multiple instances of an image control during the form load rather than to create them at design-time. One method to create a form with fifteen image controls, for example, is to lay out all fifteen image controls at design-time. Another approach could alternatively be taken to generate the same form. Only *one* image control is created at design-time, and that is indicated to be a control array by setting the image control index property to 0. Then for this form with its one control, code can be written in the form load event to load additional instances of that control into a control array at load time, by using the load statement.

This test was carried out, comparing the first method to the second. When controls are dynamically created at load time in this manner, the visible property must be set to true for the control to be visible, and the correct top and left properties must be specified for this newly created control. Even with the additional code overhead to loop through the control array, carry out the load statements, and perform the left and top initializations, this program performed faster than the counterpart that had all its image controls laid out at design-time. The code that declared additional instances of the image control by using the load statement performed approximately 10 percent faster than the program that had all the image controls pre-declared. Although this is not an enormous time savings, the speed increase could be enough to be noticed by the user in some cases. The more controls on the form, the bigger the benefit to be reaped. However, this approach does make for more code which, in turn, poses more maintenance challenges and leaves more room for bugs. Nevertheless, this observation is one to keep in mind when considering ways to speed up your program if you use many instances of the same type of control.

TIP

Runtime control array created controls load faster than design-time created controls.

There is yet another efficiency introduced by the use of dynamically loaded controls through a control array. Such controls can also be removed if they're ever needed through the unload statement. In certain cases, this allows for more efficient programs that can reduce their memory consumption even when a form is loaded by unloading particular controls.

Comparing Control Loading Between 16-Bit and 32-Bit Visual Basic Applications

32-bit Visual Basic 4.0 supports 32-bit OLE controls (commonly referred to as OCXs). Thus, its control load activity carried out is different than that of 16-bit Visual Basic 4.0, which supports both 16-bit OLE controls and VBXs (all 16 bit). Visual Basic 3.0, of course, supported only VBX controls. One other difference between applications produced in these different versions is that the application executable size will differ as well. A series of programs was converted from a Visual Basic 3.0 VBX implementation, to a Visual Basic 4.0 16-bit VBX implementation, to a Visual Basic 4.0 16-bit OLE control implementation, to a 32-bit OLE control implementation by simply changing the controls, with no code changes. The size of executables generally changed as follows:

Environment	Normalized Sizes
Visual Basic 3.0 VBX	1.00
Visual Basic 4.0 VBX	1.15
Visual Basic 4.0 16-Bit OLE Control	1.15
Visual Basic 4.0 32-Bit OLE Control	1.20

Most of the increased size of VB4 executables is simply from the switch between versions of Visual Basic. There seems to be relatively little difference between VBX and 16-bit OLE controls in terms of impact on executable size. There is a more noticeable, but still slight, difference between 16-bit and 32-bit OLE controls and their impact on executable size. It is also significant to note that the size of the run-time executive itself varies between Visual Basic 3.0, 16-bit Visual Basic 4.0, and 32-bit Visual Basic 4.0. Program size is, of course, one factor that affects load speed, but not necessarily the most significant factor.

Run-Time Executive	Normalized Sizes
Visual Basic 3.0 VBRUN300.DLL	1.00
Visual Basic 4.0 VB40016.DLL	1.77
Visual Basic 4.0 VB40032.DLL	2.31

Note: Numbers in preceding were derived from a preliminary version of Visual Basic 4.0.

As for load times themselves, general findings held consistent between all versions. In other words, it was always true that dynamically created picture controls out-performed design-time picture controls with respect to loading, that picture controls loaded faster than image controls, and that custom controls, whether VBX or OCX, introduced noticeable load delay with each additional control included.

In the test applications that were examined, 16-bit VBX programs loaded in roughly the same amount of time as similar programs based on 16-bit OCX programs. In some cases, 16-bit OCX programs did load significantly faster than the same programs using 32-bit OCXs, particularly in cases where a very large number and variety of controls was used. Standard controls showed a slight trend to load faster in 16-bit versions than in 32-bit applications, but the difference was not statistically significant. The results will be different for every application, so the information summarized here should be viewed as one set of test data and not a sweeping statement about all control load times. However, it does point out that load time considerations are very much present on Visual Basic 4.0, and not eliminated by any means in the 32-bit world. The fewer controls you have, the faster your programs will load. The more controls you have, the more overhead that takes place at load time, and the slower the performance for your end user.

Control Properties

Working with control characteristics involves using control methods and setting control properties. Most VB developers are aware of that. However, many new VB developers are not aware that controls can have default settings. Even those developers who are aware that default settings exist often think of them as little more than a code convenience. However, the following means of making an assignment based on a control property setting are *not* equivalent:

(a) strVariableA = Label

(b) strVariableA = Label.Caption

These statements achieve the same ultimate action, but in different ways. The code path traveled for each of the two assignments *is* different. Therefore, performance is different for the two methods. A simple test program was used to measure this difference. A timing was made of a sequence of code that used default property values to set a checkbox value, label caption, and textbox text. Then a timing was made of a similar sequence of code that used explicit property references (in lieu of the defaults) to set a checkbox value, label caption, and textbox text. The results clearly illustrated that assignments made to default values are faster. The explicit property assignments take roughly 25 percent longer than the default assignments. This leads to an important observation:

> **TIP**
>
> Use control default properties rather than explicitly naming those properties to improve performance.

Control properties provide a convenient way of storing data. As we have seen, these values can be used in assignments much like variables. The natural question that follows is can variables offer better performance, because they are not encumbered by control overhead? A test was carried out to address this by carrying out a repeated loop of data assignments and additions based on variables. Property values were cached to variables at the start of the test. A similar test was carried out in which control properties were used directly in the same statements in place of variables, and therefore no initial assignment to the variables of property values was required.

Therefore, the variable-based code sequence actually consisted of more lines of code to accommodate the variable initialization from the control properties. In spite of this, the property update test took over 20 times as long as the variable-based test. This test shows the value of storing control property values in variables whenever they will have to be repeatedly referenced and leads to the following observation:

> **TIP**
>
> Store control properties in variables if you will reference those properties frequently in code.

This has the familiar maintenance drawback of requiring additional development time and introducing more code to debug and maintain. On the other hand, the performance payback from any type of program that has to frequently reuse the same property value is likely to be of enough significance to show a noticeable performance improvement to the user.

Math

This section discusses how to use variables efficiently when using them in mathematical operations. A simple program was written that carries out mathematical operations using each data type along with every arithmetic operator. In the case of the integer data type, for example, a simplified code listing of the calculations can be seen in Listing 11.9.

Listing 11.9. Integer mathematical timings.

```
' Declare the variables
Dim X As Integer

' Assign the variables
X = 2 : Y = 3

' Perform the calculations
Z = X + Y
Z = X - Y
Z = X * Y
Z = X / Y
Z = X \ Y
Z = X ^ Y
Z = X Mod Y
```

Each arithmetic operation shown here was timed for each data type. The timing results for the integer, long, and single and double data types along with the arithmetic operations applied to them are summarized in Table 11.4

Table 11.4. Integer and floating-point math comparisons—normalized results.

Data Type	+	-	*	/	\	^	Mod
Integer	1.01	1.00	1.04	2.51	1.04	3.18	1.07
Long	1.06	1.06	1.37	2.61	1.53	3.19	1.50
Single	1.32	1.30	1.30	1.45	3.32	2.16	3.31
Double	1.32	1.33	1.32	1.47	3.33	2.18	3.24

These results will be used to support the conclusions that will follow regarding arithmetic operators and the data types used with them.

Integer Math is Faster than Floating-Point Math

In most cases, integer math is faster than floating-point math. This should make sense intuitively, because the computer does not have to worry about decimal points when using integers and the range of an integer is much less than that of a floating-point value. One would expect, therefore, that a mathematical operation to be carried out on an integer would require less time than a floating-point value.

Refer back to Table 11.4 for the comparison between integer and floating-point data types. Notice that, in every case except floating-point division and the exponent operators, the integer data types out-perform their floating point counterparts. Notice that integer math is faster than floating-point math by approximately 28 percent for addition, subtraction, and multiplication. The modulus operator using the integer and long data types is faster by an average of over 150 percent. These results prove that, when performing most mathematical operations on data, if you can represent that data with the *integer* and *long* data types, the performance of your code improves. Performance improves particularly when you apply the same mathematical operation over and over, such as in a loop. While you may not obtain a noticeable speed increase by replacing one floating-point subtraction with an integer subtraction, you certainly may if that operation is contained in a loop that executes one hundred times.

TIP

Integer math is faster than floating-point math.

As you can see from the table, there are two exceptions to the guideline that integer math is faster than floating-point math. These two exceptions occur when using the *floating-point division* and *exponent* operators. Each of these exceptions are significant and are discussed later.

Do Not Use Floating-Point Division with Integers

Floating-point division (represented by the "/" symbol) is different from integer division (represented by the "\" symbol). Floating-point division returns a floating-point result regardless of the data type of the two numbers being divided. Integer division, on the other hand, rounds floating-point variables being divided into integers (unless they are already integers, in which case this is not necessary) and returns an integer result. If the numbers being divided do not divide evenly, the fractional portion of the result is truncated to ensure the result is an integer. The integer result may be of data type *integer* or *long*, depending on the range of the result.

If integers are used in a floating-point division, the values are treated as floating-point values during the division. The result is a floating-point value (single or double depending on which data type is better suited for the solution). If, however, the result is stored in an integer variable, the result must be converted back into integer form. The work of converting the two integer variables to be divided into floating-point form for division and back into integer form for the result makes the cumulative time of the entire operation much slower than if floating-point variables were to be used.

Integer division, on the other hand, takes whatever variables are being divided and converts them into integer format. The variables are essentially rounded to integer numbers and considered integers or longs, depending on the range of the data. The division is an *integer* division, and the result is an integer or long, again depending on the range of the result and the most appropriate data type to use for it. If floating-point values are used with the integer division operator, the amount of time needed to round and convert the variables into integer form and then convert the result into a floating-point representation takes much more time than if floating-point division were used with floating-point variables.

Thus, whenever you divide two integer values and desire an integer result, use the integer division operator ("\") and *do not* use the floating-point division operator ("/"). If, on the other hand, you have two floating-point values and wish a floating-point result, *do not* use the integer division operator. In Table 11.5, the comparison between integer division using the integer data type versus floating-point division using the floating point data type can be seen.

Table 11.5. Integer versus floating-point division—normalized results.

Data Type	Floating-Point Division	Integer Division
Integer	2.40	1.00
Long	2.50	1.47
Single	1.39	3.18
Double	1.41	3.19

Notice that integer division using the *integer* data type is faster than floating-point division using either the *single* or *double* data type (1.00 versus 1.39 and 1.41 normalized performance, respectively). Integer division using the *long* data type takes slightly longer than floating-point division using the single or double, but only very slightly (1.47 versus 1.39 and 1.41 normalized performance). Finally, integer division using floating-point data types take much longer than integer data types performing integer division. The most common oversight for most programmers is to use the floating point division operator with integer variables. Notice that doing so incurs a needless penalty of over 140% and 70% for *integer*s and *long*s, respectively.

> **TIP**
>
> Do not use floating-point division with integers.

Do Not Use Integers with the Exponent Operator

The other exception to the guideline that states that integer math is faster than floating-point math is the use of the exponent (^) operator. The exponent operator calculates a result based on the following formula:

result = number ^ exponent

where *number* can be any data type, *exponent* can be any data type (except that *exponent* must be an integer if *number* is negative), and *result* is of type *double* or *variant*. It is very important to notice that the result defaults to the *double* data type. Even if *number* and *exponent* are both integers, the result is still converted into the floating-point, *double* data type.

The fact that the exponent operator always produces a floating-point result indicates that the operation is inherently a floating-point operation. Even if integers are used for the *number* and *exponent*, the processor still carries out floating-point math. This means that if the number and exponent are integers, they must be converted into floating-point form before the calculation can be carried out. If the *number* and *exponent* are already in floating-point form, the operation is faster because no conversions are necessary. Furthermore, if the result variable is an integer data type, an additional conversion must be performed to round the floating-point number into an integer value. A simple application was written that applies an exponent to a number for each data type. The timing results are shown in Table 11.6.

Table 11.6. Exponent operator timings—normalized results.

Number	*Exponent*	*Result*	*Relative Performance*
Integer	Integer	Double	1.47
Long	Long	Double	1.48
Single	Single	Double	1.00
Double	Single	Double	1.01

Note that the integer and long data types take approximately the same amount of time to execute, as do the single and double data types. From these data, we can conclude that when performing operations with the exponent operator, it is better to use floating-point variables for the *number, exponent,* and result in order to increase performance. It turns out that the exponent operator is one of the more time-consuming arithmetic operators in the set.

TIP

Avoid integers with the exponent operator.

Avoid Variant Math

As we have already seen, using variants typically slows down an application due to the overhead required as a result of their flexibility. One can expect that variants will typically take more time in execution than the other data types.

Consider a simple arithmetic operation between two variants, X and Y, who are assigned integer values. Table 11.7 shows what data types are returned from each operation between two variants that are represented as integers.

Table 11.7. Variant data type emulations for arithmetic operations.

Operation	X		Y		Z
Addition	Int	+	Int	=	Int
Subtraction	Int	-	Int	=	Int
Multiplication	Int	*	Int	=	Int
FP Division	Int	/	Int	=	Double
Int Division	Int	\	Int	=	Long
Exponent	Int	^	Int	=	Double
Module	Int	Mod	Int	=	Long

As you can see, the variants being added are treated as integers (that is, the *integer* or *long* data type) as well as the result variant Z, with the exception of the floating-point division and the exponent operators. One would expect, therefore, the timings for each of the operations to be equivalent to the integer data type. If you observe Table 11.8, however, you notice that the execution times are significantly greater than the integer data type where we would expect them to be close.

Table 11.8. Variant versus integer—normalized results.

Data Type	+	-	*	/	\	^	Mod
Integer	1.00	1.00	1.00	1.00	1.00	1.00	1.00
Variant	1.37	1.38	1.37	1.06	1.93	1.09	1.85

As you can see from the table, in *every* case where we would expect the performance of the variant to approximate that of the integer, we encounter a substantial percentage increase in execution time. For addition, subtraction, and multiplication we see almost 40 percent more time required. But for integer division and the mod operators, the percentages jump way up to 93% and 85%, respectively. Floating-point division and the exponent operators for the *integer* data type do not result in much difference, but this can be accounted for due to the fact that, in both cases, the variables must be converted to floating-point and then back to integer. The time required for these conversions applies equally to the variant and both integer data types and may explain why those execution times are more equal. Thus, when performing mathematical operations, it is always advisable to use the integer and floating-point data types and avoid the variant.

Multiplication Is Faster than Division

Now that data types have been discussed, you now focus on the arithmetic operators and mathematical functions themselves. This section compares multiplication to division regardless of data type. Table 11.9 summarizes the results of the multiplication and division operations for each data type.

Table 11.9. Multiplication versus division—normalized results.

Data Type	Multiplication	FP DivisionInt	Division
Integer	1.00	2.40	1.00
Long	1.31	2.50	1.47
Single	1.25	1.39	3.18
Double	1.25	1.41	3.19
Currency	1.93	2.27	3.69
Variant	1.37	2.55	1.93

Note that in every case but one, multiplication is faster than division. The only exception is multiplication and integer division of variables with the *integer* data type, which yields the same execution time in this test.

Because multiplication is faster than division, it is obviously preferable to multiply rather than divide whenever possible. Notice also that integer division using variables of the *integer* data type can actually be faster than floating point division using floating-point variables. If integer division is carried out with the *long* data type, the execution time is slightly longer than single or double floating-point division. Thus, if the two values being divided are of the integer data type, and the result is to be an integer, then integer division is faster than floating-point division. In most cases, however, when dividing two quantities, floating-point math is needed because a decimal number may result. Thus, only use integer division when you don't need or won't get a remainder, that is, decimal point.

NOTE

Strategies are presented in the book *Visual Basic Performance Tuning and Optimization* to use multiplication instead of division in applications, as well as the resultant speed increase that can be obtained. Consult this book for more information.

Graphics Controls and Methods

Windows is an environment that relies heavily on graphics. Unlike the character-based environment of MS-DOS, Windows uses a friendly graphical user interface, or GUI, that makes simple programming tasks easier for the user. The graphical interface also provides a common platform upon which all Windows applications are based.

Because graphics are such an inherent part of Windows, it is natural to assume that graphics issues can have a large impact on performance. When writing programs using Visual Basic, the programmer is presented with an easy-to-use programming interface. Using this environment, it is very easy to make extensive use of graphics, bitmaps, animation, and other techniques to enhance the appearance and functionality of an application. With the use of graphics, however, comes the responsibility to make sure they are used in the most optimal way for the sake of performance. This section points out some of the significant points to remember when working with graphics controls and methods.

TIP

Graphics created at design-time using controls are faster than using graphics methods at run-time.

When graphics controls are explicitly defined at design-time, they are faster than graphics methods (VB statements that generate graphics such as Line). On the other hand, when graphics controls are created dynamically at run-time, they are only very slightly faster than graphics methods. The total time required to use controls compared with methods depends on the quantity and type of graphics being displayed. As a rule, however, the results should favor the use of graphics controls, particularly when they are all defined and created in design mode. Keep in mind that, although the ultimate load and display time of the application that uses controls is faster than that of methods, the application that uses controls has a larger executable file size and requires more memory and resources. This is because the controls must be stored as a part of the form rather than created "on-the-fly" at run-time. The time it takes for the interpreter to implement the methods takes more cumulative time than when the graphics are "pre-defined" with a graphics control.

This does not automatically mean that you should rule out the use of graphics methods in every instance. The pros and cons of each approach must also be considered in light of the way in which they are used. One primary benefit of graphics methods is that some of the graphics *methods* can produce graphics that are impossible to create using the standard graphics controls. For example, the PSet method can plot a single point, which is impossible when using a graphics control unless you draw a very small line.

Another benefit of graphics methods is that they do not consume the memory and resources that controls do. Furthermore, a great deal of graphics can often be generated quickly using code where using controls may be otherwise cumbersome or impractical. For example, consider the case when you need to draw 100 grid lines for a graph. Rather than constructing 100 controls, it may be easier to write a simple code loop that plotted the 100 lines on the form using graphics methods. The 100 graphics controls would also take up space in memory, because they are controls that must be addressable until they are destroyed.

Graphics methods, however, are simply painted on the form and cannot be "addressed" as graphical entities like controls can. Thus, they take up much fewer resources and memory than the graphics methods do. If memory is limited, the benefits of using methods may outweigh the speed benefits of using controls. After all, when memory becomes scarce, Windows itself can bog down and make every operation in Windows run slower. Thus, speed may become an issue after all.

As expected, graphics methods also have disadvantages as compared to the other techniques. While they often paint and redisplay faster on forms, they take more processing time to create and place on the form. Furthermore, they often require more programming effort to implement. When working with graphics methods, the programmer must write code to perform simple drawing and positioning of graphics on the form. The programmer not only has the responsibility of calculating the size and position of each graphic drawn, he also must define the shape and its dimensions. Controls, on the other hand, have a predetermined shape that can be changed in code but do not *have* to be changed or specified in code. When using methods, the programmer also cannot see the graphics on the form at design-time, which is a big disadvantage when trying to put together graphics quickly. Thus, graphics controls are often easier to use and faster to display than graphics created using graphics methods. But this comes at the cost of additional memory and resource consumption, which can often be a significant issue when memory and resources are scarce.

TIP

Printing graphics to a printer takes longer than displaying those graphics on screen.

The programmer should expect that printing graphics to the printer will, in almost all cases, take considerably longer to display graphics on the screen. Video display resolutions have, over the years, been more standardized than the various printers and printer drivers out on the market.

Because the printer is a mechanical device, while the video display is essentially an electronic device, the developer should always favor providing graphics output to the screen when possible, and not just the printer.

It is wise, for example, to provide the user with a *print preview* screen in a word processing application to show the user what the document will look like out on the printer before it is actually sent there. Because it takes so much longer to print the document than to view it, the user can make changes and see on the monitor what the document will look like on the printed page. In such a manner, the user can refine the document until he gets it just the way he wants it, and then he can send it out to the printer. The user may become very frustrated if he has to wait three minutes every time he wants to print his document and make a change, not to mention all the paper he will waste in the process.

Therefore, when considering printing speed versus display speed, keep in mind that display speed is almost always faster by far, and that your application should always allow the user to see what he is about to print before it gets printed. In this manner, he can only print when he needs to and is not dependent on a slow printer for making changes to something he could do much faster by seeing it on the screen. Furthermore, by keeping the graphics resolution larger and using monochrome if a printer does not support color, the performance of the printing process can be improved dramatically.

Displaying Pictures

In addition to displaying lines and shapes, programmers often wish to incorporate pictures into their applications for animation and other visual effects. Visual Basic has several mechanisms that allow the programmer to display and manipulate pictures. Visual Basic forms have a `Picture` property that can be set to a graphics file. Furthermore, two controls can be used to display pictures inside forms. These two controls are the *PictureBox,* or *picture* control, and the *Image* control. These two controls differ somewhat in functionality and performance.

Picture Controls

Picture controls are very powerful and useful for displaying pictures. The picture control, which is located on the Visual Basic tool palette, can be selected and the programmer can place the control on the form. The programmer essentially defines the size and location of the picture control on the form. The picture control has a property called *picture* that can be set at design-time to a graphics file of format .BMP, .DIB, .ICO, and .WMF. The graphics file can also be loaded into the control at run-time, which is to be discussed later in the chapter.

When the programmer places a picture control on a form, he has control over the control's dimensions, in particular, the width and height. When a picture is loaded into the control, the picture consumes as much space as when created. In other words, if you have a bitmap that is two inches wide by two inches high, and you create a picture control four inches by four inches, the bitmap will fit into the picture control and there will be twelve square inches of space remaining in the picture control. In order to re-size the picture control so that there is no extra space, the programmer can set the AutoSize property to True, which re-sizes the bitmap just to fit around the bitmap image.

Controls such as labels and command buttons can be placed inside picture controls and, in essence, become "child controls" of the picture control, which is the parent. This makes the picture control not only a powerful mechanism for displaying pictures, but also for containing and manipulating groups of controls in addition to pictures.

Image Controls

An image control is another one of the three ways to display a picture in a Visual Basic application. In the Microsoft Programmer's Guide, an image control is defined as "a rectangular area into which you can load picture files." The picture file formats supported are .BMP, .DIB, .ICO, and .WMF. Image controls, unlike picture controls, allow the programmer to stretch, or resize, pictures so that they utilize the entire rectangular area of the image control. When using a picture control, the size of the picture being loaded into the control cannot change. With image controls, however, the Stretch property can be set to True, which automatically resizes the picture to take up the entire region of space defined by the image control.

As was true with the picture control, the bitmap is smaller than the actual control that stores the picture. The image control does not have an Autosize property like the picture control does. Thus, we cannot automatically size the control to fit the bitmap. In the case of the image control, we have to go the other way around. By setting the Stretch property to True, we can increase or decrease the size of the picture to fill up all the space in the image.

Image controls are also different from picture controls in that the programmer cannot place "child" controls inside them. Nothing can be placed inside an image control other than an image, which must be set using the Picture property or by being loaded into the control at run-time.

> **TIP**
>
> Image controls are faster than picture controls.

A test application was constructed that loads a series of picture controls which contained a bitmap, and another application loaded a series of image controls which contained the same bitmap. Timings were taken and, in all cases, the application loaded faster using the image controls than it did using the picture controls.

One of the reasons that image controls are faster is that the underlying structure of the image control is simpler than that of the picture control. A picture control is essentially a window of the type similar to a Visual Basic form. First of all, it can contain child controls like a form can.

This means that the picture control must keep track of all its "children" controls and pass windows messages to them. This requires additional complexity and processing time which are not required of the image control. Furthermore, the picture control has more properties, events, and methods than the image control. Table 11.10 shows the events for an image control.

Table 11.10. Image control events.

Click
Double-Click
DragDrop
DragOver
MouseDown
MouseUp
MouseMove

Compare this to the events for a picture control, shown in Table 11.11.

Table 11.11. Picture control events.

Click
Double-Click
DragDrop
DragOver
MouseDown
MouseUp
MouseMove
Change
GotFocus
KeyDown
KeyUp
KeyPress
LinkClose
LinkError
LinkNotify
LinkOpen
LostFocus
Paint
Resize

Having examined the much larger list of events for the picture control, you will notice several additional capabilities the picture control has that the image control does not have. Picture controls can recognize keyboard input, initiate OLE and DDE links, recognize when focus is lost, and are notified by VB when they are painted and resized. This means that Visual Basic must do more work and message handling with picture controls than it must with image controls due to the increased functionality of the picture control.

This additional processing takes extra time, which is the primary reason for the decrease in performance of the picture control versus the image control. Unlike the image control, the picture control is an actual window, which means it consumes a greater amount of resources. In some cases, it may be desirable to take advantage of the picture control's additional functionality. In such cases, functionality is traded for decreased performance. In many other cases, however, this added functionality is not needed or used. In those cases, it is certainly preferable to use an image control rather than a picture control. If the only thing you have the user do with a picture control is click on it or drag and drop it, you are needlessly wasting resources and degrading performance. The image control would be sufficient and faster. If, as in the examples presented in this chapter, you are simply displaying a picture and do not need to worry about keyboard input, OLE, and resizing and painting of the control, then the image control is clearly desirable.

The image control may also be preferred, in certain cases, for its functionality. While it is not as complex as the picture control, developers often take advantage of the "stretch" feature of the image control, which may make it the ideal candidate separate from performance considerations. Keep in mind, however, that the increase of the performance may become more dramatic as the number of controls, resolution of the pictures in those controls, and interaction between controls and the forms used to contain them increases.

Summary

This chapter has presented some of the key points and strategies to apply to Visual Basic programs to make them as efficient as possible. Having read this chapter, one would rightly conclude that the subject of performance is rather broad. The subject can, at times, be a bit daunting, but this chapter should make the subject more clear and easier to tackle. The guidelines pointed out in this chapter can be applied in a general sense, because they are a result of verification through the programs the authors have created and tested. Visual Basic 4.0 provides a great deal more functionality than its predecessor and, in many cases, better performance as well. Even though the language has been optimized, however, the programmer still shares the responsibility of writing applications that are robust, efficient, and pleasing to the user. As a result of this chapter, the authors hope this becomes more of a reality for you.

NOTE

For a much more detailed and thorough treatment of Visual Basic performance tuning and optimization, remember to consider Sams' comprehensive book on performance tuning, *Visual Basic Optimization and Performance Tuning*, by Keith Brophy and Tim Koets. This book covers a much wider range of performance issues than can be addressed here and is recommended for those who wish to have an in-depth understanding of performance issues.

Printing with Visual Basic

12

by
David Medinets

IN THIS CHAPTER

Printing is among the most complicated tasks that a Windows application programmer undertakes. Fortunately, you are using Visual Basic. Visual Basic makes printing relatively easy by hiding most of the complexity of the Windows API.

This chapter explores printing with Visual Basic by focusing on the Print dialog box, Microsoft Word, and the Printer object.

Using the Print Dialog Box

The dialog box in Figure 12.1 is an example of the Print common dialog box. It allows the user to select a printer, change its properties, select a range of pages to print, and specify the number of copies. If needed, you can modify the dialog box in various ways. For example, you could disable or hide the Print To File check box.

FIGURE 12.1.

The Print common dialog box.

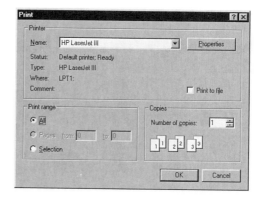

Displaying the Print Dialog Box

In the following example, the Print dialog box appears on-screen when the user clicks the File | Print menu option. The steps to create the example follow:

1. Create the File and Print menu options using Visual Basics Menu Editor.

2. Add a common dialog control to the form. The location is unimportant.

3. Right-click on the CommonDialog1 control to display its Properties dialog box(see Figure 12.2).

4. Select the Print tab and change the Copies field to 1. This action changes the default number of copies that will be in effect when a user invokes the dialog box. Click on the OK button to close the Properties dialog box.

5. Add the following code line to the click event of the Print menu option:

```
CommonDialog1.ShowPrinter
```

6. Press F5 to run your program. When you select the Print option, the Print dialog box should appear on-screen.

FIGURE 12.2.

The Common Dialogs Control Properties dialog box.

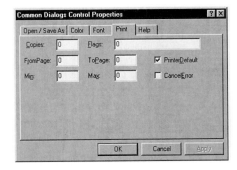

Customizing the Print Dialog Box

You can customize the Print dialog box by setting the `Flags` property of the common dialog control. Table 12.1. shows the constants you can use to set the `Flags` property.

Table 12.1. Selected constants used to set the `Flags` property.

Constant	Description
`cdlPDAllPages`	Selects the All Pages option button, which is the default.
`cdlPDPageNums`	Selects the Pages option button. This constant only works if the `Max` property of the common dialog control is greater than 0.
`cdlPDNoPageNums`	Disables the Pages option button and the associated edit control.
`cdlPDSelection`	Selects the Selection option button.
`cdlPDNoSelection`	Disables the Selection option button.
`cdlPDCollate`	Checks the Collate check box.
`cdlPDPrintToFile`	Checks the Print To File check box.
`cdlPDDisablePrintToFile`	Disables the Print To File check box.
`cdlPDHidePrintToFile`	Hides the Print To File check box.

For example, if you wanted to have the Print to Disk check box checked, the All Pages option button selected, and the Selection option button disabled, you would use the following two lines in the click method of the Print menu option:

```
CommonDialog1.Flags = cdlPDAllPages Or cdlPDPrintToFile _
       or cdlPDNoSelection
CommonDialog1.ShowPrinter
```

Some of the constants shown in Table 12.1 are mutually exclusive. For example, `cldPDAllPages`, `cdlPDPageNums`, and `cdlPDSelection` all affect the same group of option buttons. You should only use one of them at a time.

In order to enable the user to enter beginning and ending page numbers or to select the Collate check box, you must set the `Max` property of the common dialog box. Assuming that your document has seven pages, you could invoke the Print dialog box in the following manner:

```
CommonDialog1.Flags = cdlPDPageNums Or cdlPDPrintToFile _
        or cdlPDNoSelection
CommonDialog1.MAX = 6
CommonDialog1.FromPage = 0
CommonDialog1.ToPage = CommonDialog1.MAX
CommonDialog1.ShowPrinter
```

CAUTION

The `FromPage` property has a base of zero, not one. So if you have a seven-page document, the starting page is zero and the ending page is six. If the `ToPage` property is greater than the `Max` property, error number 28760 will occur and a dialog box saying `An error occurred during this operation` will be displayed.

You can find additional information about the constants used to set the `Flags` property by using the Object Browser in the Microsoft Common Dialog Control library or using the term *Flags* and looking under the topic *Flags Property (Print Dialog)* in the Visual Basic help file.

Retrieving Information from the Print Dialog Box

After the Print dialog box appears on-screen, the user makes his or her selections and then clicks on OK or Cancel. You can then retrieve the information that the user entered. Before discussing the information, let's look at the case where the user clicks the Cancel button.

Handling the Cancel Button

You can handle the Cancel button in two different ways. You can ignore it, or you can have Visual Basic generate an error that you can trap. To have Visual Basic generate an error, use the following lines of code:

```
    On Error goto CancelPrtDlg
    CommonDialog1.CancelError = True
    CommonDialog1.ShowPrinter
    ' Do stuff with user input
    ' print document
    ' exit routine
CancelPrtDlg:
    If Err.Number = 32755 Then
        ' handle cancel button
```

```
end if
' handle other errors
' exit routine
```

The second line in the preceding code sets the CancelError property to True. Then, the dialog box is displayed using the ShowPrinter method. If the user cancels the dialog box, the code immediately after the CancelPrtDlg label will be called. Otherwise, the document would be printed.

Handling the OK Button

When Visual Basic returns control to your program after the user clicks OK, several properties of the common dialog control will have been set. To find out whether the user selected to print all pages or a range of pages, use the following lines of code:

```
Dim pagesAll As Boolean
Dim pagesSome As Boolean
Dim pagesSelection As Boolean
pagesAll = (CommonDialog1.Flags And cdlPDAllPages) = cdlPDAllPages
pagesSome = (CommonDialog1.Flags And cdlPDPageNums) = cdlPDPageNums
pagesSelection = (CommonDialog1.Flags And cdlPDSelection) = cdlPDSelection
```

By using the logical AND operator, you can extract the information about a specific flag from the Flags property. When the All Pages option button is selected, PagesAll is True, and the rest of the properties are False. When the Selection option button is selected, PagesSelection *is* True, and the rest of the properties are False. If you have disabled or hidden the Page Range or Selection option buttons, you don't need to test for them.

You can test the Print to File check box with the following lines of code:

```
Dim printToFile As Boolean
printToFile = (CommonDialog1.Flags And cdlPDPrintToFile) = cdlPDPrintToFile
```

If the Print to File check box is checked, then PrintToFile is True; otherwise, it is False.

In a similar fashion, you can test the Collate check box with the following lines of code:

```
Dim collate As Boolean
collate = (CommonDialog1.Flags And cdlPDCollate) = cdlPDCollate
```

If the Collate check box is checked, then Collate is True; otherwise, it is False.

Getting the rest of the information is very straightforward. Simply look at the FromPage and ToPage properties of the common dialog control. You can retrieve the number of copies that the user selected by looking at the value of Printer.Copies.

Using Microsoft Word

Thanks to Microsoft Words OLE interface, you can take a side trip from Visual Basic and look at ways to cheat when printing. Instead of developing routines to read a file, perform word wrap, handle columns, display a print preview, and print a document, you can let Microsoft Word do the work. And if you keep Microsoft Word minimized, your user might never know!

> **CAUTION**
>
> This section was written using Microsoft Word for Windows 6.0a. If you have a different version of Word, you may need to adjust the code lines a bit for them to work.

The first step to using Microsoft Word is to allocate an object and create an instance of word.basic. To perform this step, use the following code:

```
Private Sub Form_Load()
Dim msword As Object
Set msword = CreateObject("word.basic")
...
' do things with the msword object.
...
Set msword = Nothing
End Sub
```

You can use the msword object to send WordBasic statements to Microsoft Word for execution. For example, the following lines of code will print two copies of the config.sys file:

```
Private Sub Form_Load()
Dim msword As Object
Set msword = CreateObject("word.basic")
With msword
    .AppMaximize
    .FileOpen Name:="c:\config.sys", AddToMru:=0
    .FilePrint Background:=1, Type:=0, NumCopies:=2
End With
Set msword = Nothing
End Sub
```

You can manipulate multiple documents at once by creating more objects in the Word.basic class.

Using WordBasic from within Visual Basic

The WRDBASIC.HLP file that comes with Microsoft Word is complete. However, the syntax that is used to call the WordBasic function in Visual Basic is slightly different than the one shown in the help file.

You need to be aware of two differences. The first is that parameters do not need a leading period. The second is that the assignment operator for named arguments in Visual Basic is ':='. For example, the help file topic that discusses FilePrint shows the syntax as

```
FilePrint [.Background = number] [, .Type = number] [, .NumCopies = number]
```

The corresponding Visual Basic statement is

```
msword.FilePrint Background:=1, Type:=0, NumCopies:=2
```

You can see that the changes are easy to handle.

Creating a Letter with Visual Basic

Listing 12.1 contains methods that enable you to create a new Microsoft Word document based on the Letter2 template. This project contains a form with a text control in which the user enters the main text of a letter. After entering the text, the user clicks a command button, and Microsoft Word starts. The information from the user is combined with the Letter2 template to produce a printed page.

To run the example program in Listing 12.1, follow these steps:

1. Start Visual Basic or choose File | New to clear your workspace.
2. Enter Listing 12.1 into the code window for Form1.

Listing 12.1. Create a letter using Microsoft Word.

```
Dim msword As Object

Private Sub wordDelLineWith(oldStuff As String)
    msword.StartOfDocument
    msword.EditFind Find:=oldStuff, Direction:=0, MatchCase:=0, _
        WholeWord:=0, PatternMatch:=0, SoundsLike:=0, Format:=0, Wrap:=0
    msword.StartOfLine
    msword.EndOfLine 1
    msword.EditClear
End Sub

Private Sub wordReplace(oldStuff As String, newStuff As String)
    msword.StartOfDocument
    msword.EditReplace oldStuff, newStuff, 0, 0, 0, 0, 0, 0, 1, 0, 0, 0
End Sub

Private Sub Command1_Click()
    Set msword = CreateObject("word.basic")

    With msword
        .AppMaximize
        .FileNew Template:="Letter2", NewTemplate:=0
    End With
```

continues

Listing 12.1. continued

```
    ' Replace all of the easy stuff. This is all fixed information
    wordReplace "[Company Name]", "Barside Brewery"
    wordReplace "[Street Address]", "123 Lite Road"
    wordReplace "[City, State/Province Zip/Postal Code]", "Pub City, Montana
➥43255"
    wordReplace "[Recipient Name]", "Jack Tremor"
    wordReplace "[Address]", "1414 Runner Drive"
    wordReplace "[City, State/Province Zip/Postal Code]", "Boston, MASS 12321"
    wordReplace "[Recipient]", "Jack"
    wordReplace "[Your name]", "Rose Switz"
    wordReplace "[Your position]", "Shipping Coordinator"
    wordReplace "[Typist's initials]", "dmm"
    wordReplace "[Number]", "0"
    wordDelLineWith "cc:"
    wordDelLineWith "[Type"

    With msword
        .INSERT Text1.TEXT
        .InsertPara
        .FilePrint
        .FileClose 2
    End With
    Set msword = Nothing
End Sub

Private Sub Form_Load()
    Label1.AutoSize = True
    Label1.Caption = "Enter the body of the letter below and then click on PRINT."
    Label1.Height = 200
    Label1.Left = 50
    Label1.TOP = 50

    ' Note that this control must be set as
    ' MultiLine=True & ScollBars=2 through
    ' the properties dialog box at design time.
    Text1.Height = 3000
    Text1.Left = 200
    Text1.TEXT = ""
    Text1.TabIndex = 1
    Text1.TOP = Label1.TOP + Label1.Height + 100
    Text1.Width = 4000

    Command1.Caption = " Print Letter"
    Command1.Height = 500
    Command1.Left = 50
    Command1.TabIndex = 2
    Command1.TOP = 3500
    Command1.Width = 4500

    Form1.Caption = "Letter Entry"
    Form1.Height = 4500
    Form1.Width = 4700
End Sub
```

3. Add one label, one text box, and one command button control anywhere on the form. The Form_Load method will take care of positioning them neatly.

4. Change the MultiLine property of Text1 to TRUE. Then change the ScrollBars property to 2 so that a vertical scroll bar will appear. You have to set these properties manually because you can't set them at run time.

5. Press F5 to execute the program. The form will look similar to Figure 12.3.

FIGURE 12.3.

The Letter Entry screen.

The wordDelLineWith and wordReplace methods simplify the rest of the code. You use the wordDelLineWith method to find a line containing a given string and delete it. A side effect of the search and delete is that the insertion point is positioned at the beginning of the old string. The wordReplace method takes two arguments; one is the target string to search for, and the other is the replacement string.

You might notice that the wordDelLineWith method uses named parameters to call the WordBasic EditFind statement, but the wordReplace method simply uses the parameters with no names. Both are valid ways of creating WordBasic statements. When using the no-name style, remember to provide a value for every parameter.

The application created in the preceding example follows this sequence of events:

1. The user enters the body of the letter and clicks on the Print Letter command button.

2. A new Microsoft Word document is created based on the Letter2 template.

3. The default information in the template is changed to match your needs. You could change the original template to eliminate this step.

NOTE

This technique of replacing the template information might be very useful if you are pulling the information from a database to support multiple letterheads.

4. The text from the Text1 control is inserted.

5. The document is printed and closed.

> **NOTE**
>
> Before printing the document, consider starting WordBasic's `ToolsSpelling` statement to spell check the document.

This application is very basic, but it does demonstrate how to access WordBasic. If you want additional information about WordBasic, look at the help file provided with Microsoft Word. Additional information is available on the Internet at the Microsoft World Wide Web site.

Using the *Printer* Object

Visual Basic programs don't have to use Microsoft Word to print; they can use the `Printer` object. When Visual Basic is first started, the `Printer` object is connected to the default Windows printer. This means that you don't need to initialize this object. The `Printer` object encapsulates a lot of functionality in one place and is an excellent example of how objects can make difficult programming easier.

Printing Considerations

Printing to a piece of paper is significantly different than displaying information on a form on a computer screen. Although Visual Basic has come a long way in achieving device independence, dealing with a printer requires some special attention. Here is a short list of things to keep in mind:

- A printer can run out of paper.
- A printer may be offline.
- Some printers are not capable of printing graphics or might handle graphics but no bit-block transfers. For example, plotters can handle graphic lines and boxes, but not a pixel-oriented image which would involve a bit-block transfer.
- Printers are slow.
- Multiple programs may be accessing the same printer simultaneously.

For the most part, Windows will isolate you from these errors when you use the Print Manager. The Print Manager is responsible for handling errors that arise during printing. In order to address the last concern, printing in Visual Basic takes place on a job by job basis. Each job consists of one unit of work (for example, one document or chart) that is sent to the Windows print queue. After the entire job has been sent to the queue, Windows takes care of actually printing it by sending the job to the printer.

Printer Object Basics

Before looking at the `Printer` object in detail, it may be useful to look at a simple example of how the `Printer` object is used in a Visual Basic project. The example in this section uses three methods of the `Printer` object: `Print`, `NewPage`, and `EndDoc`.

The syntax of the `Print` method is as follows:

```
Printer.Print outputlist
```

The `outputlist` parameter can be any combination of strings, functions, or variables. In short, you can place any valid expression after the `Print` method and its value will be printed. The `NewPage` and `EndDoc` methods take no arguments. You use the `NewPage` method to eject a page, reset the print position, and increment the `Printer.Page` property. You use `EndDoc` to tell the Print Manager that a print job has been transferred to the print queue and is ready for printing.

The following three lines will print the words "Hello, World!" at the top of the paper, eject the page, and end the print job.

```
Printer.Print "Hello, World!"
Printer.NewPage
Printer.EndDoc
```

The `Print` method supports the `Tab()` and `Spc()` functions that may already be familiar to you. You use the `Tab()` function to move the print position to a specific horizontal location. You use the `Spc()` function to insert a specific number of spaces into the print line. The following example shows the difference:

```
Printer.Print "00000000001111111111122222222223"
Printer.Print "12345678901234567890123456789 0"
Printer.Print "Hello, World!"; Tab(15); "Visual Basic"
Printer.Print "Hello, World!"; Spc(15); "Visual Basic"
Printer.NewPage
Printer.EndDoc
```

The printed output should look like the following:

```
00000000001111111111122222222223
12345678901234567890123456789 0
Hello, World! Visual Basic
Hello, World!            Visual Basic
```

You can see that the third line, which uses the `Tab()` function, starts the "Visual Basic" string at print position 15, and the fourth line, which uses the `Spc()` function, starts the "Visual Basic" string at print position 29.

You use the semi-colons to indicate that no space should be inserted between the item just printed and the next item. This is true even if items are on a separate line of code.

Printer Object Methods and Properties

The Printer object has a large amount of methods and properties defined for it. Table 12.2 shows all of the methods of the Printer object. Table 12.3 shows all the properties for this object.

Table 12.2. The methods of the Printer object.

Method	Description
Circle	Draws a circle, ellipse, or arc on an object. If you want the graphic to be filled, set the Printer.FillColor and Printer.FillStyle properties.
EndDoc	Informs Windows that the current print job is finished and that printing should begin.
KillDoc	If KillDoc is executed before EndDoc, then the entire print job is deleted.
Line	Draws a line or box on the page. The line is affected by the DrawWidth, DrawMode, and DrawStyle properties.
NewPage	Ejects the page and resets the print position. Also, increments the Printer object's Page property.
PaintPicture	Draws the contents of a graphics file. The supported graphics formats are BMP, WMF, EMF, ICO, and DIB.
Print	Prints any expression.
PSet	Draws a point. You can change the size of the point by using the DrawWidth property. When DrawWidth is greater than 1, the point is centered on the specified coordinates. The DrawMode and DrawStyle properties also affect the point. You can erase a point by using the BackColor property as the *color* parameter.
Scale	Defines the coordinate system used for specifying locations on the page.
ScaleX, ScaleY	Converts from one coordinate system to another.
TextHeight	Returns the height of a string. If the string contains multiple lines, the cumulative height is returned.
TextWidth	Returns the width of a string. If the string contains multiple lines, the width of the longest line is returned.

Chapter 12

Table 12.3. The properties of the `Printer` object.

Property	*Description*
ColorMode	If you set this property to vbPRCMMonochrome, then the printer will print in black and white. If you set this property to vbPRCMColor, then the printer will print in color. The default value depends on the printer driver.
Copies	The number of copies of a job to print. Remember that if more than one copy is needed, you may need to collate the pages.
CurrentX, CurrentY	The current horizontal (CurrentX) or vertical (CurrentY) coordinates for printing.
DeviceName	The name of the currently selected printer.
DrawMode	This property determines the appearance of output produced by a graphics method or the appearance of a Shape or Line control.
DrawStyle	This property determines the line style produced by graphics methods. The possibilities are Solid, Dash, Dot, Dash-Dot, Dash-Dot-Dot, Transparent, and Inside Solid. If DrawWidth is more than 1, the first five options all produce a solid line.
DrawWidth	This property determines the line width produced by graphics methods.
DriverName	The name of the printer driver for the currently selected printer.
Duplex	This property controls the use of two-sided printing.
FillColor	This property controls the color used to fill lines and circles.
FillStyle	This property controls the pattern used to fill shapes, lines, and circles.
Font	This property controls the font used to display text. You set it by using the Font object, which is discussed later in this chapter.
FontBold	This property is included for backwards compatibility and should not be used. Use the Font property instead.
FontCount	The number of fonts available in the printer.
FontItalic	This property is included for backwards compatibility and should not be used. Use the Font property instead.
FontName	This property is included for backwards compatibility and should not be used. Use the Font property instead.
Fonts(x)	This property is a list of the font names available for the printer. It works in conjunction with the FontCount property.

continues

Table 12.3. continued

Property	Description
FontSize	This property is included for backwards compatibility and should not be used. Use the Font property instead.
FontStrikethru	This property is included for backwards compatibility and should not be used. Use the Font property instead.
FontTransparent	This property controls whether background text and graphics are displayed in the spaces around characters. Changing this property does not affect items already drawn.
FontUnderline	This property is included for backwards compatibility and should not be used. Use the Font property instead.
ForeColor	The foreground color of items to be printed.
hDC	The handle to the device context of the printer.
Height	The physical height of the paper. If set at run time, it will supersede the PaperSize property.
Orientation	If this property is equal to vbPRORPortrait, then items are printed with the long edge at the left. If this property is equal to vbPRORLandscape, then items are printed with the short edge at the left.
Page	The current page number. It is incremented when the NewPage method is run or the text being printed will not fit on the current page. Graphic items will be clipped and will not cause a new page to eject.
PaperBin	The bin number where the pages being printed should be taken from.
PaperSize	The size of the paper being printed. Setting the Height or Width property of the printer automatically sets PaperSize to be user-defined.
Port	The name of the port that the printer will be using.
PrintQuality	The resolution of the printer. You can set it to vbPRPQDraft, vbPRPQLow, vbPRPQMedium, vbPRPQHigh, or the actual resolution.
ScaleHeight	The number of units for the vertical measurement of the interior of an object.
ScaleLeft	The horizontal coordinate for the next print operation.
ScaleMode	The unit of measurement for coordinates. You can set it to twips, points, pixels, and other values.
ScaleTop	The vertical coordinate for the next print operation.

Property	Description
ScaleWidth	The number of units for the horizontal measurement of the interior of an object.
TrackDefault	Determines whether the Printer object changes the printer it is connected to if the user changes the default printer setting in the Control Panel or a Print dialog box.
TwipsPerPixelX	The number of twips per pixel in the horizontal direction.
TwipsPerPixelY	The number of twips per pixel in the vertical direction.
Width	The physical width, in twips, of the paper. If set at run time, it will supersede the PaperSize property.
Zoom	The percentage by which printed output is to be scaled up or down. The printer driver, not Windows, handles this activity. Before using this property, make sure your printer driver supports it.

Aborting the Printing Process

This section explains how to let the user abort the printing process. You do this by invoking the KillDoc method when the user clicks on a Cancel button.

To run the example program in Listing 12.1, follow these steps:

1. Start Visual Basic or choose File | New to clear your workspace.
2. Enter Listing 12.2 into the code window for Form1.

Listing 12.2. Letting the user abort the printing process.

```
Dim printingCancelled As Boolean

Private Sub Command1_Click()
    printingCancelled = False
    For i = 1 To 500
        DoEvents
        If printingCancelled = True Then
            printingCancelled = False
            Exit For
        End If
        Label1.Caption = "Printing " & i
        Printer.Print i
    Next i
End Sub

Private Sub Command2_Click()
    Printer.KillDoc
    printingCancelled = True
End Sub
```

continues

Listing 12.2. continued

```
Private Sub Form_Load()
    Label1.Left = 100
    Label1.TOP = 100
    Label1.Height = 200
    Label1.Caption = ""

    Command1.Left = 100
    Command1.TOP = 400
    Command1.Caption = "Start"

    Command2.Left = 1600
    Command2.TOP = 400
    Command2.Caption = "Cancel"

    Form1.Caption = "Visual Basic Printing Test"
    Form1.Height = 2000
    Form1.Width = 4000
End Sub
```

3. Add one label and two command button controls anywhere on the form. The Form_Load method will take care of positioning them neatly.

4. Press F5 to execute the program.

You can start the printing process by clicking on the Start button. The label will indicate what number is currently being printed so that you know that something is occurring. You can stop the printing at anytime by pressing the Cancel button.

This example demonstrates a couple of important points. One is that the printing method needs to call the DoEvents method so that Windows gets a chance to process that Cancel request. In fact, if the DoEvents method is not called, the label caption will not be updated either. The other is that the printing loop needs a variable (printingCancelled) to indicate that the printing should stop.

Font Object Properties

The look of printed text is controlled by the Font object. This object has no methods, only properties. Table 12.4 lists these properties.

Table 12.4. Properties of the Font object.

Property	Description
Bold	Determines whether text is **Bold**.
Italic	Determines whether text is *italicized*.
Name	Specifies the name of the typeface to be used (For example, Arial or Courier).

Property	Description
Size	Specifies the size of the text to be used, measured in points.
StrikeThrough	Determines whether text is ~~Strikethrough~~.
Underline	Determines whether text is <u>underlined</u>.
Weight	Specifies the thickness of the strokes that make up the text. Valid values are 400 (regular) or 700 (bold).

You can set the printer for bold text with the following line of code:

```
Printer.Font.Bold = True
```

You can set the rest of the properties in a similar manner. To find out which fonts are supported by the default printer, use the following code block:

```
Printer.Copies = 1

For i = 1 To Printer.FontCount - 1
    Printer.Print i; ":"; Printer.Fonts(i)
Next i
Printer.EndDoc
```

This code prints a list of all of the typefaces supported by your default printer.

CAUTION

Notice that the first line of the code block changes the number of copies to 1. This is done because the last setting of the Copies property of the printer persists unless you change it in the Print dialog box. If the last user of the Print dialog box requested six copies, this code block would also print six copies unless you specifically set the Copies property to something else. If you don't use the Print dialog box, **always** set the Copies property explicitly.

Printing with the *Printer* Object

This section examines how to use some of the methods of the Printer object. There are too many methods to discuss them all, but these examples will give you a good head start.

Using the *PaintPicture* Method

The first example shows how to use the PaintPicture method. You can use this method to print any BMP, WMF, EMF, ICO, or DIB file. The first step is to place a PictureBox control on a form. Then, run the code in Listing 12.3 when you want to print the control's contents.

Listing 12.3. Printing a graphic using the `PaintPicture` method.

```
Picture1.picture = LoadPicture("ICONS\COMPUTER\TRASH02A.ICO")

Printer.Copies = 1
startX = 100
startY = 100
Printer.PaintPicture Picture1.picture, _
    startX, startY, Picture1.Width, Picture1.Height

nextY = startY + Picture1.Height + 200
Printer.PaintPicture Picture1.picture, _
    startX, nextY, Picture1.Width * 2, Picture1.Height * 2

nextX = startX + Picture1.Width * 2
nextY = nextY + (Picture1.Height * 4) + 200
Printer.PaintPicture Picture1.picture, _
    nextX, nextY, Picture1.Width * -2, Picture1.Height * -2

Printer.EndDoc
Printer.Copies = 1
startX = 100
startY = 100
Printer.PaintPicture Picture1.picture, _
    startX, startY, Picture1.Width, Picture1.Height

nextY = startY + Picture1.Height + 200
Printer.PaintPicture Picture1.picture, _
    startX, nextY, Picture1.Width * 2, Picture1.Height * 2

nextX = startX + Picture1.Width * 2
nextY = nextY + (Picture1.Height * 4) + 200
Printer.PaintPicture Picture1.picture, _
    nextX, nextY, Picture1.Width * -2, Picture1.Height * -2

Printer.EndDoc
```

Centering Text

To center text, you must use the `TextWidth` method of the `Printer` object in order to account for proportional fonts. The `centerText` method in Listing 12.4 shows how to find the print position needed to start printing. First, the center point of the page is found and then half of the width of the string parameter is subtracted. This calculation results in the starting print position. If you need to manipulate the font, such as changing the typeface or point size, be sure to do it before calling the `TextWidth` method.

Listing 12.4. Centering text on the printer.

```
Private Sub centerText(h As Integer, str As String)
    pageMiddle = Printer.ScaleWidth / 2
    Printer.CurrentX = pageMidle - (Printer.TextWidth(str) / 2)
    Printer.CurrentY = h
    Printer.Print str
End Sub

Private Sub Form_Click()
    Printer.Copies = 1
    centerText 1440, "This text is centered."
    centerText 2880, "This text is centered also."
    Printer.EndDoc
End Sub
```

Summary

This chapter explained how to display and interact with the Print dialog box, how to manipulate Microsoft Word, and how to use the Printer object.

Using Microsoft Word to handle print chores is a very powerful technique. You can incorporate any or all of Word's features inside your own program. Additional uses of Word might be to print labels, create tables from databases, or to automatically create indexes.

Advanced usage of the Printer object usually takes advantage of its dual nature. You can use the Print method to do text-based printer, but you can also use Line, Circle, PSet, and PaintPicture methods to do graphic-based printing.

Debugging and Testing

For the twelfth bug of Christmas, my manager said to me:

> *"Tell them it's a feature*
> *Say it's not supported*
> *Change the documentation*
> *Blame it on the hardware*
> *Find a way around it*
> *Say they need an upgrade*
> *Reinstall the software*
> *Ask for a dump*
> *Run with the debugger*
> *Try to reproduce it*
> *Ask them how they did it and*
> *See if they can do it again."*

—The Twelve Bugs of Christmas - Anon.

How many lines of that chorus have you heard before? How many of those have been in the context of lame excuses for a late or faulty project? This chapter is intended to help you avoid being in that embarrassing position.

Introduction to Debugging

There are many excellent books available dedicated to the entire philosophy of software development, for example *Code Complete* by Steve McConnell of Microsoft. I strongly encourage you to obtain and study books of this kind as they will help you to get things right the first time and save a lot of last-minute grief. It goes without saying that you should also read as much as you can of the Visual Basic 4.0 manuals *before* you start coding!

TIP
"It's easier to make correct programs efficient, than efficient programs correct." —Dominic Connor

While it's true that Visual Basic 4.0 provides you with a wealth of tools and facilities to trace bugs and eliminate them, you should clearly note that these tools only have particular relevance to the Coding and Testing stages of the development process. It is important that all the other aspects should also be attended to with equal intensity. Even the best debugging tools in the world are useless in the face of convoluted "spaghetti" code.

So, assuming you've read the debugging part of the Visual Basic 4.0 manuals, I'll complement it by spending the first few pages of this chapter on a whistle-stop tour of some of the concepts that can save you time in the long run if applied up-front, and the rest in a discussion of generic faults that you can look for in any Visual Basic program.

TIP

"Never put off till tomorrow what you can do today."

"Prevention is better than cure."

"More haste, less speed."

"You reap what you sow."

—PROVERBS

Simply speaking, project development may be split into three stages in which defects may be found and reported. The stages are as follows:

1. Specification
2. Building
   a. Program Design
   b. Coding
   c. Preliminary testing
   d. Final Testing
3. In Use by the Customer

Stages 1 and 3 usually rely on interactions between the customer and business analysts, often without any particular reference to yourself, the humble programmer. Visual Basic 4.0's debugging tools can only really help you with the later parts of Stage 2. Any significant fault that gets as far as the third stage should be treated as an indicator of critical failure of development procedure.

For the purposes of this chapter, we will assume that the specification stage has been carried out promptly and to the highest possible standard. While this is rarely true in practice, the first stage that you will probably be able to influence is the Program Design stage—to optimize your progress, you should think about debugging and testing at this stage—not at the end of the project.

One of the major enhancements to Visual Basic 4.0 has been the introduction of *class modules*, which enables you to define your own objects. I can't emphasize enough how important it is to make sure the design and definitions of these objects are correct and fixed before you start coding around them. This is even more important if you are working in a team environment where one person could change a class module without other team members finding out until much later and spending ages trying to understand why their previously tested code doesn't work properly any more.

The Purpose of Testing

> **TIP**
>
> The purpose of testing is to produce a product of impeccable commercial quality. Therefore, the intention is to find defects in the system, not to attempt to show that the system works.

The testing of each component should be aimed at causing it to fail. In addition to testing the functionality, the product should be subject to invalid input, be stressed so as to check its management of resources, and be surrounded by barriers that detect any attempt to use objects that it was not intended to access. A certain amount of this barrier functionality should also be placed within the application itself, subject to performance considerations. Be aware that removing debug code from your application is effectively creating a new version of the software—which will then need to be retested from first principles.

In practice, you will find that no substantial piece of software is ever error-free. You will also (almost invariably) find that the sooner a defect is found, the easier and cheaper it is to fix. In the worst case, regular detection of errors in production systems is invariably detrimental to your relationship with your customers.

On the other hand, an efficient testing regime speeds development by increasing the rate at which components can be successfully integrated into the system. Delivery of a quality product within the necessary time scale is crucial to the commercial success of the project.

> **TIP**
>
> Remember: The earlier the finding, the easier the fixing!

However, the recent pervasiveness of the Internet (with other networks and bulletin boards) has often tempted vendors to ship a less-than-perfect product. This is based on the idea that cheap fixes can be rapidly issued via modems. This is not a system that a quality vendor will apply as a matter of course—due to the inability to control the application of the fix (given that the user is even aware of its existence) and the impression the user will get that the vendor's software is always seriously faulty until at least the first service pack has been applied.

Encapsulation

NOTE

As a reminder to the reader, this section is not discussing OOPS concepts.

An important technique in Program Design is to encapsulate sections of the code into self-contained units whose purpose is sufficiently simple and definable that they may be rigorously tested and proved in isolation from other external considerations. Visual Basic's event-driven model and support for modular design has always guided the programmer toward this in the past—Visual Basic 4.0 extends these facilities.

It should be clear that global variables are anathema to good program design because they are effectively undocumented and invisible parameters. Global constants are not quite so bad as long as their values do in fact remain constant throughout the life of the project; any variation from this rule must be seen as a prime opportunity for errors to arise. Another potential source of errors arises when the name could equally imply a variable or a constant. For example, is EndOfList a defined constant or a true/false Boolean? You can get around the need for global constants in Visual Basic 4.0 by using Type library (a .TLB file)—just add a typelib and you instantly have access to an object's methods and properties, including constants. You don't carry any extra baggage in your .EXE—you only compile in what you use. Be aware of the implications for the system registry—see "Creating Object Applications" in Professional Features Book 1.

If well-designed, the components may also become reusable in later projects—which is the philosophy behind the .VBX (and now .OCX) components that have made Visual Basic such a successful development tool.

One of the major advances of Visual Basic 4.0 over previous versions of Visual Basic is the ability to encapsulate and include your code within libraries of reusable OLE objects. You should take every opportunity to use this facility offered by class modules. For further information, read the Visual Basic 4.0 manuals and the relevant chapters of this book. For example, consider such things as About or Password dialogs. Once you have created and tested a generic version of each of these, why should you ever have to bother doing another one? Reuse of such components also helps your projects conform to corporate look and feel guidelines of different projects, which are important from the perspective of reducing training costs when users are transferred between departments.

Component Testing

TIP

Provided that a function actually performs a meaningful operation, it must be possible to unit test it. Conversely, any function that does not perform a meaningful operation should not be a part of the system.

Removal of "unreachable code" should be a regular process for developers. There are excellent tools available for this process such as VBCompress by WhippleWare—check for the availability of a Visual Basic 4.0 version. In practice, however, you may wish to make exceptions for fully tested modules containing a set of standard, general-purpose functions where it might be less disruptive to retain the original version (instead of hacking different bits off to suit different projects that might share that module).

Testing of completed components falls into two main areas :

- Unit testing of individual components
- System testing of interactions between components

Bug tracing naturally lags behind program coding. It follows that anything you can do to minimize this time lag will tend to reduce the opportunity for the defect to disrupt you and delay your application. It's therefore essential to devise and produce a programmatic test-harness at the same time the component is designed and written. If it is not done concurrently as an integral part of the development process, it will probably never get done. A test-harness can also give you some information about the component's speed without other influences confusing the results.

There are two further benefits from early allocation of resources for testing needs. First, the flattening out of the resource requirement for the test group so it will not have to cope with a sudden influx of work. Second, as soon as the tests are in place, the developers will have an extra resource for debugging their code. Therefore, produce test programs to automatically exercise all the methods and properties exposed by the objects as part of the build process itself. Don't sign any component off or release it for public use until it has passed the full set of tests. If a change is made to common code, then all other components using that code must also be subjected to the same procedure.

Version Control and Numbering

Once the component has passed the tests it must be allocated a version number that can be read at run-time by any programs using it. From that sign-off point forward, this version of the component is effectively cast in stone and the source code for that version should be readily retrievable from a Version Control archive system. A major feature of Visual Basic 4.0 is its capability to accommodate add-ins, one of which enables links to Version Control systems. As Microsoft has decided to push the SourceSafe product, you can be sure that it will play a large part in their plans—perhaps as a basis for an object repository? In the meantime, consider whether you might be better off with a VCS that supports multiple hardware platforms.

The addition of resource files and version information is a further major improvement in Visual Basic 4.0. Previous versions required use of Borland's Resource Workshop or Desaware's VersionStamper to retrospectively add version numbers to Visual Basic-produced .EXE's (C++ components are versioned in their .RC file at final build). See Microsoft's Knowledge Base article number Q107992 for any VB3 versioning needs you may have. This is available on the Developer Network CDs or via GO MSKB on CompuServe.

If a bug is found, an extra set of tests must be added immediately to the test-harness to verify the corrected component, which then must pass the entire enlarged suite of tests before it is allocated a new version number and signed off. When the time for system issue comes around, you can then define a set of approved component versions that have been tested together for that release.

To determine whether an approved combination of components is being run, your application must then be coded with a function call to interrogate all the components at start-up. If another application has been installed since this one, overwriting one or more of your set of components, you can then display a warning to that effect and (if required) prevent the application from continuing until the correct versions are replaced. This procedure may save you hours of support calls that aren't helped by the fact that users cannot be seen as a reliable source of information about the exact nature of a fault. You can't control what other software may be running or what hardware it is running on—but that's no excuse for failing to control the aspects that are under your jurisdiction.

System and Regression Testing

System Testing is when all the fully tested and signed-off components have been assembled into a larger whole and the correctness of their interactions is verified. If possible, it is better to create subassemblies of components (which can have their own test-harness) for subsystem testing rather than throwing everything together at once. To use a biological analogy, test the branches individually before testing the whole tree.

Regression Testing is when a complete program is systematically retested after each build in order to verify that its behavior only differs from the previous build in the desired manner, and no other. It is invaluable for detecting complex defects missed by unit level tests, in that an unpredicted change in output is often an indication of error.

The only practical way to properly regression-test is to use one of the software tools that can automate the running of your application. They should include facilities to save at each stage of the run (Record mode), the states and contents of all the objects in the current form, and compare this set of master states with later builds (Playback mode) so that unintended changes manifesting themselves in user interface differences can be picked up immediately.

For example, here's an analysis of a simple Visual Basic 3.0 project's object states and menu states as evaluated by SQA TeamTest v3.0—a high-end and, compared to MS Test, fairly expensive tool. It is not clear at the time of writing (June 1995) whether TeamTest will be available for 32-bit Visual Basic 4.0 developments under Win95/NT operating systems, but this should give you an idea of what may be achieved. See Figures 13.1 and 13.2.

It's useful to get some statistics on what percentage of your system is actually being exercised by such tests—you may be surprised at how much of your system is hardly ever used.

FIGURE 13.1.

An example of a regression test tool.

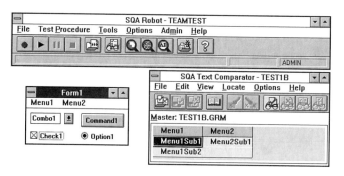

FIGURE 13.2.

An example of a regression test tool.

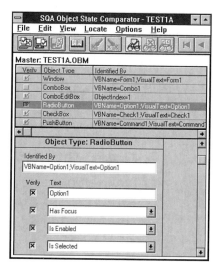

Test Plans and Resourcing

Programmers have a duty to issue components for testing only when they consider them to be entirely correct—as long as time pressures permit. However, a common misconception is that testing is somehow separate from the main process of development. This usually results in the scheduling of testing requirements not being considered as important as the scheduling of programming tasks, which leads to time and resources for testing being squeezed into a frantic last-minute panic, and any chance of efficiency and thoroughness is squandered.

If the testing is relegated to the end of the product development cycle, any time spent testing must compete with the commercial need to ship the product. The inevitable result is a product being shipped later, and with a lower level of reliability and perceived quality than could have been achieved. There is also a risk of the software being tested in too narrow a set of conditions with the effect that in highly diverse environments it may not be sufficiently resilient.

Clearly, there will be more, and less efficient, sequences in which testing can take place. Some components may require other components before they can do anything useful, so a critical path analysis proves useful. A schedule of programming tasks should be devised with this in mind and in consultation with the testing personnel. This critical path analysis helps you optimize your testing strategy by showing which portions of the project can be tested concurrently, and the extent of any rollback required in the testing procedure should a bug be discovered in previously signed-off components. It also aids you in your regular reports to your superiors.

It is therefore vital that the testing stage reached by any element of the system can be identified at any time. The validity of dependent tests will be uncertain if this is not the case.

A common problem with the hiring of testing personnel or assigning testing tasks is that testing in particular is often regarded as a menial and tedious task. In fact, it is a specialized task, requiring a good technical knowledge and a thorough understanding of the system design. Without such knowledge it is impossible to devise meaningful and efficient tests; therefore, it is essential that personnel with appropriate capabilities are made available for the whole process.

Monitors and Code Reviews

Given sufficient abilities, it is often productive for testers to have access to the source code to enable them to "rig" the code with their own monitoring and analysis tools—that is, to add temporary code to yield more information about the programs operation. However, this may be a source of political friction in some workplaces.

Nevertheless, there is nothing like the threat of public review to inspire an immediate improvement in code quality. Go for it! Find a secure area and pin regularly updated printouts of all the project's source code on the wall for the whole development team to add their comments to! You may also have an opinion on the value of some kind of reward scheme for consistent low-error coding.

When undertaking code reviews, it is important to prevent the discussion from degenerating into an argument. A publicized checklist of both preferred and unacceptable coding practices can help prevent this as well as reduce the likelihood of the faults occurring in the first place. If you're a manager, you might like to set up a spreadsheet with types of errors given a weighting (according to severity) and multiplied by the number of occurrences. You can then derive a "Code Quality Index" (whose value should tend to zero over time) for each code module once it has stabilized. Whether such practices are cost and time efficient depend on how mission-critical your software is.

Errors Independent of Business Rules

It's possible to define the characteristics of a piece of code that are necessarily incorrect, regardless of any functional specification that the code may represent.

For example, consider the following dialog box with absolutely no code behind it (see Figure 13.3).

FIGURE 13.3.

A dialog box with no code behind it that has an error.

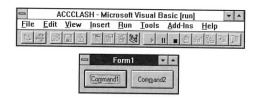

Can you see what's wrong? Yes—there's a clash of accelerator keys!

The first button has its first "m" underlined, the second button has its second "m" underlined. This program is inherently defective (unless, of course, you're trying to demonstrate hot-key clashes!).

Multiple use of accelerator assignments is not incorrect when the objects involved are always mutually invisible. For example, multiple assignments are acceptable within different menus or tab dialogs. Nevertheless, it is best to detect the possibility of a problem and discount it later instead of ignoring the possibility of error altogether.

Detection of these kinds of errors is essentially an extension of the process of syntax checking. The C language has long had tools, Lint for example, to inspect the code for generic faults. Raising the compilation Warning Level to 4 in Visual C++ does much the same job.

Tools for Generic Fault-Finding

As such tools are currently not available for Visual Basic, you must consider writing a few programs of your own, although it may not be thought an effective use of time to go too far down this road. You should prioritize your available time and resources accordingly.

By way of example, here's a simple method to find accelerator key clashes. If you've never saved a VB form in ASCII format and inspected it with Notepad, do it now! If you re-create the preceding dialog, you get something like this :

```
VERSION 4.00
Begin VB.Form Form1
   Caption         =    "Form1"
   ClientHeight    =    735
   ClientLeft      =    2970
   ClientTop       =    1980
   ClientWidth     =    2775
   Height          =    1080
   Left            =    2940
   LinkTopic       =    "Form1"
   ScaleHeight     =    735
   ScaleWidth      =    2775
   Top             =    1665
   Width           =    2835
   Begin VB.CommandButton Command2
      Caption      =    "Com&mand2"
      Height       =    495
      Left         =    1440
      TabIndex     =    1
      Top          =    120
      Width        =    1215
   End
   Begin VB.CommandButton Command1
      Caption      =    "Co&mmand1"
      Height       =    495
      Left         =    120
      TabIndex     =    0
      Top          =    120
      Width        =    1215
   End
End
Attribute VB_Name = "Form1"
Attribute VB_Creatable = False
Attribute VB_Exposed = False
```

You can read a lot more about the Visual Basic file format in the Programmers Guide manual. The essential rule of thumb to remember is that these values are occasions of properties differing from their defaults.

The lines you are interested in are these:

```
Caption         =    "Com&mand2"
Caption         =    "Co&mmand1"
```

I hope you agree that detection of multiple occurrences of characters preceded with & (except the ampersand character itself!) within lines that begin with

```
Caption        =   "
```

is not a desperately difficult task—the sort of thing that could be done in MS-DOS QBasic on a 1981 twin-floppy PC with 512K RAM! Not a Windows API in sight!

50 Possibilities for Generic Fault-Finding

There are many different faults (or at least, sub-optimal practices) that can be found by programmatic examination of the source code.

Here are 50 that I have thought of (in no particular order). See if you can think of any more. Note that some are more applicable to Windows 3.1 than Windows 95. Because it is almost certain that our applications will still have to be able to run on Windows 3.1 systems for the foreseeable future (whether native 16 bit or via Win32s) you should take that into account.

Static Tests

Some tests may be performed on the source code itself.

Is Option Explicit in all Forms/Modules?

It is extremely important to ensure that all your source files each contain the Option Explicit line.

Its purpose is to force you to declare variables before use which not only forces you to consider the scope and usage of the variables but also warns you of mistyped variable names that would otherwise auto-initialize to zero or the empty string. Also, is it a typo if a variable ends in 'l' or '1'? Use of Option Explicit should help to prevent this kind of fault, but it's happened before so it might happen to you.

Is There Adequate Use of DoEvents?

The DoEvents command allows other tasks to share the CPU within non-preemptive multitasking versions of Windows. All calls that take a substantial time to execute should have a DoEvents within or nearby.

Do All File Handles Use FreeFile?

If you open a file with a hardcoded I/O stream number, you run the risk that another routine within the program is already be using this number (or vice-versa), so always use the FreeFile command for file I/O.

Instead of doing

```
Open "myfile.txt" For Input As #1
```

do this instead,

```
Dim MyFileNumber As Integer
MyFileNumber = FreeFile
Open "myfile.txt" For Input As #MyFileNumber
```

Are Variables Given Global Scope Unnecessarily?

Visual Basic 4.0 has Typelibs and predefined constants.

If you're using products such as Help Compilers that churn out huge files of global constants, you should beware of the problems this can cause with encapsulation of your code. There have also been many large Visual Basic 3.0 projects made lame by global name or symbol table overflow.

Also note that the Global keyword has been replaced by Public in Visual Basic 4.0 (although it has been retained for reverse compatibility).

Are There Accelerator (Shortcut) Key Clashes?

This is important for applications that may have to be used without a mouse. While most people prefer to use a mouse, you should not assume that machines (especially portables) will always have a mouse attached.

As mentioned earlier in the text, it is possible to allocate the same hot-key definition to more than one object. This is not a problem for objects that are mutually invisible, such as menus and objects within different tab dialogs.

Is There Error Handling?

Is there error handling within all Subs that define Form Events, preferably within all other Subs or Functions, too?

When a line of code that is syntactically correct is run but causes an illegal operation to occur (such as division by zero), the debugger halts the interpreter if you are in design mode or the program if you are in a compiled .EXE file.

This behavior can be altered by the addition of the On Error construct that enables graceful handling of error conditions without throwing the user out and losing his data. However, you should be careful when coding error handling that you don't hide the existence of genuine coding errors from yourself by applying too much of a "blanket" approach. On Error Resume Next should always be viewed with the maximum doubt you can manage.

On the contrary, errors should be amplified as much as possible during the development process so that the error causes an immediate break in the program. It is especially useful to wrap DLL calls within their own Visual Basic functions to provide a consistent approach to this coding-error-prone interface as well as to provide comprehensive return-code handling and trapping of returned error codes. Ideally, you should leave out (or comment out) all Visual Basic-error handling code while in the development process, replacing it at the final stages of the build. Look in the MSBASIC forum on CompuServe for VBRIG by Brad Kaenel (72357,3523), which is an excellent program to "rig" your finished code with error-handlers. It has other uses for run-time analysis as I mention later. It's shareware so don't forget to GO SWREG.

See Chapter 5, "Error Trapping, Handling, and Reporting," for more details.

Are Line Lengths or Overall Sizes of Subs and Functions Not Excessive?

In general, if a sub or function is more than a couple of screensful long, you should consider breaking it down to smaller units for maintainability. Code not directly relevant to a .FRM should be moved to a .BAS module to allow faster form loading. Excessively long lines should be broken down into smaller units that can be rapidly understood as individual concepts.

Check for Recursion

Recursion is when a function calls itself. It can be very useful if it is intentional.

If not intentional, it causes havoc by going on indefinitely. The usual scenario is a set of routines calling one of the others in turn and forming a logical loop, with resulting in your program going round and round until it runs out of stack and/or memory.

Do All Referenced DLL Calls Actually Exist in the DLLs?

It is possible to declare Dynamic Link Library functions that do not actually exist in the physical DLL. This often happens when the DLL is written by a team (C++ developers) other than the Visual Basic developers and the two developments go out of sync.

As the functions are only looked for at run-time when required, this kind of omission can be missed in testing if the omitted function is only called in one or two obscure places. Be sure that the users will manage to find it, though.

Prevent these errors by using the EXEHDR tool (that comes with the Windows SDK or with VC++) to list the exported functions in all the DLLs specified in all the referenced declare lines in your code. If you find any functions that are declared but are not in the EXEHDR output, investigate immediately.

See Chapter 20 for an example of how to check that the DLL is actually the correct one.

Is Consistent Variable Naming Enforced?

It's useful to avoid data conversions wherever possible because they consume processor time and may lose accuracy.

For example, assigning the contents of a Double (a 4-byte floating-point number) into a Single (a 2-byte floating-point number) and back again replaces the second seven significant figures of the original number with random digits. Likewise, if the left hand side of a line of code is a long or an integer, you run the risk of losing accuracy if the right hand side involves floating-point variables or division because the fractional part of the answer will be lost.

There is a convention used among C programmers called *Hungarian notation* where the variable names are prefixed with a few letters to signify the datatype and possibly its intended usage. Alternatively you can use the old BASICA suffix convention of %, !, $, and so on; but this is often viewed as being a little ugly.

The point of this convention is that you can see if the datatypes match up at a glance.

Is Tab Order Logical to the User?

If the cursor jumps around the screen at random whenever Tab is pressed, it will be more difficult for the user to input data to your application. You must decide for yourself what is the most logical, but going from top/left of the screen to bottom/right is usually a good way to start.

Use Named Constants

Scattering explicitly numeric constants around your code is one of the best ways to make it unmaintainable and error prone. Anyone who wants to read your code will not have a clue what the constants are for.

If someones task is to alter a constant used in more than one place to be another value, they might easily miss one of the occurrences. There is the further complication that two numeric entities might have the same value and it will be difficult to discern which is which in the code.

It is arguable that 0 and 1 in the context of `For ptr = 1 To limit` are valid exceptions to this rule.

Spellcheck All Strings

Spelling mistakes are one of the easiest ways to reduce the users' confidence in your testing procedures due to the mistakes' visibility. You should also ensure that your warning and error messages are comprehensible.

Write a small program to extract all the lines with double-quote marks, remove the characters before the first double-quote in each line and put the remainder through the spellchecker in Word or some other word processor. Don't forget to ensure that you are also using the correct words even if the spellcheck passes. For example, look for "their" instead of "there" and vice versa.

Do this check before every formal release of your application.

In *Dim Var1, Var2 As String—Only Var2 Is a String*

This is a fault often made by C programmers who have moved on to Visual Basic. In Visual Basic, each variable has to be explicitly given a datatype, or else it takes the default datatype, which is usually variant unless altered with the Def??? function.

To make Var1 and Var2 both strings, use

```
Dim Var1 As String
Dim Var2 As String
```

You should always try to combat Visual Basic 4.0's tendency to make anything it possibly can into a variant.

Is There Maximized Use of *ByVals* on Function Calls?

The ByVal keyword is used to send a throwaway copy of the variable's data to a function instead of the variable itself. Therefore, you should always use the ByVal keyword to pass data to a function unless you specifically want the function to be able to modify that variable's data. Doing this should prevent corrupt data from "escaping" from the offending function.

There is an unusual use of the ByVal keyword in the context of passing variable-length strings to DLL functions. Because the C language uses a different internal representation of strings than Visual Basic 4.0, it is necessary to always use the ByVal keyword to instruct Visual Basic 4.0 to translate between the formats when passing or receiving variable-length string data to or from a DLL.

Fixed length strings (either stand-alone or within user-defined types) do not share this use of the ByVal keyword.

Are Variables Used Before They Are Set?

Variables must be given a value before being used. If one of these operations is missing or the order of these operations is reversed, there is almost certainly an error.

It is bad practice to rely on BASIC's feature of auto-initializing variables on first use. You don't always know when that first use will be!

Are Types and Structures Sensitive to Packing for C/C++ DLL Calls?

This is a minor optimization issue in that passed parameters must be expanded to WORD boundaries before use in a DLL.

If you arrange your user-defined types to have the 8-byte variables first (Double and Currency), followed by the 4-byte variables (Single and Long), followed by the 2-byte variable (Integer), followed by the remainder, you will naturally prealign most of your UDT contents on WORD boundaries. See the VC++ documentation (if you have it) on the /Zp parameter for more information.

Does Your Application Fully Support Multiple Instancing?

If your application cannot run perfectly alongside another instance of itself, you should check for use of App.PrevInstance in the start-up form and exit immediately if this is true.

Are There Any Variable Length Strings in User-Defined Types?

If you include a variable length string within a user-defined type and save it to disk with a Put command, you save the string's current size and memory address instead of its contents. This isn't useful for very long.

Are Global Vars Set in More Than One Place?

Global variables are anathema to function encapsulation. If they are set in more than one place you increase your lack of program control by an order of magnitude.

Is There More Than One (Non-Error) Exit Point from the Sub or Function?

If you are able to exit a routine via more than one place you will not be able to trace your program execution without a lot more care and attention. If you are stepping over functions, it won't always be obvious what was executed within the functions and what wasn't.

Are Constant Expressions and Explicitly Referenced Object Properties within Loops?

Sometimes, lines of code are able to be moved outside a loop with no change to the results produced. For example, the following Var2 line can be moved outside the For...Next loop, meaning that it is only executed once instead of a hundred times, which aids run-time performance.

```
For ptr = 1 To 100
   Var1 = Var1 + ptr
   Var2 = 10
Next ptr
```

Also, it is much quicker to get the value of a variable than to get the value of an object property, so don't refer to heavily used constant property values explicitly. Assign the property to a temporary variable and use that instead. Be sure that the property will remain constant before you do this.

For example, if you are aligning many screen objects dynamically with respect to the dimensions of the form itself, you can improve the speed by assigning the Form dimension properties to temporary variables and using the temporary variables instead.

Are There Any Single-Letter Variables?

Unless there is an agreed and pervasive local standard where single letter variables are appropriate, variable names should always be long enough to make their purpose clear (without being so long that they overflow the code window and raise the chances of typos).

For example, actuaries might prefer to use a variable N(x) in their calculations instead of AnnuityCommutationFactorNumerator(CurrentAge), but if you're sensible you'll improve your code legibility.

Are All Return Codes from Functions Checked?

A lot of DLL functions return integers to indicate whether the function executed correctly or not. If it didn't, the value of that integer indicates the nature of the failure. You should always enclose DLL calls with a Visual Basic wrapper function to handle all the possibilities smoothly.

One of the best things about Visual Basic so far has been the fact that it's almost impossible to cause a General Protection Fault if you stick to native Visual Basic code and MS-packaged VBXs. If you get a GPF in Visual Basic you can be sure there's some rogue DLL-coding lurking somewhere. It's much easier to watch the actual data flowing to and from Visual Basic to C++ if you limit the crossover point to a single instance instead of many.

Is Help Implemented Fully? Do All *HelpContextIDs* Exist in .HLP?

People use your application's Help file when they need to know certain facts to enable them to carry on with their tasks, so it is usually very frustrating to be told that the Help topic does not exist or even given the wrong Help topic altogether. Read the "Testing Help Files" chapter in the Help Compiler section of the Visual Basic 4.0 manuals for more information.

Help compilers usually generate large files of global constants to maintainably represent the set of HelpContextIDs implemented in the Help file. You should check that your application does not use any old constant names that have since ceased to have any meaning within the .HLP file.

Are All VB Specifications and Limitations Adhered To?

Read Appendix D (Specifications and Limitations) in the Visual Basic 4.0 Programmer's Guide manual. Are you likely to overflow any of the constraints mentioned there?

There Should Be No *GoTos* or *GoSubs*

On Error GoTo may be classed as a useful command in making your programs more resilient.

On the other hand, pure GoTo and GoSub are BASICA reverse compatibility commands that have no sensible use in a Windows 95 world centered around encapsulated objects. They are the surest indicator of spaghetti code you can find.

If...Then Constructs Should Cover All Possibilities

The following code is a simple example of how a logically incomplete If...Then statement has led to a function that does something only for a very limited set of input possibilities. This should happen only if you have deliberately made that choice.

```
Function MyFunct(MyParam As Integer) As String
    If MyParam = 1 Then
        MyFunct = "One"
    ElseIf MyParam = 2 Then
        MyFunct = "Two"
    End If
End Function
```

You should always ensure all possibilities are catered for, usually by including a final Else statement before each End If to catch any default cases.

Does Your Chosen Font Name Exist on the Target PC?

If you are using a special font that is not supplied as standard with Windows (for example, an unusual corporate standard font) you should ensure that the font exists on any target machine on which you install your application. This is especially important because the error returned (Property Not Found) does not particularly indicate a missing font.

Are Local Variables Given Same Names as Globals?

Here's a simple example of a project where the nature of Var1 is ambiguous without careful study of the code.

```
MODULE1.BAS
Global Var1 As String
```

```
FORM1.FRM
Private Sub Form_Load()
    Dim Var1 As Integer
End Sub
```

Use of a consistent variable naming notation (for example, Hungarian notation) helps to prevent this source of confusion.

There Should Not Be Too Many Depths of Brackets

If you find you're having to spend time with your fingers against the screen to work out what code is where within a forest of brackets, you should split the line into smaller units. This will help you debug a line because you can easily watch the temporary variables' values.

Is Inlining Possible?

If a certain function is very heavily used in only one place in your code and performance needs to be improved in that area, you might try replacing the function call with the contents of the function—enclosed with comments to state what has happened.

This saves the overhead of a (far) function call every time the *inlined* code is executed.

Are Default Properties and the *With...End With* Construct Used?

Since the first version of Visual Basic, toolbox objects have had default properties. For example, you may access the Text property of a textbox using just Text1 instead of Text1.Text.

The With...End With construct introduced with Excel 5.0 and Visual Basic 4.0 allows you to perform a similar operation with the leading qualifiers of a property value. See the Visual Basic 4.0 manual for examples.

Both of these can save some run-time interpretation overhead.

Are There Single-Line *If...Then* Constructs?

These can make it visually difficult to match Ifs with End Ifs, particularly if line indentation has been disturbed or not implemented carefully in the first place.

Is the Use of Integers Maximized?

If your code is being run on a machine without floating-point calculation hardware, you can often gain a significant speed increase by maximizing your use of integers: either the Integer, Long, or Currency datatypes. Beware of the different number of bytes that may be used for an integer—2 bytes in 16-bit systems and 4 bytes in 32-bit systems!

You can allow integers to be used for control positions by ensuring that Scalemode is set to "Twips" or "Pixels."

Beware of UNICODE Text Conventions

Programmers who have not spent much time programming for Windows NT applications are often unaware that it is dangerous to assume that a character always occupies one byte. In the UNICODE text convention used within Windows NT, each character occupies two bytes, to enable more than 256 international characters to be described.

There are many articles on this subject in recent issues of the *Microsoft Systems Journal* as well as within the MS Knowledge Base.

Here are some examples from the MS-KB library:

```
Q89295   Unicode Conversion to Integers
Q99884   Unicode and Microsoft Windows NT
Q100639  Unicode Support in the MS Foundation Class Library
Q103977  Unicode Implementation in Windows NT 3.1 and 3.5
Q109199  INF: Using Double-byte Character Sets with SQL Server
Q130052  Tips for Converting from ASCII or ANSI to Unicode
```

Beware of Date Order Conventions

The US convention for abbreviated dates is MM/DD/YY, whereas the European convention is DD/MM/YY. If you want your program to work sensibly both here and abroad for more than 12 days each year, you should consider using "mmm" as your format string within For-mat$() instead of "mm."

This is equally important for documentation, where style and meaning of phrases can be subtly different between countries. You might use UK English spelling if you are producing a specific version of your program for use there (that is, "colour" instead of "color"). Likewise, any text that refers to "Invoking the Serialization Facility" will cause great mirth among any readers who prefer to "Save the file."

See Chapter 28 ("International Issues") in the Programmer's Guide manual for more Visual Basic-specific considerations like this.

Is There Preferential Usage of Certain Controls to Save Windows Resources?

Some controls map directly to Windows control classes and so occupy resources when used. Some are internal to Visual Basic and don't. If resources are tight, you should try to use the Visual Basic ones. For example, use a label instead of a read-only textbox. Likewise the Image control is a lightweight version of the Picture control.

Are There Too Many Controls on the Same Form?

If you have too many controls on the same form, it makes the form difficult to use. If you employ dynamic positioning of controls to match form resizing, you run the risk of controls overlapping.

If you have many command buttons, you might consider the use of a Buttonbar control.

Controls that Are Never Visible or Enabled

Generally, if a control is never visible or enabled it should be removed from the project to reduce complication and Windows resource requirements. Sometimes, invisible controls may serve a useful function. For example, invisible listboxes may be used for quick-and-dirty, no-code, auto-sorting storage for small amounts of text data.

Is *ClipControls = False* Property Usable?

Use of this Form, Frame, or Picturebox property can substantially increase user interface speed by repainting only the screen image of the object that has changed instead of the whole form. Use with care, though, because lightweight controls such as Labels and Images will be painted over if they ever overlap with any Windows graphical controls.

Is Related Code Kept in Same Module?

Don't scatter related functions over many different code modules. It makes it difficult to keep track of them, particularly if they are designed to implement a replaceable programming interface.

If you've got many different systems to interface to, it's much easier to swap different complete modules in and out than to hunt around for sets of individual functions.

Is *Me.Show* Used in *Form_Load()* for Improved Start-Up Impressions?

If your application does a lot of work at start-up, it's a good idea to get something on the screen immediately to reassure the user that something is happening. If you don't have a *splash screen* such as a bitmap of your corporate logo to show, put a Me.Show statement as soon as possible in the Form_Load() function.

VB3/VBA/VBDOS Portability

If you still need to support DOS versions of your software, you will have to accommodate the mismatch in available commands between the Windows versions and the DOS version of Visual Basic (which has not been updated since 1992).

For example, many commands such as PRINT USING are missing from Windows versions while the Access database functionality is missing from the DOS version.

Are Internal Name, Symbol, and DLL Tables Overloaded?

If you read the "Code Limitations" section in the "Specifications and Limitations" section in Appendix D of the Programmer's Guide manual, you will see that Visual Basic uses internal 64K tables that hold dynamic information used at run-time. The 16-bit version has tighter limitations than the 32-bit version, so be careful if you intend to reverse-migrate from 32-bit to 16-bit.

It's worth checking to make sure large projects don't push these limits. Common causes of this include large include files of DLL declarations supplied with third-party libraries or files of global constants generated by Help compilers. Look in the MSBASIC forum on CompuServe for VBSPAC.ZIP, which is an excellent program to analyze your code for potential overflow of these tables. Check for a Visual Basic 4.0 version (as Visual Basic 3.0 did not have a separate internal table for DLL declarations).

Run-Time Tests

Some tests have to be done on the program while it is running.

Windows Resource (GDI/Usr) Usage

If your application needs to run alongside other applications such as MS Office, you should do all you can to minimize its Windows resources, because Win3.1 systems (which limit you to 64K for each of their GDI and Usr tables) will still be used for a long time yet.

Verify that the amounts of free GDI and Usr resources are the same on application exit as when it started; if not, some of your components have not been correctly unloaded.

You can even take these checks down to function level if required. There's a Windows API function (GetFreeSystemResources) that you can call at appropriate times, writing the results to a file in a RAM disk so that speed doesn't suffer too much.

```
Declare Function GetFreeSystemResources Lib "User" (ByVal SysResType As Integer)
As Integer

For GDI, call GetFreeSystemResources(1),
For Usr, call GetFreeSystemResources(2).
```

If you want to go for this in a big way, download VBRIG (an error handler, code rigger by Brad Kaenel (72357,3523)) from the MSBASIC forum in CompuServe. (It's shareware, so don't forget to GO SWREG!)

Use VBRIG to bulk-add function calls to the entry and exit points of each sub or function in the project. You can then replace his VBRIGSTD.BAS module with your own 10-line one, consisting of a call to the GetFreeSystemResources() API function followed by an append of the data to a RAM disk file. You should Open and Close the file for each Append to ensure the RAM disk file is complete should your program crash.

Note that VBRIG was deliberately coded to be reversible. It does not rig any single-line If statements used to exit functions (because this would mean altering the line itself), so you must split lines like

```
If {condition} Then Exit Function
```

into

```
If {condition} Then
    Exit Function
End If
```

otherwise, these function exit points will be missed.

Profiling

Another thing you can use a VBRIGed project for is to write the time difference between sub exits and entries to your RAM disk file. You can then perhaps home in on the slow points of the program. This is of restricted use unless the application is being run by some kind of regression test/automation tool to give completely reproducible timings.

Be careful about the results of calling small functions many times because the overhead of doing this check can take a lot longer to execute than the function contents. Remove the rigging from such functions and try again.

You can also derive the number of times each function is called. The results may surprise you if there are timer functions with intervals set too low, for example. These results are also useful for regression test purposes in that you can derive a list of the routines in your system that are *not* exercised by your test scripts and create new scripts to address the omissions.

Are There Any Unnecessarily Loaded Forms?

Try printing the names of currently loaded forms in Form_Activate() events placed in every form. You might prefer to print to a file instead of the Debug object.

```
Private Sub Form_Activate ()
    Dim ptr As Integer

    For ptr = 0 To Forms.Count - 1
        Debug.Print Forms(ptr).Caption
    Next ptr
End Sub
```

This can be important from a security point of view because if you want users to be able to partially leave the application as far as its password-screen level, you want to be sure that forms containing the last user's data do not remain in memory.

Should Forms be Modal and/or Resizeable?

Modal forms demand that the user interact with them before allowing further progress. They are useful for handling serious errors, but you should almost always use Application Modal to prevent any further interaction with the application, rather than System Modal which prevents any interaction with the whole of Windows.

Are Different Windows Color Schemes and Font Sizes Supported?

You should try at least one color scheme different from the Windows default. You should also ensure that any Windows 95 or Plug-and-Play features, such as altering the screen resolution while your application is running, do not upset its operation.

Summary

Always remember that Prevention is better than cure. You should try to design your program to be testable. Test the components of your program at the earliest opportunity before the effects of the errors have time to propagate. Read the Visual Basic 4.0 manuals and a good book on software development theory *before* you start coding.

Creating Multi-User Applications

In this chapter, you'll learn about issues you'll encounter when you design, build, and install Visual Basic applications in a multiple-user environment. The topic of creating multi-user applications is very broad, so I'll concentrate on a handful of issues in this chapter. The focus will be the following:

- **General issues in multi-user programming.** Designing for multiple users from the start, distributing and installing your multi-user programs, and shared verses local resources.

- **Writing user-configurable applications.** Techniques you can use to make sure your Visual Basic application is easy for users to customize to their needs and tastes. You'll learn how to add features like storing the user's window size and position values, allowing for customized fonts and colors, and handling user preferences for program behaviors.

- **Microsoft Jet database locking.** High-level locking methods at the database and table level, and low-level locking at the page level. You'll also review the differences between pessimistic and optimistic locking, how to use Microsoft Jet Relation objects to improve locking integrity, and how to reduce locking conflicts by installing a lock table and performing batch updates from temporary tables to the master table.

- **Microsoft Jet security.** Techniques for establishing and maintaining the Microsoft Access SYSTEM Security profiles for your Visual Basic applications. You'll also learn about the limitations of the Microsoft Jet Security system.

Before I get into the details of coding multi-user features into your Visual Basic applications, I first want to touch on some points concerning multi-user programming in general.

Looking at General Issues in Multi-User Programming

Designing and creating multi-user applications is more than just making sure that you add error handlers to trap for database update conflicts. Good multi-user applications are designed with the user in mind. Applications that are well-designed, multi-user programs enable users to modify the program environment to fit their needs and preferences. Good multi-user applications also are aware of the division between shared and localized resources. Some configuration data might be shared with all users (location of needed files, system-level control parameters, and so on). Some other configuration data might be local to the logged-in users (their security profile, the last project data they were working on, and so on). Still other configuration data might be local to the physical workstation (type of hardware available, location of non-shared resources on the workstation, and so on). Good multi-user applications take all these factors into account.

After you design your multi-user application, you need to distribute and install it. You must decide whether your application will operate only in a multi-user setting or be allowed to function as a stand-alone program. You also need to make sure your program can locate and use all the needed resources, such as printers, modems, and disk drives. Finally, you need to make sure your program can locate and use any shared or local configuration information that might be stored on the workstation or at the network level.

Designing for Multiple Users

Before you begin coding your multi-user application, you should take time to think about the various multi-user aspects of your program. Will your application use a set of centrally located files? If so, you need to provide pointers in your program that will identify the location of these files. If you hard code these values into your program, you'll have trouble when you install it somewhere else.

Typically, "pointer gathering" is done at the start of the program using INI or registry settings and internal variables. If your application opens a central database file, for example, you can load the location for an INI or registry setting into your internal variable.

> **NOTE**
>
> Throughout this chapter, I refer to *INI settings* instead of *registry values*. The examples in this chapter all use the Visual Basic 4.0 `GetSetting` and `SaveSetting` statements. In 32-bit environments, these statements modify the Windows registry file. In 16-bit environments, these statements modify named INI files. Throughout the rest of this chapter, you'll see the words "INI settings." This will refer to the values stored in the 16-bit INI files and the values stored in the 32-bit registry file.

Listing 14.1 shows a typical technique for loading data from an INI setting into an internal variable. This routine usually is executed at the start of the program to establish the basic environment for the application.

> **NOTE**
>
> Listing 14.1 assumes the existence of some global variables and some predefined functions that use the INI-related statements. This code is part of a sample program that is covered in the section "Writing User-Configurable Applications," later in this chapter.

Listing 14.1. Loading INI settings into internal variables.

```
Public Sub LoadINIVars()
    '
    ' read ini values into internal variables
    '
    ' attempt to access settings
    If OpenINI() = False Then
        Unload Me    ' oops!
    End If
    '
    cDatabase = GetIniStr("System", "Database", "c:\source\chap14\vbu1401.mdb")
    cLocalPrinter = GetIniStr("System", "LocalPrinter", "No")
    cLocalModem = GetIniStr("System", "LocalModem", "No")
    '
    ' get form size and location info
    '
    nFormWidth = GetIniStr("Forms", Me.Name + ".Width", "6800")
    nFormHeight = GetIniStr("Forms", Me.Name + ".Height", "4550")
    nFormLeft = GetIniStr("Forms", Me.Name + ".Left", "1200")
    nFormTop = GetIniStr("Forms", Me.Name + ".Top", "1300")
    '
    ' get confirmation flag
    gblConfirm = UCase(GetIniStr("system", "Confirm", "YES"))
    '
    ' get color set
    gblColorSet = UCase(GetIniStr("system", "ColorSet", "Default"))
    '
End Sub
```

If your software will be using other system resources, such as modems or printers, you need to make sure that your program can locate the resources and that it provides error handlers to take care of instances when these resources are not responding. It is usually a good idea to test for the presence of these shared resources at the start of your program. If you need a modem to perform communications tasks with your program, for example, you should attempt to open and initialize the modem at startup. If it is not responding, you can tell users about the problem before they enter a great deal of data and click the Send key.

NOTE

Throughout the chapter, the term *Windows* is used to refer to all current flavors of the Microsoft Windows operating system—including Windows 3.1, Windows for Workgroups, Windows NT, and Windows 95. In cases where differences in the various flavors of Windows systems are important, the specific Windows version is mentioned in the text. Otherwise, you can assume that the behavior or feature discussed works the same in all cases.

Lastly, your application should allow individual users to customize their program environment to fit their own preferences. Whenever possible, you should let users choose the colors and fonts they prefer. The resulting selections should be stored by the users so that each user can have his or her own set of preferences. The values typically are stored in a local INI file in the same directory that contains the Windows executable.

However, there might be cases where this is not an acceptable solution. There are times when some configuration data must be stored in a central location in order to give application administrators access to the data. In this case, the configuration data can be stored in an INI-type file in a central location. This INI-type file can contain header sections that identify the configuration data by user. The sample INI file shown in Listing 14.2 is an example of storing multiple user data in a single INI file.

Listing 14.2. INI-type file with multiple-user settings.

```
[UserA.Settings]
LocalPrinter=Yes
ModemFound=No
ColorMonitor=Yes
[UserB.Settings]
LocalPrinter=No
ModemFound=Yes
ColorMonitor=No
```

Distributing and Installing Multiple-User Programs

When you finish coding your multi-user application, there are some additional items you should plan for when you distribute and install the program. If your application assumes the existence of INI files or other resources, you need to ship the application with a default INI file or add routines to your application that will create these INI files. The configuration file creation can be a special configuration applet or a part of the user program.

Using a Configuration Applet after Installation

If you must create files that will be used by all users, it usually is best to take care of this with a special configuration program that runs independently of the user application. A good example of this is a routine to create a set of new data tables at installation time. You can write a small applet that creates the database and then creates empty tables.

The advantage of creating files of this type on-site, instead of shipping them with the application, is that users now have a method for re-creating these files without having to perform a complete installation. Also, if users want to perform an installation to refresh some damaged programs, they don't need to worry about destroying their existing data at the same time.

Listing 14.3 shows how you might write a routine to create all your data tables. This routine can be part of an initial configuration program that is run immediately after installation.

Listing 14.3. Creating fresh data tables at configuration.

```
Public Sub NewData()
    '
    ' create a new database
    '
    Dim dbFile As Database
    Dim cDBFile As String
    Dim cTable1 As String
    Dim cTable2 As String
    Dim nTemp As Integer
    '
    ' set vars
    cDBFile = "c:\source\chap14\ch1401.mdb"
    cTable1 = "CREATE TABLE Table1 (CustID TEXT(10),CustName TEXT(30),CustType
    ➥TEXT(10));"
    cTable2 = "CREATE TABLE Table2 (CustType TEXT(10),TypeName TEXT(20));"
    '
    ' kill any current database
    nTemp = MsgBox("Ready to Delete Any Existing Database?", vbInformation +
    ➥vbYesNo, "Create Database")
    If nTemp = vbNo Then
        MsgBox "Create Database Canceled"
    Else
        On Error Resume Next
        Kill cDBFile
        On Error GoTo 0
        '
        ' create empty DB
        Set dbFile = DBEngine.CreateDatabase(cDBFile, dbLangGeneral)
        '
        ' create tables
        dbFile.Execute cTable1
        dbFile.Execute cTable2
        '
        ' add additional tables, indexes, relations, etc.
        '
        MsgBox "Database has been Created"
    End If
End Sub
```

Creating User Configuration Information within the Program

For configuration data that will be specific to each user, it usually is a good idea to add configuration routines to the user program. When the program is run for the first time at a workstation, these routines should create a configuration INI file that contains default values. The user then can modify these values at any time to customize the application. Because this configuration file is local, any changes made by one user will not affect other users at other workstations.

A simple method for incorporating auto-generation of local configuration files is to automatically create and populate the local INI file at initial startup. You can store default values for all INI settings in your program or in an ASCII file that you ship with the installation. These default values can be used at startup to create any missing settings. After the settings have been created, users should be able to use their version of the program to modify the settings they want.

Listing 14.4 shows how to write an INI-file `read` function that automatically creates missing entries by checking the return value from the `GetSettings` statement. If the return value is the same as the default value, the routine assumes that Windows could not find the INI setting and immediately calls the INI-file `write` function.

> **NOTE**
>
> This routine assumes that the proper user-defined functions and global variables exist. This code is taken from an example program reviewed in the section "Writing User-Configurable Applications," later in this chapter.

Listing 14.4. A GetINI routine that writes missing items.

```
Function GetIniStr(cSection As String, ByVal cItem As String, ByVal cDefault As
➡String)
    '
    ' this routine looks for cItem
    ' in section cSection. If it
    ' is not found, the item is
    ' written using the cDefault
    ' value.
    '
    Dim cTemp As String
    '
    ' try to get it
    cTemp = GetSetting(gblIniFile, cSection, cItem, cDefault)
    '
    ' returned default? may be missing, write it to be sure
    If Trim(UCase(cTemp)) = Trim(UCase(cDefault)) Then
        SaveSetting gblIniFile, cSection, cItem, cDefault
    End If
    '
    GetIniStr = cTemp    ' set return value
    '
End Function
```

Looking at Local versus Shared Resources

Some portions of a multi-user application must be shared among all users, such as central database files. Other portions, such as the local user preference INI file, must exist on the local workstation. Still other parts of an application, such as common DLL files or other program modules, can exist in either location. You should consider the advantages and disadvantages when determining the final placement of shared application resources.

Sharing Program Code from a Network Device

Placing shared resources in a central location makes it easy to maintain an application and can reduce the total amount of storage resources occupied by your application. Suppose that your application has a total of 1.5 MB of executable modules (EXEs and DLLs). You need to roll out this application to 50 users on the same network server. If you place a single copy of the application on a shared network disk, your total program storage is only 1.5 MB. If you store the program at each workstation, however, you'll be using 75 MB of disk space for the same program.

Although saving space is nice, there is the matter of program performance to consider, too. Sharing an application over a networked disk can dramatically decrease overall performance— not just for your application, but for the entire network. If your program makes numerous calls to executables stored on the server, server traffic can skyrocket, causing even unrelated programs to become bogged down.

In situations where the installation requires that your program work in a diskless workstation environment, you have no choice but to locate your programs on the remote disk. However, because of the potential performance drain, it is recommended that you install all executables at the workstation level.

Storing DLLs and OCX/VBX Files in the Windows Directory

Whether you are working in a diskless environment or at a powerful desktop workstation, you always should store any DLL, OCX, and VBX files in the \WINDOWS\SYSTEM directory.

> **NOTE**
>
> It is possible that you will have workstations that do not have a \WINDOWS\SYSTEM directory. Users can use any name they want when they install the Windows operating system. You can use the GetWinDir API to determine the actual name of the Windows launch directory and then locate the SYSTEM folder below that. To simplify the text, this chapter refers to the *\WINDOWS\SYSTEM* directory or the *\WINDOWS* directory. Just remember that some workstations might use other names for these locations.

In fact, if you do not store this information in the \WINDOWS\SYSTEM directory, you might run into serious problems. Windows assumes that the needed DLLs and other components will be stored in the SYSTEM directory; it looks there first. If the needed item is not found in the SYSTEM directory, the directory that contains the EXE file that is currently running is checked next. If you store your components (DLLs and so on) in the same directory as the EXE file, youll be okay as long as no one installs a component with the same name (possibly a different version) in the SYSTEM directory. If this does happen, you'll spend hours trying to figure out why your program is acting weird or hanging up entirely.

Always store DLLs, OCXs, VBXs, and other similar components in the user's \WINDOW\SYSTEM directory. This greatly reduces the possibility of encountering unexplained and difficult-to-diagnose fatal errors in your multi-user applications.

Writing User-Configurable Applications

Writing programs that can be configured for user preferences is an important part of creating any multi-user application. Users should be able to configure their own colors and fonts, arrange and size forms when appropriate, and control some aspects of program behavior (skip confirmations on deletes, display or hide a toolbar on the main form, and so on).

Most of this type of information can be stored in local INI-type configuration files. In the next several sections, we'll cover the use of INI files and explore several examples of user-configurable options you should consider for your multi-user programs.

Using INI Files to Store User Configuration Information

Multi-user applications need to allow for individual customization of selected aspects of the program. In the 16-bit Windows environment (Windows for WorkGroups and Windows 3.1), details about these customizations can be stored in a related INI file in the user's \WINDOWS directory. In the 32-bit Windows environment (Windows 95 and Windows NT), this information is stored in the registry file. It is easy to read and write INI data using Visual Basic 4.0 GetSettings and SaveSettings statements. In some cases, you will also need the GetWindowsDirectory API call. These can form the basis of a valuable set of library routines you can use in all your Visual Basic programs.

> **NOTE**
>
> This section shows how to store configuration information using the GetSettings and SaveSettings statements of Visual Basic 4.0. In 16-bit systems, these Visual Basic statements will modify an associated INI file in the Windows launch directory. In 32-bit systems, these statements will modify associated registry settings in the HKEY_CURRENT_USERS\Software\VB and VBA Program Settings area. If you plan to store shared settings in a 32-bit environment, you should not use the GetSettings and SaveSettings statements because these will always modify the Windows registry on the local workstation.

Listing 14.5 shows a short set of routines that make up a library file you can use in any Visual Basic program to read and write INI entries.

> **NOTE**
>
> This code is used in several code examples throughout this chapter. A completed version of this code library can be found in the \source\chap14\ directory of the disc included with this book.

Open a new project in Visual Basic, add a BAS module to the project, and enter the code in Listing 14.5 in the declaration section of the module.

Listing 14.5. Declaring LibINI Global variables.

```
Option Explicit

'
' *** ini api declarations
'
#If Win16 Then
Declare Function OSGetWindowsDirectory% Lib "Kernel" Alias "GetWindowsDirectory"
➥(ByVal a$, ByVal b%)
#End If
'
#If Win32 Then
Declare Function OSGetWindowsDirectory Lib "kernel32" Alias "GetWindowsDirectoryA"
➥(ByVal lpBuffer As String, ByVal nSize As Long) As Long
#End If

'
Global gblIniFile As String ' name of INI file
Global gblWinDir As String  ' name of Windows launch directory
```

Now add the function that will return the Windows launch directory. Create a new function called GetWinDir and enter the code shown in Listing 14.6.

Listing 14.6. Getting the Windows Launch directory.

```
Function GetWinDir() As String
    '
    ' get the Windows launch dir
    '
    Dim cTemp As String
    Dim nTemp As Integer
    '
    cTemp = String$(255, 32)     ' reserve space
    nTemp = OSGetWindowsDirectory(cTemp, 255) ' call API
    GetWinDir = Left$(cTemp, nTemp) ' set return value
End Function
```

Now create a new function called `WriteINIStr` and enter the code shown in Listing 14.7.

Listing 14.7. Writing an INI/Registry setting.

```
Function WriteINIStr(ByVal cSection, ByVal cItem, ByVal cDefault) As Integer
    '
    ' write cKeyName into cSection
    SaveSetting gblIniFile, cSection, cItem, cDefault
    WriteINIStr = True   ' in case they ask!
    '
End Function
```

Now, create a new function called `GetINIStr` and enter the code shown in Listing 14.8.

Listing 14.8. Reading an INI/Registry setting.

```
Function GetIniStr(cSection As String, ByVal cItem As String, ByVal cDefault As
➡String)
    '
    ' this routine looks for cItem
    ' in section cSection. If it
    ' is not found, the item is
    ' written using the cDefault
    ' value.
    '
    Dim cTemp As String
    '
    ' try to get it
    cTemp = GetSetting(gblIniFile, cSection, cItem, cDefault)
    '
    ' returned default? may be missing, write it to be sure
    If Trim(UCase(cTemp)) = Trim(UCase(cDefault)) Then
        SaveSetting gblIniFile, cSection, cItem, cDefault
    End If
    '
    GetIniStr = cTemp    ' set return value
    '
End Function
```

Notice that this routine does more than just read an INI entry. If the entry is determined to be missing, this routine automatically adds that entry, using the default value supplied. This makes it very easy to automatically create fully populated INI files when a user first starts up the newly installed application.

We need to add one more routine to our library. This routine will handle differences between the 16-bit and 32-bit versions of Windows. In 16-bit environments, all settings are stored in an ASCII text file. We will need to make sure that file is present and available to our 16-bit application. In the 32-bit environment, this routine just confirms the name of the registry key we will use.

Create a new function called OpenINI and add the following code, as in Listing 14.9.

Listing 14.9. Verifying the INI Settings source file.

```
Public Function OpenINI(Optional cININame As Variant)
    '
    ' For 32-bit
    '    set gblIniFile name for registry calls
    '
    ' For 16-bit
    '    set gblIniFile name for File calls
    '    if not there, create a new one
    '
    OpenINI = True   ' assume all goes OK
    '
    If IsMissing(cININame) Then ' no parm passed?
        cININame = App.EXEName  ' set to this app
    End If
    gblIniFile = Trim(cININame) ' clean up spaces
    '
    Dim nFile As Integer        ' for file channel
    Dim cFile As String         ' for file name
    '
    ' If we're running in 16-bit environment
    ' we have to get to a file in the Windows
    ' launch directory. We'll make sure it's
    ' there and create a new one if needed.
    '
    #If Win16 Then
        On Error Resume Next    ' keep quiet about errors
        nFile = FreeFile        ' get free file channel
        cFile = gblIniFile + ".INI" ' fill out file name
        Open cFile For Input As nFile   ' try to open it
        If Err <> 0 Then        ' some error
            If Err = 53 Then    ' was it 'FileNotFound?'
                Open cFile For Output As nFile  ' create it
            Else       ' uh-oh....
                MsgBox Error$, vbCritical, "Error opening INI File - " + Str(Err)
                OpenINI = False ' we failed!
            End If
        End If
        Close nFile 'close channel
    #End If
    '
End Function
```

Save this module with the name libINI.bas. Now let's add a bit of code to the main form of the project to show how the INI library works.

First add the form-level variables shown in Listing 14.10 to the form.

Listing 14.10. Adding form-level variables.

```
Option Explicit

'
' internal vars for INI values
'
Dim cDatabase As String
Dim cLocalPrinter As String
Dim cLocalModem As String
```

Next, create a subprocedure called LoadINIVars and add the code shown in Listing 14.11.

Listing 14.11. Loading the INI/Registry values.

```
Public Sub LoadINIVars()
    '
    ' read ini values into internal variables
    '
    ' attempt to access settings
    If OpenINI() = False Then
        Unload Me    ' oops!
    End If
    '
    cDatabase = GetIniStr("System", "Database", "c:\source\chap14\vbu1401.mdb")
    cLocalPrinter = GetIniStr("System", "LocalPrinter", "No")
    cLocalModem = GetIniStr("System", "LocalModem", "No")
    '
    ' get form size and location info
    '
    nFormWidth = GetIniStr("Forms", Me.Name + ".Width", "6800")
    nFormHeight = GetIniStr("Forms", Me.Name + ".Height", "4550")
    nFormLeft = GetIniStr("Forms", Me.Name + ".Left", "1200")
    nFormTop = GetIniStr("Forms", Me.Name + ".Top", "1300")
    '
    ' get confirmation flag
    gblConfirm = UCase(GetIniStr("system", "Confirm", "YES"))
    '
    ' get color set
    gblColorSet = UCase(GetIniStr("system", "ColorSet", "Default"))
    '
End Sub
```

This routine attempts to open the INI file (16-bit only). If it is not found (and a new file couldn't be created), an error is returned and the program is halted. If OpenINI returns TRUE, the routine attempts to read three INI settings in the file. Because of the behavior of your GetINIStr function, if these settings are missing from the INI file, they will be created with the default values.

Now add one more routine to the form. This will display the INI readings captured in the LoadINIVars routine. Place the code shown in Listing 14.12 in the Form_Activate event.

Listing 14.12. Adding code to the Form Activate event.

```
Private Sub Form_Activate()
    LoadINIVars ' read INI stuff
    Me.Cls
    Me.Print "gblIniFile="; gblIniFile
    Me.Print "cDatabase="; cDatabase
    Me.Print "cLocalPrinter="; cLocalPrinter
    Me.Print "cLocalModem="; cLocalModem
    '
End Sub
```

This routine first calls the INI read routine, and then displays the results on the form. Save this form as vbu1401.frm and save the project as vbu1401.vbp. Now run the project and view the results. Your screen should look like the screen shown in Figure 14.1.

FIGURE 14.1.

Displaying INI file results.

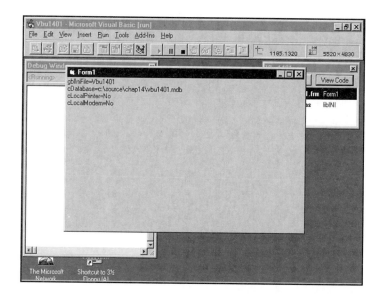

If you are running the 16-bit version of Visual Basic, you now have a new INI file in your \WINDOWS directory called vbu1401.ini. Use Notepad or some other ASCII editor to load and view this file. It should look like Listing 14.12.

If you are running the 32-bit version of Visual Basic, you now have a new set of entries in the Windows registry. Use RegEdit.EXE to open the registry and look under the key "HKEY_CURRENT_USERS\Software\VB and VBA Program Settings\vbu1401." You'll see the same values shown in Listing 14.13.

Listing 14.13. Results of 16-bit INI creation.

```
[System]
Database=c:\source\chap14\vbu14.mdb
LocalPrinter=No
LocalModem=No
```

Adjusting Window Placement and Size

A common user preference is the capability to remember the size and placement of program windows within the application. It always is annoying to have to continually rearrange windows on a screen each time you start the program. Listing 14.13 shows how this information can be stored and recalled the next time the program is started. Because this data is stored in the local INI file, multiple users can arrange their forms to their liking without affecting the forms arrangement for other users of the same application.

Add the form-level variables shown in Listing 14.14 to the declaration section of the form.

Listing 14.14. Adding Form Location variables.

```
'
' form size/location
Dim nFormWidth As Integer
Dim nFormHeight As Integer
Dim nFormLeft As Integer
Dim nFormTop As Integer
```

Now add the code shown in Listing 14.15, which will read the new INI settings at the end of the LoadINIVars routine.

Listing 14.15. Getting Form Location settings.

```
    '
    ' get form size and location info
    '
    nFormWidth = GetIniStr("Forms", Me.Name + ".Width", "6800")
    nFormHeight = GetIniStr("Forms", Me.Name + ".Height", "4550")
    nFormLeft = GetIniStr("Forms", Me.Name + ".Left", "1200")
    nFormTop = GetIniStr("Forms", Me.Name + ".Top", "1300")
    '
```

Notice that you are using the form name as part of the INI setting. This means that you can use this code to store different forms without changing your code.

WARNING

This code will not work properly if you are using multiple instances of the same form. Each of the instances will have the same name. Storing the form information using this routine would result in only one set of form values. You should consider modifying this routine to check for multi-instanced forms.

Now add the code that will use the variables to update the form properties. Add the lines shown in Listing 14.16 to the `Form_Activate` routine. Insert these lines right after the `LoadINIVars` line and before the `Me.Cls` line.

Listing 14.16. Using INI settings to resize the form.

```
'
' resize based on INI settings
'
Me.Left = nFormLeft
Me.Width = nFormWidth
Me.Height = nFormHeight
Me.Top = nFormTop
```

Finally, add the code that will update the INI file with the current form properties (see Listing 14.17). You'll do this in the `Form_Unload` event.

Listing 14.17. Saving the form location at the `Unload` event.

```
Private Sub Form_Unload(Cancel As Integer)
    '
    ' store form size & location
    '
    Dim lTemp As Long
    Dim cForm As String
    '
    cForm = Me.Name
    '
    lTemp = WriteINIStr("Forms", cForm + ".Top", Str(Me.Top))
    lTemp = WriteINIStr("Forms", cForm + ".Left", Str(Me.Left))
    lTemp = WriteINIStr("Forms", cForm + ".Width", Str(Me.Width))
    lTemp = WriteINIStr("Forms", cForm + ".Height", Str(Me.Height))
    '
End Sub
```

Now save this form and run it. The first time it runs, you'll see no change in the form's size or location. Now use your mouse to resize and move the form, and then close the form (use the standard form buttons, not the Visual Basic End button). Now restart the form. This time, the form is sized and located in the same way you left it (see Figure 14.2).

FIGURE 14.2.

Recalling the resized form.

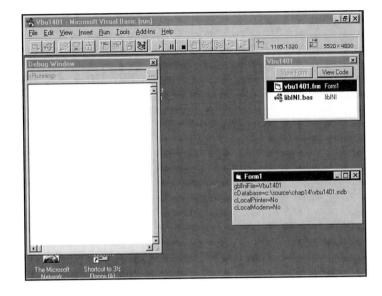

This example performs the resizing and relocating within the Form_Activate event. To keep the code simple, you usually should perform this task in the Form_Load event so that the user will not see the form move or resize.

Now use Notepad to load and view the modified vbu1401.ini file or registry entries. Your values for these settings may differ from the ones shown in Listing 14.18.

Listing 14.18. Saved Form Location settings.

```
[System]
Database=c:\source\chap14\vbu14.mdb
LocalPrinter=No
LocalModem=No

[Forms]
Form1.Width= 3210
Form1.Height= 3255
Form1.Left= 2715
Form1.Top= 1485
```

Customizing Colors

One of the most common user customizations is the capability to alter the colors displayed on the user's monitor. Providing this level of customization is essential for any good multi-user application. It also is a fairly straightforward task if you follow a short list of guidelines.

Using System Colors

The simplest way to provide users with the capability to customize the colors used within your program is to make sure your program uses the current Windows color scheme for all forms and controls. That way, whenever users change their Windows colors, your program follows suit. You can use a set of defined constants to get the current Windows color settings. Table 14.1 lists these defined constants, their values, and descriptions of what the constants represent in the Windows color scheme.

Table 14.1. System color table.

Constant	Value	Description
vbScrollBars	0x80000000	Scroll bar color
vbDesktop	0x80000001	Desktop color
vbActiveTitleBar	0x80000002	Color of title bar for active window
vbInactiveTitleBar	0x80000003	Color of title bar for inactive window
vbMenuBar	0x80000004	Menu background color
vbWindowBackground	0x80000005	Window background color
vbWindowFrame	0x80000006	Window frame color
vbMenuText	0x80000007	Color of text on menus
vbWindowText	0x80000008	Color of text in windows
vbTitleBarText	0x80000009	Color of text in caption, size box, and scroll arrow
vbActiveBorder	0x8000000A	Border color of active window
vbInactiveBorder	0x8000000B	Border color of inactive window
vbApplicationWorkspace	0x8000000C	Background color of multiple-document interface (MDI) applications
vbHighlight	0x8000000D	Background color of items selected in a control
vbHighlightText	0x8000000E	Text color of items selected in a control
vbButtonFace	0x8000000F	Color of shading on the face of command buttons
vbButtonShadow	0x80000010	Color of shading on the edge of command buttons

Constant	Value	Description
vbGrayText	0x80000011	Grayed (disabled) text
vbButtonText	0x80000012	Text color on pushbuttons
vbInactiveCaptionText	0x80000013	Color of text in an inactive caption
vb3Dhighlight	0x80000014	Highlight color for 3D display elements
vb3DDKShadow	0x80000015	Darkest shadow color for 3D display elements
vb3Dlight	0x80000016	Second lightest of the 3D colors after vb3DHighlight
vbInfoText	0x80000017	Color of text in ToolTips
vbInfoBackground	0x80000018	Background color of ToolTips

The values in Table 14.1 that you will most commonly use as the core of your color scheme are vbWindowBackground and vbWindowText for standard form background and form foreground values, respectively. These also can be used for standard control background and control foreground. You can use the vbApplicationWorkspace for the background color of your MDI forms. Use the vbHighlight and vbHightlighText values for any controls or text that should be highlighted (active input controls, selected values in a listbox, and so on). You can use any of the color values you want in your Visual Basic applications, but be sure you are not confusing the user by misapplying the color used by Windows (don't use the disabled text color (vbGrayText) for all your active input controls, for example).

Listing 14.19 shows how you can use the system color constants to set the colors for your forms. Create a new subprocedure in the vbu1401.vbp project and add this code.

Listing 14.19. Loading the current system colors.

```
Public Sub LoadSysColors()
    '
    ' load the colors from the current
    ' Windows color scheme
    '
    Dim ctlTemp As Control
    '
    ' set colors for all controls on form
    On Error Resume Next
    For Each ctlTemp In Me.Controls
        ctlTemp.BackColor = vbWindowBackground
        ctlTemp.ForeColor = vbWindowText
    Next
```

continues

Listing 14.19. continued

```
On Error GoTo 0
'
' set colors for form itself
Me.BackColor = vbApplicationWorkspace
Me.ForeColor = vbWindowText
'
End Sub
```

The code in Listing 14.18 loops through all the controls on the form and attempts to set their foreground and background colors to match the standard colors for the current color scheme. Notice the On Error Resume Next and On Error Goto 0 statements. This is done to prevent error messages from occurring if you try to set colors for controls that have no ForeColor or BackColor properties. Because the idea is to have your application change whenever the Windows color scheme changes, you do not save the colors setting in the user's INI file.

Add a line to the Form_Load event that calls the LoadSysColors routine. Place this line right after the LoadINIVars line. Now save and run the project to see the slightly different color scheme you now have for the sample program.

Using Custom Colors

If you want to give users the capability to set and retain their own color values, you need to provide an input form for them to select their desired colors. In our example, we will stick to the standard foreground and background colors for the input and form controls. Use Figure 14.3 as a guide in laying out new controls on the existing form.

FIGURE 14.3.

Laying out the custom color form.

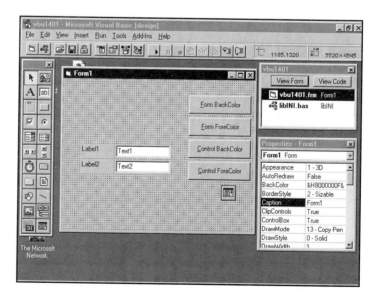

Add a single command button to the form. Set its Name property to cmdColor and then use Copy and Paste to create a command button array with four members (0..3). After adding two text controls and two label controls, add a single common dialog control. You'll use that to call up the Windows colors dialog box.

First add the form-level variables shown in Listing 14.20 to the declaration section of the default form.

Listing 14.20. Declaring constants for custom colors.

```
'
' colors
'
Dim lUserColor(4) As Long
Const vbuFormBG = 1
Const vbuFormFG = 2
Const vbuControlBG = 3
Const vbuControlFG = 4
```

Now add the code shown in Listing 14.21 to the cmdColor_Click event.

Listing 14.21. Control routine for color settings.

```
Private Sub cmdColor_Click(Index As Integer)
    '
    ' handle user color settings
    '
Select Case Index
        Case 0
            ' form back color
            CommonDialog1.DialogTitle = "Select Form Background Color"
            CommonDialog1.ShowColor
            lUserColor(Index + 1) = CommonDialog1.Color
        Case 1
            ' form fore color
            CommonDialog1.DialogTitle = "Select Form Foreground Color"
            CommonDialog1.ShowColor
            lUserColor(Index + 1) = CommonDialog1.Color
        Case 2
            ' control back color
            CommonDialog1.DialogTitle = "Select Control Background Color"
            CommonDialog1.ShowColor
            lUserColor(Index + 1) = CommonDialog1.Color
        Case 3
            ' control fore color
            CommonDialog1.DialogTitle = "Select Control Foreground Color"
            CommonDialog1.ShowColor
            lUserColor(Index + 1) = CommonDialog1.Color
    End Select
    '
    ' set object colors
    SetUserColors
    '
End Sub
```

Listing 14.21 calls the Color dialog box for each designated color value. The returned color is stored in the lUserColor array, and then the objects are updated with the current color settings.

Now add the routine that actually uses the values set by the user to set the Color properties. Create a new subprocedure called SetUserColors and add the code shown in Listing 14.22.

Listing 14.22. Update controls with selected colors.

```
Public Sub SetUserColors()
    '
    ' set the form and controls
    ' to the selected colors
    '
    Dim ctlTemp As Control
    '
    ' first the form
    Me.BackColor = lUserColor(vbuFormBG)
    Me.ForeColor = lUserColor(vbuFormFG)
    '
    ' now all controls
    On Error Resume Next
    For Each ctlTemp In Form.Controls
        ctlTemp.BackColor = lUserColor(vbuControlBG)
        ctlTemp.ForeColor = lUserColor(vbuControlFG)
    Next
    On Error GoTo 0
    '
End Sub
```

Now add the code to the Form_Unload event that will write these values out to the INI file (see Listing 14.23).

Listing 14.23. Saving the selected colors.

```
lTemp = WriteINIStr("forms", cForm + ".formBG", Str(lUserColor(lFormBG)))
lTemp = WriteINIStr("forms", cForm + ".formFG", Str(lUserColor(lFormFG)))
lTemp = WriteINIStr("forms", cForm + ".controlBG", Str(lUserColor(lControlBG)))
lTemp = WriteINIStr("forms", cForm + ".controlFG", Str(lUserColor(lControlFG)))
    '
```

And finally, add the code that reads the INI settings at startup and sets the initial color values (see Listing 14.24).

Listing 14.24. Reading the saved color settings.

```
Public Sub LoadUserColors()
    '
    ' load colors from ini file
    '
```

```
    Dim cTemp As String
    '
    cTemp = GetIniStr("Forms", Me.Name + ".formBG", Str(Me.BackColor))
    lUserColor(lFormBG) = Val(cTemp)
    '
    cTemp = GetIniStr("Forms", Me.Name + ".formFG", Str(Me.ForeColor))
    lUserColor(lFormFG) = Val(cTemp)
    '
    cTemp = GetIniStr("Forms", Me.Name + ".controlBG", Str(Text1.BackColor))
    lUserColor(lControlBG) = Val(cTemp)
    '
    cTemp = GetIniStr("Forms", Me.Name + ".controlFG", Str(Text1.ForeColor))
    lUserColor(lControlFG) = Val(cTemp)
    '
    SetUserColors
End Sub
```

Add the following line to the Form_Activate event right after the LoadSysColors line. This forces the user colors onto the form at startup:

LoadUserColors

Now save and run the vbu1401.vbp project. The first time you run this, you won't see any difference in the color scheme. After you use the command buttons to select your colors, exit the form (don't use the Visual Basic Stop button). The next time you start the program, you'll see the colors you selected instead of the original colors.

Controlling Program Behavior Options

Another way to make sure your multi-user applications are able to handle individual user configuration is to allow users to control some aspects of the program behavior. Advanced users might not need to see a confirmation message each time they attempt to update a value on-screen, for example, but novice users might like the feature. You can make this a user-configurable feature by adding a few lines of code and a new INI setting.

The code shown in Listing 14.25 adds a confirmation dialog box to the color setting command buttons. Add this code to the cmdColor_Click event. This code replaces the single SetUserColors line that is already in the routine.

Listing 14.25. Adding an optional confirmation dialog box.

```
    '
    ' check for confirmation first
    If gblConfirm = "YES" Then
        nTemp = MsgBox("Update Current Color Scheme?", vbInformation + vbYesNo,
        ➥"Color Configuration")
    Else
        nTemp = vbYes
    End If
    '
```

continues

Listing 14.25. continued

```
' if ok, then update colors
If nTemp = vbYes Then
    SetUserColors    ' set colors
End If
'
```

This code first checks to see whether a confirmation message should be sent, and then acts accordingly. Be sure to add a line at the top of the routine to initialize the nTemp variable as an integer:

```
dim nTemp as integer
```

You also need to add a new line to the declaration section:

```
dim gblConfirm as string
```

Now add the following lines to the LoadINIVars routine:

```
'
' get confirmation flag
gblConfirm = UCase(GetIniStr("system", "Confirm", "YES"))
'
```

Now save and run the project. When you attempt to change a color, you'll see a confirmation message (see Figure 14.4).

FIGURE 14.4.

Displaying the optional confirmation message.

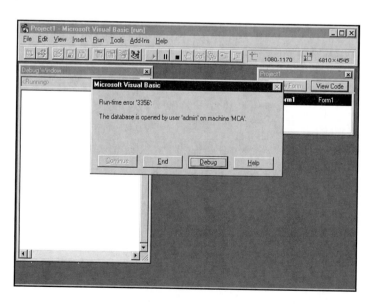

Load the vbu1401.ini file into Notepad, change the Confirm setting in the [System] section to No, and rerun the program. Now you will not see any confirmation when you attempt to change colors.

Usually applications provide check-off menu items to toggle these types of features on and off. The following listings add this menu feature to the current project. At the same time, the examples show another recommended feature for your user-configurable applications. The Preferences menu enables users to restore the original color scheme. This is highly recommended because users often will create unusable color schemes and will want to immediately restore the default values to clear out the unwanted selections.

Add one more line to the `declarations` section of the form. Place this line in the `colors` section of the listing:

```
Dim gblColorSet As String
```

Now create a subprocedure called `LoadDefaultColors` and enter the code shown in Listing 14.26. This routine resets the color variables to the initial startup values.

Listing 14.26. Loading the default colors.

```
Public Sub LoadDefaultColors()
    '
    ' load the original color set
    '
    lUserColor(vbuFormBG) = &H8000000F
    lUserColor(vbuFormFG) = &H80000012
    lUserColor(vbuControlBG) = &H80000005
    lUserColor(vbuControlFG) = &H80000008
    '
    SetUserColors
End Sub
```

Now add the code that will read the new INI setting to the `LoadINIVars` routine:

```
    '
    ' get color set
    gblColorSet = UCase(GetIniStr("system", "ColorSet", "Default"))
```

Then add the code to the `Form_UnLoad` event that will save the new INI value (see Listing 14.27). Also, wrap the lines that store the form color INI settings in an `If...Then...End If` structure. You only want to save the colors if they are the `User` settings.

Listing 14.27. Deciding which color scheme to use.

```
If gblColorSet = "USER" Then
        lTemp = WriteINIStr("forms", cForm + ".formBG", Str(lUserColor(vbuFormBG)))
        lTemp = WriteINIStr("forms", cForm + ".formFG", Str(lUserColor(vbuFormFG)))
        lTemp = WriteINIStr("forms", cForm + ".controlBG",
        ➡Str(lUserColor(vbuControlBG)))
        lTemp = WriteINIStr("forms", cForm + ".controlFG",
        ➡Str(lUserColor(vbuControlFG)))
    End If
    '
    lTemp = WriteINIStr("System", "ColorSet", gblColorSet)
```

Now add the menu to the project. Use Table 14.2 as a guide.

Table 14.2. Menu table for project vbu1401.vbp.

Caption	Menu
&File	mnuFile
E&xit	mnuFileExit
&Preferences	mnuPref
&Default Colors	mnuPrefDefaultColor
&System Colors	mnuPrefSysColor
&UserColors	mnuPrefUserColor

Now add the code shown in Listing 14.28 for each of the menu items.

Listing 14.28. Code for handling menu selections.

```
Private Sub mnuPrefDefaultColor_Click()
    '
    mnuPrefUserColor.Checked = False
    mnuPrefSysColor.Checked = False
    mnuprefdefaultcolor.Checked = True
    gblColorSet = "DEFAULT"
    LoadDefaultColors
    '
End Sub

Private Sub mnuPrefSysColor_Click()
    '
    mnuprefdefaultcolor.Checked = False
    mnuPrefUserColor.Checked = False
    mnuPrefSysColor.Checked = True
    gblColorSet = "SYSTEM"
    LoadSysColors
    '
End Sub

Private Sub mnuPrefUserColor_Click()
    '
    mnuprefdefaultcolor.Checked = False
    mnuPrefSysColor.Checked = False
    mnuPrefUserColor.Checked = True
    gblColorSet = "USER"
    LoadUserColors
    '
End Sub

Private Sub mnuFileExit_Click()
    Unload Me
End Sub
```

These routines set the proper menu check item, update the color INI variable, and update the color set itself. Now you need to modify the `Form_Activate` routine to initialize the proper color scheme at startup. Replace the calls to `LoadSysColors` and `LoadUserColors` with the lines of code shown in Listing 20.29.

Listing 20.29. Using the color setting to activate menus.

```
'
Select Case gblColorSet
    Case "DEFAULT"
        mnuPrefDefaultColor_Click
    Case "SYSTEM"
        mnuPrefSysColor_Click
    Case "USER"
        mnuPrefUserColor_Click
 End Select
'
```

Now the program will read the color set flag to determine the color set to use. If the color set flag is set to USER, the routine loads the user values from the INI file and updates the form.

Save and run the project. When you load the project, the default color scheme appears. You can change that by selecting a new scheme from the menu. You still can update the user color set and save that, too.

These are just a few examples of how you can design your application to allow multiple users to have their own customized version of your Visual Basic program. You can expand on each of the examples here to improve their flexibility and increase the number of options and features you allow your users to customize.

Examining Microsoft Jet Database Locking Issues

Probably the most frequently talked about multi-user programming issue for Visual Basic (or any other language) is that of database locking. Although all database programmers must deal with this issue in some fashion, Visual Basic programmers have the somewhat dubious honor of having to deal with database locking in a rather unique environment. The Microsoft Jet database engine provides three levels of locking within databases:

- **Database level.** Locks the entire database for only one user.
- **Table or recordset level.** Locks a complete table or all tables involved in a recordset query statement.
- **Page level.** Locks all records that reside within a physical page of data.

Those familiar with the common PC database packages (dBASE, FoxPro, Paradox, and so on) will notice that an important additional locking level is missing from this list: record-level locking. The Microsoft Jet database engine does not provide record-level locking for the native database format (Microsoft Access MDB-type databases) and only provides record-level locking when the Microsoft Jet is used to directly open compatible non-Microsoft Jet databases, such as FoxPro, Paradox, and so on.

> **NOTE**
>
> It is important to note that the Microsoft Jet database engine is not the only Microsoft data engine that currently lacks record-level locking. The most current version of Microsoft SQL Server as of this writing (6.0) is also a page-locking database engine.

In this section, you'll review the three locking levels provided by Microsoft Jet, focusing more time on the issues related to page-level locking. This chapter also contains three other techniques for reducing the occurrence of locking conflicts and speeding the processing of Visual Basic database programs. These other techniques include the use of Visual Basic Data Access Object Relation objects to improve cross-table integrity and locking, the use of a manual lock table to reduce unwanted lock conflicts when updating databases, and a method of employing temporary local batch input tables to speed data entry and reduce the need for constant access to busy database tables.

You May Not Need to Lock It

Although it is essential to understand how Microsoft Jet locking behavior affects your multi-user applications, it is even more important to know when locking is an appropriate way to solve your programming problems. Typically, locking methods are used whenever database updates (adds, edits, or deletes) occur. In these cases, the locking produces a static condition in the database until the update is completed. There are other times when your Visual Basic program might need to ensure a static database to properly perform critical operations, such as totals calculations or lengthy report production.

Although some of these problems can be solved by locking the required tables or the entire database during the operation, it is not always necessary to do so. Time-sensitive calculations and reporting can be performed on a private copy of the needed data tables. These private tables can be created at the moment the calculation or report is to be performed, and then destroyed at the end of the critical process.

Listing 14.30 shows how you can use table copies to increase integrity without using table locking when starting a lengthy set of reports for an accounting system.

Listing 14.30. Using table copies for long reports.

```
Public Sub ProcMonthEndReports()
    '
    ' create copies of required tables
    '
    db.Execute "SELECT Master.* INTO MER_Master FROM Master;"
    db.Execute "SELECT Trans.* INTO MER_Trans FROM Trans;"
    db.Execute "SELECT Orders.* INTO MER_Orders FROM Orders;"
    '
    ' now run reports
    ReportMonthlyTrans' report transactions
    ReportMonthlyOrders' report orders
    '
    ' kill temporary tables
    db.Execute "DROP TABLE MER_Master;"
    db.Execute "DROP TABLE MER_Trans;"
    db.Execute "DROP TABLE MER_Orders;"
    '
End Sub
```

Using this technique often can reduce the number of database update conflicts you encounter in your program. It also can increase processing speed because users performing updates never experience any "hits" on their tables during the reporting process. Reports also can run faster for the same reason.

If you need to perform mass updates to database tables, you cannot use the copy method because you need to act on "live" data throughout the update process. In these cases, you should consider database or table-level locking for your solution.

High-Level Locking

High-level locking schemes available within the Microsoft Jet engine include locking at the database level and at the data table or recordset level. This locking level is handy when you need to perform mass updates on one or more tables and you want to reduce the chance of encountering update conflicts during the process.

Typically, database-level locking is used when your update operation will affect more than one table in the database. A good example of this kind of operation is an update that performs mass changes to the part numbers in an inventory database. It is likely that this part number appears in not only the master parts table, but also in pending order tables, return or reject item tables, and other control and report tables. Changing the part number in just one record can affect several tables within the database. If you have a busy application (a great deal of traffic and/or many users), it's quite likely that someone will be holding at least one record that contains the part number you are updating. If so, your entire update process could be halted unless you clear all users out of the system before you start the update.

Locking at the table or recordset level typically is used when your update operation will affect multiple records within the same table or recordset. A good example of this operation is the mass removal of all records for a specific customer from the history table of a revenue accounting system. Depending on the size of the data table, this operation could affect hundreds of records. You can reduce the chance that an operation of this type will fail by locking other users out of the table before you begin.

Database Locking

You should consider using database-level locking whenever you are about to perform a mass update (or delete) operation that will affect more than one table within the database. Keep in mind that the existence of enforced database integrity relation objects can widen the effects of even a simple single-record update. If you plan on deleting a single row from the master table of a database where you have well-defined and enforced relationships to several related transaction and history tables, for example, this single delete could affect tens of records in several tables within the database. If you plan on deleting several rows from the same master table, you easily could be up for deleting hundreds of records from the database.

To lock a database, you must open it for exclusive use. This prevents any other users from opening the database until you close the database completely. You can open a database for exclusive use by setting the Exclusive property of the data control to True or by using the optional Exclusive parameter in the OpenDatabase method (see Listing 14.31).

Listing 14.31. Opening a database for exclusive use.

```
Private Sub Form_Load()
    Dim db As Database
    '
    ' open db exclusively
    Set db = WorkSpaces(0).OpenDatabase("c:\source\chap14\ch1402.mdb", True)
    MsgBox "Database Opened Successfully", vbInformation, "Open DB"
    '
End Sub
```

If you attempt to open a database exclusively and there is at least one other program that has the database open, you'll get an error 3356: Database is opened by user *username* on machine *machinename* (see Figure 14.5).

You may also get an error 3196, Couldn't use *database name*; database already in use, or an error 3045, Couldn't use *name*; file already in use.

You can add logic to your Visual Basic program that traps for these errors and tells users to attempt to open the database later. You should add this code to the startup of your application if you intend to use database-level locking anywhere in your program (see Listing 14.32).

FIGURE 14.5.

Attempting to open a locked database.

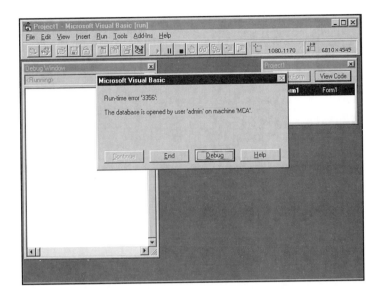

Listing 14.32. Trapping exclusive open errors.

```
Private Sub Form_Load()
    Dim db As Database
    '
    ' open db exclusively
    On Error GoTo FormLoadErr
    '
    Set db = OpenDatabase("c:\source\chap14\ch1402.mdb", True)
    MsgBox "Database Opened Successfully", vbInformation, "Open DB"
    '
    GoTo FormLoadExit
    '
FormLoadErr:
    If Err = 3356 or Err = 3196 or Err = 3045 Then
        MsgBox "Database Locked for Maintenance - Try again later", vbCritical,
        ➡"Open DB"
    Else
        MsgBox Error$, vbCritical, "Error " + Str(Err)
    End If
    Unload Me
    End
    '
FormLoadExit:
    '
End Sub
```

When you are using the Visual Basic data control to open the database with the Exclusive property set to True, you can trap for error 3196 by placing the error logic in the Error event of the data control, as shown in Listing 14.33.

Listing 14.33. Friendly message for exclusive open errors.

```
Private Sub Data1_Error(DataErr As Integer, Response As Integer)
    If DataErr = 3356 or DataErr = 3196 or DataErr = 3045 Then
        MsgBox "Database Locked for Maintenance - Try again later", vbCritical,
        ➥"open DB"
    Else
        MsgBox Error$, vbCritical, "Error " + Str(Err)
        Unload Me
        End
    End If
End Sub
```

Table and Recordset Locking

Table- and recordset-level locking should be used whenever you plan to perform mass updates on a single table or recordset (see Listing 14.34). If you plan to update all the wholesale prices in the inventory file, for example, you should lock the inventory price table before you begin.

Listing 14.34. Using table- and recordset-level locking to perform many updates.

```
Public Sub UpdatePrices()
    '
    ' update all inventory wholesale prices
    '
    Dim dbFile As Database
    Dim rsTable As Recordset
    '
    ' open db
    Set dbFile = DBEngine.OpenDatabase("c:\source\chap14\ch1402.mdb")
    '
    ' open table exclusively
    Set rsTable = dbFile.OpenRecordset("InvPrice", dbOpenTable, dbDenyRead)
    '
    ' perform mass update
    '
    On Error Resume Next    ' ignore errors
    Workspaces(0).BeginTrans ' start trans tracking
    While Not rsTable.EOF    ' for every row
        rsTable.Edit         ' start edit
        rsTable.Fields("WholesalePrice") = rsTable.Fields("WholesalePrice") * 1.05
        rsTable.Update       ' end edit
    Wend                     ' get another
    If Err = 0 Then          ' no errors
        Workspaces(0).CommitTrans    ' final update
        MsgBox "Wholesale Prices Updated", vbInformation, "Inventory"
    Else                     ' trouble
        Workspaces(0).Rollback   ' undo all edits
        MsgBox "Wholesale Price Update Failed", vbCritical, "Error " + Str(Err)
    End If
    On Error GoTo 0          ' tell me about errors!
    '
    ' close and release lock
    dbFile.Close
End Sub
```

Notice the use of transaction processing in Listing 14.33. If any error occurs during the update, the entire process can be rolled back. The use of transaction keywords is highly recommended whenever you perform mass updates to databases.

> **TIP**
>
> You might have noticed that we used a `While...Wend` loop to perform the mass update instead of using a single SQL Update query like `UPDATE InvPrice SET WholesalePrice = WholesalePrice * 1.05`. The SQL line is easier to code and much faster than the program loop. However, if you open the table with a `dbDenyRead` option, Visual Basic will not let you `Execute` an update query against the same table.

You can open a table for exclusive use by using the Visual Basic data control, setting the `Options` property to 2 (`dbDenyRead`), and filling in the `DataSource` property with the name of the table you want to lock. This can be done at design time or at runtime with Visual Basic code.

The code example in Listing 14.35 sets the `Options` property of a data control in order to perform an exclusive table open.

Listing 14.35. Opening a table exclusively with the Data control.

```
'
' set to open table exclusively
'
Data1.Options = 2
Data1.DatabaseName = c:\source\chap14\ch1402.mdb
Data1.RecordSource = InvPrice
```

If your Visual Basic program will perform any table locks, you should provide error-handling code in all your startup routines or any other location that attempts to open a table. You can trap for Error 3008, `Table tablename is exclusively locked` and Error 3009, `Couldn't lock table name; currently in use`. Add this code in the same module that contains the `OpenRecordSet` statement. If you are using the Visual Basic data control, add the error trapping logic to the `Error` event of the data control.

Locking at the recordset level affects all underlying tables used to make up the data set. If you have only one table as the source of the recordset, you will see the same effects you see when you perform a lock on a table object. However, if your recordset is the product of a complex query that contains `JOIN`s, `UNION`s, or subqueries, the lock could affect several tables at once.

For example, the query shown in Listing 14.36 contains a `JOIN` statement that combines two tables into a single query.

Listing 14.36. Example of a multi-table update.

```
SELECT [Department Name],
FirstName & " " & LastName AS Name
FROM Departments LEFT JOIN Employees
ON Departments.[Department ID] = Employees.[Department ID]
ORDER BY [Department Name];
```

This query affects two tables (Departments and Employees). If this query were used to create a locked recordset, both tables would be locked to all users.

Although multi-table recordset locking is very useful when performing mass updates, it can be annoying in a multi-user environment. Because multiple tables are affected, it often is difficult to successfully open a locked recordset in a busy application. Also, once the recordset is locked, it is possible that many users will be adversely affected by the lock operation. This can lead to numerous access denials, attempted re-reads, and time-out conditions. All this might make users think your application is coming loose at the hinges! Because the effects of a recordset lock can be far-reaching, it is recommended that you use it sparingly, if at all. If you need to perform an update on a complex, multi-table recordset, consider performing a database lock before you begin the update process.

Low-Level Locking

The lowest level of locking provided by the Microsoft Jet database engine is at the page level. A page is always 2K in size. Page locking is automatic and cannot be turned on or off through Visual Basic code or via any property settings. Each time you attempt to save or edit a record, the Microsoft Jet automatically locks a page of data.

A data page can contain one or more records, depending on the size of the record. If the data record is 2K in size, each data page contains a single data record. If the data record is 200 bytes in size, then each data page contains 10 records. If a data record is larger than 2K, Microsoft Jet locks all the pages needed to lock an entire data record.

The Microsoft Jet database engine has two forms of low-level page locking: *pessimistic* (the default) and *optimistic*. Under pessimistic locking, data pages are locked as soon as a user begins to edit a record. Under optimistic locking, data pages are locked only at the moment a user attempts to save the updated record to the database. In both pessimistic and optimistic locking, the page lock stays active until the Edit operation is completed successfully or canceled by the user.

Page-Locking Option

You can set the page-locking option (pessimistic or optimistic) by setting the LockEdits property of the record set. When LockEdits = True, pessimistic locking is in place. When LockEdits = False, optimistic locking is in place. The code examples in Listing 14.37 show how this is done.

Listing 14.37. Examples of page-level locking.

```
' setting page locking with the data control
Data1.Recordset.LockEdits = True ' pessimistic locking
Data2.Recordset.LockEdits = False ' optimistic locking
'
' setting page locking with Visual Basic code
rsObject1.LockEdits = True ' pessimistic locking
rsObject2.LockEdits = False ' optimistic locking
'
```

Pessimistic Locking

Pessimistic locking is the default page-locking method. Under the pessimistic locking scheme, pages are locked when the Edit method is invoked using Visual Basic code. If you are using the Visual Basic data control, the page is locked when the current record is selected using the reposition event. The lock stays in effect until the Visual Basic code Update or Cancel method is used or when the record pointer is advanced past the previously locked record using the data control.

Under pessimistic locking, the data pages stay locked the longest amount of time (from Edit to Update). Once USERA begins to edit a record, for example, that record cannot be edited by USERB until USERA commits an Udpate or Cancel operation to match the Edit that started the page lock. This ensures the greatest level of database integrity because both users cannot edit the same record at the same time.

The disadvantage of pessimistic locking is that the long locks increase the odds that users will encounter page-locking conflicts. This is especially true if your data tables have small record sizes. Because all locking is done in 2K increments, updates of small records result in page locks in several records at the same time. If a page contains twenty 100-byte records, for example, each time USERA edits record 1, USERB will not be able to edit records 1 through 100 (but USERB can edit record 101).

There are several possible errors that can occur within your Visual Basic program if you attempt to edit a record that is on a data page that is already locked. The most common errors you'll encounter are Error 3260 and Error 3197. Error 3260 occurs whenever you attempt to edit a record that is stored on a page that is already locked by another user or program. You can handle this error by attempting a read at another time. Error 3197 occurs when your program attempts to read a record that has been updated or deleted since you last refreshed the data set. You can handle this error by reloading the record into the data set (usually by invoking the Edit method again). Refer to Listing 14.38 as an example.

Listing 14.38. Handling page lock errors during edits.

```
Public Sub PageLockErrors(LockErr As Integer)
    '
    ' handle errors due to page locks
    '
    Static nTries As Integer
    Dim nMaxTries As Integer
    Dim nLoop As Integer
    Dim nTemp As Integer
    '
    nMaxTries = 3
    '
    Select Case LockErr
        Case 3197
            ' data changed
            rsObject.Edit      ' re-read changed record
        Case 3260, 3816
            ' currently locked
            nTries = nTries + 1 ' try again
            If nTries > nMaxTries Then   ' too manytimes?
                nTemp = MsgBox(Error, vbRetryCancel, "Error " + Str(Err))
                If nTemp = vbRetry Then ' user said try again
                    nTries = 1  ' start all over
                End If
            End If
    End Select
    '
    DBEngine.Idle   ' free up old locks
    DoEvents                 ' let messages catch up
    '
    For nLoop = 1 To 2000  ' 2000 millisecond pause
        ' empty loop
    Next nLoop
    Resume
    '
End Sub
```

Notice the use of the Idle and DoEvents methods in the error handler in Listing 14.38. These two lines allow Visual Basic and Windows to pass any backlogged messages to each other that may relate to old page locks that are no longer active.

The key to handling these errors is to trap for the error at the moment the user attempts the edit. If you are using the data control, you can place your error-handling logic in the Error event of the control. If you are using Visual Basic code, place the error handler in the same routine that invokes the Edit method (see Listing 14.39).

Listing 14.39. Basic approach to handling edit errors.

```
On error goto LocalErr
rsTable.Edit
'
' more code to edit record
'
```

```
rsTable.Update
'
Exit Sub
'
LocalErr:
Call PageLockErrors Err
```

If you are using the data control, you can place the same logic that is in the PageLockErrors routine directly into the Error event of the control, or you can call the error handler, passing the error code into the remote handler.

Optimistic Locking

Under the optimistic locking scheme, pages are locked only during the time the actual physical Update method is in operation. This is the shortest possible page-locking method. The advantage of this method is that the chance that two users will both perform updates on the same page at the same time is very small.

The main disadvantage of the optimistic locking scheme is that is it possible for two different users to edit the same record (not page) at the same time. This can result in locking errors at update time. If USERA begins to edit record 1 and then USERB begins to edit record 1, and then USERB saves record 1 back to the data set, USERA receives a locking error when attempting to save record 1 back to the data set. This is because USERB changed the data that USERA initially read; USERA has an outdated copy of record 1. The only way to remedy this situation is for USERA to abandon the update operation, read in USERB's version of the record, and start editing again (let's hope USERB doesn't do the same thing again!).

The most common locking errors received under optimistic locking are Errors 3186, 3260, and 3197. Error 3186 occurs when another user has locked the page you are attempting to update. Errors 3260 and 3197 were discussed in the preceding section, "Pessimistic Locking." Error 3186 should be handled in the same way 3260 is handled—clear any locks and try again.

Page Locks and Adding New Records

Regardless of which page-locking scheme you are using (pessimistic or optimistic), lock conflicts for adding new records always occur at the moment your program attempts to save the new record to the data set. This is the same scenario as updating an existing record under optimistic locking. Even though you might be using pessimistic locks for all existing records, you still will see update errors when users encounter page locks while adding new records.

If your application has several users entering data at the same time, you are likely to see many update errors. This is because all new records are added to the last data page of the data set. If you have five people entering new data, you have five people all attempting to lock the same data page. Also, the shorter the record, the more likely users are to see data page locks.

Sections later in the chapter show you a few techniques for reducing update conflicts.

Transactions and Locking

Page-level locking is affected by the use of the BeginTrans, CommitTrans, and RollBack methods in Visual Basic. When you are performing a transaction set, all page locks established during the transaction set are maintained from the time the BeginTrans method is invoked until the CommitTrans or Rollback method is invoked. This can lead to several page locks on one or more tables.

In Listing 14.40, every row of the data table is affected by the update within the transaction. This means that, in effect, you have created a table-level lock. If you attempt this while others have one or more pages locked, you will not be able to complete the transaction. Conversely, if you are successful, you will have locked the first page of the table for quite a long time (and the last page for a short time).

Listing 14.40. Table-level lock.

```
WorkSpaces(0).BeginTrans ' start trans tracking
While Not rsTable.EOF   ' for every row
    rsTable.Edit         ' start edit
    rsTable.Fields("Field1") = rsTable.Fields("Field1") * 1.05
    rsTable.Update        ' end edit
Wend                     ' get another
If Err = 0 Then          ' no errors
    WorkSpaces(0).CommitTrans   ' final update
    MsgBox "Table Updated", vbInformation
Else                     ' trouble
    WorkSpaces(0).RollBack  ' undo all edits
    MsgBox "Table Update Failed", vbCritical, "Error " + Str(Err)
End If
```

If you use nested transactions and/or transactions that span multiple tables, you must keep in mind that you will be placing and holding locks on all affected records until the CommitTrans or RollBack method is invoked.

Looking at Relation Objects and Locking

If you have a highly relational data design, your Microsoft Jet locking-scheme performance can be affected. If you have defined multiple relationships between tables within your database, even single-row updates can affect several rows in the database and require a number of locked pages in order to successfully complete the update operation. This can be both a blessing and a curse. It is a blessing to know that you can use Microsoft Jet to define and enforce multi-table update and delete integrity. It is a curse to know that you might be creating a page-locking demon when you build your database structure.

If you define enforced integrity relation objects within your database, you will be able to ensure that your update operations will cascade properly to all related tables within the database. This also points out the need to use transaction methods for all your critical database updates.

You can use the VisData sample application that ships with Visual Basic to create and maintain relation objects within your database (see Figure 14.6).

> **NOTE**
>
> You can find the VisData sample application in the Professional and Enterprise Editions of Visual Basic 4.0. It is stored in the "\sample\visdata" directory under the main Visual Basic install directory.

FIGURE 14.6.

Using VisData to create a relation object.

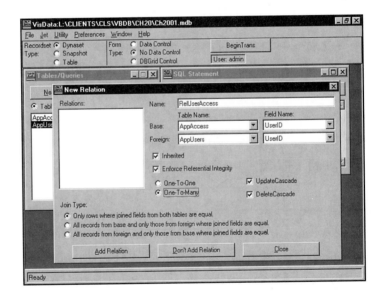

You also can create and store relation objects using Visual Basic code. Listing 14.41 creates a new database, adds two tables with indexes, and then creates a relationship object. This particular relation object enforces cascading updates and deletes to make sure any changes to the master table are reflected in the related table.

Listing 14.41. Creating a `Relation` object.

```
Private Sub cmdRelation_Click()
    On Error Resume Next
    '
    Dim dbFile As DATABASE
    Dim tdTemp As TableDef
```

continues

Listing 14.41. continued

```
Dim idxTemp As Index
Dim fldTemp As Field
Dim relTemp As Relation
Dim proTemp As Property
'
Dim cDBName As String
Dim cTblLookUp As String
Dim cTblMaster As String
Dim cIdxLookUp As String
Dim cIdxMaster As String
Dim cRelName As String
'
cDBName = "\source\chap14\ch1400.mdb"
cTblLookUp = "ValidUnits"
cTblMaster = "MasterTable"
cIdxLookUp = "PKUnits"
cIdxMaster = "PKMaster"
cRelName = "relUnitMaster"
'
' erase database if it's already there
Kill cDBName
'
' create database
Set dbFile = CreateDatabase(cDBName, dbLangGeneral, dbVersion20)
'
' create list table
' this has the stuff to lookup
Set tdTemp = dbFile.CreateTableDef(cTblLookUp)
'
' add fields to the table
Set fldTemp = tdTemp.CreateField("UnitID", dbText, 10)
tdTemp.Fields.Append fldTemp

Set fldTemp = tdTemp.CreateField("UnitDesc", dbText, 30)
tdTemp.Fields.Append fldTemp
'
' add main index to ValidUnits table
Set idxTemp = tdTemp.CREATEINDEX(cIdxLookUp)
idxTemp.PRIMARY = True
idxTemp.Required = True
Set fldTemp = tdTemp.CreateField("UnitID")
idxTemp.Fields.Append fldTemp
tdTemp.Indexes.Append idxTemp
'
' append table def to database
dbFile.TableDefs.Append tdTemp
'
' now create master table
' this table will need a reference to lookup
Set tdTemp = dbFile.CreateTableDef(cTblMaster)
'
' now add some fields
Set fldTemp = tdTemp.CreateField("MasterName", dbText, 20)
tdTemp.Fields.Append fldTemp
'
Set fldTemp = tdTemp.CreateField("MstrUnitID", dbText, 10)
```

```
        tdTemp.Fields.Append fldTemp
        '
        ' add main index to master table
        Set idxTemp = tdTemp.CREATEINDEX(cIdxMaster)
        idxTemp.PRIMARY = True
        idxTemp.Required = True
        Set fldTemp = tdTemp.CreateField("MasterName")
        idxTemp.Fields.Append fldTemp
        tdTemp.Indexes.Append idxTemp
        '
        ' append table to db
        dbFile.TableDefs.Append tdTemp
        '
        ' now set a relationship
        Set relTemp = dbFile.CreateRelation(cRelName)
        relTemp.TABLE = cTblLookUp ' table for lookups
        relTemp.ForeignTable = cTblMaster ' table to check
        Set fldTemp = relTemp.CreateField("UnitID") ' field to lookup
        fldTemp.ForeignName = "MstrUnitID"  ' field to check
        relTemp.Fields.Append fldTemp     ' add field object to relation object
        relTemp.Attributes = dbRelationUpdateCascade ' for cacading updates
        dbFile.Relations.Append relTemp ' book the completed relation object
        '
        ' enumerate the relation object
        Me.Cls
        For Each relTemp In dbFile.Relations
            For Each proTemp In relTemp.Properties
                Me.Print proTemp.Name,
                Me.Print ">";
                Me.Print proTemp.VALUE;
                Me.Print "<"
            Next
            '
            Me.Print "Relation Fields:"
            For Each fldTemp In relTemp.Fields
                Me.Print "",
                Me.Print "Name: ";
                Me.Print fldTemp.Name,
                Me.Print "ForeignName: ";
                Me.Print fldTemp.ForeignName
            Next
        Next
        '
End Sub
```

The down side of this power is that you will need to be prepared for multiple page locks when you attempt to update or delete highly dependent data objects in your database. If you want to change the CustomerID value in a master table, for example, you probably will affect a number of related transaction and history tables within the database. This will call for several page locks. If you are a good database programmer, you'll encapsulate this action within a single transaction. If you create a long transaction that spans multiple tables, you'll commit many page locks and hold them for some time before you finally complete and commit the transaction.

WARNING

Relation objects cannot be enforced in non-Microsoft Jet database formats, including attached tables. This means that you will not be able to count on Microsoft Jet to lock and update related attached tables during your database updates. If you have attached tables in your database, you must handle any relational updates within your Visual Basic code.

Using a Lock Table for Multiple Table Locking

Most programmers prefer to use the optimistic page-locking scheme. This results in the shortest locks and the least number of lock conflicts at edit time. If your application experiences heavy data entry, however, it is possible that your users will experience many update lock conflicts during peak load times. You can reduce the number of conflicts users encounter by creating a Lock table that contains information on all current locked records. By forcing your code to check this table before beginning an edit operation, you can reduce the number of update lock conflicts your users encounter under optimistic locking.

Here's how you can establish a Lock table for your application. Create a single table in your database called AppLock. This table should have four fields: UserID, TableName, RecordID, and LockStamp. The LockStamp field is a date/time field, and the rest are text fields (set their length to about 10 to 20 characters each). Each time a user attempts to edit a record in a table, the program first checks to see whether that TableName/RecordID pair is already on file in the table. If so, the user is told that the record is locked and to try again later. You could even add the user who holds the record and the time that user started his or her lock operation). If the TableName/RecordID pair was not found in the AppLock table, a new record is added to the table containing the UserID, TableName, RecordID, and current time. When the user has completed the edit work, the program can remove the record from the lock file to allow others to read the record.

NOTE

Listings 14.42 and 14.43 assume the existence of a few primer routines and some form-level or global-level variables. In order to get these routines to work properly, you need to add a routine that opens the LockTable recordset and a routine that clears out old records once the edit is done.

Listing 14.42. Function to check for locked records.

```
Public Function CheckLockTable(cTable$, cRecID$) As Boolean
    '
    ' check lock table to see if
    ' we can edit this rec
    '
    rsLockTable.FindFirst "TableName=" + cTable$ + " and RecordID=" + cRecID$
    If rsLockTable.NoMatch = False Then
        MsgBox cTable$ + "." + cRecID$ + " is Locked - Try again later.",
        ➥vbCritical, "CheckLockTable"
        CheckLockTable = False
    Else
        CheckLockTable = True
    End If
    '
End Function
```

You can place CheckLockTable function right before the Edit method in Visual Basic code or as part of the Reposition event of the Visual Basic data control (see Listing 14.43).

Listing 14.43. Checking the lock table before edits.

```
Public Sub EditRec()
    '
    ' check locks, then edit
    '
    Dim cTable As String
    Dim cRecId As String
    '
    cTable = rsEditTable.Name ' get table to lock
    cRecId = rsEditTable.Field(0) ' first field is primary key
    '
    If CheckLockTable(cTable, cRecId) = True Then
        rsEditTable.Edit
        '
        ' perform edits
        '
        rsEditTable.udpate
        ClearLock cTable, cRecId
    End If
End Sub
```

The main drawback to this approach is that updating the lock table itself can result in locking conflicts. Also, this design essentially has tripled the number of database disk operations needed to save a single record (read lock record, write lock record, read edit record, write edit record, and delete lock record). A routine like this might be overkill in a tiny data-entry application, but it works well in a large application that experiences heavy data input from multiple users.

Reducing Locking Conflicts with SQL Statements

Another way to reduce page-locking conflicts is to perform data table updates via SQL statements. The basic concept here is to use snapshots to load data onto the workstation, and then use SQL statements to actually perform the update. Finally, after the update, requery the snapshot object to get an updated picture of the data. This method works well in an environment where the centrally located data file is some distance away and the updates are rare and/or small.

The code for this kind of process might look like Listing 14.44.

Listing 14.44. Using SQL to perform single record updates.

```
Public Sub SQLProcess()
    '
    ' perform updates via SQL statements
    '
    Dim db As Database
    Dim rs As Recordset
    Dim cSQL As String
    '
    Set db = DBEngine.OpenDatabase("c:\source\chap14\ch1403.mdb")
    Set rs = db.OpenRecordset("Table1", dbOpenSnapshot)
    '
    ' add new record
    cSQL = "INSERT INTO Table1 VALUES('MCA','Weather
Ballon','FirstClass','RoundTrip');"
    db.Execute cSQL
    '
    db.Close
    '
End Sub
```

The limitations of this system include possible wait time to load the data set and the chance that the data set will be too large to fit into workstation memory. Also, even though record adds and deletes are quite easy with this method, updates can be tougher because they involve a series of SQL UPDATE statements (one for each field). Still, although this is a somewhat restrictive system, many ODBC applications still use this basic model for reading and writing remote data sources.

Using Batch Updates for Transaction Tables

One of the most annoying problems in multi-user database work is handling heavy data entry loading from multiple users. In Visual Basic Microsoft Jet, all new records are added to the last physical page in the database. If you have several users all attempting to add records at the same time, it is very likely that users will see numerous update locking conflicts because they are all trying to add records to the same physical data page.

One way to reduce the update conflicts is to have users enter their data into private temporary tables. Then, when they have completed a batch of entries, this private table can be used to update the master database table. The update can be accomplished with a SQL APPEND query, and then the temporary table can be deleted.

Listing 14.45 shows how you could structure a batch-update application.

Listing 14.45. Using SQL to perform batch updates.

```
Public Sub BatchUpdate()
    '
    ' provide temporary table
    ' for batch loading of
    ' master table
    '
    Dim dbFile As Database
    Dim rsTable As Recordset
    Dim cSQL As String
    '
    Set dbFile = DBEngine.OpenDatabase("c:\source\chap14\ch1402.mdb")
    '
    cSQL = "SELECT InvTrans.* INTO MyTrans SELECT * FROM InvTrans WHERE
    ➡InvID='JUNK';"
    dbFile.Execute cSQL
    '
    Set rsTable = dbFile.OpenRecordset("MyTrans", dbOpenTable)
    '
    ' allow user to peform batch processing on local table
    '
    cSQL = "INSERT * INTO InvTrans FROM MyTrans;"
    dbFile.Execute cSQL
    '
End Sub
```

This method works very well on applications that handle a large volume of transaction-type data entry work (accounting entries, for example). This method does not work well for data tables that act as master records that must be related to other child tables in the system (such as customer master records).

Modifying Page-Level Lock Related Settings

There are several INI/registry settings that you can adjust to control the page-level locking behavior of the Microsoft Jet database engine. These settings control the number of times Microsoft Jet will attempt to lock a page, the number of pages held in memory, and the length of time Microsoft Jet will hold unused pages in memory. Usually the default values for these settings will work fine. However, if you are having problems with your database reads and writes over a network, you might want to experiment with these settings.

When working with Microsoft Jet 2.5 data format, these settings can be placed in the [ISAM] section of your VB.INI file or the INI file that has the same name as your executable Visual Basic program. For Microsoft Jet 3.0 databases, these values can be found in the JET\3.0\ENGINES\JET folder of the registry.

> **NOTE**
>
> Some of these settings also appear in the ODBC-related INI files ODBCISAM.INI and ODBCDCCP.INI. If you are using the ODBC drivers to access your data, you may need to adjust the values in the ODBC-related INI files, too.

Table 14.3 shows the INI settings that are used to control page-lock behavior. The first column contains the complete INI setting, as it would appear in your VB.INI file including the default value. The second column contains a brief description of the setting and its meaning.

Table 14.3. Page-level lock related INI settings.

INI Key	Comment
PageTimeOut=5	Release unused data pages after 500 milliseconds.
LockedPageTimeOut=5	Release used (locked) pages after 500 milliseconds.
MaxBufferSize=512	This is the total memory cache used by Microsoft Jet. Enlarging this cache can help speed ODBC processing.
LockRetry=20	Microsoft Jet will attempt to perform a page lock 20 times before reporting an error.
CommitLockRetry=20	Microsoft Jet will attempt to commit changes to a database 20 times before returning an error. Each "commit" attempt involves executing a lock. The attempt involves executing a lock. The number of locks attempted is controlled by the LockRetry setting. The default settings will result in 20 CommitLockRetries, each attempting 20 LockRetries before Microsoft Jet will return an error. This is 400 locking attempts in all.
ReadAheadPages=16	Microsoft Jet will preload 16 data pages when reading records. Increasing this number can speed sequential processing since it reduces the number of disk operations. Excessive pages in memory can also increase the chances of update errors in optimistic locking mode since users are preloading data pages that may be edited by other users.

NOTE

For more information on modifying locking-related settings, see the Visual Basic online help under the topic locking behavior.

Implementing Microsoft Jet Security

You can add user- and group-level security to your Microsoft Jet database Visual Basic applications by installing the SYSTEM.MDA security file created when you install Microsoft Access. This system security file contains information on defined users and groups along with permission profiles. You can use a single SYSTEM file to manage multiple databases or you can use a different security file for each database or application you use.

NOTE

The Microsoft Jet Security file is called SYSTEM.MDA in the 16-bit environment and SYSTEM.MDW in the 32-bit environment. When SYSTEM.MDA appears in this chapter, keep in mind that it also refers to the SYSTEM.MDW file where appropriate.

This section covers the advantages and disadvantages of using the SYSTEM security file; you'll review the security objects and permission levels available through the SYSTEM file and you'll see some examples of how you can use Visual Basic code and the VisData sample application to create and maintain Microsoft Jet security features.

NOTE

Microsoft Jet security operations do not work with non-Microsoft Jet format databases. However, if you create an attachment to a non-Microsoft Jet database, you can maintain security for the attachment. This section focuses on Microsoft Jet format databases.

Looking at the Advantages and Limitations of Microsoft Jet Security

There are several advantages and disadvantages to using Microsoft Jet security with your Visual Basic database applications. Some programmers love the SYSTEM.MDA, but others don't. It's up to you to determine whether the SYSTEM security file will work for you and how you will use it.

The main advantage of using the SYSTEM.MDA file is that you can use the Microsoft Jet security scheme as a basis for creating secure database applications. You can define users and groups that have carefully defined permissions and you easily can enforce this security scheme within your Visual Basic program.

The primary drawback of using Microsoft Jet security is that all the security features are stored in one single file. If you lose this file (it gets erased or corrupted), you might not be able to recover your data. Also, you easily can overwrite the security file with a clean security file that gives you (or anyone else) free access to all your secured data.

You also can manage multiple databases from within a single SYSTEM.MDA file. This is a real advantage for sites that have several Visual Basic or Microsoft Access programs in production. A system administrator easily can control access rights to all Microsoft Jet databases active on the server from one single point.

The default name for the Microsoft Jet security file is SYSTEM.MDA. However, if you want to define a special security scheme for each database installed at your site, you can rename the SYSTEM.MDA file to a name more appropriate like ACCOUNTING.MDA or INVENTORY.MDA.

When you use the SYSTEM.MDA file with Visual Basic, you can secure only table and QueryDef objects. You cannot set permission rights for forms, reports, or program modules.

Even if you have designed a tight security scheme, other non-Microsoft Jet data tools (ODBC-enabled query tools) might simply ignore the SYSTEM.MDA file altogether and allow users free access to the data within your secured database.

In summary, while the SYSTEM security file is useful, you should not count on the SYSTEM.MDA file alone to properly secure your databases. Also keep in mind that other software that needs access to the database might ignore the SYSTEM security file altogether. Still other applications might use the security file, and those users will need security profiles defined in the SYSTEM file.

Identifying the Microsoft Jet Security File

The name of the security file that will be loaded by your application at startup is determined by the SystemDB setting in the INI startup file. If you are running Microsoft Access, this is stored in the Microsoft Access INI file. If you are running a specific Visual Basic application, your application can be pointed to a specific security file by using the SystemDB INI setting in your applications INI file:

```
[Options]
SystemDB=C:\MSOFFICE\ACCESS\SYSTEM.MDA
```

If your program will be running in a 32-bit environment, you can use the SystemDB property of the DBEngine to point to the SYSTEM security file:

```
DBEngine.SystemDB = "c:\msoffice\access\system.mda"
```

NOTE

The `SystemDB` property of the `DbEngine` is available only for the 32-bit version of Visual Basic 4.0. If you attempt to refer to the `SystemDB` property while running the 16-bit version of Visual Basic 4.0, you'll get an error.

Installing Microsoft Jet Security

You cannot create a Microsoft Jet security file using Visual Basic. Only Microsoft Access can create the SYSTEM.MDA file needed to define and maintain database security profiles. If you have Microsoft Access, you can copy the SYSTEM.MDA data file to a new location (your application directory) and use that as the security file for your Visual Basic application.

WARNING

Before you begin to change the SYSTEM.MDA file, be sure to make a backup copy of the SYSTEM.MDA and all the databases secured by the SYSTEM.MDA. It is possible to secure yourself right out of the system. You might not be able to gain access to any of your databases if the SYSTEM.MDA file is lost or corrupted.

Once the SYSTEM security file is in place, you can use the VisData sample Visual Basic program to create and maintain user and group objects and set permission rights for all identified `QueryDefs` and Databases (see Figure 14.7).

FIGURE 14.7.

Using VisData to create and maintain Microsoft Jet security.

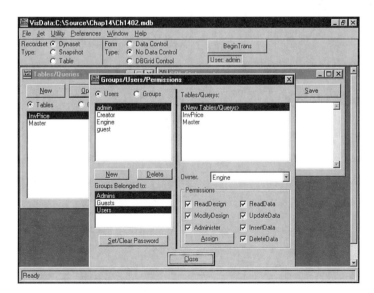

After you copy a clean SYSTEM.MDA to the application or Visual Basic directory, you must add the `SystemDB` setting to your Visual Basic and application INI files in order to be able to access the security system (see Identifying the Microsoft Jet Security File, earlier in this chapter). In other words, unless you actually tell Visual Basic applications the exact name and location of the SYSTEM security file, no security features will be in place; your data will not be secure.

> **TIP**
>
> If you want to remove security features from an application, simply remove the SystemDB setting from the INI file. Real secure, right?

Now that you have a clean SYSTEM security file and it has been activated, you are ready to start creating users and groups for your Visual Basic application.

Logging In to a Secured Database

Once the security features are in place, users will be prompted to provide a Login Name and Password each time they attempt to open a secured database (see Figure 14.8).

FIGURE 14.8.

Login dialog box for secured database.

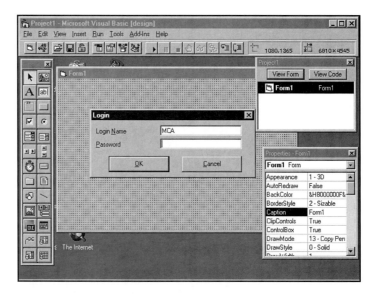

You can bypass this dialog box by setting the `DefaultUser` and `DefaultPassword` properties of the `DBEngine` object before you execute an `OpenDatabase` statement. Listing 14.46 shows how this can be done.

Listing 14.46. Bypassing the secured database login screen.

```
Private Sub Form_Load()
    '
    ' set defaults before login
    '
    On Error GoTo FormLoadErr
    '
    DBEngine.DefaultUser = "MCA"
    DBEngine.DefaultPassword = "MyPassword"
    '
    Workspaces(0).OpenDatabase ("c:\source\chap14\ch1403.mdb")
    '
    Exit Sub
    '
FormLoadErr:
        MsgBox Error$, vbCritical, "Error Opening Database [" + Str(Err) + "]"
        End
End Sub
```

In Listing 14.46, the Login Name and Password are supplied via hard coding. These could also be stored in an INI setting/registry or in another database. However, storing login information in this manner can defeat the security system. An alternate approach might be to store the UserName parameter in an INI setting and prompt the user to provide the password.

Notice also that the routine in Listing 14.46 contains an error trap. If the UserName and Password parameters are not valid for this SYSTEM.MDA, an error will be reported and the database will not be opened (see Figure 14.9).

FIGURE 14.9.

Error attempting to login to secured database.

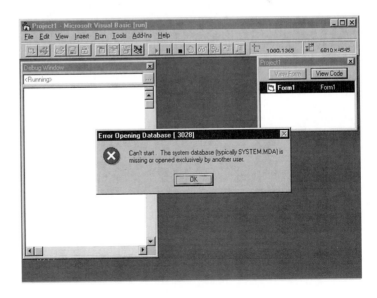

Working with Microsoft Jet Database Security Objects and Levels

The Microsoft Jet allows you to secure two data objects: Tables and QueryDefs. You toggle on or off seven permission values:

- **ReadDesign, ModifyDesign, and Administer.** These three values all control the permissions each user or group has when it comes to reading and updating the design of the database itself. Only users with ModifyDesign, for example, are able to change the structure of the database.

- **ReadData, UpdateData, InsertData, DeleteData.** These four permissions all control the level of access each user has for the defined table and QueryDef objects. Only those users with InsertData rights, for example, can add new records to a table.

There are several possible security-related error codes that Visual Basic could return. The most common ones are listed in Table 14.4.

Table 14.4. Common security-related error codes.

Error Code	Error Text
3028	Can't start your application. The system database is missing or opened exclusively by another user.
3029	Not a valid account name or password.
3030	*Account name* isn't a valid account name.
3031	Not a valid password.
3032	Can't perform this operation.
3033	No permission for *name*.

You can trap for these errors in the Error event of the Visual Basic data control. You also can check for them during data table AddNew, Edit, Update, and Delete methods.

Summary

This chapter concentrated on four challenges you will encounter when you create multi-user applications using Visual Basic 4.0:

- **General issues in multi-user programming.** Designing for multiple users from the start, distributing and installing your multi-user programs, and shared versus local resources.

■ **Writing user-configurable applications.** Techniques you can use to make sure your Visual Basic application is easy for users to customize to their needs and tastes. You learned how to add settings to users' INI files that can store form size and location and user-selected fonts and colors. You also learned how to use checked menu items to set and remember user preferences.

■ **Microsoft Jet database locking.** High-level locking methods at the database and table level, and low-level locking at the page level. You learned the differences and advantages and disadvantages of pessimistic and optimistic page locking. You learned to use Microsoft Jet relation objects to improve locking integrity, to reduce locking conflicts by installing a lock table, to perform table updates via SQL statements, and to perform batch updates from temporary tables to the master table.

■ **Microsoft Jet security system.** In the "Microsoft Jet Security" section, you learned techniques for establishing and maintaining the Microsoft Access SYSTEM security profiles for your Visual Basic applications. The section also covered the limitations of the Microsoft Jet security system.

TCP/IP, WinSock, and Visual Basic

15

*by Mike Stefanik
(of Catalyst
Software)*

IN THIS CHAPTER

With the acceptance of Transmission Control Protocol/Internet Protocol (TCP/IP) as a standard platform-independent network protocol, and the explosive growth of the Internet, the Windows Sockets API (application program interface) has emerged as the standard for network programming in the Windows environment. Visual Basic is positioned as a powerful tool for building comprehensive Internet-aware applications quickly and easily. This chapter will introduce the basic concepts behind Windows Sockets programming and get you started with your first application.

The Windows Sockets specification was created by a group of companies, including Microsoft, in an effort to standardize the TCP/IP suite of protocols under Windows. Prior to Windows Sockets, each vendor developed its own proprietary libraries, and although they all had similar functionality, the differences were significant enough to cause problems for the software developers that used them. The biggest limitation was that, upon choosing to develop against a specific vendor's library, the developer was "locked" into that particular implementation. A program written against one vendor's product would not work with another's. Windows Sockets was offered as a solution, leaving developers and their end-users free to choose any vendor's implementation with the assurance that the product will continue to work.

There are two general approaches that you can take when creating a Visual Basic program that uses Windows Sockets: code directly against the API, or use a custom control (VBX) that provides an interface to the library by setting properties and responding to events. The first approach, while possible, is not recommended. The Windows Sockets API was designed for use by C programmers, and some of the functions are fairly unpleasant to use in the Visual Basic environment. You'll end up writing a great deal of code geared toward working around the incompatibilities between the API and Visual Basic, rather than writing the code for your application. Remember, sockets programming is a means to an end, not an end in itself.

A custom control provides a more "natural" programming interface, and allows you to avoid much of the error-prone drudgery commonly associated with network programming. By dropping the control on a form, setting some properties and responding to events, you can quickly and easily write an Internet-enabled application. Because of the nature of custom controls in general, the learning curve is low, and experimentation is easy. For these reasons, you use a custom control called SocketWrench/VB to create a simple client and server application. This control was developed by Catalyst Software of Oak Park, California, and may be freely redistributed with any project. Before you get started with the control, however, you cover the basic terminology and concepts behind sockets programming in general.

Transmission Control Protocol

When two computers are to exchange information over a network, there are several components that must be in place before the data can actually be sent and received. Of course, the physical hardware must exist, which typically includes network interface cards (NICs) and wiring of some type connecting them. Beyond this physical connection, however, computers also need to use a *protocol*, which defines the parameters of the communication between them. In short, a protocol defines the "rules of the road" that each computer must follow so that all the systems in the network can exchange data. One of the most popular protocols in use today is TCP/IP.

By convention, TCP/IP is used to refer to a suite of protocols, all based on the Internet Protocol (IP). Unlike a single, local network, where every system is directly connected to another, an *internet* is a collection of networks, combined into a single, virtual network. The Internet Protocol provides the means by which any system on any network can communicate with another as easily as if they were on the same physical network. Each system, commonly referred to as a *host*, is assigned a unique 32-bit number which can be used to identify it over the internetwork. Typically, this address is broken into four 8-bit numbers separated by periods. This is called *dot-notation*, and looks something like "127.0.0.1." Some parts of the address are used to identify the network the system is connected to, and the remainder identifies the system itself. Without going into the minutia of the Internet Protocol addressing scheme, just be aware that there are three classes of addresses, referred to as "A," "B," and "C." The rule of thumb is that class A addresses are assigned to very large networks, class B addresses are assigned to medium-sized networks, and class C addresses are assigned to smaller networks (networks with less than 250 hosts).

When a system sends data over the network using the Internet Protocol, it is sent in discrete units called *datagrams*, also commonly referred to as *packets*. A datagram consists of a header followed by application-defined data. The header contains the addressing information used to deliver the datagram to it's destination, much like an envelope is used to address and contain postal mail. Like postal mail, there is no guarantee that a datagram will actually arrive at its destination. In fact, a datagram may be lost, duplicated, or delivered out of order during its travels over the network. Needless to say, this kind of unreliability can cause a lot of problems for software developers. What's really needed is a reliable, straightforward way to exchange data without having to worry about lost packets or jumbled data.

To fill this need, the Transmission Control Protocol (TCP) was developed. Built on top of IP, TCP offers a reliable, full-duplex byte stream that may be read and written to in a fashion similar to reading and writing a file. The advantages to this are obvious: the application programmer doesn't need to write code to handle dropped or out-of-order datagrams, and instead, can focus on the application itself. Because the data is presented as a stream of bytes, existing code can be easily adopted and modified to use TCP.

TCP is known as a *connection-oriented* protocol. In other words, before two programs can begin to exchange data they must establish a "connection" with each other. This is done with a three-way handshake in which both sides exchange packets and establish the initial packet sequence numbers. The sequence number is important because, as mentioned above, datagrams can arrive out of order. This number is used to ensure that data is received in the order that it was sent. When establishing a connection, one program must assume the role of the *client*, and the other the *server*. The client is responsible for initiating the connection, while the server's responsibility is to wait, listen, and respond to incoming connections. Once the connection has been established, both sides may send and receive data until the connection is closed.

User Datagram Protocol

Unlike TCP, the User Datagram Protocol (UDP) does not present data as a stream of bytes, nor does it require that you establish a connection with another program in order to exchange information. Data is exchanged in discrete units called *datagrams*, which are similar to IP datagrams. In fact, the only features that UDP offers over raw IP datagrams are port numbers and an optional checksum.

UDP is sometimes referred to as an unreliable protocol because when a program sends a UDP datagram over the network, there is no way for it to know that it actually arrived at its destination. This means that the sender and receiver must typically implement their own application protocol on top of UDP. Much of the work that TCP does transparently (such as generating checksums, acknowledging the receipt of packets, retransmitting lost packets, and so on) must be performed by the application itself.

With the limitations of UDP, you might wonder why it's used at all. UDP has the advantage over TCP in two critical areas: speed and packet overhead. Because TCP is a reliable protocol, it goes through great lengths to ensure that data arrives at its destination intact, and as a result it exchanges a fairly high number of packets over the network. UDP doesn't have this overhead and is considerably faster than TCP. In those situations where speed is paramount, or the number of packets sent over the network must be kept to a minimum, UDP is the solution.

Hostnames

In order for an application to send and receive data with a remote process, it must have several pieces of information. The first is the IP address of the system on which the remote program is running. Although this address is internally represented by a 32-bit number, it is typically expressed in either dot-notation or by a logical name called a *hostname*. Like an address in dot-notation, hostnames are divided into several pieces separated by periods, called *domains*. Domains are hierarchical, with the top-level domains defining the type of organization that network belongs to, with sub-domains further identifying the specific network.

FIGURE 15.1.

The hierarchical domain naming system.

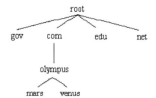

In this figure, the top-level domains are "gov" (government agencies), "com" (commercial organizations), "edu" (educational institutions), and "net" (Internet service providers). For systems located outside of the United States, the site's country code is used as the top-level domain. For example, the top-level domain for a site in Ireland is "ie".

The fully qualified domain name is specified by naming the host and each parent sub-domain above it, separating them with periods. For example, the fully qualified domain name for the "mars" host would be "mars.olympus.com". In other words, the system "mars" is part of the "olympus" domain (a company's local network) which in turn is part of the "com" domain (a domain used by all commercial enterprises).

In order to use a hostname instead of a dot-address to identify a specific system or network, there must be some correlation between the two. This is accomplished by one of two means: a local *host table* or a *name server*. A host table is a text file that lists the IP address of a host, followed by the names that it's known by. Typically this file is named hosts and is found in the same directory in which the TCP/IP software has been installed. A name server, on the other hand, is a system (actually, a program running on a system) that can be presented with a hostname and will return that host's IP address. This approach is advantageous because the host information for the entire network is maintained in one centralized location, rather than being scattered about on every host on the network.

Service Ports

In addition to the IP address of the remote system, an application also needs to know how to address the specific program that it wishes to communicate with. This is accomplished by specifying a *service port*, a 16-bit number that uniquely identifies an application running on the system. Instead of numbers, however, service names are usually used instead. Like hostnames, service names are usually matched to port numbers through a local file, commonly called *services*. This file lists the logical service name, followed by the port number and protocol used by the server.

A number of standard service names are used by Internet-based applications, and these are referred to as *well-known services*. Some common services are shown in Table 15.1.

Table 15.1. Well-known Internet services.

Service Name	Function
echo	Echoes data back to the program that sent it. This is commonly used to test an application to make sure that a network connection can be established successfully.
ftp	Transfers files between computer systems using the File Transfer Protocol.
telnet	Provides terminal emulation services for the remote host.
smtp	Sends electronic mail to a remote host by using the Simple Mail Transfer Protocol.

Remember that a service name or port number is a way to *address* an application running on a remote host. Because a particular service name is used doesn't guarantee that the service is available, just as dialing a telephone number doesn't guarantee that there is someone at home to answer the call.

Sockets

The previous sections described what information a program needs to communicate over a TCP/IP network. The next step is for the program to create what is called a *socket*, a communications end-point that can be likened to a telephone. However, creating a socket by itself doesn't let you exchange information, just like having a telephone in your house doesn't mean that you can talk to someone by simply taking it off the hook. You need to establish a connection with the other program, just as you need to dial a telephone number, and to do this you need the socket address of the application that you want to connect to. This address consists of three key parts: the protocol family, Internet Protocol (IP) address, and the service port number.

We've already talked about the IP address and service port, but what's the protocol family? It's a number used to logically designate the group that a given protocol belongs to. Because the socket interface is general enough to be used with several different protocols, the protocol family tells the underlying network software which protocol is being used by the socket. In our case, the Internet Protocol family is always be used when creating sockets. With the protocol family, IP address of the system, and the service port number for the program that you want to exchange data with, you're ready to establish a connection.

Client/Server Applications

Programs written to use TCP are developed using the *client/server model*. As mentioned previously, when two programs wish to use TCP to exchange data, one of the programs must assume the role of the client, while the other must assume the role of the server. The client application initiates what is called an *active open*. It creates a socket and actively attempts to connect to a server program. On the other hand, the server application creates a socket and passively listens for incoming connections from clients, performing what is called a *passive open*. When the client initiates a connection, the server is notified that some process is attempting to connect with it. By *accepting* the connection, the server completes what is called a *virtual circuit*, a logical communications pathway between the two programs. It's important to note that the act of accepting a connection creates a new socket; the original socket remains unchanged so that it can continue to be used to listen for additional connections. When the server no longer wishes to listen for connections, it closes the original passive socket.

To review, there are five significant steps that a program using TCP must take to establish and complete a connection. The server side would follow these steps:

1. Create a socket.
2. Listen for incoming connections from clients.
3. Accept the client connection.
4. Send and receive information.
5. Close the socket when finished, terminating the conversation.

In the case of the client, these steps are followed:

1. Create a socket.
2. Specify the address and service port of the server program.
3. Establish the connection with the server.
4. Send and receive information.
5. Close the socket when finished, terminating the conversation.

Only steps two and three are different, depending on whether it's a client or server application.

Blocking versus Non-Blocking Sockets

One of the first issues that you'll encounter when developing your Windows Sockets applications is the difference between blocking and non-blocking sockets. Whenever you perform an operation on a socket, it may not be able to complete immediately and return control back to your program. For example, a read on a socket cannot finish until some data has been sent by the remote host. If there is no data waiting to be read, one of two things can happen: the function can wait until some data has been written on the socket, or it can return immediately with an error that indicates that there is no data to be read.

The first case is called a *blocking socket*. In other words, the program is "blocked" until the request for data has been satisfied. When the remote system does write some data on the socket, the read operation finishes, and execution of the program resumes. The second case is called a *non-blocking socket*, and requires that the application handle the situation appropriately. Programs that use non-blocking sockets typically use one of two methods when sending and receiving data. The first method, called *polling*, is when the program periodically attempts to read or write data from the socket using a timer. The second, and preferred method, is to use what is called *asynchronous notification*. This means that the program is notified whenever a socket event takes place, and in turn can respond to that event. For example, if the remote program writes some data to the socket, a "Read event" is generated so that program knows it can read the data from the socket at that point.

For historical reasons, the default behavior is for socket functions to "block" and not return until the operation has finished. Under Windows this can introduce some special problems, because when the program blocks, it enters what is called a *message loop*, where it continues to process messages sent to it by Windows and other applications. Because messages are being processed, this means that the program can be re-entered at a different point, with the blocked operation "parked" on the program's stack. For example, consider a program that attempts to read some data from the socket when a button is pressed. Because no data has been written yet, it blocks, and the program goes into a message loop. The user then presses a different button, which causes code to be executed, which in turn attempts to read data from the socket, and so on. Obviously, this can pose a big problem. To resolve it, the Windows Sockets standard states that there may only be one outstanding blocked call per thread of execution. This means that, in the example given above, the second read would fail with an error indicating that a blocking operation is already in progress. While blocking sockets may be convenient in some situations, their use is generally discouraged because of the complications that they can introduce into the program.

The SocketWrench control facilitates the use of non-blocking sockets by firing events when appropriate. For example, a Read event is generated whenever the remote host writes on the socket, which tells your application that there is data waiting to be read. The use of non-blocking sockets is demonstrated in the next section, and is one of the key areas in which a control has a distinct advantage over coding directly against the Windows Sockets API.

SocketWrench/VB

The sample program covered in this chapter was developed by using the SocketWrench/VB custom control, which is included on the book's accompanying CD-ROM.

Because SocketWrench has a large number of properties, you might feel overwhelmed when you start reading through the technical reference material. Don't worry—you only need to understand how to use a handful of properties and events to get started. Once you've become more comfortable and knowledgeable about sockets programming, you'll appreciate the power and flexibility that SocketWrench gives you.

Each control that you use corresponds to one socket which may or may not be connected to a remote host. If you need access to multiple sockets, you must use multiple controls, typically as a control array. This is most commonly needed when your application acts a server and must be able to handle several connections at one time.

System Requirements

The SocketWrench control requires Microsoft Windows 3.1 or later, Visual Basic 3.0 or later, and a TCP/IP protocol stack with a Windows Sockets 1.1 compliant library. Microsoft has a free TCP/IP implementation for Windows for Workgroups 3.11 and Windows 95 includes TCP/IP as part of the base operating system.

For those systems that do not have a network connection, Catalyst Software includes a *loopback* library that supports the complete Windows Sockets API. It can be used to simulate a network connection so that applications using SocketWrench can function. Refer to the release notes for further information on installing and configuring the loopback library.

A Sample Client Program

The sample program used throughout this section is a simple tool that can be used to connect with an *echo server*, a program that echoes any data that's sent to it. Later on, you also cover how to implement your own echo server.

The first step, after starting Visual Basic, is to include the SocketWrench control in your new project. Select the File | Add File option from the Visual Basic menu. A file selection dialog box is displayed. Enter the complete pathname of the control, such as `c:\windows\system\cswsock.vbx`, after the control has been added to the tool palette. In addition to adding the control to the project, you also need to include the cswsock.bas file that was copied to the directory you specified during installation. This file is included in the same fashion as the control.

To begin, you need to start Visual Basic and create a form that has three labels, three text controls, a button, and the SocketWrench control. The form might look something like what is presented in Figure 15.2.

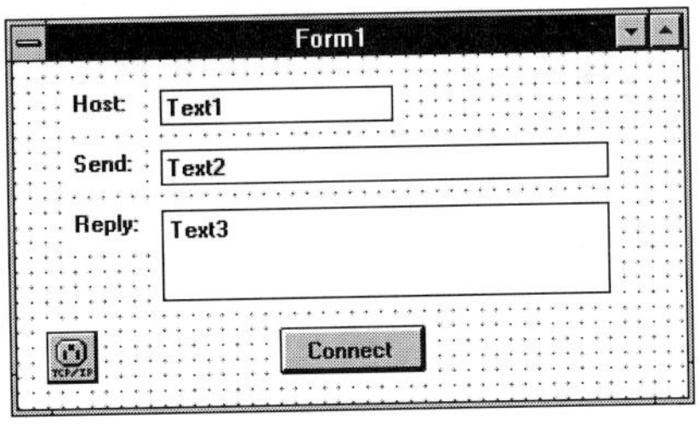

FIGURE 15.2.

Visual Basic form.

When executed, the user enters the name or IP address of the system in the Text1 control, the text that is to be echoed in the Text2 control, and the server's reply is displayed in the Text3 control. The Command1 button is used to establish a connection with the remote server. The Text2 and Text3 controls should be created with their Enabled properties initially set to False.

Some essential properties of the SocketWrench control, called Socket1, needs to be initialized. The best place to do this is in the form's Load subroutine. The code should look like this:

```
Sub Form_Load ()
    Socket1.AddressFamily = AF_INET
    Socket1.Protocol = IPPROTO_IP
    Socket1.Type = SOCK_STREAM
```

```
    Socket1.Binary = False
    Socket1.BufferSize = 1024
    Socket1.Blocking = False
End Sub
```

These six properties should be set for every instance of the SocketWrench control:

AddressFamily	This property is part of the socket address and should always be set to a value of AF_INET, which is a global constant with the integer value of 2. At this time, the Windows Sockets interface only supports the IP address family.
Protocol	This property determines which protocol is going to be used to communicate with the remote application. Most commonly, the value IPPROTO_IP is used, which means that the protocol appropriate for the socket type will be used.
Type	This property specifies the type of socket that is to be created. It may be either of type SOCK_STREAM or SOCK_DGRAM. The stream-based socket uses the TCP protocol, and data is read and written on the socket as a stream of bytes, similar to how data in a file is accessed. The datagram-based socket uses the UDP protocol, and data is read and written in discrete units called datagrams. Most sockets that you create will be of the stream variety.
Binary	This property determines how data should be read from the socket. If set to a value of True, then the data is received unmodified. If set to False, the data is interpreted as text, with the carriage return and linefeed characters stripped from the data stream. Each receive returns exactly one line of text.
BufferSize	This property is used only for stream-based (TCP) sockets. It specifies the amount of memory, in bytes, that should be allocated for the socket's send and receive buffers.
Blocking	This property specifies if the application should wait for a socket operation to complete before continuing. Setting this property to False indicates that the application does not wait for the operation to complete, and instead responds to events generated by the control. This is the recommended approach to take when designing your application.

The next step is to establish a connection with the echo server. This is done by including code in the Command1 button's Click event. The code should look like this:

```
Sub Command1_Click ()
    Socket1.HostName = Trim$(Text1.Text)
    Socket1.RemotePort = IPPORT_ECHO
    Socket1.Action = SOCKET_CONNECT
End Sub
```

The Text1 edit control should contain the name or IP address of a system with an echo server running (most UNIX- and Windows NT-based systems do have such a server). The properties that have been used to establish the connection are:

HostName	This property should be set to either the host name of the system that you want to connect to, or it's IP address in dot-notation.
RemotePort	This property should be set to the number of the port that the remote application is listening on. Port numbers below 1024 are considered reserved by the system. In this example, the echo server port number is 7, which is specified by using the global constant IPPORT_ECHO.
Action	This property initiates some action on the socket. The SOCKET_CONNECT action tells the control to establish a connection using the appropriate properties that have been set. A related action, SOCKET_CLOSE, instructs the control to close the connection, terminating the conversation with the remote server.

Both HostName and RemotePort are known as *reciprocal properties*. This means that by changing the property, another related property also changes to match it. For example, when you assign a value to the HostName property, the control determines its IP address and automatically sets the HostAddress property to the correct value. The reciprocal property for RemotePort is the RemoteService property. For more information about these properties, refer to the *SocketWrench Technical Reference,* which is included with the control.

Because the socket is non-blocking (that is, the Blocking property has been set to a value of False), the program does not wait for the connection to be established. Instead, it returns immediately and responds to the Connect event in the SocketWrench control. The code for that event should look like this:

```
Sub Socket1_Connect ()
    Text2.Enabled = True
    Text3.Enabled = True
End Sub
```

This tells the application that when a connection has been established, it is to enable the edit controls so that the user can send and receive information from the server.

Now that the code to establish the connection has been included, the next step is to actually send and receive data to and from the server. To do this, the Text2 control should have the following code added to it's KeyPress event:

```
Sub Text2_KeyPress (KeyAscii As Integer)
    If KeyAscii = 13 Then
        Socket1.SendLen = Len(Text2.Text)
        Socket1.SendData = Text2.Text
        KeyAscii = 0: Text2.Text = ""
    End If
End Sub
```

If the user presses the Enter key in the Text2 control, then that text is sent down to the echo server. The properties used to send data are as follows:

SendLen   This property specifies the length of the data being sent to the server. It should *always* be set before the data is written to the socket. After the data has been sent, the value of the property is adjusted to indicate the actual number of bytes that have been written.

SendData   Setting this property causes the data assigned to it to be written to the socket. The number of bytes actually written may be less than the amount specified in the SendLen property if the socket buffers become full.

Once the data has been sent to the server, it immediately sends the data back to the client. This generates a Read event in SocketWrench, which should have the following code:

```
Sub Socket1_Read (DataLength As Integer, IsUrgent As Integer)
    Socket1.RecvLen = DataLength
    Text3.Text = Socket1.RecvData
End Sub
```

The properties used to receive the data are as follows:

RecvLen   This property specifies the maximum number of bytes that should be read from the socket. After the data has been received, the value is changed to reflect the number of bytes actually read.

RecvData   Reading this property causes data to be read from the socket, up to the maximum number of bytes specified by the RecvLen property. If the socket is non-blocking and there is no data to be read, an error is generated.

The Read event is passed two parameters, the number of bytes available to be read, and a flag specifying if the data is urgent (also known as *out-of-band* data, the use of urgent data is an advanced topic outside the scope of this book). For more information about the Read event, please refer to the *SocketWrench Technical Reference*.

The last piece of code to add to the sample is used to handle closing the socket when the program is terminated by selecting Close on the system menu. The best place to put socket cleanup code in the form's Unload event, such as:

```
Sub Form_Unload (Cancel As Integer)
    If Socket1.Connected Then Socket1.Action = SOCKET_CLOSE
    End
End Sub
```

This should be rather self-explanatory. The only new property that has been introduced is the Connected property, which is a Boolean flag. If it is True, then a connection has been established. With all of the properties and event code needed for the sample client application completed, all that's left to do is run the program!

The first thing that you'll probably notice is that if you specify an incorrect host name or address, an error is generated and the program stops. Of course, in a real application you'd need to provide extensive error checking. SocketWrench errors start at 24,000 and correspond to the error codes used by the Windows Sockets library. Most errors occur when setting the host name, address, service port, or `Action` property.

Building an Echo Server

The next step is to implement your own echo server. To accomplish this, you modify the client application to function as a server as well. The side benefit is that this allows you to test both the client and server application on your local system.

Remember that the first thing a server application must do is *listen* on a local port for incoming connections. You know that an application is attempting to connect with you when the `Accept` event is generated for the SocketWrench control. There are two methods that you can use to accept an incoming connection: set the `Action` property to the value `SOCKET_ACCEPT`, or set the `Accept` property.

Setting the `Action` property is the simplest of the two methods. As you recall, the act of accepting a connection causes a *second* socket to be created. The original listening socket continues to listen for more connections, while the second socket can be used to communicate with the client that connected to you. When you set the `Action` property to `SOCKET_ACCEPT`, you're telling the control to *close* the original listening socket, and from that point on, the control can be used to communicate with the client. While this is convenient, it is also limiting—because the listening socket has been closed, no more clients can connect with your program, effectively limiting it to a single-client connection.

The more flexible approach is to set the `Accept` property to the value passed as an argument to the `Accept` event. However, this cannot be done by the control that is listening for connections because it is in use. You have to use another, unused control to accept the connection. The problem is, how many clients are going to attempt to connect to you? Of course, you could drop a fixed number of SocketWrench controls on your form, thereby limiting the number of connections, but that's not a very good design. The better approach is to create a *control array* which can be dynamically loaded when a connection is attempted by a client, and unloaded when the connection is closed. This is the approach that you'll take in your server code sample.

The first thing to do is to add a second SocketWrench control to your form, and make it a control array. Initially there will only be one control in the array, identified as Socket2(0). This control will be responsible for listening for client connections. Just as with the client socket control, several of the control's properties should be initialized in the form's `Load` subroutine. The new subroutine should look like this:

```
Sub Form_Load ()
    Socket1.AddressFamily = AF_INET
    Socket1.Protocol = IPPROTO_IP
    Socket1.Type = SOCK_STREAM
    Socket1.Binary = False
    Socket1.BufferSize = 1024
    Socket1.Blocking = False
```

```
    Socket2(0).AddressFamily = AF_INET
    Socket2(0).Protocol = IPPROTO_IP
    Socket2(0).Type = SOCK_STREAM
    Socket2(0).Blocking = False
    Socket2(0).LocalPort = IPPORT_ECHO
    Socket2(0).Action = SOCKET_LISTEN
    LastSocket = 0
End Sub
```

The only thing that is new here is the LocalPort property and the NextSocket variable. The LocalPort property is used by server applications to specify the local port that it's listening on for connections. By specifying the standard port used by echo servers, any other system can connect to yours and expect the program to echo back whatever is sent to it.

The LastSocket variable is defined in the general section of the Visual Basic application as an integer. It is used to keep track of the next index value that can be used in the control array.

By setting the Action property to SOCKET_LISTEN in the form's Load event, the program starts listening for connections as soon as the program starts executing. When a client tries to connect with your server, Socket2's Accept event fires. The code for this event should look like this:

```
Sub Socket2_Accept (Index As Integer, SocketId As Integer)
    Dim I As Integer
    For I = 1 To LastSocket
        If Not Socket2(I).Connected Then Exit For
    Next I
    If I > LastSocket Then
        LastSocket = LastSocket + 1: I = LastSocket
        Load Socket2(I)
    End If
    Socket2(I).AddressFamily = AF_INET
    Socket2(I).Protocol = IPPROTO_IP
    Socket2(I).Type = SOCK_STREAM
    Socket2(I).Binary = True
    Socket2(I).BufferSize = 1024
    Socket2(I).Blocking = False
    Socket2(I).Accept = SocketId
End Sub
```

The first statement loads a new instance of the SocketWrench control as part of the Socket2 control array. The next six lines initialize the control's properties, and then the Accept property is set to the value of the SocketId parameter that is passed to the control. After executing this statement, the control is now ready to start communicating with the client program.

Because it's an echo server's job to echo back whatever it is sent, we must add code to the control's Read event, which tells it that the client has sent some data to us. It looks like this:

```
Sub Socket2_Read (Index As Integer, DataLength As Integer,
                  IsUrgent As Integer)
    Socket2(Index).RecvLen = DataLength
    Socket2(Index).SendLen = DataLength
    Socket2(Index).SendData = Socket2(Index).RecvData
End Sub
```

Finally, when the client closes the connection, the socket control must also close its end of the connection. This is accomplished by adding a line of code in the socket's Close event.

```
Sub Socket2_Close (Index As Integer)
    Socket2(Index).Action = SOCKET_CLOSE
End Sub
```

To make sure that all of the socket connections are closed when the application is terminated, the following code should be included in the form's Unload event:

```
Sub Form_Unload (Cancel As Integer)
    Dim I As Integer
    If Socket1.Connected Then Socket1.Action = SOCKET_CLOSE
    If Socket2(0).Listening Then Socket2(0).Action = SOCKET_CLOSE
    For I = 1 To LastSocket
        If Socket2(I).Connected Then Socket2(I).Action = SOCKET_CLOSE
    Next I
    End
End Sub
```

The only new property shown here is the Listening property, which, like the Connected property, is a Boolean flag. If the control is listening for incoming connections, this property returns True, otherwise it returns False. This is added only as an extra "sanity check", and the property should always return True for this instance of the control.

Summary

This chapter has introduced you to the basic concepts behind socket programming, and how to use SocketWrench to get started developing your own TCP/IP applications. Although the echo client and server sample program is fairly basic, it does illustrate many of the key issues that you'll encounter when developing your own software.

PART

Unleashing Component-Based Programming

OLE for the First Time

16

by
Richard Buhrer

IN THIS CHAPTER

OLE, pronounced Olé! (like at a fiesta), and an acronym for "Object Linking and Embedding," is a standard that provides several ways for software programs to communicate with each other. Visual Basic 4.0 has fully implemented OLE 2.x and this has expanded the collection of tools available in the product. A working understanding of objects and OLE 2.x is required in order to get the greatest value from the changes in VB 4.0.

Microsoft's position is that OLE 2.x is not just object linking and embedding anymore. The second (and current version) of the standard has expanded the focus of OLE to include a standard for interapplication communication. One good way to summarize the differences between OLE 1.0 and OLE 2.x, is that 1.0 was about object linking and embedding, whereas OLE 2.0 is about objects, and linking and embedding are only one part of the picture.

Navigating This Chapter

This chapter begins with a discussion of the object linking and embedding technology. If you already have a basic understanding of OLE 2.x technology, then you might skip or skim the first section as a review. The following section discusses Visual Basic's place in the world of OLE 2.x. The third section explores Visual Basic 4.0's place as an object oriented programming language. It discusses ways to implement object oriented design techniques providing VB programmers with reusable code and bulletproof applications. The final section presents some resources for further information on object linking and embedding.

An Introduction to Objects, Linking, and Embedding

"Object" is one of the most abstract and amorphous words in the English language. Just about any entity we can talk about qualifies as an object. Webster's Dictionary defines an object in this way:

(1) ob.ject)(n)(14c)<objectum, >fr. L, neut. of ><obicere >to throw in the way, present, hinder, fr. ><ob-> in the way + ><jacere >to throw

1a: something material that may be perceived by the senses <I see an object in the distance.>

1b: something that when viewed stirs a particular emotion (as pity) <look to the tragic loading of this bed ... the object poisons sight; let it be hid —Shak.>

2: something mental or physical toward which thought, feeling, or action is directed <an object for study> <the object of my affection> <delicately carved art objects>

3: the goal or end of an effort or activity: PURPOSE, OBJECTIVE <their object is to investigate the matter thoroughly>

4: a thing that forms an element of or constitutes the subject matter of an investigation or science

5a: a noun or noun equivalent (as a pronoun, gerund, or clause) denoting the goal or result of the action of a verb

5b: a noun or noun equivalent in a prepositional phrase

What Is an Object, Anyway?

The software industry has developed several meanings of the term, "object." Marketing types have appropriated the word and turned "object-oriented" into a buzzword. Almost every major piece of software claims to be object oriented. To restore some clarity, here are some of the relevant definitions of objects:

Object-oriented software theorists understand an object to be a component of a software program that "models" or "represents" a something in the real world, like a ledger or a bicycle. Because of this correlation between real world and software objects, it is allegedly easier to construct re-usable software components and to reduce bugs by isolating one module of a program from changes in another. In order to qualify as an object, the design must support four qualities:

- Abstraction
- Encapsulation
- Polymorphism
- Inheritance

Devout OOP programmers vehemently argue whether OLE 2.x "objects" deserve the name. It's something of an irony that theorists would choose one of the most vague words in the English language and then get huffy about the imprecise use of the term. We'll explore the details of this is the third section of this chapter.

From Visual Basic's perspective, objects are combinations of code and data that function as a unit. In another sense, an object is a user interface element in Windows (or any other operating system), for example, a program window, a text box, a command button, and so on.

Finally in the pure sense of object linking and embedding, an object is a self-contained bit of information that lives in a compound document. It behaves the same regardless of the application that manages the compound document because the object determines its own behavior. Such an object has two levels of data: presentation data and native data. *Presentation data* allows the object to be viewed on screen or in print. *Native data* is the binary information stored in random access memory or on disk and underlies the presentation. In linking, the native data resides on the user's disk in a separate file or document; in embedding, the native data resides in the compound document itself.

A Short History of OLE

It is helpful to review the history of object linking and embedding, which may help clarify the muddle. This "history" might be subtitled "The Quest for Integration," because it is driven by the need to provide the end-user with tools to assemble data in different formats into cohesive presentations or documents. To make this more vivid, let's take the example of Joe User who has the following task to perform: He needs to analyze sales performance for four divisions of the company, and send this analysis along with a cover letter to all sales personnel in the company.

"The Dark Ages"

Back before the birth of graphical user interfaces, we were stuck with applications that couldn't communicate with each other.

Joe uses a flat file database, a character mode spreadsheet and a character mode word processor. To accomplish this task he opens the database program and exports a tab delimited text file containing the list of sales personnel and their addresses. Then he closes the database. He opens a spreadsheet program and creates a spreadsheet in which he constructs a summary table of sales information based on other spreadsheets. This, in itself, could get pretty tedious because the spreadsheet may not support multiple open files. He prints copies of the spreadsheet, closes the spreadsheet program, and then he opens the word processor. He types a mail merge letter laboriously, and retypes the spreadsheet information into the word processor as a table (with tab characters separating the report columns). He prints the letter several times to get the formatting and alignment just right, then he runs the mail merge. Finally, he stuffs envelopes, feeds them through a postage meter, and sends them on their way. Yes, it's easier than doing it with a ledger and a typewriter, but....

Cut, Copy, Paste

Along comes Windows, or Desqview, or a Macintosh, and Joe's work gets a little easier; he can switch between running applications and he can use a *clipboard*. He still needs to save the database information in a format his word processor can understand, but he can copy parts of the spreadsheet directly into his document. However, it needs to be reformatted to look good, and if the data in the spreadsheet changes, he has to repeat this process. It is very easy for errors to slip into the process and bosses being the way they are, well....

DDE and Links

Windows 2.1 comes with *Dynamic Data Exchange (DDE)* and *links*. Joe's word processor might even be able to read the database tables directly for the mail merge, and using Excel or some other Windows-based spreadsheet he can paste a link into his Word document that always reflects the current state of the spreadsheet data in the document. Unfortunately, DDE is slow. When Joe uses this approach, Windows often crashes mysteriously (remember UAEs, Unforgivable Application Errors), and he can only transfer text, not graphs or pictures.

Object Linking and Embedding (OLE 1.0)

Windows 3.x and OLE 1.0 comes along. Now Joe can either embed or link the spreadsheet data into his document. If he double-clicks on the embedded or linked data, the spreadsheet application launches in a separate window and Joe can edit the data directly. He can use graphs from the spreadsheet, and the data is always up to date, but the system slows to a crawl with multiple applications running, and it seems to take forever when switching between editing applications.

OLE 2.x

OLE 2.x comes along. Now when Joe double-clicks on his spreadsheet data, the toolbars and menus of the word processor change to those from the spreadsheet. When he clicks outside of the spreadsheet object, they return to the usual ones for the application. If he has both applications running, he can actually drag a selection from one application into another with his mouse. Although it feels like developing a single document in a single application, he now has the ability to develop *compound documents* that hold OLE 2.x objects from a variety of sources. Applications that support compound documents can allow him to edit the various components transparently. Additionally, instead of paper mail, he can broadcast these letters across the network as attachments to e-mail messages that can be dispatched directly from the word processor. The applications he uses are large and require a lot of memory, and he has to add more RAM to his machine. Even after adding a substantial amount of RAM, he gets these mysterious out-of-memory messages from Windows when he is really only out of *resources*. Finally, some of these maneuvers can still be pretty slow on the hardware bought just a year or two ago. Joe is now working on a network and unfortunately some of these nifty features do not work across the network.

Beyond OLE 2.x

Microsoft is promising a standard for distributed OLE so that Joe will be able to use objects across the network from applications that are actually running on other computers. This is yet to be seen.

Through OLE 2.x, computer programs are assisting users to move from a program-centric model of computing to a document-, or data-centric model. In the program-centric model, considerable learning is required to master the foibles of different programs and there are difficulties involved in presenting information in various formats (graphs, pictures, tabular data, formatted text) in the same document or presentation. In the document-centric model (which is yet to be fully realized) a user can transparently assemble information in different formats and present it to others while focusing only on meaning and content. This is a work in progress and the transition is far from complete.

The OLE 2.0 Feature Set

OLE 2.x is a complex technology that has been notoriously difficult for developers to implement. It is constructed on a layered model as shown in Figure 16.1. The upper layer describes the features available for use by (or customization for) the end user. The infrastructure describes the low level services that are managed by the operating system and by Visual Basic. For the most part, the Visual Basic programmer is shielded from these details. The grayed areas of the model are areas of special interest for Visual Basic programmers. *Interface* in OLE is a means by which two programs communicate with each other: for example, drag and drop, or programmability.

FIGURE 16.1.

The Layered model of OLE 2.x.

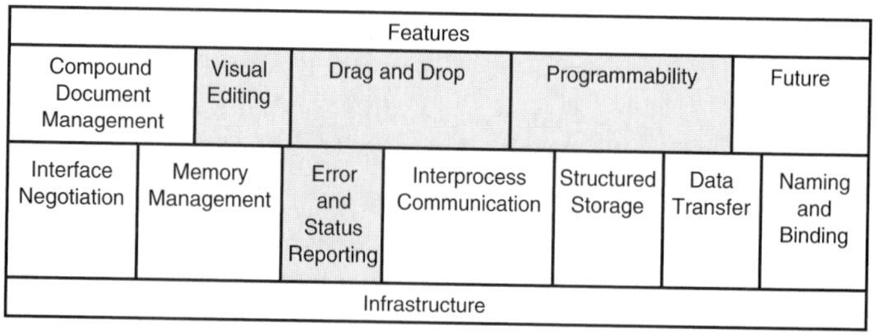

Features					
Compound Document Management	Visual Editing	Drag and Drop	Programmability		Future
Interface Negotiation	Memory Management	Error and Status Reporting	Interprocess Communication	Structured Storage	Data Transfer	Naming and Binding
Infrastructure					

OLE 2.x is based on the *Component Object Model* or *COM*. You might say that COM acts like a dating service for software components, introducing them and then slipping into the background while they communicate. It continues to work in the background managing the infrastructure services.

NOTE

The System Registry

OLE manages information about programs in a database called the *system registry*. The registry in 16-bit Windows manages only information about OLE servers: where they are located on disk, what objects they provide, and file extension information that enables File Manager to manage drag and drop. In 32-bit Windows, the registry takes over many other functions including that of initialization files (*.INI).

The registration database is contained in the REG.DAT file found in the \Windows\System directory in Windows 3.x and Windows 95 and in the \Windows\System32 directory in Windows NT. There is an application called

REGEDIT which allows users and developers to browse (and at their own risk, edit) the system registry. If you browse the system registry you will find it has a tree structure similar to an MS DOS directory tree. There are root entries with subentries with further sub-entries and finally, values. Entries and sub-entries would be analogous to directories or folders and values to files.

Visual Basic 4.0 provides four new statements for initialization file and registry information management. These are `GetSetting`, `SaveSetting`, `DeleteSetting`, and `GetAllSettings`. These functions manage initialization file entries on 16-bit Windows and registry information on 32-bit Windows. The good news is that you won't need to use API calls anymore to manage this information. It's finally native to Visual Basic.

You can find more information on this from the Visual Basic help file system or in Chapter 17 of the Programmers Guide, "Interacting with the Environment."

From the user's point of view, OLE 2.x provides the following features:

- Visual editing
- Compound documents
- Drag and drop
- OLE automation

Visual editing or *in-place activation* is how embedded or linked objects present themselves in an OLE 2.x-aware application. Instead of opening a separate window for editing, the menus and toolbars of the client application change and display the menus and toolbars of the server application.

OLE 2.x compound documents allow for nested objects, so one could place a graphic object on a spreadsheet table inside a word processing document.

Drag and drop allows the use of the mouse to transfer data from one application to another without using the Clipboard. There are three levels of drag and drop functionality in OLE 2.x:

- Interwindow dragging—Dragging an object from one application to another
- Inter-object dragging—Objects nested within objects can be dragged out of their containing objects and dropped in to other containing objects
- Dropping over icons—Objects can be dropped on resource icons like printers and mail boxes and be processed appropriately

Finally, and probably most importantly to VB programmers, OLE 2.x Automation allows objects to expose a programmable interface to OLE 2.x-aware programming and macro languages. This allows programmers to develop integrated solutions that utilize features of several applications to automate tasks for end-users.

CAUTION

Containers, Controllers, Clients, Servers?

Every few years, the folks at Microsoft change the terminology used to describe these interapplication services. Source/target, client/server, and so forth. Now the terminology has changed again and requires just a bit of clarification. An application that manages compound documents is now called a *container application*. It was formerly referred to as an OLE client. An application that provides compound document objects (formerly called a server) is now called an *object application*. You'll notice, of course, that most container applications are also object applications.

In terms of OLE automation, the client application is now called an *object controller*. The OLE automation server (which is still the legitimate term) is usually referred to simply as an *object*.

In summary, in the wonderful world of OLE 2.x there are really two types of objects: programmable objects and non-programmable objects. *Non-programmable* objects are components of compound documents. They reside in the interface between users and documents. Examples of this type of object are sounds, animations, text, spreadsheet tables, and graphics, in other words, "multimedia." *Programmable objects*, or OLE 2.x Automation objects, reside in the interface between programmers and production software. They allow themselves to be manipulated through properties and methods.

Visual Basic in the World of OLE 2.x

Visual Basic interacts with both programmable and non-programmable OLE 2.x objects. Table 16.1 describes the implementation of OLE services in Visual Basic 4.0. It includes only those services that are native to Visual Basic 4.0. Other support may be available in add-ins and third party custom controls.

Table 16.1. The implementation of OLE services in Visual Basic 4.0.

OLE 2.x service	Visual Basic Support
Visual Editing	Visual Basic forms in conjunction with the OLE container control support visual editing with toolbar and menu negotiation, that is, they allow the menus and toolbars of a Visual Basic application to update with information from server applications.

OLE 2.x service	Visual Basic Support
Compound documents	You can display compound documents in a Visual Basic form or in an OLE 2.x container control, previously called the OLE custom control in Visual Basic 3.0; however, you may not create a server application that provides OLE 2.x non-programmable objects similar to Visio drawings or Word documents.
Non-programmable objects	These can be embedded or linked to Visual Basic forms and OLE container controls.
Drag and Drop	The OLE container control can function as the target for an interapplication drag and drop maneuver.
OLE Automation	Fully supported as both a controller and as an object itself.

Visual Basic Non-Programmable Objects

Right off the bat, it's important to point out what Visual Basic cannot do: it cannot create an application that manages compound documents and provides objects to fill them. You cannot write a Visio, Microsoft WordArt, or the answer to Excel in Visual Basic, but there is interesting new support for non-programmable OLE objects in Visual Basic.

Insertable Objects

Visual Basic forms can function as OLE containers without using the OLE 2.x control. One can place objects like graphs, drawings, and sounds directly on forms. The objects will even show up in the Toolbox window, and you can draw them directly on the form in the same way that you draw controls (see Figure 16.2).

In this way, a programmer can produce an interface that uses elements from various applications for an integrated presentation on-screen, for example, in EIS (Executive Information Systems) applications (see Figure 16.3). There are several examples of this type of program in the Microsoft Office Developers Kit which is included with the Professional Edition of Visual Basic 4.0.

Although this application, developed in Visual Basic 3.0, uses OLE custom controls to contain the various elements, Visual Basic 4.0 supports drawing them directly on forms.

FIGURE 16.2.

Tools for Excel and Word are displayed in the Visual Basic 4.0 Toolbox window.

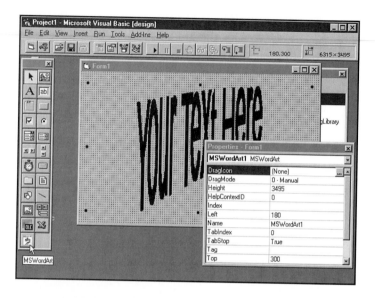

FIGURE 16.3.

An EIS application from the Office Developers Kit.

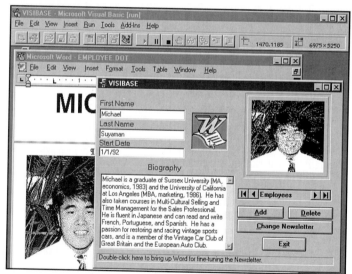

The OLE 2.x Container Control

Even though there is direct support for insertable objects on Visual Basic forms, there are additional advantages to be gained by using the OLE control.

- Objects can be created and changed at runtime.
- Menus and toolbars are able to update themselves to those of the server.

- The container can receive OLE information dropped from an interapplication drag and drop maneuver.
- The container can accept objects from the clipboard.
- The container can display objects as icons.
- The container can be bound to a database and display OLE objects stored there.
- The container provides backward compatibility with applications developed in prior versions of Visual Basic.

Example: A Trivial OLE 2.x Browser

This application consists of a single form with six controls. The controls are:

- A Windows 95 tool bar control—The toolbar has no functional buttons but is necessary in order to display the object application's toolbar.
- Three list boxes in a control array—These display some additional information about the object.
- An OLE container control—This enables changing the inserted object at runtime.
- A Windows 95 status bar control—Like the toolbar, this allows for negotiation and display of the object application's status bar.

Figure 16.4 shows the Viewer project in the development environment.

FIGURE 16.4.

The OLE Viewer form in the development environment.

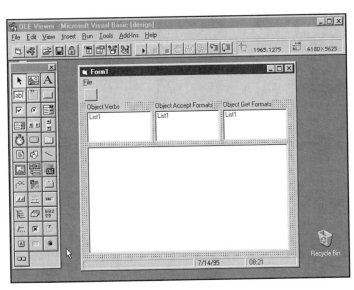

There is one menu with two submenus. Figure 16.5 shows the Menu Design window with the menus for the OLE Viewer.

FIGURE 16.5.

The Menu Design window.

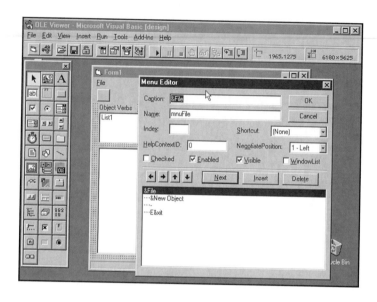

Following is the code for the entire application. Figure 16.6 shows the application running.

```
VERSION 4.00
Begin VB.Form Form1
   Caption         =   "Form1"
   ClientHeight    =   4935
   ClientLeft      =   1410
   ClientTop       =   1815
   ClientWidth     =   6060
   Height          =   5625
   Left            =   1350
   LinkTopic       =   "Form1"
   ScaleHeight     =   4935
   ScaleWidth      =   6060
   Top             =   1185
   WhatsThisButton =   -1   'True
   WhatsThisHelp   =   -1   'True
   Width           =   6180
   Begin VB.ListBox List1
      Height       =   840
      Index        =   2
      Left         =   4020
      TabIndex     =   4
      Top          =   660
      Width        =   1815
   End
   Begin VB.ListBox List1
      Height       =   840
      Index        =   1
      Left         =   2100
      TabIndex     =   3
      Top          =   660
      Width        =   1815
   End
```

```
Begin VB.ListBox List1
   Height          =    840
   Index           =    0
   Left            =    180
   TabIndex        =    2
   Top             =    660
   Width           =    1815
End
Begin VB.Label Label1
   AutoSize        =    -1  'True
   Caption         =    "Object Get Formats"
   Height          =    195
   Index           =    2
   Left            =    4020
   TabIndex        =    8
   Top             =    420
   Width           =    1365
End
Begin VB.Label Label1
   AutoSize        =    -1  'True
   Caption         =    "Object Accept Formats"
   Height          =    195
   Index           =    1
   Left            =    2100
   TabIndex        =    7
   Top             =    420
   Width           =    1620
End
Begin VB.Label Label1
   Caption         =    "Object Verbs"
   Height          =    195
   Index           =    0
   Left            =    180
   TabIndex        =    6
   Top             =    420
   Width           =    1035
End
Begin ComctlLib.StatusBar StatusBar1
   Align           =    2  'Align Bottom
   Height          =    255
   Left            =    0
   Negotiate       =    -1  'True
   TabIndex        =    5
   Top             =    4680
   Width           =    6060
   _Version        =    65536
   _ExtentX        =    10689
   _ExtentY        =    450
   _StockProps     =    68
   AlignSet        =    -1  'True
   SimpleText      =    ""
   _timers         =    2
   NumPanels       =    3
   i1              =    "Form1.frx":0000
   i2              =    "Form1.frx":010C
   i3              =    "Form1.frx":01FB
End
```

```
        Begin ComctlLib.Toolbar Toolbar1
            Align            =   1   'Align Top
            Height           =   390
            Left             =   0
            Negotiate        =   -1  'True
            TabIndex         =   1
            Top              =   0
            Width            =   6060
            _Version         =   65536
            _ExtentX         =   10689
            _ExtentY         =   688
            _StockProps      =   100
            ImageList        =   ""
            NumButtons       =   2
            i1               =   "Form1.frx":02EA
            i2               =   "Form1.frx":046A
            AlignSet         =   -1  'True
        End
        Begin VB.OLE OLE1
            Height           =   2895
            Left             =   180
            TabIndex         =   0
            Top              =   1620
            Width            =   5655
        End
        Begin VB.Menu mnuFile
            Caption          =   "&File"
            NegotiatePosition=   1   'Left
            Begin VB.Menu mnuFileNewObject
                Caption          =   "&New Object"
            End
            Begin VB.Menu mnuFileSep1
                Caption          =   "-"
            End
            Begin VB.Menu mnuFileExit
                Caption          =   "E&xit"
            End
        End
    End
End
Attribute VB_Name = "Form1"
Attribute VB_Creatable = False
Attribute VB_Exposed = False
Option Explicit

Private Sub mnuFileExit_Click()
    Unload Me
End Sub

Private Sub mnuFileNewObject_Click()
    Dim I    ' Declare counter variable.
    Dim Buffer As String 'for string manipulation
    'Clear the OLE Control if it contains an object
    If OLE1.Class <> "" Then
        OLE1.Close
    End If

    ' Display the Insert Object dialog box.
    On Error GoTo ThisWayOut
    OLE1.InsertObjDlg
```

```
On Error GoTo 0
' Update the list of available verbs.
Buffer = OLE1.Class
Me.Caption = "This is not " & _
    Left$(Buffer, InStr(Buffer, ".") - 1) & _
    " running."
OLE1.FetchVerbs ' Fetch verbs.

' Clear the list boxes.
For I = 0 To 2
    List1(I).Clear
Next
' Fill the verbs list box. Because ObjectVerbs(0) is
' the default verb and is repeated in the ObjectVerbs()
' array, start the count at 1.
For I = 1 To OLE1.ObjectVerbsCount - 1
    List1(0).AddItem OLE1.ObjectVerbs(I)
Next I

'Fill the Accept Formats list box.
For I = 0 To OLE1.ObjectAcceptFormatsCount - 1
    List1(1).AddItem OLE1.ObjectAcceptFormats(I)
Next I
' Fill the Get Formats list box.
For I = 0 To OLE1.ObjectGetFormatsCount - 1
    List1(2).AddItem OLE1.ObjectGetFormats(I)
Next I
Exit Sub
ThisWayOut:
    OLE1.Class = ""
End Sub
```

FIGURE 16.6.

The OLE Viewer application running.

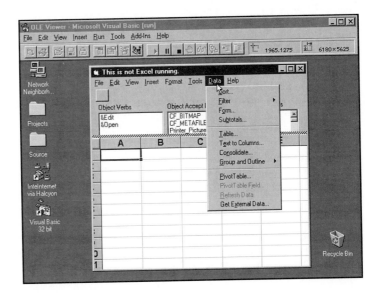

Visual Basic and Programmable Objects

I know that this borders on gushing, but OLE Automation is a magic kingdom for Visual Basic programmers. The syntax of OLE Automation is already well understood by anyone with even a passing understanding of Visual Basic. The level of integration and customization of off-the-shelf and original Visual Basic software should provide Visual Basic users with fine economic opportunities for a long time to come.

In order to appreciate the wide range of new tools in Visual Basic 4.0, this section starts with a brief discussion of some of the underlying technology of OLE Automation, and a third-party tool that is very useful for exploring the capabilities of OLE Automation servers. Then the section steps through the relevant features in Visual Basic 4.0. These include:

- Forms as objects
- Class modules
- OLE Automation server applications and dynamic link libraries
- Visual Basic Add-ins
- Controlling other applications' objects

You use a rudimentary Visual Basic application, improving it at the various stages to illustrate the uses more concretely.

Type Libraries and a Better Mousetrap

When an OLE Automation server is installed on a system, it must be registered in the system registry with information about the location of the server application or DLL and information about the objects it provides. When it is installed, the application generates a file with a distinctive extension (*.tlb, *.olb, and *.ola are usual extensions). This file contains information about the programmable object the application exposes, including constants, properties, events (in the case of OLE controls), and methods. These are defined in *object definition language* and compiled in a binary form that is not humanly readable.

In order to use the programmable objects, a programmer needs either documentation from the publisher of the software or a utility that displays the contents of the type library in an understandable format. Visual Basic for Applications and Visual Basic 4.0 contain a built-in Object Browser dialog that does this in a rudimentary way (see Figure 16.7). The first version of the Microsoft Developers Kit contained a free-standing version of the dialog as well.

There are problems with the native Object Browser dialog, though. It lists all the properties, methods, and events for a particular object in a single list box in alphabetical order without any instruction about which item is a property or method or whatever. You have the option of pasting from the dialog to your development environment but only as a declaration, for example "Const xlBar = 2". Although this is helpful as far as it goes, there is now a better alternative.

FIGURE 16.7.

The Object Browser in Visual Basic 4.0.

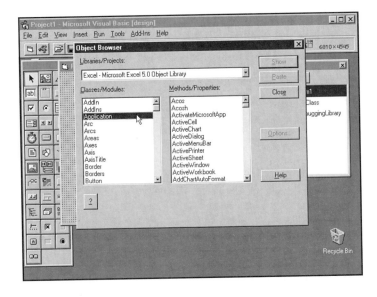

Apex Software has released a product called *VBA Companion*. This is the better mousetrap: a full-feature object browser. In addition to the services of the native object browser, VBA Companion separates properties, methods, and events into separate lists but also provides immediate access to the full range of details (see Figure 16.8). Whereas the native browser only allows you to add comments to your own objects, VBA Companion allows you to add notes or annotations to the type libraries on your system to help you with future use of the objects.

FIGURE 16.8.

VBA Companion.

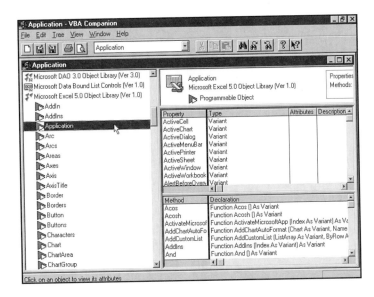

In addition to the clearer exposition of the contents of type libraries, VBA Companion allows you to paste information into your programs as comments, declarations, or statement/function templates. For example, VBA Companion copies this to the clipboard when you use the context menu:

```
xlBar
```

But when you select it and use the Edit menu's Copy command, it copies the declaration

```
Const xlBar = 2
```

Similarly, for a function or sub, when you use the context menu it copies the template for a function or statement (this example uses a method of the Arc object in Excel 5.0).

```
arc.CopyPicture(Appearance:=, Format:=)
```

When you use the edit menu it copies the declaration and adds the End Function line, a feature that Visual Basic supplies automatically but Visual Basic for Applications does not.

```
Function CopyPicture (Appearance As Variant, Format As Variant) As Variant
End Function
```

These features can be very helpful when one is struggling with object hierarchies from other applications.

Example: A "Run..." Dialog Box

To illustrate the range of OLE Automation services in Visual Basic, I have chosen the Run dialog. Frequently found in shell replacements and utilities for Windows, the Run dialog allows a user to enter a command line to be executed by Windows. Figure 16.9 shows the Run dialog from Windows 95.

FIGURE 16.9.

The Run dialog from Windows 95.

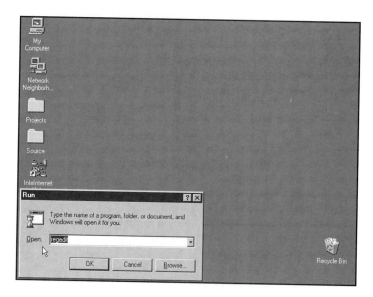

You'll step this simple dialog through the various layers of OLE Automation support in Visual Basic 4.0. The form that functions as the run dialog has an image control with an icon in it, a text box, three command buttons, and a common dialog control. Figure 16.10 shows the form for our Run dialog in the Visual Basic development environment.

FIGURE 16.10.

The form for our Run dialog.

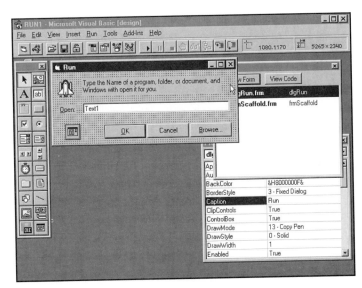

Forms as Objects

In Visual Basic 4.0, forms are fully qualified OLE objects. This means that, in addition to the event procedures and built-in properties, one can declare public variables and public functions that then function as custom methods and properties for the form. In our example there is one private and one public variable declared at the Form level.

```
Option Explicit
Public CommandLine As String
Private boolOK As Boolean
```

There are two public functions declared at the form level; the first displays the dialog and the second executes the command line that the user has chosen in the dialog.

```
Public Function Display() As Boolean
    Me.Show vbModal
    Display = boolOK
End Function

Public Function Execute() As Variant
    Dim lngResult As Long

    'This will return a variant of type error
    'if the command line does not execute successfully
    'Otherwise it returns the task ID as a variant
    'to the calling procedure.
```

```
        On Error Resume Next
        lngResult = Shell(CommandLine, vbNormalFocus)
        If Err.Number <> 0 Then
            Execute = CVErr(Err.Number)
        Else
            Execute = lngResult
        End If
End Function
```

The project contains a scaffold form with one command button on it to test the execution of the Run dialog. A scaffold form or program is software whose only reason for existing is to test modules in isolation from each other. The code in the scaffold form demonstrates the syntax to use in addressing forms as objects.

```
Private Sub cmdRun_Click()
    Dim dlg As New dlgRun
    Dim success As Variant
    success = dlg.Display()
    MsgBox success
    If success Then
        MsgBox dlg.CommandLine
        success = dlg.Execute
        MsgBox success
    End If
End Sub
```

A major side-effect of this implementation is that forms now support most of the module features in previous versions of Visual Basic. For example, variables declared as public are visible from other modules and forms by using the object.property syntax. Forms now support public or private `Declare` and `Const` statements. One can now design sophisticated Visual Basic applications that only contain forms.

NOTE

Collections

You can now develop user-defined collection objects like the `Forms` or `Controls` collections in Visual Basic.

A collection is like an array in that it contains a series of similar items. It has advantages over arrays however.

1. Collections have more flexible indexing than arrays. You can use two syntactical forms to address a member of a collection:

   ■ `Collection(index)`—The numerical index that underlies the native order of members in the collection.

   ■ `Collection!Key` or `Collection("Key")`—The key is a variant element in the member that constitutes the user-identified indexing system.

2. Collections may use less memory than arrays, especially sparse arrays.

3. Collections automatically provide methods and properties for ascertaining the count and adding or deleting elements from the collection.

4. Collections automatically manage memory allocation so you do not need to use `Redim` or `Redim Preserve` to dimension the array.

Rounding Out the Dialog with Classes

The Run dialog form can be added to any project and bring full functionality with it. With a simple dialog this would probably be adequate, but Visual Basic 4.0 goes further. In addition to greater functionality in forms, it adds the possibility for developing a new kind of module, called a *class module*, which is, simply put, a fully functional OLE Automation object. You'll change your form into a fully functional OLE Automation server by adding a class module (*.CLS) to the project.

Instead of accessing the methods of the dlgRun form directly, you'll make the form a private element in the `RunClass` and only access it through methods of the `RunClass`.

The following is the text of the class module, RunClass.cls:

```
Option Explicit

Private dlg As New dlgRun

Public Property Get CommandLine() As Variant
    CommandLine = dlg.CommandLine
End Property

Public Function Execute() As Variant
    Dim varHolder As Variant
    varHolder = dlg.Execute
    If VarType(varHolder) = vbError Then
        Execute = False
    Else
        Execute = varHolder
    End If
End Function

Public Function Run() As Variant
    Run = dlg.Display
    If Run Then dlg.UpdateCommandLines
End Function

Private Sub Class_Initialize()
    Load dlg
End Sub

Private Sub Class_Terminate()
    Unload dlg
    Set dlg = Nothing
End Sub
```

Some notes about the class module: The distinction between `Private` and `Public` properties and methods is supremely important. The underlying implementation in private methods and properties (in this case they are mostly contained in the Run dialog form) can be changed as needed, but the interface that is exposed needs to remain consistent. The advantage of a consistent interface is that the program can be changed over time and still work with OLE controllers (also called client applications) without breaking them or itself. It also demonstrates Property and Class procedures (new procedure types in Visual Basic 4.0). The Property procedures are transparent to the calling application as properties. They are addressed with simple assignment calls. Table 16.02 lists the syntax and effect of each type of Property procedure.

Table 16.2 Syntax and effect of property procedures.

Syntax	Effect
`MyProperty = NewValue`	Triggers the `Property Let` procedure
`Set MyObject = NewObject`	Triggers the `Property Set` procedure
`ThisValue = Object.Property`	Triggers the `Property Get` procedure

This type of procedure allows special processing in response to assignment statements. In this example, all that happens is that information from the private form is expressed to other elements of the program. In more complex programs, this ability could be very useful.

The second new type of procedures are `Class` procedures: `Initialize()` and `Terminate()`. These permit special processing when the object is created and destroyed. In object-oriented programming terminology, these would be called the constructor and destructor for an object. In my experience, the `Terminate` procedure is most important because it allows necessary cleanup, especially when you are using objects inside the object. This cleanup ensures that any memory assignments are freed up when the object exits.

To test this version, you are still using a scaffold application; there are some minor modifications in this version.

```
VERSION 4.00
Begin VB.Form frmScaffold
   Caption        =   "Form1"
   ClientHeight   =   4140
   ClientLeft     =   1140
   ClientTop      =   1515
   ClientWidth    =   6690
   Height         =   4545
   Left           =   1080
   LinkTopic      =   "Form1"
   ScaleHeight    =   4140
   ScaleWidth     =   6690
   Top            =   1170
```

```
Width           =    6810
Begin VB.CommandButton cmdUnload
   Caption      =    "Command1"
   Height       =    795
   Left         =    420
   TabIndex     =    1
   Top          =    1680
   Width        =    2055
End
Begin VB.CommandButton cmdRun
   Caption      =    "&Run"
   Height       =    735
   Left         =    480
   TabIndex     =    0
   Top          =    660
   Width        =    1875
End
End
Attribute VB_Name = "frmScaffold"
Attribute VB_Creatable = False
Attribute VB_Exposed = False
Option Explicit

Dim obj As New RunClass

Private Sub cmdRun_Click()

   Dim success As Variant
   success = obj.Run
   MsgBox obj.CommandLine
   success = obj.Execute
End Sub

Private Sub cmdUnload_Click()
   Unload Me
End Sub

Private Sub Form_QueryUnload(Cancel As Integer, UnloadMode As Integer)
   Set obj = Nothing
End Sub
```

Creating OLE Automation Servers with Visual Basic 4.0

Now, simply by replacing the scaffold form with a module and writing a Sub Main procedure, you have an OLE automation server that can be distributed either as an executable or, and this is quite an advance, as a dynamic link library. The ability to create dynamic link libraries in Visual Basic is limited to OLE automation servers. Nonetheless, now Visual Basic programmers can distribute to other programmers components that are written entirely in Visual Basic without exposing code and providing performance superior to compiled executables in Visual Basic.

There are three types of OLE Automation servers: in-process, out-of-process, and remote. Remote servers are not available yet; they are expected in "Cairo," the next major version of Windows NT.

Out-of-process servers run a separate executable with their own code and data memory segments. Other applications address them through a process called lightweight remote procedure calls (LRPCs). LRPCs are a little like DDE calls but are more stable and reliable. They do, however, make a hit on speed.

In-process servers run as dynamic link libraries. Each library has its own code segment but stores its data in the data segment of the calling application. There is a significant performance gain because these servers do not have to use the LRPC system for communication.

Visual Basic 4.0 32-bit professional version allows developers to create both in-process and out-of-process servers.

This is the `Sub main` procedure for our object server.

```
Attribute VB_Name = "MainModule"
Option Explicit

Sub Main()
    'Check to see if the application has
    'been launched by a curious user
    If App.StartMode = vbSModeStandalone Then
        Dim msg As String, style As Integer
        msg = "This application cannot be run " _
            & "as a stand alone executable. Sorry! " _
            & "Exiting now."
        style = vbOK + vbExclamation
        MsgBox msg, style, "rbRun.exe"
        'End '(the end statement is not supported in DLLs
    End If
End Sub
```

The message is presented as a courtesy to people who may be browsing executable files. It at least acknowledges their industry but doesn't allow them to get in trouble, or worse, delete the file because it doesn't appear to do anything.

Note that modules (both normal and class) now have properties. The class module properties deserve some explanation. Table 16.3 explains the various properties for class modules.

Table 16.3. Class module properties.

Property	Values	Comments
Instancing	0—Not Creatable 1—Creatable Single Use 2—Creatable Multi-Use	Not Creatable means you can only create instances of your server in your own project. Single Use means that you can create instances in and outside of your project but each instance requires a separate copy of the server to be run. Multi-Use allows multiple instances to share the same code segment. This the required setting for DLLs.
Name	Visual Basic's internal name for the module.	This must follow Visual Basic variable naming conventions. It is also a property of normal modules.
Public	True False	When True, your object is visible to and usable by other applications. It is the required setting for objects you publish for use by others.

Finally, after you compile your application, you need to register it on your system as an OLE 2.x server. If you use the Setup Wizard to package your application for distribution, the SETUP.EXE you create registers your application on the target system. You can register it by hand by using the REGSVR??.EXE program that ships with Visual Basic. The ?? stands for 16 or 32 depending on the target system. You run it from the command line with your server's fully qualified path and file as a parameter. The following line is the command to register the example server on your system, presuming you place it with other common DLLs in your system directory:

```
C:REGSVR32.EXE C:\WINDOWS\SYSTEM\RBRUN.DLL
```

If you publish your server as an executable file, it registers itself the first time it is run or if you run it with the /REGSERVER switch.

```
MYAPP.EXE /REGSERVER
```

This does not launch the application but registers it with the system and exposes its type library. Figure 16.11 shows the type library for the rbRun.DLL exposed in VBA Companion.

FIGURE 16.11.

The type library for rbRun.DLL in VBA Companion.

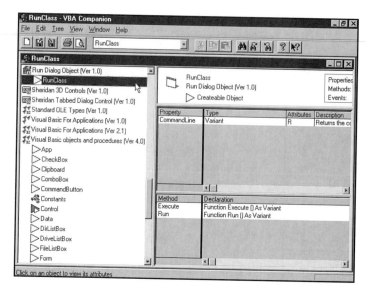

The capability of creating OLE 2.x servers is probably the most significant feature in Visual Basic 4.0. This gives Visual Basic programmers access to a whole realm of software production that is likely to become very important with the release of OLE 2.x–aware operating systems like Windows 95.

The Development Environment as an OLE Automation Controller: Creating Add-Ins

Visual Basic 4.0 takes this one step further by exposing its own type library and allowing other applications to "drive" it. This means that developers can create add-ins that customize and automate the behavior of Visual Basic's development environment. Examples of this capability ship with Visual Basic. A simple example is the Align program which aligns controls on a form, but the Data Forms Designer example shows sample code for automated form development based on a data table. The Data Manager application also functions as an add-in.

In order to transform your simple Run dialog into an add-in to Visual Basic, you need to open a new project in Visual Basic and set a reference in the Tools References dialog box to the rbRun Run Dialog object (see Figure 16.12).

In addition, you need to add two class modules and a code module to the project. Note that this project has no form modules in it.

The first class module, RunAddIn, contains the code for connecting the add-in application to Visual Basic.

FIGURE 16.12.

The References dialog box from Visual Basic 4.0.

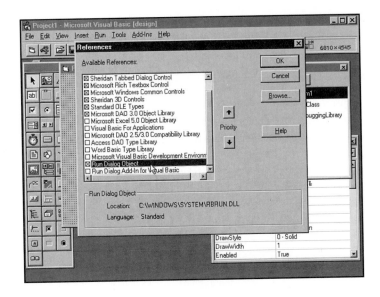

```
VERSION 1.0 CLASS
BEGIN
   MultiUse = -1  'True
END
Attribute VB_Name = "RunAddIn"
Attribute VB_Creatable = True
Attribute VB_Exposed = True
Option Explicit

'Storage for the instance of VBInstance given to us in ConnectAddIn
Dim ThisInstance As Object
'Storage for the menu and menuline objects created when the add-in adds its own
➡menu
'and menulines to Visual Basic
Dim RunMenuLine As Object
'Set up an instance of the menu line Clicked() Event Handlers
Dim RunHandler As New DoDoRunRun
'Storage for the cookies that are passed back
'from ConnectEvents
Dim RunConnectCookie As Long

Sub ConnectAddIn(VBInstance As Object)
    Set ThisInstance = VBInstance
    Set RunMenuLine = ThisInstance.AddInMenu.MenuItems.Add("Run...")
    Set RunHandler.VBInstance = VBInstance
    RunConnectCookie = RunMenuLine.ConnectEvents(RunHandler)
End Sub

Sub DisconnectAddIn(Mode As Integer)
    RunMenuLine.DisconnectEvents RunConnectCookie
    ThisInstance.AddInMenu.MenuItems.Remove RunMenuLine
    Set ThisInstance = Nothing
End Sub
```

Notice that there are module-level object values to hold references to the calling instance of Visual Basic and other variables that represent objects in the Visual Basic environment. The most significant example in this case is the MenuLine object, which represents an entry on the Add-Ins menu in the development environment. The two required procedures that the Visual Basic Add-In Manager uses to install and remove the add-in are in this module. Note that to register an add-in you store a reference to the instance of Visual Basic, create the menu lines you need, set a reference to the Visual Basic instance in the EventHandler modules (in this case, it is the other class module, DoDoRunRun (pardon the whimsy). Finally you use the ConnectEvent method of the MenuLine object to retrieve a "cookie" (actually a long pointer to a function in C or C++). To disconnect, the process is neatly reversed, removing the event connect, deleting the menu entries, and releasing the reference to Visual Basic.

The second class module, DoDoRunRun, manages the operation of the Run dialog.

```
VERSION 1.0 CLASS
BEGIN
   MultiUse = -1  'True
END
Attribute VB_Name = "DoDoRunRun"
Attribute VB_Creatable = False
Attribute VB_Exposed = True
Option Explicit

Public VBInstance As Object

Private dlg As New RunClass

Public Sub AfterClick()
    dlg.Run
    dlg.Execute
End Sub
```

The AfterClick() method of this class is required for an add-in. It represents the action taken on the Click event on the menu item. The settings for the Instancing and Public properties of this module are interesting. When a module is Instancing=3, (Creatable Multi-Use) and Public = True, the object is a Creatable OLE 2.x object. That means that it can be instanced with the New keyword in a Set or Dim statement or with the GetObject or CreateObject functions in Visual Basic. When Public = False, then the object is a programmable object, that is, it can be controlled from outside of the module, but it can't be independently instantiated. Using VBA Companion, you see this distinction of creatable versus programmable objects in all of the object hierarchies you browse. This is an important consideration in object design (a topic that needs to be dealt with elsewhere). Figure 16.13 shows the Run item on Visual Basics Tools menu, and Figure 16.14 shows the Run dialog launched.

FIGURE 16.13.

The Run dialog option on the Add-Ins menu.

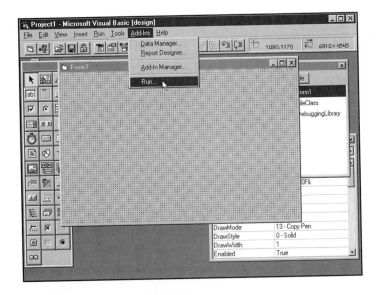

FIGURE 16.14.

The Run dialog running in the Visual Basic development environment.

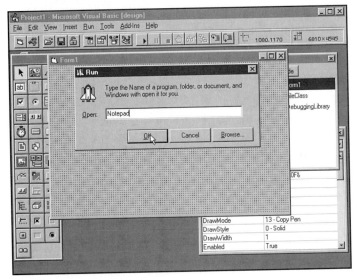

Programming Other Application Objects

Programming other application's objects is covered well in any number of references and is not a feature new to this version of Visual Basic. Suffice it to say that Visual Basic continues to be the environment of choice for customization and inter-application coordination when the applications are OLE aware.

Overview of Visual Basics OLE Features

Visual Basic 4.0 offers a range of new OLE features including support for compound document objects in forms and in the OLE container control, menu, toolbar, and status bar negotiation with OLE document objects. For programmers, the more valuable changes are in the support for OLE automation, including the ability to develop OLE automation server application and dynamic link libraries. Visual Basic utilities can now be developed in Visual Basic itself and installed in the development environment. Visual Basic now supports multiple instances so that Visual Basic can be used to debug OLE servers and add-in programs. An entire range of new business opportunities for Visual Basic programmers flows from these features.

Visual Basic and Object Oriented Programming (OOP)

Object Oriented Programming (OOP) requires the implementation of four qualities in a programming language: abstraction, encapsulation, polymorphism, and inheritance. *Abstraction* is a process of dividing your program into chunks that have a correlation with the real world problems the program is meant to solve. Rather than focusing on the function as the unit of interest, in OOP you focus on the object. This means that you can deal with more of the program at once without straining your mental faculties, so to speak.

Encapsulation is the process of making an application out of a series of black boxes which have predictable input and output, but whose inner functioning is unknown and unknowable.

Polymorphism is a more difficult concept to grasp. The bottom line is that different objects can interact without knowing before runtime what the other objects will be. A good example might be a computer game that supports different rockets. Each of these rockets exposes a trajectory property that varies with the design of the rocket. A screen painting module could interact with these rockets and access their trajectory property to paint them differently on the screen. It need not know beforehand how many of which kinds of rockets there are in order to successfully managing their presentation on screen.

The argument has raged for the life of Visual Basic about whether it qualifies as an object-oriented development tool. In the earlier versions of Visual Basic, the only claim to OOP was the use of controls and forms which had some object-oriented features in that they had both properties (data) and methods (procedures that manipulate the data). Visual Basic added a further dimension to this through the event-driven model. Events represented the interaction between the user and the objects exposed by the programmer, but for any reasonably rigorous definition of OOP, Visual Basic did not begin to qualify.

Inheritance is a process whereby one class of objects inherits all the qualities of a parent class of objects simply by reference, that is by the programmer stating in the object that it is of type X.

Many developers attempted to support OOP principles by separating data and procedures into separate code modules. Version 3.0 supported the use of Private variables and procedures. This allowed more abstraction and encapsulation; however, this was not a feature of the development environment but an innovation by programmers.

With the addition of class modules, more features of OOP are accessible to Visual Basic programmers. Abstraction and encapsulation are easily implemented with these modules. Inheritance is not supported by reference, but with careful planning of objects, one can accomplish a sort of inheritance by containment. For example, a class that managed File I/O and error checking could be included as a private member of a class that managed the file content. The second class inherits the functions of the other class by containment. Granted, this is not accomplished as simply and transparently as it is in C++, but the opportunity is at least seminally present.

Similarly, with careful design, polymorphism is supported in Visual Basic. Object references can be changed transparently, so that the same variable could represent the rocket from Apollo 13 and later represent the rocket of the space shuttle with different values in properties of the same name and with different functionality exposed in methods of the same name. In this way, the details of which object is interacting at which time need not be established until run-time.

The bottom line is that Visual Basic is evolving into an object-oriented language but does not fully embrace all the features of an OOP (at least as it is "religiously" understood). The object-oriented feature of Visual Basic, however, does present new opportunities for better architectural designs and more stable software.

Where to Go Next

OLE and object oriented design are complex topics, and both are having significant influence on the computer industry at this time. Visual Basic offers an array of tools to participate in this revolution. To realize this promise, programmers need a fairly detailed understanding of the processes involved. Visual Basic programmers have the opportunity to exploit these features without enduring the pain of C and C++ (pardon the prejudice). For further information, consider some of the following references:

For more information on OLE 2.x:

- Kraig Brockschmidt's *Understand OLE 2.0* from Microsoft Press
- *The OLE2 Programmers Reference*, from Microsoft Press

For more information on OLE Automation with Microsoft Office:

- Lee Hudspeth and Timothy-James Lee, 1995. *The Underground Guide to Microsoft Office, OLE, and VBA*. Reading, Massachusetts: Addison Wesley Publishing Company. This book takes a whimsical approach but contains all sorts of "in-the-trenches" information and understandable discussions of OLE 2.x technology.

- Apex Software, 1995. *VBA Companion.* This program has become invaluable to me in exploring the world of OLE Automation. I highly recommend it.

For in-depth discussion of object-oriented design,

- Grady Booch, 1991. *Object Oriented Design: With Applications.* Redwood City, California: Benjamin/Cummings.

Finally, for overall information on software construction and design:

- Steve McConnell, 1993. *Code Complete: A Practical Handbook of Software Construction.* Redmond, Washington: Microsoft Press.

Using Visual Basic Add-Ins

17

by
David Medinets

IN THIS CHAPTER

An *add-in* is a tool, written specifically for the Visual Basic development environment, that is designed to make life easier for the developer. Some versions of Visual Basic 4.0 come with a few such tools, for example, the Data Manager and the Report Designer. The Data Manager makes the investigation and querying of databases easier, and the Report Designer aids in preparing reports generated from databases.

You access all add-in tools through the Add-Ins menu. When Visual Basic is installed, this menu looks like Figure 17.1. You use the Add-In Manager option when you want to add other add-ins to the menu.

FIGURE 17.1.

The initial Add-Ins menu.

This chapter will explain how add-in tools link to the Visual Basic development environment. It will also show you some examples of how to create add-ins. Finally, it will explain the Visual Basic IDE OLE interface and how to create standardized dialog boxes using an add-in tool.

Within a few months after the release of Visual Basic 4.0, there is sure to be an emerging market in add-ins for developers. This chapter will help you get in on the ground floor of an entirely new programming opportunity.

Understanding Add-Ins

Add-ins can attach either temporarily or permanently to the Integrated Development Environment (IDE). The examples in this section create temporary links. The section later in this chapter, "Creating a Permanent Add-In," discusses how to create a permanent link.

Choosing Add-Ins | Add-In Manager opens the Add-In Manager dialog box shown in Figure 17.2. Checking an add-in tool adds that tool to the Add-Ins menu.

FIGURE 17.2.

The Add-In Manager dialog box.

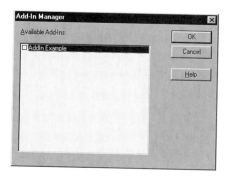

The example project that this section describes adds one menu option to the Add-Ins menu. Figure 17.3 shows the Add-Ins menu after the AddIns Example has been checked in the Add-In Manager dialog box.

FIGURE 17.3.

The Add-Ins menu with the example add-in.

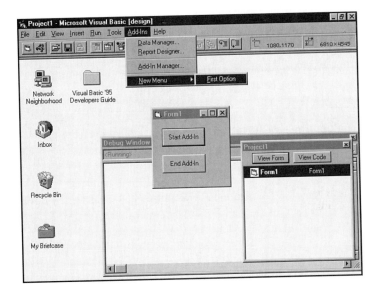

Linking to the Add-In Manager

Linking to the Add-In Manger involves two parts. The first part is to create a connector class that defines the menu structure and description of the add-in. The second part is to place an entry in the VB.INI file to indicate that the add-in is available for use.

Creating the Connector Class

Each add-in tool needs its own class module that contains the program code to link the add-in to the Add-In Manager. This code consists of, at the minimum, the ConnectAddIn event, the DisconnectAddIn event, and some global variables.

The ConnectAddIn event is called when the user selects the Add-Ins check box in the Add-In Manager dialog box. This event is responsible for adding the appropriate menu items to the Add-Ins menu by calling methods of the MenuItems collection. The following code snippet, pulled from a larger program, shows how this is done:

```
Set NewMenu = VBInstance.AddInMenu.MenuItems.AddMenu("&New Menu")
Set MenuLines = NewMenu.MenuItems.Add("&First Option")
```

The first line adds the second level menu option, and the second line adds a subsidiary menu. The new Add-Ins menu looks like Figure 17.3. Figure 17.1 shows what the original menu looked like.

At this point, the menu interface is defined. You now need to tell Visual Basic what method is attached to the menu's Click event. Each menu's Click event must be attached to a different AfterClick method. For this example, the AfterClick method is defined in the same class as the connecting method, but you don't have to do it this way.

> **NOTE**
>
> You can get around the one menu option to each AfterClick method restriction. Look at the Align sample project installed with Visual Basic to see how to do it.

You use the ConnectEvents method to link the menu option with the class of the AfterClick method. A typical line of code might look like the following:

```
ConnectID = MenuLines.ConnectEvents(Me)
```

The Me variable refers to the current instance of the class. This variable basically says to look inside the current class for the AfterClick method.

You also need to let the Add-In Manager know what description to show in the Add-In Manager dialog box. Follow these steps:

1. Open the Object Browser.
2. Select the current project in the Libraries/Project list box and your connector class in the Class/Modules list box.
3. Click on the Options button to display the Member Options dialog box.
4. Enter the description in the Description box. Figure 17.4 shows you what the Member Options dialog box looks like after the description is entered. Click the OK button when you're finished.

Setting Up the VB.INI File

In order for the Add-in Manager to be aware of an add-in, there must be an entry in the VB.INI file in either the section named [Add-Ins32] or the section named [Add-Ins16]. You can create this entry by using the WritePrivateProfileString API function as shown in the following line of code:

```
WritePrivateProfileString "Add-Ins32", "AddIn.Connector", "0", "VB.INI"
```

The first argument is the name of the section (with the square brackets), the second argument is the name of the profile string, the third is the value of the profile string, and the last is the name of the INI file.

Take a closer look at the second argument. Notice that it has two names separated by a period. The syntax of the second argument is as follows:

```
projectName.className
```

FIGURE 17.4.

Setting the connector class description in the Object Browser.

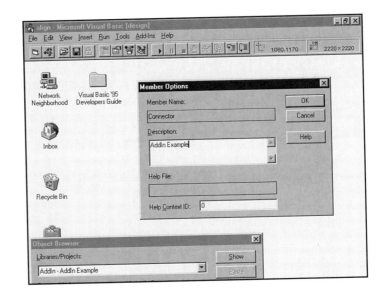

The project name is taken from the Project Name field of the Tools/Options dialog box shown in Figure 17.5. The `className` is the name of the class that implemented the `ConnectAddIn` and `DisconnectAddIn` events.

FIGURE 17.5.

The Project tab of the Tools Options dialog box.

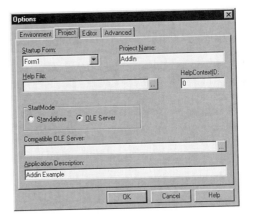

Unlinking from the Add-In Manager

When you are finished using the add-in, you need to unlink it from the Add-In Manager. Like the connection process, the unlinking process has two parts. First, you must sever the connection to the Add-Ins menu, and then you must remove the VB.INI profile string.

Removing the Connector Class

The `DisconnectAddIn` event is called when the user de-selects the add-in from the Add-In Manager dialog box. The add-in needs to call the `DisconnectEvents` method to disconnect the `AfterClick` method from the menu, as shown in the following line of code:

```
MenuLines.DisconnectEvents ConnectID
```

Then the subsidiary menu item is removed:

```
NewMenu.MenuItems.Remove MenuLines
```

Finally, the menu option in the Add-Ins menu is removed:

```
VBInstance.AddInMenu.MenuItems.Remove NewMenu
```

The `ConnectId`, `MenuLines`, `NewMenu`, and `VBInstance` variables are all variables that were assigned a value when the link to the Add-In Manager was created.

Removing the VB.INI Entry

Removing the VB.INI entry is necessary so that subsequent instances of Visual Basic will not present the developer with the add-in tool when it is not available. To remove the `Addin.Connector` string from the VB.INI file, run the following line of code:

```
WritePrivateProfileString "Add-Ins32", "AddIn.Connector", "", "VB.INI"
```

When you remove a profile string, its value must be a zero-length string.

Creating a Simple Add-In

The purpose of the simple add-in you create in this section is to display a dialog box that says "Click!" when the Add-Ins menu option is selected. To create the add-in, follow the steps in example 1.

Add-In Example 1

1. Start Visual Basic, or choose File | New to clear your workspace.
2. Select Tools | Reference and make sure that the check box next to Microsoft Visual Basic Development Environment is checked. This check box will make the VBIDE object hierarchy available to your project. This object hierarchy is described later in this chapter.
3. Enter Listing 17.1 into the code window for Form1.

Listing 17.1. FORM1.FRM from add-in example 1.

```
' Declarations for the API functions used to manipulate
' initialization files.
Private Declare Function WritePrivateProfileString _
    Lib "Kernel32" Alias "WritePrivateProfileStringA" _
    (ByVal AppName$, ByVal KeyName As Any, _
    ByVal KeyDefault As Any, ByVal FileName$) As Long

Private Declare Function GetPrivateProfileString Lib _
    "Kernel32" Alias "GetPrivateProfileStringA" (ByVal AppName$, _
    ByVal KeyName$, ByVal KeyDefault$, ByVal ReturnString$, _
    ByVal NumBytes As Long, ByVal FileName$) As Long

' This method adds a profile string to the VB.INI file. The
' instance of VB that is started will see it.
Private Sub Command1_Click()
    prof$ = String$(255, Chr$(0))

    ' If profile string is not present, return "NotFound" as the
    ' result.
    GetPrivateProfileString "Add-Ins32", "AddIn.Connector", _
        "NotFound", prof$, Len(prof$) + 1, "VB.INI"

    ' get rid of trailing blanks.
    prof$ = Left(prof$, InStr(prof$, Chr(0)) - 1)

    If prof$ = "NotFound" Then
        WritePrivateProfileString "Add-Ins32", _
            "AddIn.Connector", "0", "VB.INI"
    End If

    ' Change the directory in the next line to reflect
    ' the directory in which Visual Basic is installed.
    Shell "\vb4.32\vb32.exe", vbNormalFocus
End Sub

Private Sub Command2_Click()
    Unload Form1
End Sub

' Perform some control initialization.
Private Sub Form_Load()
    With Screen
        Left = (.Width - Width) / 2
        TOP = (.Height - Height) / 2
    End With

    Command1.Caption = "Start Add-In"
    Command2.Caption = "End Add-In"
End Sub

' Remove the profile string so that new instances
' of VB will not look for it.
Private Sub Form_Unload(Cancel As Integer)
    WritePrivateProfileString "Add-Ins32", _
        "AddIn.Connector", "", "VB.INI"
    End
End Sub
```

4. Add two command buttons to Form1. You may want to make the form small so that it does not get in the way of other windows. The Form_Load method takes care of changing their captions. Figure 17.6 shows one possible version of the form.

FIGURE 17.6.

Form1 of the add-in example 1 project.

5. Insert a class module and enter Listing 17.2.

Listing 17.2. CONNECT.CLS from add-in example 1.

```
' This class connects the add-in to the VB menu.

Dim NewMenu As VBIDE.SubMenu
Dim MenuLines As VBIDE.MenuLine
Dim ConnectID As Long
Dim thisInstance As VBIDE.Application

Sub ConnectAddIn(VBInstance As VBIDE.Application)

    Set thisInstance = VBInstance

    Set NewMenu = thisInstance.AddInMenu.MenuItems.AddMenu("&New Menu")
    Set MenuLines = NewMenu.MenuItems.Add("&First Option")
    ConnectID = MenuLines.ConnectEvents(Me)
End Sub

Sub DisconnectAddIn(Mode As Integer)
    MenuLines.DisconnectEvents ConnectID
    NewMenu.MenuItems.Remove MenuLines
    thisInstance.AddInMenu.MenuItems.Remove NewMenu
End Sub

Public Sub AfterClick()
    MsgBox "Click! "
End Sub
```

6. Press F4 to display the properties box. Set the Public property to TRUE, the Instancing property to 2 (Creatable MultiUse), and the Name property to **Connector**.

7. Select Tools | Options, and then select the Project tab in the Options dialog box. Enter **AddIn** in the Project Name text box.

8. Press F2 to start the Object Browser. Select the Connector class in the current project, and then click on the Options button. The Options dialog box appears. Enter **AddIn Example 1** as the class description.

9. Press F5 to run the project. Form1 is displayed. You should be looking at a form similar to Figure 17.6.

10. Click on the Start Add-In button. Clicking this button adds the profile string to the VB.INI file and starts a new instance of Visual Basic. The new instance of Visual Basic sees the new profile string and updates its Add-In Manager dialog box accordingly.

11. In the new instance of Visual Basic, select Add-Ins | Add-In Manager. Then check the check box next to the AddIn Example tool.

12. Select Add-Ins | New Menu | First Option. The AddIn Example tool added this new menu option. The *original* Visual Basic instance displays a message box with the words, "The Add-Ins menu option has been clicked."

13. Shut down the second instance of Visual Basic.

14. Click on the End Add-In button. Clicking this button removes the profile string from the VB.INI file so that future instances of Visual Basic don't look for a tool that is unavailable.

You can see that creating an add-in tool is somewhat involved. However, now that you have a working add-in tool, you can simply modify the AfterClick method in the Connector class module to develop a more advanced tool.

Add-In Example 2

Example 1 showed you how to create a simple add-in tool. The AfterClick method that responded to the new option on the Add-Ins menu was located in the same class as the connection methods. This example shows you how to locate the AfterClick method in a separate class. The following steps build on the code from Add-In Example 1:

1. Press F2 to start the Object Browser. Select the Connector class in the current project, and then click on the Options button to display the Options dialog box. Enter **AddIn Example 2** as the class description.

2. Add the following line of code to the CONNECT.CLS file in the declaration section:

```
Dim clickHandler As AddInClass
```

3. Add the following line of code to the CONNECT.CLS file immediately after the line that sets thisInstance to VBInstance in the ConnectAddIn method:

```
Set clickHandler = New AddInClass
```

4. Replace the line of code that sets the ConnectId variable with the following line:

```
ConnectID = MenuLines.ConnectEvents(clickHandler)
```

5. Delete the AfterClick method from the CONNECT.CLS file.

6. Add another class module to the project and call it ADDIN.CLS. Change its Name property to **AddInClass**. Then enter the code shown in Listing 17.3.

Listing 17.3. ADDIN.CLS from add-in example 2.

```
Public Sub AfterClick()
    MsgBox "click!"
End Sub
```

This example works in exactly the same way as the first example. The only difference is the location of the AfterClick event. The key to linking another class to the Connector class is that the ConnectEvents method is set to clickHandler, which holds the instance of the new class. With this information in hand, try adding a second option to the Add-Ins menu by following the steps in the next example.

Add-In Example 3

This example adds a menu option called Second Option to the Add-Ins menu. This example builds on the code in example 2. First, create a new class module called ADDIN2.CLS. Change its Name property to **AddInClass2**. Then enter the following lines of code in Listing 17.4:

Listing 17.4. ADDIN.CLS from add-in example 3.

```
Public Sub AfterClick()
    MsgBox "click two!"
End Sub
```

In the CONNECT.CLS file, change and add code as indicated by the highlighted lines in Listing 17.5:

Listing 17.5. CONNECT.CLS from add-in example 3.

```
' This class connects the add-in to the VB menu.
'
Dim NewMenu As VBIDE.SubMenu
Dim MenuLines As VBIDE.MenuLine
Dim MenuLines2 As VBIDE.MenuLine
Dim clickHandler As AddInClass
Dim clickHandler2 As AddInClass2
Dim ConnectID As Long
Dim ConnectID2 As Long
Dim thisInstance As VBIDE.Application

Sub ConnectAddIn(VBInstance As VBIDE.Application)

    Set thisInstance = VBInstance

    Set clickHandler = New AddInClass
    Set clickHandler2= New AddInClass2

    Set NewMenu = thisInstance.AddInMenu.MenuItems.AddMenu("&New Menu")
    Set MenuLines = NewMenu.MenuItems.Add("&First Option")
```

```
        Set MenuLines2 = NewMenu.MenuItems.Add("&Second Option")
        ConnectID = MenuLines.ConnectEvents(clickHandler)
        ConnectID2 = MenuLines2.ConnectEvents(clickHandler2)
End Sub

Sub DisconnectAddIn(Mode As Integer)
        MenuLines.DisconnectEvents ConnectID
        MenuLines2.DisconnectEvents ConnectID2
        NewMenu.MenuItems.Remove MenuLines
        NewMenu.MenuItems.Remove MenuLines2
        thisInstance.AddInMenu.MenuItems.Remove NewMenu
End Sub
```

The project is ready to be run. When you select the AddIn Example from the Add-In Manager, two menu options should be added to the Add-Ins menu.

Creating a Permanent Add-In

You can turn your temporary link to the Add-In Manager into a permanent one by following these steps:

1. Select File | Make EXE File and create an executable file. Make sure to click on the Options button and fill in the descriptive fields and versioning information.

2. Run the EXE file with a command line argument of /REGSERVER. For example:

   ADDIN-EXP /REGSERVER

   Where ADDIN-EXP is the name of the executable that you created in step one.

The application will start, permanently register the add-in, and then immediately close.

> **NOTE**
>
> If you distribute an add-in, each of the recipients will need to run your EXE with the /REGSERVER command line. You can avoid this requirement by using the Setup Wizard that comes with Visual Basic.

Understanding the Visual Basic IDE OLE Interface

Microsoft has turned everything in the Visual Basic project into an object of one type or another. Low-level objects, such as text boxes and labels, are combined into high-level objects, such as forms and modules, and these are in turn combined into the highest-level object, your application. Microsoft calls the application-level object App.

The *App* Object

The App object stores information about the currently executing application. It has no methods or events associated with it, only properties. The App object is available to every method in the application. In other words, it has a global scope. Table 17.1 shows a list of the properties of the App object.

Table 17.1. Properties of the *App* object.

Property	Description
Version Number Properties	
Major Minor Revision	These three properties relate to the version number of the application. They become especially important if you are making a DLL or EXE file.
Version Information Properties	
Comments CompanyName FileDescription LegalCopyright LegalTrademarks ProductName	These five properties serve to identify your application in a way people can understand. They can be set to any string value.
OLE Properties	
OLERequestPendingMsgText OLERequestPendingMsgTitle OLERequestPendingTimeout OLEServerBusyMsgText OLEServerBusyMsgTitle OLEServerBusyRaiseError OLEServerBusyTimeout	These seven properties allow you to override the default timeout values and message text of the dialog boxes that Windows uses to respond to OLE Request Pending and OLE Server situations.
Miscellaneous Properties	
Title	The name of the application as displayed in the Windows Task List.
EXEName	The name of the executable file or, if in the IDE, the project name.

Property	Description
HelpFile	The name of the help file associated with the project. Its value is usually set in the initialization section of applications.
hInstance	The handle of the instance of the application. When running in the IDE, its value is the handle of the Visual Basic instance.
Path	The value of the current path. A *path* is a list of directories where Windows can look for needed files. This property is read-only.
PrevInstance	The value of this property indicates whether a previous instance of the application is already running. You can use this property in a Load event procedure to specify whether a user is already running an instance of an application.
StartMode	This property governs whether the application runs as a standalone project (vbSModeStandalone) or as a OLE server (vbSModeAutomation).
TaskVisible	This property determines if a task is visible in the task list.

Using the App object is very straightforward. For example, you can set the HelpFile property in the following manner:

```
App.HelpFile = "c:\MYPROJ.HLP"
```

Most of the properties of the App object are blank or equal to zero until you set them yourself. However, the OLE properties are used later in this chapter.

The VBIDE Object Hierarchy

Each time that Visual Basic is started, an object of the VBIDE.Application class that contains all of the other objects in the project, except for the App object, is created. This VBIDE.Application object can be referred to as the *instance value*. When the check box in the Add-In Manager dialog box is checked, the ConnectAddIn method is called and the instance value is passed as the parameter, VBInstance. Table 17.2 shows the properties of the VBIDE.Application object. You can refer to any of these properties in your AfterClick method if you store the value of VBInstance in a global variable. The AddIn example program used the global variable called thisInstance.

Table 17.2. Properties of the `VBIDE.Application` object.

Property	Description
ActiveProject	This is an object of the class `ProjectTemplate`. You can use this property to access the current `ActiveForm` object, add new objects to the project, or determine the currently selected components.
AddInMenu	This is an object of the class `Menu`. You can use this property to modify the Add-Ins menu of a project.
Application	The `Application` object representing the current instance of Visual Basic. You don't need to use this property because `VBInstance` also represents the current instance of Visual Basic.
FileControl	The `FileControl` object of Visual Basic. Using this property allows you to register to receive all file control events. See the SPY sample project for more information.
LastUsedPath	The path used for the File dialog boxes. You can modify this property if needed.
Name	The name used in code to identify the current object. The value of this property seems to always be Microsoft Visual Basic, so you can ignore it.
Parent	The object that contains the current object. This property is useful when talking about a control object, but when the object is the application instance itself, you can ignore this property.
Version	The version number of the application the add-in is connected to. The value of this property seems to always be 4.0. You can ignore this property also, unless you need to know which version of Visual Basic is being used.

The *VBIDE.ProjectTemplate* Object

The `ActiveProject` property of the `VBIDE.Application` object is a member of the class `VBIDE.ProjectTemplate`. Table 17.3 lists the methods of the `VBIDE.ProjectTemplate` class, and Table 17.4 lists its properties.

Table 17.3. Methods of the `VBIDE.ProjectTemplate` object.

Method	Description
AddFile	This method adds a file to the project. It takes a file name as an argument. Visual Basic automatically adds the file as a form, module, or class, depending on the file extension. This method returns a string identifying the type of file added.

Method	*Description*
AddFormTemplate	This method adds a blank form to the project. The added form becomes the active form. This method returns a FormTemplate object so that you can further manipulate the form.
AddMDIFormTemplate	This method adds a MDI form to the project. The added form becomes the active form. This method returns a FormTemplate object so that you can further manipulate the form.
AddReference	This method adds a reference (.OLB file) to the project. You can specify the reference by library name or by file name.
AddToolboxProgID	This method adds a compound document object to the toolbox. The programmatic identifier of the compound document object is a required parameter.
AddToolboxTypelib	This method places the objects from a type library into the toolbox.
AddToolboxVBX	This method adds a VBX control to the toolbox. The file name of the VBX control is a required parameter.
RemoveComponent	This method removes a component from a project. It requires two parameters. The first is a Component object specifying the component to be removed. The second specifies whether to save the component before removal.

Table 17.4. Properties of the VBIDE.ProjectTemplate object.

Property	*Description*
ActiveForm	The form that is the active window. This property is a member of the FormTemplate class. If an MDI form is active or referenced, this property specifies the MDI form.
Application	The Application object representing the current instance of Visual Basic. You don't need this property because VBInstance also represents the current instance of Visual Basic.
FileName	The file name of the currently selected file.
Parent	This property points to the object that contains the current object. This property should always be equal to VBInstance.
SelectedComponents	A collection of the currently selected components. The Align sample project uses this property.

The `AfterClick` method refers to the `VBIDE.ProjectTemplate` object by using the `VBInstance.ActiveProject` variable. The most useful property is `ActiveForm`, which is a member of the `VBIDE.FormTemplate` class. The `VBIDE.FormTemplate` class is discussed in the next section.

The *VBIDE.FormTemplate* Object

The `ActiveForm` property of the `VBIDE.ProjectTemplate` object is a member of the class `VBIDE.FormTemplate`. Table 17.5 lists the methods of the `VBIDE.FormTemplate` class, and Table 17.6 lists its properties.

Table 17.5. Methods of the `VBIDE.FormTemplate` object.

Method	Description
AddMenuTemplate	This method adds a Menu object to a form. It has two required arguments. The first is a string naming the new menu. The second is the name of a ControlTemplate object representing the parent menu item. If this object is set to Nothing, the menu will be added to the end of the menu bar.
InsertFile	This method inserts code from a file into the code module of a form immediately after the declarations and before the first procedure.

Table 17.6. Properties of the `VBIDE.FormTemplate` object.

Property	Description
Application	The Application object representing the current instance of Visual Basic. You don't need this property because VBInstance also represents the current instance of Visual Basic.
ControlTemplates	The collection of all the controls on a form. This property is a member of the ControlTemplates class.
Parent	The object that contains the current object. This property should always be equal to VBInstance.ActiveProject.
Properties	The collection of all properties relating to the active form. This property is a member of the Properties class.

Property	Description
SelectedControlTemplates	The collection of all selected controls on the form. This property is a member of the SelectedControls class.

The next section shows you how to use some of these properties and methods to programmatically create a form.

Creating Standardized About Dialog Boxes

One possible use for an add-in tool might be to add standardized dialog boxes to new projects. Once you have designed a dialog box that you like, you can create an add-in tool to automatically add it to a new project.

Listings 17.6, 17.7, and 17.8 contain an entire project that demonstrates how to add new forms to your project. Listing 17.6 is the code behind Form1; it performs the INI file changes if needed. Listing 17.7 is the ADDIN.CLS file. Call its class by the name of AddInClass. Listing 17.8 is the CONNECT.CLS file. Call its class by the name of Connector.

Listing 17.6. ADDIN.CLS for adding a standard dialog box.

```
Option Explicit

Public thisInstance As VBIDE.Application
Public bar As Integer

Private Declare Function WritePrivateProfileString Lib "Kernel32" _
    Alias "WritePrivateProfileStringA" (ByVal AppName$, _
    ByVal KeyName As Any, ByVal KeyDefault As Any, ByVal FileName$) As Long

Private Declare Function GetPrivateProfileString Lib _
    "Kernel32" Alias "GetPrivateProfileStringA" (ByVal AppName$, _
    ByVal KeyName$, ByVal KeyDefault$, ByVal ReturnString$, _
    ByVal NumBytes As Long, ByVal FileName$) As Long

Private Sub Command1_Click()
    Dim prof As String

    prof = String$(255, Chr$(0))

    ' If profile string is not present, return "NotFound" as the
    ' result.
    GetPrivateProfileString "Add-Ins32", "AddIn.Connector", _
        "NotFound", prof, Len(prof) + 1, "VB.INI"
```

continues

Listing 17.6. continued

```
    ' get rid of trailing blanks.
    prof = Left(prof, InStr(prof, Chr(0)) - 1)

    If prof = "NotFound" Then
        WritePrivateProfileString "Add-Ins32", _
            "AddIn.Connector", "0", "VB.INI"
    End If

    Shell "\vb4.32\vb32.exe", vbNormalFocus
End Sub

Private Sub Command2_Click()
    Unload Form1
End Sub

Private Sub Form_Load()
    With Screen
        Left = (.Width - Width) / 2
        TOP = (.Height - Height) / 2
    End With

    Command1.Caption = "Start Add-In"
    Command2.Caption = "End Add-In"
End Sub

Private Sub Form_Unload(Cancel As Integer)
    WritePrivateProfileString "Add-Ins32", _
        "AddIn.Connector", "", "VB.INI"
    End
End Sub
```

Listing 17.7. ADDIN.CLS for adding a standard dialog box.

```
Public thisInstance As VBIDE.Application
Dim numDialog As Integer

Public Sub AfterClick()
    numDialog = numDialog + 1
' This With statement is changing the
    ' properties of a VBIDE.FormTemplate
    With thisInstance.ActiveProject.AddFormTemplate
        .Properties("BackColor") = &H800080
        .Properties("BorderStyle") = 1
        .Properties("Caption") = "About Add-In Examples"
        .Properties("ControlBox") = False
        .Properties("Height") = 2500
        .Properties("Left") = 1000
        .Properties("Name") = "AboutFrm" + Right(Str(numDialog), 1)
        .Properties("MaxButton") = False
        .Properties("MinButton") = False
        .Properties("Top") = 1000
        .Properties("Width") = 5000
```

```
        ' This With statement is changing the
        ' properties of a VBIDE.ControlTemplate
        With .ControlTemplates.Add("CommandButton")
            .Properties("Caption") = "&OK"
            .Properties("Left") = 2000
            .Properties("Width") = 1000
            .Properties("Top") = 1320
        End With

        With .ControlTemplates.Add("Label")
            .Properties("BackColor") = &H800080
            .Properties("Caption") = "Copyright 1995, SAMS"
            .Properties("ForeColor") = &H80FFFF
            .Properties("Left") = 1550
            .Properties("Height") = 250
            .Properties("Width") = 1700
            .Properties("Top") = 850
        End With

        With .ControlTemplates.Add("Label")
            .Properties("Alignment") = 2 ' center
            .Properties("BackColor") = &H800080
            .Properties("Caption") = "AddIn Examples 3 - Version 1.0"
            .Properties("ForeColor") = &H80FFFF
            .Properties("Height") = 250
            .Properties("Left") = 250
            .Properties("Width") = 4500
            .Properties("Top") = 250
        End With
    End With
End Sub
```

Listing 17.8. CONNECT.CLS for adding a standard dialog box.

```
' This class connects the add-in to the VB menu.
'
Dim NewMenu As VBIDE.SubMenu
Dim MenuLines As VBIDE.MenuLine
Dim clickHandler As AddInClass
Dim ConnectID As Long
Dim thisInstance As VBIDE.Application

Sub ConnectAddIn(VBInstance As VBIDE.Application)
    Set thisInstance = VBInstance
    Set clickHandler = New AddInClass
    Set clickHandler.thisInstance = thisInstance
    Set NewMenu = thisInstance.AddInMenu.MenuItems.AddMenu("&New Menu")
    Set MenuLines = NewMenu.MenuItems.Add("&First Option")
    ConnectID = MenuLines.ConnectEvents(clickHandler)
End Sub

Sub DisconnectAddIn(Mode As Integer)
    MenuLines.DisconnectEvents ConnectID
    NewMenu.MenuItems.Remove MenuLines
    thisInstance.AddInMenu.MenuItems.Remove NewMenu
End Sub
```

You also need to add the following line to the Connector class in the ConnectAddIn method after the line in which the clickHandler variable is set:

```
Set clickHandler.thisInstance = thisInstance
```

This example just scratches the surface of how to add a form. You can change font typefaces and size. You could also add methods or properties to the form by creating a temporary file and then using the InsertFile method of the FormTemplate class.

Summary

This chapter showed you how to create add-ins for use inside Visual Basic. Starting with a single additional menu option, you progressed to two options each invoking a different class. Then after a brief tour of the Visual Basic IDE underpinnings, you looked at how to use an add-in to create a standardized form or dialog box.

Microsoft has included the source code for an alignment add-in, as well as the code for the Data Manager add-in. Take advantage of their code to learn more about how to create your own.

In addition, don't ignore the potential profit that can be yours if you create the ultimate add-in. With a potential market of over 1.5 million programmers, even a small success can pay off big!

Understanding OLE

18

by Chuck Traywick

IN THIS CHAPTER

If you have been reading anything about software development in the past few years, you have been somewhat bombarded by OLE discussions. These next two chapters are intended to be a first start. While the space we have here does not allow an in-depth definitive work, these chapters will explain what OLE is, what it isn't, and will show you how to apply this exciting new technology. This chapter will provide an overview of OLE and will illustrate how to add OLE to your projects.

If you are new to Visual Basic and have not spent much time with the system, the concepts in this chapter may appear obscure at first. If you stick with it, however, you'll find that the results are worth the struggle.

How Do OLE and Visual Basic Work Together?

Almost everything written about Windows development discusses *objects* or *OLE* (Object Linking and Embedding). Objects are a method to help you raise the functionality and reliability of your development efforts.

Visual Basic 4.0 is an object-oriented language, which means you manipulate objects to develop programs instead of typing in a lot of code. For example, you take an existing control like the text box and place it onto a form. This text box control contains events, methods, and properties. That is, it contains data (such as the properties that you set to your needs) and code (such as the code to control the object).

These three classes of features (events, methods, and properties) to this control are pre-programmed for you. You can use these features without additional programming by following the rules laid out by the original developer (Microsoft, in this case) of this control.

The Development of OLE

In the past, programs were monolithic. You had to include all of the features you wanted as code. As the computer industry evolved, operating systems began to increase in functionality and to provide additional features that application programs could call. For example, instead of writing the code to put the data on the screen, developers could now call a built-in function of the operating system to perform this action for them. The operating system's built-in functions were called the API (Application Programming Interface).

One problem that developers encountered was inconsistency between applications on the same platform (DOS, for example). The keystrokes they used for a particular spreadsheet most likely were not the same as the keystrokes of their word processor. The emergence of Windows 3.0 solved this problem by enforcing consistency across all application interfaces.

Now that the applications looked similar, the issue was how to get them to work together. One solution was *DDE* (Dynamic Data Exchange), which is a widespread implementation that used different applications to perform different functions. Developers could now use a spreadsheet to perform calculations and a database program to store the results. They could put these multiple interfaces and applications together into one application solution.

DDE, for all of its power, was limited. It was based upon the client/server model and was message based. As a result, getting two applications to work together involved a lot of programming. To address this issue and other issues, Microsoft released OLE 1.0.

OLE 1.0 was the first major effort that was available in a widespread fashion that attempted to increase the ability of applications to work together.

OLE 1.0 was really intended to expose developers to the concepts of objects. The operating system platform at the time of OLE 1.0 shipment (such as Windows 3.0 and Windows 3.1) was not sufficient to exploit this technology but was adequate to get developers started with using it. Even Microsoft OLE between Excel and Word, for example, was not reliable in its first release. Also, OLE 1.0 did not provide a full set of APIs that allowed full implementation of the technology from a programming point of view.

OLE 2.0 is focused upon the Windows 95 and Windows NT platforms. Windows NT (in my view) is by far the more stable platform for serious OLE development. OLE 2.0 includes several enhancements that are significant. Perhaps the most significant is REMOTE OLE capability. This requires Windows 95 or Windows NT 3.51 or greater.

These two operating systems make it easier for objects to be called and used because they provide a new kind of interface at the programming level called the REGISTRY. This means that the applications that we develop can install themselves into the REGISTRY of either Windows 95 or Windows NT 3.51. Thus, these applications become part of these operating systems.

OLE 2.0 also supports components, another significant enhancement. For example, Excel 5.0 contains many objects. Older implementations of OLE would allow one call or one interface to Excel as an object. That is, Excel (the entire application) was one object. OLE 2.0 allows applications to define complex hierarchical interfaces (called "Collections" in Visual Basic 4.0 speak). This enables Excel to expose over 100 components that another application can use. For example, we could theoretically call the Excel grid control and completely control it from a Visual Basic program.

The Benefits of OLE

OLE enables you to paste data and a controlling piece of software into another application. The recipient application has *containers* that enable it to accept this new kind of interface. Now, for example, you can take the functionality of AutoCAD and paste it inside of a Visual Basic application.

How can this capability help you and your users? Consider the following example. AutoCAD is an excellent CAD (Computer-Aided Drawing) system, but it stores its data (drawing files) in a highly compressed numerical database that is proprietary. Although AutoCAD has facilities for keeping information about the drawings, it is not very good at performing traditional database functions. This is the kind of situation in which OLE can really help you and, more importantly, your end users.

You can take a simple application in Visual Basic that uses an Access database (or XBase) to store things like project name, author, description, date of last revision, and so on. On this same screen, you can place an OLE container that allows you to put the AutoCAD and the Access data together at the same time. To perform this function without OLE would take a tremendous programming effort. An example follows this section that illustrates this concept.

OLE enables you to create an application that merges data and applications from multiple sources. The authors of the different applications you use do not have to program their applications to know about each other in advance. The programmers at Autodesk (authors of AutoCAD) wrote their application to support OLE functionality as Microsoft did with Visual Basic. After both of these applications were shrink-wrapped and shipped, you could merge them into a custom solution that provides more power to the user.

The other major benefit to OLE is time savings. Not only can you accomplish the things mentioned in the previous paragraphs, but learning how to do it is not that difficult once you master some new skills.

Note that OLE requires a more powerful computer to run successfully than a normal Windows environment. The best thing you can do for your end users is to get them to a computer that is Windows NT capable (486/66 or higher with 16 M of RAM). This level of system will provide you with the speed and memory needed to effectively run OLE applications.

What Is Linking?

When you implement OLE, you can choose to embed or link an object. Linking is intended for applications where the changes in data are important. A monthly sales analysis is a good example of this type of application. You can create the charts and numbers in Excel and paste the spreadsheet object into a Word document. Each time a user loads the Word document, a current copy of the Excel data is also loaded without any additional interaction from the end user.

When you create a link, the OLE interface and Windows create a hexadecimal named file that contains the data necessary to maintain the source and destination objects together. This file also contains the data necessary for the graphic to display your image (kind of like a large thumbnail icon). The location of this file will vary based on your system setup. In Windows 3.*x*, if you defined a TEMP directory setting in your AUTOEXEC.BAT file, it would be located in this directory. If you do not make this setting, it will be in the author link location. That is, if you have a spreadsheet in Excel that includes a WORD document, the link (absent the setting above) would be in the Excel directory where the spreadsheet was started.

Since most applications in Windows will have a graphical image of some sort, the OLE function can use this image to place into the OLE container that you place upon a form.

In the AutoCAD/Access example, you can take a small image that AutoCAD created and store it in the container in the Visual Basic application. The end user can then see a thumbnail of the drawing along with the data from the Access database about the drawing name, project, and so on. When you link the object, you can now double-click on the image in the OLE container and launch AutoCAD with that image open.

Each application that supports OLE must install the features of the OLE API it supports into the Windows registry. Then any application that is OLE-compliant can use this functionality. The *registry* is a global database that enables object-oriented features of a given application to be exposed by the definitions found here. Another way of saying this is that you can extend the operating system with applications you develop by adding them to the registry! If you have not played around with the registry, select Windows' Run command and enter **Regedit** in the dialog box that appears to see what this does for you.

What Is Embedding?

Embedding is similar to linking except that the data from the source application is cloned and placed in its entirety into the destination object. Embedding is intended for documents in which the data is either static or is not going to be on the machine where the data was authored. For example, you may embed an object in a compound document that you are going to give to another user of another computer.

When you embed one object into another object, the destination object can become quite large.

Embedding is also the way to go if you're working on a network. Sometimes you can get links to work on a network, but linking is not recommended. OLE is not network tested. Microsoft is working on distributed OLE as you read this chapter; expect it soon from a dealer near you.

What Are Classes?

In traditional object-oriented definitions, a *class* is a general group of objects that share common attributes. For example, you might have a class of transportation vehicles called Vehicles. This class would share common properties, such as engine, capacity, and so on. You could then extend these properties to subclasses. This process is called *inheritance* in OOP (object-oriented programming). If you had Truck as a subclass of the Vehicle class, the Truck subclass would have the same properties (engine, capacity, and so on) as the Vehicle class because it is a subclass of the Vehicle class. The Truck subclass is said to be dependent upon the Vehicle class because it inherits some of its properties from that class.

In Visual Basic 4.0, classes are somewhat different. You define the classes you are going to use in a class module. A class module is like the code module in Visual Basic 3.0 except that the class module pertains expressly to classes. When your code calls one of the class modules, that module creates a class or an object.

Suppose that you want to create a class of object that you can use to turn on and off a light switch. You might take the following steps:

1. Start up Visual Basic 4.0 and start a new project.

2. Choose Insert | Class Module from the menu bar. Visual Basic creates a blank class module.

3. With the class module highlight bar illuminated, press F4 to bring up the properties. In the Name property, type in **SwitchPlate.**

4. Click on Form1 to activate it.

5. Draw two labels and three command buttons on Form1.

6. Set the border style for Label1 and Label2 to Fixed Single.

7. In the declarations section of Form1, type the following code:

```
Dim objX As SwitchPlate
Public BuildingA As New Form1
```

8. Activate the first command button, Command1. Double-click it to display the Code window, and then open the Event combo box and select the Click event.

9. In the Click event, insert the following code:

```
Sub Command1_Click()
    Dim LightOn As New SwitchPlate
    LightOn.SwitchStatus = 1
    Set BuildingA.LightStatus = LightOn
    BuildingA.LightStatus.TurnLightsOn 1
End Sub
```

10. Close the Code window. With Command1 still activated, press F4 to display the Properties window.

11. In the Caption property, enter the following code:

```
Light &On
```

12. Close the Properties window.

13. Click on the second command button, Command2. With this button highlighted, double-click to display the Code window for the Click event (which should be the default procedure).

14. Insert the following code:

```
Private Sub Command2_Click()
    Dim LightOn As New SwitchPlate
    LightOn.SwitchStatus = 2
    Set BuildingA.LightStatus = LightOn
    BuildingA.LightStatus.TurnLightsOn 2
End Sub
```

15. In the declarations section, add the following two code segments:

```
Property Get LightStatus() As SwitchPlate
    Set LightStatus = objX
End Property

Property Set LightStatus(x As SwitchPlate)
    Set objX = x
End Property
```

16. Activate the class module and display the declarations section. Then insert the following code:

```
Public SwitchStatus As Integer
Public Sub TurnLightsOn(x As Integer)
    Select Case x
        Case 1
            Form1.Label1.BackColor = vbYellow
            Form1.Label1.Caption = "Light On"
            Form1.Label2.Caption = ""
            Form1.Label2.BackColor = vbBlack
        Case 2
            Form1.Label2.BackColor = vbGreen
            Form1.Label2.Caption = "Light Off"
            Form1.Label1.Caption = ""
            Form1.Label1.BackColor = vbBlack
    End Select
End Sub
```

17. Activate Form1 again and click on the third command button. Press F4 to display the Properties window. In the Caption property, enter **E&XIT**.

18. Close the Properties window.

19. Double-click on the third command button to display the Code window for the Click event and enter the following code:

```
Private Sub Command3_Click()
    End
End Sub
```

20. Press F5 and see what happens.

This previous example is not complex, but it does illustrate several new features of Visual Basic 4.0. The class module you created and named SwitchPlate is a new class of object for this application. By declaring SwitchStatus in this module, you made SwitchStatus a property of SwitchPlate. You can access this property the same way you access the properties for the standard Visual Basic controls.

The LightStatus code in Form1 (both set and get procedures) creates an object at run time that has the properties of the SwitchPlate class. Each time you execute this code, you activate an instance of the SwitchPlate class. The last code segment creates a method for this class (TurnLightsOn).

You have created a new class with properties, multiple instances, and its own method. The capability to create objects with full object-oriented capability is new to Visual Basic 4.0. The ease of Visual Basic and the power of OOP is a tough combination to beat!

Imagine what you can do with this technology. You could write a standard printer header routine for reports that cannot be written with the report writer and then call the routine in other code forever. Now if you could just persuade Microsoft to allow developers to create DLLs with Visual Basic ...

How Does OLE Combine Multiple Data Types?

This chapter previously used an AutoCAD example to demonstrate how you could use OLE to combine multiple data types. In the following procedure, you create the drawing management system for AutoCAD that allows end users to select the drawing they want by looking at it from inside of AutoCAD. By following this example step by step, you can get a feel for how you can combine multiple data types and multiple application types. If you don't have AutoCAD, keep in mind that this code will also work with other OLE-compliant applications.

Start a new project and name it DrawMgt1. On Form1 (see figure 18.1), you need to place several controls. (Note that the example project in the figures is using Windows 95 as a testing platform.)

FIGURE 18.1.

The form you need to create for the drawing management program.

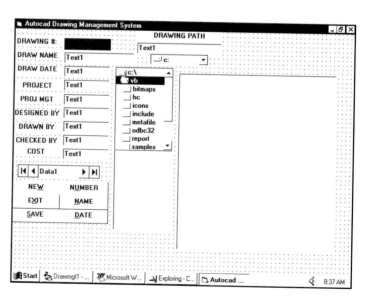

Starting from the upper left corner of the form and moving downward, the following steps describe each control you need to add:

1. Insert a text box and set its `Name` property to FDRAWNUM.

2. Insert a label to the left of the text box control and set its caption to DRAWING #:

3. Insert another text box and name this one FDRAWNAME.

4. Place a label to the left of the text box with the caption set to DRAW NAME.

5. Insert the remaining seven text boxes and name them as shown in the following code:

```
TextBox = FDRAWDATE
TextBox = FPROJECT
TextBox = FPROJMGT
TextBox = FDESIGNED
TextBox = FDRAWN
TextBox = FCHECKED
TextBox = FCOST
```

6. Insert label controls to the left of each of these text boxes you added in step 5 and set the caption properties as you see in the figure or follow this list:

DRAW DATE

PROJECT

PROJ MGT

DESIGNED BY

DRAWN BY

CHECKED BY

COST

After you set up all the controls on the form, start up Access and create a new database named WINSEM1. When Access displays your new database, create a new table named DRAWINGS with the following fields and properties:

```
PRIMARY KEY FIELD FDRAWNUM TEXT 8
FDRAWNUM TEXT 30
FDRAWDATE DATE/TIME
FPROJECT TEXT 30
FPROJMGT TEXT 30
FDESIGNED TEXT 30
FDRAWN TEXT 30
FCHECKED TEXT 30
FCOST OLE/Object
FDRAWPATH TEXT 30
```

In the Visual Basic form, insert a data control named Data1. Set the `Database` property to WINSEM1, which you just created. Then set the `Data1.Recordsource` property to the Drawings table.

Next, bind each field in the text boxes to the appropriate field in the table as follows:

TextBox: FDRAWNUM Bound To Data1.FDRAWNUM

TextBox: FDRAWNAME Bound To Data1.FDRAWNAME

TextBox: FDRAWDATE Bound To Data1.FDRAWDATE

TextBox: FPROJECT Bound To Data1.FPROJECT

TextBox: FPROJMGT Bound To Data1.FPROJMGT

TextBox: FDESIGNED Bound To Data1.FDESIGNED

TextBox: FDRAWN Bound To Data1.FDRAWN

TextBox: FCHECKED Bound To Data1.FCHECKED

TextBox: FCOST Bound To Data1.FCOST

You may notice that you do not have an OLE field for the AutoCAD drawing. This omission is related to an incompatibility between Access 2.0 and Visual Basic 3.0. Each OLE object contains a wrapper that the destination object uses to store and retrieve the sending object. Access 2.0 and Visual Basic 3.0 did not use the same wrapper, so if you are using these products, you cannot stuff an OLE object directly into an Access OLE field. This example shows a workaround for this problem that may be useful to you when you create other applications.

You now need to create six command buttons below the Data Access Object (or DAO). Create the first button using this code:

```
NAME = cmdnewdraw; CAPTION = NE&W
```

Attach the following code to the preceding button's `Click` event:

```
Private Sub cmdNewDraw_Click()
        AddedNew = "T"
    Data1.Recordset.AddNew
    cmdSaveNew.Visible = True
    Dir1.Visible = True
    Drive1.Visible = True
    File1.Visible = True
    FDRAWNUM.MaxLength = 8
    FDRAWNAME.MaxLength = 30
    FDRAWDATE.MaxLength = 8
    FPROJECT.MaxLength = 30
    FPROJMGT.MaxLength = 30
    FDESIGNED.MaxLength = 30
    FDRAWN.MaxLength = 30
    FCHECKED.MaxLength = 30
    FDRAWNUM.SetFocus
End Sub
```

Create the next button:

```
NAME = cmdexit; CAPTION = E&XIT
```

Then attach the following code to the preceding button's `Click` event:

```
Private Sub cmdExit_Click()
    End
End Sub
```

Create the next button:

```
NAME = cmdsavenew; CAPTION = &SAVE
```

Then attach the following code to the preceding button's `Click` event:

```
Private Sub cmdSaveNew_Click()
    Dir1.Visible = False
    Drive1.Visible = False
    File1.Visible = False
    cmdSaveNew.Visible = False
    Dim FileNum ' Declare variable.
    FileNum = FreeFile   ' Get a valid file number.
    YFilePath = Dir1.Path
    FileName = FDRAWNUM.Text
    sFileName = YFilePath & "\" & FileName & ".OLE"
    Open sFileName For Binary As FileNum   ' Open file to save
    FDRAWOBJ.FileNumber = FileNum   ' Set the filenumber.
    FDRAWOBJ.Action = OLE_SAVE_TO_FILE
    Data1.Recordset.Update
    Close #FileNum   ' Close the file.
    AddedNew = "F"
    Data1.Recordset.MoveLast
End Sub
```

This example doesn't implement the following three buttons, but they demonstrate how you could easily add features that would make life simpler for the end user:

```
NAME = cmdbydrawnum; CAPTION = N&UMBER
NAME = cmdbydrawname; CAPTION = &NAME
NAME = cmdbydrawdate; CAPTION = &DATE
```

On Form1, add the following code to the `Form Load` event:

```
Private Sub Form_Load()
    AddedNew = "F"
End Sub
```

At the top center of Form1, add a label named LABEL10 and set its caption to DRAWING PATH. Just below this label, insert a text box and set its name to FDRAWPATH. Below this text box insert a DriveListBox and set its name to Drive1. Just below the Drive1 control insert a DirListBox and set its name to Dir1. Double-click on the DirListBox control and attach the following code to its `Change` event:

```
Private Sub Dir1_Change()
    File1.Path = Dir1.Path   ' Set File path.
End Sub
```

Below the DirListBox control, insert a FileListBox control and set its name to FILE1. Then attach the following code to its `DoubleClick` event:

```
Private Sub File1_DblClick()
Dim xFilename As String
    FDRAWOBJ.Class = "AutocadDrawing"
    If Right(File1.Path, 1) <> "\" Then
    xFilename = File1.Path & "\" & File1.FileName
    Else
    xFilename = File1.Path & File1.FileName
    End If
    FDRAWPATH = File1.Path
    FDRAWOBJ.SourceDoc = xFilename
```

```
    FDRAWOBJ.Action = OLE_CREATE_FROM_FILE
    FDRAWOBJ.Action = OLE_ACTIVATE
    Data1.Recordset("FDrawPath").Value = xFilename
    AddedNew = "T"
End Sub
```

Create a module file (code file) and insert the following code into it:

```
Global Const OLE_CREATE_NEW = 0
Global Const OLE_CREATE_FROM_FILE = 1
Global Const OLE_COPY = 4
Global Const OLE_PASTE = 5
Global Const OLE_UPDATE = 6
Global Const OLE_ACTIVATE = 7
Global Const OLE_EXECUTE = 8
Global Const OLE_CLOSE = 9
Global Const OLE_DELETE = 10
Global Const OLE_SAVE_TO_FILE = 11
Global Const OLE_READ_FROM_FILE = 12
Global Const OLE_CONVERT_TO_TYPE = 13
Global AddedNew
Global xFilename
```

Lastly, insert a large OLE container control to the right of your drive controls and set its Name property to FDRAWOBJ. Now you're ready to run the application. Start the application, and then click on the New command button. Your screen should display something similar to Figure 18.2.

FIGURE 18.2.

The drawing management program's execution screen.

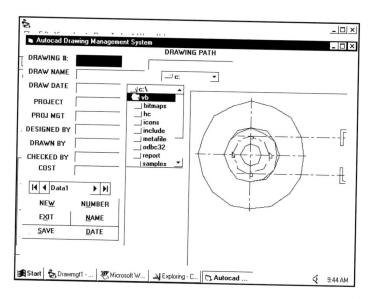

Notice that the directory box becomes illuminated, which prompts the user to find the correct directory. Watch the text box at the top of the screen and notice that the path is built as the user clicks on the directory he wants to be in. When the user double-clicks on a drawing file, AutoCAD launches, as shown in Figure 18.3.

FIGURE 18.3.

The AutoCAD drawing screen.

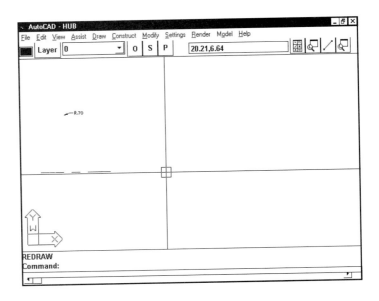

Notice that AutoCAD was invoked with the drawing that you selected. To get back to the Visual Basic application, all you need do is type **END** at the AutoCAD prompt. Now you can enter the data you want to attach to this drawing and click on Save. The Visual Basic screen now looks like Figure 18.4.

FIGURE 18.4.

The finished screen of the drawing management program.

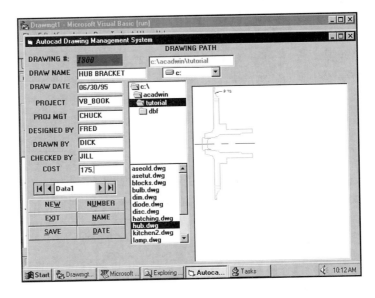

You can use the arrows on the data control to move to the drawing you want. When you find it, double-click in the OLE container and AutoCAD starts up with the drawing that you selected. When you exit AutoCAD, control returns to the Visual Basic application at the spot you left it.

> **NOTE**
>
> Before you start creating your own applications, consider the level of the machine you implement this type of application on. You need at least a 486/66 with 16M of RAM. The memory is very important.

What Is OLE Automation?

Another application of OLE is OLE Automation. OLE Automation is the capability of using features of another OLE-compliant program remotely from your Visual Basic application. For example, Microsoft Excel contains many programmable objects. You can selectively use these objects through your Visual Basic interface.

Microsoft has been embedding a script form of Visual Basic into many of their products called Visual Basic for Applications or VBA. Not all Microsoft applications are fully implemented with VBA. In the following procedure, you are going to provide an example of OLE Automation using Word Basic in Microsoft Word.

I recently worked on a system for a client (I develop custom software for corporate clients) in Visual Basic. This client manufactures large industrial equipment that it in turn sells throughout the world. This equipment is very large and complex. The quoting process is also very complex. Frequently this client must respond to formal requests for proposals with the pricing data as well as engineering and other data that is requested by the potential customer.

I developed a system to create the quote, but a simple printout was not enough of a solution for the proposal problem. Enter OLE Automation. Now the user can drag the quote they want and drop it on a Microsoft Word icon. This icon executes code that invokes Word as an object that is managed by Visual Basic. The quoting data is then sent to Word through this object management. The result is the quote data formatted in a Word document that the user can then modify as she wishes.

The following steps outline this type of program:

1. Start a new project.

2. On Form1, add three text boxes in a column.

3. Add two command buttons. Place the caption SEND on one command button. Place the caption EXIT on the other command button.

4. Attach the following code to the SEND button's `Click` event:

```
Private Sub Command1_Click()
Const MB_OK = 0, MB_OKCANCEL = 1    ' Define buttons.
Const MB_YESNOCANCEL = 3, MB_YESNO = 4
```

```
Const MB_ICONSTOP = 16, MB_ICONQUESTION = 32     ' Define Icons.
Const MB_ICONEXCLAMATION = 48, MB_ICONINFORMATION = 64
Const MB_DEFBUTTON2 = 256, IDYES = 6, IDNO = 7  ' Define other.
Dim DgDef, Msg, Response, Title ' Declare variables.

    On Error GoTo COMMAND1ERR
    Title = "OLE AUTOMATION PRINTING INSTRUCTIONS"
    Msg = "This data that is currently selected will be sent to word. " & Nl
    Msg = Msg & " Do you want to continue?"
    DgDef = MB_YESNO + MB_ICONSTOP + MB_DEFBUTTON2  ' Describe dialog.
    Response = MsgBox(Msg, DgDef, Title)    ' Get user response.
            If Response <> IDYES Then    ' Evaluate response
                Exit Sub
            End If

    MemAction = "WORD"
    MemDocType = "Ltr"
    Dim Word As Object
    Set Word = CreateObject("Word.Basic")
    SendKeys "%"
    DoEvents
    SendKeys "F"
    DoEvents
    SendKeys "N"
    DoEvents
    SendKeys "{ENTER}"
    DoEvents

    Word.Insert Chr$(13)
    DoEvents



        Word.Font "Arial", 10
        Word.LeftPara
        MemText = Text1.Text & Chr$(13)
        Word.Insert MemText
        DoEvents
        MemText = ""
        MemText = Text2.Text & Chr$(13)
        Word.Insert MemText
        DoEvents
        MemText = ""
        MemText = Text3.Text & Chr$(13)
        Word.Insert MemText
        DoEvents
        MemText = ""

        MsgBox "Go to word before you press enter"
        Set Word = Nothing
        Screen.MousePointer = 1

        Exit Sub

COMMAND1ERR:
    Msg = Error$
    MsgBox Msg
    Resume Next
End Sub
```

Your screen should look like Figure 18.5 when you execute the program.

FIGURE 18.5.

Visual Basic OLE
Automation development
screen.

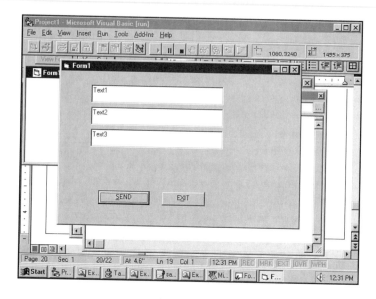

5. Add some text to the text boxes in your application.
6. Click on the SEND button. A dialog box appears, prompting you to continue.
7. Pick YES. Word starts and the contents of the three text boxes should be sent to Word (see Figure 18.6).

FIGURE 18.6.

Word showing results from
Visual Basic.

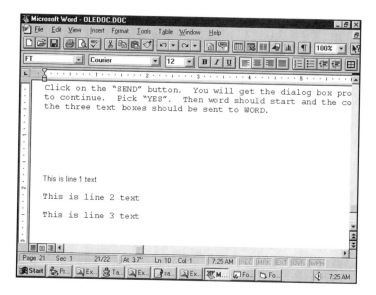

Although this example is fairly simple, you can extend its basic concepts dramatically to solve real-world problems like the one mentioned at the beginning of this section. By using other applications to solve end user problems, you can implement more sophisticated (and more reliable) systems in less time.

What Are OLE Clients?

OLE can involve multiple sources of data and the objects that control them. Your system must have a host or destination object where the control of the application resides. So far, all of the examples in this chapter use Visual Basic as the front end and host or destination application, and the objects that you use are sources or clients. For example, when you use Microsoft Word, your application is binding some of Words objects into your Visual Basic application. The Word executables do not exist in your Visual Basic application. In that sense, your application is a client of some of the Microsoft Word functionality.

Terminology is confusing now because of the convergence of many concepts and technologies. For example, client/server terms also apply to DDE and SQL data access. However, these terms mean slightly different things in each of these application areas.

Basically, one application must act as a server to another application. The requesting application is the client because it is requesting the other application (the server) to do something. For example, Word has a built-in programming language called Word Basic. When you declare Word as an object, it first has to install itself as an object when the initial installation is performed. By that I mean any application that is going to provide OLE services must install a section into the system registry to identify itself as an object and to define what services it is going to provide.

The OLE-compliant application (the one you are creating) calls upon the OLE-supplied services of Word as defined in the Registry. In other words, your code requests Microsoft Word do to something. The OLE definition makes the link between the two applications, but the actual execution of the code occurs within Word.

Note that when you activate an object, you are running the application in which the object resides. When you click on the image of an AutoCAD drawing, for example, you are executing AutoCAD with the data represented by the image. For this reason, you need at least a 486/66 with 16 M of RAM to run OLE-enabled applications.

What Is an OLE Server?

An OLE server is an application that contains objects that have been exposed to the entire system by installing a definition of what functions the application supports and how they are called. In earlier examples, both Microsoft Word and AutoCAD acted as OLE servers to the Visual

Basic application. With Visual Basic 4.0, a Visual Basic application can now register itself as an OLE-compliant application.

Many people made complaints about Visual Basic 3.0's Setup program. As a result, the Setup Wizard has been dramatically improved in version 4.0. All you need to do to get an OLE-compliant object installed into the Registry is to make your class Public when it is defined at the application level. Then choose the Setup Wizard command from the Visual Basic menu.

Use the CLASSEX example to see how this process works. You should have a folder or directory off Visual Basic named Setupkit. This example uses the kitfl32 for the 32-bit setup program. Your screen should look like Figure 18.7.

FIGURE 18.7.

The Visual Basic Setupkit screen.

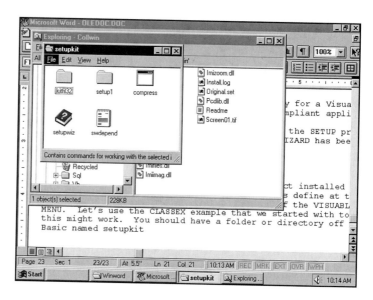

Execute the Setup icon and follow the on-screen prompts. When prompted for the DAO object (it should be something like DAO2532.tlb), point to the c:\windows\msapps\DAO directory to locate it. After compression, the system creates a SETUP.EXE file on a floppy disk (you will need two floppy disks). After the system has finished copying the program to disk, run the Setup program from the floppy disk.

You should now be able to go into the Regedit program by selecting the Run command and entering **Regedit** in the dialog box that appears. Your initial screen should look like Figure 18.8.

Open the Edit menu and select the Find command. When prompted, enter **CLASSEX** (the name of your executable file). You should now see CLASSES as an object on screen, as shown in Figure 18.9.

CLASSEX.EXE is now a part of the registry on the computer shown in Figure 18.9. What this means is that you can now execute CLASSEX without a path or icon by entering its name in the Run dialog box.

FIGURE 18.8.

The Windows 95 Registry Editor.

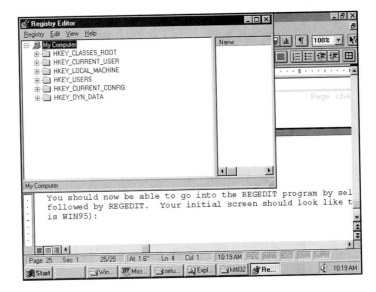

FIGURE 18.9.

The installed object in the registry.

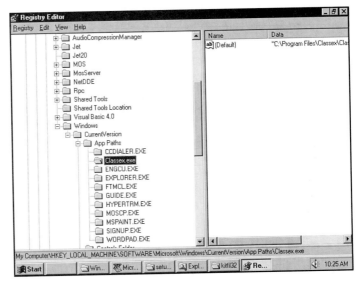

NOTE

Keep in mind that this example is using Windows 95, whose registry is almost identical to Windows NT. The registry will of course look different on older platforms. I strongly suggest you do Visual Basic 4.0 development and deployment on Windows NT or Windows 95. Many of the new Visual Basic services you will want to take advantage of are not available on older versions of Windows.

What Is In-Place Editing?

In-place editing is the capability to use an OLE compliant application to create or edit data in a VB OLE container. For example, you can run a copy of Excel inside of a VB container that you have placed on a form.

One of the biggest advantages of OLE is the ease of use it offers to end users. You can combine multiple applications and control them from Visual Basic the entire time. Take a look at Form1 in Figure 18.10.

FIGURE 18.10.

The OLE in-place editing layout screen.

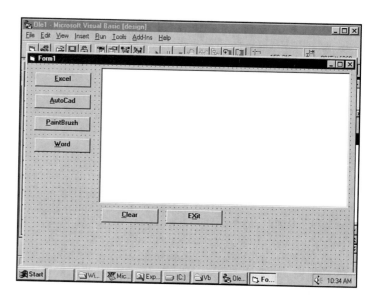

As you can see, this application allows for multiple OLE data types. To create this application, follow these steps:

1. Start a new project.
2. Add four command buttons stacked on the left side as you see in Figure 18.10.
3. To the right of these buttons, insert an OLE container.
4. Below the OLE container, add two more buttons as you see in Figure 18.10.
5. Add a code module and paste the following code into it:

```
Global Const OLE_CREATE_NEW = 0
Global Const OLE_CREATE_FROM_FILE = 1
Global Const OLE_COPY = 4
Global Const OLE_PASTE = 5
Global Const OLE_UPDATE = 6
Global Const OLE_ACTIVATE = 7
Global Const OLE_EXECUTE = 8
Global Const OLE_CLOSE = 9
Global Const OLE_DELETE = 10
```

```
Global Const OLE_SAVE_TO_FILE = 11
Global Const OLE_READ_FROM_FILE = 12
Global Const OLE_CONVERT_TO_TYPE = 13
```

6. Set the caption as follows:

```
CAPTION = EXCEL; NAME = cmdExcel
```

7. Paste in the following code to this button's `Click` event:

```
Private Sub cmdExcel_Click()
    Ole1.Class = "ExcelWorksheet"
    Ole1.SourceDoc = "C:\Excel\saledata.xls"  put in your own valid
spreadsheet name
    Ole1.SourceItem = "A1:G10"
    Ole1.Action = OLE_CREATE_FROM_FILE
    Ole1.Action = OLE_ACTIVATE
End Sub
CAPTION = AUTOCAD; NAME = cmdAutocad
Private Sub cmdAutocad_Click()
    Ole1.Class = "AutoCadDrawing"
    Ole1.SourceDoc = "C:\AcadWin\sample\psglobe.dwg"  put in your own valid
drawing name
    Ole1.Action = OLE_CREATE_FROM_FILE
    Ole1.Action = OLE_ACTIVATE
End Sub

CAPTION = PAINTBRUSH; NAME = cmdPBRUSH
Private Sub cmdPBRUSH_Click()
    Ole1.Class = "PBrush"
    Ole1.SourceDoc = "C:\VB\BitMaps\assorted\balloon.bmp" put in a valid
paintbrush file name
    Ole1.Action = OLE_CREATE_FROM_FILE
    Ole1.Action = OLE_ACTIVATE
End Sub

CAPTION = WORD; NAME = cmdWord
Private Sub cmdWord_Click()
    Ole1.Class = "Word Document"
    Ole1.SourceDoc = "C:\Winword\3DSTUDIO.DOC" put in a valid word file
    Ole1.Action = OLE_CREATE_FROM_FILE
    Ole1.Action = OLE_ACTIVATE
End Sub
```

8. Put the following captions on the command buttons below the OLE container:

```
CAPTION = CLEAR; NAME = Command1
Private Sub Command1_Click()
    Ole1.Class = " "
    Ole1.SourceDoc = " "
    Ole1.SourceItem = " "
    Ole1.Action = OLE_DELETE
End Sub
CAPTION = EXIT; NAME = Command2
Private Sub Command2_Click()
    End
End Sub
```

Now execute the program and click on the AutoCAD button.

As you can see, you now have AutoCAD running in a window of your Visual Basic application, as shown in Figure 18.11.

FIGURE 18.11.

OLE in-place editing of an AutoCAD drawing.

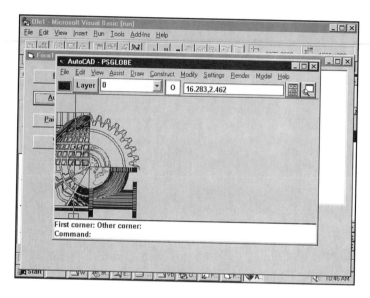

You can use AutoCAD as if you were executing the application from an icon. The difference is that you return to your Visual Basic application when you type **end**. The screen now looks like Figure 18.12.

FIGURE 18.12.

Visual Basic OLE in-place editing showing the OLE container.

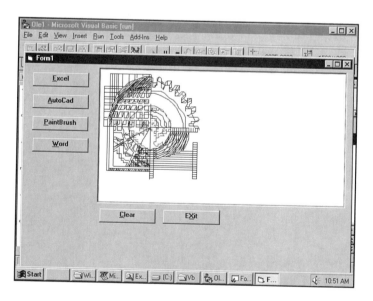

Figure 18.13 shows a screen with a Paintbrush image. As you can see, there are some slight differences in how various applications execute underneath OLE.

FIGURE 18.13.

OLE in-place editing with Paintbrush.

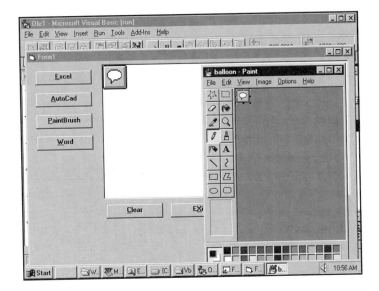

Summary

As you have seen in this chapter, OLE is a very versatile programming concept that extends itself to many types of applications and assists with many programming chores. Hopefully, the examples in this chapter have demonstrated just how powerful this technology has become. Don't be left behind; learn OLE now. The examples in this chapter are simple by design. You should be able to enter and execute them with minimal difficulty. Then you can take these examples and extend them into a real-world scenario.

Good luck!

In Process
OLE Servers

19

by Chuck Traywick

Wouldn't it be nice if you had the ability to create procedures in Visual Basic that you could call like standard DLLs? Well, guess what? Part of Visual Basic 4.0 has that exact capability. It's called In Process and Out of Process servers.

As a brief refresher, in the previous chapter, you created a class module and then compiled and installed this new class into the system registry. A *class* defines what an object is or can become. The actual object is created when you call its class or define a class in a procedure. You can call a class multiple times and create multiple instances of this class.

When you define a class, you specify what actions it can take. These actions are called *methods*. Most classes also have static fields where values can be stored; these fields are called *properties*. When you insert, for example, a text box onto a form and then press F4, a dialog box that displays the current properties of the text box control appears. Double-clicking on the text box causes a code window to appear. This code window contains a combo box that lists the events from which you can choose; these events are the methods for this object.

You can now create this same capability for extensions to Visual Basic or for use by other applications within Visual Basic. You can compile a library of functions that you can encapsulate into an In Process server that can in turn be called by multiple applications. Suppose that your applications always format the header and footer the same way when using the Printer object. You could develop a routine that formats the header and footer by accepting parameters and then call that routine from all applications that you develop. You can use this same capability to extend the operating system as well as your development tools. For example, you can now (using Windows NT 3.51 and above and Windows 95) develop an application as you would develop a general purpose query. When this application is installed, you can choose to install it into the system registry as a object. Then other applications that are OLE 2.0-compliant can paste your object into their applications.

OLE objects that are defined by In Process servers use the basic Windows messaging structure, which involves a server and a client(s) that calls the methods and properties of the server.

Understanding the Benefits of OLE Servers

OLE servers and OLE itself are not as difficult to use as some people in the computer industry would lead you to believe. If you are comfortable programming in Visual Basic, you can learn to use OLE effectively. I frequently encounter smart, capable individuals who don't try some of the new technology because someone wrote an article about how difficult it is to implement compared with what you get out of it. Experiment with this technology and try it out for yourself.

There have always been protracted discussions about the philosophy of software development. C programmers do the really hard stuff, COBOL programmers work on the everyday stuff, and so on. My advice to you is don't put yourself into a box, and don't let others put you in a box about new ideas. The whole purpose of OLE is simple: share data and code; reduce cost; and improve reliability.

OLE, as the previous chapter discussed, is not as widespread in non-shrink-wrapped applications as it is in shrink-wrapped applications. I think this is partly due to competition among vendors of shrink-wrapped applications in their feature wars. To be fair, OLE is not yet a mature technology, but that does not mean you should not use it. By the time you get a good application up and implemented, OLE will be much further along.

In my experience, most organizations take considerable time to implement new technology. For example, if your organization has 500 employees and has been in existence for awhile, then most likely you will have a wide array of computer types and users. Most organizations that I have dealt with cannot afford to throw away the equipment and training they have whenever a new technology comes along.

There is also an element of risk in investing in learning OLE and developing some applications using it because there's no way of knowing whether it will become a standard. I have absolutely no doubts that object technology is going to dominate software in the future, and I think Microsoft with OLE will have a large piece of that market when it matures. Even so, if some other concept becomes a standard, what you learn with this technology will give you a leg up on those that are waiting until the technology matures.

Some pundits believe that programming will become a task of coordinating multiple software components over the next few years. An OLE object can be a software component. Programmers are doing significant new things with OLE objects. Have you ever written any client/server applications in Visual Basic? If you have, you know how frustrating it was with version 3. Version 4 has remote data objects (RDO). The RDO control is an OLE object for connecting to remote data that is ODBC-compliant. Not only does the RDO object simplify the connection to remote data but it dramatically improves speed of the connection as well. RDO is a good example of what OLE objects can do: improve access, improve reliability, reduce programming time, and improve performance. If you start using OLE now in a meaningful way, then, as the standard matures, you will have in house expertise and working applications that will increase reliability, lower cost, and allow data to be shared more easily.

Creating an In Process Server

To see how OLE In Process servers work, try the following procedure. This procedure shows you how to create a server that displays copyright information and does a couple of other things for clients that call it. Follow these steps to create the OLE server:

1. Start up Visual Basic 4.0. Then choose File | New project.
2. Select Tools | Options.
3. Click on the Project tab at the top of the form. Your screen should look like Figure 19.1.

FIGURE 19.1.

The Project tab of a Visual Basic form.

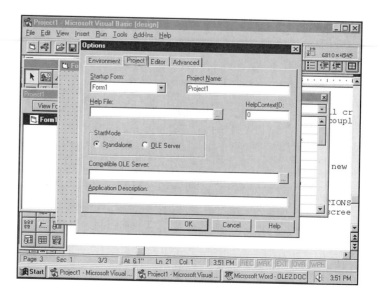

4. From the Startup Form drop-down list, pick Sub Main(). This option causes your application to start with an invisible procedure named Sub Main() instead of a visible form. Because this OLE server will be called from client applications, you don't want it to specify a form as its start module. Sub Main() is a reserved name used for this purpose.

5. In the Project Name box, enter **MyCopyRight**.

6. Select the OLE Server option button in the Start Mode box.

7. In the Application Description text box, enter **MyCopyDemo**.

8. Click the OK button on this screen to save your changes.

The Sub Main procedure you chose in step 4 above is where you can establish start-up code prior to initialization if you need or want to do so. To make this procedure work, you first need to create a code module. Follow these steps:

1. From the main Visual Basic menu choose Insert | Module.

2. While this module is on-screen, choose View | Properties.

3. From the Object drop-down list, pick General.

4. In the code window, type in **Sub Main()** followed by an Enter. Visual Basic automatically adds the End Sub to create the outline of a procedure.

5. Press F4 to view the properties window. After viewing the properties window, close the Properties dialog box by double-clicking on the close icon. You should now already be in the code window for the module you just inserted. If not, display the code window by double-clicking on the form.

6. You should now have a module that looks like Figure 19.2. This code module doesn't contain anything, but you need to create it regardless of whether you intend to use it.

7. Close the code window for `Sub Main()` by double-clicking on the close icon.

FIGURE 19.2.

The default `Sub Main` *procedure.*

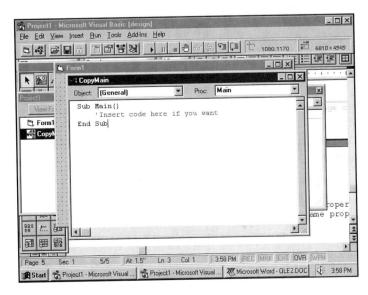

Now you need to add a class module. Remember from Chapter 18 that a class defines an object. The object itself does not get created until it is called. Then Visual Basic uses the specifications defined in the class module to create a specific instance of this class as your particular object. The OLE server creates a reference to the specific object that is created at call time. In other words, the only thing you are creating here is the outline or parameters of your object. When the class is called, a specific object that has its own life will be created using the parameters that you define here. To create a class module, follow these steps:

1. Choose Insert | Class Module. You now should have a blank Class Module code window on your screen.

2. With the Class Module window highlighted, press F4 to display this class' properties window.

3. Change the properties as follows:

```
NAME = CopyR
PUBLIC = TRUE
INSTANCING = 2 -creatable MultiUse
```

The `Name` property specifies the name of the class. Setting the `Public` property to `TRUE` means you can see the class from other applications. Setting the `Instancing` property to `2-creatable multiuse` allows the OLE server to create multiple objects. (Note that it is sometimes useful to be able to restrict an object instance to one call. You might want to make this restriction if, for example, you were to use OLE to do maintenance on a database.) These properties create a framework for your object.

Now you need to define properties and methods. If you want your properties and methods to be public, they must be defined as such. There are cases, even in an OLE server, in which you might want private variables and procedures instead. Users can read private variables, but they cannot change these variables.

Follow these steps to define the properties and methods:

1. In the Declarations section of the class module, define the following properties:

```
Option Explicit
Public Msg1 As String
Public CopyDate As Date
```

Your screen should look like Figure 19.3.

FIGURE 19.3.

The object properties.

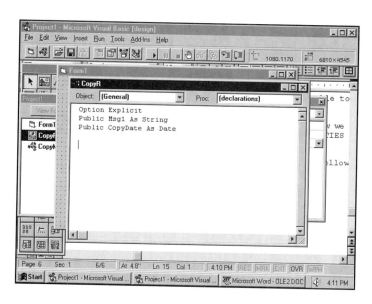

2. To create a method that gets the copyright data, choose Insert | Procedure.
3. In the Name field, enter `Copy_Date` and select the Property and Public option buttons. Because this is a property, Visual Basic automatically creates a LET (or read) function and a GET (or write) function.
4. To test what you've done so far, press Ctrl + F5. If everything is correct, you should see a running debug screen as shown in Figure 19.4. Nothing is displayed because you are testing the OLE server. Remember that the client application displays and processes the data in this example.

TIP

Always test your OLE server to see whether it will run without errors before developing your client application. If a bug exists in the server and you don't discover it until you have two pieces of code (the client and the server), the bug is more difficult to find because you have increased the number of variables.

FIGURE 19.4.

Testing the Visual Basic object.

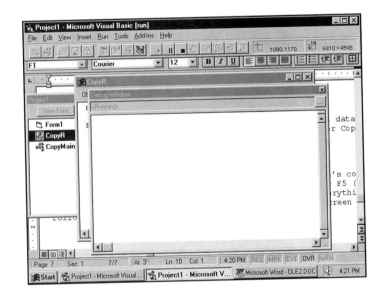

Creating the Client Application

To create the client application that will call the server you just created, follow these steps:

1. While your OLE server is still running, start another instance of Visual Basic, and then start a new project.

2. Resize the form to a smaller size and place the command buttons that are shown in Figure 19.5.

3. Define a second form that overlays the first form.

4. Change Form1's caption to `MyCompany`. Change Form2's caption to `Copyright Information`.

5. In Form2, create a text box that almost fills up the form.

6. In Form2, set the `MultiLine` property to `TRUE` and the `Visible` property to `FALSE`.

7. Create the two command buttons on Form1 shown in Figure 19.5. Set the caption on Command1 to `Show Copyright`, and set the caption on Command2 to `Hide Copyright`.

FIGURE 19.5.

Defining the client object.

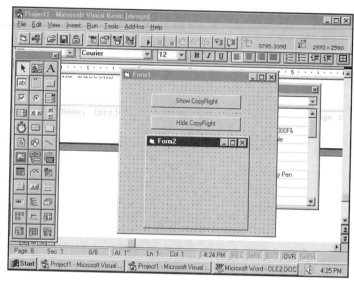

Linking the Client and the Server Applications

To create a link or reference between this client application and the server that you are calling, follow these steps:

1. Choose Tools | Reference. Your screen should look like Figure 19.6. At the bottom of the screen, you should see the server named MyCopyDemo (you may have to scroll down to see this server). Any other applications you have loaded on your computer also appear on this screen.

FIGURE 19.6.

Including a reference in your client object application.

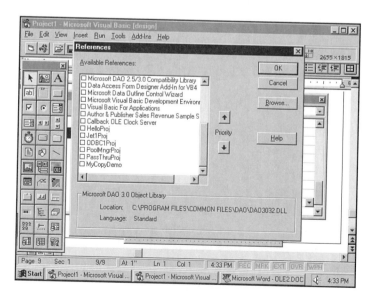

2. Click on the box to the left of MyCopyDemo and then click on OK.

3. Press F2 to display the object browser. The initial screen should show Form1 and Form2.

4. From the Library/Projects drop-down list, select MyCopyDemo. The screen shown in Figure 19.7 appears. The left window shows the CopyR class module you created earlier. The right window shows the methods(s) (in this case Copy_Date) and the properties (in this case MSG1 and CopyDate) you defined.

FIGURE 19.7.

Browsing objects in our OLE server object.

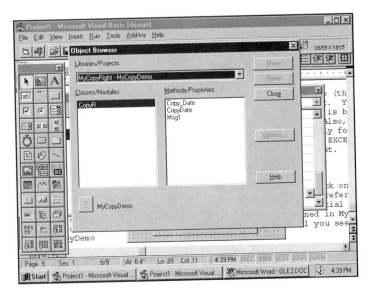

5. Press Alt+Tab to go to the OLE server you have running. Then click on the Stop button on the toolbar.

6. Highlight the class module and display its code window.

7. From the Object drop-down list, select General.

8. In the Proc window, select COPY_DATE[PropertyGet].

9. Below the Public property Get Copy_Date(), add the following:

```
Copy_Date = Format$(Now, MM/DD/YY)
```

10. Press Alt+Tab to switch to your other instance of Visual Basic and display your client application.

11. Display the code window for Form1.

12. In the Object drop-down list, pick General.

13. Make sure the Proc window says Declarations. Then add the following code:

```
Option Explicit
Dim MyRights As New CopyR
```

14. To access the CopyR class, you need to attach some code to the command buttons you placed above. Add the following code to the Form Load event on Form1:

```
Private Sub Form_Load()
    MyRights.Msg1 = InputBox("Enter your name")
End Sub
```

15. Insert the following into Command1's Click event:

```
Private Sub Command1_Click()
    Form2.BackColor = vbBlue
    Form2.Text1.BackColor = vbYellow
    Form2.Text1.TEXT = "All rights reserved by " & MyRights.Msg1 &
Chr(169) & vbCrLf & MyRights.Copy_Date
    Form2.Visible = True
End Sub
```

16. With the OLE server still running, test the client application by pressing F5. The screen shown in Figure 19.8 should appear.

FIGURE 19.8.

Testing the client object.

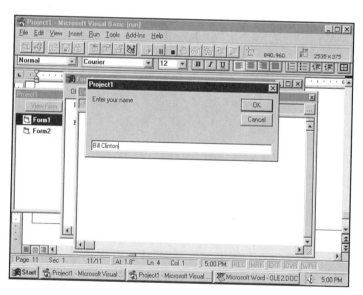

17. Enter your name and press Enter. The Form1 screen appears.

18. Click on the Show Copyright button. The screen defined by Form2 and the data called from the OLE server should appear, as shown in Figure 19.9.

This example worked because you had both the client and the server applications running at the same time. Closing the OLE server and running the client application produces an error. To prevent this error from occurring, you need to register the server application into the system registry.

FIGURE 19.9.

A running client accessing the In Process server.

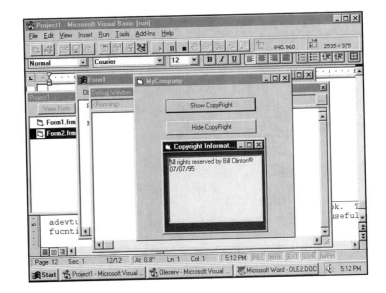

Registering Your OLE Server

To register your OLE server on the same computer you created it on, choose File | Make OLE DLL file. Enter an appropriate name and the system will register the In Process server in the system registry as shown in Figure 19.10.

> **NOTE**
>
> Be careful about the naming syntax you use. When you install these objects into the system registry, they become public names throughout your system. There are limited restrictions to names, but you do not want to create conflicts with what other applications may do. For example, you may want to have your own section in the registry for each application that installs under LOCAL_MACHINE:
> LOCAL_MACHINE;SOFTWARE;MY_APP;THIS_OPTION. This section would look like the following:
>
> ```
>         LOCAL_MACHINE
>             LOCAL_MACHINE
>                 SOFTWARE;
>                 MY_APP
>                     THIS_OPTION   OPTION 0x1
> ```
>
> Because this technology is new, developers will have to add to their applications install procedures code that checks the registry for duplicate section names in order to avoid this problem.

FIGURE 19.10.

Registering the In Process server.

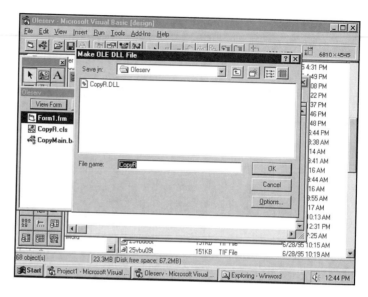

You can also create an OLE server as an executable file for installation onto a target machine by choosing File | Make EXE. When you install on your target machine, enter the following in the Run command dialog box:

```
C:\MyProg.EXE /REGSERVER
```

Figure 19.11 shows how the executable file named TARGET.EXE would look in the registry.

FIGURE 19.11.

Registering external In Process servers.

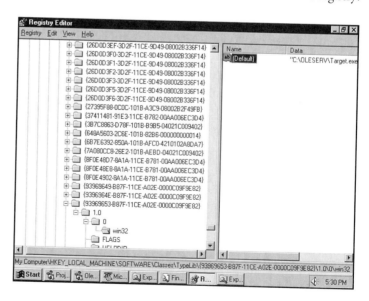

The computer shown in Figure 19.11 now has two OLE servers that do the same thing installed on it. The COPYR.DLL is located in the C:\OLESERV directory and now also is TARGET.EXE. When you run the client application again, you must first terminate the instance of Visual Basic that is running your OLE server. Then go into your client application and remove the reference to MyCopyDemo (you called your DLL COPYR.DLL). Using the Browse button, point to COPYR.DLL in the C:\OLESERV directory. When you run the application again and click on the Show Copyright button (now without the other instance of Visual Basic running), you see the screen shown in Figure 19.12. Save this OLE server project and client project as separate projects.

FIGURE 19.12.

A client application accessing a built-in In Process server.

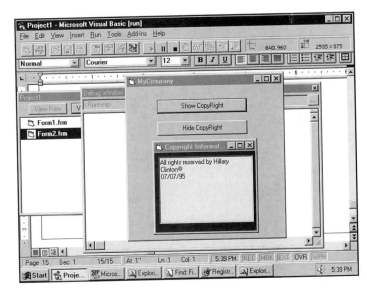

The previous application examples are defined as In Process servers because they execute in the same process space as the client that called them. In the example, you knew ahead of time that you wanted to link the copyright server to your application, so you could include a reference to it. What if that were not the case? Or what if we wanted to use some pre-existing OLE servers?

As demonstrated in the previous example, you can dramatically expand OLE servers to perform all kinds of tasks. Before you can put this technology to work, however, you need to ask yourself some questions. I do not have the space in this chapter to define all of the following characteristics, but you can use the following questions as a brief checklist of issues to resolve prior to creating your OLE servers:

- What type of OLE server do you want to call? The one in the prior example was an In Process server because it was combined with the client that called it. Is your server In Process or Out of Process (externally created)?

- Is your OLE server dependent upon your client or is your client dependent upon your server? The answer determines how and where you create the objects.

- Do you want the end user to be able to start the server? What if the user tries to start the server by clicking on it? Do you want the server to start?

- Does your server have any special interface characteristics? For example, does it display forms?

- What do you want to happen when the OLE server starts?

- What do you want to happen when the OLE server is called, such as when it creates an instance of the object of a given class?

- What do you want to happen when an object is terminated?

- How do you want the OLE server to terminate?

- Do you create the classes that your server allows in the system registry as external or internal processes?

- How do you handle errors in the server?

NOTE

OLE servers with Visual Basic 4.0 do not support in place editing. In OLE-compliant applications, you can embed, for example, an Excel form that invokes the Excel interface. Visual Basic doesn't have this capability. You can execute forms and procedures, but not complete application interfaces. For example, you could run a query that returned data to an Excel spreadsheet, but you could not run the application in its entirety within Excel.

Answering all these questions will guide you to a proper design. You also need to consider the normal programming concerns such as determining how many resources the application will consume, figuring out how large the in-memory image will be, and deciding whether to use many small objects or large DLLs that contain many objects. The answers to these questions are, of course, dependent upon the application involved.

When you start to answer the questions mentioned previously, it is helpful to look at objects in another light. Traditionally, good programming style has dictated using parametric design in many of the algorithms that you create. This design means that a set of given values that a program may use to display or get data are not coded into the program but are established in a Setup function somewhere within the system. In this way, you can think of objects as stored procedures. Like anything that you store and retrieve, you can also link these objects together into a database-like hierarchy.

When I use the term stored procedure, I don't mean it in the same vein that this term is used in SQL databases. These procedures are limited in function to specific database activities and are tied to very specific applications. Objects are like stored procedures in that they do not reside in the client software, but, unlike stored procedures, they can be called and used by a wide variety of applications and can be used throughout the system.

> **NOTE**
>
> Of note here is the last minute addition of *Remote OLE*, which is the ability to use objects across a network. Using Remote OLE, you can have multiple stored OLE objects that reside on a server that can be used repeatedly by multiple users from multiple locations. For example, you could create an In Process Server that could install onto an Windows NT server that could be pasted into client applications—like a query written in Visual Basic 4.0 that extracts data from a SQL database. Let's say you have monthly reports to create each month. The report is the same, and only the data changes. You could take this query that you create in VB as an OLE object and paste it into an Excel spreadsheet. The spreadsheet could contain graphs (showing what a wonderful job you are doing) and other functions that create your report. When you load the spreadsheet, the query would automatically execute to refresh the data and your report is done.

In traditional database nomenclature, you can have flat files, and you can have hierarchical files. This is also true of objects. You could create a set of objects that are all flat in that no one object depends upon the other. For example, you could have a set of objects that you use with the printer object. You could have a page header object, a page footer object, a print logo object, and so forth. You could call each one of these objects directly.

A hierarchical file could be something like an inventory class. The top or main class could be Inventory. Transactions could be a subclass. You could tie the Transactions subclass to the Inventory class with a Collection class. Therefore, when you refer to the Inventory class, you automatically get the Transactions class as well. For instance, in the previous example, you could get to the MSG1 object by defining a new instance of CopyR. This is because MSG1 is encapsulated within CopyR, each new instance of CopyR also creates a reference to the subclasses within this object. If you defined a new instance of Inventory, you would get all of the methods and properties of Inventory as well as all of the subclasses, properties, and methods of Transactions. Again, this is because Transactions as a class is encapsulated within Inventory. You could extend this idea dramatically to nest classes several levels deep. Of course, when you have several levels of classes, you have slower performance (because there are more classes to go through to find objects) and a larger program image size.

Keep in mind the purpose of your objects. If they become too specific, you may want to weigh the time it takes to create an object class versus the time it takes to embed the code in your application. A class or object should be a code fragment that has multiple applications and uses.

Another example may give you a better idea of how this process works. As you did in the previous example, you need to set up the project somewhat differently in order to create an OLE server. Consider Figure 19.13.

FIGURE 19.13.

*Defining an In Process
server.*

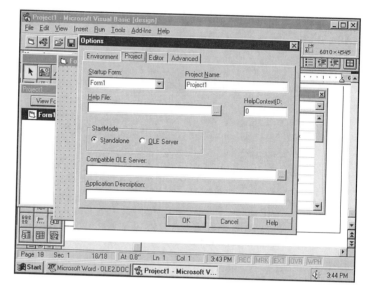

The first thing you need to do is to enter a name in the Project name box. At this point in the process, some planning is worthwhile. Remember that the project name needs to be unique when you install it into the system registry. In the previous example, you created a class CopyR. To use this class in a new client application, you could use the following code fragment:

```
PUBLIC MyNewObject As MyCopyRight.CopyR
```

This kind of code is called a fully qualified class name because it contains the project name (MyCopyRight) and the class you are creating (CopyR). Remember that most of your users' Windows applications will now have multiple definitions of unique classes for a given application. For example, I recently read that Excel 5.0 has over 100 object classes of its own. If you were to define a class that had the same name as your application, your application could crash. For this reason, you should use fully qualified class names in addition to planning out what class names you want to use.

Figure 19.14 shows an example of how not to name your projects. Remember when you created two objects earlier in the chapter and named one COPYR.DLL and the other TARGET.EXE? Next, you installed TARGET.EXE with the /REGSERVER option. As a result, you ended up with two of the same object. You can prevent such situations by planning your names and controlling versions and compiles. Even though one of our compiles was a DLL and another was as an EXE, both used the same object name. The object name is what you see here in the Visual Basic reference window.

FIGURE 19.14.

*Duplicate In Process
servers.*

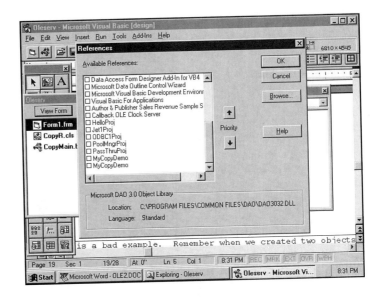

In the Start Mode box, make sure you select the OLE server option in order to create your server first. Visual Basic creates temporary entries into the system registry and creates links to any client provided that you execute two copies of Visual Basic in Design mode, the first copy being your OLE server and the second copy being your client, and perform the proper setting with the Reference function. Although you may not yet want to compile this application of your server and link it into the registry, note that Visual Basic creates temporary links for you so that you can test your client applications. This means that you do not have to permanently link server applications until you are ready to do so.

You would most likely want to make sure that your OLE server compiles and runs before launching a client to test it. This feature is built into the Visual Basic Design mode. Normally, a compiled OLE server would not start until the client called it. When you set the Start mode to OLE server, Visual Basic knows to keep your project running even though no calls are being made to it. Otherwise, the project would end immediately because there are no clients requesting it. In Development mode, it is useful to be able to execute two copies of Visual Basic, one running the server and the other running the client. If you have an OLE server running in Design mode and a client that calls it, stopping your OLE server will produce an error message that notifies you that you have dependent applications.

The vast majority of the time your start-up form will contain a Sub Main() procedure as its primary start-up mode. If you need a start-up form, you should display that form from Sub Main(). Be sure that Sub Main() is not in a class module. Also, use caution when putting forms into OLE servers. Many developers think most, if not all, of the user interface should be in the client application.

As discussed briefly in the previous example, another distinguishing feature of an OLE server is that it contains at least one class module with its Public property set to TRUE. Clients can read and write to the procedures and properties in the class module that have their Public properties set to TRUE. This applies to variables, procedures, and functions.

Extending Your OLE Server

Of course, because the OLE server is a project like any other Visual Basic project, you can extend it. To demonstrate this fact, try adding an initialize procedure for when the server you created earlier starts and ends. Follow these steps:

1. Display the OLE server that you previously created.

2. In the Project window, highlight COPYR.CLS and double-click it. You should see the screen shown in Figure 19.15.

FIGURE 19.15.

Extending an In Process server.

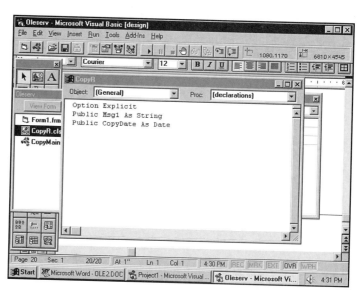

3. Display the CopyR class module. In the object window, make sure the caption states Class.

4. In the Proc: window, select the `Initialize` event.

5. Add the following statement to the `Initialize` event:

```
MsgBox "Started OLE server On: " & vbCrLf & Format$(Now, "MM/DD/YY")
```

6. Save this project and compile it to an OLE server .DLL. Replace the old COPYR.DLL in the directory that you initially created it in. If you have trouble with this procedure, delete the old COPYR.DLL and compile and save a new one.

7. Start your client application. Your screen should look like Figure 19.16. You can see that the OLE server's `Initialize` event performed its function.

FIGURE 19.16.

*Running the In Process
server with new extensions.*

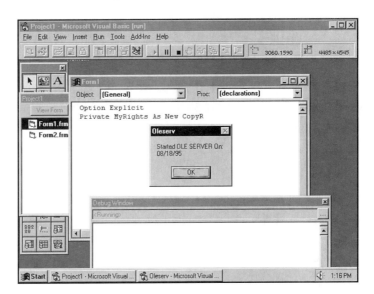

8. Click on OK to display the screen in Figure 19.17.

As you can see, you can extend existing OLE servers quite easily. Try adding another method to the OLE server by following these steps:

1. Activate the class module `CopyR`.

2. Double-click the module to display the code window.

3. Make sure General is selected in the Object drop-down list, and then enter the following code:

```
Public Property Get Legal()
Legal = "According to U.S. Copyright Law 1995"
End Property
```

4. Save your project and replace the COPYR.DLL by recompiling and using the Make DLL command on the File menu.

FIGURE 19.17.

Expanding the In Process server functionality.

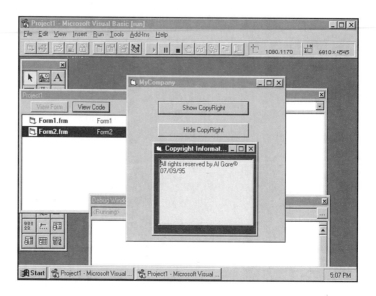

5. Add the following changes to the client applications Command1 button. You don't need to replace all of the code; just add the & vbCrLf & MyRights.Legal to the Form2.Text1.TExt = statement:

```
Form2.BackColor = vbBlue
Form2.Text1.BackColor = vbYellow
Form2.Text1.TEXT = "All rights reserved by " & MyRights.Msg1 & Chr(169)
& vbCrLf &      MyRights.Copy_Date & vbCrLf & MyRights.Legal
Form2.Visible = True
```

6. Rerun the client application; it should produce the screen shown in Figure 19.18.

FIGURE 19.18.

Adding a new method to the OLE server.

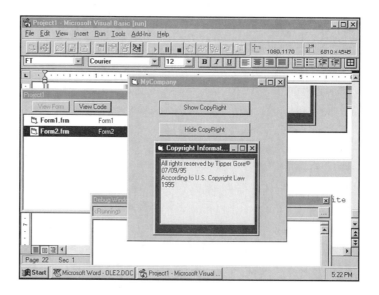

In order to create a complete OLE server, you should add a help file to assist end users and other developers that want to reuse your code. (If the code you are contemplating for an OLE server cannot be reused, you should consider whether you need to create an OLE server at all.) Follow these steps to add a help file:

1. In your OLE server project, choose Tools | Options.

2. Display the Project tab. Then specify a path and name for a help file. For example, specify c:\oleserv\oleserv.hlp. Your screen should look like Figure 19.19.

FIGURE 19.19.

Adding a help file to your In Process server.

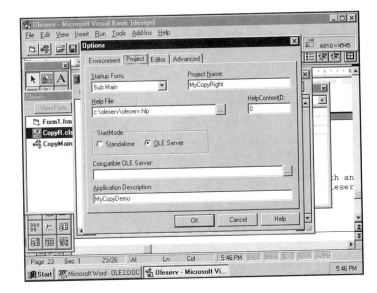

3. Open your Oleserv project and press F2 to display the object browser. Your screen should look like Figure 19.20. The left hand window shows the methods and properties for the CopyR class. If the CopyR class is not highlighted in the left window, click on it to get the correct display in the right hand window.

4. Click on Class_Initialize(Sub).

5. Click on Options. Your screen should now look like Figure 19.21.

6. Enter a description as follows:

```
This procedure is the initialization code for MyCopyRight. This procedure
shows the date that you initialized the OLE server in a dialog box.
```

7. Click on close to return to the Visual Basic editor.

The confines of this chapter do not allow me to describe all of the features you could add to your OLE server. Two important features you should add are error handling and version control. The Microsoft Visual Basic manuals present some information on these subjects, but it is best to experiment for yourself and keep in mind the problems you can avoid downstream by building in code for these two additional areas.

FIGURE 19.20.

Browsing the In Process server.

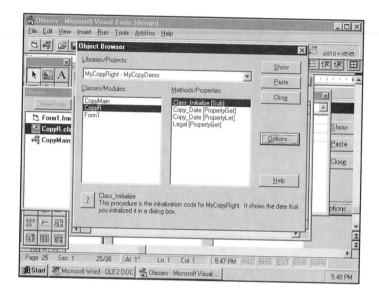

FIGURE 19.21.

Browsing elements of our server.

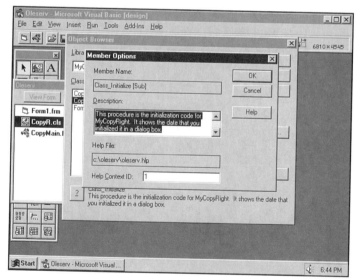

Summary

I could write a very long book just on OLE programming. Because OLE is not the main focus of this book, I will stop here with a couple of additional thoughts that may be helpful. Hopefully, you can see the tremendous potential in OLE and OLE programming. Yes, it is new. Yes, it has constraints. Yes, it has some bugs. However, I believe Microsoft will be adept at addressing these issues. If you want to move your organization forward and if you are tired of programming the same old stuff over and over again, OLE is a way to resolve both issues in an elegant fashion.

Happy coding!

Incorporating DLLs

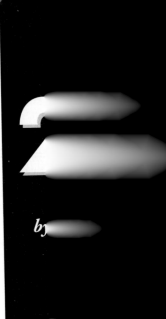

by

This chapter complements the "Calling Procedures in DLLs" chapter in the Visual Basic 4.0 Programmer's Guide by showing you how to build a simple DLL and demonstrating some of the tools that Microsoft has provided to enable you to investigate the DLL's characteristics.

This chapter does not discuss the inline OLE servers you can create within Visual Basic 4.0 because they are implemented as logically partitioned sections of the same interpreted threaded p-code, which is used for all other Visual Basic 4.0 executables. Although these inline OLE servers perform a function similar to a true OLE server (which you might be able to make if you are an expert with the latest version of the Microsoft foundation classes and the C++ language), they are not optimized machine code DLLs in any way that is commonly understood. You should consult the Visual Basic 4.0 manuals for example code and other information on inline OLE servers.

Understanding DLLs

Dynamic link libraries (DLLs) are executable modules containing functions that Windows applications can call to perform useful service tasks. DLLs play a central role in Windows applications; they make its resources and functions available to Windows applications. Actually, all Windows libraries are dynamic link libraries. These libraries are called *dynamic* because they are linked with the application that needs them at runtime, instead of being statically linked as a final act of the software's build process.

DLLs are not loaded into memory until a function in the DLL is called for the first time.

The different linking methods have different benefits. Static linking can give you a stand-alone program that you know is complete, but dynamic linking enables a modular approach in which different components can be replaced individually. The DLL approach enables components to share common executable code instead of duplicating the runtime code for each program.

From the point of view of a given DLL, any of its functions available for use by other applications are known as *exported* functions; if the DLL uses functions from other libraries, these are its *imported* functions. One DLL's exported functions are another DLL's imported functions.

> **NOTE**
>
> To further illustrate the qualities of and differences between static linked programs and dynamic linked libraries, I've included Listings 20.11 onwards at the end of the chapter, where I build one of each type of link using the minimum tools necessary. The capability to build DLLs using the fundamental tools is invaluable if you ever have to create them on a low-speed/low-memory computer that sags under the weight of a GUI-based environment.

By the way, not all DLLs have DLL file name extensions—the Windows system files have .EXE extensions, Visual Basic controls are packaged DLLs with .VBX or .OCX extensions, drivers have .DRV extensions, and fonts have .FON extensions.

You need to be careful when running programs that use DLLs because the link is not performed until runtime, which means that you might pick up the wrong DLL if you have more than one copy of the DLL on your system. I have included some sample source code (in Listing 20.3) that your main program can use to ask Windows components for their version number.

TIP

Unless a path is specified explicitly, the directory (folder) sequence Windows uses to search for DLLs follows:

1. Current directory
2. Windows directory
3. Windows system directory
4. Any of the directories in the MS-DOS PATH environment variable
5. Any directory in the list of directories mapped in a network

---

Examining the Limitations of Visual Basic

Visual Basic does not directly support pointers to variables, which causes difficulties when accessing a considerable portion of Windows API functions (which frequently pass pointers as parameters). This is not as big a problem as it might seem, however, because Visual Basic can hold the value of pointers in integer variables (usually Long values). As long as you don't need to explicitly know what the contents of a pointer mean, you can receive a pointer value from one API and pass it back into another API. As long as the first and last API calls in a sequence will take and return Visual Basic-compatible variables, respectively, you can proceed without any further complications.

Listing 20.1 shows a code example where hOldWnd% and lbhWnd% are used to validly hold the values of non-Visual Basic data because Visual Basic does not need access to the values. A Windows API call SendMessage() is used to make a Visual Basic listbox behave in a way beyond what usually is available in Visual Basic by appearing to support synchronized multiple columns. Figure 20.1 shows the resulting listbox.

FIGURE 20.1.

Using Windows APIs to extend the functionality of the Listbox control.

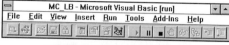

Listing 20.1. Discovering the version number of a Windows module at runtime.

```
Declare Function GetFocus Lib "user" () As Integer
Declare Function SendMessage Lib "user" (ByVal hWnd As Integer, ByVal wMsg As
➡Integer, ByVal wp As Integer, lp As Any) As Long
Declare Function PutFocus Lib "user" Alias "SetFocus" (ByVal hWnd%) As Integer

Const WM_USER = &H400
Const LB_SETTABSTOPS = WM_USER + 19

Sub Form_Click()
    Dim retVal&, R%                     'API return values
    Dim hOldWnd%, lbhWnd%               'WinCtrl handles
    Static tabs(3) As Integer

    tabs(1) = 10                        'Set up array of defined tab stops.
    tabs(2) = 70
    tabs(3) = 130

    hOldWnd% = GetFocus()               'Remember who had the focus.
    Form1.Show                          'Showing the form avoids  "Illegal
                                        ' Function Call" on 'List1.SetFocus'
    list1.SetFocus                      'Set the focus to the list box.
    lbhWnd% = GetFocus()                'Get the handle to the list box.

    'Send a message to the message queue.
    retVal& = SendMessage(lbhWnd%, LB_SETTABSTOPS, 3, tabs(1))

    R% = PutFocus(hOldWnd%)             'Restore handle to whoever had it.

    'Place some elements into the list box, separated by TAB chars:
    list1.AddItem "Last Name" + Chr$(9) + "First Name" + Chr$(9) + "Year"
    list1.AddItem "Washington" + Chr$(9) + "George" + Chr$(9) + "1789"
    list1.AddItem "Adams" + Chr$(9) + "John" + Chr$(9) + "1797"
    list1.AddItem "Jefferson" + Chr$(9) + "Thomas" + Chr$(9) + "1801"
    list1.AddItem "Madison" + Chr$(9) + "James" + Chr$(9) + "1809"
    list1.AddItem "Monroe" + Chr$(9) + "James" + Chr$(9) + "1817"
    list1.AddItem "Adams" + Chr$(9) + "John Q." + Chr$(9) + "1825"
End Sub
```

A further limitation of Visual Basic is that you have to explicitly declare your DLL function calls at design time, which makes runtime binding of unspecified device driver libraries impossible within Visual Basic alone.

Deciding Whether to Create Your Own DLLs

In order to provide the optimum design-time flexibility, Visual Basic 4.0 is implemented as an interpreter that processes semicompiled programs. The code is analyzed and internally represented so that the code can be reconstituted for display purposes, yet have a minimum interpretation overhead at runtime. Therefore, due to its interpreted nature, few of the optimizations are available that might otherwise be attempted during a true reduction to native machine code (such as that offered by the compiler shipped with Visual C++).

This limitation is not necessarily significant, because the target computer specification may be sufficiently generous to run the Visual Basic code within the user's limits of patience. However, if many iterative processes are required that take far too long to execute in spite of the careful removal of inefficiencies, you can take advantage of the superior performance of optimized pure machine code by rewriting the time-consuming sections of the program in a language that has a suitable compiler available.

Be aware, though, that the standard of programming competence and thoroughness required for writing Windows DLLs is very high. Failures of Visual Basic programs due to general protection faults (GPFs) almost always are due to rogue DLL programming—usually within libraries not supplied by Microsoft. You should try to remove all errors and warnings from your compiler output with the warning level set to the highest value available (with a few possible exceptions, such as the // comment symbol not being to the ANSI standard).

Using Mixed-Language Programming

Although there is no intrinsic reason why a DLL could not be built using a BASIC optimizing compiler, there are no vendors of Microsoft's size and presence that sell one (at least not at the time of this writing). Therefore, if you want to build a DLL to use with your Visual Basic program, you must write it in a different language. Although vendors such as Borland sell PASCAL compilers that can be used to create DLLs, Microsoft's languages of choice are C or C++, which can be compiled using Microsoft's Visual C++ product.

Building a DLL the Easy Way

Building a DLL is a much easier job these days than it used to be! The process I've put in Listings 20.11 and onwards (at the end of this chapter) used to be standard practice before visual tools such as Microsoft's Visual C++ or Borland's Pascal and C++ products for Windows became available.

To create a simple DLL using Visual C++, follow these steps:

1. Choose Project | New. The New Project dialog box appears, as shown in Figure 20.2.

FIGURE 20.2.

Visual C++—defining a new project.

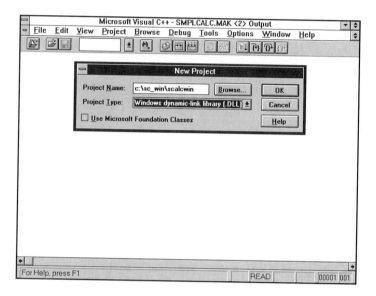

2. Type a project name in the Project Name field. Then choose the Windows dynamic-link library (.DLL) option from the Project Type drop-down list and click OK.

   If you have pre-existing completed code that you want to make into a DLL, then proceed to Step 5 below.

3. Choose Close in the New Project dialog box, then choose File | New from the main menu. A dialog box for your new code appears.

4. Type the code into the UNTITLED window and save it with a filename of your choice using File | Save As. A simple example program is shown in Figure 20.3 (with the code window maximized).

   Add this new code to the project using Project | Edit... from the main menu (whose dialog is virtually identical to that of Project | New).

   The MS-proprietary _far and _pascal keywords have been added to the declaration in order to ensure that the parameters are not 16-bit and are passed in the correct order (see Figure 20.3). In practice, you should include the WINDOWS.H header file and use the defined constants FAR and PASCAL, but I've bypassed that step here for simplicity.

5. Add the code to the project by first clicking on the desired item within the File Name list and then by clicking on the Add button (see Figure 20.4). Choose Close in the New Project dialog box when all files to be added to the project have been added.

FIGURE 20.3.

Example source code within Visual C++.

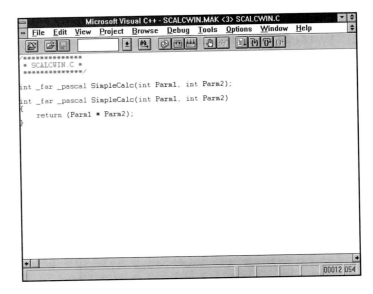

FIGURE 20.4.

Choosing files to add to the project.

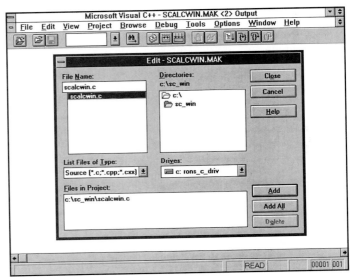

6. Choose Project | Rebuild All. Reply Yes to the `Add default definition file and edit it?` question in the message box that appears.

7. Add the names and matching Ordinal Numbers of your Exports to the EXPORTS section of the dialog that appears (as I have done with `SimpleCalc` and `@1`, respectively in Figure 20.5).

8. Then click the Save button on the main toolbar (with the diskette icon on it). You may now close this dialog if you want to tidy your screen.

FIGURE 20.5.

Adding and editing the Module Definition file.

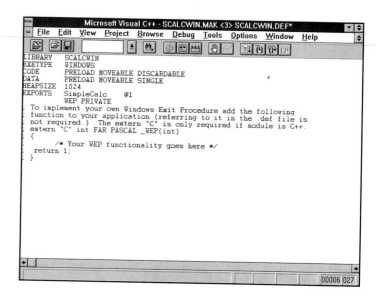

9. Choose Project | Rebuild All. You may expect to see abbreviated compiler output appear on the screen such as in Figure 20.6—if there are no errors, your DLL should be within the same directory as the project files.

10. **OPTIONAL.** If you're curious about what's going on behind the scenes, close the whole project and load the project file *<projectname>*.MAK into Notepad (or some other suitable ASCII Editor). Ignore the Do not modify comment at the top of the file and delete all the /nologo and /NOLOGO words. Save the project file, reopen it within Visual C++, and choose Rebuild All again. You will see a lot more text in the Output window; most of it is very similar to the manual compiler output shown in Listings 20.11 and following at the end of the chapter.

For 32-bit compiling, you replace the "int _far _pascal" with a single keyword "__declspec(dllexport) int" and use VC++ version 2.0 onwards instead of the 16-bit VC++ version 1.5 :

```
/**************
 * SCALC_32.C *
 **************/
__declspec(dllexport) int SImpleCalc(int Parm1,int Parm2);
__declspec(dllexport) int SImpleCalc(int Parm1,int Parm2)
{
    return (Parm1 * Parm2);
}
```

FIGURE 20.6.

Building the DLL.

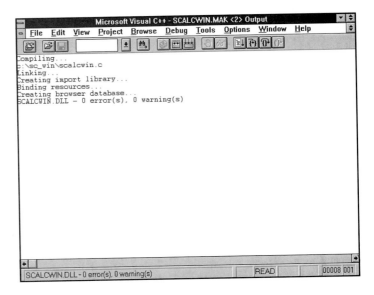

Running the DLL from Visual Basic

The DLL you just created can be declared in the code, and then run from a Visual Basic 4.0 event routine, such as the one shown in Listing 20.2 and demonstrated in Figure 20.7.

Listing 20.2. Running the DLL from Visual Basic.

```
Declare Function SimpleCalc% Lib "C:\SC_WIN\SCALCWIN" (ByVal Parm1%, ByVal
➡Parm2%)

Private Sub Label3_Click()
    Dim Parm1 As Integer
    Dim Parm2 As Integer

    Parm1 = Val(Text1.Text)
    Parm2 = Val(Text2.Text)
    Label3.Caption = Format$(SimpleCalc(Parm1, Parm2))
End Sub
```

If you are building more sophisticated DLLs, you should consider using the Resource Compiler (RC.EXE) for features such as version information. You also might want to use IMPLIB.EXE to handle imports if your DLL calls any functions from other DLLs. See the Visual C++ documentation for more information on these utility programs.

FIGURE 20.7.

Running a DLL with
Visual Basic.

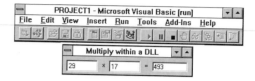

Furthermore, if you're planning to make both 16-bit and 32-bit versions of your code, you should allow for certain subtleties in the function declaration, such as that Win32 is case-sensitive regarding function names but Win16 is not. Also note that 32-bit Windows API calls often have the number 32 appended to the end of the 16-bit function name.

The best way to deal with this problem is to localize Visual Basic 4.0's logical link to the DLL to one place only by using the `Alias` keyword within the `Function` declaration. The only line of your code that will need to be altered in order to migrate to 32-bit, therefore, is the `Declare` line.

Further 16-Bit versus 32-Bit Issues

One of the trickiest issues to arise from having both 16-bit and 32-bit versions of Visual Basic 4.0 is that of ANSI strings (VB4/16—one byte per character) and UNICODE strings (VB4/32—two bytes per character).

To be sure of always using the same number of bytes, you should use the new `Byte` data type instead of `Strings`. An exception to this necessity is when a DLL is called using the established Visual Basic declaration syntax, in which all versions of Visual Basic 4.0 will use the ANSI convention to pass strings. To force the passing of UNICODE, you should copy the string to a `Byte` array and pass that instead, or you should declare the function by using a `TypeLib`.

Likewise, with user-defined types (UDTs), it is important to ensure that the UDT defined in Visual Basic is of the same size as the C structure defined in the DLL. You can do this by enforcing a strict one-to-one alignment of corresponding members in both UDTs.

The 16-bit version of Visual Basic 4.0 packs the UDT members on byte boundaries, and the 32-bit version packs the UDT members on 4-byte (DWORD) boundaries. You therefore should compile your 16-bit DLL code using a `single byte struct alignment` compiler setting and your 32-bit DLL code using the `4-byte struct member alignment` compiler setting.

You can aid full compatibility between versions by ordering the UDT members in a certain way: the >= 4-byte built-in data types first (Variant, Double, Currency, Single, and Long), followed by the remaining even-length data types, with the rest of the datatypes completing the structure. Then most of your data types (except the last-mentioned types) will be inherently impervious to this consideration.

Remember that, although integers always are two bytes long for Visual Basic and 16-bit DLLs, they are four bytes long for 32-bit DLLs. Therefore, always declare your two-byte integers as Short in your DLLs.

In Visual Basic 3.0, you can use the Visual Basic API routines to access and modify DLL data types. In Visual Basic 4.0, you should use the OLE APIs to access your DLL data types.

Table 20.1 lists some of the Visual Basic 3.0 API routines and their Visual Basic 4.0 OLE equivalents.

Table 20.1. Visual Basic 3.0 API routines and their Visual Basic 4.0 OLE equivalents.

Visual Basic 3.0 API Routine	Visual Basic 4.0 OLE Equivalent
VBArrayBounds	SafeArrayGetLBound/SafeArrayGetUBound
VBArrayElement	SafeArrayGetElement
VBArrayElemSize	SafeArrayGetElemsize
VBArrayFirstElem	N/A
VBArrayIndexCount	SafeArrayGetDim
VBCoerceVariant	VariantChangeType
VBCreateHlstr	SysAllocString/SysAllocStringLen
VBCreateTempHlstr	SysAllocString/SysAllocStringLen
VBDerefHlstr	N/A
VBDerefHlstrLen	N/A
VBDerefZeroTermHlstr	N/A
VBDestroyHlstr	SysFreeString
VBGetHlstrLen	SysStringLen
VBGetVariantType	N/A
VBGetVariantValue	N/A
VBResizeHlstr	SysReAllocStringLen
VBSetHlstr	SysReAllocString
VBSetVariantValue	N/A

Looking at Version Information

In Visual Basic 4.0, it is just as possible to save version information within executables as it always has been for DLLs via the Resource Compiler. This means that you can check all your software components at start-up to ensure that the correct combination of component-builds is available; if they are not available, the application can be terminated gracefully before anything unexpected occurs (such as a crash due to a critical component of yours having been overwritten by a third-party install program's different version of that component).

Listing 20.3 gives you some sample code so that you can read the version number of a DLL.

Listing 20.3. Sample Code to find the version number of a DLL at runtime.

```
Type VS_VERSION
    wLength             As Integer
    wValueLength        As Integer
    szKey               As String * 16 ' "VS_VERSION_INFO"
    dwSignature         As Long        ' VS_FIXEDFILEINFO struct
    dwStrucVersion      As Long
    dwFileVersionMS     As Long
    dwFileVersionLS     As Long
    dwProductVersionMS  As Long
    dwProductVersionLS  As Long
    dwFileFlagsMasks    As Long
    dwFileFlags         As Long
    dwFileOS            As Long
    dwFileType          As Long
    dwFileSubType       As Long
    dwFileDateMS        As Long
    dwFileDateLS        As Long
End Type

Declare Function GetFileVersionInfo% Lib "Ver.dll" (ByVal Filename$, ByVal
➥dwHandle&, ByVal cbBuff&, ByVal lpvData$)
Declare Function GetFileVersionInfoSize& Lib "Ver.dll" (ByVal Filename$,
➥dwHandle&)
Declare Sub hmemcpy Lib "kernel" (hpvDest As Any, hpvSrc As Any, ByVal cbBytes&)

Function HIWORD (X As Long) As Integer
    HIWORD = X \ &HFFFF&
End Function

Function LOWORD (X As Long) As Integer
    LOWORD = X And &HFFFF&
End Function

Function VerInfo$ (FullFileName$)
    Dim X As VS_VERSION
    Dim FileVer$

    BufSize& = GetFileVersionInfoSize(FullFileName$, dwHandle&)
    If BufSize& = 0 Then
        MsgBox "No Version Info available!"
        Exit Function
    End If
    lpvData$ = Space$(BufSize&)
    r% = GetFileVersionInfo(FullFileName$, dwHandle&, BufSize&, lpvData$)
    hmemcpy X, ByVal lpvData$, Len(X)

    FileVer$ = LTrim$(Str$(HIWORD(X.dwFileVersionMS))) + "."
    FileVer$ = FileVer$ + LTrim$(Str$(LOWORD(X.dwFileVersionMS))) + "."
    FileVer$ = FileVer$ + LTrim$(Str$(HIWORD(X.dwFileVersionLS))) + "."
    FileVer$ = FileVer$ + LTrim$(Str$(LOWORD(X.dwFileVersionLS)))

    VerInfo$ = FileVer$
End Function
```

Listing 20.3 can be run with a function call like this:

```
Sub Form_Load ()
    Text1.Text = VerInfo$("c:\windows\system\vbrun300.dll")
End Sub
```

See the "MS Knowledge Base" article Q112731 for more extensive information. It's available via CompuServe (GO MSKB) or via the MS Developer Network CDs.

Finding Out What's in a DLL

Some useful tools are provided within Windows and the Software Development Kit (SDK) bundled with Visual C++, which enable you to examine DLLs to find out useful things about their contents. These tools are described in the following sections.

EXEHDR

One of the most useful tools is EXEHDR.EXE, which enables you to read and print the DLL's header information in an intelligible format. Applying EXEHDR to the DLL you produced using Visual C++ above, for example, gives the output shown in Listing 20.4.

Listing 20.4. Using EXEHDR.EXE to examine a DLL.

```
C:\SC_WIN>exehdr scalcwin.dll

Microsoft (R) EXE File Header Utility  Version 3.20
Copyright (C) Microsoft Corp 1985-1993. All rights reserved.

  Library:                    SCALCWIN
  Description:                SCALCWIN.exe
  Data:                       SHARED
  Initialization:            Global
  Initial CS:IP:              seg   1 offset 00a8
  Initial SS:SP:              seg   0 offset 0000
  DGROUP:                     seg   2
  Heap allocation:            0400 bytes
  Application type:           WINDOWAPI
  Other module flags:         Contains gangload area; start: 0x140; size 0xa00

  no. type address  file  mem    flags
    1 CODE 00000160 007bd 007bd PRELOAD, (movable), (discardable)
    2 DATA 000009c0 00170 00170 SHARED, PRELOAD, (movable)


  Exports:
  ord seg offset name
    2   1  0000   WEP exported, shared data
    3   1  040e   ___EXPORTEDSTUB exported, shared data
    1   1  07b0   SIMPLECALC exported, shared data
```

Listing 20.4 demonstrates that SIMPLECALC is indeed an exported function from your DLL, along with two other Windows functions: WEP and _EXPORTEDSTUB, which were built-in automatically due to the inclusion of the /GD parameter when the source code was compiled. You also can derive from this listing an alternative means of calling the function; the first column gives the ordinal number of the function so that you can call SIMPLECALC by number as function #1 within the SCALCWIN library.

There also is an optional /VERBOSE parameter that you can apply to get even more information, such as the Windows functions that SCALCWIN.DLL uses itself (imports) as part of its operation. If you apply this parameter, you can derive that SCALCWIN uses the functions shown in Listing 20.5 from the Windows Kernel (which I have shown in both ordinal and name form).

Listing 20.5. Windows Kernel functions used by SCALCWIN.DLL.

```
KERNEL.1        (FATALEXIT)
KERNEL.3        (GETVERSION)
KERNEL.4        (LOCALINIT)
KERNEL.15       (GLOBALALLOC)
KERNEL.16       (GLOBALREALLOC)
KERNEL.17       (GLOBALFREE)
KERNEL.18       (GLOBALLOCK)
KERNEL.19       (GLOBALUNLOCK)
KERNEL.20       (GLOBALSIZE)
KERNEL.23       (LOCKSEGMENT)
KERNEL.48       (GETMODULEUSAGE)
KERNEL.91       (INITTASK)
KERNEL.102      (DOS3CALL)
KERNEL.131      (GETDOSENVIRONMENT)
KERNEL.137      (FATALAPPEXIT)
KERNEL.178      (__WINFLAGS)
```

C++ Name Mangling

While on the subject of EXEHDR, there's one important thing to mention—try renaming the C source file shown in Figure 20.3 so that it has a CPP extension instead of a C extension. If you rebuild the SCALCWIN project once more using a CPP file name, you get the error shown in Figure 20.8.

This error occurs because of C++ name mangling (or *name decoration*, as Microsoft often describes it) where the compiler appends characters to the function name for its own internal purposes—which can render the function name unrecognizable to the calling program.

It's possible to get around this linking problem by using the _export keyword on the function prototype itself, as shown in Listing 20.6 (instead of declaring the function name in the DEF linker definitions file).

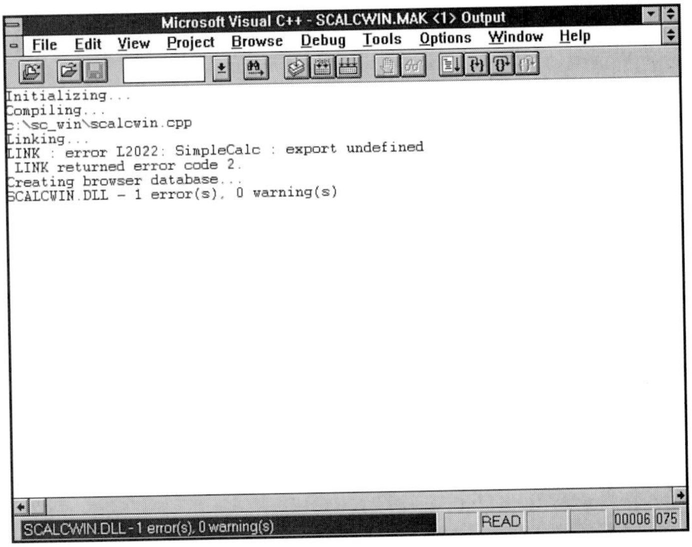

FIGURE 20.8.

Link failure caused by C++ name mangling.

Listing 20.6. Poor workaround for C++ name mangling.

```
/****************
 * SCALCWIN.CPP *
 ****************/

int _export _far _pascal SimpleCalc(int Parm1, int Parm2);

int _export _far _pascal SimpleCalc(int Parm1, int Parm2)
{
    return (Parm1 * Parm2);
}
```

However, even if you get around the linking problem, the effect of C++ name mangling is to mess up the EXEHDR Exports output, as shown in Listing 20.7.

Listing 20.7. Corrupted function name due to C++ name mangling.

```
Exports:
ord seg offset name
  1   1  0026  WEP exported, shared data
  2   1  045e  ___EXPORTEDSTUB exported, shared data
  3   1  0000  ?SIMPLECALC@@ZCHHH@Z exported, shared data
```

```
You need to add  extern "C"  to the function declaration to correct it :-
```

```
/****************
 * SCALCWIN.CPP *
 ****************/
```

continues

Listing 20.7. continued

```
extern "C" int _export _far _pascal SimpleCalc(int Parm1, int Parm2);

extern "C" int _export _far _pascal SimpleCalc(int Parm1, int Parm2)
{
    return (Parm1 * Parm2);
}
```

HeapWalker

Another useful Windows tool found in the SDK is HeapWalker, which you can use to inspect the *global heap* (the system memory that Windows uses) and local heaps used by active applications or DLLs currently loaded into memory. It's useful for analyzing any memory allocation and deallocation effects when an application creates or destroys objects, so you can use it to verify that your application cleans up after itself properly when terminated—that is, it unloads all the DLLs it has used in order to free the computer's memory for other applications.

HeapWalker also is more than a simple Windows-based dump program; it can display graphical objects correctly rather than merely displaying screensful of bytes.

To see how HeapWalker works, exit Windows and reboot your machine so that you can be sure that no orphan memory allocations remain. Run Windows and HeapWalker alone before doing anything else, and then page down until you find the entries for SHELL in the OWNER column. If the correct Sort option has been chosen, you should see something like the lines shown in Listing 20.8 (probably with different memory addresses) for Windows 3.1*x*.

Listing 20.8. HeapWalker output before invoking About dialog.

ADDRESS	HANDLE	SIZE	LOCK	FLG	HEAP	OWNER	TYPE
806BD820	176E	512		D		SHELL	Code 1
806BBDC0	1766	6752		D		SHELL	Code 2
806BB3C0	175E	2560		D		SHELL	Code 3
806B9FC0	1756	5120		D		SHELL	Code 4
806B9D80	174E	576		D		SHELL	Code 5
806B9C20	1746	352		D		SHELL	Code 6
00015900	1716	32				SHELL	Data
0004BF80	170E	1120			Y	SHELL	DGroup
0004B0C0	177E	864				SHELL	Module Database
0004D6A0	151E	128				SHELL	Private
00058960	1706	224		D		SHELL	Resource String

Minimize HeapWalker. Then choose Help | About from the main Windows menu and just cancel the resulting About dialog box. To perform this, a DLL had to be loaded; so if you maximize HeapWalker and search for the SHELL entries again, you should see that the following extra lines have appeared:

```
8071EDE0 172E    3552      D    SHELL    Code 9
00015680 150E    576       D    SHELL    Resource Dialog
00059960 1FEE    2080      D    SHELL    Resource RCdata
```

These lines show that calling a Windows function has caused memory to be allocated but not freed afterward. You might wonder what these extra memory allocations are for; to find out, just double-click on the line that interests you. If you choose the Resource Dialog line, for example, you see a screen similar to Figure 20.9.

FIGURE 20.9.

HeapWalker in action.

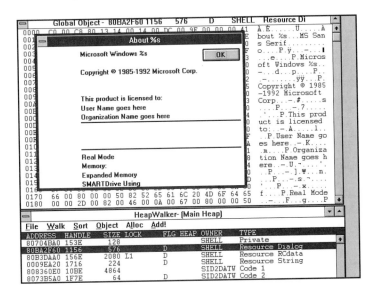

As you can see, the template for the dialog used for all the Help | About dialog boxes within Windows 3.1-supplied utilities has been located (in both graphical and as-loaded-into-memory formats). If you want to use this template within your own application, try using code like the code shown in Listing 20.9 to access the undocumented ShellAbout function.

Listing 20.9. Code to use the Windows About dialog box.

```
Declare Function ShellAbout Lib "C:\windows\system\shell.dll"
        (ByVal hWnd As Integer,
         ByVal Caption As String,
         ByVal Copyright As String,
         ByVal hIcon As Integer) As Integer      'All on one line!

Sub Form_Load ()
    HInstance% = ShellAbout(hWnd, "My Name", "My Copyright", 0)
End Sub
```

Likewise, if you choose the Resource RCData line within HeapWalker, you see a strange list of abbreviated names—none other than the credit list of Microsoft personnel responsible for Windows 3.1 development!

If you've never seen this list before, you can access the hidden list by choosing Help | About. Then press Ctrl+Shift and double-click about a millimeter to the left of the bottom left corner of the blue square in the Windows Flag icon. The first time, nothing happens. The second and third time you do it are much more interesting! The third time around gives you the results shown in Figure 20.10.

FIGURE 20.10.

Hidden Microsoft credits scrolling in Win3.1 or Win 3.11.

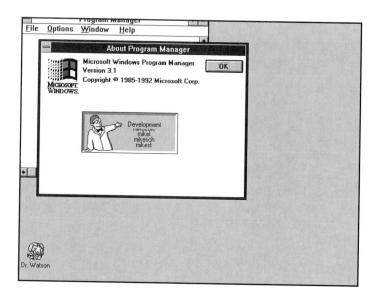

This time around, it's Bill Gates as the MC. Other times you do it, you will get other illustrious 'Softies like Steve Ballmer or T-Bear....

A curious thing to note about this feature is that the credits text is not visible if you dump SHELL.DLL to text or view it with something like the Norton Utilities. This is because the credits text is encrypted by XORing each character with &H99 (99 hex), so HeapWalker has helped you detect something particularly unusual! If you want to prove this, run the code shown in Listing 20.10.

Listing 20.10. Proving that HeapWalker can help you decrypt hidden text.

```
Sub Form_Load ()
    ShStr$ = Space$(2100)

    Open "c:\windows\system\shell.dll" For Binary As #1

    'UNCOMMENT ONE OF THESE
    'Get #1, 38722, ShStr$        'Win3.1
    'Get #1, 38067, ShStr$        'WfW3.11

    Close
```

```
   For n = 1 To 2060
      tmp = Asc(Mid$(ShStr$, n, 1))
      If tmp >= &H20 Then
         Debug.Print Chr$(tmp Xor &H99);
      ElseIf tmp = 0 Then
         Debug.Print
      End If
   Next
End Sub
```

As you can see, HeapWalker is a valuable tool that detects all sorts of objects that might be resident in memory as a result of your application's operation.

Special Note—Static versus Dynamic Linking

This section presents a detailed, behind-the-scenes account of the differences between static and dynamic linking, with an example of how to build one of each.

I will be using the same command-line tools for building both sorts—which demonstrates the similarities between the two methods and also might be useful if you are forced to use a low-speed/low-memory computer that sags under the strain of the full Visual C++ environment.

The most common examples of static-linked programs are MS-DOS ones, so I'll build a simple application where an MS-DOS BASIC program uses a simple C function to multiply two integers. I'll then implement the same functionality within Visual Basic 4.0 and a DLL, using the same command-line tools for a fair comparison.

Command-line tools, you might be saying, that's the hard way! Don't worry—it's not as hard as it looks at first sight!

Static Linking—An Example

Consider the Visual Basic-DOS program SCALCB.BAS shown in Listing 20.11. I've removed the user interface form SCALC.FRM and made it into a minimal, command-line program for the utmost simplicity.

Listing 20.11. Minimal VB-DOS program to call a C function.

```
' - - - - - - - - - - -
' SCALCB.BAS
' - - - - - - - - - - -

DECLARE FUNCTION SimpleCalc% CDECL(BYVAL Parm1%, BYVAL Parm2%)
```

continues

Listing 20.11. continued

```
DIM Parm1 AS INTEGER
DIM Parm2 AS INTEGER

INPUT Parm1
INPUT Parm2

PRINT "In BASIC, going into C..."
PRINT SimpleCalc (Parm1, Parm2)
PRINT "Back into BASIC!"
```

In summary, two variables are declared and given values by the user. They then are passed to a C function (SimpleCalc), which multiplies them and returns the answer to BASIC for output.

If you are unfamiliar with MS-DOS programming, note that a DOS program always assumes that it is the only application running and therefore does not need to specify a form to which to print. It just takes the input off the screen and throws the answer back out there afterward. Although Windows can provide multiple DOS sessions, each instance of DOS still behaves in this way within its respective window.

To compile this program, you use the BC.EXE compiler, which has a heritage going back even before Bill Gates' and Paul Allen's work with IBM in the early 1980s (when BC.EXE was known as BASCOM.EXE). This compiler is shown in Listing 20.12.

Listing 20.12. VB-DOS compiler output.

```
C:\SMPLCALC>bc scalcb /o /d;
Microsoft (R) Visual Basic (TM) for MS-DOS (R)
Compiler - Professional Edition Version 1.00
Copyright (C) 1982-1992 Microsoft Corporation. All rights reserved.

42901 Bytes Available
42410 Bytes Free

    0 Warning Error(s)
    0 Severe Error(s)
```

This produces an *object* module—a skeleton of BASIC functionality without the explicit low-level machine code attached yet. A directory listing now includes something like these lines:

```
SCALCB    BAS      298 06/06/95   15:58
SCALCB    OBJ     1340 06/06/95   15:59
```

NOTE

The /o option is a compiler directive to produce a complete, stand-alone executable (instead of producing a small executable that uses the standard runtime executable supplied with BASIC). The /d option instructs the compiler to include some runtime error-checking code so that the machine won't lock up easily if a serious coding error is made.

Table 20.2 shows the full option list for the BASIC compiler.

Table 20.2. BASIC compiler option list.

Option	Function
/?	Displays command-line options
/A	Generates assembly listing
/Ah	Enables huge dynamic arrays
/C:*n*	Sets default COM buffer size
/D	Performs runtime error-checking
/E	Enables ON ERROR checking
/Es	Enables EMS sharing
/Fpa	Enables the alternate math pack
/G2	Generates code for 286
/G3	Generates code for 386
/Ib:*n*	Sets number of ISAM buffers; requires ASCII format source file
/Ie:*n*	Reserves non-ISAM EMS
/Ii:*n*	Sets number of ISAM indexes
/MBF	Supports Microsoft Binary Format numbers
/O	Compiles stand-alone EXE
/R	Stores arrays in row-major order
/S	Disables string compression
/T	Issues no compiler warnings (Terse)
/V	Tells ON EVENT to check each statement
/W	Tells ON EVENT to check each label
/X	Enables RESUME NEXT support
/Zd	Provides limited CodeView information
/Zi	Provides full CodeView information; requires ASCII format source file

Next, consider the matching C program, SCALCC.C, shown in Listing 20.13.

Listing 20.13. A simple C function to multiply two integers.

```
/************
 * SCALCC.C *
 ************/

int SimpleCalc(int Parm1, int Parm2);

int SimpleCalc(int Parm1, int Parm2)
{
    return (Parm1 * Parm2);
}
```

In summary, two integer variables are received, multiplied, and returned to the calling program. This is compiled in a manner similar to the BASIC program shown in Listing 20.11, except that the C compiler CL.EXE is used instead. CL.EXE is supplied with Visual C++ and usually is found in the \MSVC\BIN directory. Listing 20.14 shows the compiler output.

Listing 20.14. C compiler output.

```
C:\SMPLCALC>cl /c /W4 /AL scalcc.c
Microsoft (R) C/C++ Optimizing Compiler Version 8.00c
Copyright (c) Microsoft Corp 1984-1993. All rights reserved.

scalcc.c
```

This produces another object module—this time, a skeleton of C functionality. A directory listing now includes something like these lines:

```
SCALCC    C      164 06/06/95   15:58
SCALCC    OBJ    350 06/06/95   15:59
```

NOTE

The /c option is a compiler directive to compile the code and then stop without automatically invoking the subsequent link stage. The /W4 option directs the compiler to be as strict as possible with syntax errors or warnings. The /AL option instructs the compiler to use the large memory model, which means that four bytes are allocated for code and data addresses instead of the two bytes needed for pure 16-bit applications.

To get the full list of the 140 options for the C compiler, type **cl /?** and press Enter.

The next stage is to perform the static link. The BASIC and the C skeletons are joined together; the machine code routines to actually execute the program are copied from the Visual Basic-DOS library VBDCL10E.LIB and attached to the appropriate places on the combined skeleton. This is performed with the LINK.EXE program, as shown in Listing 20.15.

Listing 20.15. Performing the Static Link.

```
C:\SMPLCALC>link

Microsoft (R) Segmented Executable Linker  Version 5.60
Copyright (C) Microsoft Corp 1984-1993. All rights reserved.

Object Modules [.obj]: scalcb.obj +
Object Modules [.obj]: scalcc.obj
Run File [scalcb.exe]:
List File [nul.map]:
Libraries [.lib]: vbdcl10e.lib
Definitions File [nul.def]:
```

This listing produces a stand-alone executable SCALCB.EXE:

```
SCALCB    EXE    37012 06/06/95   15:59
```

This executable can be run by typing **SCALCB** at the DOS command prompt and pressing Enter. See the next section for what it looks like when run.

Dynamic Linking—A Similar Example

The process to create a dynamic link library is remarkably similar to that used for static-linked programs, except a few keywords are added to the program, the compiler parameters are slightly altered, and some extra definitions are added to the link stage in a separate DEF file.

Listing 20.16 shows the altered C program. The Microsoft proprietary _far and _pascal keywords have been added to the declaration in order to ensure that the parameters are not 16-bit and are passed in the correct order. In practice, you should include the WINDOWS.H header file and use the defined constants FAR and PASCAL, but I've bypassed that here for simplicity.

Listing 20.16. C program modified for compilation as a DLL.

```
/**************
 * SCALCWIN.C *
 **************/

int _far _pascal SimpleCalc(int Parm1, int Parm2);

int _far _pascal SimpleCalc(int Parm1, int Parm2)
{
    return (Parm1 * Parm2);
}
```

This is compiled in a manner similar to the original C program, as shown in Listing 20.17.

Listing 20.17. Compiling a C program for Windows.

```
C:\SC_WIN>cl /c /W4 /ALw /GD scalcwin.c
Microsoft (R) C/C++ Optimizing Compiler Version 8.00c
Copyright (c) Microsoft Corp 1984-1993. All rights reserved.

scalcwin.c
```

As before, this listing produces an object module—this time, a skeleton of C DLL functionality. A directory listing now includes something like these lines:

```
SCALCWIN C      196 06/06/95   16:55
SCALCWIN OBJ    253 06/06/95   16:55
```

NOTE

The /ALw option is a modified form of the /AL compiler directive to compile the code for Windows; the /GD parameter automatically adds Windows library entry and exit routines. Furthermore, if you are using compilers from another manufacturer (such as Borland), you must change these parameters to the appropriate equivalents as used by that manufacturer.

An extra component that must be produced is the DLL link definitions file SCALCWIN.DEF. The contents are shown in Listing 20.18.

Listing 20.18. Link Definitions File contents.

```
LIBRARY   SCALCWIN                          ;Make a DLL...
EXETYPE   WINDOWS                           ;      ... for Windows
CODE      PRELOAD MOVEABLE DISCARDABLE      ;Build so that Windows can
DATA      PRELOAD MOVEABLE SINGLE           ;   relocate it in memory
HEAPSIZE  1024                              ;Free mem alloc'd to DLL
EXPORTS   SimpleCalc    @1                  ;Available function(s)
          WEP PRIVATE                       ;Exit Procedure properties
```

Because you are producing a DLL that is independent of the calling application, you do not need to deal with the Visual Basic calling program at this stage. You merely link the C routine to the appropriate machine code libraries, as shown in Listing 20.19.

Listing 20.19. Using LINK.EXE to make a Dynamic Link Library.

```
C:\SC_WIN>link

Microsoft (R) Segmented Executable Linker  Version 5.60
Copyright (C) Microsoft Corp 1984-1993. All rights reserved.
```

```
Object Modules [.obj]: SCALCWIN.OBJ
Run File [SCALCWIN.exe]: SCALCWIN.DLL
List File [nul.map]:
Libraries [.lib]: libw +
Libraries [.lib]: ldllcew
Definitions File [nul.def]: SCALCWIN.DEF;
```

This listing produces a dynamic link library as follows:

```
SCALCWIN DLL      2880 06/06/95    16:56
```

Figure 20.11 shows the dynamic-linked and static-linked programs running side by side.

FIGURE 20.11.

Examples of dynamic-linked and static-linked programs.

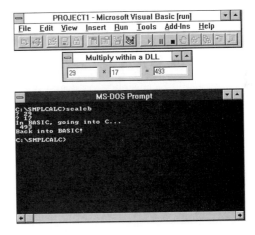

The link between the BASIC code and the C code is made at build time for the static-linked program and at runtime for the dynamic-linked program.

Summary

In this chapter, you learned that Dynamic Link Libraries (DLLs) are core-important executable files containing functions that Windows applications can call to perform useful service tasks. You should use DLLs to extend the functionality or ultimate performance of your Visual Basic applications. Check the version number of your DLL when using it. Be aware of the tools in the SDK to analyze your DLLs.

Exploiting VBXes

21

by Brad Shannon

IN THIS CHAPTER

Visual Basic extensions (VBXes) and OLE custom controls (OCXes) are extra or third-party components that can be added to your Visual Basic project. Custom controls provide additional functionality and capabilities to your application. The functionality and capabilities are built into the components. The custom controls can range from text boxes that provide additional capabilities, such as automatic text selection, to complete spreadsheets or word processing applications.

By using custom controls, you are able to greatly reduce the effort that is needed in order to add additional functions and features to your application.

Comparing 16-Bit VBXes to 32-Bit OCXes

VBX custom controls have been available since Version 1.0 of Visual Basic. VBX custom controls currently are supported in other development environments (Microsoft C++ and Delphi, for example). With the release of version 4.0 of Visual Basic, the OCX type of custom control was introduced. The OCX control is based on the OLE version 2 application model. Currently, this type of control is supported by Visual Basic 4.0 and Access 2.0. Other development platforms will be able to host OCX controls (Visual Fox Pro and Microsoft C++ 4.0, for example). OCX controls exist in both 16-bit and 32-bit models, whereas VBX controls exist only in 16-bit models.

The 16-bit version of Visual Basic supports both 16-bit OCX controls and 16-bit VBX controls. The 32-bit version of Visual Basic supports only 32-bit OCX controls.

VBX and OCX Controls

If your application is using custom controls, you must be aware of the following points and potential problems when using OCX/VBX controls. As there are many applications created with Visual Basic, there is a good chance you could find yourself in a situation similar to that described here:

- If a different version of the custom control (perhaps an older version) is installed on your system, your application may behave differently. A sure way around this problem is to check for the version number of the VBX or OCX control that your application is expecting. You can check this as part of your start-up routine. If your application finds that a version of controls is installed that it does not support or recognize, it can warn the user. The application then can provide a choice: to exit or to continue.

- VBX and OCX controls generally are not distributed with their source code to developers. If you find a problem with the control, you must find a way to work around the problem or convince the vendor to fix it.

- The VBX or OCX file is another file that must be controlled and shipped with your application.

In the next section, you learn how to retrieve the Windows version information based on the name of the file passed to it.

Adding Custom Controls to Your Project

In order to add a custom control to your application, you will need to use the Custom Controls dialog (see Figure 21.1). The contents of the Custom Controls dialog is determined based on the state of the control's insertable objects, selected items only, and check boxes. If you select controls, then all of the OCX and VBX controls that have been registered with the OLE registry will be displayed. If you select Insertable objects, all of the OLE objects that have been registered with the OLE registry will be displayed (an example of an insertable object is an Excel spreadsheet). If the control is part of the current project, an X appears at the left of the control. If a control is installed on your system, but it is not listed in the Available Controls list, you can add it to the list by clicking the Browse button. Selected items will display only the custom controls and insertable objects that are part of the current project. You are unable to remove a control from the selected item that is currently being used in your project.

FIGURE 21.1.

Illustrates the Custom Control Selection dialog.

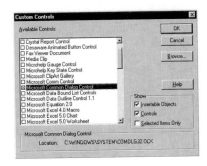

In order to add a VBX or OCX control to your project, you need to complete the following steps:

1. Choose Tools | Custom Controls.

2. Select the control that you wish to add by clicking on the box to the left of the control (for example, the Common Dialog control).

3. Once the control has been selected, a graphic representation of the control will be visible in your toolbox (see Figure 21.2).

4. Once the control is part of your toolbox, it can be used in the same manner as any other Visual Basic control.

FIGURE 21.2.

The toolbox with the newly added common Dialog control.

Standard Edition versus Professional Edition Custom Controls

The Standard Edition of Visual Basic contains five custom controls; the Professional Edition of Visual Basic contains 19 custom controls. These controls were obtained from various VBX and OCX vendors who may sell another version of the control with additional functionality. Some of the commercial counterparts to the custom controls covered in this chapter are covered in Chapter 30, "Using Third Party VBX/OCX Controls." Table 21.1 lists the controls included in each version.

Table 21.1. Controls included in Standard Edition versus Professional Edition.

Custom Control	Standard Edition	Professional Edition
3D Controls		X
Animated Button		X
Data Bound ComboBox	X	X
Data Bound Grid	X	X
Data Bound ListBox	X	X
Common Dialog	X	X
Communications		X
Crystal Reports		X
Gauge		X
Graph		X
Grid	X	X
Key State		X
MaskEdit TextBox		X
Microsoft Mail		X

Custom Control	Standard Edition	Professional Edition
MultiMedia		X
Outline		X
Picture Clipping		X
Spin		X
Tabbed Dialog		X

The 32-bit version of Visual Basic also includes controls that can be used only in Windows 95 and Windows NT 3.51 and later. These additional controls are shown in Table 21.2.

Table 21.2. Controls included for Windows 95, Windows NT 3.51 only.

Control	Function
ImageList	Enables you to store bitmap images that then can be used by the other controls listed in this table
ListView	Provides the Standard view so that you can display the contents of folders
ProgressBar	Adds the new Windows 95 type progress indicator; provides a function similar to the Gauge custom control
RichText	Displays documents in Rich Text format
Slider	Indicates a sliding scale
StatusBar	Adds the new Windows 95 status bar; provides a function similar to the KeyStats custom control
TabStrip	The Tab Strip control can be used as an alternative to tabbed dialog control supplier with the Professional Edition of Visual Basic. Additionally, the TabStrip control can be used in order to provide a group of push buttons where only one button may be depressed at any one time.
Toolbar	Adds the functionality of a toolbar to your application

Distributing Applications that Use Custom Controls

If the project you have developed includes custom controls, the files relating to these custom controls must be included when you distribute your application. The easiest method to ensure that the correct files are distributed is to use the SetupWizard application that is included with Visual Basic. Once you have completed your application, you need to perform the following steps in order to create distribution diskettes.

1. Start the SetupWizard Application by double-clicking on the SetupWizard icon contained in the Visual Basic Program Group. You will see a dialog like the one illustrated in Figure 21.3.

FIGURE 21.3.

SetupWizard startup.

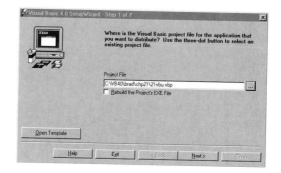

Once the SetupWizard has started, you need to supply the path to your applications project file. You can also indicate if you want your project recompiled prior to the creation of your distribution media. The SetupWizard will then read through all of the files in your project in order to determine if there are any external files that need to be included. If you have selected the compile option, the SetupWizard will also recompile your application. Once you have entered your project file name, press the Next button in order to continue to the next step.

2. Once the SetupWizard has completed step one, you will then be prompted with a list of external Data Access Engines (DBASE III, for example) that may be needed by your application (see Figure 21.4). If your application does not perform any data access or uses the Jet engine exclusively, you may skip this step; otherwise, select the appropriate items from the list. Once you have completed this step, press the Next button in order to continue to the next step.

NOTE

You can go back a step by pressing the Back button.

3. Once the SetupWizard has completed step two, you will then be prompted for the destination drive and directory for the distribution files (see Figure 21.5). You are able to place your distribution files either directly on diskette or save them to your PC's hard disk and copy them at a later date. Once you have selected the destination drive and directory, press the Next button in order to continue to the next step.

FIGURE 21.4.

SetupWizard Data Access Engine selection.

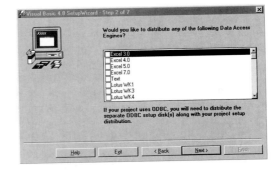

FIGURE 21.5.

SetupWizard Destination selection.

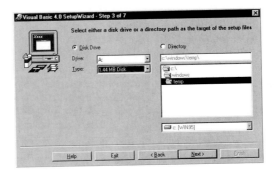

4. Once the SetupWizard has completed step three, you will then be prompted to add any needed OLE servers to the distribution files (see Figure 21.6). If your application is using OLE Servers, enter the details via the Add OLE Servers dialog. Once this is complete, press the Next button in order to continue to the next step.

FIGURE 21.6.

SetupWizard OLE Server setup.

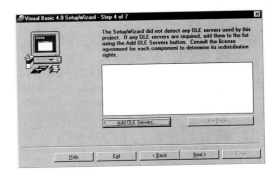

5. Once the SetupWizard has completed step four, you will be prompted with a list of files that the SetupWizard has determined that need to be distributed with your application (see Figure 21.7). If there are files included in the list that you do not wish to distribute (for example, you know they are resident on the user's Machine), clear the check box next to the file. Once you are satisfied with the files included for distribution, press the Next button in order to continue to the next step.

FIGURE 21.7.

SetupWizard OLE Server setup.

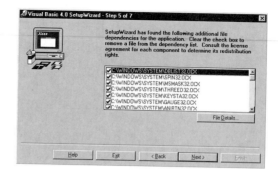

6. Once the SetupWizard has completed step five, you will be prompted for the type of application that you are distributing (see Figure 21.8). If you are distributing an OLE shared component, the component will be installed in the shared OLE components directory; otherwise, the application will be installed into a directory of the user's choice.

FIGURE 21.8.

SetupWizard OLE Server setup.

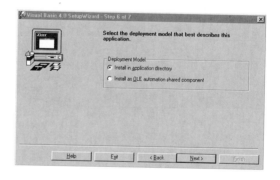

7. Once the SetupWizard has completed step six, you will be prompted with a final list of files that the SetupWizard has determined should be distributed with your application (see Figure 21.9). You are able to deselect files in the same manner as described in step five. Additionally, you can specify additional files that you may wish to distribute with your application (an example of an additional file would be a database). If you wish to add additional files, select the Add button and enter the path to the files that you wish to add. Once you have finalized the contents of your application, you should save a template that can then be used in future distribution builds by the SetupWizard.

Once you have completed this step, press the Finish button, and the SetupWizard will compress all of the distribution files and copy them to the destination that was indicated in step three. The SetupWizard will also create a setup program that can be used to install the application.

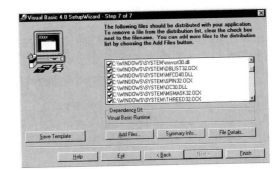

FIGURE 21.9.

*SetupWizard Files
Addition, removal.*

Using the Professional Edition Controls

The following sections discuss the main purposes of the controls and provide examples to illustrate the behaviors of these controls.

> **NOTE**
>
> The Crystal Reports Custom Control is covered in Chapter 8, "Reporting Mechanisms."

3D Controls

Six controls are included with the 3D controls:

- 3D Check Box
- 3D Frame
- 3D Command Button
- 3D Panel
- 3D Option Button
- 3D Ribbon Button

The 3D controls are similar to existing Visual Basic controls (the check box, for example). However, the 3D controls contain additional properties. Some of the enhancements over the standard Visual Basic controls follow:

- The Command button can display a picture.
- All the controls can display 3D fonts.
- The 3D panel can display text or can be used as a progress meter.
- The 3D Ribbon control can be used as command buttons, or it can be used to create pushbuttons. You can use this control to create a group of pushbuttons and allow only one of the buttons to be pressed at any one time.

- The 3D panel can have a raised or inset border.
- The border size of a 3D panel can be changed.
- The frame on the 3D Frame control can be raised or lowered.
- The 3D controls will always appear in 3D regardless of the forms Appearance property.
- The 3D controls default to a gray background.

To check out some of the capabilities of some of the 3D controls, follow these steps:

1. Using the File | New Project command, open a new project.

2. Follow the steps outlined in the "Adding Custom Controls to Your Project" section in order to add the Sheridan 3D controls to your project.

3. Double-click on the Picture control (PictureBox in ToolTips display) contained in the toolbox in order to place a Picture control on your form.

4. Include the following property settings for the Picture control:

   ```
   Align = Align Top
   Appearance = 1-Flat
   BackColor = Grey
   Left = 0
   Height = 465
   Width = 6690
   ```

5. Single-click the 3D Ribbon control contained in the toolbox (SSRibbon in ToolTips display). Draw three 3D Ribbon controls on to the picture control.

6. Include the following property settings for the 3D Ribbon button control:
   SSRibbon1

   ```
   Autosize = 2 - Autosize button to Picture
   Name = ribBold
   GroupNumber = 1
   Left = 4260
   PictureDisabled= c:\vb40\bitmaps\toolbar3\bld-dis.bmp
   PictureDn= c:\vb40\bitmaps\toolbar3\bld-mds.bmp
   Pictureup= c:\vb40\bitmaps\toolbar3\bld-up.bmp
   ```

   SSRibbon2

   ```
   Autosize = 2 - Autosize button to Picture
   Name = ribCenter
   GroupNumber = 2
   Left = 4800
   PictureDisabled= c:\vb40\bitmaps\toolbar3\cnt-dis.bmp
   PictureDn= c:\vb40\bitmaps\toolbar3\cnt-mds.bmp
   Pictureup= c:\vb40\bitmaps\toolbar3\cnt-up.bmp
   ```

   SSRibbon3

   ```
   Autosize = 2 - Autosize button to Picture
   Name = ribItalic
   ```

```
GroupNumber = 3
Left = 5280
PictureDisabled= c:\vb40\bitmaps\toolbar3\itl-dis.bmp
PictureDn= c:\vb40\bitmaps\toolbar3\itl-mds.bmp
Pictureup= c:\vb40\bitmaps\toolbar3\itl-up.bmp
```

7. Single-click the 3D Command Button control contained in the toolbox (SSCommand in ToolTips display). Draw one 3D Command Button control on the Picture control.

8. Include the following property settings for the 3D Command button control:

```
Autosize = 2 - Autosize button to Picture
Name = cmdHelp
Left = 5880
Picture= c:\vb40\bitmaps\toolbar3\hlp-up.bmp
```

9. Add the following code to the `cmdHelp_Click` event.

```
MsgBox " Help Button Was Pressed "
```

10. Double-click on the 3D Panel control (SSPanel in ToolTips display) contained in the toolbox in order to place a 3D Panel on to your form.

11. Include the following property settings for the 3D Panel control:

```
BevelInner = 1- Insert Bevel
BevelOuter = 2- Raised Bevel
BevelWidth = 1
BorderWidth =1
Caption =
FloodShowPCt = True
FloodType = 1 - From Left to Right
Height = 315
Left =  1800
Name = pnlGauge
Top = 5520
Width = 6690
```

12. Double-click on the 3D Command Button control (SSCommand in ToolTips display) contained in the toolbox in order to place a 3D Command Button on your form.

13. Include the following property settings for the 3D Command button control:

```
Caption = &Gauge
Height = 495
Left =  1920
Name = cmdGauge
Top = 3300
Width = 1215
```

14. Add the following code to the `cmdGauge_Click` event:

```
Dim x As Integer
Dim y As Integer
Screen.MousePointer = 11
' Gauge in Panel
For x = 1 To 100

pnlgauge.FloodPercent = x
If x = 49 Then
```

```
    pnlgauge.ForeColor = &HFFFFFF

End If


For y = 1 To 1000

    DoEvents

Next y

Next x

Screen.MousePointer = 0
```

15. Press the F5 key to run the project.

Once the project is running, you can click the Gauge button; the `pnlGauge` control displays a progress bar (see Figure 21.10). Clicking the Help command button displays a message box indicating that the button has been pressed. You can also see the behavior of non-grouped Ribbon buttons.

FIGURE 21.10.

Illustrates the use of the 3D Panel Control as a progress meter.

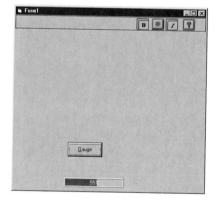

Animated Button

You use the Animated Button control to show a series of pictures to emulate animation. If you want to determine the bitmap that is displayed or to change the currently displayed bitmap, you should retrieve or change the `Value` property. You can use this control to convey a series of images to the user, much like a cartoon.

In the example in this section, you use the Animated Button control to step through the four suites available in a deck of cards. All the pictures used in this example are located in the Assorted bitmaps directory.

To use the Animated Button control, follow these steps:

1. Using the File | New Project command, open a new project.
2. Follow the steps outlined in the "Adding Custom Controls to Your Project" section to add the Desaware Animated Button control to your project.
3. Double-click on the Animated Button control (AniPushButton in ToolTips display) contained in the toolbox in order to place an Animated Button on your form.
4. Press the F4 key in order to access the property setting of the newly added Animate button. Select the Custom property. You will then be presented with a Tabbed dialog displaying the Custom properties that can be changed. Enter the following property settings:

```
General Tab 1

        Cycle - 1- By Frame
        BorderStyle - None
        PictdrawMode - Autosize

General Tab 2

        Caption - Empty String
        Speed - 32767
        Value - 1

Frame Setting Tab

        Select Frame 1
        Load file c:\vb40\bitmaps\assorted\club.bmp

        Select Frame 2
        Load file c:\vb40\bitmaps\assorted\diamond.bmp

        Select Frame 3
        Load file c:\vb40\bitmaps\assorted\heart.bmp


        Select frame 4
        Load file c:\vb40\bitmaps\assorted\spade.bmp
```

NOTE

The Bitmaps\Assorted directory is located inside the directory in which Visual Basic was installed.

5. After all of the above property settings have been completed, press the OK button.

6. Enter the following code in the `AniPushButton1_Click` event:

```
AniPushButton1.Value = 1

For x = 1 To 10000
    DoEvents
Next

AniPushButton1.Value = 2

For x = 1 To 10000
    DoEvents
Next

AniPushButton1.Value = 3

For x = 1 To 10000
    DoEvents
Next

AniPushButton1.Value = 4
```

7. Press the F5 key to run the project.

8. Click the AniButton control so that your application will cycle through the four bitmaps.

Because the displayed bitmaps are fairly small and do not take much time to load, `DoEvents` loops are needed. Otherwise, the pictures would change so quickly that you would be unable to see them. If the picture flips too slowly, decrease the counter value for the loops; if the bitmaps change too quickly, you might want to increase the delay. In order to increase or decrease the delay, alter the value of the To parameter in the `For` statements contained in the `AniPushButton1_Click` event.

Data Bound ComboBox

You can use the Data Bound ComboBox control to display the information stored in a database in a combo box without having to manually add the items, as you would if you were using an unbound combo box. You can update the contents of different fields based on the selection made in the combo box.

Suppose that you have a master record containing a code-type field (PubID), and its definition is defined in another table (Publishers). When the description of the code field (Publishers) is selected from the ListBox, the equivalent code (PubID) is updated in the master record.

The following example illustrates a combo box bound to the Publishers table. When a selection is made, the PubID field in the Titles table is updated. Follow these steps:

1. Using the File | New Project command, open a new project.

2. Follow the steps outlined in the "Adding Custom Controls to Your Project" section to add the Microsoft Data Bound List controls to your project.

3. Double-click on the Data control (Data in ToolTips display) contained in the toolbox to place a Data control on your form.

4. Include the following property settings for the Data control:

```
DatabaseName = C:\vb40\biblio.mdb
Recordsource = select * from titles
```

5. Double-click on the Data Control (Data in ToolTips display) contained in the toolbox to place a Data control on your form.

6. Include the following property settings for the Data Bound List control:

```
name = dtaList
DatabaseName = C:\vb40\biblio.mdb
Height = 1815
Left = 3780
Top = 1260
Width = 2895
Recordsource = select * from publishers
```

7. Double-click on the Data Bound ComboBox control (DBCombo in ToolTips display) contained in the toolbox to place a Data Bound ComboBox control on your form.

8. Include the following property settings for the Data Bound ComboBox control:

```
BoundColumn = PUBID
DataField = PUBID
DataControl = Data1
Height = 315
Left = 1560
ListField = name
Name = dbCompub
RowSource = dtaList
Top = 180
Width = 3135
```

9. Double-click on the TextBox control (TextBox in ToolTips display) contained in the toolbox in order to place a TextBox control on to your form.

10. Include the following property setting for the TextBox control:

```
Height = 315
Left = 1680
Name = txtPubid
Top = 1260
Width = 675
```

11. Double-click on the Label control (Label in ToolTips Display) contained in the toolbox to place a Label control on your form.

12. Include the following property setting for the Label control:

```
Caption = Publisher
Height = 195
Left = 120
Name = pnlTitle
Top = 240
Width = 1215
```

13. Double-click on the Label control (Label in ToolTips display) contained in the toolbox to place a Label control on your form.

14. Include the following property setting for the Label control:

```
Caption = Publisher ID
Height = 195
Left = 120
Name = pnlPubid
Top = 1320
Width = 1215
```

15. Add the following code to the dbcompub_Click event:

```
txtPubid.Text = dbCompub.BoundText
```

16. Press the F5 key in order to run the project.

The combo box contains the publisher's name. When the publisher's name is selected from the combo box, the PubID field is displayed in the text box (see Figure 21.11).

FIGURE 21.11.

The Data Bound combo box.

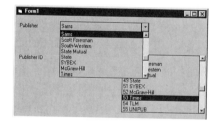

Data Bound Grid

You can use the Data Bound Grid to enable your application to display the recordset of a data control in row/column format. The contents of the recordset can be a complete table or the results of an SQL statement. You can perform the following functions on data displayed in the grid:

- Edit
- Add
- Delete
- Cut
- Copy
- Paste

You can set the contents of each column of the grid by specifying the field the column will hold. The caption for the column defaults to the name of the database field. You can change this caption to something more descriptive at design time and runtime. At runtime and design time, you can determine which features will be available to the users of your application, and you can limit the action that will be permitted on the recordset.

To understand the capabilities of the Data Bound Grid control, follow these steps:

1. Use the File | New Project command to open a new project.

2. Follow the steps outlined in the "Adding Custom Controls to Your Project" section to add the Apex Data Bound Grid control to your project.

3. Double-click on the Data control (Data in ToolTips display) contained in the toolbox to place a Data control on your form.

4. Double-click on the Data Bound Grid control (DBGrid in ToolTips display) contained in the toolbox to place a Data Bound Grid control on your form.

5. Click and drag the top-left corner of the Data Bound Grid control to the top-left corner of the form. Click and drag the bottom-right corner of the Data Bound Grid so that the Data Bound Grid occupies most of your form.

6. Include the following property settings in the Data control:

```
DatabaseName = C:\vb40\biblio.mdb
Recordsource = select * from titles order by title
```

7. Include the following property setting for the Data Bound Grid control:

```
DataSource = Data1
```

8. Press the F5 key to run the project.

When the project is running, you should see the contents of the Titles table from the BIBLIO database, in order by book title (see Figure 21.12). You can edit the records contained in the grid. Select a complete row for deletion. Add new records to the table. Resize the columns and rows. Then scroll through the complete table.

FIGURE 21.12.

Using the Data Bound Grid control.

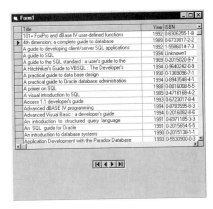

Data Bound ListBox

You can use the Data Bound ListBox control to display the information stored in a database in a ListBox without having to manually add the items, as you would if you were using an unbound ListBox. You can update the contents of different fields based on the selection made in the ListBox.

Suppose that you have a master record containing a code-type field (PubID), and its definition is provided in another table (Publishers). When the description of the code field (Publishers) is selected from the ListBox, the equivalent code (PubID) is updated automatically in the master record.

The following example illustrates a ListBox that is bound to the Publishers table. When a selection is made, the Publisher's ID is updated to the Titles table. Follow these steps:

1. Using the File | New Project command, open a new project.

2. Follow the steps outlined in the "Adding Custom Controls to Your Project" section to add the Microsoft Data Bound List controls to your project.

3. Double-click on the Data control (Data in ToolTips display) contained in the toolbox to place a Data control on your form.

4. Include the following property settings for the Data control:

```
DatabaseName = C:\vb40\biblio.mdb
Recordsource = select * from titles order by title
```

5. Double-click on the Data control (Data in ToolTips display) contained in the toolbox to place a Data control on your form.

6. Include the following property settings for the Data control:

```
name = dtaList
DatabaseName = C:\vb40\biblio.mdb
Recordsource = select name,pubid,pubid & " " & name as test from publishers
```

7. Double-click on the Data Bound ListBox (DBList in ToolTips display) contained in the toolbox to place a Data Bound ListBox control on your form.

8. Include the following property settings for the Data Bound ListBox control:

```
BoundColumn = PUBID
DataField = PUBID
DataControl = Data1
Listfield = test
Name = dblistPub
RowSource = dtaList
```

9. Double-click on the TextBox (Text in ToolTips display) contained in the toolbox to place a TextBox control on your form.

10. Include the following property setting for the TextBox control:

```
Height = 315
Left = 1680
Name = txtPubid
Top = 1260
Width = 675
```

11. Add the following code to the dbListpub_Click event:

```
txtPubid.Text = dblistPub.BoundText
```

12. Double-click on the Label control (Label in ToolTips display) contained in the toolbox to place a Label control on your form.

13. Include the following property setting for the Label control:

```
Caption = Publisher
Height = 195
Left = 120
Name = pnlTitle
Top = 240
Width = 1215
```

14. Press the F5 key to run the project.

The contents of the ListBox will be a combination of the publisher's ID and the publisher's name. When an entry is selected, the PubID field in the Titles table is updated based on the PubID of the selection made. The publisher ID is also displayed in the List Box.

The Common Dialog

You can use the Common Dialog control to enable your application to display dialog boxes consistent with those of other Windows applications. You use the Common Dialog control to prompt users to perform certain actions. The user interface elements provided by this control follow:

Element	Function
Color	Prompts the user to select or define a color.
File Open	Prompts the user to select the location and the file to open.
File Save	Prompts the user to save a file, specifying the name and location of the file being saved.
Fonts	Prompts the user to select a font.
Printer	Prompts the user to select or change the active printer or to change the printer's characteristics. An example of this would be the tray to be used for printing or the paper to be used.
WinHelp	Enables the user to evoke the WinHelp program to open a specified Windows Help file at a certain location.

NOTE

You cannot set the location in which a Common Dialog will be displayed on the screen.

To use the Common Dialog control, follow these steps:

1. Using the File | New Project command, open a new project.
2. Follow the steps outlined in the "Adding Custom Controls to Your Project" section to add the Microsoft Common Dialog control to your project.

3. Double-click on the Command Button control (CommandButton in ToolTips Display) contained in the ToolBox and place five command buttons on your form.

4. Using the property editor, set the following properties of the command buttons:

   Command Button 1

   ```
   Left = 120
   Name = cmdColor
   Top = 4260
   Width = 1215
   ```

   Command Button 2

   ```
   Left = 2760
   Name = cmdFonts
   Top = 3660
   Width = 1215
   ```

   Command Button 3

   ```
   Left = 5400
   Name = cmdHelp
   Top = 3660
   Width = 1215
   ```

   Command Button 4

   ```
   Left = 120
   Name = cmdOpen
   Top = 3660
   Width = 1215
   ```

   Command Button 5

   ```
   Left = 4080
   Name = cmdPrint
   Top = 3660
   Width = 1215
   ```

   Command Button 6

   ```
   Left = 1440
   Name = cmdSave
   Top = 3660
   Width = 1215
   ```

5. Double-click on the Common Dialog control (Common Dialog in ToolTips display) contained in the toolbox to place a Label control on your form.

6. In order to illustrate some of the functionality of the Color Common dialog, enter the following code in the cmdColor_Click event:

   ```
   CommonDialog1.DialogTitle = " Select A Color "
   CommonDialog1.Flags = &H2
   CommonDialog1.ShowColor
   MsgBox " The following Color has Been Selected " & CommonDialog1.Color
    the flag property indicates that the user will be able to define custom
   colors.
   ```

7. In order to illustrate some of the functionality of the Fonts Common dialog, enter the following code in the `cmdFonts_Click` event:

```
CommonDialog1.DialogTitle = " Select A Font "
CommonDialog1.Flags = &H40000
CommonDialog1.ShowFont
the flag property indicates that only TrueType fonts will be displayed
```

8. In order to illustrate some of the functionality of the Help Common dialog, enter the following code in the `cmdHelp_Click` event:

```
CommonDialog1.DialogTitle = " Select A Help Topic "
CommonDialog1.HelpCommand = &H4
CommonDialog1.ShowHelp
the flag property indicates that the Help on Help Function will be run
```

9. In order to illustrate some of the functionality of the File Open Common dialog, enter the following code in the `cmdOpen_Click` event:

```
CommonDialog1.DialogTitle = " Open A File "
CommonDialog1.Filter = "*.*"
CommonDialog1.FileName = "*.*"
CommonDialog1.ShowOpen
MsgBox " You have selected " & CommonDialog1.FileName & " As the file to Open"
```

10. In order to illustrate some of the functionality of the Print Common dialog, enter the following code in the `cmdPrint_Click` event:

```
CommonDialog1.DialogTitle = " Select A Printer "
CommonDialog1.Flags = &H100&
CommonDialog1.ShowPrinter
the flag property indicates to return the printer HDC once it has been
selected

MsgBox " The Selected printer has the Windows device handle of " &
CommonDialog1.hDC
```

11. In order to illustrate some of the functionality of the Save as Common dialog, enter the following code in the `cmdSave_Click` event:

```
CommonDialog1.DialogTitle = " Save A File "
CommonDialog1.Filter = "*.*"
CommonDialog1.FileName = "*.*"
CommonDialog1.Flags = &H2&
CommonDialog1.ShowSave
MsgBox " You have selected " & CommonDialog1.FileName & " As the file to Save
to "
the flag property indicates the user will be prompted if an existing file has
been selected
```

12. Press the F5 key to run the project.

When the project is running, you are able to see the behavior of all the available common dialog boxes. When you open or save a file, a message box appears indicating that the file was selected (see Figure 21.13). When a color is selected from the colors Common Dialog box, the Windows internal representation of the color will be displayed in a message box. The Help dialog box takes the user to Windows Help. When a Printer is selected from the printers Common Dialog box, the Windows device context ID for that printer will be displayed in a message box. The Font dialog box tells the user which font is selected.

FIGURE 21.13.

The Save As File dialog box.

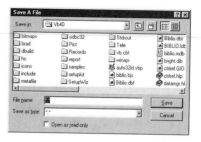

Communications

You can use the Communications control to enable your application to communicate through the serial ports of the computer on which it is running. You must use one control for each serial port that you want to control. You are able to control the following aspects of the device (modem) attached to the serial port of your computer where your application is running:

- Data Line Speed
- Communication Protocol
- Indicate to the modem that the computer is ready to accept input from the modem
- Indicate to the modem that the computer is ready to send information to the modem
- Retrieve the data that has been sent to the modem from another source
- Transfer data from the computer to the modem, thus allowing the modem to send data to another source
- Control all aspects of communication between two devices

The Communications control can be used to develop applications as simple as telephone dialer or as complicated as a complete communications package.

The following example illustrates the use of the Communications control to dial a telephone number. Follow these steps:

1. Use the File | New Project command to open a new project.

2. Follow the steps outlined in the "Adding Custom Controls to Your Project" section to add the Microsoft Comm control to your project.

3. Double-click on the Communication control (MSComm in ToolTips display) contained in the toolbox to place a Label control on your form.

4. Double-click on the Command Button (CommandButton in ToolTips display) contained in the toolbox to place a Command Button control on your form.

5. Include the following property setting for the Command Button control:
   ```
   Name = cmdHangUp
   Caption = "&Hang Up"
   Height = 395
   ```

```
Left = 4380
Top =   3480
Width = 1215
```

6. Double-click on the Command Button (CommandButton in ToolTips display) contained in the toolbox to place a Command Button control onto your form.

7. Include the following property setting for the Command Button control:

```
Name = cmdDial
Caption = "&Dial"
Height = 395
Left = 2940
Top = 3480
Width = 1215
```

8. Double-click on the ComboBox control(ComboBox in ToolTips display) contained in the toolbox to place a ComboBox control on your form.

9. Include the following property setting for the ComboBox control:

```
Name = comParity
Height = 315
Left = 3000
Style = 2  'Dropdown List
Top = 2880
Width = 1755
```

10. Double-click on the ComboBox control(ComboBox in ToolTips display) contained in the toolbox to place a ComboBox control on your form.

11. Include the following property setting for the ComboBox control:

```
Name = comStopBits
Height = 315
Left = 3000
Style = 2  'Dropdown List
Top = 2400
Width = 1755
```

12. Double-click on the ComboBox control(ComboBox in ToolTips display) contained in the toolbox to place a ComboBox control on your form.

13. Include the following property setting for the ComboBox control:

```
Name = comDataBits
Height = 315
Left = 3000
Style = 2  'Dropdown List
Top = 1920
Width = 1755
```

14. Double-click on the ComboBox control (ComboBox in ToolTips display) contained in the toolbox to place a ComboBox control on your form.

15. Include the following property setting for the ComboBox control:

```
Name = comLineSpeed
Height = 315
Left = 3000
Style =   2  'Dropdown List
Top = 1440
Width = 1755
```

16. Double-click on the ComboBox control (ComboBox in ToolTips display) contained in the toolbox to place a ComboBox control on your form.

17. Include the following property setting for the ComboBox control:

```
Name = comCommPort
Height = 315
Left = 3000
Style = 2   'Dropdown List
Top = 960
Width = 1755
```

18. Double-click on the Label control (Label in ToolTips display) contained in the toolbox to place a Label Control on your form.

19. Include the following property setting for the Label control:

```
Name = txtNumber
Height = 300
Left = 3000
Top = 480
Width = 2355
```

20. Double-click on the Label control (Label in ToolTips display) contained in the toolbox to place a Label Control on your form.

21. Include the following property setting for the Label control:

```
Name = lblParity
Caption = "Parity"
Height  = 300
Left = 420
Top = 2880
Width = 2175
```

22. Double-click on the Label control (Label in ToolTips display) contained in the toolbox to place a Label Control on your form.

23. Include the following property setting for the Label control:

```
Name = lblStopBits
Caption = "Stop Bits"
Height = 300
Left = 420
Top  = 2400
Width = 2175
```

24. Double-click on the Label control (Label in ToolTips display) contained in the toolbox to place a Label Control on your form.

25. Include the following property setting for the Label control:

```
Name = lblDataBits
Caption = "Data Bits"
Height = 300
Left = 420
Top = 1920
Width = 2175
```

26. Double-click on the Label control (Label in ToolTips Display) contained in the toolbox to place a Label Control on your form.

27. Include the following property setting for the Label control:

```
Name = lbl_lineSpeed
Caption = "Line Speed"
Height = 300
Left = 420
Top  = 1440
Width = 2175
```

28. Double-click on the Label control (Label in ToolTips display) contained in the toolbox to place a Label Control on your form.

29. Include the following property setting for the Label control:

```
Name = lblCommPort
Caption = "Communication Port"
Height = 300
Left = 420
Top = 960
= 2175
```

30. Double-click on the Label control (Label in ToolTips display) contained in the toolbox to place a Label Control on your form.

31. Include the following property setting for the Label control:

```
Name = lblNumber
Caption = "Number To Dial"
Height = 295
Left = 420
Top = 480
Width = 2175
```

32. Add the following code to the `Form_Load` event:

```
comCommPort.AddItem "Com1:"
comCommPort.AddItem "Com2:"
comCommPort.AddItem "Com3:"
comCommPort.AddItem "Com4:"

comDataBits.AddItem "8"
comDataBits.AddItem "7"

comLineSpeed.AddItem "19200"
comLineSpeed.AddItem "14400"
comLineSpeed.AddItem "9600"
comLineSpeed.AddItem "4800"
comLineSpeed.AddItem "2400"
comLineSpeed.AddItem "1200"

comParity.AddItem "N- None"
comParity.AddItem "O - Odd"
comParity.AddItem "E - Even"
comParity.AddItem "E - Mark"
comParity.AddItem "S - Space"

comStopBits.AddItem "1"
comStopBits.AddItem "1.5"
comStopBits.AddItem "2"
```

33. Add the following code to the `comCommPort_Click` event:

```
Select Case comCommPort.TEXT

    Case "Com1:"

        MSComm1.CommPort = 1

    Case "Com2:"

        MSComm1.CommPort = 2

    Case "Com3:"

        MSComm1.CommPort = 3

    Case "Com4:"

        MSComm1.CommPort = 4

End Select
```

34. Add the following code to the `cmdDial_Click` event:

```
If Len(comCommPort.TEXT) = 0 Then

    MsgBox " You must Select a Communications Port prior to Dialing"
    Exit Sub

End If

If Len(txtNumber.TEXT) = 0 Then

    MsgBox " You Have Not Entered a Number Dial "
    Exit Sub

End If

MSComm1.Settings = comLineSpeed.TEXT & "," & Mid$(comParity.TEXT, 1, 1) & ","
& comDataBits.TEXT & "," & comStopBits.TEXT
MSComm1.PortOpen = True
MSComm1.Output = "ATDT" & "9," & txtNumber.TEXT & Chr$(13) ' Dial the
requested number
```

35. Add the following code to the `cmdHangUp_Click` event:

```
MSComm1.Output = "ATH0" + Chr$(13)
MSComm1.PortOpen = False
```

36. Press the F5 key to run the project.

Once the project is running, you can select the Com: port that the modem is attached to. Additionally, you can set the communication protocol that the modem will employ (this will have no effect on the example; it is only included for illustration). If you enter the telephone number that you want to dial in to the TextBox and press the Enter key, the number will be dialed for you. In order to disconnect the modem, press the Hang Up button.

Gauge

You use the Gauge control to indicate the progression or status of a process. The gauge can be a horizontal or vertical bar that fills as the process takes place, or it can be a needle-type indication, much like that of a speedometer. You control the position of the gauge's progress by the Value property. If the Value property exceeds the Gauge control's Maximum property, the value is reset to the value of the Maximum property. If the Value property is less than the Minimum property value, the Value property is reset to the value of the Minimum property.

To learn how to use the Gauge control, go through the steps in the following procedure to create a gauge to indicate progress via a clock-like indicator. The picture used in this example is located in the Gauge directory. Follow these steps:

1. Using the File | New Project command, open a new project.

2. Follow the steps outlined in the "Adding Custom Controls to Your Project" section to add the Microhelp Gauge control to your project.

3. Double-click on the Gauge control (Gauge in ToolTips display) contained in the toolbox to place a Gauge on your form.

4. Press the F4 key to access the property setting of the newly added Gauge. Select the Custom Property. You will be presented with a Tabbed dialog displaying the custom properties that can be changed. Enter the following property settings:

   General Tab 1

   ```
   InnerTop = 20
   InnerBottom = 20
   InnerLeft = 20
   InnerRight = 20
   Max = 100
   Min = 0
   NeedleWidth = 2
   Style = 3  Full Needle
   ```

   Pictures Tab
   Select the **Picture** Property and select the circclock.bmp.

5. Using your mouse, click and drag the lower-right edge of the Gauge control so that you are able to fully view the clock bitmap.

6. Double-click on the Command Button control (CommandButton in ToolTips display) contained in the toolbox to place a Command Button control on your form.

7. Enter the following code in the command1_Click event:

   ```
   Dim x As Integer
   Dim y As Integer

   Screen.MousePointer = 0

   For x = 1 To 100

       Gauge1.Value = x
   ```

```
For y = 1 To 1000

        DoEvents

    Next y

Next x

Screen.MousePointer = 0
```

8. Press the F5 key to run the project.

Click the Command button. The needle on the graph moves around the clock (see Figure 21.14), indicating the progress of your operation. You might want to add a text panel to indicate the percentage of completion.

FIGURE 21.14.

The Gauge control.

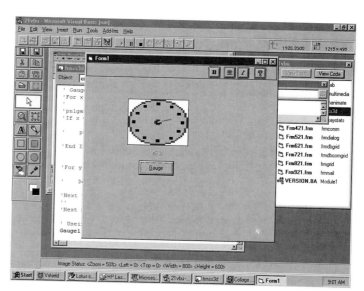

Graph

You can use the Graph control to quickly present numerical information graphically. The Graph control provides the following types of pre-built graphs:

- 2D pie
- 3D pie
- 2D bar
- 3D bar
- Gantt

- Line
- Log/line
- Area
- Scatter
- Polar
- High-low comparison

When designing your application, you can preview the types of graphs by setting the `RandomData` property to On. After you create a graph in your application, you can print it or copy it to the Clipboard for use in another application. Because the Graph control uses a graphical drawing engine in addition to the VBX or OCX control, all changes to the data used by the graph are reflected in the graph almost immediately.

The following example will illustrate the different types of graphs that can be created using the Graph control. The Data used for the graph is provided using the `QuickData` property of the Graph control. To create the sample application using the Graph control, follow these steps:

1. Using the File | New Project command, open a new project.

2. Follow the steps outlined in the "Adding Custom Controls to Your Project" section to add the Pinnacle-BPS Graph control to your project.

3. Double-click on the Graph control (Graph in ToolTips Display) contained in the toolbox to place a Graph control on your form.

4. Include the following property setting for the Graph control:

```
Name = Graph1
Height = 4215
Left = 60
Top = 0
Width = 6615
BorderStyle = 1
RandomData = 0
ColorData = 0
```

5. Double-click on the Label control (Label in ToolTips display) contained in the toolbox to place a Label control on your form.

6. Include the following property setting for the Label control:

```
Name = lblGraph
Caption = "Graph Type"
Height  = 375
Left = 240
Top = 4680
Width = 1215
```

7. Double-click on the ComboBox control (ComboBox in ToolTips display) contained in the toolbox to place a ComboBox control on your form.

8. Include the following property setting for the ComboBox control:

```
Name= comGraph
Height = 315
Left = 2100
Style =  2   'Dropdown List
Top = 4680
Width  = 4275
```

9. Enter the following code in the Form_Load event:

```
Dim sTAB As String
Dim sCRLF As String
Dim sTestData As String
sTAB = Chr$(9)
sCRLF = Chr$(13) + Chr$(10)
sTestData = "11" & sTAB & "12" & sTAB & "13" & sCRLF & "5" & sTAB & "6" &
sTAB_ & "7" + sCRLF & "20" & sTAB & "21" & sTAB & "22" & sCRLF
Graph1.QuickData = sTestData

Graph1.LegendText = " HardWare"
Graph1.LegendText = " SoftWare"
Graph1.LegendText = " Services "
Graph1.LabelText = "USA"
Graph1.LabelText = "Europe"
Graph1.LabelText = "Asia"

comGraph.AddItem "1 - 2D Pie"
comGraph.AddItem "2 - 3D Pie"
comGraph.AddItem "3 - 2D Bar"
comGraph.AddItem "4 - 3D Bar"
comGraph.AddItem "5 - Gantt"
comGraph.AddItem "6 - Line"
comGraph.AddItem "7 - Log/Lin"
comGraph.AddItem "8 - Area"
comGraph.AddItem "9 - Scatter"
comGraph.AddItem "10 - Polar"
comGraph.AddItem "11 - H1C"
comGraph.ListIndex = 3
```

10. Enter the following code in the comGraph_Click event:

```
Graph1.GraphType = CInt(Mid$(comGraph.TEXT, 1, 2))
Graph1.DrawMode = 2 ' Force the Graph to Re-Draw
```

11. Depress the F5 key to run the project.

When the project is running, you will see the data presented as a 3D Bar Graph, as shown in Figure 21.15. You can change the type of graph by selecting a different format from the ComboBox.

FIGURE 21.15.

Using the Graph control.

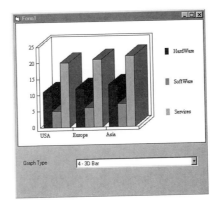

Grid

You can use the Grid control to display data in a row-and-column format. Unlike the Data Bound Grid control, the Grid control requires that you add data to control using the AddItem method. All editing of the data contained in the grid must be handled by the application. You can place both text and pictures in the cells of the grid. Once the application is running, the user can scroll through the data, resize rows and columns, and select multiple rows of data on which actions supported by your application can be performed.

The following example shows you how to load a grid from the data stored in the Titles table of the BIBLIO database. To use the Grid control, follow these steps:

1. Using the File | New Project command, open a new project.
2. Follow the steps outlined in the "Adding Custom Controls to Your Project" section to add the Microsoft Grid Gauge control to your project.
3. Double-click on the Grid control (Grid in ToolTips Display) contained in the toolbox to place a Command Button control on your form.
4. Click and drag the top-left corner of the Grid control to the top-left corner of the form. Click and drag the bottom-right corner of the Grid so that the Grid occupies most of your form.
5. Include the following property setting for the Grid control:

    ```
    Cols= 3
    ```
6. Enter the following code in the Form_Load event:

    ```
    Dim ws As WorkSpace
    Dim db As Database
    Dim rs As Recordset

    Screen.MousePointer = 11
    ```

```
Set ws = DBEngine.CreateWorkspace("ws1", "ADMIN", "")
Set db = ws.OpenDatabase("C:\vb40\biblio.mdb", False, False)
Set rs = db.OpenRecordset("select * from Titles order by title",
dbOpenDynaset)

rs.MoveLast
Grid1.Rows = rs.RecordCount + 2
rs.MoveFirst

Grid1.Row = 0

Grid1.Col = 0
Grid1.Text = "PUBID"
Grid1.ColWidth(0) = 1000


Grid1.Col = 1
Grid1.Text = "Year"
Grid1.ColWidth(1) = 1000

Grid1.Col = 2
Grid1.Text = "Title"
Grid1.ColWidth(2) = 3000

Grid1.Row = 1
Do While rs.EOF = False

    Grid1.Col = 0

    If Not IsNull(rs("pubid")) Then

        Grid1.Text = rs("pubid")

    End If

    Grid1.Col = 1

    If Not IsNull(rs("year published")) Then

        Grid1.Text CStr(rs("year published"))

    End If

    Grid1.Col = 2

    If Not IsNull(rs("title")) Then

        Grid1.Text = rs("title")

    End If

    rs.MoveNext
    Grid1.Row = Grid1.Row + 1

Loop

Screen.MousePointer = 0
```

7. Press the F5 key to run the project.

When the project is running, you can see some of the data contained in the Titles table of the BIBLIO database, as shown in Figure 21.16. You can resize the rows and columns of the grid.

FIGURE 21.16.

Using the Grid control.

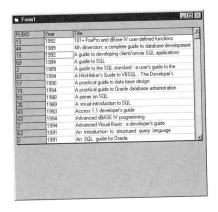

Key Status

The Key Status control enables you to monitor the status of these keys: Caps Lock, Scroll Lock, Num Lock, and Insert. The status of these keys generally is displayed in an application to give the user a quick reference to each key's status. Generally, the status is displayed at the bottom of an MDI form.

To see how the Key Status control works, create a status bar that displays the status of certain keys at the bottom of an MDI form. Follow these steps:

1. Using the File | New Project command, open a new project.

2. Follow the steps outlined in the "Adding Custom Controls to Your Project" section to add the Microhelp Key State control to your project.

3. Follow the steps outlined in the "Adding Custom Controls to Your Project" section to add the Sheridan 3D controls to your project.

4. Using the Insert | MDI Form command, add an MDI form to your project.

5. Double-click on the Picture control (Picture in ToolTips Display) contained in the toolbox to place a Picture control on your form.

6. Select the `Align` property of the Picture control and set it to align `Bottom`.

7. Double-click on the Key Status control (MhState in ToolTips display) contained in the toolbox to place four Key Status controls on your form.

8. Include the following property settings for the Key Status controls:

   Key Status 1

   Name - Keyins
   Style - 2- Insert Key

```
Key Status 2
```

Name - Keycaps
Style - 0- Caps Lock

```
Key Status 3
```

Name - Keynes
Style - 1- Num Lock

```
Key Status 4
```

Name - KeyScroll
Style -   3 - Scroll Lock

9. Select the 3D panel control (SSPanel in ToolTips display) from the toolbox and draw four panels on the Picture control.

10. Include the following property settings for the 3D Panel controls:

```
3D Panel  1
```

Name - pnlins
BevelInner - 0-No Bevel
BevelOuter - 1-Inset Bevel
BevelWidth - 2
BorderWidth - 2
Top - 60
Left - 6060
Height - 315
Width - 555

```
3D Panel 2
```

Name - pnlcaps
BevelInner - 0-No Bevel
BevelOuter - 1-Inset Bevel
BevelWidth - 2
BorderWidth - 2
Top - 60
Left - 3960
Height - 315
Width - 555

```
3D Panel 3
```

Name - pnlnum
BevelInner - 0-No Bevel
BevelOuter - 1-Inset Bevel
BevelWidth - 2
BorderWidth - 2
Top - 60
Left - 4620
Height - 315
Width - 555

```
3D Panel 4
```

```
Name - pnlscrl
BevelInner - 0-No Bevel
BevelOuter - 1-Inset Bevel
BevelWidth - 2
BorderWidth - 2
Top - 60
Left - 5340
Height - 315
Width - 555
```

11. Select the Timer control from the toolbox (Timer in ToolTips display) from the toolbox and draw a timer on the Picture control.

12. Include the following property setting for the Timer control:

    ```
    Interval = 1000
    ```

13. Enter the following code in the `Timer1_Timer` event:

    ```
    ' Caps Lock Key

    If keycaps.Value = True Then

        pnlcaps.Caption = "Cap"

    Else

        pnlcaps.Caption = ""

    End If

    ' Num Lock Key

    If keynum.Value = True Then

        pnlnum.Caption = "Num"

    Else

        pnlnum.Caption = ""

    End If

    ' Scroll Lock

    If keyscrl.Value = True Then

        pnlscrl.Caption = "Scrl"

    Else

        pnlscrl.Caption = ""

    End If

    ' Insert Key
    If keyinsert.Value = True Then

        pnlins.Caption = "Ins"
    ```

```
    Else

        pnlIns.Caption = "Ovr"

    End If
```

14. Press the F5 key in order to run the project.

While your project runs, the current status of the Caps Lock, Scroll Lock, Num Lock, and Insert keys is displayed at the bottom of the MDI form (see Figure 21.17). If these keys are enabled, you see Cap, Num, Scrl, and Ins in the status line. If the keys are not enabled, the keys box in the status line appears blank. When the status of one of these keys changes, the display is updated accordingly.

FIGURE 21.17.

Using the Key Status control.

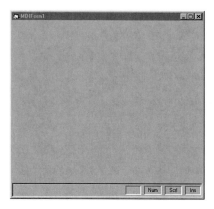

MaskEdit TextBox

The MaskEdit TextBox control provides the same basic functionality as that of the TextBox control included with Visual Basic. Properties have been added, however, to format the data displayed in the text box. The MaskEdit TextBox control also provides additional properties to indicate the behavior of text stored in the control when it is copied from the text box.

To define a MaskEdit TextBox control in order to display date-related information, follow these steps:

1. Using the File | New Project command, open a new project.
2. Follow the steps outlined in the "Adding Custom Controls to Your Project" section to add the Microsoft MaskEdit TextBox control to your project.
3. Double-click on the MaskEdit TextBox control (MaskEdBox in ToolTips display) contained in the toolbox to place a MaskEdit TextBox control on your form.

4. Select the `Custom Control` property of the MaskEdit TextBox control and indicate the following property settings:

```
Mask =
Format = MMMM-DD-YYYY
name= txtDate
Width 2200
```

5. Add the following code to the `Form_Load` event:

```
txtDate.Text = Now
```

6. Press the F5 key to run the project.

As illustrated in Figure 21.18, the MaskEdit TextBox control now contains the current date in the format MMMM-DD-YYYY. Once you have finished this example, save your project because we will be building on it in order to illustrate another custom control.

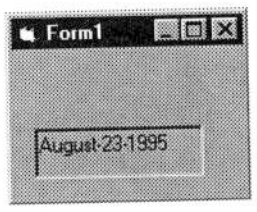

FIGURE 21.18.

*Using the MaskEdit
TextBox control.*

Microsoft Mail

You must use two controls to create a mail-enabled application: MAPIsession and MAPImessage.

> **NOTE**
>
> For a more in-depth look at a mail-enabled application, see Chapter 25, which concentrates on the Mail API.

> **NOTE**
>
> You must have access to Microsoft Mail and a Microsoft Mail server in order to use the MAPIsession and MAPImessage controls.

You use the MAPIsession control to establish a session between your application and the Microsoft Mail server. No events are associated with the MAPIsession control. All interaction between the control and the Mail server takes place through the methods of the control. Two methods are applicable to the MAPIsession control: Signon (Establish a Session) and Signoff (End a Session). These two methods are used to manage the mail session.

Listing 21.1 illustrates establishing a session and signing off from the session using the MAPIsession control.

Listing 21.1. MAPIsession control.

```
MAPISession1.Username= "MAIL1"
MAPISession1.Password= "Password"
MAPISession1.LogonUI= False    'suppress the Logon Dialog
MAPISession1.Newsession= True   'Establish a new session
MAPISession1.downloadmail= true    'Download all mail when signed on
MAPISession1.signon  'sign on to the Mail server

'Perform Mail-related tasks
MAPISession1.signoff  sign off the Mail server
```

The MAPImessage custom control enables users to manipulate their messages (using Add, Edit, and Delete) and the Address Book. You can manipulate messages only after a MAPIsession has been established through the MAPIsession custom control. No events are associated with the MAPImessage control; all interaction between the control and the Mail server takes place through the messages and properties of the control.

The following methods are available in the MAPImessage control:

Method	Function
Compose	Prepares a new message
Copy	Copies an existing message to a new message
Delete	Deletes an existing message
Fetch	Retrieves an existing message for viewing
Forward	Forwards an existing message to another Mail user
Reply	Creates a new message and addresses it to the location of the message to which it is replying
ReplyAll	Creates an empty message addressed to the person and all other users copied on the originating message
ResolveName	Performs a check on all addressees of the message to ensure that they are valid addresses
Save	Saves the current message
Send	Sends a copy of the current message to all addressees
Show	Displays the Address Book

Listing 21.2 shows the steps you should follow to generate a message.

Listing 21.2. Generating a message.

```
MAPIMessages1.compose  'Prompt the user to generate a new message

'User enters address and destination of the Message
```

```
MAPIMessage.ResolveName   'Check all Address are Valid

if ERR <> 0 then

    MsgBox "Address ERROR"

end if

MAPIMessage.send(false)   'Send the message without the Dialog

MAPIMessage.Save   'Save the Current Message
```

MultiMedia

You use the MultiMedia control to open and play one of the many types of MultiMedia files. The following capabilities are supported by the MultiMedia control:

- Playing AVI video files
- Playing MM movie files
- Playing CDs
- Playing and recording digital audio tapes
- Playing and recording digital videos
- Playing and recording videotapes
- Playing and recording Wave audio files

> **NOTE**
>
> In order to create or use MultiMedia applications, your system must contain the correct hardware (such as a CD-ROM and a Sound Card).

> **NOTE**
>
> For a more in-depth look at MultiMedia, see Chapter 9, which concentrates on the MultiMedia applications.

You use the MultiMedia control to control the playback of the devices or files through a VCR-like user interface. To set up a MultiMedia control to play an audio compact disc, for example, follow these steps:

1. Using the File | New Project command, open a new project.
2. Follow the steps outlined in the "Adding Custom Controls to Your Project" section to add the Microsoft MultiMedia control to your project.

3. Double-click on the MultiMedia control MMControl in ToolTips display) contained in the toolbox to place a MultiMedia control on your form.

4. Include the following property settings for the MultiMedia control:

```
BackVisible= False
Devicetype = CDAUDIO
EjectEnabled = True
NextEnabled = True
PauseEnabled = True
PlayEnabled = True
PrevEnabled = True
RecordVisible= False
StepVisible = False
StopEnabled = True
```

5. Add the following code to the From_Load event:

```
MMControl1.Command = "open"   open the MM Device
```

6. Add the following code to the mmcontrol1_NextClick event:

```
MMControl1.Track = MMControl1.Track + 1
```

7. Add the following code to the MMControl1_PlayClick event:

```
MMControl1.Track = 1
```

8. Add the following code to the MMControl1_PrevClick event:

```
MMControl1.Track = MMControl1.Track - 1
```

9. Add the following code to the MMControl1_StatusUpdate event:

```
txtTrack.Text = " Track " & MMControl1.Track & " of " & MMControl1.Tracks & "
Tracks
```

10. Double-click on the TextBox control (TextBox in ToolTips display) contained in the toolbox to place a TextBox control on your form.

11. Include the following property setting in the TextBox control:

```
Name = txtTrack
Height = 495
Left = 2280
Top = 780
Width = 1215
```

12. Press the F5 key to run the project. Figure 21.19 illustrates the MultiMedia control as it would appear on your display.

13. Insert an audio CD into your CD drive.

14. Click the Play button on the MultiMedia control.

The CD starts to play. You can Click the Move Forward button to move to the next song, or you can Click the Move Back button to move to the preceding song. Click the Eject button to open the CD drive door.

Click the Stop button before you end the project; otherwise, the CD continues to play.

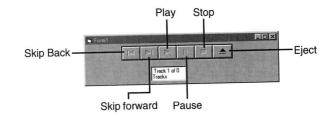

FIGURE 21.19.
Using the MultiMedia control.

Outline

You use the Outline control to group data into a hierarchical structure and to provide a visual indication of that structure.

The application used in this section uses the Publisher table as the master table or top level of the outline. The child or secondary level of the outline is Titles. The link between the two levels is the publisher's ID. Using that link, you can select the publisher to identify all the titles it has published.

To create the sample application using the Outline control, follow these steps:

1. Using the File | New Project command, open a new project.
2. Follow the steps outlined in the "Adding Custom Controls to Your Project" section to add the Microsoft Outline control to your project.
3. Double-click on the Outline control (Outline in ToolTips display) contained in the toolbox to place a MultiMedia control on your form.
4. Click and drag the top-left corner of the Outline control to the top-left corner of the form. Click and drag the bottom-right corner of the Outline control so that the Outline control occupies most of your form.
5. Add the following code to the Form declarations section:

```
Dim ws As Workspace
Dim db As Database
```

6. Add the following code to the Form_Load event:

```
Dim rs As Recordset
Set ws = DBEngine.CreateWorkspace("ws1", "Admin", "")
Set db = ws.OpenDatabase("c:\vb40\biblio.mdb", False, False)
Set rs = db.OpenRecordset("Select * from publishers order by name",
dbOpenDynaset)
'load the Publishers into the OutLine control

Do While rs.EOF = False

    If Not IsNull(rs("name")) Then

        Outline1.AddItem rs("name")

    End If
```

```
        rs.MoveNext
    Loop
```

7. Add the following code to the `Outline1_DblClick` event:

```
Dim rs As Recordset
Dim rspub As Dynaset

If Outline1.Indent(Outline1.ListIndex) <> 1 Then
    Exit Sub
End If

If Outline1.HasSubItems(Outline1.ListIndex) = False Then

    Set rspub = db.OpenRecordset("select * from publishers where name ='" &
Outline1.List(Outline1.ListIndex) & "'", dbOpenDynaset)

    If rspub.RecordCount > 0 Then

        Set rs = db.OpenRecordset("select * from titles where pubid = " &
rspub("pubid"), dbOpenDynaset)

        If rs.RecordCount = 0 Then

            Exit Sub

        End If

        Do While rs.EOF = False

            Outline1.AddItem rs("title"), Outline1.ListIndex + 1
            Outline1.Indent(Outline1.ListIndex + 1) = 2
            rs.MoveNext

        Loop


    End If

End If

Outline1.Expand(Outline1.ListIndex) = True
```

8. Add the following code to the `Outline1_Keypress` event:

```
Select Case KeyAscii

Case 13

    If Outline1.Expand(Outline1.ListIndex) = False Then

        Outline1_DblClick

    Else

        Outline1.Expand(Outline1.ListIndex) = False

    End If

End Select
```

9. Press the F5 key to run the project.

When the project starts, you see a list of publishers (see Figure 21.20). When you double-click on the publisher's name, a list of related books appears. When you click on the minus sign (–), the list collapses. If subitems are associated with the publisher, a plus sign (+) appears next to the publisher's name. If you click on the plus sign, the list expands.

FIGURE 21.20.

Using the Outline control.

Picture Clipping

You use the Picture Clipping control to select a bitmap from a file containing multiple bitmap images. You can use the Picture Clipping control to design bitmaps for each of the states of a button that appear in a toolbar. In order to reduce the physical number of files, the bitmaps are combined into one file. To access the pictures in your application, you use the Picture Clipping control to select the appropriate bitmap based on the state of the button.

To create the sample application using the Picture Clipping control, follow these steps:

1. Using the File | New Project command, open a new project.

2. Follow the steps outlined in the "Adding Custom Controls to Your Project" section to add the Microsoft PictureClip control to your project.

3. Double-click on the PictureClip control (PictureClip in ToolTips display) contained in the toolbox to place a PictureClip control on your form.

4. Include the following property settings for the PictureClip control:

```
Name = PictureClip1
Left = 300
Top = 300
Rows = 4
Cols = 6
Picture = c:\vb40\book\chp21\toolbar.bmp
```

5. Follow the steps outlined in the "Adding Custom Controls to Your Project" section to add the Sheridan 3D Controls to your project.

6. Double-click on the 3D Command Button control (SSCommand in ToolTips Display) contained in the toolbox to place two 3D Command Buttons on your form.

7. Include the following property settings for the PictureClip control:

3D Command button 1

```
Name = cmdPrint
Height = 495
Left = 240
Top = 120
Width = 1215
AutoSize =   2
```

3D Command button 2

```
Name = cmdHelp
Height = 495
Left = 1860
Top = 120
Width = 1215
AutoSize = 2
```

8. Add the following code to the Form_Load event:

```
cmdHelp.picture = PictureClip1.GraphicCell(6)
cmdPrint.picture = PictureClip1.GraphicCell(5)
```

9. Press the F5 key to run the project.

When the project starts, bitmap number 5 from the picture clip control will be loaded as the picture for the cmdPrint command button; picture number 6 will be loaded as the picture for the cmdHelp button (see Figure 21.21).

FIGURE 21.21.

Using the PictureClip control.

Spin

You use the Spin control with another control to give the user a visible method of incrementing or decrementing a value in an associated control.

NOTE

The following example builds on the example presented in the MaskEdit TextBox section.

To use the Spin control with the MaskEdit TextBox control, follow these steps:

1. Open the project containing the MaskEdit control example using the File | Open project command.

2. Follow the steps outlined in the "Adding Custom Controls to Your Project" section to add the Outrider SpinButton control to your project.

3. Double-click on the SpinButton control (SpinButton in ToolTips display) contained in the toolbox to place a SpinButton control on your form.

4. Set the `Name` property to spnDate.

5. Add the following code to the `spnDate_Spindown` event:

   ```
   txtDate.Text = CVDate(txtDate.Text) - 1
   ```

6. Add the following code to the `spnDate_Spinup` event:

   ```
   txtDate.Text = CVDate(txtDate.Text) + 1
   ```

7. Press the F5 key to run the project.

Once the project is running, click the Spin buttons (see Figure 21.22). When you click the Spin Up button, the value of the date increases. When you click the Spin Down button, the value of the date decreases.

FIGURE 21.22.

Using the Spin control.

Tabbed

The Tabbed Dialog control provides a Tabbed dialog box (see Figure 21.23), much like those seen in other Microsoft products (Word, for example). The Tabbed Dialog control enables you to grant users access to a large amount of information on one form without needlessly cluttering up the screen. By using the Tabbed Dialog control, you can group similar items together and allow the users to quickly switch between the types of items they want to access.

FIGURE 21.23.

Word 6.0 Tabbed dialog box.

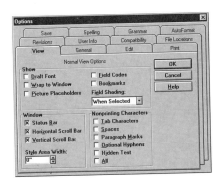

The following example will utilize a Tabbed dialog in order to display information from the BIBLIO database. Tab one will contain publisher information; Tab two will contain book information. When you select the book tab, you will see only books relating to the publisher currently displayed on Tab one.

To create the sample application using the Tabbed Dialog control, follow these steps:

1. Using the File | New Project command, open a new project.

2. Follow the steps outlined in the "Adding Custom Controls to Your Project" section to add the Sheridan Tabbed Dialog control to your project.

3. Double-click on the Tabbed Dialog control (SSTab in ToolTips display) contained in the toolbox to place a Tabbed Dialog control on your form.

4. Include the following property settings for the Tabbed Dialog control:

```
Name = SSTab1
Height = 3075
Left = 0
Top = 0
Width = 6195
TabsPerRow = 3
Tabs =  2
Style = 0
```

In order to place controls on a specific tab, you need to first select the tab where the controls are to be placed, then double-click the control that you want to place on the tab.

5. Double-click on the Data control (Data in ToolTips display) contained in the toolbox to place a Data control on your Tabbed dialog.

6. Include the following property settings for the Data control:

```
Name = dtaPublishers
Caption = "Publishers"
DatabaseName = "c:\vb40\biblio.mdb"
Height = 300
Left = 420
RecordSource = "Publishers"
Top =   2580
Width = 5475
```

7. Double-click on the TextBox control (Data in ToolTips display) contained in the toolbox to place a TextBox control on your Tabbed dialog.

8. Include the following property settings for the TextBox control:

```
Name = txtState
DataField = "State"
DataSource = "dtaPublishers"
Height = 375
Left =  4740
Top  = 2100
Width = 1215
```

9. Double-click on the TextBox control (Data in ToolTips display) contained in the toolbox to place a TextBox control on your Tabbed dialog.

10. Include the following property settings for the TextBox control:

```
Name = txtCity
DataField = "City"
DataSource = "dtaPublishers"
```

```
Height = 375
Left = 2340
Top = 2100
Width = 1215
```

11. Double-click on the TextBox control (Data in ToolTips display) contained in the toolbox to place a TextBox control on your Tabbed dialog.

12. Include the following property settings for the TextBox control:

```
Name = txtAddress
DataField = "Address"
DataSource = "dtaPublishers"
Height = 735
Left = 2340
Top = 1260
Width = 3675
```

13. Double-click on the TextBox control (Data in ToolTips display) contained in the toolbox to place a TextBox control on your Tabbed dialog.

14. Include the following property settings for the TextBox control:

```
Name = txtName
DataField = "Name"
DataSource = "dtaPublishers"
Height = 315
Left = 2340
Top = 780
Width = 3675
```

15. Double-click on the Label control (Label in ToolTips display) contained in the toolbox to place a Label control on your Tabbed dialog.

16. Include the following property settings for the Label control:

```
Name = lblState
Caption = "State"
Height = 300
Left = 3840
Top = 2160
Width = 735
```

17. Double-click on the Label control (Label in ToolTips display) contained in the toolbox to place a Label control on your Tabbed dialog.

18. Include the following property settings for the Label control:

```
Name = lblCity
Caption = "City"
Height = 300
Left = 540
Top = 2160
Width = 1215
```

19. Double-click on the Label control (Label in ToolTips display) contained in the toolbox to place a Label control on your Tabbed dialog.

20. Include the following property settings for the Label control:

```
Name = lblAddress
Caption =   "Address"
```

```
Height =    300
Left =    540
Top =    1260
Width =    1215
```

21. Double-click on the Label control (Label in ToolTips display) contained in the toolbox to place a Label control on your Tabbed dialog.

22. Include the following property settings for the Label control:

```
Name = lblPublisher
Caption =    "Publisher"
Height =    295
Left =    540
Top =    780
Width =    1215
```

23. Double-click on the Data control (Data in ToolTips display) contained in the toolbox to place a Data control on your Tabbed dialog.

24. Include the following property settings for the Data control:

```
Name= dtaBooks
Caption = "Books"
DatabaseName = "c:\vb40\biblio.mdb"
Height = 300
Left = 420
Options = 0
RecordSource = "Titles"
Top = 2640
Width = 5475
```

25. Double-click on the TextBox control (Data in ToolTips Display) contained in the toolbox to place a TextBox control on your Tabbed dialog.

26. Include the following property settings for the TextBox control:

```
Name = txtDescription
DataField =    "Description"
DataSource =    "dtaBooks"
Height =    315
Left =    2280
Top =    1080
Width =    3675
```

27. Double-click on the TextBox control (Data in ToolTips Display) contained in the toolbox to place a TextBox control on your Tabbed dialog.

28. Include the following property settings for the TextBox control:

```
Name = txtTitle
DataField = "Title"
DataSource = "dtaBooks"
Height = 315
Left = 2280
Top = 660
Width = 3675
```

29. Double-click on the Label control (Label in ToolTips Display) contained in the toolbox to place a Label control on your Tabbed dialog.

30. Include the following property settings for the Label control:

```
Name= lblDescription
Caption = "Description"
Height = 300
Left = 360
TabIndex = 12
Top = 1140
Width = 1215
```

30. Double-click on the Label control (Label in ToolTips display) contained in the toolbox to place a Label control on your Tabbed dialog.

31. Include the following property settings for the Label control:

```
Name = lblTitle
Caption = "Title"
Height = 300
Left =  360
Top = 720
Width = 1215
```

32. Add the following code to the `Form_Load` event:

```
SSTab1.TabCaption(0) = "Publishers"
SSTab1.TabCaption(1) = "&Books"
```

33. Add the following code to the `SSTab1_Click` event:

```
If PreviousTab = 0 Then

    dtaBooks.RecordSource = "select * from titles where pubid= " &_
dtaPublishers.Recordset("pubid")
    dtaBooks.Refresh
End If
```

34. Press the F5 key to run the project.

Once the project is running, select a publisher using the Data Control on the first tab (see Figure 21.24). Select the second Tab, and you should now be able to move through the books from the publisher on the first Tab.

FIGURE 21.24.

Using the Tabbed dialog.

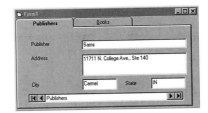

Summary

In this chapter, you looked at what custom controls are, and how you can use them in your projects to improve the application's user interface and its functionality. You also looked at some brief examples using the controls bundled with Visual Basic. Chapter 30 looks at some of the available third-party controls.

IV

PART

Unleashing Visual Basic 4.0 with Other APIs and Software

Using the Windows 95 API

22

by David Medinets

IN THIS CHAPTER

This chapter will look at the Windows 95 *API* or *Application Programming Interface*. The Windows 95 API consists of a large number of functions that Microsoft has made available for you to use. Usually, an API function does something that is part of the operating system. For example, determining the display resolution or finding out how much memory is available.

Visual Basic wraps the Windows 95 API into an easy-to-program environment. When you display a command button, Visual Basic translates your requests into function calls to the API. Normally, you don't need to worry about what the API consists of.

Sometimes, however, Visual Basic does not allow you to use a specific operating system function call. When this happens, you need to call the API yourself. This chapter will show you how to do this.

API functions are located inside *DLL* files. A DLL, short for *Dynamic Link Library*, is a collection of functions located in a single file. Windows 95 knows how to find a specific function inside a DLL file. In order to tell Visual Basic which DLL file the API function that you need is, use the Declare statement. The Declare function links the function name with the DLL file and tells Visual Basic what parameters an API function needs and what type of data it returns, if any.

This chapter is not an exhaustive listing of the over 1,300 available Windows 95 API functions; instead, it will show you how some functions can be used in real-life situations. Table 22.1 lists the API functions mentioned in this chapter and the listing number in which the function is used. A copy of each listing has been included on the CD-ROM provided with this book.

Table 22.1. API functions discussed in this chapter.

API Function	Code Listing (Page Number)	Short Description
CloseHandle	Listing 22.6, p. 646	This function terminates a thread or process.
CreateFontIndirect	Listing 22.8, p. 651	This function creates a logical font that can be selected as the current font for any device.
CreateProcessA	Listing 22.6, p. 646	This function executes a given file starting a new process and thread. It is important to close both the thread and the process using the CloseHandle function.

API Function	*Code Listing (Page Number)*	*Short Description*
DeleteObject	Listing 22.8, p. 651	This function frees all memory associated with an object. An object can be a font, pen, palette, and so on.
GetCurrentDirectory	Listing 22.3, p. 641	This function returns the current directory.
GetPrivateProfileInt	Listing 22.5, p. 643	This function returns an integer value from a private INI file.
GetPrivateProfileString	Listing 22.5, p. 643	This function returns a value from a private INI file.
GetProfileInt	Listing 22.5, p. 643	This function returns an integer value from the WIN.INI file.
GetProfileString	Listing 22.5, p. 643	This function returns a value from the WIN.INI file.
GetSystemDirectory	Listing 22.3, p. 641	The function returns the system subdirectory under the main Windows directory. The system directory contains such files as DLLs, drivers, and font files.
GetSystemMetrics	Listing 22.2, p. 639	This function returns the height and width of various Windows elements and the values of various system configuration values.
GetTempPath	Listing 22.3, p. 641	This function returns the directory Windows uses as temporary storage.

continues

Table 22.1. continued

API Function	Code Listing (Page Number)	Short Description
GetVersionEx	Listing 22.1, p. 638	This function returns information about the version number of Windows.
GetWindowsDirectory	Listing 22.3, p. 641	This function returns the directory in which Windows was installed.
GetWindowRect	Listing 22.4, p. 642	This function returns the corner coordinates of a given object.
hread	Listing 22.12, p. 659	This function reads blocks (can be > 64K) of data from files.
hwrite	Listing 22.12, p. 659	This function writes blocks (can be > 64K) of data to files.
lclose	Listing 22.12, p. 659	This function closes files.
LZClose	Listing 22.6, p. 646	This function closes files opened with the LZOpenFile function.
LZCopy	Listing 22.6, p. 646	This function copies a file opened with LZOpenFile.
LZOpenFile	Listing 22.6, p. 646	This function opens a file that might be compressed.
LZRead	Listing 22.6, p. 646	This function reads from a compressed file as if it were not compressed.
LZSeek	Listing 22.6, p. 646	This function positions the file pointer in a compressed file as if the file were not compressed.
OpenFile	Listing 22.12, p. 659	This function creates, opens, or deletes a file.

API Function	Code Listing (Page Number)	Short Description
ReleaseCapture	Listing 22.11, p. 657	This function releases the mouse capture for the current thread and restores normal mouse input processing.
SelectObject	Listing 22.8, p. 651	This function selects an object for use in a given device context.
SetCapture	Listing 22.11, p. 657	This function allows the current thread to capture all mouse events.
SetCursorPos	Listing 22.4, p. 642	This function sets the mouse pointer position.
TextOut	Listing 22.8, p. 651	This function displays text using a given device context.
WaitForSingleObject	Listing 22.6, p. 646	This function waits for a process, thread, or object to get into a desired state.
WritePrivateProfileString	Listing 22.5, p. 643	This function writes an application/key value profile string to a private INI file.
WriteProfileString	Listing 22.5, p. 643	This function writes an application/key value profile string to the WIN.INI file.

API Functions Can Be Dangerous!

As you look at the examples in this chapter and explore the rest of the API, remember that some API functions are very dangerous. (For example, the menu API functions clash with Visual Basic.) *Save your work often!* If you have trouble, look at the following list for ideas:

- **Check your parameter data types.** Make sure that the data types of your parameters match those of the `declare` statement for the API function you are using. Don't forget the `ByVal` keyword if needed.

- **Check your parameter values.** If necessary, print the values of the parameters in the debug window. Then you can verify that the values are meaningful in the context of the current API call.

- **Check your return data types.** Frequently, return values from one API function are passed to another. If the return data types are incorrect, Visual Basic can get confused and your system will lock-up, or the infamous Global Protection Fault message will appear. Also, remember to check the return value to see if an error occurred.

- **Initialize strings to have a specific length.** Also, make sure that they are long enough. Usually, 255 is the longest string you will need. Check your API reference. You can create a fixed-length string with a declaration like this:

`Dim stringTemp As String * 20`   You can also use the `space` function to allocate space for a string. Using the `space` function has this advantage: you can use it to allocate up to roughly two billion characters. Yup, I said *two billion!* Of course, if you allocate more memory than you have physical RAM, you use virtual RAM and hard disk space. A variable-length string is defined like this:

`Dim stringTemp As String`

`stringTemp = space(1000000)`

- **Use the `Option Explicit` statement in the declarations section of all modules.** Including this statement ensures that all variables in your program have been explicitly declared. This approach short-circuits the tendency of many Visual Basic programmers to let the compiler choose a default variable data type.

- **Check the DLL.** If Visual Basic says that it can't find the API function in the DLL you specified, maybe you have the wrong DLL. The WINAPI.TXT file that shipped with the beta version of Visual Basic 4.0 said that the `SelectObject` API function was located in USER32.DLL when it was really located in GDI32.DLL.

Changes to API since Windows 3.1

Most of the changes to API are because of the need to support 32-bit operations. Many functions have been added to support the new functionality of the Windows 95 operating system. Additional OLE functionality has also been added. Following is a short list of changes that affect how API calls are made:

- The most pervasive change is that long data types are used instead of integer data types in most API calls. This change affects both return values and parameters.

- The names of the DLLs have changed. For example, USER.DLL is now USER32.DLL. Glance at the Windows system directory to see the new filenames.

- Visual Basic 4.0 handles empty strings differently than the previous version. Declare a string as follows so that you can use it in place of the null pointer as a parameter to API functions:

```
Dim sNull As String
```

- The PictureBox control has been enhanced with the PaintPicture method. This method can be used to replace calls to the BitBlt and StrechBlt API functions.

- Quite a few old API calls have been upgraded with the addition of Ex to the API function name. This change was done to add Win32 support. If fact, much of the documentation for Win32 and Windows NT API calls is valid for Windows 95 also.

- The System Registry (instead of an initialization file) is used to hold profile information and temporary values between program instances.

- Allocating memory using the API is no longer necessary in most cases. Most of the time, you can use the space function to allocate a string when you need memory. This technique is demonstrated in "Copying Large Files," later in this chapter.

Tricks with Windows

The following sections are devoted to short topics that allow you to interact with the Windows operation system.

Getting System Version Information

Sometimes, it is nice to know the version of Windows your program is running in. The recommended method for doing this is to use the GetVersionEx API function. Listing 22.1 shows how to call the function. The main difference between GetVersionEx and the older GetVersion function is that the major and minor version numbers are split into separate structure members.

The GetVersionEx function also lets you determine which type of Windows platform your program is running on: Win32s, Windows, or Windows NT. Listing 22.1 shows you how to check for each platform type.

Listing 22.1. The `GetVersionEx` API function.

```
Option Explicit

Private Type OSVERSIONINFO
        dwOSVersionInfoSize As Long
        dwMajorVersion As Long
        dwMinorVersion As Long
        dwBuildNumber As Long
        dwPlatformId As Long
        szCSDVersion As String * 128
End Type

'  dwPlatformId defines:
Private Const VER_PLATFORM_WIN32s = 0
Private Const VER_PLATFORM_WIN32_WINDOWS = 1
Private Const VER_PLATFORM_WIN32_NT = 2

Private Declare Function GetVersionEx Lib "kernel32" _
    Alias "GetVersionExA" _
    (lpVersionInformation As OSVERSIONINFO) As Long

Private Sub Form_Load()
    Dim v As OSVERSIONINFO

    v.dwOSVersionInfoSize = Len(v)

    GetVersionEx v
    MsgBox "Major Version = " & v.dwMajorVersion
    MsgBox "Minor Version = " & v.dwMinorVersion
    MsgBox "Build Number = " & v.dwBuildNumber
    If v.dwPlatformId = VER_PLATFORM_WIN32s Then MsgBox "Win32s"
    If v.dwPlatformId = VER_PLATFORM_WIN32_WINDOWS Then MsgBox "Windows"
    If v.dwPlatformId = VER_PLATFORM_WIN32_NT Then MsgBox "Windows NT"
End Sub
```

CAUTION

The WINAPI.TXT file in the beta version of Visual Basic shows the `GetVersionEx` declaration with the `lpVersionInformation` parameter being passed as by value. This is incorrect; Visual Basic does not allow you to pass user-defined structures this way. Use the `Declare` statement as shown in Listing 22.1.

Getting System Information

Several API functions allow you to access information about the Windows system your program is running on. The program in Listing 22.2 prints out all the information available from the `GetSystemMetrics` function. There are 45 different pieces of information you can access using this one function.

Listing 22.2. The `GetSystemMetrics` API function.

```
Private Const SM_CXSCREEN = 0
Private Const SM_CYSCREEN = 1
Private Const SM_CXVSCROLL = 2
Private Const SM_CYHSCROLL = 3
Private Const SM_CYCAPTION = 4
Private Const SM_CXBORDER = 5
Private Const SM_CYBORDER = 6
Private Const SM_CXDLGFRAME = 7
Private Const SM_CYDLGFRAME = 8
Private Const SM_CYVTHUMB = 9
Private Const SM_CXHTHUMB = 10
Private Const SM_CXICON = 11
Private Const SM_CYICON = 12
Private Const SM_CXCURSOR = 13
Private Const SM_CYCURSOR = 14
Private Const SM_CYMENU = 15
Private Const SM_CXFULLSCREEN = 16
Private Const SM_CYFULLSCREEN = 17
Private Const SM_CYKANJIWINDOW = 18
Private Const SM_MOUSEPRESENT = 19
Private Const SM_CYVSCROLL = 20
Private Const SM_CXHSCROLL = 21
Private Const SM_DEBUG = 22
Private Const SM_SWAPBUTTON = 23
Private Const SM_RESERVED1 = 24
Private Const SM_RESERVED2 = 25
Private Const SM_RESERVED3 = 26
Private Const SM_RESERVED4 = 27
Private Const SM_CXMIN = 28
Private Const SM_CYMIN = 29
Private Const SM_CXSIZE = 30
Private Const SM_CYSIZE = 31
Private Const SM_CXFRAME = 32
Private Const SM_CYFRAME = 33
Private Const SM_CXMINTRACK = 34
Private Const SM_CYMINTRACK = 35
Private Const SM_CXDOUBLECLK = 36
Private Const SM_CYDOUBLECLK = 37
Private Const SM_CXICONSPACING = 38
Private Const SM_CYICONSPACING = 39
Private Const SM_MENUDROPALIGNMENT = 40
Private Const SM_PENWINDOWS = 41
Private Const SM_DBCSENABLED = 42
Private Const SM_CMOUSEBUTTONS = 43
Private Const SM_CMETRICS = 44

Private Declare Function GetSystemMetrics Lib "user32" _
    (ByVal nIndex As Long) As Long

Private Sub logMetric(nIndex As Long, name As String, desc As String)
    Dim ret As Long

    ret = GetSystemMetrics(nIndex)
    Printer.Print name; " = "; ret; Tab(30); "' "; desc
End Sub
```

continues

Listing 22.2. continued

```
Private Sub Form_Load()
    logMetric SM_CXSCREEN, "SM_CXSCREEN", "Screen width in pixels"
    logMetric SM_CYSCREEN, "SM_CYSCREEN", "Screen height in pixels"
    logMetric SM_CXVSCROLL, "SM_CXVSCROLL", "Vertical scroll arrow width"
    logMetric SM_CYHSCROLL, "SM_CYHSCROLL", "Horizontal scroll arrow height"
    logMetric SM_CYCAPTION, "SM_CYCAPTION", "Caption bar height"
    logMetric SM_CXBORDER, "SM_CXBORDER", "Window border width"
    logMetric SM_CYBORDER, "SM_CYBORDER", "Window border height"
    logMetric SM_CXDLGFRAME, "SM_CXDLGFRAME", "Dialog window frame width"
    logMetric SM_CYDLGFRAME, "SM_CYDLGFRAME", "Dialog window frame height"
    logMetric SM_CYVTHUMB, "SM_CYVTHUMB", "Vertical scroll thumb height"
    logMetric SM_CXHTHUMB, "SM_CXHTHUMB", "Horizontal scroll thumb width"
    logMetric SM_CXICON, "SM_CXICON", "Icon width"
    logMetric SM_CYICON, "SM_CYICON", "Icon height"
    logMetric SM_CXCURSOR, "SM_CXCURSOR", "Cursor width"
    logMetric SM_CYCURSOR, "SM_CYCURSOR", "Cursor height"
    logMetric SM_CYMENU, "SM_CYMENU", "Menu bar height"
    logMetric SM_CXFULLSCREEN, "SM_CXFULLSCREEN", "Full screen client area width"
    logMetric SM_CYFULLSCREEN, "SM_CYFULLSCREEN", "Full screen client area height"
    logMetric SM_CYKANJIWINDOW, "SM_CYKANJIWINDOW", "Kanji window height"
    logMetric SM_MOUSEPRESENT, "SM_MOUSEPRESENT", "Mouse present flag"
    logMetric SM_CYVSCROLL, "SM_CYVSCROLL", "Vertical scroll arrow height"
    logMetric SM_CXHSCROLL, "SM_CXHSCROLL", "Horizontal scroll arrow width"
    logMetric SM_DEBUG, "SM_DEBUG", "Debug version flag"
    logMetric SM_SWAPBUTTON, "SM_SWAPBUTTON", "Mouse buttons swapped flag"
    logMetric SM_RESERVED1, "SM_RESERVED1", "Reserved"
    logMetric SM_RESERVED2, "SM_RESERVED2", "Reserved"
    logMetric SM_RESERVED3, "SM_RESERVED3", "Reserved"
    logMetric SM_RESERVED4, "SM_RESERVED4", "Reserved"
    logMetric SM_CXMIN, "SM_CXMIN", "Minimum window width"
    logMetric SM_CYMIN, "SM_CYMIN", "Minimum window height"
    logMetric SM_CXSIZE, "SM_CXSIZE", "Minimize/Maximize icon width"
    logMetric SM_CYSIZE, "SM_CYSIZE", "Minimize/Maximize icon height"
    logMetric SM_CXFRAME, "SM_CXFRAME", "Window frame width"
    logMetric SM_CYFRAME, "SM_CYFRAME", "Window frame height"
    logMetric SM_CXMINTRACK, "SM_CXMINTRACK", "Minimum window tracking width"
    logMetric SM_CYMINTRACK, "SM_CYMINTRACK", "Minimum window tracking height"
    logMetric SM_CXDOUBLECLK, "SM_CXDOUBLECLK", "Double click x tolerance (3.1)"
    logMetric SM_CYDOUBLECLK, "SM_CYDOUBLECLK", "Double click y tolerance (3.1)"
    logMetric SM_CXICONSPACING, "SM_CXICONSPACING", "Horizontal icon spacing (3.1)"
    logMetric SM_CYICONSPACING, "SM_CYICONSPACING", "Vertical icon spacing (3.1)"
    logMetric SM_MENUDROPALIGNMENT, "SM_MENUDROPALIGNMENT", "Left or right menu
drop (3.1)"
    logMetric SM_PENWINDOWS, "SM_PENWINDOWS", "Pen extensions installed (3.1)"
    logMetric SM_DBCSENABLED, "SM_DBCSENABLED", "DBCS version of USER32 installed"
    logMetric SM_CMOUSEBUTTONS, "SM_CMOUSEBUTTONS", "Number of buttons on mouse"
    logMetric SM_CMETRICS, "SM_CMETRICS", "SM_CMETRICS"

    Printer.NewPage
    Printer.EndDoc
End Sub
```

Using the `GetSystemMetrics` function is simple. All the action in Listing 22.2 occurs in the `logMetric` subroutine. This subroutine calls the `GetSystemMetrics` function and then prints the result to the Printer object. For more information about the Printer object, see Chapter 12, "Printing with Visual Basic."

You can also use the API to locate information about what directories Windows is using. For example, the `GetWindowsDirectory` API function lets you know the directory in which Windows was installed. Listing 22.3 shows how to use the four API functions that get information about the directories Windows is using.

Listing 22.3. The get directory API functions.

```
Private Declare Function GetCurrentDirectory Lib "kernel32" _
        Alias "GetCurrentDirectoryA" (ByVal nBufferLength As Long, _
        ByVal lpBuffer As String) As Long

Private Declare Function GetSystemDirectory Lib "kernel32" _
    Alias "GetSystemDirectoryA" (ByVal lpBuffer As String, _
    ByVal nSize As Long) As Long

Private Declare Function GetTempPath Lib "kernel32" _
    Alias "GetTempPathA" (ByVal nBufferLength As Long, _
    ByVal lpBuffer As String) As Long

Private Declare Function GetWindowsDirectory Lib "kernel32" _
    Alias "GetWindowsDirectoryA" (ByVal lpBuffer As String, _
    ByVal nSize As Long) As Long

Private Sub Form_Load()
    Dim curDir As String
    Dim sysDir As String
    Dim tmpDir As String
    Dim winDir As String

    curDir = Space(500)
    sysDir = Space(500)
    tmpDir = Space(500)
    winDir = Space(500)
    curDir = Left(curDir, GetCurrentDirectory(Len(curDir), curDir))
    sysDir = Left(sysDir, GetSystemDirectory(sysDir, Len(sysDir)))
    tmpDir = Left(tmpDir, GetTempPath(Len(tmpDir), tmpDir))
    winDir = Left(winDir, GetWindowsDirectory(winDir, Len(winDir)))
    MsgBox curDir
    MsgBox sysDir
    MsgBox tmpDir
    MsgBox winDir
End Sub
```

> **NOTE**
>
> The `Declare` statement for the `GetCurrentDirectory` function in the WINAPI.TXT file of the beta version of Visual Basic was missing the `Alias` clause. Without the `Alias` clause, Visual Basic cannot find the function inside the DLL.

Moving the Mouse Pointer

Occasionally, you find a feature in a program's user interface that you want to duplicate. This happened to me a little while ago: Every time a dialog box popped up, the mouse pointer was located on the most likely command button—a nifty feature. Although the WINAPI.TXT file (in the beta version of Visual Basic) does not have an entry for the `SetCursorPos` API function, the code in Listing 22.4 uses Windows 3.1 as a base to show how you can declare the `SetCursorPos` function.

To run the program in Listing 22.4, create a form with two command buttons. Then copy the code from the CD-ROM. After starting the program, click the first command button. The cursor should automatically move to the second command button.

Listing 22.4. Moving the mouse pointer with CURSOR.BAS.

```
Private Type POINTAPI
        x As Long
        y As Long
End Type

Private Type RECT
        left As Long
        top As Long
        Right As Long
        Bottom As Long
End Type

Private Declare Function SetCursorPos Lib "user32" _
    (ByVal x As Long, ByVal y As Long) As Long

Private Declare Function GetWindowRect Lib "user32" _
    (ByVal hwnd As Long, lpRect As RECT) As Long

Dim p As POINTAPI
Dim r As RECT
Dim rWidth As Long, rHeight As Long

Private Sub Command1_Click()
    GetWindowRect Command2.hwnd, r

    rWidth = r.Right - r.left
    rHeight = r.Bottom - r.top
    SetCursorPos r.left + (rWidth / 2), r.top + (rHeight / 2)
End Sub
```

The `GetWindowRect` function is called to get the screen coordinates of the corners of the second command button. The coordinates of the center of the button are then found and `SetCursorPos` is called.

Using Initialization Files

Windows 3.1 used initialization (INI) files to hold information used when Windows and other applications were started. INI files contained information such as the default printer, starting directories, and the last bookmark viewed in a file. In short, whatever information the program wanted to remember from one invocation to the next was stored in the INI file.

Microsoft no longer recommends the use of INI files because Windows 95—and Windows NT—use a *System Registry* to store initialization information. However, you still need to know about INI files to interact with Windows 3.1 programs and, perhaps, to read information from the WIN.INI file.

Although there are ten API functions that deal with INI files, this section discusses only six of them (three that work with the WIN.INI file and three that work with private or application INI files). Each of the functions is used in Listing 22.5 to show you how to interact with them.

The format of an INI file looks like this:

```
[VB Unleashed]                                    ' <== Section Name
Chapter Number = 25 - Using the Windows 95 API.   ' <== Key Name & value
...
[next section]                                     ' <== Section Name
...
```

Each INI file is a series of section names and key names with their values.

Listing 22.5. Accessing INI files with PROFILE.FRM.

```
Option Explicit

Private Declare Function GetProfileInt Lib "kernel32" _
    Alias "GetProfileIntA" (ByVal lpAppName As String, _
    ByVal lpKeyName As String, ByVal nDefault As Long) As Long

Private Declare Function GetProfileString Lib "kernel32" _
    Alias "GetProfileStringA" (ByVal lpAppName As String, _
    ByVal lpKeyName As String, ByVal lpDefault As String, _
    ByVal lpReturnedString As String, ByVal nSize As Long) As Long

Private Declare Function WriteProfileString Lib "kernel32" _
    Alias "WriteProfileStringA" (ByVal lpszSection As String, _
    ByVal lpszKeyName As String, ByVal lpszString As String) As Long

Private Declare Function GetPrivateProfileInt Lib "kernel32" _
    Alias "GetPrivateProfileIntA" (ByVal lpApplicationName As String, _
    ByVal lpKeyName As String, ByVal nDefault As Long, _
    ByVal lpFileName As String) As Long
```

continues

Listing 22.5. continued

```
Private Declare Function GetPrivateProfileString Lib "kernel32" _
    Alias "GetPrivateProfileStringA" (ByVal lpApplicationName As String, _
    ByVal lpKeyName As String, ByVal lpDefault As String, _
    ByVal lpReturnedString As String, ByVal nSize As Long, _
    ByVal lpFileName As String) As Long

Private Declare Function WritePrivateProfileString Lib "kernel32" _
    Alias "WritePrivateProfileStringA" _
    (ByVal lpApplicationName As String, ByVal lpKeyName As String, _
    ByVal lpString As String, ByVal lpFileName As String) As Long

Dim secName As String
Dim keyName As String
Dim prvName As String

Private Sub Form_Load()
    Dim keyValue As String

    secName = "VB Unleashed"
    keyName = "Chapter Number"
    prvName = "sams.ini"
    keyValue = "22-Using the Windows 95 APIs"

    testProfile

    WriteProfileString secName, keyName, keyValue
    testProfile

    WriteProfileString secName, keyName, ""
    testProfile

    testPrivateProfile

    WritePrivateProfileString secName, keyName, keyValue, prvName
    testPrivateProfile

    WritePrivateProfileString secName, keyName, "", prvName
    testPrivateProfile
End Sub

Private Sub testProfile()
    Dim lChapNum As Long
    Dim sChapNum As String

    lChapNum = GetProfileInt(secName, keyName, 10)

    sChapNum = Space(50)
    GetProfileString secName, keyName, "10", sChapNum, Len(sChapNum)

    MsgBox "Chapter Int = " & lChapNum
    MsgBox "Chapter Str = " & sChapNum
End Sub
```

```
Private Sub testPrivateProfile()
    Dim lChapNum As Long
    Dim sChapNum As String

    lChapNum = GetPrivateProfileInt(secName, keyName, 10, prvName)

    sChapNum = Space(50)
    GetPrivateProfileString secName, keyName, "10", sChapNum, Len(sChapNum),
prvName

    MsgBox "Private Chapter Int = " & lChapNum
    MsgBox "Private Chapter Str = " & sChapNum
End Sub
```

NOTE

The `Declare` statement for `GetPrivateProfileString` in the WIN.INI file in the beta version of Visual Basic has the `lpKeyName` parameter as `Any`. It should be declared as `ByVal lpKeyName as String`.

The `Declare` statement for `WritePrivateProfileString` in the WIN.INI file in the beta version of Visual Basic has the `lpString` parameter as `Any`. It should be declared as `ByVal lpString as String`.

You can see that the functions for the WIN.INI file and the private files parallel each other. The program in Listing 22.5 first calls the `testProfile` function. The `testProfile` function looks for a section called `VB Unleashed` and then for the key name `Chapter Number` in WIN.INI. These won't be found; therefore the default value of 10 is returned and displayed in a message box.

Next, the `WriteProfileString` function is called to create the section name, key name, and key values in the WIN.INI file. The `testProfile` function is called again to verify that the entries were correctly created.

Then the `WriteProfileString` function is called to delete the entries just added. And the `testProfile` function is called to verify that the entries were deleted.

The code performs the same operations using a private INI file called SAMS.INI. If the SAMS.INI file does not exist, the `WritePrivateProfileString` function creates it.

This section has not discussed the `GetProfileSection`, `WriteProfileSection`, `GetPrivateProfileSection`, or `WritePrivateProfileSection` API functions. However, if you want to explore their use, you will find the constant `vbNullChar` to be invaluable. To read or set an entire section of an INI file, the API function needs a series of NULL-terminated strings, with the last string terminated by two NULLs. You can append the vbNullChar constant directly to a string to represent the NULL character.

Using Compressed Files

One of the more intriguing sets of API functions are located in the LZ32 DLL file. This file contains the Windows decompression API functions. You can use these functions to decompress files that were compressed using the COMPRESS executable. All files whose extensions end in an underscore (for example, FIGHT.IN_) have been compressed. Usually, files are compressed to save room on a diskette; the files are expanded during application installation.

However, the LZ32 DLL library also contains two functions (lzseek and lzread) that allow you to manipulate a compressed file as if it were normal size. This means that you can use a compressed file to hold inventory parts and still use normal routines to extract the data. Unfortunately, the API function only lets you read from the compressed file. To create, modify, or insert information, you first must expand the file, then make the change and recompress the file.

Still, the ability to use compressed databases, even in a read-only fashion, is valuable. In addition, the compression can act as a rudimentary encryption. It is possible that only another programmer will catch on to the idea that the file has been compressed instead of encrypted.

Listing 22.6 shows the class definition of COMPRESSION. It has routines to compress, expand, and read a file. If you are entering the code by hand, set the class module Name to "Compression" and set its Public flag to TRUE.

Listing 22.6. The COMPRESSION.CLS class used to work with compressed files.

```
Option Explicit

Private Const OF_READ = &H0
Private Const OF_CREATE = &H1000
Private Const OFS_MAXPATHNAME = 128

Private Const NORMAL_PRIORITY_CLASS = &H20&
Private Const INFINITE = -1&

' OpenFile() Structure
Private Type OFSTRUCT
        cBytes As Byte
        fFixedDisk As Byte
        nErrCode As Integer
        Reserved1 As Integer
        Reserved2 As Integer
        szPathName(OFS_MAXPATHNAME) As Byte
End Type

Private Type STARTUPINFO
    cb As Long
    lpReserved As String
    lpDesktop As String
    lpTitle As String
    dwX As Long
    dwY As Long
```

```
        dwXSize As Long
        dwYSize As Long
        dwXCountChars As Long
        dwYCountChars As Long
        dwFillAttribute As Long
        dwFlags As Long
        wShowWindow As Integer
        cbReserved2 As Integer
        lpReserved2 As Long
        hStdInput As Long
        hStdOutput As Long
        hStdError As Long
End Type

Private Type PROCESS_INFORMATION
        hProcess As Long
        hThread As Long
        dwProcessID As Long
        dwThreadID As Long
End Type

Private Declare Function WaitForSingleObject Lib "kernel32" (ByVal _
        hHandle As Long, ByVal dwMilliseconds As Long) As Long

Private Declare Function CreateProcessA Lib "kernel32" (ByVal _
        lpApplicationName As Long, ByVal lpCommandLine As String, ByVal _
        lpProcessAttributes As Long, ByVal lpThreadAttributes As Long, _
        ByVal bInheritHandles As Long, ByVal dwCreationFlags As Long, _
        ByVal lpEnvironment As Long, ByVal lpCurrentDirectory As Long, _
        lpStartupInfo As STARTUPINFO, lpProcessInformation As _
        PROCESS_INFORMATION) As Long

Private Declare Function CloseHandle Lib "kernel32" (ByVal _
        hObject As Long) As Long

Private Declare Function LZCopy Lib "lz32.dll" (ByVal _
        hfSource As Long, ByVal hfDest As Long) As Long

Private Declare Function LZOpenFile Lib "lz32.dll" Alias "LZOpenFileA" _
        (ByVal lpszFile As String, lpOf As OFSTRUCT, ByVal style As Long) _
        As Long

Private Declare Function LZSeek Lib "lz32.dll" (ByVal _
        hfFile As Long, ByVal lOffset As Long, ByVal nOrigin _
        As Long) As Long

Private Declare Function LZRead Lib "lz32.dll" (ByVal _
        hfFile As Long, ByVal lpvBuf As String, ByVal cbread _
        As Long) As Long

Private Declare Sub LZClose Lib "lz32.dll" (ByVal hfFile As Long)

Private expandedName As String
Private compressedName As String

Property Get fileName() As String
        fileName = expandedName
End Property
```

continues

Listing 22.6. continued

```
Property Let fileName(fName As String)
    expandedName = fName
End Property

Public Sub compress()
    Dim p As PROCESS_INFORMATION
    Dim s As STARTUPINFO
    Dim procStatus As Long

    ' Initialize the STARTUPINFO structure:
    s.cb = Len(s)

    ' Start the shelled application:
    ' make sure that close upon exit is checked.
    CreateProcessA 0&, "setupkit\compress -r " & expandedName, _
        0&, 0&, 1&, _
        NORMAL_PRIORITY_CLASS, 0&, 0&, s, p

    ' Wait for the shelled application to finish:
    WaitForSingleObject p.hProcess, INFINITE

    CloseHandle p.hThread
    CloseHandle p.hProcess

    compressedName = Left(expandedName, _
        Len(expandedName) - 1) & "_"
End Sub

Public Sub expand()
    Dim openStruct As OFSTRUCT

    hSource& = LZOpenFile(compressedName, openStruct, OF_READ)

    ' Note: Do not use expName$ you will get a access violation.
    ' take care to pre-allocate space.
    hDestination& = LZOpenFile(expandedName, openStruct, OF_CREATE)
    ret& = bytesOfDest = LZCopy(hSource&, hDestination&)
    LZClose hDestination&
    LZClose hSource&
End Sub

Public Sub read(recNum As Long, recLen As Long, recBuf As String)
    Dim openStruct As OFSTRUCT

    hSource& = LZOpenFile(compressedName, openStruct, OF_READ)
    LZSeek hSource&, recLen * (recNum - 1), 0
    LZRead hSource&, recBuf, recLen
    LZClose hSource&
End Sub
```

The compress function is interesting because it starts a subprocess with the COMPRESS executable. This subprocess is affected by the properties associated with the COMPRESS.EXE file (especially the close_window_on_exit flag), which you can view on the Program tab of the Properties dialog box). Figure 22.1 shows the Properties dialog box. Display this dialog box by opening the Windows Explorer program, locating the COMPRESS.EXE file in the setupkit subdirectory under the Visual Basic directory, right-clicking on the file, and selecting the Properties menu option. Then, click on the Program tab. You will see the `Close_Window_on_Exit` checkbox. Make sure that it is checked so that the window will close when the compress program is finished running.

FIGURE 22.1.

The Properties dialog box for COMPRESS.EXE.

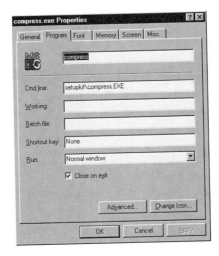

Listing 22.7 shows the program that uses the COMPRESSION class. It uses a form with two text boxes and two command buttons. Place the text boxes one above the other; place the buttons side by side.

When the program starts, only the button labeled Create Testfile is active. Pressing it makes the program create a test file of 26 fixed-length records in a file called TESTFILE.DAT. The file is then compressed. A message box displays, allowing you time to look at both the TEXTFILE.DAT file and the compressed version, TEXTFILE.DA_.

The next step is the deletion of the original data file; you are again prompted to check the files. After you click OK, the compressed file is expanded so that you can verify that the act of compression did not lose any data.

The final actions of the Create Testfile button are to activate the second button, deactivate itself, and read the first compressed record.

Listing 22.7. COMPRESS.FRM: Using the COMPRESSION class.

```
Option Explicit

Private Type Record ' Define user-defined type.
    ID As String * 3
    Name As String * 20
End Type
```

continues

Listing 22.7. continued

```
Dim MyRecord As Record
Dim recIdx As Long
Dim recBuf As String * 100
Dim F As New COMPRESSION

Private Sub Command1_Click()
    Dim idx As Long

    F.fileName = "testfile.dat"

    Open F.fileName For Random As #1 Len = Len(MyRecord)

    For idx = 0 To 25
        MyRecord.ID = CStr(idx) + 1
        MyRecord.Name = "*" & String(18, idx + Asc("A")) & "*"
        Put #1, , MyRecord
    Next idx

    Close #1

    F.compress

    MsgBox "textfile.dat has been compressed...Go Look! Then click OK."
    Kill "testfile.dat"

    MsgBox "testfile.dat has been deleted...Go Look! Then click OK."
    F.expand
    MsgBox "textfile.da_ has been expanded...Go Look! Then click OK."

    Command1.Enabled = False
    Command2.Enabled = True

    readRec
End Sub

Private Sub Command2_Click()
    If recIdx > 26 Then recIdx = 1
    readRec
End Sub

Private Sub Form_Load()
    Command1.Caption = "Create TestFile"
    Command2.Caption = "Next Record"
    Command2.Enabled = False
    recIdx = 1
End Sub

Private Sub readRec()
    F.read recIdx, Len(MyRecord), recBuf

    MyRecord.ID = Left(recBuf, 3)
    MyRecord.Name = Mid(recBuf, 4)
    Text1.text = MyRecord.ID
    Text2.text = MyRecord.Name
    recIdx = recIdx + 1
End Sub
```

When you click the Next Record button, the next record is read. If the end of the records are reached, the method cycles back to the first record.

The readRec method is at the heart of the record-reading activity. It uses the read method of the COMPRESSION class to fill a buffer with the data located at record number recIdx. Then the record buffer is parsed to fill the MyRecord structure.

Displaying Rotated Fonts

Visual Basic can display text only along the 0° axis, from left to right. It is sometimes useful to be able to display fonts in other orientations. For example, if text relates to several controls, you may want to display the related text vertically.

By using Windows 95 API functions, you can rotate fonts. The class module in Listing 22.8 defines the ROTATEFONT class. Its main function, dispText, displays text at any angle.

Listing 22.8. How to display text along any axis with ROTATEFONT.CLS.

```
Option Explicit

Private Const OUT_DEFAULT_PRECIS = 0
Private Const OUT_STRING_PRECIS = 1
Private Const OUT_CHARACTER_PRECIS = 2
Private Const OUT_STROKE_PRECIS = 3
Private Const OUT_TT_PRECIS = 4
Private Const OUT_DEVICE_PRECIS = 5
Private Const OUT_RASTER_PRECIS = 6
Private Const OUT_TT_ONLY_PRECIS = 7
Private Const OUT_OUTLINE_PRECIS = 8

Private Const CLIP_DEFAULT_PRECIS = 0
Private Const CLIP_CHARACTER_PRECIS = 1
Private Const CLIP_STROKE_PRECIS = 2
Private Const CLIP_MASK = &HF
Private Const CLIP_LH_ANGLES = 16
Private Const CLIP_TT_ALWAYS = 32
Private Const CLIP_EMBEDDED = 128

Private Const DEFAULT_QUALITY = 0
Private Const DRAFT_QUALITY = 1
Private Const PROOF_QUALITY = 2

Private Const DEFAULT_PITCH = 0
Private Const FIXED_PITCH = 1
Private Const VARIABLE_PITCH = 2

Private Const ANSI_CHARSET = 0
Private Const DEFAULT_CHARSET = 1
Private Const SYMBOL_CHARSET = 2
Private Const SHIFTJIS_CHARSET = 128
Private Const HANGEUL_CHARSET = 129
```

continues

Listing 22.8. continued

```
Private Const CHINESEBIG5_CHARSET = 136
Private Const OEM_CHARSET = 255

' Font Families
'
Private Const FF_DONTCARE = 0      '  Don't care or don't know.
Private Const FF_ROMAN = 16        '  Variable stroke width, serifed.

' Times Roman, Century Schoolbook, etc.
Private Const FF_SWISS = 32        '  Variable stroke width, sans-serifed.

' Helvetica, Swiss, etc.
Private Const FF_MODERN = 48       '  Constant stroke width, serifed or sans-serifed.

' Pica, Elite, Courier, etc.
Private Const FF_SCRIPT = 64       '  Cursive, etc.
Private Const FF_DECORATIVE = 80 '  Old English, etc.

' Font Weights
Private Const FW_DONTCARE = 0
Private Const FW_THIN = 100
Private Const FW_EXTRALIGHT = 200
Private Const FW_LIGHT = 300
Private Const FW_NORMAL = 400
Private Const FW_MEDIUM = 500
Private Const FW_SEMIBOLD = 600
Private Const FW_BOLD = 700
Private Const FW_EXTRABOLD = 800
Private Const FW_HEAVY = 900

Private Type LOGFONT
        lfHeight As Long
        lfWidth As Long
        lfEscapement As Long
        lfOrientation As Long
        lfWeight As Long
        lfItalic As Byte
        lfUnderline As Byte
        lfStrikeOut As Byte
        lfCharSet As Byte
        lfOutPrecision As Byte
        lfClipPrecision As Byte
        lfQuality As Byte
        lfPitchAndFamily As Byte
        lfFaceName As String * 32
End Type

Private Declare Function CreateFontIndirect Lib "gdi32" _
    Alias "CreateFontIndirectA" (lpLogFont As LOGFONT) As Long

Private Declare Function SelectObject Lib "gdi32" _
    (ByVal hDC As Long, ByVal hObject As Long) As Long

Private Declare Function TextOut Lib "gdi32" Alias "TextOutA" _
    (ByVal hDC As Long, ByVal x As Long, ByVal y As Long, _
    ByVal lpString As String, ByVal nCount As Long) As Long
```

```
Private Declare Function DeleteObject Lib "gdi32" _
    (ByVal hObject As Long) As Long

Private font As LOGFONT

Private Sub Class_Initialize()
    font.lfHeight = 10
    font.lfWidth = 0
    font.lfEscapement = 0
    font.lfPitchAndFamily = FF_MODERN
    font.lfCharSet = ANSI_CHARSET
    font.lfQuality = PROOF_QUALITY
    font.lfWeight = FW_NORMAL
    font.lfFaceName = ""
End Sub

Public Sub setPointSize(ps As Long)
    font.lfHeight = ps
End Sub

Public Sub setAngle(angle As Long)
    font.lfEscapement = angle * 10
End Sub

Public Sub dispText(hDC As Long, text As String, x As Long, y As Long)
    Dim hFont As Long
    Dim hOldFont As Long

    hFont = CreateFontIndirect(font)
    hOldFont = SelectObject(hDC, hFont)
    TextOut hDC, x, y, text, Len(text)
    hFont = SelectObject(hDC, hOldFont)
    DeleteObject hFont
End Sub
```

Listing 22.8 has quite a few constants defined for controlling which font is used with the TextOut API function. Before looking at the listing in detail, look at the program that uses the ROTATEFONT class; see Listing 22.9. Figure 22.2 shows the results of this program.

Listing 22.9. Using the ROTATEFONT class, example 1.

```
Private Sub Form_Click()
    Dim font As New ROTATEFONT

    font.setPointSize 36
    font.setAngle 10
    font.dispText Form1.hDC, "Frank and Burgers", 10, 100
    font.setAngle 5
    font.dispText Form1.hDC, "Frank and Burgers", 10, 100
    font.setAngle -5
    font.dispText Form1.hDC, "Frank and Burgers", 10, 100
    font.setAngle -10
    font.dispText Form1.hDC, "Frank and Burgers", 10, 100
End Sub
```

FIGURE 22.2.

The output of using the
ROTATEFONT class,
example 1.

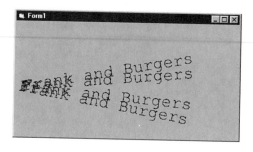

This first example shows that you have to do several things to display rotated text. First, you must define a variable as New ROTATEFONT. Then you must set the PointSize and Angle. Finally, you call the dispText method to print the text. Notice that you can use negative angles as well as positive ones when specifying the axis to use.

It is important to note that the display functions are called from the Click method and not the Load method. If you place the same code in the Load method, nothing is displayed on the form because the form has not yet finished being initialized.

Example 2 in Listing 22.10 shows the effect of printing using all four points of the compass. Figure 22.3 shows the results of this small program.

Listing 22.10. Using the ROTATEFONT class, example 2.

```
Private Sub Form_Click()
    Dim font As New ROTATEFONT
    font.setPointSize 14
    font.setAngle 0
    font.dispText Form1.hDC, "Frank and Burgers", 200, 150
    font.setAngle 90
    font.dispText Form1.hDC, "Frank and Burgers", 200, 150
    font.setAngle 180
    font.dispText Form1.hDC, "Frank and Burgers", 200, 150
    font.setAngle 270
    font.dispText Form1.hDC, "Frank and Burgers", 200, 150
End Sub
```

NOTE

The ROTATEFONT class can used with any object for which you can obtain an hDC value. This includes Forms and PictureBox objects as well as the Printer object.

Now let's go back and look briefly at Listing 22.8, where the ROTATEFONT class was defined. To use the TextOut API function, Windows must know which font it should use to display the text. You can describe a *logical font* using the LOGFONT structure. A logical font can be thought of as a font description. When Windows actually needs to display the font, the best font available is used. Windows cannot choose a font to use until it knows which device will be used to display the text. The font selected for displaying on a monitor might be different from what is used to display the same logical font on a printer. Table 22.2 describes the different members of the LOGFONT structure.

FIGURE 22.3.

The output of using the
ROTATEFONT *class,*
example 2.

Table 22.2. Members of the LOGFONT structure.

Member Name	Description
lfHeight	This member specifies the height, in logical units, of the font. Windows will find the largest font that does not exceed lfHeight.
lfWidth	This member specifies the *average* width, in logical units, of characters in the font. If zero, Windows will use the aspect ratio of the device to determine the closest font match.
lfEscapement	This member specifies the angle, in tenths of a degree, relative to the bottom of the page. Not all devices support this ability.
lfOrientation	This member specifies the orientation, in tenths of a degree, of each character's base line relative to the bottom of the page. Not all devices support this ability.
lfWeight	The member specifies the weight of the font. Although any number from 0 to 1,000 is valid (constants starting with *FW* are supplied), only 400 for Normal weight and 700 for Bold is supported. Any value over 550 is displayed as bold.
lfItalic	This member, when set to TRUE, specifies an italicized font.
ifUnderline	This member, when set to TRUE, requests an underlined font.
lfStrikeout	This member, when set to TRUE, requests a font with a strikeout line.

continues

Table 22.2. continued

Member Name	Description
lfCharSet	This member specifies the character set to be used for the font. ANSI_CHARSET, OEM_CHARSET, SYMBOL_CHARSET, and UNICODE_CHARSET are the currently defined values.
lfOutPrecision	This member specifies how closely the output must match the requested font. OUT_CHARACTER_PRECIS, OUT_DEFAULT_PRECIS, OUT_STRING_PRECIS, and OUT_STROKE_PRECIS are the defined values.
lfClipPrecision	This member specifies how to clip characters that display partially outside the clipping region. CLIP_CHARACTER_PRECIS, CLIP_DEFAULT_PRECIS, and CLIP_STROKE_PRECIS are the defined values.
lfQuality	This member specifies how carefully Windows is to be in matching the logical font to a physical font. DEFAULT_QUALITY, DRAFT_QUALITY, and PROOF_QUALITY are the defined values.
lfPitchAndFamily	This member specifies both the pitch and the family of the typeface. Typically, the values DEFAULT_PITCH, FIXED_PITCH, or VARIABLE_PITCH are ORed with FF_DECORATIVE, FF_DONTCARE, FF_MODERN, FF_ROMAN, FF_SCRIPT, or FF_SWISS.
lfFaceName	This member specifies the typeface of the font. If NULL, a default typeface is used.

The default values of the logical font are set in the Class_Initialize function in the ROTATEFONT class module. Functions are provided to allow the programmer to change the default characteristics. This implementation of rotated text is very primitive. No thought has been given to checking whether the device has the capability to display rotated text or to changing the orientation of text.

Displaying ToolTips

One of the most recent enhancements to the user interface is the ToolTip. A *ToolTip* is the little window that pops up when you hold the mouse cursor over an icon or menu item for more than a second or so.

To duplicate this feature in Visual Basic, you must be able to capture mouse events while the cursor is over an object. The SetCapture API function sends all mouse events to a window (specified by hWnd). It is important to remember that each Visual Basic control is considered a window so that each control can potentially issue the SetCapture function.

The SetCapture function captures *all* mouse events, even those for other processes. Therefore, it is important to call the ReleaseCapture API function when the mouse moves away from your window.

The code in Listing 22.11 shows how this is done. The following line is used to determine whether the mouse has moved away from the Command1 control:

```
If x > Command1.Width Or x < 0 Or y > Command1.Height Or y < 0 Then
```

The ReleaseCapture function is also called if the Command1 control is clicked.

The TOOLTIP form consists of two command buttons, one picture box, and a timer. These can be placed anywhere on the form. The appearance property of the picture box should be set to 0 to eliminate the 3-D effect. This must be done at design time.

Listing 22.11. Displaying ToolTips with TOOLTIP.FRM.

```
Option Explicit

Private Declare Function SetCapture Lib "user32" _
    (ByVal hwnd As Long) As Long

Private Declare Function ReleaseCapture Lib "user32" () As Long

Private Sub Command1_Click()
    Timer1.Enabled = False
    ReleaseCapture
    Picture1.Visible = False
End Sub

Private Sub Command1_MouseMove(Button As Integer, _
    Shift As Integer, x As Single, y As Single)

    If x > Command1.Width Or x < 0 Or y > Command1.Height Or y < 0 Then
        Timer1.Enabled = False
        ReleaseCapture
        Picture1.Visible = False
    Else
        If Not Picture1.Visible Then
            Timer1.Enabled = True
            SetCapture Command1.hwnd
        End If
    End If

End Sub

Private Sub Form_Load()
    Picture1.BackColor = Form1.BackColor
    Picture1.Visible = False
    Timer1.Interval = 250
    Timer1.Enabled = False
End Sub
```

continues

Listing 22.11. continued

```
Private Sub Timer1_Timer()
    Dim font As New ROTATEFONT
    Dim hlpText As String

    hlpText = "Help me!"
    Picture1.Width = Picture1.TextWidth(hlpText) + 100
    Picture1.Height = Picture1.TextHeight(hlpText) + 100
    Picture1.TOP = Command1.TOP + Command1.Height + 20
    Picture1.Left = Command1.Left + (Command1.Width / 2)
    Picture1.Visible = True
    Picture1.Cls

    font.setPointSize 12
    font.dispText Picture1.hDC, hlpText, 2, 2

    Timer1.Enabled = False
End Sub
```

NOTE

This program requires the ROTATEFONT class module from Listing 22.8.

This code makes no pretense to be elegant. Everything is hard-coded to demonstrate the steps needed to display the ToolTip. To make real use of these concepts, create a control array and have one routine handle the ToolTips. You may want to store the help strings in a resource file or an array so that they can be easily changed as your program changes. In addition, you can make the picture box prettier by changing the font, background colors, or maybe displaying a "thought balloon" around the text.

Copying Large Files

This section shows how to use the OpenFile, hread, hwrite, and lclose API functions to copy files. Although you can use the FileCopy statement to copy files, the routine in Listing 22.12 is better for the following reasons:

- It can copy files up to 2 gigabytes in size. This ability is rapidly becoming important as hard disks become larger and larger.

- It can create a second copy of the file without rereading the original. This can be useful if you are creating multiple backup copies.

- It takes advantage of any disk caches and memory management that Windows uses. You don't have to worry about where the memory is coming from—it is all virtual.

Listing 22.12 includes two functions: `firstCopy` and `additionalCopy`. They are used in the following manner:

```
firstCopy "vb.gid", "vb.one"
additionalCopy "vb.two"
```

To use these routines in your own Visual Basic program, use the Insert | Module menu option to add a module to your project. Call this module HUGECOPY.BAS and then copy the code from the CD-ROM file for Listing 22.12.

When testing the routines, try copying smaller files first. If a problem develops, you will find out quicker.

Listing 22.12. Copying large files with HUGECOPY.BAS.

```
' Constants with OpenFile API call.
Private Const OF_WRITE = &H1
Private Const OF_READ = &H0
Private Const OF_CREATE = &H1000

' Structure filled in by OpenFile API call.
Private Type OFSTRUCT
        cBytes As Byte
        fFixedDisk As Byte
        nErrCode As Integer
        Reserved1 As Integer
        Reserved2 As Integer
        szPathName(128) As Byte
End Type

' declarations for the API functions that this class uses.
Private Declare Function OpenFile Lib "kernel32" _
    (ByVal lpFileName As String, _
     lpReOpenBuff As OFSTRUCT, _
     ByVal wStyle As Long) As Long

Private Declare Function hread Lib "kernel32" Alias "_hread" _
    (ByVal hFile As Long, lpBuffer As Any, ByVal lBytes As Long) As Long

Private Declare Function hwrite Lib "kernel32" Alias "_hwrite" _
    (ByVal hFile As Long, ByVal lpBuffer As String, ByVal lBytes As Long) As Long

Private Declare Function lclose Lib "kernel32" Alias "_lclose" _
    (ByVal hFile As Long) As Long

Private inpOFS As OFSTRUCT
Private outOFS As OFSTRUCT
Private myBuf As String
Private size As Long

Public Sub firstCopy(inp As String, out As String)
    Dim hInp As Long
    Dim hOut As Long
```

continues

Listing 22.12. continued

```
        size = FileLen(inp)
        myBuf = String(size, "*")
        hInp = OpenFile(inp, inpOFS, OF_READ)
        hOut = OpenFile(out, outOFS, OF_CREATE Or OF_WRITE)
        If (hInp <> -1 And hOut <> -1) Then
            hread hInp, ByVal myBuf, size
            hwrite hOut, ByVal myBuf, size
        End If
        lclose hOut
        lclose hInp
End Sub

Public Sub additionalCopy(out As String)
    Dim hOut As Long

    hOut = OpenFile(out, outOFS, OF_CREATE Or OF_WRITE)
    If (hOut <> -1) Then
        hwrite hOut, ByVal myBuf, size
    End If
    lclose hOut
End Sub
```

This module is pretty simple. The only tricky points are that the size variable must be global to the module so that the additionalCopy function can see it and that the space function is used to allocate memory.

You can use the space function to read an entire database into memory. Then you can access it with the various string-manipulation functions (left, middle, right, and instr). In fact, searching a file for a phrase becomes much easier if the file is entirely in memory.

The following sections discuss the four API functions used by the HUGECOPY code module.

The *OpenFile* API Function

The OpenFile API function can be used to open, create, or delete a file; it can also be used to test for a file's existence. First, let's look at the syntax of the function; then you will see how to control which action it performs. The syntax is as follows:

```
Private Declare Function OpenFile Lib "kernel32"
    (ByVal lpFileName As String, _
    lpReOpenBuff As OFSTRUCT, _
    ByVal wStyle As Long) As Long
```

As you can see, the OpenFile function is located in the file KERNEL32.DLL, takes three parameters, and returns a long value. The return value is a file handle if a file was successfully opened or created. If the action to be performed was to check a file's existence or delete a file, the return value is irrelevant unless an error occurred. The return value is HFILE_ERROR (−1) if an error has occurred.

The parameter `lpFileName` is the name of the file on which the function is to perform an action.

The parameter `lpReOpenBuff` is the address of an `OFSTRUCT` structure that is to be valued by the `OpenFile` function. This structure, shown here, has only three interesting members:

```
Private Type OFSTRUCT
        cBytes As Byte
        fFixedDisk As Byte
        nErrCode As Integer
        Reserved1 As Integer
        Reserved2 As Integer
        szPathName(OFS_MAXPATHNAME) As Byte
End Type
```

The `fFixedDisk` member is set to nonzero if `lpFileName` is on a fixed disk. The `szPathName` member holds the full path of the file. The `nErrCode` member is set to the error code if the `OpenFile` action fails. Table 22.3 shows a list of the possible error codes that `nErrCode` can be set to. Some of the error codes in Table 22.3 do not directly relate to copying with the `HUGECOPY` module; however it is good to see the wide range of possible errors so that you can plan other uses for the `OpenFile` function.

> **NOTE**
>
> Comments have been added to Table 22.3 only where the Public Constant names are not clearly indicative of the error.

Table 22.3. Possible error codes for the `OpenFile` API function.

Constant Name	Value	Description
ERROR_INVALID_FUNCTION	1&	
ERROR_FILE_NOT_FOUND	2&	
ERROR_PATH_NOT_FOUND	3&	
ERROR_TOO_MANY_OPEN_FILES	4&	
ERROR_ACCESS_DENIED	5&	
ERROR_INVALID_HANDLE	6&	
ERROR_ARENA_TRASHED	7&	There was a problem with the storage control blocks.
ERROR_NOT_ENOUGH_MEMORY	8&	There was not enough storage space to process the action.
ERROR_INVALID_BLOCK	9&	The storage control block address was invalid.

continues

Table 22.3. continued

Constant Name	Value	Description
ERROR_BAD_ENVIRONMENT	10&	
ERROR_BAD_FORMAT	11&	An attempt was made to load a program with an incorrect format.
ERROR_INVALID_ACCESS	12&	The access code was invalid.
ERROR_INVALID_DATA	13&	
ERROR_INVALID_DRIVE	15&	The system can't find the requested drive.
ERROR_CURRENT_DIRECTORY	16&	A directory that is attached to can't be deleted.
ERROR_NOT_SAME_DEVICE	17&	The system can only move a file from one directory to another on the same disk drive. You attempted to move a file to another disk drive.
ERROR_NO_MORE_FILES	18&	
ERROR_WRITE_PROTECT	19&	The media on which the file was to be written or created is write-protected.
ERROR_BAD_UNIT	20&	The system can't find the requested device.
ERROR_NOT_READY	21&	The requested device is not ready.
ERROR_BAD_COMMAND	22&	The requested device does not understand the requested action.
ERROR_CRC	23&	The action caused a data error.
ERROR_BAD_LENGTH	24&	The requested command has the wrong length.
ERROR_SEEK	25&	The requested device could not find an area on the media it was searching.
ERROR_NOT_DOS_DISK	26&	The requested device could not be accessed.
ERROR_SECTOR_NOT_FOUND	27&	The requested device could not find a section on the media it was searching.
ERROR_OUT_OF_PAPER	28&	The printer is out of paper.
ERROR_WRITE_FAULT	29&	The system could not write to the requested device.
ERROR_READ_FAULT	30&	The system could not read from the requested device.
ERROR_GEN_FAILURE	31&	The requested device is not functioning.

Constant Name	Value	Description
ERROR_SHARING_VIOLATION	32&	The requested file is currently being used by another process.
ERROR_LOCK_VIOLATION	33&	The requested file is currently locked, in whole or part, by another process.
ERROR_WRONG_DISK	34&	The wrong floppy disk is in the drive. This error can occur when installing software from floppy disk.
ERROR_SHARING_BUFFER_EXCEEDED	36&	The system has too many shared files open and can't open another.
ERROR_NOT_SUPPORTED	50&	The system does not support the network request specified.
ERROR_REM_NOT_LIST	51&	The remote computer requested is not available.
ERROR_DUP_NAME	52&	A duplicate name exists on the network.
ERROR_BAD_NETPATH	53&	The requested network path was not found.
ERROR_NETWORK_BUSY	54&	
ERROR_DEV_NOT_EXIST	55&	The requested network resource of device is no longer available.
ERROR_TOO_MANY_CMDS	56&	The network BIOS command limit has been reached.
ERROR_ADAP_HDW_ERR	57&	A network adapter hardware error has been detected.
ERROR_BAD_NET_RESP	58&	The requested server can't perform the action.
ERROR_UNEXP_NET_ERR	59&	An unexpected network error has occurred.
ERROR_BAD_REM_ADAP	60&	The remote adapter is not compatible.
ERROR_PRINTQ_FULL	61&	The printer queue is full.
ERROR_NO_SPOOL_SPACE	62&	The spooler has run out of space on the server for the queue.
ERROR_PRINT_CANCELLED	63&	The file that was waiting to be printed has been deleted.
ERROR_NETNAME_DELETED	64&	The requested network name is no longer available.
ERROR_NETWORK_ACCESS_DENIED	65&	

continues

Table 22.3. continued

Constant Name	Value	Description
ERROR_BAD_DEV_TYPE	66&	The network resource type is not correct.
ERROR_BAD_NET_NAME	67&	The requested network name can't be found.
ERROR_TOO_MANY_NAMES	68&	The name limit for the local network adapter card has been exceeded.
ERROR_TOO_MANY_SESS	69&	The network BIOS session limit has been exceeded.
ERROR_SHARING_PAUSED	70&	The remote server has been paused or is being started.
ERROR_REQ_NOT_ACCEP	71&	The network request was not accepted.
ERROR_REDIR_PAUSED	72&	The requested printer or device has been paused.
ERROR_FILE_EXISTS	80&	
ERROR_CANNOT_MAKE	82&	The requested directory or file could not be created.
ERROR_FAIL_I24	83&	A failure has occurred during an interrupt 24 call.
ERROR_OUT_OF_STRUCTURES	84&	There is no storage space left in which to process this request.
ERROR_ALREADY_ASSIGNED	85&	The local device is already in use.
ERROR_INVALID_PASSWORD	86&	The network password was incorrect.
ERROR_INVALID_PARAMETER	87&	
ERROR_NET_WRITE_FAULT	88&	A write fault has occurred on the network.

The last parameter of the OpenFile function is wStyle. It is used to tell OpenFile which actions to perform. The basic actions are OF_CREATE, OF_DELETE, OF_EXIST, OF_READ, OF_VERIFY, and OF_WRITE (see Table 22.4).

You can also use _ to modify the basic actions. For example, you can use OF_PROMPT to tell Visual Basic to prompt the user for a filename if the requested file is not found.

Table 22.4. Possible actions for the OpenFile API function.

Constant Name	Value	Description
OF_READ	&H0	This flag opens the file for read access only.
OF_WRITE	&H1	This flag opens the file for write access only.

Constant Name	Value	Description
OF_READWRITE	&H2	This flag opens the file for read and write access.
OF_SHARE_COMPAT	&H0	This flag opens the file in compatibility mode, which allows any program on the same computer to open the file any number of times.
OF_SHARE_EXCLUSIVE	&H10	This flag opens the file and prevents other programs from either reading or writing the file.
OF_SHARE_DENY_WRITE	&H20	This flag opens the file and prevents other programs from writing to it.
OF_SHARE_DENY_READ	&H30	This flag opens the file and prevents other programs from reading from it.
OF_SHARE_DENY_NONE	&H40	This flag opens the file without denying other programs read or write access to the file.
OF_PARSE	&H100	This flag causes the system to fill the OFSTRUCT buffer with information.
OF_DELETE	&H200	This flag causes the file to be deleted.
OF_VERIFY	&H400	This flag causes the system to compare the date and time in the OFSTRUCT buffer with that of the file. The value HFILE_ERROR (−1) is returned if the time and date are different.
OF_CANCEL	&H800	This flag adds a Cancel button to the dialog box OF_PROMPT uses.
OF_CREATE	&H1000	This flag creates a new file. If the file already exists, it is overwritten.
OF_PROMPT	&H2000	This flag causes the system to display a dialog box if the named file does not exist. The dialog box asks the user to insert into drive A a disk that contains the file.
OF_EXIST	&H4000	This flag opens the file and then closes it to see whether the file exists. It does not change the last-modified date of the file.
OF_REOPEN	&H8000	This flag opens the file using the information in the OFSTRUCT buffer.

The system looks for the file using the following search criteria:

1. The current directory.
2. The Windows directory (the directory containing WIN.COM), whose path the GetWindowsDirectory function retrieves.

3. The Windows system directory (the directory containing such system files as GDI.EXE), whose path the `GetSystemDirectory` function retrieves.

4. The directory containing the executable file for the current task; the `GetModuleFileName` function obtains the path of this directory.

5. The directories listed in the `PATH` environment variable.

6. The list of directories mapped in a network.

The *hread* API Function

The `hread` API function is used to read data from an open file into a buffer in memory. It can handle blocks of data greater than 64K. The syntax is as follows:

```
Private Declare Function hread Lib "kernel32" Alias "_hread" _
    (ByVal hFile As Long, lpBuffer As Any, ByVal lBytes As Long) As Long
```

The `hread` function is located in the KERNEL32.DLL file, takes three parameters, and returns a long value. The return value is the number of bytes read or `HFILE_ERROR` (−1).

The `hFile` parameter is the file handle of an open file. In the example in Listing 22.12, the handle was the return value of the `OpenFile` function.

The `lpBuffer` parameter is the location of a buffer to receive the data from the file. Make sure that the buffer is initialized before this function is called.

The `lBytes` parameter is the number of bytes of data to read. If the return value is less that `lBytes`, the end of the file was reached before all of the requested data was read.

The *hwrite* API Function

The `hread` API function is used to read data from an open file into a buffer in memory. It can handle blocks of data greater than 64K. The syntax is as follows:

```
Private Declare Function hwrite Lib "kernel32" Alias "_hwrite" _
    (ByVal hFile As Long, ByVal lpBuffer As String, ByVal lBytes As Long) As Long
```

The `hwrite` function is located in the KERNEL32.DLL file, takes three parameters, and returns a long value. The return value is the number of bytes written or `HFILE_ERROR` (−1).

The `hFile` parameter is the file handle of an open file. In the example in Listing 22.12, the handle was the return value of the `OpenFile` function.

The `lpBuffer` parameter is the location of the buffer whose contents are to be written to the file.

The `lBytes` parameter is the number of bytes of data to write.

The *lclose* API Function

The lclose API function is used to close an open file. Its syntax is as follows:

```
Private Declare Function lclose Lib "kernel32" Alias "_lclose" _
    (ByVal hFile As Long) As Long
```

The lclose function is located in the KERNEL32.DLL file, takes one argument, and returns a long value. The return value is zero for successful completion or HFILE_ERROR (–1) if the system could not close the file.

Summary

This chapter covered many different types of API functions. And yet, in reality, it barely scratched the surface of the functionality available to you with the Windows API library.

One piece of advice: before looking for a solution using an API function, either look for a way that Visual Basic can perform the task (you may have overlooked something in the manuals) or see whether an existing OCX can perform the task for you. Spending time debugging API calls can be frustrating and takes away time from your main programming task.

Windows Games

by

Do you remember where you were in the early eighties? I do. I was at the arcade. The arcade craze was at its height, and computer games were the coolest thing in the world. At least, they were the coolest thing in *my* world. I was addicted.

But my love of arcade games didn't end with getting the highest score on Kix or Zaxxon. I wanted to do more than play in these stark, magical, interactive worlds. I wanted to create them. My parents encouraged my obsession by buying me a TRS-80 Model 1 when I was 12. Before long, I had a complete Pac-Man clone running. Well, complete except for the ghosts. It was a pretty dull game without the ghosts. But when I tried to add a ghost, the game slowed down to a crawl. My problem was Basic. I loved the Basic programming language because it was fairly easy to use (much easier than, say, assembly language). But Basic didn't work so well as a game programming language.

Later, I wrote a Q-bert clone on my Commodore 64. He was beautiful. He hopped from one cube to the next and when he hopped in the wrong direction, he fell into the unfathomable nothingness at the bottom of my screen. But, once again, when I added the first bouncing bad guy, the whole thing slowed to a crawl—all because of Basic.

Then I went to college and learned all kinds of nifty things like C and Pascal and Ada. These were real languages, compiled languages with manly code. Never again would I have to return to the wimpy Basic of my youth. Or so I was told.

But Basic came back. And here I am writing games in it again. The difference is that Basic is better (and faster) now. Today's Basic, in its Visual Basic incarnation, is a surprisingly good gaming platform that strikes an ideal balance between development speed, broad capabilities, and execution speed. It has support for everything you need. And, although you probably won't see the next DOOM written in Visual Basic (at least not until Visual Basic is compiled), you can do some pretty amazing stuff with this language.

This chapter shows you some of that stuff and explains how you can take advantage of it, not only in killer games, but in educational and multimedia programs as well.

The Top Ten Visual Basic Gaming Features

I love David Letterman. Even after being out of college these past several years, I've never been able to shake the urge to stay up late, eat junk food, and watch Letterman. It's a perfect end to the day. So in honor of my favorite talk-show host, this chapter will be in the form of a top ten list.

Here, now, I have in my left hand, a copy of tonight's top ten list. Tonight's category, Top Ten Visual Basic Features for Windows Game Development...

10. Win32 and DCI

 9. Visual Interface

 8. Quick Development Time

7. Win32 sndPlaySound

6. Timers

5. Collision Detection

4. Win32 API Joystick Commands

3. The Media Control Interface (MCI)

2. The PaintPicture Method and ImageList Control

1. Real Objects

Win32 and DCI

Not too long ago, the phrase "Windows game development" would be considered by most serious gaming folks to be a contradiction in terms. Windows was just too slow. It tried to be all things to all people and provide a nice, easy uniform interface to a broad variety of hardware. Although this setup was very convenient for most applications, it was death to games. Games always try to squeeze the most performance out of whatever platform they run on, and Windows didn't give them much flexibility. As a result, Windows game development stayed on the Solitaire and Minesweeper level for the greater part of the life of Windows 3.0 and 3.1.

After Windows 3.1 had been on the market for some time, an interesting thing happened. Both Intel and Microsoft had been working, more or less independently, on different ways of accessing video hardware more directly. They finally came together and created Device Control Interface (DCI). This was an interface that Windows *drivers*, not Windows applications, could use to access the hardware more directly and therefore get better performance.

Out of DCI grew a new application level interface called WinG. WinG evaluates the hardware of the target environment when you first install an application, and then uses that evaluation to choose what methods are the fastest for managing information. WinG achieves its performance boost by integrating and relying heavily on DCI. WinG promises to bridge the gap between the waning Windows 3.1 and the new Windows 95 and Windows NT 32-bit environments because the same WinG API works in all three.

Because DCI is so incredibly powerful, Microsoft made it a standard part of the Windows API. Now that DCI is integrated with Win32, both Windows NT and Windows 95 can leverage it to give them, in many cases, near-DOS performance in a device-independent environment.

With WinG, Windows 95 also has backward compatibility with all those games and multimedia titles written for WinG on Windows 3.1. WinG doesn't provide any performance boost to Win32, however. In fact, behind the scenes, WinG ends up doing nothing more than making its own Win32 calls. So if your focus is Windows 95 and Windows NT applications, you don't need to worry about WinG. All the performance you need for almost any application is built into the system already.

Microsoft is dedicated to making Windows *the* killer game platform. With that in mind, they are working on something called the Windows Game SDK. It will be an API created specifically to support the efforts of the game developer. It will, of course, be built on top of the already powerful Win32/DCI interface and will become an integrated part of the operating system. Finally, the PC platform will have native game support!

The Visual Interface

Much has been made of Visual Basic's visual interface and how it empowers the developer. This interface, known as a Visual Development Environment (VDE), is simply an extension of the Windows paradigm. In Word Processing, for example, WYSIWYG allowed you to view your document, while you're creating it, as it will look when it is printed out. Likewise, visual development enables you to design an application and, at the same time, see how it'll look when the user runs it.

This capability is especially important when you're developing games and multimedia applications. For example, it's tedious to determine the exact X and Y location where a sprite should appear and then figure the difference to the next location, and so on. It is much easier to simply drop the sprite on the form and then note its coordinates and move it. This allows you to see the changes and how it should appear.

Quick Development Time

Tied closely with visual development is the by-product of quick development time. Before the reviews, before the side-by-side evaluations, usually-conservative corporate developers quickly picked up Visual Basic and put it to use right away. Why? Corporations today need quick results and flexibility to prepare for change in the future. Visual Basic offers both of these things.

The game programming environment is not all that different. If anything, the heat is simply turned up. Each game company wants to have the hottest games out there on the market today. Every day that the *next-level* product is in development is a day of tremendous sales lost.

At the same time, the advent of the CD-ROM as the standard gaming platform, replacing the cramped space of the cartridge and floppy disk has freed developers from worrying so much about storage space. The endless march of hardware toward faster and faster processors has relieved developers from having to worry so much about the speed of every single instruction. These trends, combined with the market pressure, have caused teams of game programmers who used to be very C and assembly language-oriented to look toward class libraries and high level tools in order to develop the games more quickly.

That is not to say that the next game of the year will be written in Visual Basic. Its interpreted environment is still too slow for the most cutting edge stuff. However, many in-house multimedia projects, as well as corporate and commercial release projects, are already using it to build kiosks, hypermedia lookup systems and, yes, even some games. As development time becomes a higher priority and the combined efforts of Windows and Visual Basic produce an increasingly viable platform, the trend toward Visual Basic will only grow stronger.

Win32 *sndPlaySound*

Good sound can't make a bad game good, but it can make a good game great and a great game excellent. Unfortunately, the only sound support Visual Basic offers is Beep. In order to play a sound effect, you must use Win32 and a function called sndPlaySound. This single function provides a great deal of flexibility and is all you'll need for most of your WAV playing needs.

The declaration for this function looks like this:

```
Declare Function sndPlaySound Lib "winmm" _
Alias "sndPlaySoundA" (ByVal lpszSoundName As String, _
ByVal uFlags As Long) As Long
```

> **NOTE**
>
> You can include WIN32API.TXT as a module in your application to automatically declare all the Win32 functions and to declare constants you might need when calling them.

The first thing the function does is search for an entry in the [sounds] section of the registry to see whether it has an entry matching lpszSoundName. If not, the function assumes that lpszSoundName is the name of a WAV file and begins looking for it on the hard drive. It looks in the current directory, the Windows and Windows\System directories, and then works through the path and the network drives. If it finds the file, it plays the file. If not, it plays the default system beep. You can also specify a path as part of lpszSoundName.

uFlags determines how the sound is played. The following constants are the most commonly specified. They are combined by adding the values together and sending the result in uFlags.

```
'  flag values for uFlags parameter
Public Const SND_SYNC = &H0
Public Const SND_ASYNC = &H1
Public Const SND_NODEFAULT = &H2
Public Const SND_MEMORY = &H4
Public Const SND_LOOP = &H8
Public Const SND_NOSTOP = &H10
```

SND_SYNC, which is the default, causes the function to wait until the sound is done before returning control. SND_ASYNC is the opposite—it requests that control be returned to the calling function as soon as possible. Most games will have you using SND_ASYNC everywhere.

SND_NODEFAULT requests that the function do nothing if it cannot find the associated file. This request stops Visual Basic from playing the default beep. SND_MEMORY indicates that lpszSoundName is a pointer to an image of a WAV file already in memory.

SND_LOOP allows you to play a WAV file over and over again. You must also specify SND_ASYNC when you specify SND_LOOP. When you want the WAV file to stop playing, you just call sndPlaySound again with lpszSoundName set to the empty string (""). By the way, you can call sndPlaySound with NULL for the lpszSoundName anytime you want to stop a playing sound.

SND_NOSTOP indicates that you don't want to interrupt a currently playing sound, if there is one. If there is, the sndPlaySound function will quit and return False. SND_NOSTOP helps to prevent you from interrupting important sounds with less important ones.

The following lines of code demonstrate how these arguments work together:

```
rc = sndPlaySound("c:\windows\media\chimes.wav", SND_ASYNC)
```

The above line plays the WAV file in the specified directory and returns control to the calling function without waiting for the sound to finish playing.

```
rc = sndPlaySound("pretty.wav", SND_ASYNC + SND_LOOP)
```

The above line plays the specified WAV file again and again, without waiting for the sound to finish playing before returning control to the sndPlaySound function. Remember that you always have to use SND_ASYNC with SND_LOOP.

```
rc = sndPlaySound("",SND_ASYNC)
```

The above line stops the current WAV file from playing.

Timers

Timers are probably the simplest control on the Visual Basic palette. You just set the interval and the timer executes the code just that often. For their simplicity, timers are amazingly broad in their application.

The first and most obvious use for timers in games is for the main game loop. Games traditionally work by looping and doing things at (very quick) regular intervals. The code must move the sprites, check for collisions among the sprites, verify game parameters (to see whether the score should increase or the game should end) and update the screen all in a fraction of a second. That's the challenge of game programming. With timers, you can meet this challenge.

Timers are useful in other ways, too. To pause a game, just set the Enabled attribute of the timer for the main loop to False. To monitor the status of a device or anything else in your application, just set the timer's interval to check the device or status at whatever interval you like and write the code to do it. You can even use timers to animate an application's icon when the application is minimized.

Collision Detection

Okay, I admit, this isn't really a Visual Basic feature, but if you are going to implement games in any environment, you have got to know about basic collision detection. *Collision detection* is the process of determining which sprites in your world have bumped into each other. If you have a dozen sprites on the screen, you don't have to go through too many permutations to figure out that you are talking about a lot of potential collisions. Even though the most important stuff in the game seems to happen when things collide, figuring out when these collisions occur isn't always easy. It isn't always quick either.

Suppose that your game has a spaceship with lots of odd bits sticking out here and there. How do you find out if any of its parts are overlapping with any of the parts of the equally oddly shaped ships of the bad guy? The best answer is you don't. You fake it. If you have a finite amount of time to check all of your potential collisions, you must simplify the problem. You do this with a bounding box.

A *bounding box* is a box that encircles your sprite and defines its place. If any other sprite's bounding box is found partially inside your sprite's bounding box, the two will be considered touching, even if no actual graphic parts are hitting each other. The reason for this is that it's much quicker and easier to tell whether one box is touching another box than it is to tell whether two graphic parts are touching.

If you're worried that by using a bounding box you're sacrificing accuracy for speed and simplicity, keep in mind that this bounding box technique is really quite accurate, and the number of times that it gives a false positive response is too low to worry about. One technique you can use to reduce the possibility of errors even further is to reduce the size of your bounding box. Make the box even smaller than the outer edges of your sprite. This reduction causes some false negatives (saying there is no collision, when there was a slight one), but usually you can find a balance so good that the user will never be able to tell the difference. In fact, here's a routine to do it:

```
Type ScreenObject
     X As Integer
     Y As Integer
     Height As Integer
     Width As Integer
End Type

Private Function Collision(Obj1 As ScreenObject, Obj2 As ScreenObject) As Integer

' These are variables for holding the X and Y position of
' the lower-right corners of the objects
Dim LowerX1 As Integer, LowerY1 As Integer
Dim LowerX2 As Integer, LowerY2 As Integer
```

```
Dim Collided As Integer

' Find the lower right corners of the objects
LowerX1 = Obj1.X + Obj1.Width - 1
LowerY1 = Obj1.Y + Obj1.Height - 1

LowerX2 = Obj2.X + Obj2.Width - 1
LowerY2 = Obj2.Y + Obj2.Height - 1

Collided = True

If ((LowerX1 < Obj2.X) Or (Obj1.X > LowerX2) Or _
    (LowerY2 < Obj2.Y) Or (Obj1.Y > LowerY2)) Then
        Collided = False
  End If

Collision = Collided

End Function
```

The function accepts two user-defined type variables that each give the X, Y, height, and width a sprite. The function returns a simple True or False indicating whether there has been a collision between the two. The function determines whether there has been a collision by assuming a collision has occurred and then setting out to disprove it. If the function cannot disprove it, then the collision must have happened. This backwards method turns out to be just as accurate and much faster than any other way you might approach the problem.

When you're writing your game, your initial inclination might be to just loop through all the sprites and check for collision with every other sprite. Even when using bounding boxes, this process can very quickly turn your application into a dog. To reduce the sheer number of collision tests that you have to do, ask yourself two questions for each collision:

1. Is it possible?
2. Do I care?

First, is it physically possible that this sprite that only runs across the top of my screen could run into the player who is constrained in the lower half of the screen? If not, then forget it! Don't waste your time checking things that couldn't possibly happen.

Second, does it matter if these two sprites ran into each other? Does anything really occur when an alien shot from one ship hits an alien shot from another ship? If you are not going to change anything if a collision occurs, you don't need to find out whether one has happened.

Win32 API Joystick Commands

Although Visual Basic doesn't have built-in commands that allow you to access the joystick, you do have full access to the Win32 joystick commands from Visual Basic. The commands you will use most often are joyGetDevCaps and joyGetPos, which are explained in the following sections.

joyGetDevCaps

You use joyGetDevCaps to get information about the joystick capabilities and calibration. When working with a gaming application, you will want to call joyGetDevCaps in your initialization code so that you have the information later when you need it.

The declaration for joyGetDevCaps is as follows:

```
Declare Function joyGetDevCaps Lib "winmm" Alias "joyGetDevCapsA" _
(ByVal id As Long, lpCaps As JOYCAPS, _
ByVal uSize As Long) As Long
```

Because some systems can have two joysticks connected, you must specify the ID number of the joystick that you want information on. The two constants that you can use are:

```
Global Const JOYSTICKID1 = 0
Global Const JOYSTICKID2 = 1
```

The second parameter in the declaration is used to pass a structure by reference that will receive the information from the external function. The third parameter is the size of the filled-in structure, in bytes. You can do a Len(), which sends your JOYCAPS variable to figure out what to send for uSize.

The structure's definition looks like the following:

```
Type JOYCAPS
    wMid As Long
    wPid As Long
    szPname As String * 25
    wXmin As Long
    wXmax As Long
    wYmin As Long
    wYmax As Long
    wZmin As Long
    wZmax As Long
    wNumButtons As Long
    wPeriodMin As Long
    wPeriod Max As Long
End Type
```

The information this structure gathers is as follows:

- The manufacturer identification number
- The product identification number
- The product name (in a null-terminated string)
- The minimum X position of the joystick
- The maximum X position of the joystick
- The minimum Y position of the joystick
- The maximum Y position of the joystick
- The minimum Z position of the joystick

- The maximum Z position of the joystick
- The number of buttons supported
- The smallest polling interval supported when the joystick is captured by a window
- The largest polling interval supported when the joystick is captured by a window

> **NOTE**
>
> The last two items of information may be confusing to you. Using other Win32 functions, you can capture the joystick to a particular window so that it sends events to that window when anything happens with the joystick. Although this setup may sound ideal, you can't do it from Visual Basic because you have no way of capturing the associated Windows events.

The most important bits of information here are the minimums and maximums on each of the different axes. You may be surprised to find the Z axis included because most gaming joysticks don't support Z-axis movement. This specification is, no doubt, anticipating future input devices that will have this movement.

When you ask a joystick where it is, it doesn't just tell you that it is being pulled right or left. It gives you a number. In order for that number to make any sense, you have to know what the maximum and minimum X and Y values that the joystick supplies are. Then you can make an estimate of how far left or right the joystick is being pulled and adjust the action in the program accordingly. You must call the `joyGetDevCaps` function at the beginning of your program so you'll have a context for understanding the numbers sent to you when you get information from the joystick.

The other bit of information that will be interesting to you is the number of buttons the joystick supports. Most joysticks today support at least two, and some support as many as three or four. You may want to give the user the flexibility of assigning meaning to any extra joystick buttons.

joyGetPos

You use `joyGetPos` to get the current position of the joystick. You will call `joyGetPos` again and again, probably as a part of the processing done in a timer to determine the current joystick position and update the action accordingly.

The declaration for `joyGetPos` looks like the following:

```
Declare Function joyGetPos Lib "winmm" Alias "joyGetPos" _
(ByVal id As Long, lpInfo As JOYINFO) As Long
```

This declaration receives a joystick identification number just as `joyGetDevCaps` did to identify the joystick for which you want position information. It also takes a user-defined type as an argument by reference to pass back the information you want.

`JOYINFO` looks like the following:

```
Type JOYINFO
    wXpos As Long
    wYpos As Long
    wZpos As Long
    wButtons As Long
End Type
```

`JOYINFO` gives you a number for each axis and then a long indicating which buttons are pressed. As I mentioned before, you can understand the number passed for each axis by looking at the minimum and maximum numbers for that axis, which you obtained at the beginning of the application.

How does `JOYINFO` pass all the button information in one long? The information is encoded in the bits. The first bit specifies the first button, the second bit specifies the second button, and so on. So if the first button was being pushed, you would receive 00000001, or a decimal 1, in the least significant byte of the long. If the first and third buttons were being pressed, you'd get 00000101 or a decimal 5. The easiest way to decode these numbers is with the constants provided:

```
Global Const JOY_BUTTON1 = &H0001
Global Const JOY_BUTTON2 = &H0002
Global Const JOY_BUTTON3 = &H0004
Global Const JOY_BUTTON4 = &H0008
```

All you have to do to find out about any particular button is enter the following code:

```
If (lJoyInfo.wButtons AND JOY_BUTTON1) Then
```

The AND in the above code does a bitwise AND with the mask and returns a value other than zero only if that bit is set.

The Media Control Interface (MCI)

The Media Control Interface is an easy-to-use interface to the many multimedia devices that are connected to your user's system. Visual Basic has a control that gives you a very flexible way of using the MCI. Win32 also has a command called `mciSendString()` that provides an English-like text interface to MCI. This command enables you to completely avoid all the device-specific details and simply make MCI work.

Chapter 9, "Multimedia," is completely devoted to covering the MCI control and the `mciSendString()` command. In addition, that chapter provides numerous examples of the language to get you started using it.

For game programming, you are most likely to use this interface to play background music in the form of MIDI files. So, before I leave this topic, let me show you a series of commands that will play MIDI files.

When you want to begin playing the music, execute these commands:

```
OPEN MYSONG.MID TYPE SEQUENCER ALIAS SEQ
PLAY SEQ FROM 0
```

These commands open a MIDI file called MYSONG and play it from the beginning. When you want to stop the music, execute the following command:

```
STOP SEQ
```

To start up the music again where you left off, use the following command:

```
PLAY SEQ
```

When you have stopped the music and are ready to close the application, be sure and close the MIDI file first with this command:

```
CLOSE SEQ
```

For more information on exactly how to send these strings and what the mciSendString() command does, see the chapter on multimedia (Chapter 9).

The *PaintPicture* Method and *ImageList* Control

The PaintPicture method and ImageList control are new with Visual Basic 4.0. They go a long way toward making your sprite creation and utilization as simple as possible. They are so important that I've devoted a complete chapter to them. See the Animation chapter (Chapter 10) for more information on these items and a really cool quote from Walt Disney.

Real Objects

It has been a long time coming, but finally Visual Basic is a truly object-oriented environment. That is, it allows you to create your own classes and then create new objects from those classes. The classes can have their own functions and data structures. The following sections explain how classes work and demonstrate how you can put them to work in a game.

How Classes Work

Choose Insert | Class Module in your application. A new code window appears on-screen, much as it does for a regular module. In it you can now declare functions and procedures as well as data structures, just as you would for a form. You will notice one object called Class and two methods for it: Initialize and Terminate. These methods are executed when your class is first instantiated (turned into an object) and when the object is destroyed. Once you create a class module, you can't simply call functions from it the way you do a normal module. You have to remember that a class is just a definition of an object. You have to create an actual object to work with before you can start calling its functions.

To create an object, you would use the following code:

```
Dim NewObject As New MyClass
```

This code assumes you have created a class module called `MyClass`. If you wanted to call a procedure called `DoIt` in `MyClass`, you would enter the following:

```
MyClass.DoIt
```

A class is a very flexible mechanism. Remember that because this is a class and you instantiate objects from it, you can create as many identical objects as you like. They will have identical functions, procedures and data structures, but each will have its own copy of data in the data structures.

If you are a hard-core Visual Basic person, you might regard this new feature as a minor expansion of capabilities, but don't gloss over this one lightly. Classes can have the power to significantly alter the way you design and develop your applications. In earlier versions of Visual Basic, you were forced to create either global- or form-level functions that did all the work of your application. Now you can segment your application functionality and data into components that make sense for your problem. This capability is especially useful in game programming.

A Gaming Example

Imagine that you want to create a Q-bert-style video game. In case you don't remember, Q-bert was a ball-shaped creature with legs that hopped around on cubes arranged in the form of a pyramid. When he landed on top of a cube, the cube would change color. When he changed the color of all the cubes, he got to go to the next level. Of course, there were meanies jumping around on the pyramid too who killed the hapless hero if he landed on the same cube with them.

The following might be a rough outline of the application's flow:

> Query: Does anybody want to move?
>
> Movement phase: Loop through the movement of all currently jumping pieces at once. Loop through the complete jump.
>
> Collision Detection: Is the hero on the same cube as meanie? If so, kill the hero.
>
> Did the hero land on a cube that hasn't already had its color changed? If so, change the color and add points.
>
> Are all the cubes' colors changed on the board? If so, do the following:
>
> - Add points
> - Clear board
> - Set up next board
> - Display board
> - Place hero on board
> - Restart the meanies

Now that you have a rough idea of what the main loop of the program will look like, you are likely to start thinking in terms of procedures you need to write. Don't. Instead, think in terms of objects. What objects are involved with the application? The hero is an object. The meanies are objects. Even the game board itself is an object.

When you have a rough idea of what objects are involved, begin thinking about the objects. Each object has properties and methods. *Properties* are the data associated with that object that either may or may not be accessed by other objects (your choice). *Methods* are simply the procedures and functions in the object.

What kinds of things should the hero be able to do? He should be able to check user input to see whether he should jump from this cube to another. What kinds of data will he want to keep? He needs to monitor his X and Y location and which direction he is facing. The meanies have much the same data and procedures, except that instead of checking user input to decide to jump, they will check some clever little algorithm you have cooked up.

For the board, you might want a procedure that changes a cube's color, a function like IsLevelComplete, and a procedure that does everything necessary to take the user to the next level. You will also need an internal 2-D array that represents the game board and can be used to update the screen.

You begin to see how an application divides itself up among its objects. There are no hard and fast rules on how this is done; in fact, many volumes have been written on this topic with no clear agreement. The most important thing about the process of creating objects and segmenting your functionality is to remember that it is iterative. You will start with a rough idea and then shape it over time into your master application. Hopefully, the new object-oriented paradigm will also make your code more modular. With modular code, the next time you start a game that is similar to this one, you'll be able to drop in the appropriate objects and start off half-finished.

Summary

This chapter has been a wild romp through a broad variety of topics that are important to the Visual Basic game developer. Not only did we talk about animation and sound but also about collision detection and object-oriented design. There is a lot more to learn, but hopefully this foundation will serve you well.

Microsoft Office

24

by Conrad Scott

The addition of the Visual Basic for Applications (VBA) language into Visual Basic 4.0 opens up a new frontier for Visual Basic applications. This frontier allows you to incorporate the full functionality of applications such as Microsoft Excel and Word directly into Visual Basic applications. This incorporation is accomplished through OLE automation. This chapter explores the interaction between Visual Basic 4.0 and Microsoft Office and outlines methods for incorporating this powerful functionality into applications developed in Visual Basic 4.0.

The OLE Container Control

The OLE container control provides a method of displaying and manipulating Microsoft Office (and other graphical) objects directly from your Visual Basic application. A container as it is applied to Visual Basic is an item (usually a control) that contains another item. For example, if I place a frame control on a form and then place a text box inside of it, the frame is a container to the text box. Using this same principle, you can add a Microsoft Excel spreadsheet or a Microsoft Word document directly to a Visual Basic form using the OLE Container control. The spreadsheet or document is contained within the OLE Container control.

To display another application's object in your application, that object must be visible to Visual Basic. There are two types of objects available for use by Visual Basic applications: custom controls and references. *Custom controls* mirror the controls available with Visual Basic 3. The Visual Basic 4.0 version of the custom control has the extension OCX (instead of VBX). In Visual Basic 3, the File | Add File menu option was selected to insert a custom control into an application. In Visual Basic 4.0, this method has been simplified: select Tools | Custom Controls from the main menu. A dialog box appears, providing a list of all custom controls and insertable items available for use by Visual Basic applications (see Figure 24.1). An example of an insertable item is a Microsoft Excel chart. Although the chart is not an OCX object, it is a tangible object that can be added to an application. Once an OCX or OLE object is included in a Visual Basic application, its properties and methods can be accessed directly from code. To include a control or an OLE object, simply select its checkbox in the dialog box. Once you have selected the items you want to include in your application, choose OK. The items you select are added to the Visual Basic toolbar.

NOTE

There are 2 types of objects that can be added to a Visual Basic Project: Custom controls (select Tools | Custom Controls... from the VB menu) and OLE objects exposed by other applications (select Tools | References... from the VB menu).

You can use one of two methods when you want to include an object in a Visual Basic application using the OLE control: linking or embedding.

FIGURE 24.1.

The Visual Basic Custom Controls dialog box displays the available OCX controls and OLE objects.

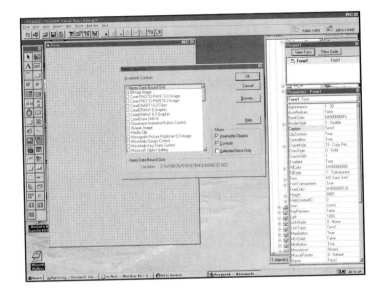

Linking

Linking allows you to directly edit an object's data from within Visual Basic. When you link, the object in the OLE container is linked directly to the data it is accessing. Any actions taken on the data from the OLE control act on the original data. For example, use linking if you want to allow your users to edit a Microsoft Word document directly from Visual Basic and directly apply any changes made to the document in Visual Basic to the Word document file. To achieve this, follow these steps:

1. Add an OLE control to your form (double-click the OLE control in the toolbox to add it to the form). The Insert Object dialog box appears.

2. Select the Create From File option on the left side of the dialog box. An edit box and a Browse button appear.

3. Click the Browse button; a common dialog box appears (see Figure 24.2). Select any Microsoft Word document.

4. Select the Link checkbox in the Insert Object dialog box.

5. Choose OK.

    At this point, the contents of the document are displayed in the control. If nothing seems to be visible, stretch the control to display a wider area of the document. Now run the Visual Basic application and double-click the document within the OLE control. This action brings up Microsoft Word and displays the document.

6. Close Microsoft Word. At this point, you should be viewing your Visual Basic form. This form displays the contents of the Word document in the OLE control. Stop Visual Basic.

FIGURE 24.2.

The Insert Object dialog box after the Create From File option is selected. Select the Link checkbox to link the OLE control to its data. Leave this checkbox deselected to store a copy of the data in the control.

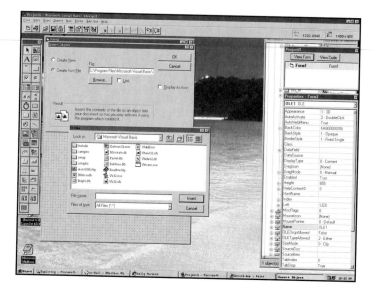

These steps have established a link with the Word document's data using the OLE control. Imagine that the document is updated by another user after you displayed it with your OLE control. To view the changes made to the document, use the OLE control's update method. Do the following:

1. Add a command button to the form.
2. Double-click the command button and add the following code:

   ```
   OLE1.Update
   ```

3. Run Visual Basic. The OLE control displays the current contents of the Word document.
4. Open Microsoft Word and then open the document displayed in the Visual Basic application.
5. Make noticeable change to the document, save the changes and close Microsoft Word. (If you tile your Visual Basic and Word windows, the results of this example are easier to see.)
6. Switch to Visual Basic. Notice that the document is displayed in the original format (as it was before you changed the document in step 5). Click the command button.

The data displayed in the OLE control is updated to reflect the changes you made to the document.

In this case, the OLE control is directly connected to the original data. Clicking the command button updates the data displayed in the control. You can also change the document directly from the Visual Basic application by following these steps:

1. Run the Visual Basic application.

2. Double-click the OLE control. A copy of Microsoft Word is run (if it isn't running already) and the document is displayed. If Microsoft Word is already running, the document is displayed in the existing copy and any other open documents are available through Word's Window menu.

3. Make a noticeable change to the document, save the change, and close Word.

4. View the updated data in the Visual Basic application's OLE control.

The updated data is displayed in the OLE control. In this example, you are acting directly on the original data. Any changes made by the application are made to this data; any changes made to this data by other applications can be viewed by the application by using the update method (that is, by clicking the command button).

Embedding

The second method through which the OLE control displays data is *embedding*. When you embed an object, the control maintains a copy of the data within itself. This is a *private* copy of the data and is not inherently available to other applications. If changes are made to the data, the original data is unaffected. Here are the steps for embedding a Word document into an application:

1. Add an OLE control to your form. The Insert Object dialog box appears.

2. Select the Create From File option on the left side of the dialog box. An edit box and a Browse button appear.

3. Click the Browse button; a common dialog box appears. Select a Microsoft Word document.

4. Choose OK.

The primary difference between the steps for linking and those for embedding is the selection of the Link checkbox. Because the preceding steps did not select the Link checkbox, you are provided with a copy of the data. When this copy is updated, the original data remains unchanged.

If you close the application without saving the data, the data within the OLE control is lost. To save your copy of the data, use the SaveToFile method. The following code saves the contents of the OLE control to a file:

```
Private Sub cmdSaveToFileOLE_Click()
    iFileNum = FreeFile
    Open "C:\PROJECTS\PROJECT1\REPORT.TXT" For Binary Lock Write As x
    OLE1.SaveToFile iFileNum
    Close iFileNum
End Sub
```

The preceding code saves the contents of the control to a file. To get the contents from the file and place them into the control, use the `ReadFromFile` method. The following sample code accomplishes this:

```
Private Sub cmdReadFromFileOLE_Click()
    iFileNum = FreeFile
    Open "C:\PROJECTS\PROJECT1\REPORT.TXT" For Binary Lock Write As x
    OLE1.ReadFromFile iFileNum
    Close iFileNum
End Sub
```

It is important to note here that the file must be opened for Binary when you both read and write the file. Because this is the case, the file should be edited only from within Visual Basic. Additionally, only data placed in the file using the `SaveToFile` method can be retrieved using the `ReadFromFile` method.

The data from multiple objects can be saved to the same file. It is important to understand, however, that the data must be removed from the file in the same order in which it was added. If you do not remove the data in the proper order, the data you display (if the data displays at all) will be incorrect. This is logical because the data is stored in a file. Once an object's data is written to the file, the file pointer is at a certain position. The data for additional objects is added beginning with the first byte after the end of the last object's data. The `ReadFromFile` method does not allow you to specify where in the file you begin reading data.

OLE versus DDE

If you have used DDE in the past, you may be wondering what differences exist between DDE and OLE and when each is appropriate. OLE is a far better standard than DDE and is the preferred method for use whenever possible. DDE is a method of exchanging only textual information. When you request data from an application using DDE, you receive the data and the data only. On the other hand, OLE offers the use of any objects an application exposes. For example, if you request data from a Word document using DDE, you receive the data and nothing more. If you use OLE, you receive the data and, in addition, you are afforded the use of Word's spelling checker. Using OLE Automation, you can borrow the functionality of the spelling checker from Word. Borrowing the spelling checker eliminates the need to incorporate a spell-check utility in your Visual Basic application.

The key is to understand that the end user must also be able to access any objects you incorporate into an application. Using the Word example, the user is required to have a copy of Microsoft Word installed on his or her system for your application to successfully access the spelling checker (or any other object Microsoft Word exposes).

OLE and Microsoft Excel

In OLE Automation, an application exposes its objects to other applications for use. For example, Microsoft Excel exposes a spreadsheet object. An instance of the spreadsheet object can be created by other applications and the properties and methods of the spreadsheet can then be accessed. Each object exposed in OLE Automation has a hierarchy. This hierarchy is the path through which an object and its properties and methods are accessed. This is not an unfamiliar concept. In Visual Basic, a picture box is accessed through its form. To access the picture box, you must call the form, as shown here:

```
Form1.Picture1.BackColor = RGB(255,255,255)
```

This code changes the `backcolor` property of the picture control contained on `Form1`. OLE Automation operates in the same manner. An Excel workbook has in its hierarchy a spreadsheet object. This spreadsheet object has cells. A range of cells can be selected on a spreadsheet object by using the `Range` property. To access a range of cells on a spreadsheet that is a part of a workbook, use the following code:

```
objSpreadSheet1.Range(objSpreadSheet1.Cells(1, 2), objSpreadSheet1.Cells(1, 5))
```

To access an object's properties and methods, an instance of the object must first be created. In the previous example, `objSpreadSheet1` is an instance of a spreadsheet object that Microsoft Excel exposes. In the next section of this chapter, you create an Excel application piece by piece directly from Visual Basic. Each step adds an object that Excel exposes and then manipulates its properties and methods.

Creating an Excel Application from Visual Basic

If you want to create a spreadsheet, you must follow the hierarchy of Excel. To create the spreadsheet, you must first create an instance of Excel and then an instance of an Excel workbook. Each of these elements of Excel are objects Excel exposes. The following example creates an instance of Excel and adds a workbook to the Excel instance:

```
'Declare the Excel object variable
Dim objApp As Object
'Declare a workbook object
Dim objWorkBook As Object
'Set the application object to an instance of Excel
Set objApp = CreateObject("Excel.Application")
'Set the workbook object to a new workbook using the add method.
Set objWorkBook = objApp.WorkBooks.Add
```

This instance of Excel is an OLE object that Excel exposes. You can access any of the properties and methods of the Excel object using OLE Automation. In this case, we created a workbook using the workbook's `Add` method. Notice that each of the objects is assigned a variable (`objApp` and `objWorkBook`). These variables are then used to address the created object.

The Excel instance and the workbook are now objects in memory. These objects are not yet visible. Once you create a workbook, you are provided with several spreadsheets by default. Imagine that you want to manipulate the first spreadsheet in the workbook. Before you can manipulate it, you have to declare an object to represent it. Referring to the object hierarchy, add the following code:

```
'Declare a spreadsheet object
Dim objSpreadSheet As Object
'Set the spreadsheet object to the first (active) sheet of the excel workbook.
Set objSpreadSheet1 = objApp.ActiveWorkbook.ActiveSheet
```

This code creates a new spreadsheet object and gives it the focus. It also assigns the application workbook's active sheet the variable objSpreadSheet1. This eliminates the need to continually refer to an ever increasing hierarchy of items directly.

You can use the following code to assign a value to the Font.Size property:

```
objApp.ActiveWorkBook.ActiveSheet.Range.Font.Size = 14
```

However, if you assign the spreadsheet range a variable name (objSpreadSheetRange) with the statement Dim objSpreadSheetRange = objApp.ActiveWorkBook.ActiveSheet.Range, you can accomplish what the preceding line of code did by using this shorter line:

```
objSpreadSheetRange.Font.Size = 14
```

This next example selects a range of cells through Visual Basic code:

```
Set objSpreadSheet1Range = objSpreadSheet1.Range(objSpreadSheet1.Cells(1, 1),
objSpreadSheet1.Cells(36, 16))
```

Now change the color of the selected cells (the preceding statement stored the range of cells in the objSpreadSheet1Range variable):

```
objSpreadSheet1Range.Interior.Color = RGB(125, 125, 125)
```

This statement used the color property to change the color of the cells (seems logical). However, it is important to note that in the hierarchy of Excel, the spreadsheet range does not have a color property. The spreadsheet range does have an Interior object, however, and this object has a color property. The following line results in runtime error 1000:

```
objSpreadSheet1Range.Color = RGB(125, 125, 125)
```

The error occurred because the range does not have a color property; the statement failed to access the color property through the Interior object. This understanding of objects and their hierarchy is one of the most important concepts in OLE Automation.

The proper statement to set this property is:

```
objSpreadSheet1Range.Interior.Color = RGB(125, 125, 125)
```

While you are manipulating cells in a spreadsheet, change the font characteristics. The following example assumes that you have selected some cells. The example sets the font size of the cell and applies a bold look:

```
objSpreadSheet1Range.Font.Size = 12
objSpreadSheet1Range.Font.Bold = True
```

In this example, the font size (`Font.Size`) and boldness (`Font.Bold`) of the selected range of cells that belong to the spreadsheet (`objSpreadSheet1Range`), that belongs to the workbook (`objWorkBook`), that belongs to the application (`objApp`) is changed. How are you doing?

> **NOTE**
>
> Microsoft Excel provides a list of the hierarchy of objects in its Help file. From the main Excel menu, choose Help | Contents. Then choose the Programming with Visual Basic jump to display a screen entitled Visual Basic Reference. Choose the Microsoft Excel Object Model topic to display the list of objects Excel exposes to other applications. An item that contains a red arrow can be expanded to reveal additional objects contained by that item.

Imagine that you have created an instance of Excel (an Excel object) and that you have also created a workbook. By default, this workbook contains several spreadsheets; you have set the focus to the first spreadsheet. Now imagine that you want to add some command buttons to the spreadsheet. The following code adds several command buttons to the spreadsheet. It sets the positions of the buttons, sets the font to bold, and sets the size of the text on the button to 8 point:

```
For X = 33 To 153 Step 30
        objSpreadSheet1.Buttons.Add 153, X, 80, 24
        objSpreadSheet1.Buttons.Font.Bold = False
        objSpreadSheet1.Buttons.Font.Size = 8
    Next X
```

The reason that the `For` loop runs from 33 to 153 is that these are positions used to set the command buttons to the desired positions. Now that you have added command buttons to the spreadsheet, add the desired text:

```
objSpreadSheet1.Buttons(1).TEXT = "SelectA1"
objSpreadSheet1.Buttons(2).TEXT = "SetCells"
objSpreadSheet1.Buttons(3).TEXT = "ClearCells"
objSpreadSheet1.Buttons(4).TEXT = "SelectCells"
objSpreadSheet1.Buttons(5).TEXT = "SetActiveCell"
```

To provide functionality to the command buttons, create a module of functions to attach to the buttons. Create the module in your Visual Basic application. The saved module is added to the Excel application with the following code:

```
Set objModule1 = objWorkBook.Modules.Add(, objSpreadSheet1, 1)
objModule1.Activate
objModule1.InsertFile filename:="C:\PROJECTS\MODULE1.TXT"
```

The module is a text file created in Excel and is simply a text file that contains functions. It is also possible to create the functions in a Visual Basic module and export that module to the Excel application as a text file. The following section lists the contents of the module.

The Excel Module

The functions in the module added to the Excel application demonstrate some of the automation capabilities of VBA. These functions can just as easily be implemented directly from Visual Basic.

The first function selects the cell at location A:1

```
Sub SelectA1()
    'This function selects cell A1
    Range(Cells(1, 1), Cells(1, 1)).Select
End Sub
```

The next function selects 10 rows down and 10 columns to the right from the currently selected cell:

```
Sub SelectCells10X10()
    'Selects 10 rows and 10 columns adjacent to the active (currently selected)
    'cell.
    iRow = 10                             'set number of rows to move to 10
    iCol = 10                             'set number of columns to move to 10
    Selection.Resize(iRow, iCol).Select 'select the cells
End Sub
```

The following function is similar to the preceding one but it prompts the user for the number of cells to be selected in both directions:

```
Sub SetActiveCell()
    'Changes the position of the active cell by the number of rows and columns
    'selected.
    Dim iRow, iCol
    iRow = InputBox("Enter the number of rows to move", "Enter Rows", 1)
    iCol = InputBox("Enter the number of columns to move", "Enter Columns", 1)
    iRow = Abs(iRow)                      'use the InputBox function to set the
                                          'number of rows
    iCol = Abs(iCol)                      'use the InputBox function to set the
                                          'number of rows
    Selection.Offset(iRow, iCol).Select 'select the new cell
End Sub
```

The next function places a value in cells A1 through A10. These values are formatted using the properties bold, italic, and so on. Note that the With...End With statement is used here. This statement allows you to refer to an object without continually retyping its name:

```
Sub SetCellValueAndFormat()
    'Sets the value in the first 20 cells of column A to the current value of x and
    'makes the 'font bold,italic and underlined. .Offset(x, 0).Select selects the
    'next cell in the column.
    Range(Cells(1, 1), Cells(1, 1)).Select
    For x = 1 To 20                       'begin Loop
        With ActiveCell                   'working on the active cell
            .Value = x - 2                'set the value in the cell to the current value
                                          'of x
            .Font.Size = 10               'set the font size to 14
```

```
        .Font.Bold = True          'set the cell font to bold
        .Font.Italic = True        'italicize the cell text
        .Offset(1, 0).Select       'Select the next cell down (A1, A2, A3, etc.)
      End With                     'close the With statement
    Next x                         'Loop to the next x value
End Sub
```

The next function clears the values placed in the cells with the `SetCellValueAndFormat` function and also resets the formatting:

```
Sub ClearCellValueandFormat()
    'Clears the values and formatting set in the function SetCellValueandFormat()
    Range(Cells(1, 1), Cells(1, 1)).Select
    For x = 1 To 20                'begin Loop
        With ActiveCell           'working on the active cell
            .Value = ""           'set the value in the cell to NULL
            .Font.Bold = False    'turn off the bold
            .Font.Italic = False  'turn off the italics
            .Offset(1, 0).Select  'Select the next cell down (A1, A2,etc.)
                                  '.Offset(rows,columns).Select
        End With                  'close the With statement
    Next x                        'Loop to the next x value
End Sub
```

Once you add the module to your application-to-be, attach the functions to the command buttons on the spreadsheet. This is accomplished with the `OnAction` property:

```
objSpreadSheet1.Buttons(1).OnAction = "SelectA1"
objSpreadSheet1.Buttons(2).OnAction = "SetCellValueAndFormat"
objSpreadSheet1.Buttons(3).OnAction = "ClearCellValueAndFormat"
objSpreadSheet1.Buttons(4).OnAction = "SelectCells10X10"
objSpreadSheet1.Buttons(5).OnAction = "SetActiveCell"
```

So far, you have created and formatted a spreadsheet. The following instructions add some additional data to the spreadsheet that is used later to create a chart.

First, label the spreadsheet data:

```
'Set the range of cells that we will be working with (one cell).
Set objSpreadSheet1Range = objSpreadSheet1.Range(objSpreadSheet1.Cells(3, 2), _
objSpreadSheet1.Cells(3, 2))
'Place the Chart Data label in the selected cell.
objSpreadSheet1Range.Characters.Caption = "Chart Data:"
```

Next, place the data for the chart on the spreadsheet:

```
For X = 4 To 13
        'Set the range of cells. The range is 1 cell and changes each time through
        'the loop.
        Set objSpreadSheet1Range = objSpreadSheet1.Range(objSpreadSheet1.Cells(X,
     ➡2), _objSpreadSheet1.Cells(X, 2))
        'This is a bogus value (X * 5) to be placed in the current cell.
        sValue = X * 5
        'Place the value in the cell.
        objSpreadSheet1Range.Characters.Caption = sValue
    Next X
```

Before wrapping up the spreadsheet portion of the application, add a Microsoft Word document to your spreadsheet. To do this, you must first select the size of the document. This is done by selecting a range of cells for the document's location:

```
Set objSpreadSheet1Range = objSpreadSheet1.Range(objSpreadSheet1.Cells(4, 2), _
objSpreadSheet1.Cells(13, 2))
```

Next, add the document to the spreadsheet. The following line of code adds the document and displays the contents of a Microsoft Word file:

```
objSpreadSheet1.OLEObjects.Add filename:="C:\PROJECTS\OLE.DOC"
```

You can manipulate the size of the Word document in the following manner:

```
objSpreadSheet1.OLEObjects(1).Height = 200
objSpreadSheet1.OLEObjects(1).Width = 250
objSpreadSheet1.OLEObjects(1).TOP = 30
objSpreadSheet1.OLEObjects(1).Left = 300
```

This completes the spreadsheet portion of the application. To summarize, you have created an Excel object and added a workbook to that object. The workbook automatically provided several spreadsheets; you set the focus to the first spreadsheet and formatted it (with colors, fonts, and so on). Then you added command buttons and attached the functions in a module to the command buttons. You then created some data for the yet-to-be-created chart to access. Finally, you added a Microsoft Word document object to the spreadsheet and displayed a Word document file in the object.

Creating an Excel Chart

The next step is to create a chart for the application. The following line of code adds the chart:

```
Set Chart1 = objWorkBook.Charts.Add(, objSpreadSheet1, 1)
```

Next, you have to point the chart to the data on the spreadsheet:

```
Chart1.ChartWizard Source:=objSpreadSheet1Range
```

The Excel Chart object provides the ChartWizard object to completely format the chart. The wizard's properties and methods provide the same level of manipulation you can achieve manually.

And there you have it: a completed application. The only thing left to do is to set the application to Visible so that it can be seen. These lines of code make the application and the chart visible:

```
objApp.Visible = True
Chart1.Visible = True
```

When the application appears, you want the user to see the spreadsheet; add this line to display the first spreadsheet and give it the focus:

```
objSpreadSheet1.Activate
```

Now that you are finished creating the application, it is very important that you destroy the object variables you have created. If you are familiar with GDI functions, you know that if you create a brush and do not destroy it, you have a serious memory leak. It is the same with objects: If you do not destroy object variables, you will cause your users great distress. The following lines destroy the object variables created so far:

```
Set objApp = Nothing
Set objWorkBook = Nothing
Set objSpreadSheet1 = Nothing
Set objSpreadSheet1Range = Nothing
Set Chart1 = Nothing
```

Also remember to consider the creation of objects when debugging OLE Automation code. In this example, the Excel application is not rendered visible until nearly the last line. If you continually step through your code creating objects, but break before you delete them, you will quickly run out of memory. Additionally, when you exit Windows, you are asked whether or not you want to save the changes made to the newly created application. If this occurs, answer No.

Putting It All Together

Listing 24.1 shows the complete application. It is important to note that this application starts with nothing. It creates an instance of Excel, adds objects and code to it, and creates a fully functional Excel application directly from Visual Basic.

Listing 24.1. The Excel application.

```
Function CreateWorkBook()
    Dim objApp As Object
    Dim objWorkBook As Object
    Dim objSpreadSheet As Object
    Screen.MousePointer = 11
    Set objApp = CreateObject("Excel.Application")
    Set objWorkBook = objApp.WorkBooks.Add
    Set objSpreadSheet1 = objApp.ActiveWorkbook.ActiveSheet
    Set objSpreadSheet1Range = objSpreadSheet1.Range(objSpreadSheet1.Cells(1, 1), _
    ➡objSpreadSheet1.Cells(36, 16))
    objSpreadSheet1Range.Interior.Color = RGB(0, 255, 255)
    Set objSpreadSheet1Range = objSpreadSheet1.Range(objSpreadSheet1.Cells(3, 4), _
    ➡objSpreadSheet1.Cells(14, 5)) 'row/column
    objSpreadSheet1Range.Interior.Color = RGB(125, 125, 125)
    Set objSpreadSheet1Range = objSpreadSheet1.Range(objSpreadSheet1.Cells(1, 2), _
    ➡objSpreadSheet1.Cells(1, 2))
    objSpreadSheet1Range.Font.Size = 12
    objSpreadSheet1Range.Font.Bold = True
    objSpreadSheet1Range.Characters.Caption = _
"Visual Basic 4 Unleashed - Chapter 2 - Microsoft Office Application developed from
➡within Visual Basic"
    For X = 33 To 153 Step 30
        objSpreadSheet1.Buttons.Add 153, X, 80, 24
```

continues

Listing 24.1. continued

```
        objSpreadSheet1.Buttons.Font.Bold = False
        objSpreadSheet1.Buttons.Font.Size = 8
    Next X
    objSpreadSheet1.Buttons(1).TEXT = "SelectA1"
    objSpreadSheet1.Buttons(1).OnAction = "SelectA1"
    objSpreadSheet1.Buttons(2).TEXT = "SetCells"
    objSpreadSheet1.Buttons(2).OnAction = "SetCellValueAndFormat"
    objSpreadSheet1.Buttons(3).TEXT = "ClearCells"
    objSpreadSheet1.Buttons(3).OnAction = "ClearCellValueAndFormat"
    objSpreadSheet1.Buttons(4).TEXT = "SelectCells"
    objSpreadSheet1.Buttons(4).OnAction = "SelectCells10X10"
    objSpreadSheet1.Buttons(5).TEXT = "SetActiveCell"
    objSpreadSheet1.Buttons(5).OnAction = "SetActiveCell"
    Set objModule1 = objWorkBook.Modules.Add(, objSpreadSheet1, 1)
    objModule1.Activate
    objModule1.InsertFile filename:="c:\temp\temp3\module1.txt"

(The file name is the same as the Visual Basic module created earlier)
    'Chart
    Set objSpreadSheet1Range = objSpreadSheet1.Range(objSpreadSheet1.Cells(3, 2), _
    ➡objSpreadSheet1.Cells(3, 2))
    objSpreadSheet1Range.Characters.Caption = "Chart Data:"
    For X = 4 To 13
        Set objSpreadSheet1Range = objSpreadSheet1.Range(objSpreadSheet1.Cells
        ➡(X, 2), _objSpreadSheet1.Cells(X, 2))
        sValue = X * 5
        objSpreadSheet1Range.Characters.Caption = sValue
    Next X
    Set objSpreadSheet1Range = objSpreadSheet1.Range(objSpreadSheet1.Cells(4, 2), _
    ➡objSpreadSheet1.Cells(13, 2))
    objSpreadSheet1.OLEObjects.Add filename:="c:\winword\moving.doc"
    objSpreadSheet1.OLEObjects(1).Height = 200
    objSpreadSheet1.OLEObjects(1).Width = 250
    objSpreadSheet1.OLEObjects(1).TOP = 30
    objSpreadSheet1.OLEObjects(1).Left = 300
    objSpreadSheet1.OLEObjects.Add classtype:="MSGraph"
    Set Chart1 = objWorkBook.Charts.Add(, objSpreadSheet1, 1)
    Chart1.ChartWizard Source:=objSpreadSheet1Range
    objApp.Visible = True
    Chart1.Visible = True
    objSpreadSheet1.Activate
    Set objApp = Nothing
    Set objWorkBook = Nothing
    Set objSpreadSheet1 = Nothing
    Set objSpreadSheet1Range = Nothing
    Set Chart1 = Nothing
    Screen.MousePointer = 0
End Function
```

When you run this application, a fully functional Microsoft Excel application is created. This application is included on the CD-ROM that accompanies this book. Once the application is created, the user can manually exit the application and save changes. Saving the changes creates a permanent copy of the application. If you want to close and destroy the application using Visual Basic code, do the following:

```
Sub CloseExcel()
 iRet% = MsgBox("Click OK to close spreadsheet or Cancel to leave spreadsheet
open", _1, "Close Spreadsheet")
    If iRet% = 2 Then Exit Sub
    objSpreadSheet.Application = Nothing
    Set objSpreadSheet = Nothing
End Sub
```

When you create a spreadsheet from Visual Basic, a copy of Excel may already be open. To let Windows know that you are destroying an Excel instance created by Visual Basic, use the `CloseExcel()` function (see the preceding code). Do not use `objSpreadSheet.Application.Quit`. Because Windows is unsure whether a copy of Excel was already open, this second approach merely flashes the title bar. Only when the application is given the focus does the Save Changes dialog box appear.

Accessing an Existing Excel Application

Once the application is created, you can access it without re-creating it. In the same way, any previously created spreadsheet can be accessed with Visual Basic. The following example opens a preexisting spreadsheet and adds a chart:

```
Sub GetReportData()
 Dim X As Integer
    'The GetObject function retrieves an OLE automation object from a file.
    Set objSpreadSheet = GetObject("c:\msoffice\excel\conrad.xls")
    'Set up values for the chart. This is done by prompting the user for values.
    For X = 1 To 5
        Do
            iValue = InputBox("Enter a value", "Create Chart", 0)
            Loop Until CStr(Val(iValue)) = iValue
            objSpreadSheet.Cells(1, X).VALUE = iValue
    Next X%
    'Show the application
    objSpreadSheet.Application.Visible = True
    objSpreadSheet.Parent.Windows(1).Visible = True
End Sub
```

Notice that because this code does not create any objects (it merely retrieves an existing object using the `GetObject` function), you do not have to destroy any objects on completion of the program.

Microsoft Word

In the first part of this chapter, you created an Excel application totally independent of Visual Basic. In this section, you incorporate the functionality of Microsoft Word into Visual Basic. In the next section, you use OLE Automation to borrow objects that Microsoft Word exposes, eliminating the need to create functionality in your application that is already available in Word.

The best method to use to create the code that objects from Microsoft Word can understand (WordBasic) is to record the commands you need in a Word macro. To record a macro in Word, select Tools | Macro from the main menu. The Macro dialog box displays.

Enter a name for the macro in the Macro Name text box and click Record. The Record Macro dialog box appears (see Figure 24.3). Click OK in this dialog box to begin recording the macro. A small window appears with a Stop and a Pause button (place the mouse over one of the buttons and a ToolTip appears). Once you have finished recording the macro, click the Stop button.

FIGURE 24.3.

The Microsoft Word Macro dialog box. Use the macro recorder to create code you can copy to Visual Basic.

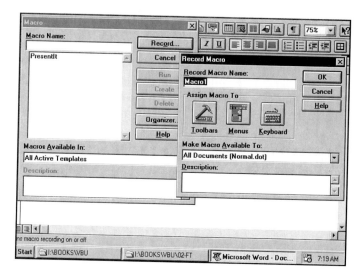

Select Tools | Macro from the main menu again. Click the name of the macro you just created in the list box and click Edit. A new Word document appears, containing the WordBasic code for the macro. With small modifications, this code can be incorporated into the Visual Basic application.

The following fragment of code was created by the macro recorder when I saved an open file with a new name:

```
FileSaveAs .Name = "NEW.DOC", .Format = 0, .LockAnnot = 0, .Password = "",_
 .AddToMru = 1, .WritePassword = "", .RecommendReadOnly = 0, .EmbedFonts = 0, _
.NativePictureFormat = 0, .FormsData = 0
```

This fragment was created when I selected **File** | Page Set**u**p and manipulated some of the page properties:

```
FilePageSetup .Tab = "3", .PaperSize = "1", .TopMargin = "1" + Chr$(34), _
.BottomMargin = "1" + Chr$(34), .LeftMargin = "1.25" + Chr$(34), .RightMargin =
"1.25" + Chr$(34)
```

Selecting Help | Search for Help On creates this WordBasic code:

```
HelpSearch
```

With some manipulation, you can import this code into Visual Basic and manipulate objects Word exposes without creating code from the ground up. It does not take very long to learn the basic functions of Word. The following section creates an instance of the Microsoft Word application and uses many of the objects, properties, and methods Word exposes.

Creating a Word Application

In the `form_load` procedure, you must set a `filename` variable. This is the file to be created with this application:

```
Private Sub Form_Load()
    Dim sFileName as String
    sFileName = "C:\PROJECT\APP.DOC"
End Sub
```

First, create a variable to hold the text box string:

```
Dim sText As String
```

The next step is to create an instance of Microsoft Word. This object is created using the `CreateObject()` function:

```
Dim objWord As Object
Set objWord = CreateObject("word.basic")
```

Now set up an error handler. The reason for this error handler is that Microsoft Word sets the `err` variable to something other than 0 when it completes certain operations. For example, the spelling checker object returns error code 51 when the spell check completes successfully. Without the error handler, Visual Basic pops up an error dialog box.

```
On Error GoTo ErrorHandler
```

Here is the error handler:

```
ErrorHandler:
        Select Case Err
            Case 51     'The spelling checker completed successfully.
                Resume Next
            Case 5003    'A disabled command was selected
                MsgBox "That Command is not available at this time (disabled)"
            Case Else
                MsgBox Error$
        End Select
```

The next step is to get the text the user entered in the text box and place it in a variable:

```
sText = Text1.TEXT
```

Now clear the Clipboard and place the contents of the sText variable into the Clipboard. This text will be added to the newly created document. The 1 in the `Clipboard.SetText` statement indicates that the format of what is being placed on the Clipboard is text:

```
'Clear the clipboard
Clipboard.Clear
'Copy the text in Text1 to the clipboard.
Clipboard.SetText sText, 1
```

Next, check the Clipboard to ensure that the text is there. If there is no text, the user may not have entered anything in the text box. In this case, exit the subprocedure.

```
'There is text on the clipboard
If Clipboard.GetFormat(vbCFText) Then
```

You access the Word object using the `With... End With` statement.

```
With objWord
```

First, create a new Word document:

```
.FileNew
```

The next step is to paste the contents of the Clipboard into the newly created document:

```
.EditPaste
```

Now that you have added text to the document, spell check it. When the spell check is complete, assuming all words are spelled correctly, the `err` variable is 51.

```
.ToolsSpelling
```

Now that the spelling check is complete, select the text and copy it to the Clipboard. The text will be retrieved later by the Visual Basic application that you are creating and placed back into the text box:

```
.EditSelectAll
.EditCopy
```

Now save the newly created document as a file and close the Word document:

```
.FileSaveAs sFileName
.FileClose 2
End With
```

The final step of this subprocedure is to destroy the Word object and set the text box back to blank:

```
Set objWord = Nothing
Text1.TEXT = ""
```

Then retrieve the spell-checked text and place it back into the text box:

```
Text1.TEXT = Clipboard.GetText(vbCFText)
```

In summary, you created an instance of a Microsoft Word object, added a new document, and pasted the contents of the Clipboard to the document. Then you spell-checked the text, saved the document (creating a new document file), and placed the spell-checked text back on the Clipboard. Finally, you pasted the Clipboard contents back into our Visual Basic application's text box. Listing 24.2 shows the finished product.

Listing 24.2. A Word application.

```
Private Sub CreateWordDocument()
    'sFilename is the file that we are going to create.
    Dim sFileName As String
    sFileName = "D:\test.doc"
```

```
'sText is what we will place in the file (the contents of the text box)
Dim sText As String
'Create an instance of Word
Dim objWord As Object
Set objWord = CreateObject("word.basic")
'Prevents errors when spelling checker completes OK.
On Error GoTo ErrorHandler
sText = Text1.TEXT
'Clear the clipboard
Clipboard.Clear
'Copy the text in Text1 to the clipboard
Clipboard.SetText sText, 1
'Check the clipboard to ensure that the text is there
If Clipboard.GetFormat(vbCFText) Then
        'Using the word object
        With objWord
                'Select File ¦ New from the menu to create a new document
                .FileNew
                'Paste the contents of the clipboard into the document
                .EditPaste
                'Spell check the document. If the spell check is successful, error 51
                'occurs.
                .ToolsSpelling
                'Select the text
                .EditSelectAll
                'Copy it to the clipboard
                .EditCopy
                'Save the word document (this creates a file)
                .FileSaveAs sFileName
                'Close the word document
                .FileClose 2
        End With
    Else
        'No text was in the text box
        MsgBox "There is nothing to save."
    End If
    'Destroy the Word object
    Set objWord = Nothing
    'Reset the text box to blank
    Text1.TEXT = ""
    Exit Sub
ErrorHandler:
        Select Case Err
            Case 51
                Resume Next
            Case 5003
                MsgBox "That Command is not available at this time (disabled)"
            Case Else
                MsgBox Error$
        End Select
End Sub
Private Sub GetTextFromClipboard()
    Text1.TEXT = Clipboard.GetText(vbCFText)
End Sub
```

Summary

This chapter outlined some of the ways applications developed in Visual Basic 4.0 can interact with Microsoft Office. A fully functional Excel application was created using only code from Visual Basic. This application contained a spreadsheet with buttons attached to macros. A chart was added to the application as was a module of functions that performed basic operations on the spreadsheet. Finally, a Microsoft Word document that displayed the contents of a document was embedded into the application.

Another application was created using OLE Automation and Microsoft Word. This Visual Basic application used the objects Word exposes to create a Word application and document, send text to the document, spell check the document, and return it to Visual Basic. The Microsoft Word document was then saved as a file.

This chapter provided the base on which you can develop creative, interactive applications that incorporate the OLE Automation objects Microsoft Office exposes.

Using the MAPI Interface with Visual Basic 4.0

25

by Michael Amundsen

Electronic mail capabilities are fast becoming a "must-have" feature for desktop applications. Most network installations today have at least one mail server. Some offices even have multiple mail and messaging platforms all running on the same network. Design specifications for custom applications often includes the capability to send program output to other locations via electronic transfer as one of the basic requirements of the system.

In this chapter, you'll learn how to use the Microsoft Mail Application Programmer Interface (MAPI) to add electronic mail capabilities to your Visual Basic applications. First, you'll get a quick overview of the MAPI interface itself. Then you'll review the two Visual Basic controls you can use to create MAPI applications with Visual Basic. Finally, you'll work through programming examples of the three most common MAPI applications: *electronic mail (e-mail) applications*, *mail-aware applications*, and *mail-enabled applications*.

When you complete this chapter, you'll have a good understanding of the Microsoft MAPI interface and the Visual Basic MAPI controls. You will also be able to design and build applications that can use the MAPI interface to provide mail services from within your Visual Basic programs.

An Overview of the MAPI Interface

The *Mail Application Programming Interface (MAPI)* is a set of API calls that has become the de facto standard for creating e-mail-capable applications for the Windows environment. The MAPI standards provide a high-level set of tools for linking any Windows application with electronic mail message services. You can use these tools to create client applications that can compose, send, and receive electronic messages with any other valid address recognized by the mail server.

The real advantage of using MAPI is that most of the mail servers on the market today recognize and comply with the MAPI standard. If you write your program using MAPI, it will work with Microsoft Mail and Microsoft Exchange without any programming changes at all. You can also expect it to work with non-Microsoft products like Novell's Group Wise, Lotus cc:Mail, and any other e-mail system that is MAPI compatible.

There are two major components to any messaging system: the *server component* and the *client component*. In typical network installations, the mail server usually operates from a single workstation somewhere on the network. One or more client applications can run on the individual workstations connected to the network. The mail server handles all messaging requests generated by the mail client application. MAPI acts as a translator between your Visual Basic client program and the mail server that processes all electronic messages. This chapter deals with the *client side* of electronic mail applications.

Because MAPI is a high-level set of standards, there are really only a handful of basic operations to learn before you can start designing and building mail-aware applications. Along with a core set of functions, there are several support functions you can use to increase the feature set of your Visual Basic mail applications. You'll learn about the core services and the support routines later in this chapter. But first, take a look at the different types of MAPI applications that exist today.

Common MAPI Applications

The topic of mail applications includes a wide range of applications. Any program that can interact with the underlying mail services can be thought of as a mail application. This can range from simple programs that allow users to send and receive one-line messages on up to major systems that are capable of automatically transferring large amounts of data to any location in the world. For the purposes of this chapter, mail applications can be divided into three main groups:

- Electronic Mail (e-mail) applications
- Mail-aware applications
- Mail-enabled applications

Even though all these programs provide some level of interaction with the available mail services, they each have their own set of features that set them apart.

E-mail programs are applications that act as a front-end to the mail server. These applications allow users to create, read, and send messages to each other. Usually, e-mail programs also allow users to define and maintain a list of commonly used e-mail addresses. While all e-mail programs allow users to compose and send text messages, most also provide features for sending binary files such as graphic images, spreadsheets, and so on. These nontext portions of the message are called *attachments*.

Mail-aware applications are programs that provide electronic send and/or receive services as a part of their basic feature set. Mail-aware software is able to use the available mail services much in the same way programs use available printers, modems, or storage media (disk drives, CD-ROMs, and so on). For example, most office suite applications (word processing, spreadsheet, and so on) provide a "Send" feature on the main menu of all their programs. Basically, whatever documents you can create with the program can be sent to other locations using the mail services available on the network.

The third class of applications goes even further in providing mail services as part of their basic structure. These applications are usually referred to as *mail-enabled applications*. These applications use mail services to perform all or part of their primary task. Even more important, users may not even know they are using the mail services. The use of mail services is embedded in the very design of the application. A good example of a mail-enabled application is a trouble call program that prompts users to enter details about a customer service complaint and then automatically forwards the information to one or more individuals who can then act on the request. The person entering the data may not be aware that the information is forwarded on to others using the same network services that are used to send company e-mail messages.

A Typical MAPI Session

The MAPI standards define a small set of core routines for providing mail services to client applications. The core services can be divided into two groups:

- **Session Services.** All tasks related to locating and connecting to (and disconnecting from) the mail services provider.
- **Message Services.** All tasks related to sending and receiving messages via the mail services provider. This also includes creating and maintaining the list of valid message addresses recognized by the mail services provider.

In a typical MAPI session, you need to first establish a connection to the mail server. This involves providing a valid user address and password for the mail server that you are attempting to communicate with. If the user name and password are valid for this mail server, MAPI will return a unique session ID number that will be used in all communications between your Visual Basic program and the mail server.

Once the MAPI session is established, your program has access to the message services provided by the mail server. The core services provided by MAPI-compliant systems include:

- Access messages currently in the Inbox
- Compose a new message
- Send messages
- Save, copy, and delete messages
- Display the Address Book
- Access attachments, including Object Linking and Embedding (OLE) attachments
- Resolve a recipient name during addressing
- Perform reply, reply-all, and forward actions on messages

This list of message services is provided to the client application by the mail server. In other words, the client application tells the server that the client wants to compose a new message. The server then provides all the functionality needed to compose the message. When the client asks for a list of valid addresses, the server provides the list and lets the client select one or more names as the destination address for the message. Finally, when the client tells the server to deliver the message, the server takes the address list and forwards the composed message to each address in the destination list.

The key concept to keep in mind here is that the mail server is performing all the tasks—not the client program. You can write a simple electronic mail program by sending a handful of service requests to the mail server. In fact, later in this chapter, you learn how to create a ten-line Visual Basic program that can compose and send an e-mail message to any valid address.

You can also gain access to MAPI functions that allow your Visual Basic program to provide replacements for many of the high-level MAPI services. You can create your own message input screen, then supply the completed message to the mail server for addressing and delivery. You could also provide your own addressing services and simply tell the mail server to forward the completed and fully addressed message to the appropriate location.

To sum up, no matter how much your Visual Basic program requests of the mail server, the same set of functions must always occur when dealing with the MAPI interface. All MAPI sessions involve the following set of operations:

- Log on to the mail server
- Perform message services such as read, compose, address, and/or send messages
- Log off from the mail server

The rest of this chapter will show you how you can use the MAPI controls that ship with Visual Basic 4.0 Professional Edition to perform the preceding tasks. You will also learn how to use the MAPI controls to create the three types of mail applications (e-mail, mail-aware, and mail-enabled).

The Visual Basic MAPI Controls

> **NOTE**
>
> Throughout the rest of this chapter, there are example programs that illustrate the use of the MAPI controls to create mail-aware applications with Visual Basic 4.0. These example programs will only run correctly on a workstation that has a MAPI-compliant mail server available. If you have the network version of Microsoft Mail, Microsoft Mail for Windows for Workgroups, or Microsoft Exchange Mail, or any other fully MAPI-compliant system up and running in your environment, you will have no problem running the examples in this chapter. If you do not have access to MAPI services, you can still get a lot out of this chapter, but you will not be able to run the examples.

Visual Basic 4.0 Professional Edition ships with two OCX controls that provide access to all the MAPI services you'll need to create fully functional electronic mail applications using Visual Basic. The MAPI Session control provides access to everything you'll need to sign on and sign off any MAPI-compliant server. The MAPI Message control provides access to the MAPI routines that allow you to read, compose, address, and send messages using the session established with the MAPI Session control. This section of the chapter will review the MAPI-related properties and methods of each of these controls.

The *MAPI Session* Control

The MAPI Session control is used to establish a link between your Visual Basic program (the mail client) and the electronic mail server. The MAPI-compliant mail server must be installed and available to the Visual Basic client program. If your program will run on a traditional network server, the mail server may be Microsoft Mail installed on a network workstation. If you are running Windows for Workgroups or Windows 95, Microsoft Mail or Microsoft Exchange (Windows 95 only) can act as a mail server. There are other mail servers available for both file server and peer-to-peer networks.

There are two methods and seven properties for the MAPI Session control that are directly MAPI related. The following two sections identify these components of the MAPI Session control, their meaning, and their use in Visual Basic programs.

Methods of the *MAPI Session* Control

There are only two MAPI Session methods: SignOn and SignOff. The SignOn method is used to begin a MAPI session. By default, the SignOn method provides a log-in dialog box that prompts the user for valid log-in information. The exact nature of the log-in dialog box depends on the mail server. The Microsoft Mail log-in dialog box prompts the user for a valid username and password (see Figure 25.1).

FIGURE 25.1.

Default log-in dialog box for Microsoft Mail.

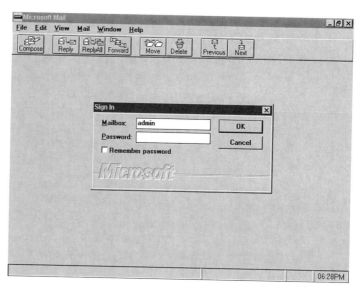

The default log-in dialog box for the Microsoft Exchange Mail product simply asks the user to select the desired mail services profile (see Figure 25.2).

FIGURE 25.2.

Default log-in dialog box for Microsoft Exchange Mail.

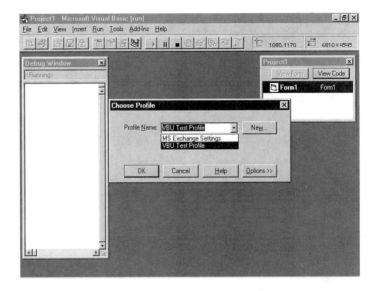

If a valid username and password are supplied via the SignOn method, the MAPI Session control returns a unique value in the SeesionID property. This unique value is used in all message transactions to identify the link between the client application and the mail server. You'll learn more about the SessionID property in the next section.

The SignOff method of the MAPI Session control does just what you'd expect. You use the SignOff method to safely end your link to the mail server. There is no dialog box associated with the SignOff method.

In order to use the MAPI Session control methods, you must first place the MAPI Session control on a Visual Basic form. The form is invisible at run-time and is used only to provide the methods and properties needed to establish a MAPI session between your Visual Basic program and the mail server.

As an example of the MAPI Session control, start a Visual Basic project. Use the Tools | Custom Controls menu item to add the Microsoft MAPI controls to your project. Place a MAPI Session control on the form and add the following code to the form load event.

Listing 25.1. MAPI session SignOn and SignOff.

```
Private Sub Form_Load()
    '
    ' smallest e-mail program
    '
    MAPISession1.SignOn
    MAPISession1.SignOff
    End
    '
End Sub
```

Save the form as vbu2501.frm and the project as vbu2501.vbp and run the project. You'll see the default log-in dialog box provided by your mail server. After you sign in, the Visual Basic program immediately signs you out and ends. You'll add more features as you go along.

Properties of the *MAPI Session* Control

The MAPI Session control has seven MAPI-related properties. These properties all deal with options that you can set to control the behavior of the control at log-in time.

The Action property can be used to invoke the sign-on or sign-off methods. This property was present in Visual Basic 3.0 and has been replaced by the SignOn and SignOff methods discussed earlier.

The DownloadMail property is used to control whether new messages are downloaded from the mail server at log-in time. By default, all new messages are forced to the user's mail box at log-in time. You can set this property to False to prevent this from happening. In the following code example, the DownloadMail property has been set to False before invoking the SignOn method.

Listing 25.2. Disabling mail download at SignOn.

```
Private Sub Form_Load()
    '
    ' smallest e-mail program
    '
    MAPISession1.DownloadMail = False ' dont get new mail
    MAPISession1.SignOn
    MAPISession1.SignOff
    End
    '
End Sub
```

The LogonUI property can be used to turn off the default log-in screen provided by the mail server. You can set this property to False to suppress the mail server from presenting the log-in screen when you invoke the SignOn method. If you set this property to False, you must supply valid data in the UserName and Password properties, or an error will be reported.

You can use the NewSession property to force the creation of a new MAPI session, even if a MAPI session already exists for this workstation. By default, the SignOn method will attempt to locate any current MAPI interface session before attempting to log into the mail server. When you set the NewSession parameter to True, the SignOn method will create a second MAPI session link with the mail server. Listing 25.3 shows how you can accomplish this.

Listing 25.3. Forcing a new session at `SignOn`.

```
Private Sub Form_Load()
    '
    ' smallest e-mail program
    '
    MAPISession1.DownloadMail = False    ' dont get new mail
    MAPISession1.NewSession = True       ' force a unique session
    MAPISession1.SignOn
    MAPISession1.SignOff
    End
    '
End Sub
```

The `Password` and `UserName` properties should be set to valid values if you want to bypass the default log-in screen. If you supply a `UserName` but leave the `Password` property blank, the `SignOn` method will force the log-in dialog box to appear to fill out the missing information. If, however, the `LogonUI` property is set to `False`, no dialog box will appear, and an error will be returned.

If you are using the Microsoft Exchange Mail Client, you only need to provide a valid Profile Name. Microsoft Exchange Mail will ignore any value in the `Password` property. If you are using the Microsoft Mail client (network or workgroup version), you will need to supply both the `UserName` and the `Password` properties if you want to bypass the default log-in dialog box.

Listing 25.4 shows how to perform an automatic log-on for Microsoft Mail. If you want to log on to Microsoft Exchange, replace the UserName with a valid Exchange profile name (MS Exchange Settings is the default) and leave the Password property blank.

Listing 25.4. Automatic log-in at session `SignOn`.

```
Private Sub Form_Load()
    '
    ' smallest e-mail program
    '
    MAPISession1.DownloadMail = False    ' dont get new mail
    MAPISession1.NewSession = True       ' force a unique session
    MAPISession1.UserName = "MCA"        ' username for mail
    MAPISession1.Password = "PASSWORD"   ' users password
    MAPISession1.SignOn
    MAPISession1.SignOff
    End
    '
End Sub
```

The `SessionID` property is a read-only property available only at run time that contains the unique session ID number of a completed link between your Visual Basic program and the mail server. This session ID value must be used in all transactions to the mail server. This value is used to set the `SessionID` of the `MAPI Message` control before attempting to access the message services provided by the mail server.

In Listing 25.4, you'll see an added message box that shows the unique MAPI Session Handle.

> **NOTE**
>
> In Listing 25.5, the UserName is set to VBU Profile. The default Exchange profile is called MS Exchange Profile. You can use any valid profile that has been defined for your system.

Listing 25.5. Auto log-in to Microsoft Exchange.

```
Private Sub Form_Load()
    '
    ' smallest e-mail program
    '
    MAPISession1.DownloadMail = False     ' don't get new mail
    MAPISession1.NewSession = True        ' force a unique session
    MAPISession1.UserName = "VBU Profile" ' username for mail
    MAPISession1.Password = ""            ' users password
    MAPISession1.SignOn
    MsgBox Str(MAPISession1.SessionID)    ' show unique session handle
    MAPISession1.SignOff
    End
    '
End Sub
```

Modify the UserName and, if needed, the Password properties to contain valid log-in data for your mail server. Then save and run the project. You will see a message box that shows the unique session handle for the MAPI link (see Figure 25.3).

FIGURE 25.3.

Displaying the SessionID of a MAPI Link.

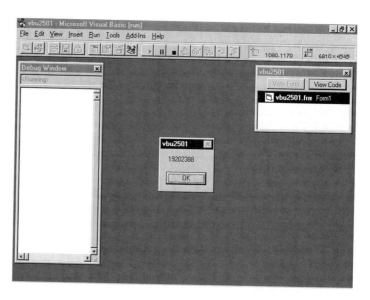

The *MAPI Message* Control

The MAPI Message control gives your Visual Basic program access to all the message services available from the mail server with which your program has established a session. The MAPI Message control provides services for reading, composing, addressing, and sending mail messages. You can perform all major mail operations simply by requesting the service from the server.

The MAPI Message control has four primary responsibilities:

- Create and send messages
- Read any new messages
- Delete any old messages
- Maintain the address list

There are 11 methods and over 30 properties of the MAPI Message control that are MAPI-related. These methods and properties are reviewed briefly here. You can find additional documentation on each of the MAPI Message properties in the Visual Basic online help files.

Methods of the *MAPI Message* Control

There are 11 methods for the MAPI Message control. These methods fall into four general categories:

- **Create and Send Messages.** Uses the Compose, Copy, Forward, Reply, Reply All, and Send methods
- **Reading Messages.** Uses the Fetch method.
- **Managing Old Messages.** Uses the Save and Delete methods.
- **Maintaining the Address List.** Uses the Show and ResolveName methods.

The message creation methods account for six of the 11 methods. Of these six, you only need to know two before you can create a functional e-mail application. The Compose method clears out the edit buffer area and prepares a clean slate for the creation of a new message. The Send method will attempt to send the new message to the address supplied. If an address or message is not supplied, the Send method will force the mail server to present the default message compose form to the user.

In other words, you can create a complete e-mail composer by adding only two lines to the code you started earlier in this chapter. The following code in Listing 25.6 is all you need to be able to create a Visual Basic application that can compose and send e-mail messages. Start a new Visual Basic project and add the MAPI Session and the MAPI Message controls to the form. Then add the following code to the Form_Load event.

Listing 25.6. Complete e-mail composer.

```
Private Sub Form_Load()
    '
    ' smallest e-mail program
    '
    MAPISession1.SignOn      ' log into MAPI server
    MAPIMessages1.SessionID = MAPISession1.SessionID
    '
    MAPIMessages1.Compose    ' clear buffers
    MAPIMessages1.Send True ' show default form
    '
    MAPISession1.SignOff     ' exit MAPI server
    End
    '
End Sub
```

Now save the form as vbu2502.frm and the project as vbu2502.vbp and run the program. You'll be prompted for a log-in, and then you'll see the default compose form. Figure 25.4 shows what comes up if you are using Microsoft Exchange Mail.

FIGURE 25.4.

The default compose form for Microsoft Exchange.

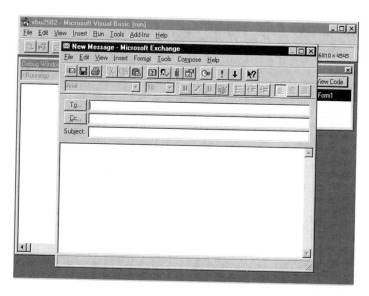

Notice that you have a highly functional e-mail program with very little coding. Use this form to send yourself a message. You'll use other Visual Basic code to read the message later in this chapter.

You can use the other message creation methods (Copy, Forward, Reply, and ReplyAll) to load the compose buffer with messages that have been sent to you by others. You can then use the default compose dialog box to edit the old message and send it just as you would a new message you created from scratch. The Forward, Reply, and ReplyAll methods also alter the subject line to reflect the action. For example, when you use the Forward method, the mail server will add FW: to the beginning of the subject line. The Reply and ReplyAll methods place RE: at the start of the subject line.

The code in Listing 25.7 takes the first message in the user's Inbox and copies it to the compose buffer with FW: on the subject line.

Listing 25.7. Forwarding a message.

```
Private Sub Form_Load()
    '
    ' smallest e-mail program
    '
    MAPISession1.SignOn    ' log into MAPI server
    MAPIMessages1.SessionID = MAPISession1.SessionID
    '
    MAPIMessages1.Fetch      ' get meesages
    MAPIMessages1.Forward    ' forward the current message
    MAPIMessages1.Send True ' send it
    '
    MAPISession1.SignOff    ' exit MAPI server
    End
    '
End Sub
```

You can use the Fetch method to tell the mail server to send your Visual Basic program all the messages that are currently on file in the Inbox for the logged-in user. The following code example fetches all the messages for the user and then uses the MsgCount property to find out how many messages are actually on file.

Listing 25.8. Getting a message count.

```
Private Sub Form_Load()
    '
    ' smallest e-mail program
    '
    MAPISession1.SignOn    ' log into MAPI server
    MAPIMessages1.SessionID = MAPISession1.SessionID
    '
    MAPIMessages1.Fetch      ' get all messages into inbox
    MsgBox Str(MAPIMessages1.MsgCount)  ' show number of msgs
    '
    MAPISession1.SignOff    ' exit MAPI server
    End
    '
End Sub
```

You can use the Delete method to remove messages from the user's collection. The Delete method can also be used to remove a single recipient from a list of addresses or to remove a single attachment from a list of currently attached files. The following code in Listing 25.9 removes the current message from the user's collection.

Listing 25.9. Deleting a message.

```
Private Sub Form_Load()
    '
    ' smallest e-mail program
    '
    MAPISession1.SignOn      ' log into MAPI server
    MAPIMessages1.SessionID = MAPISession1.SessionID
    '
    MAPIMessages1.Fetch      ' get all messages into inbox
    MsgBox Str(MAPIMessages1.MsgCount)
    MAPIMessages1.Delete     ' get rid of first message
    MsgBox Str(MAPIMessages1.MsgCount)
    '
    MAPISession1.SignOff     ' exit MAPI server
    End
    '
End Sub
```

Finally, you can tell the mail server to show you a list of all the mail server addresses on file by invoking the Show method. You can also use the Show method to display details of the current message recipient (if this is supported by the MAPI mail server). The following code in Listing 25.10 will display the current mail server address list.

Listing 25.10. Displaying the Address Book.

```
Private Sub Form_Load()
    '
    ' smallest e-mail program
    '
    MAPISession1.SignOn      ' log into MAPI server
    MAPIMessages1.SessionID = MAPISession1.SessionID
    '
    MAPIMessages1.Show       ' show the addresss list
    '
    MAPISession1.SignOff     ' exit MAPI server
    End
    '
End Sub
```

Properties of the *MAPI Message* Control

The MAPI Message control has more than 30 MAPI-related properties. I will go through a quick review of them here. You can find more detailed information on each of the MAPI Message control properties by consulting the topic "MAPI Message Control" in the Visual Basic on-line help file.

The MAPI Message control properties can be divided into several groups. Each group contains a set of properties that all deal with the same aspect of the message services provided by the mail server. Table 25.1 shows the MAPI-related properties, divided by service group.

Table 25.1. MAPI-related properties of the `MAPI Message` **control.**

Group	Property	Description
Address	AddressCaption	Allows you to set the caption of the Address Book dialog box.
	AddressEditFieldCount	Use this property to set the number of edit buttons available on the Address book dialog box.
	AddressLabel	If you use only one edit button (To:), you can set the button label with this property.
	AddressModifiable	When set to `True`, allows the user to modify the contents of the address book. Default is `False`.
	AddressResolveUI	When set to `True`, presents a dialog box to help the user resolve rejected addresses. Use this property in conjunction with the `ResolveName` method. Default is `False`.
Attachment	AttachmentCount	Contains the number of attachments for the current message.
	AttachmentIndex	Pointer to the current attachment in the list.
	AttachmentName	File name of the attachment pointed to by the `AttachmentIndex` property.
	AttachmentPathName	Contains full path name of the current attachment.
	AttachmentPosition	Position (in characters) where the attachment is located within the message body.
	AttachmentType	Indicates the type of the current attachment. Valid values are `DATA` (data file), `EOLE` (embedded OLE object), and `SOLE` (static OLE object).
Fetch	FetchMsgType	Contains the type of message to look for when executing the `Fetch` method. Not commonly used by current products.
	FetchSorted	Controls sort order when building message collection. Set to `True` for First In, First Out sort order. Set to `False` to sort by user's Inbox Setting. Default is `False`.

continues

Table 25.1. continued

Group	Property	Description
	FetchUnreadOnly	Set to True to get only the unread messages into the user's collection. If False, all messages for the user's ID are loaded into the local set. Default is True.
Message	MsgConversationID	Contains internally generated ID that keeps track of all messages in a related "thread." You can use this value to collect all related messages into a single group.
	MsgCount	Contains the total number of messages in the set.
	MsgDateReceived	Date the current message was received.
	MsgID	Internally generated unique ID value.
	MsgIndex	Pointer to the current message in the message collection.
	MsgNoteText	This is the actual body of the message (less any attachments).
	MsgOrigAddress	Address of the originator (sender) of the current message.
	MsgOrigDisplayName	Contains the "display name" associated with the MsgOrigAddress property.
	MsgRead	Flag to indicate that the message has been read by the user to which it was addressed. When set to True, the user has read the message.
	MsgReceiptRequested	Flag to indicate that a return receipt has been requested by the sender. When set to True, the sender wants a confirmation that the message has been successfully delivered.
	MsgSent	Flag to show that the message has been sent to the mail server for delivery. This flag is updated by the server, not the client.
	MsgSubject	The text line that identifies the subject of the message.
	MsgType	Contains the message type code. Currently, all MsgType code is left null or empty to indicate an Interpersonal Message (IPM).

Group	Property	Description
Recipient	RecipAddress	Address of the current recipient (could be a list of 'em!).
	RecipCount	Contains the number of recipients for the current piece of mail.
	RecipDisplayName	The "display name" associated with address in the address book.
	RecipIndex	Points to the current recipient in the list.
	RecipType	Shows what type of recipient is currently pointed to by the RecipType flag. OrigList = 0 (the message editor); 1 = a (person in the TO: address list; 2 = a (person on the Carbon Copy list); 3 = a (person on the BccList/blind Carbon Copy list).
Other	Action	Carry-over from Visual Basic 3.0—use the new methods instead.
	SessionID	Contains the value of the SessionID generated by the MAPI Session control. You must update this property before you can perform any Message operations.

You can use these properties to modify the behavior of the MAPI dialog boxes supplied by the mail server. For example, you can change the caption of the address list, change the number of buttons that appear on the list, even change the caption of the To: button. You can also use these properties to add increased functionality to your Visual Basic mail applications by honoring attached documents, allowing the use of blind carbon copy recipients, and so on.

There are a number of things you can do with the numerous properties of the MAPI Message control, but one of the most useful is the capability to create e-mail attachments. That is the subject of the next section.

Creating E-Mail Attachments

Creating e-mail attachments is very useful and very easy to do with the MAPI Message control and Visual Basic 4.0. Attachments can be simple text files, word processing documents, and even databases. For this example, you'll attach a system file from a user's work station and prepare a message to send to the help desk at a large corporation.

There are four property values you need to set in order to successfully create an e-mail attachment. These four properties are:

- **AttachmentPathName.** This contains the complete file name as it is used by the operating system (c:\config.sys or \\server\directory1\file.ext).

- **AttachmentName.** This is a text string that appears under the attachment icon in the message.

- **AttachmentType.** This flag tells the server what type of attachment you are using. Visual Basic constants for this property are mapData (a data file), mapEOLE (an embedded OLE object), and mapSOLE (a static OLE object).

- **AttachmentPosition.** This is an integer value that contains the exact character position in the message text that the attachment icon is to appear.

> **NOTE**
>
> If you plan on adding multiple attachments to the message, you'll also need to use the AttachmentCount and AttachmentIndex properties to fetch the attachments when you read the message.

You can add an attachment to any valid message in the compose buffer. The following code example creates a new message and adds the workstation's CONFIG.SYS file as an attachment. Modify the FormLoad event of vbu2502.frm to match the code in Listing 25.11.

Listing 25.11. Creating an e-mail attachment.

```
Private Sub Form_Load()
    '
    ' smallest e-mail program
    '
    MAPISession1.SignOn      ' log into MAPI server
    MAPIMessages1.SessionID = MAPISession1.SessionID
    '
    MAPIMessages1.Compose    ' clear buffer
    MAPIMessages1.MsgSubject = "User's CONFIG.SYS File"
    MAPIMessages1.MsgNoteText = "Here is the CONFIG.SYS File" + Chr(13) + " "
    '
    MAPIMessages1.AttachmentPosition = Len(MAPIMessages1.MsgNoteText)
    MAPIMessages1.AttachmentType = mapData
    MAPIMessages1.AttachmentName = "System Configuration File"
    MAPIMessages1.AttachmentPathName = "C:\CONFIG.SYS"
    '
    MAPIMessages1.Send True ' send it
    '
    MAPISession1.SignOff     ' exit MAPI server
    End
    '
End Sub
```

Now save and run the vbu2502.vbp project. After logging into the mail server, you'll see a form appear with the C:\CONFIG.SYS file already attached to the message (see Figure 25.5).

FIGURE 25.5.

Viewing an added attachment to the message.

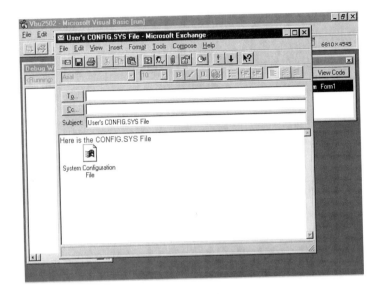

In the final three sections of this chapter, you will create three different MAPI applications using Visual Basic 4.0. Each application will illustrate the three types of mail applications:

- Electronic mail (e-mail) applications
- Mail-aware applications
- Mail-enabled applications

Creating E-Mail Applications with Visual Basic 4.0

In this first programming example, you'll build a very simple electronic mail application that will get any new messages sent to the user and will allow the user to edit, store, and/or delete those messages. The user will also be able to create and maintain addresses in their personal address book.

This application will require very little in the way of Visual Basic code and only two forms are needed. The first form will be the main form that the user sees. This form will contain a list of all the messages in the user's Inbox and a set of buttons giving the user access to the various message services. Refer to Figure 25.6 and Table 25.2 for layout details.

FIGURE 25.6.

*Laying out the main form
for the Simple Mail Tool.*

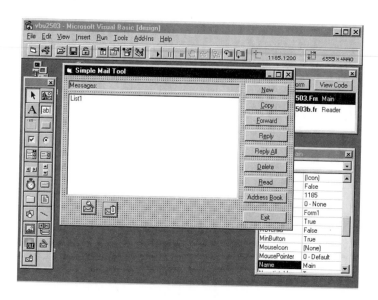

Table 25.2 shows a control array containing nine command buttons. Add the first button, then copy and paste the other eight buttons on the form.

Table 25.2. Control table for the main form of the Simple Mail Tool.

Control	Property	Setting
Form	Name	Main
	Caption	Simple Mail Tool
	Height	4440
	Left	1380
	Top	1710
	Width	6555
Command Button	Name	Command1(0)
	Caption	&New
	Height	300
	Left	5100
	Top	120
	Width	1200

Control	Property	Setting
Command Button	Name	Command1(1)
	Caption	&Copy
	Height	300
	Left	5100
	Top	540
	Width	1200
Command Button	Name	Command1(2)
	Caption	&Forward
	Height	300
	Left	5100
	Top	960
	Width	1200
Command Button	Name	Command1(3)
	Caption	R&eply
	Height	300
	Left	5100
	Top	1380
	Width	1200
Command Button	Name	Command1(4)
	Caption	Reply &All
	Height	300
	Left	5100
	Top	1800
	Width	120
Command Button	Name	Command1(5)
	Caption	&Delete
	Height	300
	Left	5100
	Top	2220
	Width	1200

continues

Table 25.2. continued

Control	Property	Setting
Command Button	Name	Command1(6)
	Caption	&Read
	Height	300
	Left	5100
	Top	2640
	Width	1200
Command Button	Name	Command1(7)
	Caption	Address &Book
	Height	300
	Left	5100
	Top	3060
	Width	1200
Command Button	Name	Command1(8)
	Caption	E&xit
	Height	300
	Left	5100
	Top	3600
	Width	1200
List Box	Name	List1
	Height	2790
	Left	120
	Top	480
	Width	4815
Label	Name	Label1
	BorderStyle	1 - Fixed
	Caption	Messages:
	Height	255
	Left	120
	Top	120
	Width	4815
MAPI Session	Name	MAPISession1
MAPI Message	Name	MAPIMessages1

Now you can add the code behind the controls. First add the code that will perform the MAPI Session log-on. Place the code in Listing 25.12 in the FormLoad event of the form.

Listing 25.12. Start session and get messages.

```
Private Sub Form_Load()
    '
    ' attempt signon
    '
    On Error GoTo FormLoadErr
    '
    MAPISession1.SignOn ' tell server to log me in
    MAPIMessages1.SessionID = MAPISession1.SessionID
    GetMessages         ' get lots of messages
    '
    Exit Sub
    '
FormLoadErr:
    MsgBox Error$, vbCritical, "Error Code " + Str(Err)
    Unload Me
    End
End Sub
```

This routine calls a module to get the messages (GetMessage). I'll define that in just a bit. Next, add the code in Listing 25.13 to the Form_Unload event.

Listing 25.13. End MAPI session.

```
Private Sub Form_Unload(Cancel As Integer)
    '
    On Error Resume Next
    MAPISession1.SignOff
    '
End Sub
```

Now it's time to create a new Sub procedure called GetMessages. The routine in Listing 25.14 will fetch the messages from the mail server and load the subject lines into the list control for you to view.

Listing 25.14. Load messages into Visual Basic List control.

```
Public Sub GetMessages()
    '
    ' get all unread stuff from this user
    '
    Dim x As Integer
    Dim cLine As String
    '
```

continues

Listing 25.14. continued

```
    On Error GoTo GetMessagesErr
    '
    MAPIMessages1.Fetch        ' get messages from server
    '
    List1.Clear                ' clear local list control
    If MAPIMessages1.MsgCount > 0 Then  ' got at least one?
        For x = 0 To MAPIMessages1.MsgCount - 1
            MAPIMessages1.MsgIndex = x        ' move pointer
            cLine = MAPIMessages1.MsgSubject    ' get subject
            List1.AddItem cLine        ' add to list control
        Next x
    End If
    '
    Exit Sub
    '
GetMessagesErr:
    MsgBox Error$, vbCritical, "Error Code: " + Str(Err)
    Unload Me
    '
End Sub
```

The next routine you need is the one that responds to the command button array. Because you built the control array, you can place all the real substantial commands in one module. Place the code in Listing 25.15 in the Command1_Click event.

Listing 25.15. Event code for Command Button array.

```
Private Sub Command1_Click(Index As Integer)
    '
    ' handle user clicks
    '
    On Error GoTo Command1ClickErr
    '
    Dim nTemp As Integer
    '
    Select Case Index
        Case 0
            ' new message
            MAPIMessages1.Compose      ' clear compose buffer
            MAPIMessages1.Send True    ' start server dialog
        Case 1
            ' copy message
            MAPIMessages1.MsgIndex = List1.ListIndex    ' point to msg
            MAPIMessages1.Copy         ' copy in to compose buffer
            MAPIMessages1.Send True    ' start server dialog
        Case 2
            ' forward message
            MAPIMessages1.MsgIndex = List1.ListIndex    ' point to msg
            MAPIMessages1.Forward      ' copy as forwarded in to buffer
            MAPIMessages1.Send True    ' start dialog
        Case 3
            ' reply to message
            MAPIMessages1.MsgIndex = List1.ListIndex    ' point to msg
```

```
              MAPIMessages1.Reply       ' copy as reply into buffer
              MAPIMessages1.Send True ' start server dialog
         Case 4
             ' reply to all senders
             MAPIMessages1.MsgIndex = List1.ListIndex   ' point to msg
             MAPIMessages1.ReplyAll  ' copy as reply all into buffer
             MAPIMessages1.Send True ' start server dialog
         Case 5
             ' delete message
             nTemp = MsgBox("Delete Current Message?", vbYesNo, "Delete Message")
             If nTemp = vbYes Then       ' if confirmed delete
                 MAPIMessages1.MsgIndex = List1.ListIndex     ' point to msg
                 MAPIMessages1.Delete       ' tell server to delete msg
                 GetMessages               ' refresh local list
             End If
         Case 6
             ' read message
             MAPIMessages1.MsgIndex = List1.ListIndex     ' point to msg
             Reader.Show vbModal      ' start read form
         Case 7
             ' address book
             MAPIMessages1.Show        ' show book
         Case 8
             ' exit program
             nTemp = MsgBox("Exit Program?", vbInformation + vbYesNo, "Program
             ➡Exit")
             If nTemp = vbYes Then     ' if confirmed exit
                 Unload Me             ' shut down
             End If

    End Select
    '
    Exit Sub
    '
Command1ClickErr:
    MsgBox Error$, vbCritical, "Error Code: " + Str(Err)
    '
End Sub
```

The only thing you have left to do here is to add a line of code to the List1_DblClick event.
The line of code in Listing 25.16 will fire off the Click event for the Read button each time the
user double-clicks on an item in the list.

Listing 25.16. Activate message read from List control.

```
Private Sub List1_DblClick()
    Command1_Click 6      ' read message
End Sub
```

Save this form as vbu2503.frm and the project as vbu2503.vbp. You can run this if you wish.
You can perform all the tasks except reading existing messages. You'll add that form next.

Add a new form to the project. Use Figure 25.7 and Table 25.3 to complete the form layout.

FIGURE 25.7.

Laying out the reader form.

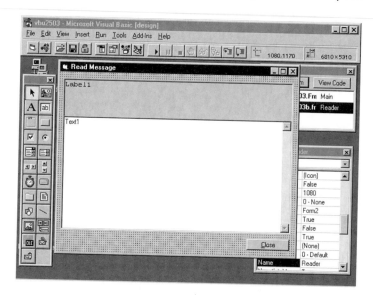

Table 25.3. Control table for the Reader form.

Control	Property	Setting
Form	Name	Reader
	Caption	Read Message
	Height	5310
	Left	1080
	Top	1170
	Width	6810
Label	Name	Label1
	BorderStyle	1 - Fixed
	Font	MS LineDraw, 10pt
	Height	1035
	Left	120
	Top	180
	Width	6435
Text Box	Name	Text1
	Height	3075
	Left	120
	MultiLine	-1 True

Control	Property	Setting
Text Box	ScrollBars	2 - Vertical
	Top	1200
	Width	6435
Command Button	Name	Command1
	Caption	&Close
	Height	300
	Left	5340
	Top	4440
	Width	1200

You need only three code pieces for this form. The first occurs in the Form_Load event. The code in Listing 25.17 loads the label and the text controls.

Listing 25.17. Load current message for reading.

```
Private Sub Form_Load()
    '
    ' load message into form
    '
    On Error GoTo FormLoadErr

    Label1 = "Date:      " + Main.MAPIMessages1.MsgDateReceived + Chr(13)
    Label1 = Label1 + "From:      " + Main.MAPIMessages1.MsgOrigDisplayName +
    ➡Chr(13)
    Label1 = Label1 + "Subject:  " + Main.MAPIMessages1.MsgSubject + Chr(13)
    '
    Text1 = Main.MAPIMessages1.MsgNoteText
    '
    Exit Sub
    '
FormLoadErr:
    MsgBox Error$, vbCritical, "Error Code: " + Str(Err)
    Unload Me
End Sub
```

The only other things you'll need are a line behind the Exit button and a line to disable data entry in the text control. First, add to code in Listing 25.18 behind the Exit button.

Listing 25.18. Unload Message Reader form.

```
Private Sub Command1_Click()
    Unload Me
End Sub
```

Now add the following line of code in Listing 25.19 to the KeyPress event of the Text box control. This code will ignore any attempts to type within the control.

Listing 25.19. Ignore keyboard during Message Read.

```
Private Sub Text1_KeyPress(KeyAscii As Integer)
    KeyAscii = 0    ' ignore all keys
End Sub
```

Save this form as vbu2503b.frm and run the project. After responding to the MAPI Log-In dialog box, you'll see the main form (see Figure 25.8).

FIGURE 25.8.

Running the Simple Mail Tool.

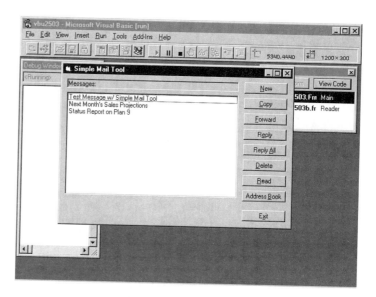

You now have a fully functional mail front end with less than 100 lines of code! Of course, you could spice this up with other features and goodies, too.

Creating Mail-Aware Applications with Visual Basic 4.0

The next category of MAPI applications is the mail-aware application. This is a program that offers mail services as an "added feature." A good example of this is the Send option in Word, Excel, Access, and the other Microsoft Office programs.

Making your Visual Basic programs "mail-aware" is about the same as making them aware of a printer. Usually, you can add a Send option to the main menu and treat the output to the mail server the same way you produce output to the printer. It is possible that you may have to create an interim ASCII text file that you can then import into the message text using the clipboard or a few lines of Visual Basic code. All in all, it's quite easy.

For this example, you'll borrow the code from a sample program that ships with Visual Basic 4.0 Standard Edition: the MDI sample application. This can be found in the `samples\mdi\` folder within the main Visual Basic folder. If you do not have this application or if you want to leave your copy alone, you can find another copy of it in the `\vbu\chap25\mdi` folder on the CD-ROM shipped with this book.

This MDI application is a simple project that creates a multi-document editor that can save documents as ASCII files. To make this system mail-aware will require a few lines of code behind a Send... menu item in one form.

Load the MDI project and open the NOTEPAD form. First, add the `MAPI Session` and `MAPI Message` controls to the bottom of the form. Next, add a separator line and a Send... menu item just after the Save As... menu item (see Figure 25.9).

FIGURE 25.9.

Modifying the NOTEPAD form.

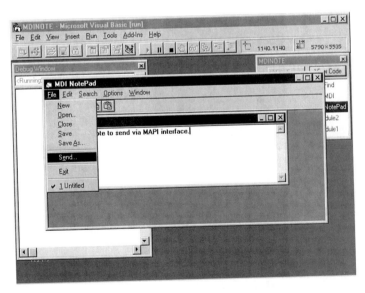

Finally, add the code in Listing 25.20 to the `mnuFileSend_Click` event. This is all the code you need to make this application mail-aware.

Listing 25.20. MAPI Send routine for NOTEPAD.

```
Private Sub mnuFileSend_Click()
    '
    ' log onto mail server
    ' start mail compose session
    ' log off mail server
    '
    On Error GoTo mnuFileSendErr
    '
    '
    MAPISession1.DownloadMail = False   ' dont check box
    MAPISession1.SignOn       ' start mail session
    MAPIMessages1.SessionID = MAPISession1.SessionID
    '
    ' handle sending msg
    MAPIMessages1.Compose     ' clear buffer
    MAPIMessages1.MsgNoteText=Me.Text1 ' move text to message
    MAPIMessages1.MsgSubject = Me.Caption ' get subject
    MAPIMessages1.Send True ' show server dialog
    '
    MAPISession1.SignOff      ' end mail session
    '
    Exit Sub
    '
mnuFileSendErr:
    MsgBox Error$, vbCritical, "Mail Send Error " + Str(Err)
    On Error Resume Next
    MAPISession1.SignOff
    '
End Sub
```

Notice that the DownloadMail property is set to skip over checking the Inbox. The Inbox isn't important here; you just want to send this document to someone via the mail server. The message text and message subject are set using data from the input form.

Now save and run the project. Begin to edit a new document (see Figure 25.10).

When you are done editing the text, select the Send... menu item to send the document out. You'll see the default compose form appear with the text and subject already supplied (see Figure 25.11).

There is a way to "bury" the mail features even deeper into this application. You really only need a way to tack on an address to this document. The following code shows a modified routine that calls only the address dialog and then sends the document out.

FIGURE 25.10.

Using the MDI application.

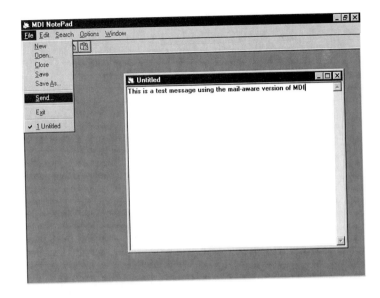

FIGURE 25.11.

The MDI text ready to address and send.

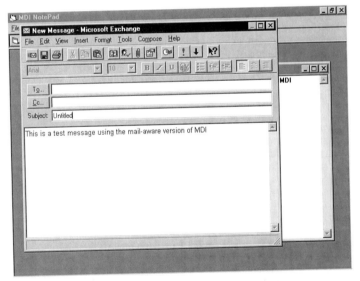

NOTE

In the code in Listing 25.21, it is possible for the user to call the address book and exit it without selecting a valid address. This will be reported as an error when the Send method is invoked. To prevent the error, you could add a check the RecipAddress property before invoking the Send method.

Listing 25.21. Sending NOTEPAD using Address Book.

```
Private Sub mnuFileSend_Click()
    '
    ' log onto mail server
    ' start mail compose session
    ' log off mail server
    '
    On Error GoTo mnuFileSendErr
    '
    MAPISession1.DownloadMail = False   ' dont check box
    MAPISession1.SignOn      ' start mail session
    MAPIMessages1.SessionID = MAPISession1.SessionID
    '
    ' handle sending msg
    MAPIMessages1.Compose    ' clear buffer
    MAPIMessages1.MsgNoteText = Me.Text1   ' get text
    MAPIMessages1.MsgSubject = Me.Caption  ' get subject
    MAPIMessages1.Show       ' get address
    MAPIMessages1.Send       ' send without dialog
    '
    MAPISession1.SignOff     ' end mail session
    '
    Exit Sub
    '
mnuFileSendErr:
    MsgBox Error$, vbCritical, "Mail Send Error " + Str(Err)
    On Error Resume Next
    MAPISession1.SignOff
    '
End Sub
```

Save and run this project. When you select the Send... menu, you now will see only the address dialog before the program sends your document out to the server.

As you can see, it's not at all difficult to add mail features to your existing applications.

Creating Mail-Enabled Applications with Visual Basic 4.0

The final category of mail applications to demonstrate is the "mail-enabled" type. This is a program that has mail services as a basic part of its structure. In this case, you will build a single form that will handle trouble call reports and route the message to an appropriate person for resolution. This is a very simplistic version of a mail-aware application, but it will touch on the main points.

FIGURE 25.12.

Laying out the mail enabled Trouble Call form.

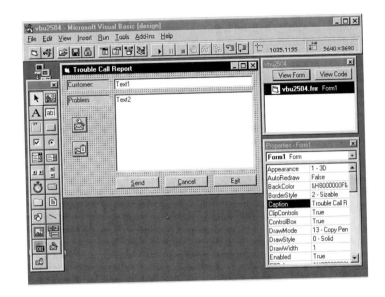

Use Figure 25.12 and Table 25.4 to lay out the simple trouble call data entry form.

Table 25.4. Control table for the Trouble Call form.

Controls	Property	Setting
Form	Name	frmTrouble
	Caption	Trouble Call Report
	Height	3690
	Left	1035
	Top	1155
	Width	5640
Label	Name	Label1
	Borderstyle	1 - Fixed
	Caption	Customer:
	Height	300
	Left	120
	Top	120
	Width	1200

continues

Table 25.4. continued

Controls	Property	Setting
Label	Name	Label2
	Borderstyle	1 - Fixed
	Caption	Problem:
	Height	300
	Left	120
	Top	540
	Width	1200
Text Box	Name	Text1
	Height	300
	Left	1440
	Top	120
	Width	3915
Text Box	Name	Text2
	Height	2115
	Left	1440
	Multi-Line	True
	ScrollBars	2 - Vertical
	Top	540
	Width	3915
Command Button	Name	Command1(0)
	Caption	&Send
	Height	300
	Left	1440
	Top	2820
	Width	1200
Command Button	Name	Command1(1)
	Caption	&Cancel
	Height	300
	Left	2820
	Top	2820
	Width	1200

Controls	Property	Setting
Command Button	Name	Command1(2)
	Caption	E&xit
	Height	300
	Left	4200
	Top	2820
	Width	1200
MAPI Session	Name	MAPISession1
MAPI Message	Name	MAPIMessages1

This time, you'll write four standalone routines that you can call from the main form control events. First, create a new Sub procedure called DOMAPILogOn and add the code in Listing 25.22.

Listing 25.22. MAPI Log On procedure.

```
Public Sub DoMAPILogOn()
    '
    ' attempt to log on to mail services
    '
    On Error GoTo DoMAPILogOnErr
    '
    MAPISession1.DownloadMail = False
    MAPISession1.UserName = "MS-Mail Only"
    MAPISession1.SignOn
    MAPIMessages1.SessionID = MAPISession1.SessionID
    Exit Sub
    '
DoMAPILogOnErr:
    MsgBox Error$, vbCritical, "Error Code: " + Str(Err) + " [DoMAPILogOn]"
    Unload Me
    End
End Sub
```

Notice that we are supplying a predefined user name in this routine. As long as this is a valid login name, Microsoft Exchange will automatically log the user in without any dialog box appearing. This value could be stored in an INI/Registry setting or in a database. The key here is that you are establishing the link to messaging services without asking for input from the user.

> **WARNING**
>
> The code example here contains Microsoft Exchange Profile and Recipient Address values that may not be valid at your location. Replace these values with ones that will work for your MAPI server. Using incorrect address and profile values will result in error reports from your Visual Basic application.

Now create a new Sub procedure called DoMAPILogOff and enter the code in Listing 25.23.

Listing 25.23. MAPI Log Off Procedure.

```
Public Sub DoMAPILogOff()
    '
    ' log off mapi services
    '
    On Error Resume Next
    MAPISession1.SignOff
    '
End Sub
```

Nothing special here. It's just the standard log out of the messaging server. The next routine is the one that sends the message without bothering the user again. Create a Sub procedure called DoMAPISend and add the code in Listing 25.24.

Listing 25.24. MAPI Send Procedure

```
Public Sub DoMAPISend()
    '
    ' put together message and
    ' ship it out
    '
    On Error GoTo DoMAPISendErr

    MAPIMessages1.Compose
    MAPIMessages1.MsgSubject = "Trouble Report for " + Me.Text1
    MAPIMessages1.MsgNoteText = Me.Text2
    MAPIMessages1.RecipAddress = "MS:COMTRAX/PO1/mca"
    MAPIMessages1.Send
    '
    Exit Sub
    '
DoMAPISendErr:
    MsgBox Error$, vbCritical, "Error Code: " + Str(Err) + " [DoMAPISend]"
    Exit Sub
End Sub
```

Here, we clear the compose buffer, work up the subject line, load the text, and then address it ourselves. The recipient address can be stored in the program, in INI/Registry settings, or in a database. More sophisticated programs would allow configuration routines to modify this parameter as needed—maybe even send the message to different (or multiple) people, depending on the type and severity of the trouble call. All this logic can be kept in your Visual Basic application and used to perform messaging services without requiring the user to know anything about e-mail or electronic messaging.

Add this final `Sub` procedure in Listing 25.25 to clear out the input fields for data entry.

Listing 25.25. Clearing the Input form.

```
Public Sub ClearForm()
    '
    ' clear this form for next input
    '
    Text1 = ""
    Text2 = ""
End Sub
```

Now that the core routines are done, you need to place some code at the key events in the form. Listing 25.26 contains the code pieces for the `Form_Load` and `Form_Unload` events.

Listing 25.26. `Form Load` and `Unload` events.

```
Private Sub Form_Load()
    DoMAPILogOn
    ClearForm
End Sub

Private Sub Form_Unload(Cancel As Integer)
    DoMAPILogOff
End Sub
```

Finally, add the `Select Case` structure to handle the command buttons as in Listing 25.27.

Listing 25.27. Main control code for Button array.

```
Private Sub Command1_Click(Index As Integer)
    '
    ' handle user clicks
    '
    Select Case Index
        Case 0
            ' send out report
            DoMAPISend
            ClearForm
        Case 1
            ' cancel this report
            ClearForm
        Case 2
            ' exit this program
```

continues

Listing 25.27. continued

```
            Unload Me
    End Select
    '
End Sub
```

Save this form as vbu2504.frm and the project as vbu2504.vbp. Now run the program. Assuming you have added valid login and recipient address data, your program will log itself in without prompts and then show the data entry form (see Figure 25.13).

FIGURE 25.13.

Running the mail-enabled Trouble Call Report.

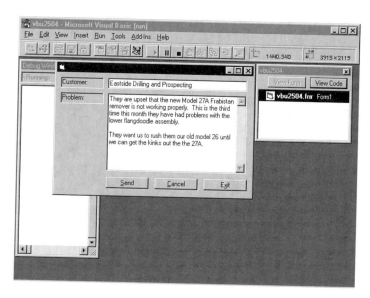

When you press the Send key, the data will be packaged up and sent to the predetermined e-mail location.

As mentioned earlier, this is a very simple mail-enabled application. There is no limit to the types of applications you can develop using the MAPI controls to provide messaging services for your Visual Basic programs.

Summary

This chapter covered several general issues concerning the MAPI message standard. The key points are:

- MAPI is the *de facto* messaging interface standard.
- You can use MAPI to provide generic, portable message and e-mail services for your Visual Basic applications.

- Services like user log-in and log-out, reading, composing, addressing, and sending messages are requested by the client application and provided by the server application.

- There are three broad categories of MAPI applications. They are e-mail programs (e-mail is the primary function), mail-aware applications (messaging is an added feature), and, mail-enabled applications (messaging is embedded into the design of the application).

You learned that there are two Visual Basic MAPI controls. The `MAPI Session` control provides user log-in and log-out services for linking the Visual Basic client application with the mail server. The `MAPI Message` control provides all other message services including reading, composing, addressing, and sending electronic messages and attachments.

Lastly, you learned how to use the Visual Basic MAPI controls to build three sample applications. These applications illustrated the differences between the three main categories of messaging programs: e-mail, mail-aware, and mail-enabled.

Using TAPI

26

*by Edward B.
Toupin*

Telephony is a technology that allows your computer to work directly with the telephone network. The Windows Telephony Application Programming Interface (TAPI) allows you, the programmer, to easily develop applications that provide telephony services to Microsoft Windows users.

To encompass all of the capabilities of telephony, TAPI supports speech and data transmission as well as a variety of terminal devices, complex connection types, conference calls, call waiting, and voice mail. Because TAPI isolates applications from the morass of operations required on the telephone network, you can easily develop network-independent applications. For the user, the API is hardware/connection-independent, thus allowing configuration to be very flexible.

This chapter explores a wide range of functionality available to business users and developers through the integration of the desktop computer with the telephone. Understanding telephony under Windows is important because the availability of Windows Telephony support will soon become a key factor in the selection of telephony hardware. By using Visual Basic, you will learn how to use TAPI to explore Windows Telephony for new applications that will improve services and productivity.

The advantages of using TAPI are as follows:

- Windows Telephony is centered around the desktop systems consisting of a single PC and telephone.

- Windows Telephony provides a link between call control and existing Windows data communications features.

- Windows Telephony allows multiple applications to share telephony devices.

- Windows Telephony is a superset of the standard existing telephone network capabilities that we use everyday, thus providing for hardware and network independence.

- Windows Telephony service providers can expose special telephone network features to applications.

- Windows Telephony is based on the C language with which Windows programmers are familiar. Visual Basic developers can integrate this functionality right into their Visual Basic applications.

- Windows Telephony provides easy access to telephone features through the Windows graphical user interface.

What Is TAPI?

With many of the existing telephone connections in the world, the *Plain Old Telephone Service* (POTS) handles the connection and transmission of voice and data while in the local portion of a phone system. This local portion, or *loop*, exists between the user's telephone and the central office (CO). Within this loop, voice is transmitted in analog format and a modem must convert the digital computer data to analog. Digital networks are gradually replacing analog in the local loop to conform with the existing digital connections between the different COs (see Figure 26.1).

FIGURE 26.1.

*Central offices connect your
telephone to the larger
telephone system for
communications with other
telephone users.*

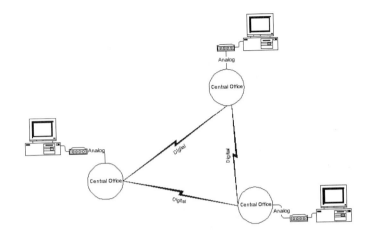

TAPI provides a means of application development that supports POTS and other communications mediums. Using TAPI for communications over POTS is straightforward because POTS is a simple technology. Other mediums for communications supported by TAPI allow you to take advantage of advanced types of data transmission. One such medium is called ISDN (Integrated Services Digital Network), which is expected to grow significantly in availability over the next few years.

> **TIP**
>
> As ISDN connections propagate, users will be able to transmit data to the person with whom they are simultaneously speaking.

ISDN has the following advantages over POTS:

- ISDN data travels from one end of the ISDN network to the other in digital format, thus maintaining lower error rates than analog transmission.

- Speeds of up to 128 kilobytes per second (Kbps) are possible on ISDN, compared with today's maximum dial-up modem data rates of 28.8 Kbps.

- ISDN lines can provide three or more simultaneous channels for voice and data.

- The ISDN communications standard is accepted internationally.

In addition to ISDN, you can use TAPI to develop applications that utilize the services of T1/E1 and Switched 56. Switched 56 provides 56 Kbps throughput over dial-up telephone lines and is becoming available throughout the U.S. and in many other countries. This medium requires special equipment, and though its connection capabilities are limited to calls to other specially equipped facilities, its high speed and low pricing make it a good choice for data communications. T1/E1 service is similar to Switched 56 in that it is a digital transmission medium; however, it runs at much higher speeds in the range of 1.5 Mbps (megabytes per second). T1/E1 service is provided generally as dedicated lines over which digital data is transmitted (see Figure 26.2).

FIGURE 26.2.

TAPI allows transparent, medium-independent communications over analog POTS as well as any of the existing digital networks available.

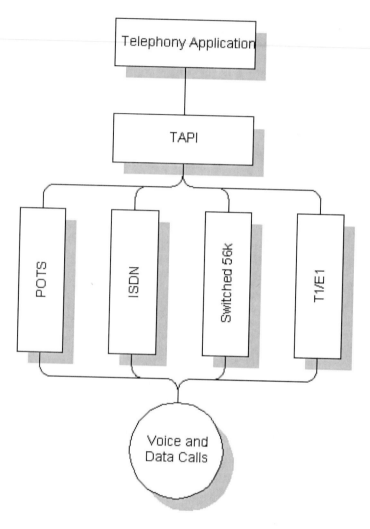

Switched 56 and T1/E1 are data-only services and are transparent to TAPI-enabled applications. Applications use standard methods for placing calls and let the service provider handle the transfer of the phone number to the telephone network. To the application, the Switched 56 line appears as a channel that supports digital service at the 56 Kbps rate because the medium over which calls are made only carries digital data.

In addition to standard POTS and digital services, you can use TAPI with services such as CENTREX, which provides for centralized network services, such as conferencing, without requiring specialized communications equipment. You also can use TAPI with digital *Private Branch Exchanges* (PBXs), which provide communications for small areas, such as office buildings or organizations. Because TAPI is network-independent, development of a PBX application is the same as that of a POTS application, which means you can use an application that was developed for POTS within a PBX environment without any code changes.

Advantages of Windows Telephony

The emergence of local-area networks (LANs) expanded the role of the desktop computer from just a personal productivity tool to a means of sharing information and resources within workgroups and departments. With LANs came e-mail, which made the desktop computer an important business communications medium.

The next logical step in the expansion of desktop computers is to integrate them with the telephone. To make this step, Intel, Microsoft, and several major telecommunications, PC, and software companies created TAPI. This API brings the function of the telephone to the desktop computer and, with the availability of cellular telephone technology, provides a means of implementing the portable office.

Everyone involved with the telephony and computing industries will benefit from the widespread distribution and use of TAPI. Application developers will have access to a standard API, which provides telephony network and hardware independence on the most popular operating system platform. Developers can now focus on the end product, not the intricacies of low-level communications, and need not be concerned with being tied to a particular hardware platform. Telephony network, switch, and hardware vendors can focus on the area of their expertise, hardware, and switching without having to come up to speed on Windows application development. With TAPI, third parties can develop a full range of applications, thus expanding the market for telephony hardware for PC platforms and PCs with integrated telephony capabilities.

End users, the main targets of any development, will benefit because their investments in software and telephony hardware are protected by the interchangeability of components. Competition in telephony application software means that a wide variety of programs will be available at competitive prices, and commercial developers will continue to create new features in order to meet growing user needs.

The idea of integrating communications and data is to make things more efficient for the end user. With TAPI, users can efficiently manage their voice calls and control their data-transfer operations. The following are just some of the possibilities:

- Personal information managers (PIMs) that provide automated dialing, voice mail management, and collaborative computing over telephone lines
- Integrated messaging and information management through connection to database managers, spreadsheets, and word processors over the telephone network
- Integrated conferencing and call managers to manage conference calls or the morass of complicated phone features provided by phone service providers

TIP

In the near future, video as well as audio conference calls will be available at the desktop.

- Drag-and-drop data transmission that allows users to drag and drop file icons to transmit files from a local disk to that of a remote machine
- TAPI applications that provide access to information services such as CompuServe and the Internet

> **NOTE**
>
> One of the futures for TAPI involves the new idea of telecommuting. Through TAPI-enabled applications users could work at home and have their entire office transparently available over the telephone network.

TAPI and Other Telephony Approaches

Of course, TAPI is not the first telephony application programming interface in the industry. In developing TAPI, its creators tried to address some of the issues raised by other similar applications. These issues include the following:

- **Specific Platforms.** Many attempts at a telephony interface yielded special hardware that was not expandable, did not meet requirements for general computing needs, and was incompatible with standard operating systems.
- **Larger Call Centers.** Most TAPI-style interfaces concentrate on large call center operations where call routing equipment is directly associated with a PBX and mainframe computer for an entire department. These call centers provide call management by handling call routing on behalf of a caller or third-party.
- **Single Application Focus.** Many TAPI-style interfaces focus on one application and are unable to handle multiple PC applications that share telephony resources.
- **Single Switching Platform.** Many of the current telephony APIs require you to use the PBX and associated hardware of the switch manufacturer that developed the API. This approach has narrowed the market for any particular application written in conformance to these APIs.
- **Unfamiliar Programming Model.** Many existing telephony APIs are based on special languages or involve data structures and messaging models that are unfamiliar to experienced Windows programmers.

In contrast to previous telephony APIs, TAPI provides the basis for the widespread integration of telephony and personal computers by including the following characteristics:

- **Generic Platforms.** Because TAPI is built on the Microsoft Windows foundation, Windows Telephony uses standard hardware and software.
- **Desktop Focus.** TAPI assumes that the desktop computer is one endpoint of each call, thereby simplifying the API and making it easier for programmers to learn and use.

- **Media Stream Access.** Windows Telephony manages the routing of different data on a given media, which allows you to use existing Windows functions for data communications, fax, audio input and output, and other media streams.

- **Multiple Application Support.** TAPI allows multiple applications to share telephony devices and to cooperatively control telephone calls.

- **Network Independence.** Because Windows Telephony is designed to be independent of specific telephone network capabilities, it can handle all possible networks.

- **Familiar Programming Model.** TAPI is based on C functions, libraries, data structures, and messages, which are familiar to Windows programmers. Developers can create TAPI-enabled applications using standard Windows development and testing tools.

The Windows Telephony API Architecture

TAPI's standard application programming interface enables users and application developers to take advantage of the many capabilities and services of the underlying network without having to worry about how that network is structured. TAPI allows application programs to control telephony functions such as establishing, answering, and terminating a call. The API also allows applications to take advantage of supplementary functions, such as hold, transfer, conference, and call park, found in PBXs and other phone systems. In addition to standard telephone functionality, the API provides access to features specific to certain telephone systems and can accommodate future telephony features and networks as they become available.

In conjunction with its network independence, TAPI also functions independently of the connection method used between the computer and the telephone. This independence provides maximum flexibility in the integration of the PC with the telephone system. For example, you can connect a PC to the telephone network, as shown in Figure 26.3, to provide a means of directly communicating over the telephone network or to act as a call center for third-party call routing.

FIGURE 26.3.

TAPI allows you to connect a PC directly to a telephone network to act as a call center controller to handle third-party call routing.

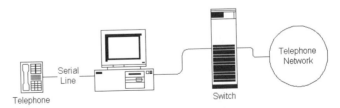

You can also connect the PC through a programmable telephone handset, as shown in Figure 26.4, in order to utilize the services of the phone to connect to the telephone network. Such phones may contain the capability of allowing you to record memos on the answering device incorporated in the handset body, for example. Applications that control such devices communicate with them using the phone functions that allow you to set the switchhook, control ringing, control volume, and so forth directly in the phone device itself.

FIGURE 26.4.

TAPI allows you to connect a PC directly to a telephone to use the services of the telephone network.

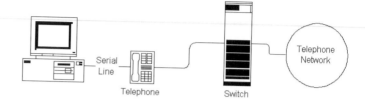

Multiple PCs can also share telephony resources through a LAN-based voice server, as shown in Figure 26.5, in order to maximize the use of telephony and existing network resources. This voice server distributes data to appropriate PCs from the telephone network. Device sharing for voice digitizers, fax machines, and data modems is also available if such devices are installed on the server.

FIGURE 26.5.

TAPI allows you to use your PC as a voice server to answer incoming voice calls.

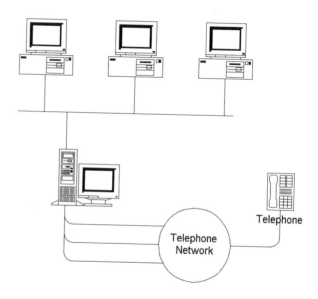

Finally, you can connect a server through a telephone network switch, as shown in Figure 26.6, as another method of resource sharing and call routing. In this model, multiple PCs are connected to the server to access information retrieved from the telephone network. TAPI operations invoked at any of the client computers are forwarded over the LAN to the host, which uses a third-party switch-to-host link protocol to implement the client's call-control requests. The switch provides the interface to the telephone network, and the LAN server provides the interface for all the PC client operations.

Each implementation may require a different connection model in order to take advantage of the different capabilities. For example, conferencing applications require a connection such as the one shown in either Figure 26.3 or Figure 26.5 in order for the PC to gain access to the information transmitted over the phone line. In this way, TAPI can access and distribute the information to all connecting devices.

FIGURE 26.6

TAPI allows you to connect a PC as a server across the telephone network.

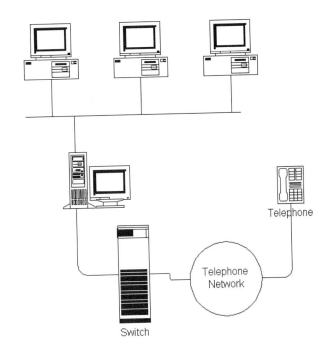

Telephone

Telephone Network

Switch

TAPI and WOSA

To provide seamless integration into the Microsoft Windows operating system, the Windows Telephony API was incorporated as part of the Windows Open Services Architecture (WOSA). This architecture provides a single set of interfaces to implement computing services that are accessed through Windows APIs. As a full enterprise-oriented implementation, WOSA includes services for data access, messaging, software licensing, connectivity, and financial services.

The WOSA model provides an abstraction layer to computing resources as a back-end for the front-end application. The front-end application accesses the services of the primary API while the back-end service accesses the computing resources.

Services such as the Windows Telephony API consist of two interfaces. The primary interface is the developer API that allows you to develop applications that utilize the services of TAPI. The second interface is an abstraction layer known as a *service provider interface* (SPI). The SPI is used to establish the connection and communicate with a specific telephone network. TAPI supplies a Telephony DLL component, called TAPI.DLL, which resides between the Telephony API and the Telephony SPI. TAPI-compliant applications call TAPI functions managed by TAPI.DLL, which in turn route the calls to the appropriate service provider for execution. Figure 26.7 shows the relationship between the Windows Telephony API (TAPI) and the Windows Telephony SPI (TSPI).

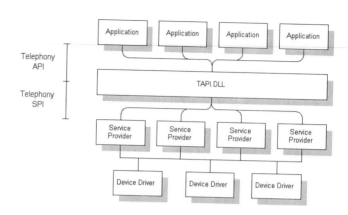

Multiple TAPI-enabled applications can operate simultaneously to use one or more service providers. In addition, multiple service providers can be used, as long as they access different hardware devices. When the service provider is installed, you can specify the mapping between each service provider and its hardware using the Windows Telephony Control Panel applet. Some service providers may contain a device-driver component, but, in general, service providers are separate and above the drivers, as shown in Figure 26.7.

TAPI Architecture

The functional interfaces for the TAPI and the service providers combine to provide a generic view of the underlying telephone networks to all TAPI-enabled applications. This generic view is known as *virtualizing* the environment for both applications and service providers. TAPI-enabled applications can send requests to what appears to be a single large service provider that supports a wide selection of devices. In reality, the service provider can be multiple service providers that provide different types of services.

When multiple service providers interact with a single application, each service provider is only aware of its own interactions with an application. TAPI.DLL hides the interactions that occur between an application and other service providers, which makes each service provider think it is the only service provider in the system. TAPI.DLL also hides the interactions between applications and service providers from other applications, which makes each application think that it is the sole user of the system.

In Figure 26.8, TAPI.DLL resides as the interface between applications and the Telephony infrastructure. TAPI.DLL handles all transactions that occur with regard to requests and incoming events between applications and service providers.

The solid arrows in the figure show that several different applications can use a device controlled by one service provider at the same time. TAPI.DLL allows both applications to open the device without concern for contention. These applications can also elect to become aware of one another if necessary so that they can cooperate and communicate with one another through TAPI.DLL. The service providers are not concerned with communication between multiple applications because they think only one application is using their services.

FIGURE 26.8.

The TAPI architecture.

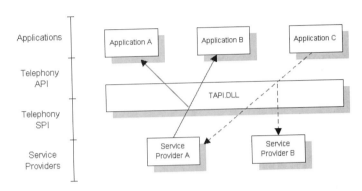

The dashed arrows in Figure 26.8 show that multiple service providers can interact with the same application. Each service provider only interacts with TAPI.DLL so that TAPI.DLL can merge the event streams from both service providers into a single stream for the application. Service providers do not need to be concerned about the details of cooperating with one another or even the existence of other service providers.

Device Classes

To simplify the underlying network, the TAPI programming model abstracts heterogeneous real-world objects such as telephones, modems, and telephone lines into device classes. Device classes allow developers to present devices as a uniform set that TAPI can access in a consistent manner. The abstraction of devices into classes also increases the longevity of TAPI by providing a framework of device classes that can support future equipment.

TSPI defines two device classes for device abstraction—the *line device class* and the *phone device class*. A line device is any device that appears as a telephone network to TSPI, and a phone device is any device that appears as a telephone to TSPI. TSPI defines a collection of functions and messages for each of these device classes and manages the mapping of this abstraction layer into the real-world device.

In addition to the line and phone device classes, Telephony includes *call objects*. Line and phone objects are statically defined, but call objects are dynamically created based on call activities. A call object represents an actual communication instance or call as the endpoint of a connection to one or more remote parties. A call object is bound to a line and is created as required for outbound or inbound calls (see Figure 26.9).

FIGURE 26.9.

Call objects are instances of inbound or outbound calls connected to a line or phone.

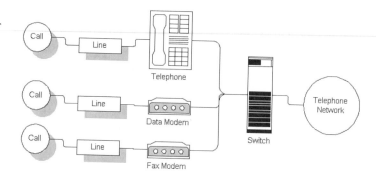

Service Levels

Service levels provide different kinds of access to TAPI. Figure 26.10 gives you a idea of how the three available service levels, basic, supplementary, and extended, overlap.

FIGURE 26.10.

Telephony service levels provide different types of functionality for TAPI-enabled applications.

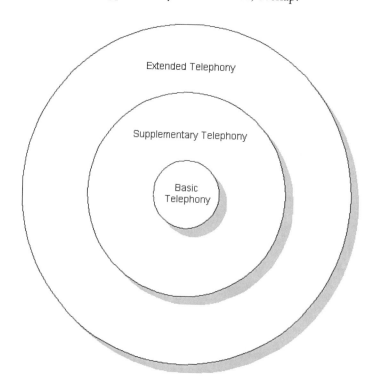

The elementary level of service is called *Basic Telephony*; it provides the minimum set of functions for POTS. Because all service providers support the basic Telephony functionality, applications that access this service level will work with any TAPI service provider. You use Basic Telephony for simple access to a telephone network. If you plan on writing PBX phone systems or ISDN connectivity solutions, you need to look at the Supplementary Telephony service level.

> **NOTE**
>
> Because phone device control is not directly offered by all service providers, phone device services are not a part of Basic Telephony.

Supplementary Telephony services are the services defined by the API above Basic Telephony. These services include features found on modern PBXs, such as hold, transfer, conference, and park. Applications can access a device using TAPI for the set of supplementary services provided. Service providers provide a Supplementary Telephony service only if it can implement the function as defined by TAPI; otherwise, the feature is provided as an Extended Telephony service.

The third service level is called *Extended Telephony,* and it provides special purpose API extensions for access to service provider functions not defined by TAPI. Extended services include all extensions to the API defined by a particular service provider. TAPI's extension mechanism allows service-provider vendors to define new values for some data types and bit flags and to add fields to most data structures. TAPI interprets these extensions by using the service provider's Extension ID. The Extension ID identifies the set of supported extensions; these extensions may cross several manufacturers.

Address Assignments

A TAPI address is the complete telephone number of a telephone, fax machine, or other device that can receive calls. These addresses are assigned to a TAPI-controlled line in the setup operation for a service provider. In the simplest scenario, each line has only one address. However, it's not unusual for a line to have several addresses as with ISDN (see Figure 26.11).

Telephony-enabled applications use Telephony services as a *first-party call control* model. This model requires that service providers allow applications to control telephone calls as the initiator or the recipient of a call. Following this model, applications can make calls to an address, be notified about inbound calls from an address, answer inbound calls, invoke switch features such as hold, transfer, conference, pickup, and park, and can detect and generate DTMF (Dual Tone Multiple Frequency) tones for signaling remote equipment (see Figure 26.12).

FIGURE 26.11.

Line addressing allows identification of line devices for TAPI.

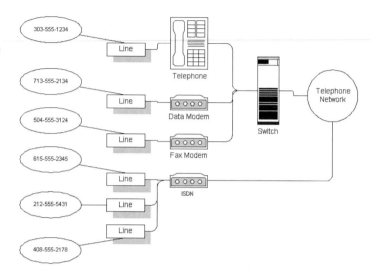

> **NOTE**
>
> For reference, *third-party call control* means that Telephony applications are not the endpoint of a call. The third-party call-control model allows an application to route calls between the caller and party being called.

FIGURE 26.12.

TAPI uses the first-party call control model for establishing calls.

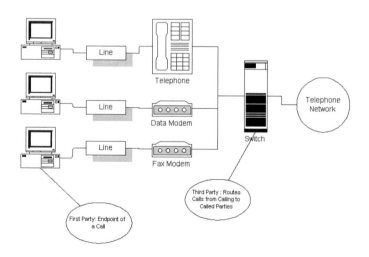

The format of the phone number used to initiate a call depends on where the call comes from. To make calls from a portable computer, you can use a single address book, even when calling from different locations or telephony environments. Corporations can keep master address books available to all employees even though they might be in different area codes because TAPI's address translation capabilities determine how to contact a specific number based on the current location designated by the user. TAPI handles the dialing differences of different phone regions without requiring changes to the user's address book. The Windows Telephony applet in the Windows Control Panel manages all of the information regarding location and address translation. This applet can also manage telephone calling card information and dialing procedures.

Media Access

TAPI provides control for the *media mode* of line and phone devices only and does not have support for handling the actual data transferred in a call. To handle this data, known as a *media stream*, you must incorporate functions from other APIs into telephony applications. To perform the information management operations, TAPI works in conjunction with other Windows-based services such as the Media Control Interface (MCI) or other data APIs. This division of control enables TAPI to work with existing audio or data applications (see Figure 26.13).

FIGURE 26.13.

TAPI works in conjunction with other APIs to manage the data transferred in a media stream.

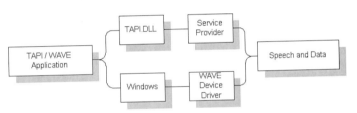

To determine the type of media stream, the Telephony SPI defines a function that allows the caller to retrieve the appropriate media device to be opened and used through the associated media API. For example, for line devices, TAPI.DLL uses the Telephony SPI to establish a connection to another station. Once the connection is established, TAPI.DLL can retrieve the MCI device associated with the call device and can then use the MCI device to play back and record audio data over the connection. Similarly, if the media stream is from a fax or data modem, the TAPI client would retrieve a fax or data modem device associated with the call and then use a fax API or a data modem API to manage the media stream.

To properly manage media stream types, the Telephony SPI reports media stream type changes to TAPI.DLL. This process is referred to as *call classification*. To determine the type of media stream, a service provider may filter the media stream for energy or tones that characterize the media type. Alternatively, the service provider may determine the media type by using information exchanged in messages over the network, such as the use of distinctive ringing, the caller's identification number, or the identification number of the party being called.

Assisted Telephony

To minimize the work involved in managing TAPI-enabled applications, *Assisted Telephony* provides an easy-to-use mechanism for making phone calls without requiring the developer to become a telephony expert. The remainder of this chapter explains how to access TAPI resources from Visual Basic applications using Assisted Telephony.

Figure 26.14 illustrates the way an Assisted Telephony application, a call manager, and a Full Telephony application relate to TAPI.DLL and the service provider. As you will notice, Assisted Telephony applications require a call manager because they cannot directly control calls. Once the call manager has established the connection, the call manager turns control of the connection over to the original application. In the case of a Full Telephony application, the application has total control over call requests and connection management and does not require intervention by an intermediate call manager.

FIGURE 26.14.

Full telephony applications directly manage the media stream while assisted telephony applications require an intermediate call manager.

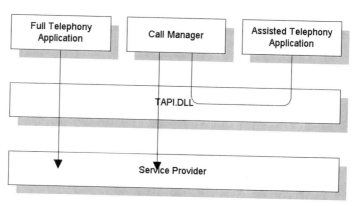

An example of how you can use Assisted Telephony is the integration of a spreadsheet application with an online database service. The spreadsheet application could contain a button or menu selection that would contact the online service and download information from a stock quote service into the cells of the spreadsheet. Using Assisted Telephony, the spreadsheet application passes the phone number to the call manager, which in turn places the call to the stock quote service (see Figure 26.15).

Assisted Telephony is responsible for establishing the line and, via the call manager, completing the call. The call manager then sends a return code to the spreadsheet about the status of the call request. Once the call manager connects to the online service, the spreadsheet application takes control and manages the incoming data. After all the data has been transferred, the call is terminated.

FIGURE 26.15.

Using Assisted Telephony, a spreadsheet application can call an online service and download information.

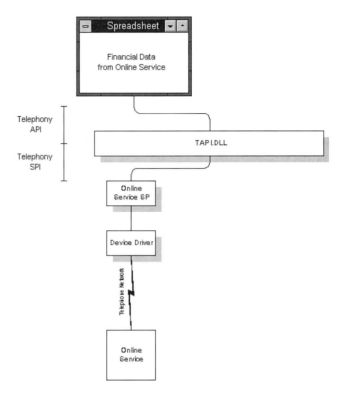

Visual Basic TAPI Applications

Now that you know some of the basics of Windows Telephony, you can use Visual Basic to develop an application capable of initiating calls. The examples in this section use Assisted Telephony to develop such an application, but you can also use the procedures outlined here to develop an application that can receive calls using the Full Telephony API.

The first point to note when developing Visual Basic TAPI applications is that there are no immediate include files created to allow you to access TAPI.DLL. In order to incorporate an external function located in TAPI.DLL into your Visual Basic application, you must define the function internally. The next few sections take you step-by-step through two examples, and then examine some of the other functions available to you via TAPI.

Making a Call

The simplest Assisted Telephony operation is `tapiRequestMakeCall()`. This TAPI function allows you to establish a connection by passing a phone number (otherwise known as a TAPI address) to a call manager for dialing purposes. The sample code for this function uses a phone number entered by the user on the command line and dials that number.

To begin this development endeavor, you must first declare the function and constants used by that function. You should place these declarations in a module containing global declarations for the entire application, as shown in Listing 26.1.

Listing 26.1. Declarations required to access an external TAPI.DLL function.

```
Declare Function tapiRequestMakeCall Lib "TAPI32.DLL" _
(ByVal lpszDestAddress As String, ByVal lpszAppName As String, _
ByVal lpszCalledParty As String, ByVal lpszComment As String) _
As Long

Global Const TAPIERR_NOREQUESTRECIPIENT = -2&
Global Const TAPIERR_REQUESTQUEUEFULL = -3&
Global Const TAPIERR_INVALDESTADDRESS = -4&
```

The declarations in Listing 26.1 inform Visual Basic that a function that you require resides externally in the library called TAPI32.DLL—the 32-bit version of TAPI.DLL. The parameters that are to be passed to the function are to be passed by value, meaning that the value passed to the function in Visual Basic is the value passed to the TAPI.DLL function. In contrast, `ByRef` informs Visual Basic to pass arguments as pointers, or references, to values.

From the declaration of `tapiRequestMakeCall()`, the `lpszDestAddress` parameter specifies a destination address of the call request and contains the phone number. The `lpszAppName` specifies the name of the application originating the call. The `lpszCalledParty` specifies the called party's name. The `lpszComment` parameter specifies a comment about the call.

The reason for declarations is to provide an association between a Visual Basic internal call and a function residing in an external library. This association allows you to call external functions within Visual Basic as though they were native to Visual Basic. Once you create these associations, you can write the code required to perform the desired TAPI operations.

> **TIP**
>
> You can create declarations for external functions in the other APIs available under Windows in addition to TAPI. You also have access to RAS for remote access, MCI for multimedia extensions, and any number of other integrated features of the operating system.

Listing 26.2 first extracts the phone number entered on the application's command line, `phone_num$ = Command$`. The program then verifies that a number has been provided on the command line by checking the length of the string in `phone_num$`. If a phone number is provided in `phone_num$`, the `tapiRequestMakeCall(phone_num$, "", phone_num$, "")` function is called to access the call manager and make the call. The first parameter, as shown in the declaration of Listing 26.1, is the address to be assigned to a line. This address is the number that will be dialed when the function executes. The third parameter, as you will notice, is the same variable. In this case, you are merely assigning the phone number as the called party's identification for tracking and notification purposes.

Listing 26.2. Code to call a number provided on the command line.

```
Sub Form_Load ()
    phone_num$ = Command$

    i = Len(phone_num$)
    If i = 0 Then End

    retval& = tapiRequestMakeCall(phone_num$, "", phone_num$, "")
    If retval& = 0& Then End

    infostr$ = "Unable to dial " + phone_num$ + "because"

    Select Case retval&
    Case TAPIERR_NOREQUESTRECIPIENT
        infostr$ = infostr$ + "a call-manager is unavailable."
    Case TAPIERR_REQUESTQUEUEFULL
        infostr$ = infostr$ + "the Windows Telephony dialing queue is full."
    Case TAPIERR_INVALDESTADDRESS
        infostr$ = infostr$ + "the phone number is invalid."
    Case Else
        infostr$ = infostr$ + "of an unknown problem."
    End Select

    MsgBox infostr$

End Sub
```

Once the function is called, the TAPI.DLL is initialized and the function is called internal to TAPI. At this point, TAPI initializes the call manager in order to make the call and establish a connection for use by the Visual Basic application (see Figure 26.16). If an error should occur, as represented by a non-zero result, a message box, using `MsgBox`, is displayed to comment about the error.

FIGURE 26.16.

The Windows Telephony Dialer is the default call manager available to call on behalf of applications utilizing Assisted Telephony.

With Assisted Telephony, the `tapiRequestMakeCall()` function takes into account a number of operations that would otherwise have to be performed by a Full Telephony application at the lower level of the TAPI. Assisted Telephony performs the following operations for you in order to minimize the amount of work required to establish and perform a call:

1. **Determining the Call Type/Media Mode.** The user must tell the application what kind of call to make. The user specifies the transmission of data in order to transmit a specified file to another user.

2. **Initializing TAPI.** The application establishes a means of communication between itself and TAPI. This establishment process involves the registration of a *callback function* from the application with TAPI so that TAPI knows how to send responses back to the application. This callback function is a function internal to the application that, once registered, is called by TAPI to submit call status information to the application.

3. **Obtaining a Line.** The application next obtains a handle to a telephone line that can support the desired type of call.

4. **Placing the Call.** Once the application has opened the line device, it places the call by specifying the address (the phone number) and the media mode. If dialing completes successfully, TAPI uses the callback function to inform the application about the call's progress.

5. **Sending Data.** After a line is available and a connection is established, the application can send the media stream. The application accomplishes this by giving control back to the user who initiates data transmission. Because TAPI functions continue to manage the opened line as well as the call, actual transmission is started and controlled by other Windows applications.

6. **Ending the Call.** When the transmission is complete, the application receives a `LINE_CALLSTATE` message, which informs the application that the state of a line device has changed (has been disconnected, in other words).

As you can see from the list, Full Telephony applications are a bit more complex than Assisted Telephony applications. For most applications you create with Visual Basic, Assisted Telephony will provide you with the basic requirements for a TAPI-enabled application.

Retrieving Country and City Code Information

Occasionally, you will have to extract country- and city-specific information in order to allow your application to assist in properly formatting telephone numbers and offering these as defaults when new numbers are entered in a phone book entry or database record. The function that gets this information is called `tapiGetLocationInfo()` and is declared within Visual Basic as follows :

```
Declare Function tapiGetLocationInfo Lib "TAPI32.DLL" _(ByVal lpszCountryCode As
➥String, ByVal lpszCityCode As String) As Long
```

The `lpszCountryCode` parameter contains a string variable where the country code for the current location will be returned. You should allocate at least eight bytes to hold the string. The call will place an empty string (\0) in the argument variable if the country code has not been set.

The `lpszCityCode` parameter contains a string variable where the city area code for the current location will be returned. As with the country code, you should allocate at least eight bytes to store the values. The call will place an empty string (\0) in the argument variable if the city code has not been set.

In Listing 26.3, you see that two string variables are declared statically for 10 bytes. These variables are passed as arguments to the `tapiGetLocationInfo()` function in order to retrieve the country and city codes from TAPI. Once retrieved, the information is displayed in a simple message box as a result of the call to `MsgBox`.

Listing 26.3. Retrieving the city and country code from TAPI.

```
Private Sub Form_Load()
    Dim lpszCountryCode, lpszCityCode As String * 10

    retval& = tapiGetLocationInfo(lpszCountryCode, lpszCityCode)

    MsgBox lpszCountryCode + "/" + lpszCityCode
End Sub
```

Accessing Telephony Media

On the disk included with this book, you will find a file called `vbtapi32.txt`. This file contains the declarations required to access TAPI from Visual Basic so that you can immediately begin developing state-of-the-art TAPI-enabled applications. The functions are separated into Assisted Telephony and Full Telephony functions and also include global definitions for use within your applications. To use this file, add it to your project list by selecting the File | Add File menu selection.

Of the methods declared in the included file, pay close attention to those shown in Listing 26.4. You will use these primary functions whenever you implement the Assisted Telephony you were exposed to in Listings 26.1 through 26.3.

Listing 26.4. Assisted Telephony Visual Basic declarations.

```
Declare Function tapiRequestMakeCall Lib "TAPI32.DLL" _
(ByVal lpszDestAddress As String, ByVal lpszAppName As String, _
ByVal lpszCalledParty As String, ByVal lpszComment As String) As Long

Declare Function tapiRequestMediaCall Lib "TAPI32.DLL" _
(ByVal hWnd As Integer, ByVal wRequestID As Integer, _
ByVal lpszDeviceClass As String, ByVal lpDeviceID As String, _
ByVal dwSize As Long, ByVal dwSecure As Long, _
ByVal lpszDestAddress As String, ByVal lpszAppName As String, _
ByVal lpszCalledParty As String, ByVal lpszComment As String) As Long

Declare Function tapiRequestDrop Lib "TAPI32.DLL" _
(ByVal hWnd As Integer, ByVal wRequestID As Integer) As Long

Declare Function tapiGetLocationInfo Lib "TAPI32.DLL" _(ByVal lpszCountryCode As
String, ByVal lpszCityCode As String) As Long
```

The code in Listing 26.4 uses the tapiRequestMakeCall() and the tapiGetLocationInfo() functions described in the previous sections, as well as the tapiRequestMediaCall() function. The tapiRequestMediaCall() function requests a media call for accessing one of the media streams (such as voice, fax, or data). The request is passed to an application that has been registered with the API as a recipient of such requests. The TAPI_REPLY Windows message informs the application about the success or failure of the request. Once the call is established, the media stream becomes active and control is turned over to the application through the media control API.

> **NOTE**
>
> Do not confuse Windows device classes with media modes. A *media mode* describes the format of information on a call, and a device class defines a Windows API used to manage the media stream.

The hWnd parameter of the function specifies the window handle of the application. From Visual Basic, this handle can be the hWnd property of the form in which the function is being called (for example, Form1.hWnd). The wRequestID parameter provides an identifier, which you provided during development, that identifies the current call request. The value supplied for this argument is used in a later call to the tapiRequestDrop() function to disconnect the line. As shown in Listing 26.4, this function takes the same hWnd argument and the wRequestID used to establish the call.

The lpszDeviceClass is the name of the device class that identifies the media type for the requested call. Table 26.1 lists the most common device classes. The first portion of a name identifies the API used to manage the device class, and the second portion is typically used to identify a specific device type extension or subset of the overall API (such as mci/wave or mci/midi). For those classes that do not have a second portion, such as comm, the entire API is used for the desired operation.

Table 26.1. Device classes available for `tapiRequestMediaCall()`.

Device Class Name	Description
comm	Serial Device API or Comm Port
wave	Wave Audio
mci/midi	Midi Sequencer
mci/wave	Wave Device Control
tapi/line	TAPI Line Device
tapi/phone	TAPI Phone Device
ndis	Network Driver Interface

The lpDeviceID parameter specifies the name of the media device that corresponds to the media stream of the requested call. This device is associated with the device class specified in lpszDeviceClass. Such devices include the Windows Media Player, which allows you to manipulate the wave and midi class media streams. The dwSize parameter is the length of the lpDeviceID string in bytes.

The dwSecure parameter specifies the security of the media call. If the value is set to 0, the call is not required to be secure, and features such as call waiting are not disabled and are allowed to interfere with the media stream on the call. If dwSecure is set to 1, the call is required to be secure, which causes all features that could interrupt the media stream to be disabled.

As with the tapiRequestMakeCall() function, the lpszDestAddress, lpszAppName, lpsz-CalledParty, and lpszComment specify the phone number and associated identifiers that identify the line address and the call. Of these arguments, only lpszDestAddress is required in order to establish a call.

Summary

Windows Telephony is a simple but powerful technology that allows you to easily develop applications that link your computer directly with the telephone network. The Windows Telephony Application Programming Interface (TAPI) contains all of the functions available for you to transparently access the underlying network and easily develop applications that provide telephony services to Microsoft Windows users. The examples in this chapter discussed the Assisted Telephony functions of tapiRequestMakeCall() and tapiGetLocationInfo(),which provide an excellent foundation for accessing and utilizing the other Windows Telephony from Visual Basic.

PART

Unleashing Database Programming

The Data Control

by *Brad Shannon*

27

IN THIS CHAPTER

This chapter will cover the various properties, methods, and events of the Data control. There will be examples provided throughout in order to illustrate the capabilities of the control.

What Is the Data Control?

The Data control is a component of Visual Basic that allows your application to interact with databases of different formats. Using the Data control, you can open a database and define the contents of the underlying Recordset.

A *Recordset* is a collection of records that are extracted from the database and then manipulated by the Data control. There are three types of Recordsets: dynaset, snapshot, and table. Each of these Recordsets has a variety of properties and methods that you can apply to it. This chapter and Chapter 28, "The Access Jet Engine," discuss the properties and methods of the Data control and the underlying Recordset.

> **NOTE**
>
> The constants used in the chapter are now included in the Visual Basic Environment. There is no need to include an external Constants.txt file.

Through the Data control's RecordSource and RecordSourceType properties, you define the Recordset that your application will work with. Using the Data control, you can view, edit, and update records in the underlying Recordset. You cannot use the Data control to delete records or create a new database.

The Data control supports the following database formats:

- MS Access
- Btrieve
- dBASE
- Excel
- FoxPro
- Paradox
- Text files
- ODBC

MS Access is the most flexible format of database to use with Visual Basic because MS Access and Visual Basic share the same database engine (called Jet).

Bound Controls and the Data Control

Using a combination of bound controls and the Data control, you can create an application that will allow you to move through the records in a Recordset. You can edit these records or add new records to the Recordset with a minimum of programming effort.

Bound controls provide direct access to the contents of a field in a database. The fields that are available to the bound control are defined by Recordset contained in the Data control. The DataSource and DataField properties are used in order to define the contents of a bound control.

Bound controls support all of the Standard Visual Basic text editing and formatting properties and methods. Additionally, bound controls support the DataSource, DataField, and DataChanged properties. The DataSource property is a read/write property at both run time and design time that refers to the Data control that is resident on the same form as the bound control. The DataField property is a read/write property at both run time and design time that refers to a field contained in the Recordset held by the Data control. The DataChanged property is a read-only, run-time property that is used in order to determine whether a change has been made to the underlying Recordset through a bound control. Any changes you make to the contents of the bound controls will be automatically updated to the Recordset whenever the record pointer of the Data control is altered either through the use of the Data control's record movement buttons or through actions performed in your application.

The Data control provides navigation buttons (shown in Figure 27.1) for you to use to move through records.

FIGURE 27.1.

The Data control navigation buttons.

Moves to the first record in the Recordset

Moves to the last record in the Recordset

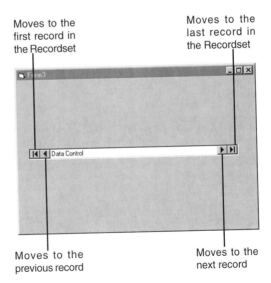

Moves to the previous record

Moves to the next record

The following example shows how to use the Data control and bound text boxes to display and edit values stored in the TITLES table of the BIBLIO.MDB database that is supplied with Visual Basic. Follow these steps:

1. Open a new project.
2. Place the following controls on the form:

Control	Name	Caption	Top	Left	Width	Height
Form	form1	Bound Form	1515	1920	6810	5190
Data control	data1	Data control 1	3360	0	6495	300
Label	lblpubid	Pub ID.	180	180	1215	285
Label	lblyear	Year Pub.	180	3660	1215	285
Label	lblIsbn	ISBN	600	180	1215	285
Label	lblTitle	Title	1020	180	1215	285
Label	lblSubject	Subject	1440	180	1215	285
Label	lblDescription	Description	1860	180	1215	285
Label	lblComments	Comments	2280	180	1215	285
Label	lblNotes	Notes	2700	180	1215	285
Textbox	txtPubid		180	1560	855	285
Textbox	txtYear		180	5040	855	285
Textbox	txtIsbn		600	1560	1635	285
Textbox	txtTitle		1020	1560	4635	285
Textbox	txtSubject		1440	1560	4635	285
Textbox	txtDescription		1860	1560	4635	285
Textbox	txtComments		2280	1560	4635	285
Textbox	txtNotes		2700	1560	4635	285
Command	cmdExit	E&xit	4080	5400	795	295

3. Set the following properties for the `Data1` Data control:

    DataBaseName: **BIBLIO.MDB**
    RecordSource: **Titles**

NOTE

The BIBLIO.MDB database referred to throughout this chapter can be found in the directory containing Visual Basic.

4. Set the `DataSource` and `DataField` properties for the text boxes that you have added to the form.

You set the DataSource property by entering the name of the Data control. In this case, type **data1** or select it from the combo box that appears in the DataSource property list box. After you set the DataSource property, you set the DataField property by entering the name of the field into the underlying Recordset or by selecting the name of the field from the combo box that appears in the DataField property. The following is the code that results from this step:

TextBox **Txtpubid**

```
    DataSource = data1
    DataField =  pubid
```

TextBox **Txtyear**

```
    DataSource = data1
    DataField =  Year Published
```

TextBox **Txtisbn**

```
    DataSource = data1
    DataField = ISBN
```

TextBox **Txttitle**

```
    DataSource = data1
    DataField = Title
```

TextBox **Txtsubject**

```
    DataSource = data1
    DataField = Subject
```

TextBox **Txtdescription**

```
    DataSource = data1
    DataField = Description
```

TextBox **Txtcomments**

```
    DataSource = data1
    DataField = comments
```

TextBox **Txtnotes**

```
    DataSource = data1
    DataField = notes
```

5. In the Click event for the cmdExit control, enter the following line:

    Unload Me

6. Run the project. A window much like the one shown in Figure 27.2 should appear.

You can use the Data control's record navigation buttons to move through all of the records contained in the titles Recordset. Additionally, you can make changes to the contents of the Recordset by altering the information contained in the text boxes and using the Data control to change the current record.

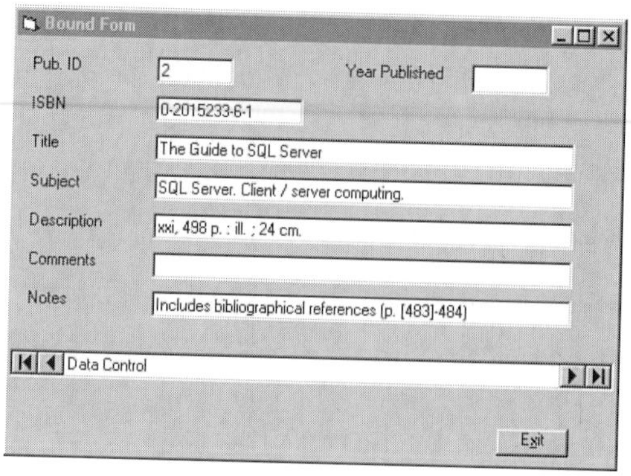

FIGURE 27.2.

*The bound fields illustrates
the Data control.*

The preceding example is a very simple examination of the capabilities of the Data control. The rest of this chapter builds on this example in order to fully explore the different properties, methods, and events available to the Data control.

Additional Properties Provided with the Data Control

The Data control supports all of the standard properties, such as control placement, that are associated with Visual Basic controls. It also supports properties that relate to data manipulation. You can manipulate these data manipulation properties for read/write access at both design and run time. The following sections describe each of the data manipulation properties.

Align

You use the `Align` property to determine the location of the Data control in relation to the form at run time as well as design time. You can align the Data control with the top, left, bottom, or right edge of the form. You also can choose to have no alignment and place the control anywhere on the form. The default value of the `Align` property is no alignment.

Add the following line to the `Form_Load` event or make the change using the properties editor and run your project:

```
Data1.align= 2
```

The Data control should now be aligned along the button of the form under the Exit button.

BOFAction

The `BOFAction` property determines what action the Data control takes when the `BOF` (beginning of file) property of the `Recordset` is true. `MoveFirst` and `BOF` are the two possible settings for the `BOFAction` property.

The MoveFirst setting causes the Data control to reposition the Recordset to the first record in the set and make it the current record when the BOF condition is true. To set the BOFAction property to this setting at run time, use the following expression (data1 represents the name of the Data control):

```
data1.BOFaction= vbBOFActionMoveFirst
```

If the BOFAction property is set to BOF, the Data control takes no action when the BOF condition is true. At this point, there is no current record and any attempt to edit the displayed record results in a No Current Record error message. If the Data control is visible, then the move to previous navigation button is disabled. To set the BOFAction property to this setting at run time, use the following expression (data1 represents the name of the Data control):

```
data1.BOFaction= vbBOFActionBOF
```

> **NOTE**
>
> The default of the BOFAction property is to move to the first record. In most circumstances, this action is the desired result as it ensures that you have a valid current record.

To demonstrate the behavior of the BOFAction property, perform the following steps.

1. Add the following line to the Form_Load event or use the properties editor to make the change:

   ```
   data1.BOFAction= vbBOFActionBOF
   ```

2. Add a check box control with the following properties to the form:

   ```
   Name  = chkbof
   Caption =  BOF Reached
   Enabled= false
   Top = 3660
   Left=  180
   Height = 295
   Width = 1875
   ```

3. Add the following to the Data1.reposition event:

   ```
   If Data1.Recordset.BOF = True Then

           chkbof.Value = vbchecked

   Else

           chkbof.Value = vbunchecked

   End If
   ```

4. Run your project.

5. Select the move to first record navigation button on the Data control. The TextBoxes on the form will now display the contents of the fields of the first record in the Recordset.

6. Select the move to previous record navigation button on the Data control. The previous record button should now be dimmed, indicating that you are at the BOF. At this point, the Data control no longer has a valid record pointer. The BOF check box will also be selected, providing another indication that you are in the BOF state (see Figure 27.3).

    If at this point you were to make a change to the displayed record and subsequently try to move to a different record using one of the navigation buttons on the Data control, you would receive a run-time error because you tried to update an invalid record.

    Once you have ended the application, Reset the BOFAction property back to the MoveFirst setting.

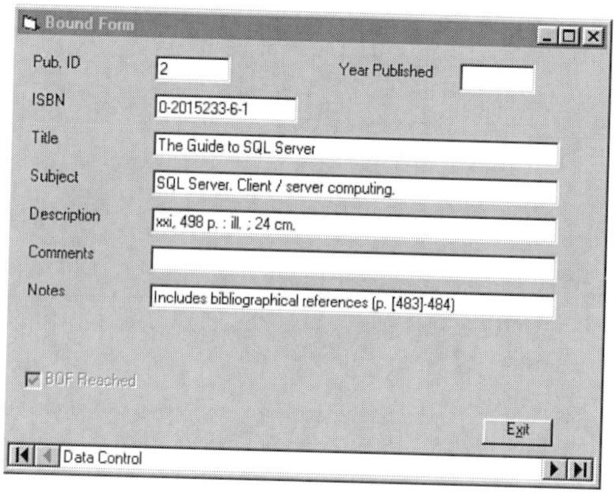

FIGURE 27.3.

This is how a screen looks when you are at the beginning of a file.

Connect

You use the Connect property when you are accessing databases from a program other than MS Access. The Connect property specifies the type of database that you are connecting to. Note that only files of the specified type are displayed in the Database Selection dialog box. If you are connecting to an ODBC database, for example, you need to specify ODBC in the Connect property and perhaps supply additional information such as USERID and PASSWORD. The additional information depends on the type of ODBC database you're using. (The ODBC database driver supplies further information on the connect string for ODBC databases.)

The following is an example of an expression that sets the Connect property at run time:

```
data1.connect= " dBASE III;"
```

DataBaseName

The contents of the DataBaseName property depend on what type of database you're connecting to. If you are connecting to an MS Access database, the property contains the name of the database that contains the tables you want to access. If you are connecting to a Btrieve database, the property contains the name of the Btrieve Data Definition file relating to the tables you want to access. If you are connecting to an ODBC database, the property is blank because the name of the data source is determined by settings in the Connect property. For all other supported databases, the DataBaseName property is set to the directory that contains the files that contain the data you want to access. To select the database file or the directory from a file selection dialog box, select the (...) in the properties editor.

> **NOTE**
>
> If you change the DataBaseName property at run time, you must execute the Refresh method in order for the change to take effect.

Follow these steps to learn how the DataBaseName property works:

1. Remove the reference to the DataBaseName property of the Data control.

2. Add the following lines to the Form_Load event in your project:

```
dim filepath as string
filepath="c:\vb40\"
data1.databasename= filepath&"biblio.mdb"
data1.refresh
```

> **NOTE**
>
> The value assigned to the file path variable should be the directory in which Visual Basic is installed.

3. Run your project. The project should behave in the same manner as when you examined the behavior of the BOFAction property.

> **NOTE**
>
> In a real-world application, the path to the database would probably be stored as a public variable that is initialized as part of your application start up. It is good practice to keep the file path of your data files external to your application, either in an application INI file or in a separate database. Doing this provides additional flexibility in the setting up and distribution of your application. The initial setting of the path could be a task completed by your installation program.

EOFAction

The EOFAction property determines what action the Data control takes when the EOF (end of file) property is true. MoveLast, EOF, and AddNew are the possible settings for this property.

The MoveLast setting causes the Data control to reposition the Recordset to the last record and make that record the current record when the Data control encounters an EOF condition of true. The following expression demonstrates how to specify this setting at run time (data1 is the name of the Data control):

```
data1.EOFAction= vbEOFActionMoveLast
```

The EOF setting causes the Data control to take no action when the EOF condition is true. At this point, there is no current record and any attempt to edit the displayed record results in a No Current Record error message. If the Data control is visible, the move to the next record button is disabled. To specify this setting at run time, use the following expression:

```
data1.EOFAction= vbEOFActionEOF
```

The AddNew setting causes the Data control to add a new record to the table and make that record the current record when the EOF condition is true. To specify this setting at run time, use the following expression:

```
data1.EOFaction= vbEOFActionAddNew
```

> **NOTE**
>
> The default action of the EOFAction property is to move to the last record in the Recordset when an EOF condition of true occurs. In most circumstances, this setting is the one you want because it ensures that you have a valid current record and gives you better control of the circumstances in which records can be added.

Follow these steps to use the AddNew setting of the EOFAction property:

1. Add the following line to the Form_Load event or use the properties editor to make the appropriate change to the EOFAction property:

   ```
   dat1.EOFaction= vbEOFActionAddNew
   ```

2. Add a check box control to the form with the following properties:

   ```
   Name  = chkEof
   Caption =  EOF Reached
   Enabled= false
   Top = 3660
   Left= 2340
   Height = 295
   Width = 1875
   ```

3. In the Data1.Reposition event, add the following:

```
If Data1.Recordset.EOF = True Then

    chkeof.Value = vbchecked

Else

    chkeof.Value = vbunchecked

End If
```

4. Run your project.

5. Select the move to last record button on the Data control. The last record in the Recordset is displayed.

6. Select the move to the next record button on the Data control, the Data control automatically adds a new blank record to the Recordset. Enter relevant data into the text boxes.

7. Select the move to the next record button. The contents of the newly created record are added to the Recordset, and you are positioned on another new record.

Exclusive

The Exclusive property determines whether your application is opening the database for exclusive use, which means no other users can access the database. You can set this property to true (no other users can access the database) or false (other users are able to access the database). The following expression shows how you can set this property at run time:

```
dim filepath as string
filepath="c:\vb40\"
data1.databasename= filepath&"biblio.mdb"
data1.exclusive= true
data1.refresh
```

NOTE

If you change the Exclusive property at run time, you must execute the Refresh method in order for the change to take effect.

To practice using the Exclusive property, perform the following steps:

1. Change the Exclusive property to true by using the properties editor.

2. Run your project.

3. While your project is running, open the BIBLIO database using the data manager application that is distributed with Visual Basic or MS Access. When you try to access the file, you should receive a message indicating that the file cannot be opened.

4. Exit your project and reset the Exclusive property back to false.

Options

The Options property specifies the characteristics of the Recordset that is created by the Data control. This property is predominantly used in a multi-user environment. The following constants are available in order to set the options at run time:

- **dbDenywrite**. This constant ensures that the other users in a multi-user environment cannot write any changes to the records contained in the Recordset.

- **dbDenyRead**. This constant ensures that other users are unable to read records contained in the Recordset. This setting applies only to the table type Recordset.

- **dbReadOnly**. With this constant in place, the Recordset is opened as read only and no changes can be made.

- **dbAppendOnly**. This constant lets you add records to the Recordset, but it prevents you from updating or deleting existing records.

- **dbInconsistent**. On a joined Recordset, this constant lets you update only those fields that do not affect the join condition.

- **dbSQLPassThrough**. If you are using an ODBC database, such as SQL Server or Oracle, this constant specifies that SQL expression that is used to create the Recordset be executed on the Server as opposed to using the Access database engine.

- **dbForwardOnly**. This constant sets the Recordset so that the only movement possible is forward (only the MoveNext method will have any effect). You cannot set this option on a Data control.

- **dbSeeChange**. This constant causes a trappable error if another user is making a change to the record that is currently being edited by someone else.

You can select multiple options by adding these constants together. By using the following expression to set the Options property at run time, for example, you can ensure that you have exclusive usage of the records in your Recordset:

```
dim filepath as string
filepath="c:\vb40\"
data1.databasename= filepath&"biblio.mdb"
data1.option= dbDenywrite + dbreadonly
data1.refresh
```

> **NOTE**
>
> If you change the Options property at run time, you must execute the Refresh method in order for the change to take effect.

ReadOnly

The ReadOnly property indicates whether the Recordset opened with the Data control can be edited. The following is an example of an expression you could use to set this property at run time:

```
dim filepath as string
filepath="c:\vb40\"
data1.databasename= filepath&"biblio.mdb"
data1.readonly= True
data1.refresh
Prevents any changes being made to the DataBase
```

To practice using the ReadOnly property, perform the following steps.

1. Add the following line to the Form_Load event or change the property by using the properties editor.

   ```
   data1.readonly= True
   ```

2. Run your project.

3. Use the move to the last record button on the Data control to move to the end of the Recordset.

4. Select the move to the next record button, which should, based on our previous setting, add a new record. An error message saying that the Recordset is read only appears.

5. Exit your project and set the ReadOnly property back to false and reset the EOFAction property back to the MoveLast setting.

> **NOTE**
>
> If you change the ReadOnly property at run time, you must execute the Refresh method in order for the change to take effect.

RecordsetType

The RecordsetType property determines that type of Recordset that the Data control creates. The following constants are available to define the Recordset at run time:

- **vbRStypetable**. This constant opens a table-type Recordset.
- **vbRSTypeDynaset**. This constant opens a dynaset-type Recordset.
- **vbRSTypeSnapshot**. This constant opens a snapshot-type Recordset.

In the following example, the code defines a snapshot type of Recordset:

```
dim filepath as string
filepath="c:\vb40\"
data1.databasename= filepath&"biblio.mdb"
data1.recordsettype= vbRSTypeSnapShot
data1.refresh
```

Each of the Recordset types contains different methods and properties. Subsequent chapters discuss the methods and properties associated with each Recordset type.

RecordSource

The RecordSource property determines the source of the records that make up the Recordset that is held by the Data control. This RecordSource property can contain the name of a table stored in the database, an SQL statement selecting the table and the fields that are to be part of the Recordset, or the name of a QueryDef that is stored in your database.

> **NOTE**
>
> Setting the RecordSource property to a QueryDef is only supported with MS Access databases.

> **NOTE**
>
> If you change the RecordSource property at run time, you must execute the Refresh method in order for the change to take effect.

Perform the following steps to practice changing the RecordSource:

1. Add a new form to your project named form4.
2. In the Project Options dialog box, change the start-up form to Form.
3. Add a Data control to the form; all relevant properties will be set at run time.
4. Add a Data Bound Grid with the following properties to the form:
   ```
   DataSource : Data1
   Top = 60
   Left=  60
   Height = 2895
   Width = 6675
   ```
5. Add a combo box control with the following properties to the form:
   ```
   Name  = comField
   Top = 3120
   Left=  1560
   Height = 315
   Width = 1875
   ```

6. Add a Label control with the following properties to the form:

```
Name= lblField
Caption= Order By
Top= 3180
Width = 1215
Height= 285
left = 180
```

7. Add the following code to the Form_Load event:

```
Sub Form_Load

Dim filepath As String
    dim x as integer
    filepath = "c:\vb40\"
Data1.DatabaseName = filepath & "biblio.mdb"
Data1.RecordSource = "select * From titles order by pubid ,[year published]"
 Data1.Refresh


    For x = 0 To Data1.Recordset.Fields.Count - 1

        comfield.AddItem Data1.Recordset.Fields(x).Name

    Next x

end sub
```

8. Add the following code to the comfield_Click event:

```
Private Sub comfield_Click()

    If comfield.Text <> "Comments" Then
        Data1.RecordSource = "select * From titles order by [" &
comfield.Text & "]"
        Data1.Refresh
    End If

End Sub
```

9. Run your project.

The Recordset as displayed in the Grid is ordered based on the field that you select for the combo box control (see Figure 27.4). The only exception to this rule would be if you selected the Comments field. In this case, the Recordset order would not change because it is impossible to order a Recordset by a memo type field.

FIGURE 27.4.

Illustrates the Recordset after it has been sorted by title.

> **NOTE**
>
> If you are unsure of the field names that will be used to order a Recordset, place "[]" around the field names. Otherwise, a runtime error will occur if a field name contains embedded spaces.

Recordset

As previously discussed, a Recordset is a collection of records that is held by the Data control. The RecordSource property of the Data control determines the source of the data contained in the Recordset. The RecordsetType property of the Data control determines the type of the Recordset that the Data control will contain. Through the Recordset property, you are able to manipulate the properties and methods of the Recordset associated with the Data control in the same way that you manipulate a Recordset object. Chapter 28, "The Access Jet Engine," discusses the various properties and methods that apply to the Recordset object.

Perform the following steps to practice using the Recordset property:

1. Make a copy of the Form1 form and name it Form2.
2. In the Project Options dialog box, change the start-up form to Form2.
3. Alter the Form2 caption to Unbound Form.
4. Remove the information that bounds the text boxes to the Data control by resetting the DataField and DataSource properties to blanks.
5. Add the following code to the Data1_Reposition event:

```
Private Sub Data1_Reposition()


If Data1.Recordset.BOF = True Then

    chkbof.Value = vbChecked
    Exit Sub

End If

If Data1.Recordset.EOF = True Then

    chkeof.Value = vbChecked
    Exit Sub

End If

    chkbof.Value = vbUnchecked
    chkeof.Value = vbUnchecked
```

```
txtcomments.Text = getfield(Data1.Recordset, "comments")
txtdescription.Text = getfield(Data1.Recordset, "description")
txtnotes.Text = getfield(Data1.Recordset, "notes")
txtpubid.Text = getfield(Data1.Recordset, "pubid")
txtsubject.Text = getfield(Data1.Recordset, "subject")
txttitle.Text = getfield(Data1.Recordset, "title")
txtyear.Text = getfield(Data1.Recordset, "[year published]")
txtisbn.Text = getfield(Data1.Recordset, "isbn")

End Sub
```

6. In the General section of Form2, add the following function:

```
Function getfield(rs As Recordset, cfield As String) as variant
If IsNull(rs.Fields(cfield).Value) Then

    Select Case rs.Fields(cfield).Type

        Case dbBoolean

            getfield = False

        Case dbByte To dbDate

            getfield = 0

        Case dbLongBinary

            getfield = 0&

        Case dbMemo, dbText

            getfield = ""

    End Select


Else

    getfield = rs.Fields(cfield).Value

End If

End Function
```

7. Run your project.

When you select the Data control's navigation buttons, the text boxes on the display will be filled using the data from the Titles Recordset. The update of the controls occurs during the Data1_Reposition event. The purpose of the Getfield function is to retrieve the value of the field in the Recordset. If the value of the field is #NULL#, the default null value based on the type of the field is returned. If the field is numeric, for example, it returns 0. If the field is a string type field, it returns blank. Otherwise, the contents of the field are returned.

NOTE

Trying to return a #NULL# value to a text box results in a run-time error.

8. After you complete this example, change the start-up form in your project back to FORM1, as you will be using this form for the remaining examples.

Additional Events Provided with the Data Control

The Data control supports all of the standard events, such as Drag, and mouse movement events that are associated with Visual Basic controls. In addition to the standard events, the Data control supports events that relate to data manipulation. This section describes the events that relate to data manipulation.

Error

The Error event occurs when there is a data access error that is not related to any of your code and therefore cannot be trapped by standard Visual Basic error handling. An example of this type of error would be if the design time properties that have been set up in the Data control become invalid at run time, for example, if a field name has been changed but the DataField property in the related text box has not been altered. The Error event consists of two parts. DateErr is the error code representation of the error that occurred. Response is the response that you want to make in the error condition.

The following constants are available to set the response:

- **vbDataErrContinue**. This constant continues executing the program.
- **vbDataErrDisplay**. This constant displays an error dialog box.

To practice handling an error event, make the following changes to your project:

1. Change the start-up form of your project to Form1.
2. Change the DataField property of the TxtIsbn control to "test."
3. Add the following code to the Data1_Error event:

```
Private Sub Data1_Error(DataErr As Integer, Response As Integer)

    If DataErr > 0 Then

        MsgBox " The Following Error Occurred " & DataErr & " " & Error$

    End If


End Sub
```

4. Run your project.

You will now receive a message box prior to your Form_Loading that indicates that an item was not found in the fields collection.

Reposition

The Reposition event occurs when a new record becomes the current record. The event can occur as a result of the selection of one of the record navigation buttons on the Data control or when the record is changed in your code through the use of one of the move or find methods of the Data control or Recordset. The Reposition event has no parameters. The Reposition event differs from the Validate event in that the Validate event occurs before the current record has been changed and the Reposition event occurs after the new record has been made current. You would use the Reposition event in order to perform an operation each time that the current record in the Recordset has been changed. The Unbound Form example under the earlier Recordset heading in the chapter illustrated this kind of situation.

Validate

The Validate event occurs prior to the current record in the Recordset changing. The following parameters are available in the Validate event:

- **Save**. This parameter indicates if any of the bound controls' data has changed. The value of this parameter is determined via the DataChanged property in the bound controls on the form. A value of true indicates that there has been a change in at least one of the bound controls on the form. A value of false indicates that no changes have been made to the bound controls.

- **Action**. This parameter represents the action that has caused the Validate event.

The following constants are available in order to determine what action triggered the Validate event:

- **vbDataActionMoveFirst**. The user has selected the move to the first record button on the Data control, or the MoveFirst method has been executed against the Recordset held by the Data control.

- **vbDataActionMovePrevious**. The user has selected the move to the previous record button on the Data control, or the MovePrevious method has been executed against a Recordset held by the Data control.

- **vbDataActionMoveNext**. The user has selected the move to the next record button on the Data control, or the MoveNext method has been executed against the Recordset held by the Data control.

- **vbDataActionMoveLast**. The user has selected the move to the last record button on the Data control, or the MoveLast method has been used against the Recordset held by the Data control.

- **vbDataActionAddNew.** The AddNew method has been used against the Recordset held by the Data control, or the user has attempted to move past the EOF position of the Recordset when the EOFAction property has been set to AddNew.

- **vbDataActionUpdate.** The Update method has been used against the Recordset held by the Data control.

- **vbDataActionDelete.** The Delete method has been used against the Recordset held by the Data control.

- **vbDataActionFind.** One of the find methods has been used against the Recordset held by the Data control.

- **vbDataActionBookmark.** The Bookmark property of the Recordset held by the Data control has been changed.

- **vbDataActionClose.** The Close method has been used against the Recordset held by the Data control.

- **vbDataActionUnload.** The form containing the Data control has had the Unload method applied to it.

- **VbDataActionCancel.** Undoes changes to bound controls caused by the foregoing actions.

To practice handling a Validate event, make the following changes to your project:

1. In Form1, change the DataField property of the txtIsbn control back to isbn.
2. Add the following code to the Data1_Validate event:

```
If Save = False Then

    Exit Sub

End If


If MsgBox(" Save Changed Record ", vbYesNo, "", "", 0) = vbNo Then
    Action = 0
    Exit Sub

End If
```

3. Run your project.
4. Change the contents of a number of fields in the current record.
5. Use the Data control to move to another record or try to unload the form. You will be prompted in order to determine whether you want to save the changes (see Figure 27.5).
6. Select Yes to save your changes. Select No to ignore the changes.

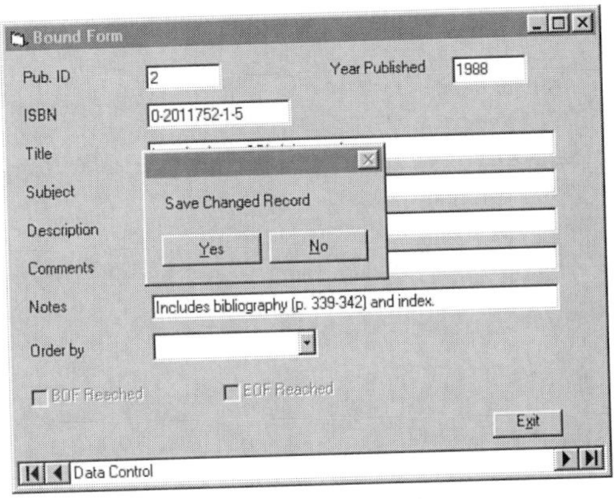

FIGURE 27.5.
Updating a record often causes a dialog box to appear.

Additional Methods Provided with the Data Control

The Data control supports all of the standard methods, such as Z-Order, and Drag methods that are associated with Visual Basic controls. In addition to the standard methods, the Data control supports methods that relate to data manipulation. The following sections discuss these data manipulation methods.

Refresh

The Refresh method is used in a variety of ways with the Data control. This chapter used the Refresh method in order to effect changes to the underlying Recordset after a property in the Data control had been changed. In addition to the examples previously illustrated, you must invoke the Refresh method in order to place a newly added record into the correct order in a currently open Recordset. You need to invoke the Refresh method because the default position for the newly added record is at the end of the Recordset. In addition, the Refresh method is needed in order to allow the newly added record to be visible to other users of a similarly created Recordset. The same would also be true of editing a field that was part of the order by clause in an SQL statement or changing a field that composed the index of a table. In a multi-user environment, it is important to ensure that an update is always executed after adding, changing, or deleting records so that all users have access to an up-to-date database.

NOTE

If you are using transaction controls, you must ensure that a Refresh method is not used inside a BeginTrans/CommitTrans block since this action will cause a runtime error.

To practice using the Refresh method, make the following changes to your project:

1. Add the following command button to your form:

```
Name= cmdadd
Caption= &Add
Top= 4080
Width = 795
Height= 295
left = 4440
```

2. Add the following command button to your form:

```
Name= cmdrefresh
Caption= &Refresh
Top= 4080
Width = 855
Height= 295
left = 3420
```

3. Add the following code to the Cmdadd_Click event:

```
data1.Recordset.addnew
```

4. Add the following code to the Cmdrefresh_Click event:

```
data1.refresh
```

5. Run your project.

6. Press the Add button; a blank screen appears.

7. Enter the data for the new record into the available text boxes.

8. Select the move to the next record button to save your record and move to the next record.

9. Move to the previous record, and note that your new record is not there.

10. Move to the last record in the Recordset, and note that this is the record that you entered.

11. Select the Refresh button. The Refresh method causes the Data control to rebuild its underlying Recordset and position the current record to the first record in the set. Your newly added record now appears in the correct position of the Recordset.

UpdateControls

The UpdateControls method will reset the bound controls to the values they had prior to any editing. This method provides the same effect as re-reading the current record. An example of using the UpdateControls method would be when the user decides that he does not want to save any changes that have been made.

To practice using the UpdateControls method, make the following changes to your project:

1. Add the following to the data1_Validate event:

```
data1_Validate (action as integer , save as integer)


if save= false then

    exit sub

endif

if msgbox (" Save Changed Record ",vbyesno,"","",0)= vbNo then

    data1.updatecontrols
    exit sub

endif
```

2. Run your project.
3. Change a number of fields in the current record.
4. Use the Data control to move to another record or try to unload the form. You are prompted in order to determine whether you want to save the changes.
5. Select Yes to save your changes. Select No to ignore the changes.

UpdateRecord

The UpdateRecord method causes the contents of the bound controls to be updated to the database. This method allows you to save any changes and keep the record current. In contrast, previous examples used the Data control to save the record changes only when the record pointer was changed.

To practice using the UpdateRecord method, make the following changes to your project:

1. Add the following command button to your form:

```
Name= cmdupdate
Caption= &Update
Top= 4080
Width = 855
Height= 295
left = 2460
```

2. Add the following code to the cmdupdate_Click event:

```
data1.updaterecord
```

3. Run your project.
4. Make a change to the currently displayed record.
5. Select the Update button. The changes that you have made to the record are saved, and the changed record remains the current record (see Figure 27.6).

FIGURE 27.6.

The final appearance of the bound control form.

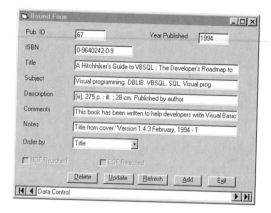

Using the Data Control with Non-Access Databases

The Data control enables you to access databases other than MS Access databases. To access an external(non-MS Access) database, you must make an entry in the Connect property that matches the type of database you are trying to access. Once you have connected to the external database, it will behave like a native Access database.

Perform the following steps in order to practice connecting to an external database:

1. Using either MS Access or the Visdata sample application that comes with Visual Basic, export the TITLES table contained in the BIBLIO.MDB MS Access database to a DBASE III format file named TITLE.DBF. Save the exported file to same directory as BIBLIO.MDB.

2. Make a copy of the Form1 form and name it Form3.

3. In the Project Options dialog box, change the start-up form to Form3.

4. Alter the form caption for Form3 to Bound DBASE.

5. Make the following changes to the Data control's properties:
   ```
   Connect = DBASE III;
   DataBase= The Directory where the TITLE.DBF resides.
   RECORDSOURCE= title
   Ensure that the Recordsettype is set to Dynaset.
   ```

6. Remove the existing code from the Form_Load event and add the following code:
   ```
   sub Form_Load
   Dim x As Integer

   Data1.Refresh
   ```

```
For x = 0 To Data1.Recordset.Fields.Count - 1
    comfield.AddItem Data1.Recordset.Fields(x).Name
Next x

end sub
```

7. Run the project.

Note that the application behaves in the same manner as when an MS Access format database was used.

NOTE

When you are using non-MS Access databases, you must use the SQL syntax of the attached database, not that of MS Access.

Using the Data Control to Delete Records

So far in this chapter, you have looked at all of the properties, methods, and events that are associated with the Data control. However, there has not been an example presented on how records are removed from a Recordset. The reason for this is that there is not a delete type of action provided with the Data control. The following example will build upon the final bound control example and add a method in order to delete a record from the underlying Recordset.

Make the following changes to your project:

1. Set the start-up form in your project to Form1.

2. Add the following command button to your form:

```
Name= cmdDelete
Caption= &Delete
Top= 4080
Width =855
Height= 295
left = 1440
```

3. Add the following code to the cmdDelete_Click event

```
data1.Recordset.delete
cmdrefresh_Click
```

4. Run your project.

When you select the Delete button, the currently displayed record is deleted and the Recordset is updated. You could perform the same steps to provide the same functionality to the Bound DBASE form.

Summary

This chapter covered the various properties, methods, and events of the Data control. The examples provided have used simple examples in order to illustrate the capabilities of the control. The final version of the form you created allowed you to sort, display, edit, delete, and add records to the TITLES table of the BIBLIO database as well as that of the external TITLE.DBF file.

In addition to the Data control, you had a very brief look at the Recordset property of the Data control. The Recordset property is very powerful as it allows you to fully exploit the properties and methods of the Jet database engine.

In the following chapter, you will see additional properties and methods that can be applied to Data Access Objects. You can apply the majority of these properties and methods to the Data control through the use of the Recordset property.

The Access Jet Engine

28

by Brad Shannon

The Jet engine is the database management system used by Visual Basic and Microsoft Access. The Jet engine is responsible for the retrieval and storage of data in users' databases. The Jet engine supplied with Visual Basic comes in the following three forms:

- **16-bit version of Jet version 2.5.** This version includes all the new features available in the Jet engine and also provides backwards compatibility with applications created using either Jet 1.1 or Jet 2.0 architecture. Jet 2.5 is compatible with databases created using all version up to and including Access version 2.5.

- **32-bit version of Jet version 2.5/3.0 compatibility layer.** This version includes all the new features available in the Jet engine and also provides backwards compatibility with applications created using either Jet 1.1 or Jet 2.0 architecture. Jet 2.5 is compatible with databases created using all version up to and including Access version 2.5. This 32-bit version is provided to ease the conversion of your applications to Jet 3.0.

- **32-bit Jet version 3.0.** This version is not 100 percent backwards compatible with the previous version of the Jet engine. You may have to modify some areas of your application to take full advantage of the new engine and its features. The Jet 3.0 engine is compatible with databases created using the 32-bit version of Microsoft Access .

The Jet engine is a collection of objects controlled by your application. The objects are used to access and manipulate information contained in a database used by your application. The collection of objects is referred to as *Data Access Objects*, or the DAO layer. The following objects make up the DAO layer:

- DBEngine
- Workspace
- Database
- TableDef
- Field
- Index
- QueryDef
- Parameter
- Recordset
- Relation
- Error

These objects—and the properties and methods associated with them—are covered in this chapter.

To ensure that the Data Access Objects are available to your project, select the appropriate DAO library (such as Microsoft DAO 3.0 Object Library) from the Tools | References selection dialog box.

DAO Supplied with the Professional Edition versus Standard Edition

The Standard edition of Visual Basic contains a 32-bit version of the Jet engine. With the Standard edition, you cannot directly manipulate the DAO—you can only use the built-in Data control and data bound controls in order to manipulate data stored in a Jet database.

> **NOTE**
>
> To create a database with the Standard edition of Visual Basic, you can use either the Data Manager application distributed with the Standard edition of Visual Basic or the 32-bit version of MS Access.

The Professional edition of Visual Basic contains two versions of the Jet engine:

- Version 2.5, a 16-bit version of the Jet Engine that provides all the new features of the DAO while maintaining backwards compatibility with applications created using Visual Basic 3.0.
- Version 3.0, a 32-bit version of the Jet engine that provides all the new features of the DAO.

> **NOTE**
>
> The 32-bit version of the DAO does not support any of the older methods contained in Visual Basic 3.0. For example, the older CreateDynaset method has been replaced in the 32-bit version with the CreateRecordset method.

Bound Controls versus the Jet Engine

In the preceding chapter, you saw how the Data control allows you to quickly create an application to view or edit existing records. However, you cannot use the Data control to add, delete, or change many of the underlying properties of the recordset. To make these changes, you must drop down to the DAO layer.

Data Access Object Model

The Data Access Object (DAO) model is a hierarchy of objects and collections (see Figure 28.1). In order to access the information displayed in Figure 28.1, search the Help file supplied with Visual Basic for the topic Jet Database Engine.

FIGURE 28.1.

The Data Access Object model is a hierarchy.

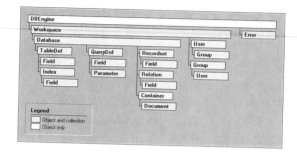

The following sections discuss each of the objects or collections that make up the Data Access Object model.

DBEngine Object

The DBEngine object is the top layer of the DAO. All other objects and collections are contained in the DBEngine object. Although you do not have to define the DBEngine in your application, you cannot have more than one instance of this object in your application. The DBEngine object contains and defines the Workspace and Error objects and collections.

> **NOTE**
>
> At any one time, you can run a maximum of 10 applications that use the Jet engine.

DBEngine Object Properties

The following properties are available for use by the DBEngine object:

- **DefaultUser/DefaultPassword.** This property provides the default user information for all created workspaces. This information is used only when the user information is not supplied during the creation of a workspace. The property needs to be set only when working with secured MS Access databases. This property is provided for backward compatibility. Use the User and Password properties of the Workspace to maintain future compatibility.

- **IniPath.** The IniPath property is used to set or retrieve the path to the file containing the location of the ISAM.DLL files. The files are needed by Visual Basic to open non-Access-based databases. The IniPath property must be set before any event that initializes the database engine or a runtime error will occur.

NOTE

The behavior of the `IniPath` property varies between the 32-bit and 16-bit versions of Windows. In the 16-bit version, the setting of the ISAM DLL affects all applications currently running on the user's computer. In the 32-bit system, the setting affects only the current application.

- ▪ **LoginTimeout.** This property specifies the period of time that the Jet engine should wait for a response from a login request to an ODBC database.

- ▪ **Version.** The `Version` property is a read-only property that returns the version of the `DBEngine` currently in use.

DBEngine **Object Methods**

The following methods are available to the `DBEngine`:

- ▪ **CompactDatabase.** The `CompactDatabase` method defragments your database, allowing it to use space more efficiently and improving data access performance. It is possible to change the database version using the `CompactDatabase` method. However, this method cannot convert nontabular information stored in the database.

- ▪ **CreateWorkspace.** The `CreateWorkspace` method creates a workspace that can later be used to open databases. When you create a new workspace, that workspace is added automatically to the Workspace collection. The `CreateWorkspace` method uses the following three parameters:

Parameter	Description
Name	The `Name` parameter defines the name of the new workspace. The name of each workspace must be unique.
Userid	The `Userid` parameter defines the user creating the workspace.
Password	The `Password` parameter defines the user's password. `Userid` and `password` are needed only for secured MS Access databases.

Once a workspace has been created, you cannot change any of its properties.

The following example shows the creation of a workspace on an unsecured database:

```
Dim wstest As Workspace
Set wstest = DBEngine.CreateWorkspace(0)
```

If the database is secured, you must include the following expression to create the workspace:

```
wstest = DBEngine.CreateWorkspace("testworkspace", "User1", "password1")
```

■ **Idle.** The Idle method provides the database engine with the necessary time to perform housekeeping tasks. These tasks were not previously possible during a period of heavy database activity. Use of the Idle method is important in a multiuser environment because it ensures that all writes have been made. Using the Idle method's optional dbFreeLocks parameter forces the database engine to release all the currently held read locks to be released, freeing previously held memory. Using the Idle method is similar to using the DoEvents statement in your application to allow other system events to occur.

Note: If your operations are part of a transaction, there is no need to invoke the Idle method because the equivalent action is provided by the CommitTrans method, which is discussed later.

■ **RegisterDatabase.** The RegisterDatabase method records the ODBC connect information in the ODBC.INI file. The driver for the ODBC source reads this information and uses it to open a connection to the database. Because the database must be registered only once, it is perhaps a better idea to use the Windows Control Panel-based OBDC application to register your database. Alternatively, include the registration as part of you application setup.

■ **RepairDatabase.** The RepairDatabase method attempts to correct errors in a corrupt MS Access database. If a database is damaged, you will receive a trappable error when you try to open the database.

Note: You should compact a database that has been repaired to ensure that the database is no longer fragmented.

Workspace **Object/Collection**

The Workspace object allows you to open databases so that you can perform operations on the database object. You can have multiple workspaces in an application.

The Workspace object contains and defines the User, Group, and Database objects and collections.

> **NOTE**
>
> Once you have created a workspace and added it to the Workspace collection, you cannot alter any of its properties.

Workspace **Object Properties**

The following properties are available to the Workspace object:

■ **Count.** The Count property is used to indicate the number of workspaces contained in the Workspace collection. If the count equals 0, there are no workspaces contained in the Workspace collection.

- **Name.** The Name property is used to assign a meaningful name to the workspace.
- **Username and Password.** The UserName parameter defines the user creating or owning the Workspace. The Password parameter defines the user's password.

  The Username and Password properties are needed only when working with secured MS Access databases.

Workspace Object Methods

The following methods are available to the Workspace object:

- **BeginTrans, CommitTrans, and RollBack.** The BeginTrans, CommitTrans, and RollBack methods are all used as part of a transaction block. Reasons for using these methods are as follows:

  - For speed. Because all writes are deferred until the CommiTrans method is executed, using the method speeds up write access considerably.

  - To maintain the integrity of a database transaction. If part of a transaction cannot be completed, you can use the RollBack method to return the database(s) to the state they were in just before the BeginTrans statement.

In the following code example, the Notes field in the Titles table of the BIBLIO database is set to Test Notes when the Yes button is selected from the MsgBox that is displayed.

```
Dim wstitle As Workspace
Dim dbbiblio As Database
Dim rstitles As Recordset

Set wstitle = DBEngine.CreateWorkspace("title", "Admin", "")
Set dbbiblio = wstitle.OpenDatabase("c:\vb40\biblio.mdb", False, False)
Set rstitles = dbbiblio.OpenRecordset(" select * from titles", dbOpenDynaset)

If rstitles.RecordCount = 0 Then
    Exit Sub
End If

wstitle.BeginTrans

Do While rstitles.EOF = False
    rstitles.Edit
    rstitles("notes") = "Test Notes "
    rstitles.Update
    rstitles.MoveNext

Loop
If MsgBox("Do you wish to Save the Changes you have Made ", vbYesNo, "", "",
➥0) = vbYes Then
    wstitle.CommitTrans
Else
    wstitle.Rollback
End If
```

■ **Close.** The Close method closes the specified workspace and removes it from the Workspace collection. If an attempt is made to close the default workspace, an error is generated.

■ **CreateDatabase.** The CreateDatabase method is used to create a new MS Access database and assign it to a Database object. When creating the database, you can specify the following information:

■ Language-specific information that relates to the collating method used by the database.

■ The target version of MS Access that the database is compatible with.

■ Whether the database is to be encrypted.

Once the database has been created, it does not contain Data Access objects. These must be created by your application or by using a database-manipulation tool such as MS Access.

The following example shows the creation of a new MS Access database using a general collating order. The database is created as a Jet 3.0 (32-bit) or Jet 2.5 (16-bit) database depending on the version of the DAO used in your project.

```
Dim wstitle As Workspace
Dim dbnew As Database

Set wstitle = DBEngine.CreateWorkspace("title", "Admin", "")
Set dbnew = wstitle.CreateDatabase("c:\vb40\new.mdb", dblangGeneral)
```

■ **CreateGroup.** The CreateGroup method is used to create a new Group security object. The CreateGroup method has two parameters:

Parameter	Description
Name	Represents the name to be assigned to the new Group object.
PID	Represents the group account to be assigned to the new Group object.

■ **CreateUser.** The CreateUser method is used to create a new User security object. The CreateUser method has three parameters:

Parameter	Description
Name	Represents the name to be assigned to the new User object.
PID	Represents the account to be assigned to the new User object.
Password	Represents the password to be used by the new User object.

■ **OpenDatabase.** The OpenDatabase method opens a physical database and assigns it to a Database type object. The OpenDatabase method uses the following parameters:

Parameter	Description
Dbname	If the database is a Microsoft Access–type database, the Dbname property contains the name and the path to the database. If the database is an ODBC-type database, the Dbname property can either be a valid ODBC source name or can be left blank (so that a dialog box of existing ODBC sources will be displayed). If the database is a replaceable ISAM-type database, the directory in which the database files reside is specified. If the database to be opened is a Btreive-type database, the name of the database definition file is specified.
Exclusive	This parameter is used to open the database for exclusive use by your application. If the database is currently in use by another user, a trappable error is generated when you try to access it.
Read-only	This parameter is used to open the database so that the user cannot make changes to the data in the database.
Connect	The Connect property provides additional information needed to open ODBC-type databases. An example of additional information that may be needed for an ODBC database would be Datasource, Userid, and password.

The following code sample opens the BIBLIO.MDB database as a read-only database:

```
Set dbbiblio = wstitle.OpenDatabase("c:\vb40\biblio.mdb", False, True)
```

The following code sample opens the TITLE.DBF file created in the previous chapter (please note that the IniPath property of DBEngine must have been previously set):

```
Set dbbiblio = wstitle.OpenDatabase("c:\vb40", False, TRUE,"DBASEIII;")
Set rstitles = dbbiblio.OpenRecordset(" select * from title", dbOpenDynaset)
```

The following sample code prompts you to select a valid ODBC data source when opening the database:

```
Set dbbiblio = wstitle.OpenDatabase("", False, TRUE,"ODBC;")
```

Database **Object/Collection**

The Database object allows you to manipulate databases residing on your computer or on a network. The Database object contains and defines the TableDef, QueryDef, and Recordset objects and collections.

Database Object/Collection Properties

The following properties are available to the Database object/collection:

- **CollatingOrder.** The CollatingOrder property is read-only at runtime. The CollatingOrder corresponds to the sort order of the language-specific value that was used when the database was created. If you want to change this value, you must compact the database and specify a new CollatingOrder.

- **Connect.** The Connect property is read-only at runtime. The value of the Connect property corresponds to the Connect string used when then database was opened.

- **Count.** The Count property indicates the number of Database objects contained in the Database collection. If Count equals 0, there are no databases contained in the Database collection.

- **Name.** The database Name property is read-only at runtime. The value of the Name property corresponds to the name of the physical database used when the database was opened or assigned to a data control.

- **QueryTimeout.** The QueryTimeout property specifies the period of time the Database object should wait for a response from an ODBC database.

- **RecordsAffected.** The RecordsAffected property is read-only; it indicates the number of records that were changed, added, or deleted as a result of an action query performed on the Database object.

  The following example displays a message box that shows the number of record that would change if the Yes button in the message box is selected. Note that if Yes is selected, the Notes field in the Titles table contains Test Notes for all records.

```
Dim wstitle As Workspace
Dim dbbiblio As Database
Dim rstitles As Recordset
Dim csql As String

Set wstitle = DBEngine.CreateWorkspace("title", "Admin", "")
Set dbbiblio = wstitle.OpenDatabase("c:\vb40\biblio.mdb", False, False)
Set rstitles = dbbiblio.OpenRecordset(" select * from titles", dbOpenDynaset)

If dbbiblio.Transactions = True Then
    wstitle.BeginTrans
End If

csql = " update titles set notes = 'Test Notes' "
dbbiblio.Execute csql, dbFailOnError

If MsgBox("There have been " & dbbiblio.RecordsAffected & " Records changed
Do you wish to Save the Changes you have Made ", vbYesNo, "", "", 0) = vbYes
Then
    If dbbiblio.Transactions = True Then
        wstitle.CommitTrans
    End If
Else
```

```
    If dbbiblio.Transactions = True Then
        wstitle.Rollback
    End If
End If
```

■ **Transactions.** The Transactions property is read-only at runtime. The value of the property can be either TRUE or FALSE, indicating whether the Database object supports transaction processing.

Note: You should always make sure that the Database object supports transactions before executing any transaction-related methods.

The following example checks whether or not transactions are allowed for a Database object. If they are, the actions performed on the Database object are part of a transaction block. Otherwise, the transaction block is ignored.

```
sub begintransaction (ws as workspace, db as database)

if db.transaction= true then
    ws.BeginTrans
endif

end sub
```

■ **Updatable.** The Updatable property is read-only at runtime. The value of the property can be either TRUE or FALSE, indicating whether any changes can be made to the underlying Database object. The value of this property is determined by the choice options used in creating the Database object.

The following example checks the Updatable property to determine whether or not an edit action can be completed:

```
Dim wstitle As Workspace
Dim dbbiblio As Database
Dim rstitles As Recordset

Set wstitle = DBEngine.CreateWorkspace("title", "Admin", "")
Set dbbiblio = wstitle.OpenDatabase("c:\vb40\biblio.mdb", False, True)
Set rstitles = dbbiblio.OpenRecordset(" select * from titles", dbOpenDynaset)

If dbbiblio.Updatable = True Then
    rstitles.Edit
Else
    MsgBox ("This Database Object Is Read Only ")
End If
```

■ **Version.** The Version property is read-only at runtime. This property indicates the version of the DAO engine that was used to create the database. This property differs from the DBEngine property in that you can open any version of a Microsoft database with the DBEngine version 3.0.

The following example displays the version of the DBEngine and the version of the BIBLIO.MDB database. With the 16-bit version of Visual Basic, the version of the DBEngine should be 2.5 and the version of the BIBLIO.MDB database should be 2.0. With the 32-bit version of Visual Basic, the version of the DBEngine would be 3.0, and the version of the BIBLIO.MDB database would be unchanged.

```
Dim wstitle As Workspace
Dim dbbiblio As Database
Dim rstitles As Recordset

Set wstitle = DBEngine.CreateWorkspace("title", "Admin", "")
Set dbbiblio = wstitle.OpenDatabase("c:\vb40\biblio.mdb", False, True)

MsgBox " The Version of the DBEngine is " _
& DBEngine.Version & ". The version of the " _
& dbbiblio.Name & " Database is " _
& dbbiblio.Version & "."
```

Database Object/Collection Methods

The following methods are available to the `Database` object/collection:

■ **OpenRecordset/CreateDynaset/CreateSnapshot/OpenTable.** The `OpenRecordset` method is a replacement for the `CreateDynaset`, `CreateSnapshot`, and `OpenTable` methods provided in Visual Basic 3.0. The `CreateDynaset`, `CreateSnapshot`, and `OpenTable` methods are provided only for compatibility purposes. It is recommended that you use the `OpenRecordset` method because it provides additional functionality. The `OpenRecordset` method uses the following parameters:

Parameter	Description
Source	The `Source` parameter indicates the contents of the recordset. The `Source` parameter can be a table contained in the database, a record-returning SQL statement, or an existing QueryDef contained in the `Database` object.
Type	The `Type` parameter indicates the type of recordset you want to open. The following constants are available for use as the `Type` parameter:
	`dbOpenTable` A table-type recordset is created.
	`dbOpenDynaset` A Dynaset-type recordset is created.
	`dbOpenSnapShot` A snapshot-type (Read-only Dynaset) recordset is created.
	The default type of recordset to open is a table-type recordset.
Options	The `Options` parameter further defines the characteristics of the recordset you are creating. The following constants are available for use with the `Options` parameter (you can combine options by adding them together using the + sign between constants):
	`dbDenyWrite` Other users cannot make any changes to the records contained in your recordset.

dbDenyRead	Other users cannot read any of the records contained in your recordset. This option applied only to recordsets created with the dbOpenTable type.
dbReadOnly	The recordset is opened as read-only and no changes can be made.
dbAppendOnly	You can add records to the recordset. You cannot update or delete existing records. This option applies only to recordsets created with the dbOpenDynaset type.
dbConsistent	On a joined recordset, only fields that do not affect the join condition can be updated. This option applies only to recordsets created with the dbOpenDynaset type.
dbInconsistent	On a joined recordset, all fields including those responsible for the join can be up dated. This option applies only to recordsets created with the dbOpenDynaset type.
dbForwardOnly	A snapshot-type recordset is created, which supports only the MoveNext record move-ment method.
dbSQLPassThrough	If you are using an ODBC database (for example, SQL Server or Oracle), the SQL expression used to created the recordset is executed on the server instead of using the Access database engine.
dbSeeChange	Use this option to cause a trappable error if another user tries to make a change to the record currently being edited.

The following examples use the OpenRecordset equivalents in place of the older-style CreateDynaset, CreateSnapshot, and OpenTable methods:

```
Dim wstitle As Workspace
Dim dbbiblio As Database
Dim rstitles As Recordset
Dim dstitles As Dynaset
Dim sntitles As Snapshot
Dim tbltitles As Table
Set wstitle = DBEngine.CreateWorkspace("title", "Admin", "")
Set dbbiblio = wstitle.OpenDatabase("c:\vb40\biblio.mdb", False, True)

' old method to create a Dynaset Object
Set dstitles = dbbiblio.CreateDynaset("Select * from titles")
'New Method to Open a Dynaset Type Recordset
Set rstitles = dbbiblio.OpenRecordset(" select * from titles", dbOpenDynaset)
```

```
' old method to create a Table Object
Set tbltitles = dbbiblio.OpenTable("titles")
'New Method to Open a Dynaset Type Recordset
Set rstitles = dbbiblio.OpenRecordset("titles", dbOpenTable)

' Old method to create a SnapShot Object
Set sntitles = dbbiblio.CreateSnapshot("Select * from titles")
'New Method to Open a Dynaset Type Recordset
Set rstitles = dbbiblio.OpenRecordset(" select * from titles",
➥dbOpenSnapShot)
```

An additional benefit to using the Recordset object is that when you are creating functions to retrieve data (see Chapter 27, "The Data Control"), you need only one function to handle all types of recordsets. On the other hand, if you work with the older methods, you need one function for each of the different recordset types (snapshot, Dynaset, and table).

■ **CreateProperty.** The `CreateProperty` method allows you to add additional properties to the `Database` object. The additional properties then become members of the Property collection.

The `CreateProperty` method has the following four parameters:

Parameter	Description
Name	The `Name` parameter provides identification for the new property.
Type	The `Type` parameter identifies the type of data to be stored by new property.
Value	The `Value` parameter provides the initial value of this property when the property object is created.
FDDL	The value of this parameter indicates whether the property being created is a Data Definition Language object. If this value is set to `TRUE`, the object cannot be modified or deleted unless the user has `dbSecWrite` definition.

The following example adds a Boolean `Dirty` property to the Database object and sets its default value to `TRUE`:

```
Dim wstitle As Workspace
Dim dbbiblio As Database
Dim propdirty As Property

Set wstitle = DBEngine.CreateWorkspace("title", "Admin", "")
Set dbbiblio = wstitle.OpenDatabase("c:\vb40\biblio.mdb", False, False)
' Create the New Property
Set propdirty = dbbiblio.CreateProperty("dirty", dbBoolean, True, False)
' Save the Property definition

dbbiblio.Properties.Append propdirty

Debug.Print propdirty.Value
```

```
propdirty.Value = false

Debug.Print propdirty.Value
```

■ **CreateQueryDef.** The CreateQueryDef method creates a new QueryDef that is stored in your database. Once the query has been created, it can be used to create recordsets from the database.

The CreateQueryDef method has the following parameters:

Parameter	Description
Name	The Name parameter provides the name of the newly created QueryDef. It is the name that is used in all other references to the QueryDef.
SQLtext	The SQLtext parameter contains the SQL statement to be executed when the QueryDef is run.

The following sample code creates a new QueryDef and uses the newly created QueryDef to create a recordset:

```
Dim wstitle As Workspace
Dim dbbiblio As Database
Dim qrynew As QueryDef
Dim rstitles As Recordset

Set wstitle = DBEngine.CreateWorkspace("title", "Admin", "")
Set dbbiblio = wstitle.OpenDatabase("c:\vb40\biblio.mdb", False, False)
' Create a New QueryDef
Set qrynew = dbbiblio.CreateQueryDef("new", "Select * from titles where pubid
➡= 13")
' Load The Recordset based on the New Query
Set rstitles = dbbiblio.OpenRecordset("new", dbOpenDynaset)
```

■ **CreateRelation.** The CreateRelation method creates a Relation object. The Relation object enables the Jet engine to provide referential integrity between two TableDefs or two QueryDefs. The Relation object and collection are covered in more depth later in this chapter.

The CreateRelation method has the following parameters:

Parameter	Description
Name	The Name parameter provides the name of the newly created Relation object. It is the name used in all other references to the Relation object.
Table	The Table parameter represents the parent table in the relationship.
ForeignTable	The ForeignTable parameter represents the child table in the relationship.

Parameter	Description
Attributes	The Attributes parameter further defines the characteristics of the relationship you are creating. The following constants are available for use with the Attributes parameter (you can combine options by adding them together, using the + sign between constants):

dbRelationUnique	Indicates to the Jet engine that there is a one-to-one relationship between the parent and child tables. That is, there cannot be multiple records in the child table that relate to only one record in the parent table.
dbRelationDontEnforce	Indicates to the Jet engine that there is no referential integrity between the two tables.
dbRelationInherited	This type of relationship applies only to attached tables. It indicates to the Jet engine that the relationship integrity is maintained externally.
dbRelationLeft	Indicates to the Jet engine that for every record in the parent table there can be multiple records in the child table.
dbRelationRight	Indicates to the Jet engine that for every record in the child table there can be multiple records in the parent table.
dbRelationUpdateCascade	Indicates to the Jet engine that when the value of a field relating a parent table to a child table changes, the changes should also be made to all records in the child table.
dbRelationDeleteCascade	Indicates to the Jet engine that when a record in the parent table is deleted, all the records in the child table should also be deleted.

The following sample code creates a new Relation object between the Publishers table and the Titles table in the BIBLIO.MDB database. The relationship is based on the PUDID field present in both tables. This relationship allows multiple titles per publisher and supports cascaded updates and deletions.

```
Dim wstitle As Workspace
Dim dbbiblio As Database
Dim relnew As Relation
Dim fld1 As Field

Set wstitle = DBEngine.CreateWorkspace("title", "Admin", "")
Set dbbiblio = wstitle.OpenDatabase("c:\vb40\biblio.mdb", False, False)
' Create a New Relation

Set relnew = dbbiblio.CreateRelation("new", "publishers", "titles", _
dbRelationLeft + dbRelationUpdateCascade + dbRelationDeleteCascade)
' Set the parent table field for the Relation
Set fld1 = relnew.CreateField("pubid")
' Set the Child Table field for the Relation
fld1.ForeignName = "pubid"
' Update the Fields portion of the Relations Collection

relnew.Fields.Append fld1

' Update the New Relation to the Relations Collection

dbbiblio.Relations.Append relnew
```

■ **CreateTableDef.** The CreateTableDef method creates a new table in the Database object. If you try to create a table with the name of an existing table, a trappable error occurs.

The CreateTableDef method has the following parameters:

Parameter	Description
Name	The Name parameter indicates the name of the newly created table.
Attributes	The Attributes parameter further defines the characteristics of the table you are creating. The following constants are available for use with the Attributes parameter:
dbAttachExclusive	Indicates that the table is an attached table and can be opened only for exclusive use.
dbAttachSavePWD	Indicates that the user ID and password for the attached table should be saved for use in subsequent access to the table.
dbSystemObject	Indicates that the table is a System table provided by the Jet engine. Tables of this type can be opened only as read-only.
dbHiddenObject	Indicates that the table is a Hidden table provided by the Jet engine. Tables of this type are temporary tables and can be opened only as read-only.

Parameter	Description	
	dbAttachedTable	Indicates that the table is an attached table from a non-ODBC source.
	dbAttachedODBC	Indicates that the table is an attached table from an ODBC source.
SourceTableName	If you are connecting an external table to the current Database object, this parameter should contain the actual name of the table in the external source.	
Connect	The Connect parameter is needed only when you are accessing non-Microsoft Access databases. The needs of the Connect property are specific to the type of database to which you are connecting. Further information about the Connect string for ODBC types of databases is supplied with the ODBC database driver.	

The following sample code adds the table Books to the BIBLIO.MDB database. The table contains two fields: Title and Author.

```
Dim wstitle As Workspace
Dim dbbiblio As Database
Dim newtable As TableDef
Dim fld1 As Field
Dim fld2 As Field

Set wstitle = DBEngine.CreateWorkspace("title", "Admin", "")
Set dbbiblio = wstitle.OpenDatabase("c:\vb40\biblio.mdb", False, False)

' creates a table if Data Base specified in Parameter 1

Set newtable = dbbiblio.CreateTableDef("books")

' add the fields to the tabledef Object

Set fld1 = newtable.CreateField("")

fld1.Name = "Title"
fld1.Type = dbText
fld1.Size = 30

newtable.Fields.Append fld1

Set fld2 = newtable.CreateField("")
fld2.Name = "Author"
fld2.Type = dbText
fld2.Size = 30
```

```
newtable.Fields.Append fld2

' Now add the table definition to the database object
' - - - - - - - - - - - - - - - - - - - - - - - - - - - - - - - - - - - - - - -

dbbiblio.TableDefs.Append newtable
```

■ **Execute.** The Execute method allows you to run an action QueryDef or action SQL statements on the Database object. The Execute method is used to run non-record-returning action queries.

Note: To enhance your application's performance, nest Execute statements between BeginTrans and CommiTrans statements.

The Execute method has the following parameters:

Parameter	Description		
Source	Can be a non-record-returning SQL statement or non-record-returning QueryDef.		
Options	The Options parameter further defines the characteristics of the SQL or QueryDef you are running. The following constants are available for use with the Options parameter:		
	dbDenyWrite	This option does not allow other users to make changes to the affected records until the Execute statement is completed.
	dbInconsistent	This option allows changes to fields in tables that have been joined in a relationship.
	dbConsistent	This option disallows changes to fields in tables that have been joined in a relationship.
	dbSQLPassThrough	This option indicates to the Jet engine that the QueryDef or the SQL text should be passed on to the ODBC database for processing there.
	dbFailonError	This option specifies that if there is an error at some point during the Execute statement, a RollBack of all changes automatically occurs.
	dbSeeChanges	This option causes an error to be generated if another user is editing a record that is to be affected by the QueryDef or SQL text statement.

The following sample code resets the Notes field in the Titles table to the comment
`This is a Test`. If you do not want to make the changes permanent, select the No
option from the message box and all the changes are rolled back.

```
Dim wstitle As Workspace
Dim dbbiblio As Database
Dim rstitles As Recordset
Dim csql As String

Set wstitle = DBEngine.CreateWorkspace("title", "Admin", "")
Set dbbiblio = wstitle.OpenDatabase("c:\vb40\biblio.mdb", False, False)
Set rstitles = dbbiblio.OpenRecordset(" select * from titles", dbOpenDynaset)
wstitle.BeginTrans

csql = " update titles set notes = 'Test Notes' "
dbbiblio.Execute csql, dbFailOnError

'the following statement must be entered on one line

If MsgBox("There have been " & dbbiblio.RecordsAffected & "Records changed_
   Do you wish to Save the Changes you have Made ", vbYesNo, "", "", 0) = vbYes
Then
     wstitle.CommitTrans
Else
     wstitle.Rollback
End If
```

■ **ExecuteSql.** The `ExecuteSql` method is used only against ODBC-type databases. This
method is provided for compatibility with earlier versions of Visual Basic. The only
difference between the `Execute` method and the `ExecuteSql` method is that the
`ExecuteSql` method returns the number of rows affected. As with the `Execute` method,
the SQL to be executed must be a non-record-returning SQL statement.

The `Execute` method has only one parameter: `SQLstatement`, an SQL statement that
does not return any records.

After successful completion of `ExecuteSql`, the number of rows affected is returned, as
shown in the following example. If this code was run against an ODBC-type database,
the number of records that were changed would be contained in the nrows field.

```
dim nrows as long
csql = " update titles set notes = 'Test Notes' "
nrows = dbbiblio.ExecuteSQL(csql)
```

TableDef Object/Collection

The `TableDef` object allows you to manipulate the structure of the tables in the database. The
`TableDef` object contains and defines the `Field` and `Index` objects and collections.

TableDef Object/Collection Properties

The following properties are available to the `TableDef` object/collection:

- **Attributes.** This property is read-only at runtime. The `TableDef`'s attributes are determined when the table is created by using the `CreateTableDef` method of the `Database` object.

- **Connect.** This property is read-only at runtime. The `TableDef`'s Connect property is determined when the table is created by using the `CreateTableDef` method of the `Database` object.

- **Count.** The `Count` property indicates the number of `TableDef` objects contained in the `TableDef`'s collection. If `Count` equals 0, there are no `TableDefs` contained in the `TableDef` collection.

- **DateCreated and LastUpdated.** The `DateCreated` and `LastUpdated` properties are both read-only at runtime. The `DateCreated` property contains the date and time of the table's creation; the `LastUpdated` property contains the date and time of the last modification.

- **Name.** The `Name` property is read-only at runtime. The `Name` property contains the name of the table as it was defined by the `CreateTableDef` method of the `Database` object.

- **RecordCount.** The `RecordCount` property is a read-only property that contains the total number of records in the table defined by the `TableDef` object.

- **SourceTableName.** The `SourceTableName` property is read-only at runtime for all tables in the `TableDef` collection. This property is Read/Write for an external table (at least until the table is added to the `TableDef` collection).

- **Updatable.** The `Updatable` property indicates whether or not changes can be made to the `TableDef` object. This property returns `TRUE` if changes can be made. For attached tables, this value is always `FALSE`.

- **ValidateRule.** The `ValidateRule` property indicates the conditions that must be met before a new or changed record can be successfully saved to the table. Using this property, you can allow the Jet engine to perform validation of your data.

- **ValidationText.** The `ValidationText` property specifies the text to be displayed when the results of `ValidateRule` return `FALSE`.

TableDef Object/Collection Methods

The following methods are available to the `TableDef` object/collection:

- **Append.** The `Append` method adds a new `TableDef` object to the TableDef collection.

- **CreateField.** The `CreateField` method defines the characteristics of a field that will become part of the `TableDef` object.

The `CreateField` method has the following parameters:

Parameter	Description
Name	The name associated with the field.
Type	The type of field you are creating. The following constants are available for use with the `Type` parameter. The size of the field can be automatically determined by the type of the field you are creating:

dbDate	Indicates that the field will contain date/time information (default size: 8).
dbText	Indicates that the field can contain any type of character with a maximum length of 255 characters (default size: 1 to 255).
dbMemo	Indicates that the field can contain any character or an OLE object up to a maximum size of 1.2 gigabytes (default size: 0)
dbBoolean	Indicates that the field can contain TRUE/FALSE or Yes/No values (default size: 1).
dbInteger	Indicates that the field can contain whole numbers in the range of −32,768 to 32,767. Additionally, an integer field can be used to contain Boolean data (default size: 2).
dbLong	Indicates that the field can contain whole numbers in the range −2,147,483,648 to 2,147,483,647 (default size: 4).
dbCurrency	Indicates that the field can contain currency type information. The maximum size of the value can be 11 numbers to the left of the decimal and 4 numbers to the right of the decimal. The number of decimals is fixed for each value in this type of field (default size: 8).
dbSingle	Indicates that the field can contain single precision floating-point numbers (default size: 4).
dbDouble	Indicates that the field can contain double-precision floating-point numbers (default size: 8).
dbByte	Indicates that the field can contain positive integers in the range 0 to 255 (default size: 1).
dbLongBinary	Indicates that the field can contain OLE objects (default size: 0).

The following sample code creates a field named Month in the Titles table:

```
Dim wstitle As Workspace
Dim dbbiblio As Database
Dim tbltitles As TableDef
Dim fld1 As Field

Set wstitle = DBEngine.CreateWorkspace("title", "Admin", "")
Set dbbiblio = wstitle.OpenDatabase("c:\vb40\biblio.mdb", False, False)
' Get the Existing Table Definition
Set tbltitles = dbbiblio!Titles
' Create Field object.
Set fld1 = tbltitles.CreateField("month", dbText, 12)
    ' Append MyField to Fields collection.
tbltitles.Fields.Append fld1
```

NOTE

Notice the use of the ! character when setting the TableDef. It is used because we are accessing a member of a collection.

- **CreateIndex.** The CreateIndex method is used to create a new Index object. The CreateIndex method has only one parameter: Name, which defines the name used to refer to the index.

    The following sample code creates an index on the newly created Month field in the Titles table:

```
Dim wstitle As Workspace
Dim dbbiblio As Database
Dim indx1 As Index
Dim fld1 As Field
Dim tbltitles As TableDef

' Create the Workspace
Set wstitle = DBEngine.CreateWorkspace("title", "Admin", "")
' Open the Database
Set dbbiblio = wstitle.OpenDatabase("c:\vb40\biblio.mdb", False, False)
' Open the Table Definition
Set tbltitles = dbbiblio!Titles
' Create the new Index object.
Set indx1 = tbltitles.CreateIndex("nonthindx")
' define the index field
Set fld1 = indx1.CreateField("month")
' Define the index as non primary, non unique, and non required
indx1.Unique = False
indx1.Primary = False
indx1.Required = False
indx1.Fields.Append fld1 ' Save Index definition by appending it to Indexes
➥collection.
tbltitles.Indexes.Append indx1
```

- **CreateProperty.** The CreateProperty method allows you to add additional properties to the TableDef object. The additional properties become members of the Property collection.

The CreateProperty method has the following parameters:

Parameter	Description
Name	The Name parameter provides identification for the property being created.
Type	The Type parameter identifies the type of data to be stored by the property being created.
Value	The Value parameter provides the initial value of the property being created.
FDDL	The value of this parameter indicates whether the property being added is a Data Definition Language object. If this value is set to TRUE, the object cannot be modified or deleted unless the user has dbSecWrite definition.

The following sample code adds a Contents property using the CreateProperty method to the Title TableDef object and sets its default value to Test:

```
Dim wstitle As Workspace
Dim dbbiblio As Database
Dim proptext As Property
Dim tbltitle As TableDef

Set wstitle = DBEngine.CreateWorkspace("title", "Admin", "")
Set dbbiblio = wstitle.OpenDatabase("c:\vb40\biblio.mdb", False, False)
Set tbltitle = dbbiblio!titles
' Create the New Property
Set proptext = tbltitle.CreateProperty("contents", dbText, "Test", False)

' Save the Property definition

tbltitle.Properties.Append proptext
Debug.Print proptext.Value
proptext.Value = " testing property"
Debug.Print proptext.Value
```

■ **Delete.** The Delete method removes a TableDef object from the TableDef collection.

■ **OpenRecordset.** The OpenRecordset method opens a Recordset object from a TableDef object. The difference between the OpenRecordset method for a TableDef and the OpenRecordset method for a Database is that when opening a recordset from a TableDef, you cannot specify the Source parameter. Instead, all records from the TableDef are returned in the recordset.

The `OpenRecordset` method has the following parameters:

Parameter	Description
Type	The `Type` parameter indicates the type of recordset you want to open. The following constants are available for use with the `Type` parameter:
	`dbOpenTable` A table-type recordset is created.
	`dbOpenDynaset` A Dynaset-type recordset is created.
	`dbOpenSnapShot` A snapshot-type (read-only Dynaset) recordset is created.
	The default type of recordset to open is a table-type recordset.
Options	The `Options` parameter further defines the characteristics of the recordset you are creating. The following constants are available for use with the `Options` parameter. You can combine options by adding them together, using the + sign between constants.
	`dbDenyWrite` Other users cannot make changes to the records contained in your recordset.
	`dbDenyread` Other users cannot read any of the records contained your recordset. This option applies only to recordsets created with the `dbOpenTable` type.
	`dbReadOnly` The recordset is opened as read-only; no changes can be made.
	`dbAppendOnly` You can add records to the recordset; you cannot update or delete existing records. This option applies only to recordsets created with the `dbOpenDynaset` type.
	`dbConsistent` On a joined recordset, only fields that do not affect the join condition can be updated. This option apples only to recordsets created with the `dbOpenDynaset` type.
	`dbInconsistent` On a joined recordset, all fields including those responsible for the join can be updated. This option apples only to recordsets created with the `dbOpenDynaset` type.
	`dbForwardOnly` A snapshot-type recordset is created that supports only the `MoveNext` record movement method.

Parameter	Description
dbSQLPassThrough	If you are using an ODBC database (such as SQL Server or Oracle), the SQL expression used to create the recordset is executed on the server instead of using the Access database engine.
dbSeeChange	This option causes a trappable error if another user makes a change to the record currently being edited.

The following sample code creates a recordset from the `TableDef` of the Titles table:

```
Dim wstitle As Workspace
Dim dbbiblio As Database
Dim proptext As Property
Dim tbltitle As TableDef
Dim rstitle As Recordset
' open the Workspace
Set wstitle = DBEngine.CreateWorkspace("title", "Admin", "")
' open the Database
Set dbbiblio = wstitle.OpenDatabase("c:\vb40\biblio.mdb", False, False)
' Set the Table Definition
Set tbltitle = dbbiblio!titles
' Open the RecordSet
Set rstitle = tbltitle.OpenRecordset(dbOpenDynaset)
```

- **Refresh.** The `Refresh` method ensures that the collection is complete and up to date.

- **RefreshLink.** The `RefreshLink` method ensures that the information contained in attached tables is complete and up to date.

Note: It is good practice to perform a `Refresh` after you have performed a `RefreshLink` to ensure that all the collections have been updated.

Field Object/Collection

The `Field` object allows you to directly manipulate the data stored in the database. It is through the `Field` object that data is read and placed in fields.

Field Object/Collection Properties

The following properties are available to the `Field` object/collection:

- **AllowZeroLength.** The value of the `AllowZeroLength` property is read/write until the field you are creating has been added to the Fields collection. Once the field is added to the collection, the `AllowZeroLength` property becomes read-only. The `AllowZeroLength` property determines whether the value of the field can be an empty string. If the value of this property is `TRUE`, any attempt to place a null value in this field results in a runtime error.

■ **Attributes.** The value of the `Attributes` property is read/write until the field you are creating has been added to the Fields collection. Once the field is added to the collection, the `Attributes` property becomes read-only. The `Attributes` property allows you to define additional information about the field's characteristics. The value of the `Attributes` property can be a made up of a combination of the following constants:

Constant	Description
dbFixedField	Indicates that the length of the field is fixed. This is the default setting for all numeric fields.
dbVariableField	Indicates that the length of a field is variable. This is the default setting for all text fields.
dbAutoIncrField	Indicates that the field is numeric. This field cannot be changed and contains a value that is automatically assigned by the Jet engine. This type of field is supported only by Microsoft Access databases.
dbUpdateableField	Indicates that the value in the field can be changed.
dbDescending	If the field is part of an Index collection, this attribute indicates that the field is sorted in descending order.

■ **CollatingOrder.** The `CollatingOrder` property is a read-only property that indicates the method in which the field is to be sorted. See the `CollatingOrder` property of the `Database` object, earlier in this chapter, for more information.

■ **Count.** The `Count` property indicates the number of `Field` objects contained in the Field collection. If `Count` equals 0, there are no fields contained in the Field collection.

■ **DataUpdateable.** The `DataUpdateable` property is a read-only property that indicates whether the contents of the field can be changed.

■ **DefaultValue.** The `DefaultValue` property is read/write at runtime until the field you are creating has been added to the Field collection. Once the field is added to the collection, the value of the `DefaultValue` property is read-only. `DefaultValue` contains the value automatically assigned to a field when a new record in a table containing that field is added.

■ **ForeignName.** The `ForeignName` property refers to the name of the field in a table.

■ **Name.** The `Name` property is read/write at runtime until the field you are creating has been added to the Field collection. The `Name` property identifies the field so that the field can be accessed by your application.

■ **OrdinalPosition.** The `OrdinalPosition` property is read/write at runtime until the field you are creating has been added to the Field collection. Once the field is added to the collection, the `OrdinalPosition` property becomes read-only. `OrdinalPosition` represents where in the Field collection the field you are creating is to appear.

■ **Required.** The Required property is read/write at runtime until the field you are creating has been added to the Field collection. Once the field is added to the collection, the Required property becomes read-only. The Required property indicates that the value of the field must not contain a #NULL# value. If no value is supplied, a trappable runtime error is generated.

■ **Size.** The Size property is read/write at runtime until the field you are creating has been added to the Field collection. Once the field is added to the collection, the Size property becomes read-only. The Size property indicates the maximum size of data that can be stored in the field. The maximum size of a field is limited by the type of data the field can store (for example, a dbText field can contain a maximum of 255 bytes of data). If your application makes an attempt to place more data than is allowed by the field, a trappable runtime error is generated.

■ **SourceField.** The SourceField property is read/write at runtime until the field you are creating has been added to the Field collection. Once the field is added to the collection, the SourceField property becomes read-only. SourceField indicates the original name of a field in an attached table.

■ **SourceTable.** The SourceTable property is read/write at runtime until the field you are creating has been added to the Field collection. Once the field is added to the collection, the SourceTable property becomes read-only. The SourceTable property indicates the name of the attached table containing the field.

■ **Type.** The Type property is read/write at runtime until the field you are creating has been added to the Field collection. Once the field is added to the collection, the Type property becomes read-only. The Type property indicates the type of field that has been defined. You can use the Type property to determine what the contents of the field should be.

The following constants are available for use with the Type property. The size of the field is automatically determined by the type of the field you are creating.

Constant	Description
dbDate	Indicates that this field will contain date/time information (default size: 8).
dbText	Indicates that this field can contain any type of character with a maximum length of 255 characters (default size: 1 to 255).
dbMemo	Indicates that the field can contain any character or an OLE object up to a maximum size of 1.2 gigabytes (default size: 0).
dbBoolean	Indicates that the field can contains TRUE/FALSE or Yes/No values (default size: 1).
dbInteger	Indicates that the field can contain whole numbers in the range −32,768 to 32,767. Note that an integer field can be used to contain Boolean data as well (default size: 2).

Constant	Description
dbLong	Indicates that the field can contain whole numbers in the range −2,147,483,648 to 2,147,483,647 (default size: 4).
dbCurrency	Indicates that the field can contain currency-type information. The maximum size of the value can be 11 numbers to the left of the decimal and 4 numbers to the right of the decimal. The number of decimals is fixed for each value in this type of field (default size: 8).
dbSingle	Indicates that the field can contain single-precision floating-point numbers (default size: 4).
dbDouble	Indicates that the field can contain double-precision floating-point numbers (default size: 8).
dbByte	Indicates that the field can contain positive integers in the range 0 to 255 (default size: 1).
dbLongBinary	Indicates that the field can contain OLE objects (default size: 0).

■ **ValidateOnset.** The ValidateOnset property is read/write at runtime until the field you are creating has been added to the Field collection. Once the field is added to the collection, the ValidateOnset property becomes read-only. The ValidateOnset property determines at what point the field-level validation is carried out. If the value of the property is TRUE, the validation defined by the validation rule of the field takes places when the value of the field is modified. If the value of the property is FALSE, the validation occurs as part of the update method of the recordset.

Note: The ValidateOnset property and all other validate properties are available only when using the new type of recordset objects.

■ **ValidateRule.** The ValidateRule property is read/write at runtime until the field you are creating has been added to the Field collection. Once the field is added to the collection, the ValidateRule property becomes read-only. The ValidateRule property defines the validation that the Jet engine is to perform on your data. The timing of the validation is defined by the setting of the ValidateOnset property.

■ **ValidationText.** The ValidationText property is read/write at runtime until the field you are creating has been added to the Field collection. Once the field is added to the collection, the ValidationText property becomes read-only. The ValidationText property defines the message displayed to the user if the contents of the field do not pass the ValidateRule.

■ **Value.** The Value property is read/write at runtime. The Value property retrieves or sets the value of a field at runtime.

Note: When retrieving data from a Field object, ensure that you do not try to assign a #NULL# value to a Visual Basic control. Doing so causes a runtime error.

The following example shows how you can view the properties of all of the fields contained in the BIBLIO.MDB database supplied with Visual Basic:

1. Open a new project.
2. Add a form to the project.
3. Place the following controls on the form:

Control	Name	Caption	Top	Left	Width	Height
FORM	Form1	Bound Form	1240	1635	6495	5190
Label	ldlfieldname	Field Name	240	180	1215	285
Label	lblfieldtype	Field Type	240	3300	1215	285
Label	lblposition	Position	720	180	1215	285
Label	lblsize	Size	720	3300	1215	285
Label	lslsourcefield	Source Field	1200	180	1215	285
Label	lblsourcetable	Source Table	1200	3300	1215	285
Label	lblvalue	Value	1680	180	1215	285
Label	lblattributes	Attributes	2100	180	1215	285
Label	lblcollating	Collating Order	2100	3300	1215	285
Label	lbldefault	Default Value	2520	180	1215	285
Label	lblvalidaterule	Validate Rule	180	5040	1215	285
Label	lblvalidatetext	Validation Text	2940	1560	1215	285
CheckBox	chkdataupdateable	Upateable	3540	180	1755	285
CheckBox	chkrequired	Required	3540	2160	1335	285
CheckBox	chkallowzerolength	Allow Zero Length	3540	3780	1875	285
CheckBox	chkvalidate	Validate on Set	3900	180	1875	285
Command	cmdend(1)	E&xit	4320	5440	795	295
TextBox	txtname		240	1680	1515	295
TextBox	txttype		240	4740	1515	295
TextBox	txtordinalposition		720	1680	1515	295
TextBox	txtsize		720	4740	1515	295
TextBox	txtsourcefield		1200	1680	1515	295
TextBox	txtsourcetable		1200	4740	1515	295
Textbox	txtvalue		1680	1680	4635	295
TextBox	txtattributes		2100	1680	1515	295
TextBox	txtcollatingorder		2100	4740	1515	295
TextBox	txtdefaultvalue		2520	1680	2355	295

Control	Name	Caption	Top	Left	Width	Height
TextBox	txtvalidaterule		2940	1680	1515	295
TextBox	txtvalidationtext		2940	4740	1515	295

4. Add a frame to the form and place these additional controls on the Frame control:

Control	Name	Caption	Top	Left	Width	Height
Frame	frame1		0	0	6735	4755
Label	lbltable	Table	660	240	1215	295
Label	lblfield	Field	1740	240	1215	295
Combo Box	comtable		660	2880	1875	300
Combo Box	comfield		1740	2880	1875	300
Command	cmdend(0)	E&xit	4320	5460	795	295
Command	cmdpoperties	&Properties	4320	4380	795	295

5. Add the following code to the Form_load event:

```
Dim wstitle As Workspace
Dim dbbiblio As DATABASE
Dim X As Integer

Set wstitle = DBEngine.CreateWorkspace("title", "Admin", "")
Set dbbiblio = wstitle.OpenDatabase("c:\vb40\biblio.mdb", False, False)

For X = 1 To dbbiblio.TableDefs.Count - 1
    If dbbiblio.TableDefs(X).Attributes <> dbSystemObject - 2 And
dbbiblio.TableDefs(X).Attributes <> dbReadOnly Then
        comtable.AddItem dbbiblio.TableDefs(X).Name
    End If
Next
```

6. Add the following code to the comtable_click event:

```
Dim X As Integer

comfield.Clear

Set rstitles = dbbiblio.OpenRecordset(comtable.Text, dbOpenTable)

For X = 1 To rstitles.Fields.Count - 1
    comfield.AddItem rstitles.Fields(X).Name
Next
```

7. Add the following code to the cmdproperties_click event:

```
Dim rstitles As Recordset

If Len(comfield.Text) = 0 Or Len(comtable.Text) = 0 Then
    Exit Sub
End If

Frame1.Visible = False

Set rstitles = dbbiblio.OpenRecordset(comtable.Text, dbOpenTable)
```

```
If rstitles.RecordCount = 0 Then
    Exit Sub
End If

rstitles.MoveFirst

If Not IsNull(rstitles(comfield.Text)) Then
    txtnotes.Text = rstitles(comfield.Text).Value
End If

txttype.Text = rstitles(comfield.Text).Type
txtsourcetable.Text = rstitles(comfield.Text).SourceTable
txtsourcefield.Text = rstitles(comfield.Text).SourceField
txtsize.Text = rstitles(comfield.Text).Size
txtattributes.Text = rstitles(comfield.Text).Attributes
txtcolattingorder.Text = rstitles(comfield.Text).CollatingOrder
txtdefaultvalue.Text = rstitles(comfield.Text).DefaultValue
txtvalidaterule.Text = rstitles(comfield.Text).ValidationRule
txtvalidationtext.Text = rstitles(comfield.Text).ValidationText

If rstitles(comfield.Text).Required = True Then
    chkrequired.Value = vbChecked
Else
    chkrequired.Value = vbUnchecked
End If

If rstitles(comfield.Text).DataUpdatable = True Then
    chkdataupdateable.Value = vbChecked
Else
    chkdataupdateable.Value = vbUnchecked
End If

If rstitles(comfield.Text).AllowZeroLength = True Then
    chkAllowZeroLength.Value = vbChecked
Else
    chkAllowZeroLength.Value = vbUnchecked
End If

If rstitles(comfield.Text).ValidateOnSet = True Then
    chkvalidate.Value = vbChecked
Else
    chkvalidate.Value = vbUnchecked
End If

txtordinalposition.Text = rstitles(comfield.Text).OrdinalPosition
txtname.Text = rstitles(comfield.Text).Name
```

8. Add the following code to the cmdend_click event:

```
If index = 1 Then
    Frame1.Visible = True
    Exit Sub
End If

Unload Me
Set form228 = Nothing
```

9. Now run the project. Select a table from the Tables combo box and then select a field from the Fields combo box (see Figure 28.2). When you click the Properties button, you see all the properties for the selected field (see Figure 28.3).

FIGURE 28.2.

Field selection .

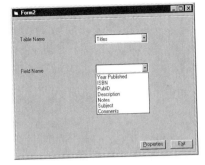

FIGURE 28.3.

Properties of the selected field.

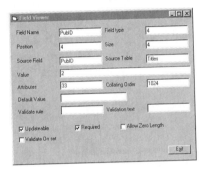

Field Object/Collection Methods

The following methods are available to the `Field` object/collection:

- **Append.** The `Append` method is used to add a new `Field` object to the Field collection.
- **AppendChunk.** The `AppendChunk` method is used to assign a string field exceeding 255 bytes.
- **CreateProperty.** The `CreateProperty` method allows you to add additional properties to the `Field` object. The additional properties become members of the Property collection.

  The `CreateProperty` method has the following parameters:

Parameter	Description
Name	The value of the `Name` parameter provides identification for the new property.
Type	The `Type` parameter identifies the type of data to be stored by the new property.
Value	The `Value` parameter provides the initial value of the property you are adding.
FDDL	The value of this parameter indicates whether the property being added is a Data Definition Language object. If this value is `TRUE`, the object cannot be modified or deleted unless the user has `dbSecWrite` definition.

- **Delete.** The Delete method is used to remove a field from the Field collection.
- **FieldSize.** The FieldSize method returns the size of a large field (greater than 255 bytes). Use this method in conjunction with the AppendChunk and GetChunk methods.
- **GetChunk.** The GetChunk method retrieves the contents of a large field (greater than 255 bytes) and assigns it to a string variable.
- **Refresh.** The Refresh method ensures that the collection is complete and up to date.

Index Object/Collection

The Index object contains all the information relating to indexes that exist for tables in the database. The Index object contains and defines the Field objects and collections.

Index Object/Collection Properties

The following properties apply to the Index object/collection:

- **Count.** The Count property indicates the number of Index objects contained in the index collection. If Count equals 0, there are no indexes contained in the Index collection.
- **Foreign.** The Foreign property indicates whether the Index has been created on a attached table. This property is read-only at runtime.
- **IgnoreNulls.** The IgnoreNulls property is read/write at runtime until the index has been added to the index collection. Once the index is added to the collection, the IgnoreNulls property becomes read-only. The IgnoreNulls property indicates whether any of the values contained in the key fields of the index can contain a #NULL# value. If the IgnoreNulls property is set to FALSE, and the Required property is set to TRUE, a runtime error is generated when any of the fields making up the index is #NULL#.
- **Name.** The Name property of an index is read/write at runtime until the index has been added to the Index collection. Once the index is added to the collection, the Name property becomes read-only. The Name property is used to access indexes in your application.
- **Primary.** The Primary property of an index is read/write at runtime until the index has been added to the Index collection. Once the index is added to the collection, the Primary property becomes read-only. The Primary property indicates that this index is the main index for the table. The primary index must have a unique value for all records. You cannot assign #NULL# values to a primary index.

■ **Required.** The Required property of an index is read/write at runtime until the index has been added to the Index collection. Once the index is added to the collection, the Required property becomes read-only. The Required property indicates that the Value property for each of the fields making up the index expression of your table cannot be a #NULL# value.

■ **Unique.** The Unique property of an Index is read/write at runtime until the index has been added to the Index collection. Once the index is added to the collection, the Unique property becomes read-only. The Unique property indicates that the values contained in the fields making up the index must be unique for each record in the table. If the values are not unique, a runtime error is generated. The Unique property is automatically set to TRUE when an Index is defined as the primary index.

Index Object/Collection Methods

The following methods apply to the Index object/collection:

■ **Append.** The Append method is used to add a new Index object to the Index collection.

■ **CreateField.** The CreateField method is used to define the index expression to be used on the table.

In the following sample code, an Index object is created for the Titles table using the Month field:

```
Dim wstitle As Workspace
Dim dbbiblio As Database
Dim indx1 As Index
Dim fld1 As Field
Dim tbltitles As TableDef

' Create the Workspace
Set wstitle = DBEngine.CreateWorkspace("title", "Admin", "")
' Open the Database
Set dbbiblio = wstitle.OpenDatabase("c:\vb40\biblio.mdb", False, False)
' Open the Table Definition
Set tbltitles = dbbiblio!Titles
' Create the new Index object.
Set indx1 = tbltitles.CreateIndex("nonthindx")
' define the index field
Set fld1 = indx1.CreateField("month")
' Define the index as non primary, non unique, and non required
indx1.Unique = False
indx1.Primary = False
indx1.Required = False
indx1.Fields.Append fld1 ' Save Index definition by appending it to Indexes
collection.
tbltitles.Indexes.Append indx1
```

■ **CreateProperty.** The CreateProperty method allows you to add additional properties to the Index object. The additional properties become members of the Property collection.

The `CreateProperty` method has the following parameters:

Parameter	Description
Name	The value of the `Name` parameter provides identification for the property you are creating.
Type	The `Type` parameter identifies the type of data to be stored by the property you are creating.
Value	The `Value` parameter provides the initial value of the property you are creating.
FDDL	The value of this parameter indicates whether the property being created is a Data Definition Language object. If this value is set to `TRUE`, the object cannot be modified or deleted unless the user has `dbSecWrite` definition.

- **Delete.** The `Delete` method removes an `Index` object from the Index collection.
- **Refresh.** The `Refresh` method ensures that the collection is complete and up to date.

QueryDef Object/Collection

The `QueryDef` object allows you to manipulate the queries stored in your database. The `QueryDef` object contains and defines the `Field` and `Parameter` objects and collections.

QueryDef Object/Collection Properties

The following properties are available to the `QueryDef` object/collection:

- **Connect.** The `Connect` property is needed only when you are accessing a non-Microsoft Access database. The value of the `Connect` property depends on the type of database to which you are connecting. If you are connecting to an ODBC database, specify `ODBC` in the `Connect` property and also supply any additional information such as USERID and PASSWORD. The additional information depends on the type of ODBC database. Further information about the `Connect` string for ODBC databases is supplied with the ODBC database driver.

- **Count.** The `Count` property indicates the number of `QueryDef` objects contained in the QueryDef collection. If `Count` equals 0, there are no `QueryDefs` contained in the QueryDef collection.

- **DateCreated and LastUpdated.** The `DateCreated` and `LastUpdated` properties are both read-only at runtime. The `DateCreated` property contains the date and time of the QueryDef's creation; the `LastUpdated` property contains the date and time of the last modification.

■ **LogMessages.** The LogMessages property indicates whether the messages received during execution of a QueryDef against an ODBC database are to be recorded. The LogMessages property must be added to the QueryDef object using the CreateProperty method, as shown in the following example:

```
Dim wstitle As Workspace
Dim dbbiblio As Database
Dim qrynew As QueryDef
Dim rstitles As Recordset
Dim propmessages As Property

Set wstitle = DBEngine.CreateWorkspace("title", "Admin", "")

Set dbbiblio = wstitle.OpenDatabase("", False, False,"ODBC;")
' Create a New QueryDef
Set qrynew = dbbiblio.CreateQueryDef("new", "Select * from titles where pubid
= 13")
' Load The Recordset based on the New Query
Set rstitles = dbbiblio.OpenRecordset("new", dbOpenDynaset)

Set propmessages = qrynew.CreateProperty("logmessages", dbBoolean, True,
False)
' Save the Property definition

qrynew.Properties.Append propdirty
' Set the Query to Log messages
qrynew.Logmessages= true
```

■ **Name.** The Name property of a QueryDef is read/write at runtime until the QueryDef has been added to the QueryDef collection. Once the QueryDef is added to the collection, the Name property becomes read-only. The Name property provides the primary identification method for the QueryDefs in your application.

■ **ODBCTimeout.** The ODBCTimeout property specifies the length of time the Jet engine will wait for a reply from an ODBC database before returning a time-out error to your application.

■ **RecordsAffected.** The RecordsAffected property is a read-only property that indicates the number of records changed, added, or deleted as a result of an action query performed by the QueryDef object.

■ **ReturnsRecords.** The ReturnsRecords property indicates whether a SQLPassThrough query is expected to return records to the application or whether it is an action query.

■ **SQL.** The SQL property sets or reads the SQL contained in the QueryDef object.

The following sample code uses the SQL property to change the expression used to create the recordset:

```
Set qrynew = dbbiblio.CreateQueryDef("new", "Select * from titles where pubid
➡= 13")
qrynew.SQL = " Select from titles where pubid=1"
' Load The Recordset based on the New Query
Set rstitles = dbbiblio.OpenRecordset("new", dbOpenDynaset)
```

■ **Type.** The Type property indicates the type of QueryDef you want to open or create. The following constants are available for use as the Type parameter (you can combine Type constants for the QueryDef by adding them together, using the + sign between constants):

Constant	Description
dbQSelect	The query is to select a number of records and return them to the application with no changes.
dbQAction	The query is to perform an action on the underlying recordset. The action may be to add a record update record or delete records. An action query does not return rows.
dbQCrosstab	The query is not to alter any of the data in the underlying recordset; it does, however, return summary data.
dbQDelete	The query is to perform a delete action. A delete query does not return any records.
dbQUpdate	The query is to perform an update on records in the underlying recordset. An update query does not return any records.
dbQAppend	The query is to add records to the underlying recordset. An append query does not return any records.
dbQMakeTable	The query is to create a new table definition based on a table definition currently stored in the recordset. A make table query does not return any records.
dbQDDL	The query is used to make changes to the structure or index of an existing table. A DDL query does not return any records.
dbQSQLPassThrough	The query is not processed by the Jet engine; instead, all processing is passed on to the database server. If a passthrough query returns records to the application, the records returned are read-only.
dbQSetOperation	The query is to return records from multiple tables based on a join condition. The returned recordset is read-only.
dbQSPTBulk	This option is used in conjunction with the PassThrough method to indicate that the query will not return any records.

■ **Updateable.** The Updateable property indicates whether any changes can be made to the QueryDef object.

QueryDef Object/Collection Methods

The following methods are available to the QueryDef object/collection:

- **Append.** The Append method is used to add a new QueryDef object to the QueryDef collection.

- **Close.** The Close method closes the QueryDef and reclaims any memory it may have been using.

- **CreateProperty.** The CreateProperty method allows you to add additional properties to the QueryDef object. The additional properties become members of the Property collection.

  The CreateProperty method has the following parameters:

Parameter	Description
Name	The value of the Name parameter provides identification for the property you are creating.
Type	The Type parameter identifies the type of data to be stored by the property you are creating.
Value	The Value parameter provides the initial value of the property you are creating.
FDDL	The value of this parameter indicates whether the property being added is a Data Definition Language object. If this value is set to TRUE, the object cannot be modified or deleted unless the user has dbSecWrite definition.

- **Delete.** The Delete method removes a QueryDef object from the QueryDef collection.

- **Execute.** The Execute method allows you to run an action QueryDef or action SQL statements on the Database object. The Execute method is used to run non-record-returning action queries.

  Note: For best performance, nest the Execute method between BeginTrans and CommiTrans statements.

  The Execute method has only one parameter: Options. The Options parameter is used to further define the characteristics of the SQL or QueryDef you are running. The following constants are available for use with the Options parameter:

Constant	Description
dbDenyWrite	This option does not allow other uses to make changes to the affected records until the Execute statement is complete.
dbInconsistent	This option allows changes to fields in tables that have been joined in a relation.

Constant	Description
dbConsistent	This option disallows changes to fields in tables that have been joined in a relation.
dbSQLPassThrough	This option indicates to the Jet engine that the QueryDef or SQL text should be passed on to the ODBC database for processing there.
dbFailonError	This option specifies that if an error occurs during the Execute statement, a roll back of all changes will automatically occur.
dbSeeChanges	This option causes an error to be generated if another user is editing a record to be affected by the QueryDef or SQL text statement.

The following sample code resets the Notes field in the Titles table to the comment This is a Test. If you do not want to make the changes permanent, select the No option from the message box; all the changes will be rolled back.

```
Dim wstitle As Workspace
Dim dbbiblio As Database
Dim Qrynew as QUERYDEF
Dim rstitles As Recordset

Set wstitle = DBEngine.CreateWorkspace("title", "Admin", "")
Set dbbiblio = wstitle.OpenDatabase("c:\vb40\biblio.mdb", False, False)
Set rstitles = dbbiblio.OpenRecordset(" select * from titles", dbOpenDynaset)
Set qrynew = dbbiblio.OpenQueryDef("new")

qrynew.sql= "update titles set notes = 'Test Notes'"

wstitle.BeginTrans

qrynew.Execute dbfailonError

If MsgBox("There have been " & qrynew.RecordsAffected & " Records changed Do
you wish to Save the Changes you have Made ", vbYesNo, "", "", 0) = vbYes
Then
    wstitle.CommitTrans
Else
    wstitle.Rollback
End If
```

OpenRecordset. The OpenRecordset method creates a Recordset object from a QueryDef object. The difference between the OpenRecordset method for a QueryDef and that available for a Database object is that when opening a recordset from a QueryDef, you cannot specify the Source parameter.

The OpenRecordset method of the QueryDef object has the following parameters:

Parameter	Description
Type	The `Type` parameter specifies the type of recordset you want to open. The following constants are available for use with the `Type` parameter:
	`dbOpenTable` — A table-type recordset is created.
	`dbOpenDynaset` — A Dynaset-type recordset is created.
	`dbOpenSnapShot` — A snapshot-type (read-only Dynaset) recordset is created.
	The default type of recordset to open is a table-type recordset.
Options	The `Options` parameter further defines the characteristics of the recordset you are creating. The following constants are available for use with the `Options` parameter (you can combine the available options by adding them together, using the + sign between constants).
	`dbDenyWrite` — Other users cannot make changes to the records contained in your recordset.
	`dbDenyread` — Other users cannot read any of the records contained your recordset. (This option apples only to recordsets created with the `dbOpenTable` type.)
	`dbReadOnly` — The recordset is opened as read-only and no changes can be made.
	`dbAppendOnly` — You can add records to the recordset; however, you cannot update or delete existing records. (This option apples only to recordsets created with the `dbOpenDynaset` type.)
	`dbConsistent` — On a joined recordset, only fields that do not affect the join condition can be updated. (This option apples only to recordsets created with the `dbOpenDynaset` type.)
	`dbInconsistent` — On a joined recordset, all fields including those responsible for the join can be up dated. (This option apples only to recordsets created with the `dbOpenDynaset` type.)
	`dbForwardOnly` — A snapshot-type recordset is created that supports only the `MoveNext` record-movement method.

Parameter	Description
dbSQLPassThrough	If you are using an ODBC database (such as SQL Server or Oracle), the SQL expression used to created the recordset is executed on the server instead of using the Access database engine.
dbSeeChange	This option causes a trappable error if another user is making a change to the record currently being edited.

The following sample code creates a recordset based on a QueryDef:

```
Dim wstitle As Workspace
Dim dbbiblio As Database
Dim proptext As Property
Dim tbltitle As TableDef
Dim qrynew As QueryDef
Dim rstitle As Recordset
' open the Workspace
Set wstitle = DBEngine.CreateWorkspace("title", "Admin", "")
' open the Database
Set dbbiblio = wstitle.OpenDatabase("c:\vb40\biblio.mdb", False, False)
' Set the QueryDef  Definition
Set qrynew = dbbiblio.OpenQueryDef("new")
qrynew.SQL = " Select * from titles "
' Open the RecordSet
Set rstitle = qrynew.OpenRecordset(dbOpenDynaset)
```

■ **Refresh.** The Refresh method ensures that the collection is complete and up to date.

Parameter Object/Collection

The Parameter object allows you to specify parameters to be used by the QueryDef object.

Parameter Object/Collection Properties

The following properties are available to the Property object/collection:

■ **Count.** The Count property indicates the number of Parameter objects contained in the Parameter collection. If Count equals 0, there are no parameters contained in the Parameter collection.

■ **Name.** The Name property of a parameter is read/write at runtime until the parameter has been added to the Parameter collection. Once the parameter is added to the collection, the Name property becomes read-only. The Name property is the primary method of identification for Parameter object in your application.

■ **Type.** The Type property is read/write at runtime until the parameter has been added to the Parameter collection. Once the parameter is been added to the collection, the Type property becomes read-only. The Type property indicates the type of parameter being defined. Use the Type property to determine what the contents of the parameter should be.

The following constants are available for use with the Type parameter. The size of the parameter is automatically determined by the type of field you are creating.

Constant	Description
dbDate	Indicates that the field is to contain date/time information (default size: 8).
dbText	Indicates that the field can contain any type of character with a maximum length of 255 characters (default size: 1 to 255).
dbMemo	Indicates that the field can contain any character or an OLE object up to a maximum size of 1.2 gigabytes (default size: 0).
dbBoolean	Indicates that the field can contains TRUE/FALSE or Yes/No values (default size: 1).
dbInteger	Indicates that the field can contain whole numbers in the range −32,768 to 32,767. Note that an integer field can be used to contain Boolean data as well (default size: 2).
dbLong	Indicates that the field can contain whole numbers in the range −2,147,483,648 to 2,147,483,647 (default size: 4).
dbCurrency	Indicates that the field can contain currency-type information. The maximum size of the value can be 11 numbers to the left of the decimal and 4 numbers to the right of the decimal. The number of decimals is fixed for each value in this type of field (default size: 8).
dbSingle	Indicates that the field can contain single-precision floating-point numbers (default size: 4).
dbDouble	Indicates that the field can contain double-precision floating point numbers (default size: 8).
dbByte	Indicates that the field can contain positive integers in the range 0 to 255 (default size: 1).
dbLongBinary	Indicates that the field can contain OLE objects (default size: 0).

■ **Value.** The Value property is read/write at runtime. The Value property is used to retrieve or set the value of a Parameter object at runtime.

Parameter Object/Collection Methods

The following method is available to the `Parameter` object/collection:

■ **Refresh.** The `Refresh` method ensures that the collection is complete and up to date.

Recordset Object/Collection

The Recordset collection allows you to manipulate the records contained in the tables of the `Database` object. The `Recordset` object contains and defines the `Field` object and collection.

Recordset Object/Collection Properties

The following properties are available to the `Recordset` object/collection.

> **NOTE**
>
> The properties available to `Recordset` objects vary based on the type of recordset created. If a property is not supported by a specific type of recordset, this is noted at the end of the description of the property.

■ **AbsolutePosition.** The `AbsolutePosition` property represents the current record's count from the beginning of the recordset. If there are no records present in the recordset, the value of `AbsolutePosition` is -1. It is possible (but not recommended) to position the recordset at a specific record by assigning the record number to this property. If the record does not exist, a trappable error occurs. If the current record is deleted, the `AbsolutePosition` property contains an invalid record number.

Note: The first record in a recordset is 0.

This property is not available for table-type recordsets.

The following example shows the use of the `AbsolutePosition` property to move through a recordset:

```
Dim wstitle As Workspace
Dim dbbiblio As Database
Dim rstitles As Recordset
Set wstitle = DBEngine.CreateWorkspace("title", "Admin", "")
Set dbbiblio = wstitle.OpenDatabase("c:\vb40\biblio.mdb", False, True)

Set rstitles = dbbiblio.OpenRecordset(" select * from titles", dbOpenDynaset)
rstitles.AbsolutePosition = 1
```

■ **BOF.** The `BOF` property is read-only at runtime. This property is used to determine whether the recordset is in the beginning-of-file (BOF) position. When the `BOF` property is `TRUE`, any attempt to move backwards in the recordset results in a runtime error.

The following example generates an error at runtime:

```
if dstitles.BOF= true then
    dstitles.moveprevious
endif
```

- **Bookmark.** The `Bookmark` property contains a unique value for each record in the recordset. You can use the `Bookmark` property to mark your current position in a recordset and later use the saved bookmark to return to the original record. The following example shows the use of `Bookmark` property in order to save the current position in the recordset and return to that position after a move operation.

```
dim sbookmark as string
' save the Bookmark
sbookmark= dtitles.bookmark
' change the record pointer
dstitles.movenext
' Restore the Record pointer to the previously saved bookmark.
dstitles.bookmark= sbookmark
```

- **BookMarkable.** The `BookMarkable` property indicates whether the current recordset supports bookmarks. Although all Microsoft Access databases support bookmarks, not all installable ISAMs support bookmarks. If you work with non-Microsoft-Access databases, verify that the recordset supports bookmarks before trying to read or restore the `Bookmark` property.

- **CacheSize.** The `CacheSize` property defines the number of records in the recordset to be stored in a local cache. The `CacheSize` property applies only to an ODBC-type data source.

  This property is not available for table-type or snapshot-type recordsets.

- **CacheStart.** The `CacheStart` property defines the first cacheable record in the recordset. The `CacheStart` property applies only to an ODBC-type data source.

  This property is not available for table-type or snapshot-type recordsets.

- **Count.** The `Count` property indicates the number of `Recordset` objects contained in the Recordset collection. If `Count` equals 0, there are no recordsets contained in the Recordset collection.

- **DateCreated, LastUpdated, and LastModified.** The `DateCreated`, `LastUpdated`, and `LastModified` properties are read-only at runtime. The `DateCreated` property contains the date and time of the `Recordset`'s creation; the `LastUpdated` property contains the date and time of the last modification; the `LastModified` property contains the bookmark to the record that was last most recently added or changed.

  All three properties are not available for snapshot-type recordsets; the `DateCreated` and `LastModified` properties are not available on Dynaset-type recordsets.

- **EditMode.** The `EditMode` property is read-only at runtime. It can be used to determine the state of the current record. The following constants can be used in order to determine the state of the `EditMode` property.

Constant	Description
dbEditNone	No editing is currently taking place on this record.
dbEditinProgress	The Edit method has been used on the recordset and the current record is currently being changed.
dbEditAdd	The AddNew method has been used on the recordset and the current record is currently being added to the recordset.

- **EOF.** The EOF property is read-only at runtime. This property is used to determine whether the recordset is in the end-of-file (EOF) position. When this property is TRUE, any attempt to move forward through the recordset results in a runtime error.

  The following sample code generates an error at runtime:

  ```
  if dstitles.EOF= true then
      dstitles.movenext
  endif
  ```

- **Filter.** The Filter property further specifies which records are to be contained in the recordset. Using the Filter property is similar to using the WHERE clause in an SQL statement.

  This property is not available for table-type recordsets.

- **Index.** The Index property sets the active index of a recordset. The chosen index determines the order in which the records appear in the recordset. The recordset must have an active index before you can use the Seek method.

  This property is not available for snapshot-type or Dynaset-type recordsets.

- **LockEdits.** The LockEdits property specifies which locking mechanism is used by the Jet engine. You can use one of two types of locking:

  - If LockEdits is set to TRUE, a 2K page of records containing the current record is locked between the execution of the Edit or AddNew method and the Update method. This approach is sometimes called *pessimistic locking*.

  - If LockEdits is set to FALSE, a 2K page of records containing the current edit record is locked only when the Update method is used. This approach is sometimes called *optimistic locking*.

    This property is not available on snapshot-type recordsets.

- **Name.** The Name property is read/write at runtime until the recordset has been added to the Recordset collection. Once the recordset is added to the collection, the Name property becomes read-only. The Name property provides the primary identification for the recordset in your application.

- **NoMatch.** The NoMatch property is read-only at runtime. The NoMatch property indicates whether the result of a search using either the Find or Seek method was successful.

Following is an example of the use of the NoMatch property:

```
' save the Bookmark
dstitles.findfirst "pubid =13"
if dstitles.nomatch= true then
    ' record was found
else
    ' record was not found
endif
```

■ **PercentPosition.** The PercentPosition property represents the approximate record position of the record as a percentage of the total records in the table. If no records are present in the recordset, the value of this property is -1. You can position a recordset to a specific record by assigning a percentage value to the PercentPosition property. If the record does not exist, a trappable error occurs. If the current record is deleted, the PercentPosition property contains an invalid record pointer.

Note: The first record in a recordset is 0.

■ **RecordCount.** The RecordCount property is read-only at runtime. The property represents the exact number of records in a table-type recordset. For a Dynaset-type or snapshot-type recordset, the RecordCount property indicates only the highest record number that has been visited. If no records are in the recordset, the value of this property is 0.

■ **Restartable.** The Restartable property is read-only at runtime. You can use this property to determine whether the recordset supports the ReQuery method.

This property is not available for table-type recordsets.

■ **Sort.** The Sort property is used to reorder the records in the recordset. Using the Sort property is similar to using the ORDER BY clause in an SQL statement.

This property is not available for table-type recordsets.

■ **Transactions.** The Transaction property is read-only at runtime. It is used to determine whether the recordset can support use of the BeginTrans, CommitTrans, and RollBack methods.

This property is not available for snapshot-type recordsets.

■ **Type.** The Type property is read-only at runtime. It is used to determine the type of recordset currently being used. The following constants are returned by the Type property in order to determine the type of the current recordset.

Constant	Description
dbOpenTable	Indicates a table-type recordset.
dbOpenDynaset	Indicates a Dynaset-type recordset.
dbOpenSnapShot	Indicates a snapshot-type recordset.

■ **Updateable.** The Updateable property indicates whether any changes can be made to the recordset. This property always returns FALSE on snapshot-type recordsets.

■ **ValidateRule.** The ValidateRule property is read/write at runtime until the recordset has been added to the Recordset collection. Once the recordset is added to the collection, the ValidateRule property becomes read-only. The ValidateRule property indicates the type of record validation to be performed on the recordset. You can use this property to allow the Jet engine to perform the validation of your data.

■ **ValidationText.** The ValidationText property is read/write at runtime until the recordset has been added to the Recordset collection. Once the recordset is added to the collection, the ValidationText property becomes read-only. The ValidationText property specifies the text that displays when the conditions set in the ValidateRule property are not met.

Recordset Object/Collection Methods

The following methods are available to the Recordset object/collection:

■ **AddNew.** The AddNew method prepares an empty record that is added to the end of the recordset when the Update method is used. If the recordset is repositioned before the Update method is used, the added record is lost. Record locking defaults to pessimistic unless you set the LockEdits property to FALSE.

This method is not available for snapshot-type recordsets.

The following example adds a new record to the Titles table. The Refresh method repositions the new record in the recordset.

```
' set optimistic locking
rstitles.lockedit= false
' add a new record
rstitles.addnew
rstitles("pubid")= 6
rstitles.("title") = "New Book "
' Update the new record
addnew.update
' refresh the recordset in order to reposition the new record
rstitles.refresh
```

■ **CancelUpdate.** The CancelUpdate method cancels any changes pending to the recordset caused by the Edit or AddNew method.

This method is not available for snapshot-type recordsets.

The following example cancels an AddNew method so that no changes are made to the recordset:

```
' set optimistic locking
rstitles.lockedit= false
' add a new record
rstitles.addnew
```

```
rstitles("pubid")= 6
rstitles.("title") = "New Book "
' Cancel the Record addition
addnew.Cancelupdate
```

- **Clone.** The Clone method enables you to create a copy of an existing recordset. The Clone method is useful when you need multiple copies of the same recordset to maintain different record positions.

  This method is not available for snapshot-type recordsets.

  The following example clones the rstitles recordset to create a new recordset based on the contents of the first:

  ```
  dim rstitleclone as recordset
  set dstitlesclone= rstitles.clone()
  ```

- **Close.** The Close method closes the recordset and reclaims any memory it may have been using.

- **CopyQueryDef.** The CopyQueryDef method creates a duplicate of the QueryDef used to create the recordset. If the recordset was not created using a QueryDef, a #NULL# value is returned.

  This method is not available for table-type recordsets.

- **Delete.** The Delete method deletes the current record in the recordset. When a record is deleted, the current record pointer becomes invalid. If there is no current record when the Delete method is used, a trappable error occurs.

  This method is not available for snapshot-type recordsets.

  The following example generates a runtime error because there is no valid record pointer:

  ```
  If rstitles.RecordCount = 0 Then
       rstitles.DELETE
  End If
  ```

- **Edit.** The Edit method prepares a existing record for modification. If the recordset is repositioned before the Update method is used, the changes are lost. Record locking defaults to pessimistic unless you set the LockEdits property to FALSE. Once the record has been edited and updated, it remains the current record.

  This method is not available for snapshot-type recordsets.

  The following example edits an existing record:

  ```
  ' set optimistic locking
  rstitles.lockedit= false
  ' add a new record
  rstitles.edit
  rstitles("pubid")= 6
  rstitles.("title") = "New Book "
  ' Update the new record
  addnew.update
  ```

- **FillCache.** The FillCache method is used to fill the previously allocated cache of the recordset with records from the database. When using the FillCache method, you must specify the number of records to retrieve as well as the record number at which the retrieval is to begin. The FillCache method applies only to ODBC-type data sources.

  This method is not available for table-type or snapshot-type recordsets.

- **FindFirst.** The FindFirst method is used to search forward from the first record in a recordset to find the first record that meets the specified criteria. If the Find method locates the record, the NoMatch property is set to FALSE and the found record is made the current record. If no match is found, the record pointer is positioned to the first record in the recordset and the NoMatch property is set to TRUE. The FindFirst criteria expression works in the same way as the WHERE clause in an SQL statement.

  This method is not available for table-type recordsets.

  The following example locates the first record in the recordset where pubid equals 13.

  ```
  dstitle.findfirst "pubid= 13"
  if nomatch= false
     ' the record was found
  else
     ' the record was not found
  endif
  ```

- **FindLast.** The FindLast method is used to search forward from the first record to locate the last record in a recordset that meets the specified criteria. If the Find method locates the record, the NoMatch property is set to FALSE and the found record is made the current record. If there is no match, the record pointer is positioned to the first record in the recordset and the NoMatch property is set to TRUE. The FindLast criteria expression works as the WHERE clause in an SQL statement.

  This method is not available for table-type recordsets.

- **FindNext.** The FindNext method is used to search forward from the current record to locate the next record in a recordset that meets the specified criteria. If the Find method locates the record, the NoMatch property is set to FALSE and the found record becomes the current record. If there is no match, the record pointer is positioned to the first record in the recordset and the NoMatch property is set to TRUE. The FindNext criteria expression works the same way as the WHERE clause in an SQL statement.

  This method is not available for table-type recordsets.

- **FindPrevious.** The FindPrevious method is used to search backwards from the current record to locate the first record in a recordset that meets the specified criteria. If the Find method locates the record, the NoMatch property is set to FALSE and the found record is made the current record. If there is no match, the record pointer is positioned to the first record in the recordset and the NoMatch property is set to TRUE. The FindLast criteria expression works the same way as the WHERE clause in an SQL statement.

  This method is not available for table-type recordsets.

NOTE

If any of the Find methods are used on an empty recordset, a trappable error occurs.

- **Move.** The Move method is used to move a specified number or records from either the beginning of the recordset or from a specified starting point. If the EOF property is TRUE, any attempt to move forward causes a trappable error. If the BOF property is TRUE, any attempt to move backward causes a trappable error.
- **MoveFirst.** The MoveFirst method moves to the first record in a recordset.
- **MoveLast.** The MoveLast method moves to the last record in a recordset.
- **MoveNext.** The MoveNext method moves to the next record in a recordset. If the EOF property is TRUE before the MoveNext method is attempted, a trappable error occurs.
- **MovePrevious.** The MovePrevious method moves to the previous record in a recordset. If the BOF property is TRUE before the MovePrevious method is attempted, a trappable error occurs.

NOTE

If any of the Move methods are used on an empty recordset, a trappable error occurs.

- **OpenRecordset.** The OpenRecordset method creates a new Recordset object from an existing Recordset object. Unlike the OpenRecordset method of a Database object, you cannot use the OpenRecordset method of a Recordset object to specify the source of the new Recordset object. Instead, all records contained in the existing recordset are returned in the new recordset.

    The OpenRecordset method has the following parameters:

Parameter	Description
Type	The Type parameter specifies the type of recordset you want to open. The following constants are available for use with the Type parameter:
	dbOpenTable A table-type recordset is created.
	dbOpenDynaset A Dynaset-type recordset is created.
	dbOpenSnapShot A snapshot-type (read-only Dynaset) recordset is created.
	The default type of recordset to open is a table-type recordset.

Parameter	Description
Options	The Options parameter further tunes the characteristics of the recordset you are creating. The following constants are available for use with the Options parameter (you can combine the available options by adding them together, using the + sign between constants):
	dbDenyWrite — Other users cannot make any changes to the records contained in your recordset.
	dbDenyread — Other users cannot read any of the records contained your recordset. (This option apples only to recordsets created with the dbOpenTable type.)
	dbReadOnly — The recordset is opened as read-only; no changes can be made.
	dbAppendOnly — You can add records to the recordset; however, you cannot update or delete existing records. (This option apples only to recordsets created with the dbOpenDynaset type.)
	dbConsistent — On a joined recordset, only fields that do not affect the join condition can be updated. (This option apples only to recordsets created with the dbOpenDynaset type.)
	dbInconsistent — On a joined recordset, all fields— including those responsible for the join— can be updated. (This option apples only to recordsets created with the dbOpenDynaset type.)
	dbForwardOnly — A snapshot-type recordset is created that supports only the MoveNext record movement method.
	dbSQLPassThrough — If you are using an ODBC database (such as SQL Server or Oracle), the SQL expression used to create the recordset is executed on the server instead of using the Access database engine.
	dbSeeChange — This option causes a trappable error if another user is making a change to the record currently being edited.

The following example creates a new recordset from an existing recordset:

```
Dim wstitle As Workspace
Dim dbbiblio As Database
Dim proptext As Property
Dim rstitle As Recordset
Dim rsnewAs Recordset
' open the Workspace
Set wstitle = DBEngine.CreateWorkspace("title", "Admin", "")
' open the Database
Set dbbiblio = wstitle.OpenDatabase("c:\vb40\biblio.mdb", False, False)
' Open the original recordset
set rstitle= wstitle.openrecordset("select * from titles",dbOpenDynaset)
' Open the RecordSet
Set rsnew = qrynew.OpenRecordset(dbOpenTable)
```

■ **Refresh.** The Refresh method ensures that the collection is complete and up to date.

■ **ReQuery.** The ReQuery method re-executes the query originally used to create the recordset.

This method is not available for table-type recordsets.

■ **Seek.** The Seek method is used to locate the first record in an indexed table-type recordset that matches the specified criteria. The specified criteria must mach the index expression used to create the index.

This method is not available for Dynaset-type or snapshot-type recordsets.

■ **Update.** The Update method is used to update any changes made to a record after the Edit or AddNew method was used on the recordset. If the Update method is used before an AddNew or Edit method, a trappable error occurs. During the Update method, validation rules are checked and errors are indicated if the validation fails.

To ensure that all locks are removed after the update, use the IDLE method of the DBEngine object with the FreeLocks parameter.

Relation Object/Collection

The Relation collection allows you to define table-level relations in your database. The Relation object contains and defines the Field object and collection.

Relation Object/Collection Properties

The following properties are available to the Relation object/collection:

■ **Attributes.** The Attributes property is read/write at runtime until the relation has been added to the Relation collection. Once the Relation object is added to the collection, the Attributes property becomes read-only.

The following constants are available for use with the `Attributes` property:

Constant	Description
dbRelationUnique	Indicates to the Jet engine that a one-to-one relationship exists between the parent and child tables. There cannot be multiple records in the child table related to only one record in the parent table.
dbRelationdontEnforce	Indicates to the Jet engine that there is no referential integrity between the two tables.
dbRelationInherited	This type of relationship applies only to attached tables. It indicates to the Jet engine that the relationship integrity is maintained externally.
dbRelationLeft	Indicates to the Jet engine that for every record in the parent table there can be multiple records in the child table.
dbRelationRight	Indicates to the Jet engine that for every record in the child table there can be multiple records in the parent table.
dbRelationUpdateCascade	Indicates to the Jet engine that when the value of a field relating a parent table to a child table changes, the changes should also be made to all records in the child table.
dbRelationDeleteCascade	Indicates to the Jet engine that when a record in the parent table is deleted, all the records in the child table should also be deleted.

- **Count.** The `Count` property is used to indicate the number of `Relation` objects contained in the Relation collection. If `Count` equals 0, there are no relations contained in the Relation collection.

- **ForeignTable.** The `ForeignTable` property is read/write at runtime until the relation has been added to the Relation collection. Once the `Relation` object is added to the collection, the `ForeignTable` property becomes read-only. The `ForeignTable` parameter is the child table in the relation.

- **Name.** The `Name` property is read/write at runtime until the relation has been added to the Relation collection. Once the `Relation` object is added to the collection, the `Name` property becomes read-only. The `Name` property indicates how the relation is to be addressed in the application.

- **Table.** The `Table` property is read/write at runtime until the relation has been added to the Relation collection. Once the `Relation` object is added to the collection, the `Table` property becomes read-only. The `Table` parameter is the parent table in the relation.

Relation Object/Collection Methods

The following methods are available to the Relation object/collection:

- **Append.** The Append method adds a new Relation object to the Relation collection.
- **CreateField.** The CreateField method is used to define the characteristics of a field that will become part of the relation. The parameters for the CreateField method are identical to those of the CreateField method of the Index object, described earlier in this chapter.
- **Delete.** The Delete method removes a Relation object from the Relation collection.
- **Refresh.** The Refresh method ensures that the collection is complete and up to date.

Error Object/Collection

The Error collection allows you to set and return error codes and error messages throughout your application.

Error Object/Collection Properties

The following properties are available to the Error object/collection:

- **Count.** The Count property indicates the number of errors contained in the Error collection. If Count equals 0, there are no errors contained in the Error collection.
- **Description.** The Description property specifies a text description that is displayed to the user when the error occurs.
- **HelpContext and HelpFile.** If valid HelpFile and HelpContext IDs are specified, the help file is opened and positioned to the topic defined by the HelpContext ID when the error occurs.
- **Number.** The Number property specifies an error number to identify the error that has occurred.
- **Source.** The Source property indicated to the user where in the application the error occurred.

Error Object/Collection Methods

The following methods are available to the Error object/collection:

- **Clear.** The Clear method is used in order to clear all of the properties associated with the Error object.
- **Raise.** The Raise method is used in order to indicate an error at runtime.

The `Raise` method has the following parameters:

Parameter	Description
Number	The `Number` parameter is used to specify an error number in order to identify the error that has occurred.
Source	The `Source` parameter is an optional parameter that is used to identify the application that caused the error.
Description	The `Description` parameter is an optional parameter that is used in order to provide a text description of the error that occurred.
HelpFile	The `HelpFile` parameter is an optional parameter that is used in order to provide the name of the help file containing additional information on the error that has occurred.
HelpContext	The `HelpContext` parameter is an optional parameter that is used in order to provide a topic ID in the specified help file, where further information on the error can be found.

Summary

This chapter covered the various properties, methods, and events of the DAO. The examples provided have shown how the DAO can be used in order to manipulate the data stored in databases, as well as the underlying structure of the database.

Open Database Connectivity (ODBC)

Open Database Connectivity (ODBC) is a standard developed by Microsoft to simplify the development of applications that may have to target a variety of Database platforms. ODBC is implemented through a collection of database drivers that are provided by Microsoft and third-party database vendors. ODBC database drivers provide your application with the capability to utilize a variety of database formats through the use of driver libraries. When using ODBC databases, it is possible to support more than one database format using the same application source code. In order to switch databases, you would only need to switch ODBC drivers.

Examining the Levels of ODBC Compliance

All ODBC-type databases are SQL-based. The developers of the ODBC drivers decide to which level of the ODBC specification the driver will be compliant. For a driver to be compliant, it must support all aspects of that level. There are three levels of ODBC driver compliance:

1. **Core.** This level contains all the tools needed to perform the following tasks:
   - Opening and closing a database
   - Supporting ODBC core data types
   - Executing supported core-level SQL statements
   - Retrieving and updating data
   - Supporting the use of database level transactions
   - Providing error information when an error condition exists

2. **Level 1.** This consists of all the core functionality plus additional tools that can be used on the database. The additional functionality consists of the following:
   - Executing supported level 1 SQL statements
   - Supporting ODBC level 1 data types
   - Providing information about connections to the database
   - Retrieving or writing partial data to a field
   - Retrieving statistical and structural information about the database and its objects
   - Retrieving information about the data types supported by the database
   - Retrieving database driver information—the version of the database driver, for example

3. **Level 2.** This consists of all of the core functionality, level 1 functionality, and the additional tools that can be used on the database. The additional functionality consists of the following:
   - Providing information about connections to the database and all the other available data sources (such as other ODBC databases) installed on the users PC
   - Executing supported level 2 SQL statements

- Supporting ODBC level 2 data types
- Providing a description for parameters in an SQL statement
- Providing a scrollable cursor
- Retrieving information from the database catalog
- Retrieving and executing stored procedures contained in the database
- Retrieving and setting index information contained in the database
- Using a translation DLL when working in a multilanguage database

The ODBC driver developer generally provides information regarding the level of compatibility of the drivers, as well as functions, methods, and data types that are supported. It also is possible for your application to determine the level of conformance by using the following ODBC API calls (all ODBC API calls are located in the ODBC.DLL library included with Visual Basic):

- **SQLGetInfo.** Returns information about the database driver, as well as connection information.
- **SQLGetFunctions.** Returns the functions supported by the database driver.
- **SQLGetTypeInfo.** Returns the data types supported by the database driver.

Using ODBC, it is possible to have one application that can host a variety of database platforms using the same application code. This is accomplished through the use of ODBC database drivers that support the target database. With ODBC, it is possible to create an application based on one ODBC-based database engine. After that application has been completed, you then can substitute an alternative ODBC-based database engine and your application will perform all its operations against the new ODBC-based database engine.

Looking at the Benefits of ODBC

The primary benefit of ODBC is that it enables your application to be database independent. To achieve the maximum benefit from ODBC, you must decide early in the design stage whether this is the route you want to follow. You must follow certain rules to fully exploit the ODBC layer.

ODBC allows the developer to create an application using a locally available ODBC-compliant database (Oracle, for example). After the application is completed, the process to move the application to another ODBC database (an SQL server, for example) is as simple as changing the ODBC connect string in the OpenDataBase function.

Listings 29.1 through 29.3 provide examples in order to illustrate the different methods available for opening an ODBC-type database. The methods illustrated here utilize the different parameters that can be used in conjunction with the OpenDatabase method of a Workspace object for ODBC databases.

Listing 29.1. Opening an ODBC database, prompting the user to select the database.

```
Dim db As DataBase
Dim ws As WorkSpace
Set ws = DBEngine.CreateWorkspace("ws1", "ADMIN", "")

Set db = ws.OpenDatabase("", False, False, "ODBC;")
```

This example prompts the user to select from a list of previously defined ODBC data sources. The user will be prompted as the final step in opening the database. After the user selects a database, the database opens using the security information provided in the `CreateWorkspace` statement. If the user chooses the Cancel option, a trappable error is generated.

FIGURE 29.1.

The ODBC selection dialog box.

Listing 29.2. Opening an ODBC database, prompting for password only.

```
Dim db As Database
Dim ws As Workspace
Dim sconnect As String
Set ws = DBEngine.CreateWorkspace("ws1", "ADMIN", "")

sconnect = "DataBase=BIBLIO;UID=ADMIN;PWD=ADMIN"

Set db = ws.OpenDatabase("BIBLIO", False, False, "ODBC;" & sconnect)
```

Listing 29.2 opens the BIBLIO database and associates it to the data source type ORACLE. The user ID, ADMIN, and an empty password field are displayed. The user will have to enter a valid password prior to the database being opened. If the database cannot be opened, a trappable error is generated.

NOTE

The connect string varies between different ODBC drivers.

Listing 29.3. Opening an ODBC database, prompting for the Userid and password.

```
Dim db As Database
Dim ws As Workspace
```

```
Dim sconnect As String
Set ws = DBEngine.CreateWorkspace("ws1", "ADMIN", "")

sconnect = "DataBase=BIBLIO;UID=;PWD="

Set db = ws.OpenDatabase("BIBLIO", False, False, "ODBC;" & sconnect)
```

Listing 29.3 opens the BIBLIO database and associates it to the data source type ORACLE. Because the User ID and the password items have been omitted, a database Logon dialog box is displayed (see Figure 29.2). If the user chooses the Cancel option, a trappable error is generated. If the database cannot be opened, a trappable error is generated.

FIGURE 29.2.

The database Logon dialog box.

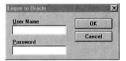

Using ODBC with the Data Control

Utilizing the Data control or Data Access objects, you are able to manipulate an ODBC data source in the same manner as that of native Microsoft Access databases.

Before you can access an ODBC database, you first must set up the database using the ODBC application shipped as part of Visual Basic. You can find this application in the Windows Control Panel or in the Visual Basic program group.

To set up an ODBC source, perform the following steps (this example assumes that the ORACLE Version 7.1 ODBC driver has been installed on your system, but these steps would apply to all ODBC drivers):

1. Double-click on the ODBC configuration option, which is contained in the Windows Control panel application.

2. When the ODBC configuration application has started, you will be presented with a list of the ODBC data sources that are currently set up on your PC. Select the Add button to add a new ODBC data source.

3. You will now be presented with a list of ODBC drivers that are currently installed on your system. Double-click on the ORACLE71 ODBC Driver.

4. Once you have selected the ORACLE71 driver, you will then be presented with a dialog box similar to that displayed in Figure 29.3

5. In the Data Source field, you enter the name of the data source as it is used in your application. For this example, enter **BIBLIO**.

6. In the Description field, type **Chapter 29**.

FIGURE 29.3.

The ODBC Oracle Setup dialog box.

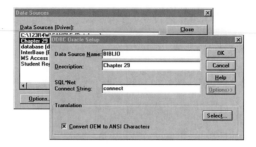

7. In the SQL *Net Connect String field, type **connect**. This will provide the Oracle driver with the location of the Oracle server. The information contained in this field is generally the name of the File server on which the Oracle Database server is installed. For additional information on the connect string, see the Oracle SQL *Net documentation supplied with your Oracle server.

> **NOTE**
>
> The above SQL *Net setting is specific to Oracle and may be different for other ODBC drivers. Other database drivers may require additional or different information. The driver specific requirements will be provided with the ODBC documentation, provided by the vendor.

8. Once you have completed the Setup, press the OK button to exit the ODBC data source Configuration utility. You will then be returned to the data source selection display. Your new data source will now be visible. Press the Close button in order to exit the ODBC configuration utility.

Examining Specific Properties Used with an ODBC Database

The properties, methods, and events of the Data control have been fully described in Chapter 27, "The Data Control." The following section will deal only with the properties, methods, and events that are specific to the use of the Data control with ODBC types of databases.

Connect

When connecting to an ODBC database, you must specify ODBC in the Connect property, and perhaps supply additional information such as user ID and password, as well as any additional information necessary dependent on the type of ODBC database you are using. Further information on the Connect string for ODBC databases is supplied in the ODBC database driver documentation.

To set the `Connect` property at design time, enter the `Connect` string using the Property Editor.

To set the `Connect` property at runtime, use the following expression:

```
data1.connect= "OBDC;Database= BIBLIO;UID=ADMIN;PWD=ADMIN"
```

NOTE

To utilize an ODBC database in your application, it must have been previously registered. The steps you need to take to register a data source have been outlined in the section "Using ODBC with the Data Control."

DatabaseName

If you are using an ODBC type of database, this property must be left blank.

To set this property at design time, clear any entry contained in the `DatabaseName` property.

To set this property at runtime, use the following expression:

```
data1.DatabaseName=""
```

Options

When using an ODBC database, you can set the Data control so that all SQL statements will be executed on the database server and not interpreted by the Jet Engine (the default Database engine supplied with Visual Basic). You would need to use the `Options` setting in the following situations:

- The SQL statement used to create the record set to be held by the Data control contained SQL statements that were not recognized by the Jet Engine.
- You are trying to execute a stored procedure on the databases server to create your record set.

To set the `Options` property at design time, enter the `dbSQLPassThrough` constant into the `Options` property using the Property Editor.

To set this property at runtime, use this expression:

```
data1.options= dbSQLPassThrough
```

NOTE

If you use `SQLPassThrough`, you cannot use any of the `Find` methods on the recordset that has been created.

Looking at an Example of a Bound ODBC Database

This section provides an example of opening an ORACLE database that is a copy of the BIBLIO database. This example is based on the bound controls example discussed in Chapter 27.

> **NOTE**
>
> The example uses an Oracle database that is an exact copy of the BIBLIO database supplied with Visual Basic.

1. Using the File | New Project command, open a new project.
2. Add the controls listed below to your form either by double-clicking their representation in the toolbar or by selecting the control and drawing it on the form. Once all the controls have been added to the form, access their property setting and make the following changes:

Control	Name	Caption	Top	Left	Width	Height
FORM	Form1	Bound Form	1515	1920	6810	5190
Data	Data1	Data control	3360	0	6495	300
Label	lblPubid	Pub ID.	180	180	1215	285
Label	lblYear	Year Pub.	180	3660	1215	285
Label	lblIsbn	ISBN	600	180	1215	285
Label	lblTitle	Title	1020	180	1215	285
Label	lblSubject	Subject	1440	180	1215	285
Label	lblDescription	Description	1860	180	1215	285
Label	lblComments	Comments	2280	180	1215	285
Label	lblNotes	Notes	2700	180	1215	285
TextBox	txtPubid		180	1560	855	285
TextBox	txtYear		180	5040	855	285
TextBox	txtIsbn		600	1560	1635	285
TextBox	txtTitle		1020	1560	4635	285
TextBox	txtSubject		1440	1560	4635	285
TextBox	txtDescription		1860	1560	4635	285
TextBox	txtComments		2280	1560	4635	285
TextBox	txtNotes		2700	1560	4635	285
Command	cmdExit	E&xit	4080	5400	795	295

3. Set the following properties for the Data1 Data control:

```
Connect= ODBC;DATABASE=BIBLIO;UID=Admin;PWD=Admin
DatabaseName =
RecordSource = Select * from titles
```

4. Set the DataSource and DataField properties for the text boxes as indicated in Listing 29.4 for the text boxes that were added to the form in step two.

   You set the DataSource property by entering the name of the Data control—in this case, **data1**—or by selecting it from the combo box that appears in the DataSource property. After you set the DataSource property, you select the DataField property associated with the bound control by entering the name of the field in the underlying record set or selecting it from the combo box that appears in the DataField property.

Listing 29.4. Additional TextBox property settings.

```
TextBox txtPubid
   DataSource = data1
   DataField =  Pubid
TextBox   txtYear
   DataSource = data1
   DataField =  Year Published
TextBox txtIsbn
   DataSource = data1
   DataField = Isbn
TextBox txtTitle
   DataSource = data1
   DataField = Title
TextBox txtSubject
   DataSource = data1
   DataField = Subject
TextBox txtDescription
   DataSource = data1
   DataField = Description
TextBox txtComments
   DataSource = data1
   DataField = Comments
TextBox txtNotes
   DataSource = data1
   DataField = Notes
```

5. In the Click event for the cmdExit control, enter the following line:

   `Unload Me`

6. Press the F5 key in order to run the project.

A window like the one shown in Figure 29.4 appears. Using the Data control's record navigation buttons, it is possible to move through all of the records contained in the title's recordset. Additionally, you can make changes to the contents of the recordset by altering the information contained in the text boxes and using the Data control to change the current record.

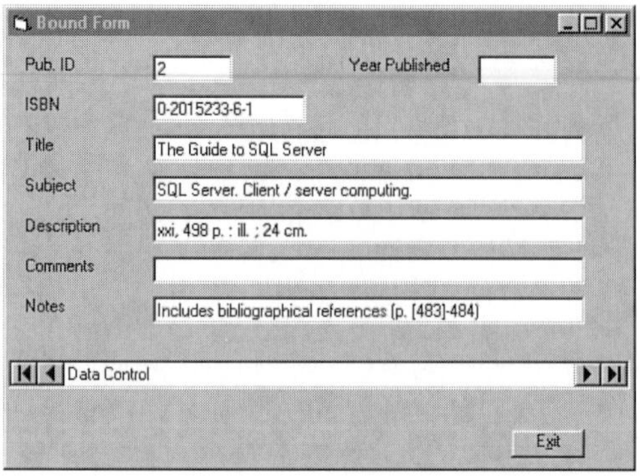

FIGURE 29.4.

Output from the bound Oracle database.

As you can see, you were able to switch the database that this application was using to another database with only changes being made to the Connect, DatabaseName, and the RecordSource properties.

Using ODBC with Data Access Objects

You can use *Data Access Objects (DAOs)* to manipulate an ODBC database in the same manner as that of Microsoft Access databases. Primarily, this section will cover aspects of the DAO that are of particular importance when dealing with ODBC types of databases. For a detailed look at the other facilities available in the Data Access Object, please refer to Chapter 28, "The Access Jet Engine."

Specific Properties of the DAO Used with an ODBC Database

The following properties of the DAO are to be used in conjunction with ODBC types of databases. Many of the properties examined here are to be used only with ODBC types of databases, hence they were only briefly covered in Chapter 28.

CacheSize

The CacheSize property of the Recordset object defines the number of records in the record set that should be stored in a local cache. The CacheSize property is not available on table or Snapshot types of recordsets.

CacheStart

The CacheStart property of the Recordset object defines the first cacheable record in the record set. This property is not available on table or Snapshot types of recordsets.

Connect

When opening a QueryDef (stored procedure) that is contained in an ODBC database, you need to specify ODBC in the Connect string, and perhaps supply additional information such as user ID and password. The additional information that needs to be specified depends on the type of ODBC database. The additional information that must be supplied in the Connect string for the ODBC database is supplied in the ODBC database driver documentation.

ExecuteSQL

The ExecuteSQL method of the database object is used only with ODBC-type databases. This method is provided for compatibility with earlier versions of Visual Basic. The ExecuteSQL method returns the number of rows affected. The SQL contained in the ExecuteSQL method must be a nonrecord-returning SQL statement.

The Execute method has the SQLStatement parameter, which is a nonrecord-returning SQL statement.

Listing 29.5 illustrates the use of the ExecuteSQL method.

Listing 29.5. "Bulk" Update Query using the ExecuteSQL method.

```
Dim db As Database
Dim ws As Workspace
Dim sconnect As String
Dim rs As Recordset
Dim nrows As Long
Dim csql As String
' Now open the DataBase
Set ws = DBEngine.CreateWorkspace("ws1", "ADMIN", "")

sconnect = "DataBase= BIBLIO,UID=ADMIN,PWD=Admin"

fSet db = ws.OpenDatabase("BIBLIO", False, False, "ODBC;" & sconnect)

Set rs = db.OpenRecordset("select * from titles", dbOpenDynaset, dbSQLPassThrough)

csql = " update titles set notes = 'Test Notes' "
nrows = db.ExecuteSQL(csql)
```

If this code were run against an ODBC-based database, the number of modified records would be contained in the nrows field.

FillCache

The FillCache property of the Recordset object fills the previously allocated cache of the recordset with records from the database. When using the FillCache property, you must specify the number of records to retrieve, as well as the record number at which the retrieval is to begin. The `FillCache` property is not available on table or Snapshot types of record sets.

Listing 29.6 illustrates the use of the `CacheSize` and `CacheStart` properties and the `FillCache` method of a recordset created from an ODBC data source. The `FillCache` method will fill the cache with 25 records, starting with record 25 in the `rs` recordset.

Listing 29.6. Cache properties and methods of ODBC based recordset.

```
Dim db As Database
Dim ws As Workspace
Dim sconnect As String
Dim rs As Recordset

Set ws = DBEngine.CreateWorkspace("ws1", "ADMIN", "")
' Now open the DataBase
Set db = ws.OpenDatabase("BIBLIO", False, False, "ODBC;" & sconnect)

Set rs = db.OpenRecordset("select * from titles", dbOpenDynaset, dbSQLPassThrough)

rs.CacheSize = 25
rs.CacheStart = rs.Bookmark
rs.FillCache rs.CacheSize, rs.CacheStart
```

LoginTimeout

The `LoginTimeout` property of the `DBEngine` object instructs the Jet Engine how long it should wait for a response to a Login request from an ODBC database. The `LoginTimeout` property defaults to 20 seconds. If you want your application to wait an indefinite period of time, set the value to 0.

LogMessages

You use the `LogMessages` property to indicate whether the messages received during execution of a `QueryDef` against an ODBC database should be logged. The `LogMessages` property must be added to the `QueryDef` object using the `CreateProperty` method. All the logged messages are stored in an ADMIN-xx table.

Listing 29.7 illustrates the use of the `LogMessages` property method.

Listing 29.7. Adding the `LogMessages` property to an ODBC based recordset.

```
Dim ws As Workspace
Dim db As Database
Dim qrynew As QueryDef
Dim rstitles As Recordset
Dim propmessages As Property
```

```
Dim sconnect As String
Set ws = DBEngine.CreateWorkspace("title", "Admin", "")

Set db = ws.OpenDatabase("BIBLIO", False, False, "ODBC;" & sconnect)
' Create a New QueryDef
Set qrynew = db.CreateQueryDef("new", "Select * from titles where pubid = 13")
' Set the connect information for the Query
sconnect = "DataBase= BIBLIO,UID=ADMIN,PWD=Admin"

qrynew.Connect = sconnect
' Load The Recordset based on the New Query
Set rstitles = db.OpenRecordset("new", dbOpenDynaset)

Set propmessages = qrynew.CreateProperty("logmessages", dbBoolean, True, False)
' Save the Property definition

qrynew.Properties.Append propmessages
' Set the Query to Log messages
qrynew.logmessages = True
```

ODBCTimeout

The ODBCTimeout property of the QueryDef object indicates the length of time the Jet Engine waits for a reply from an ODBC database before returning a time-out error to your application. The default value for the QueryTimeOut property is 60 seconds. To force the QueryDef not to time-out, set the property to 0. The value of the ODBCTimeout overrides the value set for the QueryTimeOut property of the database object.

OpenDataBase

The OpenDataBase method or the WorkSpace object creates a connection between your application and the ODBC database and assigns it to a database type object. The OpenDataBase method contains the following parameters:

- **Dbname.** The name of the ODBC data source to be opened.
- **Exclusive.** Opens the data source and stops other users from accessing the data source at the same time as your application. If the data source currently is open by another user, a trappable error is generated.
- **Read-only.** Opens the data source, but does not allow any changes to be made to the data it contains.
- **Connect.** When opening an ODBC database, you need to specify ODBC in the connect string, and perhaps supply additional information such as user ID and password. This additional information depends on the type of ODBC database. Further information on the connect string for ODBC databases is supplied with the ODBC database driver documentation.

Listing 29.8 illustrates the opening of a registered Oracle database. If the database is not registered, a trappable error is generated.

Listing 29.8. Opening of an ODBC type of database.

```
Dim db As Database
Dim ws As Workspace
Dim sconnect As String
Set ws = DBEngine.CreateWorkspace("ws1", "ADMIN", "")

sconnect = "DataBase=BIBLIO;UID=ADMIN;PWD="

Set db = ws.OpenDatabase("BIBLIO", False, False, "ODBC;" & sconnect)
```

Option

The Option parameter of the OpenRecordset, CreateDynaset, CreateSnapshot, OpenTable, and Execute methods of the DataBase, QueryDef, and Recordset objects must be set to dbSQLPassThrough if you want the SQL statements associated with the creation of the object to be processed on the database server and not be interpreted by the Jet Engine. This option is needed in the following situations:

- The SQL statement used to create the recordset, to be held by the record set, contains SQL statements not recognized by the Jet Engine.
- To create the recordset, a stored procedure must be executed on the database server.

Listing 29.9 shows how to use the dbSQLPassThrough option when creating a record set from an ODBC data source. This causes the SQL statement to be passed on to the database server for processing.

Listing 29.9. Creation of a Recordset using the dbSQLPassThrough option.

```
Dim db As Database
Dim ws As Workspace
Dim sconnect As String
Dim rs As Recordset
' Now open the DataBase
Set ws = DBEngine.CreateWorkspace("ws1", "ADMIN", "")

sconnect = "DataBase= BIBLIO,UID=ADMIN,PWD=Admin"

Set db = ws.OpenDatabase("BIBLIO", False, False, "ODBC;" & sconnect)

Set rs = db.OpenRecordset("select * from titles", dbOpenDynaset, dbSQLPassThrough)
```

QueryTimeout

You use the `QueryTimeout` property or the `DataBase` object to set the amount of time the `DataBase` object waits for a response to a query issued by the `execute` or `ExecuteSQL` method of the `DataBase` object. The value of the `QueryTimeout` property applies to all SQL (such as `ExecuteSQL`) requests made to the ODBC data source. The `QueryTimeout` property defaults to 60 seconds.

RegisterDataBase

The `RegisterDataBase` method of the `DBEngine` records information associated with the data source. This information includes the name of the data source, the type of data source, and the driver library that will be used to access the data source. This information is then stored in the ODBC.INI file. The driver for the ODBC source reads this information and uses it to open the connection to the data source. Because the data source needs to be registered only once, it is perhaps a better idea to use the ODBC function located in the Windows Control Panel to register your database, or to include the registration as part of your application setup.

The `RegisterDataBase` method has four parts to it:

1. The name of the data source that will be used by the `OpenDataBase` method.
2. The name of the ODBC driver.
3. Whether you want the Register DataSource dialog box to appear. A setting of True causes the ODBC DataSource Registration dialog box to be displayed in order to prompt the user for additional information, or to verify that the data has been entered correctly.
4. The attributes associated with the database driver. An example of the attributes would be the SQL *Net location that would have to be specified for an Oracle database.

Listing 29.10 illustrates the steps necessary to register the BIBLIO data source of the type of ORACLE.

Listing 29.10. Registering an ODBC type database.

```
Dim db As Database
Dim ws As Workspace
Dim sconnect As String

sconnect = "network1"

DBEngine.RegisterDatabase "BIBLIO", "ORACLE", True, sconnect

' Now open the Database
Set ws = DBEngine.CreateWorkspace("ws1", "ADMIN", "")

sconnect = "DataBase= BIBLIO,UID=ADMIN,PWD=Admin"

Set db = ws.OpenDatabase("BIBLIO", False, False, "ODBC;" & sconnect)
```

DAO Methods Inappropriate for Use with ODBC Databases

The following methods of the Data Access Object `DBEngine` cannot be used with an ODBC type of database:

- **Compact DataBase.** The `Compact` method of the DAO is designed to rearrange the data contained in a Jet database so that all of the data is stored in a contiguous manner. If this functionality is needed with ODBC databases, it is supplied by the supplier of the database.

- **RepairDataBase.** The `RepairDataBase` method of the DAO is designed to correct any errors that may occur with Jet-based databases. Because the DAO cannot be expected to be familiar with the internal structure of all database available, you are unable to use this method on ODBC-type databases. The supplier of your database server should have provided software to perform similar actions to the `RepairDataBase` method.

You are also unable to use the following database object creation methods, as each database handles the creation of its object in a different manner:

- `CreateQueryDef`—Create Query Definition
- `CreateRelation`—Create Table Relationship
- `CreateTableDef`—Define a Table

As mentioned earlier, the supplier of your database software will include separate tools that will enable you to perform these functions.

Using ODBC with the ODBC API

Using the API effectively bypasses all Jet Engine interaction with the ODBC database. When using the ODBC API, you cannot use the native Visual Basic Data control or any of the bound control features of Visual Basic.

All the functions contained in the ODBC API are contained in the ODBC.DLL library.

Using the ODBC API is beyond the scope of this book, but I will touch briefly on some of the most important functions contained in the ODBC API. The majority of the calls outlined here are provided in the core level of compliance. You can find more detailed information in the Microsoft ODBC SDK Guide. Where possible, the Visual Basic equivalents are listed:

- **SQLAllocConnect.** Allocates a connection handle in the database defined by the allocation handle returned from the `SQLAllocEnv` function.

    Visual Basic equivalent: `CreateWorkspace` method performed on the `DBEngine` object

■ **SQLAllocEnv.** Allocates a handle that connects to the ODBC data source. This must be the first call made prior to executing any additional calls to the ODBC API.

Visual Basic equivalent: DBEngine

■ **SQLAllocStmt.** Establishes a memory handle used by any SQL calls to the ODBC driver. This API must be run prior to any SQL statements being executed against the ODBC database.

Visual Basic equivalent: **Declare a String** variable that will contain an SQL statement

■ **SQLBinCol.** Allocates memory to receive values of a result set created by an SQLExecute or SQLExecuteDirect series of API calls.

Visual Basic equivalent: N/A

■ **SQLCancel.** Cancels any processing currently occurring as the result of an SQLExecute or SQLExecuteDirect series of API calls.

Visual Basic equivalent: N/A

■ **SQLColAttributes.** Returns the same information as that of SQLDescribeCol, except that it cannot access the bookmark column(0).

Visual Basic equivalent: Properties available in the Fields collection

■ **SQLConnect.** Establishes the connection with the ODBC data source.

Visual Basic equivalent: OpenDataBase method performed on the WorkSpace object

■ **SQLDescribeCol.** Returns data type, column name, number of decimals, if it is a numeric field, and whether a #NULL# value is valid in this column. This function also can retrieve information based on the bookmark column(0).

Visual Basic equivalent: Properties available in the Fields collection, the Bookmark property of a Recordset object

■ **SQLDisconnect.** Disconnects the connection and releases the memory associated with a connection to the ODBC database opened as a result of SQLConnect.

Visual Basic equivalent: Close method applied to a DataBase object

■ **SQLError.** Returns additional error information in the event of an error occurring in any of the previously executed API calls.

Visual Basic equivalent: Error collection contained in the DBEngine object

■ **SQLExecute.** Executes the SQL previously set up using the SQLPrepare API call.

Visual Basic equivalent: Execute method performed on a DataBase or QueryDef object

■ **SQLExecuteDirect.** Provides the functionality of the SQLPrepare and SQLExecute API calls.

Visual Basic equivalent: Execute method performed on a DataBase or QueryDef object

■ **SQLFetch.** Returns all the data from the current row in the record set where the SQLBinCol API has allocated memory.

Visual Basic equivalent: Returning the Value property from a Field object to a variable

■ **SQLFreeConnect.** Closes the connection and releases the memory associated with a connection opened as a result of `SQLAllocConnect`.

Visual Basic equivalent: `Close` method applied to a `Workspace` object

■ **SQLFreeEnv.** Closes the ODBC environment and frees all memory associated with the environment opened as a result of an `SQLAllocEnv` statement.

Visual Basic equivalent: Closing the `DBEngine`, this can be accomplished only by ending the project

■ **SQLFreeStmt.** Frees all memory previously allocated to the SQL, closes the created record set, and removes any of the created cursors.

Visual Basic equivalent: N/A

■ **SQLGetCursorName.** Returns the name of the cursor associated with the data returned as the result of an `SQLExecute` API call.

Visual Basic equivalent: N/A

■ **SQLGetFunctions.** Returns the functions supported by the database driver.

Visual Basic equivalent: N/A

■ **SQLGetInfo.** Returns information about the database driver, as well as connection information.

Visual Basic equivalent: `Version` property of the `DataBase`, `DBEngine` object

■ **SQLGetTypeInfo.** Returns the data types supported by the database driver.

Visual Basic equivalent: N/A

■ **SQLNumResultsCol.** Returns the number of columns in the record set returned by an `SQLExecute` or `SQLExecuteDirect` series of API calls.

Visual Basic equivalent: N/A

■ **SQLPrepare.** Prepares an SQL statement for execution on the ODBC server.

Visual Basic equivalent: **Define an SQL** statement and assign it to the SQL variable

■ **SQLRowCount.** Returns the number of rows affected by an `SQLExecute` and `SQLExecuteDirect` series of API calls. The values are returned only if the SQL that was executed resulted in an action type of query.

Visual Basic equivalent: `RecordsAffected` property of a `DataBase` or `QueryDef` object

■ **SQLSetCursorName.** Assigns a name to the cursor associated with the data returned as the result of an `SQLExecute` API call.

Visual Basic equivalent: N/A

■ **SQLTransac.** Commits or rolls back a series of SQL statements.

Visual Basic equivalent: `CommitTrans`, or `RollBack` method applied to a `Workspace` object

Putting the API Calls Together

When using the ODBC API, there are certain steps that must be performed each time that a session is to be established with the database server. The following functions are necessary to perform the steps:

1. **SQLAllocEnv.** This API call will initiate the conversion between your application and the ODBC driver manager. Additionally, this function will allocate memory that will be used to store a handle to the driver manager. This function must be used prior to any other ODBC API function being used.

2. **SQLAllocConnect.** Using the information that is retrieved by the SQLAllocEnv function, this function will allocate memory that will be used to store a handle to the database connection.

3. **SQLConnect.** Using information that has been retrieved by the SQLAllocConnect function, this function will perform the connection as well as logon to the specified database.

Listing 29.11 illustrates the use of the preceding ODBC API functions in order to establish a session and open a database.

> **NOTE**
>
> All of the ODBC API functions return a value indicating whether the API function was successful, The following constants should be added to a public module contained in your project:
>
> ```
> Public Const SQL_SUCCESS = 0
>
> Public Const SQL_ERROR = -1
>
> Public Const SQL_SUCCESS_WITH_INFO = 1
>
> Public Const SQL_INVALID_HANDLE = -2
>
> Public Const SQL_NO_DATA_FOUND = 100
> ```

Listing 29.11. Opening an ODBC Data Source.

```
Sub OpenOdbcSource()
Dim nenv As Long
Dim nok As Integer
Dim cdatasource As String
Dim suserid As String
Dim spassword As String
```

continues

Listing 29.11. continued

```
nok = SQLAllocEnv(nenv)
If nok <> SQL_SUCCESS Then

    MsgBox "An Error Occured During the Allocation of the ODBC Environment"
    Exit Sub

End If

nok = SQLAllocConnect(nenv, nconnect)

If nok <> SQL_SUCCESS Then

    MsgBox "An Error Occured During the Allocation of ODBC Connections"
    Exit Sub

End If
        ' change the following 3 lines for your environment
cdatasource = "BIBLIO"
suserid = "ADMIN"
spassword = "PASSWORD"


nok = SQLConnect(nconnect, cdatasource, Len(cdatasource), suserid, Len(suserid),
spassword, Len(spassword))

If nok <> SQL_SUCCESS Then

    MsgBox "An Error Occured During the Conection to the ODBC Database"
    Exit Sub

End If

MsgBox " You have sucessfully connected to the ODBC Database"

End Sub
```

After you have opened the ODBC database, you can manipulate the data contained in the database. The following functions are necessary to select all of the records from a table (in this example, it is a table named Currencies):

1. **SQLAllocStmt.** This API call will allocate a handle to the area in memory that will be used to store the result of SQL statements issued against the ODBC database. This memory will also be associated with the database connection that was obtained using the SQLAllocEnv API call.

2. **SQLExecDirect.** This API call will execute the SQL statement that has been passed to it and return the result set to the handle that was obtained by the SQLAllocStmt API call.

Listing 29.12 illustrates the statements that are needed in addition to those in Listing 29.11 to create a recordset from the currency table stored in this ODBC database.

Listing 29.12. Opening a recordset using the ODBC API.

```
Dim nsql As Long
Dim csql As String

nok = SQLAllocStmt(nconnect, nsql)

If nok <> SQL_SUCCESS Then

    MsgBox "An Error Occured Allocating the SQL Results Handle"
    Exit Sub

End If

csql = " Select * from currency"

nok = SQLExecDirect(nsql, csql, Len(csql))

If nok <> SQL_SUCCESS Then

    MsgBox "An Error Occured Excuting the SQL Statment"
    Exit Sub

End If
MsgBox "SQL Completed Sucessfully "
SQLNumResultsCol
```

After you have created an ODBC recordset, you can extract data from the table in order to place the information either into controls on a form or into variables that will be used later in your application. The following are the calls that are necessary to read the data from the fields contained in the recordset.

1. **SQLFetch.** This API call retrieves a row of data from the recordset that was created by the SQL statement. In order to retrieve the row you need to specify the handle that was obtained by the SQLAllocStmt API call.

2. **SQLGetData.** This API call retrieves the data contained in the columns of the recordset that was created by the SQL statement. In order to retrieve the data, you need to know which column of the recordset you want to retrieve, the type of data contained in that column, as well as the length of the data field.

Listing 29.13 illustrates the statements that are necessary in addition to those in Listings 29.11 and 29.12 to retrieve the value of a field from a recordset and to display it in a message box.

Listing 29.13. Retrieving a Fields value from a recordset using the ODBC API.

```
Dim cdata As String
Dim nlong As Long
Const SQL_C_CHAR = 1
nok = SQLFetch(nsql)
```

continues

Listing 29.13. continued

```
If nok <> SQL_SUCCESS Then

    MsgBox "An Error Occured Obtaining the SQL Result Set"
    Exit Sub

End If
nok = SQLGetData(nsql, 1, SQL_C_CHAR, cdata, 30, nlong)

If nok <> SQL_SUCCESS Then

    processerror nenv, nconnect, 0

    MsgBox "An Error Occured Obtaining the Field Value"
    Exit Sub
Else
    MsgBox "The Following data was retreived " * cdata

End If
```

In the event of an error occurring during any of the ODBC API functions, the SQLError function will provide you with additional information in order to further diagnose the problem. In order to retrieve additional error information, you need to specify the following information for the SQLError function:

■ The handle to the driver manager that was previously obtained by SQLAllocEnv API function.

■ The handle to the database connection that was previously obtained by the SQLAllocConnect API function.

■ If the error occurred as the result of an SQL statement, the handle to the SQL statement that was previously obtained by the SQLAllocStmt API function should be specified.

■ The Maximum length that should be allocated for the returned error text.

The function will then return the following information:

■ The current state of the ODBC driver.

■ The ODBC driver error code.

■ Any text associated with the error code.

The example contained in the opening and closing of an ODBC Data Source section illustrates the use of the SQLError function.

When closing an application that is using the ODBC API, you must manually close all of the connections that were opened when initiating the application. The functions and steps involved in closing the connections consist of the following:

1. **SQLDisconnect.** The SQLDisconnect function will remove the link between your application and the ODBC data source. You must supply this function with the database connection handle that was obtained by the SQLConnect API function.

2. **SQLFreeConnect.** The SQLFreeConnect function will remove the handle to the database driver that was previously established using the SQLConnect API function. You must supply this function with the database connection handle that was obtained by the SQLConnect API function.

3. **SQLFreeEnv.** The SQLFreeEnv function will remove the handle to the driver manager that was previously established using the SQLAlocEnv API function.

Opening and Closing an ODBC Data Source

The following example illustrates the opening and closing of an ODBC database using the ODBC API. Follow the steps listed here to create the example application(note that this is a 16-bit example):

1. Using the File | New Project command, open a new project.

2. Double-click on the Command Button control (CommandButton in ToolTips display) contained in the ToolBox in order to place a Command Button on your form.

3. Include the following property settings for the Command Button control:

   Caption = &Open ODBC

   Name = cmdOpenOdbc

4. Add the following to the general section of the form:

   ```
   Dim nenv As Long
   Dim nconnect As Long
   ```

5. Enter the following code into the cmdOpenOdbc_Click event:

   ```
   Dim nok As Integer
   Dim cdatasource As String
   Dim suserid As String
   Dim spassword As String

     'change the following 3 lines for your environment

   cdatasource = "BIBLIO"
   suserid = "ADMIN"
   spassword = "PASSWORD"

   nok = sqlallocenv(nenv)
   If nok < SQL_SUCCESS Then

       processerror nenv, nconnect, 0
       Exit Sub
   ```

```
End If

nok = sqlalloconnect(nenv, nconnect)

If nok < SQL_SUCCESS Then

    processerror nenv, nconnect, 0
    Exit Sub

End If


nok = SQLConnect(nconnect, cdatasource, Len(cdatasource), suserid,
Len(suserid), spassword, Len(spassword))

If nok < SQL_SUCCESS Then
    processerror nenv, nconnect, 0
    Exit Sub

End If
```

6. Double-click on the Command Button control (CommandButton in ToolTips display) contained in the ToolBox in order to place a Command Button on your form.

7. Include the following property settings for the Command Button control:

    Caption = &Close ODBC
    Name = cmdCloseOdbc

8. Enter the following code into the cmdCloseOdbc_Click event:

```
Dim nok As Integer
nok = SQLDisconnect(nconnect)

If nok < SQL_SUCCESS Then

    processerror nenv, nconnect, 0
    Exit Sub

End If

nok = SQLFreeConnect(nconnect)

If nok < SQL_SUCCESS Then

    processerror nenv, nconnect, 0
    Exit Sub

End If

nok = SQLFreeEnv(nenv)
```

```
If nok < SQL_SUCCESS Then

    processerror nenv, nconnect, 0
    Exit Sub

End If
```

9. Create the following subroutine in the general declaration section of the form:

```
Sub processerror(nenv As Long, nconnect As Long, nstatement As Long)

Dim nok As Integer
Dim csqlstate As String
Dim snativeerror As Long
Dim serrormessage As String * 255
Dim nerrormsg As Integer

nok = SQLError(nenv, nconnect, nstatement, csqlstate, snativeerror,
serrormessage, Len(serrormessage), nerrormsg)

MsgBox " the following Error" & serrormessage & " occurred Number " &
snativerror

End Sub
```

10. Using the Insert | Module command, add a BAS module to your project.

11. Enter the following declarations to the BAS module:

```
Declare Function sqlallocenv Lib "odbc.dll" (ByVal phenv As Long) As Integer
Declare Function sqlalloconnect Lib "odbc.dll" (ByVal henv As Long, phdbc As
Long) As Integer

Declare Function SQLConnect Lib "odbc.dll" (ByVal hdbc As Long, ByVal szDSN
As String, ByVal cbDSN As Integer, ByVal szUID As String, ByVal cbUID As
Integer, ByVal szAuthStr As String, ByVal cbAuthStr As Integer) As Integer

Declare Function SQLError Lib "odbc.dll" (ByVal henv As Long, ByVal hdbc As
Long, ByVal hstmt As Long, ByVal szSqlState As String, pfNativeError As Long,
ByVal szErrorMsg As String, ByVal cbErrorMsgMax As Integer, pcbErrorMsg As
Integer) As Integer

Declare Function SQLDisconnect Lib "odbc.dll" (ByVal hdbc As Long) As Integer

Declare Function SQLFreeConnect Lib "odbc.dll" (ByVal hdbc As Long) As
➡Integer
Declare Function SQLFreeEnv Lib "odbc.dll" (ByVal henv As Long) As Integer
```

12. Press the F5 key to run the project.

When the project is running, you can connect the ODBC data source as defined in the cmdOdbcConnect_Click event. If an error occurs during the connect, you will receive a message box containing the complete text of the error. Once you have opened a connection, you then can perform additional operations on the database using the examples presented earlier in this section. Press the Close button, and the connection to the database will be closed.

Summary

In this chapter, you looked at the features of ODBC as well as some of the benefits of ODBC. You learned to use a Data control to open an Oracle type database. You also explored the properties and methods of the Data control and the Data Access Objects that apply specifically to ODBC databases. Finally, you looked at a few of the ODBC API calls, their Visual Basic equivalents, as well as some examples illustrating the functionality of the ODBC API.

Using Third-Party VBX/OCX Controls

30

by Brad Shannon

IN THIS CHAPTER

In addition to the VBX/OCX controls supplied with Visual Basic, there is a wealth of controls available from third-party vendors. This chapter will cover some of the VBX/OCX controls that are available from third-party vendors.

Introduction to Third-Party VBXes

Third-party custom controls have been available since the introduction of Visual Basic Version 1.0. There are currently hundreds of controls available that perform almost any function that you could imagine. In this chapter, we will look at some of the commercial products available from Crescent SoftWare, Sheridan SoftWare, Apex SoftWare, Visual Components, and a public domain custom control. The current release of Visual Basic (4.0) supports three types of custom controls—16-Bit VBX, 16-Bit OCX, and 32-Bit OCX. The professional edition of Visual Basic, contains custom controls that have been licensed to Microsoft by a variety of third-party control vendors. The vendors and the controls provided in the professional edition are as follows:

> Data Bound Grid—supplied by Apex
> Crystal Report Control—supplied by Crystal Reports
> Animated Button Control—supplied by Desaware SoftWare
> Communications Control—supplied by Crescent SoftWare
> Key State Control—supplied by MicroHelp
> Gauge Control—supplied by MicroHelp
> 3D Controls—supplied by Sheridan SoftWare
> Tab Control—supplied by Sheridan SoftWare
> Graph control—supplied by Bits per Second
> Spin Button—supplied by Outrider systems

Benefits of Third-Party Custom Controls over the Controls Bundled with Visual Basic

For the most part, the controls that are supplied with Visual Basic can be used in order to emulate the functionality contained in most of the third-party custom controls. You would, however, need to design this functionality for each application that would use this feature. An example of this would be a ToolBar. While it is possible to design a ToolBar using a Picture control, command buttons, and bitmaps, you would have to perform this step for each project that needed a ToolBar. If you had a ToolBar custom control, you would simply add the control to your project, make a few property changes and that would be it. This is a simple example. The following example will help to illustrate an area where a custom control can be used to a greater advantage. You would like all the text in a TextBox to be selected when the user accesses the field. In order to perform this task in Visual Basic, you would need to add a GETSELTEXT statement to each of the text boxes GotFocus event. Alternatively, you may use a third-party custom control that contains a property that would allow this to be done automatically for you.

No matter which version of Visual Basic you are using, the best method available to further enhance your applications is through the use of third-party controls. Third-party custom controls are available for simple controls such as a replaceable text boxes, with additional properties right up to full-fledged spreadsheet type of controls.

During the discussion of custom controls, no mention will be made of standard Visual Basic properties or events that are supported by the controls. Most of the custom controls listed here support all of the standard Visual Basic properties and events.

Crescent SoftWare QuickPack Plus

Crescent SoftWare's QuickPack for Windows package consists of the following custom controls:

CSInvis

The CSInvis control is an invisible button control. This control is used when you want to define areas in a picture (HotSpots) that users could select through the click of the mouse when they require additional information.

CSPict

The CSPict control provides additional properties and methods when used with the Picture control supplied with Visual Basic.

By using the CSPict control, the following additional functionality is added to the Picture control:

- 3D borders
- Support for drag and drop from the File manager to the Picture control
- Provides the capability that allows the picture to be scrollable

CSDialog

The CSDialog control is a combination of six common dialogs that can be used in your application.

The common dialogs included are:

- File Open/File Save
- Find Text/Replace Text
- Color selection
- Fonts selection
- Printer selection

Because the dialogs are separated into different controls, you are able to concentrate only on the properties and methods that are relevant for the type of dialog that you are creating.

With Visual Basic, all of the functionality appears in one control.

CSForm

The CSForm control adds additional functionality to the forms in your application, as follows:

- Creates scrollable forms
- Provides events in order to receive notification of system events that have occurred. These include changes to colors, printers, and the WIN.INI file.
- When the memory available to Windows becomes low or fragmented, an event is triggered.
- Provides additional functionality in order to allow your application to be tiled or cascaded from the Windows task list dialog.

CSCalendar

The CSCalendar control provides the user with a graphic representation of a calendar from which dates can be selected.

CSMeter

The CSMeter control provides a progress bar indicator to indicate the progression of a long operation. The gauge can be used to represent a horizontal or vertical filing process.

CSopt

Using the CSopt control, it is possible to create a framed group of option buttons. In order to accomplish this same task in Visual Basic, you would need to use a frame control and one or more option buttons.

CSPictur

The CSPictur control is similar to the picture control supplied with Visual Basic. The CSPictur control adds the following functionality to your application:

- The ability to load pictures in the following formats:
  - Windows Bitmaps (BMP)
  - CompuServe Graphics Interchange files (GIF)
  - PC-Paintbrush files (PCX)
  - Targa files (TGA)
- The CSPictur control can be bound to a database field.
- You are able to zoom the image in as well as out.
- If the size of the picture exceeds the size of the control, scroll bars are automatically provided in order to indicate that there is additional information to be viewed.

CSSpin

The CSSpin control is used in conjunction with another control in order to provide the user with a visible method of increasing or decreasing the value of an associated control. The CSSpin control adds the following functionality to your application:

- The ability to bind the spin button to a field in a database.
- The ability to display an adjacent text box that is automatically updated as the value of the spin button is changed.
- 2D or 3D display of the spin button.
- The ability to set the value of the increments, when the spin button is depressed.

CSText

The CSText control is a combination of seven controls.

1. A TextBox that accepts and formats text input.
2. A TextBox that accepts and formats numeric double values.
3. A TextBox that accepts and formats numeric long values.
4. A TextBox that accepts and formats numerical currency values.
5. A TextBox that accepts and formats numerical date values.
6. A TextBox that accepts and formats numerical time values.
7. A Label control.

The controls listed provide the following enhancements over the controls supplied with Visual Basic.

1. All controls can be DataBound.
2. All of the controls can appear in 3D.
3. All the controls can have either a raised, sunken, or flat border.
4. All of the TextBox controls have a `FocusSelect` property that enables all of the text contained in the TextBox to be selected when the control receives focus.
5. All of the TextBox controls can operate in overstrike mode as well as insert mode.
6. All of the TextBox controls support a display-only property.
7. All of the TextBox controls support edit masks that format the contents of the control.
8. All of the controls support either left, right, or center justification of the contents contained in the control.
9. The numeric and date types of TextBoxes support an upper and lower limit. If the data entered does not fall within the defined range, an out of range event is triggered that allows your application to trap the error.
10. The non-numeric TextBox control can be set up to convert all of the text entered into uppercase.

CSChklist

Using the CSChklist control, it is possible to create a framed group of check boxes. In order to accomplish this same task in Visual Basic, you would need to use a frame control and one or more check boxes.

CSCombo

The CSCombo control is similar to the standard ComboBox supplied with Visual Basic. The following additional features have been provided in order to enhance the control:

■ You are able to bind the ComboBox to a database.
■ You can search the contents of the combo for specific criteria and automatically select the result of the search.

CSCommand

The CSCommand control is similar to the standard command button supplied with Visual Basic. The following additional features have been provided in order to enhance the control:

■ You are able to display a picture as part of the command button.

■ You are able to bind the button to a database and specify the action that will be performed on the current record when the button is pressed.

CSGroup

The CSGroup control provides the same functionality as the Frame control supplied with Visual Basic. The following additional features have been provided in order to enhance the control:

■ You are able to display a 3D caption.

■ You are able to set the alignment of the caption.

CSVlist/QPList

The CSVlist and QPList controls are similar to the standard ListBox control supplied with Visual Basic. The following additional features have been provided in order to enhance the control:

■ You are able to bind the listboxes to a database.

■ You can search the contents of the list for specific criteria and automatically select the result of the search.

■ There is no restriction to the amount of data that can be stored in a CSVlist box.

CurTime

The CurTime Control provides your application with a continuously updating clock. The time is displayed to the user through a 3D panel-type control. Additionally the CurTime control contains an alarm function.

QPRO DLL

Also provided with QuickPack is the QPRO DLL. This library is provided in the form of a Windows-callable DLL. Contained in the DLL are over 350 powerful routines that can be called from your application. The DLL provides routines that could be programmed in Visual Basic; however, some of the functions provided return information that is not accessible to Visual Basic. All of the routines have been written in either Assembler or C so there will not be any performance impact in using the routines. The routines are grouped into the following areas:

■ Array manipulation routines

■ Low-level DOS functions

■ Statistical function

■ File input and output routines

■ Memory manipulation routines

- Numeric manipulation routines
- String manipulation routines
- Wrappers for some of the well-used Windows API calls

Figure 30.1 illustrates some of the controls contained in the QuickPack Package.

FIGURE 30.1.

QuickPack Package controls.

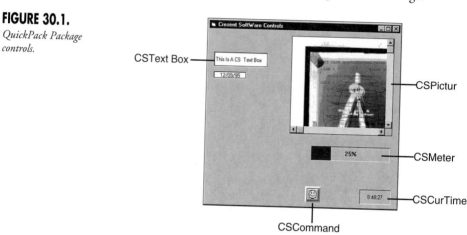

Crescent SoftWare QuickPack Plus can be ordered from:

Crescent SoftWare
11 Bailer Avenue
Ridgefield, CT USA 06877
Telephone (203) 438-5300
Fax (203) 431-4626

Sheridan SoftWare Designer Widgets

The Designer Widgets package provides custom controls to visually enhance your application. The Designer Widgets package is made up of the following custom controls.

SSFormFX

The SSFormFX control is used to enhance the appearance of the forms in your application. The control can be used to add the following functionality to your application:

- Create 3D form title bars and captions.
- Change the colors, fonts, and height of the forms caption. You are also able to have multiline form captions.

- Change the colors of the background as well as the shadow of the forms caption.

- Include a bitmap or metafile picture as part of the forms caption.

- Adjust the appearance of the Forms Control box control button, as well as the minimize and maximize buttons.

- Enable your application to ensure that the forms are always kept on top (for example, the Clock application supplied with MS Windows).

Figure 30.2 illustrates the use of the custom control in order to provide 3D minimize, maximize, and a smaller 3D control panel selector.

FIGURE 30.2.

3D Minimize and Maximize custom controls.

SSIndexTab

The SSIndexTab control provides a tabbed dialog much like that found in other Windows applications. The tab control allows you to organize a large amount of information on one form without needlessly cluttering up the screen. Using the tab control, you are able to group like items together, and allow the user to quickly switch between the item types. The control can be used to add the following functionalities to your application:

- The number of rows of tabs, as well as the number of tabs per row is definable.

- The appearance of the tab control at design time is the same as that at run time. There is no need to place tabs on a frame and then rearrange the frames as tabs are selected. To add controls to a tab, you would selected the tab at run time. To place the controls on the selected tab, add your controls that select the next tab.

- You are able to include pictures as part of the tabs caption.

- The tabs can be set so that they appear at the top, bottom, left, or right of the control.

- The caption, or picture, on the active tab can be modified to draw attention to it.

- You are able to disable individual tabs without having to disable the complete control.

Figure 30.3 illustrates the use of the Tab control to display titles, publishers, and author information from the BIBLIO database.

FIGURE 30.3.

Tab control.

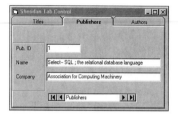

SSToolbar

This SSToolbar control provides a full-featured dockable ToolBar much like that seen in other Windows applications. Figure 30.4 illustrates the appearance of this ToolBar. The dockable ToolBar provides the following features to enhance your applications:

- There is set of supplied bitmaps that can be used to provide pictures for the ToolBar. There is also a ToolBar editor provided that allows the use of your own bitmaps in the creation of the ToolBar.

- You are able to assign shortcut keys to each of the buttons on the ToolBar, similar to what you can do with the menus in the Visual Basic environment.

- Balloon help can be assigned to each button. The delay prior to the balloon help appearing can be set during design time.

- In addition to the balloon help, you are able to trap the balloon help delay in order to display additional information in a status bar panel.

- You are able to create fixed ToolBars at the top, bottom, left, or right of the form. You are also able to create floating ToolBars. The ToolBar can be undocked, allowing the user to position the ToolBar based on his or her preferences.

FIGURE 30.4.

SSToolbar ToolBar control.

Sheridan SoftWare Designer Widgets can be ordered from:

Sheridan SoftWare
35 Pinelawn Road Suite 206E,
Melville, NY USA 11747
Telephone (516) 753-0985
Fax (516) 753-3661

Message Blaster Custom Control

The Message Blaster Custom Control is a freeware control that was developed by Ed Staffin of Microsoft consulting services. You can obtain the control as well as samples that illustrate its many uses from the following locations:

- CompuServe—Log on to forum MSL and search for the SmallCap.exe file.
- Logon to the Microsoft Download service and search for the SmallCap.exe file.
- The Internet—Log on to the `ftp:ftp.microsoft.com` server as `Anonymous` and change to the `softlib\mslfiles` directory. You will then be able to download the file.
- You may also be able to locate the sample on a local bulletin board that deals with Visual Basic programming.

Windows is a message-driven environment. If you were developing an application in C or C++, you would decide which of the Windows messages your application would act upon, and ignore the ones you felt were of no importance. In the Visual Basic environment this decision has been made for you. It is not possible using Visual Basic to redefine the messages that a particular control or application will respond to. For example, in Visual Basic it is not possible to enable a MDIForm to react to a double-click from the mouse on its area.

With the advent of the Message Blaster control your application has the opportunity to respond to the messages received from Windows prior to Visual Basic intercepting them.

NOTE

It should be noted that it is unwise to override any of the default Visual Basic message handling, as unpredictable results will occur.

The sample applications that are supplied with the Message Blaster Custom Control illustrate how the control could be used to display a reduced-sized control box, much like that of the Visual Basic ToolBox. Figure 30.5 illustrates the output from the SmallCap sample provided with the Message Blaster control.

FIGURE 30.5.

Message Blaster control.

Message Blaster Small Form Caption

Sheridan SoftWare Data Widgets

The Data Widgets package provides custom controls that allow you to have much more flexibility when editing and displaying data in your application. The Sheridan Data Widgets package is made up of the following custom controls.

SSDataCommand

The SSDataCommand DataBound command button provides the following features:

- The ability to bind the DataBound command button to a data control either on the current form or to a data control on a another form that is currently loaded.
- Support for 2D or 3D display.
- Can be used to provide record navigation in the same manner as the buttons provided on the standard data control supplied with Visual Basic.

SSHData/SSVData

The SSHData/SSVData Enhanced Data Controls are used with the data control that is supplied with Visual Basic. There are two controls contained in the enhanced data control, one control displays horizontally, and the other displays vertically. The enhanced data controls provide the following features:

- The ability to bind the enhanced data controls to a data control either on the current form or to a data control on another form that is currently loaded.
- In addition to the standard navigational buttons supplied on the standard data control, there are two other buttons: one for moving forward a predetermined number of rows and another for moving back the same number of predetermined rows. The number of rows is defined by your application.
- The default pictures on the navigational buttons can be changed.
- Provides a button to save a bookmark, and another to return to the previously set bookmark.

SSDataGrid

The SSDataGrid DataBound grid control provides the following features:

- The ability to bind to a data control either on the current form or to a data control on another form that is currently loaded.
- Displays the contents of the underlying recordset to which the control
- Supports in-place editing of the displayed records.

■ There is no limit to the size of table that can be displayed, as the grid only loads the displayed record into memory.

■ Provides add, update, and delete facilities without the need of programming these features.

■ Supports the placement of drop-down list controls directly on the grid. The contents of the drop-down lists can be derived from the same data control as the DataBound grid or another control on the form.

■ Each column and its heading can be individually formatted in accordance with the information that is being displayed.

■ Support for 2D or 3D display.

■ The grid can be partially in unbound mode to provide calculated columns based on the data displayed in the grid. Alternatively, the grid can be operated completely in unbound mode using data supplied by your application.

SSDataCombo

The SSDataCombo Data Bound ComboBox control provides the following features:

■ The ability to bind the ComboBox to a data control either on the current form or to a data control on another form that is currently loaded.

■ The Edit portion and the drop-down portion of the ComboBox can be bound to different fields in the same table or to different fields in different tables.

■ The drop-down section of the ComboBox can display multiple columns.

■ Each column and its heading can be individually formatted in accordance with the information that is being displayed.

■ Support for 2D or 3D display.

■ The SSDataCombo can be partially in unbound mode, in order to provide calculated columns based on the data displayed in the combo. Alternatively, the SSDataCombo can be operated completely in unbound mode using data supplied by your application.

■ There is no limit to the size of table that can be displayed, as the SSDataCombo only loads the displayed record into memory.

SSDropDown

The SSDropDown control can only be used with the DataControl grid control. The drop-down list control provides the following features:

■ The ability to bind the drop-down list to a data control either on the current form or to a data control on another form that is currently loaded.

- Each column and its heading can be individually formatted in accordance with the information that is being displayed.

- Support for 2D or 3D display.

- The drop-down list can be partially in unbound mode, in order to provide calculated columns based on the data displayed in the drop-down list. Alternatively, the drop-down list can be operated completely in unbound mode using data supplied by your application.

- There is no limit to the size of table that can be displayed, as the drop-down list only loads the displayed record into memory.

SSDataOption

The SSDataOption Bound option button provides the following features:

- The ability to bind the option button to a data control either on the current form or to a data control on another form that is currently loaded.

- Support for 2D or 3D display.

- Each button in a group of option buttons can be used to represent different values of the same field as opposed to only a true/false value.

Figure 30.6 illustrates the use of the Data widgets to display the contents of the Titles table from the BIBLIO database.

FIGURE 30.6.

Data widgets.

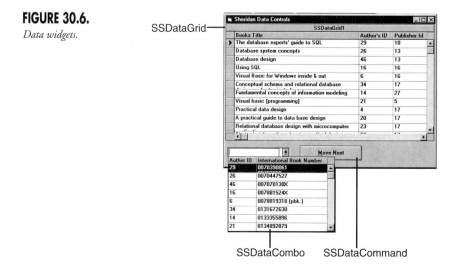

Sheridan SoftWare Data widgets can be ordered from:

Sheridan SoftWare
35 Pinelawn Road Suite 206E
Melville, NY USA 11747
Telephone (516) 753-0985
Fax (516) 753-3661

In addition to these tools, a layout editor is also provided to define and format the contents of the columns displayed in the ComboBox, grid control, and the drop-down list.

Visual Components Formula One

The Formula One custom control is a tool that gives your application all of the functionality of a spreadsheet package. The Formula One control provides the following features:

- The capability to read and write Excel 5.0 format spreadsheet files as well as workbook files.
- The capability to connect to ODBC-type databases such as SQL server and Oracle.
- Validation rules to ensure that the correct data has been entered.
- The capability to automatically fill an area of the spreadsheet with common items such as dates, days of the week, and so on.
- The capability to specify column widths as well as row heights.
- Built-in support for many common spreadsheet functions.
- A formula editor that allows the contents of formulas to be checked for correctness.
- The capability to redisplay the data contained in the spreadsheet in a graphical method.
- Drop-down lists can be stored directly in cells.

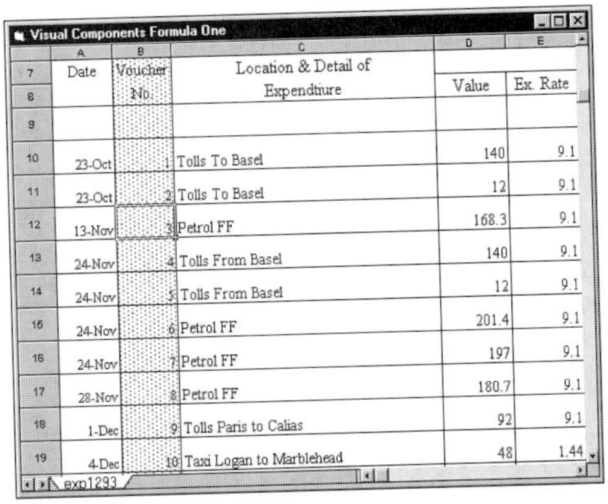

FIGURE 30.7.

Formula One controls.

Figure 30.7 illustrates the use of the Formula One control to design a spreadsheet.

Visual Components Formula One can be ordered from:

Visual Components
15721 College Blvd
Lenexa, KS USA 66219
Telephone (913) 599-6500
Fax (913) 599-6597

Apex TrueGrid

The TrueGrid control is a data grid control that can be either be operated bound to a database or unbound.

The TrueGrid control provides a wide range of functionality through a large range of properties and methods. The following list illustrates the major features that are supported by the TrueGrid control:

- The capability to bind the grid to a data control either on the current form or to a data control on another form that is currently loaded.
- The capability to split the grid (much like that of an Excel spreadsheet) and update the contents on either side of the split.
- Records displayed in the grid can be edited, deleted, or added in-place.
- No limit on the size of table that can be displayed, because the grid only loads the displayed records into memory.
- All changes to the recordset that is contained in the data control will be reflected in the grid.
- Row and cell highlighting can be tailored for each element of the grid.
- Each column and its heading can be individually formatted for display in accordance with the information that is being displayed.
- Validation for data entry can be defined on a column-by-column basis.
- You are able to use all Visual Basic functions in order to provide editing of the data contained in the columns.
- A selectable drop-down list can be added to the column.
- The capability to easily add drag-and-drop capabilities between two TrueGrid controls.
- A column editor is provided to define the contents of the columns contained in the grid.
- The capability to specify automatic translation of value stored in the grid. An example of this would be to display the expression True/False as opposed to the numeric representation.

Figure 30.8 illustrates the use of the TrueGrid control to design a spreadsheet.

FIGURE 30.8.

TrueGrid control.

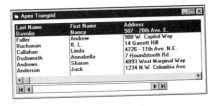

Apex TrueGrid can be ordered from:

> Apex SoftWare Corporation
> 4516 Henry Street
> Pittsburgh, PA USA 15213
> Telephone (412) 681-4343
> Fax (412) 681-4384

Sheridan SoftWare Calendar Widgets

The Calendar Widgets package provides custom controls that allow you to have much more flexibility when editing and displaying date and time, based on information in your application. The Sheridan Calendar Widgets package is made up of the following custom controls.

SSMonth

The SSMonth control provides the following features:

- Displays dates in a month format much like that of a calendar.
- Special days (such as holidays, vacation days, and weekends) can be displayed in a different format from that of other dates. You can assign pictures to individual days or to all days of a specific type.
- The ability to view up to three months at a time. The months can be viewed either in a horizontal or vertical format.
- A scroll bar allows you to move the display month by month or year by year.
- The control can be displayed either as a 2D control or a 3D control.
- You can the bind the MonthView control to a Visual Basic data control. When the calendar is bound, the selected date will be altered in order to match the date that is stored in the database.
- The ability to disable access to individual days or days of the week in order to keep them from being displayed or edited.

■ The capability to select which day will represent the beginning of the week.

■ The date that has been selected as well as today's date is indicated by two command buttons in the scroll bar area. This allows you to quickly switch calendar views between these two dates.

■ The capability to specify a picture that will appear above the calendar display portion of the control.

Figure 30.9 illustrates the use of the Calendar control used to display one month. All Saturdays will be displayed in blue, and all Sundays will be displayed in red. The button on the left represents today's date. The button on the right represents the date that has been selected.

FIGURE 30.9.

Calendar control.

SSYear

The SSYear control contains the following features:

■ All of the features contained in the SSMonth control.

■ The ability to display a complete year.

■ The ability to specify the starting month of the year displayed.

Figure 30.10 illustrates the use of the Year View control to display a complete year. All Saturdays will be displayed in blue and all Sundays will be displayed in red. Public holidays are indicated in green. The button on the left represents the date today. The button on the right represents the date that has been selected.

FIGURE 30.10.

Year View control.

SSDateCombo

The SSDateCombo control contains the following features:

- The capability to increment and decrement the date displayed using a spin button control.
- When the drop-down portion of the control is selected, a full-featured version of the SSMonth control is displayed, providing an easy method of selecting a date.
- You can bound the control to a Visual Basic data control. When the Date ComboBox is bound, the date that is displayed or altered will be reflected in the underlying recordset.
- The control can be displayed either as a 2D control or a 3D control.
- Dates can be displayed in any format. The default is based on the Windows International setting.
- The height of both the text portions of the ComboBox and the drop-down MonthView can be adjusted.
- An error event is available in order to trap invalid date entries.

Figure 30.11 illustrates the use of the Date ComboBox control for the entry of a date.

FIGURE 30.11.

Date ComboBox control.

SSDay

The SSDay DayView control contains the following features:

- Displays a daily time schedule.
- Allows you to schedule appointments during the day.
- Multiple items can be assigned for each period.
- The capability to specify the start and end times as well as the interval per period.
- The control can be displayed either as a 2D or a 3D control.
- A complete Day view is provided in order to quickly identify free periods.
- The capability to add pictures to tasks in order to provide a specific reminder.

Figure 30.12 illustrates the use of the DayView control in order to manage a daily schedule.

FIGURE 30.12.

DayView control.

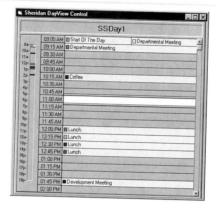

Sheridan SoftWare Calendar Widgets can be ordered from:

Sheridan SoftWare
35 Pinelawn Road Suite 206E
Melville, NY USA 11747
Telephone (516) 753-0985
Fax (516) 753-3661

Summary

In this chapter we have examined the advantages of using third-party controls as well as major features of some of the custom controls that are currently available. In the move to Visual Basic 4.0 and the switch to OCX controls, the number of controls that are available will increase and their functionality will continue to grow. Additional information on available custom controls can be found from the following sources:

The *Companion Products* booklet supplied with Visual Basic.

The *Visual Basic Programmers Journal*, *Dr. Dobbs Journal*, and *Byte* magazines, as well as many other periodicals.

Creating, Modifying, and Maintaining Databases

by

Most application programs need to store some kind of data. Visual Basic gives the application program developer many options in this area. With the rich VBA language, a programmer can create and read low-level disk files directly; or through API calls, the programmer can read and edit INI files. But for more powerful and maintainable data storage and retrieval, it is Visual Basic's database management capabilities that come into play.

This chapter covers some Visual Basic database fundamentals. It starts with an introduction to the database concept and ends with some useful comments on keeping a database in good shape. Along the way, you will see some examples that create a database and modify it.

Looking at Database Fundamentals

In the simplest conceptual terms, a computer database is just an electronic filing cabinet. Unlike an old-fashioned filing cabinet, however, a well-designed database facilitates automated retrieval and management of the data stored in it.

In practice, a computer database is a collection of tables. Tables hold items that are described by the same list of characteristics. For example, the tblCandidate table in the database of Figure 31.1 contains people's names and other information. Each person whose name is stored in the database has a record in that table that describes their first name, last name, middle initial, and a few other items. The point however, is that each person is described by the same list of characteristics—their name, and so on. It is only the values of those characteristics that change from record to record. For example, the first name and last name of each person is stored, but all persons do not have the same name.

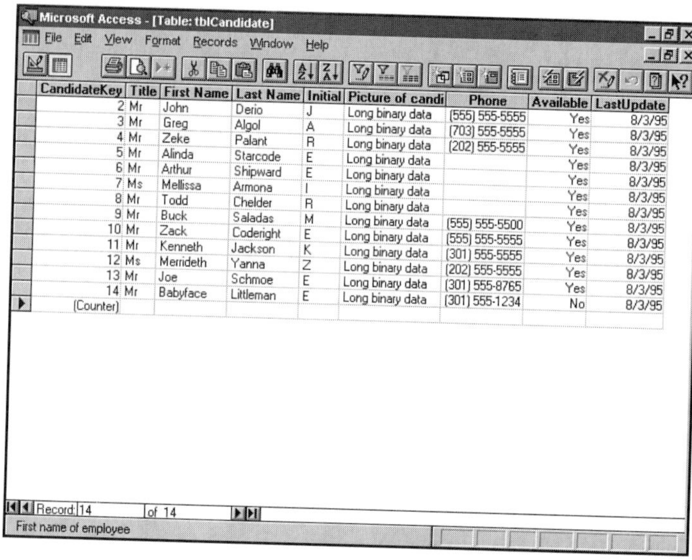

FIGURE 31.1.

The tblCandidate table from the BTS (Best Team Selector) database. BTS is a sample program on the CD-ROM that accompanies this book.

In the language of SQL databases, a record also is known as a *row*, and a field also is known as a *column*. Figure 31.2 shows the data in the tblCandidate table, which shows why these terms so readily lend themselves. The records appear as rows, and the fields are stacked as columns.

FIGURE 31.2.

The tblCandidate table showing columns and rows.

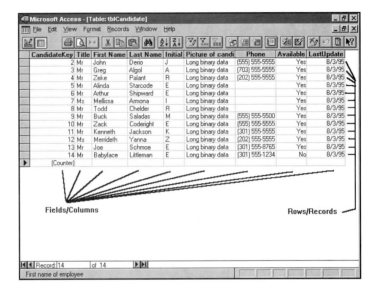

Although a complex definition for a relational database exists, the practical concept is this: In a *relational database*, tables are related to other tables through their fields. In the BTS sample program, the tblCandidate table is related to the tblCandidateSkill table through the CandidateKey field, which they both share. In other words, when the value of a field in one table record matches the value of a designated field in another table record, those records are related. Table relationships do not happen automatically. It is up to the database designer to designate fields between tables that relate to each other.

> **NOTE**
>
> Today's common database is a hierarchy of structures. A *database* is a collection of tables. A *table* is a collection of records. A *record* is a collection of fields. A *field* is the smallest unit of information that a database holds.

Understanding SQL

Sometimes pronounced *sequel*, SQL stands for *Structured Query Language*. It has become the *de facto* interface to relational database management systems and is a database interface available in most of today's development tools. Visual Basic 4.0 supports SQL for its database operations.

> **NOTE**
>
> A commonly used abbreviation for *relational database management system* is RDBMS. In some cases, the term DBMS is used, which just means *database management system*. The Jet Engine is the RDBMS for Visual Basic 4.0 when using Access (MDB) databases. When using ODBC, the RDBMS is either the ODBC driver itself or the database server managing the database.

SQL is not a language in the same sense that Basic or C/C++ are languages. Basic and C/C++ are general-purpose languages used to build programs by creating loops and conditions that are executed in a procedural fashion. The XBase dialects (dBASE, Clipper, and FoxPro) are in the same category as Basic and C/C++, although they are targeted at database management. A SQL statement, however, is not a sequentially executing list of instructions. Instead, each SQL statement is a complete query that tells an RDBMS what results you want, not necessarily every detail about how to get those results. The RDBMS translates your query into whatever steps are necessary to fulfill your request.

Webster's New World Dictionary defines a query as "a question." That's pretty much what the word means in SQL. Instead of phrasing SQL questions in English, however, you phrase them using the SQL language. You can go a considerable distance just by knowing how to apply the following keywords:

SELECT   Specifies the table columns (fields) you want to know about.

FROM   Specifies the rows of data to which the query applies. (In the examples used in this chapter, this is where you specify the source table. In more complex examples, like those in Chapter 32, "Unleashing SQL," this is where you embed other SQL queries.)

WHERE   Specifies conditions that limit the number of table rows returned.

Some simple examples showing how to apply these keywords follow; here, the Best Team Selector database is used. (See Chapter 38, "Unleashing LAN Programming," for more information on this database. The database is available on the CD-ROM that accompanies this book.)

The following code returns a list of all the candidates' first names:

```
SELECT    tblCandidate.FirstName
FROM      tblCandidate;
```

To return the first name of every available candidate, use this code (availability is defined in the tblCandidate table by the Yes/No field "Available"):

```
SELECT    tblCandidate.FirstName
FROM      tblCandidate
WHERE     ((tblCandidate.Available=True));
```

To return the first and last name of each available client, just modify the select portion of the SQL statement to get the following:

```
SELECT     tblCandidate.FirstName, tblCandidate.LastName
FROM       tblCandidate
WHERE      ((tblCandidate.Available=True));
```

To return ALL fields of the available candidates, use the following code:

```
SELECT *
FROM tblCandidate
WHERE ((tblCandidate.Available=True));
```

You can try out these examples by adding a data control to a new form and placing the example SQL query into the RecordSource property. The DatabaseName property should be set to the MAKETEAM.MDB. You can see the result of the query by placing a DBList on the form and setting the RowSource property to the name of your data control and the ListField property to the name of the field you want to display.

> **NOTE**
>
> The MAKETEAM.MDB file is the database used by the Best Team Selector program and can be found on the CD-ROM that accompanies this book. MAKETEAM.MDB contains all the tables described in the preceding examples.

There is also another class of SQL queries usually referred to as *action queries*. In the strictest sense, these are not really questions, although in most environments they return an answer with regard to the success or failure of the query:

ALTER TABLE	Alters an existing database table.
CREATE INDEX	Creates an index for an existing database table.
CREATE TABLE	Creates a new database table.
DELETE	Deletes records from a table.
INSERT INTO	Inserts records into a table.
UPDATE	Updates records in a table.

The CREATE TABLE, CREATE INDEX, and ALTER TABLE action query keywords are known as *Data Definition Language* statements, sometimes abbreviated as DDL. These are not supported by Visual Basic 4.0 on non-Jet engine databases. In practice, unless your application needs to create or modify a database (other than at the record level) you will not use these commands. If you do need these actions, Visual Basic supports them through methods of the data control and through SQL Passthrough. In general, you may want to create and edit your databases with other tools or at minimum with Visual Basic's Data Manager.

To create a simple database that contains one table by using the Visual Basic Data Manager, follow these steps:

1. From the Add-Ins menu, select Data Manager.
2. From the Data Manager File menu, select New Database.
3. For the database File name, enter **People** and click Save.
4. Press the New button to create a new table.
5. Fill in the fields of the Add Table dialog to match those of Figure 31.3. Once you've filled in the screen, press the > button to move the new field into the list box. This list box shows all the fields that are part of the table.

FIGURE 31.3.

The Add Table dialog box.

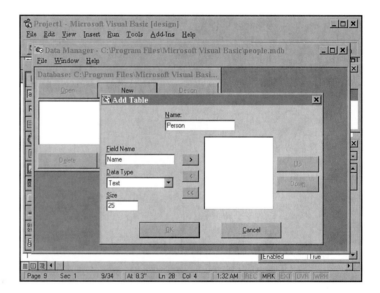

6. Create another field and call it State. This field should also be of type text, but it should only be of length 2.
7. Press the > button to move the State field into the list box and then click the OK button.
8. You can now add records to the database table you've defined by selecting the table, as shown in Figure 31.4, and by clicking the Open button.

The remaining action query commands—INSERT INTO, DELETE, and UPDATE are subject only to restrictions of the particular database or table to which they are applied. Some simple examples, which again use the BTS database, follow.

FIGURE 31.4.

Adding records to a table.

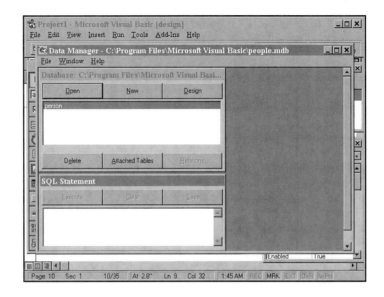

To create a record in the tblCandidate table with Bobby as the FirstName field and Demo as the LastName field, use this code:

```
INSERT INTO    tblCandidate(FirstName,LastName)
VALUES         ("Bobby","Demo");
```

This code deletes the Bobby Demo record from the tblCandidate table:

```
DELETE    *
FROM      tblCandidate
WHERE     (tblCandidate.FirstName="Bobby")
          AND (tblCandidate.LastName="Demo");
```

To change the last name of all Bobby Demo records in the table, use this code:

```
UPDATE    tblCandidate
SET       [tblCandidate.LastName] = "Ademo"
WHERE     (tblCandidate.FirstName="Bobby")
          AND (tblCandidate.LastName="Demo");
```

We've only touched on the SQL language here. For more comprehensive coverage, turn to Chapter 32.

Choosing a Database Back End

Database back end is a common term these days that refers to the type of database used by a program. The back-end part of the phrase stems from the fact that the database is usually not something the users see directly on their desktops. They interact with the database in whichever ways their programs enable them. The particular database in use by the program is of no particular intellectual importance to them if the program they use gives them what they want.

As with most modern Windows development tools, you are not limited to one type of database system when using Visual Basic 4.0—you can use Access, various XBase flavors, Excel and many others for database storage. Visual Basic's ODBC and OLE 2 support enables it to access any database compatible with the ODBC or OLE 2 standard. These databases include Microsoft SQL Server, Oracle, and Sybase. Oracle has both OLE 2 and ODBC drivers. Sybase is accessible through ODBC.

You can choose from two groups of database back ends: ISAM and client/server. ISAM stands for *Indexed Sequential Access Method*, and just about any popular database that is not configured as client/server falls into this category. ISAM databases include the dBASE (DBF) types, Access (MDB), and many others. The distinguishing characteristic of ISAM databases is that they are directly manipulated in every way by the computer running the query program.

> **TIP**
>
> If you decide to use an ISAM database with your Visual Basic 4.0 program, Access can be a good choice because it is directly controllable by Visual Basic's Jet engine. All other ISAM databases go through additional layers of processing.

Client/server databases, on the other hand (as the name implies), reside on something manipulated at the most basic levels by an RDBMS server. The client interacts with the database by making requests to the RDBMS, which the server then carries out. Oracle, Sybase, and Microsoft SQL Server are some popular client/server databases available today.

If you need a database scheme for use by one computer at a time, ISAM is usually an obvious choice. Among its benefits are more straightforward development and maintenance issues. Depending on the type of system hardware and software function, ISAM also can respond faster than a client/server approach.

However, if you are developing a database application for use by several computers simultaneously and fault-tolerance is a very important factor, client/server schemes should be considered. In the ISAM implementations, generally any computer writing to the database has the opportunity to physically corrupt it. In a multiuser environment, this can mean that everyone is exposed to the instability of just a few user computers. If a corruption can be fixed, all users may have to log out while the database is repaired.

If the RDBMS server in a client/server scheme is well designed and maintained, physical database corruption is less likely. Only the server itself can physically corrupt the database, and if the server is well designed and maintained, this would be unusual. Unlike user PCs, access to the configuration of the server usually is tightly controlled.

In general, the following rules apply when the user or users will be writing to a database in an application:

Database Situation	Comment
Small, single-user database	ISAM is the best choice. Simple to implement and can be the fastest solution.
Small database with few simultaneous users	ISAM may not be a bad choice. See the later section, "Keeping Your Database Healthy."
Small database with many simultaneous users	No easy answer here. If the number of transactions is small, ISAM may be adequate. However, if fault prevention is paramount, RDBMS client/server is the only real choice.
Huge, single-user database	Most RDBMS servers are optimized in ways that significantly enhance performance of the SQL queries.
Huge database with many simultaneous users	A client/server RDBMS may be the only way to implement this system with acceptable performance and reliability.

Sharing Your Database

The RDBMS nature of Visual Basic 4.0 database interaction goes a long way toward simplifying multiuser database access. On the surface, sharing client/server databases is just a matter of appropriate definitions at the server level by the Database Administrator (DBA), and sharing ISAM databases is a matter of placing the database in a network directory and applying the OpenDatabase method without setting exclusive access to True. For quick and simple shared database applications, this can be enough to share a database, because the Jet engine and the client/server RDBMS can handle multiple users behind the scenes.

Looking a little deeper however, there are some subtle issues that can have tremendous impact on the usability and performance of a shared database application. The following items are of particular relevance to both ISAM and client/server implementations:

- Table indexes
- Refresh frequency
- Transactions
- Pessimistic versus optimistic locking
- Page locking versus record locking

Every time a table is written to, its indexes must be updated. If there are many indexes or the indexes are very complex or large, the update can significantly impact the total number of operations and time dedicated to the transaction. In an ISAM environment, this means more opportunity for a physical database corruption by the user's machine. In both a client/server RDBMS and an ISAM environment, it can mean slower processing. It is generally a good idea to keep indexes as few and simple as possible, although the inclination is to index everything to cover all the "what if someone asks for..." situations. Ironically, the increased risk of corruption in an ISAM environment from excess indexes also translates into longer down time for repairs. (Compacting an MDB and packing a DBF causes re-creation of every index associated with the affected tables. Compacting and packing of ISAM databases is explained in the "Keeping Your Database Healthy" section of this chapter.) In general, smaller and fewer is better where indexes are concerned.

Although Visual Basic 4.0 does a good job of shielding the mundane issues of shared data access from the application developer, a fundamental fact cannot be ignored when multiple users read and write to the same database: Data cannot be assumed to stay static. This means that it is a good programming practice to issue the Idle method periodically to update program record sets and release unneeded read locks.

Read locks are issued by some databases to ensure that related records are not altered. Sometimes these are set automatically by database management systems, and sometimes they are set at runtime by program code. The Idle method can be used to free those locks sooner than they might otherwise be freed when issued with the dbFreeLocks parameter. (There is a detailed explanation of this method and what it does in the Visual Basic help file under the keyword "idle.")

All users of the shared database benefit when locks are removed, because a lock can interfere with another user's update request. The user issuing an Idle benefits by getting a refresh of the database. This is especially relevant if the user program is displaying a list of table items and some of those items have been modified or removed in the time that the list was displayed originally.

Transactions help performance of a shared database application in two significant ways:

1. Proper use of transactions improves the responsiveness of the database for all users; in particular, it improves the performance of the machine incorporating transaction processing.
2. Proper use of the transactions ensures logical data integrity even in the event of some program failures.

Transactions are implemented in Visual Basic 4.0 by the BeginTrans, RollBack, and CommitTrans methods. Start a transaction by applying the BeginTrans method to your database workspace. Until Visual Basic 4.0 executes a Rollback or CommitTrans method on that workspace, it will not actually "write" any updates to the shared database. Instead, all updates are stored in RAM and in temporary files. If your application will update many records in a batch process, the shared database will be impacted only once when the CommitTrans method is issued at the end, instead of during each iteration of the batch.

In the case of a batch update failure, an issue to the Rollback method on the database workspace prevents any of the pending updates from affecting the shared database. This is especially significant when changes to one part of a database are only meaningful if updates in other parts take place simultaneously. A Rollback command can be issued via an On Error construction, as illustrated in Listing 31.1, to correct for unanticipated errors during processing.

Listing 31.1. Sample structure for a batch processing database procedure with RollBack.

```
Sub BatchDatabaseUpdate(MyDB as Database)
    MyDB.BeginTrans     'Start the transaction block.
    On Error Goto BatchDatabaseUpdate_Undo
    ...
    ... Batch Processing
    ...
    MyDB.CommitTrans  'Commit all the batch processing.
    Exit Sub
BatchDatabaseUpdate_Undo:
    MyDB.Rollback     'Undo the transaction block.
End Sub
```

An important concept when dealing with multiuser database updates is that of pessimistic versus optimistic locking. A *pessimistic locking scheme* is one in which a database application assumes that unless it "locks out" other users from a particular record, another user will try to modify it while the program needs to use it exclusively. (Read locking falls somewhat into the pessimistic locking umbrella.) An *optimistic locking scheme* applies the opposite philosophy: It cheerfully assumes that no one will interfere with the record while it does exclusive processing. These two schemes are of particular significance in the case of a record edit. A pessimistic scheme would issue a lock on a record as soon as the Edit method is issued. This lock would exist for the duration of the edit. In fact, the user could walk away from the machine after starting the edit, and unless the program has a built-in time-out feature, the lock would persist until the user comes back and issues the Update method. The advantage for the user here is that there is no chance something will happen to the record while the user is editing it. Any defined relationships this record might have in the database are not going to change. This ensures that the user update will not conflict with the database constraints when the database update is performed.

However, the downside to pessimistic locking is obvious: No one else can update that record or perform other exclusive operations on the database if they impact that record in any way. Visual Basic 4.0 is pessimistic by default for some databases.

The optimistic locking alternative is more multiuser-database friendly. Optimistic locking can be implemented in Visual Basic 4.0 by setting the LockEdits property of the database to False. A well designed, multiuser database that allows extended-use edits of its data generally should employ optimistic record locking to reduce impact on other system users. Listing 31.2 shows a construction that implements optimistic locking on a modal form called frmEditRecord through a Visual Basic Data control called Data1.

NOTE

The likelihood of having a problem with pessimistic locking in a multi-user environment is very complex to determine. The essential factors in this case are the number of users that will edit the database simultaneously and the structure of the database itself. A thorough discussion of these issues is beyond the scope of this chapter. Arguably, optimistic locking can be the most user friendly when implemented properly.

Listing 31.2. Procedure to illustrate an implementation of optimistic locking for a multiuser environment.

```
- - - - - - - - - - - - - - - - - - - - - - - - - - - - - - - - - - - - - - - - - - - - - - - - - - - - - -
'This subroutine just illustrates the concept of using optimistic
'record locking. In practice, unless a modal edit window
'is desired the DataChanged property check and logic would
'be on the OK or SAVE button of the edit form itself.
- - - - - - - - - - - - - - - - - - - - - - - - - - - - - - - - - - - - - - - - - - - - - - - - - - - - - -
Sub FriendlyEdit()
    Dim Done
    Done = FALSE
    Data1.LockEdits = FALSE
    While Not Done
        Data1.Edit
        frmEditRecord.Show 1     'Modal edit form.
        If Data1.DataChanged Then
            'Not safe to write back - may overwrite someone else.
            Beep
            MsgBox "Someone changed the record data.",48,"Changed"
            Data1.UpdateControls 'Load controls with new data.
        Else
            'Safe to write changes back.
            Data1.Update
            Done = TRUE
        Endif
    Wend
End Sub
```

A very subtle database-sharing issue lies in the physical type of locking that an RDBMS employs. There are two types: record-level locking and page-level locking. *Record-level locking* is implemented by the DBF types (dBASE and FoxPro, among others) and some client/server

RDBMSs (Oracle is one). A record-level locking scheme locks only those records that need to be locked in order for a particular exclusive operation to take place. *Page-level locking* schemes, on the other hand, lock entire sections of a database to lock a record. The locked section is the *page* or *pages* of the database that contain the record. Pages do not usually correspond to records in size, so several records are included in a single page, or records can span pages. Microsoft SQL Server, Access, and BTrieve are three page-locking databases.

The logic behind a page-locking implementation is that of speed: Less computing is required of the DBMSs to identify and mark the section of the database that contains the target record. For reasons beyond the scope of this chapter, page calculation is computationally simple for the RDBMS. The downside of this scheme is the unnecessary and somewhat unpredictable locking of unrelated records. Page-locking systems, more than any others, need to ensure quick turnaround on locks. It can be quite unacceptable in a large, multiuser page-locking database to employ pessimistic locking because it may lock neighboring records for significantly long periods of time. If you use a page-locking database, you may need to pay particular attention to the dynamics of your application and the relative size of the table records to the table page sizes.

Designing Your Database

The subject of relational database design can be extremely complex. However, there are some fundamentals. A good place to begin is with database normalization.

Normalization is the process of removing redundancies in a database scheme. In the language of relational databases, there are five standard normal forms. The last two are rarely applied, difficult to describe, and difficult to understand. For this reason, I will only discuss the first three in detail. The fourth and fifth forms are only listed here with limited explanation.

Normal Form	Function
1	Eliminates repeating groups. Different items belong in separate tables, and each table should have a primary key.
2	Eliminates redundant data. If a field depends on only part of a multifield key, remove it to a separate table.
3	Eliminates columns not dependent on a key. If fields do not contribute directly to the description of a key, move those fields to a new table.
4	Isolate independent multiple relationships.
5	Isolate semantically related multiple relationships.

Each normal form builds on the one before it; in other words, a database that meets the requirements of third normal form also satisfies normal forms 2 and 1.

An example of a completely non-normalized database is a database consisting of one table containing the names of people with skills they possess (see Figure 31.5). Because this is a single table, a person with more than one skill appears more than once in the table. In each record, the name and other information identifying the person is repeated. To normalize this database, you could remove the fields describing the skills to a new table. The new "tblPeople" table would now use the "PeopleKey" as a foreign key into the new "tblPeopleSkill" table (see Figure 31.6). (*Foreign key* is just a fancy term for a field or group of fields that are used to "lookup" values in another table.)

FIGURE 31.5.

A non-normal form database.

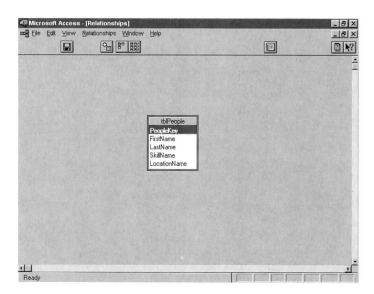

The database in the above example is still not in second normal form, because the tblPeopleSkill table lists the name of the skill although the unique key into the table is PeopleKey + SkillKey and SkillName only applies to SkillKey. As a result, the skill name is repeated in the table each time more than one person has a particular skill. To place the database into second normal form, you remove the SkillName field from the table and place it into a new table to which the SkillKey is a foreign key. Figure 31.7 shows the result of changing the tables from Figure 31.6 as described.

The database is now in second normal form, but not third because the tblPeople table contains fields that are not really about people. The LocationName field is an attribute independent of the PeopleKey field, so you can move it to its own table and replace LocationName with LocationKey. Figure 31.8 illustrates this change.

FIGURE 31.6.

The first normal form tblPeople, and the tblPeopleSkill database.

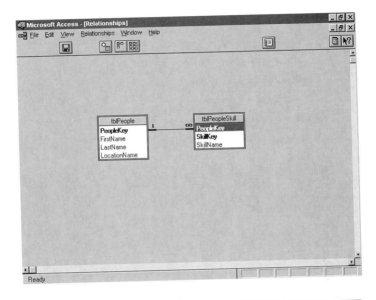

FIGURE 31.7.

The second normal form tblPeople, tblPeopleSkill, and the tblSkill database.

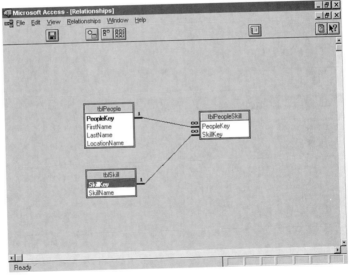

Normalization can be a good exercise when designing a database because it forces a bit of rigor into the analysis. The elegance of normalization is that it reduces the data stored in the database to its smallest logical components. The cost, however, is sometimes an excess of tables and indexes for a database. In general, fewer tables and fewer indexes can mean less database application overhead. Many databases eventually are denormalized to improve performance. It is not unusual to normalize an original design to the third level and then denormalize it back to the first form to reduce disk storage needs and to improve access time.

FIGURE 31.8.

The third normal form of our database. You now have four tables: tblPeople, tblPeopleSkill, tblSkill, and tblLocation.

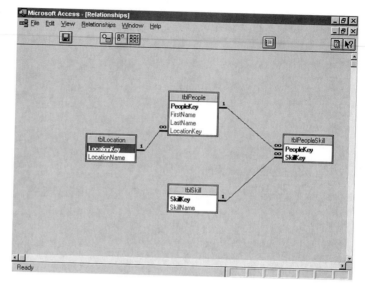

One more fundamental relational database design element is that of the relationship definitions themselves. In general, there are three types:

- **One to One.** One record in a table has one and only one record that relates to it in another table. Having this kind of relationship usually implies a need to normalize the database.

- **One to Many.** One record in a table has one or many records that relate to it in another table. Very common database relationship. Figure 31.8 illustrates several of these relationships. In that figure, the 1 at the "tblLocation" table and the infinity symbol at the "tblPeople" table indicate that for any record in the "tblPeople" people table, there is only one matching record in the "tblLocation" table. This is Microsoft Access's diagram convention.

- **Many to Many.** A free-for-all. Any number of records in one table match any number of records in another table, and vice versa. This can be difficult to maintain programmatically.

There are variations on the preceding relationship types with respect to whether at least one record is required or not. In other words, some tools allow the specification that at least one record must exist in the many side of a one to many relationship. By the same token, some tools allow a one to many relationship to have zero records on the many side. Figure 31.9 shows the generic symbols sometimes used to illustrate these relationships in database diagrams.

If you are using a client/server RDBMS, these relationships can be defined in the database and enforced by the RDBMS. When using ISAM databases with Visual Basic 4.0, maintenance of relationships relies entirely on the program code.

FIGURE 31.9.

Generic database diagram relationship symbols.

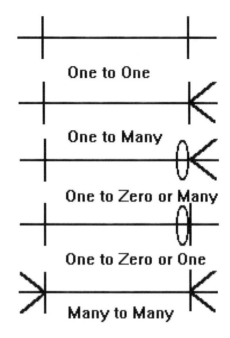

Creating Your Database

Unless your program has to create a database at runtime, the best way to create your database for use with Visual Basic 4.0 is to use the Data Manager application or to use a database tool designed for that database. Following are some ISAM database tools:

Database Type	Database Tool
Access	Microsoft Access
dBASE	Borland Visual dBASE
FoxPro	Microsoft Visual FoxPro
Paradox	Borland Paradox for Windows

Most client/server databases come with their own tools for use by the DBA and are of varying quality and usability. If you are working with client/server databases and do not like the tools that come with them, or you just want to take a step up in relational database design, several third-party relational database tools are available that create databases for you after you design them interactively in their environment. Most of the larger mail-order software vendors carry a few tools.

If you choose to create a database from within Visual Basic 4.0 code, there are two ways to do it: You can use the Visual Basic 4.0 methods or if your RDBMS supports it, the SQL language directly. The Visual Basic 4.0 methods can create only Access-type databases (MDB). Listing 31.3 creates an Access database with three tables similar to those of the BTS program found on the CD-ROM. Figure 31.10 shows the result of this code listing.

Listing 31.3. Sample Visual Basic 4.0 code that illustrates creation of tables and indexes in a database.

```
'----------------------------------------------------------------------
'Sample code to create a three table Access database.
'----------------------------------------------------------------------
Sub CreateTestDB()

'Define the variables we will use.
Dim MyDB As DATABASE, MyWs As Workspace
Dim tblC As TableDef, tblS As TableDef, tblCS As TableDef
Dim fldC(3) As Field, fldS(4) As Field, fldCS(5) As Field
Dim idxC As Index, idxS As Index, idxCS As Index
Dim fldTemp As Field
Dim DBName As String

'Create the database in the same directory as application.
DBName = App.Path + "\TEST.MDB"
Set MyWs = DBEngine.Workspaces(0)
Set MyDB = MyWs.CreateDatabase(DBName, dbLangGeneral, dbVersion20)

'Create the tables of the database.
Set tblC = MyDB.CreateTableDef("tblCandidates")
Set tblS = MyDB.CreateTableDef("tblSkill")
Set tblCS = MyDB.CreateTableDef("tblCandidateSkill")

'Create the fields of the Candidates table.
Set fldC(0) = tblC.CreateField("CandidateKey", dbLong)
fldC(0).Attributes = dbAutoIncrField
Set fldC(1) = tblC.CreateField("FirstName", dbText)
fldC(1).Size = 20
Set fldC(2) = tblC.CreateField("LastName", dbText)
fldC(2).Size = 25

'Create the fields of the Skills table.
Set fldS(0) = tblS.CreateField("SkillKey", dbLong)
fldS(0).Attributes = dbAutoIncrField
Set fldS(1) = tblS.CreateField("Name", dbText)
fldS(1).Size = 20

'Create the fields of the Relationship table.
Set fldCS(0) = tblS.CreateField("CandidateSkillKey", dbLong)
fldCS(0).Attributes = dbAutoIncrField
Set fldCS(1) = tblS.CreateField("CandidateKey", dbLong)
Set fldCS(2) = tblS.CreateField("SkillKey", dbLong)

'Now append fields to Candidate table and then to DB.
tblC.Fields.Append fldC(0)
tblC.Fields.Append fldC(1)
tblC.Fields.Append fldC(2)
MyDB.TableDefs.Append tblC
```

```
'Now append fields to Skills table and then to DB.
tblS.Fields.Append fldS(0)
tblS.Fields.Append fldS(1)
MyDB.TableDefs.Append tblS

'Now append fields to Relationship table and then to DB.
tblCS.Fields.Append fldCS(0)
tblCS.Fields.Append fldCS(1)
tblCS.Fields.Append fldCS(2)
MyDB.TableDefs.Append tblCS

'Now add an index to the Candidates table.
Set idxC = tblC.CREATEINDEX("idxCandidateKey")
idxC.PRIMARY = True
idxC.UNIQUE = True
Set fldTemp = idxC.CreateField("CandidateKey")
idxC.Fields.Append fldTemp
tblC.Indexes.Append idxC

'Now add an index to the Skills table.
Set idxS = tblS.CREATEINDEX("idxSkillKey")
idxS.PRIMARY = True
idxS.UNIQUE = True
Set fldTemp = idxS.CreateField("SkillKey")
idxS.Fields.Append fldTemp
tblS.Indexes.Append idxS

'Now add an index to the relationship table.
Set idxCS = tblCS.CREATEINDEX("idxCandidateSkillKey")
idxCS.PRIMARY = True
idxCS.UNIQUE = True
Set fldTemp = idxCS.CreateField("CandidateSkillKey")
idxCS.Fields.Append fldTemp
tblCS.Indexes.Append idxCS

'Create relationship C to CS
Dim relCtoCS As Relation
Set relCtoCS = MyDB.CreateRelation("CtoCS")
relCtoCS.TABLE = "tblCandidate"
relCtoCS.ForeignTable = "tblCandidateSkill"
Set fldTemp = relCtoCS.CreateField("CandidateKey")
fldTemp.ForeignName = "CandidateKey"
relCtoCS.Fields.Append fldTemp
MyDB.Relations.Append relCtoCS

'Create relationship S to CS
Dim relStoCS As Relation
Set relStoCS = MyDB.CreateRelation("StoCS")
relStoCS.TABLE = "tblCandidate"
relStoCS.ForeignTable = "tblCandidateSkill"
Set fldTemp = relStoCS.CreateField("SkillKey")
fldTemp.ForeignName = "SkillKey"
relStoCS.Fields.Append fldTemp
MyDB.Relations.Append relStoCS

End Sub
```

FIGURE 31.10.

Diagram of tables created by Listing 31.3.

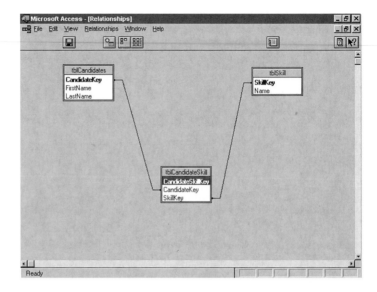

> **NOTE**
>
> Although Visual Basic 4.0 now allows complete control of Access database security features, it does not support creation of a secure database. Secure Access databases need a SYSTEM.MDW file, and Visual Basic 4.0 doesn't provide a facility to build one at runtime. To create a secure database, you need to use another tool, such as Microsoft Access.

As Figure 31.10 illustrates, Listing 31.3 creates three tables in the database and each has a defined relationship to one of the others. Because Visual Basic 4.0 does not support the creation of non-Jet engine databases, you have to use other tools to create an initial database. In the case of some ISAM databases, this is just a matter of creating a blank directory and placing the individual database files into it.

> **NOTE**
>
> The Jet engine database does not support SQL statements that define or alter the structure of non-Jet engine databases. If you want to use SQL for those operations, you have to use SQL Passthrough commands that your particular RDBMS accepts.

> **TIP**
>
> If your intent is just to provide the user with a blank database, you do not have to create it at runtime. Instead, you can take the approach implemented in BTS, which is to ship a blank database and then at runtime copy that blank database to a new name. The advantages follow:
>
> - **Reduced version control complexity.** The database design you implement (and change) during development does not impact the new database creation functionality of your program.
>
> - **Capability to determine contents of "blank" database without recoding the Visual Basic program.** In the case of BTS, the TEMPLATE.MDB can be pre-populated with whatever data is appropriate for a new instance of the database. The users creating a new database in BTS then get a copy that already has the settings they wanted to begin with. (For BTS, users may want to have a particular listing of skills in every database, for example.)

Modifying Your Database

There are fundamentally two ways to modify the structure of existing databases within Visual Basic 4.0 if you choose not to use a dedicated database tool. One way is to use Visual Basic 4.0 database methods, and the other is to use SQL action queries. The Visual Basic methods are the same ones employed in the `CreateTestDB()` function in Listing 31.3.

Visual Basic 4.0 does not support action queries that modify database structure, so any SQL commands you use for that purpose have to be handled entirely by your RDBMS. The SQL action queries would be of the Alter Table variety, but would depend on the RDBMS you use.

Working with Your Database

Visual Basic 4.0 programs can work with database data through native Visual Basic methods, SQL action queries, or OLE 2. Although Oracle has released an OLE 2 interface to its RDBMS, ODBC and native Visual Basic methods are the more common ways to interact with database data; those ways are focused on in this section.

If you have the professional version of Visual Basic 4.0, you can open database objects entirely through code. With both the standard and professional versions, you can open database objects through the data control. Details of the data control are covered in Chapter 27, so I won't cover that here. Instead, let's jump right into working with the BTS database to create and edit `tblCandidate` records:

1. Start a new project and get a blank form. You can do this by selecting New Project from the Visual Basic File menu. A blank form then appears automatically.

2. Place a Data control on your form. You can do this by double-clicking on the data control icon displayed in your Visual Basic toolbox (see Figure 31.11).

FIGURE 31.11.

The Data control.

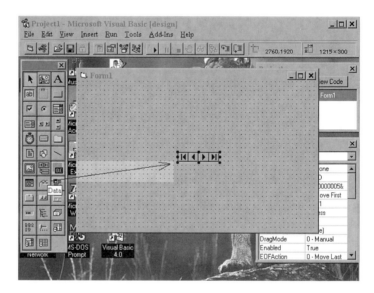

3. Assuming that the MAKETEAM.MDB file from the sample BTS program is already on your drive, edit the `Data1` properties as follows:

```
DatabaseName        Maketeam.mdb
Name                Data1
RecordSource        tblCandidate
```

4. Place two `TextBox` controls on your form. Edit the properties so that all have a data source of `Data1`. Set the `DataField` property of one to `Title`, another to `FirstName`, and the value for the last control to `LastName`.

5. Add four `CommandButton` controls to your form and edit the properties as in the following code:

```
Command1
Caption        &Add
Name           cmdAdd

Command2
Caption        &Delete
Name           cmdDelete
```

```
Command3
Caption          &Undo
Name             cmdUndo

Command4
Caption          &Quit
Name             cmdQuit
```

6. Place the following code into your form (You can get to the code module by double-clicking on any unused area of the form):

```
Private Sub cmdAdd_Click()
    cmdDelete.Enabled = False
    Data1.Recordset.AddNew
End Sub

Private Sub cmdDelete_Click()
    Data1.Recordset.Delete
    Data1.Recordset.MoveFirst
End Sub

Private Sub cmdUndo_Click()
    Data1.UpdateControls
End Sub

    Private Sub cmdQuit_Click()
    End
    End Sub

Private Sub Data1_Reposition()
    cmdDelete.Enabled = True
End Sub
```

7. Add some labels to the TextBox controls by editing their caption properties so that they look like those of Figure 31.12. You can run this program by pressing F5 while in Visual Basic.

The simple form created in the preceding seven steps demonstrates how to add, delete, edit, and undo database changes. The edit functionality, in this case, is handled by the data control and requires no special coding.

NOTE

This example does not consider the data integrity of the MAKETEAM.MDB database. If it did, it also would delete skills associated with candidates when the candidates are deleted.

To perform batch updates on your database, SQL is sometimes a good choice. Visual Basic 4.0 SQL is covered in detail in Chapter 32. Only a simple example is shown here to illustrate one way to execute such a query.

FIGURE 31.12.

The final screen.

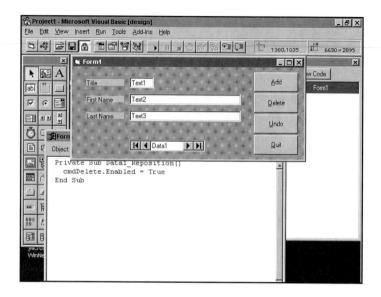

Follow these steps using the add/edit/delete/undo form created earlier. These steps will add SQL batch processing to the form:

1. Add another `CommandButton` control to your project from the previous Add/Edit/Delete screen.

2. Edit the properties of the button to be the following:

   ```
   Command1
   Caption      &Kill All
   Name         cmdKillAll
   ```

3. Place the following code into your form:

   ```
   Private Sub cmdKillAll_Click()
       Dim r, style
       style = vbYesNo + vbCritical + vbDefaultButton2
       r = MsgBox("Delete all candidates?",style,"WARNING")
       If r = vbYes Then
           Data1.Database.Execute "DELETE * FROM tblCandidate"
           MsgBox "All candidates deleted."
       End If
   End Sub
   ```

Now when you run the form, you have a "Kill" button. Click on it to delete all the records in the tblCandidates table.

Keeping Your Database Healthy

Whatever database scheme you implement, periodic backup is cheap insurance that can pay huge dividends should anything ever go wrong. Backup strategies depend on the type of database and the circumstances of the implementation.

If your application uses an ISAM database, backup can be as simple as a periodic PKZIP of the database files. In the case of a shared ISAM database, all users have to log out during this process. If you have the space for it, this is a good idea even on systems that have tape backups, because backup tapes can be somewhat unreliable.

Client/server RDBMSs can be more complex to back up, and the process may be unique to the hardware on which your RDBMS resides. Although a well-designed RDBMS can be very stable, not keeping current backups can be foolish.

There are two types of database corruption: physical and logical. A *physical* database corruption is when the format of the database files are in some way adulterated. A *logical* corruption is when a relationship constraint is not preserved or a table restriction is not adhered to. An example of a logical corruption is leaving a field blank when the database requires a non-null value. Examples of physical corruption are a malformed record or an improperly updated index.

As discussed earlier, shared ISAM databases are physically manipulated by the users' machines. In the case of Visual Basic 4.0 database programs, the manipulations are through the Jet Engine or an ODBC driver. If the user computer has a malfunction during a write operation or some user software derails and writes inappropriate data to the shared database files, a database corruption can take place.

Some database corruptions can linger undetected for some time and cause other corruptions and user program crashes. A good practice for any ISAM database, and in particular any shared ISAM databases, is to periodically "repair" them. For non-Access (MDB) databases, you need to use an appropriate utility for that database type or system. In the case of DBF type databases, a common repair function is a "pack." (Pack in the xBase world removes records marked for deletion and rebuilds indexes.) Visual Basic 4.0 does not include a pack utility. It can, however, repair Access databases with the `DBEngine.CompactDatabase` method. There is no harm in repairing a healthy database, but there is much potential harm in letting a corrupt database continue to serve application users.

Unless a logical database corruption contradicts a stored logical definition in the database itself, a general-purpose repair utility will not detect it. (An example of a logical requirement that is not defined in a database would be in the case of a dBASE database where one table record depends on the existence of a record in another table. Because dBASE databases do not store any relationship information, a pack or third party repair program would have no way of knowing this requirement.) For this reason, it is always a good idea to define all relationships and database constraints within the database instead of within your program code whenever possible. Some ISAM databases, such as the DBF type, do not support constraint storage, but the Access (MDB) type does. All client/server RDBMS systems support constraint definition within the database.

Summary

This chapter introduced some database fundamentals, covered some practical considerations, and touched on the power of SQL. For more details on the SQL language and discussion on how to apply it, turn to Chapter 32.

Unleashing SQL

32

by Frank Font

IN THIS CHAPTER

Everybody in the database world is talking about, has talked about, or will be talking about SQL. *SQL* stands for *Structured Query Language*. The reason it's such a hot topic is that this "query language" can express very complex database operations concisely and nonprocedurally. This is particularly significant when working in a client/server environment, as you will see in Chapter 33, "Visual Basic 4.0 and Client/Server Programming." However, as working with SQL in Visual Basic 4.0 demonstrates, client/server is not required to benefit from the power of SQL.

This chapter starts with a little background information about SQL and its standards. It then goes into a comparison of SQL database access versus other methods. The chapter uses introductory concepts and terms at first, but then moves into more advanced topics toward the end. Along the way, you will see examples that can be coded in Visual Basic 4.0.

If you are not already comfortable with general database concepts and the terminology commonly used when discussing them, now may be a good time to review Chapter 31. That chapter introduces many of the concepts that this chapter assumes the reader already knows.

Most of the examples in this chapter, as with Chapters 31 and 33, refer to the database of the BTS program. This program and its database are described in Chapter 36. Sample code for this program and its database can be found on the CD-ROM that accompanies this book.

Some SQL History and Background

Although it had its roots in IBM labs as far back as the late 1960s, SQL as a database interface language first was implemented commercially by Oracle in 1979. By 1986, when the ANSI committee published its first SQL standards, it was available from several other vendors and was growing in popularity. ANSI updated the standard in 1989 and then again in 1992. SQL-92 is the latest ANSI version of the SQL language. Among other things, the latest standard details language extensions for the creation and modification of databases.

The level of SQL-92 compliance you can expect in your Visual Basic 4.0 programs depends on the driver and database system you use. The Jet Engine database generally is only SQL-89 compliant, with some extra functionality and keywords not in that standard. This means that some databases, such as Access and FoxPro, do not support all the newer features and keywords when used directly though the Jet Engine.

If you are using SQL on an ODBC ISAM database, the level of support is entirely dependent on the ODBC driver and may be completely SQL-92 compliant. If you are using client/server, the degree of compliance is determined by your RDBMS. Most of the newer RDBMS servers, such as Oracle7, Sybase, and Microsoft SQL Server support SQL-92 extensions.

Harnessing the Power of SQL

You can do in one SQL statement what could take an entire program to do with procedural data access methods. Sometimes, particularly in the case of client/server environments, letting the RDBMS carry out the request specified by a SQL statement is faster than constructing a program to do the same job yourself step by step. Listing 32.1 shows you a simple example.

Listing 32.1. Iterative database manipulation.

```
'------------------------------------------------------------
'Example of a table update via iterative methods.
'Visits each record of the tblCandidate Table because no
'assumption with respect to record order is made.
'
'This procedure assumes the following:
'1. Data1 control is on the form and is set to query
'   the BTS sample program database.
'------------------------------------------------------------
Sub DoUpdateBySteps()

    Dim MyCriteria As String

    ' Open recordset.
    Data1.RecordSource = "tblCandidate"
    Data1.Refresh

    'Count the matching records.
    MyCriteria = "Title = 'Mr'"
    Data1.Recordset.FindFirst MyCriteria
    Do Until Data1.Recordset.NoMatch
        Data1.Recordset.Edit
        Data1.Recordset!Available = False
        Data1.Recordset.UPDATE
        Data1.Recordset.FindNext MyCriteria
    Loop    ' End of loop.

End Sub
```

This procedure sets the Available field to `False` for each tblCandidate record with a Title value of "Mr." The simpler procedure shown in Listing 32.2 accomplishes the same thing with one SQL action query.

Listing 32.2. SQL database manipulation.

```
UPDATE      tblCandidate
SET         Available = FALSE
WHERE       Title = 'Mr';
```

You can issue this action query from a Visual Basic program, as shown in Listing 32.3.

Listing 32.3. SQL database manipulation coded in Visual Basic 4.0.

```
'--------------------------------------------------------------
'Example of a table update via a single SQL statement.
'Only records containing 'Mr' are visited if an index starting
'with the Title field exists. Otherwise, all records are visited
'by the RDBMS.
'
'This procedure assumes the following:
'1. Data1 control is on the form and is set to query
'   the BTS sample program database.
'--------------------------------------------------------------
Sub DoUpdateBySQL()  Dim SQL As String

    'Define the query.
    SQL = "UPDATE tblCandidate "
    SQL = SQL + "SET Available = FALSE "
    SQL = SQL + "WHERE Title = 'Mr'"

    'Execute the query.
    Data1.DATABASE.Execute SQL, dbFailOnError

End Sub
```

> **NOTE**
>
> It is important to use the dbFailOnError option, as in the preceding code sample, when employing the Execute method to carry out your SQL action queries. This ensures that a trappable error is generated if any of the actions specified in the SQL statement cannot be carried out. This option is also important if you are wrapping your statements into transactions. Transactions are discussed in Chapter 33.

The effect of using Listing 32.1 at runtime depends on the type of database that the table it updates resides in. If the table is in an ODBC database, each iteration *may* require a new ODBC query at the Jet Engine level. Translation: Slow performance that gets noticeably slower as the database increases in size. The routine could be optimized by making sure that the records are first sorted by Title. Then the code can be rewritten so that only the "Mr" records are visited. However, in a multi-user environment, runtime database sorting or index creation can be impractical if not impossible. If the index with the particular sort you need does not already exist, you are out of luck.

In contrast, the SQL example sends the complete instruction of your desired action in one step to the database driver. If an appropriate index exists, it is used to speed the operation. The specific nature of the execution depends on your database:

■ If the database is native Jet (MDB), the Jet Engine interprets the instruction and executes it directly.

- If the database is ODBC ISAM, the ODBC driver for the database interprets the instruction and executes it.

- If the database is client/server, the RDBMS server receives the instruction and carries it out on its CPU. This frees up the user workstation while the query is carried out.

Sometimes a SQL approach is not only faster to execute, but also simpler to code. For example, if you want to create a list of skills that no candidate in the tblCandidate table has, you can write a single SQL statement or a program to iterate through the tables. To code this iteratively, you, the programmer, would have to check *each* record of the tblSkill table against the tblCandidateSkill table to see if it was already in use. Listing 32.4 is such a program. However, the Jet RDBMS of Visual Basic 4.0 is smart enough to know and deliver what you want when it sees the SQL statement of Listing 32.5. All the benefits and issues that applied to the code of Listings 32.2 and 32.3 apply here also.

Listing 32.4. Filtered list created iteratively.

```
'------------------------------------------------------------
'Show skills in a list box using iterative methods.
'All skills that the candidate does not have are shown.
'
'This procedure assumes the following:
'1. Data1 control is on the form and is set to query
'    the BTS sample program database.
'2. List1 control is on the form.
'------------------------------------------------------------
Sub ListNewSkillsBySteps(CandidateKey As Long)
    Dim MyCriteria As String
    Dim Count As Integer

    'Clear the list box.
    List1.Clear

    ' Open recordsets.
    Data1.RecordSource = "tblSkill"
    Data1.Refresh
    Data2.RecordSource = "tblCandidateSkill"
    Data2.Refresh

    'Build the list.
    Count = 0
    Data1.Recordset.MoveFirst
    Do Until Data1.Recordset.EOF

        'Define the search criteria.
        MyCriteria = "CandidateKey = " + Str$(CandidateKey) + _
            " AND SkillKey = " + Str$(Data1.Recordset!SkillKey)
        Data2.Recordset.FindFirst MyCriteria
        If Data2.Recordset.NoMatch Then
            'Add the skill to the list since candidate doesn't have it.
            List1.AddItem Data1.Recordset!Name, Count
            Count = Count + 1
        End If
```

continues

Listing 32.4. continued

```
        Data1.Recordset.MoveNext
    Loop    ' End of loop.

End Sub
```

It is important to note that the program of Listing 32.4 uses two data controls. One is for the table that holds the skill names, and one is for the table that defines the skills a candidate possesses. Compare Listing 32.4 to the procedure shown in Listing 32.5, which needs only one data control. The result is that the SQL method in this case is not only easier to code, it may also use fewer workstation resources. (Since the amount of resources used depends heavily on the type of RDBMS employed, the database, and several other factors, a blanket statement that such SQL statements will always use fewer resources cannot be made.)

Listing 32.5. Filtered list created via SQL.

```
'-------------------------------------------------------------------
'Show skills in a list box using a SQL statement.
'All skills that the candidate does not have are shown.
'
'This procedure assumes the following:
'1. Data1 control is on the form and is set to query
'   the BTS sample program database.
'2. DBList1 is on the form with RowSource as Data1.
'-------------------------------------------------------------------
Sub ListNewSkillsBySQL(CandidateKey As Long)
    Dim SQL As String

    'Define the query.
    SQL = "SELECT DISTINCTROW tblSkill.Name"
    SQL = SQL + " FROM tblSkill LEFT JOIN"
    SQL = SQL+ " tblCandidateSkill ON tblSkill.SkillKey"
    SQL = SQL + " = tblCandidateSkill.SkillKey"
    SQL = SQL + " WHERE tblSkill.SkillKey NOT IN"
    SQL = SQL + " (SELECT tblCandidateSkill.SkillKey"
    SQL = SQL + "  FROM tblCandidateSkill"
    SQL = SQL + "  WHERE tblCandidateSkill.CandidateKey"
    SQL = SQL + " = " + Str$(CandidateKey) + ")"

    'Execute the query.
    Data1.RecordSource = SQL
    Data1.Refresh

    'Fill the listbox.
    DBList1.ListField = "Name"
    DBList1.Refresh

End Sub
```

Although the SQL statement in Listing 32.5 is complex, its performance can be tremendously better than that of the iterative method. The fact that some statements are complex should not be a significant deterrent to implementing SQL in Visual Basic programs, because there are several ways to create these statements automatically using third-party tools. Even if the statements are constructed manually, the payback in the performance of the application can be well worth the effort.

Now look at one more example that illustrates the potential for simplification and performance enhancement, as shown in Listing 32.6.

Listing 32.6. Count candidate skills iteratively.

```
'------------------------------------------------------------------
'Pass in the key of the candidate. Return the number of skills
'that candidate has. Processes record by record.
'
'This function assumes the following:
'1. Data1 control is on the form and is set to query
'   the BTS sample program database.
'------------------------------------------------------------------
Function HowManySkillsBySteps(CandidateKey As Long) As Integer
    Dim SkillsCount As Integer
    Dim MyCriteria As String

    'Initialize the counter.
    SkillsCount = 0

    ' Open recordset.
    Data1.RecordSource = "tblCandidateSkill"
    Data1.Refresh

    'Count the matching records.
    MyCriteria = "CandidateKey = " + Str$(CandidateKey)
    Data1.Recordset.FindFirst MyCriteria
    Do Until Data1.Recordset.NoMatch
        SkillsCount = SkillsCount + 1
        Data1.Recordset.FindNext MyCriteria
    Loop      ' End of loop.

    'Return the result.
    HowManySkillsBySteps = SkillsCount
End Function
```

The function in Listing 32.6 counts the number of skills a specified candidate possesses. This is done by finding the first skill and then iterating through each skill until all skills have been processed. Contrast that process to the SQL version shown in Listing 32.7.

Listing 32.7. Count candidate skills via SQL.

```
' - - - - - - - - - - - - - - - - - - - - - - - - - - - - - - - - - - - - - - - -
'Pass in the key of the candidate. Return the number of skills
'that candidate has. Process via single SQL query.
'
'This function assumes the following:
'1. Data1 control is on the form and is set to query
'   the BTS sample program database.
' - - - - - - - - - - - - - - - - - - - - - - - - - - - - - - - - - - - - - - - -
Function HowManySkillsBySQL(CandidateKey as Long) As Integer

    Dim SQL As String

    'Define the query.
    SQL = "SELECT count(*) as [Total] FROM tblCandidateSkill"
    SQL = SQL + " WHERE tblCandidateSkill.CandidateKey = " + _
        Str$(CandidateKey)

    'Execute the query.
    Data1.Recordset = SQL
    Data1.Refresh

    'Return the result.
    HowManySkillsBySQL = Data1.Recordset![Total]

End Function
```

The BTS database does not have many skills assigned to any candidate, so the counts are not very large. If a count operation is executed on a large database, or there are many records to count, the performance of the SQL implementation can be remarkably better than that of the procedural method.

Examining the Dangers of SQL

The power of the SQL language to generate very complex results is also a source of danger. It is sometimes easy to forget that the requests defined by SQL statements will be carried out at some point by a computer somewhere. If the database is in a client/server environment, then that computer is the RDBMS server. Otherwise, the computer carrying out the SQL request is the user's machine.

There are many factors that can make a query execute inefficiently. In general, one way to ensure efficient query execution is to make sure your databases are properly indexed. If you are using SQL Passthrough, you also might want to order your statements in the best way for your particular RDBMS. Specifics vary from database to database. Consult the documentation of your RDBMS or your DBA, if you have one.

Additionally, if your database is on a network or you have a client/server database, network bandwidth is a consideration. To reduce the impact of data access on network bandwidth, it is best to return as few rows as possible. If you have a large set of data that a user needs to browse, consider requesting only a portion of that data at a time as the user needs to see it. Otherwise, the application user might need to wait as the entire data set is downloaded before seeing any of it.

> **NOTE**
>
> Network bandwidth is usually a reference to the amount of traffic that a network system can handle. Having high bandwidth is a good thing. Moving information across your network reduces available bandwidth while that information is transferring.

In general, however, properly constructed SQL queries combined with well-designed databases can be the best solutions for network environments or situations with low bandwidth (see Figure 32.1). The best old-style procedural access methods cannot compete with the best SQL access methods, with respect to bandwidth requirements on large database systems.

FIGURE 32.1.

Moving information from the server to the client.

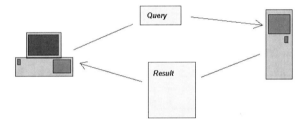

Understanding Some Common Terms

Before getting into the mechanics of SQL syntax, it helps to be familiar with some of the subject matter language. Table 32.1 lists some of the common terms you may run across.

Table 32.1. SQL terms and their meanings.

Term	Description
Attribute	See description of "Column." This term has fallen out of favor lately, but is still in use.
Action query	A SQL query that modifies database contents or structure.
ANSI	American National Standards Institute. A recognized source of standards for industry and government.

continues

Table 32.1. continued

Term	Description
Column	Smallest item of information in a database. Also known as a *field* of a table. Sometimes called an *attribute*. Same as "Field."
Field	See explanation of "Column." Most familiar term to XBase programmers.
Foreign key	A table column or a group of columns that represent a value meant to relate the record in which it resides to a record or records of another table.
Index	A structure implemented by a DBMS to more quickly access table records. Indexes are defined by the database designer and maintained by the RDBMS from that point on.
Join	A combination of one or more tables produced by a `Select` statement. Tip: Not all RDBMSs support the same syntax for these operations. For example, Microsoft SQL Server accepts *= and =* as indicators for two types of joins, but the Jet Engine does not recognize this syntax.
Key	A column or group of columns that contain values used for grouping or filtering.
Null	In SQL, this literally means *nothing*, as in nothing is stored. When a field contains a NULL value, its contents mean nothing. NULL is not the same as blank. Some languages, including Visual Basic, include special functions such as `IsNull()` to test for NULL values.
Primary key	A table column or a group of columns that represents a unique value in each row of the table. In other words, the *primary key* value for a record identifies one and only one record of a table.
Query	In the most general sense, this is just a SQL statement.
Record	Also known as a table row. This is a collection of fields. Information in a table is stored in records.
Row	Also known as a table record. This is a collection of columns. Information in a table is stored in rows.
SQL	Structured Query Language. As discussed in the earlier parts of this chapter, SQL is a language designed to describe database operations concisely. It can be used extensively for database access in Visual Basic 4.
Table	The component of a database that contains rows and columns. The columns are individual fields, and the rows are records of fields.
View	Generally, another name for a query that returns a set of columns and rows. Usually associated with stored queries, but the precise meaning varies between RDBMS vendors.

Using SQL Syntax

The SQL language is very rich. Entire books exist that discuss nothing but SQL syntax and its subtleties. A very detailed discussion of the particulars is beyond the scope of this book.

An excellent source of the SQL language structure is available in the Visual Basic 4.0 Help system. Use Tables 32.2 through 32.4 to identify some SQL keywords that address your needs, and then refer to the Help system associated with the keyword for syntax details.

Table 32.2. Important SQL keywords for retrieving data.

Keyword	Abbreviated Function Description
ALL	This is a qualifier used in other SQL statements to tell the RDBMS to return all records specified in a query. The RDBMS assumes this by default. (This keyword also can be replaced by the * symbol in most queries when used in the SELECT portion of the query.) This keyword also plays a role in subqueries.
ANY	Used in subqueries.
ASC	Ascending order. Used with ORDER BY clause.
AVG	Returns the arithmetic mean of a set of values contained in a field of the query. Used with SELECT.
COUNT	Counts the number of records returned by a query.
DESC	Descending order. Used with ORDER BY clause.
DISTINCT	Removes duplicate results from a query. Also see DISTINCT ROW in the Help system.
FIRST	Returns a field from the first record of a query. Used with SELECT.
FROM	Part of the SELECT query structure. Defines the source of information for a query.
GROUP BY	Used in a SELECT query to group records. Allows use of aggregate functions, such as SUM, to generate summary records for each group in the returned data set.
HAVING	When using the GROUP BY clause in a SELECT, this clause limits the returned groups to those with a particular set of qualities.
IN	An operator that tells the RDBMS to see whether the item to the left of the IN keyword is "in" the set to the right. See the complex query of Listing 32.5 for an example combining IN with NOT.
INNER JOIN	Type of join where only records that match by some criterion between two tables are included in the result set.

continues

Table 32.2. continued

Keyword	Abbreviated Function Description
JOIN	A type of SELECT operation that combines one or more tables to return a result that contains fields from both tables. Several types of joins exist. The two broad categories of joins are OUTER JOINS and INNER JOINS.
LAST	Returns a field from the last record of a query. Used with SELECT.
LEFT JOIN	Type of join that produces a set where all the records from the table to the left of this keyword are included and only some of the records from the table to the right are included. This is a type of outer join.
MAX	Returns the maximum value of a query. Used with SELECT.
MIN	Returns the minimum value of a query. Used with SELECT.
ORDER BY	Sorts the data set in a SELECT. Tip: If you have a common ORDER BY setting in your application, create an index that sorts the data in the same order.
PIVOT	Used in crosstab query definitions with the TRANSFORM statement to return a view of a database in a more compact form. The resulting view can use calculated fields as column headings.
RIGHT JOIN	Type of join where all the records from the table to the right of this keyword set are included and only some of the records from the table to the left are included. This is a type of outer join and, in a sense, is the opposite of a LEFT JOIN.
SELECT	Fundamental keyword for defining a query that returns data.
STDEV	Standard deviation for a population sample. Used with SELECT.
STDEVP	Standard deviation for a population. Used with SELECT.
SUM	Sums the set of values resulting from a query. Used with SELECT.
TOP	Causes a SELECT to return only the top records of a query. For example, you can use this keyword to specify that you want only the top 10 results. All others are ignored and are not returned by the query.
TRANSFORM	Used in crosstab query definitions. See description of PIVOT.
UNION	A SQL operator that combines the results of two or more SELECT queries or tables. Sometimes considered a type of outer join.
VAR	Statistical variance of a population. Used with SELECT.
VARP	Statistical variance of a population sample. Used with SELECT.
WHERE	Part of the SELECT query structure. Restricts rows returned by the query.

Table 32.3. Important SQL keywords for changing data.

Keyword	Abbreviated Function Description
DELETE	Fundamental keyword to remove records from a table.
FROM	Used as a clause in the DELETE statement to identify the target tables.
INSERT INTO	Inserts new records into a database table.
SELECT	Used with INSERT INTO statement when inserting records based on records of another table.
SET	Used with the UPDATE keyword to set field values of selected records.
UPDATE	Fundamental keyword for defining a query that changes records in a table.
VALUES	Used with INSERT INTO to specify the values that the inserted record should have when only one record will be added.
WHERE	Used as a clause in UPDATE and DELETE statements.

In general, the Jet Engine does not support SQL commands on non-Jet databases that alter a database structure. For this reason, some of the commands in the following table will only work if your RDBMS can handle them in the form of a SQL passthrough. The following table is presented with the Visual Basic method alternatives.

Table 32.4. Important SQL keywords to change a database structure.

Keyword	Abbreviated Description	VB Method
ALTER TABLE	Changes the design of a table.	CreateTableDef
CONSTRAINT	Defines a relationship between tables of a database. This allows the RDBMS to prevent operations that may damage the logical integrity of the database.	CreateRelation
CREATE INDEX	Fundamental keyword to remove records from a table.	CreateIndex
CREATE TABLE	Creates a table in the current database.	CreateTableDef
DROP COLUMN	Deletes a field from a table.	Delete
DROP INDEX	Deletes an index from a database table. Generally works with the Execute method.	Delete
DROP TABLE	Deletes a table from a database. Generally works with the Execute method.	Delete
SELECT INTO	Creates a new table based on the result of a SELECT type query. The new table contains the selected records.	NA
WHERE	Used as a clause in UPDATE and DELETE statements.	NA

A Tip for Access Users

If you are using Access 2.0, you can copy/paste the SQL generated for your queries into Visual Basic by highlighting the statements in SQL view of Access and then pasting them into your application or a text file. If you would like to save your query SQL statements directly into a file, add the Access Basic program shown in Listing 32.8 to your MDB and execute it in Access 2.0 by passing in the query name and the name of the file you want the SQL statement saved to.

Listing 32.8. Access 2.0 program to save SQL statements.

```
'------------------------------------------------------------------
'Access 2.0 Basic procedure to save a generated SQL statement
'directly to a file.
'------------------------------------------------------------------
Sub WriteSQL (qryName$, fileName$)
    Dim db as Database
    Dim qd as QueryDef
    Set db = dbengine(0) (0)
    Set qd = db.OpenQueryDef(qry)
    Open fn$ For Output As 1
    Write #1, qd.sql
    Close #1
    MsgBox "Wrote"  & qryName$ &  "to"  & fileName$
EndSub
```

Looking at Simple Query Examples

Sometimes the best way to understand something is to see it in simple terms. With that thought, let's look at some simple examples of SQL queries that use the BTS database. All these examples can be executed with Visual Basic procedures like those of Listings 32.3 and 32.5 of the first section in this chapter.

Reminder: BTS is the "Best Team Selector" program of Chapter 36. Its database is used extensively in the examples of this chapter. Full source code for that program, and its database, can be found on the CD-ROM that accompanies this book.

The SQL query that lists the first and last name of all candidates in the tblCandidate table follows. The result is ordered by first name:

```
SELECT    FirstName, LastName
FROM         tblCandidate
ORDER BY    FirstName;
```

To return only those candidates that have a title of "Ms," use the following code:

```
SELECT    FirstName, LastName
FROM         tblCandidate
WHERE    Title = "Ms"
ORDER BY    FirstName, LastName;
```

To return the names and codes of all the available skills in the tblSkill table, use the following query:

```
SELECT     Name,SkillKey
FROM         tblSkill
ORDER BY    Name;
```

To see the names of all candidates with the skill with code value 1, you can issue this SQL command:

```
SELECT     FirstName, LastName
FROM         tblCandidate INNER JOIN tblCandidateSkill
ON         tblCandidate.CandidateKey = tblCandidateSkill.CandidateKey
WHERE      tblCandidateSkill.SkillKey = 1;
```

The main elements of the preceding statement are the INNER JOIN and the WHERE clause. A join "joins" two tables to produce a new kind of record that contains fields from both tables. An "inner join" keeps *only* those records that exist in both tables. In this case, the join occurs on the CandidateKey field that both the tblCandidate and tblCandidateSkill tables share. Since the WHERE clause filters the resulting join to records that have a skillkey value of 1, we get what we want.

If you want to see a table that mixes all skills and job titles, you can execute a union, as shown in the following code:

```
SELECT     Name,LastUpdate
FROM       tblJobTitle
UNION
SELECT     Name,LastUpdate
FROM         tblProject;
```

To count the number of candidates in the system, you can run the following query:

```
SELECT     COUNT(*)
FROM         tblCandidate;
```

To count only available candidates, you can run a query with a WHERE clause as follows:

```
SELECT     COUNT(*)
FROM         tblCandidate
WHERE      Available = TRUE;
```

You can group the available candidates by title and get a summary count of each title group by using the following query. The resulting table has two columns. A new column called "Total" is created to the right of the "Title" column. The "Total" column contains the result of the COUNT(Title) function:

```
SELECT     Title, COUNT(Title) AS Total
FROM         tblCandidate
WHERE      Available = TRUE
GROUP BY    Title;
```

Looking at Some Simple Action Query Examples

The following action query updates all records of the tblCandidate table so that all "Ms" titles are replaced with "Dr:"

```
UPDATE    tblCandidate
SET       Title = "Dr"
WHERE     Title = "Ms";
```

To ensure that every "Mr" candidate has a rating of at least 7 for any skill that they are listed as having, use the following query:

```
UPDATE    tblCandidateSkill
SET       Rating = 7
WHERE     Rating < 7
AND       Title = "Mr";
```

The following example creates a new candidate. Notice that no CandidateKey is specified, because this field is defined as a *counter* type. The RDBMS, in this case, automatically creates a new CandidateKey for any new record:

```
INSERT INTO
tblCandidate(Title,FirstName,LastName,MiddleInitial,Phone,Available,LastUpdate)
VALUES
("Mr", "Delamato", "Kode", "I", "(555) 999-9999", TRUE, Now);
```

To delete the skills of all the candidates in the system, you can issue a SQL command like the following:

```
DELETE    *
FROM      tblCandidateSkill;
```

To delete only the skills of those with a title of "Mr," you can use the following:

```
DELETE    *
FROM      tblCandidateSkill INNER JOIN tblCandidate
ON        tblCandidateSkill.CandidateKey = tblCandidate.CandidateKey
WHERE     tblCandidate.Title="Mr";
```

If you only want to delete skills of "Mr" candidates that are unavailable, you could use the following code:

```
DELETE    *
FROM      tblCandidateSkill INNER JOIN tblCandidate
ON        tblCandidateSkill.CandidateKey = tblCandidate.CandidateKey
WHERE     tblCandidate.Title="Mr"
AND       tblCandidate.Available=FALSE;
```

You can archive the candidates into a new table called arcCandidate by using this code:

```
SELECT    *
INTO      arcCandidate
FROM      tblCandidate;
```

Examining Some Advanced Concepts

Now it's time to take a closer look at some of the more complex aspects of SQL constructions and concepts. In particular, you'll learn about the following items:

- Inner joins
- Outer joins
- Stored queries
- Subqueries
- Relationships/constraints
- Table indexes

The *inner join* is the type of join most people find easiest to understand initially. In this type of join, the result is a table that *only* contains records from *both* tables. This also is known as a *natural join*. Figure 32.2 illustrates why the term *inner* applies: The only records used are "inside" both tables.

FIGURE 32.2.

A conceptual diagram of an inner join.

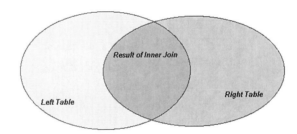

The outer joins pretty much come in two flavors: left and right. The left and right refer to the relative placement of the joining tables in the SQL command that joins them. In a *left join*, the table specified to the left of the keyword has *every* record output to the result set. The table on the right only contributes to the result set record if it relates to the left table. If there are fields from both tables in the result set, and the second table does not relate to the left table, the fields from the second table are set to NULL for that record. In a *right join*, the same logic applies, but this time it is the table to the right that outputs all its records.

Figure 32.3 shows why these are considered outer joins: The result set includes records that are "outside" the domain of one of the tables.

Joins and other queries can be stored at design time in some databases. One type that does not support stored queries is the original dBASE type. Most of the client/server RDBMSs and the Access database type do support stored queries. A *stored query* is a query that already has been defined and is stored in the database itself. This is in contrast to all the examples so far, which code the query in the Visual Basic program. The advantage of a stored query is that, in some cases, its execution plan already has been defined to some degree.

FIGURE 32.3.

A conceptual diagram of a left join.

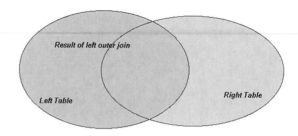

To understand this, you need to know what steps Visual Basic goes through when you issue a SQL command at runtime through an Execute method. The steps are something like this:

1. The driver parses the SQL text into its logical parts for processing.

2. The driver translates the logical components into an execution plan.

3. The driver follows the execution plan to construct the result.

4. The driver returns the result to Visual Basic.

In this case, the driver could be the Jet Engine, a client/server RDBMS, or an ODBC driver. Depending on the complexity of the SQL query and the circumstances of the application, the first and second steps may have a marginal impact on performance. A stored query already has been through step 1 and, in some cases, has been through most of step 2. When you execute a stored query, the database driver picks right up at step 2 to create the result you want.

The data control accepts stored queries as its record source. Storing a join query for later use can be a good practice to implement when you know in advance what the join needs to be. Even when you are not able to hard code the query entirely—to show a subset of a join where that subset is defined at runtime, for example—you still can store a query and access it from your application with a parameter. To use parameter queries, define the query as having a parameter when you create it. (See the help system for detail on the PARAMETERS keyword and how to use it with Jet Engine queries in Visual Basic. Non-Jet parameter queries may have vendor specific syntax.)

A *subquery* is a Select statement nested inside another query. This is a powerful feature of the SQL language that enables a query to do what otherwise could take several queries and temporary tables to accomplish. The ListSkillsBySQL() procedure of Listing 32.5 uses a subquery to return all the skills that a candidate *does not have*. For clarity, take a look at it in Listing 32.9 outside the Visual Basic syntax.

Listing 32.9. Query with subquery.

```
SELECT DISTINCTROW tblSkill.Name
FROM      tblSkill LEFT JOIN tblCandidateSkill
ON        tblSkill.SkillKey = tblCandidateSkill.SkillKey
WHERE     tblSkill.SkillKey NOT IN
          (SELECT tblCandidateSkill.SkillKey
           FROM    tblCandidateSkill
           WHERE   tblCandidateSkill.CandidateKey = #);
```

The # in the subquery in Listing 32.9 is substituted with the CandidateKey of the candidate in question at runtime by the Visual Basic program before executing the query. (The query will not run with "#" in it.) Conceptually, the gist of why the query in Listing 32.9 works follows:

1. The main SELECT body builds a result that contains ALL skills.

2. The driver executes the subquery to produce a set of skills that the candidate already has.

3. The WHERE clause then removes all skills in the set produced by the subquery. Removing all skills the candidate already has from the complete set of skills leaves you with *only* those skills the candidate *does not* already have.

An important relational feature that not all databases share, but all current client/server RDBMSs and the Access type do share, is the definition of *relationships* or *constraints*. Both terms are used interchangeably to describe the definition of table relationships within an RDBMS. Visual Basic 4.0 supports the definition of relationships through the CreateRelation method on Jet databases. It does not, however, support the definition of relationships in Jet databases that involve attached tables. Presently, the dBASE database type does not support defined relationships.

> **NOTE**
>
> For more detail on the CreateRelation method, consult the Visual Basic help system. However, unless you need to create database relationships at runtime, you are better off using a third-party tool or the Visual Basic Data Manager Add-In because they can be easier to work with.

Defining relationships is a key ingredient to maintaining referential integrity of a database. Once a relationship is defined, the RDBMS can check the validity of application requests to modify the database. In the case of client/server RDBMSs, the system can prevent the modification of the database if doing so would contradict a defined relation.

> **NOTE TO ACCESS USERS**
>
> The Access programming environment enforces relationships defined in an MDB, but Visual Basic does not. For example, although the BTS database requires a matching CandidateKey to exist in the tblCandidate table for any tblCandidateSkill record, it is possible to execute "DELETE * FROM tblCandidate" and orphan all the tblCandidateSkill records in the process.

Automatic referential integrity maintenance of the database by the RDBMS has the advantage of keeping coding errors from damaging the logical relationships of the database.

Although the specifics of when a database driver uses an index to assist in a query is very dependent on the way the driver itself is designed, in general the following is true:

1. If an index exists with the same order of fields as in an ORDER BY clause, the index is used to speed processing.

2. Some drivers only use one index per query. (SQL Server 4.2 is an example.)

The advantage of using an index on a SELECT query is that of speed: The index is a structure that tells the RDBMS directly where to find the records it needs. Without an index, it must visit each record until it finds what it seeks.

Indexes are not free, however. Otherwise, there would be no reason not to index every field in every table in every way. The price is paid when the database is updated and in disk space. In the case of ISAM databases, there also can be a price to pay in reliability. Indexes should be created judiciously. If there is consistently an ORDER BY clause that uses the same chain of fields to sort a selection and that selection can be large, it may be a good argument to create an index with the same ordered fields. You can create indexes at runtime in Visual Basic 4.0 via the CreateIndex method. (As with most database definition issues, however, you should use the Database Manager Add-In or a database-specific tool to do this.)

Working with Complex SQL Queries

Now let's dive into a few nasty looking SQL queries that do quite a bit of processing in one fell swoop.

Listing 32.10 shows a SQL query that returns a table with all used skills across the top as column headings, and all the candidate names along the left margin as rows. Each row has a 1 in any column that represents a skill the candidate of that row has.

Listing 32.10. Crosstab query.

```
TRANSFORM Count(tblSkill.SkillKey) AS CountOfSkillKey
SELECT tblCandidate.FirstName
FROM tblCandidate INNER JOIN (tblSkill INNER JOIN tblCandidateSkill ON
tblSkill.SkillKey = tblCandidateSkill.SkillKey) ON tblCandidate.CandidateKey =
tblCandidateSkill.CandidateKey
GROUP BY tblCandidate.FirstName, tblCandidate.CandidateKey
PIVOT tblSkill.Name;
```

To create more candidates automatically, you can execute the SQL query shown in Listing 32.11. It creates a new record for every existing candidate and appends it to the tblCandidate table. Each new candidate shares everything with its source record, with the exception that the CandidateKey is unique to the table and the first name is now "2." The CandidateKey is defined as a counter type and is the primary key, so the Jet Engine fills in that value

Listing 32.11. A query that creates test data.

```
INSERT INTO tblCandidate ( Title, FirstName, LastName, MiddleInitial, Picture,
Phone, Available, LastUpdate )
SELECT DISTINCTROW tblCandidate.Title, "2"
AS FirstName, tblCandidate.LastName, tblCandidate.MiddleInitial,
tblCandidate.Picture, tblCandidate.Phone, tblCandidate.Available,
tblCandidate.LastUpdate
FROM tblCandidate;
```

> **TIP**
>
> You can create a lot of test data with very few iterations of the type of action query shown in Listing 32.11. Each new execution of that query doubles the size of the database. Starting with 10 records, you would need to run it only 10 times to have 10,240 new records in the table.

Optimizing Your Queries

As mentioned in the "Examining Some Advanced Concepts" section, proper use of indexes and stored queries can increase performance of Visual Basic queries. A few other items also play a particularly obvious role in query optimization.

To reduce the number of rows returned by a query in a particular subquery, use the DISTINCTROWS or DISTINCT predicate with your SELECT statement. This produces a shorter table when duplicate records otherwise would appear. Listing 32.5 earlier in this chapter illustrates the use of the DISTINCT predicate.

If you are using an ISAM database locally, set the Exclusive database access mode to TRUE. If you are using a data control, this is a property. If you are using OpenDatabase methods, this is a parameter. Exclusive database access is much faster but can be implemented only when the database will not be shared.

Do not use ORDER BY unless you need to order the result. For example, an ORDER BY clause in the subquery of Listing 32.5 of this chapter would cause unnecessary processing, because the result of the subquery is only used internally to filter out records of the main query and is not displayed itself.

Use SQL queries instead of iterative methods whenever a result involves more than one table. Otherwise, you may need multiple data controls or data objects. In some cases, this can result in more open connections. More data controls and connections can reduce resources available to your program and other programs on your system.

> **NOTE**
>
> When the Jet Engine is given queries to apply against MDB or DBF files, it tries something called "Rushmore Optimization." This is a technology Microsoft inherited from the original creators of FoxPro that can speed up non-client/server queries considerably. All queries cannot be optimized by the Jet Engine this way, but some, if not most, can be converted into forms that can. If you are using MDB (Access) or DBF databases in your project, check the Visual Basic Help system and documentation for details that can help you ensure your queries run with Rushmore Optimization as much as possible.

Making RDBMS-Specific Enhancements

As mentioned earlier, most client/server RDBMSs go beyond the specifications of SQL-92 by adding enhanced functions. In some cases, SQL-92 specifications are violated in the interest of enhancing RDBMS functionality or performance. The only way to know what features are available with your RDBMS is to review its documentation or contact someone knowledgeable on the subject with respect to your RDBMS.

In particular with client/server RDBMSs, there are significant database-optimization features available to the DBA (Database Administrator) that are not SQL standard. Microsoft SQL Server, for example, supports a technology they call *clustered* indexing, which can improve data lookup times in larger tables by essentially "grouping" related files near each other on the server's disk. Oracle supports what they call *interleaving*, which gives a performance boost in large databases by factoring in characteristics of the disk storage system to improve physical access to the data.

Other nonstandard features that are available in SQL Server, Oracle, and other client/server RDBMSs are *triggers* and *stored procedures*. Triggers and stored procedures are programs that can be stored on the database server. When properly used, they can improve operation of a database noticeably by off-loading some of the business logic from the user computer to the database server. Client/server issues are discussed more thoroughly in the next chapter.

Summary

This chapter introduced many significant SQL concepts and terms. Along the way, it illustrated some ways to use SQL in Visual Basic 4. Although this chapter shows that SQL can be applied powerfully to both ISAM and client/server databases, Structured Query Language shines most in the client/server environment. For an introduction to client/server concepts, turn to Chapter 33, "Visual Basic 4.0 and Client/Server Programming."

Visual Basic 4.0 and Client/Server Programming

33

by Frank Font

This chapter presents some of the concepts and issues of client/server development with Visual Basic 4.0. Some illustrative examples are used. This chapter also introduces some common terms used in client/server development.

The Concept of Client/Server

At least two computers exist in the basic client/server environment: the *client*, which interacts directly with the user, and the *server*, which processes queries and returns results. This architecture is sometimes referred to as *two tier* (see Figure 33.1). Visual Basic is a tool that can be used to create programs on the client computer. Commercially available RDBMS servers, such as Oracle, SQL Server, and so on are used to process the queries that the Visual Basic client program issues.

FIGURE 33.1.

An example of two-tier architecture.

Client RDBMS Server

In two-tier implementations, the business rules are incorporated into the client machine or the server, or they are shared by both. In a three-tier client server solution, a third computer is inserted between the client machine and the server to implement some or all of the business logic (see Figure 33.2). This frees up the resources of the server to focus more exclusively on directly fulfilling query requests, and it reduces the burden on the client machine. The software running on the middle computer sometimes is referred to as *middleware.* There are very few standards in this relatively new area, and Visual Basic 4.0 does not readily support development of middleware. This chapter therefore focuses on the two-tier model.

FIGURE 33.2.

An example of three-tier architecture.

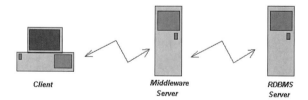

Client Middleware Server RDBMS Server

In contrast to a client/server database system, an *ISAM (Indexed Sequential Access Method)* database forces all processing to be done by the user computer. Some common databases that fall into this category are the XBase types (dBASE and FoxPro, among others) and the Microsoft Access database. For more detail on ISAM databases, turn back to Chapter 31, "Creating, Modifying, and Maintaining Databases."

NOTE

Btrieve is a hybrid database system that can be configured for both local use and server managed use. It has features of both an ISAM database and a client/server database system. Since it is not entirely a client/server RDBMS, I will not focus on it here.

Examining the Benefits of Client/Server Systems

A well-designed client server system can have several advantages over an ISAM database system:

- Better referential integrity enforcement
- Less network traffic
- Parallel processing
- Scalability (an ability to grow as needs increase)

The referential integrity of a database can be better maintained with a client/server RDBMS for the following reasons:

- The RDBMS can be designed to understand the referential needs of the database and then will automatically enforce those rules. The rules are independent of user applications and are thus not subject to logical corruption from ill-behaving user programs. ISAM, on the other hand, relies *entirely* on the user program to maintain the logical database integrity. A poorly designed ISAM database program or ill-behaved workstation can damage the referential integrity of its database, which it may be sharing with other computers.

- Unlike ISAM database programs that rely on the user program to directly update the database files when modifying data, a client/server RDBMS carries out those operations itself. Because the server carries out all changes and the user computer does not directly affect the database files, a user computer crash or user system corruption will not physically corrupt the database. In a sense, the database is insulated from ill-behaved user machines.

Network traffic can be reduced when using a client/server RDBMS solution. In an ISAM application, all record access is carried out by the user program. Any search or series of updates requires the user computer to receive unrelated database records and index information over the network so that it can locate the proper spot in which to make the change it needs. In simple terms, this means that an ISAM database has *substantial* irrelevant transactions over the network. A client server solution, on the other hand, executes its database operations first by sending a query that describes exactly what it wants done, and then receiving through the network *only* exactly what it wanted. No irrelevant network traffic is generated under ideal conditions. Query and connection considerations exist when using Visual Basic 4.0, which impact on the degree of idealized communication between the client computer and the RDBMS server. These considerations are discussed later in the section Creating a Nice Client.

Because queries are carried out by the RDBMS computer independently of the client computer, a degree of parallel processing is already taking place. While the query is being fulfilled, the user computer is available to focus on other computational tasks. This is not the same as multitasking, which Windows already does. This is better. In multitasking, parallel processing is only *simulated* by switching between application program instructions behind the scenes so that it seems as though everything is running at once. The key to the difference here is *seems to be running at once*. With one CPU doing everything, this is only a trick. With two independent CPUs, there is no trick: parallel processing is real. When using a Visual Basic 4.0 query on an ISAM database, that query is executed in its entirety by the user computer. When a client/server RDBMS is used to execute a user query, the user machine is free to work on other tasks.

Some commercial RDBMS servers—such as Oracle, SYBASE, and MS SQL Server—are able to utilize more than one CPU on the server computer. This capability gives those RDBMS servers a scalability not available to ISAM database applications. If you develop a client/server application using Visual Basic and your database server is scaleable with respect to CPUs, you can increase query performance and server responsiveness *without* recoding your program as you add users and clients. If your RDBMS supports it, you can replace your server hardware with a multi-CPU PC and transfer the existing database to it. This process is transparent to your Visual Basic client/server application.

A Look at Possible Disadvantages of Client/Server Systems

All the advantages of client/server systems do not come free. Unlike ISAM database applications, the client/server model introduces at least one other machine into the picture that must be configured and debugged in order for the solution to work. Although development of a client application using ODBC for client/server connectivity can be straightforward and not much different from development of an ISAM program, each RDBMS server is at least slightly different from other vendor versions and requires specialized knowledge about that system.

Depending on the size and needs of a project, it may be wise to have a dedicated Database Administrator (DBA) who works exclusively with the database server to configure it and maintain the databases. Most RDBMS servers today still need or greatly benefit from periodic tuning. Tuning steps and procedures are not standard across server platforms.

Getting Started with Client/Server Development

There are three versions of Visual Basic 4.0: Standard, Professional, and Enterprise. The Enterprise version adds enhancements specifically geared for client/server developers. However, you can use any version to work with client/server databases through ODBC.

In general, although the order can be different, these are the steps you should take to create an application for a three-tier client/server architecture:

1. Design and implement a database on the server.
2. Design and implement the business rules in the middleware server.
3. Design and implement an application for the user.

Creating an application for a two-tier architecture only requires steps 1 and 3. Since there are few standards for interfacing to the middleware layer of a three-tier architecture, I will focus on the two-tier model here.

Several tools are available from third parties to assist with the design and implementation of a database on RDBMS servers. These tools make the job easier by providing graphical interfaces and generating the SQL creation commands for you. The exact process of implementing databases on RDBMS servers varies from vendor to vendor. You should consult your vendor's documentation for the details. If you are lucky and have one, however, you can just ask your DBA to create the database for you.

After your database is designed and implemented on your server, you are ready to connect to it via ODBC. To access your server via this method, you have to ensure that the proper ODBC driver is installed on your system. ODBC drivers are available from several sources, one of which is usually the RDBMS vendor. Some companies, such as Intersolve, sell developer packages that contain drivers for many RDBMS systems, including Oracle and SQL Server.

You can access your database directly through ODBC or indirectly if your database tables are attached to an Access-type MDB file. Attaching your tables to an Access MDB file has several advantages—including those of performance—over directly accessing tables through code and ODBC. An attached table is managed by the Visual Basic Jet Engine so that its connection information is preserved between queries. If this information is not preserved, every query has to reestablish authorization with the target database before the query can be executed.

Looking at the Advantages of Passthrough Queries

If you are using ODBC, you can issue RDBMS-specific commands by employing ODBC passthrough queries. This technique, sometimes referred to as SQL PassThrough, bypasses the

Microsoft Jet database engine and sends your commands directly to the RDBMS. If your RDBMS supports stored procedures, you will need to use this technique to run them. (A stored procedure is a small program stored on the server.)

The reason cutting Jet out of the picture can be an advantage is that, in its effort to help processing along, the Jet engine sometimes ends up creating more network traffic and stealing work from the RDBMS server.

Extra network traffic is created when the Jet engine shares action query processing by requesting data in chunks from the server to process it locally. Anything modified is then sent back to the server for storage. In an idealized client/server scenario, this doesn't happen; the server does all the processing with no back and forth transmission of the work in process. ODBC passthrough ensures reduced network overhead by moving all the processing to the server. Only the result comes back to the user computer.

Looking at the Disadvantages of Passthrough Queries

Like most things, passthrough queries have a price. A fundamental disadvantage of implementing applications that rely heavily on passthrough queries is reduced portability. If the passthrough commands are RDBMS specific, you may need to recode these queries to use the application with a different RDBMS.

Since passthrough queries are not analyzed by the Jet engine, they have to be coded exactly as the RDBMS expects to see them. Some SQL queries, such as joins in particular, vary in structure from vendor to vendor. The common interface presented by Jet is an advantage that leaves when passthrough is relied on heavily.

Not only is the element of a common SQL interface reduced when Jet is removed from the processing, losing Jet can also mean you lose some query functionality. Jet allows native Visual Basic functions in query constructions. RDBMS servers do not have access to the Visual Basic parser, so Visual Basic's intrinsic functions, such as `Now()` and `Mid$()`, are not available.

Although most major RDBMSs have functions similar to the ones Visual Basic allows in Jet queries, they have no way of integrating parameterized query prompting into a Visual Basic program. A parameterized query through the Jet engine can accept the parameter directly from the user or a program variable. An RDBMSs parameter query value must be supplied directly as a literal in the passthrough string.

Another possible disadvantage is that passthrough queries only return snapshots. Snapshots are not updatable. As a result, if there is anything in the result of a passthrough query that requires update, another query has to be issued.

Creating a Nice Client

Two terms heard frequently with describing client applications are *fat client* and *thin client*. A fat client is one that incorporates many business rules into the user application. A thin client relies more significantly on the server or a middleware server for its business rule logic. Visual Basic client/server applications can be fat or thin clients. Some of the factors that determine the mode are obvious and some are subtle.

Assuming that the BTS database was implemented in a client/server RDBMS, a simple example of a fat client would be an application that returns the entire contents of the tblCandidate database and filters out all non Mr records at the user workstation to display the Mr entries. Such a query follows:

```
SELECT * FROM tblCandidate;
```

Alternatively, a thin version of this application might issue the following query:

```
SELECT * FROM tblCandidate WHERE tblCandidate.Title = Mr;
```

The significance of this difference is that in the fat client version, the server had less logical processing to execute but more raw data to transmit. Additionally, the user machine had more processing to execute in the fat client version.

In general, it is better to develop thin clients for the following reasons:

- Business logic stored on the server in the form of stored procedures and triggers is available to *all* client server applications that use the database.
- Network traffic is reduced when the RDBMS returns only the rows needed by the user program.
- Processing burden on the user machine is reduced when a query is as precise as possible.

If your RDBMS supports stored procedures and triggers, such as Oracle and SQL Server, you can use them to help keep your client thin. Stored procedures and triggers are programs that execute on the server itself. They usually are written in the language provided by the server system for that purpose. The particulars of their implementation are unique to the server you use, so consult your DBA or system documentation.

Some processing automatically is performed locally, even by the Jet Engine under some circumstances in Visual Basic 4.0. In particular, the Jet Engine may process some joins locally, causing increased network traffic and slower performance. Consult the Visual Basic 4.0 manuals for the specific situations in which this can happen.

Visual Basic 4.0 for Client/Server Development

There are several reasons to consider Visual Basic 4.0 for client/server development:

- Limited specialized knowledge of client/server databases is required.
- The Visual Basic language is easy to pick up and to train new programmers in.
- ODBC provides transparent accessibility to multiple RDBMS servers.
- Visual Basic has one of the best screen designers available.

With few exceptions, creating client/server applications in Visual Basic requires no special knowledge beyond that required to create ISAM database applications. The most significant exceptions are those with respect to configuring the RDBMS server, but that is actually independent of the application development itself in a logical sense. An office with a dedicated DBA and a Visual Basic programmer can begin creating client/server applications without any special training beyond that which they already have to perform non-Visual Basic client/server development.

Visual Basic's support for ODBC makes it possible to develop generic client/server applications that can work with multiple database back end solutions. In fact, unless ODBC passthrough is used, porting a Visual Basic client/server program to another back end is only a matter of selecting a different ODBC driver on the user workstation. If the ODBC driver information is not explicitly coded into the application or stored in an MDB attached table, no program change is necessary.

Visual Basic was one of the first Windows application development tools to have a genuinely intuitive and powerful screen designer. Given that a very significant amount of development time can be spent laying out the user interface and that users form significant impressions from the way the application is presented, this is a very significant factor in a tool's usability. With the advent of version 4, Visual Basic has enhanced the designer by enabling the form layout to lock down after it is set to the designer's liking. Additionally, the right button on the mouse now provides ready access to Control properties, which make configuration even faster and easier. Although some other tools—notably, Delphi from Borland—have recently made significant inroads into screen designer usability, Visual Basic still has one of the easiest and most intuitive screen designers available.

Summary

This chapter introduced some of the concepts and techniques of client/server development with Visual Basic 4.0. It focused on the common factors of this type of development without going into much detail about specific RDBMS systems or techniques. For more information on client/server RDBMS systems, consult your particular system's documentation.

PART

VI

Putting It All Together

Help Files

34

by Mark Steven Heyman

IN THIS CHAPTER

Most commercially viable Windows Applications provide their own Help Systems. Adding custom help to your applications might seem a tall order, almost like writing another whole program. In fact, however, most applications use the built-in Windows help system and only provide a Help file (HLP) which that system can use. In this chapter, you'll see how to create such a Help file.

You'll also gain an understanding of context-sensitive help in this chapter, and see how to incorporate it into your Visual Basic applications. You'll learn how to add to your Help system a secondary window, which may be used to display glossaries, lists, sample code, or other information to be viewed concurrently with the main Help text.

In addition, this chapter examines different ways of adding graphic images to your Help files. You'll come to understand what is meant by "hot spots," and see how they may be used to jump between related Help topics. You'll also get a chance to create some hypergraphics, a special kind of graphics which may contain multiple hot spots, each of which may be used to jump between topics, pop-up windows, or execute Help macros.

The last topic covered in this chapter is Help Macros. You'll receive a brief introduction to the more than 50 macros available in the WinHelp application, and see how many of them may be invoked to customize the way WinHelp works in conjunction with your own Help files.

Creating a Windows Help File

A Windows Help File is a specially compiled file with the HLP extension; it may be used with the built-in Windows help system to display help information pertaining to your Visual Basic application. The user may select an item from the Help Contents, then view, search, and navigate the various Help screens by jumping from one topic to another. In addition to "topic-jumping," custom Help Systems often provide pop-up windows that give more detailed information about a particular keyword, without actually jumping to another help page.

The process of creating your own custom help file can be broken down into four distinct steps. Here they are:

1. Create the HelpText File (or Topic File) in RTF Format.
2. Create the Help Project File (HPJ).
3. Compile the Help File using the Help Compiler and Project File.
4. Attach the Help File to your Visual Basic Application.

Each of these steps is discussed and demonstrated in this chapter.

The Help Text or Topic File is created with an editor, such as Microsoft Word, that is capable of saving text in the RTF format; it contains topics that are linked together via hypertext "jump phrases" or special hypergraphics (discussed later in this chapter). Without linking, the topics in a Help file would be isolated islands of information; a user could not move from one topic to another. The most convenient way of linking topics is to create hypertext that enables users to jump between topics or display a pop-up window. Such topic-jumps serve a purpose similar to cross-references in a book. These jumps consist of specially coded text or graphics that cause the WinHelp application to display another topic in the main Help window.

The Project File is a simple ASCII text file, with an extension of HPJ. The project file is used to pass information regarding the current Help project to the Help Compiler. This information includes the name and location of the RTF Topic file or files, the directory location of any required bitmaps, errorlog specifications and warning levels, context-sensitive help information, and the location, size, and color of the Help System window.

How to Create the Help Text: Contacts.Rtf

To create the Help text file you must use an editor that is capable of saving files in the Rich Text Format (RTF). Microsoft Word is such a program, and will be used here. You're going to be working with underlined (Ctrl+U), double-underlined (Ctrl+Shift+D), and hidden text (Ctrl+Shift+H), so it's not a bad idea to reveal all formatting codes while you create your RTF file.

In the Topic file, jump phrases (hypertext jumps) are double-underlined; they are followed immediately by a "tag" phrase (or context string), which is formatted as hidden text. In the Help window, hypertext jumps appear underlined and on color monitors appear green. For example, a double-underlined phrase Export A File appears as Export A File in green text to the user.

Here, in general, are the steps required to establish a word or phrase as a jump in the topic file:

1. Place the insertion point at the place in the text where you want to enter the jump phrase.
2. Select the double-underline (or strikethrough) feature of your editor.
3. Type the jump word or words in double-underlined format.
4. Turn off double-underlining and select the editors hidden text feature.
5. Type the context string (or jump tag) assigned to the topic that is the target of the jump.

CAUTION

When coding jumps, be careful not to include spaces between the double-underlined text and the hidden text. Also be careful not to format paragraph marks accidentally as hidden text. If you do, a compiler error or warning will occur.

Now it's time to start Word and create your new help system's topic file. For the examples in this chapter, a Contact Manager system will be used. Figure 34.1 presents the Contact Manager Help Contents screen, the first page of Contacts.Rtf:

FIGURE 34.1.

The Help Text File: Contents screen.

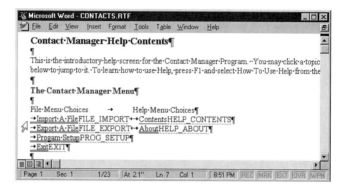

The first thing to notice here is the use of double-underlining. As already mentioned, words or phrases that are double-underlined here will appear as green, single-underlined jump phrases (or hypertext) in your Help System. When the user clicks on them, control will jump to the page represented by the "jump tag," which is the hidden label immediately following the double-underlined jump phrase. (All codes are revealed here, so hidden text shows up with a light, dotted underline, as you can see in Figure 34.1.) This is important: the jump tag must follow the jump phrase immediately, no spaces, and it must be hidden. In the example seen previously, "Import A File" is the jump phrase, "FILE_IMPORT" is the hidden tag; "Export A File" is the phrase, "FILE_EXPORT" is the tag, and so on.

Once your Help Contents screen is completed, start a new page (in Word press Ctrl+Enter). The text for each jump page must be written on a separate word processing page. You connect the jump page text to the jump phrase by using the jump tag with a custom footnote symbol. In fact there are three custom footnote symbols you may use, each invoking a different Help System feature. They are summarized here, in Table 34.1, and discussed in detail immediately afterward:

Table 34.1. Help Text File: Custom footnote symbols.

Symbol	Description
#	Connects a jump page to its jump phrase by referencing the jump tag.
$	References the jump page title, which will then appear in the Help System's Search list box.
K	References a keyword with which the user may search for a topic.

The (#) footnote symbol is used to connect a help topic page with its related jump tag. In this way, jump tags identify each topic in the Help system. Each tag must be unique—you can assign it to only one topic in the Topic File. Assigning a jump tag gives a topic an identifier that you can use to create jumps to that topic or to display it in a pop-up window. Although the Help Compiler can successfully compile topics that don't have a jump tag, the user of the Help system can't display them unless they contain keywords (see next section). Although a jump tag has a practical limitation of 255 characters, you should keep the tags short so they are easier to enter into your Topic Files.

The ($) footnote symbol is used to identify a Help Topic Title. In your custom Help System, the title of a topic usually appears at the beginning of the topic, and in the Bookmark menu and Search list box, if the topic contains keywords. To place the title at the beginning of the topic, type it as the first paragraph. You must define code for the title in a footnote for the title to appear correctly in the Bookmark menu and the Search dialog. Although the Help Compiler doesn't require that a topic have a title footnote, only those topics in the main Help window or a secondary window that do have a title footnote appear correctly in the Bookmark menu.

The (K) footnote symbol specifies topic keywords, which may be used to search for related topics. The WinHelp application lists matching topics by their titles (as defined in the title footnote) in the Search dialog box. The keyword search facility serves the same purpose as the index in a book. Because a keyword search is often the fastest way for users to access Help topics, you'll probably want to assign keywords to most topics in your Help system. You may specify more than one keyword per topic by separating them with semi-colons in the topic footnote. Here's how a keyword footnote for a topic entitled Opening Text Files might appear:

```
K open;opening;text file;ASCII;existing;text only;documents
```

TIP

You should specify a keyword footnote only if the topic has a title footnote, because the title of the topic appears in the Search dialog box when the user searches for the keyword. Topics that do not have titles but that are accessible through keywords are listed as >>Untitled Topic<< in the list at the bottom of the Search dialog box.

Take a look at Figure 34.2, which shows the primary jump pages and associated footnote symbolism you should add to Contacts.Rtf.

As you can see, the custom footnote symbol(s) must be the first item(s) on the jump page, followed by the Help Topic Title, and any other help text. To place a footnote using Word, you select Footnote from the Insert menu, which brings up the Footnote and Endnote dialog box. You want to use a Custom symbol here, so click the Custom Mark option button and enter one of the three symbols described previously in Table 34.1 (the # is required to connect a tag to a jump phrase, and should be entered first). When OK is clicked, the screen will split into two windows, with the jump page above, and footnotes below. You may then enter the appropriate jump tag, if you're inserting the # footnote, or any other text reference, such as a title or search keyword. Here's Figure 34.3 for comparison.

FIGURE 34.2.

The Help Text File: Jump screens.

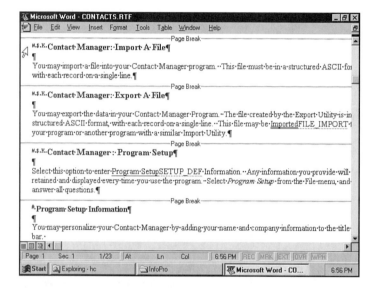

FIGURE 34.3.

The Help Text File: inserting custom footnotes.

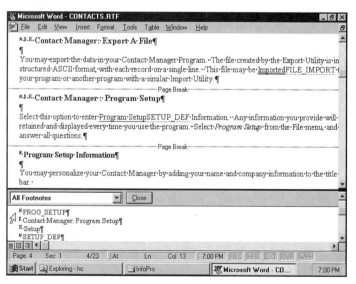

Here, the arrow is pointing to the first of three footnotes associated with the Program Setup help screen. Notice the actual footnote symbols, side by side, in the Program Setup text page in the upper window. This is a valid jump page; its title will appear in the Help Search list box; and Setup will serve as a search keyword.

There's something else to notice in Figure 34.3. In the Contact Manager: Program Setup help page, the phrase "Program Setup" is single-underlined, and there's a hidden tag "SETUP_DEF" associated with it. When a phrase is single-underlined in your RTF file, the phrase will appear in green, with a light dotted underline, in your running Help System. Rather than jumping to another page, a click to this phrase will pop up a small window displaying a definition or additional information. The phrase's hidden tag must still be referenced in a footnote on a separate page containing the pop-up window's text. (You can see this clearly in Figure 34.3).

NOTE

Pop-up windows need not be limited to definitions, although it's important to keep the text brief, because the main purpose of a pop-up window is to display definitions or notes that don't distract the user from the main topic.

Okay, that's it for the first version of your Help Text file (you'll add much more to this file over the rest of this chapter). If you're working along with this chapter, you should save the file as Contacts.RTF (again, it must be saved in the RTF format). The next step, Step 2, is to create the Help Project file.

Creating the Help Project File: Contacts.HPJ

The Help Project file is a simple text file that contains information to be passed to the Help Compiler. You may use your favorite text editor to create it. Figure 34.4 shows what it looks like for the first version of your new Help System.

FIGURE 34.4.

The Help Project File: Contacts.HPJ.

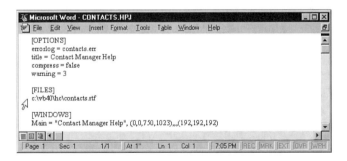

All you're doing in the [OPTIONS] section is specifying an error log for any help compiler errors that may be generated; and you're setting an associated warning level. You're setting the Help System's title bar, and indicating that no special file compression should take place.

The [FILES] section contains the fully qualified path to your Help Text file. If you're working along with the book, provide your own path here. The last section, [WINDOWS], contains a single line that sets the Help Window's size, position, and color.

That's it for Step 2. Save the file as Contacts.Hpj. Now it's compile time.

Compiling the Help File: Contacts.HLP

The third step is the easiest. To create your Contacts.HLP file, you use the Windows Help Compiler, a copy of which is included with Visual Basic's Professional Edition. The Help Compiler is located in the HC sub-directory of your VB installation directory. Open a DOS Window and locate the HC directory. At the prompt type:

```
HC Contacts.HPJ
```

and press Enter. (Be sure to pass the correct name and location of your Help Project file. This example assumes the file is in the HC directory). You may get some error messages or warnings during the compile process. If so, they will most likely be due to problems with your RTF file, such as improperly hidden or referenced tags. There's no penalty for compiling more than once, so fix the RTF source and try again.

> **TIP**
>
> It's not a bad idea to keep your help-related files in the same directory, at least during the development phase. In fact, the HC directory of the VB40 directory is a good place to keep them, because you'll need to run the Help Compiler (HC.EXE) located there. Another tip is to create a batch file containing the call to the compiler, HC Contacts.HPJ, in this case. It's then a simple matter to compile (and re-compile, as necessary) by running the batch file from the File Manager or the Windows 95 Explorer.

The fourth and final step in setting up your own Custom Help System is to attach Contacts.HLP to your Visual Basic application, in this case the Contact Manager program.

Attaching the Help File to the Contact Manager Program

This next step is where the rubber meets the road. If you're working along with the book, start a new project and add the form Contacts.FRM to it. You'll find this form, along with its associated database, CONTACTS.MDB, in the Chapter 34 section of the CD.

NOTE

The Contacts form contains a Data Control whose DataBaseName property is set to "C:\VB40\SAMS\CONTACTS.MDB." If you decide to place CONTACTS.MDB in a different directory, you'll need to change the DataBaseName property accordingly. If you want the Contact Manager program to be fully functional, be sure to incorporate into your project the CrystalReport, CommonDialog, and MSComm controls, as well as all the data types and constants contained in the VBU_CH34 module.

The first place to attach your new Help file is in the Project's Options dialog box, which may be accessed by selecting Tools | Options from the Visual Basic menu. Locate the Help File text box by clicking the Project tab and enter the full path to Contacts.HLP. This will allow the user to get Help by pressing F1, in addition to accessing it through the Help Menu. (While you're here, you might want to make sure that frmContacts is the Startup Form.)

Next, create a standard code module called VBU_CH34. You need to add one DECLARE (for the API WinHelp() function), and a few helpful constants, to your VBU_CH34 module's general declarations section. Feel free to use the API Text Viewer, if you find it easier than typing. Here's what must be added to VBU_CH34's general declarations section:

```
'   Help engine declaration — All on one line.
Declare Function WinHelp Lib "user32" Alias "WinHelpA" (ByVal hwnd As Long, ByVal
lpHelpFile As String, ByVal wCommand As Long, ByVal dwData As Long) As Long

'   Useful Constants which may be passed to WinHelp()
Public Const HELP_CONTEXT = &H1              'Display topic identified by number in
dwData
Public Const HELP_QUIT = &H2                ' Terminate help
Public Const HELP_INDEX = &H3               ' Display index
Public Const HELP_HELPONHELP = &H4          ' Display help on using help
Public Const HELP_SETINDEX = &H5            ' Set an alternate Index, if needed
Public Const HELP_KEY = &H101               ' Display topic for keyword in dwData
Public Const HELP_MULTIKEY = &H201          ' Lookup keyword in alternate table
```

Now use the Menu Editor to add a Help menu to the Contact Manager form. The Help menu will contain just two items, as seen in Table 34.2.

Table 34.2. Design time settings—Help menu for Contact Manager.

Visual Basic Object	*Property*	*Design Time Setting*
Form	Name	frmContacts
Menu Control	Name	mnuHelp
	Caption	&Help

continues

Table 34.2. continued

Visual Basic Object	Property	Design Time Setting
Sub-Menu Item	Name	mnuContents
	Caption	&Contents
Sub-Menu Item	Name	mnuAbout
	Caption	&About Contact Manager...

Now here's the code to be added to mnuContent's Click event; it consists of a call to the API function WinHelp():

```
Private Sub mnuContents_Click()
RV = WinHelp(frmContacts.hWnd,"c:\vb40\hc\contacts.hlp", HELP_INDEX,CLng(0))
End Sub
```

Here the first argument is the main form's Windows handle, which is just frmContact's hWnd property. The second argument points to the precise location of the compiled Help file. The third argument indicates that the Help contents (or Index) screen is to be displayed; and the fourth may be used to provide context-sensitive help based on which program object the user was focused on when F1 was pressed (context-sensitive help is covered later in this chapter).

That's all there is to it. Now when you run your Contact Manager program, and select Contents from the Help menu (or Press F1), this is what you'll see (see Figure 34.5).

FIGURE 34.5.

The Help File In Action: Help Contents.

When you click on the green, single-underlined keyword "Program Setup," and click on the dotted underlined keyword, you'll see this (see Figure 34.6).

FIGURE 34.6.

The Help File In Action: Program Setup Jump screen.

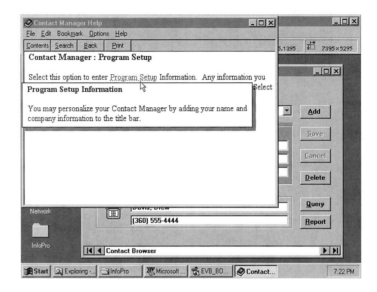

Once you're in the Help System, you may use all the features you're familiar with, such as searching, stepping back, printing, or jumping to the top-level contents screen. When you're done with Help, exit in any of the usual ways.

In your testing, you may have noticed that it's possible to quit your program and still leave the Help System on the screen. This is because the WinHelp application is a stand-alone, shared resource available to all Windows programs. As a result, your program's Help System has limited control over the WinHelp application. You may, however, force WinHelp to quit at the same time your own program is shut down. To do this, add the following line to frmContact's Unload event procedure:

```
Private Sub Form_Unload(Cancel As Integer)
RetVal = WinHelp(hWnd, dummy$, HELP_QUIT, 0)
End Sub
```

Here you make another call to WinHelp, except, this time, the third argument is a constant, which politely informs WinHelp that its services are no longer needed (the second argument is just a "dummy" place-holder).

That's it. You now have the beginnings of a full-blown Custom Help System. More importantly, you've acquired the skills to add simple custom help to all of your Visual Basic applications. In the next part of this chapter, you'll see how to enhance your Help System by adding context-sensitivity and a secondary window.

Creating Context-Sensitive Help

In this section you'll add context-sensitive Help to your Contact Manager program. You'll also see how to redirect Help information to a second window, one that operates independently of the main help screen. In the process, you'll learn how to work with the [MAP] and [WIN-DOWS] sections of the Help project file.

You're probably already familiar with the notion of context-sensitive help. If you've ever selected a Windows application object and then pressed F1 to find out more about it, you've used the application's context-sensitive help feature. The application is smart enough to determine which object has the focus, read the object's *context reference* (see the next section), and send it to WinHelp, which in turn displays the appropriate help topic.

Creating Context References

In developing context-sensitive Help, you're required to establish a set of context references so that WinHelp and your application pass the correct information back and forth. In Visual Basic applications, the *context reference* is a unique number, stored in the HelpContextID property, which corresponds to a particular object—for example, to a menu item, form, control, or screen region. You can assign HelpContextIDs arbitrarily, but they must be unique for each object and you should not change them afterward.

You then use these HelpContextIDs (or context numbers) to create links between your application and the corresponding Help topics. This is done by listing your topic file's jump tags, along with the associated object's HelpContextID, in the [MAP] section of the Help project file (HPJ). When writing the [MAP] section, you can use either decimal or hexadecimal numbers to specify context numbers, but be sure to separate jump tags and context numbers by an arbitrary amount of white space, using either space characters or tabs.

The following example illustrates two formats you can use in your project file's [MAP] section.

```
[MAP]

dcmb_scr    30          ; Jump tags and decimal numbers representing
dmxi_scr    31          ; unique HelpContextIDs...
dmni_scr    32
dri_scr     33
dtb_scr     34

Edit_Window     0x0001  ; Or work a little harder and use Hex,
Control_Menu    0x0002   ; if there's a good reason...
Maximize_Icon      0x0003
Minimize_Icon      0x0004
Split_Bar     0x0005
Scroll_Bar      0x0006
Title_Bar     0x0007
Window_Border      0x0008
```

CAUTION

Be sure to assign a unique context number to each jump tag. Assigning the same context number to more than one jump tag generates a compiler error. The Help Compiler also generates a warning message if a context string appearing in the [MAP] section is not defined in the RTF topic file, or files.

Secondary Help Windows

A *secondary help window* is one that operates independently of the main help screen. It may be sized, moved, scrolled through, or closed at the user's discretion. Secondary windows may display any help topic defined in the RTF Topic file, and are often used to show a list, such as a help glossary, or examples of code, or any other topic the user might like to view simultaneously with the main help text.

As you saw earlier in this chapter, the [WINDOWS] section of the Help project file defines the size, location, and colors for the primary Help window. It's also where you may specify the dimensions and other attributes of any secondary window types you might want to use.

Window characteristics are defined using the following syntax:

```
typename = caption, (hpos, vpos, width, height), sizing, (rgb), (ns_rgb), top
```

Here's a list describing each parameter:

typename	Specifies the type of window that uses the defined attributes. For the primary Help window, this parameter is main. For a secondary window type, this parameter can be any unique name up to eight characters other than main. Any jumps that display a topic in a secondary window give this unique type name as part of the jump.
caption	The caption that appears on the title bar of different types of secondary windows. For the main Help window, this caption is given by the Help TITLE option in the [OPTIONS] section of the Help project file.
hpos, vpos	Horizontal and vertical position, respectively, of the window's upper-left corner. WinHelp uses a 1024 x 1024 coordinate system (starting at 0,0) and maps this coordinate system onto the resolution of the video card displaying the Help file.

width, height	Gives the default width and height of a secondary window. The width and height, like the x and y positions, are based on the resolution of the video adapter (as indicated for the *hpos* and *vpos* parameters in the preceding description).
sizing	Specifies how a secondary window is sized when WinHelp first opens it. This parameter is 0 for normal size and 1 for maximized. If the value is 1, WinHelp ignores the *hpos, vpos, width,* and *height* parameters given in the type definition.
rgb,ns_rgb	Three comma-delimited, three-digit values giving the background colors for the window and nonscrolling region (if any) in the window. The three digits represent the red, green, and blue (RGB) components of the color. If these colors are not given, the scrolling and nonscrolling areas are displayed with the normal system colors in the background.
top	Specifies whether a secondary window always remains on top of all other windows. This parameter is optional. If not specified, the secondary window normally moves behind other windows. If the value is 1, WinHelp keeps the secondary window on top of other windows.

The following example shows the format of the [WINDOWS] section in a sample Help project file:

```
[WINDOWS]
main = "Sample Help System", (0,0,1023,1023),,, (192,192,192)
glossary = "Sample Glossary", (222,206,725,486),,, (192,192,192), 1
```

This section sets the color of the nonscrolling region of the main Help window to gray. It also defines a type of secondary window named glossary with the following characteristics:

- Caption Sample Glossary in the title bar.
- Upper-left corner at (222, 206).
- Length of 725 and width of 486 (in WinHelp coordinates).
- Displayed in normal size (0).
- Gray background (192, 192, 192) for the nonscrolling region.
- Appears on top of all other windows.

Later in this chapter, you'll set up a secondary help window for your Contact Manager program, and see how to send information to it.

Adding Context-Sensitive Help to an Application

The first step in adding context-sensitive Help to your Visual Basic application is to open your project's Options Dialog Box (select Options from the Tools menu, and click the Project tab). Enter the name of your Help file in the Help File text box, or click the ellipsis to browse for it.

This setting can be a file name or a full path and file name; it indicates the file to be started when the user presses F1 from within your VB application. For now, during the development phase, use the full path. Here's how the project Options Dialog Box might look (see Figure 34.7).

FIGURE 34.7.

Adding context-sensitive help to your VB project.

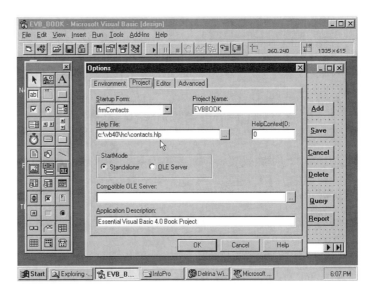

TIP

For best results after delivery, put the Help File in the same directory as your application and specify only the name of the Help File in the Help File text box. That way, you can keep the same setting for the Help File text box for each site using your application, and allow users to install the application in the directory of their choice.

The next step is to set the `HelpContextID` Property for any forms or controls you wish to be context-sensitive. This property is available for Visual Basic forms and for controls that can get focus (for example, text boxes, option groups, combo boxes, and frames). It is not available for controls that can't get focus, such as lines, labels, and graphs. The `HelpContextID` Property sets the identifying number for a topic in the custom Help file specified in the project's Help File option. The setting for the `HelpContextID` Property must be a Long integer between 0 and 2,147,483,647.

Table 34.3 displays the `HelpContextID` settings for significant controls on your Contact Manager's main form.

Table 34.3. HelpContextID settings—the Contact Manager form.

Visual Basic Object	Property	Design Time Setting
Form	Name	frmContacts
	HelpContextID	0
Menu Item	Name	mnuImport
	HelpContextID	1
Menu Item	Name	mnuExport
	HelpContextID	2
Menu Item	Name	mnuSetup
	HelpContextID	3
TextBox	Name	txtCode
	HelpContextID	4
DBCombo	Name	dbcContacts
	HelpContextID	5
Frame Control	Name	fraCompany
	HelpContextID	6
Frame Control	Name	fraContact
	HelpContextID	7
Command Button	Name	cmdAdd
	HelpContextID	8
Command Button	Name	cmdSave
	HelpContextID	9
Command Button	Name	cmdCancel
	HelpContextID	10
Command Button	Name	cmdDelete
	HelpContextID	11
Command Button	Name	cmdQuery
	HelpContextID	12
Command Button	Name	cmdReport
	HelpContextID	13

Notice that you're giving a HelpContextID to the frames surrounding the company and contact information fields, rather than to each field individually. The idea is to have a single Help

Topic for each of the field groups. The containership hierarchy comes into play here: When a user presses F1 for help, Visual Basic checks to see if the current object has a HelpContextID; if it doesn't, VB looks for a HelpContextID in the object's container, and so on, back to form level. In this way, a user may be focused on any field within the company frame, for example, and the proper help topic will be displayed when he or she presses F1.

> **NOTE**
>
> If users press F1 while in a form, control, or group for which there is no context-sensitive Help, the default topic for the Help file specified in the project options dialog is displayed. If no help file has been assigned for the project, the default topic for the Help file specified in your applications .INI file is displayed.

You must now modify your help project's HPJ file. Here's how it should look at this point:

```
[OPTIONS]
errorlog = contacts.err
title = Contact Manager Help
compress = false
warning = 3

[FILES]
c:\vb40\hc\contacts.rtf

[WINDOWS]
Main = "Contact Manager Help", (0,0,750,1023),,,(192,192,192)
Second = "Secondary Window", (512,512,511,511),,,(192,192,192),1

[MAP]
FILE_IMPORT     1
FILE_EXPORT     2
PROG_SETUP      3
CODE_FIELD      4
CONTACTS_DD     5
COMPANY_FRAME       6
CONTACT_FRAME       7
ADD_BTN     8
SAVE_BTN        9
CANCEL_BTN      10
DELETE_BTN      11
QUERY_BTN       12
REPORT_BTN      13
```

You must also add the new topics shown in Figures 34.8 and 34.9 to your Contacts.RTF file; and each new topic must be appropriately footnoted to link it with the corresponding jump tag. Remember, in the RTF topic file, each topic must appear on a separate page. The jump tag is shown in parentheses. Figure 34.10 shows the results for comparison.

FIGURE 34.8.

Help Topics to add to Contacts.RTF.

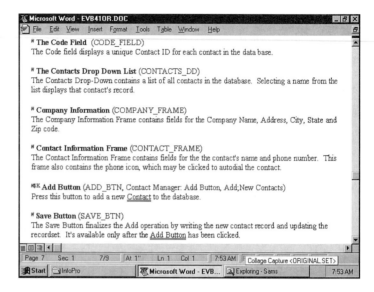

FIGURE 34.9.

Help Topics to add to Contacts.RTF (continued).

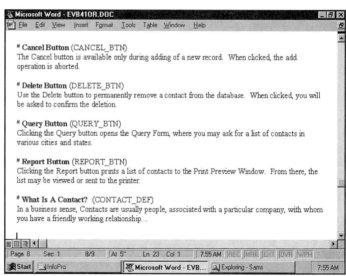

Notice the double-underlining in the Add and Save button topics. In the Add topic, the word "Contact" is double-underlined, as is "Add Button" in the Save topic. In both cases, topic jumps are indicated, but the jump tags associated with these hypertext phrases are formatted as hidden, remember, so you don't see them in the topics listed previously. Figure 34.11 presents how they'll look when formatting codes are revealed in Microsoft Word.

FIGURE 34.10.

Contact Manager Context-Sensitive Help Topics.

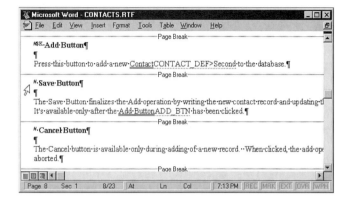

FIGURE 34.11.

More Hidden Jump Tags.

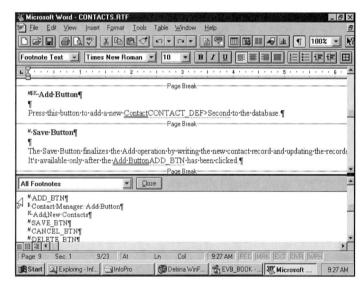

Jumps to a Secondary Window

When you create a jump to another topic, the WinHelp application assumes you want to display the topic in the main Help window. But you can code the jump to display the new topic in a secondary window. Use this syntax to code a jump that displays a topic in a secondary window:

```
JumpTag>windowname
```

Immediately following the jump tag of the new topic is a greater than (>) sign followed by the name of the secondary window.

Now look again at Figure 34.11. The jump to the ADD_BTN topic is nothing new, but notice the jump tag for the double-underlined phrase "Contact" in the Add topic. Here, you're jumping to a new topic, CONTACT_DEF, but you're displaying it in your secondary window, rather than the main help screen.

Now it's time to re-compile your Help file, then run the Contact Manager program. You should thoroughly test your new context-sensitive help feature. Notice that you may click on a field and press F1 to get related help information. Rather than clicking command buttons (thereby executing their code), it might be better to test their context-sensitivity by using the Tab key to cycle through them, pressing F1 as you go. Be sure to see your secondary window in action by clicking the "Contact" hypertext in the Add Button topic. Here, in Figure 34.12, is a sample session:

FIGURE 34.12.

The secondary Help window in action.

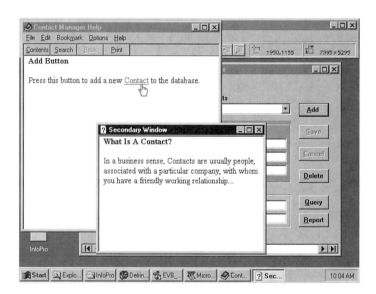

Help Graphics and Hypergraphics

You can increase clarity and add interest to a Help system by using graphics. There are some easy ways to add graphic images to your Help files. In this section, you'll receive a brief review of graphics types, and you'll be introduced to a special kind of graphics called hypergraphics, which may be used like hypertext to jump between help topics.

You can include four types of graphics in your Help system. Table 34.4 describes each of the four types.

Table 34.4. Help File graphics types.

Graphic Type	Description
Bitmap	A *bitmap* defines an image as a pattern of dots (pixels). A bitmap has the extensions .BMP or .DIB. Also called paint-type or raster graphics.
Metafile	A *metafile* defines an image as coded lines and shapes. A metafile has the extension .WMF. Only files that are compatible with Microsoft Windows version 3.0 or later can be included in the Help file. Also called draw-type or vector graphics.
Hypergraphic	A bitmap or metafile that contains at least one "hot spot." Hot spots are areas on the graphic that may be used to jump to Help topics or execute Help macros (covered later in this chapter), just like hypertext. An entire graphic may be used as a single hot spot. If a hypergraphic is to contain more than one hot spot, or if only part of the graphic is to be "hot," you must edit it using the Hotspot Editor (SHED.EXE). A hypergraphic usually has the extension .SHG.
MRB	A multiple-resoultion-bitmap (MRB) is compiled from several bitmaps with different screen resolutions by the Multiple-Resolution Bitmap Compiler (MRBC.EXE). A multiple-resolution bitmap has the extension .MRB.

NOTE

In this section you'll work with three bitmap files: EMDASH.BMP, PHONE.BMP, and SMOKES.BMP. The first, EMDASH.BMP, is located in the Visual Basic Help Compiler directory, \VB40\HC. It's recommended that you copy the other two to that location as well. PHONE.BMP and SMOKES.BMP are found in the \VB40\BITMAPS\ASSORTED directory.

There are two methods for including graphics in a Help file. You may place the bitmap or metafile directly in the topic file; or you may place a bitmap or metafile *reference* in the topic file. In this section you'll explore the advantages and disadvantages of each method.

Placing a Graphic Directly

The easiest way to place a graphic into a Help topic file is to import the graphic or metafile directly from the Windows Clipboard into Word for Windows. You then simply paste the graphic where you want it to appear in the Help topic file. You may format your text so it's positioned below or beside the graphic. When you save the Help topic file in rich-text format (RTF), and re-compile your Help file, the pasted bitmaps and metafiles are automatically included.

There are a few advantages to this method: it's simple, requiring only basic word processing skills; you're able to see the graphic whenever you work in the Help topic file; and you don't have to enter the graphic's location in the Help project file.

The disadvantages of this method are many in comparison. Here's a list:

- You can use only Word for Windows in creating your topic files.
- You can use only *inline graphics*, which are treated the same as a character, and therefore limit the ways you can display text and graphics. For example, it's not possible to wrap text *around* an inline graphic.
- Graphics pasted directly into a Word document increase the time needed to scroll or save the topic file.
- You can't change the graphic inside Word for Windows. Instead, you must modify it in your graphics application and then reimport it.
- You can't paste hypergraphics (graphics created with the Hotspot Editor) in topic files.
- Including the same graphic directly at multiple locations in the topic file adds multiple copies of the graphic to the compiled Help file, increasing its size.

Inserting a Graphic by Reference

To insert a graphic into a Help topic by reference, you include special "embraced" text that tells the WinHelp application the name of the bitmap file or metafile and how to position it with respect to related Help topic text. There are many advantages to including Help file graphics by reference:

- You can create your Help file with any text editor that produces RTF files.
- You have the widest range of options for displaying text and graphics. For example, you can treat the graphic as a character, or you can wrap text around the graphic's left or right edge.
- You can change the graphic without having to reimport it into the Help topic file. The references are pointers to the graphic files. The Help Compiler inserts the actual graphics only when you compile the Help file.
- Graphic references are the only way you can include hypergraphics (created with the Hotspot Editor) in your topic files. You cannot paste hypergraphics directly into your RTF file.
- Including the same graphic by reference at multiple locations in a topic file adds only one copy of the graphic in the compiled Help file, thereby keeping the size of the file to a minimum.

There are really only two slight disadvantages to the reference method of including graphics in your Help files: You can't see the graphic when you work in the topic file, and you have to enter the locations of the graphic files in the Help project file. Although entering graphic locations in the Help project file is a simple task, any mistakes will cause errors at compile time.

Because the advantages of the reference method far outweigh those of the direct paste method, and because importing and pasting is more a word processing issue than a programming one, the rest of this chapter will focus on including graphics by reference.

Method of Including Graphics by Reference

Placing a graphic by reference is a two-step process. First, you enter the reference text in the topic file where you want the graphic to appear. Then you enter the location of the graphic file in the Help project (.HPJ) file. One advantage to moving all your help graphics files to the same directory (as was suggested in a note at the beginning of this chapter) is that you may inform the compiler of their location by adding a single line to your Help project file. This line identifies the directory where bitmaps and other help-related graphics will be stored. Here's the listing of CONTACTS.HPJ, with the new line formatted in bold:

```
[OPTIONS]
errorlog = contacts.err
title = Contact Manager Help
compress = false
warning = 3
BMROOT = C:\VB40\HC

[FILES]
c:\vb40\hc\contacts.rtf

[WINDOWS]
Main = "Contact Manager Help", (0,0,750,1023),,,(192,192,192)
Second = "Secondary Window", (512,512,511,511),,,(192,192,192),1

[MAP]
FILE_IMPORT       1
FILE_EXPORT       2
PROG_SETUP        3
CODE_FIELD        4
CONTACTS_DD       5
COMPANY_FRAME     6
CONTACT_FRAME     7
ADD_BTN           8
SAVE_BTN          9
CANCEL_BTN       10
DELETE_BTN       11
QUERY_BTN        12
REPORT_BTN       13
```

Now, here's the syntax for creating references to graphics not directly included in a topic file:

```
{Command FileName}
```

Notice the "squiggly" braces; they are required. *FileName* is the name of the graphic file, and you *do not* include a path. The following table (see Table 34.5) lists the three *commands* you can use in creating a graphic reference.

Table 34.5. Graphic reference commands.

Command	Description
bmc	Aligns the graphic as a character. This command is used when you'd like the graphic to appear as a single character in a line of text, as a bullet or an em-dash, for example.
bml	Aligns the graphic at the left margin, and allows text to wrap or flow along the graphic's right edge.
bmr	Aligns the graphic at the right margin; text wraps along the graphic's left edge.

With all three commands, the compiled Help file contains a single copy of the graphic data separate from any related text. The *FileName* given in the graphic reference includes only the file name, not the file's full path. The Help project (.HPJ) file contains all the path information for graphics included by reference.

Aligning Graphics as Characters

The Help Compiler treats a graphic inserted with a bmc reference as a character. After compiling the Help file, graphics aligned as characters appear on the type baseline at the location of the reference command. The graphic actually becomes part of the paragraph, so any formatting applied to the paragraph also applies to the graphic. Text appearing above and below doesn't wrap around the graphic, but the size of the graphic may increase the line space between the line containing the graphic and the preceding line in the text.

> **CAUTION**
>
> Don't specify negative line spacing for a paragraph that has a bmc graphic reference. If you do, the graphic might appear on top of the paragraph when the WinHelp displays the topic.

A bullet or other special symbol is a good use of a graphic as a character. Here is how a bmc reference might appear in a Help topic file, using a small bitmap, BULLET.BMP, as the bullet in a bulleted list:

```
{bmc bullet.bmp} The Add Button is used to add a new contact.
{bmc bullet.bmp} The Cancel Button aborts the Add operation.
```

Aligning Graphics at the Left Margin

The Help Compiler places a bml graphic along the left margin. Text wraps automatically along the right edge of the image. Text is aligned with the graphic's upper-right corner, so any white space saved at the top of the image affects the way text appears in relation to the graphic. Normally, a bml reference appears at the beginning of a paragraph, which ensures proper wrapping of text around the graphic's right edge. The following example shows a typical bml reference:

```
{bml bozo.bmp}This paragraph text follows the bitmap reference...
```

Unless you want the first line of text to appear indented, do not put any space characters between the bml reference and the paragraph text.

You can also put a bml reference at the end of a paragraph. When you code a bml reference this way, WinHelp wraps the text up to the end of the paragraph, and then displays the graphic. After you compile the Help file, the image appears under the text and to the left. Here's an example usage:

```
This paragraph text precedes the bitmap reference.{bml bozo.bmp}
```

Aligning Graphics at the Right Margin

The Help Compiler places a bmr graphic along the right margin. Text automatically wraps along the image's left edge. Under normal circumstances, you would place bmr references at the beginning of a paragraph. This ensures proper wrapping of text around the image's left edge. Here's an example of a valid bmr graphic reference:

```
{bmr smokes.shg}Click the part of the cigarette you want to know more about.
```

Here, in Figure 34.13, is how such a graphic reference might look in your Help system:

You can also place a bmr reference at the end of a paragraph. In this case, the text is wrapped up to the end of the paragraph, and then the graphic is displayed beneath the text and to the right. Here's an example of such a reference:

```
This paragraph text precedes the right-aligned bitmap.{bmr name.bmp}
```

FIGURE 34.13.

A right-aligned graphic and text.

Hot-Spot Graphics

You can do much more with graphics in your Help file than simply display them. The WinHelp application allows you to use graphics as hot spots. This means you can use graphics, such as icons or buttons, as jumps to particular topics or as hot spots for pop-up windows or to execute Help macros.

It's time to make some enhancements to your Contact Manager's Help system. You'll edit the first page of your CONTACTS.RTF file to include a list of command buttons, each preceded by an em-dash bitmap graphic. The em-dash and the accompanying text will become a hot spot for jumping to the appropriate Help topic.

Figure 34.14 is a screen-shot of your modified Help topic file's first page, with the arrow pointing to the new hot spots.

Notice the double-underlining, which indicates that you're creating hot spots for jumping to a new topic page, rather than opening a pop-up window. Here are the steps to follow in coding a graphic reference as a jump-topic (or pop-up window) hot spot:

1. Enter the graphic reference (**bmc**, **bml**, or **bmr**) in the topic file where you want the jump. Be sure you've already created the topic text (and set its jump tag).

2. Select the entire graphic reference, including the file name and opening and closing braces.

3. Format the graphic reference as double-underlined text to create a jump. (Or format the graphic reference as single-underlined text to create a hot spot for a pop-up window.)

4. Type the jump tag of the destination topic immediately following the graphic reference.

5. Format the jump tag as hidden text.

FIGURE 34.14.

Using graphics as hot spots.

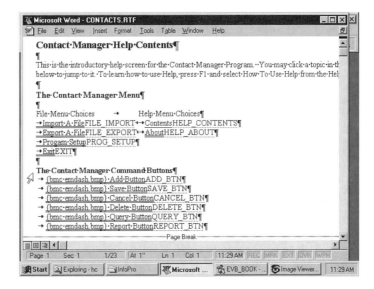

Now you'll follow these steps in adding a hot spot graphic to your Contact Information topic, which you created earlier in this chapter. Locate that topic in CONTACTS.RTF. Here, in Figure 34.15, is how it will look once you've added the phone.bmp reference as a hot spot.

FIGURE 34.15.

The phone bitmap hot spot.

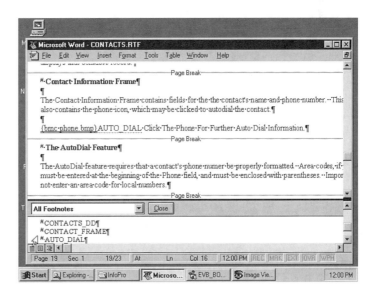

You can see how the phone bitmap reference is double-underlined, and you can see the hidden jump tag "AUTO_DIAL." You'll need to create the AutoDial topic page, which is also visible in Figure 34.15, and be sure to register its jump tag as a # symbol footnote. (See the arrow in the footnote pane of Figure 34.15 for reference.)

Once you have your new hot spots properly coded, re-compile your Help file and try it out. You should be able to jump to each button's Help topic by clicking either the em-dash bitmap or the associated hypertext. You'll also be able to click the phone graphic in the Contact Information topic, and be transported to the AutoDial Help page.

Hotspots and Hypergraphics

The preceding section showed you how to create a single hot spot in a graphic. Multiple hot spots can make the graphics in your Help file even more useful. To create more than one hot spot within a single graphic, you must create a *hypergraphic*.

A hypergraphic is a graphic (bitmap or metafile) with embedded hot spots that users can click to:

■ Jump to another Help topic.

■ Display a pop-up window.

■ Activate a Help macro.

■ Activate routines in external dynamic-link libraries (DLLs).

You create hypergraphics with the Hotspot Editor (SHED.EXE). This tool is conveniently located in the \VB40\HC directory, where the rest of your help-related files are currently stored. You can use the Hotspot Editor to open a bitmap (.BMP), a device-independent bitmap (.DIB), or a Windows metafile (.WMF), and add hot spots to the existing graphic image. It then saves the graphic as a hypergraphic (.SHG) file.

> **CAUTION**
>
> Because the Hotspot Editor is not a drawing or painting program, you must create the actual graphic outside the Hotspot Editor. Once you save a graphic as a hypergraphic, you can't open it again with a drawing or painting program. Therefore, it's not a bad idea to make copies of graphics files you intend to convert to hypergraphics.

Follow these general steps to create a hypergraphic:

1. Open a bitmap or metafile in the Hotspot Editor.
2. Draw hot-spot locations in the graphic.
3. Define attributes for each hot spot in the graphic.
4. Save the graphic as a hypergraphic.

Once you define the hot spots, the graphic is ready to be included by reference in any RTF topic file, from where it may be compiled into your Help file.

You'll work with the Hotspot Editor in this section, but first you will add three new topic pages to your CONTACTS.RTF. One topic will have a jump tag of HOT_SPOTS and be titled "Hot Spots and Hypergraphics"; it will have a title $ footnote, as well as a keyword K footnote containing the search words "Hotspots;Hypergraphics." The other two topic pages will have only jump tag footnotes, SMOKE_ONLY and FILTER_ONLY, which will allow them to be displayed, when called upon, in a pop-up window. Here, in Figure 34.16, is what they'll look like in your RTF topic file.

FIGURE 34.16.

The hotspot and hypergraphics topics.

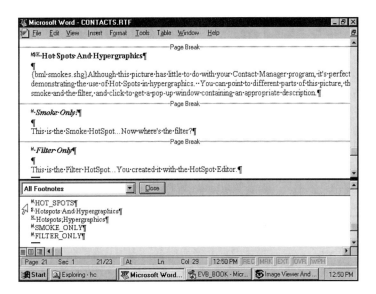

There are a couple of new things to notice here. First, your left-aligned bitmap reference is to SMOKES.SHG, which indicates that you're using a hypergraphic file (you haven't created it yet, but you will soon). The second thing to note is that there is no double-or single-underlining, and no hidden jump tags. This is because all of the jumping will be handled by setting hot spot attributes in the Hotspot Editor, which is what you'll do next.

Using the Hotspot Editor

Before you can add hot spots to a graphic, you must open it in the Hotspot Editor.

After opening a graphic in the Hotspot Editor, you can create hot spots that link to topics, pop-up windows, or macros. When you compile with the Help Compiler, the hot spots you define become part the completed Help file.

A hot spot can be any rectangular area within the graphic. You draw hot spots on the graphic as you would a rectangle in any Windows drawing or painting program.

Here are the general steps to follow in creating a hot spot:

1. Click the location on the graphic where you want to anchor one corner of the hot spot.
2. Drag the mouse until the rectangle encloses the area you want to define as the hot spot. The box stretches from the anchor point to the position of the mouse and expands and contracts as you move the mouse.
3. When the hot-spot rectangle is the desired size, release the mouse button.

After you release the mouse button, the hot-spot rectangle displays eight sizing handles, indicating the currently selected hot spot. You can use the sizing handles to resize the rectangle.

After creating a hot spot, you must define the attributes that determine what happens when a user clicks the hot spot. To define these attributes, you use the Attributes dialog box, which is discussed next.

Defining Hotspot Attributes

Follow these general steps in defining hot spot attributes:

1. Select the hot spot, or create a new one.
2. Click the hot spot with the right mouse button to display the Attributes dialog box.
3. For a jump or pop-up window, enter the jump tag for the destination jump or pop-up window topic in the Context String box. For a Help macro, enter the macro in the Context String box (Help macros are covered later in this chapter).
4. Choose the type of hot spot you want to create from the Type list. Valid types are Jump, Pop-up, and Macro.
5. Choose Visible or Invisible for the display attribute. If you want to make the hot-spot region visible to users (it will appear with a bounding rectangle), choose Visible from the Attribute list.
6. If you want to change the default name assigned to the hot spot, edit the hot-spot identifier.
7. If you want to change the size or location of the hot spot, edit the bounding box coordinates.
8. Choose OK.

The attributes defined for the hot spot now appear in the Hotspot Editor status bar.

The Attributes dialog box allows you to maintain important binding information about each hot spot you create. Here in Table 34.6 is a summary of the information contained in the Attributes dialog box.

Table 34.6. Hotspot attributes.

Field	*Description*
Context string	Specifies binding information for the hot spot. Can be either a jump tag (context string) or a macro.
Type	Indicates the type of action taken when the user selects the hot spot. You can jump to another topic, display a topic in a pop-up window, or run a Help macro.
Attribute	Specifies whether the hot spot is visible or invisible in the Help window. Hot spots are always visible in the Hotspot Editor.
Hotspot ID	Specifies a unique identifier for the hot spot. The hot-spot name is used internally by the Hotspot Editor and helps you identify hot spots in the Select dialog box. The Hotspot Editor automatically assigns an incremental number to the hot-spot name; however, you can type in a unique name.
Bounding Box	Displays the coordinates for the hot-spot rectangle: left, right, top, and bottom. The coordinates are measured in pixels and are restricted to the size of the graphic image.

Now it's time to create your first hypergraphic. Open the Hotspot Editor (SHED.EXE in \VB40\HC). Select File Open from the menu, then locate SMOKES.BMP, which should be in the same directory. Follow the preceding steps to define two hot spots, as you see them in Figure 34.17:

FIGURE 34.17.

Defining hotspots with the Hotspot Editor.

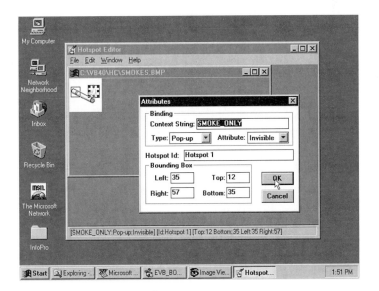

Figure 34.17 shows the bounding rectangles for Hotspot 1 and Hotspot 2. It also shows the Attribute dialog box for Hotspot 1, which is the rectangle surrounding the smoke from the cigarette. The attributes for Hotspot 2, the cigarette filter, will be very similar. Obviously, the Bounding Box coordinates will be different, and the jump tag (or context string) will be FILTER_ONLY, rather than SMOKE_ONLY.

Once the hot spots are drawn, and their proper attributes defined, save it as SMOKES.SHG, to indicate that it's a hypergraphic containing multiple hot spots. (You'll also want to be sure to name it SMOKES.SHG because that's the filename you use as your topic file reference.)

That's it for hypergraphics. Close the Hotspot Editor, if you like, to clear the decks a little. You'll now need to re-compile your Help file. When that's done, fire up your Contact Manager program and thoroughly test your new, improved, custom Help system. Because you added keywords for the Hotspot and Hypergraphics topic, you'll be able to locate it easily by using WinHelp's search feature. You'll be able to click on your hypergraphic's smoke, or filter, and get a nice pop-up window, like that seen in Figure 34.18.

FIGURE 34.18.

Hypergraphic hot spots in action.

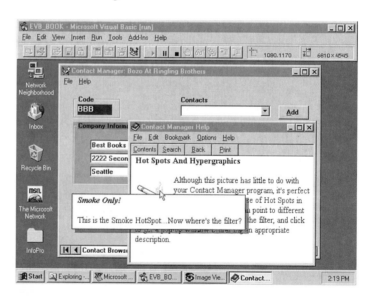

Using Help Macros

More functionality can be added to your Contact Manager Help system by calling on the Windows Help macros, which you can use to customize the way the WinHelp application works with your Help files. There are more than 50 available macros that can be used.

Help macros are routines built into the WinHelp application that allow you to further customize your own Help systems. Using macros, you can add and remove custom buttons and menus, change the function of buttons and menu items, execute applications from within Help, and even execute functions from external dynamic-link libraries (DLLs).

The following series of tables constitute a categorized list of WinHelp macros and their descriptions. If a particular macro may be called using an abbreviated form, the abbreviation is given in parentheses at the end of the description.

Use the following macros (see Table 34.7) to access standard Help buttons, to create new buttons, or to modify button functionality and appearance.

Table 34.7. Button Manipulation macros.

Macro	*Description*
Back	Displays the previous topic in the Back list.
ChangeButtonBinding	Changes the current function of a Help button. (CBB)
Contents	Displays the Contents topic of the current Help file.
CreateButton	Creates a new button and adds it to the tool bar. (CB)
DestroyButton	Removes a button from the tool bar.
DisableButton	Disables a button on the tool bar. (DB)
EnableButton	Enables a disabled button. (EB)
History	Displays the history list.
Next	Moves to the next topic in a browse sequence.
Prev	Displays the previous topic in a browse sequence.
Search	Opens the Search dialog box.
SetContents	Designates a specific topic as the Contents topic.

The following macros may be used to access standard Help menu items, to create new menus, or to modify the performance of existing menus and menu items.

Table 34.8. Menu Manipulation macros.

Macro	*Description*
About	Shows the About dialog box.
Annotate	Displays the Annotate dialog box.
AppendItem	Appends a menu item to the end of a custom menu.
BookmarkDefine	Displays the Bookmark Define dialog box.
BookmarkMore	Displays the Bookmark dialog box.
ChangeItemBinding	Changes the assigned function of a menu item. (CIB)
CheckItem	Displays a check mark next to a menu item. (CI)

continues

Table 34.8. continued

Macro	Description
CopyDialog	Opens the Copy dialog box.
CopyTopic	Copies the current topic to the Clipboard.
DeleteItem	Removes a menu item from a menu.
DisableItem	Disables a menu item. (DI)
EnableItem	Enables a disabled menu item. (EI)
Exit	Exits the WinHelp application.
FileOpen	Displays the Open dialog box.
HelpOn	Displays the How To Use Help file.
InsertItem	Inserts a menu item at a given position on a menu.
InsertMenu	Adds a new menu to the Help menu bar.
Print	Sends the current topic to the printer.
PrinterSetup	Displays the Print Setup dialog box.
SetHelpOnFile	Specifies a custom How To Use Help file.
UncheckItem	Removes a check mark from a menu item. (UI)

It's often convenient to use macros in creating links between Help topics. You might, for example, decide to create a button which, when clicked, jumps to a Glossary or terms, or example code. You may use the following macros to create hypertext links to specific Help topics.

Table 34.9. Hypertext Link macros.

Macro	Description
JumpContents	Jumps to the Contents topic of a specific Help file.
JumpContext	Jumps to the topic with a specific context number. (JC)
JumpHelpOn	Jumps to the Contents of the How To Use Help file.
JumpId	Jumps to the topic with a specific jump tag. (JI)
JumpKeyword	Jumps to the first topic containing a specified keyword.
PopupContext (PC)	Displays the topic with a specific number in a pop-up window.
PopupId (PI)	Displays the topic with a specific jump tag in a pop-up window.

The remaining auxiliary macros are used to control or modify the behavior and appearance of the Help windows; to add or remove keyboard accelerators; to run external applications; and to manage and manipulate bookmarks.

Table 34.10. WinHelp Auxiliary macros.

Macro	Description
CloseWindow	Closes the main or secondary Help window.
FocusWindow	Changes the focus to a specific Help window.
HelpOnTop	Places all Help windows on top of other windows.
PositionWindow	Sets the size and position of a Help window.
AddAccelerator	Assigns an accelerator key to a Help macro. (AA)
RemoveAccelerator	Removes an accelerator key from a Help macro. (RA)
ExecProgram	Starts an application. (EP)
RegisterRoutine	Registers a function within a DLL as a Help macro. (RR)
DeleteMark	Removes a marker added by SaveMark.
GotoMark	Jumps to a marker set by SaveMark.
IfThen	Executes a Help macro if a given marker exists.
IfThenElse	Executes one of two macros if a given marker exists.
IsMark	Tests whether a marker set by SaveMark exists.
Not	Reverses the result returned by IsMark.
SaveMark	Saves a marker for the current topic and Help file.

A Closer Look at the Macros

In this section you'll get a closer look at several of the macros listed in the tables above, many of which you'll be using in the "How To Run Help Macros" section of this chapter. The look will include complete definitions, parameters, and usage examples.

CreateButton()

The CreateButton macro (or CB) is used to define a new button and display it in your Help system's button or tool bar. Here's how it's used:

```
CreateButton(ButtonId, Caption, Macro)
```

The `ButtonId` argument is a name that WinHelp uses to identify the button. This name must appear in quotation marks, and may be referred to in the DisableButton or DestroyButton macro, if you want to remove or disable the button, or in the `ChangeButtonBinding` macro if you want to change the macro that the button runs in certain topics.

The second argument, `Caption`, is the text that appears on the button. This name must appear in quotation marks. To designate a letter for Alt Key access, place an ampersand (&) before it.

The `Macro` argument is the Help macro or macro string that is run when the user chooses the button. The macro must appear in quotation marks. Multiple macros in a macro string must be separated by semicolons (;).

Here's an example of the CreateButton macro. This call creates a new button labeled Clowns that jumps to a topic with the jump tag LIST_CLOWNS in the CIRCUS.HLP file when the button is chosen:

```
CreateButton("CLOWNS_BTN", "&Clowns", "JumpId(`circus.hlp', `LIST_CLOWNS')")
```

Notice the use of single quotes within double-quoted strings here. The third argument is a double-quoted string representing another macro. In fact, you're calling one macro from within another. This is perfectly legal as long as you don't mismatch quotes and double-quotes.

> **CAUTION**
>
> When using single quotes in your macros, remember that there's a difference between a left single quote ('), which appears below the tilde (~) on your keyboard, and a right single quote, which is the apostrophe ('). These quotes must be properly matched and balanced or the Help Compiler will squawk.

DisableButton()

The DisableButton macro (or DB) is used to dim or "gray out" a particular button when it is unavailable to the user. The syntax is simple, and here it is:

```
DisableButton(ButtonId)
```

The *ButtonId* is the identifier assigned to the button in the CreateButton macro. The button identifier must appear in quotation marks. A button disabled by the DisableButton macro cannot be used in the topic until an EnableButton macro is run.

EnableButton()

This macro, abbreviated EB, re-enables a button disabled with the DisableButton macro.

Here's its simple syntax:

```
EnableButton("ButtonId")
```

Here, as with all button-manipulation macros, *ButtonId* is the identifier assigned to the button in the CreateButton macro. Again, *ButtonId* must appear in quotation marks.

DestroyButton()

This macro removes a button added with the CreateButton macro, causing it to disappear from your Help system's button bar. Here's how you call it:

```
DestroyButton(ButtonId)
```

Again, *ButtonId* is the identifier assigned to the button in the CreateButton macro. The button identifier must appear in quotation marks. The button identifier cannot duplicate an identifier used for one of the standard Help buttons.

InsertMenu()

The InsertMenu macro adds a new menu to the Windows Help menu bar. Here's its syntax:

```
InsertMenu("MenuId", "Caption", MenuPosition)
```

MenuId is the name that WinHelp uses to identify the menu; it must be enclosed in quotation marks. You'll use this identifier in the AppendItem macro (see next) to add menu items (commands) to the menu.

The Caption argument is the name for the menu that WinHelp displays on the menu bar. This name is case sensitive and must be enclosed in quotation marks. Within the quotation marks, place an ampersand (&) before the character you want to use for the menu's accelerator key.

MenuPosition is a number specifying the position on the menu bar that the new menu name will have. This number must be an integer. Positions are numbered from left to right, with position 0 being the leftmost menu. WinHelp's default menu contains File, Edit, Bookmark, Options, and Help, numbered 0 through 4, respectively.

The following example uses the InsertMenu macro to add a menu named Utilities to WinHelp's default menu:

```
InsertMenu("Menu_Utils", "&Utilities", 3)
```

Now Utilities will appear as the fourth menu on the Windows Help menu bar, between the Bookmark and Options menus. In this case, the user may press Alt+U to access the menu.

CAUTION

Be sure that the accelerator key you assign to a menu is unique. If you assign a key that conflicts with another menu accelerator key, WinHelp displays an Unable to add menu error message and ignores the macro.

AppendItem()

This macro is used to add menu items to the end of a menu created with the InsertMenu macro. Here's how it looks:

```
AppendItem("MenuId", "ItemId", "Caption", "Macro")
```

MenuId is the name used in the InsertMenu macro to create the menu. This name must be enclosed in quotation marks. The new item is added to the end of this menu.

The *ItemId* is the name that WinHelp uses to identify the menu item. This name is case sensitive and must be enclosed in quotation marks.

Caption is the name that is displayed on the menu for the item. This name is case sensitive and must be enclosed in quotation marks. As usual, you may use an ampersand (&) before the letter you want to use for the item's accelerator key.

Macro is Help macro or macro string that executes when the user chooses the menu item. The macro must be enclosed in quotation marks. Separate multiple macros in a string with semicolons (;).

Here's an example of how the AppendItem macro might be used to add an item to the Utilities menu created in the previous example:

```
AppendItem("Menu_Utils", "New_Item", "E&xample", "JI(`sample.hlp',`eg_012_topic')")
```

Choosing the menu item causes a jump to a topic with the eg_012_topic jump tag in the SAMPLE.HLP file. Note that the letter *x* serves as the accelerator key for this menu item.

JumpId()

This macro jumps to the topic with the specified jump tag in the specified Help file. Here's how it's used:

```
JumpId("FileName", "JumpTag")
```

FileName is the name of the Help file (.HLP) containing the jump tag. The file name must appear in quotation marks. If WinHelp does not find this file, it displays an error message and does not perform the jump.

JumpTag is the jump tag of the topic in the destination file. The jump tag must appear in quotation marks. If the tag does not exist, WinHelp jumps to the contents topic for that file instead.

The following example is the JumpId macro to jump to a topic with GLOSSARY as its jump tag in the Help file named CONTACTS.HLP:

```
JumpId("CONTACTS.HLP", "GLOSSARY")
```

> **TIP**
>
> You can use the JumpId macro to display topics in secondary windows by adding the window name to the *FileName* parameter, as in this example:
>
> ```
> JumpId("Circus.hlp>BigTop", "Lion_List")
> ```
>
> The topic identified by the Lion_List jump tag would appear in the BigTop secondary window.

ExecProgram()

This macro, abbreviated EP, launches a Windows-based application from within your custom Help system. Here's the syntax:

```
ExecProgram("CommandLine", DisplayState)
```

Here, *CommandLine* is the command line for the application to be executed. The command line must appear in quotation marks. WinHelp searches for this application in the current directory, followed by the Windows directory, the user's path, and the directory of the currently displayed Help file.

The DisplayState argument is a value indicating how the application is displayed when executed. A value of 0 indicates normal, 1 indicates minimized, and 2 indicates maximized.

Here's an example of the ExecProgram macro in action; it runs the Windows NotePad program in its normal window size:

```
ExecProgram("notepad.exe", 0)
```

CloseWindow()

This macro closes the specified window, which is either the main WinHelp window or a secondary window. Its syntax is simple:

```
CloseWindow(WinName)
```

Here, *WinName* is the name of the window to close. The name main is reserved for the primary Help window. For secondary windows, the window name is defined in the [WINDOWS] section of the .HPJ file. This name must appear in quotation marks.

The following macro closes the secondary window named Glossary:

```
CloseWindow("Glossary")
```

HelpOn()

This simple macro displays the Using Help file for the WinHelp application (same as the Using Help command on the Help menu). It requires no arguments and is called directly, like this:

```
HelpOn()
```

How to Run Help Macros

Help macros can be run when WinHelp first opens a Help file; when the user selects a particular topic in the Help file; and when the user chooses a button, menu item, or hot spot containing a macro. In this section you'll explore all three ways to run macros while adding extra functionality to your Contact Manager's Help system.

If a macro appears in the [CONFIG] section of your Help project file (.HPJ), WinHelp runs that macro when it first opens the Help file. If more than one macro is listed in the [CONFIG] section, they are executed in their listed order.

Open CONTACTS.HPJ and add the following lines at the bottom of the file, beneath the [MAP] section:

```
[CONFIG]
InsertMenu("Menu_Tools", "&Tools", 4)
AppendItem("Menu_Tools","Calc_Item","&Calculator", "EP(`calc.exe',0)")
AppendItem("Menu_Tools","Note_Item","&NotePad","EP(`notepad.exe',0)")

CB("Glos_Btn","&Glossary","JumpId(`Contacts.hlp>Second',`GLOSSARY')")
CB("Help_Btn","&Help","HelpOn()")
CB("Exit_Btn","E&xit","Exit()")
```

You're accomplishing a lot here, in very few lines. The first macro creates a new menu called Tools in the fifth position of the default Help menu, that is, after Options but before Help. The next two macros add items to the new Tools menu, and specify what should happen when the items are selected. In this case, you'll run the Windows calculator or notebook programs by calling the ExecProgram macros, shortened to EP here. (Again, pay close attention when entering the single quotes.)

The next three macros add buttons to WinHelp's default button bar. The first CB macro (remember, CB is short for CreateButton) creates a Glossary button which, when chosen, will cause a jump to the topic tagged GLOSSARY (which you'll define in the next section) in your Help file named CONTACTS.HLP. But that's not all that happens here. Notice that the first argument contains a > symbol, which redirects the topic output to your secondary help window. This way the user will have the glossary displayed in its own independent window.

The last two macros are much simpler. You're creating a button that will launch WinHelp's own Help On Help search window; and you're giving the user a button that will provide an alternate way of exiting your Help system. Macros that control Help buttons, menus, or menu items remain in effect until the user quits WinHelp or opens a new Help file.

If a Help macro is called in a topic footnote, WinHelp runs that macro automatically whenever the user jumps to the topic. A user can jump to a topic by clicking a hypertext label or graphic hot spot; by clicking the Back button or a browse button; and by selecting the topic from the history list or keyword search list.

To call a macro from a topic footnote, you use the special footnote symbol (!), an exclamation mark. Now open CONTACTS.RTF, and add a new page at the bottom. This is where you'll define your Glossary topic. Refer to Figure 34.19 for the topic text (which is obviously not a complete glossary at this point), and for the associated footnotes.

FIGURE 34.19.

The glossary topic and footnotes.

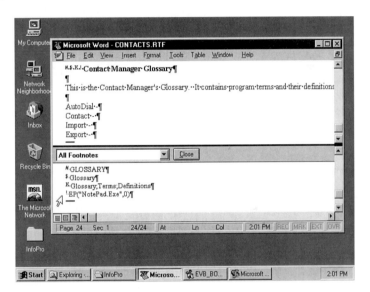

Almost everything here will be familiar to you (you've worked with such displays many times in this chapter). But there is something new to notice: the topic's last footnote, indicated by the arrow, is set with the ! symbol and identifies the macro to run when this GLOSSARY topic is first displayed. In this case, you've anticipated that the user might appreciate having a place to jot down notes, so you'll open the Windows Notepad automatically.

Help macros can also be run from hot spots within a topic. WinHelp runs a hot-spot macro whenever the user chooses the hot spot containing that macro. A hot spot containing a macro is formatted like any other hot spot. The text or bitmap reference used for the macro is double-underlined, and the macro (preceded by an exclamation point) is formatted as hidden text.

In CONTACTS.RTF, move to the first page, the Help Contents. What you'll do here is add a new bit of hypertext that, instead of jumping to a topic, will execute the About() macro, which simply displays your Help system's own About dialog box. Here, in Figure 34.20, is how the Contents page will look.

FIGURE 34.20.

Running the About() macro from hypertext.

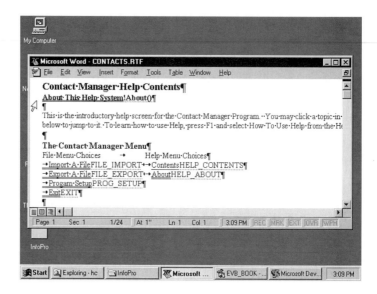

Notice the arrow pointing to the new hot spot, in this case a hypertext label. The text is double-underlined, and the About() macro is called immediately after it. Don't forget to precede the macro with an exclamation point, and format the call as hidden text.

That's it for running Help macros from your custom Help system. You should now re-compile and start up the Contact Manager program for testing. Be sure to admire and test all your new buttons and menu items, and notice that the NotePad starts up whenever you switch to the Glossary topic. Here's Figure 34.21, showing your enhanced Help system in action.

FIGURE 34.21.

The Macro-Enhanced Help System.

Summary

In this chapter, you created a custom help system for a Contact Manager application. You saw that it isn't necessary to write a help program of your own, that you may instead compile a Windows-compatible HLP file containing help text (including hypertext "jumps") specific to your application. The information in this file is then presented to the user through Windows' own WinHelp application.

You also acquired an understanding of context-sensitive help, and saw how it may be added to your Visual Basic applications. You learned how to redirect Help text to a secondary window, one that operates independently of the main help screen, and which may be used to display glossaries, lists, sample code, or any other information the user may wish to view concurrently with the main help text.

This chapter also examined different ways of adding graphic images to your Help files. You saw that you may set up references to your images, so that they may be used as hot spots for jumping between related Help topics. In addition, you were introduced to a special kind of graphics called hypergraphics, which may contain multiple hot spots, each of which may be used to jump between topics, or pop up windows, or execute Help macros.

Finally, you received a brief introduction to the more than 50 Help macros available in the WinHelp application. You were given a detailed look at several of the more commonly used macros, and saw how they may be invoked to customize the way WinHelp works in conjunction with your own Help files.

Creating a Stand-Alone Database Application

35

by Ross Rothmeier

Most applications fill a specific need. A common need is an application that enables its users to access their information the way they want. These applications usually use stand-alone databases. When expressing this need to a developer, the user might say something like, "I just want a database that keeps track of my customers."

Taking this request and converting it into an application using Visual Basic is a process that involves the following four steps:

- Getting the requirements
- Designing the database
- Developing a functional prototype
- Coding and testing

This chapter explains in detail how to perform each of these steps.

Getting the Requirements

Whether you are developing this application for yourself or someone else, your first job as a developer is to find out what this person's needs are and map them into some kind of specification. Without a specification, it is hard to tell when a project is finished and even harder to explain to someone else that it is.

Try to find out what kind of data the potential user (the client for the sake of this project) has in mind. Names and addresses are common and pretty easy to add to a project, but there are often special things that are trivial to put in at the beginning of a project and a nightmare to add in at the end, such as a shipping charge that may change how invoicing is done. Talk with the client using a pencil and paper. Draw sample screens and reports. As you discuss what the client needs to do, keep a running list of fields and things the application should do. The following list gives some examples of how the information you get from a client turns into design considerations:

- **"I want the database to store the customer's name, address, and phone number."** This request is the beginning of a customer data table. The client will need to enter these customers and change information about them, so you will need to design a data entry screen as well.

- **"I want to enter orders from my customers."** To meet this request, you will design a data entry screen, an order table, and probably a report.

- **"I want to keep track of what customers have ordered."** This request means another data table and at least one screen for viewing it. Chances are good that your client will want to edit this information as well, so you may need to add another data entry screen.

- **"I want to know what customers have paid and what they owe."** To meet this request, you need to add another data table and another data entry screen. After your client discusses this issue some more, he will probably also want to be able to print a statement of the customer's account, which means you have to add a report to this application, too.

■ **"The application should be user-friendly."** I have never known anyone to ask for a user-hostile application (and be willing to use it), but this request still provides some useful information. When someone starts using buzzwords like *user-friendly* and *GUI*, that person is expressing some knowledge of the industry. Your best bet is to develop your interface using standard conventions.

■ **"I am running Windows 3.1 on a 33-MHz 486SX computer with 14-inch VGA monitor and a 200 megabyte hard drive."** Even though bigger and faster computers are getting cheaper, there are many computers like this example still in use (there are many computers that are less powerful, too). It is extremely important to consider your target system before designing an application, especially a database. This client's computer is relatively slow, and the hard drive is probably nearly full. Your application will have to be tuned to perform acceptably in your client's environment.

With the requirements and design considerations in mind, you will start to get an idea of the processes your client wants the computer to do for him. These processes, when mapped out, would look something like Figure 35.1.

FIGURE 35.1.

The high-level process flow.

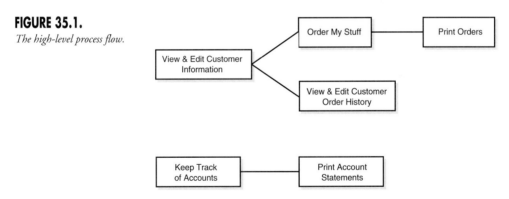

Designing the Database

The database is the heart of this application, so you should spend some time thinking about how the data should be arranged. Start by writing down the kinds of information you believe the application will need for the various processes. In this example application, you need information about a customer's demographics, orders, and account status. As you break down these general areas, you find that each contains a lot of specific data. List the specific pieces of data in each general category. You may find that a general category has several subcategories. By breaking the data into general categories, you are designing tables for a relational database.

Organizing Data into Tables

Organizing data into groups is the beginning of the table. Each element in a table will be a field. In general, a good relational design will not have a field appear in more than one table. Each table should also have a key.

The customer information table is probably the center of this application. It should contain demographic information and anything you will need whenever you refer to a customer, as shown in Table 35.1.

Table 35.1. The CustMain table.

Field	Data type	Length	Comments
CustomerNum	Counter	16	Primary key, ascending
First name	Text	16	
Last name	Text	20	
Company name	Text	50	
Street	Text	30	
P.O. Box	Text	5	
Suite/apartment	Text	30	
City	Text	16	
State	Text	2	
Zip code	Text	10	
Primary phone	Text	14	
Secondary phone	Text	14	
Contact person name	Text	10	
Current balance	Currency	16	This value will be referred to frequently in the application

NOTE

Performance and a perfect database design are often trade-offs. Because you are targeting a relatively slow computer, the current balance will be a stored value in the main customer table. A more pure design approach would be to calculate the current balance as needed and store it in a variable, but this approach could cause a performance bottleneck when calculating balances for a screen full of customers.

In this case, the trade-off was made for performance on another screen where the current balance and the order details for all customers are displayed at the same time. Loading the screen and calculating the current balance for each customer took longer as the number of customers and orders increased, but using a precalculated current balance did not result in performance degradation.

The next major group of information has to do with orders. The client needs to know who bought what, when the customer bought it, how much the client charged, and how much the customer paid. Table 35.2 demonstrates how you might organize this information into a table.

Table 35.2. The Orders table.

Field	Data type	Length	Comments
CustomerNum	Number	Long	Key field
Date	Date		Date of delivery
Description	Text	35	
Quantity	Number	Double	
Charge	Number	Double	Money the customer owes
Credit	Number	Double	Money the customer paid
OrderNum	Counter		Primary key

Creating Tables for Reporting

Reports are not always a developer's favorite part of an application. Keeping track of pages, lines, alignment, and fonts requires a lot of work. You can write your own reports using Visual Basic. If, however, you want to save a ton of work and put out some pretty snazzy reports, use the Report Designer (also known as Crystal Reports for Visual Basic, Crystal Reports, or just plain Crystal).

NOTE

All examples and discussion of Crystal Reports are based on the version 3 add-in shipped with Visual Basic 95.

Crystal makes report development easy, but using it can get tricky if you don't set up the tables for easy reporting. Add Tables 35.3, 35.4, 35.5, and 35.6 to your application. The reason for these tables will become apparent when you create the reports.

Table 35.3. CustOrdMst: The master order report table.

Field	Data type	Length	Comments
Customer number	Numeric	Long	First part of primary key
Order number	Numeric	Long	Second part of primary key
Invoice date	Date		

Table 35.4. CustordDtl: Information for the detail section of the orders report.

Field	Data type	Length	Comments
OrderNum	Numeric	Long	Key, and first part of primary key
Counter	Counter	Long	Second part of primary key
Product	Text	30	
Quantity	Numeric	Integer	
Price	Currency		
Subtotal	Currency		
Tax	Currency		
Deposit	Currency		
Total	Currency		

Table 35.5. The Billing table: Information used to produce account statements.

Field	Data type	Length	Comments
CustomerNumber	Numeric	Long	Key field
CompanyName	Text	50	
LastName	Text	20	
FirstName	Text	16	
Address	Text	30	
Apt	Text	30	
POBox	Text	5	
City	Text	16	
State	Text	2	
Zip	Text	10	
StatementDate	Date		
CompanyGreeting	Text	80	

Table 35.6. The Company Information table: Information on the owner of the person using the custom application.

Field	Data type	Length	Comments
CompanyName	Text	50	
Address1	Text	50	
Address2	Text	50	
City	Text	32	
State	Text	50	
Zip	Text	10	
Phone	Text	14	
FAX	Text	14	
CompanySlogan	Text	50	

Picking a Primary Key

Even if you are careful to properly group data in each table, you may find that there is no elegant way to uniquely identify a customer. This identification is very important in a relational database because a unique key is the common thread that connects two or more tables. You may think that you can easily create a good key using some or all of the information you have about the customer. This approach, however, is likely to generate a large, multifield key (which slows performance) and depend on the user entering certain information about every customer he has (and sometimes you don't know everything about a customer).

The main customer table should have a unique key to identify customers so that the program can retrieve a specific customer's information. The order table should have a unique key so that the program can retrieve a unique order. The best approach to defining a primary key in these cases is to assign an arbitrary number to each customer and order. The Customer table has a field called CustomerNum, and the Order table has a field called OrderNum. When you create these tables, you assign these fields the special attribute of counter, which is a long integer with some special properties. This attribute causes Visual Basic to assign a unique key each time a record gets added to the database. Getting Visual Basic to perform this task requires a little code, which is shown and explained in a later section called "Adding a Customer Record."

Tying Tables Together with Keys

Keys are the threads that tie all the tables in a relational database together. Keys are also required when using certain data constructs (like snapshots) that this application uses. For example, you will be retrieving customer orders through the relationship of CustomerNum in the CustMain table and the Orders table. This field must have the exact same name and data type in each table in order for the relationship to work. Keys are also helpful, making the database application easy to maintain and understand by making it more consistent and showing (graphically, if you are using Microsoft Access) how the data is related.

Creating the Database Using the Data Manager

Visual Basic comes with a very powerful add-in called the Data Manager. Using the Data Manager, you can create and modify the database. You can also add and modify the data in it.

> **NOTE**
>
> Even though the Data Manager is an easy tool to use, you may find that using Microsoft Access is an easier way to create a database for a Visual Basic application. Both tools use the same principles, but Microsoft Access has many useful features that the Data Manager does not have, such as the database documenter, the ability to view multiple tables at one time, and a great SQL builder. But if you just want to create a database, the Data Manager is quite capable of the task.

Using the Data Manager, create the tables you outlined in the design. After creating the tables, activate the counter attributes for the counter fields, as shown in Figure 35.2.

FIGURE 35.2.

Making CustomerNum a counter field in CustMain.

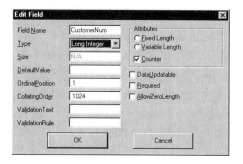

After setting the counter attribute, make this field the primary key by editing the field properties and adding an index, as shown in Figure 35.3.

FIGURE 35.3.

Setting the primary key for CustMain.

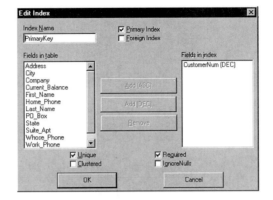

Developing a Functional Prototype

With a list of requirements from the client, the process flow diagram, and a database design, you have enough material for a specification that shows what this application will do and how it will do it. With this specification, you are ready to construct a database and a functional prototype.

A prototype is a model of the application. If you have a database to work with, you may even be able to put some real working features in your prototype without writing any code. You should avoid writing code for a prototype whenever possible. If you want to show a feature that will require code, just put together a few forms that convey the idea and use a function key to display them. Don't get too attached to a prototype. You will be changing it.

Adding a Startup Screen

Using the process flow as a roadmap, start designing the screens needed to complete a process. One thing the process flow did not show that the user will need is a place to start. To help the user out, add a startup screen called Cover_scr.

A startup screen helps organize an application, and it is a convenient place to put initialization routines and things like a screen for typing in who the company is and a way to exit the application. The startup screen (Cover_scr.frm) for this application allows the user to do the following:

- Get to a screen that allows them to access specific customer information
- Get to a screen that allows them to review general account information
- Get to a screen that allows them to type in information about the company
- Exit the application

FIGURE 35.4.

The process flow with a starting place.

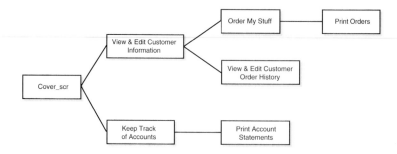

FIGURE 35.5.

The Cover_Scr form.

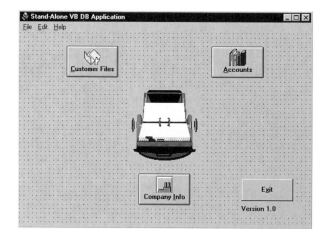

The Cover_scr is where the users can select which part of the application they want to use. This design allows you to add features to the application later on by adding a button. The two features you will add in the beginning will give access to customer information and to general account information. Table 35.7 lists the properties of the Cover_scr form.

Table 35.7. Cover_scr properties.

Property	Setting	Comments
Appearance	1-3d	
Name	Cover_scr	
Background Color	&H00C0C0C0& (light gray)	For 16-bit VGA, this is a safe color.

Property	Setting	Comments
Maximize	False	In a 640×480 world, the controls will not look centered on the screen if you allow the user to change the size of the window. There are elastic custom controls that can solve this problem.
Icon	(Icon)	Because this form is also the startup form (see Figure 35.5), this form's icon is the icon that will be used for the program in the program group.

To make the Cover_scr form the starting form for the application, select Tools | Options and click on the Project tab. The first field on the Project screen is a drop-down list of all the forms in the project (see Figure 35.6).

FIGURE 35.6.

Setting the Cover_scr as the startup form.

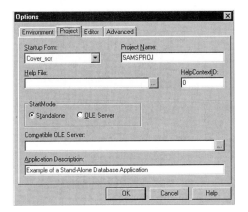

Putting a version number on a startup screen can be helpful when you start modifying the application. You know as soon as you start the application what version you are running. This version number is also helpful if a user ever calls you about the software. If you have updated the software, you will want to know what version that person is using. You can add the version number to the screen by inserting a label and specifying the version number in the label's Caption property.

Graphics can make a screen more approachable. Putting a company logo in the center of the startup screen adds a professional touch. The graphic on Cover_Scr is a picture box control with a graphic (rolodex.wmf from the Windows Meta Files (.WMF) included with Visual Basic 95 to be exact).

Most Windows applications have a menu bar even if there are on-screen buttons that do the same thing. A menu bar is part of the standard look and feel of a Windows application. You don't need to add code to the menu bar at this time, but the menu bar completes the look of the startup form so the client will get an idea of what the final product will look like. To create a menu bar, choose Tools | Menu Editor. Figure 35.7 shows the menu for Cover_scr.

FIGURE 35.7.

The menu bar for Cover_scr.

The Prototype Customer Information Screens

The first thing your client talked about was getting at customer information. Figure 35.8 highlights this portion of the specification you created earlier in the chapter.

FIGURE 35.8.

The processes related to a specific customer.

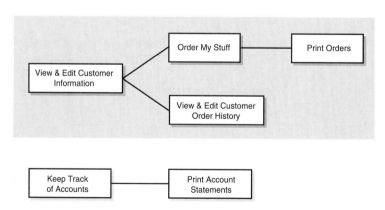

In a prototype, you are trying to convey how this application will look and how the user will go from one screen to another. From the Cover_scr, a user presses the Customer Files (btnCustMain) to display the Customer Information screen (see Figure 35.9). A user will also expect to see the pointer turn into an hourglass if this process takes a few seconds (which it probably will on that 486SX). Even though the prototype should have a minimum amount of code in it, you will need code to display screens. Entering the code in Listing 35.1 for each button makes the prototype much easier to demonstrate; you also will need this code in the final version of the application. Table 35.8 lists the btnCustMain properties.

Listing 35.1. Displaying the Customer Information screen.

```
Private Sub btnCustMain_Click()
    MousePointer = 11 ' hourglass
    Custinf.Show
End Sub
```

Table 35.8. btnCustMain properties.

Property	Setting	Comments
Name	btnCustMain	This is an SSCommand control. 
Caption	&Customer Files	The &C in Customer makes Alt+C the key combination for this button.
Picture	(Icon)	This icon is folder05.ico from the Office subdirectory.

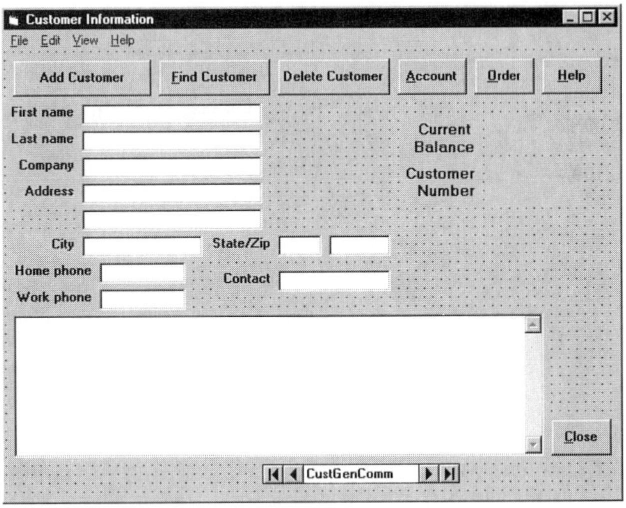

FIGURE 35.9.

The Customer Information (CustInf) form.

The main customer information screen answers more of the requirements than any other screen. In this screen, the user enters, changes, and deletes customer information. The user can also enter a note about the customer in this form and see the current customer balance. Table 35.9 lists the properties for this form.

Table 35.9. CustInf properties.

Property	Setting	Comments
Name	CustInf	A plain old form.
KeyPreview	True	Allows the form-level KeyPress event to preview keystrokes before the controls do.
MaxButton	False	Keeps the form from getting larger than it was designed to.

The buttons on the Customer Information screen display other screens of information about the customer. For example, if the user clicks the Account (btnAccount) button, a Customer Account screen appears (see Figure 35.10). Table 35.10 lists the properties for the Account button.

Table 35.10. btnAccount properties.

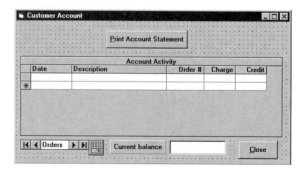

Property	Setting	Comments
Name	btnAccount	CommandButton object.
Caption	&Account	Establishes Alt+A as the key combination.
Tabstop	False	The user can tab through data entry fields only.

FIGURE 35.10.

The Customer Account (frmCusta.frm) form.

The Customer Account form contains a data-bound grid control. To access the database using the grid, you must first add a data control on the form. Table 35.11 lists the properties for the Orders data control. When bound to the data control, the grid will have access to the field names and data types in the underlying recordset.

Table 35.11. Orders properties.

Property	Setting	Comments
Name	Orders	Data control object. 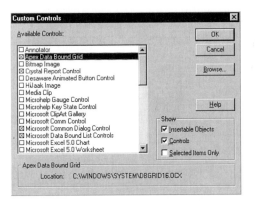
Caption	Orders	Makes the control easier to recognize on the screen.
DatabaseName	C:\VBPROJ\SAMS\VB4DB.MDB	This is the default name. You can assign another by changing the Database_name variable in the Cover_scr load subroutine.
Recordsource	Orders	Table in the database to bind to.
RecordsetType	1-Dynaset	This grid will make changes to the underlying table.
Visible	False	The default property is True.

In order to add the data-bound grid to the form, the grid must be in the toolbox. If it is not, you must add it to the project. Choose Insert | Custom Controls. In the Custom Controls dialog box (see Figure 35.11), you can select which controls you want to be active in your project. After adding the grid to the form, configure its properties as listed in Table 35.12.

FIGURE 35.11.

Adding the data bound control to the project.

If you use particular custom controls frequently, add them to your AUTO16LD.VBP file for 16-bit environments or AUTO32LD.VBP file for 32-bit development environments.

Table 35.12. OrdersGrid properties.

Property	*Setting*	*Comments*
`Caption`	`Account Activity`	
`ColumnHeaders`	`True`	Puts the field names at the top of the columns.
`DataMode`	`Bound`	
`DataSource`	`Orders`	The Orders data control.
`Name`	`OrdersGrid`	This is a data-bound grid. 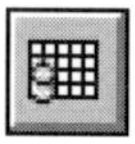
`TabIndex`	`4`	
`TabStop`	`True`	
`Visible`	`True`	

To print the current status of a customer account, you will use a report. To create the Print Account Statement button in the Customer Account screen, add the Crystal Reports control to the project the same way you added the grid for the Account Activity control. Using a word processor, you can create a mock report to show how the account statement will look (see Figure 35.12). Clicking the Close button should take the user back to the Customer Information screen.

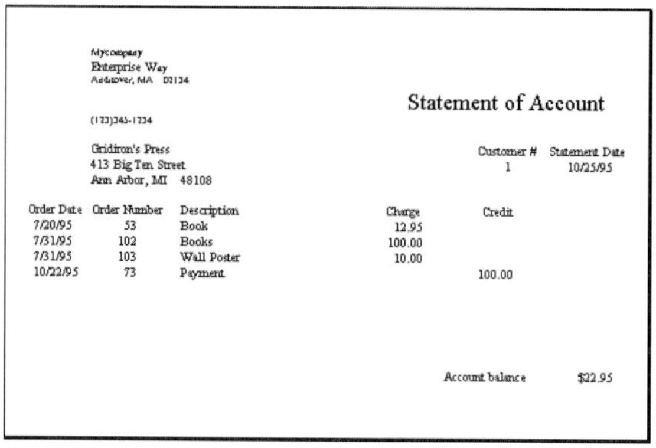

Mycompany
Enterprise Way
Andover, MA 02134

Statement of Account

(123)345-1234

Gridiron's Press
413 Big Ten Street
Ann Arbor, MI 48108

Customer # 1 | Statement Date 10/25/95

Order Date	Order Number	Description	Charge	Credit
7/20/95	53	Book	12.95	
7/31/95	102	Books	100.00	
7/31/95	103	Wall Poster	10.00	
10/22/95	73	Payment		100.00

Account balance $22.95

FIGURE 35.12.
Prototype statement of account.

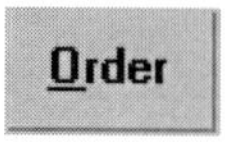

From the Customer Information screen, the user can click the Orders (btnOrder) button to display the Place Order screen shown in Figure 35.13. Table 35.13 lists the properties for this button. The user places an order from the current customer on the Place Order screen by typing it into the grid labeled Current Order.

Table 35.13. btnOrder properties.

Property	Setting	Comments
Caption	&Order	Specifies Alt+O as the key combination.
Name	btnOrder	Command button.
TabStop	False	Only tabs through data entry fields.

FIGURE 35.13.

The Place Order screen.

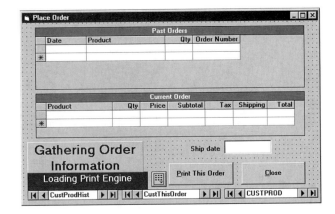

To print the order, the user clicks the Print This Order button. The actual order form will be developed using the Report Manager (Crystal Reports version 3 is included with the Visual Basic's professional edition). You must place a Crystal Reports control on the form. This control is not required for a prototype, but having it on the form will affect the time it takes to load the form. Adding the control now gives you an idea of how long this screen will take to paint. Set the control's Name property to rptOrderTicket.

Printing the order is not necessary in the prototype, but showing how the final order form will look is. Using any word processor, you can create an order form. As you create the mock order form, you may want to make note of the fields you will be using from the report table.

If the user clicks the Find Customer (btnFindCust) button on the Customer Information screen, a Lookup Customer screen appears (see Figure 35.15). Table 35.14 lists the properties for this button.

FIGURE 35.14.

The prototype order printout.

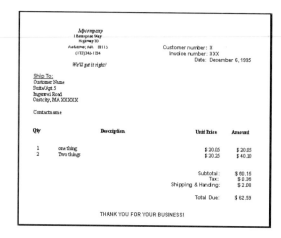

Table 35.14. btnFindCust properties.

Property	Setting	Comments
Caption	&Find Customer	Sets Alt+F as the key combination.
Name	btnFindCust	Command button. 
TabStop	False	Only tabs through data entry fields.

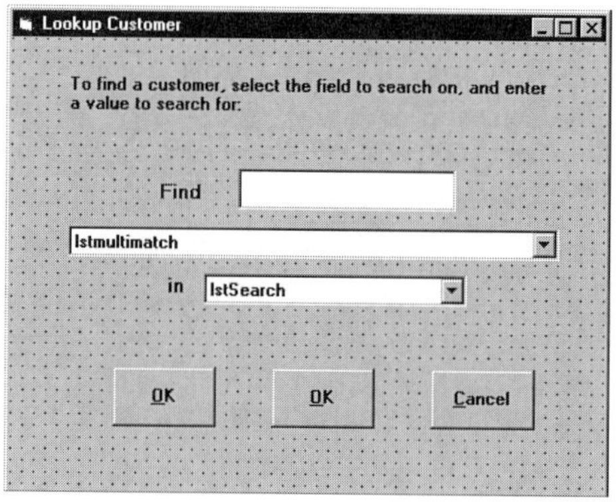

FIGURE 35.15.

The Lookup Customer form.

The user selects the customer for the Customer Information screen from the Lookup Customer form. This form is really two forms in one. Several of the controls start out invisible when the form is first shown (lstMultiMatch and the middle OK button). The user types in a value in the Find text box, selects a field to search on from the lstSearch list box, and clicks OK (only one OK button will be displayed at run time). If the application finds more than one match to the user's selection criteria, then the multimatch list box of this form is activated. This functionality all has to be programmed later. The essential message to the user here is that this is a lookup screen. The fields you will be searching on are Customer Number, Address, Company, or Last Name.

The Prototype General Accounts Screen

The second part of this application's specification relates to account information, as shown in Figure 35.16.

FIGURE 35.16.

The processes related to all accounts.

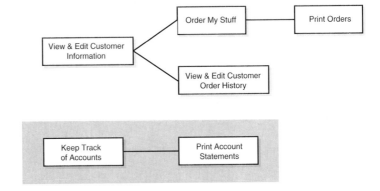

The General Accounts process starts back at the Cover_Scr, or startup screen when the user clicks on the Accounts (btnAccounts) button. Table 35.15 lists the properties for this button. By adding the code in Listing 35.2, you can cause the Account form to appear on-screen.

Table 35.15. btnAccounts properties.

Property	Setting	Comments
Name	btnAccounts	This is an SSCommand control.
Caption	&Accounts	This specifies Alt+A as the key combination for this button.
Picture	(Icon)	This is books04.ico from the Writing subdirectory.

Listing 35.2. Displaying the general accounts form.

```
Private Sub btnAccounts_Click()
    MousePointer = 11 'hourglass
    frmAccounts.Show
End Sub
```

Seeing all of the customer information at once is important to the client so he gets an overview of the accounts. The Accounts form (see Figure 35.17) is designed to show details about the accounts on the left-hand side of the screen and the current balance of each account on the right-hand side. By using two grids, you can show both pieces of information. You will have to write code to synchronize the two grids. You can reuse the statement of account report from the customer account section of the application.

FIGURE 35.17.

The Accounts form.

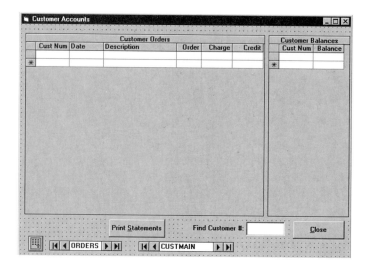

Eventually, there may be a lot of customer records on this screen. To help the user find a particular customer number, there is a data entry field at the bottom of the screen to search for a specific customer number.

Other Screens

The Cover_scr form has two other buttons on it—Company Information and Exit. There is also a picture box in the middle of the form that you will use to display an About box that shows all the legal stuff and the author's logo. These elementary forms should also be discussed in a prototype demonstration.

Coding and Testing the Application

While showing the prototype, your client may come up with other requirements and features. Before coding and testing an application, make sure you have designed the screen and discussed the things that will happen when each button is pressed, each field is changed, and all of the major features are discussed so that you both understand how the application will look and work. If this process requires several discussions, you may be able to develop parts of the application that have remained stable, but there is a risk that a yet unknown feature may require modification to anything you do.

Creating the Startup Code

The Form Load event is a good place to put code that changes the orientation of the form because this event is only executed when the form is first displayed. Most other form-based code is in the Activate event, which is invoked whenever the form becomes the active window. If something changes the data that an inactive form is displaying, the Activate event can refresh the data (or just the controls) without having to reload the form. Code in this event improves performance by reducing the amount of screen painting needed to update data. If the user moves the form while running the application, the form remains where he put it until it is unloaded.

Because Cover_scr is the starting point for the application (you set it up as the startup form earlier), you can use the load routine to check the working environment and database to make sure everything is in order. If there is a trappable, correctable error, it can be handled here (see Listing 35.3):

Listing 35.3. Getting this application off the ground.

```
Private Sub Form_Load()
    ...
    If Not Database_name Then
        Database_name = "\vbproj\sams\vb4db.mdb"
    End If
    On Error GoTo Error_db

' Open single user (default).
    Set CustDB = OpenDatabase(Database_name)
    Exit Sub

Error_db:
    Select Case Err
        Case 3049 ' Possible corrupt database
            errmsg = Err.Description & "  To attempt repairing the database, press
OK.
To Abort, press CANCEL"
            response = MsgBox(errmsg, vbOKCancel, "Database Error")
            If response = vbOK Then
                MousePointer = 11
                DoEvents
                Cover_scr.Print "Re-indexing tables..."
                RepairDatabase Database_name
                Cover_scr.Print "Optimizing tables..."
                CompactDatabase Database_name, "\tmpdb.mdb"
                Cover_scr.Print "Resetting tables..."
                Kill Database_name
```

continues

Listing 35.3. continued

```
                    Name "\tmpdb.mdb" As Database_name
                    Cover_scr.Refresh
                    MousePointer = 0
                    Resume
            End If

        Case Default
            errmsg = Err.Description & "  Press Yes to continue anyway (could be
risky),
No to exit.  Continue anyway?"
            response = MsgBox(errmsg, vbYesNo + vbDefaultButton2, "Database Error")
            If response = vbYes Then
                Resume ' Attempt to continue
            Else
                End ' Shut down the application
            End If
    End Select
End Sub
```

> **NOTE**
>
> You also can perform error handling by writing and calling a central error handler.
> The programmer's decision becomes Do I centralize all errors or put code related to a
> particular activity in one place? In this case, and throughout this sample application,
> all errors are handled in the routine in which they can occur. This method makes all
> properties of the Err object available to you when you are writing damage control code.
> If you choose to write a central error handler, you will have to save the Err object
> properties in variables and pass them to the error handler.

To make code maintenance easier, each menu item calls the corresponding button's Click event
subroutine. That way, if anything special has to happen when a screen is displayed, all of the
code is in one place. For example, the Customers item on the Edit menu calls the Click subroutine for the btnCustMain button. Listing 35.4 gives the code for this action.

Listing 35.4. Coordinating menu items and buttons.

```
Private Sub mnuEditCustomers_Click()
    Call btnCustMain_Click
End Sub

Private Sub btnCustMain_Click()
    MousePointer = 11 ' hourglass
    Custinf.Show 1 'modal
End Sub
```

The only minor exception to this rule is the About this application item on the Help menu. This item calls the `Click` event subroutine for the picture box rather than a button.

Whenever the cover_scr is activated, the pointer is reset to the default state for the form. This resetting allows you to set the cursor to be an hourglass when you unload a form, so the user knows something is happening. You can then turn the cursor back into a pointer when the unload is complete and the new form is reactivated. The `Activate` event on all forms in this sample application has this feature. Listing 35.5 provides the necessary code.

Listing 35.5. Resetting the pointer.

```
Private Sub Form_Activate()
    ' Reset to the default  pointer when returning to this form.
    MousePointer = 0
End Sub
```

Adding a Customer Record

The user can add a new customer to the database by clicking the Add Customer button (or using the menu) in the CustInf form. Adding a customer to the database means adding a unique customer number to the CustMain table. Because the customer number is a counter field, you just look for an unused number or increase the last number in the file by one by entering the following code:

```
Private Sub btnAddCust_Click()
    ' Look in the customer table for an unused customer number.
    Set CustMainTbl = CustDB.OpenTable("CUSTMAIN")
    CustMainTbl.Index = "PrimaryKey"
    indexval = 1
    CustMainTbl.Seek "=", indexval
    While (CustMainTbl.NoMatch = False)
        indexval = indexval + 1
        CustMainTbl.Seek "=", indexval
    Wend
```

Once the number has been established, you can add a record to the CustMain table, put the new customer number into the key field, and update the file:

```
    ' Add this new customer to the customer table
    CustMainTbl.AddNew
    CustMainTbl.Fields("CustomerNum") = indexval
    CustMainTbl.UPDATE
```

After adding the record, you make it the current record:

```
    ' Make this new customer number the current customer_number
    Customer_number = indexval
    txtCustomerNum.TEXT = Customer_number
    ' Make this newly created record our current record
    Qcriteria = "SELECT * FROM CUSTMAIN WHERE CustomerNum = " & Customer_number
    Set CustmainDynaset = CustDB.CreateDynaset(Qcriteria)
```

The CustmainDynaset is a global dynaset that is referenced by the Orders and CustAccount forms.

Finding an Existing Customer Record

Find Customer

A user can look up an existing customer by clicking on the Find Customer button in the CustInf form. Clicking this button displays the Lookup form. This form is actually two forms in one. It is both the form for entering selection criteria for finding a customer, and the form for selecting a specific customer if more than one customer matches the given criteria.

The lstSearch combo box lists the criteria the user may type to find a customer. This list is set in the Form_Load event subroutine. Using the AddItem method, you add the Customer Number, Address, Company, and Last Name fields from the database.

Most users prefer to use the Enter key to move between fields on a form. To accommodate this, all of the text boxes on this form have Keypress event subroutines that convert a press of the Enter key to a tab. These subroutines move the focus to the control with the next highest tab index:

```
If KeyAscii = 13 Then
        SendKeys "{tab}"
        KeyAscii = 0
    End If
```

In the case of the combo box control, the user presses the Enter key to select an item from the list. If you just mapped the keypress to be a tab, the only way a user could select an item from the list would be with a mouse click, which is unintuitive. If the user tried to press Enter to select a highlighted item, the cursor would jump to the next control on the form. To prevent this situation, use the KeyDown event to trap the keypress and force the cursor to move to the next field on the screen, as shown in Listing 35.6.

Listing 35.6. Making the selection process in a combo box move the cursor to the next field.

```
Private Sub lstSearch_KeyDown(KeyCode As Integer, Shift As Integer)
    If KeyCode = KEY_RETURN Then
        btnFindCust(0).SetFocus
    End If
End Sub
```

Once the user has entered the selection criteria, you need an event that indicates that the user is finished and it is time to use that criteria to search the database. The Lookup form has two OK buttons when viewed in Design mode. Only one of these buttons will be visible at run time. The leftmost OK button (named btnFindCust) is visible when the form is initially displayed (see Figure 35.18). This button is used to find a customer that matches the selection criteria. Clicking on this button is the event that begins the database search.

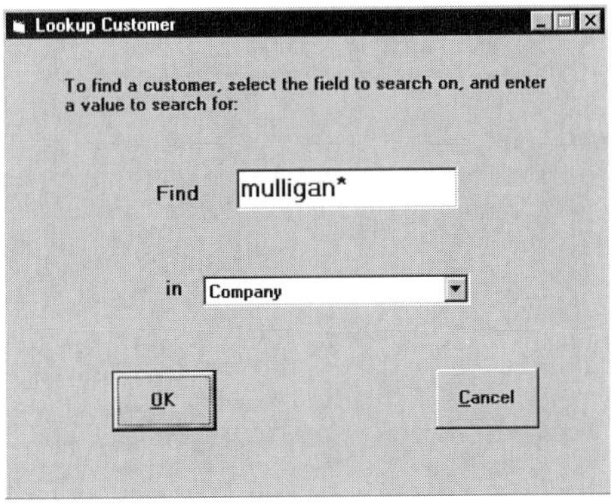

FIGURE 35.18.

The initial Lookup form.

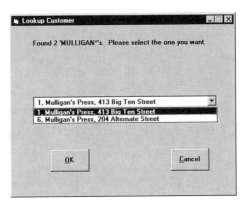

The second OK button (named btnOK2) is used to select a specific customer if more than one matched the selection criteria (see Figure 35.19).

FIGURE 35.19.

The Multimatch Lookup form.

The btnFindCust (the left OK) `Click` subroutine determines which field the user typed as the selection criteria, converts the value in the txtCustID field to the appropriate data type, and then calls the `FindCust` function.

The `FindCust` function uses SQL to select a record (or records) from the CustMain table, puts the records in the CustmainDynaset, and returns an integer (interpreted as True or False) to indicate whether any records match the selection criteria. Listing 35.7 shows the code that makes this sequence happen.

Listing 35.7. Finding customers in the database.

```
Private Function FindCust(ByVal CustID As String, SrchField) As Integer

     'If there is no active record,
     'then return without doing anything
     If Len(CustID) = 0 Or Len(SrchField) = 0 Then
         FindCust = False
         Exit Function
     Else
         ' Set one criteria if the user is searching by Number
         If SrchField = "CustomerNum" Then
             Qcriteria = "SELECT * FROM CUSTMAIN WHERE " & SrchField & " = " &
CustID & ";"
         Else
         ' Set a different criteria for an non-numeric searches
             Qcriteria = "SELECT * FROM CUSTMAIN WHERE " & SrchField & " LIKE """ &
CustID & """;"
         End If

         ' Create the dynaset
         Set CustmainDynaset = CustDB.CreateDynaset(Qcriteria)

         ' Check for a successful record search.
         ' Populate the fields on the screen if a record is found.
         If CustmainDynaset.RecordCount = 0 Then
             ' Could not find the customer,
             ' so reset the Dynaset back to the original customer.
             ' If there was no original customer, then just get out.
             If Len(tmpCustNum) = 0 Then
                 FindCust = False
                 Exit Function
             End If

             Qcriteria = "SELECT * FROM CUSTMAIN WHERE CustomerNum" & " = " &
Customer_number & ";"
             Set CustmainDynaset = CustDB.CreateDynaset(Qcriteria)
             FindCust = False
         Else
             ' Get to the last record so we can determine how
             ' many matches there were.
             CustmainDynaset.MoveLast

             ' Found more than 1 match
             If CustmainDynaset.RecordCount > 1 Then
                 Customer_number = tmpCustNum
                 FindCust = CustmainDynaset.RecordCount
             Else
                 ' Found only 1 match
                 Customer_number = CustmainDynaset.Fields("CustomerNum")
                 FindCust = True
             End If
         End If
     End If
End Function
```

You can interpret the integer that the FindCust method returned in three ways:

■ If no customers were found, you tell the user nothing matched and give him an opportunity to try again:

```
        MsgBox ("Can not find " & lstSearch & " '" & txtCustID & "' in the
database.")
        txtCustID.TEXT = ""
        Customer_number = tmpCustNum
        MousePointer = 0
        Exit Sub
```

■ If one and only one record matched, then the Lookup screen is unloaded, and the Customer Information screen is redrawn with the information in the CustmainDynaset.

■ If there were two or more matches to the selection criteria, the Lookup form changes and becomes the Multimatch form:

```
    ' Get the correct number of records by going to the last one
        CustmainDynaset.MoveLast
        'Tell the user how many were found.
        Label1.Caption = "Found " & CustmainDynaset.RecordCount & " '" &
UCase(txtCustID.TEXT) & "'s.  Please select the one you want."

        ' Turn off the parts of the screen that don't apply now.
        lblFind.Visible = False
        lblin.Visible = False
        txtCustID.Visible = False
        lstSearch.Visible = False
        btnFindCust(0).Visible = False
        lblFind.Enabled = False
        lblin.Enabled = False
        txtCustID.Enabled = False
        lstSearch.Enabled = False
        btnFindCust(0).Enabled = False

        ' Activate & place the lstMultiMatch control and  associated
        ➥controls.
        lstmultimatch.Visible = True
        lstmultimatch.Enabled = True
        btnOK2.Visible = True
        btnOK2.Enabled = True
        btnOK2.Left = 1080
        btnOK2.TOP = 3360
```

Now that the Lookup form is the Multimatch form, the same basic things happen as before except that you do not have to search the CustMain table for any selection criteria.

The lstmultimatch combo box contains the list of matches to the query. To make it easier to fit on a screen, only the customer's number, first name, last name, company name, and address are displayed in this list:

```
    'Make sure the list empty before adding items to it.
    lstmultimatch.Clear

    ' Go to the beginning of the dynaset and populate the list.
    CustmainDynaset.MoveFirst
```

```
         ' Put a default value in the control
            addcriteria = Str$(CustmainDynaset.Fields("CustomerNum"))
        If IsNull(CustmainDynaset.Fields("First_Name")) <> True Then
            addcriteria = addcriteria & ", " &
            ➡CustmainDynaset.Fields("First_Name")
        End If
        If IsNull(CustmainDynaset.Fields("Last_name")) <> True Then
            addcriteria = addcriteria & " " &
            ➡CustmainDynaset.Fields("Last_Name")
        End If
        If IsNull(CustmainDynaset.Fields("Company")) <> True Then
            addcriteria = addcriteria & ", " &
            ➡CustmainDynaset.Fields("Company")
        End If
        If IsNull(CustmainDynaset.Fields("Address")) <> True Then
            addcriteria = addcriteria & ", " &
            ➡CustmainDynaset.Fields("Address")
        End If
        lstmultimatch.TEXT = addcriteria
        ListCount = 0
        While CustmainDynaset.RecordCount > ListCount
            addcriteria = Str$(CustmainDynaset.Fields("CustomerNum"))
            If IsNull(CustmainDynaset.Fields("First_Name")) <> True Then
                addcriteria = addcriteria & ", " &
                ➡CustmainDynaset.Fields("First_Name")
            End If
            If IsNull(CustmainDynaset.Fields("Last_name")) <> True Then
                addcriteria = addcriteria & " " &
                ➡CustmainDynaset.Fields("Last_Name")
            End If
            If IsNull(CustmainDynaset.Fields("Company")) <> True Then
                addcriteria = addcriteria & ", " &
                ➡CustmainDynaset.Fields("Company")
            End If
            If IsNull(CustmainDynaset.Fields("Address")) <> True Then
                addcriteria = addcriteria & ", " &
                ➡CustmainDynaset.Fields("Address")
            End If
            lstmultimatch.AddItem addcriteria
            CustmainDynaset.MoveNext
            ListCount = ListCount & 1
        Wend
    End If
End If
```

Once the user selects an item from the list, you call the FindCust routine to fill in the CustmainDynaset again:

```
' Get the customer number from the listbox text
srchCustNumstr = Mid$(lstmultimatch.TEXT, 1, custnumlen)
srchCustNum = Val(srchCustNumstr)

' Use the customer number to create the dynaset.
foundcust = FindCust(ByVal srchCustNum, "CustomerNum")
If foundcust = True Then
    MousePointer = 0
    Unload frmLookup
    Exit Sub
Else
```

Displaying Customer Information on the Screen

Putting values from a populated CustmainDynaset onto the screen is done though the form's `Activate` subroutine. Whenever the form is activated, the `UpdateInfo` subroutine updates all the fields in the dynaset based on the current customer number. This process is fairly simple, but be careful not to put a null value on the screen—referencing a null value will generate a run-time error. To avoid this problem, the `UpdateInfo` routine explicitly checks for a null value in the dynaset field. If there is a null value, the field is given a blank value:

```
Private Sub UpdateInfo()
    ...
    'Check for existence of data in the fields to
    ' avoid the invalid use of null error.
    If IsNull(CustmainDynaset.Fields("First_Name")) = False Then
        txtFirstName = CustmainDynaset.Fields("First_Name")
    Else
        txtFirstName.TEXT = ""
    End If
    ...
```

Changing Customer Information

The Customer Information screen is based on the CustmainDynaset, but changes to the data are updated in the database as soon as the cursor leaves the field. Each field on the CustMain form has a `LostFocus` event subroutine that calls the `UpdateField` subroutine, as shown in Listing 35.8.

Listing 35.8. A general purpose SQL update routine for the CustMain table.

```
' This subroutine Updates any field in the CUSTMAIN table.
Private Sub UpdateField(ByVal FldText As String, fldName As String)
Dim SqlUpdateDynaset
    ...
    If Len(FldText) <> 0 Then
        ' Change the value in the table field
        SqlUpdateDynaset = "UPDATE CUSTMAIN SET " & fldName & " = """ & FldText &
""""
    Else
        ' Set the value in the table field to blank
        SqlUpdateDynaset = "UPDATE CUSTMAIN SET " & fldName & " = NULL"
    End If

    ' Put the rest of the update string on.
    SqlUpdateDynaset = SqlUpdateDynaset & " WHERE CustomerNum = " & Customer_number
    CustDB.Execute SqlUpdateDynaset
End Sub
```

An SQL update statement is used to modify the field using the `Execute` method on the database. This technique is so fast that even 386SX machines show no noticeable delay when updating the field. There are a few pitfalls to using SQL in this case, however; the following list explains how to avoid them.

- You must enclose the text string passed to the Execute method in double quotes (" "). If you refer to a field, it must be in double quotes too, which means you must put double-quotes in the string. To do this, put the double quotes in double quotes. Three sets of double quotes (" ") are passed to Jet as a single double quote (").

- To clear a field, replace its value with NULL. To pass NULL in the string, use the keyword NULL. Do not pass two sets of double quotes () in this case. You will get a syntax error at run time for mismatched quotes.

Similar rules apply to apostrophes. Examples of how to handle quotes of all kinds are in the btnFindCust_Click and FindCust routines in the sample application for this chapter.

Placing an Order

Order

The Order screen has a lot of controls on it, including two data-bound grids. The longest potential response time in the entire application is the Activate event on this form. In addition to the hourglass pointer, you give the user a little information about what is going on by displaying a panel with a special status message on it, as shown in Figure 35.20. This panel is invisible by default. It is set to visible at the beginning of the Activate subroutine, and then set to invisible again at the end of the Activate routine.

FIGURE 35.20.

pnlDelivMsg.

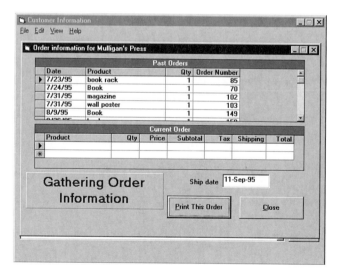

The only grid that gets data from the database when the form is loaded is the Product Order History grid. The grid is bound to the data control that is bound to the CustProdHist table.

To subset the data in the data controls dynaset, modify the RecordSource property using an SQL statement:

```
    ' Set up the Product history data control
    SQLCustProdHistInq = "Select * from CustProdHist where CustomerNum = " &
Customer_number & ";"
    CustProdHist.RecordSource = SQLCustProdHistInq
    CustProdHist.Refresh
```

The Current Order grid is tied to the CustThisOrder table, which should be cleared out (just in case there were any records left from a prior order). You should also put in a new record for this customer to ensure that there is a current record if the user starts entering data in the grid:

```
' Clear out any old orders
CustDB.Execute ("Delete * from CustThisOrder")
' Insert a record in the CustThisOrder.
Set CustThisOrderTbl = CustDB.OpenTable("CustThisOrder")
CustThisOrderTbl.AddNew
CustThisOrderTbl.Fields("CustomerNum") = Customer_number
CustThisOrderTbl.UPDATE
CustThisOrder.Refresh
```

As the user types information into the Current Order grid, data is automatically put into the CustThisOrder table in the database. The only information on the screen is for the current customer. The customer number is not on the grid, but it is a field in the underlying table. You use the BeforeUpdate event to write the customer number into the CustThisOrder table, as shown in Listing 35.9. Every time the user updates data in the grid, this routine is invoked.

Listing 35.9. Getting the customer number in the record when it is not displayed on the grid.

```
Private Sub ThisOrder_BeforeUpdate(Cancel As Integer)
     CustThisOrder.Recordset.Fields("CustomerNum") = Customer_number
End Sub
```

Once the user has typed in the order, he can print an order form showing the order. Clicking the Print this Order button kicks off the ordering process. The Click event could take a few seconds to update the tables and load Crystal Reports. To keep the user informed, a status message is placed over the buttons. Listing 35.10 shows the code for this message.

Listing 35.10. Processing an order.

```
Private Sub btnPrintOrder_Click()
    ...
    lblPrntMsg.Left = 4200
    lblPrntMsg.TOP = 3620
    lblPrntMsg.Visible = True  puts a message on the screen saying the Print Engine
is loading
    btnPrintOrder.Visible = False
    btnDelTickets.Visible = False
```

While this message is on the screen, four tables are updated before the Crystal Reports object is loaded: one for order history, one for accounting, and two for the report. The report needs two tables because the order may have multiple items. The first table is for information about the order; the second is for information about each item in the order. The report itself links these tables at run time. Linking these tables makes it possible to print a report with multiple-record detail sections and a one-record header.

As the orders table is updated, the primary key field OrderNum (which is defined as a counter) is automatically incremented by the database engine (Jet). In order to retrieve this number, you search for the highest number in the table. This number represents the most recent order:

```
' Add a record to ORDERS.  This must be done before the CUSTORDMST
' record is added because an order number is needed.
OrdersTbl.AddNew
OrdersTbl.Fields("CustomerNum") = Customer_number
OrdersTbl.Fields("Date") = txtDelDate.TEXT
OrdersTbl.Fields("Description") = CustThisOrder.Recordset.Fields("Product")
OrdersTbl.Fields("Charge") = CustThisOrder.Recordset.Fields("Total")
OrdersTbl.UPDATE

' Now retrieve the order number of the order just placed in ORDERS
OrdersTbl.Index = "PrimaryKey"
OrdersTbl.Seek "<=", 9999999
```

The reporting tables are updated until there are no more detail items in the CustThisOrder table:

```
' Populate the CUSTORDMST table
CustOrdMstTbl.AddNew

CustOrdMstTbl.Fields("CustomerNum") = Customer_number
CustOrdMstTbl.Fields("InvoiceDate") = txtDelDate.TEXT
CustOrdMstTbl.Fields("OrderNum") = OrdersTbl.Fields("OrderNum")
CustOrdMstTbl.UPDATE
' Populate the CUSTORDDTL table.  One record for each record contained
' in CUSTTHISORDER
CustThisOrderTbl.MoveFirst
While (CustThisOrderTbl.EOF = False)
    CustOrdDtlTbl.AddNew
    CustOrdDtlTbl.Fields("OrderNum") = OrdersTbl.Fields("OrderNum")
    CustOrdDtlTbl.Fields("product") = CustThisOrderTbl.Fields("product")
    ...
    CustOrdDtlTbl.Fields("Total") = CustThisOrderTbl.Fields("Total")
    CustOrdDtlTbl.UPDATE
```

Although most people are very careful to make sure their hard drives are free of unnecessary data, even the most diligent user would find it tedious to monitor the Order History table and delete old records for every customer in the database. To help out, a small piece of code keeps the Order History table from taking over the user's hard drive:

```
' Now add a record to CustProdHist.  To keep the the filesize
' down, limit the history to the last 10 records.
If (Flag = False) Then
    ' "Flag" is False which means I have not yet checked to see if
```

```
       ' there are 10 unique orders for the current customer.
       buffer = "SELECT DISTINCT OrderNum, CustomerNum, Date_Delivered FROM
       ➥CustProdHist WHERE "
       buffer = buffer & "((CustProdHist.CustomerNum = " &
       ➥Str(Customer_number) & ")) "
       buffer = buffer & " Order By Date_Delivered"
       Set dynset = CustDB.CreateDynaset(buffer)
       If (dynset.RecordCount > 0) Then
           dynset.MoveLast
       End If
       If (dynset.RecordCount >= 10) Then
           dynset.MoveFirst
           deldate = dynset.Fields("Date_Delivered")
           If deldate Then
               buffer = "Delete * From CustProdHist Where CustomerNum =
" & Str(CustProdHistTbl.Fields("CustomerNum")) & " AND "
               buffer = buffer & "Date_Delivered = " &
               ➥dynset.Fields("Date_Delivered")
               CustDB.Execute (buffer)
           Else
               buffer = "Delete * from CustProdHist where CustomerNum =
" & Str(CustProdHistTbl.Fields("CustomerNum")) & " AND "
               buffer = buffer & "product = NULL"
               CustDB.Execute (buffer)
           End If
       End If
       Flag = True
   End If

   CustProdHistTbl.AddNew
   CustProdHistTbl.Fields("CustomerNum") = Customer_number
   CustProdHistTbl.Fields("Date_Delivered") = txtDelDate.TEXT
   CustProdHistTbl.Fields("product") = CustThisOrderTbl.Fields("Product")
   CustProdHistTbl.Fields("Qty") = CustThisOrderTbl.Fields("Qty")
   CustProdHistTbl.Fields("OrderNum") = OrdersTbl.Fields("OrderNum")
   CustProdHistTbl.UPDATE
   CustThisOrderTbl.MoveNext
Wend
```

To print the report, the `Action` property of the Crystal Report object is set to 1:

```
' Kick off the report.
rptOrderTicket.ReportFileName = "c:\vbproj\sams\ordtick.rpt"
rptOrderTicket.WindowTitle = "Printing Order Ticket"
rptOrderTicket.Destination = 0 '1=printer, 0=screen
rptOrderTicket.Action = 1
```

After the report is printed (or removed from the screen), the buttons return to normal and the status message is invisible again. Because there is now another order to display, the CustProdHist data control has to be refreshed, which automatically updates the bound OrderHistoryGrid:

```
lblPrntMsg.Visible = False
btnPrintOrder.Visible = True
btnDelTickets.Visible = True
CustProdHist.Refresh
   ...
Exit Sub
```

Creating the Order Ticket Report

The major benefit of using a report writer is all the code you don't have to write. The report writer doesn't take care of all the necessary code, but it should handle the pagination, printing, and formatting issues while you deal with the data. The Order Ticket report draws fields from the application database, formats them, and places them on the report.

The header section of the Order Ticket report shows the company name. The first two lines are straight out of the database: CoInf.CompanyName and CoInf.Address1. The user probably entered information in both of these fields. The third and fourth lines, however, may be blank. To avoid printing a blank line if the company does not have a second address line, the third line is a formula field, as shown in Listing 35.11 To create a formula field, select Formula from the Insert item on the Crystal Reports menu bar. When the Crystal Reports editor comes up, you may write Visual Basic-like code that defines what should go in a field (or line) on the report.

Listing 35.11. Crystal Report code to format an address line.

```
if length({CoInf.Address2}) > 0 then
    {CoInf.Address2}
else
    TrimRight ({CoInf.City}) + ", " + TrimRight ({CoInf.State}) + "    " +
{CoInf.Zip}*
```

The CustOrdMst table drives the order. One entry in the CustOrdMst table generates one report. The customer's name and address come from the CustMain table through a link between it and the CustOrdMst table, as shown in Figure 35.21.

FIGURE 35.21.

Linking the CustOrdMst table to the CustMain table in Crystal Reports.

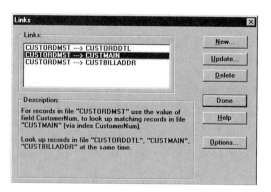

The detail section of the report lists the items in the customer's order. Through a link to the CustOrdMst table, the report finds all of the entries in the CustOrdDtl table and places them in the detail section of the report.

The bottom of the detail section of the report summarizes the financial information in order by using special summary fields. To create a summary field in Crystal Reports, click on the field you would like to summarize and choose Insert | Summary. The screen shown in Figure 35.22 appears.

FIGURE 35.22.

Creating a summary field in Crystal Reports.

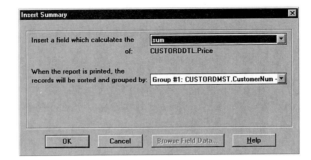

TIP

The following are some tips for making your experience with Crystal Reports (version 3) more pleasant:

Make sure you use fonts that are on the system or include the ones you want when you distribute your application (within copyright restrictions). If your report has a font that is not on the system running it, a substitute (probably Courier) will be used.

Make sure the appropriate .DLLs for Crystal Reports are distributed with your application.

If your application is going to print labels on a dot-matrix printer, your biggest challenge will be the continuous feed. Crystal Reports (version 3) automatically puts a form feed at the end of each page. Compensating for this action is almost not worth it. You may decide to write to the printer object directly and not use a Crystal Report for this feature.

Learn how to use formulas. They allow you to format text and conditionally put values on the report, making it look polished and professional. Several useful ones are included in the reports in this sample application.

Creating the Customer Account Form

The Customer Account form is pretty lean compared to the other forms on the CustInf form. The frmCusta form loads quickly, so the hourglass pointer is a sufficient signal to the user that

Account

things are happening. When the form is loaded, the data control is filled with order information about the current customer by setting the RecordSource property with an SQL statement:

```
orders.RecordSource = "Select * From Orders Where CustomerNum = " &
Str(Customer_number) & " Order By Date DESC;"
```

The Order By clause sorts the entries by descending date order so the top of the grid will show the most recent activity.

Each time the form is activated or an entry is either added or changed on the Orders grid, the current balance is recalculated and placed in the txtCurrentBalance text field:

```
' Calculate and put the current balance on the screen.
Call CalculateCurrentBalance
txtCurrentBalance = CurrentBalance
```

The CalculateCurrentBalance subroutine is a public subroutine that adds all of the charges and credits in the Orders table for the customer number passed to it. Then this subroutine updates the global variable CurrentBalance and the CustMain table field Current_Balance (see the section on the main module later in this chapter).

Like the Orders form, the Accounts form customer number is implied and therefore not displayed on the grid. To update the database, the customer number has to be added before the record is written. The Orders grid has a BeforeUpdate event routine (see Listing 35.12) that does just this.

Listing 35.12. Making sure the key field is updated even though it is not displayed on the grid.

```
Private Sub OrdersGrid_BeforeUpdate(Cancel As Integer)
     orders.Recordset.Fields("CustomerNum") = Customer_number
End Sub
```

After the record has been written, the current balance is calculated and the text field showing it is updated, as shown in Listing 35.13.

Listing 35.13. Making sure the current balance is updated when the data is updated.

```
Private Sub OrdersGrid_AfterUpdate()
    Call CalculateCurrentBalance
    txtCurrentBalance = CurrentBalance
End Sub
```

If a record is deleted, the balance has to be recalculated as well:

```
Private Sub OrdersGrid_AfterDelete()
    OrdersGrid.SetFocus
```

```
CalculateCurrentBalance
txtCurrentBalance = CurrentBalance
 ...
```

If the last record is deleted, then a single record is placed into the grid as a placeholder until the user enters data in the grid:

```
If (orders.Recordset.RecordCount = 0) Then
    orders.Recordset.AddNew
    orders.Recordset.Fields("CustomerNum") = Customer_number
    CalculateCurrentBalance
    OrdersGrid.SetFocus
    Exit Sub
End If

orders.Recordset.MoveFirst
orders.Refresh
```

Creating the Account Statement Report

The Account Statement is designed to be placed in a windowed envelope. The return address is printed in small fonts on the upper left and the delivery address is in larger type just below it. Several fields in the delivery address imply text like P.O. Box or Suite/Apt #. Formulas in the report determine if there is a value in the P.O. Box field, for example, and then place the implied text in front of the data in the field, as shown in Listing 35.14.

Listing 35.14. Crystal Reports code to format an address line.

```
TrimRight({BILLING.Address}) + " PO Box " + {BILLING.POBox}
```

Printing the Account Statement is much like printing the Order report. The main report table is the Billing table. In this report, all of the detail items come from the Orders table, and the detail information comes from the Billing table. Because the Orders table already has all of the information needed for the report, the only table that the application has to update is the Billing table.

Each entry in the Orders table for a customer in the Billing table will get a report. This setup makes it possible to share this report with the other accounting section of this application, the Customer Accounts form.

Creating the frmAccounts Form

The Customer Accounts form (called frmAccounts) shows both summary and detail information about the customers served by this business. Whenever this form is activated, the two grids are populated by the values in the data controls they are bound to and the focus is set to the Orders grid, as shown in Listing 35.15.

Listing 35.15. Defining the data controls and setting up the grids on the accounts form.

```
Private Sub Form_Activate()
    ...
    orders.DatabaseName = Database_name
    orders.RecordSource = "Select * from ORDERS Order By CustomerNum, Date DESC;"
    custmain.DatabaseName = Database_name
    custmain.RecordSource = "Select * from CUSTMAIN order by CustomerNum;"

    custmain.Refresh
    orders.Refresh
    ...
End Sub
```

When the Orders grid has the focus, the CustMain grid gets a cursor put next to the customer being referenced. When a user places the cursor on a field in the Orders grid to look at the details of a customer account, a pointer is put next to the CustMain grid showing the total balance for the account. Listing 35.16 shows the code for these actions.

Listing 35.16. Synchronizing the two grids when the Orders grid has the focus.

```
Private Sub OrdersGrid_GotFocus()
    ...
    If (orders.Recordset.RecordCount = 0) Then
        ' The following DoEvents is necessary.
        DoEvents
        orders.Recordset.AddNew
        orders.Recordset.Fields("CustomerNum") = Customer_number
    End If

    ' If this is the first time the grid has the focus, populate the billing
    ' fields from an existing record or enter a new record in CustBillAddr.
    If (FirstTimeFocus = True) Then
        Set Tbl = CustDB.OpenTable("CustBillAddr")
        Tbl.Index = "PrimaryKey"
        Tbl.Seek "=", Customer_number
        If (Tbl.NoMatch = True) Then
            Tbl.AddNew
            Tbl.Fields("CustomerNum") = Customer_number
            Tbl.UPDATE
        End If
    End If
End Sub
```

There is no implied customer number for a record in the customer grid, so the user is required to enter it. When the user adds or changes a record in the Orders grid, the current balance may also change so it must be recalculated, as shown in Listing 35.17.

Listing 35.17. Updating the current balance and CustMain grid when an order is added.

```
Private Sub OrdersGrid_RowColChange(ByVal LastRow As String, ByVal LastCol As
Integer)
    ...
    CalculateCurrentBalance (CurrentCustomerNumber)

    ' Update the current balance in CUSTMAIN
    Set CustMainTbl = CustDB.OpenTable("CustMain")
    CustMainTbl.Index = "PrimaryKey"
    CustMainTbl.Seek "=", CurrentCustomerNumber
    If (CustMainTbl.NoMatch = False) Then
        CustMainTbl.Edit
        CustMainTbl.Fields("Current_Balance") = CurrentBalance
        CustMainTbl.UPDATE
        custmain.Refresh
    End If

    ' Synchronize the CustMain grid with the Orders grid
    If orders.Recordset.RecordCount <> 0 Then
        If (IsNull(orders.Recordset.Fields("CustomerNum")) = False) Then
            CurrentCustomerNumber = orders.Recordset.Fields("CustomerNum")
            buffer = "CustomerNum = " & orders.Recordset.Fields("CustomerNum")
            custmain.Recordset.FindFirst buffer
            CustMainGrid.Refresh
        End If
    End If
    ...
End Sub
```

Similarly, if a user deletes a record from the Orders grid, the current balance has to be recalculated (see Listing 35.18).

Listing 35.18. Recalculating the current balance after deleting a record from the Orders grid.

```
Private Sub OrdersGrid_AfterDelete()
    ...
    CalculateCurrentBalance (Val(Customer_number))
    ...
End Sub
```

On the CustMain side of the screen, the user may click on a customer number and make the Orders grid cursor move to the first order for that customer (see Listing 35.19).

Listing 35.19. Synchronizing two grids when the CustMain grid has the focus.

```
Private Sub CustMainGrid_RowColChange(ByVal LastRow As String, ByVal LastCol As
Integer)
    ...
    ' Synchronize the Orders grid with the CustMain grid
    If orders.Recordset.RecordCount <> 0 Then
        If custmain.Recordset.RecordCount = 0 Then
            'custmain.Recordset.Refresh
        End If

        If (orders.Recordset.Fields("CustomerNum") <>
custmain.Recordset.Fields("CustomerNum")) Then
            ' Only synchronize if records exist in ORDERS for this customer
            Set OrdersTbl = CustDB.OpenTable("Orders")
            OrdersTbl.Index = "CustomerNum"
            OrdersTbl.Seek "=", custmain.Recordset.Fields("CustomerNum")
            If (OrdersTbl.NoMatch = False) Then
                buffer = "CustomerNum = " &
custmain.Recordset.Fields("CustomerNum")
                orders.Recordset.FindFirst buffer
            End If
        End If
    End If
End Sub
```

If there are a lot of customers in the CustMain grid and the user just wants to get to a specific customer quickly, the user can enter the customer number in the CustomerNumberField text box. When the user presses Enter or leaves the field, the Lost Focus event is triggered and the CustMain cursor is reset to the customer number the user typed.

Printing Statements for All Customers

The same report you use to print statements for one person is used to print statements for everyone, but the setup is a little different. You create a snapshot containing customers that have a non-zero balance (there's no point in printing a statement with nothing in it). The billing table is then populated with one record for each of the customers in the snapshot, as shown in Listing 35.20.

Listing 35.20. Printing the account statement.

```
Private Sub Command2_Click()
    ...
    ' Retrieve all records from CUSTMAIN where the current balance is greater
    ' than 0.
    Set RecSet = CustDB.CreateSnapshot("Select * From CUSTMAIN Where
Current_Balance > 0.0;")
    ...
    RecSet.MoveFirst
    While (RecSet.EOF = False)
        Screen.MousePointer = 11
```

```
         ' Remove any records existing in BILLING
         CustDB.Execute ("Delete * From BILLING")

         BillingTbl.AddNew
         BillingTbl.Fields("CustomerNumber") = RecSet.Fields("CustomerNum")
         BillingTbl.Fields("CompanyName") = RecSet.Fields("Company")
          ...
         BillingTbl.Fields("StatementDate") = Date

         BillingTbl.UPDATE
         rptBilling.ReportFileName = "c:\vbproj\sams\statemnt.rpt"
         rptBilling.Destination = 0    ' 1=Output to Printer, 0=Screen
         rptBilling.Action = 1
         RecSet.MoveNext
         Screen.MousePointer = 0
    Wend
    Exit Sub

billerr:
    MsgBox (Err.Description)
End Sub
```

When the report is invoked, a new report will be printed for each person in the Billing table.

NOTE

For the benefit of this demonstration, the report is being sent to the screen. In a real setting, it would make more sense to print to the printer rather than make the user press the Print button for each report. To do this, change the line that sends the output to the screen

```
rptBilling.Destination = 0    ' 1=Output to Printer, 0=Screen
```

so that it sends output to the printer

```
rptBilling.Destination = 1    ' 1=Output to Printer, 0=Screen
```

Creating the Company Information Form

Both of the reports in the system get information about the customers from the CustMain table and information about the company from the CoInfo table. The Company Information form is about as simple as a data entry form gets in Visual Basic. The `Activate` procedure populates the CoInfo data control with the records (there is only one) from the CoInfo table:

```
Private Sub Form_Activate()
Dim SQLinq
     ' Reset to the default  pointer when returning to this form.
     MousePointer = 0

     SQLinq = "SELECT * FROM COINF;"
     datCoInfo.RecordSource = SQLinq
```

```
        datCoInfo.Refresh
        If datCoInfo.Recordset.RecordCount <> 0 Then
            Exit Sub
        Else
            datCoInfo.Recordset.AddNew
            datCoInfo.Recordset.UPDATE
        End If
End Sub
```

All of the fields on this screen are data-bound text boxes. As the user moves the cursor through the fields on the screen, the data control automatically updates the underlying table. To allow the user to press Enter to move the cursor from one field to another, a form-level Keypress event subroutine translates the Enter key to the Tab key (see Listing 35.21).

Listing 35.21. Trapping the Enter key to make it a tab at the form level.

```
Private Sub Form_KeyPress(KeyAscii As Integer)
    If KeyAscii = 13 Then
        SendKeys "{tab}"
        KeyAscii = 0
    End If
End Sub
```

> **NOTE**
>
> You must set the forms Keypreview property to True for this subroutine to work. Otherwise, this code won't be invoked.

The Company Information form is a simple form, but it gives the user the flexibility to change how the company looks on the reports in the system, which is a valuable feature.

Putting Your Signature on the Application with the About Box

The About box is standard in most Windows applications. It is often used to sign your work, make legal statements, and provide general information about the application.

An About box can be as simple as a small form with your name and the name of the application. If your client calls you with questions or problems, it can be helpful to include the version number and system information (like available memory or disk space) on this screen, too.

Creating the Main Module

There is a lot less code in a Visual Basic application than there is in other languages, but you will still need some plain old-fashioned code. The MAIN.BAS module is where you set global variables and enter general subroutines and functions (see Listing 35.22). You should try to minimize your use of global variables because they take up memory and resources. But if you find that you are passing the same variable around, consider making that variable global.

Listing 35.22. Global declarations.

```
' Allow the user to set the database location
Global Database_name
Global CustDB As DATABASE

' Snapshot for Custmain table
Global CustmainSnapshot As Snapshot
Global CustmainDynaset As Dynaset

' Customer number is the key to the database
Global Customer_number

' Customer balance
Global CurrentBalance As Double
```

The subroutines in the MAIN.BAS are general functions that can be called by subroutines in one or more forms.

The `CalculateCurrentBalance()` is a subroutine that is called from the Customer Account form and the General Accounting form. It is the single place that the customer balance is calculated and the only routine that changes the `CurrentBalance` global variable. It is also the only routine that changes the Current_Balance field in the CustMain table. All this is accomplished with just a few lines of code and some SQL. A single SQL statement accesses the Orders table in the database, adds up the charges and the credits for the current customer, and puts all the information into a snapshot (see Listing 35.23).

Listing 35.23. The `CalculateCurrentBalance` subroutine.

```
Public Sub CalculateCurrentBalance()
    Dim RecSet As Snapshot
    Dim buffer As String
    Dim CustOrdTbl As TABLE
    Dim charge
    Dim credit
    Dim Tbl As TABLE

    ' Get all of the customers orders and subtract
    ' the credits from the charges.
    Set CustOrdTbl = CustDB.OpenTable("Orders")
    buffer = "Select Sum(Charge),Sum(Credit) From Orders Where CustomerNum = " &
Str(Customer_number) & ";"

    Set RecSet = CustDB.CreateSnapshot(buffer)
```

continues

Listing 35.23. continued

```
    ' If there is no value, then the value is considered zero.
    If (IsNull(RecSet.Fields(0))) = True Then
        charge = 0
    Else
        charge = RecSet.Fields(0)
    End If
    If (IsNull(RecSet.Fields(1))) = True Then
        credit = 0
    Else
        credit = RecSet.Fields(1)
    End If
    ' Set the gloabal variable
    CurrentBalance = charge - credit

    ' close the order table
    CustOrdTbl.Close

    ' Now update the main customer table.
    Set Tbl = CustDB.OpenTable("CustMain")
    Tbl.Index = "PrimaryKey"
    Tbl.Seek "=", Customer_number
    If (Tbl.NoMatch = False) Then
        Tbl.Edit
        Tbl.Fields("Current_Balance") = CurrentBalance
        Tbl.UPDATE
    End If
    Tbl.Close
End Sub
```

Running and Testing the Application

Most developers tend to run the application as pieces get developed. By the time all the forms and reports are completed and the database looks like it is getting updated properly, the application is probably fairly stable. A quick last test is to create an executable file. Visual Basic programs run differently as executable files than they do when they are interpreted in the development environment. The process of creating an executable file demonstrates some errors that do not occur in the interpreted world. To create an executable version of your application, select the MAKE.EXE file item from the File option on the menu bar.

> **TIP**
>
> The following are some tips on debugging and testing:
>
> Turn off error handling when debugging a procedure (On Error Goto 0) so that Visual Basic can tell you what it thinks the problem is.

Set a breakpoint several lines before the line of code that is causing the error, and add a watch for what is causing the problem. Anything you write in Visual Basic can be watched, even database field values in a recordset.

If you suspect a corrupt database is the cause of your problem, use the Repair Database option from the Data Manager's File menu. Sometimes the Compact Database option can help, too.

Save early; save often. Always back up what you have before trying to fix a bug. There is nothing quite as demoralizing as working on a problem only to find you've made things worse and can't even get back to what was bad in the first place. At the very least, copy all of your .FRM files to a safe place. If you need to bring back an old version of a form, you can copy it back.

Refer to Chapter 13 for a more thorough discussion about debugging techniques.

All source and project files for the 16-bit version of this application are on the CD-ROM included with this book. They are intended for learning purposes only. The sample project for this chapter was developed using the 16-bit Visual Basic programming environment under Windows 3.1.

Summary

In this chapter, you learned what questions to ask when developing an application for the user. You learned how to design a database and develop a functional prototype. You also learned how to code and test an application. Finally, you discovered the best way to test and run an application.

Optimum Selection Database System

36

by Frank Font

The program discussed in this chapter is included on the CD-ROM as the Best Team Selector. Figure 36.1 shows the Best Team Selector program main screen. In a small and hopefully interesting way, it demonstrates some of the power that Visual Basic 4.0 brings the programmer. As many developers have discovered, there is always a way to make Visual Basic do what you want.

FIGURE 36.1.

Main screen of the Best Team Selector program.

This chapter will dissect this moderately complex database application to study the use of several VB4 programming techniques and data access methods. In particular, we will take a close look at how this program implements some of the following:

- Splash Screen
- A Windows 95 Tab Interface
- Runtime Data Control Manipulation
- Synchronized DBList Controls
- Text and Picture Controls
- Form Management
- Pointer Simulation
- Branch and Bound Algorithm

But before we get into those details, let's spend a little time looking at what this program does and doesn't do.

The Concept

As implied by its name, Best Team Selector (BTS) analyzes a database of candidates and reports a combination that makes a best team to staff a project. Candidates are described by the skills they possess. Projects are described by the skills needed to tackle them. This program could be used to find a best team to work on a technology project, as illustrated by the sample database supplied with the program, or a best fantasy baseball team, football team, you name it. For instance, you could describe the skills your favorite baseball players possess, describe the skills a baseball team needs by position, press the Select Best Team button, and presto: You have an awesome fantasy baseball team. The gist is this: If team members can be described by the skills they possess, and the things the teams do can be described by the skills needed to do them, you can use this program to pick a team for you.

> **NOTE**
>
> If you have not done so already, now is a good time to copy the program from the CD-ROM into a directory that you can edit. For example, you may wish to create a directory on your C drive called BTS and copy all the program files to it. Once off the CD-ROM, you can load the project into VB by opening the MAKETEAM.VBP project file. To see the program run from the VB4 environment, select Start With Full Compile from the Run menu or press Ctrl+F5. When the program starts, it automatically loads the sample database.

In the sample database *Frank's Virtual Workshop*, many of the skills are technology-oriented, such as VB Programming. Each skill a candidate has is rated on a scale from 1 to 10 with 10 being the best, and 1 being, well, really bad. To see the skills of our hypothetical candidates, select the Candidates tab and then the Detail subtab. You can view each candidate in the database by pressing the left and right arrows of the data control called Candidate Scroll.

The candidate skills come from a master list of skills available through the Skills tab. Press the Skills tab to switch into that tab page. This is where you define any skill you think might matter. Skills from the master list are assigned to candidates back on the Candidates tab page. The skills themselves have no rating, only the ability of a candidate to apply a skill is rated.

Job titles are described on the Titles tab screen. A *title* is just a group of skills lumped together and given a name. The sample database, Frank's Virtual Workshop, defines a *software tester* as someone who has some skill in *English Writing and Regression Testing*.

Projects are just tasks that require people with certain skill sets. In BTS, those skill sets are identified by job title. In the sample database, the Superstore Billing System project requires two Programmer/Analysts, one Computer Graphic Artist, and one Software Tester.

Pressing the Select Best Team button on the Teams tab screen for the sample Superstore Billing System project comes back with the following list:

```
Title                          Name
Computer Graphic Artist        Mellissa Armona
Programmer/Analyst             Greg Algol
Programmer/Analyst             John Derio
Software Tester                Todd Chelder
```

Although there are other teams in this database that may be just as good, there is no better team. A program that finds all best teams could be a lot slower to execute than this one, but could be built from the code in this Best Team Selector. The programming involved to do that is beyond the scope of this presentation.

How to Use the Program

To begin a new analysis, select New from the file menu. This gives you a blank database. Alternatively, select an existing database and modify it to your needs. For example, you could start with the sample database and alter the candidates to reflect your scenario if you want to start with the skills already defined there.

If your database does not already have the relevant skills for your projects, start by adding them. Once you have defined most of the skills, figure out the types of jobs members of your team would perform and give each type a name. Each job type is named and defined in the Titles section of the program. Titles are defined by the skills attributed to them.

At this point you may either enter your candidate information or define your projects. Candidates are described by the information on the Detail subscreen of the Candidate tab page. Skills are attributed to each candidate from the list of skills entered earlier into the database. Each skill is assigned with a rating, where 10 is the best, and 1 is the worst. Projects are defined by the titles that are needed to work on them.

Once your database is populated with Candidates and Projects, you are ready to find optimal teams. Do this by selecting the Team tab page and then identifying the project of interest from the combo box (see Figure 36.2).

Pressing the Select Best Team button brings up the Settings form that lets you specify whether or not you only want *exact* skill matches to be considered. This means that if exact skill matches are required, a candidate that is missing *any* skill defined for a title will *not* be considered for that title. This may cause a result where no team can be picked because none of the available candidates can do a particular job by that strict requirement. If exact matches are not required, all candidates are considered for all jobs. However, for every skill a candidate does not have, a huge disadvantage is attributed to that candidate. The result is that better fitting candidates are more readily considered for the jobs that they fit well, but all jobs will be filled as long as breathing bodies are available.

FIGURE 36.2.

The starting of the selection process.

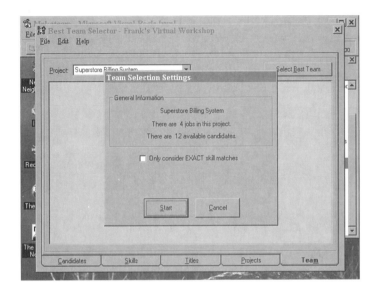

Because the BTS program only reports one best team, you can fiddle around a bit with the scenarios by making some employees unavailable for consideration. This is easily done by toggling the Available checkbox for the candidate on the Detail subtab screen of the Candidate tab page.

Team selections are overwritten every time a new team is selected. When a team is selected, a cost is displayed. This cost value can be used for comparison between teams of the same project. No printing capabilities have been built into this sample program.

> **NOTE**
>
> This sample program has not been tested rigorously enough to ensure faultless operation. You should restrict its use to entertainment purposes only.

Pointing to User-Defined Data Structures

Unlike some other languages, such as C/C++ and Pascal, Visual Basic does not support a pointer datatype that you can use for general referencing purposes in your programs.

In the loosest sense, the general concept of a pointer datatype is that it does not contain any data directly that is of particular use to a program, but rather that it points to something that might be of interest. For example, an integer datatype holds a number that a program can use to store a value of some importance. Conceptually, a pointer might be used to point to that integer. If the program accessed the pointer, it would really just be accessing the value of the integer it is pointing to.

Best Team Selector simulates the functionality of a pointer datatype to pass the user-defined type `memjrec_t` to and from procedure and functions. Just as a real pointer would tell the program where to find a structure, the index to an array of user defined types does the same. The reason for doing this is that BTS has to allocate and deallocate `memjrec_t` nodes as it calculates possible candidate combinations.

The MEM.BAS file (module frmMEM) contains all the procedures used to implement this simulation. VB programmers that take a close look at that module will notice that the allocation of memory is simulated by the simplest means—a sequential search of the `memPool()` array. This is okay for small memory sizes, but very inefficient for larger pools. If you want to boost the performance of BTS significantly, this is a good place to spend some time.

The Heap

A *heap* in computer science terms is a type of memory structure that keeps its contents sorted. The BTS program does not really implement a heap, as a close look at the code in HEAP.BAS shows, but it does present the interface routines that could wrap a real heap in VB.

Heaps are usually implemented as linked structures, although they can be implemented in arrays. Simulating linked structures is facilitated by the routines in MEM.BAS.

If you really want to wring performance out of the BTS program, this is also a section that will give a lot of return on time invested. There are many books that explain heap structures. A good university bookstore should have several data structure books that describe heap implementations.

Looking at the Branch and Bound Algorithm

There are several ways to solve optimization problems like the ones that BTS is built for. A general type of algorithm that could do it is known as *back tracking*. In this method, a program systematically constructs combinations until it has constructed every possible one. At that point, the program knows from brute force which combination was the best. That's great only if you have very few members to experimentally combine.

To get an idea how analyzing all combinations can quickly become an intractable problem, look at the numbers in the following table.

Number of Candidates	Size of a Team	Total Combinations
1	1	1
2	1	2
4	2	4
8	2	28
8	4	70
16	2	120
16	4	1,820
16	8	12,870
32	2	496
32	4	35,960
32	8	10,518,300
32	16	601,080,390
64	32	approx. 18×10^{18}

This table is only meant to give an idea of how bulky the problem can become. In reality, calculating the number of possible team member combinations is more complicated. Because the BTS program allows a candidate to qualify for more than one type of position, the total number of combinations can actually be substantially more than indicated in the table. In fact, the actual number of team solutions can be more like a permutation calculation than a combination calculation. To illustrate what this can mean, the permutations of 64 candidates where there are 32 on a team is approximately 48×10^{51}. (That's 48 followed by 51 zeros! Translation: Man that's a big number.)

The Branch and Bound algorithm reduces the number of combinations it builds by taking smart guesses at which might prove fruitful, and which might not. A well-designed Branch and Bound implementation will not waste much time on bad combinations. Because fewer combinations are sampled, the Branch and Bound can be faster than the Backtracking alternative. In some cases, this can mean the difference between an answer in a million years and an answer within the hour.

A very simplified Branch and Bound algorithm looks like this:

1. Initialize everything.
2. If we have found a best combination, print the result and end.
3. Form another combination by adding a candidate to an existing partial team that has potential to be the best.
4. If step 3 could find no more potential team members, fail. Otherwise, go to step 2.

The BB() function in the MINIMIZE.BAS file implements those steps. Step 1 is carried out by function AnswerNode(). Step 3 is carried out by function Expand(). Let's get an overview of how these functions do their jobs.

The AnswerNode() function determines if the current candidate was the last possible addition to a team by comparing its job count number to the total number of jobs required on the team. Because the program keeps track of team additions by incrementing a job count, when these figures match, the team is filled. The Branch and Bound algorithm only builds teams that can be the best, so the fact that we have a complete team implies we have a best team.

The Expand() function is more difficult to understand. The loosest explanation is that it creates a node representing the addition of another team member for each possible type of team member addition at that particular point in time. Of special significance, and where the power of the Branch and Bound algorithm springs, is that each new node is assigned an estimated cost. The estimated cost of each node determines whether the algorithm will pursue combinations derived from that node.

Estimating the cost can be a very complex topic in its own right and there are many ways to do it. The BTS program approaches the task by figuring a matrix of each candidate vs. each job. This matrix contains the cost of the candidate doing every job. Because the engine of this program is designed to minimize the total cost of a team and the inputs specify 10 as better than 9 and so forth, the higher numbers are translated to lower numbers up front by the CalcCost() function. The job cost estimates are then computed by taking the minimum value of each row, where each row of the matrix represents a particular job on the team. The InitMinsTable() carries out this process.

The logic of applying the minimum values to predict the total cost is this: If we add up all the minimums from a filled job down to the last job, we have an estimate that *can be no worse* than any real result. Since the real cost is never less than this sum-based estimate, a large minimum sum indicates a poor combination choice.

Nodes are kept in memory, ready for plucking by lowest cost. Using a heap for this is a good solution because we can efficiently find the lowest cost node when we need it. We pluck the lowest cost node to figure new team possibilities and then repeat the process. By this means we end up constructing a team that can be no worse than any other.

This trek only superficially explains the Branch and Bound concept. For a detailed explanation and discussions of related concepts that are touched on here, you should consider purchasing a good fundamental algorithms book. Most university and college bookstores carry them.

Managing Your Forms

There are two general form management approaches. A popular choice is the Multiple Document Interface, MDI method, where the program forms are contained within a parent form. Alternatively, a program can go the Single Document Interface, SDI, route as this one does.

An SDI interface, more than an MDI, requires the programmer to decide the following basic construction/flow items up front:

1. Will there be a main form?
2. Will several forms be available at once?

In BTS, the answer to the first question is yes, and the answer to the second is no. This is a relatively easy way to implement a VB program. BTS implements the results to preceding questions 1 and 2 by following these rules:

1. The main form is never unloaded or hidden during normal operation.
2. All sub-forms are displayed in Modal fashion so that nothing can be done on other forms while the sub-form is presented for input.

As illustrated by the single line of the `HelpAbout_Click()` function in the `frmMain` module:

```
frmAbout.Show 1
```

The 1 after the method keyword Show forces VB to wait until that form is no longer visible before allowing input to other forms. In other words, `frmAbout` is a modal form. All the sub-forms of this application are loaded in the same way (see Figure 36.3).

FIGURE 36.3.

The ABOUT form selected from the HELP menu.

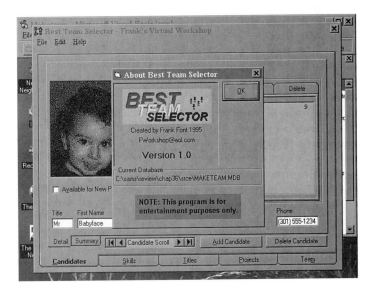

Make a Splash

As with most programs heavy on database access and loaded with custom controls, BTS can take a little while to load. Few things confuse some users more than starting a program and then seeing nothing happen for several seconds or more. In the old days, that was enough to make some people reboot.

The most common way to entertain the user while their program loads is to paint a Splash screen first and then start loading and setting up whatever program modules are to do business with the user. Making this type of screen and displaying it first is fun and easy in VB4. Here's how it's done in BTS:

1. Select Options from the Tools menu of the VB form designer and click on the Project tab. Set Startup Form to Sub Main.

2. Create a module in your project, call it anything you want, and create a subroutine called MAIN in it. The one in BTS is located in the MAIN.BAS module and contains only the following line:

   ```
   frmSplash.show
   ```

   This loads the BTS splash screen, in this case called `frmSplash` (see Figure 36.4).

FIGURE 36.4.

The SPLASH screen at design time.

3. Now comes the neat trick: VB is funny about painting when it is busy executing our code so we force it to paint the splash screen before it begins the heavy work of loading and configuring our program. The code in the BTS splash screen that does this is as follows:

   ```
   Private Sub Form_Initialize()
       'Center the form on the screen.
   ```

```
            Left = (Screen.width - Width) / 2
            TOP = (Screen.Height - Height) / 2

            'Set the hourglass pointer.
            MousePointer = 11

            'Display version information on label control.
            lblVersion.Caption = "Version"  + gProgramVersion
    End Sub

    Private Sub Form_Activate()
            'Force Windows to display our screen before moving on.
            frmSplash.Refresh

            'Start the main program loading and configuring from this point on.
            Load frmMain
            frmMain.show
    End Sub
```

In the BTS case, frmMain is the only thing that needs to load and show. If there were other modules that might be displayed frequently during program operation, we would load them here, also.

4. Unload the splash screen from the last module of the program that you load. Because BTS only has one module to load at start time, we unload the splash screen and restore the mouse pointer with the following two lines in the Form_Activate procedure of the frmMain form:

```
            Unload frmSplash
            MousePointer = 0
```

That's all there is to it. Just keep in mind that the splash screen should not have too many controls or be very large because this might slow down its load time. It would be silly to need a splash screen for your splash screen.

Why Use Tabs

Because it's easy. Easy to implement, and —okay, some people may not agree with this—easy to use. Each tabbed screen in this program could have been implemented as a separate form but that would have required code to manage those forms. Instead, each screen is just laid onto a pane of an SSTab control. The tab control does the display management for you.

Some users love tabs, some hate tabs. Some folks are not sure if they love or hate them. One thing is for sure however, we will see more tabs because Windows 95 uses them throughout its utilities. My guess is that as people become more familiar with using this interface, they will move on to other areas to complain about. Users always have to complain.

To see how the main tab control is configured in this program, press the right mouse button over the Candidates tab while in design mode and pick properties from the popup menu that appears. This displays the Sheridan Tabbed Dialog Control Properties interface, which is not the same one you get when you press F4 on a selected SSTab but is more intuitive to work with. You see here that each tab screen has a TabCaption, which is the text you see at the bottom of the BTS program. The number of tabs supported by the control is simply set by the Tab Count property. If you view the properties of the tab control nested into the Candidates tab screen with the Detail and Summary tab labels, you will notice that its Style is set to the Windows 95 Property Page so that the tab labels bunch over to the left. The main tab control spreads its tab labels across the entire width of the screen because there is room to do it. Likewise, the tabs in the Skills of Candidate area of this same screen cover the width of the tab page section. The full spread style is Microsoft Office Tabbed Dialog, named after the fact that this style is employed in the Microsoft office software that began shipping back in 1994.

When building your programs, treat each tab screen as a form in the sense that it contains the controls you wish to use. Drop 'em, size 'em, configure 'em, and move onto the next tab screen. It's that simple.

At runtime, you can tell what tab the user is on by reading the TAG property of your Tab control. The tab values will match those visible in the property display at design time. The SSTab control on the Candidate Detail tab page has the following code on the Click event:

```
Private Sub tabCandidateSkill_Click(PreviousTab As Integer)
  Dim thekey
  thekey = lstCandidateSkill.BoundText

  Select Case tabCandidateSkill.Tab
  Case 0
    'List
    If Len(CStr(txtCandidateKey)) > 0 Then
      If txtCandidateKey > -1 Then 'Flag that no candidate is selected.
        'We have a candidate so list his/her skills.
        On Error Resume Next
        dbaCandidateSkill.RecordSource = "Select * From qryCandidateSkillRating
Where CandidateKey=" + txtCandidateKey
        dbaCandidateSkill.Recordset.Requery
        dbaCandidateSkill.UpdateControls
        lstCandidateSkill.Refresh      'Due to Beta6 trouble.
        dbaCandidateSkill.Refresh      'Due to Beta6 trouble.
      End If
    End If
  Case 1  'Add
    'Add
    cboAddSkill = ""
    txtAddRating = gDefaultRating
  Case 2  'Edit
    'Get the current record.
    If IsNull(thekey) Or Len(Trim$(thekey)) < 1 Then
      MsgBox "No candidate skill is selected.", 64, gProgramTitle
      tabCandidateSkill.Tab = 0
    Else
      dbaCandidateSkill.Recordset.FindFirst "CandidateSkillsKey=" + Str$(thekey)
      txtEditSkill = dbaCandidateSkill.Recordset![Name]
      txtEditRating = dbaCandidateSkill.Recordset![Rating]
    End If
  Case 3
    'Delete
    If IsNull(thekey) Or Len(Trim$(thekey)) < 1 Then
      MsgBox "No candidate skill is selected.", 64, gProgramTitle
      tabCandidateSkill.Tab = 0
```

```
        Else
            dbaCandidateSkill.Recordset.FindFirst "CandidateSkillsKey=" + Str$(thekey)
        End If
    End Select
End Sub
```

When the Click event is triggered, the Tab value is already set to the new page. Although the preceding code example does not need this, you can tell where the user was before by reading the value of the PreviousTab parameter. This is a feature not readily available when using separate forms instead of a tab interface.

The Database

Figure 36.5 shows the tables and relationships of the database used by the BTS program. The relationships among tables are represented by the lines connecting the matching fields. A relationship of one-to-many is represented by a number 1 on the one side and an infinity symbol on the many side.

FIGURE 36.5.

MAKETEAM database relationship diagram.

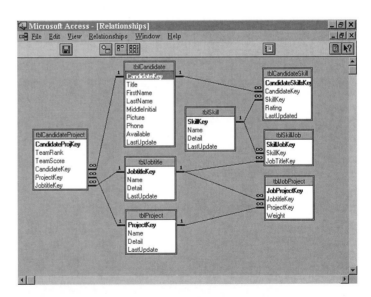

TIP

Although it is possible to create a database design using VB4 and its tools, other tools are available that make that job easier. This database was created using Access 2.0.

The candidate records are in their own table. Likewise, there is a table for skills and a table for projects. Connecting these tables are linking tables that relate the contents of the tables to each other. For example, tblCandidateSkill is a table that links skills from tblSkill to candidates from tblCandidate. Figures 36.6 through 36.8 show the structure detail of these particular tables.

FIGURE 36.6.

Detail of Candidates table.

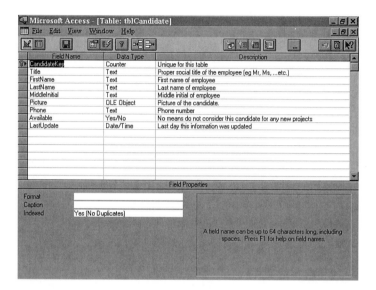

FIGURE 36.7.

Detail of Skills table.

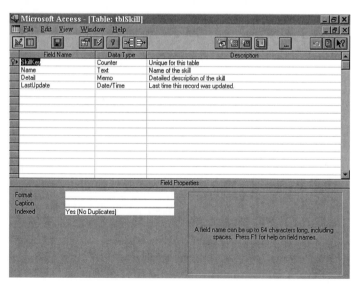

FIGURE 36.8.

Detail of linking table for candidates and their skills.

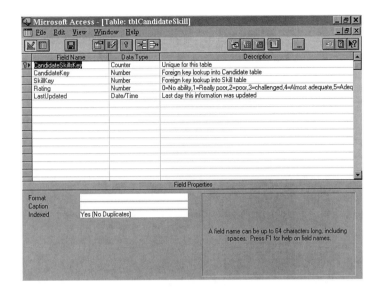

Although the BTS program uses an Access 2.0 database structure, there is no reason this database could not be implemented in any number of other schemes. However, Access has an advantage within VB that it is handled directly by the Jet engine and thus runs faster than *some* others.

Getting to the Data

Although some database access is done in BTS through dynamically declared data objects, most of the access is handled through VB Data controls. These controls have the advantage of convenience.

At design time, the DatabaseName property of every Data control was left blank. Otherwise, the program will try to load a database at whatever directory was used during development. Instead of hardcoding a directory, the program sets the datasource of all the main Data controls to the application directory as follows:

```
'--------------------------------------------------------
'Open the selected database.  Returns FALSE if error.
'--------------------------------------------------------
Public Function SetDatabase(AP As String) As Boolean

  On Error GoTo SetDatabase_SomethingBad

  'Open main database.
  gMainDBName = AP
  Set gMainDB = Workspaces(0).OpenDatabase(gMainDBName)

  'Adjust the data controls to proper path.
  dbaCandidate.DatabaseName = gMainDBName
```

```
    dbaCandidateSkill.DatabaseName = gMainDBName
    dbaSkills.DatabaseName = gMainDBName
    dbaJobProject.DatabaseName = gMainDBName
    dbaProject.DatabaseName = gMainDBName
    dbaJobtitle.DatabaseName = gMainDBName
    dbaCandidateProject.DatabaseName = gMainDBName
    dbaSkillJob.DatabaseName = gMainDBName

    'Refresh all the controls.
    dbaCandidate.Refresh
    dbaCandidateSkill.Refresh
    dbaSkills.Refresh
    dbaJobProject.Refresh
    dbaProject.Refresh
    dbaJobtitle.Refresh
    dbaCandidateProject.Refresh
    dbaSkillJob.Refresh

    SetDatabase = True   'Successful.
    Exit Function

SetDatabase_SomethingBad:
    SetDatabase = False 'Unsuccessful.

End Function
```

The SetDatabase function is called both at startup with the default database name of MAKETEAM passed as the parameter. It also runs when the user elects to open a new database. When it runs, this function sets a global dynamic data access object called gMainDB to the selected database to simplify ad-hoc data access throughout the program. In particular, the GENSQL.BAS module contains three general purpose data access routines that are usually called with gMainDB as a parameter. These routines are as follows:

```
'------------------------------------------------------------------
'Returns number of records in set defined by the "From" and "Where".
'------------------------------------------------------------------
Function SQLResultCount(MyDB As DATABASE, From$, Where$) As Long
  Dim MyData As Recordset, SQL$
  SQL$ = "Select count(*) as [total] from " + From$ + _
        IIf(Len(Trim$(Where$)) > 0, " where " + Where$, "")
  Set MyData = MyDB.OpenRecordset(SQL$, dbOpenDynaset)
  If MyData.RecordCount = 0 Then
    SQLResultCount = 0
  Else
    MyData.MoveLast
    SQLResultCount = MyData![total]
  End If
End Function


'------------------------------------------------------------------
'Returns value of field named in "aField$" of "MyDB" after applying the
'"From" and "Where" portions of the SQL statement.
'This only returns the value in last record.  If the record is not
'found, the empty string is returned.
'------------------------------------------------------------------
Function SQLResultStr(MyDB As DATABASE, aField$, From$, Where$) As String
  Dim MyData As Recordset, SQL$
```

```
    SQL$ = "Select " + aField + " as [result] from " + From$ + _
        IIf(Len(Trim$(Where$)) > 0, " where " + Where$, "")
    Set MyData = MyDB.OpenRecordset(SQL$, dbOpenDynaset)
    If MyData.RecordCount = 0 Then
      SQLResultStr = ""       'Send empty string.
    Else
      MyData.MoveLast
      SQLResultStr = MyData![result]
    End If
End Function

'------------------------------------------------------------------
'Returns sum of values in "SumField" of "MyDB" after applying the
'"From" and "Where" portions of the SQL statement.
'------------------------------------------------------------------
Function SQLResultSum(MyDB As DATABASE, SumField As String, From$, Where$) As Long
    Dim MyData As Recordset, SQL$
    SQL$ = "Select sum(" + SumField + ") as [total] from " + From$ + _
        IIf(Len(Trim$(Where$)) > 0, " where " + Where$, "")
    Set MyData = MyDB.OpenRecordset(SQL$, dbOpenDynaset)
    If MyData.RecordCount = 0 Then
      SQLResultSum = 0       'Send empty string.
    Else
      MyData.MoveLast
      SQLResultSum = MyData![total]
    End If
End Function
```

These general purpose functions require just a few parameters to carry out some otherwise tediously coded syntax queries. The MINIMIZE.BAS module uses them extensively for data processing. In the case of BTS, the MyDB parameter is always set to the gMainDB data access object.

Synchronizing DBList Controls

The BTS program has several instances of lists that control other lists. For example, the Titles tab page has a list of existing titles on the left and a list of skills for the selected title at the right. The synchronization is done by using a Text box as follows:

- Assign the Datasource of the text box to the same as the datasource of the master DBList.

- Assign the Datafield of the text box to be the unique key for the table.

- On the change event of the text box, call procedures that alter the Rowsource property of the slave DBList. In the case of the BTS program, this alteration is usually the insertion of a SQL query that filters all list elements to those that match the key value in the text box.

- Issue a Refresh to the slave DBList.

One issue to watch out for when using this synchronization method is that VB will trigger the Change event of the text box as it loads the form. To keep your code from trying to synchronize a list with an invalid key value, you may want to place a flag value, such as -1, into the text box at design time. Then at runtime, you can check for this value and exit your processing during the form load.

Although most of the DBLists could have been implemented with data-aware Grid controls, none were available at the time this program was written. However, if you have access to DBGrid controls you may want to use them in your projects instead of DBList. The DBGrid control dynamics are very similar to those of the DBList, but they display multiple columns with greater ease.

Displaying Database Pictures

Visual Basic 4.0 can directly bind the Image and Picturebox controls to an OLE type BLOB field for graphic display and entry. The advantage of using the Image control is that it uses fewer system resources and displays faster than the picture control. The disadvantage is that it does not crop the input image. To keep odd-size images from spilling into the form space, BTS uses the Picturebox control.

Picture setting in BTS is done through the Copy/Paste method. To add a picture to a Candidate record in BTS, follow these steps:

1. Load your picture into the Paint program and copy it by selecting Copy from the Edit menu.

2. Select the BTS picture box by clicking on it with the mouse pointer.

3. Select the Paste option from the BTS Edit menu.

The code that implements this functionality also handles the cut/copy/paste functionality for all the other controls in the BTS program. The subroutines from BTS are attached to the menu and are as follows:

```
Private Sub editCut_Click()
  ' First do the same as a copy.
  editCopy_Click
  ' Now clear contents of active control.
  If TypeOf Screen.ActiveControl Is TextBox Then
    Screen.ActiveControl.SelText = ""
  ElseIf TypeOf Screen.ActiveControl Is ComboBox Then
    Screen.ActiveControl.TEXT = ""
  ElseIf TypeOf Screen.ActiveControl Is PictureBox Then
    Screen.ActiveControl.picture = LoadPicture()
  ElseIf TypeOf Screen.ActiveControl Is ListBox Then
    Screen.ActiveControl.RemoveItem Screen.ActiveControl.ListIndex
  Else
    ' No action makes sense for the other controls.
  End If
End Sub

Private Sub editCopy_Click()
  Clipboard.Clear
```

```
   If TypeOf Screen.ActiveControl Is TextBox Then
      Clipboard.SetText Screen.ActiveControl.SelText
   ElseIf TypeOf Screen.ActiveControl Is ComboBox Then
      Clipboard.SetText Screen.ActiveControl.TEXT
   ElseIf TypeOf Screen.ActiveControl Is PictureBox Then
      Clipboard.SetData Screen.ActiveControl.picture
   ElseIf TypeOf Screen.ActiveControl Is ListBox Then
      Clipboard.SetText Screen.ActiveControl.TEXT
   Else
      ' No action makes sense for the other controls.
   End If
End Sub


Private Sub editPaste_Click()
   If TypeOf Screen.ActiveControl Is TextBox Then
      Screen.ActiveControl.SelText = Clipboard.GetText()
   ElseIf TypeOf Screen.ActiveControl Is ComboBox Then
      Screen.ActiveControl.TEXT = Clipboard.GetText()
   ElseIf TypeOf Screen.ActiveControl Is PictureBox Then
      Screen.ActiveControl.picture = Clipboard.GetData()
   ElseIf TypeOf Screen.ActiveControl Is ListBox Then
      Screen.ActiveControl.AddItem Clipboard.GetText()
   Else
      ' No action makes sense for the other controls.
   End If
End Sub
```

The naming convention for menus in the BTS program is to prefix the menu options with the menu name. So, editCopy_Click is the Click event handler for the Copy function of the Edit menu.

Summary

The BTS program applies some complex coding concepts to identify an optimal project team. Some explanation of the Branch and Bound algorithm and other computer science esoterica are explored here as they apply to Visual Basic 4.0, although in brief form.

The chapter also covers more bread and butter Visual Basic 4.0 development items implemented in BTS, such as employing a splash screen and accessing a database through code and data controls. These and other topics were discussed with examples.

Creating Your Own Screen Savers

37

by Bill Hatfield

Screen savers have taken on a life of their own in the computer industry. These whimsical distractions originally were created for a serious purpose: to stop phosphor burn-in of text or graphics on a monitor. Have you ever seen a monitor on a computer or (very often) an ATM that looks as though you can see a shadow of its title screen or main menu, even when something else is being displayed? This shadow is the result of displaying that same screen for hours on end and permanently burning its image into the monitor.

Obviously, this is not a good thing. So someone, somewhere, decided to blank the screen after a while to keep this from happening. But this made the users think the computer had shut itself off. So the developer created an animated display to make it clear that the computer was, in fact, still alive. And this was the beginning of something big.

Although today, modern color monitors are not really at risk of anything like phosphor burn-in, screen-savers have become a big business. Developers always seem to have a surplus of creativity and are just looking for nooks and crannies where they can express it. And they have exploited this blank computer screen to the hilt for all sorts of complex geometric designs, 3D rendering, animations, video clips, and cartoons. And users have bought them up. They enjoy watching as much as developers enjoy creating. In the computer industry, screen savers have come to express the triumph of creativity over mundane productivity.

Making Your Own Screen Saver

Isn't it difficult to create your own screen saver? Don't you have to muck about with difficult system coding to integrate with the Windows environment? Actually, no. Although there is some complexity when creating screen savers in C or C++, Visual Basic makes it very easy.

In this chapter, I will walk you through the process of creating a screen saver of your own. Once you have the basic structure down, your imagination is your only limit in creating exciting new screen savers of your own. Create them for yourself, your co-workers, or share them with the rest of the world for fun or for profit.

Laying the Foundation

As you may have noticed, Windows screen savers have the extension SCR, and they are placed in the Windows subdirectory. They are recognized and displayed as options in the Display Properties dialog box on the Screen Saver tab.

These SCR files are nothing mysterious. In fact, they are nothing more than EXE files that have been renamed! And Windows handles calling these disguised EXEs whenever they should be invoked. So you don't even have to worry about when the screen saver should start up. All of that is handled for you by Windows.

So what *do* you have to worry about? Well, to create a very simple screen saver, just two things:

- Displaying your screen saver graphics
- Recognizing valid interruptions and releasing control back to Windows

Taking the First Steps

Your first step is to start a new project that has one form and one module. In the module, create a procedure called `Main` that receives no arguments, and set it to be the first thing called on startup. You do this by choosing Tools | Options and then working in the Project tab of the Options dialog box, in the Startup Form drop-down list (see Figure 37.1).

FIGURE 37.1.

Setting the Main procedure to be the first thing called.

You want to execute a procedure first thing, because you want to do some checking before you go to the trouble of loading a form. The code for `Main` is shown in Listing 37.1.

Listing 37.1. The `Main` procedure.

```
Sub Main()

If App.PrevInstance Then End

If InStr(Command, "/s") > 0 Then
    CursorOff
    frmScreenSaver.Show
ElseIf InStr(Command, "/c") > 0 Then
    MsgBox "No setup necessary for this screen saver", _
        vbOKOnly + vbInformation, "Boxes Screen Saver"
End If
End Sub
```

First off, you want to check to see whether there is another instance of the program running. If there is, get out.

Otherwise, you call the `Command` function to find out whether any command-line arguments were passed when the screen saver was called. Why would Windows call the screen saver with command-line arguments? To let you know what it wants you to do. Windows might want you to simply display the screen saver. If this is the case, it sends you an /s. But when the user clicks the Settings button in the Display Properties dialog box (see Figure 37.2), Windows calls your screen saver with a /c. Because I want to focus on creating a simple screen saver to start, a message box explaining that there is no setup necessary is all you need for that case.

FIGURE 37.2.

After the user clicks the Settings button, the screen saver is called with the /c command-line argument.

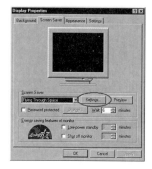

Hiding the Mouse Pointer

If Windows does request the actual screen saver (with /s in the command line), then you want to turn off the cursor (the mouse pointer) and display the screen saver. You don't want the ugly mouse pointer obscuring the user's view of your beautiful creation, do you? So you need to create a new procedure called CursorOff. There isn't a Visual Basic command that enables you to do this, so you will have to resort to the ShowCursor() Win32 API function. Put the following code in your module's Declarations section:

```
Declare Function ShowCursor Lib "user32" (ByVal bShow As Long) As Long
```

ShowCursor accepts one value. If the value is False (0), it hides the cursor, and if it is True (non-zero), it shows the cursor. Simple, yes? Well, not quite so simple.

When Windows first starts up, it creates a cursor-display counter and sets it to 0. The mouse pointer is displayed when the counter is 0 or greater. If ShowCursor(False) is called, the counter is decremented, putting it at –1. This causes the cursor to disappear, because any counter value below 0 hides the cursor. But then, suppose that another task in Windows makes a call to ShowCursor(False). The counter is decremented again to –2. The cursor was invisible before and remains invisible. Then that task finishes whatever it was doing and does a ShowCursor(True). This increments the display counter back up to –1. But because this is still less than zero, it still is not displayed. Finally, the first task that made the call to ShowCursor(False) finishes up and does a ShowCursor(True). The counter is incremented to 0, and finally the mouse pointer appears again. Make sense? Windows wants to be sure that all the tasks work well together. If task 1 turns off the cursor and task 2 turns it off and back on, task 1 will expect that it is still off until it turns it back on.

It works the same way in the other direction. Several calls to ShowCursor(True) cause the cursor-display counter to increment to higher and higher positive values. Only an equal number of ShowCursor(False) calls actually cause the cursor to disappear.

The catch is that you really, really want it to disappear, regardless of what the display counter is. But, at the same time, you don't want to disturb the counter for other applications. Listing 37.2 shows the CursorOff procedure that will do what you want.

Listing 37.2. The `CursorOff` procedure.

```
Public Sub CursorOff()
Dim CurrentCursorDepth As Integer

CurrentCursorDepth = ShowCursor(False)
giCursorDepth = CurrentCursorDepth + 1  'Restore original value
Do While CurrentCursorDepth > -1
    CurrentCursorDepth = ShowCursor(False)
Loop

End Sub
```

The first thing you do is call ShowCursor(False) and receive its return code into CurrentCursorDepth. ShowCursor() returns the value of the display counter after it is changed by the call, so you increment the value and put the result in giCursorDepth to return it to the original cursor-display value before you touched it. That way, you can restore it back to this original value later, when CursorOn is called. giCursorDepth is a global defined in the Declarations section of the module:

```
Global giCursorDepth As Integer
```

Next, you loop while the current cursor depth is greater than –1. In other words, regardless of where it is now, get it less than 0. If it already is less than zero, this top-tested loop does not execute.

While we're on this topic, let's look at the CursorOn procedure (see Listing 37.3).

Listing 37.3. The `CursorOn` procedure.

```
Public Sub CursorOn()
Dim CurrentCursorDepth As Integer

CurrentCursorDepth = ShowCursor(True)
Do While CurrentCursorDepth < giCursorDepth
    CurrentCursorDepth = ShowCursor(True)
Loop
End Sub
```

First, you increment the counter with the ShowCursor(True) and capture the new CurrentCursorDepth. Then the loop tests to see whether the display counter is back where it belongs. If it isn't, it does ShowCursor(True) statements until it is. So you turned the cursor off and back on again without disturbing the cursor-display counter.

Creating the Screen Saver Form

Look back at Listing 37.1. Before we jumped into our discussion on CursorOn and CursorOff, we were looking at the Main procedure. If Windows passes an /s command line argument, that's your cue to display the actual screen saver. After the cursor is turned off, the code displays frmScreenSaver.

I told you to start off this project by creating a module and a form. So far, we've been talking about the module. Now let's look at the form.

The first thing you will want to do is to name your form frmScreenSaver, because that is what you are showing in the Main procedure. You also will want to change some of the following properties.

Property	Value
BackColor	Black
BorderStyle	None
ControlBox	False
MaxButton	False
MinButton	False
ScaleMode	Pixel
WindowState	Maximized

Next, drop a timer on the form. Leave the default name Timer1, but change the interval to 1,000.

There is no Titlebar True/False property, but changing the BorderStyle to None and the ControlBox, MaxButton, and MinButton to False effectively gets rid of the title bar for you. So, once the window is maximized, it covers everything else on-screen and provides a large blank slate to do your magic.

Finally, you might want to create an icon for your form. If you associate it with the form's Icon property, you'll be able to choose it as the application's icon when you generate an EXE.

When you are done setting up your window, it should look like Figure 37.3.

FIGURE 37.3.

The frmScreenSaver form.

Setting Up the Timer Event (The Fun Part)

Just so there won't be any doubt, we have now arrived at the fun part. This is where you loosen the tie and let your creative juices flow. The Timer event gets executed once a second. You can make that much quicker, if you like, by adjusting the Interval property. The number there is in milliseconds, but you probably aren't going to get much code to execute in a millisecond, so be reasonable in how low you set this property.

Regardless of the interval value, you now have a place to write code that will happen every so often. What do you want to do? Just for the sake of example, I created a very simple graphics routine. My Timer event code is in Listing 37.4.

Listing 37.4. My `Timer` event.

```
Private Sub Timer1_Timer()
Dim X1, Y1, X2, Y2 As Integer

Randomize

X1 = Rnd * (ScaleWidth - 1) + 1
Y1 = Rnd * (ScaleHeight - 1) + 1
X2 = Rnd * (ScaleWidth - 1) + 1
Y2 = Rnd * (ScaleHeight - 1) + 1
ForeColor = RGB(Rnd * 255 + 1, Rnd * 255 + 1, Rnd * 255 + 1)
Line (X1, Y1)-(X2, Y2), , BF
End Sub
```

After declaring some variables and seeding the random number generator, you create a couple of random coordinates in your window's workspace and set the ForeColor property to a random color. Then, using the Line command's BF option, you draw a filled-in box with the upper-left and lower-right corners defined by the random coordinates. Nothing too amazing here but, like I said, we'll keep it basic this time around and once you get the hang of it, you can jazz it up all you want.

Waking Up

The Timer event continues to fire indefinitely unless we stop it somehow. And how are most screen savers stopped? By a mouse click or a keystroke. Listings 37.5 and 37.6 show you what should be in your MouseDown and KeyDown events.

Listing 37.5. The `MouseDown` event.

```
Private Sub Form_MouseDown(Button As Integer, Shift As Integer, _
   X As Single, Y As Single)
EndScreenSaver
End Sub
```

Listing 37.6. The `KeyDown` event.

```
Private Sub Form_KeyDown(KeyCode As Integer, Shift As Integer)
EndScreenSaver
End Sub
```

And what does `EndScreenSaver` look like? It's a procedure defined in the module that takes no parameters. See Listing 37.7.

Listing 37.7. The `EndScreenSaver` procedure.

```
Public Sub EndScreenSaver()
CursorOn
End
End Sub
```

And that's all there is to it. There's just one more thing. Normally, a screen saver goes away even if you just move the mouse. Shouldn't you put something in the `MouseMove` event? Yes, and that is in Listing 37.8.

Listing 37.8. The `MouseMove` event.

```
Private Sub Form_MouseMove(Button As Integer, Shift As Integer, _
   X As Single, Y As Single)
Static OldX As Integer
Static OldY As Integer

If (OldX > 0 And OldY > 0) And _        'If this isn't the first time and
   (Abs(X - OldX) > 3 Or Abs(Y - OldY) > 3) Then    'there is a big move
      EndScreenSaver
End If
OldX = X
OldY = Y
End Sub
```

You probably were expecting a routine as simple as the one for the `MouseDown` and `KeyDown` events. This one adds a bit of code to verify that the mouse has, in fact, moved more than a pixel or two. Why bother to do this? Several reasons.

First, and most intuitive, you don't necessarily want an accidental touch of the mouse to cause the screen saver to go away. Verifying that there has been a significant change since the last MouseMove event does this.

Second, for some reason, when a window first is opened, Windows triggers a MouseMove event on it. This is not normally a problem. But it would be here, of course. The screen saver would end as soon as it starts. Verifying that there has been an actual mouse position change before you kill the screen saver fixes the problem.

Finally, Windows does another weird thing (keeping a list?). If you set the wait time in the Display Properties dialog box on the Screen Saver tab to two minutes, for example, Windows waits for two minutes without interruption before executing your screen saver (see Figure 37.4). So far so good. But then, every two minutes after that time, Windows will trigger a MouseMove event on your screen saver. For no reason at all. But again, testing to be sure the mouse did move in the MouseMove event solves the problem.

FIGURE 37.4.

The wait time in the Display Properties dialog box, on the Screen Saver tab.

Generating the Finished Product

That's it! You now have a working product. If you try running it, you might be sad to see that it does nothing. That's because, you will recall, it is looking for a command-line argument: a /c to change its settings or an /s to display the screen saver. To test it, choose Tools | Options. The Options dialog box appears. From here, choose the Advanced tab. In the Command Line Arguments field, type **/s** (see Figure 37.5).

FIGURE 37.5.

Specifying a command-line argument for design-time execution.

This edit enables you to simulate passing a command-line argument when you run an application at design time. By using /s, you can view the actual screen saver. (Trying /c would show you only the little message box you created, saying that no setup is necessary for this screen saver.)

Now when you run the screen saver, you should see a black screen with lots of pretty (or not so pretty, as the case may be) boxes appearing about once a second before your eyes.

Now you are ready to create the final executable. Creating a screen saver executable is not that different from creating any other executable. First, save your work. (You were doing that all the way along, weren't you?) Then choose File | Make EXE File to display the Make EXE File dialog box (see Figure 37.6).

FIGURE 37.6.

The Make EXE File dialog box.

If you click the Options button, you see the EXE Options dialog box, as shown in Figure 37.7.

FIGURE 37.7.

The EXE Options dialog box.

Here, you can specify an icon (by choosing an icon already assigned to one of the forms), a version number, comments, company name, product name, and so on. Fill all this out as you like. There is one crucial thing you must do here, though. Set the application title to this:

```
SCRNSAVE: Boxes
```

This line lets Visual Basic know that this application is to be generated as a screen saver. Click OK in the EXE Options dialog box to return to the Make EXE File dialog box. The only thing left is to make sure that the file is generated with an SCR extension. Do this by explicitly entering the extension. When you are done, the file name edit control should contain this:

```
Boxes.SCR
```

That's it. Click OK, and your new screen saver is generated. After it finishes, copy the screen saver to the Windows directory and then right-click on your desktop. Choose Properties from the pop-up menu and then click the Screen Saver tab after the Display Properties dialog box appears. Pull down the Screen Saver drop-down list and scroll up to find Boxes. Choose it. Click Preview. You should see the Boxes screen saver at work.

Now set the wait time to one minute, click OK, and wait. Soon, boxes again fill your field of view. You've done it. Good work.

Adding a Configuration Dialog Box

Now you have a template for creating any screen saver you can imagine. What will you do first? A good place to start would be to add a Configuration dialog box that is displayed after the user clicks Settings from the Screen Saver tab in the Display Properties dialog box.

You probably can figure out how to do this without my help at all, right? All you need to do is create a new form—call it frmSetup. What sort of configuration makes sense for the Boxes screen saver? How about providing an option to add a beep every time a box comes up? We'll call this new feature BeepBox. Nothing like a little aural stimulation to go with those fetching boxes.

Figure 37.8 shows an example of frmSetup.

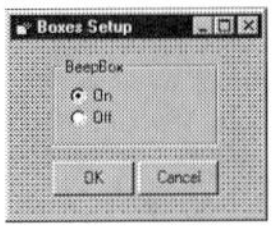

FIGURE 37.8

The layout of frmSetup, providing access to the nifty new BeepBox feature.

Very simple. The thing that's not so simple is this: where are you going to store this setting? A global variable won't work. Your program is going to end and then be called with an /s parameter a second time before you actually display the screen saver. You'll have to go to an INI file. Add these two lines to your module's Declaration section (Listing 37.9).

Listing 37.9. Declarations for the profile functions.

```
Declare Function WritePrivateProfileString Lib "kernel32" _
    Alias "WritePrivateProfileStringA" _
    (ByVal lpApplicationName As String, _
    ByVal lpKeyName As Any, ByVal lpString As String, _
    ByVal lpFileName As String) As Long
Declare Function GetPrivateProfileString Lib "kernel32" _
    Alias "GetPrivateProfileStringA" _
    (ByVal lpApplicationName As String, _
    ByVal lpKeyName As Any, ByVal lpDefault As String, _
    ByVal lpReturnedString As String, ByVal nSize As Long, _
    ByVal lpFileName As String) As Long
```

If you haven't used these functions before, here's a quick explanation of how they work. (If you have, feel free to skip the next few paragraphs.)

What's a Profile?

A *profile* is another name for an INI file. INI files are used by Windows and lots of Windows applications to store information from one run to the next—things like configuration settings, preferences, and screen layouts. Because this is so commonly done by so many applications, Windows has provided a standardized profile layout and an easy way to access profile data. The format looks like Listing 37.10.

Listing 37.10. An example INI file.

```
[Graphics]
Color=5
XPos=100
YPos=300

[Text]
Title=The Man About Town
CursorPos=15
CursorRow=7
```

And so on. You are looking at the contents of a single profile that has a file name with the extension INI. Notice that the file is divided into one or more sections. Each section has one or more *variable=value* entries. The variables are called *Keys* and the values can be strings or numerics. All data in a profile is stored this way.

To access and change data in a profile, you use the two Win32 API functions declared in Listing 37.9. `WritePrivateProfileString` adds or changes information in the profile. The arguments you send to it follow (in order):

- The section name (`lpApplicationName`)
- The variable or key name (`lpKeyName`)
- The string value you want to set the key to (`lpString`)
- The file name of the profile (`lpFileName`)

If the section or key doesn't exist, it is created in the profile.

`GetPrivateProfileString` is the counterpart read function, and its parameters follow:

- The section name
- The key
- A default value to return if the key isn't found
- A variable passed by reference to receive the value held in the key

- The maximum size of the string variable passed by reference
- The file name of the profile

Remember that strings always are passed by reference and that the use of `ByVal` in a declaration indicates that a C-style, null-terminated string is passed rather than a Visual Basic-style string.

> **WARNING**
>
> Be careful when using `GetPrivateProfileString` or any external function that expects a string variable to be passed by reference. You cannot pass a dynamic string variable that was just declared. You must either pass a fixed-length string or create a dynamic string and fill it with spaces long enough to contain the returned string plus one character for a C null end-string character. C doesn't know how to deal with Visual Basic's dynamic string structure, so be sure that you give it enough room to work with.

Adding the Configuration Code

So now that you have `GetPrivateProfileString` and `SetPrivateProfileString` at your disposal, what should the OK and Cancel button `Click` events in your Setup dialog look like? See Listings 37.11 and 37.12.

Listing 37.11. The OK button `Click` event for frmSetup.

```
Private Sub cmdOK_Click()
Dim i As Long
Dim sValue As String
If optBeepBoxOn.VALUE = True Then
    sValue = "TRUE"
Else
    sValue = "FALSE"
End If

i = WritePrivateProfileString("Screen Saver.Boxes", _
    "BeepBox", sValue, "CONTROL.INI")

Unload Me

End Sub
```

Listing 37.12. The Cancel button `Click` event for frmSetup.

```
Private Sub cmdCancel_Click()
Unload Me
End Sub
```

After the user clicks OK, the code checks to see which option button was clicked and sets sValue to TRUE or FALSE appropriately. Then a WritePrivateProfileString sets a key called BeepBox in a section of the CONTROL.INI file called Screen Saver.Boxes to sValue. Normally, it is a bad idea to use the system INI files like WIN.INI, SYSTEM.INI, and CONTROL.INI to keep application-specific information. It usually is best to keep that stuff in an application-specific INI file. But screen savers are an exception. Almost every screen saver has a section with the header Screen Saver.name in the CONTROL.INI. You could have made your own INI file, but this is a more standardized way of doing it.

And don't forget to add Listing 37.13 to the frmSetup Open event.

Listing 37.13. The frmSetup Open event.

```
Private Sub Form_Load()
Dim sBeepBox As String
Dim i As Long
Dim iSize As Integer

sBeepBox = "        " ' 8 spaces
iSize = 8
i = GetPrivateProfileString("Screen Saver.Boxes", "BeepBox", _
    "TRUE", sBeepBox, iSize, "CONTROL.INI")

If UCase(Left(sBeepBox, 4)) = "TRUE" Then
    optBeepBoxOn.VALUE = True
Else
    optBeepBoxOff.VALUE = True
End If

End Sub
```

The inverse function, GetPrivateProfileString, is called to get the value, and the option boxes are set appropriately. Notice that I put eight spaces into sBeepBox before passing it. Be sure to always give your strings more room than they need when they are passed by reference to an external function.

Integrating the BeepBox Feature

Okay, now you have a Configuration dialog box that enables the user to choose an option and remembers what the user chose. Now all that's left is to make the application use that information. First, declare a new global in the module's Declarations section:

```
Global giBeepBox As Integer
```

Add appropriate lines to your Main procedure so that it looks like Listing 37.14.

Listing 37.14. The updated `Main` procedure.

```
Sub Main()
Dim sBeepBox As String
Dim i As Integer
Dim iSize As Integer

If App.PrevInstance Then End

sBeepBox = "        " ' 8 spaces
iSize = 8
If InStr(Command, "/s") > 0 Then
    CursorOff
    i = GetPrivateProfileString("Screen Saver.Boxes", "BeepBox", _
        "TRUE", sBeepBox, iSize, "CONTROL.INI")
    If UCase(Left(sBeepBox, 4)) = "TRUE" Then
        giBeepBox = True
    Else
        giBeepBox = False
    End If
    frmScreenSaver.Show
ElseIf InStr(Command, "/c") > 0 Then
    frmSetup.Show
End If

End Sub
```

If you are to run the screen saver, you get the `BeepBox` value from the profile and set the `giBeepBox` flag. Now in `frmScreenSaver`, Timer1's `Timer` event should look like Listing 37.15.

Listing 37.15. Timer1's new `Timer` event.

```
Private Sub Timer1_Timer()
Dim X1, Y1, X2, Y2 As Integer

X1 = Rnd * (ScaleWidth - 1) + 1
Y1 = Rnd * (ScaleHeight - 1) + 1
X2 = Rnd * (ScaleWidth - 1) + 1
Y2 = Rnd * (ScaleHeight - 1) + 1
ForeColor = RGB(Rnd * 255 + 1, Rnd * 255 + 1, Rnd * 255 + 1)
Line (X1, Y1)-(X2, Y2), , BF
If giBeepBox = True Then Beep
End Sub
```

The only change is the last line, which beeps for the new box, if it is supposed to.

That's it. Make a new SCR file, move it to the Windows directory, and give it a try! Depending on the WAV you have set as your system beep, you will find the new BeepBox feature to be somewhere on a scale between mildly annoying to completely maddening. Good thing there's an option to turn it off!

Future Enhancements

Screen savers are easy to create in Visual Basic, once you get the structure down. You can use this code as a starting point to move on to bigger and better things. Here are some suggestions for future enhancements:

- Create splashier or more creative displays (it shouldn't be too tough to be beat the BeepBox feature in creativity).
- Create a scrolling text display that tells would-be visitors where you've gone or when you'll be back.
- Add a password to protect the screen from unintended onlookers.
- Add a feature that allows others to leave notes for you that you can read when you get back.

But most important, have fun!

Summary

In this chapter, you have walked through all the steps necessary to create a basic screen saver. It's not difficult, but there are some quirks. Now you have the tools you need to let your creativity run wild. Enjoy!

Unleashing LAN Programming

38

by Mark Steven Heyman

Shakespeare would have called it the dark backward and abysm of time—the dimly remembered, pre-Win95 days of yestermonth—when Visual Basic programmers who wanted to explore and manipulate the network resources underlying their applications were forced to link to the network provider's own Windows DLLs (Novell's NWNETAPI.DLL, for example), assuming these even were available. As you might imagine, this method of LAN resource management is at best tolerable—when a network consists of a single provider protocol. But in today's world, where it is not uncommon for a LAN (or WAN) to include two, three, or more distinct network protocols, this scheme becomes ponderous if not wholly unworkable.

With the introduction of Windows 95 and Windows NT, the creation and management of multi-protocol networks (as well as the creation of Windows applications to take full advantage of them) has been simplified greatly. A variety of network protocols and services can coexist under Windows 95 or NT, with no notion of primary or secondary networking software. Remote disk drives and printers can each be served by different network protocols—all under the watchful eye of the Win32 API. Under Windows 95, for example, drive E could be on a Windows NT server, drive G could be a NetWare server, and drive W could be a CD-ROM on a Sun Systems workstation across a WAN. The difference between local and network printers similarly has disappeared. The Win32 API offers the same basic programming interface for networking, regardless of the underlying software protocol and topology.

What this means to you, the Visual Basic programmer, is that your 32-Bit Visual Basic programs can call the network functions in the Microsoft Win32 application programming interface (API). These functions enable you to implement networking capabilities *without making adjustments for a particular protocol provider or physical network configuration.* In other words, the Win32 network functions are *network independent.* Your Visual Basic applications can use these functions to add and cancel network connections and to retrieve information about the current configuration of the physical network. In addition, the Win32 API implements a version of the NetBIOS network interface for applications that require it.

> **NOTE**
>
> In addition to using the network functions, your application's processes also can use the Win32 API implementations of mailslots and named pipes to communicate with one another. These topics will not be covered in this chapter, but for more information, see the discussions of mailslots and pipes in the online documentation for the Win32 SDK.

The Network Hierarchy

In this chapter, you'll be introduced to a dozen or so Win32 API functions (the Windows Network or WNet* functions) that can be called from your Visual Basic applications. (The asterisk in WNet* is a wild card character, indicating that all the function names begin with the same four letters.) But first, in order to familiarize yourself with the network jargon you'll encounter, take a look at Figure 38.1, which shows the structure of a typical multi-provider network.

FIGURE 38.1.

A typical multi-provider network.

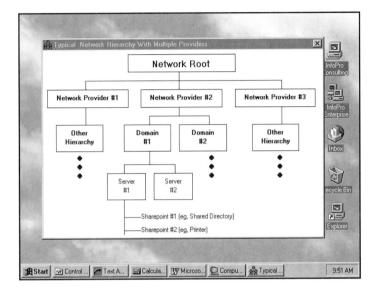

In Figure 38.1, the hierarchy for Microsoft Advanced Server resources is shown in detail as Network provider #2. Network resources from other providers (#1 might be Novell, for example, while #3 is Banyan) have different hierarchical systems. However, your Visual Basic application does not need information about the hierarchy before it begins to work with a network. It can proceed from the network root (that is, the topmost *container resource*) and retrieve information about the network's other resources as that information is required. Resources that do not contain other resources are regarded as *objects*. Sharepoint #1 and sharepoint #2 in Figure 38.1 are objects. A *sharepoint* is an object accessible across the network, such as a printer or shared directory.

> **NOTE**
>
> Network resources that contain other resources are called *containers*. An NT Advanced Server Domain is a container, as are any physical servers within it. In Figure 38.1, container resources are shown in boxes.

The Windows Network Functions

Windows 3.1 (and Windows For Workgroups) included the following protocol-independent network management functions (they did not, however, take advantage of 32-bit architecture):

- **WNetAddConnection().** Enables the calling application to connect a local device, such as a drive letter or printer port, to a network resource, such as a shared directory or printer. A successful connection is *persistent*, meaning that Windows automatically restores the connection at the next logon.

- **WNetCancelConnection().** Breaks an existing network connection.

- **WNetGetConnection().** Retrieves the name of the network resource associated with a local device, such as a specific drive letter.

The Win32 API supports these functions and has added the following network and network resource enumeration functions:

- **WNetAddConnection2().** Makes a connection to a network resource, using the NETRESOURCE structure (in Visual Basic, a custom data type). This function can be used to make persistent and non-persistent network connections. It supersedes the WNetAddConnection function.

- **WNetCancelConnection2().** Breaks an existing network connection. It also can be used to remove persistent network connections that currently are not connected. This function supersedes WNetCancelConnection.

- **WNetConnectionDialog().** Displays a general network browsing dialog box for connecting to network resources.

- **WNetDisconnectDialog().** Displays a general network browsing dialog box for disconnecting from network resources.

- **WNetGetUser().** Retrieves the current default user name or the user name used to establish a particular network connection.

- **WNetGetUniversalName().** Takes a drive-based path for a network resource and obtains a data structure that contains a more universal form of the name.

- **WNetGetLastError().** Retrieves the most recent extended error code (discussed later in this chapter) set by a Windows network function.

- **WNetOpenEnum().** Starts a listing of network resources or existing connections.

- **WNetEnumResource().** Continues a network-resource enumeration started by the WNetOpenEnum function.

- **WNetCloseEnum().** Ends a network resource enumeration started by the WNetOpenEnum function.

Your Visual Basic applications can use these network functions to browse, add, or cancel network connections anywhere in the hierarchy. By starting at the network root, the resources from all network providers can be listed for documentation or manipulation.

The Windows network functions enable your application to explore and manage network connections directly, or to give direct control of the network connections to your users. To call these functions, you must link to the multiple-provider router library (MPR.LIB). The following section discusses and demonstrates how to use many of these functions in your Visual Basic applications.

Function Declarations and the API Text Viewer

First, start a new Visual Basic project, add a new standard code module, and name it VBUCODE. Next, you'll add some function declarations to your new module with the help of the API Text Viewer. The API Text Viewer is a great little tool included with Visual Basic 4.0. You can use it to paste long and cumbersome function declarations, constants, and custom data types into your Visual Basic modules. The API Text Viewer is located in the Visual Basic 4.0 group. In fact, there may be two of them there: one for 16-bit development and one for 32-bit projects. In this chapter, you'll be working with the Win32 API. From the Viewer's File menu, select Load Text File and load Win32Api.Txt. This process takes a while, so be patient. There's a lot of stuff here.

> **CAUTION**
>
> After the API text file is first loaded, you may be asked if you want to convert the text file to a database for faster loading. In the beta copy of Visual Basic 4.0, answering Yes to this question caused the system to hang. The problem may well be fixed in your version of Visual Basic 4.0, but... well, you're on your own here.

After the file is loaded, select Declares from the API Type drop-down list. In the Available Items list, locate WNetAddConnection and double-click it to add it to the Selected Items list. Do the same for WNetCancelConnection. Your screen should look something like Figure 38.2.

FIGURE 38.2.

The Win32 API Text Viewer.

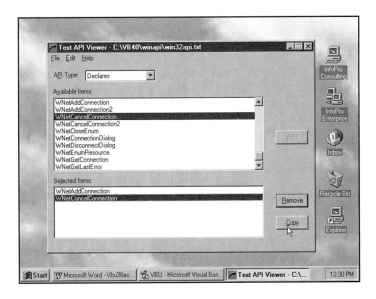

After the functions are selected in the Selected Items list, click the Copy button to copy them to the Clipboard. Then switch to your VBUCODE module and paste them in. That's all there is to it. This way, you're ensured of getting an accurate declaration, no matter how long and cumbersome the statement. Just minimize the API Text Viewer for now—you'll need it again later.

The next step is to rename your project's default form (Form1) to something a little more descriptive—frmVBNet, for example. This form will provide an interface for connecting to, and disconnecting from, network resources.

> **NOTE**
>
> All the examples in this chapter were created using the 32-bit version of Visual Basic 4.0, on a Windows 95 computer in a peer-to-peer relationship with a Pentium system running Windows NT Workstation, Version 3.51.

Figure 38.3 shows how the Visual Basic IDE (Integrated Development Environment), including frmVBNet, will look once you've completed the form's visual implementation.

FIGURE 38.3.

The Connecting to Network Resources dialog box.

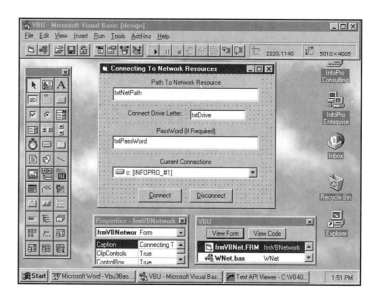

Now complete the visual design of your new form, referring to Table 38.1 for significant objects and suggested settings.

Table 38.1. Design time settings—the Network Connection form.

Visual Basic Object	Property	Design Time Setting
Form	Name	frmVBNet
	Caption	Connecting To Network Resources
TextBox	Name	txtNetPath
TextBox	Name	txtDrive
TextBox	Name	txtPassWord
Drive List Box	Name	Drive1
Command Button	Name	cmdConnect
	Caption	&Connect
	Default	True
Command Button	Name	cmdDisconnect
	Caption	&Disconnect

Program Overview

As you probably have surmised, this form enables the user to connect to a network resource, such as a shared directory, by providing the resource's network path and an available drive letter. Because some network resources might be password protected, there's also a TextBox control for entering the password. The DriveList control will be used to verify a successful connection, as well as to select a current resource for disconnection.

You've already DECLARED the WNetAddConnection and WNetCancelConnection functions you'll need. Now it's time to take a closer look at these functions, and to put them into action.

The *WNetAddConnection* Function

This function enables your application to connect a local device to a network resource. A successful connection is always persistent, meaning that Windows automatically attempts to restore the connection at the next logon. Here's the syntax, followed by a discussion of the parameters and possible error conditions:

```
lngRetVal = WNetAddConnection(strRemoteName,strPassword,strLocalName)
```

Here, the strRemoteName parameter is a string variable that specifies the complete path to the desired network resource. The parameter strPassword specifies the password to be used to make a connection, if one is required. This parameter is usually the password associated with the current user. If the string is empty, no password is used. The last parameter, strLocalName, is a string variable that identifies the name of the local device to be redirected, such as F or LPT1. If this string is NULL, a connection to the network resource is made, but no local device is redirected.

If the connection is successful, the value returned by this function, lngRetVal, is equal to the value of the constant ERROR_SUCCESS (which can be located, along with any other constants mentioned in this chapter, under Constants in the API Text Viewer and pasted into your VBUCODE module).

If the function fails and no connection is made, the return value is an error code constant. Table 38.2 lists the most likely error codes for the WNetAddConnection function.

Table 38.2. WNetAddConnection error codes.

Constant	Meaning
ERROR_ACCESS_DENIED	Access is denied
ERROR_ALREADY_ASSIGNED	The device specified in the strLocalName parameter already is connected
ERROR_BAD_DEV_TYPE	The device type and the resource type do not match
ERROR_BAD_DEVICE	Value specified in strLocalName is invalid
ERROR_BAD_NET_NAME	Value specified in the strRemoteName parameter is not valid or cannot be located.
ERROR_BAD_PROFILE	User profile is in an incorrect format
ERROR_CANNOT_OPEN_PROFILE	System is unable to open the user profile to process persistent connections
ERROR_DEVICE_ALREADY_REMEMBERED	An entry for the device specified in strLocalName is already in the user profile
ERROR_EXTENDED_ERROR	A network-specific error occurred
ERROR_INVALID_PASSWORD	Specified password is invalid
ERROR_NO_NET_OR_BAD_PATH	Operation cannot be performed because either a network component is not started or the specified name cannot be used
ERROR_NO_NETWORK	No network is present

The *WNetCancelConnection* Function

This simple function breaks an existing network connection. Here's its syntax:

```
lngRetVal = WNetCancelConnection(strName,bForce)
```

Here, the parameter strName is a string variable containing the name of the redirected local device (F or LPT1, for example) or the network resource to be disconnected. When strName specifies a redirected local device, only the specified redirection is broken, and Windows will not restore the connection during ensuing logon operations. When this parameter specifies a remote network resource, the connection to that remote network resource is broken.

The bForce parameter is a Boolean value indicating whether the disconnection is to occur even if there are open files or uncompleted jobs on the connection. If this parameter is FALSE, the function fails if there are open files or jobs, and an appropriate error code is returned.

If the function succeeds, the return value, lngRetVal, is ERROR_SUCCESS. If the function fails, the return value may be an error listed in Table 38.2 or Table 38.3.

Table 38.3. WNetCancelConnection **error codes.**

Constant	Meaning
ERROR_DEVICE_IN_USE	The specified device is in use by an active process and cannot be disconnected
ERROR_NOT_CONNECTED	The name specified by the strName parameter is not a redirected device, or the system is not currently connected to the device specified by the parameter
ERROR_OPEN_FILES	There are open files or uncompleted processes, and the bForce parameter is FALSE

Adding Code to Your Network Connection Form

It's time to add some spark to your new Network Connection form. The action occurs when cmdConnect or cmdDisconnect is clicked. Listings 38.1 and 38.2 are the documented listings for those two event procedures.

Listing 38.1. cmdConnect's Click **event procedure.**

```
Private Sub cmdConnect_Click()
Dim ServerText As String, PassWordText As String     ' Useful variables
Dim DriveLetter As String

Dim Msg As String                    ' For returned error message.
Dim Succeed As Long                  ' For long value returned by functions.

ServerText = UCase$(txtNetPath) ' Network resource name
PassWordText = txtPassWord      ' Password for the resource
DriveLetter = txtDrive          ' Get drive letter
```

continues

Listing 38.1. continued

```
Succeed = WNetAddConnection(ServerText, PassWordText, DriveLetter)

If IsSuccess(Succeed, Msg) = True Then      ' Call custom function
                                            ' with returned value
                                            ' to test for success
                                            ' and/or get error message.

    Drive1.Refresh                          ' If successful connect,
                                            ' show new connection in
                                            ' drive list box.

Else                                        ' Function not successful
    MsgBox Msg, , "Visual Basic Unleashed!" ' so display error.

End If

End Sub
```

Listing 38.2 shows the code to be added to cmdDisconnect's Click event. Notice that you select the drive to be disconnected by picking it from the DriveList drop-down list.

Listing 38.2. cmdDisconnect's Click event procedure.

```
Private Sub cmdDisconnect_Click()
Dim DriveLetter As String, Msg As String
Dim Succeed As Long

DriveLetter = Mid$(Drive1.Drive, 1, 2)              ' Get drive letter.

Succeed = WNetCancelConnection(DriveLetter, True)   ' Send it to the
                                                    ' CancelConnection
                                                    ' function, along
                                                    ' with a TRUE to
                                                    ' force the
                                                    ' disconnect, even
                                                    ' with open files
                                                    ' and/or processes.

If IsSuccess(Succeed, Msg) = True Then              ' If successful,
    Drive1.Refresh                                  ' refresh drive list

Else

    MsgBox Msg, , "Visual Basic Unleashed!"         ' Otherwise, display
                                                    ' the error message.

End If

End Sub
```

Listing 38.3 shows the IsSuccess() function, which is really just a specialized error handler. This code should be added to your VBUCODE module.

Listing 38.3. The IsSuccess() function.

```
Function IsSuccess(ReturnCode As Long, Msg As String) As Boolean

If ReturnCode = ERROR_SUCCESS Then

    IsSuccess = True

Else

    IsSuccess = False

    Select Case ReturnCode

      Case ERROR_INVALID_FUNCTION:
         Msg = "Function is not supported."
      Case ERROR_OUTOFMEMORY:
         Msg = "Out of Memory."
      Case ERROR_BAD_NET_NAME:
         Msg = "Invalid Network Resource Name."
      Case ERROR_NO_RESOURCE_NAME:
         Msg = "Must Enter A Valid Network Resource Name."
      Case ERROR_INVALID_PASSWORD:
         Msg = "The Password was Invalid."
      Case ERROR_ACCESS_DENIED:
         Msg = "A Security Violation Occurred."
      Case ERROR_ALREADY_CONNECTED:
         Msg = "Local Device Already Connected."
      Case ERROR_CONNECTION_UNAVAIL:
         Msg = "The Resource Is Not Shared."
      Case ERROR_ALREADY_ASSIGNED:
         Msg = "Local Drive Identifier Is In Use."
      Case ERROR_BAD_USERNAME:
         Msg = "No Such User."
      Case ERROR_INVALID_PRINTER_NAME:
         Msg = "No Such Printer."
      Case ERROR_LOCAL_DRIVE:
         Msg = "Can't Disconnect Local Drive."
      Case ERROR_INTERNAL_ERROR:
         Msg = "Internal Error!"
      Case Else:
         Msg = "Unrecognized Error " + Str$(ReturnCode) + "."
   End Select
End If
End Function
```

Finally, you'll need to set up the ERROR constants referred to in the IsSuccess() function. Add the lines shown in Listing 38.4 to your VBUCODE module, using the API Text Viewer if you find it easier.

Listing 38.4. Common network error codes.

```
Public Const ERROR_SUCCESS = 0&
Public Const ERROR_INVALID_FUNCTION = 1&
Public Const ERROR_ACCESS_DENIED = 5&
Public Const ERROR_OUTOFMEMORY = 14&
Public Const ERROR_ALREADY_CONNECTED = 52&
Public Const ERROR_BAD_NETPATH = 53&
Public Const ERROR_UNSHARED_RESOURCE = 67&
Public Const ERROR_BAD_NET_NAME = 67&
Public Const ERROR_ALREADY_ASSIGNED = 85&
Public Const ERROR_INVALID_PASSWORD = 86&
Public Const ERROR_BUFFER_OVERFLOW = 111&
Public Const ERROR_BAD_PATHNAME = 161&
Public Const ERROR_ALREADY_EXISTS = 183&
Public Const ERROR_NO_RESOURCE_NAME = 487&
Public Const ERROR_CONNECTION_UNAVAIL = 1201&
Public Const ERROR_BAD_PROVIDER = 1204&
Public Const ERROR_BAD_PROFILE = 1206&
Public Const ERROR_EXTENDED_ERROR = 1208&
Public Const ERROR_INVALID_PASSWORDNAME = 1216&
Public Const ERROR_INTERNAL_ERROR = 1359&
Public Const ERROR_INVALID_PRINTER_NAME = 1801&
Public Const ERROR_BAD_USERNAME = 2202&
Public Const ERROR_LOCAL_DRIVE = 2250&
```

It's time to test your form, assuming that you're working in a network environment. Be sure frmVBNet is your project's StartUp form, and then run your program. Test your form by trying various connections and disconnections. If the functions are not successful, you should get an appropriate error message. If they are successful, you'll be able to drop down the DriveList box and verify the connection, or disconnection, as the case may be.

Figure 38.4 shows a sample session where the connection was successful.

FIGURE 38.4.

The Network Connection form in action.

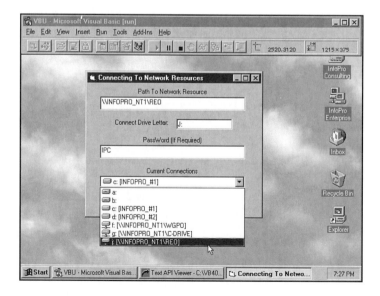

In Figure 38.5, you see the results of an attempt to connect to an unshared directory.

FIGURE 38.5.

*A failed connection
attempt.*

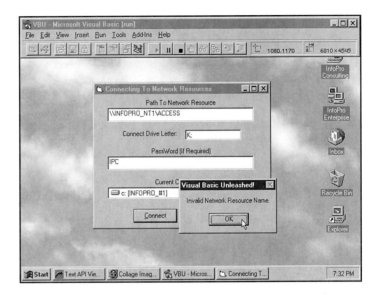

The *WNetAddConnection2* Function

One of the disadvantages of plain ol' `WNetAddConnection` is that you have no control over the type of connection you make—that is, whether it's *persistent.* (Remember that a persistent connection is one that is "remembered" by Windows, and is automatically re-established at the next logon. Connections made with `WNetAddConnection` are persistent.)

Using `WNetAddConnection2`, you can specify a persistent connection or one that is valid only for the current session. The price you pay for this is a little more complexity in making the call. As you'll see in the following discussion, `WNetAddConnection2` requires a custom data type, `NETRESOURCE`, as one of its parameters. You need to add the type definition and constants shown in Listing 38.5 to your VBUCODE module.

Listing 38.5. The `NETRESOURCE` custom data type.

```
Type NETRESOURCE

        lngScope As Long            ' To specify scope during enumeration.
        lngType As Long             ' Defines the type of resource.
        lngDisplayType As Long      ' How resources will be displayed.
        lngUsage As Long            ' Specifies the resource usage.
        strLocalName As String      ' Local device for the connection.
        strRemoteName As String     ' Indicates the network resource.
        strComment As String        ' For a provider-supplied comment.
        strProvider As String       ' Name of provider who owns the resource.
```

continues

Listing 38.5. continued

```
End Type

Public Const RESOURCETYPE_ANY = &H0        ' These are some useful
Public Const RESOURCETYPE_DISK = &H1       ' constants to be used
Public Const RESOURCETYPE_PRINT = &H2      ' with many of the WNet
Public Const RESOURCETYPE_UNKNOWN = &HFFFF ' functions.
Public Const CONNECT_UPDATE_PROFILE = &H1
```

Now here's the syntax for WNetAddConnection2, followed by a detailed discussion of all its parameters:

```
lngRetVal=WNetAddConnection2(nrCon,strPassword,strUserName,lngConnect)
```

The first parameter, nrCon, is a NETRESOURCE structure (in Visual Basic, a custom data type) that provides details of the proposed connection. It contains information about the network resource, the local device to be redirected, and the network resource provider. When calling WNetAddConnection2, you must specify the members of the NETRESOURCE data type shown in Table 38.4.

Table 38.4. Required NETRESOURCE members.

Member	Description
lngType	Specifies the type of network resource to connect to. If strLocalName points to a non-empty string, this member can be one of the constants RESOURCETYPE_DISK or RESOURCETYPE_PRINT. If strLocalName is NULL or empty, lngType can be RESOURCETYPE_DISK, RESOURCETYPE_PRINT, or RESOURCETYPE_ANY.
strLocalName	A string that specifies the name of a local device to be redirected, such as "X:" or "COM1". The case of the string is unimportant. If the string is empty or NULL, the function makes a connection but does not redirect the resource to a local device.
strRemoteName	A string that specifies the network resource to connect to. This string must adhere to the network provider's naming conventions.
strProvider	Specifies the network provider to connect to. If strProvider is NULL or empty, the operating system attempts to determine the correct provider by parsing the string pointed to by strRemoteName.
	If this member is not NULL, the operating system attempts to make a connection only to the named network provider.
	You should set this member only if you know for sure which network provider you want to use. Otherwise, let the operating system determine which provider the network name maps to.

The WNetAddConnection2 function ignores the other members of the NETRESOURCE structure.

The second parameter expected by WNetAddConnection2, strPassword, is a string that specifies a password to be used in making the network connection, if one is required. If this string is NULL, the function uses the current default password associated with the user specified by strUserName. If strPassword is an empty string, the function does not use a password.

The third parameter, strUsername, is a string that specifies a user name to be used in making the connection. If strUserName is NULL, the function uses the resource's default user name. The strUserName parameter is specified when users want to connect to a network resource for which they have been assigned a user name or account other than the default user name or account.

The final parameter, lngConnect, is used to specify connection options. When this parameter is set to CONNECT_UPDATE_PROFILE, the network resource connection is remembered, and Windows automatically attempts to restore the connection when the user logs on. If this parameter is 0, the user's profile is not updated and Windows will not automatically restore the connection at logon.

As with other WNet* functions, the return value, lngRetVal, is ERROR_SUCCESS if the function is successful in making the connection. If the function fails, the return value is an error code from one of the ERROR CODE tables in this chapter. Table 38.5 describes two additional errors associated with this function.

Table 38.5. WNetAddConnection2 error codes.

Constant	Meaning
ERROR_BUSY	The router or provider is busy, possibly congested or initializing. The function should be retried.
ERROR_CANCELLED	The connection attempt was canceled by the user through a dialog box from one of the network resource providers, or by a called resource or other process.

Finally, Listing 38.6 shows how your new form's cmdConnect Click event might look if you were using WNetAddConnection2 to connect to a network disk resource and make the connection persistent.

Listing 38.6. The Revised cmdConnect Click event.

```
Private Sub cmdConnect_Click()
Dim ServerText As String, PassWordText As String
Dim DriveLetter As String, UserName As String
```

continues

Listing 38.6. continued

```
Dim Msg As String
Dim Succeed As Long

Dim nrConnect As NETRESOURCE                    ' Get NETRESOURCE var.

nrConnect.lngType = RESOURCETYPE_DISK           ' Set resource type.
nrConnect.strLocalName = txtDrive               ' Get drive letter.
nrConnect.strRemoteName = UCase$(txtNetPath)    ' Path to resource.
nrConnect.strProvider = ""                       ' Unknown provider.

PassWordText = txtPassword                       ' Get password.
UserName = ""                                     ' Default user.

Succeed = WNetAddConnection2(nrConnect, PassWordText, UserName,
CONNECT_UPDATE_PROFILE)      ' Here's the call, all on one line.
                             ' Set the last parameter to 0, if you
                             ' don't want a persistent connection.


If IsSuccess(Succeed, Msg) = True Then

    Drive1.Refresh
Else
    MsgBox Msg, , "Visual Basic Unleashed!"

End If

End Sub
```

CAUTION

If you intend to test WNetAddConnection2 and WNetCancelConnection2 in your current project, be sure to use the API Text Viewer to add the function declarations to your VBUCODE module. Otherwise, the functions will not be known to Visual Basic.

The *WNetCancelConnection2* Function

The WNetCancelConnection2 function is very similar to WNetCancelConnection, but has a little more punch. WNetCancelConnection2 requires three arguments. The first is the resource identifier; the second is either 0 or CONNECT_UPDATE_PROFILE; and the third indicates whether the connection should be broken if files are open or processes are uncompleted.

Listing 38.7 shows how you might use WNetCancelConnection2 to break a connection during the current session, and not have any effect on that connection's persistence (or lack of persistence) at the next logon.

Listing 38.7. The Revised `cmdDisconnect Click` **event.**

```
Private Sub cmdDisconnect_Click()
Dim DriveLetter As String, Msg As String
Dim Succeed As Long

DriveLetter = Mid$(Drive1.Drive, 1, 2)   ' Get drive letter from list.
                                         ' You might want to get this
                                         ' from the txtDrive TextBox
                                         ' instead.

Succeed = WNetCancelConnection2(DriveLetter,0,False) ' Don't update the
                                                     ' user's connection
                                                     ' profile, and
                                                     ' don't force the
                                                     ' break if files
                                                     ' are open.

If IsSuccess(Succeed, Msg) = True Then
   Drive1.Refresh
Else
   MsgBox Msg, , "Visual Basic Unleashed!"
End If

End Sub
```

The *WNetConnectionDialog* Function

The WNetConnectionDialog function displays a general resource browsing dialog box. It's very useful if all you require is a simple, predefined interface for making network connections. WNetConnectionDialog saves you the hassle of having to design and implement your own dialog box. Listing 38.8 shows how it's used.

Listing 38.8. The Call To `WNetConnectionDialog()`.

```
lngRetVal = WNetConnectionDialog(hWinHandle,lngResourceType)
```

The first parameter, hWinHandle, is a handle to the window which will own the dialog box. In Visual Basic, this is simply your calling form's hWnd property. The second parameter, lngResourceType, specifies which type of resource, or resources, to browse. The value of lngResourceType is one of the RESOURCETYPE constants: RESOURCETYPE_DISK or RESOURCETYPE_PRINT.

If the function succeeds, the return value, lngRetVal, is ERROR_SUCCESS. If the user cancels the dialog box, it is 0xFFFFFFFF, and no connection is made. As usual, the return value is an error code if the function fails.

> **NOTE**
>
> If the user chooses OK in the dialog box, the requested network connections are attempted. If the function attempts to make a connection and the network provider returns the message ERROR_INVALID_PASSWORD, Windows prompts the user to enter a password, which then is used to make another connection attempt.

The *WNetDisconnectDialog* Function

The WNetDisconnectDialog function displays a general browsing dialog box for breaking current network connections. The syntax and parameters are nearly identical to those of WNetConnectionDialog. Here's how the function is used:

```
lngRetVal = WNetDisconnectDialog(hWinHandle,lngResourceType)
```

You now should use the API Text Viewer to paste declarations for these two functions into your VBUCODE module. To test the Connect and Disconnect dialog functions, you'll add a simple form to your current project. Call it frmDialogs and make it the project's StartUp form. The form consists of two CommandButtons, and a Frame enclosing two OptionButtons, as displayed in Figure 38.6.

FIGURE 38.6.

The Connections Dialog Boxes form.

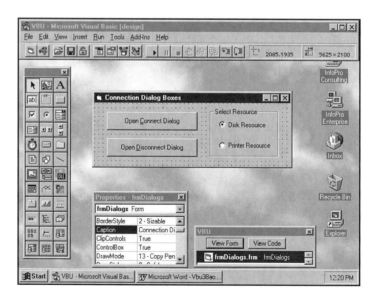

Table 38.6 shows your new form's significant objects and property settings. Use it to complete the visual implementation of frmDialogs.

Table 38.6. Design time settings—the Connection Dialog Boxes form.

Visual Basic Object	Property	Design Time Setting
Form	Name	frmDialogs
	Caption	Connection Dialog Boxes
Command Button	Name	cmdConnectDialog
	Caption	Open &Connect Dialog
Command Button	Name	cmdDisconnectDialog
	Caption	Open &Disconnect Dialog
Frame	Name	fraResources
	Caption	Select Resource
OptionButton	Name	optDisk
	Caption	Disk Resource
	Value	True
OptionButton	Name	optPrinter
	Caption	Printer Resource

By now, you probably have discerned the purpose of this form. It enables you to select a resource type, disk, or printer; and then open the corresponding Connect or Disconnect dialog box by clicking the appropriate CommandButton. Listing 38.9 shows the code for cmdConnectDialog's Click event.

Listing 38.9. cmdConnectDialog's Click event procedure.

```
Private Sub cmdConnectDialog_Click()
Dim Succeed As Long                          ' For return value.
Dim Resource As Long                         ' For resource type.

If optDisk Then                              ' If optDisk is True,
    Resource = RESOURCETYPE_DISK             ' use disk constant,
Else                                         ' otherwise,
    Resource = RESOURCETYPE_PRINT            ' use print constant.
End If

Succeed = WNetConnectionDialog(hWnd, Resource)   ' Here's the call.
                                             ' Notice the use
                                             ' of hWnd, the
                                             ' calling window's
                                             ' handle, which is
                                             ' just frmDialogs'
                                             ' hWnd property.

End Sub
```

Listing 38.10 shows cmdDisconnectDialog's nearly identical Click event procedure.

Listing 38.10. cmdDisconnectDialog's Click event.

```
Private Sub cmdDisconnectDialog_Click()
Dim Succeed As Long
Dim Resource As Long

If optDisk Then
   Resource = RESOURCETYPE_DISK
   Else
   Resource = RESOURCETYPE_PRINT
End If

Succeed = WNetDisconnectDialog(hWnd, Resource)

End Sub
```

You're ready to test. Figures 38.7 and 38.8 show some sample sessions.

FIGURE 38.7.

The Printer Connect dialog box in action.

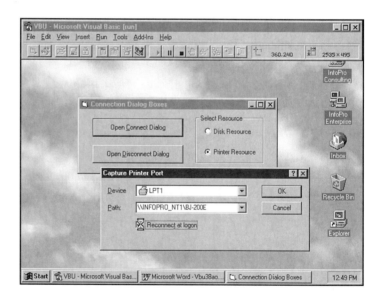

FIGURE 38.8.

The Disk Disconnect dialog box in action.

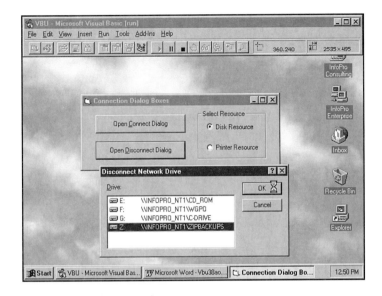

The *WNetGetUser* Function

The WNetGetUser function retrieves the current network user name, or the user name used to establish a current network connection. Here is WNetGetUser's syntax, followed by a discussion of all parameters:

```
lngRetVal = WNetGetUser(strLocalName,strUserName,lngBuffer)
```

Here, strLocalName is a string that specifies the name of the local device to return the user name (for "LPT2" or "L:", for example), or the name of a network resource to which the user has made a connection. If strLocalName is NULL, Windows returns the name of the current user. If this parameter is a valid network resource and the user is connected to that resource using different names, the network provider might not be able to resolve which user name to return. In this case, the provider can choose arbitrarily from the possible user names.

The second parameter, strUserName, is a blank-space string variable that receives the user name. It must be big enough to contain the returned user name. The last parameter, lngBuffer, is a long variable that specifies the size, in characters, of the variable indicated by strUserName. If the call fails because the buffer is too small, the function returns a value equal to the error code constant ERROR_MORE_DATA, and lngBuffer contains the required buffer size.

Again, if the function succeeds, the value returned to lngRetVal is ERROR_SUCCESS. If the function fails, the return value is an error code that can be evaluated and subsequently displayed.

The *WNetGetConnection* Function

The WNetGetConnection function retrieves the name of the network resource currently associated with a particular local device. Here is how it's used:

```
lngRetVal = WNetGetConnection(strLocalName,strRemoteName,lngBuffer)
```

The strLocalName parameter is a string variable that specifies the name of the local device whose network resource name is to be returned.

The second parameter, strRemoteName, is a blank space string variable that receives the remote resource name used to make the connection. The last parameter, lngBuffer, is a long variable that specifies the size, in characters, of the variable indicated by strRemoteName. If the function is not successful because the lngBuffer is too small, WNetGetConnection returns a value equal to the error code constant ERROR_MORE_DATA, and lngBuffer contains the required buffer size.

As with all the WNet* functions, if WNetGetConnection succeeds, the value returned to lngRetVal is ERROR_SUCCESS.

If the function fails, the return value is one of the previously discussed error codes, which you can capture and display.

Using *WNetGetUser* and *WNetGetConnection*

In this section, you'll put your understanding of the WNetGetUser and WNetGetConnection functions to use. First, add another form to your current project, call it frmNetInfo, and make it the project's StartUp form.

Now refer to Figure 38.9 and Table 38.7 to complete the visual design of your new form.

FIGURE 38.9.

frmNetInfo in Design mode.

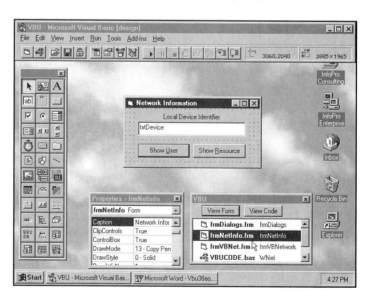

Table 38.7. Design time settings—the Network Information form.

Visual Basic Object	Property	Design Time Setting
Form	Name	frmNetInfo
	Caption	Network Information Form
TextBox	Name	txtDevice
	TabIndex	0
Command Button	Name	cmdShowUser
	Caption	Show &User
	Default	True
Command Button	Name	cmdShowResource
	Caption	Show &Resource

This form enables the user to enter a local device ID, such as LPT1: or Z:, and to receive the user name or network resource name associated with the device. (Don't forget to add the function declarations for WNetGetUser and WNetGetConnection to your VBUCODE module.) Listing 38.11 shows the code to add to the Click event procedures for cmdShowUser and cmdShowResource.

Listing 38.11. cmdShowUser's Click event procedure.

```
Private Sub cmdShowUser_Click()
Dim GetUser As Long                  ' For the return value.
Dim DeviceID As String               ' Local device.
Dim UserName As String               ' To receive user name.
Dim lngName As Long                  ' User name buffer size.

Dim Msg As String                    ' For MsgBox display.

UserName = Space(25)
lngName = Len(UserName)

DeviceID = txtDevice

GetName = WNetGetUser(DeviceID, UserName, lngName)   ' The call.

'Now prepare and display the user information.
Msg = "Device " + DeviceID + vbCrLf + "Is Being Used By " + UserName
MsgBox Msg, , "Network User Information"
End Sub
```

Listing 38.12 shows cmdShowResource's Click event.

Listing 38.12. cmdShowResource's Click event procedure.

```
Private Sub cmdShowResource_Click()
Dim GetResource As Long                    ' RetVal
Dim DeviceID As String                     ' Local device.
Dim ResourceName As String                 ' For resource name.
Dim lngResource As Long                    ' Buffer size.

Dim Msg As String                          ' For MsgBox.

ResourceName = Space(50)
lngResource = Len(ResourceName)

DeviceID = txtDevice

GetResource = WNetGetConnection(DeviceID, ResourceName, lngResource)

'Now prepare and display the resource information.
Msg = "Device " + DeviceID + vbCrLf + "Connected To: " + ResourceName
MsgBox Msg, , "Network Resource Information"

End Sub
```

Okay, go ahead and test your form on your own network. See Figures 38.10 and 38.11 for sample output. Figure 38.11 shows some resource connection information, as displayed by the frmNetInfo program.

FIGURE 38.10.

Network user information.

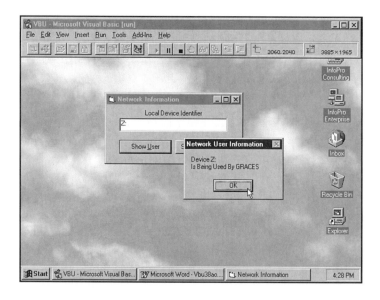

FIGURE 38.11.

Network connection information.

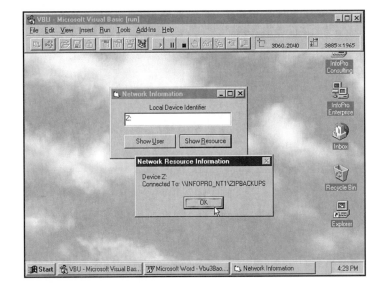

The *WNetGetLastError* Function

The final function you'll cover in this chapter is the WNetGetLastError function. This function retrieves the most recent extended error code set by a Windows network function. An *extended error code* is network-specific; that is, it is supplied by a particular network provider—Novell or Banyan, for example—and therefore contains error information that pertains only to that provider's network protocol.

Here's the syntax for the WNetGetLastError function:

```
lngRetVal = WNetGetLastError(lngCode,strDesc,lngDesc,strName,lngName)
```

The first parameter, lngCode, is a long variable that receives the network-specific error code reported by the provider software.

The next parameter, strDesc, receives the string describing the error. The parameter lngDesc specifies the size, in characters, of strDesc. If the variable is too small for the error string, the string is truncated. A variable of at least 256 characters is recommended.

The fourth parameter, strName, is a string variable that receives the name identifying the network provider that threw the error. The fifth and last parameter, lngName, sets the size, in characters, of the strName parameter.

If the function successfully obtains the last error reported by the network provider, the return value is ERROR_SUCCESS.

A Custom Extended Error Handler

WNetGetLastError should be used when any Windows network function returns ERROR_EXTENDED_ERROR. As mentioned earlier, this function returns detailed error information that is network specific, including a string for reporting errors that are not described by any existing Windows error code.

Now, in this final section, you'll enhance your IsSuccess() function, the simple error handler you created earlier in this chapter so that it can handle extended as well as standard error codes. In the process, you'll create a new custom function called ExErrorHandler. Listing 38.13 shows you what should be added to your VBUCODE module.

Listing 38.13. The ExErrorHandler() function.

```
Function ExErrorHandler() As String

Dim strRetVal As String            ' For returned error message.

Dim ExRV As Long                   ' For value returned by function.
Dim ExEC As Long                   ' Stores the error code.
Dim ExED As String                 ' Stores the error description.
Dim ExDS As Long                   ' The size of description variable.
Dim ExPR As String                 ' Stores the provider name.
Dim ExPS As Long                   ' The size of the provider variable.

ExED = Space(256)                  ' Initial values
ExDS = Len(ExED)
ExPR = Space(30)
ExPS = Len(ExPR)

ExRV = WNetGetLastError(ExEC, ExED, ExDS, ExPR, ExPS)   ' The call.

If ExRV = ERROR_SUCCESS Then       ' Check for success.
                                   ' If successful, build network
                                   ' specific error message to be
                                   ' returned to IsSuccess function.

strRetVal = "Extended Error Information" + vbCrLf + vbCrLf
strRetVal = strRetVal + "Error Code: " + CStr(ExEC) + vbCrLf
strRetVal = strRetVal + "Error Description: " + ExED + vbCrLf
strRetVal = strRetVal + "Network Provider: " + ExPR

Else                                          ' Otherwise,
strRetVal = "Unable To Process Extended Error!"   ' Return generic msg.

End If

ExErrorHandler = strRetVal          ' Return message to IsSuccess()

End Function
```

Now your new function, ExErrorHandler(), is called from the IsSuccess() function you created near the beginning of this chapter. It is called only when one of your WNet* functions returns an ERROR_EXTENDED_ERROR value. Listing 38.14 shows the code for IsSuccess(), with the call to ExErrorHandler printed in bold.

Listing 38.14. The revised IsSuccess() function.

```
Function IsSuccess(ReturnCode As Long, Msg As String) As Boolean

   If ReturnCode = ERROR_SUCCESS Then
      IsSuccess = True
   Else
      IsSuccess = False
      Select Case ReturnCode

         Case ERROR_INVALID_FUNCTION:
            Msg = "Function is not supported."
         Case ERROR_OUTOFMEMORY:
            Msg = "Out of Memory."
         Case ERROR_BAD_NET_NAME:
            Msg = "Invalid Network Resource Name."
         Case ERROR_NO_RESOURCE_NAME:
            Msg = "Must Enter A Valid Network Resource Name."
         Case ERROR_INVALID_PASSWORD:
            Msg = "The Password was Invalid."
         Case ERROR_ACCESS_DENIED:
            Msg = "A Security Violation Occurred."
         Case ERROR_ALREADY_CONNECTED:
            Msg = "Local Device Already Connected."
         Case ERROR_CONNECTION_UNAVAIL:
            Msg = "The Resource Is Not Shared."
         Case ERROR_ALREADY_ASSIGNED:
            Msg = "Local Drive Identifier Is In Use."
         Case ERROR_BAD_USERNAME:
            Msg = "No Such User."
         Case ERROR_INVALID_PRINTER_NAME:
            Msg = "No Such Printer."
         Case ERROR_LOCAL_DRIVE:
            Msg = "Can't Disconnect Local Drive."
         Case ERROR_INTERNAL_ERROR:
            Msg = "Internal Error!"

         Case ERROR_EXTENDED_ERROR:      ' If Extended error, call
            Msg = ExErrorHandler()       ' ExErrorHandler() for
                                         ' processing and building
                                         ' a network-specific error
                                         ' message.

         Case Else:
            Msg = "Unrecognized Error " + Str$(ReturnCode) + "."
      End Select
   End If
End Function
```

If you intend to use some version of this function in your applications, don't forget to paste the WNetGetLastError declaration into a standard code module.

Summary

In this chapter, you learned that the introduction of Windows 95 and Visual Basic 4.0 has greatly simplified the creation of Windows applications that can take full advantage of the networks on which they run. Now your 32-bit Visual Basic programs can call the WNet* network functions in the Microsoft Win32 application programming interface (API). These functions enable you to explore and manage mixed-protocol networks without making adjustments for a particular network software or topology. The Win32 network functions therefore enable your Visual Basic applications to be network independent.

You were introduced to all 13 WNet* functions, and you spent some time exploring nine of them in detail. You created a form that enables you to connect and disconnect network resources using WNetAddConnection and WNetCancelConnection, and then you modified that form to use the more powerful WNetAddConnection2 and WNetCancelConnection2 functions. You used WNetConnectionDialog and WNetDisconnectDialog to display predefined dialog boxes for facilitating network connections and disconnections, and you created a Network Information form, using WNetGetUser and WNetGetConnection, which enabled you to retrieve and display network user and resource names. Finally, you used WNetGetLastError to create a custom extended error handler, which enables you to evaluate and display network-specific error information.

IN THIS PART

Appendixes

Visual Basic versus Other Languages

A

by Greg Perry

If you have programmed using other programming languages before, you might be wondering how Visual Basic 4.0 compares to those languages in speed, power, flexibility, and ease of use. This appendix surveys several popular languages in use today and discusses how Visual Basic 4.0 responds to the challenge of meeting or surpassing those languages' capabilities.

Instead of comparing Visual Basic 4.0 to other languages command by individual command, this appendix discusses the main attributes of the languages and shows you how Visual Basic 4.0 supports or does not support those language attributes. By studying the comparisons you will be able to understand Visual Basic 4.0's strengths and weaknesses against these other languages. Visual Basic 4.0 is not necessarily the best language for every job. Although your specific application's requirements will ultimately determine whether or not you should use Visual Basic 4.0 or something else, this appendix will help you make the language decision.

The Other Basics

The roots of Visual Basic 4.0 date back to the early 1960s when, at Dartmouth University, two college professors set out to develop a programming language and environment in which non-programming students could write programs using a language easier than COBOL or FORTRAN. The result was BASIC whose acronym name stands for *Beginner's All-purpose Symbolic Instruction Code*—an acronym that is more difficult to remember than most of the commands in the language!

Not only was BASIC easier to learn than the other languages of the time; it was easier to use. Instead of being a compiled language, the novice student programmers could write their programs and execute those programs within the same interactive environment. BASIC was the first widely-used interpreted language. Here are the steps programmers then needed to write and execute a compiled, non-interpreted language program:

1. Write the program.
2. Compile the program.
3. Link the program.
4. Run the program.

These four steps were more time-consuming in the days of old than today because many of today's compiled language environments help shelter the programmer from the second and third steps. When BASIC was developed, each of these four steps required tedious commands that were often not understood by those using them. Interpreted BASIC honed those steps down to these two:

1. Write the program.
2. Run the program.

The primary problem with the early BASIC language was its lack of structure. The BASIC language really is not that much easier to *learn* than other languages, but it's easier to *use*. The original BASIC language was rigid and did not support the free-form control structures available in most of today's languages including Visual Basic 4.0. Listing A.1 contains a BASIC program listing. Now that you've learned Visual Basic 4.0 you will notice these items about the program:

- Line numbers are required at the left of each statement.

- The remarks are rigid and do not easily help describe surrounding code.

- Variable names are virtually meaningless due to their limited length (some versions of BASIC allowed for variable names that contained only two letters)

NOTE

BASIC was written long before windowed environments were available.

Listing A.1. A BASIC program must follow unstructured and rigid coding rules.

```
10 REM A PROGRAM TO CALCULATE FACTORIALS
20 F = 1
30 PRINT "WHAT IS YOUR NUMBER";
40 INPUT N
50 REM STEP THROUGH THE NUMBERS FROM ONE
60 REM TO THE USER'S ENTERED VALUE
70 FOR I = N TO 1 STEP -1
80 F = F * I
90 NEXT I
100 PRINT
110 PRINT "THE FACTORIAL IS"; F
120 END
```

As you've seen throughout this book, the language format of Visual Basic 4.0 greatly surpasses this rigid style of BASIC. The two languages are so greatly different that a side-by-side comparison is unneeded at this stage. No vendor currently supports the old style of the BASIC language. The importance of discussing BASIC comes in learning the roots of Visual Basic 4.0 and in understanding why Microsoft designed Visual Basic 4.0 to work the way it does.

How important was BASIC to the design of Visual Basic 4.0? Some might think that BASIC is so far from Visual Basic 4.0's capability that there is no need to make the comparison. The truth is that the old interpreted BASIC played a major role in Visual Basic 4.0's current design.

Not only are many of the same language commands supported in both languages, such as For-Next loops, assignment statements, and If-Else comparison statements, but Microsoft designed Visual Basic 4.0 to be an interpreted language. Although a Windows-based language must be event driven (see the next section for more discussion on event driven versus procedural languages), the BASICs that came before Visual Basic 4.0 had a direct impact on the make-up of Visual Basic 4.0.

In today's programming world, the idea of an interpreted language is often scoffed at until someone sees Visual Basic 4.0 in action. Interpreted languages are inherently slower than compiled languages. Applications are often time critical and must run as fast as possible. Knowing this, developers often forego Visual Basic 4.0 in favor of a much more difficult language such as Visual C++. (A later section in this appendix compares Visual Basic 4.0 to C++ languages.) These developers often forget the following points:

- Computers are getting faster every day, not slower. As the speed of computers increases, the speed differences between running compiled and running interpreted programs becomes less and less critical.

- The time it takes to develop programs is often *much* more costly to developers and end-users than speed difference costs of the completed running programs.

- Despite the fact that compiler developers are making compilers easier to use, interpreted languages require far fewer system resources, fewer programmer-controlled options, and a smaller learning curve than using an interpreted language such as Visual Basic 4.0.

Microsoft added *BASICA* and a version of *GWBASIC* (standing, respectively, for *BASIC Advanced* and *Gee-Whiz BASIC*) to the MS-DOS operating system starting with the very first IBM PC. The success of PCs and MS-DOS compatibles ensured that those versions of BASIC were available to the masses of computer users.

Over the years, Microsoft improved upon the original line-numbered uppercase BASIC language. In the early 1980s, Microsoft developed *QuickBasic*, a compiled version of BASIC that finally eliminated the line numbers and turned the BASIC language into a language that professional developers began to take seriously. QuickBasic survived four major versions and improvements. By adding more control statements such as While options, ElseIf, and Case statements, and by improving the language's readability by supporting separate sub-programs and external routines, the BASIC language continued to thrive whereas it may have withered away without the improvements.

Beginning with MS-DOS 5.0, Microsoft introduced *QBasic*, an interpreted version of QuickBasic that included a full-screen editor and added the structured control statements that were so popular in QuickBasic. It was not until Windows 95 appeared that Microsoft failed to add an interpretive BASIC-like programming language to a major operating system product.

QUICKBASIC: THE NOW-FORGOTTEN COMPILED BASIC

Why did Microsoft introduce the QuickBasic compiler, improve the language through four versions, and then revert back to interpreted languages such as QBasic and Visual Basic and eliminate all support for a compiled QuickBasic? Perhaps Microsoft thinks that the interpreted environment is simply too appealing for novice programmers. In spite of the increased responsibilities of compiler users, however, the QuickBasic environment made the task of compiling and running programs almost as easy as using interpreted languages.

Microsoft may have dropped QuickBasic because of the timing of Windows. As Windows gained more popularity during the 1980s there was less and less reason to support a compiled MS-DOS language, albeit a well-written language, such as QuickBasic. Microsoft left QBasic in their operating system for several years after QuickBasic faded into the background but did not improve upon QBasic significantly since its first release in MS-DOS 5.0.

NOTE

One of the biggest language failures in computer history was *Visual Basic for DOS*. In the early 1990s, Microsoft produced an MS-DOS version of Visual Basic that supported the same visual interface as Windows only doing so in the MS-DOS mode. Programmers who wanted a Windows-like full-screen interactive interface could have that interface in MS-DOS. Sadly for Microsoft (and for MS-DOS program developers), Visual Basic for DOS appeared just at the time that Windows took off strongly; the need for an MS-DOS programming environment died along with Visual Basic for DOS in just a few short months. The surprising thing is that Visual Basic for DOS was a true compiler and yet never achieved the success or use that any one of Microsoft's interpreted BASIC languages achieved.

Table A.1 presents an overview of some of the specific feature comparisons between Visual Basic 4.0 and many of the BASIC languages that appeared over the years.

Table A.1. Visual Basic 4.0 compared to the other BASICs.

Visual Basic 4.0	*BASICs*
No line numbers needed.	Line numbers often needed.
Long variable names.	Short variable names.

continues

Table A.1. continued

Visual Basic 4.0	*BASICs*
True parameter passing between subprograms by value and by address.	Limited argument passing between complete programs via the CHAIN statement.
Full support for the Windows environment.	No support for Windows, only for MS-DOS.
Stand-alone programs possible using the Visual Basic 4.0 run-time DLL file (inside the Windows environment).	Requires the BASIC environment to any program.
Advanced file I/O support including indexed files.	Sequential and random access file I/O supported supported but no keyed access or other advanced database and file access available.
Full-featured debugging system included with Visual Basic 4.0.	Limited debugging tools.

Mainframe COBOL and Visual Basic 4.0

In the mainframe/PC combination environment found in many of today's corporations, many programming shops are faced with using both a mainframe language and then supplementing that language with a PC-based language for the smaller work areas. The most popular high-level mainframe language still in use today is COBOL.

There are several PC-based COBOL languages on the market. The problem with many PC COBOL compilers is their support for Windows. Although there are COBOL compilers that support Windows program development, COBOL was never designed to be used in a graphical user environment. Instead of using a COBOL compiler for your mainframe application and a PC-based COBOL compiler for your PC applications, you should probably stick with COBOL for the mainframe and use Visual Basic 4.0 for your PC applications, whether or not you ever need to interface those applications to the mainframe.

COBOL was originally designed to be a procedural language. Procedural languages work well in text-based data-processing environments because procedural languages respond to sequential events. When a Windows screen appears, with command buttons, option buttons, scroll bars, and dropdown listboxes, the program reacting to that user's screen must be event-driven to handle whatever action the user performs next. A language such as COBOL simply cannot handle the interactions a Windows program needs.

About the only advanced user-interface allowed in traditional COBOL is a menu selection. Suppose that you display a five-element menu for the user. The menu might offer the user the following choices:

1. Add a customer record

2. Remove a customer record

3. Change a customer record

4. Print a customer detail report

5. Terminate the program

The user might enter one of five values in response to this menu. Some might think that, in an archaic sense, a text menu offers a primitive form of an event-driven user interface because the user might enter any one of five values (ignoring error conditions for now which are special events in and of themselves in a proper event-driven environment). Nevertheless, such a menu is a procedural screen interface element because the code needed to handle the menu is standard decision-making code as shown here:

```
GO TO ADD-CUST-PARA,
      REMOVE-CUST-PARA,
      CHANGE-CUST-PARA,
      PRINT-REPORT-PARA,
      END-PGM-PARA
DEPENDING ON USER-RESPONSE.
```

In the Visual Basic 4.0 environment, an option button might control the action requested by the user. A pull-down menu might be available for a printed report. The user might display an existing customer record, and then, decide to change one or more values from that record. Instead of writing procedural code in Visual Basic 4.0 to handle each event that might happen, the programmer writes one routine for each event and does not worry about the order in which those events may or may not happen. Also, the tedious task of selecting the correct event is out of the user's hands; in other words, nowhere in the program does the programmer have to look to see what the user decides to do. When the user changes a record, Windows automatically triggers that field's change event and the code written for that particular event executes.

The lack of event-driven support is not the only reason COBOL programmers should move to Visual Basic 4.0 when writing Windows applications. The *most* time-consuming task in COBOL is the *least* time-consuming task in Visual Basic 4.0: designing and developing the user-interface.

COBOL programmers must master the design and programming of user-interface screens and reports. Listing A.2 contains a partial listing of a COBOL program's screen output design. To produce a full screen of output, a COBOL programmer must type many line-by-line descriptions, called *PIC clauses*, for the screens. (If the COBOL program produces printed output, the programmer must also write tedious descriptions for the reported output lines as well.) The PIC clauses can be bug-prone. COBOL programmers often have to compile their programs many times, adjusting PIC clauses over and over, until their screens display or accept data in a desired format and layout.

> **CAUTION**
>
> Despite its length, Listing A.2 describes only two formats for output: titles and data. If fields for user input of values are needed, or if additional kinds of detail lines might appear on the screen, additional sets of PIC clauses are required. It is not unusual for a single COBOL program to contain twenty pages of PIC clause listings. A Visual Basic 4.0 program requires no such text listings no matter how many extensive Visual Basic 4.0 user screens are required.

Listing A.2. An example of tedious COBOL PIC clauses.

```
*   The following code describes part of a COBOL screen.
*   This code would appear before a COBOL program's
*   procedure division but after the identification and
*   environment divisions. The purpose of this code is
*   to show how a COBOL programmer must tediously describe
*   every line of a user's screen.
WORKING-STORAGE DIVISION.
01 Detail-Line-Descsripts-1.
     03 PCodeTop            PIC X(7)    VALUE 'Product'.
     03 FILLER              PIC X(30)   VALUE SPACES.
     03 NSoldTop            PIC X(6)    VALUE 'Number'.
     03 FILLER              PIC XXX     VALUE SPACES.
     03 UPriceTop           PIC X(4)    VALUE 'Unit'.
     03 FILLER              PIC XXXX    VALUE SPACES.
     03 EPriceTop           PIC X(8)    VALUE 'Extended'.
*
01 Detail-Line-Descsripts-2.
     03 PCodeBot            PIC X(5)    VALUE 'Code'.
     03 FILLER              PIC X(5)    VALUE SPACES.
     03 PName               PIC X(12)   VALUE 'Product Name'.
     03 FILLER              PIC X(16)   VALUE SPACES.
     03 NSoldBot            PIC X(4)    VALUE 'Sold'.
     03 FILLER              PIC X(4)    VALUE SPACES.
     03 UPriceBot           PIC X(5)    VALUE 'Price'.
     03 FILLER              PIC X(5)    VALUE SPACES.
     03 EPriceBot           PIC X(5)    VALUE 'Price'.
*
01 Detail-Line-Data.
     03 FILLER              PIC XX      VALUE SPACES.
     03 ProdCode            PIC X(4).
     03 FILLER              PIC X(5)    VALUE SPACES.
     03 ProdName            PIC X(25).
     03 FILLER              PIC XXX     VALUE SPACES.
     03 NumSold             PIC 999.
     03 FILLER              PIC X(3)    VALUE SPACES.
     03 PriceEach           PIC S9999V99.
     03 FILLER              PIC XX      VALUE SPACES.
     03 ExtPrice            PIC S99999V99.
```

Visual Basic 4.0 programmers do not use code to describe their screens. Instead, as you've seen throughout this book, Visual Basic 4.0 programmers literally create their applications by pointing and clicking with the mouse. If a text box control does not appear in the correct place the programmer only has to drag the control to the correct location. If a listbox is not large enough to display enough items at one time, the programmer can increase the size of the listbox by dragging the listbox control's edge with the mouse.

NOTE

You can print a textual description of your Visual Basic 4.0 form (File | Print) and that description does not look much different from a listing of COBOL PIC clauses. The difference lies in the *timing* of the listing. To produce a full-screen of output in COBOL you must first write the tedious text that describes the PIC clauses that produce the output. In Visual Basic 4.0 you first use the mouse and toolbox to design your form. Visual Basic 4.0 then produces the printed description of that screen that you can use as system documentation. It is much easier and faster, and less error-prone, to design a screen using the mouse than to design the screen using text descriptions.

COBOL's procedure division contains COBOL code that processes the data in the same way that Visual Basic 4.0 procedures process data. Much of COBOL's procedure code is taken up with the displaying and inputting of user data, a task not needed inside Visual Basic 4.0 programs due to the Window's event-handling and the graphical controls already described. The remaining commands in the two languages are actually rather similar in many ways.

Both COBOL and Visual Basic 4.0 contain selection statements that execute certain routines based on data values. Visual Basic 4.0's If-ElseIf statement is virtually identical to COBOL's IF-THEN-ELSE statement. COBOL contains OPEN and CLOSE file I/O commands that mirror those in Visual Basic 4.0.

Once a COBOL programmer accepts the event-driven environment found in Visual Basic 4.0, and once a COBOL programmer understands that a WORKING-STORAGE SECTION describes variables, whereas Visual Basic 4.0 programs require variable-definition statements such as DIM, and once a COBOL programmer learns how to place and adjust controls using the toolbox, the COBOL programmer will find a one-to-one correspondence in almost every COBOL statement to an equivalent Visual Basic 4.0 statement.

Both COBOL and Visual Basic 4.0 certainly have their own particular language idioms and individual statements but the COBOL programmer will not have much trouble understanding the procedural control language of Visual Basic 4.0. The PERFORM statement executes COBOL subroutines just as Call and even Gosub execute Visual Basic 4.0 routines. The breakdown of large COBOL programs into sections and paragraph prepares the would-be Visual Basic 4.0 programmer well for the smaller event procedures found in Visual Basic 4.0.

The primary caveat for newly converted COBOL programmers to the Visual Basic 4.0 environment primarily lies in the separation of data once the COBOL programmer masters the screen-generating window controls. Although COBOL programmers are perhaps the best structured programmers in existence, they are used to a programming environment where every data value is global to the program and available at all times. The secret behind a powerful Visual Basic 4.0 program's success lies in the hiding of data in local variables. In Visual Basic 4.0, a variable available in one routine may be local to that routine and not visible for a different routine. The definition of all data inside a COBOL program's data division makes that data visible to *all* routines in the subsequent code. Once the COBOL programmer masters the Visual Basic 4.0 programming environment and toolbox controls, that programmer should concentrate on learning how local and global data works inside a Visual Basic 4.0 program. The rest of the language will then pose no major conversion complications.

Table A.2 presents an overview of some of the specific feature comparisons between Visual Basic 4.0 and COBOL.

Table A.2. Visual Basic 4.0 compared to COBOL's significant features.

Visual Basic 4.0	COBOL
Straightforward language using simple keyword commands and data definition statements.	Wordy language producing long listings for simple programs.
Provides full support for Windows.	Provides no applications support for Windows applications unless you purchase a COBOL compiler that includes non-standard library calls to Windows routines. Even then you are not assured that your software investment will be valid as subsequent versions of Windows become available.
Supports (with optional installation features) all the same advanced file I/O operations as COBOL.	Supports most common and powerful file I/O operations.
Data definitions are performed close to their actual usage in the program.	Data definitions appear toward the beginning of a program listing only, making debugging and program authoring somewhat of a book keeping chore.
Local and global variables are supported.	Only global data values are available.

Visual Basic 4.0	COBOL
No line-terminating character required.	A line-terminating character (a period) required after each executable statement.
Free-form flow of code.	Strict column placement of many sections and paragraph headings.
De facto support for graphics through common commands that have been available for many incarnations of BASIC	Lack of standardized graphics support for PC or mainframe hardware.
Programs are interpreted.	Programs are compiled.

C and Visual Basic 4.0

C differs from Visual Basic 4.0 like night differs from day. C is a small programming language. Where ANSI C has fewer than 35 keywords, Visual Basic 4.0 has over 200. The C programmer must rely heavily on special symbolic character operators that perform much of the work in the language. Where Visual Basic 4.0 uses a keyword command to compare two values, the C language uses a special operator in certain instances.

Unlike COBOL, C is primarily a PC-based language. Although C is available on most mainframe and minicomputers today, C's small size made C the ideal language for PCs during the 1980s when ample PC memory and disk space were scarce. The use of C in writing PC-based programs grew tremendously in the decade of the 1980s. Now that the memory and disk storage capacity of PCs rival those of the computer giants in the early 1980s, C's inertia (and its successor, C++, discussed in this appendix's final section) makes C a major player in PC languages today. Almost every data processing shop writing PC-based code, whether for Windows or still for the MS-DOS environment, must make the C-or-Visual Basic 4.0 decision. Both languages offer advantages and disadvantages that complement each other.

Despite its small language, C is difficult to learn when compared to Visual Basic 4.0. C is cryptic and Visual Basic 4.0 is verbose. Even well-written C code can be confusing to an expert, whereas well-written Visual Basic 4.0 code can be somewhat self-documenting. Despite its small vocabulary, C requires time to master, but a programmer can begin writing Visual Basic 4.0 programs quickly.

The size and learning curve of the two languages are not the only considerations one must make when deciding between C and Visual Basic 4.0. C programs are compiled whereas Visual Basic 4.0 programs are interpreted. Although the compile versus interpret arguments were presented earlier in this appendix's first section discussing BASIC, the development discussion is more critical when discussing C over the earlier BASIC languages. C is an extremely efficient language. C's speed virtually rivals assembly language speed when written with efficiency in mind. In time-critical applications, such as embedded code found in automated test systems and flight simulators, C's speed is critical to the success of the application. There is no way to consider Visual Basic 4.0 in such an application despite today's fast computers.

Given the huge speed advantage that C offers over Visual Basic 4.0, speed is *rarely important* these days to most final Windows applications. Nobody wants sluggish applications, and a Windows application is often many times slower than an equivalent MS-DOS application. Nevertheless, Visual Basic 4.0 was never intended to be used in time-critical applications. It was intended to be used to produce powerful Windows applications very quickly. Visual Basic 4.0 provides the ability to write user screens and prototypes during the program's design *and the programmers can then turn those screens and prototypes into final working applications quickly.*

The C programming language was originally the primary language used when writing Windows applications. Perhaps the speed of C was the reason for the selection of C as the original de facto standard Windows language. C, however, is a terrible language for designing Windows program prototypes. C is a terrible language for moving from design to finished product quickly in the Windows environment. In addition to a slow development cycle, the learning curve for the C language is only the first step in writing Windows programs using C; the detailed and tedious architecture of a Windows program must be fully understood by C programmers before a single simple Windows program can be written in C.

When writing a Windows program, you've got to consider the design ease and speed of development for that program. A simple C program that does nothing more than display a three-word phrase requires over one hundred C statements and a huge understanding of Windows internal function calls and architecture. The same program requires about ten mouse clicks and one or two lines of code when using Visual Basic 4.0. Developers simply cannot ignore the learning curve advantages and development time improvements that Visual Basic 4.0 provides over C.

When writing Windows programs using C, the C programmer must not only write code to process data and respond to controls, but the C programmer must also control the Windows environment and check for all the conditions expected by and of the user. Visual Basic 4.0 hides most of the standard Windows interaction from the programmer. Although the Visual Basic 4.0 programmer can modify control properties, check for all property values, manage the window's display, and handle mouse movements and keyboard input, the Visual Basic 4.0 programmer does not have to mess with all those tedious details because so much of the Visual Basic 4.0 environment does this work for the programmer. Of course, that buffering of responsibility is one reason why Visual Basic 4.0 runs slower than C programs (in addition to Visual Basic 4.0's interpreted nature).

The advantage that C programmers realize when writing Windows programs is the low-level availability of the system that C accesses. Through function calls and bitwise operators, C lets the programmer program down on the computer's "bare metal." Although Visual Basic 4.0

does provide support for low-level programming, through hex constants, internal function calls, and bitwise-like manipulating keywords such as AND, OR, XOR, EQV, and NOT, the typical Visual Basic 4.0 programmer needs none of these low-level language tools and will be through writing and testing scores of Windows programs before a C programmer can finish debugging a single program.

At programming conferences around the country, the C versus Visual Basic 4.0 discussion often arises. The lecturer often responds to the arguments being presented for and against both languages like this: "Design and prototype your application using Visual Basic 4.0. Once your users sign off on the specs, then take those specifications and write your efficient projects using straight C."

The problem is that, as hinted at earlier in this section, when you design user screens and prototype your programs using Visual Basic 4.0, with fully-working menus, controls, and dialog boxes that are so easy to produce using the Visual Basic 4.0 development environment, *you have almost completed the application!* Of course, depending on the data processing required behind the scenes, there may still be many hours of programming left to tie those Windows prototype elements together. Nevertheless, you will have those same elements to tie together in C which makes the process more difficult and lower-level. At of the time of this writing, there is no reliable Visual Basic 4.0-to-C screen and prototype converter that transforms Visual Basic 4.0 screens, menus, and controls, into their C equivalents. Even if there were such a conversion method the time required to find the C programming hooks needed to tie the controlling elements together would be too costly to justify the effort in many programming projects.

Early releases of Windows did not include a free Visual Basic run-time distribution package. Early Visual Basic developers had to ensure that the Visual Basic runtime system, such as VBRUN200.DLL was placed in the user's Windows directory before the user ran Visual Basic programs. Windows 95 contains the runtime DLL file needed to run Visual Basic 4.0 applications. Visual Basic 4.0 developers no longer have to fear the user being without the needed runtime code. Although Visual Basic 4.0 programs are not truly compiled programs, they are as tamper-proof as compiled programs are when converted to .EXE files through Visual Basic 4.0's Run menu. The speed of today's machines makes lack of speed an unimportant Visual Basic 4.0 issue. Yesterday's advantages to the C language simply cannot be justified today in most situations where the C versus Visual Basic 4.0 question arises.

> **NOTE**
>
> C is not the same language as C++. There are some valid arguments to be made for developing Windows applications in some versions of C++ as described in the final section of this appendix.

Table A.3 presents an overview of some of the specific feature comparisons between Visual Basic 4.0 and C.

Table A.3. Visual Basic 4.0 compared to C's significant features.

Visual Basic 4.0	*C*
Straightforward language using simple keyword commands and data definition statements.	Cryptic language using more operators and symbols than keywords.
Different I/O commands for each device written to or read from making programs hardware (PC) dependent.	Similar I/O functions used for all I/O devices the program communicates with making programs more portable across different hardware platforms.
Assembly language function calls and internal Windows calls are available through the `Call`.	Assembly language function calls and internal Windows calls available by direct linking of those routines once you compile them.
Easier to learn for beginners. A programming novice can write complete Windows applications in a brief time.	Much more difficult for the novice programmer. Once the novice finally masters the fundamentals of C, the user still has a long training period ahead to learn the art and skill of writing simple Windows applications in C.
All of the internal Windows routines are available.	All of the internal Windows routines are available.
No support for MS-DOS applications.	Direct support for both Windows and MS-DOS applications.
String variables fully supported.	No string variable support.
Much slower during runtime.	Virtually the same speed as low-level assembly language.

Pascal: A Language Whose Potential Has Gone

Pascal offers most of the advantages of C although C produces slightly faster runtime code than Pascal. Pascal is a fairly small language. It is often a system-dependent language although today's de facto standard PC version of Pascal, Borland Pascal, discussed in a moment, runs extremely well on PCs under the Windows environment.

Pascal was designed in the 1970s to be a major player in the small-computer market. It was thought by some that Pascal would take over most other programming languages due to its structured approach, data flexibility, ease of use (once mastered) over more rigid programming languages of the day such as COBOL and FORTRAN, and its small size. In short, Pascal was going to be what C actually became in reality: The language that was going to be used by virtually every programmer.

During the 1970s and into the 1980s, Pascal did succeed in turning many programming communities into Pascal-only shops. Developers used Pascal in early PC software when assembly language development could not be justified. Sad for many people, however, Pascal surprised the language stalwarts by virtually dying out to make room for C. In the span of a year or two during the mid-1980s, C streaked past Pascal as the language of choice and Pascal almost died completely.

Almost. Borland International, never let Pascal die completely. Almost single-handedly, Borland's Turbo Pascal kept Pascal inside many programming circles, despite the fact that the programming community favored C (and still does by a large factor). About the time that Microsoft released the first version of Visual Basic, Borland released an *object-oriented* Pascal called *Turbo Pascal With Objects* and new life surged into the Pascal language.

> **NOTE**
>
> Today C++ is such a more popular and widely-used object-oriented programming (*OOP*) language than Pascal with objects, that a more formal discussion of OOP is left for the next section that discusses C++.

As Microsoft added features and support to Visual Basic, Borland continued to hone Turbo Pascal (along with their Turbo C and Turbo C++ languages). Today, it is rare to find a Windows programming magazine or journal that does not contain at least one article or reference to a Windows program written in Turbo Pascal. Pascal, however, suffers the same fate that C suffers when developing Windows programs: Despite its respect as a well-written, structured, efficient, small programming language, it is precisely that detailed advantage that makes Pascal almost *too sharp* of a tool to use in favor of Visual Basic 4.0. Development time is simply too costly in most programming shops and the backlog of programming projects is too huge to ignore for developers to realize benefits using Pascal (or its object-oriented cousin) in Windows development.

> **NOTE**
>
> Programmers will find that the conversion of procedural sections of code between Visual Basic 4.0 and Pascal is simple. Both languages support similar data definitions, controlling commands, looping statements, and string support. The only major language difference that will appear is your compiler's support for Windows programs. Turbo Pascal, for example, performs Windows interactions much differently from Visual Basic 4.0.

There are some Pascal die-hards who, using the tools available in such languages as Turbo Pascal with Objects, truly can develop Windows applications more quickly than C programmers. The compiled speed advantages of Pascal over Visual Basic 4.0 also cannot be ignored in some specific time-critical applications. Nevertheless, all the Visual Basic 4.0 advantages over C still apply to Pascal. Pascal is a high-level language that often acts like a low-level one. Development in Pascal can be time-consuming. The visual nature of today's Pascal languages, such as the new versions of Turbo Pascal, still do not hold a candle to development speed possible under Visual Basic 4.0.

The sheer number of C and C++ programmers over Pascal programmers help ensure that Pascal will remain in the secondary programming community and stay out of most mainstream data processing organizations. Pascal is an excellent tool for learning to program correctly and many universities rightly require students to pass Pascal before venturing into "real" languages of C and C++. Although there will probably always be those who make Pascal their development language of choice, those number of people are dwindling as the number of Visual Basic 4.0 programmers increase.

Table A.4 presents an overview of some of the specific feature comparisons between Visual Basic 4.0 and Pascal.

Table A.4. Visual Basic 4.0 compared to Pascal's significant features.

Visual Basic 4.0	Pascal
Straightforward language using simple keyword commands and data definition statements.	Also a fairly straightforward language for beginners to learn and provides a more structured approach to programming fundamentals than Visual Basic 4.0 does.
Machine- and hardware-dependent. Almost every device requires a different command making portability difficult. In the Windows environment, the *only* environment Visual Basic 4.0 is designed for, this dependence is trivial.	Machine- and hardware- independent through the use of standard I/O files. In the Windows environment, this portability, however, becomes trivial.

Visual Basic 4.0	Pascal
An interpreted language.	A compiled language. Speed is automatically faster as a result.
Code can be bloated due to runtime DLL library required.	Most programs compile into small executable files.
No support for MS-DOS applications.	Direct support for both Windows and MS-DOS applications.
Advanced data structures, such as records, are fully supported.	Advanced record data structures are supported.
No line-terminating character required.	A line-terminating character (semicolon) required after each executable statement.
Full de facto standard support for PC graphics hardware due to time Visual Basic has been available.	Full de facto standard support for PC graphics hardware due to the time PC-based Turbo Pascal has been available.

C++: The True Visual Basic 4.0 Opponent

The C++ language contains all the advantages and disadvantages of C—and then some. C++ is efficient. Despite more advanced compiler required for the language, today's C++ programs are almost exactly as efficient as similar C programs. A C programmer can learn the fundamental differences between C and C++ in a matter of a few minutes of study. The complete discussion in this appendix's section on the C language applies to C++. The differences begin to appear when one adds object-oriented programming to the C and C++ mixture. C++ is an improved C language, with additional support for object-oriented technology.

OOP is much more important to C++ than it is to Pascal. Although the OOP hooks that Borland gave to Turbo Pascal with Objects breathed new life into Pascal and kept the language active longer than it may have stayed active otherwise, the OOP in C++ took over the programming world in a frenzy. Today, programmers are scrambling to add C++/OOP notches to their programming tool belts.

There are two heavy-hitting C++ Windows development tools on the market today and they are Microsoft's *Visual C++* and Borland's *Borland C++*. There are several other C++ Windows development languages offered by other vendors but Microsoft and Borland get the most sales numbers with tools used by programmers who can produce reliable, quick, efficient, and effective Windows programs.

Before learning why Visual C++ and Borland C++ are the major contenders to Visual Basic 4.0, you should get an idea of the nature of object-oriented languages. Although complete books have been written to explain OOP, here are some of the fundamentals that separate an OOP language from a non-OOP language:

- In theory (although not always in practice), programs written using OOP technology should be faster to write and easier to modify.

- Through OOP technology known as *data abstraction*, your data values act more like their real-world counterparts. Instead of creating a data structure containing the same information as a customer record as you would do in Visual Basic 4.0, for example, an OOP customer representation (an example of an *object*) would act in the program just like a customer that can be added to the company's books, changed, deleted, or printed on a report. The code that describes, initializes, and uses that customer will use commands that behave like real-world interactions you would perform with customers; your programs will contain such commands as GetCustomer and ChangeCustomerData. The end result is be an OOP program that often reads like a physical representation of the data bringing the programmer closer to the data and removing layers of buffering between data and the real-world physical counterparts that the data represents.

- A part of OOP technology called *inheritance* makes extending capabilities of existing OOP program sections and data values easier. Therefore, you are able to reuse pieces of programs in other programs, building new programs as you might build a modular home.

- OOP programs are safer due to an OOP technology called *encapsulation*. Through encapsulation, only portions of a program or routine that needs access to a data value gets access to that value. The concept of local and global data values goes far beyond the usual terminology when you add the encapsulation ability.

OOP is not necessarily a major language change. Instead, it is more of an approach to data and programs that should, whenever fully implemented, make programmers more productive. There is one major drawback to C++ and the OOP combination, however, and that is the learning curve needed to master C++ and OOP.

Add to the learning curve of C the equal, and often more time consuming, learning curve needed to master OOP skills. While the beginning programmer moves at a snail-like pace through his or her introductory programming language to C, to C++, and finally to OOP-based C++, other programmers using Visual Basic 4.0 will have produced so much productive, working, and debugged code that the C++/OOP programmer will wonder where to sign up for Visual Basic 4.0 classes!

Due to the learning curve and the added burden of interfacing to a Windows programming environment by using a C-like language, C++ would not be a major contender in the world of Windows programming if it were not for a new use for OOP that Microsoft and Borland quickly introduced into their C++ Windows programming products: *application frameworks*.

An application framework is a tool, implemented using OOP technology, that lets you quickly develop a Windows program shell, complete with menus and controls, to which you then can add underlying C++ code that links the controls together and also add your own data processing specifications to the application. The end result will turn a shell of a Windows application (the prototype) into a complete working application.

Borland's application framework is called *ObjectWindows Library* and Microsoft's application framework is called the *Microsoft Foundation Classes*. Although the market does not always determine the best tools for a given job, especially in the field of computers, Microsoft seems to be leading the sales and the majority of Windows development using C++ seems to be done today using the Microsoft's Visual C++ development system.

Where does Visual Basic 4.0 fit into this C++ language discussion? These C++ application framework tools help bridge the gap between the novice programmer and advanced Windows applications. You'll remember from an earlier section that C programmers cannot quickly produce running prototype Windows applications and initial working code due to the complexity of writing Windows programs in C. Therefore, many developers forego using C for Windows development these days due to the power of Visual Basic 4.0.

CAUTION

Despite the similar names, Visual Basic 4.0 and Visual C++ have very little in common. The interfaces, languages, and ease of application development, are extremely different between the two languages.

The application framework seems to level the programming playing field somewhat. Using the application frameworks, a C++ programmer can develop working prototypes of Windows programs virtually as quickly as the Visual Basic 4.0 developer. Therefore, users can more quickly accept or reject program designs (one of the typical bottlenecks in most program development projects) and projects can more quickly be completed. Once the menus, controls, and user interfaces are in place, the programmer uses the C++ underlying language to connect the controls and to add the application-specific calculations and procedural requirements.

Major software developers are using these C++ application frameworks, especially Visual C++, to develop their programs for distribution. The development time is cut down from the typical C-based Windows development environment because

1. The programmers quickly develop prototypes (application shells) using the application framework.
2. The OOP advantages of C++ over C and most other procedural languages make extending that application framework and shell easier than could be done without the tools of OOP. Instead of low-level C code being used to add the meat behind the applications, the extensible object-oriented code makes adding the final glue to the framework easier than possible without OOP's tools.

However, there is one problem that still lurks in the C++/OOP application framework development system that you should understand before throwing out Visual Basic 4.0 for a new copy of Visual C++ or Borland C++: Although the application framework makes initial application development (the application's design and shell) simple, you *must* understand the in-depth relations of object orientation before you can do anything more with the application's shell. You must master the mechanics of C++'s inheritance, abstraction, and encapsulation features before you are able to add one line of code to the application's shell created by the framework. Therefore, despite the tremendous advantages that these application frameworks provide for those already skilled in advanced OOP programming techniques, these frameworks still do little for the introductory programmers and for the non-OOP programmers who want to produce Windows programs quickly.

In addition to mastering OOP technology in depth, the C++/OOP programmer must also be versed in the Windows internal routines supported by these framework development systems. Visual C++ and Borland C++ support hundreds and hundreds of Windows function calls. Although many of these calls have been simplified for the frameworks (unlike the poor C Windows programmer who must master the hundreds of Windows internal function calls with no simplification), the Windows developer using a C++/OOP framework must eventually get acquainted with hundreds of supported Windows routines that size windows, draw graphics, support mouse controls, and perform all the other mundane and critical Windows responses needed in even fairly simple Windows applications.

Visual Basic 4.0 does not require the steep learning curve that these major development tools require. It is true that with major development systems, such as Borland C++ and Visual C++, programming communities can be extremely productive and write extremely advanced and major Windows applications that run efficiently and as true compiled applications. Visual Basic 4.0's interpreted nature simply does not support major developments such as Microsoft Excel or WordPerfect for Windows. For those programming shops with major programming talents, the C++ application frameworks are the definite tools of choice.

Table A.5 presents an overview of some of the specific feature comparisons between Visual Basic 4.0 and C++ with OOP capabilities.

Table A.5. Visual Basic 4.0 compared to C++'s significant features.

Visual Basic 4.0	*C++ with OOP*
Straightforward language using simple keyword commands and data definition statements.	Cryptic language using more special operators and symbols than keywords of C's nature.
Different I/O commands for each device written to or read from making programs hardware (PC) specific.	Similar I/O functions used for any I/O device the program communicates with, making programs more portable across different hardware platforms.

Visual Basic 4.0	*C++ with OOP*
Assembly language function calls and internal Windows calls are available through the `Call` statement.	Assembly language function calls and internal Windows calls are available by direct linking of those routines once you compile them.
Easier to learn for beginners. A programming novice can write complete Windows applications in a brief time.	Much more difficult for the novice programmer. Once the novice finally masters the fundamentals of C, the programmer then must master C++, then OOP techniques, then the programmer must learn the applications framework, *and then* the internal Windows function calls supported by the framework.
All of the internal Windows routines are available.	All of the internal Windows routines are available and simplified due to the framework (although there are many one must master).
No support for MS-DOS applications.	Direct support for both Windows and MS-DOS applications using C++ (application frameworks generally support only Windows applications, however).
Much slower during runtime.	Virtually the same speed as low-level assembly language.
Quick application prototyping is possible. The final glue of the application, along with the application's data processing specifics, are easy to add.	Quick application prototyping is possible. The final glue of the application, along with the application's data processing are easy to add *but only for those who master OOP technology and many internal Windows functions.*

Summary

You've made it this far through the book so you obviously have a strong interest in using Visual Basic 4.0 to create Windows applications. You are probably already using Visual Basic 4.0 for some application development.

This appendix tried to answer a few questions you may have had concerning the acceptability of Visual Basic 4.0 as a serious Windows development tool as opposed to other languages you can use. If you have some or extensive background in other languages and are fairly new to the Visual Basic 4.0 environment, perhaps this appendix helped you categorize several of the other popular languages still in use and compare those languages with Visual Basic 4.0.

Online Resources for Visual Basic and Other Microsoft Products

B

by Bradley L. Jones

For up-to-date information and support, there are a number of areas where you can look online. These areas include the following:

- CompuServe Forums
- Usenet Newsgroups
- FTP
- Microsoft Aliases
- Microsoft Bulletin Board System

CompuServe Forums

Microsoft has a number of forums that they facilitate on CompuServe. This provides an area where direct interaction with members of Microsoft can occur. Additionally, most of the forums are frequented by others who are experts on the different Microsoft products. Although there are no additional fees for joining most of the forums, regular CompuServe connect charges apply. `GO MICROSOFT` will get you started. Table B.1 presents a list of forums.

Table B.1. CompuServe forums.

Location	Forum	Description
`GO DEVCAST`	DevCast	DevCast information. DevCasts are quarterly demonstrations by Microsoft with technical information aimed at developers.
`GO FOXFORUM`	Fox Software	Information on Microsoft's Visual Fox and other Fox database products.
`GO MDKB`	Developer	Technical articles about Knowledge Base Microsoft products, information on bugs and fixes, and answers to frequently asked questions.
`GO MSACCESS`	Microsoft Access	Information on Microsoft Access.
`GO MSBASIC`	Basic Languages	Information on Microsoft's Basic Languages family of products, including Visual Basic.
`GO MSDNLIB`	Developer Network Forum	Technical articles and sample code.
`GO MSDS`	Developer Forums	Interactive dialog with a worldwide community of Microsoft customers, facilitated by Microsoft.

Location	Forum	Description
GO MSL	Software Library	Binary files, sample code, device drivers, patches, technical specifications, and utilities.
GO MSLANG	C and Other Languages	Information on Microsoft C, Visual C++, Assembler, and other Microsoft languages and utilities.
GO MSMFC	MFC Library	Information on the Microsoft Foundation Class (MFC) library.
GO MSNETWORKS	Client Server Computing	Information on Microsoft networking systems.
GO MSSQL	MS SQL Server	Information for Microsoft SQL Server.
GO MSTECHED	Tech*Ed	Tech*Ed conference information. Microsoft Tech*Ed is a conference aimed at integrators, developers, support people, and technical managers. Tech*Ed conferences generally focus on Microsoft products.
GO MSWIN	MS Windows	Information on Microsoft Windows.
GO MSWIN32	Win32 SDK	Exchanges information on the Microsoft Windows NT Win32 SDK, Windows NT DDK, and Win32 API issues on other platforms.
GO MSWRKGRP	MS Workgroups	Information on Microsoft's workgroup applications and systems. This includes MAPI.
GO PLUGPLAY	Plug and Play	Information on Plug and Play hardware.
GO PROGMSA	MS Programming Apps	Information on Microsoft applications programming languages and tools. This includes the Microsoft Excel SDK.
GO WINEXT	Windows Extensions	Information on extensions to Microsoft Windows. This includes TAPI, WOSA/XRT, WOSA/XFS, Windows for Workgroups SDK, Far East SDK, Arabic/Hebrew SDK, Pen SDK, and ODBC.

continues

Table B.1. continued

Location	Forum	Description
GO WINMM	Windows	Information on Windows multimedia Multimedia platforms, including Video for Windows, Viewer, and the Microsoft Sound System.
GO WINNT	MS Windows NT	Information for Microsoft Windows NT.
GO WINOBJ	Windows Objects	Information on Microsoft Windows Objects, Object Linking and Embedding (OLE).
GO WINSDK	Windows SDK	Product support and information for the Microsoft Windows SDK and DDK.

Usenet Newsgroups

The Usenet newsgroups are available for information on specific topics. Unlike CompuServe, there are not necessarily Microsoft personnel monitoring these areas. Table B.2 lists many of the newsgroups available.

Table B.2. Usenet newsgroups.

Address	Description
comp.os.ms-windows.announce	A moderated newsgroup that provides announcements and news about Windows-based applications, drivers, events, and so on.
comp.os.ms-windows.programmer.tools	Discussion about Windows-based development tools.
comp.os.ms-windows.programmer.win32	Discussion about developing for the Win32 API.
comp.os.ms-windows.programmer.misc	Discussion on the Windows-based programming and development issues that don't fit into the other newsgroups.
comp.os.ms-windows.apps	Discussion about applications for the different versions of Windows, including NT.

Address	Description
comp.os.ms-windows.setup	Discussions on Windows setup and configuration.
comp.os.ms-windows.nt.setup	Discussion on Windows NT setup and configuration.
comp.os.ms-windows.misc	Discussion on Windows issues that don't fit into the other newsgroup areas.
comp.os.ms-windows.nt.misc	Discussion on Windows NT issues that are not discussed in other news groups.
comp.os.ms-windows.advocacy	Discussion for comparisons and arguments about the Windows operating systems verses other operating systems.
comp.binaries.ms-windows	Discussion and distribution of Window operating system binary files. These files include shareware, drivers, and more.

FTP

Microsofts FTP server, FTP.Microsoft.COM (198.105.232.1), enables anonymous FTP login. The server provides the Microsoft Driver Library and the Microsoft Knowledge Base.

Microsoft Internet Addresses (Aliases)

Table B.3 contains aliases at Microsoft that are accessible via Internet e-mail.

Table B.3. Microsoft aliases.

Address	Description	Notes
3D-IHV@Microsoft.COM	3D DDK issues	Display hardware vendors wanting information on 3D DDI (Device Driver Interface).
DCI-IHV@Microsoft.COM	DCI issues	Display hardware vendors wanting information on the Microsoft and Intel DCI specification.

continues

Global@Microsoft.COM	Internationalization issues	Windows ISV issues on Microsoft internationalization system strategy.
IHV@Microsoft.COM	IHV issues	Independent hardware vendor issues on Microsoft overall systems strategy.
MAPI@Microsoft.COM	MAPI issues	Windows ISV issues on MAPI issues.
MMDInfo@Microsoft.COM	Multimedia issues	Windows-based multimedia developer issues.
MSDN@Microsoft.COM	Microsoft Developer Network	Nontechnical communications with the Microsoft Developer Network group.
NTIdea@Microsoft.COM	Windows NT	Product suggestions product suggestions on the features and functionality of Windows NT and Windows NT Advanced Server.
PlayList@Microsoft.COM	Plug and Play	Independent hardware announcement list vendors wanting to be placed on a mailing list for updates to the Plug and Play specifications.
Telephon@Microsoft.COM	TAPI issues	Windows ISV issues on TAPI issues.

Microsoft BBS

Microsofts bulletin board system is called the *Microsoft Download Service* (MSDL). This BBS contains sample programs, device drivers, patches, software updates, and programming aids. It is available via modem by calling (206) 936-6735.

INDEX

X-Z

Add to Your Sams Library Today with the Best Books for Programming, Operating Systems, and New Technologies

The easiest way to order is to pick up the phone and call

1-800-428-5331

between 9:00 a.m. and 5:00 p.m. EST.
For faster service please have your credit card available.

ISBN	Quantity	Description of Item	Unit Cost	Total Cost
0-672-30602-6		Programming Windows 95 Unleashed (Book/CD)	$49.99	
0-672-30474-0		Windows 95 Unleashed (Book/CD)	$39.99	
0-672-30611-5		Your Windows 95 Consultant	$19.99	
0-672-30685-9		Windows NT 3.5 Unleashed	$39.99	
0-672-30765-0		Navigating the Internet with Windows 95	$25.00	
0-672-30568-2		Teach Yourself OLE Programming in 21 Days (Book/CD)	$39.99	
0-672-30619-0		Real-World Programming with Visual Basic (Book/CD)	$45.00	
0-672-30594-1		Programming WinSock (Book/Disk)	$35.00	
0-672-30440-6		Database Developer's Guide with Visual Basic 3 (Book/Disk)	$44.95	
0-672-30453-8		Access 2 Developer's Guide, 2nd Edition (Book/Disk)	$44.95	
0-672-30596-8		Develop a Professional Visual Basic Application in 14 Days (Book/CD)	$35.00	
0-672-30737-5		World Wide Web Unleashed, 2E	$39.99	
❏ 3 ½" Disk		Shipping and Handling: See information below.		
❏ 5 ¼" Disk		TOTAL		

Shipping and Handling: $4.00 for the first book, and $1.75 for each additional book. Floppy disk: add $1.75 for shipping and handling. If you need to have it NOW, we can ship product to you in 24 hours for an additional charge of approximately $18.00, and you will receive your item overnight or in two days. Overseas shipping and handling adds $2.00 per book and $8.00 for up to three disks. Prices subject to change. Call for availability and pricing information on latest editions.

201 W. 103rd Street, Indianapolis, Indiana 46290

1-800-428-5331 — Orders   1-800-835-3202 — FAX   1-800-858-7674 — Customer Service

Book ISBN 0-672-30837-1

WHICH ONE HAS THE BEST REPORTING TOOL?

THEY ALL DO.

 To find the reporting tool that's the first choice of Microsoft® and over 80 other software experts, just turn on your PC. Because as a Visual Basic® user, you have Crystal Reports 2.0 or 3.0 built into your software—right at

your fingertips! Crystal Reports' VBX and Report Engine DLL allow for fast, seamless integration into your data-

base applications. And now, with Crystal Reports 4.5, you get hot new features that allow you to generate presentation quality reports with even greater speed and control.

The number one reporting tool is even better...now with 32-bit technology.

- 16 or 32-bit Report Designer & Report Engine. Great for Windows 3.1, 95, NT.
- 16 or 32-bit OLE Control (OCX), full VBX and 40 new engine calls (>80 total).
- 2-10 times faster report processing.
- Crystal Reports' Experts for automatic report creation.
- 12 fully-integrated graph styles.
- Easier to use interface. And much, much more.

Order Crystal Reports 4.5 today—risk-free.

There's never been a better time to upgrade to Crystal Reports 4.5. As a Visual Basic user, you qualify for a special upgrade price of just $199. (That's a $200 savings.) Try it for 60 days and if you're not completely satisfied, you may return it for a full refund. Order today— and make the reporting tool of the experts your tool of choice.

CRYSTAL
A Seagate Software Company

Call now and get Crystal Reports version 4.5 for just $199. 1-800-877-2340

PLUG YOURSELF INTO...

MACMILLAN INFORMATION SUPERLIBRARY™

que — NRP

SAMS PUBLISHING — alpha books

Hayden Books — Brady

que COLLEGE — ADOBE PRESS

THE MACMILLAN INFORMATION SUPERLIBRARY™

Free information and vast computer resources from the world's leading computer book publisher—online!

FIND THE BOOKS THAT ARE RIGHT FOR YOU!

A complete online catalog, plus sample chapters and tables of contents give you an in-depth look at *all* of our books, including hard-to-find titles. It's the best way to find the books you need!

- ● STAY INFORMED with the latest computer industry news through our online newsletter, press releases, and customized Information SuperLibrary Reports.

- ● GET FAST ANSWERS to your questions about MCP books and software.

- ● VISIT our online bookstore for the latest information and editions!

- ● COMMUNICATE with our expert authors through e-mail and conferences.

- ● DOWNLOAD SOFTWARE from the immense MCP library:
  - Source code and files from MCP books
  - The best shareware, freeware, and demos

- ● DISCOVER HOT SPOTS on other parts of the Internet.

- ● WIN BOOKS in ongoing contests and giveaways!

TO PLUG INTO MCP: → WORLD WIDE WEB: **http://www.mcp.com**

GOPHER: gopher.mcp.com

FTP: ftp.mcp.com

Home Page   What's New   Bookstore   Reference Desk   Software Library   Macmillan Overview   Talk to Us

What's on the CD-ROM

The companion CD-ROM contains source code from the book, plus more than 45 third-party controls for use with Visual Basic, including: full versions of API Vision Lite, InstallShield Express, TrueGrid Professional, the TX-TEXT Control, and Crescent Software's Transition Wizard.

Windows 3.1 Installation Instructions

1. Insert the CD-ROM disc into your CD-ROM drive.

2. From File Manager or Program Manager, choose Run from the File menu.

3. Type `<drive>\setup` and press Enter, where `<drive>` corresponds to the drive letter of your CD-ROM. For example, if your CD-ROM is drive D:, type `D:\SETUP` and press Enter.

4. Installation creates a program manager group named "Visual Basic 4 Unleashed." To browse the CD-ROM, double-click on the "Visual Basic 4 Unleashed" icon inside this program manager group.

Windows 95 Installation Instructions

1. Insert the CD-ROM disc into your CD-ROM drive.

2. From the Windows 95 desktop, double-click on the "My Computer" icon.

3. Double-click on the icon representing your CD-ROM drive.

4. Double-click on the icon titled "SETUP.EXE" to run the installation program.

5. Installation creates a program group named "Visual Basic 4 Unleashed." To browse the CD-ROM, press the Start button and select "Visual Basic 4 Un-leashed." Then select "Visual Basic 4 Unleashed" to run the browser program for the CD-ROM.

NOTE: The browser program requires at least 256 colors. For best results, set your monitor to display between 256 and 64,000 colors. A screen resolution of 640×480 pixels is also recommended. If necessary, adjust your monitor settings before using the CD-ROM.